WordPerfect® 5.1:
The Complete Reference

WordPerfect® 5.1:
The Complete Reference

Karen L. Acerson

Osborne McGraw-Hill

Berkeley New York St. Louis San Francisco
Auckland Bogotá Hamburg London Madrid
Mexico City Milan Montreal New Delhi Panama City
Paris São Paulo Singapore Sydney
Tokyo Toronto

Osborne **McGraw-Hill**
2600 Tenth Street
Berkeley, California 94710
U.S.A.

Osborne/McGraw-Hill offers software for sale. For information on software, translations, or book distributors outside of the U.S.A., write to Osborne **McGraw-Hill** at the above address.

A complete list of trademarks appears on page 1297.

WordPerfect 5.1: The Complete Reference

7890 DOC 9987654321

ISBN 0-07-881634-3

To Alan, Bruce, and Pete for their constant support and friendship

Why This Book Is for You 1

ONE   Installation and Setup 3

TWO   WordPerfect Basics 23

THREE   Commands and Features 71

FOUR   Desktop Publishing with WordPerfect 1071

FIVE   Printer Program 1103

SIX   Advanced Macro and Merge Commands 1129

A   WordPerfect Character Sets 1219

B   WordPerfect Files 1225

C   Differences Between 5.0 and 5.1 1239

D   Differences Between 4.2 and 5.1 1251

E   Graphics Images 1265

F   Conversion Tables 1269

G   Latest Enhancements 1289

Index 1301

CONTENTS AT A GLANCE

Forward, xxxi

Introduction, xxxv

Acknowledgements, xxxiii

Why This Book Is for You, 1

ONE Installation and Setup **3**

System Requirements, 3
  Disk Space, 3
  Memory, 4
  Mice Supported by 5.1, 4
Installing WordPerfect, 5
  Starting the Install
    Program, 6
  Notes About Install, 13
Using a 5.0 Printer
  Definition, 13
    Copying Fonts, 14
Selecting Fonts, 15
Setup Options, 16

Selecting a Mouse, 16
Pull-Down Menus, 17
Colors/Fonts
  /Attributes, 18
Backup, 18
Document Management/
  Summary, 18
Initial Codes, 20
Print Options, 20
Location of Files, 20
Using 5.0 Files, 21
Options for Starting
  WordPerfect, 22

TWO WordPerfect Basics **23**

Template and
  Keystrokes, 23
  Help, 25
  Cancel, 27
  Miscellaneous
    Keystrokes, 28
Starting WordPerfect, 31
  Two Disk Drives, 31
  Hard Disk, 32
  Error Messages, 32
  Status Line, 33
  Absolute
    Measurement, 34
Word Processing
  Concepts, 35
  Clean Screen, 35
  Menus and Prompts, 37
  WordPerfect Codes, 40
  Hard and Soft Codes, 42
  Pagination, 42
  Default Settings, 44

What You See Is What
  You Get, 45
Virtual Memory,
  Document Size, and
  Switching Disks, 46
Creating Documents, 47
  Entering Text, 47
  Centering, 48
  Indenting, 48
  Boldface, 49
  Underlining, 49
  Italics, Double
    Underlining, and
    Other Attributes, 49
  Changing Fonts, 50
  Moving the Cursor, 51
  Correcting Mistakes, 52
  Editing, 53
  Formatting, 57
  Printing, 60
  Filing, 62

TABLE OF CONTENTS

Common Questions, 66
Exiting WordPerfect, 65

Checking the
Spelling, 58

T H R E E   **Commands and Features** **71**

Addition, 71
   Keystrokes, 71
   Hints, 72
   Applications, 73
   Related Entries, 73
Advance, 73
   Keystrokes, 74
   Hints, 74
   Applications, 75
   Related Entries, 76
Align Text, 76
   Options, 76
ALT Key, 78
Appearance, 79
   Related Entries, 79
Append, 80
   Keystrokes, 80
   Hints, 80
   Related Entries, 81
"Are Other Copies of
   WordPerfect Running?"
   Error Message, 81
   Reasons, 81
   Solutions, 82
Arrow Keys, 83
ASCII Text Files, 83
   Related Entries, 83
Attributes, 83
Autoexec.Bat File, 84
   Keystrokes, 84
   Applications, 85
   Related Entries, 85
Automatically Format and
   Rewrite, 86

   Keystrokes, 86
   Hints, 86
   Applications, 86
   Related Entries, 87
Automatic Font Change, 87
   Keystrokes, 88
   Hints, 89
   Related Items, 89
Automatic References, 90
Backspace Key, 90
   Keystrokes, 90
   Options, 90
   Hints, 91
   Related Entries, 91
Backup, 91
   Keystrokes, 92
   Hints, 94
   Related Entries, 95
Banners, 95
   Keystrokes, 96
Base Font, 96
   Keystrokes, 96
   Hints, 96
   Related Entries, 97
Baseline Placement for
   Typesetters, 97
   Keystrokes, 97
   Hints, 98
   Applications, 98
   Related Items, 98
Beep Options, 99
   Keystrokes, 99
   Hints, 99
   Related Entries, 100

Binding Options, 100
    Keystrokes, 101
    Hints, 102
    Related Entries, 103
Block, 103
    Keystrokes, 103
    Options, 105
    Hints, 110
    Related Entries, 110
Block Protect, 111
    Keystrokes, 111
    Hints, 112
    Applications, 113
    Related Entries, 113
Bold, 113
    Keystrokes, 114
    Hints, 115
    Related Entries, 117
Borders, 117
    Keystrokes, 117
    Applications, 121
    Related Entries, 121
Bullets, 123
    Keystrokes, 123
    Hints, 124
    Related Entries, 125
Calculations, 125
Cancel, 125
    Keystrokes, 125
    Hints, 126
    Related Entries, 126
Cancel a Print Job, 126
    Keystrokes, 127
    Hints, 127
    Related Entries, 128
"Can't Find Correct Copy of
  WP" Error Message, 128
    Reasons, 128
    Solution, 128

Capitalization, 129
    Keystrokes, 129
    Hints, 129
    Related Entries, 130
Captions, 130
    Keystrokes, 130
    Hints, 132
    Applications, 133
    Related Entries, 133
Carriage Return, 133
Cartridges and Fonts, 134
    Keystrokes, 134
    Hints, 140
    Related Entries, 140
Center Page from Top to
  Bottom, 140
    Keystrokes, 140
    Hints, 141
    Applications, 141
    Related Entries, 143
Center Text, 143
    Keystrokes, 143
    Hints, 145
    Applications, 146
    Related Entries, 146
Centimeters, 146
    Related Entries, 148
Change Directory, 148
    Keystrokes, 148
    Hints, 149
    Related Entries, 150
Characters Per
  Inch, 150
Clear Tabs, 151
Codes, 151
    List of Codes, 152
    Related Entries, 161
Colors/Fonts/Attributes, 161

Keystrokes, 162
Hints, 167
Related Entries, 169
Colors, Print, 169
Keystrokes, 169
Hints, 170
Related Entries, 171
Columns, 171
Keystrokes, 173
Hints, 175
Applications, 183
Related Entries, 185
Comments, 185
Keystrokes, 185
Hints, 187
Applications, 187
Related Entries, 188
Compare Documents, 188
Keystrokes, 188
Hints, 188
Applications, 190
Related Entries, 190
Compatibility, 191
Keystrokes, 191
Hints, 191
Related Entries, 196
Compose, 196
Keystrokes, 197
Hints, 200
Related Entries, 201
Concordance, 201
Keystrokes, 201
Hints, 203
Related Entries, 205
Condense Documents, 205
Conditional End of
Page, 205
Keystrokes, 206

Hints, 206
Applications, 207
Related Entries, 208
CONFIG.SYS, 208
Continuous Paper, 208
Control Printer, 209
Keystrokes, 209
Options, 210
Hints, 212
Related Entries, 212
Convert Program, 213
Keystrokes, 213
Options, 214
Shortcuts, 217
Applications, 218
Related Entries, 218
Copy, 218
Keystrokes, 219
Hints, 219
Applications, 221
Related Entries, 221
Copy Files, 221
Keystrokes, 221
Hints, 222
Related Entries, 222
Count Lines, 222
Count Words, 223
Create a Directory, 223
Keystrokes, 223
Hints, 223
Related Entries, 224
"Critical Disk Error
Occurred" Error Message,
224
Reason, 224
Solutions, 224
Cross-References, 225
Keystrokes, 225

Hints, 227
Related Entries, 229
CTRL Key, 229
    Keystrokes, 230
    Related Entries, 232
CURSOR.COM Program,
    232
    Keystrokes, 232
    Hints, 232
Cursor Keys, 233
    Keystrokes, 233
    Hints, 236
    Related Entries, 237
Cursor Speed, 237
    Keystrokes, 237
Cut Text and Columns, 238
Dashes, 238
    Keystrokes, 238
    Applications, 239
    Related Entries, 240
Date and Time, 240
    Keystrokes, 240
    Hints, 241
    Applications, 243
    Related Entries, 243
dBASE, 244
    Keystrokes, 244
    Hints, 245
    Related Entries, 246
DCA Format, 246
    Keystrokes, 246
    Hints, 247
    Related Entries, 248
Decimal/Align Character,
    248
    Keystrokes, 248
    Hints, 248
    Related Entries, 249
Decimal Tabs, 249
    Keystrokes, 249

Hints, 250
Related Entries, 251
Default Directory, 251
    Keystrokes, 251
    Hints, 252
Default Settings, 252
Delete, 252
    Keystrokes, 252
    Hints, 252
    Applications, 253
    Related Entries, 253
Delete a Directory, 254
    Keystrokes, 254
    Hints, 254
    Related Entries, 255
Delete Codes, 255
    Keystrokes, 255
    Hints, 255
    Applications, 258
    Related Entries, 258
Delete Files, 258
    Keystrokes, 258
    Hints, 259
    Related Entries, 259
Dictionary, 260
DIF, 260
    Keystrokes, 260
    Hints, 260
    Related Entries, 261
Directories, 261
    Related Entries, 262
"Disk Full" Error Message,
    263
    Reasons, 263
    Solutions, 264
    Related Entries, 264
Disk Space, 264
    Keystrokes, 265
    Hints, 265
    Related Entries, 266

Display Pitch, 266
    Keystrokes, 266
    Hints, 267
    Applications, 267
    Related Entries, 268
Display Print Jobs, 268
    Keystrokes, 268
    Hints, 268
    Applications, 269
    Related Entries, 269
"Divide Overflow" Error
  Message, 269
    Reasons, 269
    Solutions, 269
Document Compare, 270
Document Format, 270
    Keystrokes, 270
    Options, 270
    Related Entries, 272
Document Management
  /Summary, 272
    Keystrokes, 272
    Hints, 276
    Related Items, 278
Document Size, 279
    Keystrokes, 279
    Hints, 279
    Related Entries, 279
Document Summary, 279
DOS Command, 280
    Keystrokes, 280
    Hints, 280
    Related Entries, 281
DOS Text Files, 281
    Keystrokes, 281
    Hints, 282
    Applications, 283
    Related Entries, 283
Dot Leader, 283
    Keystrokes, 284

Hints, 284
Double Spacing, 285
Double Underlining, 285
    Keystrokes, 286
    Hints, 286
    Related Entries, 286
Downloading Fonts, 286
Drawing Lines and
  Boxes, 286
Editing Documents, 287
    Keystrokes, 287
    Related Entries, 288
Edit-Screen Options, 288
    Keystrokes, 288
    Options, 289
    Related Entries, 291
Encrypting a File, 291
END Key, 291
    Keystrokes, 291
    Related Entries, 292
Endnotes, 292
    Keystrokes, 292
    Hints, 294
    Related Entries, 300
ENTER Key, 300
    Keystrokes, 300
    Hints, 301
    Related Entries, 302
Envelopes, 302
    Keystrokes, 302
    Hints, 303
    Related Items, 305
Environment, 305
    Keystrokes, 305
    Options, 306
    Related Entries, 308
Equations, 308
    Keystrokes, 310
    Hints, 312
    Commands, 315

Applications, 345
 Related Items, 353
Erase, 353
Error Messages, 354
 Hints, 354
 Related Entries, 355
ESC Key, 355
 Keystrokes, 355
 Hints, 357
 Applications, 357
 Related Entries, 358
Excel, 358
 Keystrokes, 358
 Related Items, 359
Exit, 359
 Keystrokes, 359
 Hints, 360
 Related Entries, 360
Expanded Memory, 361
 Hints, 361
 Related Items, 363
Extended
 Search/Replace, 363
Extra-Large Print, 363
 Keystrokes, 364
 Hints, 364
 Related Entries, 365
Fast Save, 365
 Keystrokes, 365
 Hints, 365
Figures, 366
 Related Entries, 367
"File Creation Error" Error
 Message, 367
Filenames, Long and
 Short, 368
Filing Documents, 368
 Related Entries, 369
Find Files, 369
 Keystrokes, 369

Hints, 371
 Related Items, 374
Fine Print, 374
 Keystrokes, 374
 Hints, 375
 Related Entries, 375
Fixed Line Height, 375
Flush Right, 375
 Keystrokes, 376
 Hints, 378
 Applications, 378
 Related Entries, 378
Fonts, 378
 Keystrokes, 379
 Hints, 382
 Related Entries, 384
Footers, 385
 Keystrokes, 385
 Hints, 386
 Applications, 386
 Related Entries, 386
Footnotes, 386
 Keystrokes, 387
 Hints, 388
 Related Entries, 394
Force Odd/Even Page, 394
 Keystrokes, 395
 Hints, 395
 Applications, 395
 Related Entries, 395
Foreign Languages, 396
Format, 396
 Keystrokes, 396
 Options, 397
 Hints, 400
 Related Entries, 401
Form Letters and Forms
 Fill-in, 402
Forms, 403
Function Keys, 403

Generate, 404
Global Search and Replace, 404
Go to, 405
    Keystrokes, 405
    Hints, 407
    Related Entries, 407
Go to DOS or Shell, 407
    Keystrokes, 407
    Hints, 408
    Related Entries, 409
Graphics Boxes, 409
    Keystrokes, 411
    Options, 414
    Hints, 435
    Applications, 439
    Related Entries, 443
Graphics Lines, 444
    Keystrokes, 444 443
    Options, 447
    Hints, 450
    Applications, 450
    Related Entries, 452
Graphics Screen Type, 454
    Keystrokes, 454
    Hints, 455
Graphics Utilities, 456
    Keystrokes, 456
    Hints, 458
Hand-Fed Paper, 462
    Sending the Printer a "Go", 462
    Top Margin, 462
    Hand Feeding with Laser Printers, 462
    Related Entries, 463
Hanging Paragraphs and Indents, 463
    Keystrokes, 463
    Hints, 463

Applications, 464
    Related Entries, 465
Hard Hyphen, 466
    Keystrokes, 466
    Hints, 466
    Applications, 466
    Related Entries, 467
Hard Page, 467
    Keystrokes, 467
    Hints, 467
    Applications, 467
    Related Entries, 468
Hard Return, 468
    Keystrokes, 468
    Hints, 469
    Related Items, 469
Hard Return Display Character, 469
    Keystrokes, 469
    Related Entries, 471
Hard Space, 471
    Keystrokes, 471
    Hints, 471
    Applications, 471
    Related Entries, 472
Headers, 472
    Keystrokes, 472
    Hints, 473
    Applications, 479
    Related Entries, 480
Help, 480
    Keystrokes, 481
    Hints, 482
    Applications, 484
    Related Entries, 484
Hidden Text, 484
Highlighting Text, 484
    Related Entries, 484
HOME Key, 485
    Keystrokes, 485

Related Entries, 487
Horizontal Lines, 487
Hyphenation, 487
  Keystrokes, 488
  Hints, 489
  Related Items, 494
Hyphenation Zone, 495
Inches, 495
Indent, 495
  Keystrokes, 495
  Hints, 496
  Applications, 496
  Related Entries, 497
Index, 497
  Keystrokes, 498
  Hints, 501
  Related Entries, 503
Initial Base Font, 503
  Keystrokes, 504
  Hints, 504
  Related Entries, 505
Initial Codes, 505
  Keystrokes, 505
  Hints, 506
  Applications, 507
  Related Entries, 507
Initial Settings, 507
  Keystrokes, 508
  Options, 508
  Related Entries, 512
Initialize Printer, 513
  Keystrokes, 513
  Hints, 513
  Related Entries, 514
INS Key, 514
  Keystrokes, 514
  Hints, 515
  Applications, 515
  Related Entries, 515
Install, 515

Keystrokes, 515
  Related Entries, 516
Italics, 516
  Keystrokes, 516
  Hints, 517
  Applications, 517
  Related Entries, 518
Justification, 518
  Keystrokes, 518
  Hints, 520 551
  Applications, 522
  Related Items, 522
Keep Text Together, 523
  Related Entries, 523
Kerning, 523
  Keystrokes, 524
  Hints, 524
  Applications, 525
  Related Entries, 525
Keyboard Layout, 525
  Keystrokes, 525
  Hints, 534
  Applications, 545
  Related Entries, 545
Labels, 545
  Keystrokes, 545
  Hints, 551
  Applications, 555
  Related Entries, 558
Landscape Printing, 558
  Keystrokes, 559
  Hints, 560
  Related Entries, 560
Language, 560
  Keystrokes, 561
  Hints, 562
  Applications, 564
  Related Entries, 565
Large Print, 565
  Keystrokes, 565

Hints, 566
Related Entries, 566
Leading, 567
Keystrokes, 567
Hints, 567
Applications, 568
Related Entries, 569
Leaving WordPerfect, 569
Left Indent, 569
Left Margin Release, 569
Keystrokes, 570
Hints, 570
Related Entries, 570
Letter Spacing, 571
Letterhead, 571
Two-Page Letters, 571
Creating
Letterhead, 572
Related Entries, 572
Line Draw, 572
Keystrokes, 574
Hints, 576
Related Entries, 577
Line Format, 578
Keystrokes, 578
Options, 579
Hints, 581
Related Entries, 581
Line Height, 581
Keystrokes, 582
Hints, 582
Applications, 583
Line Numbering, 583
Keystrokes, 583
Options, 584
Hints, 585
Applications, 586
Related Entries, 589
Lines per Inch, 589
List, 590

Related Entries, 590
List Files, 590
Keystrokes, 591
Hints, 592
Options, 595
Related Entries, 601
Lists, 601
Keystrokes, 602
Hints, 605
Related Entries, 606
Location of Files, 606
Keystrokes, 607
Hints, 608
Related Entries, 610
Lock and Unlock
Documents, 610
Keystrokes, 610
Hints, 611
Related Entries, 612
Long Document Names, 612
Keystrokes, 613
Hints, 614
Related Entries, 615
Look at a File, 615
Keystrokes, 616
Hints, 618
Related Entries, 618
Look up a Word, 619
Lotus 1-2-3, 619
Lowercase Text, 619
Macros, 619
Keystrokes, 620
Options, 626
Hints, 632
Applications, 636
Related Entries, 645
Mail Merge, 645
Related Entries, 646
Mailing Labels, 646
Mapping the Keyboard, 646

Margin Release, 646
Margins, Left and
    Right, 647
    Keystrokes, 647
    Hints, 647
    Related Entries, 649
Margins, Top and Bottom,
    650
    Keystrokes, 650
    Hints, 650
    Related Entries, 651
Mark Text, 651
    Keystrokes, 652
    Options, 652
    Hints, 656
    Related Entries, 656
Master Document, 657
    Keystrokes, 657
    Hints, 660
    Applications, 660
    Related Entries, 661
Math, 661
    Keystrokes, 662
    Hints, 669
    Applications, 670
    Related Entries, 671
Menu Options, 672
    Keystrokes, 672
    Hints, 673
    Related Entries, 674
Menus and Messages, 674
    Mnemonic Choices, 674
    Prompts and
        Messages, 675
    Yes/No Questions, 675
    Exiting a Menu, 676
    Inserting Codes and
        Changing Modes, 676
Merge, 677
    How Merge Works, 677

Keystrokes, 679
Simple Merge
    Options, 685
    Hints, 691
    Related Entries, 697
Merge Codes, 698
Merge/Sort, 698
Minus Key, 698
MODE Command, 698
    Keystrokes, 699
    Hints, 699
    Related Entries, 699
Modems, 699
    Keystrokes, 699
    Related Entries, 701
Move, 701
    Keystrokes, 701
    Hints, 707
    Related Entries, 710
Mouse Support and
    Pull-Down Menus, 710
    Keystrokes, 710
    Hints, 714
Moving the Cursor, 722
Multiple Copies, 722
    Keystrokes, 722
    Hints, 722
    Related Entries, 723
Multiple Pages, 723
    Keystrokes, 723
    Hints, 724
    Related Entries, 724
Name Search, 724
    Keystrokes, 725
    Hints, 725
    Applications, 725
    Related Entries, 725
Network Support, 726
    Options, 726
    Related Entries, 730

New Page, 730
New Page Number, 730
   Keystrokes, 730
   Hints, 731
   Applications, 732
   Related Entries, 733
Newspaper-Style
  Columns, 733
"Not Enough Memory"
  Error Message, 733
   Reasons, 733
   Solutions, 734
NUM LOCK Key, 735
   Keystrokes, 735
Number of Copies, 735
   Keystrokes, 736
   Hints, 736
   Related Entries, 736
Numbering Lines, 736
Numbering Paragraphs, 737
Orientation, 737
Original Document
  Backup, 737
Other Format Options, 737
   Keystrokes, 738
   Related Entries, 741
Outline Printing, 741
   Keystrokes, 741
   Hints, 741
   Related Entries, 742
Outlines, 742
   Keystrokes, 743
   Hints, 746
   Options, 748
   Related Entries, 758
Overstrike, 758
   Keystrokes, 758
   Hints, 759
   Applications, 759
   Related Entries, 760

Page Breaks, 760
   Hints, 761
   Applications, 762
   Related Entries, 762
Page Format, 762
   Keystrokes, 763
   Options, 764
   Hints, 766
   Related Entries, 766
Page Numbering, 766
   Keystrokes, 767
   Hints, 770
   Applications, 771
   Related Entries, 774
Page Up/Down, 774
Pagination, 775
Paper Size/Type, 775
   Keystrokes, 775
   Hints, 778
   Related Entries, 782
Paragraph Numbering, 782
   Keystrokes, 782
   Hints, 783
   Applications, 787
   Related Entries, 788
Parallel Columns, 788
Password Protection, 789
Path For Downloadable
  Fonts and Printer
  Files, 789
   Related Entries, 789
Pitch, 789
Postscript Printing, 790
   Setting Up the
    Printer, 790
   Soft Fonts, 791
   Advantages of a
    PostScript
    Printer, 791
   Related Entries, 793

Preview a Document, 793
Print, 793
    Keystrokes, 793
    Hints, 796
    Related Entries, 805
Print Format, 805
Print Options, 806
Print to Disk, 806
    Keystrokes, 807
    Hints, 809
    Applications, 809
    Related Entries, 809
Printer Command, 810
    Keystrokes, 810
    Hints, 811
    Related Entries, 812
Printer Control, 813
Printer Selection, 813
Proportional Spacing, 813
    Related Entries, 814
Protect a Block of Text, 815
Protect a Document, 815
PRTSC Key, 815
Pull-Down Menus, 815
    Keystrokes, 816
    Hints, 816
    Related Entries, 818
"Put WP 2 Disk Back in
  Drive" Error Message,
  818
    Reasons, 819
    Solutions, 819
    Related Entries, 820
Quality of Print, 820
    Keystrokes, 820
    Hints, 820
    Applications, 821
Quit Printing, 821
Ram Drives, 821

Rectangular Move and
  Copy, 822
Redline, 822
    Keystrokes, 822
    Hints, 824
    Related Entries, 825
References, 825
Reformatting, 826
Remove Redline and
  Strikeout, 826
    Keystrokes, 826
    Hints, 827
    Related Entries, 828
Rename a File, 828
    Keystrokes, 828
    Hints, 829
    Related Entries, 829
Repeat Value, 829
Replace, 830
    Keystrokes, 830
    Hints, 830
    Applications, 834
    Related Entries, 834
Restart the Printer, 834
    Keystrokes, 834
    Hints, 835
    Related Entries, 835
Restore Deleted Text, 835
Retrieve, 835
    Keystrokes, 836
    Hints, 837
    Related Entries, 839
Retrieve Text From the
  Clipboard, 840
Return, 840
Reveal Codes, 840
    Keystrokes, 840
    Hints, 842
    Related Entries, 842
Reverse Search, 843

Rewrite the Screen, 843
    Keystrokes, 843
    Hints, 843
    Applications, 844
    Related Entries, 844
Right Align Text, 844
Right Indent, 844
Right Justification, 844
Rotate Text, 845
Ruler Line, 845
    Keystrokes, 845
    Hints, 846
    Applications, 846
    Related Entries, 847
Rush a Print Job, 847
    Keystrokes, 847
    Related Entries, 848
Save, 848
    Keystrokes, 848
    Hints, 849
    Related Entries, 853
Screen, 853
    Keystrokes, 853
    Options, 854
    Related Entries, 855
Search, 855
    Keystrokes, 855
    Hints, 856
    Applications, 858
    Related Entries, 858
Search and Replace, 859
Search For a File, 859
Selecting a Printer, 859
    Keystrokes, 860
    Hints, 866
    Related Entries, 870
Select Records From a
    Merge File, 870
Set Tabs, 870
Setup, 870

Keystrokes, 871
Options, 871
Hints, 884
Related Entries, 884
Shading, 885
Shadow Borders, 886
Shadow Printing, 886
    Keystrokes, 887
    Hints, 887
Sheet Feeders, 887
    Keystrokes, 888
    Hints, 888
    Related Entries, 889
Shell, 889
    Keystrokes, 890
    Hints, 891
    Applications, 892
    Related Entries, 893
Short Form, 893
Size Attribute Ratios, 893
    Keystrokes, 894
    Hints, 894
    Applications, 895
    Related Entries, 895
Size of Print, 895
    Related Entries, 896
Skip Language, 897
Small Caps, 897
    Keystrokes, 897
    Hints, 898
    Related Entries, 898
Small Print, 898
Soft Page, 898
    Related Entries, 899
Sort and Select, 899
    Keystrokes, 900
    Options, 902
    Hints, 910
    Applications, 912
    Related Entries, 912

Spacing, 913
    Keystrokes, 913
    Hints, 913
    Related Entries, 914
Special Characters, 915
    Keystrokes, 915
    Hints, 915
    Related Entries, 917
Spell, 917
    Keystrokes, 917
    Options, 920
    Other Options, 923
    Hints, 924
    Applications, 928
    Related Entries, 929
Spell Program, 929
    Keystrokes, 929
    Options, 930
    Hints, 936
    Related Entries, 936
Split the Screen, 937
Spreadsheet Importing and
    Linking, 937
    Keystrokes, 937
    Hints, 943
    Related Entries, 945
Start a New Page, 945
Start WordPerfect, 945
    Keystrokes, 945
    Options, 946
    Hints, 951
    Related Entries, 952
Status Line Display, 952
Stop Printing, 952
    Keystrokes, 953
    Hints, 953
    Related Entries, 954
Strikeout, 954
    Keystrokes, 954
    Hints, 955

    Related Entries, 955
Styles, 956
    Keystrokes, 957
    Hints, 962
    Applications, 968
    Related Entries, 972
Subdocuments, 972
Summary, 972
Superscript and
    Subscript, 973
    Keystrokes, 973
    Hints, 973
    Applications, 973
    Related Entries, 974
Supplementary
    Dictionary, 974
Suppress, 974
    Keystrokes, 975
    Hints, 976
    Related Entries, 977
Switch, 977
    Keystrokes, 977
    Hints, 978
    Related Entries, 978
Tab Align, 979
    Keystrokes, 979
    Hints, 980
    Applications, 980
    Related Entries, 981
Tab Key, 981
    Keystrokes, 981
    Hints, 981
    Related Entries, 983
Table of Authorities, 983
    Keystrokes, 983
    Hints, 989
    Related Entries, 992
Table of Contents, 992
    Keystrokes, 993
    Hints, 996

Related Entries, 998
Table Box, 998
Tables, 998
    Keystrokes, 1000
    Options, 1004
    Hints, 1020
    Applications, 1022
    Related Entries, 1028
Tabs, 1029
    Keystrokes, 1029
    Hints, 1031
    Related Entries, 1033
Target, 1034
Text Boxes, 1034
Text Columns, 1034
Text In/Out, 1034
    Options, 1034
    Related Entries, 1037
Text Screen Type, 1037
    Keystrokes, 1038
    Hints, 1039
    Related Entries, 1039
Thesaurus, 1039
    Keystrokes, 1040
    Hints, 1041
    Related Entries, 1043
Timed Backup, 1043
Totals, 1043
Transparencies, 1043
Tutorial, 1044
    Keystrokes, 1044
    Hints, 1045
Type Through, 1045
Typeover, 1045
    Keystrokes, 1045
    Hints, 1046
    Related Entries, 1046
Undelete, 1046
    Keystrokes, 1046
    Hints, 1047

Related Entries, 1048
Underline, 1048
    Keystrokes, 1048
    Options, 1049
    Hints, 1050
    Related Entries, 1053
Units of Measure, 1053
    Keystrokes, 1054
    Hints, 1055
Unlock a Document, 1056
Uppercase Text, 1056
Vertical Lines, 1056
Very Large Print, 1057
View Document, 1057
    Options, 1057
    Hints, 1058
Widow/Orphan
  Protection, 1059
    Keystrokes, 1060
    Hints, 1060
    Related Entries, 1061
Windows, 1061
    Keystrokes, 1061
    Hints, 1062
    Related Entries, 1063
Word and Letter
  Spacing, 1063
    Keystrokes, 1063
    Hints, 1064
Word Count, 1065
    Keystrokes, 1065
    Hints, 1065
    Related Entries, 1065
Wordperfect Files, 1066
Wordperfect Startup
  Options, 1066
Word Search, 1066
Word Spacing Justification
  Limits, 1066
    Keystrokes, 1066

Hints, 1067
Related Entries, 1067
WordStar, 1067
"WP Disk Full" Error
  Message, 1068

Reasons, 1068
Solutions, 1069
Related Entries, 1069

F O U R   **Desktop Publishing with WordPerfect 1071**

Types of Documents, 1071
Desktop Publishing
  Terms, 1072
    Fonts, 1073
    Word and Letter
      Spacing, 1074
    Kerning, 1075
    Leading or Line
      Height, 1076
    Rules or Graphics
      Lines, 1077
    Graphics Boxes, 1079
    Shading or
      Screens, 1080

    Bullets, 1080
    Em and En
      Dashes, 1081
    Styles or Tags, 1081
    Cross-References, 1082
Method for Creating a
  Document, 1082
Sample Documents, 1083
    Newsletters, 1084
    Announcement, 1094
    Brochures, 1097
    Letterhead, 1097
    Overheads and
      Transparencies, 1097

F I V E   **Printer Program 1103**

Introduction, 1104
Files That Can Be Edited
  with the Printer
  Program, 1105
Starting the Printer
  Program, 1106
    Hard Disk, 1106
    Two Disk Drives, 1108
    Printer Files from Older
      Versions, 1108
Function Keys and
  Help, 1109
    Exiting the Printer
      Program, 1110
    Help, 1110

Organization of the Printer
  Program, 1111
Uses for the Printer
  Program, 1113
    Automatic Font
      Changes and
      Substitute
      Fonts, 1113
    Character Map, 1118
    Kerning and
      Proportional Spacing
      Tables, 1118
    Copying Fonts from
      One File to
      Another, 1122

Entering Codes, 1125
Startup Options, 1126
  /MONO, 1127

/UPDATE, 1127
/UNITS = *n*, 1127
/CP = *n*, 1127

S I X   **Advanced Macro and Merge Commands 1129**

Differences Between Macros
  and Merges, 1129
    Accessing Macro
      Commands, 1130
    Accessing Merge
      Commands, 1133
Variables, 1135
    Inserting a Variable in a
      Macro or
      Merge, 1136
Expressions, 1137
    Operators, 1138
    A Final Word of
      Caution, 1142
A Description of Each
  Macro and Merge
  Command, 1143
    Document a Macro or
      Merge, 1143
    Macros for Cursor and
      Block Shortcuts, 1144
    Inserting the Date in a
      Macro or
      Merge, 1146
    Pausing and Prompting
      for Information, 1146
    Storing and Using
      Information in a
      Variable, 1152
    Data Validation, 1155
    Marking a Location or
      Subroutine, 1157

Branching with {IF}
  Commands, 1160
Branching with {CASE}
  Commands, 1165
Looping, 1168
Checking the State of
  WordPerfect, 1176
Using "System"
  Information, 1177
Chaining, Nesting, and
  Substituting, 1180
Displaying a Macro or
  Merge, 1195
Stopping, Quitting,
  Breaking, and
  Restarting, 1197
Error Checking, 1199
Debugging
  Commands, 1202
Converting Keys,
  Characters, and
  Numbers, 1203
Fields and
  Records, 1211
Miscellaneous Merge
  Commands, 1212
Appearance of Macro
  Prompts, 1215
Positioning Macros on the
  Screen, 1217

APPENDIX A   WordPerfect Character Sets 1219

WordPerfect ASCII
  Set, 1219
Multinational 1, 1220
Multinational 2, 1220
Box Drawing, 1220
Typographic Symbols, 1221
Iconic Symbols, 1221
Math/Scientific, 1221

Math/Scientific
  Extension, 1222
Greek, 1223
Hebrew, 1223
Cyrillic, 1223
Japanese, 1224
User-Defined, 1224

APPENDIX B   WordPerfect Files 1225

Files on Master Disks, 1225
  Program 1/2, 1225
  Spell/Thesaurus, 1226
  PTR Program
    /Graphics, 1226
  Install/Learn
    /Utilities, 1227
Files Installed to Hard
  Drive, 1229
  WP Program Files, 1229
  Graphics Drivers, 1229,
    1230
  Help Files, 1230
  Utility Files, 1230
  Graphics Images, 1230
  Learn and
    Tutorial, 1231
  Keyboard/Macro
    Files, 1232

Dictionary
  /Thesaurus, 1232
Style Files, 1232
Printer Files and PTR
  Program, 1233
Files Installed to 720K
  Floppy Disks, 1233
  WordPerfect 1, 1233
  WordPerfect 2, 1233
  Speller, 1234
  Thesaurus, 1234
  Install/Utilities, 1234
  Macros/Keyboards, 1234
  Font/Graphics, 1235
  Learning/Images, 1235
  Printer (.ALL)
    Files, 1236
  PTR Program, 1236
Other Files, 1236

APPENDIX C   Differences Between Version 5.0 and 5.1 1239

Interface Changes, 1239
  The Template, 1240
  Prompts, 1240
  Pull-Down Menus, 1240
  Mouse Support, 1241

Entering
  Measurements, 1241
New Features, 1242
  Tables, 1242

Spreadsheet
   Support, 1243
Equation Editor, 1244
Special Characters, 1244
Labels and Paper
   Size/Type, 1244
Merge, 1245
Descriptive
   Filenames, 1246
Text Drivers, 1246
Enhanced Features, 1246
Install, 1246
Dictionary-Based
   Hyphenation, 1247

Context-Sensitive
   Help, 1247
Outlining, 1247
Relative Tabs, 1248
Dormant Hard
   Return, 1248
Justification, 1248
Graphics, 1249
Page Numbers, 1249
Keyboard Layout, 1249
Printing Changes, 1250
Shell Support, 1250

APPENDIX D   **Differences Between 4.2 and 5.1** **1251**

Function Key
   Changes, 1252
Menus and Messages, 1254
Units of Measurement, 1254
Selecting Printers, 1256
Fonts, 1257
Types of Paper, 1258
Setup and Initial
   Settings, 1259

Styles, 1260
Special Characters, 1260
Macro Changes, 1261
   Converting 4.2
      Macros, 1262
Converting Files
   from 4.2, 1262
Conclusion, 1263

APPENDIX E   **Graphics Images** **1265**

APPENDIX F   **Conversion Tables** **1269**

Transferring Files, 1288

APPENDIX G   **The Latest Enhancements** **1289**

Border Options, 1289
Characters, 1291
Equations, 1291
Expanded Memory, 1292

Graphics, 1292
Keyboard, 1293
List Files, 1293
Merge, 1293

Mouse, 1293
Printing, 1294
Sort, 1294
Spell, 1294
Spreadsheet, 1294

Tabs, 1295
Text In/Out, 1295
Text Screen Type, 1295
Two Disk Drives, 1296

Index 1301

One morning in August 1983, Dan Lunt, WordPerfect's vice-president of marketing, and I were feeling sorry for ourselves because we wanted to hire a certain person away from IBM and knew we couldn't afford her (WordPerfect was then a small company of about 30 employees). As I stepped out of Dan's office, I saw a young woman waiting in the lobby. After talking with her long enough to find out that she was a secretary at Brigham Young University and was helping professors learn Word-Perfect (not many people knew the program well at the time), I ushered her into Dan's office and we offered her a job on the spot.

We never regretted the decision. Karen started as our third customer support employee, and because of her enthusiasm for and knowledge of all WordPerfect products, she quickly became the designated demonstrator and trainer for large and important accounts. When she wasn't traveling, she worked in almost every department of the company. When motherhood nudged her into semi-retirement, she helped the publications department write product documentation and then accepted a position as manager of the customer support department. We reluctantly accepted her resignation when she left to have a second child. Although she is no longer an "official" employee, Karen continues to be heavily involved with the company.

Karen probably knows WordPerfect better than anyone else (except me) and has an almost fanatical devotion to the product. I heartily recommend her book to anyone who wants to learn more about Word-Perfect.

W.E. Peterson
Executive Vice President
WordPerfect Corporation

There are two things that make up a great deal of my life: my family and WordPerfect. There sometimes seems to be very little difference between the two because WordPerfect is very much my family. I would also not be able to be as involved with WordPerfect without the support of my family.

My parents, Richard and Mary Jane Cozzens, deserve the highest praise for making sure I was always motivated in the right direction. My husband, Jeff, has always been there with much encouragement and pride. And while my children, Mark, Kimberly, and Lisa, have grown to hate the word "deadline," they each have helped in their own special way.

This book is more accurate and understandable because of my friend, confidant, editor, and sister, Jennifer Nelson. She's amazing and I appreciate all the help she's given me, not only with this book, but with any crazy project that I might be involved in.

The people who work at WordPerfect are also a large part of my family. They have taught and helped me through the years and I am grateful for their support. There are too many to mention, but they know who they are. I would especially like to thank the brilliant developers, dedicated testers, and hard-working support personnel who have made WordPerfect what it is today.

As far as putting the book together, the team at Osborne/McGraw-Hill made an impossible task almost enjoyable. Their dedication and attention to detail is greatly appreciated. I would especially like to thank Roger Stewart for making sure I knew what I was doing, Laurie Beaulieu for her patience and friendship, and Kathy Krause for making sure it looked great.

ACKNOWLEDGMENTS

xxxiii

WordPerfect is the undisputed leader in word processing, not only in the United States but around the world. It has almost every feature imaginable but is still easy to use for those who are just learning word processing.

WordPerfect is for those who want to create simple letters and memos. It is also for those who want graphics, tables, equations, and other desktop publishing features. In other words, the program is designed to satisfy users of all levels—you don't have to learn the more advanced features until you're ready for them.

About This Book

This book is for all WordPerfect users, those who are making a transition from a previous version of WordPerfect, a typewriter, or another word processor, as well as those who have used the program for many years. It is a comprehensive reference that teaches the basics and provides the most up-to-date information available on 5.1, the latest version of WordPerfect.

This book is designed in much the same way as the WordPerfect program itself. You can learn the individual features as you need them and see how they relate to other features. The book describes the installation process, teaches you the basics, then provides the more advanced features as you need them.

How This Book Is Organized

WordPerfect 5.1: The Complete Reference is composed of two introductory chapters, encyclopedic command and feature reference, and further chapters with more detailed information for advanced WordPerfect users. Here is a quick summary of each chapter and appendix.

Chapter 1, "Installation and Setup" shows you how to install Word-Perfect if you have not already done so. Even if WordPerfect is already installed, you may want to read this chapter so you can see the many options for customizing WordPerfect to fit your needs.

Chapter 2, "WordPerfect Basics," shows new users how to begin using WordPerfect and also serves as a refresher for those who are more experienced. It leads you through the steps of creating, editing, formatting, printing, and filing a document and checking for correct spelling. Also included is a section that addresses some of the questions new users often have.

Chapter 3, "Commands and Features," is a comprehensive reference that provides information for every key, feature, and command in Word-Perfect. Each entry includes a description of the feature, the keystrokes required, hints, suggested applications, and related entries for the feature.

Chapter 4, "Desktop Publishing with WordPerfect," discusses several desktop publishing features and explains how they can be used in WordPerfect. The examples will give you ideas on how to use graphics boxes, graphics lines, kerning, and other features to your advantage.

Chapter 5, "Printer Program," introduces you to the Printer (PTR) program that can be used to create or change printer definitions and fonts.

Chapter 6, "Advanced Macro and Merge Commands," teaches you how to use the more advanced commands available in macros and merges. These commands can be used to create customized applications and to streamline repetitious tasks.

Appendix A, "WordPerfect Character Sets," presents all the characters that can be printed in WordPerfect.

Appendix B, "WordPerfect Files," gives a description of the files included with WordPerfect and the "group" with which they are installed.

Appendix C, "Differences Between 5.0 and 5.1," describes the new features that have been included with version 5.1.

Appendix D, "Differences Between 4.2 and 5.1," helps ease the transition for those upgrading from version 4.2.

Appendix E, "Graphics Images," includes a printout of each of the 30 clip-art graphics images included with WordPerfect.

Appendix F, "Conversion Tables," compares the terms used in WordStar, MultiMate, Microsoft Word, and DisplayWrite to those used in WordPerfect. A glance at the tables found in this appendix will help you see the differences in concepts and language between popular word processing programs.

Appendix G, "Latest Enhancements," gives you a list of enhancements that have been included in the latest "interim release" of version 5.1 that may not appear in the WordPerfect documentation or the main text of this book.

Conventions Used in This Book

All function keys and other keys on the keyboard (such as ENTER, TAB, BACKSPACE, HOME, and DEL) are printed in small caps. If you see two keys with a dash between them, as in Format (SHIFT-F8), you should hold down the first key and lightly touch the second. If you see two keys with a comma separating them, you should press the keys one after the other — not simultaneously.

Whenever you see a menu of choices, WordPerfect lets you select either a number or a mnemonic choice. For example, you could choose **7** or **M** for Margins on the Line Format menu. This book shows both of these choices in bold so you can use the one that is easiest for you. You will also see the mnemonic choice in a black box on all screens in the book.

If you are using a mouse or prefer pull-down menus, you will want to refer to the entry in Chapter 3 titled "Mouse Support and Pull-Down Menus." This section will help you feel more comfortable with this alternate interface.

These and other conventions have been summarized in this table:

Instruction	Procedure
Type **Sincerely,**	Type the boldfaced text (upper- or lowercase is acceptable)
Enter **WP**	When the word "Enter" precedes an instruction, type the boldfaced text and press ENTER. (If the computer does not act on a command, it is probably waiting for you to press the ENTER key. You may type upper- or lowercase letters.)
Press Bold (F6)	Press the F6 function key (not F and then 6 on the regular keyboard)
Press Center (SHIFT-F6)	Hold down the SHIFT key and press the F6 function key. Keys that should be pressed at the same time are connected by a dash
HOME,↑	Press the HOME key, then the up arrow key. Keys that should be pressed in succession (not simultaneously) are separated by commas

Maintenance Releases

WordPerfect Corporation releases "interim releases" every two or three months to fix problems or add smaller features. You can find information about the features that have been added in Appendix G, "Latest Enhancements."

As of this printing, there was only one interim release since version 5.1 was first released on November 6, 1989. This interim release is dated 1/19/90. If you have a question as to which version you have, press Help (F3) and look in the upper-right corner.

The latest version of the software is available from WordPerfect Corporation for approximately $15-$25, depending on the number of disks needed. You can contact WordPerfect Corporation at (801) 225-5000 and ask about their Software Subscription Service, which ships the latest version of the software to you within a week after it has been released.

Additional Help from Osborne/McGraw-Hill

Osborne/McGraw-Hill provides top-quality books for computer users at every level of computing experience. To help you build your skills, we suggest that you look for the books in the following Osborne series that best address your needs.

The "Teach Yourself" Series is perfect for people who have never used a computer before or who want to gain confidence in using program basics. These books provide a simple, slow-paced introduction to the fundamental uses of popular software packages and programming languages. The "Mastery Skills Check" format ensures your understanding concepts thoroughly before you progress to new material. Plenty of examples and exercises (with answers at the back of the book) are used throughout the text.

The "Made Easy" Series is also for beginners or users who may need a refresher on the new features of an upgraded product. These in-depth introductions guide users step-by-step from the program basics to intermediate-level usage. Plenty of "hands-on" exercises and examples are used in every chapter.

The "Using" Series presents fast-paced guides that cover beginning concepts quickly and move on to intermediate-level techniques and some advanced topics. These books are written for users already familiar with computers and software who want to get up to speed fast with a certain product.

The "Advanced" Series assumes that the reader is a user who has reached at least an intermediate skill level and is ready to learn more sophisticated techniques and refinements.

"The Complete Reference" Series provides handy desktop references for popular software and programming languages that list every command, feature, and function of the product along with brief but detailed descriptions of how they are used. Books are fully indexed and often include tear-out command cards. "The Complete Reference" series is ideal for both beginners and pros.

"The Pocket Reference" Series is a pocket-sized, shorter version of "The Complete Reference" series. It provides the essential commands, features, and functions of software and programming languages for users of every level who need a quick reminder.

The "Secrets, Solutions, Shortcuts" Series is written for beginning users who are already somewhat familiar with the software and for experienced users at intermediate and advanced levels. This series provides clever tips, points out shortcuts for using the software to greater advantage, and indicates traps to avoid.

Osborne/McGraw-Hill also publishes many fine books that are not included in the series described here. If you have questions about which Osborne books are right for you, ask the salesperson at your local book or computer store, or call us toll-free at 1-800-262-4729.

Other Osborne/McGraw-Hill
Books of Interest to You

We hope that *WordPerfect 5.1: The Complete Reference* will assist you in mastering this fine product, and will also pique your interest in learning about other ways to better use your computer.

If you're interested in expanding your skills so you can be even more "computer efficient," be sure to take advantage of Osborne/M-H's large selection of top-quality computer books that cover all varieties of popular hardware, software, programming languages, and operating systems. While we cannot list every title here that may relate to Word-Perfect and to your special computing needs, here are just a few books that complement *WordPerfect 5.1: The Complete Reference.*

1-2-3 Release 2.2 Made Easy, by Mary Campbell, takes you through all the basics of working with Lotus 1-2-3 Releases 2.0, 2.01, and 2.2, the popular spreadsheets for the IBM PC and compatible computers. From beginning concepts to intermediate techniques, you'll learn 1-2-3 as you follow "hands-on" lessons filled with examples and exercises. Also see *1-2-3 Release 3 Made Easy* if you have Lotus 1-2-3 Release 3.0.

1-2-3: From 2 to 3, by The LeBlond Group, helps current users of 1-2-3 Releases 2.0, 2.01, or 2.2 make the jump to Release 3.0. Organized by task, this book allows you to quickly locate the information you need to use Release 3's commands, features, and functions in business applications.

If you're looking for intermediate-level books on Lotus 1-2-3, see *Using 1-2-3 Release 2.2,* by The LeBlond Group, or *Using 1-2-3 Release 3,* by Martin S. Matthews and Carole Boggs Matthews. Both are fast-paced, hands-on guides that quickly cover basics before discussing intermediate techniques and even some advanced topics. *Using 1-2-3 Release 2.2,* is a book/disk package that also features an add-in word processor to use with Lotus 1-2-3. It is written by Geoff LeBlond, author of an outstanding book on using 1-2-3 that has sold over one million copies.

For all PC-DOS and MS-DOS users from beginners who are somewhat familiar with the program to veteran users, *DOS: The Complete Reference, Second Edition,* by Kris Jamsa covers any DOS version up to 3.3. This book provides comprehensive coverage of every DOS command and feature. Whether you need an overview of the disk operating system or a reference for advanced programming and disk management techniques, you'll find it here.

Disk Offer

All the macros, files, and tables mentioned in this book are available on disk for $15. This disk also includes many macros and examples not included in the book. You can order the disk by calling this toll-free number:

1-800-937-EASY (3279)

VISA, MasterCard, American Express, and C.O.D. orders are accepted.

If you prefer to order the disk with a bank check or money order, you can do so by writing to this address:

> "The Complete Reference" Supplementary Disk
> 93 S. Mountainway Drive
> Orem, UT 84058

You should note which type of disk (5¼" or 3½") you desire and make all checks or money orders payable to Karen L. Acerson.

Osborne/McGraw-Hill assumes no responsibility for this offer. This is solely the offer of Karen L. Acerson and not of Osborne/McGraw-Hill or WordPerfect Corporation. Please allow four to six weeks for delivery.

There are literally dozens of books available on WordPerfect, and it is sometimes difficult to tell which book is best for you.

If you want to know everything from the basics of WordPerfect to the most advanced features in the program, you will need this book. Unlike other books, this book does not refer you to the WordPerfect manual or other sources when more advanced information is needed. In fact, those who work in the Customer Support Department at WordPerfect Corporation refer to this book as "The Bible for WordPerfect." Those who teach WordPerfect have also used the book to help them pass the tests given by WordPerfect Corporation in order to become a Certified Instructor.

Even though the size of this book may be intimidating, the organization of the book makes it easy to find the information you need. You will find the basic information at the beginning of the book while the more advanced information is at the end. All the features from A to Z can be found in the middle section, making it almost unnecessary to look up a feature in the table of contents or index.

Beginners will enjoy the step-by-step approach, while those who are more advanced will appreciate the technical tips and notes that help make them WordPerfect experts.

Learn More About WordPerfect

Here is an excellent selection of other Osborne/McGraw-Hill books on WordPerfect that will help you build your skills and maximize the power of the word processor you have selected.

The benefits of upgrading are revealed in *WordPerfect: From 5.0 to 5.1* by Karen Acerson. All the new features of Release 5.1 are discussed so you'll know exactly which have changed and how to use them.

If you are just beginning WordPerfect 5 and you are unfamiliar with other word processors or even with a computer, see *Teach Yourself WordPerfect 5*, by Mary Campbell, a simple introduction to the essentials of WordPerfect 5 with plenty of hands-on exercises.

If you are a beginning WordPerfect 5.1 user looking for an in-depth guide that leads you from basics to intermediate-level techniques, see *WordPerfect 5.1 Made Easy,* by Mella Mincberg. If you are using WordPerfect 5.0, look for Mincberg's *WordPerfect Made Easy, Series 5 Edition,* or *WordPerfect Made Easy* if you have release 4.2.

For a quick-paced book that covers basics before concentrating on intermediate-level skills and even some advanced topics, see *Using WordPerfect, Series 5 Edition* by Gail Todd. Macintosh users can refer to *Using WordPerfect for the Macintosh* by Daniel Rosenbaum.

WordPerfect: The Complete Reference, Series 5 Edition, by Karen Acerson, serves the same purpose as this volume but for WordPerfect 5.0 users. Acerson's *WordPerfect: The Complete Reference* covers release 4.2.

For a quick reference of only the essential commands, see *WordPerfect 5: The Pocket Reference*, by Mella Mincberg, or *WordPerfect: The Pocket Reference*, also by Mella Mincberg, covering release 4.2.

WordPerfect: Secrets, Solutions, Shortcuts, Series 5 Edition, by Mella Mincberg, is jam-packed with tips, tricks, and hints for beginners or experienced users.

If you're an experienced WordPerfect 5 user looking for books to help you refine your skills, see *Advanced WordPerfect, Series 5 Edition*, by Eric Alderman and Lawrence Magid, which covers macros, mathematical capabilities, integrating WordPerfect with other software, and more. Also see *Getting the Most from WordPerfect 5*, by Ruth Halpern, for creating customized macros, handling desktop publishing, and using other sophisticated features.

Installation and Setup

This chapter gives you information about the system requirements needed to run WordPerfect 5.1, explains how to install WordPerfect, and discusses setup options that can help you customize the WordPerfect program to fit your specific needs. Information about installing and running WordPerfect on a network is also included.

SYSTEM REQUIREMENTS

Disk Space

Although a hard disk is recommended for WordPerfect 5.1, the program will also run on systems with 720K (kilobyte) floppy disk drives. If you have a computer with 3 1/2-inch or high-density 5 1/4-inch disk drives, you will be able to run WordPerfect 5.1.

If you have a hard disk and want to load all the WordPerfect 5.1 disks, you will need approximately 4 MB (4 megabytes) of free disk space. You can save space by not installing the learning files (those used in the on-line tutorial and workbook) or by installing the learning files and deleting them later. Another disk saver is to select only the necessary printer files at installation time. The minimum amount of hard disk space needed is approximately 2.5 MB. For a list of all files, see Appendix B.

The more disk space you have available, the more room you have for your documents. When you are editing a document, WordPerfect uses as much memory as possible for the document. When the computer runs out of memory, WordPerfect uses *virtual files*, which keep pieces of the document on disk and continually swap pieces in and out of memory as you scroll through the document. If you are limited in both memory and disk space, the size of your documents may be limited.

WordPerfect automatically keeps the virtual files where WP.EXE and WP.FIL are located. If you are using a floppy disk system with WordPerfect in drive A, that is where the virtual files will normally be kept. Because of this design, WordPerfect lets you switch data disks in drive B. If you do not plan to switch disks in drive B (for the Speller or the Thesaurus, for example) and you need to edit larger documents, you can redirect the virtual files to drive B and have more disk space available for larger files. To do so, you would type the following to start WordPerfect:

    wp/d-b:

Memory

You will need at least 384K of free memory (a total of at least 512K). If you have a network, you will need at least 640K to load DOS, the network software, and WordPerfect. If you do not have more than 512K, you will also be limited in the number of Terminate-Stay Resident (TSR) programs that can be loaded.

WordPerfect includes a number of mouse drivers built into the program so that you will not have to load an external mouse driver (MOUSE.COM) and use valuable space in memory. See the next section for more information about mouse drivers.

WordPerfect can also use expanded memory and supports both the 3.2 and 4.0 Lotus/Intel/Microsoft (LIM) specifications. If you want to know more about how WordPerfect 5.1 uses expanded memory, see "Expanded Memory" in Chapter 3, "Commands and Features." You may also want to refer to "Options for Starting WordPerfect" at the end of this chapter.

Mice Supported by 5.1

The following mouse drivers are currently supported by WordPerfect and more may be added in subsequent releases. If your mouse is not listed, you can specify that you want to use the MOUSE.COM driver (also shown in the list).

> CH Products Roller Mouse (PS/2)
> CH Products Roller Mouse (Serial)
> IBM PS/2 Mouse
> Imsi Mouse, 2 button (Serial)
> Imsi Mouse, 3 button (Serial)
> Kensington Expert Mouse (PS/2)
> Kensington Expert Mouse (Serial)
> Keytronic Mouse (Bus)
> Keytronic Mouse (Serial)
> Logitech Mouse (Bus)
> Logitech Mouse (Serial)
> Logitech Mouse, 3 button (PS/2)
> Microsoft Mouse (Bus)
> Microsoft Mouse (Serial)
> Mouse Driver (MOUSE.COM)
> Mouse Systems Mouse, 3 button (Serial)
> MSC Technology PC Mouse 2 (Serial)
> Numonics Mouse (Serial)
> PC-Trac Trackball (Serial)

Options for selecting a mouse are discussed later in this chapter.

Installing WordPerfect

Please note that you *must* use the Install program that comes with WordPerfect—you cannot just copy the files to a hard disk. All the program files have been compressed into very few files so they can fit on ten floppy disks. As you install WordPerfect, the files are expanded to make them usable. The following list gives the names of the disks:

> Program 1
> *Program 2
> Install/Learn/Utility 1
> *Install/Learn/Utility 2

Spell/Thesaurus 1
*Spell/Thesaurus 2
PTR Program/Graphics 1
*PTR Program/Graphics 2
Printer 1
Printer 2
*Printer 3

*Not shipped with 3½″ disks

Starting the Install Program

The Install program is found on the Install/Learn/Utility 1 disk. Insert the disk into drive A (or B) and type the following:

a: install

If you are using drive B, type **b:install**. If you need to exit the program at any time, you will be returned to the proper menu item or prompt when you restart the program.

The first question asks if you want to continue with the installation. Because the Install program (INSTALL.EXE) is copied along with the other files during installation, this question is included to keep you from entering the WordPerfect installation program if you meant to start the installation process for a different program.

You are then asked if you are installing to a hard disk. If you answer Yes, you will see the menu shown in Figure 1-1, listing the choices for installing, updating, or copying the WordPerfect files. If you answer No, a message tells you that you need ten blank floppy disks and lets you exit the program so you can prepare them. The following list gives the names that WordPerfect tells you to use as labels for the blank disks:

WordPerfect 1
WordPerfect 2
Install/Utilities
Learning/Images
Macros/Keyboards
Speller

Thesaurus
PTR Program
Fonts/Graphics
Printer (.ALL) Files

Appendix B, "WordPerfect Files," lists all of the disks and the files that
are copied to these disks during installation. If you choose to continue,
the Install program displays the menu shown in Figure 1-1.

Although help is not available in the main menu, it is displayed for
each option thereafter. If you need further help during the process, you
can call WordPerfect's toll-free installation support line at (800) 533-
9605.

Basic

If you are new to computers, you may want to choose this first option.
The program assumes that you want all program files copied from drive

```
Installation

    1 - Basic         Perform a standard installation to C:\WP51.

    2 - Custom        Perform a customized installation.  (User selected
                      directories.)

    3 - Network       Perform a customized installation onto a network.
                      (To be performed by the network supervisor.)

    4 - Printer       Install updated Printer (.ALL) File.

    5 - Update        Install updated program file(s).

    6 - Copy Disks    Install every file from an installation diskette to a
                      specified location.  (Useful for installing all the
                      Printer (.ALL) Files.)




Selection: 2
```

Figure 1-1.   The Install program's main menu

A (or B) into a directory on your hard disk called C:\WP51. If that directory does not exist, Install creates it for you. If you are installing WordPerfect on floppy disks, Install automatically copies the disks from drive A to B (or vice versa if you started Install from drive B).

As soon as all the disks have been copied, Install checks your CONFIG.SYS and AUTOEXEC.BAT files to see that they include the proper commands (FILES = 20 in the CONFIG.SYS file and PATH = C:\WP51 in the AUTOEXEC.BAT file). If you modify these files, you will be prompted to reboot your system so the new changes will be in effect when the Install program starts WordPerfect and selects your printer. After rebooting, enter the Install program again (type **a:install**), and it will return you to the place at which you rebooted.

As the last step of the installation process, you are prompted to select a printer. After you insert the Printer disk, a list similar to the one shown in Figure 1-2 will appear. You can choose the Name Search option and type the name of your printer, press PGDN to see more printer selections, or use the arrow keys to move through the list. When you see your printer among the list, select it by entering the number next to the

```
  1  Acer LP-76                         Printers marked with '*' are
  2  AEG Olympia Compact RO             not included with shipping
  3  AEG Olympia ESW 2000               disks. Select printer for
  4  AEG Olympia Laserstar 6            more information.
  5  AEG Olympia Startype
  6  Alphacom Alphapro 101
  7  Alps Allegro 24
  8 *Alps Allegro 24 (Additional)
  9  Alps ALQ200 (18 pin)
 10  Alps ALQ200 (24 pin)
 11  Alps ALQ224e
 12 *Alps ALQ224e (Additional)
 13  Alps ALQ300 (18 pin)
 14  Alps ALQ300 (24 pin)
 15  Alps ALQ324e
 16 *Alps ALQ324e (Additional)
 17  Alps P2000
 18 *Alps P2000 (Additional)
 19  Alps P2100
 20 *Alps P2100 (Additional)
 21  Alps P2400C
 22  Amstrad DMP 4000

N Name Search; PgDn More Printers; PgUp Previous Screen; F3 Help; F7 Exit;
Selection: 0
```

Figure 1-2.   A sample list of printer selections

printer's name. If you do not see your printer on the list, call (801) 225-5000 for alternate printer definitions that you can use or to see if one has been defined since the initial release of version 5.1. You can also write to SoftCopy, Inc., c/o Printer Drivers, 81 N. State Street, Orem, UT 84057.

After you select a printer from the list, Install copies the appropriate printer file (a file with the extension .ALL that contains several printer definitions) to the specified location. You are then asked if you want to select more printers (up to three with the Install program). If you do, the Install program keeps track of the .ALL files that have already been copied so that if the additional printer selections are found in the same printer file, it will save time by not copying them again. Read "Using a 5.0 Printer Definition" later in this chapter if you decide to use a printer driver that you used with version 5.0 (not suggested).

After you have selected all printers, Install starts WordPerfect. You are asked if you want to enter your license number so that it will be displayed when you press Help (F3). Then the printer definitions from the printer file are selected, the help screens about the printers are displayed, and you exit WordPerfect and the Install program.

Custom

If you are familiar with your computer, you may want to choose this option. In addition to letting you select your own directories (for example, if you want to copy the WordPerfect program files to a directory other than C:\WP51), this option also lets you choose whether you want the Install program to check and modify your CONFIG.SYS and AUTO-EXEC.BAT files. Figure 1-3 displays the menu that appears if you choose to do a custom installation.

If you choose the Install Files To option, you will see the screen that is shown in Figure 1-4. If you change the directory for the first item, WordPerfect Program, the directory for all other options also changes. You can then select each option and enter a different directory. The directories specified will also be copied to the Location of Files menu inside WordPerfect as part of the installation process.

The Install Disks option on the Custom Installation menu does the actual copying and decompressing. When this option has finished, you

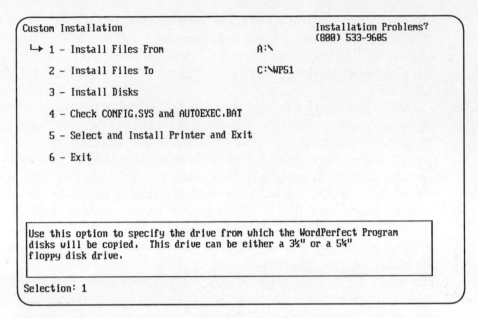

Figure 1-3.   Custom Installation menu

can have the Install program check the CONFIG.SYS and AUTOEX-EC.BAT files for necessary commands (FILES=20 in the CON-FIG.SYS file and PATH=C:\WP51 in the AUTOEXEC.BAT file). The Install program will inform you if the commands do not exist or if the FILES= command is set too low and then offer to modify the files for you. If changes are necessary, you will be prompted to reboot. After rebooting, start the Install program again (type **a:install**), and Word-Perfect will return you to the place from which you rebooted.

If you prefer to use a printer driver (.PRS file) that you have been using with version 5.0 (not suggested), skip the Select and Install Printer option, and choose Exit instead. If you want to select the new printer driver shipped with version 5.1, choose the Select and Install Printer option, and follow the process as described for the Basic Installation option. Converting a 5.0 printer driver for use with 5.1 is explained later in this chapter under "Using a 5.0 Printer Definition."

The first time you start WordPerfect (whether as part of Install or not), you are asked if you want to enter your license number so that it

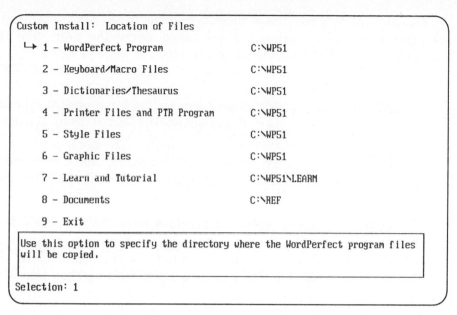

Figure 1-4.   The menu for specifying the location of files

will be displayed when you press Help (F3). This will make it convenient to locate your license number when you are updating your software or ordering interim releases.

Network

If you want to run WordPerfect in a network environment, you no longer need to purchase a separate network version. The information necessary for running WordPerfect on a network is included in the regular WordPerfect package. You do, however, need to purchase a license from WordPerfect Corporation for each additional station. Each license comes with a keyboard template and full documentation. The suggested retail price for each additional station is $295.

To install WordPerfect on a network, choose option 3 from the main menu. The resulting menu is exactly like the Custom menu but with one exception: It includes an option that checks for or creates an environment (WP{WP}. ENV) file. If it does not exist, Install can create it for you. You are then prompted for the information that will be included in this file. The first menu asks which type of network software is installed. After selecting an option, you are asked where the setup files (files ending with .SET) for all users on the network will be located.

Two lines of information are then stored in the WP{WP}.ENV file:

/NT=n	NT means "network," and n represents the number of the network selected from the list of networks.
/PS=dir	PS means "place for setup," and dir represents the directory where the .SET files will be stored.

As WordPerfect is started, it checks for the WP{WP}.ENV file. If that file is found, WordPerfect assumes that you are running under a network and asks for a *username* of up to three characters. These three characters are used to create a .SET file specifically for that user so that each person on the network can select his or her own setup options (screen colors, mouse driver, initial codes, cursor speed, and so on).

The user's setup file is named WP{*xxx*}.SET, where *xxx* represents the three characters that were entered as the username. If fewer than three characters were entered, an underline character is used instead. On a stand-alone, single-user system, the SET file is named WP{WP}. SET.

If a network version has been selected, a few additional prompts and menu options will appear that are applicable only in a network environment. You will also be able to print on printers attached to the network.

If the network software is not running, a message will notify you, but WordPerfect will start anyway. You can run WordPerfect as a stand-alone version by entering **wp/sa** to start WordPerfect.

Printer

If you receive updated printer disks from WordPerfect Corporation to fix problems or provide new features for your printer driver, you will want to update the appropriate printer file (the file with the .ALL extension). The Printer option lets you copy the file into the directory that was specified for printer files at the time of the original installation.

Update

WordPerfect Corporation updates the WordPerfect program with minor enhancements and bug fixes every few months. If you receive one of these interim releases, you can use this option to update the Word-Perfect program files as well as the Spell/Thesaurus disks, the PTR Program/Graphics disks, or any other program disk.

Copy

If you prefer to copy all files from an installation disk to a specified location (hard or floppy disk), use this option. Because a DOS COPY command will copy the files in their compressed and unusable form, you will need to use this option instead so they can be expanded at the same time. This option is especially useful to a network supervisor who needs to copy all the files from all the floppy disks.

Notes About Install

When you install WordPerfect, a file named WP51.INS is created and placed in the directory where the WordPerfect program files are kept. The file is used to store information about such options as Location of Files. This information is then used during subsequent installations so that WordPerfect will know where to copy updated files. It is also used to keep track of the point at which you left the Install program so that you can return there when Install is restarted.

Using a 5.0 Printer Definition

If you have created a customized printer driver (.PRS file) in Word-Perfect 5.0, you may not want to repeat the process again for version

5.1. If you have made only minor changes to the .PRS file, you may want to use the new printer definition included with 5.1 to take advantage of the new features.

If you plan to use a 5.0 printer definition, you will first need to convert it to 5.1 format with the PTR program. Before doing so, make sure that you have copied the PTR program from the PTR Program/Graphics disk during installation. If you have not done so, start the Install program, choose option 2 for Custom, type 3 for Install Disks, and follow the prompts displayed on the screen. When you are finished, follow these steps below:

1. Go to the directory in which the PTR program is located (which is C:\ WP51, unless you specified a different directory during installation) and type **ptr** to start the program.

2. Press Retrieve (SHIFT-F10) and enter the full pathname of the .PRS file. For example, **c:\wp50\custom.prs** would retrieve the file CUSTOM.PRS from the WP50 directory. You will see the following message along with other warnings about converting the file:

Printer file is an old version--Convert to new format? (Y/N)

3. Type **Y** to convert the file to 5.1 format.

4. Press Exit (F7) and type **Y** to save the new printer file. When the printer filename is displayed, you can enter a new pathname (for example, change \WP50\CUSTOM.PRS to \WP51\CUSTOM.PRS) so that WordPerfect will find the printer definition in the \WP51 directory. If you do not enter a new pathname, you should tell WordPerfect where to find the printer file by entering the directory in the Location of Files menu in Setup (SHIFT-F1).

Copying Fonts

If your 5.0 printer driver contains customized fonts that were created with third-party software such as that from Bitstream or Glyphix, that information will be converted to 5.1 format if you follow the steps just given. However, if you want the latest printer definition included with version 5.1 and do not want to re-create the fonts, you can copy those fonts to the new definition with the Printer (PTR) program (see Chapter 5, "Printer Program," for more information).

Selecting Fonts

If you have elected not to use a printer definition from 5.0, you will want to select additional fonts, cartridges, or print wheels that you may have purchased for your printer. To do so, you will need to start Word-Perfect. If WordPerfect will not start, see "Options for Starting WordPerfect" at the end of this chapter.

1. Press Print (SHIFT-F7) and then choose **S** for Select a Printer.

2. With the cursor on the appropriate printer selection, choose **3** for **E**dit.

3. Choose **4** for **C**artridges and Fonts.

4. Choose **2** to Change the **Q**uantity if necessary (for example, if you have added more memory to your printer).

5. Move the cursor to the appropriate font category (Cartridges, Soft Fonts, Print Wheels, and so on) and press ENTER to select fonts from that category. You may have to enter other levels, because some categories have the fonts divided into even more categories (such as different groups of soft fonts).

6. Mark each font with an asterisk (*) if it will be present when the print job begins, or use a plus sign (+) if you want the font to be loaded or unloaded during a print job. Some categories (such as Cartridges) will not display the + option, because you cannot load or unload the fonts (cartridges) during printing.

7. When you are finished selecting all available fonts, press Exit (F7). The message "Updating fonts" is displayed while WordPerfect stores information about each font. This information is used to determine which fonts will be used for automatic font changes (fine, small, large, very large, extra large, italics, and so on).

8. Press Exit (F7) three times until you reach the main editing screen.

See "Automatic Font Changes" in Chapter 3, "Commands and Features." for more information about controlling the size of fonts that are selected for automatic font changes.

Setup Options

You can change more than 50 options in the Setup menu. In fact, almost every feature in WordPerfect has some type of "default" that you can change to suit your preferences. For example, by default all margins are set to 1 inch, the filename is displayed on the status line, and graphics are set to print in medium quality. If you want to change any of these settings, you can do so in the Setup menu and have the settings saved in the WP{WP}.SET file (or WPxxx.SET, where xxx represents the user-name for those running on a network).

To enter the Setup menu, press Setup (SHIFT-F1). The options have been categorized into sections, as shown in Figure 1-5. Every option is explained under "Setup" in Chapter 3. The following sections in this chapter cover a few settings that you might want to be aware of.

Selecting a Mouse

If you have a mouse, WordPerfect assumes that you will be using the MOUSE.COM driver supplied with the mouse. If you would prefer to use an internal driver supplied in WordPerfect (and save the memory otherwise taken by MOUSE.COM), press Setup (SHIFT-F1) and choose 1 for Mouse. The only option you will probably want to change (at least until you start using the mouse) is the first one, Type. If you do not see your mouse on the list (supported mice are listed at the beginning of this chapter), leave MOUSE.COM as the selection. Press Exit (F7) until you return to the document.

```
Setup
       1 - Mouse

       2 - Display

       3 - Environment

       4 - Initial Settings

       5 - Keyboard Layout

       6 - Location of Files








Selection: 0
```

Figure 1-5.   Setup menu options

Pull-Down Menus

If you do not have a mouse, you can press ALT-= to display the menu bar
and the pull-down menus. Another option in the Setup menu lets you
choose to press ALT by itself (instead of pressing ALT-=). To select this
option, press Setup (SHIFT-F1), choose **2** for **Display**, **4** for **Menu Options**, **4**
for **Alt Key Selects Pull-Down Menu**, and then type **Y**.

While you are in a document, you can press and then release the ALT
key to display the menu bar across the top of the screen. The only
drawback is that it is easier to bring up the menu bar by mistake. For
example, if you decide to block a section of text, hold down ALT, and then
change your mind before pressing the F4 function key, letting up the ALT
key will bring up the menu bar. This is easily corrected, however, by
immediately pressing ALT again to remove the menu bar from the screen
(it works as a toggle switch).

Other options associated with the menu bar and the pull-down
menus are also included in this menu. You can change the colors for the
regular text as well as the mnemonic letter selection, choose to have the
menu bar displayed at all times, and include a line to separate the menu
bar from the document.

When you are finished, continue to press Exit (F7) until you return to the document.

Colors/Fonts/Attributes

If you have a color monitor and want to change the colors, press Setup (SHIFT-F1), choose **2** for **D**isplay, **1** for **C**olors/Fonts/Attributes, and then **1** for **S**creen Colors. If you have an EGA or VGA monitor, you can also choose to display *one* of the following: underlining, italics, small caps, or 512 characters (instead of the normal 256). If you choose one of these options, note that you are limited to 8 colors instead of the original 16. The option for using 512 characters is especially useful if you type technical documents that contain many special characters.

Backup

WordPerfect 5.1 is set to save your documents to a backup file every 30 minutes. If you want to change the frequency between backups, press Setup (SHIFT-F1) and choose **3** for **E**nvironment, **1** for **B**ackup, and then **1** for **T**imed Backup. Enter the number of minutes between each backup, and press Exit (F7) until you return to the document.

The directory in which the backup files will be kept is displayed in this menu, but it can only be changed in the Location of Files menu (also an option) in the Setup menu. This topic is discussed later in this chapter.

The backup files are named WP{WP}.BK1 or WP{WP}.BK2, depending on whether the document is being edited in Doc 1 or Doc 2. If you have two documents in memory at the same time, only the document currently being edited is backed up. You should also know that the backup files are deleted if you exit WordPerfect normally; they are only saved in the event of a power failure or if you have to reboot while in WordPerfect. Always be sure to save your document before exiting WordPerfect.

Document Management/Summary

If you deal with a large number of documents and want a better way to organize them, press Setup (SHIFT-F1), and choose option **3** for **E**nvironment, and then **4** for **D**ocument Management/Summary. The options shown in Figure 1-6, combined with the Short/Long Display option and Find option in the List Files menu, will help you identify the contents of documents.

If you want the document summary screen to appear when you first save a document, answer Yes to option 1, Create Summary on Save/Exit. The information entered in a document summary can help you find specific files while you are in the List Files (F5) menu. For example, you could use the information to find all files that were created between certain dates and typed by a specific typist. If you don't want to create a summary when a file is saved, you can press Cancel (F1) to skip the process.

If you answer Yes to the third option, Long Document Names, you will be prompted for a long document name (up to 68 characters) and a document type each time the document is saved. (You will also be required to enter a standard DOS filename, but one is suggested for you.) The descriptive name and document type can be displayed in the List Files (F5) menu by choosing option 5 for Short/Long Display and then 2 for Long Display.

The fourth option on the Document Management/Summary menu lets you specify a default document type (such as Letter or Memo). The

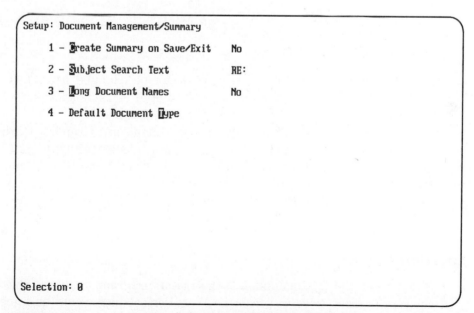

Figure 1-6.   Document Management/Summary options

first three characters of the document type will also be used as the suggested extension for the standard DOS filename (for example, JONES.LET would be the suggested filename if Letter were the document type).

Press Exit (F7) until you return to the document.

Initial Codes

The Initial Codes option lets you insert codes that will affect all documents created from that point forward (such as default margin settings and left justification). To insert these codes, press Setup (SHIFT-F1) and type **4** for Initial Settings and then **5** for Initial Codes. Enter the codes as you normally would in a regular document.

The following are just a few options that you might want to consider changing:

Justification	Left
Widow/Orphan	Yes
Paragraph Number Definition	Choose from paragraph, outline, or legal numbering

Print Options

Any options found on the printer menu can be changed permanently. From the Setup menu, choose option **4** for Initial Settings and then **8** for Print Options. The options shown in Figure 1-7 appear.

Two options that you might want to change are Graphics Quality and Text Quality, depending on whether you prefer printing draft or final copies most of the time. The Number of Copies and Size Attribute Ratios options are new to 5.1 and are explained in detail in Chapter 3, "Commands and Features."

Location of Files

If you chose the Custom option in the Install program, you were able to choose the directories in which the WordPerfect files would be copied.

The names of the directories were also entered in this menu as part of the installation process. If you chose the Basic Installation option, all files (except the learning files) were copied into the C:\WP51 directory.

To change any of these directories (including the directory to be used for backup files and the default directory to be used for saving and retrieving documents), press Setup (SHIFT-F1), choose option **6** for Location of Files from the Setup menu, and enter the directory to be used. If the directory does not yet exist, you will need to create it first. For more information, see "Create a Directory" in Chapter 3.

Using 5.0 Files

Documents created in WordPerfect 5.0 or 5.1 can be retrieved directly into either version without conversion. If a WordPerfect 5.1 document includes codes that cannot be converted to 5.0, such as table or merge

```
Setup: Print Options

    1 - Binding Offset              0"

    2 - Number of Copies            1
        Multiple Copies Generated by   WordPerfect

    3 - Graphics Quality            Medium

    4 - Text Quality                High

    5 - Redline Method              Printer Dependent

    6 - Size Attribute Ratios - Fine   60%
        (% of Normal)        Small    80%
                             Large    120%
                        Very Large    150%
                       Extra Large    200%
                    Super/Subscript    60%




Selection: 0
```

Figure 1-7.   Print Options in the Setup menu

codes, the code will appear as [Unknown] when it is retrieved into WordPerfect 5.0. (To be fully downward-compatible with version 5.0, you may want to obtain the most up-to-date version of 5.0.) The [Unknown] code will be converted to its original function when the document is retrieved into WordPerfect 5.1 again. The Save As option on the Text In/Out (CTRL-F5) menu lets you save a document in 5.0 format and strip out any [Unknown] codes.

Options for Starting WordPerfect

Although you can start WordPerfect by typing **WP** at the DOS prompt, there are 17 other ways to start WordPerfect. All of them are described in detail under "Start WordPerfect" in Chapter 3, but here are a couple of options that may be necessary in order to start WordPerfect:

WP/NC (No Cursor)	Try this option to start WordPerfect if it will not start at all. It disables the Cursor Seed feature (which may have a conflict with a TSR program or hardware). You can try combining this option with /NK (explained next) if WordPerfect still doesn't start.
WP/NK (No Keyboard)	If WordPerfect starts but then locks up at the opening screen, you might try this option. It is used to disable the enhanced keyboard calls that may not be recognized by some compatibles or TSR programs. If you still cannot start Word-Perfect, try combining it with the /NC option (**WP/NK/NC**).
WP/NE (No Enhanced Memory)	If your expanded memory is not fully compatible with WordPerfect, you may need to start Word-Perfect with this option, disabling the expanded memory.

WordPerfect Basics

This chapter teaches you how to use WordPerfect by explaining the word processing concepts used by the program, rather than by teaching you exact keystrokes. If you have used a previous version of Word-Perfect, you may want to continue reading this chapter, or you can turn to Appendix C for a summary of the differences between versions 5.0 and 5.1. If you are just beginning to use WordPerfect, you will also want to check the last section in this chapter for answers to common questions.

After reading this chapter, you can move on to Chapter 3, "Commands and Features," for detailed instructions about using each feature.

Template and Keystrokes

WordPerfect uses a template (a plastic overlay) that fits over the function keys to label its features, as shown in Figure 2-1. Four functions are assigned to each key, and they are printed in black, blue, green, and red. When you want to access a feature printed in black, press the function key by itself. For the functions printed in green, hold down the SHIFT key and press a function key. (The SHIFT keys on your keyboard might be labeled with an arrow pointing upward instead of with the word "SHIFT.") Functions printed in blue require use of the ALT key in addition to the function key, and those printed in red require the CTRL key.

In each case, hold down the SHIFT, ALT, or CTRL key, but press the function key lightly. This light touch is necessary because all the keys (except SHIFT, ALT, and CTRL) are repeating keys. If you see messages or menus flash on and off, you have held a function key down too long. To

LEGEND:

CTRL + function key

SHIFT + FUNCTION KEY

ALT + Function key

Function key alone

Shell	Spell	Screen	Move	Text In/Out	Tab Align	Footnote	Font	Merge/Sort	Macro Define	Reveal Codes	Block
SETUP	←SEARCH	SWITCH	→INDENT←	DATE/OUTLINE	CENTER	PRINT	FORMAT	MERGE CODES	RETRIEVE		
Thesaurus	Replace	Reveal Codes	Block	Mark Text	Flush Right	Columns/Table	Style	Graphics	Macro		
Cancel	Search→	Help	→Indent	List	Bold	Exit	Underline	End Field	Save		

Figure 2-1.   Two types of WordPerfect templates used to label function keys

demonstrate this, hold down the INS key, which is below the numeric keypad. The word "Typeover" will flash on and off in the lower left corner of the screen. Press a function key as you would any other key when typing, and it will turn on or off just once.

Two important keys on the WordPerfect template are Help (F3) and Cancel (F1). Other important, commonly used keys are explained in "Creating Documents" later in this chapter.

Help

When you press Help (F3), you will see the message shown in Figure 2-2, which tells you how to choose from two types of help.

Note: If you chose not to copy the help file during installation, you will see the message "WPHELP.FIL not found." If you installed (copied) the help file to a floppy disk, you are given the opportunity of inserting that disk into a drive and then entering the driver letter. If the help file is located in a different directory on your hard drive, enter the full pathname of that directory.

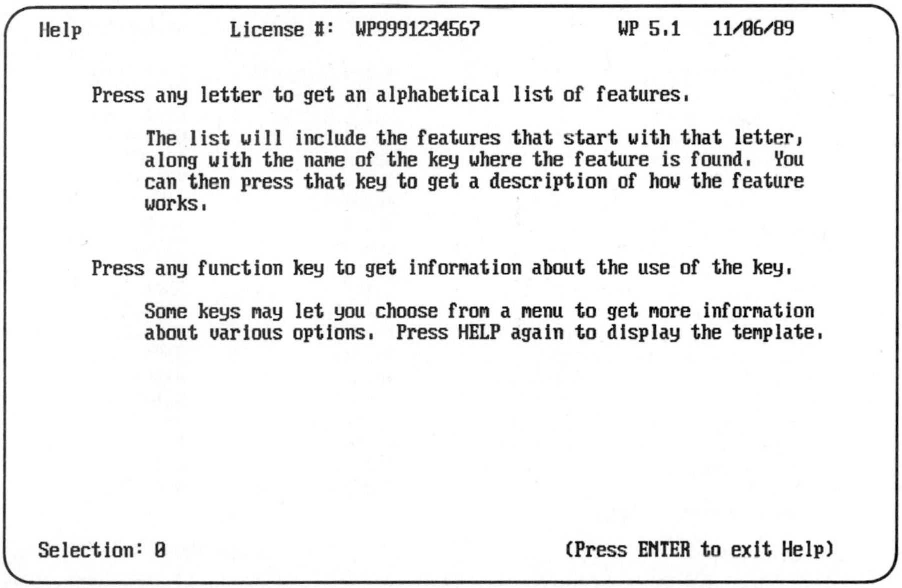

```
Help            License #:  WP9991234567          WP 5.1   11/06/89

     Press any letter to get an alphabetical list of features.

          The list will include the features that start with that letter,
          along with the name of the key where the feature is found.  You
          can then press that key to get a description of how the feature
          works.


     Press any function key to get information about the use of the key.

          Some keys may let you choose from a menu to get more information
          about various options.  Press HELP again to display the template.










     Selection: 0                              (Press ENTER to exit Help)
```

Figure 2-2.   The initial help screen

If you have entered your license number the first time you started WordPerfect (usually during the installation process), that number is displayed at the top of the screen. The date shown in the upper right corner of the screen indicates the date of your WordPerfect program. When you call WordPerfect's support department, you are usually asked for this date to determine if the problem has been fixed and whether or not you need to upgrade the software to a later release.

You can see an alphabetized list of WordPerfect features, along with their corresponding function keys, by typing a letter from "A" to "Z." This is particularly useful, because not all features are listed on the template. If you cannot find a feature listed on the template (such as Margins), press Help (F3) and then type the letter for that feature (**M**, in this case). As shown in Figure 2-3, features beginning with the letter "M" are listed, along with the function key used to invoke each feature and the name that WordPerfect has assigned to that function key.

After pressing Help (F3), you can also press a function key to learn more about that key. You will then see a short description of the

```
┌──────────────────────────────────────────────────────────────────────┐
│  Features [M]                    WordPerfect Key    Keystrokes         │
│                                                                        │
│  Macro Commands                  Macro Commands     Ctrl-PgUp          │
│  Macro Commands, Help On         Macro Definition   Ctrl-F10           │
│  Macro Editor                    Macro Editor       Ctrl-F10           │
│  Macros, Define                  Macro Define       Ctrl-F10           │
│  Macros, Execute                 Macro             Alt-F10            │
│  Macros, Keyboard Definition     Setup              Shft-F1,5          │
│  Mail Merge                      Merge/Sort         Ctrl-F9,1          │
│  Main Dictionary (Location Of)   Setup              Shft-F1,6,3        │
│  Manual Hyphenation              Format             Shft-F8,1,1        │
│  Map, Keyboard                   Setup              Shft-F1,5,8        │
│  Map Special Characters          Setup              Shft-F1,5          │
│  Margin Release                  Shft-Tab           Shft-Tab           │
│  Margins - Left and Right        Format             Shft-F8,1,7        │
│  Margins - Top and Bottom        Format             Shft-F8,2,5        │
│  Mark Text For Index (Block On)  Mark Text          Alt-F5,3           │
│  Mark Text For List (Block On)   Mark Text          Alt-F5,2           │
│  Mark Text For ToA (Block On)    Mark Text          Alt-F5,4           │
│  Mark Text For ToC (Block On)    Mark Text          Alt-F5,1           │
│  Master Document                 Mark Text          Alt-F5,2           │
│  Math                            Columns/Tables     Alt-F7,3           │
│  More... Press m to continue.                                          │
│                                                                        │
│  Selection: 0                          (Press ENTER to exit Help)      │
└──────────────────────────────────────────────────────────────────────┘
```

Figure 2-3.   A list of features beginning with "M" in help screen

feature. You can continue pressing function keys (or letters) and reading the help message for each without ever leaving help. When finished, press ENTER or the space bar.

Cancel

Cancel (F1) is used for two purposes: to cancel a procedure or to restore deleted text. If you are in a menu or if a feature is in progress, such as a search operation or a macro, press Cancel (F1) to leave the menu or cancel the procedure. You may have to press the Cancel key more than once to return to your text. If you see "Macro Def" flashing in the lower left corner of the screen, Cancel will not work; instead, press Macro Def (CTRL-F10) again to turn it off. If you are not in a menu, Cancel will restore any or all of the last three deletions. When you press Cancel (F1) to "undelete" text, the last deletion is shown in reverse video (highlighted) at the cursor and a message appears at the bottom of the screen, as shown in Figure 2-4.

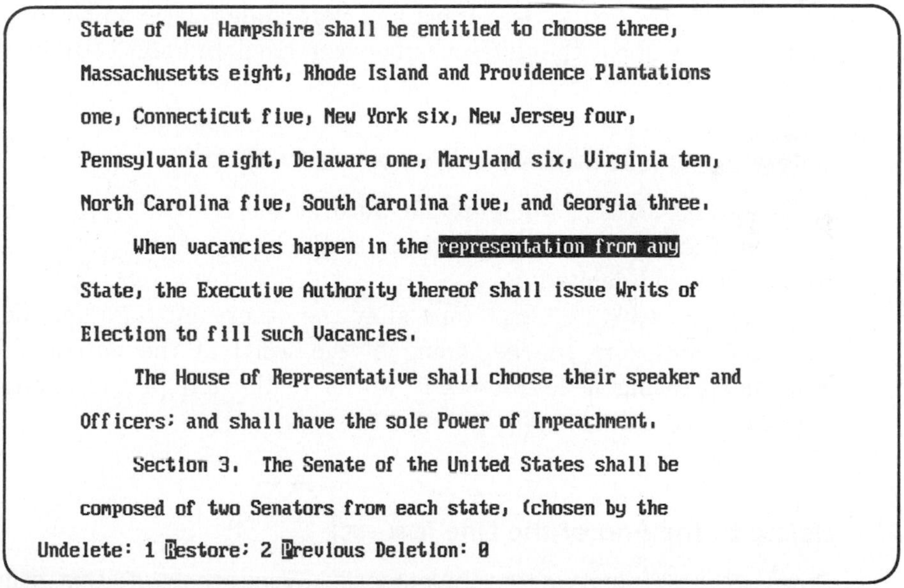

```
State of New Hampshire shall be entitled to choose three,
Massachusetts eight, Rhode Island and Providence Plantations
one, Connecticut five, New York six, New Jersey four,
Pennsylvania eight, Delaware one, Maryland six, Virginia ten,
North Carolina five, South Carolina five, and Georgia three.
    When vacancies happen in the representation from any
State, the Executive Authority thereof shall issue Writs of
Election to fill such Vacancies.
    The House of Representative shall choose their speaker and
Officers; and shall have the sole Power of Impeachment.
    Section 3.  The Senate of the United States shall be
composed of two Senators from each state, (chosen by the
Undelete: 1 Restore; 2 Previous Deletion: 0
```

Figure 2-4.   The screen after pressing Cancel

Choose **1** to **R**estore the deleted text or **2** to show the **P**revious deletion. Up to three deletions can be displayed. If you decide not to restore the deletion, press Cancel or ENTER.

Miscellaneous Keystrokes

Other keys that have special features are listed at the bottom or the side of the template. The following descriptions of special features and the keystrokes that invoke them will help familiarize you with their functions. You can find detailed information about each item in Chapter 3, "Commands and Features." In the following descriptions, two keys separated by a hyphen (-) should be pressed together. If the keys are separated by a comma (,) press the second key after the first.

Hard Page Break (CTRL-ENTER)

WordPerfect automatically inserts a page break, referred to as a *soft page break*, at the end of each page as you type. If you want to force a page break, press CTRL-ENTER. A line of double dashes appears, designating a *hard page break*. See "Hard and Soft Codes" later in this chapter to learn more about the difference between hard and soft page breaks.

Delete Word (CTRL-BACKSPACE and HOME, BACKSPACE)

Pressing CTRL-BACKSPACE deletes the word at the cursor. If you continue pressing these keys together, words to the right of the cursor will be moved over and deleted.

Pressing HOME, BACKSPACE (one after the other, not together) deletes from the cursor to the beginning of the word at the cursor. If you continue pressing HOME, BACKSPACE, words to the left of the cursor are deleted.

Delete to the End of the Line (CTRL-END)

Press CTRL-END (number 1 on the numeric keypad) to delete text from the cursor to the end of the line.

Delete to the End of the Page (CTRL-PGDN)

To delete text from the cursor to the end of the page, press CTRL-PGDN. You are asked to confirm this type of deletion.

Word Left/Right (CTRL-← and CTRL-→)

You can move to the previous or next word by pressing CTRL and the left or right arrow (← or →), respectively.

Screen Up/Down (− and + or HOME, ↑ and HOME, ↓)

Press − on the numeric keypad to move to the top of the screen and + (also on the keypad) to move to the bottom of the screen. If you continue pressing the key, the cursor moves through the text one screen at a time. Pressing HOME, ↑ and HOME, ↓ will also move you through the document one screen at a time.

Page Up/Down (PGUP or PGDN)

These keys move the cursor to the previous or next page.

Home (HOME)

The HOME key is used with other keys to move through large sections of text. Press HOME and any arrow key to move to the outside edges of the text on the screen. For example, press HOME, ↑ to go to the top of the screen and HOME, ← to go to the left side of the screen.

To move to the extreme edges of the document, press HOME twice, and then press the appropriate arrow key. Thus, HOME, HOME, ↑ takes you to the beginning of the document, and HOME, HOME, ↓ moves the cursor to the end of the document. If your margins are wider than the screen, HOME, HOME, → or HOME, HOME, ← moves the cursor to the far right or far left margin, respectively.

Pressing HOME, HOME, HOME, ↑ moves the cursor to the beginning of the document *before* all codes, whereas HOME, HOME, ↑ moves the cursor *after* all beginning codes. See "Cursor Keys" in Chapter 3 for other options that are available for moving the cursor.

Go To (CTRL-HOME)

When you press CTRL-HOME, "Go to" appears at the lower left corner of the screen. Enter a number, and the cursor will move to the top of that page. If you enter a nonexistent page number, the cursor will move to the top of the last page. After pressing Go To, you can type a character instead of a number, and the cursor will move to the next occurrence of that character. You can also press the space bar, a period, or ENTER to move by word, sentence, or paragraph, respectively, because the cursor finds the next occurrence of a space, period, or hard return.

Pressing Go To twice moves the cursor to its previous location. You could use this feature if you moved to page 20, for example, and then decided that you wanted to go back to your original location but forgot where it was.

When you are working with columns or tables, Go To is used with ← and → to move from column to column.

Escape (ESC)

As in most programs, ESC is used to "escape" from a menu or a situation. If you are in a WordPerfect menu, pressing ESC also returns you to your text. However, if there is not a menu on your screen, ESC performs a different and useful function. When you press ESC, the message "Repeat Value = 8" appears in the lower left corner of the screen. The next key that you press will be repeated 8 times. You can enter another number to replace the 8, repeating the next key that many times. For instance, you can press ESC, type 20, and then press ↑ to move up 20 lines. You can also repeat a macro a specified number of times (for more information, see "Macros" in Chapter 3). Pressing Cancel (F1) or ESC again removes the "Repeat Value = 8" message from the screen.

You can change the default from 8 to any other number during an editing session by pressing ESC, typing the number, and then pressing ENTER. For more information, see "ESC Key" in Chapter 3.

Left Margin Release (SHIFT-TAB)

Pressing SHIFT-TAB moves the cursor to the previous tab. If you are already at the left margin, this option works as a left margin release and moves the cursor to a tab setting in the left margin.

When you are working with the Outline feature, you can use TAB to change the outline number to the next level and SHIFT-TAB to return to the previous level. Pressing SHIFT-TAB in a table moves the cursor to the previous cell.

Soft Hyphen (CTRL-HYPHEN)

When WordPerfect hyphenates words for you or assists in hyphenating words, it inserts a *soft hyphen*. If, after additional editing, the word no longer needs to be hyphenated, the hyphen will not appear on the screen. If you type a word that might need to be hyphenated, or if WordPerfect inserts a hyphen in the wrong location, you can insert a soft hyphen at the exact location at which you want the hyphen to occur. WordPerfect would then use this hyphen instead of suggesting a soft hyphen of its own. With the automatic hyphenation provided by Word-Perfect, however, it is not likely that you will ever need to use this feature.

Starting WordPerfect

If you have not installed WordPerfect, refer to Chapter 1, "Installation and Setup," before you read this section.

Two Disk Drives

You can run WordPerfect 5.1 on a two-disk-drive system only if you have two high-density 5 1/4-inch disk drives, two 3 1/2-inch disk drives, or a combination of the two.

Start your computer. It is suggested that you use drive A for WordPerfect and drive B as the default for storing and retrieving files. With the WordPerfect 1 disk in drive A and a disk for files in drive B, enter the following commands at the prompts shown:

A>**b:**
B>**a:wp**

This makes drive B the default for storing and retrieving files and then causes your system to look to drive A for the WordPerfect program. When you save or retrieve files, you will need to enter only the name of the file; you do not have to type B: at the beginning of the filename each time.

Because WordPerfect is so large, the entire program cannot fit on one disk. WP.EXE has been divided into two separate files: WP.EXE and WP.FIL. WP.EXE is on the WordPerfect 1 disk, and WP.FIL is on the WordPerfect 2 disk (along with other files). You need to start the program with the WP 1 disk and then, when prompted, insert the second disk and press any key when ready.

Hard Disk

If you have the WordPerfect program installed as suggested in Chapter 1, "Installation and Setup," you should be able to start by typing **wp** at any DOS prompt.

If you chose not to have the Install program add the \WP51 directory to the PATH command in the AUTOEXEC.BAT file, the program may not be found unless you add it manually. To correct the situation, run the Install program again, and ask that it check the AUTOEXEC.BAT. Add \WP51 (or other directory, if you are using a different directory for the program files) to the path.

Error Messages

If you have a power failure or system failure while you are running WordPerfect, or if you turn your machine off without pressing Exit (F7), you will see the message "Are other copies of WordPerfect currently running? (Y/N)" when you try to start WordPerfect. Each time you start

WordPerfect, it attempts to create temporary files. If it finds that the temporary files already exist (they were not closed properly with the Exit key), you are asked this question.

To start WordPerfect normally, type **N** for No, and WordPerfect will be started. If you are on a network system or want to have more than one copy of WordPerfect in memory (only possible if you have expanded memory), type **Y** and then specify which directory should be used for the new set of temporary files. Users on a network system are not usually asked this question, because their passwords are used to create unique temporary files.

If you have the Timed Backup feature on during a power or system failure, you may see a message telling you that a backup file exists. You can then either rename or delete the backup file so that WordPerfect can back up the current document in the backup files.

If you want to retrieve the backup files, you can either rename them and then retrieve them using the new name, or you can retrieve the backup file, which is called WP{WP}.BK1 or WP{WP}.BK2.

Status Line

When you first enter WordPerfect, you will see a status line at the bottom of the screen, as shown here:

```
                                              Doc 1 Pg 1 Ln 1" Pos 1"
```

This line tells you the current location of the cursor (the blinking dash in the upper left corner of the screen). "Doc" displays "1" or "2," depending on which document you are editing (you can have two documents in memory at once); "Pg" indicates the page number; "Ln" tells you how far the cursor is from the top of the page; and "Pos" tells you how far the cursor is from the left side of the page. Note that the last two indicators, "Ln" and "Pos," are displayed in inches. These settings can also be displayed in centimeters, points (a common typesetting measurement, with 72 points per inch), or WordPerfect 4.2 units using lines and characters.

You can press Switch (SHIFT-F3) to switch between two documents. The document number on the status line will change from "Doc 1" to "Doc 2" or vice versa. The page number following "Pg" changes when you reach a soft page break (at approximately Ln 10") or after you press Hard Page (CTRL-ENTER) to force a page break. The line number following "Ln" changes when you press ENTER to create a new line or press ↓ to move down through lines. You cannot move down using ↓ if there is no text to move through, however.

The position of the cursor ("Pos") changes as you type text or press the space bar. As you reach Pos 7.5", the line will wrap. The number of characters that will fit on a line depends on the font size, paper size, and margins. "Pos" is also used to indicate if the CAPS LOCK key is on ("POS" is shown in uppercase) or NUM LOCK is on ("Pos" flashes on and off temporarily). The position number is displayed in boldface if bold is on ("**Pos 1**"), with an underline if underlining is on ("**Pos 1**"), or both boldface and underlined if both are on ("**Pos 1**"). For users who have a color monitor, the number may be shown in a different color, depending on the color that you have selected for that attribute. See "Colors/Fonts/Attributes" in Chapter 3, "Commands and Features," for more information about changing the color for these and other items.

When working with text columns, "Col" is added to the beginning of the status line to indicate the column in which the cursor is located. You can have as many as 24 text columns. When in a table, "Cell" is added, indicating the current cell.

If you have saved and named a document, the status line also shows the full pathname (drive, directory, and filename) of the current document in the lower left corner of the screen. This area is also used to display messages, warnings, and one-line menus.

Absolute Measurement

WordPerfect works in absolute measurements, which means that you do not have to calculate the number of characters that will fit on a line or the number of lines that will fit on a page. You can change fonts many times on a line or within a page, and WordPerfect will automatically make the horizontal and vertical adjustments. If you have selected a larger font, WordPerfect will make the necessary adjustments; lines and page breaks will occur more often than if you used a smaller font, where more characters could fit on a line and page.

By default, all settings (such as tabs, margins, and columns) are set in inches. Because the status line is also displayed in inches, you can tell exactly where the cursor is on the page. If you prefer, you can use centimeters or points, or even return to the way the status line was displayed in version 4.2 (although this is not recommended). See "Units of Measure" in Chapter 3 for details about making this type of change.

Word Processing Concepts

This section introduces you to some of the word processing concepts used by WordPerfect and should help you understand more about the program. Use the tutorial provided with the WordPerfect package to reinforce these concepts. Because it is an on-screen, interactive tutorial, it can teach you exact steps much better than if you were to read the same steps in a book.

To use the tutorial, insert the WordPerfect 1 disk in drive A and the Learning/Images disk in drive B, and enter the following at the A>DOS prompt:

    b:tutor

When prompted, remove the WordPerfect 1 disk and insert the Word-Perfect 2 disk.

If you are using a hard disk and asked that the learning files be copied during installation, they would normally be copied to a directory named \WP51\LEARN unless you specified otherwise. Change to that directory and enter **tutor** to start the tutorial. See "Tutorial" in Chapter 3 for details.

Clean Screen

There is no "main menu" when you first enter WordPerfect. With other word processors, you usually have to open a document and name it. WordPerfect lets you create a document, check the spelling, print it, and then clear the screen without having to name or save it. This ability saves steps and disk space for short notes, memos, and letters that do not need to be saved for future use.

If you are accustomed to seeing a list of files as the opening menu, press List (F5) and ENTER upon entering WordPerfect. Among many other options, the List Files menu lets you highlight a file and retrieve it to the screen. If you press List (F5) and do not retrieve a document, press Exit (F7) to leave the menu and begin working on a new document.

Because of WordPerfect's clean-screen approach and few menus, it might seem difficult to find a feature or know what features exist. Even after working with WordPerfect for some time, you might not realize all that it can do, and the features may seem hidden.

One of the easiest ways to find out what features are available, as well as which function keys invoke which features, is to take some time and press each key. Some function keys, such as Bold (F6) and Underline (F8), act as on/off toggle keys. Other function keys show a full-screen menu, as shown in Figure 2-5, or prompt you for more information, as shown here:

```
Document to be saved:
```

You cannot harm your computer by pressing keys. Cancel (F1) will return you to your document from any menu without invoking a feature. The only way you can destroy files already saved on the disk is by pressing List (F5), pressing ENTER to view the directory, highlighting a file, choosing 2 to delete it, and then typing Y to confirm the deletion. All five steps are necessary to delete a file, and you are not likely to do them accidentally. You could replace a file on the disk by attempting to save another document with the same filename, but because you cannot have two files with the same name, you are asked if you want to replace the previous file with the new one. This question helps protect your documents by giving you an opportunity to think about the action and enter a different filename.

Another way of locating a feature easily is by using WordPerfect's pull-down menus. These menus can be used with or without a mouse and are easily displayed by clicking the right button on a mouse or pressing ALT-= (near the BACKSPACE key). You can then look through 9 categories instead of 40 function keys. The next section tells you more about using the pull-down menus.

Menus and Prompts

Although WordPerfect does not use a main menu to guide you through the process of creating a document, other menus appear when you press certain function keys. Each option on a menu is numbered or lettered so that you can type the number or letter without pressing ENTER to make your selection. For example, in the Line Format menu, you can choose either **7** or **M** for Margins.

You also have the option of using pull-down menus to make your selections. To display the menu bar shown here, press ALT-= on the keyboard, or click the right mouse button.

To remove the menu bar, press ALT-=, or click the right button on the mouse again.

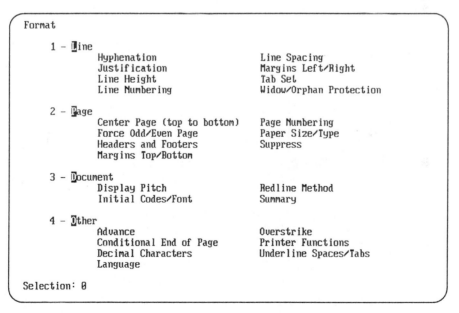

```
Format

    1 - Line
                Hyphenation                 Line Spacing
                Justification              Margins Left/Right
                Line Height                Tab Set
                Line Numbering             Widow/Orphan Protection

    2 - Page
                Center Page (top to bottom)  Page Numbering
                Force Odd/Even Page          Paper Size/Type
                Headers and Footers          Suppress
                Margins Top/Bottom

    3 - Document
                Display Pitch               Redline Method
                Initial Codes/Font          Summary

    4 - Other
                Advance                     Overstrike
                Conditional End of Page     Printer Functions
                Decimal Characters          Underline Spaces/Tabs
                Language

Selection: 0
```

Figure 2-5.　　The full-screen menu that is displayed when you press Format (SHIFT-F8)

File Edit Search Layout Mark Tools Font Graphics Help

To display the pull-down menus associated with each of the categories listed on the menu bar, move the mouse pointer to the desired
category and click the left button. A pull-down menu appears, as shown
in Figure 2-6. Continue moving the pointer to the desired options and
clicking the left button to select them. You can also hold down the left
button and drag it across the menus to display each menu separately.
Releasing the left button selects the highlighted feature. If you do not
want to select a feature, move the mouse pointer outside the menus and
release the left button.

If you do not have a mouse, you can use the arrow keys or type the
mnemonic letter associated with each feature to move through the
pull-down menus. Press ENTER or type the mnemonic letter to select an
option.

Clicking the right button or pressing Cancel (F1) backs you out one
menu at a time, whereas Exit (F7) can be used to remove all menus from
the screen.

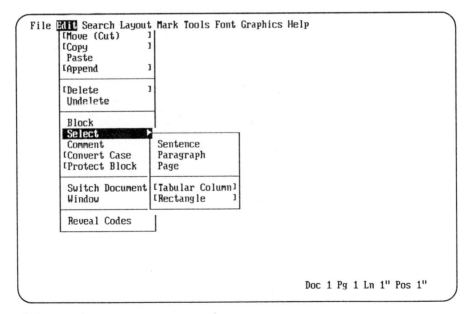

Figure 2-6.   A sample pull-down menu

See "Mouse Support" in Chapter 3, "Commands and Features," for details about using a mouse to position the cursor, scroll through the document, and highlight a block of text.

When you select options from a menu, there is always a "default" answer. Even though you can always use Cancel (F1) or Exit (F7) to leave a menu, you can press any key listed on the menu, other than the numbers or letters, to leave the menu. For example, if you have a menu listing six choices, you can press any key other than 1 through 6 (or any mnemonic choices) to leave the menu. Depending on your preferences, you might find it easiest to press ENTER or the space bar to leave a menu, rather than using Cancel or Exit.

WordPerfect will prompt you to answer Yes/No questions. When this happens, you will see "Yes (No)" or "No (Yes)" displayed on the screen. The "safest" answer always appears first, and the alternative is displayed in parentheses. For example, if you press Exit (F7), you will see "Save document? **Y**es (**N**o)." Notice that "Yes" is first, to indicate that it is the default answer. You can type any key other than **N** to save the document. Even if you do type **N**, you can press Cancel (F1) to return to the document without exiting.

WordPerfect will sometimes display a filename, pathname, or search string when you are saving a document, listing files, or searching. When this happens, you can enter new characters, edit the displayed name, or press ENTER to accept what is already displayed. For example, if you press Save (F10) and you have previously saved the document, the current filename will appear. You can press ENTER to accept that name, enter a new name, or edit the displayed name. You can change C:\WORK\ MINUTES.JAN to C:\WORK\ MINUTES.FEB by moving the cursor to the "J," deleting "JAN," and entering **FEB**.

A common mistake that new users make is to type **Y** rather than pressing ENTER to accept the displayed name when saving a file. If you do this, you can probably find the lost file under the name "Y" on your disk.

Another type of menu that commonly appears in WordPerfect is a "list" menu. When you select printers, fonts, or styles, or look in the List Files menu, you will see a list of items. In any of these menus, you can choose **N** for **N**ame Search and begin typing the name of the printer, font, style, or file. As soon as you type the first character, the cursor will move to the printer, font, style, or file beginning with that character. As you continue typing characters, the cursor will go to the name in the list that matches the entered name.

WordPerfect Codes

As you type a WordPerfect document, the text on the screen will look like it does when it is printed. Dot commands and control characters are not used, and therefore will not clutter the screen or cause text to misalign. Each key that you press is recorded either on the screen or "behind the scenes." The codes used to format a document are hidden so they will not clutter the regular text on the screen. They are sent to the printer, along with the document, to give the printer instructions for formatting the document.

You can reveal the codes and the regular text with Reveal Codes (ALT-F3), as shown in Figure 2-7. A reverse-video ruler bar, showing the current margin and tab settings, divides the screen. The upper half of the screen displays the regular text, and the lower half shows the location of codes in the text.

Note: If you have a CGA gray scale monitor and do not see reverse video, see "Colors/Fonts/Attributes" in Chapter 3 to adjust your screen.

```
                   THE CONSTITUTION OF THE UNITED STATES

                              PREAMBLE


          We the people of the United States, in Order to form a more

    perfect Union, establish Justic, insure domestic Tranquility,

    provide for the common defense, promote the general Welfare, and
                                              Doc 1 Pg 1 Ln 1" Pos 1"
    {   ▲   ▲   ▲   ▲   ▲   ▲   ▲   ▲  ₒ▲   ▲   ▲   ▲   }   ▲   ▲
    [Ln Spacing:2][Center][BOLD]THE CONSTITUTION OF THE UNITED STATES[bold][HRt]
    [Center][UND]PREAMBLE[und][HRt]
    [HRt]
    [Tab]We the people of the United States, in Order to form a more[SRt]
    perfect Union, establish Justic, insure domestic Tranquility,[SRt]
    provide for the common defense, promote the general Welfare, and



    Press Reveal Codes to restore screen
```

Figure 2-7.   Text and embedded codes displayed by pressing Reveal Codes (ALT-F3)

You can also start WordPerfect with WP/MONO to force WordPerfect to use the settings for a monochrome system.

Most of the codes used by WordPerfect are easy to interpret. In Figure 2-7, [Ln Spacing:2] indicates double-spacing, [BOLD] shows where boldface was turned on, [bold] in lowercase shows where boldface was turned off, and [HRt] indicates a hard return (where you pressed ENTER). The location of the cursor is shown in reverse video. If the cursor is resting on a character or code, that character or code will appear in reverse video.

You can enter menus, make selections, and see the code inserted immediately while in Reveal Codes. You can also type any amount of text, move text, switch documents, and even exit WordPerfect while still in Reveal Codes. To return the screen to normal editing, press Reveal Codes (ALT-F3) instead of pressing the space bar, ENTER, or Exit (F7). If pressed when in Reveal Codes, these keys will insert a space, a hard return, or start the exit procedure.

While in the normal editing screen (not Reveal Codes), if you are using BACKSPACE or DEL, you might see a message such as "Delete [BOLD]? No (Yes)" displayed in the lower left corner of the screen. This message tells you that you have run into a code, and WordPerfect wants to know if it should be deleted. If you want to delete the code, type **Y**. If you do not want to delete it (or if you do not understand the message), press any other key (even the DEL key) to accept the default, No, and the cursor will skip over the code rather than deleting it.

The easiest way to delete codes is to press Reveal Codes (ALT-F3), move the cursor to the code, and then press DEL. Although this takes two extra keystrokes (pressing Reveal Codes both to get into and out of the screen), you are not asked to confirm the deletion.

When you become accustomed to WordPerfect, you will be familiar with the location of the codes without having to use Reveal Codes, especially since you were probably the one who inserted them (unless you are editing someone else's document). Some codes, such as center, bold, and underline, give an indication of their location on the screen.

If you are using → and ← to move the cursor and you run into a code, the cursor will not seem to move on the screen but will actually be moving over the code. If you go to the beginning or the end of a word that is shown in boldface or is underlined, you can watch the "Pos" number while moving the cursor. It will also be shown in boldface or underlined when the cursor moves over the code. Then, depending on which side of the code the cursor is on, you can use BACKSPACE or DEL to delete the code and type **Y** to confirm the deletion.

Hard and Soft Codes

In WordPerfect, a return or new line that you insert is usually referred to as a *hard return*. This term is used to differentiate between the hard return code [HRt] that is inserted when you press ENTER, and the soft return code [SRt] that is automatically inserted by WordPerfect during word wrap.

If you type a document and press ENTER at the end of each line and later want to add or delete text, the document will not reformat correctly because of the [HRt] codes that force the line to break. Instead, when you type, you should let WordPerfect wrap the text to the next line. When text is edited, soft returns are removed if they are no longer needed.

WordPerfect inserts a soft page break (indicated by a line of dashes across the screen) when it reaches the bottom margin (see Figure 2-8). If you have page numbers, headers, footers, or footnotes, WordPerfect will automatically subtract the amount of space needed for these features and insert a page break at the appropriate place. Previous to version 5.0, a soft page break would normally be inserted at line 54. With versions 5.0 and 5.1, the number of lines that will fit on the page depends on the size of the page, the top and bottom margin settings, and the height of the font or fonts being used. Again, this is done automatically; no manual calculations are necessary.

A page break that you insert manually is a hard page break, which appears as [HPg] in Reveal Codes. If you type a page that has a small amount of text, such as a title page, you can press Hard Page (CTRL-ENTER) to go immediately to the next page, rather than pressing ENTER until you reach the bottom margin. A hard page break is indicated by a double line of dashes on the screen (see Figure 2-9).

Like soft returns, soft pages are readjusted automatically during editing. Hard returns and hard pages remain in their exact location until you manually delete them with BACKSPACE or DEL.

Pagination

WordPerfect is document-oriented rather than page-oriented: You can see text across page breaks, rather than having to "put a page away"

```
direct.  The Number of Representatives shall not exceed one for

every thirty Thousand, but each State shall have a least one

Representative; and until such enumeration shall be made, the State
_____
of New Hampshire shall be entitled to choose three, Massachusetts

eight, Rhode Island and Providence Plantations one, Connecticut

five, New York six, New Jersey four, Pennsylvania eight, Delaware

one, Maryland six, Virginia ten, North Carolina five, South

Carolina five, and Georgia three.

     When vacancies happen in the representation from any State,

the Executive Authority thereof shall issue Writs of Election to

fill such Vacancies.

     The House of Representatives shall choose their speaker and
C:\USA\CONST                                  Doc 1 Pg 6 Ln 3.67" Pos 7.4"
```

Figure 2-8.   A soft page break

```
                              PREAMBLE


     We the people of the United States, in Order to form a more

perfect Union, establish Justice, insure domestic Tranquility,

provide for the common defense, promote the general Welfare, and

secure the Blessings of Liberty to ourselves and our Posterity, do

ordain and establish this Constitution for the United States of

America.

=================================================================================
                             ARTICLE I.
     Section 1.     All legislative Powers herein granted shall be

vested in a Congress of the United States, which shall consist of

a Senate and House of Representatives.
C:\USA\CONST                                       Doc 1 Pg 1 Ln 1" Pos 1"
```

Figure 2-9.   A hard page break

before retrieving another. The repagination step that is required by some word processors is also eliminated. You can change the length of the page (up to a maximum of 54 inches), and WordPerfect will still continue to break the page automatically.

You can move across page breaks easily by using ↑ and ↓. If you want to move one page at a time, use PGUP or PGDN. To go to a particular page, press Go To (CTRL-HOME) and then enter the number of the page.

Default Settings

When you enter WordPerfect, you can start typing immediately because the format (such as margins, tabs, and page size) has been preset. You can change the format as many times as you want in a document. When you make changes to the format, codes are inserted and affect the text from that point on. When you clear your screen to begin work on a new document, the standard defaults are once again in effect.

The defaults for some of the more common format settings are

Format Item	Default Setting
Margins	
Left	1 inch
Right	1 inch
Top	1 inch
Bottom	1 inch
Tabs	Every half-inch
Spacing	Single-spacing
Justification	Full
Page size	8.5 × 11
Page numbering	None

Table 2-1.   Default Settings

listed in Table 2-1. You can choose your own defaults with the Word-Perfect Setup menu (for details, see "Initial Codes" in Chapter 3).

What You See Is What You Get

WordPerfect is not a "graphics" program; it displays each character in a fixed pitch. Because each character has a set amount of space, Word-Perfect cannot show proportional spacing, superscripts, right justifica-tion, or italics during normal editing. Although this may seem limiting, the program is much faster when you are creating and editing docu-ments.

WordPerfect does provide an alternative that makes it easy to differentiate the various attributes (such as bold, underlining, italics, and superscript) by letting you choose a distinct color for each one. If you do not have a color monitor, you can show them as boldface, underlined, or in reverse video. If you have a graphics card with RAM fonts (such as a Hercules Graphics Card Plus or the Hercules InColor Card), you can display up to 12 attributes on the screen during normal editing. Even though the space for each character does not change, Hercules has customized each of the 12 fonts to take a small part of the space or all the space to display superscript, subscript, fine, large, or extra-large print. The company has also customized some of the fonts so they appear to be in italics, small caps, or strikeout (with a line drawn through that font). If you prefer to show 512 characters on the screen instead of the normal 256 characters, you can use 6 of the fonts instead of all 12. For details, refer to "Colors/Fonts/Attributes" in Chapter 3.

WordPerfect also has a View feature (previously called Preview) that shows right justification, headers and footers, footnotes, page num-bers, and line numbering on the screen. If you have *any* type of graph-ics card, you can see a true representation of how the document will look when it is printed. Although there is no editing available in this screen, you can view the full page or two facing pages, or you can scale the page to 100 percent or 200 percent of the printed copy. The size and type of fonts are displayed, showing, for example, the difference between 10 point and 24 point, as well as the difference between serif and sans serif fonts, such as Times and Helvetica, respectively. You can see true proportional spacing, redline, strikeout, italics, double-underlining, su-perscript, subscript, and any graphics that might have been incorpo-rated into the document.

Virtual Memory, Document Size, and Switching Disks

At some time, you might see a question or statement regarding Word-Perfect's *overflow files*. These are temporary files that are created automatically on the disk each time you start WordPerfect; they are closed when you exit WordPerfect.

As you learned in Chapter 1, "Installation and Setup," the document that you see on your screen is in memory. When memory is filled, the document spills into overflow files on disk. As a document increases in size, so do the virtual files. Any text above the cursor that needs to be stored is kept in the top virtual file, and the text below the cursor is stored in the bottom virtual file. The names for these files are WP}WP{.TV1 and WP}WP{.BV1 for document 1, and WP}WP{.TV2 and WP}WP{.BV2 for document 2.

Overflow files, along with other temporary files, are stored on the same drive and directory as the WordPerfect program file WP.EXE. See "Starting WordPerfect" in Chapter 3, "Commands and Features," for information about storing these overflow files elsewhere.

Because of the virtual memory design, the size of a document is limited only by memory and the amount of disk space available. Although it is recommended that you work with smaller files, you can increase the size of documents by adding more memory or disk space. If you have two floppy disk drives, not much memory, and you have not redirected the overflow files to a disk other than the one containing WordPerfect, the size of your documents will be limited. This is true because there is limited space on the WordPerfect disk.

When using two floppy disk drives, you should always leave the WordPerfect 2 disk in its drive (usually drive A) after the initial startup with the WordPerfect 1 disk. You can, however, swap disks in the other drive. If you plan to use the Speller or the Thesaurus, you will need to replace the data disk with the appropriate Speller or Thesaurus disk at the right time. If you have expanded memory, you might consider loading all of WordPerfect into memory so you can remove the Word-Perfect 2 disk and use that drive for the Speller or Thesaurus. For more information, see "Starting WordPerfect" in Chapter 3.

If you have a RAM drive, you can copy the temporary files, the Speller or Thesaurus there to make them run faster and eliminate disk switching. See "RAM Drives" in Chapter 3 for details.

Creating Documents

This section presents the basic steps in creating a WordPerfect document.

Entering Text

As you enter text, remember that WordPerfect is designed to do most tasks for you automatically. If you attempt to do the same things manually, you will find yourself having to do extra work with a document after you have made only a small number of editing changes.

The first basic rule is that you should not press ENTER unless you want to end a paragraph, make a short line, or create a blank line. WordPerfect will wrap text to the next line when you reach the right margin. If you accidentally press ENTER, you can immediately press BACKSPACE to delete the extra line.

WordPerfect will insert text as you type. Any text after the cursor is pushed to the right and is reformatted as the new text is added. If you want to type over existing text, press INS, and the word "Typeover" will appear on the status line. Press it again to return to inserting text.

You can also retrieve other documents (or parts of documents, as explained later in this chapter) at the cursor location. If you know the name of a document, press Retrieve (SHIFT-F10) and enter the document name. If the file is not in the default drive and directory, enter the full pathname (drive, directory, and filename). If you do not know the filename, press List (F5) and ENTER to see an alphabetical list of the files in the default drive and directory. Move the cursor to the file you want to retrieve and choose **1** for **R**etrieve. If you retrieve a file and happen to have a file on your screen, you are asked if you want to retrieve the file into the current document. If you do not want this to happen, type **N** for No, and return to the document and clear the screen.

WordPerfect automatically formats a document for the printer that is currently selected. This lets you print the document on several different printers without having to make formatting changes manually.

The following features are commonly used in word processing. Other features, such as decimal tabs, superscripting, double-underlining, using the Thesaurus, footnotes, text columns, and inserting the current date and time are explained in detail in Chapter 3, "Commands and Features."

Centering

WordPerfect will, upon your command, automatically center titles and headings between the left and right margins. While at the left margin, press Center (SHIFT-F6), type the heading, and press ENTER to turn off centering and move to the next line.

If you want to center text that you have already typed, move the cursor to the beginning of the line and press Center. If the text is not centered immediately, insert a hard return by pressing ENTER at the end of the line being centered.

Indenting

There are several ways to indent text, as shown in Figure 2-10. You can use the TAB key to move the cursor to the next tab stop (tabs are preset

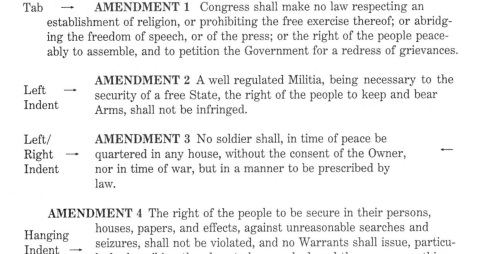

Tab → **AMENDMENT 1** Congress shall make no law respecting an establishment of religion, or prohibiting the free exercise thereof; or abridging the freedom of speech, or of the press; or the right of the people peaceably to assemble, and to petition the Government for a redress of grievances.

Left → Indent **AMENDMENT 2** A well regulated Militia, being necessary to the security of a free State, the right of the people to keep and bear Arms, shall not be infringed.

Left/ Right → Indent **AMENDMENT 3** No soldier shall, in time of peace be quartered in any house, without the consent of the Owner, ← nor in time of war, but in a manner to be prescribed by law.

Hanging Indent → **AMENDMENT 4** The right of the people to be secure in their persons, houses, papers, and effects, against unreasonable searches and seizures, shall not be violated, and no Warrants shall issue, particularly describing the place to be searched, and the persons or things to be seized.

Figure 2-10.   Options for indenting text

at every half-inch). The TAB key on your keyboard might be labeled with two arrows facing in opposite directions (⇌). This key can be used to indent the first line of a paragraph or to move to a specific tab stop.

Pressing →Indent (F4) indents and wraps each line to a tab stop until you press ENTER. You can use this option for numbered paragraphs that have the number at the left margin and the following text indented. If you try to indent each line manually with TAB and later add or delete text, you will have tabs in the middle of lines. Instead, use Indent at the first line, and WordPerfect will wrap subsequent lines to the appropriate tab stop.

Pressing →Indent← (SHIFT-F4) indents each line from the left and right margins. This feature is useful when you are creating displayed quotations and centered paragraphs. Pressing ENTER returns you to the normal margins.

You can also create a hanging indent, in which the first line "hangs" farther out than the rest of the lines, by pressing either of the Indent keys and then releasing the first line back to the previous tab stop by pressing Left Margin Release (SHIFT-TAB).

Boldface

If you want a section of text to be printed in boldface, press Bold (F6), type the text to be in boldface, and then press Bold again. If you want to boldface text that has already been typed, move the cursor to either the beginning or the end of the text, press Block (ALT-F4), move the cursor to the opposite end of the text (the block of text will be highlighted), and then press Bold (F6).

Underlining

The steps for underlining text are similar to those for boldfacing text, except that F8 is used instead of F6. Press Underline (F8), type the text, and then press Underline again. To underline existing text, block the text with ALT-F4 and then press Underline.

Italics, Double Underlining, and Other Attributes

Other attributes, such as italics, strikeout, and double-underlining, are also available and can be activated with Font (CTRL-F8). Because there are many different attributes, they are divided into two categories: Size and Appearance. The attributes shown in the following illustration are found under Size :

```
1 Suprscpt; 2 Subscpt; 3 Fine; 4 Small; 5 Large; 6 Vry Large; 7 Ext Large: 0
```

The remaining attributes are classified under Appearance :

```
1 Bold 2 Undln 3 Dbl Und 4 Italc 5 Outln 6 Shadw 7 Sm Cap 8 Redln 9 Stkout: 0
```

Note that Bold and Underline appear on this menu, as well as on the F6 and F8 function keys. When you choose any of these attributes, both the beginning and ending codes are inserted, and the cursor is left between them. You can reenter the menus and turn the attribute off, but it is easier to press → to move the cursor over the ending code instead.

Changing Fonts

You can change the font as many times as you like without changing margins, tabs, page length, and so on, because of the absolute measurements used in WordPerfect.

To change fonts, press Font (CTRL-F8) and choose 4 for Base Font. The list of fonts available for your printer will appear. Move to the desired font, and press ENTER to select that font. The Size and Appearance attributes on the menu are dependent on the base font that has been selected. For example, if Helvetica 12pt were the base font, the Helvetica 12pt Italic font would be automatically selected for italic, Helvetica 12pt Bold would be selected for boldfaced text, and so on. Large print might be 14pt, very large might be 18pt, and extra large could be 24pt, again depending on the available fonts.

If you print the document on a different printer, WordPerfect will use the attributes available for that printer and match the fonts as closely as possible.

Moving the Cursor

Table 2-2 summarizes the options for moving the cursor that were discussed previously in this chapter. If you do not have an enhanced keyboard with arrow keys that are separate from the arrow keys on the numeric keypad, you may see numbers inserted instead. If this happens, press NUM LOCK to turn the "number lock" feature off. You can then use the arrows shown on the numeric keypad to move the cursor. Other cursor keys that are used less often are listed in Table 2-3.

Keystrokes	Movement
↑	Move up one line
↓	Move down one line
→	Move right one character
←	Move left one character
CTRL- →	Move to the beginning of the next word
CTRL- ←	Move to the beginning of the previous word
−	Move to the top of the screen; continue pressing to move to the top of each previous screen
+	Move to the bottom of the screen; continue pressing to move to the bottom of each following screen
HOME,↑	Same as − (screen up)
HOME,↓	Same as + (screen down)
HOME,→	Move to the end of the line
HOME,←	Move to the beginning of the line
END	Same as HOME, HOME, → (end of line)
PGUP	Move to the beginning of the previous page
PGDN	Move to the beginning of the next page
HOME, HOME, HOME,↑	Move to the beginning of the document before all codes
HOME, HOME,↑	Move to the beginning of the document after codes
HOME, HOME,↓	Move to the end of the document
HOME, HOME, →	Move to the far right of the document (useful for documents that are wider than the screen)
HOME, HOME, ←	Move to the far left of the document after all codes
HOME, HOME, HOME, ←	Move to the far left of the document before all codes
CTRL-HOME	Go to .... Enter a number to go to that page or a character to go to the next occurrence of that character (you can also use ENTER or the space bar to go to the next hard return or space)

Table 2-2.   Cursor Movement Keys

Keystrokes	Movement
CTRL-HOME, CTRL-HOME	Go to the previous cursor position
ESC,↑	Move up eight lines. ESC can also be combined with ↑, ↓, →, ←, PGUP, PGDN, –, and + to move in that direction eight times
CTRL-HOME,↑	Go to the top of the current page or column
CTRL-HOME,↓	Go to the bottom of the current page or column
CTRL-HOME, →	In columns or tables, moves to the next column to the right
CTRL-HOME, ←	In columns or tables, moves to the previous column to the left
CTRL-HOME, HOME, →	Moves to the far right text column or cell in a table
CTRL-HOME, HOME, ←	Moves to the far left text column or cell in a table

Table 2-3.   Less Frequently Used Cursor Movement Keys

The cursor will move only through text and codes. When you reach the end of a document, you can create blank space and move down by pressing ENTER.

Correcting Mistakes

Table 2-4 summarizes the keystrokes that you can use to delete text. Remember that you can delete codes, hard page breaks, and blank lines exactly as you would delete regular text. You can also use any of the delete keys in the Reveal Codes (ALT-F3) screen.

You can delete sentences, paragraphs, or any amount of text by using Block (ALT-F4) to highlight the amount of text to be deleted. After pressing Block, you can type a period to highlight to the end of the sentence, ENTER to highlight to the end of the paragraph, or PGDN to highlight to the end of the page. After the block has been defined, press BACKSPACE or DEL and type **Y** to confirm the deletion. As a precaution against accidentally deleting large amounts of text, you are asked for confirmation when you are doing a block delete and when you are deleting to the end of the page.

If you delete text accidentally, press Cancel (F1) and then choose **1** to **R**estore the deleted text or **2** to show the **P**revious Deletion. If you

Keystrokes	Deletion
BACKSPACE	Deletes text to the left
DEL	Deletes text at the cursor (appears to delete to the right)
CTRL-BACKSPACE	Deletes the word at the cursor; continue pressing to delete words to the right of the cursor
HOME, BACKSPACE	Deletes from the cursor to the beginning of the current word; continue pressing to delete words to the left of the cursor
HOME, DEL	Deletes from the cursor to the end of the current word; continue pressing to delete words to the right of the cursor
CTRL-END	Deletes text from the cursor to the end of the line
CTRL-PGDN	Deletes text from the cursor to the end of the page; you are asked to confirm this type of deletion

Table 2-4.   Keystrokes Used for Deleting Text

want to restore the deleted text in a different location, move the cursor to the appropriate location and press Cancel (F1). You can use this method as an alternative for moving text (see the following section of this chapter and "Move" in Chapter 3). If you use the Undelete feature to move text, however, remember that only the last three deletions can be restored.

Editing

One of the nicest advantages to using a word processor is being able to manipulate the text on the screen with little or no retyping. You can edit text as you enter it or make changes to a previously saved document on disk.

When you retrieve a file from disk, you are retrieving a copy of the original file. If you decide not to keep the changes made to the copy on the screen, you can clear the screen, and the original on disk will remain untouched. Or, after making changes, you can save the file and replace the original on disk.

The rest of this section provides short explanations of some of the more commonly used editing features in WordPerfect.

Block

You can do many things with a block of text, such as boldface, underline, or delete it. You can also assign other attributes to a block, such as italics, fine print, large print, small caps, or double-underlining. You can change a block of text to uppercase or lowercase, center it, print it, save it to a new file, or append it to another file. Many other options are discussed under "Block" in Chapter 3. One of the most valuable uses of the Block feature is to cut and paste text. You can move as much text as you want without regard for page boundaries, and the remaining text is reformatted automatically.

Use the following steps to cut or copy text from one location to another:

1. With the cursor at one end of the text to be moved, press Block (ALT-F4). "Block on" flashes in the lower left corner of the screen.

2. Move the cursor to the opposite end of the text. The block will be highlighted.

3. Press Move (CTRL-F4).

4. Choose **1** for **B**lock.

5. Choose **1** to **M**ove the block (cut it from the current location) or **2** to **C**opy the block. Other options allow you to delete the block or append it to another file.

6. The message at the bottom of the screen prompts you to move the cursor to the new location and press ENTER to retrieve the block.

If, while moving to the new location, you want to cancel the move, press Cancel (F1). You can still retrieve the text at any location by pressing Retrieve (SHIFT-F10) and then pressing ENTER without entering a filename. The text that is moved or copied is saved in memory and can be retrieved repeatedly until another block of text is moved or copied. If it helps, you can imagine the name of the block being held in memory as "enter," because you can press ENTER for the name of the document to be retrieved.

Switching Between Documents

You can have two documents in memory at one time, and pressing Switch (SHIFT-F3) lets you move between them. When you switch between documents, you will see a full screen for each document. If you want to split the screen and display both documents simultaneously, press Screen (CTRL-F3), choose **1** to select Window, and then enter the number of lines that you want to use for the current document. Enter **11** if you want to split the screen evenly. You can also press ↑ or ↓ rather than entering a number to divide the screen. When you want to see a full screen again, press Screen (CTRL-F3), type **1** for Window, and then enter **24** or ↓ until the ruler line disappears.

When you press Switch (SHIFT-F3) to move between the two documents, the triangles indicating tab settings point to the document being edited, as shown in Figure 2-11. To cut or copy text between the two documents, define the block to be moved, press Move (CTRL-F4), select an option, choose **1** to Move or **2** to Copy, press Switch (SHIFT-F3), position the cursor, and then press ENTER to retrieve the text. The only additional step is pressing Switch.

Search

When editing a document, you can spend a lot of time looking for a certain word, phrase, or code such as a margin change. You can use Search (F2) and ← Search (SHIFT-F2) to search forward and backward, respectively, for both text and WordPerfect codes.

After pressing Search (F2), enter the string of characters for which you are searching, and then press Search (F2) again to start the search. Note that uppercase finds only uppercase, whereas lowercase finds both uppercase and lowercase. If you press ENTER to start the search, it will display the hard return code, [HRt]. Delete the code if it is not wanted, or WordPerfect will try to find the search string and a hard return together.

You can search for a code by pressing the appropriate function key that usually inserts the code into regular text. For example, if you want

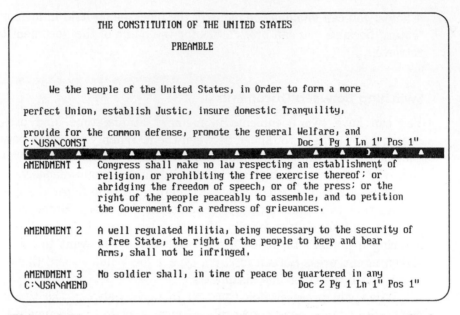

Figure 2-11.   Tab-setting indicators pointing to the document being edited

to search for a boldface code, press Bold (F6) to insert the bold code. Typing **[BOLD]** would find those exact characters—not the code.

When Search finds the search string, it places the cursor immediately after (to the right of) the word, phrase, or code. This is important to remember, because when you search for a code and want to delete it, you can immediately press BACKSPACE and confirm the deletion without first pressing Reveal Codes (ALT-F3) to see if the code is to the left of the cursor.

Replace

The Replace feature is like Search, except that you can replace the search string with something else. You can even use this feature to search for the string without replacing it with anything and delete all occurrences of the string. This is useful for removing all spacing changes, margins changes, and so on.

Follow these steps to do a search and replace:

1. Press Replace (ALT-F2).

2. Type **Y** if you want to confirm each replacement or **N** to do a global replacement.

3. Type the search string. Do not press ENTER unless you want to search for the [HRt] code.

4. Press Search (F2) to continue.

5. Type the replacement string. Skip this step if you want the search string to be deleted.

6. Press Search (F2) again to start the replacement. If you are asked to confirm each replacement, the cursor will stop at each occurrence. Type **Y** or **N** to replace or not replace each occurrence, respectively.

Formatting

You can format a document before, during, or after typing. Format codes are inserted at the current location of the cursor. When you insert a code into your text, WordPerfect uses the setting from that point forward until it finds another code telling it to change. For example, if you wanted double-spacing from the beginning of the document, you would move the cursor to the beginning of the document and change the spacing there. If you had text such as a quote that needed to be single-spaced, you would set single-spacing at the beginning of the quote and change back to double-spacing after the quote.

When you want a certain format for the entire document, set the format at the beginning of the document. Go to the top of a page to change the format for that particular page.

WordPerfect includes all formatting options on the Format (SHIFT-F8) key. When you press it, the menu shown in Figure 2-12 appears. The first item, Line, contains options that generally affect lines (margins, tabs, spacing, justification, line numbering, and so on); the second item, Page, contains options that affect a page (page size, numbering, headers and footers, and so on); the third item, Document, contains options that affect the entire document (initial font, initial codes, and so on); and the fourth item, Other, lets you choose from several miscellaneous commands. See "Format" in Chapter 3 for details about using these options.

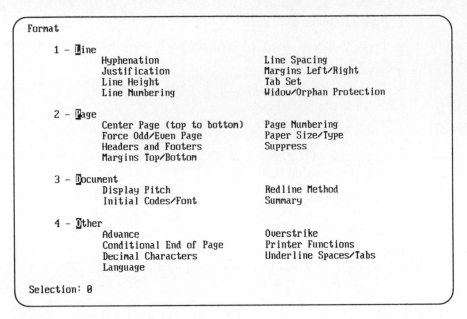

Figure 2-12.   Format menu

Checking the Spelling

WordPerfect's Speller is extremely fast and efficient. In fact, you should consider checking the spelling of your documents as a routine step in creating a document. The Speller contains approximately 125,000 words, including medical and legal terms.

If you have two disk drives, replace the data disk with the Speller disk (usually in drive B). Do not replace the WordPerfect 1 disk with the Speller disk. Press Spell (CTRL-F2), and the Speller menu will appear, as shown in Figure 2-13. If you press Spell before inserting the Speller disk, you will see the error message "WP{WP}US.LEX not found." Choose 1 for Enter **P**ath, and then type the location for the dictionary (if the disk is in drive B, type **B:**).

If you have a hard disk, press Spell (CTRL-F2), and the Speller menu will appear, as shown in Figure 2-13. If you see the error message telling you that the dictionary file is not found, choose 1 for Enter **P**ath, and then enter the location where the dictionary can be found (for example, **C:\DICT\WP**). To avoid this error message in the future,

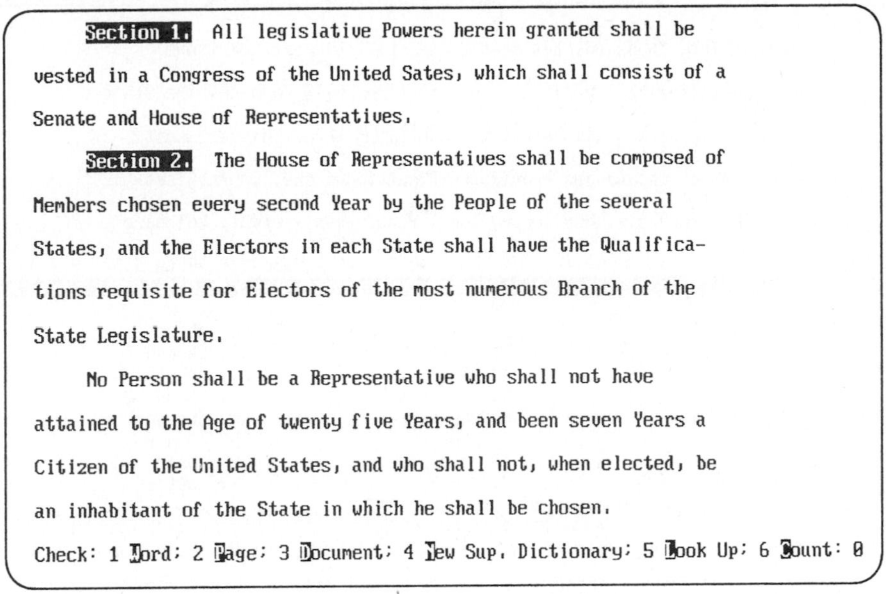

```
┌─────────────────────────────────────────────────────────────────┐
│    ███████████  All legislative Powers herein granted shall be    │
│                                                                   │
│   vested in a Congress of the United Sates, which shall consist of a │
│                                                                   │
│   Senate and House of Representatives.                            │
│                                                                   │
│    ███████████  The House of Representatives shall be composed of │
│                                                                   │
│   Members chosen every second Year by the People of the several   │
│                                                                   │
│   States, and the Electors in each State shall have the Qualifica-│
│                                                                   │
│   tions requisite for Electors of the most numerous Branch of the │
│                                                                   │
│   State Legislature.                                              │
│                                                                   │
│       No Person shall be a Representative who shall not have       │
│                                                                   │
│   attained to the Age of twenty five Years, and been seven Years a │
│                                                                   │
│   Citizen of the United States, and who shall not, when elected, be │
│                                                                   │
│   an inhabitant of the State in which he shall be chosen.         │
│                                                                   │
│   Check: 1 Word; 2 Page; 3 Document; 4 New Sup. Dictionary; 5 Look Up; 6 Count: 0 │
└─────────────────────────────────────────────────────────────────┘
```

Figure 2-13.   Speller menu

specify the location of the dictionary with Setup (SHIFT-F1), and then choose 6 for Location of Files. See "Spell" in Chapter 3 for further information.

You will usually choose option 2 to check the current Page or 3 to check the entire Document. Other options listed are explained in detail in the "Spell" section of Chapter 3. After you choose option 2 or 3, the first word not found in the dictionary will be highlighted, and the menu shown in Figure 2-14 will be displayed. Type the letter corresponding to the correct spelling, and the misspelled word will be replaced. If the correct spelling is not listed, it may be listed in a subsequent screen. Press ENTER if you are prompted to see more choices, or choose 1 to skip the word once, 2 to skip the word for the rest of the document, 3 to add the word to a supplementary dictionary, 4 to edit the word manually, 5 to look up the word, or 6 if you want to ignore all words containing numbers. The choices displayed are not always spelled correctly. The speller transposes characters, adds and deletes characters, and uses as much of a word pattern as possible to give you the choices. It also tries to find a phonetic match: If you spell "schizophrenic" as "skitsofrenik," the correct spelling will be displayed.

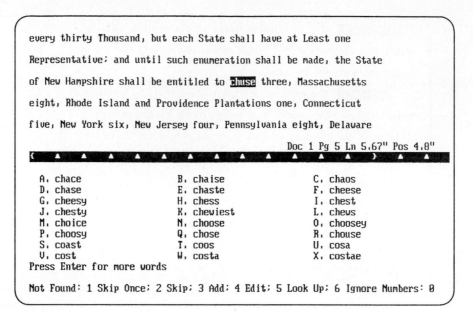

Figure 2-14.   The menu that is displayed when a word is not found

When you choose option 5 to look up a word, you are asked for the word pattern. Type as many of the characters as you know, filling in the blanks with the *, -, and ? wildcard characters. An asterisk (*) or hyphen (-) can be used in place of any number of characters, and a question mark (?) can be used for a single character. Although the hyphen is not documented in the WordPerfect manual, it is available. You can also type the word as it sounds, and WordPerfect will display phonetic choices.

Follow the same basic procedure to use the Thesaurus. Place the appropriate Spell/Thesaurus disk in drive B if you have two disk drives, press Thesaurus (ALT-F1), and follow the menu shown on the status line. The name of the Thesaurus file is WP{WP}US.THS. For details, see "Thesaurus" in Chapter 3.

Printing

WordPerfect lets you print and edit at the same time. If you send several files to the printer, they are assigned a number and are held in a

```
Print

    1 - Full Document
    2 - Page
    3 - Document on Disk
    4 - Control Printer
    5 - Multiple Pages
    6 - View Document
    7 - Initialize Printer


Options

    S - Select Printer                    HP LaserJet Series II
    B - Binding Offset                    0"
    N - Number of Copies                  1
    U - Multiple Copies Generated by      WordPerfect
    G - Graphics Quality                  Medium
    T - Text Quality                      High




Selection: 0
```

Figure 2-15.   Print menu

print queue. If you press Print (SHIFT-F7), you will see the menu shown in Figure 2-15. In addition to printing the full document or the current page, you can print a document from disk, enter the menu that controls the printer, print selected pages from the current document, view the document before printing, or initialize the printer (download all soft fonts and set up the forms for the selected printer). Also on the menu are other print options, such as selecting the printer, choosing the binding width and number of copies (and what generates the number of copies), as well as choosing the quality of print for both text and graphics.

The Control Printer menu available with option 4 lets you control the print jobs held in the queue. You can cancel print jobs, rush a print job, display more print jobs that might be in the queue, and stop or start the printer.

There are three ways to print a document. One is to print directly from the screen without having to save the document first:

1. Press Print (SHIFT-F7).

2. Choose **1** to print the Full Document or **2** to print the current **Page**. The document will be saved in a temporary print file; you can continue editing the same document or another one.

The other two methods print documents already saved on the disk. You can do this by choosing option **3** for **D**ocument on Disk, or from the List Files menu by pressing List (F5), moving to the document to be printed, and choosing **4** for **P**rint.

If you are working on a document and want to print the latest version, print from the screen rather than from the disk, unless you have just saved the document.

Filing

You can save a document at any time. Press Save (F10), and then enter the filename (up to 8 characters with an optional 3-character extension). The file will be saved automatically to the default drive and directory. If you want to save it to a different drive and directory, enter the full pathname. When you press Save (F10), the document is left on the screen.

If you want to save the document and clear the screen, press Exit (F7). Type **Y** to save the document, enter the filename, and type **N** when asked if you want to exit WordPerfect. When you make changes to a file and attempt to save it with the same filename that you used before, you are asked if you want to replace the former file. If you type **N** for No, you can enter a different name.

You might encounter an error message when trying to save a file. "File creation error" means that you have used illegal characters in a filename or that you have exceeded the maximum number of files that can be saved to the root directory (the limit varies from computer to computer but is usually 112). If you see "Disk full," replace the data disk with one that has available space, or press List (F5) and delete any unnecessary files. An error message telling you that the drive door may be open lets you close the door and retry, or cancel and return to the document.

Another option available in WordPerfect 5.1, Long Document Names, lets you name documents with up to 68 characters. This is in addition to the standard, 8-character DOS name. For more information, see "Long Document Names" and "Document Management/Summary" in Chapter 3.

WordPerfect has a very complete method of managing your files. List (F5) can be used to display all or selected files in each directory, change the default directory, and even create or delete directories. While in the List Files menu, you can retrieve, delete, rename, print, look at, copy, or search through files to find a particular file.

After pressing List (F5), press ENTER to see a list of the files in the displayed (default) drive and directory. Figure 2-16 gives an example. (See "List Files" in Chapter 3 for information about looking into a different drive and directory.) The top of the menu shows the current date, time, and directory. If you have a document in memory, the document size (in bytes) is displayed, as well as the amount of disk space available and the amount of space that is being used by the files in that particular directory.

Any subdirectories and the parent directory are listed first. You can move the cursor to any of these directories, press ENTER to see the directory's pathname, and then press ENTER again to see the list of files in that directory. You can wander through directories without ever leaving the List Files menu.

List Files has a Name Search feature. If you know the name of a file, you can type **N** to turn the feature on and then type the filename.

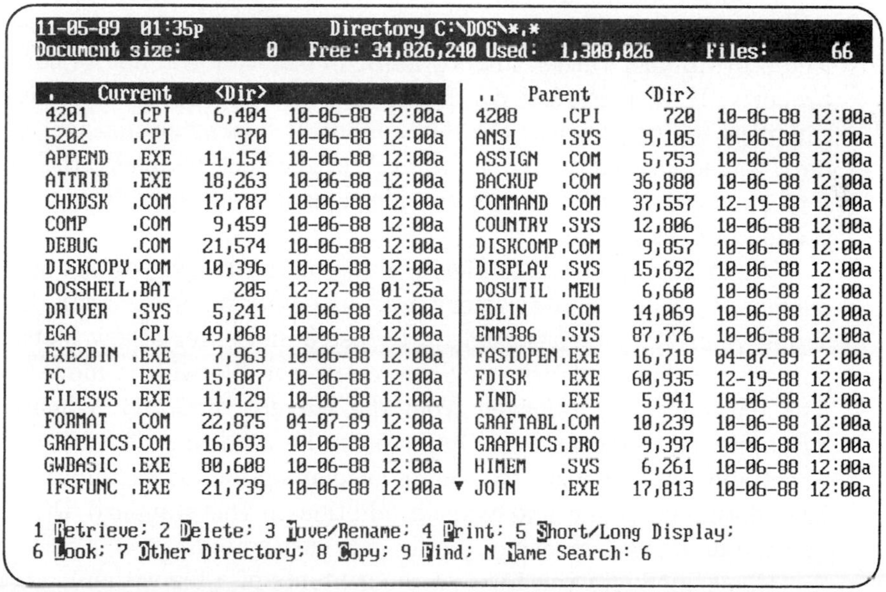

```
11-05-89  01:35p              Directory C:\DOS\*.*
Document size:       0   Free: 34,826,240  Used:   1,308,026     Files:     66

.     Current   <Dir>                  ..    Parent    <Dir>
4201    .CPI    6,404  10-06-88 12:00a   4208    .CPI     720  10-06-88 12:00a
5202    .CPI      370  10-06-88 12:00a   ANSI    .SYS   9,105  10-06-88 12:00a
APPEND  .EXE   11,154  10-06-88 12:00a   ASSIGN  .COM   5,753  10-06-88 12:00a
ATTRIB  .EXE   18,263  10-06-88 12:00a   BACKUP  .COM  36,880  10-06-88 12:00a
CHKDSK  .COM   17,787  10-06-88 12:00a   COMMAND .COM  37,557  12-19-88 12:00a
COMP    .COM    9,459  10-06-88 12:00a   COUNTRY .SYS  12,806  10-06-88 12:00a
DEBUG   .COM   21,574  10-06-88 12:00a   DISKCOMP.COM   9,857  10-06-88 12:00a
DISKCOPY.COM   10,396  10-06-88 12:00a   DISPLAY .SYS  15,692  10-06-88 12:00a
DOSSHELL.BAT      205  12-27-88 01:25a   DOSUTIL .MEU   6,660  10-06-88 12:00a
DRIVER  .SYS    5,241  10-06-88 12:00a   EDLIN   .COM  14,069  10-06-88 12:00a
EGA     .CPI   49,068  10-06-88 12:00a   EMM386  .SYS  87,776  10-06-88 12:00a
EXE2BIN .EXE    7,963  10-06-88 12:00a   FASTOPEN.EXE  16,718  04-07-89 12:00a
FC      .EXE   15,807  10-06-88 12:00a   FDISK   .EXE  60,935  12-19-88 12:00a
FILESYS .EXE   11,129  10-06-88 12:00a   FIND    .EXE   5,941  10-06-88 12:00a
FORMAT  .COM   22,875  04-07-89 12:00a   GRAFTABL.COM  10,239  10-06-88 12:00a
GRAPHICS.COM   16,693  10-06-88 12:00a   GRAPHICS.PRO   9,397  10-06-88 12:00a
GWBASIC .EXE   80,608  10-06-88 12:00a   HIMEM   .SYS   6,261  10-06-88 12:00a
IFSFUNC .EXE   21,739  10-06-88 12:00a ▼ JOIN    .EXE  17,813  10-06-88 12:00a

1 Retrieve; 2 Delete; 3 Move/Rename; 4 Print; 5 Short/Long Display;
6 Look; 7 Other Directory; 8 Copy; 9 Find; N Name Search: 6
```

Figure 2-16.   List Files menu

As soon as you type a character, the cursor moves to the files that begin with that character. Continue typing the characters in the name to narrow the search to a specific file. Press ENTER or an arrow key to leave Name Search and return to the normal List Files options.

If you can remember only part of a filename, you can press Search (F2) and enter the part of the filename that you know. Pressing Search (F2) again will search for any file in the directory that contains those characters, regardless of whether they are at the beginning of the filename or not.

Of course, you can also use the cursor keys to move by file or by screen, or to move to the beginning or the end of the list.

If you choose 1 to **R**etrieve a file and there is already a document on the screen, WordPerfect will ask you if you want to retrieve that document into the current document on the screen. Type **N** if you do not want to combine the two documents, return to the document, and clear the screen before retrieving the second file. You will also be able to tell if a document is in memory by checking the document size at the top of the screen to make sure there is not a document in memory (if the document size is zero, a document is not currently on the screen). Press Exit (F7) if you want to leave the List Files menu without retrieving a file.

If you retrieve a version 4.2 document, all formatting codes are converted if possible to version 5.1 codes. Because the fonts were selected by number rather than by name in 4.2, they will not be converted properly. If WordPerfect 5.1 encounters a font change, it will insert a comment telling you that the font cannot be converted and will need to be changed manually. If you want WordPerfect to insert the correct fonts, you can create a conversion file as explained in the "Compatibility" section of Chapter 3.

When you choose 2 to **D**elete a file or directory, you are asked to confirm the deletion. A directory must be empty before you can delete it. To **M**ove or Rename a document, choose 3 and enter a new filename. If you enter a different drive and directory, the file will be moved to the new directory and removed from the current directory. Choose 4 to **P**rint the file to the printer. Option 5 can be used to switch between the Short and Long Display. The Long Display option displays files by their long document name and type in addition to the standard DOS name and the date and time when the file was last edited.

Choosing 6 lets you **L**ook at the contents of a file without retrieving it. While looking at the file, you can use ↑ , ↓ , or Search (F2) to move through the text. You can also choose the options displayed at the bottom of the screen, which tell you to choose **1** to see the Next Document or **2** to see the Previous Document. Pressing Exit (F7) returns you to the original list of files. Option **6** is the default answer in this menu, which means that you can also press ENTER to Look at the highlighted file.

Choosing **7** for Other Directory lets you specify another directory as the default directory. If you enter the name of a nonexistent directory, you are asked if you want to create a new directory. Choosing **8** lets you Copy a file to another drive and directory.

You can use option **9** to Find specific files. The options and menus there let you search through all or selected files for a word or a phrase, files created between certain dates, or files that were created or typed by a particular person. For details, see "Find Files" in Chapter 3.

You can mark files with an asterisk (type * while a file is highlighted) and then delete, print, copy, or search through all the marked files. Press Exit (F7) or Cancel (F1) to leave the List Files menu.

Exiting WordPerfect

Always use Exit (F7) when you want to leave WordPerfect. If you turn your computer off without exiting, you will see error messages the next time you try to start WordPerfect, indicating the presence of overflow or backup files that were left open.

Lost clusters (a term used by DOS) can also eat up valuable disk space. To correct this problem, insert the DOS disk in drive B and type **chkdsk/f a:** at the B> prompt. Type **N** if asked if you want the lost clusters converted to files. If you are using a hard disk, type **chkdsk/f** at the DOS prompt.

When you press Exit (F7), you are always asked if you want to save the document, regardless of whether you just saved it or not. If you did not make changes to the file since the last time you saved it, a message is displayed on the right side of the status line indicating that the text was not modified.

Save (F10) leaves the document on the screen, while Exit (F7) lets you clear the screen for another document or exit WordPerfect. After you choose whether the file is to be saved, you will see the message "Exit WP? No (Yes)." Type **Y** to exit WordPerfect. Any other key will clear the screen so you can begin working on another document. If you change your mind and want to return to the document on the screen, press Cancel (F1) before typing **Y** or **N**.

If you have two documents in memory and attempt to exit Word-Perfect, you will be placed in the second document. If this happens, repeat the exit procedure.

If there are print jobs remaining in the print queue, you will be asked if you want to cancel them. If you type **N**, you will remain in WordPerfect and can exit after they are printed.

Common Questions

What if I delete text by mistake?

Restore deleted text by pressing Cancel (F1) and then choosing **1** for **R**estore. If you made other deletions in the meantime, choose **2** to see **P**revious deletions until you find what you are looking for. Remember that you can restore only the last three deletions.

How do I find out how to do a footnote?

The basic steps for each feature can be found in the help screens. Press Help (F3), and then press the function key that you have questions about. If you do not know which function key invokes that feature, press the first letter of the feature after pressing Help, and all the features beginning with that letter will be listed. In this case, you would press Help (F3) and choose **F** for **F**ootnote. Note that the feature is found on Footnote (CTRL-F7); press that key to read about using footnotes.

How do I go to page 25 without pressing PGDN 25 times?

You can go to any page by pressing Go To (CTRL-HOME) and entering the number of the page.

How do I know where my files are being saved?

Press List (F5), and the default drive and directory will be displayed. Press ENTER to look at the files or Cancel (F1) to return to the document.

What do I do when I see an error message on the screen?

Check "Error Messages", or look under the specific error message in Chapter 3, "Commands and Features," for solutions.

How can I tell where I am in the document?

The status line in the lower right corner of the screen tells you the page, line, and position of the cursor.

Where is the main menu?

There is not a main menu in WordPerfect. Instead, you can immediately begin creating documents or use Retrieve (SHIFT-F10) to retrieve a document from disk.

   The List Files menu, available by pressing List (F5) and ENTER, is similar to the main menus of other programs.

Where do I find out what all these codes in Reveal Codes mean?

Most codes are self-explanatory. However, if you don't understand a particular code, check the "Codes" section in Chapter 3 for a description.

How do I delete codes?

The easiest way is to press Reveal Codes (ALT-F3), move the cursor to the code, and press DEL. Press Reveal Codes (ALT-F3) to return to the regular screen.

When do I press ENTER?

You should press ENTER at the end of a paragraph or a single line. Let WordPerfect wrap multiple lines for you. If you see an instruction that prompts you for a name or a number, type the name or number and press ENTER.

Do I have to repaginate each time I make changes to a document to make sure the right number of lines are on each page?

No. WordPerfect breaks lines and pages for you automatically.

I prefer 1 1/2-inch margins. How do I change margins permanently so that I don't have to set them for every document?

See "Initial Codes" in Chapter 3 for information about changing default settings.

I'm not sure which key to use to get out of a WordPerfect menu. Should I use Cancel (F1), Exit (F7), ENTER, or the space bar?

Use the key that is most natural for you. If you decide to use ENTER, keep in mind that in the List Files menu, ENTER lets you look at a file. Use one of the other options to exit the List Files menu. Also remember that you need to press Reveal Codes (ALT-F3) to get out of the Reveal Codes screen.

I pressed Exit (F7) and typed N when asked if I wanted to save the document. However, it is still on my screen and I've decided to save it. How do I get rid of the question "Exit WP?" without losing the document?

Press Cancel (F1). You can then follow the steps for saving the document.

I turned on full justification, but the right side of the text is still ragged, not even. When I enter the Line Format menu, it says it's set to Full. How can I tell when it is on or off?

WordPerfect comes with full justification on, but you cannot see it on the screen. If it displayed full justification on the normal editing screen, you would lose some of the speed that WordPerfect is known for.

You can press Format (SHIFT-F8) and choose 1 for Line at any time to confirm whether it is on or off. The View feature on the Print menu (SHIFT-F7) will display right justification on the screen, but no editing is allowed in the View screen.

How large can my documents be?

A document is limited by the amount of disk space available. Smaller files (less than 75 pages) are easier to work with because the larger a document, the longer it takes to scroll through it.

How do I insert text into a paragraph?

Move your cursor to the place where the text is to be inserted, and begin typing. You do not have to press the INS key first. Text is automatically reformatted as you insert the new text.

I made changes to a document, but I have decided that I want to go back to the original. Can I?

Yes. If you save a document, the original remains untouched on the disk. When you retrieve a document, you are retrieving a copy. To go back to the original, clear the screen by pressing Exit (F7) and answering **N** to the question "Save document?" and **N** to "Exit WP?" You can then retrieve another copy of the original document.

There are so many options to choose from. For instance, you can move and retrieve text several different ways. Which is the best way?

There is no best way. Use the method that is easiest for you. Some ways require fewer keystrokes, while others (even if they have the same number of keystrokes) may be easier for you to remember.

I want to take out all margin changes in my document. What is the easiest way?

Rather than searching for each margin change and deleting it manually, use the Replace (ALT-F2) feature. You can search for a margin change and replace it with nothing, thus deleting it.

Can I keep working while printing?

Yes. You can work on the same or a different document. If you send the document on the screen to the printer, it makes a temporary copy of the document and prints that copy. You can continue making changes, but the changes that are not included in the temporary copy will not be printed.

I keep getting multiple copies of a document on the screen. Is the computer making the copies and saving them in the file?

The problem usually arises when you have a document on your screen and go into the List Files menu and retrieve the same or another document. You might also have used Save (F10) and assumed that it would also clear the screen. Save saves the document, but it remains on the screen for future editing. Use Exit (F7) to save the document and clear the screen.

What if my computer locks up and I cannot exit WordPerfect, and none of the keys seem to work? Do I lose my work on the screen?

Although such an occurrence is rare, the computer may lock up because it encounters something it does not understand. When this happens, you cannot exit properly from WordPerfect. You have to turn the computer off and back on, or reboot by pressing CTRL-ALT-DEL. The document on your screen will be lost.

To protect you from losing much work, WordPerfect comes with its Timed Backup feature on. This backs up the document into a file named WP{WP}.BK1 or WP{WP}.BK2, depending on which document (Doc 1 or Doc 2) is being used. You can adjust the number of minutes between each backup or use Save (F10) often. See "Backup" in Chapter 3 for more information.

When is it safe to turn off the computer?

After you press Exit (F7) and answer the "Save document?" question, type **Y** in response to the "Exit WP?" message. You should then see the DOS prompt (B:> and C:\WP51> are examples). You can then turn off the computer.

If you are running WordPerfect Library, you are returned to the Shell menu. If there are no programs in memory (indicated by an asterisk next to the program name), you can turn off the computer. If there are programs in memory, press Exit (F7) again and answer the questions that follow.

Commands and Features

This chapter is an exhaustive A through Z reference guide to all Word-Perfect menus, keys, commands, and features. Each entry includes a short description, a list of keystrokes, helpful hints, and special applications, as well as a list of related entries for further reading.

Although each topic is listed under its WordPerfect name, you can usually look up a feature's generic equivalent for a reference to the correct entry.

ADDITION

WordPerfect's Math feature lets you add a column of numbers. If the column of numbers exists in a WordPerfect table, you can use the Math feature in tables to add the column of numbers.

Keystrokes

To add a single column of numbers, you do not have to define math columns first; however, you do have to turn on Math.

1. Press Columns/Tables (ALT-F7).

2. Choose 3 for Math.

3. Choose 1 for On.

4. Press TAB and type the first number. It is aligned automatically at the decimal point.

5. Press ENTER to move to the next line, and repeat steps 4 and 5 until all numbers are entered.

6. On a blank line below the column of numbers, press TAB once again, type +, and press ENTER.

7. Press Columns/Tables (ALT-F7) and choose **3** for **Math**.

8. Choose **4** for Calculate.

Your screen will look similar to the one shown in Figure 3-1.

Hints

You must have at least one tab setting for the previous example to work. However, if you are using the defaults set by WordPerfect, you do not have to make changes.

If you want to enter a negative value in the column, enclose the number in parentheses, as shown in Figure 3-1.

```
    45.00
   302.75
    (2.43)
   256.77
    35.98
    98.21
    56.84

   793.12+

Math                                    Doc 1 Pg 1 Ln 2.33" Pos 1.8"
```

Figure 3-1.   Using Math to add a column of numbers

The example just given shows how one column of numbers can be added. You can add several columns vertically by separating each column with a tab (alignment codes are automatically inserted) and placing a + below each column. It is best to set tabs first when doing this.

WordPerfect's Math feature can also add across columns as long as you define the math columns first.

WordPerfect's Tables feature lets you add any number of cells. You are not limited to adding rows or columns and can include any cell in a formula. See "Tables" in this chapter for more information.

Applications

You can use the Addition feature for a quick calculation and then delete the column or include it in the document. Because the + sign is considered a math code, it will not be printed with the document.

To enter the + sign, use the + key at the top of the keyboard. If you have NUM LOCK on, you can also use the + key on the numeric keypad.

You can also underline or double-underline the last number in the column to set it off from the total. If you want the number underlined, either press Underline (F8) before and after typing the number or press Block (ALT-F4) and underline the number after you have entered it. See "Underline" in this chapter for more information.

Related Entries

Math
Tables
Underline

ADVANCE

The Advance feature can be used to advance the printer up, down, left, or right a specific distance from the current position. You can also advance to an exact horizontal or vertical position on the page.

Keystrokes

1. Press Format (SHIFT-F8).

2. Choose 4 for Other.

3. Choose 1 for Advance. The following options appear:

```
Advance: 1 Up; 2 Down; 3 Line; 4 Left; 5 Right; 6 Position: 0
```

4. Select the desired option. Keep in mind that options 1, 2, 4, and 5 advance the printer a specific distance from the current position, whereas options 3 and 6 advance the printer to an exact vertical or horizontal position, regardless of the current location.

5. After selecting an option, you are prompted for a measurement. For example, if you choose option 1 for Up, you will see the following prompt:

```
Adv. up 0"
```

6. Enter a measurement and then press Exit (F7) to leave the menu and return to the document.

Hints

With Advance, the cursor will not change position on the screen; however, the "Ln" and "Pos" numbers on the status line will reflect the change. For reassurance, press Reveal Codes (ALT-F3) to see that the appropriate code (AdvUp:n, AdvDn:n, AdvLft:n, AdvRgt:n, AdvToLn:n, or AdvToPos:n) has been inserted at the current location. Pressing Reveal Codes (ALT-F3) again will return you to a full editing screen.

If you type a number without specifying the type of measurement (inches, centimeters, points, and so on), the default unit of measurement will be used. For example, if you enter **2** and the default is inches, the printer will be advanced 2 inches. To use a different unit of measurement for the setting, follow the number with the appropriate abbreviation: **c** for centimeters, **p** for points, **v** for vertical lines, **h** for horizontal spaces, or **w** for WP 5.0 units. WordPerfect will convert the setting to the default unit of measurement. If you use the v or h abbreviation, lines and column positions are figured according to the current font. Since WP units are figured at 1200 per inch, measurements can be precise.

The Superscript and Subscript options found on Fonts (CTRL-F8) are also used to advance a character or group of characters slightly above or below the current line. The amount of vertical movement depends on the font being used. If you want a more or less pronounced movement, use the Advance Up and Advance Down options instead.

If you need to print one or more characters in the same position, consider using the Overstrike feature instead of Advance Left or Advance Right. See "Overstrike" in this chapter for details.

Applications

Instead of inserting several hard returns (lines), you can use Advance to move down a certain distance. Advance is also useful when you are using graphics lines to help place the text a specific distance up or down from the line.

Because WordPerfect takes care of horizontal and vertical spacing for the height and width of the font being used, pressing ENTER and the space bar gives different results from font to font. For example, if you are using a 13pt font, pressing ENTER advances down the page farther than if you were using a 6pt font. Although some of this can be controlled with the Line Height option, Advance lets you advance to a specific position without having to figure the line height required to reach that position. You will probably use Advance often in creating newsletters and other types of desktop publishing applications.

If your printer has not been defined to take advantage of automatic kerning (the ability to move characters incrementally closer to create a better "fit"), you can use the Advance Left and Advance Right options to kern characters manually. For example, if you wanted to kern the "W" and "o" in "WordPerfect," you could advance the printer slightly to the left just after typing the "W" and just before typing the "o." If you use Advance Left and Advance Right to kern characters manually, you might want to specify the measurement in WP units (1200 per inch) to achieve the exact movement needed. To do this, type the number followed by "w."

You could use Advance to advance to the bottom line of the page and label pages rather than pressing ENTER repeatedly or creating a footer.

Related Entries

Line Height
Superscript and Subscript

ALIGN TEXT

Text can be aligned at tab settings or at the right margin.

Options

For details about each of the following options, see the specific entries in this chapter.

Decimal Tabs

This option aligns characters at a decimal point (period), as shown here:

```
    5.90      67.80      35.42
  150.34       2.30   3,456.00
   23.32        .54      20.00
     .03     324.18     836.51
```

Tab Align (CTRL-F6)

This option aligns text at a decimal point or any designated character, such as, ":", shown here. This option can be used without setting a decimal tab.

```
              MEMO
   DATE:
     TO:
   FROM:
SUBJECT:
```

Tabs

This option sets tabs to align text on a decimal point, or it can be used to center-, left-, or right-align text at any particular tab setting, as shown here:

```
  The text      The text              The text
     at         at                          at
    this        this                      this
tab setting    tab setting          tab setting
is centered    is left-aligned     is right-aligned
```

Flush Right (ALT-F6)

This option aligns text at the right margin, as shown here:

```
                        Mr. Robert B. Jones
                        4532 Westwood Lane
                         Detroit, MI 78787
```

To Whom It May Concern:

Please send information about your product to the address
listed above. Thank you in advance for your assistance.

Justification

This option can be set to justify (align) text at the left margin or the right margin, to center the text between the margins, or to justify text at the left and right margins, as shown here:

PREAMBLE

We the people of the United States, in Order to form a more perfect Union, establish Justice, insure domestic Tranquility, provide for the common defense, promote the general Welfare, and secure the Blessings of Liberty to ourselves and our posterity, do ordain and establish this Constitution for the United States of America.

Tables

Each cell or column in a table can have its own type of justification or alignment. For example, you could have a row of cells containing a centered title for the table and a column of numbers aligned at the decimal point, as shown below. See "Tables" for details.

Quarter	1989	1990
First	3,456.13	6,502.78
Second	3,890.99	7,982.34
Third	4,520.64	8,328.21
Fourth	5,788.03	10,829.30

Math

When you use Math, numbers are automatically aligned at the decimal point in numeric columns, as illustrated here:

INVOICE

5	Flags	30.00	150.00
5	Flag Poles	545.00	2,725.00
250	Stars	1.89	472.50
65	Stripes	5.95	386.75
			3,734.25

ALT KEY

The ALT key has no function when it is used alone. When used with the function keys, it executes the features printed in blue on the template.

You can assign any special character, WordPerfect function, or macro to an ALT- or CTRL-key combination with WordPerfect's remappable Keyboard feature. See "Keyboard Layout" in this chapter for more information.

You can also choose to have the ALT key display the pull-down menus. See "Mouse Support and Pull-down Menus" in this chapter for details.

APPEARANCE

Appearance is the second option that is displayed when you press Font (CTRL-F8). It gives you several choices for controlling how text will appear when it is printed. These options include Bold, Underline, Double Underline, Italics, Outline, Shadow, Small Caps, Redline, and Strikeout.

Note: Bold and Underline are also found on the F6 and F8 function keys.

When you turn on the option, both a beginning and ending code are inserted, and the cursor rests on the ending code. After you type the text, you can press → to move past the ending code and turn off the feature, rather than entering the menu and choosing the option again to turn it off.

You can also define a block of text and then choose one of the Appearance options for that block. Appearance, like the Size option, modifies the current font (the last base font or initial font).

Colors or other attributes can be assigned to each option to help distinguish it from regular text. See "Colors/Fonts/Attributes" in this chapter for more information.

Related Entries

Block
Bold
Colors/Fonts/Attributes
Double Underlining
Fonts
Italics

Outline Printing
Redline
Shadow Printing
Small Caps
Strikeout
Underline

APPEND

The Append feature is used to add a block of text to the end of an existing file.

Keystrokes

1. To define a block, move the cursor to one end of the text to be appended and press Block (ALT-F4).

2. Move the cursor to the opposite end of the block.

3. Press Move (CTRL-F4).

4. Choose **1** for **B**lock, **2** for Tabular Column, or **3** for **R**ectangle. (You will most likely want to choose option 1, **B**lock, unless you are working with tabbed columns or a rectangular section of text defined from one corner to the opposite corner.)

5. Type **4** for Append.

6. Enter the name of the file to which the block is to be appended. If you enter the name of a nonexistent file, a file will be created for you.

Hints

Any formatting codes included in the block are also appended to the file. If there are no formatting codes included, the block uses the format of the file.

If the block includes a graphics box that contains text, the text will be appended; any graphics image in the block will not be appended.

See "Move" in this chapter for information about inserting a block of text within a document rather than at the end.

Related Entries

Block
Move

"ARE OTHER COPIES OF WORDPERFECT RUNNING?" ERROR MESSAGE

This message might be displayed when you are trying to start Word-Perfect. The following sections explain why the error message occurs and what you can do to prevent it from appearing.

Reasons

When WordPerfect is started, several temporary files are opened. Some files are used to save cut or copied text, deleted text, and backups. Other files, sometimes referred to as overflow files, hold parts of large documents that cannot fit in memory. If you turn off the computer without first using Exit (F7), the temporary files are left open. The next time WordPerfect is started, it finds these open files. Because WordPerfect cannot distinguish between files left open after an improper exit and those used by another copy of WordPerfect, you are asked if there are other copies of WordPerfect running.

As has been suggested, you could have WordPerfect loaded more than once. If you have expanded memory and WordPerfect Library, you could have two different WordPerfect options on the menu. This lets you have four documents in memory at once instead of two. You can also accomplish this using DESQview, TopView, and other windowing programs such as Microsoft Windows.

If you do not have any of these programs but still have expanded memory, you can press Shell (CTRL-F1) and choose 1 for **G**o to DOS (or **G**o to Shell if the WordPerfect Library's Shell program is running), and then enter **WP** at the DOS prompt. Another copy would then be loaded. Each copy of WordPerfect, however, must have its own set of temporary overflow files.

You might also get the error message if a network is not set up properly (for example, if a single-user copy is being run on a network).

Solutions

If you are sure that no other copies of WordPerfect are running, type **N** in answer to the question, and WordPerfect will be started. This lets WordPerfect overwrite the temporary files.

Always remember to use Exit (F7) to leave WordPerfect. When you see a DOS prompt (such as A:>, B:>, or C:\>) or return to a Shell menu, you can turn off the computer.

If you want to have a second copy of WordPerfect running, type **Y**. The following message is then displayed, telling you that a new directory must be specified:

Directory is in use. New WP Directory: C:\WP51\

Notice that the current directory being used is displayed. Do not press ENTER to accept that directory. It is shown as a reminder that it is currently being used so that the name will not be entered as the new directory.

Remember that each copy of WordPerfect must have its own set of overflow files. If you specify the same directory, the overflow files will become corrupted. Also, if you use the same directory for more than one copy of WordPerfect and exit one copy, you might see the error message "Insert WP 2 disk back into drive and strike any key to continue." This is displayed because the overflow files were closed when the first copy was exited. Therefore, when the second copy of WordPerfect tried to access them, it could not find them and assumed that you had removed the WordPerfect 2 disk. If this happens, you will have to reboot.

ARROW KEYS

See "Cursor Keys."

ASCII TEXT FILES

All WordPerfect files are saved in ASCII (American Standard Code for Information Interchange) format. However, they are not readable by most other programs, because WordPerfect uses the extended ASCII characters as program codes.

   If you need to transfer files to and from other programs, you should use Text In/Out (CTRL-F5) to save and retrieve DOS text files (text without codes). Because codes for such features as headers, footers, footnotes, and endnotes, all of which contain text, would also be stripped from the document, you could consider printing the document to a file on disk. All text normally included with a code is "printed" to the file as if it were regular text. Information for this option is found under "Print to Disk."

   See "DOS Text Files" for details on saving and retrieving DOS text (ASCII) files.

Related Entries

   DOS Text Files
   Print to Disk
   Text In/Out

ATTRIBUTES

WordPerfect sometimes refers to the options found under Font (CTRL-F8) as *attributes*. If you have a monochrome screen, you will be given the choice of assigning various screen attributes (rather than colors or screen fonts) to each option (italics, small caps, fine print, and so on). See "Colors/Font/Attributes" in this chapter for complete instructions on selecting these screen attributes for any type of monitor.

AUTOEXEC.BAT FILE

The AUTOEXEC.BAT file contains a batch of DOS commands that are executed automatically each time the computer is started. When installing WordPerfect, you can have the Install program check the contents of the AUTOEXEC.BAT file and add the WordPerfect directory name to the PATH statement. This enables you to start WordPerfect from any directory.

You can also use the WPINFO program that is included with WordPerfect to view the contents of your AUTOEXEC.BAT file. This file is copied during installation along with other utility files.

If you want to create or edit the AUTOEXEC.BAT file (or any other DOS file) from within WordPerfect, follow the steps presented in the next section.

Keystrokes

The first step in the procedure prevents lines from wrapping when the file is retrieved.

1. Press Format (SHIFT-F8), choose **1** for **L**ine, and choose **7** for **M**argins. Enter **0** and **0** for the left and right margins. (WordPerfect may change the margins to the minimum margins allowed for your printer.) Press Exit (F7) to exit the menu.

2. Press Text In/Out (CTRL-F5).

3. Choose **1** for DOS **T**ext.

4. Choose **2** to **R**etrieve a file. (This option converts each carriage return/line feed to a hard return.)

5. When asked for the name of the file to be retrieved, enter

a:\autoexec.bat if you are using two disk drives or
c:\autoexec.bat if you are using a hard disk.

6. If the file is found, it is displayed on the screen for editing. If you see the message "ERROR: File not found," you can create the file.

7. Make the necessary changes to the existing file, or if you are creating a new AUTOEXEC.BAT file, enter the commands to be included. The following is a sample AUTOEXEC.BAT file:

```
echo off
prompt $p-$g
path c:\;c:\library;c:\wp51;c:\plan;c:\system;c:\wp51\learn
```

8. Press Text In/Out (CTRL-F5) and choose 1 for DOS Text. The file should not be saved as a regular WordPerfect file with Save (F10).

9. Choose 1 for Save and, depending on the system being used, enter **a:\autoexec.bat** or **c:\autoexec.bat**. If the name is already displayed, press ENTER and type **Y** to replace the existing file.

10. Press Exit (F7) and type **N** twice. Do not save the document in the usual way, or it will be saved in WordPerfect format rather than DOS text format.

Applications

The AUTOEXEC.BAT file lets you store commands so you do not have to enter them each time the computer is started. If you enter a DOS command repeatedly, consider placing it in a batch file. Other batch files can be created using the same steps. You can use up to eight characters and the .BAT extension to name a batch file.

Related Entries

DOS Text Files
Text In/Out

AUTOMATICALLY FORMAT AND REWRITE

WordPerfect is set to reformat automatically when text is added or deleted. You can speed up the text display slightly by turning this option off. Text would then be reformatted as the cursor passes through it.

Keystrokes

1. Press Setup (SHIFT-F1).

2. Choose **2** for **D**isplay.

3. Choose **6** for **E**dit-Screen Options.

4. Choose **1** to select the Automatically Format and Rewrite option.

5. Choose **Y** or **N** to turn the option on or off, respectively.

6. Press Exit (F7) when you have finished.

Hints

If you turn this option off, you can reformat manually by moving the cursor through the text with ↓ , Screen Down (+ on the numeric keypad or HOME, ↓), or PGDN. You can also rewrite the entire screen at once by pressing Screen (CTRL-F3) twice.

Applications

It is particularly useful to turn this option off when you are working with side-by-side newspaper columns, where there is constant reformatting when text is added or deleted.

Related Entries

Columns
Rewrite the Screen

AUTOMATIC FONT CHANGES

WordPerfect refers to the Size and Appearance categories on the Font (CTRL-F8) key as *automatic font changes*. The fonts that are selected for these attributes (Small, Large, Extra Large, Italics, Shadow, and so on) are chosen for you by WordPerfect.

When you select a printer, either through Install or by pressing Print (SHIFT-F7) and then choosing **S** for Select a Printer, WordPerfect checks the list of "built-in" fonts and decides which fonts would be best for Small, Large, Extra Large, and so on for *each* font on the list. Because there are not usually many built-in fonts available in a printer, there may not be much of a distinction (if any) between sizes.

Since you may have purchased cartridges, soft fonts, or print wheels for your printer, you will want to edit the printer selection and let WordPerfect know that those fonts are available. Each time new fonts are selected, WordPerfect updates the automatic font changes for each font according to certain percentages:

Fine	60%
Small	80%
Large	120%
Very Large	150%
Extra Large	200%
Super/Subscript	60%

This means that a 10pt font (72 points/inch) would have the following automatic font changes (if they were available):

Fine	6pt
Small	8pt
Large	12pt
Very Large	15pt
Extra Large	20pt
Super/Subscript	6pt

Because 15pt and 20pt are not common point sizes, 14pt and 18pt fonts will most likely be chosen if they are among the list of available fonts.

Keystrokes

If you want to control the size of fonts chosen, you can do so by specifying the percentage in the Setup menu.

1. Press Setup (SHIFT-F1) and choose **4** for Initial Settings.

2. Choose **8** for **P**rint Options.

3. Choose **6** for **S**ize Attribute Ratios and enter the percentages accordingly.

4. Press Exit (F7) when you are finished.

If you have a PostScript printer, the changes just made will take effect immediately. If you don't have a PostScript printer, you will need to update the automatic font changes with the new percentages. The following steps assume you have already selected all the available cartridges and fonts for the printer. If you have not, skip these steps and go to the next paragraph.

1. Press Print (SHIFT-F7).

2. Choose **S** for **S**elect a Printer.

3. With the cursor highlighting the desired printer selection, choose **7** for **U**pdate.

4. When asked if you want new automatic font changes, type **Y**.

5. Press Exit (F7) until you return to the document.

If you have not yet selected cartridges and fonts for the printer, you will need to do so in order for the Size Attribute Ratio to take effect.

1. Press Print (SHIFT-F7) and choose S for Select a Printer.

2. With the cursor highlighting the desired printer selection, choose 3 for Edit.

3. Choose 4 for Cartridges and Fonts.

4. Move the cursor to the appropriate font category and press ENTER to select fonts from that category.

5. Mark all fonts that are available and press Exit (F7) until you leave the Cartridges and Fonts screen.

You will see a message on the screen that says "Updating fonts," which means WordPerfect is reselecting the automatic font changes using the new percentages.

Hints

If you have a Postscript printer (or another type of printer that scales any font to a specific size), you will get the exact size specified. If you don't, WordPerfect will select the font that is the closest in size to the specified percentage.

If you want to have ultimate control over the automatic font changes, you can use the Printer (PTR) program to edit the printer (.PRS) file and select the fonts manually. See Chapter 5, "Printer Program," for more information about using the PTR program.

Related Items

Fonts
Size Attribute Ratios
See also Chapter 5, "Printer Program"

AUTOMATIC REFERENCES

WordPerfect 5.1 has changed the name of the Automatic Reference feature to Cross-Referencing. See "Cross-References" later in this chapter for complete instructions for using the feature.

BACKSPACE KEY

The BACKSPACE key deletes characters to the left of the cursor.

Keystrokes

The BACKSPACE key is in the same position as that key on a typewriter. However, BACKSPACE on your keyboard deletes characters, rather than moving over text as it does on most typewriters. If you want to move the cursor to the left (a nondestructive backspace), use the left arrow key (←).

Press BACKSPACE once to delete the character to the left of the cursor. Continue pressing the key to delete more than one character to the left.

Options

The BACKSPACE key can be used in combination with other keys to delete a larger group of text.

Delete the Word at the Cursor

Press CTRL-BACKSPACE to delete the word at the cursor. Continue pressing this key combination to delete words at (to the right of) the cursor.

Delete the Word to the Left of the Cursor

Press HOME, BACKSPACE to delete from the cursor position to the beginning of the current word. Continue pressing HOME, BACKSPACE to delete words to the left of the cursor.

Delete a Block of Text

After defining a block with Block (ALT-F4), press BACKSPACE (or DEL) and type **Y** to delete the highlighted text. Type **N** to leave the block.

Hints

The BACKSPACE key can also be used to delete blank lines (hard returns), spaces, and codes.

If you are deleting in the regular screen and a code is encountered, you might be asked to confirm the deletion, depending on the code encountered. Type **Y** to delete the code, or press any other key (including BACKSPACE) to skip over the code. Codes such as [Tab] and [→Indent] do not need a confirmation because they are easily inserted in the document.

The BACKSPACE key deletes codes without confirmation when you are in Reveal Codes. (The same keystrokes apply when you are deleting text in Reveal Codes.)

If the Typeover feature is on, BACKSPACE replaces the character to the left of the cursor with a space.

Related Entries

Delete
Delete Codes
Typeover
Undelete

BACKUP

The Timed Backup feature periodically saves the documents on the screen to a temporary backup file every 30 minutes (or whatever amount of time you specify) to guard against power or machine failure.

The Original Document Backup feature can be used to save the previous draft of a document, or you can use the Copy option in the List Files menu to back up your files manually.

Keystrokes

Timed Backup and Original Backup

1. Press Setup (SHIFT-F1).

2. Choose 3 for **E**nvironment.

3. Choose 1 for **B**ackup Options. Figure 3-2 shows the screen that appears.

4. Choose 1 to turn Timed Document Backup on or off, or to change the amount of time between each backup. Choose 2 to turn on the

```
Setup: Backup

     Timed backup files are deleted when you exit WP normally.  If you
     have a power or machine failure, you will find the backup file in the
     backup directory indicated in Setup: Location of Files.

        Backup Directory

     1 - Timed Document Backup              Yes
         Minutes Between Backups            30


     Original backup will save the original document with a .BK! extension
     whenever you replace it during a Save or Exit.

     2 - Original Document Backup           No




Selection: 0
```

Figure 3-2.   Backup options

Original Document Backup feature. See the "Hints" section for a description of how Original Document Backup works.

If you type **Y** for Timed Document Backup, enter the number of minutes that you want between each backup (the default setting is every 30 minutes). See "Hints" for suggestions. If you have specified the backup directory with the Location of Files option (also on the Setup menu), the drive and directory being used for the backup files will be displayed. If there is no directory listed, the drive or directory containing WP.EXE will be used. See the following steps for help in changing the backup directory.

5. Press ENTER twice to return to the Setup menu. Do not press Exit (F7), or the cursor will return to the document instead.

6. Choose **6** for **L**ocation of Files.

7. Choose **1** for **B**ackup Files, and enter the full pathname for the backup files. Only the timed backup files will be kept there; the original backup files will be kept in their original directories. Press Exit (F7) when you are finished.

Retrieve the Backup Files

1. Press List (F5).

2. Enter the drive and directory containing the backup files.

3. Move the cursor to the backup file to be retrieved (WP{WP}.BK1, WP{WP}.BK2 for the timed backup files, or a file with extension .BK! for the original backup files).

4. Choose **1** to **R**etrieve the file.

If you do not retrieve the backup file, you will see a message informing you of its presence the next time WordPerfect attempts to make another backup. You will be given a chance to rename or delete the file, or you can cancel and retrieve the file as previously explained.

Manual Backup

1. Press List (F5).

2. Press ENTER if you want to back up the files in the displayed drive and directory, or enter the drive and directory containing the files to be backed up.

3. Move the cursor to each file to be copied, and press * to mark the file. If you want to back up all the files, press Mark Text (ALT-F5).

4. Choose 8 to select Copy.

5. Choose **Y** in answer to the question "Copy marked files?" If you type **N**, WordPerfect will assume that you want to copy the file highlighted by the cursor.

6. "Copy all marked files to:" appears. Enter the drive and directory to which the files should be copied.

If you get a "Disk Full" error message, replace the backup disk with another disk. WordPerfect will continue copying the remaining files that would not fit on the first disk to the second. Repeat the process if there is not enough room on subsequent disks.

Hints

You can also use the DOS COPY command to back up files without using WordPerfect.

The number of minutes that you enter for the timed backup should be equal to the number of minutes of work you are willing to lose. For example, if you want to make sure that you never lose more than 15 minutes of work, set the number of minutes between backups to 15. If you are working with documents that are longer than 100 pages, you may want to increase the time, however, because the longer the document, the longer it takes to back it up.

At each timed backup, document 1 is saved to a file named WP{WP}.BK1 and document 2 is saved to WP{WP}.BK2, depending on the location of the cursor. If the cursor is in document 1, only that document will be backed up. If you are using WordPerfect on a network, the backup files will be found under the name WP*xxx*}.BK1 or WP*xxx*}.BK2, where *xxx* represents the 3-character username entered when starting WordPerfect.

When you clear the screen to begin working on a new document or exit WordPerfect properly using Exit (F7), the temporary backup file is deleted. Use Save (F10) to permanently save a document.

How Original Document Backup Works

When a file is saved and a file with the same name exists, you are asked if you want to replace the "original" document. If you type **Y**, the original is named with a .BK! extension, the new copy is saved, and then the original with the .BK! extension is deleted. This process protects you from a power failure during a save. However, if you choose the Original Document Backup option, the original with the .BK! extension is not deleted during the save process but is saved so you can keep the previous draft of the document on disk.

Files that do not have a unique first name (as in LETTERS.JAN and LETTERS.FEB) use the same backup file (LETTERS.BK!). In this case, the most recent file is the one saved in the backup file.

If you do not want the .BK! original backup file to be created, you can start WordPerfect with the /NB startup option (WP/NB) for "no backup." Because twice as much disk space as the size of the actual file is needed when backing up a file, this option was added to eliminate the creation of the .BK! file. If you have Original Document Backup on and then start WordPerfect with the /NB option, the .BK! file will not be created, because the /NB option takes precedence.

Related Entries

Location of Files
Setup

BANNERS

If you are running WordPerfect on a network, you can have banners printed at the beginning of each document to identify the job being printed and the person printing it.

Keystrokes

1. Press Print (SHIFT-F7).

2. Choose **A** for Banners.

3. Type **Y** or **N**, depending on whether or not you want banners printed.

4. Press Exit (F7) when you are finished.

BASE FONT

WordPerfect formats all documents for the initial font that was selected when the printer was selected. The other options on the Font key (Large, Small Print, Italics, and so on) are based on that particular font. If you want to change the base font, follow the steps in the next section.

Keystrokes

1. At the point where you want the change to take place, press Font (CTRL-F8).

2. Choose **4** to select Base **F**ont. The list of fonts displayed varies from printer to printer. If you have not selected a printer, you will see an error message. Select a printer before continuing (see "Selecting a Printer" in this chapter for instructions).

3. Move the cursor to the desired font. If you know the name of the font, you can press Search (F2) and type the font's name so the cursor can move to that font.

4. Press ENTER to select the font.

Hints

The list of fonts that you see depends on the cartridges or fonts that you chose when you selected printers. Most printers come with several internal fonts, but if you have additional cartridges or soft fonts, you will need to select them before they are displayed on the list of available fonts. See "Cartridges and Fonts" in this chapter for details.

You can also choose an initial font that will be used for all documents. See "Initial Base Font" later in this chapter for help in designating an initial font to be used for all documents.

If you choose Helvetica 12pt as the base font, italics would be done in Helvetica 12pt Italics, bold would be done in Helvetica 12pt Bold, and so on. Depending on the available list of fonts, fine print might be Helvetica 8pt, small could be 10pt, large might be 14pt, very large might be 18pt, and extra large might be 24pt. If there are no other Helvetica fonts chosen, you will get the typeface that most closely resembles Helvetica. See "Fonts" in this chapter to learn more about selecting fonts.

Related Entries

Cartridges and Fonts
Fonts
Initial Base Font
Selecting a Printer

BASELINE PLACEMENT FOR TYPESETTERS

WordPerfect normally places the top of the first line of text at the top margin. This means that the top of a capital "X" on the first line would meet the top margin setting. The Baseline Placement for Typesetters option lets you set the baseline at the top margin, which means that the *bottom* of a capital "X" would be at the top margin setting.

The Baseline Placement for Typesetters setting takes effect only if the line height is set to a fixed measurement.

Keystrokes

1. Move the cursor to the beginning of the document or to the point at which the change is to take place.

2. If the line height is not set at a fixed measurement, press Format (SHIFT-F8); type **1** for **L**ine, **4** for **L**ine Height, and **2** for **F**ixed; and then enter a setting. Even though the measurement is displayed in inches, you can change it to point sizes. For example, if you will be using a 12pt font, you might want to enter **14p** so there will be 2 points of leading (space) between each line. Press Exit (F7) when you are finished.

3. Press Format (SHIFT-F8) and choose **4** for **O**ther.

4. Choose **6** for **P**rinter Functions.

5. Choose **5** for **B**aseline Placement for Typesetters.

6. Choose **Y** to place the first baseline at the top margin or **N** to return to the standard setting.

7. Press Exit (F7) when you are finished.

Hints

You can select this option at any time in a document and it will affect only the text from that point forward. When you choose to have the option on, the code [BLine:On] is inserted into the document at that point. [BLine:Off] is inserted when you turn the option off. If you do not have a fixed line height, the option will not take effect.

Applications

If you are sending your document to a typesetter, you may want to select this option to follow standard typesetting guidelines.

Related Items

Leading
Line Height

BEEP OPTIONS

WordPerfect makes your computer beep when it wants to make you aware of a search failure, when an error has occurred, or when a hyphenation choice needs to be made. WordPerfect gives you the option of turning the beep on or off.

Keystrokes

1. Press Setup (SHIFT-F1).

2. Choose **3** for **E**nvironment.

3. Choose **2** for Beep Options. The following menu appears (note the default settings):

```
Setup: Beep Options

     1 - Beep on Error          No

     2 - Beep on Hyphenation    Yes

     3 - Beep on Search Failure No
```

4. Choose the desired options and type **Y** or **N**.

5. When you have finished, press Exit (F7) to leave the menu and return to the document.

Hints

If you answer **Y** to the "Beep on search failure" message, you will also hear a beep when Replace is finished.

Beep During Printing

When you are using hand-fed paper or are changing print wheels or cartridges, WordPerfect beeps to let you know when the printer needs to be sent a "Go." If you want a beep to sound in other printing situations, you can use the Wait, Beep, and Prompt commands in the

Printer program to stop, beep, and display a message, respectively, in the Control Printer menu. Sending a "Go "clears the message and printing will continue.

Beep During a Macro or Merge

You can insert a {BELL} command in a macro or merge to alert people running the macro or merge of any error conditions or to prompt them to enter information during a pause. See "Macros" and "Merge" in this chapter for more information about using the {BELL} command.

Related Entries

    Error Messages
    Hyphenation
    Macros
    Merge
    Replace
    Search

BIBLIOGRAPHIES

See "Hanging Paragraphs and Indents" in this chapter.

BINDING OPTIONS

When you are printing pages for double-sided copies or if you are printing with the Double Sided Printing option (found on the Paper Size/Type menu), you can use the Binding Offset feature to shift the printing to the right on odd pages and to the left on even pages to allow space for binding along the spine of the document.

Another option on the Paper Size/Type menu lets you choose to use either the left side of the page (alternating left and right, as just described) or the top edge, where the binding offset is added to the top and bottom of the page.

Keystrokes

Changing the Binding Offset

The binding offset is the amount of space that will be used to determine how much is added to the left margin on odd pages and subtracted from the left margin on even pages. If the binding edge is set to the top edge, the measurement is added to the top or bottom margin.

1. Press Print (SHIFT-F7).

2. Choose **B** for **B**inding Offset.

3. Enter the width.

4. Print the document as you would normally (choose **1** to print the **F**ull Document on the screen, **2** to print the current **P**age, or **3** to print a **D**ocument on Disk).

5. Return the Binding Offset option to the original setting if you do not want to affect the printing of other documents.

Changing the Binding Edge

1. Press Format (SHIFT-F8).

2. Choose **2** for **P**age.

3. Choose **7** for Paper Size/Type.

4. Move the cursor to the paper type for which you want to change the binding edge, and type **5** to **E**dit that selection. You can also type **2** to **A**dd a new selection to the list, at which time you can change the binding edge. (If you are adding a new selection to the menu, you are first asked for the type of paper.) A menu similar to the one shown in Figure 3-3 appears.

5. Choose **7** for **Binding Edge**. The following choices appear:

```
Binding Edge: 1 Top; 2 Left: 0
```

6. Choose **1** for Top and **2** for Left.

7. Press Exit (F7) to leave the menu, and choose **1** to Select the form or press Exit (F7) again if you do not want to select the form but want to have the binding edge set for that form in the future.

Hints

The Binding Offset feature lets you decide how much to add to or subtract from the left or top margins. The amount specified will be added to the left or top margins on odd pages and subtracted from the

```
Format: Edit Paper Definition

        Filename            HPLASEII.PRS

    1 - Paper Size          8.5" x 11"

    2 - Paper Type          Standard

    3 - Font Type           Portrait

    4 - Prompt to Load      No

    5 - Location            Continuous

    6 - Double Sided Printing    No

    7 - Binding Edge        Left

    8 - Labels              No

    9 - Text Adjustment - Top    0"
                      Side       0"

Selection: 0
```

Figure 3-3.   The Binding Edge option in the menu used to edit a paper type

left or top margins on even pages. You will need to set the margins wide enough so that the text will not print off the page after the binding adjustment is made.

If you want to allow extra space for binding but will not be making double-sided copies, change the left margin rather than the Binding Offset.

Related Entries

Paper Size/Type

BLOCK

Block (ALT-F4) is used to identify a section of text that will be moved, copied, deleted, underlined, and so on. You can also use a mouse to highlight a block of text.

Keystrokes

Defining a Block with a Mouse

1. Move the mouse pointer to one end of a block.

2. Press and hold down the left button on the mouse.

3. Drag the mouse to the opposite end of the block and release the left button.

You can now press the right button on the mouse to bring up the menu bar for the pull-down menus and use the left button on the mouse to select a block operation (bold, underline, move, mark for table of contents, and so on) or choose any block option with the function keys.

Using Block (ALT-F4) to Define a Block

1. Move the cursor to one end of the block (either the beginning or the end).

2. Press Block (ALT-F4). "Block on" flashes on the status line. (If you have a Hercules graphics card with RamFont, "Block on" appears but does not flash.)

3. Move the cursor to the opposite end of the block. The text is highlighted in reverse video, as shown in Figure 3-4. If text appears in bold instead, you can change to reverse video in the Colors/ Fonts/Attributes menu. See "Colors/Fonts/Attributes" in this chapter for details.

4. Perform a block operation.

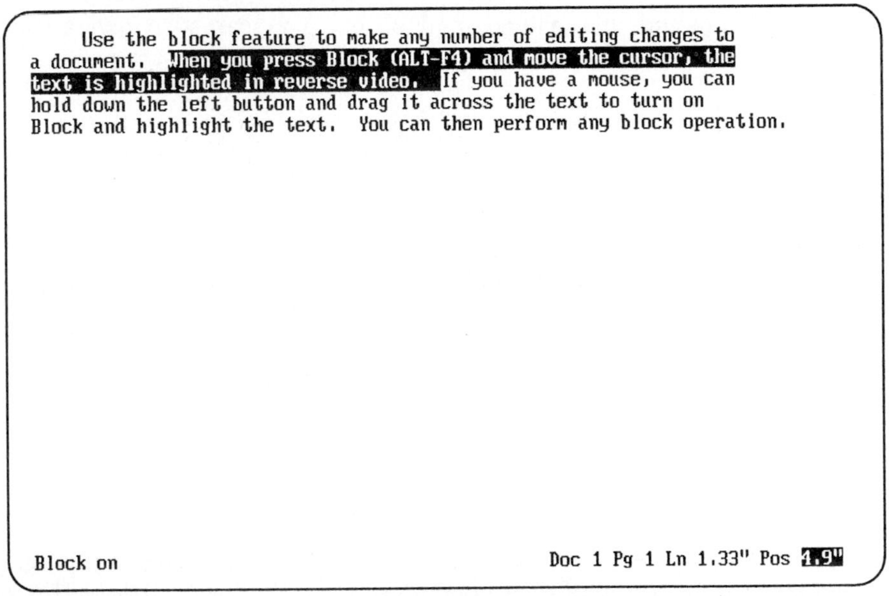

```
    Use the block feature to make any number of editing changes to
a document.  When you press Block (ALT-F4) and move the cursor, the
text is highlighted in reverse video.  If you have a mouse, you can
hold down the left button and drag it across the text to turn on
Block and highlight the text.  You can then perform any block operation.




Block on                                    Doc 1 Pg 1 Ln 1.33" Pos 4.9"
```

Figure 3-4.   A block of highlighted text

With Block, you can highlight by word, sentence, line, or paragraph. Press Block (ALT-F4) and use the following keys to highlight particular sections of text:

Space bar	Highlight the next word
Period	Highlight from the cursor to the end of the sentence
↑ or ↓	Highlight line by line
ENTER	IIighlight from the cursor to the end of the paragraph (text is highlighted up to the next [HRt] code)
Search (F2)	Search for and highlight to the end of the search string

You can also type any character, and the cursor moves to the next occurrence of that character. If the character is not found within approximately the next 2000 characters, you will hear a beep and the cursor will remain at the current location.

Options

The most commonly used Block applications are discussed first.

Bold or Underline a Block

Define a block, and then press Bold (F6) or Underline (F8). A [BOLD] or [UND] code is inserted at the beginning of the block, and a [bold] or [und] code is inserted at the end.

Assigning Other Attributes to a Block

After defining a block, you can press Font (CTRL-F8), choose 1 for Size or 2 for Appearance, and then choose an attribute such as italics, fine print, strikeout, or double-underlining. Assigning an actual font or color to a block is not an option, because there are no ending codes.

The following options appear when you choose Size. Note that Superscript and Subscript appear on this menu:

1 Superscpt; 2 Subscpt; 3 Fine; 4 Small; 5 Large; 6 Vry Large; 7 Ext Large: 0

The following options are listed under the Appearance category. Redline and Strikeout (formerly found on the Mark Text key) are found in this category:

1 Bold 2 Undln 3 Dbl Und 4 Italc 5 Outln 6 Shadw 7 Sm Cap 8 Redln 9 Stkout: 0

Delete a Block

Define a block, and then press BACKSPACE or DEL. Confirm the deletion by typing **Y**.

Move a Block

Define a block, press Move (CTRL-F4), choose **1** for **B**lock, and then choose **1** for **M**ove. Move the cursor to a new location in the document, and press ENTER to retrieve the text. You can press Cancel (F1) to cancel the procedure at any time. Pressing Retrieve (SHIFT-F10) and then ENTER retrieves the cut block if you canceled the operation before retrieving the text. See "Move" in this chapter for more information.

If you have an enhanced keyboard, you can press CTRL-DEL after defining a block instead of pressing Move and the subsequent keystrokes.

Copy a Block

Follow the steps for moving a block, except choose **2** for **C**opy instead of **1** for **M**ove. If you have an enhanced keyboard, you can press CTRL-INS after defining the block.

Attach a Style to a Block of Text

After defining a block of text, press Styles (ALT-F8), highlight the desired style, and then press ENTER to assign the style to that block. Although a paired style is more likely to be assigned to a block (style on and style off codes are inserted at the beginning and end of the block), open styles can also be assigned. The open style would appear at the beginning of the block.

Protect a Block from Page Breaks

Define a block, press Format (SHIFT-F8), and then type **Y** to keep a block from being split between two pages. See "Block Protect" in this chapter for more information.

Save a Block

This feature is useful for saving often-used paragraphs or text. Define a block, press Save (F10), and then enter the name of a file. If you enter the name of a file that is already on disk, you are asked if you want to replace the existing file with the block.

Although undocumented, you can press ENTER without entering a filename to save an "unnamed" block in memory. To retrieve the block, press Retrieve (SHIFT-F10) and again press ENTER without entering a filename. Remember, however, that the last Move/Copy text kept in memory will be replaced. This temporary file will be deleted when you exit WordPerfect.

Append a Block

To add a block of text to the end of a file on disk without first retrieving the file, define the block, press Move (CTRL-F4), choose **1** for **B**lock and **4** for **A**ppend, and then enter the name of the file. The block is appended to the file, and the text remains on the screen.

Center or Flush-Right a Block

Define a block, press Center (SHIFT-F6) or Flush Right (ALT-F6), and then type **Y** to confirm the action. A [Just:Center] or [Just:Right] code is inserted at the beginning of the block, and the current justification setting is inserted at the end of the block. All text between these two codes will either be centered or right-aligned, depending on the option chosen. See "Center Text" and "Flush Right" in this chapter for more information.

Print a Block

Define a block, press Print (SHIFT-F7), and then type **Y** to confirm the action.

Change a Block to Uppercase or Lowercase

Define a block, press Switch (SHIFT-F3), and then choose **1** to change to Uppercase or **2** to switch to Lowercase. If you include the ending punctuation of the previous sentence and choose **2** for Lowercase, the first character in the sentence will remain in uppercase.

Mark Text for Table of Contents, Lists, Index, and Table of Authorities

Define a block, press Mark Text (ALT-F5), and then choose **1** for ToC (Table of Contents), **2** for List, **3** for Index, or **4** for ToA (Table of Authorities). After choosing an option, follow the directions that are displayed on the screen. See the applicable sections in this chapter for detailed instructions.

Replace Text or Codes in a Block

The Replace feature usually works from the cursor position to the end of the document. If you want to use the feature in a specific block of text, define a block and press Replace (ALT-F2). See "Replace" if you need further assistance in answering the prompts.

Check the Spelling in a Block

Define a block, and then press Spell (CTRL-F2). See "Spell" in this chapter for information about checking a word, a page, or a document.

Sort a Block

If you have a list of items within a document that you want sorted, or if you do not want title headings to be included in a sort, block the items to be sorted and then press Merge/Sort (CTRL-F9). Choose the applicable options, and then choose **1** for **P**erform Action. The sorted list replaces the former block.

If the sort routine comes up with a blank screen, you probably used the Select feature in the Sort menu and no records were found that satisfied the selection criteria. Press Cancel (F1), and then choose **1** to **R**estore the original block.

Blocking a Column

WordPerfect has several types of columns: newspaper, parallel, and tabbed. You can use Block in any type of column, just as you would in regular text. The following are options for using Block to cut or copy tabbed columns or rectangular blocks.

Move/Copy Tabular Columns   You must have at least one tab between each column to use this option. Place the cursor at the beginning of the first line of the column to be moved or copied. Press Block (ALT-F4). Move the cursor to the last line in the column (if you want to move or copy more than one column, move the cursor to the right into the next column). A regular block, rather than the column, is highlighted until you press Move (CTRL-F4) and choose **2** for **T**abular Column. The columns, including the tabs preceding the columns, are highlighted. Choose **1** to **M**ove, **2** to **C**opy, or **3** to **D**elete the block. Move the cursor to the new location and then press ENTER. See "Move" for more information.

Rectangular Block   Although most often used in tabbed columns, the rectangular block can be used in any type of text. A rectangular block is not dependent on tabs to define columns; it is defined from corner to corner. With the cursor at one corner (upper left or lower right), press Block (ALT-F4).

Move the cursor to the opposite corner, press Move (CTRL-F4), and then choose **3** for **R**ectangle. Only the rectangle is highlighted. Choose **1** to **M**ove, **2** to **C**opy, or **3** to **D**elete the rectangle. If you choose to move or delete, any remaining text is moved to the left. Move the cursor to the new location and press ENTER to retrieve the rectangle.

Note: Be sure to have a hard return rather than a soft return at the end of each line of text in the block to prevent automatic reformatting.

Hints

Block is turned off after every block operation. If you decide not to perform a block operation and want to turn off Block, you can either press Block (ALT-F4) again or Cancel (F1). If you are using a mouse, you can turn Block off by clicking the left button.

If you find yourself redefining the same block of text for more than one function (for example, you want the block both underlined and in boldface), you can redefine the block more easily by pressing Block (ALT-F4) to turn Block back on and then pressing Go To (CTRL-HOME) twice to return the cursor to the point at which Block was originally turned on. These keystrokes could also be stored as a macro.

Be aware that WordPerfect codes can be included in a block. You might want to press Reveal Codes (ALT-F3) if you are not sure of the cursor's location in relation to the codes. You can turn Block on after you enter the Reveal Codes screen; the location is marked in Reveal Codes with the [Block] code.

Related Entries

Append
Block Protect
Bold
Center Text
Columns
Copy
Delete
Double Underlining
Flush Right
Index
Italics
Lists
Lowercase Text

Mark Text
Move
Outline Printing
Print
Redline
Replace
Save
Spell
Strikeout
Styles
Superscript and Subscript
Switch
Table of Contents
Underline
Uppercase Text

BLOCK PROTECT

Block Protect is used to prevent a block of text from being split between two pages.

Keystrokes

1. Move the cursor to one end of the text.

2. Press Block (ALT-F4).

3. Move to the opposite end.

4. Press Format (SHIFT-F8).

5. Type **Y** to confirm that you want the block protected. [Block Pro:On] and [Block Pro:Off] codes are inserted at the beginning and end of the block.

Hints

If the end of the page happens to fall within a protected block, Word-Perfect will search for the last hard return preceding the [Block Pro:On] code and change it to a page break. However, if that hard return is also protected in another block, it will cause problems. Therefore, when you are protecting consecutive blocks of text, it is important to leave an unprotected hard return between the blocks. If you remember to define your block from the first character in the block to the last character in the block, you should not have a problem.

Widow/Orphan

If a block refuses to be protected (as with two- and three-line para-graphs), it may be conflicting with the Widow/Orphan feature. You can turn off this feature temporarily by moving the cursor above the text to be protected, pressing Format (SHIFT-F8), choosing **1** for Line and **9** for Widow/Orphan Protection, and then typing **N**.

Parallel Columns with Block Protect

The Parallel Columns with Block Protect option uses the block protect codes to protect a group of columns from being split between two pages. When columns are turned on, a [Block Pro:On] code is inserted just before the [Col On] code. When columns are turned off, a [Block Pro:Off] code is inserted just before the [Col Off] code. The following shows how the codes are inserted to end the first group and begin a new one:

[Block Pro:Off][Col Off]
[HRt]
[Block Pro:On][Col On]

Do not disturb the block protect and column on/off codes when editing documents, or the columns may not be protected properly. If you want parallel columns to cross page breaks, use the regular Parallel Columns option. See "Columns" in this chapter for more information.

Protecting Footnotes and Graphics Boxes

You cannot use Block Protect in footnotes or endnotes. However, the Footnote Options menu lets you specify how many lines should be kept together before they are continued on to the next page.

When working with graphics boxes, you can attach a graphics box to a paragraph. In any of the graphics box option menus, you can specify the minimum offset from the paragraph so that if a graphics box cannot fit on the same page with the amount of offset you have specified in the main menu, the box will use the minimum offset to try to keep both the paragraph and the graphics box on that page. If it still cannot be accomplished, both the paragraph and the graphics box will be moved to the next page.

Applications

Use Block Protect for a block that must always stay together, no matter how much text is added and deleted within the block.

Use Conditional End of Page to protect a specific number of lines, as in a title or heading and the first two lines of a paragraph immediately following it.

You can use Block Protect to keep a page break from splitting a table or chart in which the number of lines may increase or decrease later.

Related Entries

Conditional End of Page
Footnotes
Graphics Boxes
Widow/Orphan Protection

BOLD

Bold (F6) is used to produce dark, heavy print at the printer and brighter text on the screen. When printed, it adds emphasis to titles and headings.

Keystrokes

Bold Text As You Type

1. Press Bold (F6) to turn on Bold. Note that the position number on the status line is shown in a higher intensity (or in a different color on a color monitor). See "Hints" if you do not see an indication of Bold on the screen.

2. Type the text.

3. Press Bold (F6) to turn off Bold.

Bold Text After It Has Been Typed

1. Move the cursor to one end of the text to be boldfaced.

2. Press Block (ALT-F4) to turn on Block.

3. Move the cursor to the opposite end of the text to be boldfaced. The text is highlighted as you move the cursor through it.

4. Press Bold (F6).

Remove Bold

1. Move to the beginning or end of the boldfaced text.

2. Press Reveal Codes (ALT-F3) to view the text and codes.

3. Locate the bold-on code, [BOLD], or bold-off code, [bold], and move the cursor so that either code is highlighted.

4. Press DEL to delete the code.

5. Press Reveal Codes (ALT-F3) to return to normal editing.

After you become more familiar with WordPerfect codes, you can tell where the bold code is located by watching the position number on the status line. You can then delete the codes from the regular editing screen.

Hints

When you press Bold (F6) to turn on the Bold feature, the bold-on and bold-off codes are both inserted at the same time—the cursor remains between the two codes. When you press Bold (F6) again to turn off Bold, no code is inserted; instead, the cursor moves over the code. You can use a cursor movement key such as → , END, or ↓ to move the cursor past the bold-off code and accomplish the same purpose as turning off Bold.

In addition to being on the F6 function key, Bold is found on the Font (CTRL-F8) key under the Appearance option.

If you have a section of boldfaced text but decide that you want only part of it to remain bold, move the cursor to the end of the text that you want to remain bold, and press Bold (F6). A bold-off code, [bold], and bold-on code, [BOLD], are inserted, and the cursor remains on the [BOLD] code, as shown here:

```
{   ▲   ▲   ▲   ▲   ▲   ▲   ▲   ▲   ▲   ▲   ▲   ▲   }   ▲   ▲
[Center][BOLD]THIS IS THE TITLE IN BOLD[bold][BOLD][HRt]
[HRt]
[Tab]It is a common mistake to type the title and forget to turn[SRt]
off bold.  To correct this, move the cursor to the end of the title[SRt]
or text that is to remain in bold and press Bold (F6).  This[SRt]
illustration shows how the bold off code [bold] and bold on code[SRt]
[BOLD] are inserted.  Press DEL and type Y to delete the [BOLD][SRt]
code at the cursor to turn off bold for the rest of the text.[bold]



Press Reveal Codes to restore screen
```

WordPerfect automatically inserts the [BOLD] code because it senses that the text to the right is in bold and assumes that you want to keep it that way. Press DEL to delete the [BOLD] code to the right, and type **Y** if you are asked to confirm the deletion. Boldface is removed from the text to the right of the cursor.

Adjusting Bold on the Screen

Monochrome Monitor   Bold text should appear in a higher intensity on a monochrome monitor. If you cannot see the difference, use the brightness and contrast controls to adjust the intensity levels. Setup

(SHIFT-F1) lets you set the screen attribute for bold. See "Colors/ Fonts/Attributes" in this chapter for more information.

Color Monitor   Bold text is displayed in a different color when you are using a color monitor. To change the color, press Setup (SHIFT-F1), choose 2 for **D**isplay and 1 for Colors/Fonts/Attributes, and then choose the option to set colors (because these menus are customized for your hardware, the option to select colors may differ from system to system). If you are using a Hercules In Color Card, you can choose the colors for the background, foreground, underlining, strikeout, and cursor. When you have finished, press Exit (F7).

Press Switch (SHIFT-F3) to switch to document 2 and set the colors there, or press Move (CTRL-F4) if you want to copy the colors from the other document.

If bold text blinks in reverse video, some other program has set the monitor as a single-color monitor with a MODE BW80 command at DOS. Exit WordPerfect, enter **mode co80** to return the "mode" to color, and then reenter WordPerfect. (For Tandy computers, the command is MODE COLOR.) If you have this problem often, especially after running Lotus 1-2-3, consider putting the MODE CO80 command in the batch file used to start WordPerfect.

Moving Bold Text

If text is moved from a boldfaced sentence or paragraph, [BOLD] and [bold] codes are inserted at the beginning and at the end of the block so that the text will remain in bold when it is retrieved. However, if you retrieve the boldfaced block into another boldfaced section of text, Bold will be turned off following the inserted block. This is because the bold-off code at the end of the block supersedes the bold-off code at the end of the original section. If this happens, you can block the text that was "unbolded" and then press Bold (F6).

Using Typeover and Line Draw with Bold

Typeover will not type over codes, nor are codes allowed to type over other characters. If you are using Line Draw to draw a box around text, it is best to type the bold text first and then draw the box around it later. If you want to boldface text that is already inside a box, use Block to highlight the text and then use Bold.

Boldfacing at the Printer

Some printers print bold by doing two or more passes with the printer, whereas some move the print head slightly to the right and reprint the character (called "shadow printing"). Other printers, such as laser printers, may use a bold font.

If you are not satisfied with the way boldface text is printed, check the printer manual for options and modify the printer driver (see Chapter 5, "Printer Program").

Printer Switch Settings

If boldfaced text is printed as shown in the following illustration, check the internal switch settings (sometimes referred to as DIP switches) and make sure that the switch for Auto LF (automatic line feed) is off. If it is on, both WordPerfect and the printer are sending line feeds.

If your bolded text looks like this when it prints, check the
         bolded
Auto LF switch in the printer and make sure it is off.

Related Entries

Block

BORDERS

If your printer has graphics capabilities, you can place borders or graphics images around your page. Border styles include single, double, dashed, dotted, thick, and extra-thick lines.

You can place horizontal or vertical lines of any thickness in any location on the page, including in a header or footer. See "Graphics Lines" in this chapter for more details.

Keystrokes

Selecting the Border Style for a Graphics Box

The method discussed here can be used to create a border around a graphics image.

1. Press Graphics (ALT-F9). The following choices appear:

```
1 Figure; 2 Table Box; 3 Text Box; 4 User Box; 5 Line; 6 Equation: 0
```

2. Type a number from 1 to 4 or choose option 6, depending on the type of graphics box you will be creating.

3. Choose **4** for **O**ptions. Note that you can choose a different border style for each side. If you choose a different type of graphics box, the type of border styles already selected will vary (for example, a text box is set to print a thick line on the top and bottom borders).

```
Options: Figure

    1 - Border Style
        Left                    Single
        Right                   Extra Thick
        Top                     Single
        Bottom                  Extra Thick
```

4. Choose **1** for **B**order Style.

5. Choose the border style from the following choices for the left, right, top, and bottom borders:

```
1 None; 2 Single; 3 Double; 4 Dashed; 5 Dotted; 6 Thick; 7 Extra Thick: 0
```

If you want to create a three-dimensional drop-shadow look, as shown in Figure 3-5, choose Thick or Extra Thick for two adjoining sides (right and bottom, for example) and Single for the remaining two sides.

6. Press Exit (F7) to return to the document.

Now that you have set the border style, you can create the type of graphics box that you want. The selected border style will stay in effect for that particular type of graphics box until you change it again. If you need further help, see "Graphics Boxes" in this chapter.

Placing a Border Around a Page

The following instructions will put the selected border style around each page of the document. If you plan to use this type of feature often, you may want to consider creating an open style and including the following steps in that style. The style can then be retrieved and selected at the beginning of the document. See "Styles" in this chapter for more information about creating, saving, and retrieving styles.

Move to the beginning of the document before following these steps.

1. Decrease the left, right, top, and bottom margins to the point at which you want the border lines placed on the page. For example, if you want the border placed one-half inch from all sides, set all margins at .5".

2. Create a header (either header A or header B) so the border will be placed on every page. You can skip this step if you want the border to be placed on only the current page.

Figure 3-5.   A three-dimensional drop-shadow border created by selecting a thick or extra-thick border for two adjoining sides

3. Press Graphics (ALT-F9), choose 4 for User Box (although you can choose any option), and then choose 4 for Options. Choose 1 to select the Border Style for each side of the box, as explained in the previous section.

4. To create the box, press Graphics (ALT-F9), choose 4 for User Box (or another box of your choice), and then choose 1 for Create.

5. You will now need to set the placement of the box so that it will expand to fill the current margins on the page. To do so, choose 4 for Anchor Type and then 2 for Page. When asked how many pages to skip, enter 0.

Next, choose 5 for Vertical Position and then 1 for Full Page. Choose 6 for Horizontal Position, 1 for Margins, and 4 for Full so it will print the full length of the page and from the left to the right margins. Note that the size of the box changes to fit the margins on the page.

6. The last option on this menu to be changed is option 8, for Wrap Text Around Box. This option should be set to No so the text will print over the box and not wrap to the next page.

7. The menu options should look something like the ones set in Figure 3-6. Press Exit (F7) to return to the header (or the document if you are not including the box in a header).

8. Because you cannot change the top and bottom margins in a header, you may want to press ENTER to create extra space between the top border of the box and the first line of text.

9. Press Exit (F7) to leave the header.

10. Create a footer that contains a [HRt] code. Press ENTER once if you want addditional space between the bottom line of text and the bottom border.

11. After exiting the footer, change the left and right margins to the ones that you want used for the regular text in the document.

If you did not place the box in a header, step 10 is not necessary. Instead, you might consider using the Center Page feature immediately

```
┌─────────────────────────────────────────────────────────────────────────┐
│ Definition: User Box                                                      │
│                                                                           │
│     1 - Filename                                                          │
│                                                                           │
│     2 - Contents            Empty                                         │
│                                                                           │
│     3 - Caption                                                           │
│                                                                           │
│     4 - Anchor Type         Page                                          │
│                                                                           │
│     5 - Vertical Position   Full Page                                     │
│                                                                           │
│     6 - Horizontal Position Margin, Full                                  │
│                                                                           │
│     7 - Size                7.5" wide x 9" high                           │
│                                                                           │
│     8 - Wrap Text Around Box Yes                                          │
│                                                                           │
│     9 - Edit                                                              │
│                                                                           │
│                                                                           │
│                                                                           │
│ Selection: 0                                                              │
└─────────────────────────────────────────────────────────────────────────┘
```

Figure 3-6.   Settings for placing an empty graphics box around a page

after the graphics box code so that text on the page will be centered between the top and bottom margins.

If you have a version of WordPerfect dated 1/19/90 or later, there is an option in the Format: Other menu that lets you specify the width and shading for the borders.

Applications

Figure 3-7 shows a page surrounded by a box with single borders on the left and right and extra-thick borders on the top and bottom of the page.

If you want to include a border on only the top and bottom of the page, you might consider placing horizontal lines in a header and footer. See "Graphics Lines" in this chapter for instructions.

Related Entries

Footers
Graphics Boxes
Graphics Lines

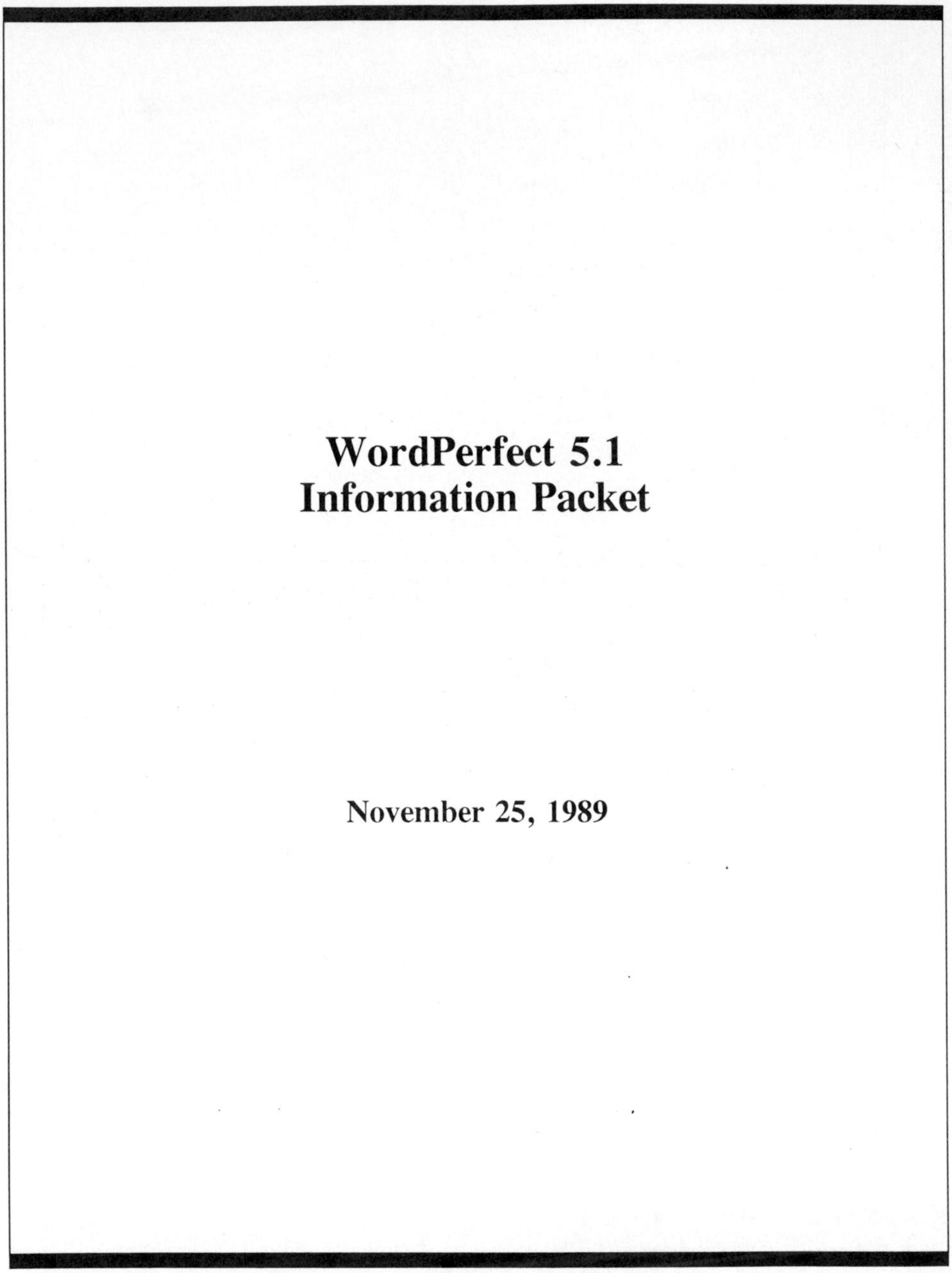

**WordPerfect 5.1
Information Packet**

November 25, 1989

Figure 3-7.   A page with single borders at the sides and extra-thick borders
at the top and bottom of the page

Headers
Margins, Left and Right
Margins, Top and Bottom
Styles

BULLETS

WordPerfect can print any type of bullet included in the WordPerfect character sets (all characters are listed in Appendix A). You can also have a bulleted outline and choose any character for the bullet characters. The most common way to insert a bullet is to use the Compose (CTRL-2) feature.

Keystrokes

Creating a Bullet

To insert a bullet into a document, follow these steps:

1. Press Compose (CTRL-2). Use the 2 at the top of the keyboard, not F2 or the 2 on the numeric keypad.

2. Type the two characters on the left to create the type of bullet displayed on the right. The following are some examples of characters that can be used. Appendix A includes other options.

*.	•
**	●
*o	○
*O	○

Bulleted Outlines

Before creating a bulleted outline, you need to choose that type of outline.

```
Paragraph Number Definition

  1 - Starting Paragraph Number              1
        (in legal style)
                                         Levels
                               1    2    3    4    5    6    7    8
  2 - Paragraph                1.   a.   i.   (1)  (a)  (i)  1)   a)
  3 - Outline                  I.   A.   1.   a.   (1)  (a)  i)   a)
  4 - Legal (1.1.1)            1    .1   .1   .1   .1   .1   .1   .1
  5 - Bullets                  •    o    -    ■    *    +    ·    x
  6 - User-defined

  Current Definition          I.   A.   1.   a.   (1)  (a)  i)   a)
  Attach Previous Level            No   No   No   No   No   No   No

  7 - Enter Inserts Paragraph Number         Yes

  8 - Automatically Adjust to Current Level  Yes

  9 - Outline Style Name

Selection: 0
```

Figure 3-8.   Paragraph and Outline Numbering Definition menu

1. Press Date/Outline (SHIFT-F5).

2. Choose **6** for **D**efine. The menu shown in Figure 3-8 appears.

3. Choose **5** for **B**ullets, or if you want to use different bullet characters, choose **6** for **U**ser-defined. If you chose option **6**, enter the bullet character to be used for each level. You can use any character (other than A, a, 1, I, or i). Press Compose (CTRL-2) to enter bullet characters as described previously.

4. Press Exit (F7) when you have finished, choose **4** for **O**utline, and then choose **1** to turn outline **O**n.

Continue pressing ENTER to insert a bullet for the first item in the outline. Press TAB when you want to change to the next level or SHIFT-TAB to change to the previous level.

Hints

You can also press ALT and then type a number on the numeric keypad to insert a bullet character. Use the following numbers to insert the characters shown on the right:

ALT-7   ●

ALT-9   ○

ALT-248   ○

ALT-249   ·

Related Entries

Outline
Special Characters

CALCULATIONS

See "Addition," "Math," or "Tables," in this chapter.

CANCEL

Use Cancel (F1) to back out of menus and prompts or to cancel a procedure. If a menu is not on the screen or a Macro, Merge, Search, or other function is not in progress, Cancel is used to restore deleted text.

Pressing the middle button on a three-button mouse is the same as pressing Cancel (F1). If your mouse has only two buttons, press both buttons simultaneously to cancel.

Keystrokes

Cancel Menus and Prompts

When you are in a WordPerfect menu or prompt, press Cancel (F1) to return to the previous menu or to return to the document if you are in a first-level menu. This works in the pull-down menus as well as in any other WordPerfect menu.

Cancel a Procedure

During execution of a Macro, Merge, Search, or Replace function, press Cancel (F1) to cancel the procedure.

If you are asked to hyphenate a word, you can press Cancel (F1) instead of ESC if you do not want the word hyphenated. The word is then wrapped to the next line and the code [/] is inserted at the beginning of the word so it will not be presented for hyphenation again.

Restore Deleted Text

1. Position the cursor where you want the last deletion to be restored.

2. Press Cancel (F1). The last deletion is highlighted.

3. Choose **1** to **R**estore the deletion or **2** to show a **P**revious Deletion. The last three deletions can be displayed and restored.

Hints

A deletion in WordPerfect is a group of consecutive deletions before any other key (including a cursor movement key) is pressed. Any combination of deletion keys can be used in one deletion.

Related Entries

Cancel a Print Job
Macros
Merge
Replace
Search
Undelete

CANCEL A PRINT JOB

You can cancel a single print job or all print jobs in the queue.

Keystrokes

1. Press Print (SHIFT-F7).

2. Choose 4 to select the Control Printer option.

3. Choose 1 for Cancel Job(s). Continue with one of the following options.

Cancel Current Print Job   The current print job number is displayed. Press ENTER.

Cancel Other Print Job   Type the job number for the print job to be canceled and then press ENTER.

Cancel All Print Jobs   Type * (rather than a number) for all print jobs. Type **Y** to confirm the cancellation.

Hints

The printer may not stop printing immediately, because it needs to empty its buffer first. You may see the message "Press "C" to cancel job immediately." If you type **C**, the print file is deleted and no additional data is sent to the printer. You can manually clear the buffer by turning the printer off and then on after the print job has been canceled.

If you wait long enough after canceling a print job, the printer will clear the buffer and reset itself automatically. However, if you typed **C** in answer to the message, you may see a warning that if you cancel the print job using this method, you may have to initialize the printer again because WordPerfect will reset the printer.

Rather than canceling print jobs so another job can be printed first, use option **2** for **R**ush a print Job.

If you need to stop the printer because of jammed paper or other temporary problems, use option **5** for **S**top printing. The current print job remains in the queue and will start at the beginning when the printer is sent a Go. If you do not want to start at the beginning, cancel the print job and start the printing on a specific page. See "Print" in this chapter for specifics.

Related Entries

Print
Rush a Print Job
Stop Printing

"CAN'T FIND CORRECT COPY OF WP" ERROR MESSAGE

If you see this error message, enter the full pathname of WordPerfect's location followed by the WP.EXE filename. If WordPerfect is found in a directory named WP51, you would enter **c:\wp51\wp.exe**.

Reasons

If you see this error message, you might have one of the following situations:

• If you are using DOS version 2.*x*, it might appear once, but it should never appear again after you have answered the question the first time.

• You might be using DOS version 2.*x* with an AT, Compaq DeskPro 286, or another AT-compatible computer. You should run only DOS version 3.*x* or above on an AT-compatible computer.

• If you are using DOS version 3.*x*, you might have mixed 2.*x* and 3.*x* files. To check this, exit WordPerfect with Exit (F7) not Shell (CTRL-F1). When the DOS prompt appears, enter **ver**. The version of DOS is displayed. Next, run COMMAND.COM by entering **command** at the DOS prompt. These commands should both display the same version of DOS.

Solution

You should have to respond to this error message only once (if ever). If you are using an AT or AT compatible, verify that you are running only DOS version 3.*x*. If versions of DOS are mixed, recopy COMMAND.COM from the DOS master disk onto the boot disk and reboot.

CAPITALIZATION

You can capitalize text as you type or after you have entered it.

Keystrokes

Capitalize While Typing

To capitalize a single character, hold down either SHIFT key and type the character. To capitalize several characters, press CAPS LOCK, type the text, and then press CAPS LOCK again to turn it off. While CAPS LOCK is on, "Pos" on the status line is shown in caps ("POS").

Capitalize Text After It Has Been Typed

1. Move the cursor to one end of the text that is to be in uppercase.

2. Press Block (ALT-F4) to turn on Block.

3. Move the cursor to the opposite end of the block.

4. Press Switch (SHIFT-F3).

5. Choose **1** to change the block to Uppercase.

Hints

If you press SHIFT while CAPS LOCK is on, any letter that is typed will be lowercase rather than uppercase. If you have the Repeat Performance program by WordPerfect Corporation, you can disable this "reverse CAPS LOCK" and always get uppercase characters, even if you press the SHIFT key accidentally.

The CAPS LOCK key only affects the letters "A" through "Z." If you want a character such as the ampersand (&) or the quotation mark ("), usually obtained by pressing SHIFT and another key, you will still need to press the SHIFT key.

Related Entries

Block
Switch

CAPTIONS

Graphics boxes (figures, tables, text boxes, user boxes, and equations) can include a caption above or below the box. You can also choose whether to have the caption appear inside or outside the border.

Keystrokes

Changing the Caption Position and Style

1. Press Graphics (ALT-F9).

2. Type a number from 1 to 4 or choose option **6** to select the type of graphics box to be created.

3. Choose **4** for **O**ptions. A menu similar to the one shown in Figure 3-9 appears. Each type of graphics box has different settings in this menu.

4. Options 6 and 7 control the style and position of the caption. Each type of graphics box (figure, table box, text box, user-defined box, and equation) has its own default settings, as shown here:

Figure	[BOLD]Figure 1[bold]	Below box, outside borders
Table Box	[BOLD]Table 1[bold]	Above box, outside borders
Text Box	[BOLD]1[bold]	Below box, outside borders
User Box	[BOLD]1[bold]	Below box, outside borders
Equation	[BOLD](1)[bold]	Right side of box

5. If you want the caption to be underlined, italicized, uppercase, or in some other style, choose option **6** and enter the new style, including the name and the number 1, if desired. Keep in mind that

```
Options: Figure

    1 - Border Style
            Left                        Single
            Right                       Single
            Top                         Single
            Bottom                      Single
    2 - Outside Border Space
            Left                        0.167"
            Right                       0.167"
            Top                         0.167"
            Bottom                      0.167"
    3 - Inside Border Space
            Left                        0"
            Right                       0"
            Top                         0"
            Bottom                      0"
    4 - First Level Numbering Method   Numbers
    5 - Second Level Numbering Method  Off
    6 - Caption Number Style           [BOLD]Figure 1[bold]
    7 - Position of Caption            Below box, Outside borders
    8 - Minimum Offset from Paragraph  0"
    9 - Gray Shading (% of black)      0%

Selection: 0
```

Figure 3-9.   Caption options for each type of graphics box

the number 1 represents any number. Even though a 1 is included in the Table Box caption style, it will be printed in Roman numerals as shown in option 4 on the menu, First Level Numbering Method.

6. Choose 7 for **P**osition of Caption. After you select an option to have the caption appear above or below the box, a second prompt appears, asking if you want the caption outside or inside the borders. Make the appropriate selection. If you are selecting the position for an equations box, you can choose to have the caption printed above, below, to the left, or to the right of the equation.

7. After selecting other applicable graphics box options, press Exit (F7) to return to the document.

Entering a Caption

Choosing the position and style of a caption does not mean that the caption will automatically be included with every graphics box. The following steps will let you insert a caption when you are creating a graphics box:

1. Press Graphics (ALT-F9).

2. Type a number from 1 to 4 or choose option **6**, depending on the type of graphics box that you want to create.

3. Choose **1** for Create. The Graphics Box Definition menu appears, as shown in Figure 3-10.

4. Choose **3** to enter a Caption. The default caption style is inserted.

5. Press Exit (F7) to accept the displayed caption, edit it and include text of your own, or delete it and enter a different caption. Because the text shown is really a code, the exact text in the code cannot be edited. If you delete the caption that was displayed initially, you can insert it again by pressing Graphics (ALT-F9) while in this screen.

6. Finish choosing the graphics options on the menu and press Exit (F7) when you have finished. See "Graphics Boxes" if you need more assistance.

Hints

When editing a caption, you can leave the caption at the left side of the graphics box, press Center (SHIFT-F6) just before the caption to center it

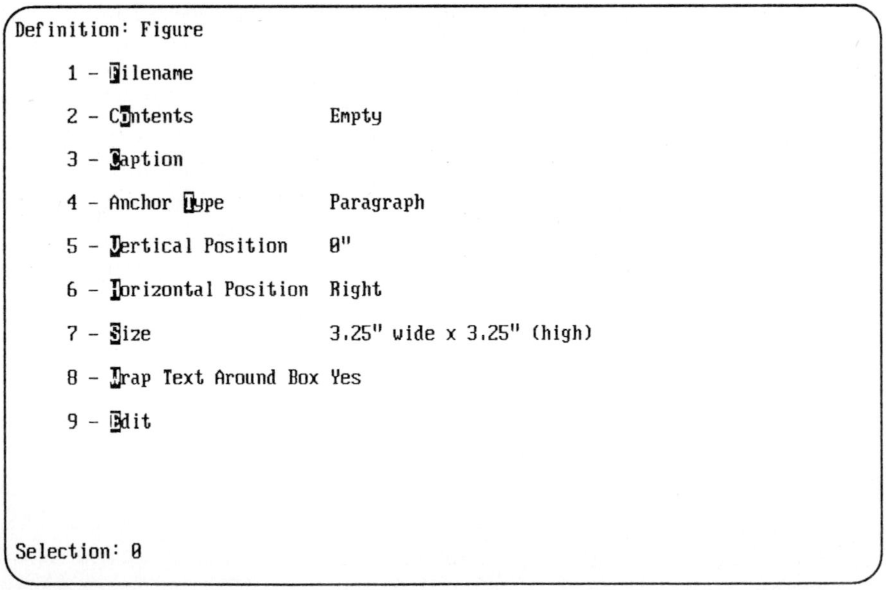

```
Definition: Figure

      1 - Filename

      2 - Contents          Empty

      3 - Caption

      4 - Anchor Type        Paragraph

      5 - Vertical Position  0"

      6 - Horizontal Position  Right

      7 - Size               3.25" wide x 3.25" (high)

      8 - Wrap Text Around Box  Yes

      9 - Edit

Selection: 0
```

Figure 3-10.   Graphics box definition menu

over or under the graphics box, or press Flush Right (ALT-F6) to place it against the right side of the graphics box. The caption is printed in the initial font or in the font that is current when graphics box options are selected. If you find that the caption is being printed in an unusual font, check the document's initial base font by pressing Format (SHIFT-F8), choosing 3 for **D**ocument, and then choosing 3 for Initial Base Font. Select the appropriate font from the list. You can also select a different font or attribute for the caption with Font (CTRL-F8).

There is no practical limit on the amount of text that can be placed in a caption.

Each type of a graphics box has its own set of options. The option settings affect that particular type of graphics box until another option code is encountered.

Applications

A caption could read as follows:

Figure 1.   First Quarter Sales of 1990

You can also format the same caption a little differently, as shown here:

Figure   1.
First Quarter Sales of 1990

Related Entries

Fonts
Graphics Boxes
Initial Base Font

CARRIAGE RETURN

See "ENTER."

CARTRIDGES AND FONTS

When selecting a printer, you can also select the fonts, cartridges, or print wheels available for that printer.

Keystrokes

Selecting Cartridges and Fonts

When you select a printer during the installation process, it selects only the internal fonts that are available in that printer. If you purchase extra cartridges, soft fonts, or print wheels, you will need to inform WordPerfect of their presence so they will also appear on the list of fonts.

1. Press Print (SHIFT-F7).

2. Choose S for the Select Printer option.

3. Move the cursor to the desired printer selection and choose 3 for Edit.

4. Choose 4 for Cartridges and Fonts. You will see a screen that is similar to the one shown in Figure 3-11. The options that appear on this menu are dependent on your type of printer. If your printer cannot accept downloaded soft fonts, the Soft Fonts option will not appear.

5. Before selecting the fonts, make a note of the quantity in the upper right corner. If you have two cartridge slots and only one is indicated, you can choose option 2 to Change the Quantity and increase that number. If you have more than 350K of memory in your printer, you can increase the quantity for the Soft Fonts option as well.

6. Move the cursor to any of the options listed (usually Cartridges, Print Wheels, or Soft Fonts).

7. Choose 1 to Select the fonts. Your screen should look like the one shown in Figure 3-12, in which a list of cartridges available for the

```
Select Printer: Cartridges and Fonts

Font Category                          Quantity          Available

Built-In
Cartridges                                2                 2
Soft Fonts                              350 K             350 K




NOTE: Most items listed under the Font Category (with the exception of Built-In)
are optional and must be purchased separately from your dealer or manufacturer.

In order to print soft fonts marked '*', you must run the Initialize Printer
option in WP each time you turn your printer on.

If soft fonts are not located in the same directory as your printer files, you
must specify a Path for Downloadable Fonts in the Select Printer: Edit menu.

1 Select; 2 Change Quantity; N Name search: 1
```

Figure 3-11.   A menu for selecting cartridges and fonts

```
Select Printer: Cartridges                         Quantity
                                        Total:        2
                                    Available:        2

                                                   Quantity Used

HP A Courier 1                                          1
HP B Tms Proportional 1                                1
HP Bar Codes & More                                    1
HP C International 1                                    1
HP D Prestige Elite                                    1
HP E Letter Gothic                                     1
HP F Tms Proportional 2                                1
HP Forms Etc.                                          1
HP G Legal Elite                                       1
HP Global Text                                         1
HP Great Start                                         1
HP H Legal Courier                                     1
HP J Math Elite                                        1
HP K Math Tms                                          1
HP L Courier P&L                                       1
HP M Prestige Elite P&L                                1

Mark:  * Present when print job begins        Press Exit to save
                                              Press Cancel to cancel
```

Figure 3-12.   A partial list of cartridges available for the HP Series II printer

HP Series II printer is displayed.

If you select the Soft Fonts category, you will most likely see a screen similar to the one shown in Figure 3-13, in which soft fonts are divided into "font libraries." This, along with the built-in font library, enables WordPerfect to share sets of fonts among certain printers to provide more efficient use of disk space and eliminate unnecessary duplication. Move the cursor to the desired category and choose 1 to Select it. You will then see a list of fonts available in that font library, as shown in Figure 3-14.

8. Move the cursor to each cartridge or font that will be present when the print job begins, and type *. (The Initialize Printer option on the Print (SHIFT-F7) menu can be used to download all soft fonts marked as "Present when print job begins.") If you use the * to mark soft fonts, the amount of memory used for that font (displayed in the right column) is subtracted from the available quantity above. You will not be able to continue marking fonts with an * if you run out of memory (as indicated by the number in the upper right corner).

Also note the total number of fonts that you can select in the upper right corner (if applicable). As you select fonts, this number is decremented to keep you from selecting more fonts than the limitation allows.

9. Move the cursor to each font that can be loaded and unloaded (swapped) during a print job, and type +. Because most printers do not have cartridges that can be swapped, this option is not listed for cartridge fonts. However, print wheels can be swapped and can be marked with a + to indicate that they are available. If you do not want to take up more of the printer's memory than is absolutely necessary, you can use the option for soft fonts that will be used occasionally. The printer will then download them as needed.

10. Press Exit (F7) when you have finished (you may need to press it more than once). The message "Updating font:" will appear on the status line. This message indicates that WordPerfect is checking the information about each font and is determining how automatic font changes are to be made (when changing to fine, small, extra large, italics, and so on).

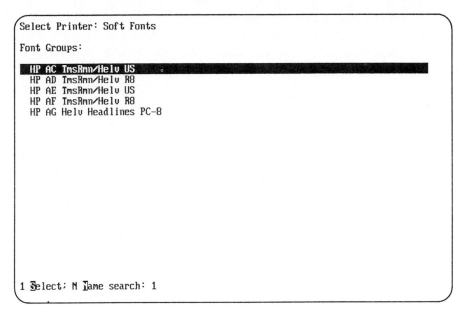

```
Select Printer: Soft Fonts

Font Groups:

   HP AC TmsRmn/Helv US        o
   HP AD TmsRmn/Helv R8
   HP AE TmsRmn/Helv US
   HP AF TmsRmn/Helv R8
   HP AG Helv Headlines PC-8




1 Select; N Name search: 1
```

Figure 3-13.   A screen showing soft font libraries

```
Select Printer: Soft Fonts              Quantity    * Fonts
                             Total:        350 K       32
                         Available:        350 K       32

HP AC TmsRmn/Helv US                        Quantity Used

   (AC) Helv  6pt                              8 K
   (AC) Helv  6pt (Land)                       8 K
   (AC) Helv  6pt Bold                         8 K
   (AC) Helv  6pt Bold (Land)                  8 K
   (AC) Helv  6pt Italic                       8 K
   (AC) Helv  6pt Italic (Land)                8 K
   (AC) Helv  8pt                              9 K
   (AC) Helv  8pt (Land)                       9 K
   (AC) Helv  8pt Bold                        11 K
   (AC) Helv  8pt Bold (Land)                 11 K
   (AC) Helv  8pt Italic                      10 K
   (AC) Helv  8pt Italic (Land)               10 K
   (AC) Helv 10pt                             13 K
   (AC) Helv 10pt (Land)                      13 K
   (AC) Helv 10pt Bold                        13 K
   (AC) Helv 10pt Bold (Land)                 13 K

Mark:  * Present when print job begins         Press Exit to save
       + Can be loaded/unloaded during job    Press Cancel to cancel
```

Figure 3-14.   A sample list of soft fonts in one font library

When you return to the menu that is used for editing a printer selection, continue to the next sections for instructions about specifying the location of soft fonts (so WordPerfect can find them when downloading them to the printer) and selecting an initial base font.

Specifying the Location of Soft Fonts

If you have selected soft fonts for your printer, you will need to tell WordPerfect where those soft fonts are located so it can download them to the printer.

1. While in the menu used to edit a printer selection (shown in Figure 3-15), choose **6** for Path for **D**ownloadable Fonts and Printer Command Files.

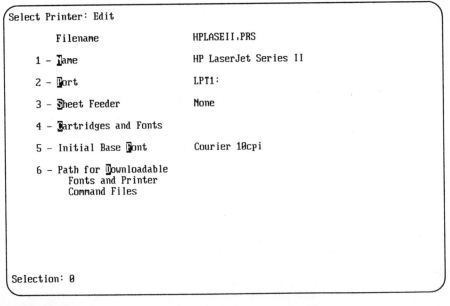

Figure 3-15.   The menu used to edit a printer selection

2. Enter the pathname (drive and directory) where the soft fonts are located. If you kept the soft fonts in a directory called FONTS on your hard disk, you would enter **c:\fonts**.

Selecting an Initial Base Font

WordPerfect has automatically selected a base font that will be used by all documents (unless you specify a different font in the document). This will usually be a 10-pitch font. Follow these steps to select a different font:

1. From the menu used to edit a printer selection (shown in Figure 3-15), type **5** for Initial Base Font.

2. The list of available fonts in your printer is displayed. The same list of fonts appears when you press Font (CTRL-F8) from within the document.

3. Move the cursor to the font to be selected and press ENTER.

The font selected as the initial base font will be used for each new document created from that point on. The selection will be stored with each document and can be changed for each document by pressing Format (SHIFT-F8), choosing **3** for Document, and then choosing **3** for Initial Base Font.

Downloading Soft Fonts

If you have selected soft fonts for your printer, you will need to download them to the printer before they can be used.

1. If you are still in the menu used for editing a printer selection, press Exit (F7) twice to return to the Print menu. If you are in the regular editing screen, press Print (SHIFT-F7).

2. Choose **7** to Initialize the Printer.

3. Choose **Y** to Proceed with Printer Initialization.

All fonts that were marked with an asterisk (*) to show that they would be present when the print job begins will be downloaded to the printer. If you look in the Control Printer menu, you will notice that the process is similar to printing a file. If you see the message "File not found," you probably have not specified the correct path for the downloadable fonts. If this is the case, follow the steps just given.

Hints

The fonts you select will be the ones that appear when you press Font (CTRL-F8) and choose **4** for **B**ase Font. You can scroll through the list and select the highlighted font by pressing ENTER.

This list can be updated at any time if you add to your collection of cartridges, soft fonts, or print wheels.

Related Entries

Fonts
Selecting a Printer

CENTER PAGE FROM TOP TO BOTTOM

The Center Page command centers a single page vertically between the top and bottom margins.

Keystrokes

1. Press Go To (CTRL-HOME) and then ↑ to move the cursor to the top of the page.

2. Press Format (SHIFT-F8).

3. Choose **2** for **P**age.

4. Choose **1** for Center Page.

5. Choose **Y** to insert the [Center Pg] code.

6. Press Exit (F7) to leave the menu and return to the document.

Hints

Before you choose the Center Page command, the cursor must be at the beginning of the page before any text. Pressing Go To (CTRL-HOME) and ↑ moves the cursor to the top of the page before all codes and text. Pressing Reveal Codes (ALT-F3) shows the location of codes in relation to the cursor.

When you choose the Center Page option, the [Center Pg] code is inserted at the location of the cursor and centers only the current page. If you want other pages centered vertically as well, you need to insert this command at the top of each page that you want centered.

If you want the Center Page command to work correctly, you should have no hard returns before the first line or after the last line of text on the page. If extra lines are included, they will also be centered.

Use Center (SHIFT-F6) to center a line at a time between the left and right margins. Use Center Justification (press Format (SHIFT-F8), and choose **1** for **Line**, **3** for **Justification**, and **2** for **Center**) to center all lines from that point until another justification option is selected.

Center Page with Hand-Fed Paper

If you are printing on hand-fed paper, WordPerfect does not add a top margin. Instead, it assumes that you allow for the top margin when you feed the paper into the printer. When printing a centered page, continue to allow for the standard top margin when feeding the paper into the printer.

Applications

You can place the Center Page command in a macro or style for single-page letters. You can also use it at the beginning of title pages, as shown in Figure 3-16.

Humanities 101
Professor Green
Section 21

The Renaissance

Ms. Sharon Brown
November 25, 1990

Figure 3-16.   A title page created with the Center Page command

Related Entries

Center Text
Justification

CENTER TEXT

Center (SHIFT-F6) is used to center text between the left and right margins or to center text over a specific position.

The Justification feature in WordPerfect lets you center a large section of text between the left and right margins without having to press Center (SHIFT-F6) for each line.

You can also include dot leaders from the left margin to the centered text.

Keystrokes

Center Between Margins

1. Move the cursor to the left margin.

2. Press Center (SHIFT-F6). The cursor is centered between the current margins.

3. Type the text to be centered.

4. Press ENTER to turn off centering and move to the next line.

Center Existing Text

1. Move the cursor to the beginning of the line.

2. Press Center (SHIFT-F6).

3. Press ↓ and the line is centered. (If the cursor does not move down and the line is not centered, there is no hard return [HRt] code at the end of the line. Press END to move to the end of the line, and press ENTER to center the line.)

Center an Existing Block of Text

If you have several lines of text to center, you can center a block instead of one line at a time.

1. Move the cursor to one end of the block to be centered.

2. Press Block (ALT-F4) to turn on Block.

3. Move the cursor to the opposite end of the block.

4. Press Center (SHIFT-F6).

5. Type **Y** when asked "[Just:Center]? No (Yes)."

A [Just:Center] code is placed at the beginning of the block, and a code indicating the current justification is inserted at the end of the block. For example, if you had left justification on and centered a block, the [Just:Left] code would be placed at the end of the block so the text following the centered block would be left-justified.

Center a Line with a Dot Leader

1. Press Center (SHIFT-F6).

2. Type the text to be centered.

3. Press Center (SHIFT-F6) again. A dot leader will appear from the left margin (or text at the left) leading to the centered text.

To add a dot leader after the text has been typed, move the cursor anywhere in the centered line and press Center (SHIFT-F6).

Centered Tabs

You can insert a centered tab anytime, regardless of the current tab setting. Press HOME and then Center (SHIFT-F6) to move the cursor to the next tab setting and center any text typed thereafter. If you want to insert a dot leader as well, press HOME, HOME, Center (SHIFT-F6).

The [CNTR TAB] code is inserted if this feature is used.

Centering Text at a Specific Position

If you use the space bar or press TAB to move to a specific position, you can then press Center (SHIFT-F6) and text will be centered at that point instead of being centered between the left and right margins.

Remove Centering

To remove centering, delete the [Center] code shown in Reveal Codes (ALT-F3). You can also remove centering from the normal screen by moving the cursor to the first character in the centered text, pressing BACKSPACE, and typing **Y** when asked to confirm the deletion.

Hints

When you press Center, a [Center] code is inserted. Pressing ENTER, TAB, or Flush Right (ALT-F6) turns off centering.

Text can be centered between the margins even if there is text at the left or right margin, as shown in the following illustration:

Monthly Department Newsletter

Volume I Number 9	Confidential	November 25, 1989

Place the cursor at the end of the first line, and then press Center (SHIFT-F6). If you are more than one space from the end of the line, the text will be centered at that position rather than between the margins. The text at the right in the example was entered with Flush Right (ALT-F6).

See "Tabs" for more information about centering text at a tab setting. WordPerfect also has an option to center a page vertically between the top and bottom margins; for more information, see "Center Page from Top to Bottom" in this chapter.

Drawing Lines Around Centered Text

You cannot draw a box around centered text with Line Draw. Instead, use a table or place text in a graphics box. See "Tables" and "Graphics Boxes" for more information.

Applications

You can use Center for titles and headings in regular documents or columns. Figure 3-17 shows how Center can be used before and within columns. Center can also be used to center a caption above or below a graphics box. See "Captions" and "Graphics Boxes" in this chapter for more information.

Related Entries

Block
Captions
Center Page from Top to Bottom
Columns
Graphics Boxes
Tabs

CENTIMETERS

You can use inches, centimeters, points, or WordPerfect (WP) units to make formatting changes. If you are more comfortable working with centimeters, you can change the way WordPerfect displays the cursor's

Bill of Rights

The first ten amendments form what is know as the
"Bill of Rights" ratified on December 15, 1791.

One

Congress shall make no law respecting an establishment of religion, or prohibiting the free exercise thereof; or abridging the freedom of speech, or of the press; or the right of the people peaceably to assemble, and to petition the Government for a redress of grievances.

Two

A well regulated Militia, being necessary to the security of a free State, the right of the people to keep and bear Arms, shall not be infringed.

Three

No Soldier shall, in time of peace be quartered in any house, without the consent of the Owner, nor in time of war, but in a manner to be prescribed by law.

Four

The right of the people to be secure in their persons, houses, papers, and effects, against unreasonable searches and seizures, shall not be violated, and no Warrants shall issue, but upon probably cause, supported by Oath or affirmation, and particularly describing the place to be searched, and the persons or things to be seized.

Five

No person shall be held to answer for a capital, or otherwise infamous crime, unless on a presentment or indictment of a Grand Jury, except in cases arising in the land or naval forces, or in the Militia, when in actual service in time of War or public danger; nor shall any person be subject for the same offense to be a witness against himself, nor be deprived of life, liberty, or property, without due process of law; nor shall private property be taken for public use, without just compensation.

Six

In all Criminal prosecutions, the accused shall enjoy the right to a speedy and public trial, by an impartial jury of the State and district wherein the crime shall have been committed, which district shall have been previously ascertained by law, and to be informed of the nature and cause of the accusation; to be confronted with the witnesses against him; to have compulsory process for obtaining witnesses in his favor, and to have the Assistance of Counsel for his defense.

Seven

In suits at common law, where the value in controversy shall exceed twenty dollars, the right of trial by jury shall be otherwise re-examined in any Court of the United States, than according to the rules of the common law.

Eight

Excessive bail shall not be required, nor excessive fines imposed, nor cruel and unusual punishments inflicted.

Nine

The enumeration in the Constitution, of certain rights, shall not be construed to deny or disparage others retained by the people.

Ten

The Powers not delegated to the United States by the Constitution, nor prohibited by it to the States, are reserved to the States respectively, or to the people.

Figure 3-17.   A page created using the Center command before and within columns

position on the status line as well as the unit of measurement used to enter and display format settings. See "Units of Measurement" in this chapter for details.

If you do not want to change the overall unit of measurement but need to set a single option in centimeters, you can type **c** after a measurement and it will be converted to the default unit of measurement. For example, if you wanted to set left and right margins of 3cm, you could enter **3c**. It would be converted to 1.18" if inches were the default unit of measurement.

Related Entries

Units of Measure

CHANGE DIRECTORY

You can change the default directory for saving and retrieving files from within WordPerfect or from DOS.

Keystrokes

Change the Default Directory Permanently

1. Press Setup (SHIFT-F1).

2. Choose **6** for Location of Files.

3. Choose **7** for Documents.

4. Enter the drive and directory to be used as the location for all documents.

5. Press Exit (F7) to return to the document.

Change the Directory Temporarily

1. Press List (F5).

2. Type = to change the default directory.

3. Enter the pathname for the new directory (as in **b:**, **c:\wp51** and **c:\personal\letters**).

4. Press Cancel (F1) to set the new directory and return to the document, or press ENTER to see the list of files within that directory.

If you enter the List Files menu and decide to change the default directory, you can do it in the List Files menu (rather than leaving that menu and following the previous steps).

1. After pressing List (F5) and then ENTER to see the list of files, choose **7** for **O**ther Directory.

2. Enter the pathname for the new directory.

3. Press ENTER to see the list of files within the new directory.

4. Press Exit (F7) to return to the document.

You can also move the cursor to the directory in the List Files menu that is to be used as the new default; type **7**, and press ENTER.

Hints

If you enter the name of a directory that does not exist, you are asked if you want to create a new directory. Type **Y** or **N**.

While in the List Files menu, you can move from one directory to another without changing the default directory. You can move up the tree structure by moving the cursor to " .. Parent < DIR >" (as shown in Figure 3-18) and pressing ENTER twice. If you are in a directory called C:\LEARN, the parent directory is the root directory (\). If you are in a directory called C:\PERSONAL\LETTERS, the parent directory is \PERSONAL.

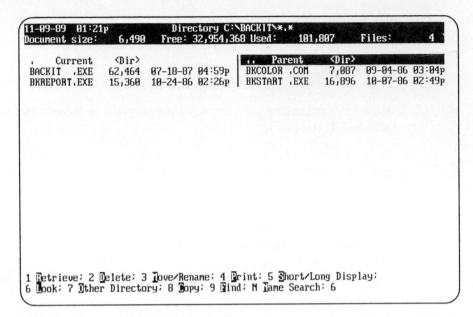

```
11-09-89  01:21p              Directory C:\BACKIT\*.*
Document size:    6,490   Free: 32,954,368 Used:    101,807    Files:      4

.   Current    <Dir>              ..   Parent    <Dir>
BACKIT  .EXE   62,464  07-18-87 04:59p  BKCOLOR .COM    7,007  09-04-86 03:04p
BKREPORT.EXE   15,360  10-24-86 02:26p  BKSTART .EXE   16,096  10-07-86 02:49p












1 Retrieve; 2 Delete; 3 Move/Rename; 4 Print; 5 Short/Long Display;
6 Look; 7 Other Directory; 8 Copy; 9 Find; N Name Search: 6
```

Figure 3-18.   Moving to the parent directory by selecting ".. Parent <DIR>" and pressing ENTER twice

You can also move down the tree structure to look into subdirectories. For instance, if you are in the root directory, you might see a List Files menu similar to the one shown in Figure 3-19. You can move the cursor to any directory listed and press ENTER twice to see the files in that subdirectory.

Related Entries

Directories

CHARACTERS PER INCH

With WordPerfect you do not need to specify the number of characters per inch (also called "cpi" or "pitch") when you are choosing a font.

The pitch is displayed with the font name itself in the list of fonts. See "Fonts" in this chapter for more information. If you need to specify the pitch, see "Word and Letter Spacing" in this chapter for details.

CLEAR TABS

See "Tabs"

CODES

WordPerfect codes control how a document is formatted and printed. When you choose a WordPerfect feature such as Bold, Underline, Indent, or Footnote, a code is placed in the document at the cursor's location. These codes are not visible within the text so that the text on the screen will look more like the printed document. However, there is

```
11-09-89  01:23p            Directory C:\*.*
Document size:    6,484  Free: 32,952,320 Used:   1,071,744    Files:      90

.    Current   <Dir>              ..    Parent    <Dir>
BACKIT   .     <Dir>  07-29-89 03:47p   BOOK     .     <Dir>  07-29-89 03:47p
CLIENTS  .     <Dir>  07-29-89 03:48p   CNEW     .     <Dir>  08-29-89 03:37p
DOS      .     <Dir>  07-24-89 07:59a   DRAW     .     <Dir>  07-28-89 10:31p
GAMES    .     <Dir>  07-29-89 03:48p   GRAPHICS .     <Dir>  10-07-89 05:47p
INSET    .     <Dir>  09-18-89 02:00p   KAREN    .     <Dir>  07-29-89 03:49p
LETTERS  .     <Dir>  10-07-89 05:48p   LIBRARY  .     <Dir>  07-29-89 03:50p
MACROS   .     <Dir>  07-29-89 04:23p   MOUSE    .     <Dir>  07-29-89 12:05p
NEW      .     <Dir>  08-29-89 02:46p   NEWBOOK  .     <Dir>  08-03-89 12:33p
NEWDATA  .     <Dir>  07-29-89 04:23p   PERSONAL .     <Dir>  07-29-89 04:24p
PLAN     .     <Dir>  07-28-89 10:24p   REF      .     <Dir>  10-30-89 05:05p
SCREENS  .     <Dir>  09-12-89 05:40p   TOOLS    .     <Dir>  10-21-89 05:01p
USA      .     <Dir>  11-04-89 04:41p   UTILITY  .     <Dir>  07-24-89 08:00a
WP50     .     <Dir>  07-29-89 04:25p   WP51     .     <Dir>  07-28-89 10:19p
ZAP      .     <Dir>  07-29-89 04:41p   {LF}FM   .DIR   2,975  11-05-89 04:36p
{ME}     .MES  4,096  07-29-89 10:26p   {ME}1    .MEB  43,008  07-29-89 10:27p
{ME}1    .MET      0  07-29-89 10:26p   {WP}LEX  .SUP     264  06-09-87 11:27p
4201     .CPI  6,404  10-06-88 12:00a   4208     .CPI     720  10-06-88 12:00a
42MACROS.MAC   3,705  08-30-88 03:23p ▼ 5202     .CPI     370  10-06-88 12:00a

1 Retrieve; 2 Delete; 3 Move/Rename; 4 Print; 5 Short/Long Display;
6 Look; 7 Other Directory; 8 Copy; 9 Find; N Name Search: 6
```

Figure 3-19.   List Files menu in the root directory showing several subdirectories (marked with "<DIR>")

usually an indication on the screen that the function has been chosen (for example, the text will be boldfaced, underlined, or indented, or a number for a footnote will be inserted).

If you want to see the text with the codes, press Reveal Codes (ALT-F3). The screen will be split, showing a ruler line with the regular screen above it and the text with codes below it. Figure 3-20 shows a Reveal Codes screen. The text is shown as regular text, whereas codes are shown in boldface. Also note that the location of the cursor in Reveal Codes is shown in reverse video. Press Reveal Codes (ALT-F3) to return to the full-screen display.

You can type, insert codes, or delete while in Reveal Codes. In fact, you can do anything in the Reveal Codes screen that you can do in the regular editing screen. See "Reveal Codes" in this chapter for more information.

List of Codes

The following list shows all the WordPerfect codes as they appear on the Reveal Codes screen. In the code designations, *n* represents a

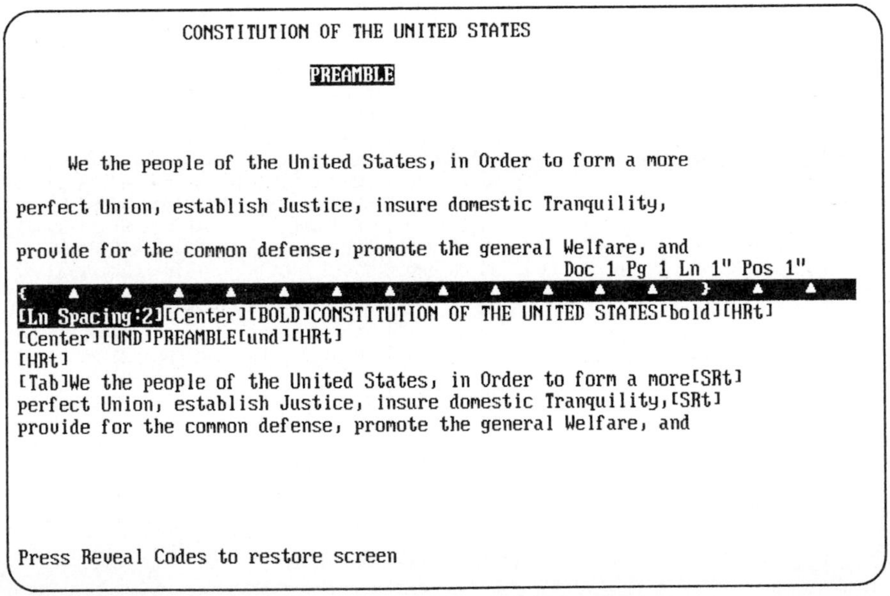

```
                    CONSTITUTION OF THE UNITED STATES
                              PREAMBLE


      We the people of the United States, in Order to form a more

perfect Union, establish Justice, insure domestic Tranquility,

provide for the common defense, promote the general Welfare, and
                                        Doc 1 Pg 1 Ln 1" Pos 1"
{  ▲   ▲   ▲   ▲   ▲   ▲   ▲   ▲    ▲   ▲   ▲   }   ▲   ▲
[Ln Spacing:2][Center][BOLD]CONSTITUTION OF THE UNITED STATES[bold][HRt]
[Center][UND]PREAMBLE[und][HRt]
[HRt]
[Tab]We the people of the United States, in Order to form a more[SRt]
perfect Union, establish Justice, insure domestic Tranquility,[SRt]
provide for the common defense, promote the general Welfare, and



Press Reveal Codes to restore screen
```

Figure 3-20.   The Reveal Codes screen showing both text and codes below

number or text that may appear in the code.

Code	Meaning
▌	Cursor position
[ ]	Hard space
[-]	Hard hyphen
-	Soft hyphen
[/]	Cancel hyphenation (inserted by canceling a hyphenation request or pressing HOME, /)
[AdvDn:n]	Advance down from current location
[AdvLft:n]	Advance left from current location
[AdvRgt:n]	Advance right from current location
[AdvToLn:n]	Advance to specific vertical position
[AdvToPos:n]	Advance to specific horizontal position
[AdvUp:n]	Advance up from current location
[BLine:On]	Baseline Placement on
[BLine:Off]	Baseline Placement off
[Block]	Beginning of block
[BlockPro:Off]	Block Protect off
[BlockPro:On]	Block Protect on
[BOLD][bold]	Bold (begin and end)
[Box Num]	Code used in graphics box captions to indicate the placement of the graphics box number
[Cell]	Cell marker in a table
[Center]	Centering
[Center Pg]	Center page from top to bottom
[Cndl EOP:n]	Conditional end of page (n = number of lines)

Code	Meaning
[Cntr Tab]	Centered tab
[CNTR TAB]	Centered tab inserted manually by pressing HOME, Center (SHIFT-F6)
[Col Def:Type;n;n, . . .]	Column definition (Type = Newspaper, Parallel, or Parallel/Block Protect; first n = number of columns; remaining n = left and right margins for each column)
[Col On][Col Off]	Beginning and end of columns
[Color:n]	Change print color (n = color name)
[Comment]	Comment in document
[Date:n]	Date/time code (n = format)
[DBL UND][dbl und]	Double underlining (begin and end)
[Dec Tab]	Decimal tab
[DEC TAB]	Decimal tab inserted manually with Tab Align (CTRL-F6)
[Decml/AlgnChar:a,b]	Decimal/alignment character (a = decimal character, b = thousands separator)
[DefMark:Index,n]	Index definition (n = format)
[DefMark:List,n:n]	List definition (first n = list number, second n = type of page numbering)
[DefMark:ToA,n]	Table of authorities definition (n = section number)
[DefMark:ToC,n;n,n . . .]	Table of contents definition (first n = number of levels, subsequent n = type of page numbering for each level)
[Dorm HRt]	Dormant hard return

Code	**Meaning**
[DSRt]	Deleteable soft return used by WordPerfect to wrap a line when a space cannot be found to convert to a regular [SRt] and when hyphenation is off
[EndDef]	End of index, list, table of contents, or table of authorities definition
[EndMark:List,n]	End marked text (n = list number)
[EndMark:ToC,n]	End marked text (n = ToC level)
[Endnote:n;[Note Num]*text*]	Endnote (n = endnote number)
[Endnote Placement]	Location for endnotes
[End Opt]	Endnote options
[Equ Box:n;*filename*;*caption*]	Equation box (n = number, *filename* = name of file in equation; *caption* = position and caption)
[Equ Opt]	Equation box options
[EXT LARGE][ext large]	Extra-large font change (begin and end)
[Fig Box:n]	Figure box (n = figure number)
[Fig Opt]	Figure options
[FINE][fine]	Fine-print font change (begin and end)
[Flsh Rgt]	Flush right
[Font:n]	Font change (n = font name)
[Font:*n]	Converted font change (n = font name)
[Footer A;n;*text*]	Footer definition (A = either A or B, n = occurrence)
[Footnote:n;[Note Num]*text*]	Footnote (n = footnote number)
[Force:n]	Force odd or even page (n = odd or even)
[Ftn Opt]	Footnote options

Code	Meaning
[Header *A;n;text*]	Header definition (*A* = either A or B, *n* = occurrence)
[HLine:*n,n* ...]	Horizontal graphics line (*n* = horizontal position, vertical position, length, width, and shading)
[HPg]	Hard page
[Hrd Row]	Hard row in tables inserted by pressing Hard Page (CTRL-ENTER) while in a table
[HRt]	Hard return
[HRt-SPg]	Hard return that is currently being used as a soft page break
[Hyph On][Hyph Off]	Hyphenation on and off
[HZone:*n,n*]	Reset hyphenation zone (*n* = left, right)
[→Indent]	Beginning of indent
[→Indent←]	Beginning of left/right indent
[Index:*heading;sub heading*]	Index mark
[Insert Pg Num:*n*]	Insert page number (*n* = page number style)
[ISRt]	Inserted soft return (press HOME, ENTER to insert). Used to wrap a line when hyphenation is not desired; useful for wrapping words separated with a slash (for example, Colors/Fonts/Attributes) or after an em or en dash
[ITALC][italc]	Italics (begin and end codes)
[Just:*n*]	Justification (*n* = Left, Center, Right, or Full)
[Just Lim:*n*]	Justification limits
[Kern:On][Kern:Off]	Kerning on and off codes
[L/R Mar:*n,n*]	Left and right margin setting
[Lang:*n*]	Change to specified language, where *n* = one of the following:

Code	Meaning
	CA Catalan
	CZ Czechoslovakian
	DK Danish
	NL Dutch
	OZ English-Australia
	UK English-United Kingdom
	US English-United States
	SU Finnish
	CF French-Canada
	FR French-France
	DE German-Germany
	SD German-Switzerland
	GR Greek
	IS Icelandic
	IT Italian
	NO Norwegian
	BR Portuguese-Brazil
	PO Portuguese-Portugal
	RU Russian
	ES Spanish
	SV Swedish
[LARGE][large]	Large font (begin and end codes)
[Leading Adj:a,b]	Leading Adjustment (a = Primary [SRt], b = Secondary [HRt])
[Link End]	End of spreadsheet link
[Link:*filename;range;cells*]	Beginning of spreadsheet link
[Ln Height:n]	Line height setting (n = Auto or Fixed setting)
[Ln Num:On][Ln Num:Off]	Beginning and end of line numbering
[Ln Spacing:n]	Line spacing (n = spacing)
[←Mar Rel:n]	Left margin release (n = positions moved)

Code	Meaning
[Mark:List,*n*]	Begin marked text for list (*n* = list number)
[Mark:ToC,*n*]	Begin marked text for table of contents (*n* = ToC level)
[Math Def]	Definition of math columns
[Math On][Math Off]	Beginning and end of Math
[!]	Formula calculation
[t]	Subtotal entry
[+]	Do subtotal
[T]	Total entry
[=]	Do total
[*]	Do grand total
[N]	Negate
[Mrg:END FIELD]	End of a merge field
[Mrg:END RECORD]	End of a merge record
[Mrg:*n*]	Merge code (*n* = code)
[New * Num:*n*]	Code used to restart numbering (* = End, Ftn, Fig, Tbl, Txt, Usr, or Equ, and *n* = the new number)
[Note Num]	Code used in footnotes and endnotes
[Outline On][Outline Off]	Beginning and end of outlining
[Outline Lvl *n type*]	Outline style (*n* = level number and *type* = Open Style, Style On, or Style Off)
[OUTLN][outln]	Begin and end of outline printing
[Overstk:*n*]	Overstrike (*n* = string of characters to print in the same position)
[Paper Sz/Typ:*n,name*]	Paper size and type code used to select forms (*n* = width and height, *name* = type of form)
[Par Num:Auto]	Automatic paragraph/outline number

Code	Meaning
[Par Num Def]	Paragraph numbering definition
[Par Num:n]	Fixed paragraph number (n = level number)
[Pg Numbering:n]	Set position for page numbers (n = position)
[Pg Num:n]	New page number (n = number)
[Pg Num Style:n]	Page-number style (n = style)
[Ptr Cmnd:n]	Printer command (n = printer command)
[REDLN][redln]	Redline (begin and end)
[Ref(ID):n]	Reference marker (n = Pg, Par, Ftn, End, Fig, Tbl, Txt Box, Usr Box, Equ Box, depending on the type of reference)
[Rgt Tab]	Right-aligned tab
[RGT TAB]	Right-aligned tab inserted with HOME, Flush Right (ALT-F6)
[Row]	Marks a new row in a table
[SHADW][shadw]	Shadow printing (begin and end)
[SMALL][small]	Small font change (begin and end)
[SM CAP][sm cap]	Small caps (begin and end)
[SPg]	Soft new page
[SRt]	Soft return
[STKOUT][stkout]	Strikeout (begin and end)
[Style On][Style Off]	Style on and off codes
[Subdoc:n]	Subdocument (n = filename)
[Subdoc Start][Subdoc End]	Beginning and end of subdocument after document has been expanded
[SUBSCPT][subscpt]	Subscript (begin and end)
[Suppress:n]	Suppress page format options (n = formats)
[SUPRSCPT][suprscpt]	Superscript (begin and end)
[Tab]	Left-aligned tab

Code	Meaning
[TAB]	Left-aligned tab (overrides current type of tab) inserted manually by pressing HOME, TAB. Can be used in tables or outlining where TAB is usually used to go to the next cell or level
[Tab Set:*type:n,n* ...]	Tab setting (*type* = Rel (relative) or Abs (absolute) and *n* = tab settings)
[Target (ID)]	Target used in automatic references
[T/B Mar:*n*]	Set top margin in half lines
[Tbl Box:*n*]	Table box (*n* = table number)
[Tbl Def:*n;n,n,n* ...]	Table definition (first *n* = table number, second *n* = number of columns, subsequent *n*'s = widths of each column)
[Tbl Off]	End of table
[Tbl Opt]	Table options
[ToA:*n*;short form;Full Form]	Mark table of authorities with full form (*n* = section number)
[ToA:*n*;short form;]	Mark table of authorities with short form (*n* = section number)
[Text Box:*n*;*filename*;*caption*]	Text box (*n* = text box number)
[Txt Opt]	Text box options
[UND][und]	Underline (begin and end)
[Undrln:Spaces,Tabs]	Underline spaces and/or tabs
[Usr Box:*n*]	User box (*n* = box number)
[Usr Opt]	User box options
[Vline:*n,n* ...]	Vertical graphics line (*n* = vertical position, horizontal position, length of line, width, and shading)
[VRY LRG][vry lrg]	Very large font change (begin and end)

Code	Meaning
[W/O On][W/O Off]	Widow/orphan on and off codes
[Wrd/Ltr Spacing:n,n]	Word and letter spacing (first n = word spacing, second n = letter spacing)

Related Entries

Reveal Codes

COLORS/FONTS/ATTRIBUTES

If you have a color monitor, you can select a background color and a different color for the text (referred to as the "foreground" color). You can also choose a background and foreground color for attributes such as italics, fine print, and redline. If you do not have a color monitor, you can still choose various screen attributes, even though color is not available.

If you have a Hercules RamFont card, you can select various screen fonts instead. For example, italics will appear as italics on screen, and large print will appear in a larger font.

WordPerfect categorizes monitors into four groups: monochrome, CGA, EGA/VGA, and Hercules with RamFont. The following discussion describes each category and the possibilities for each.

With a monochrome monitor, you can choose to have any of the attributes displayed in bold, underline, reverse video, or blinking.

If you have a CGA monitor, you can choose from 16 foreground and 8 background colors. Underlining is displayed as a different color rather than having underline actually appear on the screen.

EGA monitors have two text modes. In one mode, the EGA acts like a CGA monitor, with which you can choose from 16 foreground and 8 background colors. In the other mode, you can give up 8 of the 16 foreground colors used for text and display one of the following instead:

Underline
Italics
Small caps
512 characters (instead of the standard 256)

If you give up 8 colors, however, they are the high-intensity colors — you will not be able to show bold as bold, but as a different color instead.

If you select the option to display 512 characters instead of 256, you will be able to see more math and Greek symbols (as well as other special characters) on the screen during editing. (See "Special Characters" in this chapter for more information about entering characters not found on the keyboard.)

There are two Hercules RamFont display cards: the Hercules Graphics Card Plus for monochrome monitors and the InColor Card for EGA monitors. Either card can be put into two text modes. In the first mode, the card acts like a monochrome monitor, with just one normal font (even if it is connected to EGA monitor). The second mode is RamFont mode, in which the card can display up to 3072 characters. These characters are divided into 12 screen fonts, each having 256 characters, or into 6 fonts, each having 512 characters. The card can also display bold, underline, strikeout, and block (reverse video). The InColor Card also lets you select the colors for foreground, background, cursor, underline, strikeout, and bold.

Keystrokes

The following steps for selecting different colors will vary depending on the type of monitor or graphics card available: monochrome, CGA, EGA/VGA, or Hercules. If you want to check the type of monitor currently selected, see "Graphics Screen Type" in this chapter.

Selecting Colors, Fonts, or Attributes

1. Press Setup (SHIFT-F1).

2. Choose 2 for Display.

3. Choose 1 for Colors/Fonts/Attributes.

4. The menu you see will depend on your monitor type. If you have a monochrome screen, you will go directly to the menu that lets you determine how the attributes are to be displayed — boldface, under-

lined, block (reverse video), blinking, or a combination of these screen attributes.

If you have a CGA color monitor, you will see a menu option asking if you want fast text display. Choose **2** to select that option, and type **Y**. If you see flickering, or "snow," on your screen after answering this question, choose this option again and type **N**.

If you have an EGA or VGA graphics card, you will see the following menu:

```
Setup: Colors/Fonts

    1 - Screen Colors

    2 - Italics Font, 8 Foreground Colors

    3 - Underline Font, 8 Foreground Colors

    4 - Small Caps Font, 8 Foreground Colors

    5 - 512 Characters, 8 Foreground Colors

  *6 - Normal Font Only, 16 Foreground Colors
```

Note that you can choose to have one font and all 16 colors, or you can give up 8 colors and have underline, italics, small caps, or 512 characters appear on the screen while editing.

If you have a Hercules RamFont card, you are asked if you want 12 screen fonts with 256 characters in each font, 6 screen fonts with 512 characters, or the normal font only, as shown selected in the following example:

```
Setup: Fonts/Attributes

    1 - Screen Attributes

    2 - 12 Fonts, 256 Characters

    3 - 6  Fonts, 512 Characters

  *4 - Normal Font Only

    5 - Foreground/Background Colors
```

5. After selecting the fast text option for your CGA or the mode for your EGA or RamFont, you are ready to select colors, attributes, or fonts for the different WordPerfect attributes, such as italics, super-script, and extra large. If you have a monochrome monitor, you should be in the Setup: Attributes menu, as shown in Figure 3-21.

If you have a CGA, EGA, or VGA, or if you have a monitor with the Hercules RamFont, choose **1** for **S**creen Colors or Attributes to enter the menu. The Colors/Fonts/Attributes menu contains the options available for that type of monitor. If you have an EGA or VGA graphics card, each category (underline, italics, small caps, and 512 characters) has its own set of colors.

Figure 3-22 shows the menu for CGA, EGA, and VGA monitors, and Figure 3-23 indicates the options for a Hercules card.

6. The WordPerfect attributes are listed in the far left column. The capabilities available for your monitor are listed in the center columns, and the Sample column shows which colors, fonts, and attributes you have selected. The Sample column shows the changes immediately so that you can see how your selection will appear on the regular screen.

```
Setup: Attributes
Attribute            Blink  Bold  Blocked  Underline  Normal  Sample
Normal                 N      N      N         N         Y     Sample
Blocked                N      N      Y         N         N     Sample
Underline              N      N      N         Y         N     Sample
Strikeout              N      Y      N         N         Y     Sample
Bold                   N      Y      N         N         Y     Sample
Double Underline       N      N      N         N         Y     Sample
Redline                N      N      N         N         Y     Sample
Shadow                 N      N      N         N         Y     Sample
Italics                N      N      N         N         Y     Sample
Small Caps             N      N      N         N         Y     Sample
Outline                N      N      N         N         Y     Sample
Subscript              N      N      N         N         Y     Sample
Superscript            N      N      N         N         Y     Sample
Fine Print             N      N      N         N         Y     Sample
Small Print            N      N      N         N         Y     Sample
Large Print            N      N      N         N         Y     Sample
Very Large Print       N      N      N         N         Y     Sample
Extra Large Print      N      N      N         N         Y     Sample
Bold & Underline       N      Y      N         Y         N     Sample
Other Combinations     N      N      N         N         Y     Sample

Switch documents; Move to copy settings       Doc 1
```

Figure 3-21.   Monochrome screen attributes

```
Setup: Colors          A B C D E F G H I J K L M N O P
                       A B C D E F G H I J K L M N O P
Attribute              Foreground  Background   Sample
Normal                     H           B        Sample
Blocked                    H           E        Sample
Underline                  B           H        Sample
Strikeout                  A           D        Sample
Bold                       P           B        Sample
Double Underline           B           D        Sample
Redline                    E           H        Sample
Shadow                     B           H        Sample
Italics                    O           B        Sample
Small Caps                 E           D        Sample
Outline                    F           D        Sample
Subscript                  E           H        Sample
Superscript                F           H        Sample
Fine Print                 A           F        Sample
Small Print                H           F        Sample
Large Print                E           A        Sample
Very Large Print           D           A        Sample
Extra Large Print          H           A        Sample
Bold & Underline           P           H        Sample
Other Combinations         A           G        Sample

Switch documents; Move to copy settings      Doc 1
```

Figure 3-22.   Choosing colors for a CGA, EGA, or VGA monitor

```
Setup: Fonts/Attributes
Attribute           Font  Reverse  Bold  Underline  Strikeout  Sample
Normal               1       N      N        N          N      Sample
Blocked              1       Y      N        N          N      Sample
Underline            1       N      N        Y          N      Sample
Strikeout            1       N      N        N          Y      Sample
Bold                 1       N      Y        N          N      Sample
Double Underline     2       N      N        N          N      Sample
Redline              1       N      Y        N          N      Sample
Shadow               1       N      N        N          N      Sample
Italics              3       N      N        N          N      Sample
Small Caps           4       N      N        N          N      Sample
Outline              5       N      N        N          N      Sample
Subscript            6       N      N        N          N      Sample
Superscript          7       N      N        N          N      Sample
Fine Print           8       N      N        N          N      Sample
Small Print          9       N      N        N          N      Sample
Large Print          A       N      N        N          N      Sample
Very Large Print     B       N      N        N          N      Sample
Extra Large Print    C       N      N        N          N      Sample
Bold & Underline     1       N      Y        Y          N      Sample
Other Combinations   1       Y      N        N          N      Sample

Switch documents; Move to copy settings      Doc 1
```

Figure 3-23.   Font selections for graphics cards with RamFont

Setting	Font
1	Normal
2	Double underline
3	Italics
4	Small caps
5	Outline
6	Subscript
7	Superscript
8	Fine print
9	Small print
A	Large print
B	Very large print
C	Extra large print

Table 3-1.   Number/Letter Assignments for a Hercules RamFont Card

Move through the columns and make the desired changes. If you have a color monitor, the color selections available are displayed at the top of the menu. If you have a Hercules RamFont card, Table 3-1 will help you enter the proper number or letter for the desired font. Note that you also have combinations of reverse video (block), bold, underline, and strikeout available.

7. When you have finished, you can press Switch (SHIFT-F3) to set the colors, fonts, and attributes for document 2. After switching to document 2, you can press Move (CTRL-F4) to copy the settings from document 1 to document 2. When prompted, type **Y** to confirm the decision or **N** to not copy the settings.

8. Press Exit (F7) to return to the document. If you have an EGA, VGA, or Hercules RamFont card, you will be returned to the menu that lets you choose the "mode" (normal font, normal and underline, 6 fonts with 512 characters, and so on).

If you have the Hercules InColor Card, you will need to choose option **5** to set the **Foreground/Background Colors**. After typing **5**, you will see the following:

```
Setup: Foreground/Background Colors

     Foreground Color   8

     Background Color   2

     Cursor Color       63

     Underline Color    5   (RamFont mode only)

     High Intensity     63   (Normal text mode only)
```

Move to each option and enter a number from 1 to 64, or use ← and → to change the color for each option. If you have chosen "normal" mode (as selected in the previous menu), you can choose the color for boldface, but not for strikeout. If you are in RamFont mode, the opposite is true. Press Exit (F7) when you are finished.

9. Press Exit (F7) to return to the document if you are not already there, or continue by choosing another mode and selecting the colors, fonts, or attributes for each mode. Each mode has different settings, and they are stored separately. This is important if you have a monitor that can switch modes (VGA or EGA) and if you want to switch between those modes.

Hints

Display options do not affect the way the attribute is printed. For example, if you want to have italics appear underlined, the text will be underlined on the screen but will be printed in italics.

You can turn on as many attributes at as you want at one time, but many of the attributes cannot be displayed on the screen at the same time. These attribute combinations (other than bold and underline) will use the Other Combinations attribute unless you have a Hercules card with RamFont. Press Reveal Codes (ALT-F3) if you have a question about which attribute is being used.

All changes to the Setup menu (including color settings) are saved in the file WP{WP}.SET. If you are running a network version of WordPerfect, the WP*XXX*} is changed to match the three characters that you entered when you started WordPerfect. For example, if you entered the initials AEB when starting WordPerfect, your settings are saved in the file WPAEB}.SET.

The settings for each mode are saved separately, so if you change modes, the colors, fonts, or attributes are also reselected for that particular mode.

Some attributes cannot be changed because they are a function of the monitor itself. For example, a monochrome monitor will automatically turn on boldface if you select bold; you cannot change the display for bold on a monochrome monitor.

If you change how normal text is displayed, it may affect other lines that use normal text. For example, with a Hercules RamFont card, you can choose to have underlining as the Normal font. However, the Bold option would also change: Boldface text is normal text that is displayed in bold with the RamFont capabilities.

Some single-color monitors, such as the AT&T, can display the underline as underline. Others, such as Compaq, might need to use reverse video. (You might try entering the command **mode und on** from DOS to see if it will allow underlining on your Compaq monitor. You need the MODE.COM file on the disk to run this command.)

If you have a graphics card that can display more than the standard 25 rows and 80 columns, you can select that type of display within WordPerfect. See "Text Screen Type" in this chapter for details.

Colors Not Holding

When you exit WordPerfect, the screen is restored to the original mode that existed before WordPerfect was run. This is necessary because other programs might not be able to run in color. Some programs, such as Lotus 1-2-3, change the screen from color to single-color mode but do not return it to the original mode.

If you find that the colors you selected are not returning when you reenter WordPerfect, another program might have reset the mode. Enter **mode co80** (or **mode color** for a Tandy computer) to return to color. Remember that you need the MODE.COM file on the appropriate disk to run this command.

If you need to reset the mode often, consider putting the instructions in a batch file used to start WordPerfect or try selecting a different Text Screen Type.

/MONO Option   If you want to force WordPerfect to treat your monitor as a monochrome monitor, start WordPerfect with the /MONO switch (**wp/mono**). All colors and screen fonts will be ignored. Text may then be more readable.

Hints

WordPerfect will support every capability your monitor has to offer. Because of this, there are many choices, and things may be a little more difficult to understand than you had expected. Just remember that you can keep changing options and checking the result in the Sample column until you are satisfied with the setup.

Related Entries

Colors, Print
Graphics Screen Type
MODE Command
Text Screen Type

COLORS, PRINT

WordPerfect supports colors on several popular color printers.

Keystrokes

1. Press Font (CTRL-F8).

2. Choose **5** for Print Color. The menu shown in Figure 3-24 appears, showing each color option available and the percentage of red, green, or blue used for that color.

3. Select the desired color.

4. Press Exit (F7) or ENTER to return to the document.

Hints

When you select a color printer, a help message will tell you which colors are supported and the limitations that might exist. If a printer does not have a specific color, it may print a combination of red, blue, and green to get the desired effect.

If you have a color monitor, you can select colors to represent each WordPerfect attribute on the screen. These colors do not affect the print color. See "Colors/Fonts/Attributes" in this chapter for more information about selecting screen colors.

```
Print Color

                              Primary Color Mixture
                              Red      Green    Blue

            1 - Black         0%       0%       0%
            2 - White         100%     100%     100%
            3 - Red           67%      0%       0%
            4 - Green         0%       67%      0%
            5 - Blue          0%       0%       67%
            6 - Yellow        67%      67%      0%
            7 - Magenta       67%      0%       67%
            8 - Cyan          0%       67%      67%
            9 - Orange        67%      25%      0%
            A - Gray          50%      50%      50%
            N - Brown         67%      33%      0%
            0 - Other

            Current Color     0%       0%       0%




Selection: 0
```

Figure 3-24.   Print Color menu

Related Entries

Colors/Fonts/Attributes
Selecting a Printer

COLUMNS

Several options are available for creating columns of text. You can use tabs, tables, newspaper-style columns, and parallel columns. Use newspaper columns for text that flows from one column to the next, even when you make editing changes. Newsletters are one of the most common uses of newspaper columns, as shown in Figure 3-25.

Use parallel columns when you do not want added or deleted text in one column to affect another, but want the columns to stay parallel to each other. Parallel columns can extend across page breaks or they can be protected from being split across page breaks by using Parallel with Block Protect columns. Script writers often use parallel columns to keep the "action" part of a script with the dialogue, as shown here:

Lights flicker, then go out. Camera picks up Jane as she frantically feels for the light switch.	Jane: "I can't find the light switch!"
She finds the switch and tries to turn on the lights. They don't come on.	Jane: "Bob ... Bob ... The lights are out. Did you hear me? Are you there?
Camera searches, then picks out Bob crumpled in the corner of the room.	Bob moans and says, "Yes, I hear you. The power must be out. Check with Randy next door. And get some help—quick!"

Use parallel columns if you want text to wrap within a column but want the look of tabbed columns.

The Tables feature can also be used to create parallel columns that will not be separated between pages. You can turn off the lines that are automatically placed around a table.

If you have questions about which option to use, see "Tabs" and "Tables" in this chapter for examples and steps.

Corporate Update

| *Volume III Number 1* | *Internal Communication* | *January 4, 1990* |

Welcome to the New Year!

1989 was a very good year and all indications point to 1990 being even better. We are predicting sales to double and profits to soar.

During 1989 we opened several overseas offices, built three new buildings, introduced several new products, and received rave reviews on our old ones.

We wish you every success in your personal goals and career and are grateful to have you as part of the winning team. May 1990 be our best year ever!

New Home for Marketing

As of January 15, the Marketing department will move into building six.

All mail normally sent to the marketing department should be addressed to building six. A new phone book will be distributed before the end of the month, listing new addresses and phone numbers for those involved in the move.

Insurance Update

If you are admitted to a hospital for any reason, please specify your employer upon admittance. The billing departments of all hospitals have been advised of our insurance coverage and are aware of the information needed to process a claim.

Don't forget that, when filing your first claim each year, one fully completed claim form must be submitted for each family member. Subsequent claims may be submitted with only a receipt for services rendered (unless the claim is accident-related, in which case a fully completed claim form is required.

Insurance Questions?

All questions regarding company insurance policies—coverage, eligibility, and reimbursements—should now be directed to Mary in Accounting at extension 304.

Business Card Orders

All employees who will be attending the computer convention and need to reorder business cards are requested to do so before January 25. Please call Laurie with your order.

Travel Policies

Due to recent changes in the company travel policies and procedures, an authorization number is needed before airline tickets can be issued. If you will be traveling for the company, please have your travel form filled out and signed by your supervisor prior to submitting it to May in Accounting. She will then give the authorization number to the travel agent.

Training Classes

The next session of product training classes begins on

Figure 3-25.   Newspaper columns

Keystrokes

If necessary, change the left and right margins: Press Format (SHIFT-F8), choose **1** for **Line** and **7** for **Margins**, and then enter the new left and right margins. These settings are used to calculate evenly spaced columns.

Defining Newspaper or Parallel Columns

1. Press Columns/Tables (ALT-F7).

2. Choose **1** for **Columns**. The following choices appear:

```
Columns: 1 On; 2 Off; 3 Define: 0
```

3. Choose **3** for **Define**. The menu shown in Figure 3-26 appears.

4. This menu is preset for two newspaper columns with one-half inch (1/2") of space between the columns. If you do not need to make changes to this setting, move to the next step. If you do need to change the type of columns, choose **1** for **Type** and select one of the choices shown here:

```
Column Type: 1 Newspaper; 2 Parallel; 3 Parallel with Block Protect: 0
```

The difference between Parallel and Parallel with Block Protect is that parallel columns can continue over a page break. Parallel with Block Protect will not allow a page break to split the group of columns.

Choose **2** for **Number of Columns** if you want more than two columns. Enter the number of columns; as many as 24 columns across the screen are allowed.

Even though the distance between columns is not displayed, it is always calculated at one-half inch. To change the amount of space (often referred to as "gutter space"), choose **3** for **Distance Between**

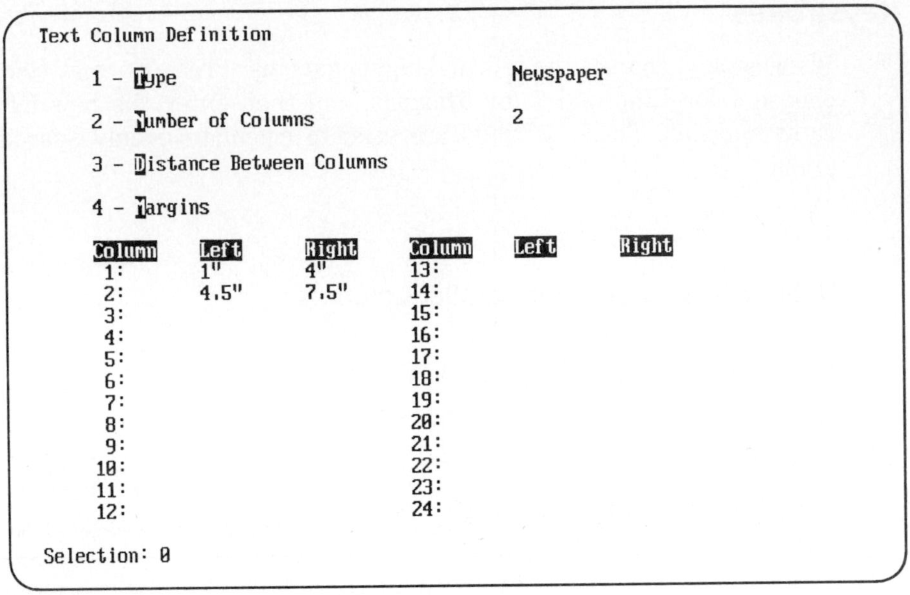

```
┌─────────────────────────────────────────────────────────────┐
│ Text Column Definition                                        │
│                                                               │
│     1 - Type                           Newspaper              │
│                                                               │
│     2 - Number of Columns              2                      │
│                                                               │
│     3 - Distance Between Columns                              │
│                                                               │
│     4 - Margins                                               │
│                                                               │
│    Column   Left     Right    Column   Left     Right         │
│      1:     1"       4"         13:                           │
│      2:     4.5"     7.5"       14:                           │
│      3:                         15:                           │
│      4:                         16:                           │
│      5:                         17:                           │
│      6:                         18:                           │
│      7:                         19:                           │
│      8:                         20:                           │
│      9:                         21:                           │
│     10:                         22:                           │
│     11:                         23:                           │
│     12:                         24:                           │
│  Selection: 0                                                 │
└─────────────────────────────────────────────────────────────┘
```

Figure 3-26.   Menu used to define columns

Columns, and enter the new measurement. You do not have to choose this option if you want to set columns of unequal width.

As you change the number of columns and the distance between columns, the left and right margins for each column are calculated and displayed below. If you need to change any of the settings (if you want columns of different widths, for example), you can choose 4 for **M**argins and enter the left and right margins for each column.

5. When you are finished, press Exit (F7).

6. You are returned to the initial Columns menu, where you can choose 1 to turn Columns **O**n. If you want to turn the columns on at a later time, press Exit (F7).

Turning Columns On and Off

Before turning Columns on, you have to define them. Remember that if you need only two newspaper columns, you can enter the Columns menu and then immediately press Exit (F7) to accept those settings.

After defining columns, you can turn them on or off at any time.

1. Press Columns/Tables (ALT-F7).

2. Choose **1** for **Columns**.

3. Choose **1** for **On** or **2** for **Off**.

When you turn on Columns, you will see "Col 1" on the status line. As you move from column to column, the column number on the status line will change as well.

Entering Text in Columns

If you have defined newspaper columns, you will most likely type text until you reach the end of the first column. The text will then wrap to the next column.

If you want to end a column before it reaches the bottom of the page, press Hard Page (CTRL-ENTER) to start the next column. This is also how you start the next column in a section of parallel columns. Once you reach the end of one column and want to start the next column, press Hard Page (CTRL-ENTER).

After all the columns on the page are filled, the cursor moves to the next page and continues in columns.

Moving Between Columns

If you have an enhanced keyboard with cursor keys in the middle (between the letter keys and numeric keypad), you can press ALT-→ to move to the column to the right, or ALT-← to move to the column to the left. If you are working with parallel columns, pressing ALT-↑ and ALT-↓ moves you to the section of parallel columns above or below.

If you do not have an enhanced keyboard, you can press Go To (CTRL-HOME) and then ← or → to go to the column to the left or right. See "Hints" for more options.

Hints

When you have defined your columns, the following code is placed in the document:

[Col Def:Type;$n;n,n;n,n;$. . .]

The type of columns is identified by "Newspaper," "Parallel," or "Parallel/Block Pro" in the columns definition code. The first number (*n*) represents the number of columns. The remaining numbers indicate the left and right margins for each column. A [Col On] code is displayed in Reveal Codes where columns are turned on, and a [Col Off] code is inserted where columns are turned off.

Most formatting options are available when you are in columns, including font and spacing changes. The spacing can be changed within columns, giving those who need a single-spaced column on the left and a double-spaced column on the right the ability to create such columns.

Moving from Column to Column

Most cursor keys function the same as they do when you are not working in columns. If you press HOME and either ← or → , the cursor will go to the far left or far right margin of the *current* column instead of the far left or right of the screen. The following options are available for moving the cursor among columns and on the screen.

Arrow Keys   The arrow keys work within columns just as they do in normal text. However, pressing → will make you travel across and down the column and eventually into the next column. Pressing ← will move you up and to the left in the column and eventually into the previous column. Pressing ↑ and ↓ move you up and down within the same column.

Go To, ← or →   Pressing Go To (CTRL-HOME) displays "Go to" at the bottom of the screen. Press ← to go to the previous column or → to move to the next column.

Go To, HOME, ← or →   After pressing Go To (CTRL-HOME) to display "Go to" on the screen, you can press HOME and then either ← or → to move to the far left or far right column, respectively.

Go To, ↑ or ↓   Moves to the top or bottom of the current column, respectively.

Turning Columns On and Off

You cannot turn Columns on if you have not yet defined any. If you attempt to do so, you will see the message "ERROR: No text columns defined."

You can turn Columns on and off throughout a document as many times as you like and even have standard text and multiple columns within the same document. To turn Columns off within a document, press Columns/Tables (ALT-F7) and choose 2 for Off. You do not have to turn off Columns at the end of the document if the entire document is in columns. Parallel columns turn off and on automatically to achieve the parallel effect.

Although different column definitions can exist on the same page, you cannot define columns in Columns mode. You first need to turn off Columns, create the new column definition, turn on Columns, and then continue.

You can turn on columns before or after you have entered. In fact, you might find it easier (and faster) to create and edit a document first and then move to the beginning of the text and turn Columns on.

If a document is in columns and you want to change it back to the standard left and right margins, move the cursor to the [Col On] code and delete it.

Drawing Lines Between Columns

If you have a laser or dot-matrix printer, you can use Graphics (ALT-F9) to draw horizontal or vertical lines between or around columns. See "Applications" for steps or "Graphics Lines" for more information.

Increasing the Speed of Columns

In versions prior to 4.1, WordPerfect did not display columns side by side. Instead, a page break was used to separate columns and "Col n" was included on the status line to show which column the cursor was in. Text in columns was reformatted as quickly as text that was not in columns.

When WordPerfect Corporation decided to display columns side by side on the screen, there was a noticeable delay when you added or deleted text or when automatic reformatting took place. To help with the problem, a feature was added to allow you to turn off automatic reformatting. If you turn off this feature, the screen will reformat only when the cursor is moved down through the text; if you turn it on, reformatting is done when you press a single cursor key. To turn this option off, press Setup (SHIFT-F1), choose **2** for **Display**, **6** for **Edit-Screen Options**, **1** for **Automatically Format and Rewrite**, and then type **N**.

You can also speed the display of columns if you choose not to display them side by side. They will still remain in the correct horizontal position, but they will be separated by page breaks. If you want to set the option to display columns on separate pages, press Setup (SHIFT-F1), choose **2** for **Display**, **6** for **Edit-Screen Options**, and **7** for **Side-by-side Columns Display**; and then type **N** to show that you do not want columns displayed side by side on the screen. If you type **N**, reformatting takes place at the normal speed of text not in columns.

Changing the Number of Columns

If you need to change the number of newspaper columns, place the cursor just after the previous [Col Def] code and redefine the columns. The columns will readjust automatically. Changing the number of parallel columns is explained later in this section.

Moving Columns

When you block text and press Move (CTRL-F4), you will see an option asking if you want to move tabular columns. This option should not be used to move text in newspaper or parallel columns. If you want to move sections of text, use the regular Block-Move procedure. See "Move" in this chapter for complete information.

Converting Parallel Columns to a Table

If you want to convert parallel columns to a table, follow these steps:

1. Block the section of columns to be converted with Block (ALT-F4).
2. Press Columns/Tables (ALT-F7).

3. Choose **2** for **T**ables.

4. Choose **1** for **C**reate. The following prompt will appear:

Create Table from: 1 Tabular Column; 2 Parallel Column: 0

5. Type **2** for **P**arallel Column, and the table will be drawn around the columns. The menu used to edit a table will also be displayed at the bottom of the screen.

6. Make any necessary changes to the table and press Exit (F7) when you are finished.

If you convert parallel columns to a table, you can easily switch (move) columns. See "Tables" in this chapter for more information.

If you convert parallel columns to a table, you cannot return to normal parallel columns by deleting the table definition. You can, however, turn off the lines that are normally drawn around the table and return to the parallel columns "look."

Column Limitations

Although you cannot currently create footnotes while in columns, you can create endnotes. If you have text containing footnotes and turn on Columns at the beginning of that text, the footnotes will be converted to endnotes automatically and without warning.

You cannot define tables while in Columns mode. You can, however, create a graphics box with Graphics (ALT-F9) and create a table within that box. This technique would also allow text to wrap around a table or let you place multiple tables side by side on a page.

If you have a table in a document, you should not define and turn on Columns above that table. If you do, the table definition will be deleted without warning and the text will be converted to tabular text.

You can define and enter columns while in a text box, as shown in Figure 3-27. In this example, the document is entered in two columns, while three columns are entered in the text box. Neither column definition affects the other.

Selecting a Printer

As the last step of the installation process, you will be prompted to select a printer. A printer will not actually be selected, but the appropriate printer file containing the printer definition will be copied. After inserting the Printer disk, a list of printers appears. The names of some of the most popular printers supported by WordPerfect is shown in Figure 1-3.

You can choose the Name Search option and type the name of your printer, press PgDn to see more printer selections, or use the arrow keys to move through the list. When you see your printer among the list, select it by entering the number next to the printer's name. If you do not see your printer on the list, call (801) 225-5000 for alternate printer definitions that can be used or to see if one has been defined since the initial release of version 5.1. You can also write to:

SoftCopy, Inc.
c/o Printer Drivers
81 N. State Street
Orem, UT 84057

After selecting your printer from the list, Install copies the appropriate printer file (an .ALL file containing several printer definitions) to the specified location. You are then asked if you want to select more printers (up to three using the install program). If you do, the install program keeps track of the .ALL files that have already been copied so that if the additional printer selections are found in the same printer file, it will save time by not copying them again.

Read the section about "Using a 5.0 Printer Definition" if you decide to use a printer driver that was used with version 5.0.

After all printers have been selected, Install starts WordPerfect (you are asked if you want to enter your license number so it will be displayed when you press Help (F3)), selects the printer definition(s) from the printer file, displays the help screen(s) about the printer(s), then exits WordPerfect and the Install program.

Using a 5.0 Printer Definition

If you have created a customized printer driver (.PRS file) in WordPerfect 5.0, you may not want to repeat the process again for version 5.1. Because the format of the .PRS files are not compatible between versions, you will need to convert the 5.0 printer file to 5.1 format using the PTR Program.

Alphacom Alphapro 101	Centronics PagePrinter 8	Epson FX-286
Alps Allegro 24	Citizen 120D/180D	Epson FX-80/100
Alps ALQ200/300 (24 pin)	Citizen 5200/5800	Epson FX-85/185
Alps ALQ224e/324e	Citizen Premiere 35	Epson FX-850/1050
Alps P2000	Citizen Tribute 124/224	Epson FX-86e/286e
Alps P2100	Cordata LP300X	Epson LQ-1500
Alps P2400C	Dataproducts LZR-1260	Epson LQ-2550
Apple LaserWriter IINTX	Destiny PageStyler	Epson LQ-500
Apple LaserWriter IINT	Diablo 620	Epson LQ-800/1000
Apple LaserWriter Plus	Diablo 630 ECS	Epson LQ-850/1050 (N9)
Apple LaserWriter	Diablo 630	Epson LQ-850/1050
AST TurboLaser	Diablo 635	Epson LQ-950
Brother HL-8e	Diablo Advantage D25	Epson LX-800
Brother HR-15XL	Diconix 150 Plus	Epson LX-810
Brother HR-20	Digital LJ250	Fortis DP600S
Brother HR-35	Digital LJ252	Fortis/Dynax DH45
Brother HR-40	Digital LN03 Plus	Fortis/Dynax DX15
Brother Twinriter 6	Digital LN03	Fortis/Dynax DX21
C.ITOH F10-40 Printmaster	Digital LN03R	Fortis/Dynax DX25
C.ITOH F10-40 Starwriter	(ScriptPrinter)	Fortis/Dynax DX41
Canon BJ-130	Digital PrintServer 40	Fujitsu DL2400/2600/3400
Canon LBP-8 A1/A2	EiconScript	Fujitsu RX7100PS
Canon LBP-8II/T/R	Epson Apex-80	Fujitsu SP 320
Canon LBP-8III	Epson DFX-5000	HP DeskJet Plus

Figure 1-3 List of Printers (continued on next page)

Figure 3-27.   A document in which columns have been used inside a graphics box

You can sort items within columns, but because you might get unpredictable results, save the document first.

Parallel Columns with Block Protect

When you choose the Parallel Columns with Block Protect option, a Block Protect code is placed at the beginning of the first column and at the end of the last column. The Block Protect codes keep the columns together without letting a soft page break split the group. If you choose to use regular parallel columns, no Block Protect codes are inserted, and columns can cross page breaks.

When you turn on parallel columns with Block Protect, the codes [BlockPro:On][Col On] are inserted together at the beginning of the first column. When you press CTRL-ENTER between columns, an [HPg] code is inserted into the text but is not visible on the screen. At the end of the last column, CTRL-ENTER does not insert an [HPg] code. Instead, the following codes are inserted to end the first group of parallel columns, insert a blank line, and begin the second group:

    [BlockPro:Off][Col Off]
    [HRt]
    [BlockPro:On][Col On]

If you want to add text to the last column in a group, do not place the cursor between the [Block Pro:Off] and [Col Off] codes. In fact, you might want to leave Reveal Codes (ALT-F3) on when editing so you do not accidentally move or delete a Block Protect code.

If you are in parallel columns and want to convert to normal text, you must delete the [Col On] code at the beginning of each parallel section. You should also delete the [BlockPro:On] code. Instead of manually searching for the codes, use the Replace feature to search for them and replace them with nothing. When parallel columns are returned to normal text, a hard page code, [HPg], appears between each "column." You could then use the Search feature to search for a hard page and replace it with something else, such as a hard return.

Changing the Number of Parallel Columns

The easiest way to change the number and location of columns is to first convert the columns into a table. The steps for that process are listed earlier in this section. Once the columns are in a table, you can easily add, delete, and move columns and rows. Be aware, however, that if you convert parallel columns to a table, you cannot convert them back again. If you decide to redefine parallel columns instead, save the file first, because it is easy to make a mistake during the process. If you add a column, the new column is added at the end of the group by inserting a hard page code, [HPg]. If you want to add a column within the group rather than at the end, you will need to use Block (ALT-F4) to move text from one column to another.

If you want to remove a column, first remove the text from that column and then redefine the columns. Extra [HPg] codes are automatically deleted, leaving the correct number of columns.

If you need more than 24 text columns, determine which columns do not require word wrap, and set tabs within those columns.

Moving and Copying Tabbed Columns

Again, it is easiest to work with columnar data in a table. If you want to convert columns separated by tabs to a table, block the text to be converted, press Columns/Table (ALT-F7), choose 2 for Tables, and then choose 1 for Create. When asked for the type of text to be converted to a table, choose 1 for Tabular Column.

You can delete the tables definition code and return to tabular text at any time.

If you want to leave the text as tabular text instead of converting it to a table, you can still use the choices found on Move (CTRL-F4) for moving or copying tabular columns or rectangles. See "Move" in this chapter for more information.

Moving the Cursor in Tabbed Columns

Unlike parallel or newspaper columns, you can move through tabbed columns just as you would through normal text. However, if you prefer to jump over the text to the next tab setting, press INS to turn on Typeover mode. Pressing TAB in this instance will move you to the next tab setting rather than inserting a [Tab] code and will help you move across columns quickly.

Applications

Most WordPerfect owners use newspaper columns to create newsletters. The sample shown in Figure 3-28 includes vertical graphics lines between columns. The first column was ended with Hard Page (CTRL-ENTER) before it reached the end of the page.

The following steps will help you place vertical lines between columns:

1. Make sure that the Columns feature is on and that the cursor is at the beginning of the first column.

2. Press Graphics (ALT-F9).

3. Choose 5 for Line.

4. Choose 2 for a Vertical line.

5. Choose 1 for Horizontal Position.

6. Choose 3 to place the line Between Columns. The following prompt appears:

```
Place line to right of column: 1
```

7. Enter the number of the column and press ENTER to return to the document.

These steps place a vertical line from the top margin to the bottom margin. If you want to start the line at any other position, choose 2 for Vertical Position, and then choose 5 for Set Position. The cursor's current position will be displayed. Press ENTER to accept that setting or enter a different one. You can then choose option 3 for Length of Line and adjust that as well.

If you have more than two columns and you want vertical lines between the others, repeat the steps just given, entering the appropriate column number. Be sure that you are in Columns mode when you are defining a vertical line, or the line will appear at the right margin. See Chapter 4, "Desktop Publishing with WordPerfect," for more information about using newspaper columns.

Corporate Update

Volume III Number 1   *Internal Communication*   *January 4, 1990*

Welcome to the New Year!

1989 was a very good year and all indications point to 1990 being even better. We are predicting sales to double and profits to soar.

During 1989 we opened several overseas offices, built three new buildings, introduced several new products, and received rave reviews on our old ones.

We wish you every success in your personal goals and career and are grateful to have you as part of the winning team. May 1990 be our best year ever!

New Home for Marketing

As of January 15, the Marketing department will move into building six.

All mail normally sent to the marketing department should be addressed to building six. A new phone book will be distributed before the end of the month, listing new addresses and phone numbers for those involved in the move.

Insurance Update

If you are admitted to a hospital for any reason, please specify your employer upon admittance. The billing departments of all hospitals have been advised of our insurance coverage and are aware of the information needed to process a claim.

Don't forget that, when filing your first claim each year, one fully completed claim form must be submitted for each family member. Subsequent claims may be submitted with only a receipt for services rendered (unless the claim is accident-related, in which case a fully completed claim form is required.

Insurance Questions?

All questions regarding company insurance policies—coverage, eligibility, and reimbursements—should now be directed to Mary in Accounting at extension 304.

Business Card Orders

All employees who will be attending the computer convention and need to reorder business cards are requested to do so before January 25. Please call Laurie with your order.

Travel Policies

Due to recent changes in the company travel policies and procedures, an authorization number is needed before airline tickets can be issued. If you will be traveling for the company, please have your travel form filled out and signed by your supervisor prior to submitting it to May in Accounting. She will then give the authorization number to the travel agent.

Training Classes

The next session of product training classes begins on

Figure 3-28.   Vertical graphics lines between newspaper columns

See "Border" in this chapter for a method of placing a border around the entire page.

Related Entries

Borders
Graphics Lines
Line Draw
Move
See also Chapter 4, "Desktop Publishing with WordPerfect"

COMMENTS

Sometimes referred to as "hidden text," comments can be placed throughout your document without being printed.

Keystrokes

Create a Comment

To create a comment, follow these steps:

1. Press Text In/Out (CTRL-F5).

2. Choose **4** for Comment.

3. Choose **1** for Create a Comment. A double-lined box labeled as a document comment appears on the screen.

4. Type the text for the comment.

5. Press Exit (F7) when you are finished.

The comment is displayed on the screen where the cursor was located and is enclosed in a box, as shown in Figure 3-29.

Change a Block of Text to a Comment

To create a comment from existing text follow these steps:

1. Position the cursor at one end of the text and press Block (ALT-F4).

2. Move the cursor to the opposite end of the block.

3. Press Text In/Out (CTRL-F5). The following prompt appears:

   Create a comment? No (Yes)

4. Type **Y** to convert the block to a comment.

Change a Comment to Text

The following steps change a comment to regular, printable text:

1. Move the cursor just below the comment to be changed to text.

2. Press Text In/Out (CTRL-F5) and type 4 for Comment.

3. Choose **3** to Convert the comment to Text.

```
on the Journal of each House respectively.  If any Bill shall not
be returned by the President within ten Days (Sundays excepted)
after it shall have been presented to him, the Same shall be a Law,
in like Manner as if he had signed it, unless the Congress by their
Adjournment prevent its Return, in which Case it shall be a Law.

┌────────────────────────────────────────────────────────────┐
│ Question for Final Exam:                                     │
│ How many days does the President have to veto a bill?        │
└────────────────────────────────────────────────────────────┘

     Every Order, Resolution, or Vote to which the Concurrence of
the Senate and House of Representatives may be necessary (except on
a question of Adjournment) shall be presented to the President of

                                    Doc 1 Pg 1 Ln 3.67" Pos 7.5"
```

Figure 3-29.   A boxed comment

Hints

When a comment is inserted into the document, the [Comment] code is visible when you press Reveal Codes (ALT-F3). If you need to edit the text in a comment, move the cursor just after (below) the comment to be edited. Press Text In/Out (CTRL-F5) and choose 4 for Comment and 2 for Edit. If there is not a comment to the left of the cursor, the first comment after the cursor will be edited. Press Exit (F7) when you are finished.

By default, WordPerfect has been set to display comments on the screen. Remember that they will not print, regardless of whether they are displayed or not. You can choose not to display comments by pressing Setup (SHIFT-F1) and choosing 2 for Display, 6 for Edit-Screen Options, then 2 for Comments Display. Type **N** if you do not want the comments displayed or **Y** if you do want them displayed. If you want to delete a comment permanently, move the cursor above the comment and press DEL, or move just below the comment and press BACKSPACE. You are asked to confirm the deletion. You will then see the message

Delete [Comment]? No (**Yes**)

Type **Y** for Yes or **N** for No. If you want to search for a comment, press Search (F2), press Text In/Out (CTRL-F5), and then choose 1 for Comment. Press Search (F2) again to start the search.

If you are looking at a file from the List Files menu, comments are not displayed.

Applications

When you are editing a document for someone else, you can use the Comment feature to make comments directly within a file. During further editing, these comments can be converted to text or deleted as the changes are made in the document. If more than one person is editing a document, each person can insert his or her name and the date in the comment so that the author can track suggestions and responses.

Related Entries

Text In/Out

COMPARE DOCUMENTS

WordPerfect has a feature that lets you compare a document on the screen with one on disk and then insert redline and strikeout marks automatically when differences are found.

Keystrokes

1. After retrieving a document from disk and revising it, press Mark Text (ALT-F5).

2. Choose **6** for **G**enerate.

3. Choose **2** for **C**ompare Screen and Disk Documents and Add Redline and Strikeout.

4. You will be prompted to enter the name of the file on disk to be used for the comparison. If the file on the screen was originally retrieved from the disk, that filename is displayed automatically. Press ENTER to accept that name, or enter a different one.

5. A counter will appear in the lower left corner to show that progress is being made.

Hints

If text was added to the document on screen, that text will be redlined. If text was found on disk that was not in the document on screen, that text would be copied from disk to the document on the screen with strikeout marks through it. If a section of text has been moved to another location in the document, "The Following Text Was Moved" will be placed just before the text that was moved and "The Preceding Text

THE CONSTITUTION OF THE UNITED STATES

PREAMBLE

We the people of the United States, in order to form a more perfect Union, establish

Justice,———— We the masses of the United States, in order to form a more perfect

establishment, maintain Justice, insure domestic Tranquility, provide for the common

Defense, promote the general Welfare, and secure the Blessings of Liberty to ourselves and

our Posterity, do ordain and establish this Constitution for the United States of America. do

ordain this Constitution for the United States of America.

Figure 3-30.   The result of a compared document with redline and strikeout
added

Was Moved" just after that particular section. If any changes were made
in the text that was moved, those changes will also be shown with the
redline and strikeout markings. Figure 3-30 shows a document that has
had redline and strikeout marks inserted automatically as a result of the
Compare feature.

WordPerfect compares the document phrase by phrase, instead of
word by word or character by character. A phrase is defined as a section
of text from a comma, period, colon, semicolon, question mark, exclamation, or hard return [HRt] code to the next. Therefore, if any text is
added or deleted in a phrase, the entire phrase is redlined or struck out.

Removing Redline and Strikeout Marks

If you decide to remove the redline markings and delete the text
marked for strikeout, press Mark Text (ALT-F5), choose **6** for **G**enerate,
and choose **1** for **R**emove Redline Markings and Strikeout Text from
Document.

To add redline and strikeout marks of your own, press Font (CTRL-
F8), choose **2** for **A**ppearance, and choose **8** for **R**edln (redline) or **9** for

Stkout (strikeout). Type the text to be marked for redline or strikeout, and then press → to move past the redline-off [redln] or strikeout-off [stkout] code.

If the text has already been typed, block the text using Block (ALT-F4), press Font (CTRL-F8), choose **2** for **A**ppearance, and then choose **8** for **R**edln or **9** for **S**tkout.

To determine how redline markings will print, press Format (SHIFT-F8), choose **3** for **D**ocument, and then choose **4** for **R**edline Method. The following options appear, with Printer Dependent being the default answer:

```
Redline Method: 1 Printer Dependent; 2 Left; 3 Alternating: 1
```

You can choose to have redline print the way WordPerfect has defined your printer to print it (usually shown with a shaded background or font change) or with a character in the left margin, or you can have the character alternate between the left and right margins depending on whether it is being printed on an odd or even page. If you select the Left or Alternating option, you can specify the character to be used. The vertical bar ¦ is automatically displayed as a suggestion.

Applications

If you revise a contract, you can quickly compare the revised document on screen with the original on disk and have the redline and strikeout markings inserted automatically, rather than having to mark each phrase manually.

Related Entries

Redlining
Strikeout

COMPATIBILITY

You can retrieve any 5.0 or 4.2 document into WordPerfect 5.1 without converting it. If you need to reverse the process and transfer files from 5.1 into 5.0, no conversion needs to be done. If a 5.1 document contains codes that are new to 5.0, they will be converted into [Unknown] codes. When the document is retrieved back into version 5.1, the [Unknown] codes will convert back to their original function.

If you prefer to have the [Unknown] codes stripped from the file or would like to save a 5.1 document into 4.2 format, you can do so with options found on Text In/Out (CTRL-F5).

Keystrokes

1. Press Text In/Out (CTRL-F5).

2. Choose **3** for Save As. The following options appear:

```
1 Generic; 2 WordPerfect 5.0; 3 WordPerfect 4.2: 0
```

Choose the Generic option if you want to save the file in a format that can be used by another type of word processor (similar to a DOS text file, with soft return [SRt] codes converted to spaces and tabs converted to DOS tabs).

3. Choose **2** for WordPerfect 5.0 or **3** for WordPerfect 4.2 format.

4. Enter a filename.

You will be returned to your document when you are finished.

Hints

Converting 4.2 Files to 5.1

When a 4.2 document is retrieved into version 5.1, it is automatically converted to the new format. However, because of several incompatibilities (fonts are numbered in 4.2 and named in 5.1, measurements for margins and paper size are different, there are no sheet-feeder bin-number codes in 5.1, and so on), WordPerfect can use a conversion (.CRS) file to help translate some of the 4.2 codes to those that can be understood by 5.1.

The conversion file is a regular file created in WordPerfect. When the file is saved, it should be named so that it matches the printer (.PRS) file. For example, if you use the HP LaserJet Series II printer for both 4.2 and 5.1, and the printer file in 5.1 is named HPLASE-II.PRS, you would create a conversion file named HPLASEII.CRS. WordPerfect will look for such a file when retrieving a 4.2 document and make the necessary conversions.

All commands that can be included as options in the .CRS file are described here:

FO	Font on
FF	Font off
BN	Bin number
SZ	Paper size
CH	Character
BC	Beginning codes
MB	Margin bias
IP	Initial pitch

When entering these commands, enter the abbreviation for the code (for example, FO), the command as it appears in 4.2, an equal sign (=), and then the 5.1 code followed by a hard return [HRt] code. For example, if Font 3*, 13 pitch in WordPerfect 4.2 was a Times Roman 12pt font, you would enter the command **FO 3*,13**, choose Times Roman 12pt from the list of fonts, and then press ENTER when you are finished. In Reveal Codes, the command might look like the following:

FO 3*,13 = [Font:Times Roman 12pt][HRt]

The FF (font-off) command can be used if you are using attributes instead of a font change. For example, if your version of 4.2 used font 2 as italics, you could insert the [ITALC] code as the font-on code and [italc] as the font-off code. To insert the commands in the conversion file, you could turn on Block just after the = for FO, move the cursor just after the = for FF, and choose Italics. The [ITALC] code would then be inserted whenever there was a font 2 change in the 4.2 document, and the italics-off code, [italc], would be inserted just before any other font change.

The BN command can be used to choose a 5.1 paper size/type to replace the sheet-feeder bin command used in 4.2. For example, if you have envelopes in the third bin in the sheet feeder, you could use the BN command to choose the envelope form.

You would enter the code as follows:

BN 3 = [Paper Sz/Typ:9.5″ x 4″,Envelope]

If the margins are not converting properly from 4.2 to 5.1, you can use the SZ command to specify the size of paper that is being used. You might want to use this command if you were using an unusual paper size (such as 14″ x 8.5″). You would enter the command as follows:

SZ = [Paper Sz/Typ:14″ x 8.5″,Standard]

You can use the CH (character) command if you had assigned a nondisplayable character, such as a copyright or registered trademark symbol, to a displayable character in 4.2. For example, the copyright character might have been available in 4.2 only by choosing font 5 and using ALT-9 (©) to represent the character. The printer definition would have mapped the copyright symbol to the same character and would have printed it correctly.

To convert the characters used in 4.2 (such as © in font 5) to version 5.0 section and character numbers (4,23), you would use Compose (CTRL-2) to enter the numbers after the equal sign.

CH 5,9 = [■:4,23][HRt]

You can use the BC command to insert any codes at the beginning of the converted document. This is helpful if you had changed any of the default settings with the /S option in 4.2 and wanted them inserted in the 5.1 document. If you wanted Widow/Orphan Protection on, and the margins in the 4.2 documents were always 15 and 80, you could enter a BC command as shown here:

BC = [W/O On][L/R Mar:1.5″,0.5″]

The MB command represents a margin bias. In version 4.2, users had to compensate for any unprintable zone by decreasing the left margin. With 5.1, the unprintable zone is taken into account in the printer file so that changes to margins and other adjustments are no longer necessary. If you subtract an unprintable zone of .25″ in 4.2 (setting a left margin at 7 instead of 10), you can use the following command in the conversion file so that .25″ is added to all left margin settings, tabs, indents, column definitions, and line number settings:

MB = .25″[HRt]

The IP (initial pitch) command is useful when you have chosen a 12-pitch font as the default font using 4.2's Setup menu. Those who have done so have probably also changed their default margins and tab settings to reflect 12 characters per inch (margins at 12 and 90, and tabs starting at 2 instead of 0). By specifying the initial pitch in the format shown here, you can have WordPerfect assume that margins and tabs are also based on 12 pitch and convert them accordingly:

IP = 12

Converting 5.1 Files to 4.2

WordPerfect also looks for a .CRS file when you save a 5.1 file as a 4.2 document with Text In/Out (CTRL-F5). The commands for converting documents both ways are included in the same .CRS file. When you enter the following commands, the WordPerfect 5.1 codes are on the left side of the equal sign (=) and the 4.2 equivalents are on the right.

There are six commands that are similar to the ones already discussed:

FT Font

AO Attribute on

AF Attribute off

BP Bin paper

WC WordPerfect character

MB Margin bias

You can repeat any of the commands as many times as necessary. For example, if you use many different fonts, you may want to use the FT command several times to specify which 4.2 font should be selected for each base font in 5.1.

To convert a 5.1 base font to a 4.2 font/pitch setting, use the FT command. In Reveal Codes, it would appear in the following manner:

FT[Helv 12pt] = 3,13*[HRt]

Use the asterisk if the 5.1 font is proportionally spaced.

If you prefer to use attributes instead of a base font, use the AO and AF commands. For example, if you have used [LARGE] throughout your document, you can convert it to a specific font. When the [large] off code is encountered, the font can return to the standard base font.

AO[LARGE] = 5,8[HRt]
AF[large] = 3,13*[HRt]

You can insert bin number codes into the 4.2 document for specific paper sizes and types. For example, if you keep your envelopes in bin 3, you can use the following command:

BP[Paper Sz/Typ:9.5″ x 4″,Envelope] = 3

WC is similar to the CH command described earlier, but it converts a WordPerfect 5.1 character back to its 4.2 equivalent. Using the earlier example, where the copyright symbol is mapped to character 9 in font 5, the command would appear as:

    WC[•:4,23] = 5,9[HRt]

If you have already entered a margin bias (MB) for the 4.2-to-5.1 conversion, you do not need to enter it again; the same setting is used in both conversions.

Converting Multiple Files

Instead of retrieving or saving one document at a time, you can use the appropriate options in the Convert program to convert multiple files. The Convert program will also look for and use a .CRS file that matches the current printer selection.

Related Entries

    Convert Program

COMPOSE

The Compose feature lets you quickly insert a special character into your document. If you use a character often, you may want to map or assign it to a key combination, such as ALT-B for a bullet (•), with the Keyboard Layout/Mapping feature so you don't have to create it each time you need it. See "Keyboard Layout/Mapping" in this chapter for more information.

Like the "dead" key on dedicated word processors, the Compose feature lets you type a character followed by a diacritical mark to display a special character on screen. You can also type two characters to create a digraph or other symbol, or look up the desired character in Appendix A, "WordPerfect Character Sets," and enter the section and character number to create a special character.

Keystrokes

1. Press CTRL-2 (use the 2 found on the numbered keys across the top of the keyboard). Note that no prompt or help message appears. If you are in the normal editing screen (not in a menu), you can also use CTRL-V, which displays the prompt "Key=."

2. Three options are available:

a. Type a character and then a diacritical mark. The following diacritical marks can be used in conjunction with another character:

´	Acute
`	Grave
¨	Umlaut
~	Tilde
v	Caron
^	Circumflex
- (dash)	Crossbar
_ (underscore)	Macron
,	Cedilla
;	Ogonek
.	Dot above
:	Centered dot
o or @	Ring above
/	Slash
\	Stroke

The following characters are examples of how these diacriticals can be used:

´ and e	é
` and a	à
¨ and u	ü

~ and n	ñ
v and g	ğ
ˆ and a	â
- and T	Ŧ
_ and N	N̄
, and c	ç
; and u	ų
. and e	ė
: and l	l·
o and a	å
/ and o	ø
\ and L	Ł

b. Type two characters to create a digraph (a pair of letters representing a single sound) or other symbols such as a bullet, ™, or © symbol. The following table shows some of the possibilities available. In some cases more than one combination can achieve the same result.

* and .	•	Small solid bullet
* and *	●	Medium solid bullet
* and o	◦	Small hollow bullet
* and O	○	Medium hollow bullet
P and ¦	¶	Paragraph sign
/ and 2	½	One-half
/ and 4	¼	One-fourth
--	—	Em dash
m-	—	Em dash
n-	-	En dash
t and m	™	Trademark
T and M	™	Trademark
r and o	®	Registered trademark

R and O	®	Registered trademark
c and o	©	Copyright
C and O	©	Copyright
r and x	℞	Prescription
R and x	℞	Prescription
o and x	¤	General currency symbol
Y and =	¥	Japanese yen
- and L	£	Pound sterling
P and t	Pt	Pesetas
c and /	¢	Cent
??	¿	Upside-down ?
!!	¡	Upside-down !
A and E	Æ	AE digraph
a and e	æ	ae digraph
I and J	IJ	IJ digraph
i and j	ĳ	ij digraph
O and E	Œ	OE digraph
o and e	œ	oe digraph
s and s	ß	German double "s"
< and <	«	Left double guillemet
> and >	»	Right double guillemet
+ and -	±	Plus or minus
< and =	≤	Less than or equal to
> and =	≥	Greater than or equal to
= and =	≡	Equivalent
~ and ~	≈	Approximately equal to
/ and =	≠	Not equal to
a and o	å	"A" with a ring
f and -	ƒ	Integration
a and =	a̲	"A" underscore
o and =	o̲	"O" underscore

c. WordPerfect has assigned all characters to different "sets" and has given each character a number within that set. You can insert the special character in the document by using the Compose feature and typing the number of the set, a comma, and then the number for the character. Press ENTER as the last step. Before using this option, you will need to locate the set and character numbers in Appendix A, "WordPerfect Character Sets."

Hints

See "Keyboard Layout" and "Mapping the Keyboard" in this chapter if you want to assign a special character to a key combination such as ALT-B or CTRL-T.

Your monitor will display at least 256 of the possible 1500 characters. If you have a graphics printer (laser or dot matrix), you can print all of the special characters available. The following tips explain how you can display more than 256 characters on the screen and tells you how to print the special characters.

Displaying Special Characters

If you have an EGA, a VGA, or a Hercules Graphics Plus or InColor Card, you can choose to display 512 characters on the screen instead of the standard 256.

If a character cannot be displayed, a small box will appear instead. Pressing Reveal Codes (ALT-F3) and moving your cursor to the small box displays the character set and character number that you entered.

Printing Special Characters

If you have a graphics printer (laser or dot matrix), WordPerfect will print every available character. If a character is not found in the current font, WordPerfect checks the list of automatic font changes to see if you have entered a font for that particular character set. If not, it begins scanning the substitute fonts for the special character. (See Chapter 5, "Printer Program," for more information about automatic font changes and substitute fonts.) If the character is not found in either location, WordPerfect prints it (or the part of the character that cannot be found) as a graphics character.

If either the Text or Graphics Quality option in the Print (SHIFT-F7) menu is set to High, the character will be printed in high quality. If both are set to anything less than High, the character will be printed in the quality selected for Graphics Quality. If either is set to Do Not Print, the graphics characters will not print.

Characters printed graphically take up memory in the printer. If you hear a beep during printing, press Print (SHIFT-F7) and then choose 4 for Control Printer to check for a "Not Enough Memory" error message. If you continue the print job, the remaining characters that could not be printed because of lack of memory are printed as spaces. Printing characters as graphics characters takes quite a bit longer than printing text characters.

Related Entries

Keyboard Layout
Mapping the Keyboard
Special Characters
See also Appendix A, "WordPerfect Character Sets"

CONCORDANCE

A *concordance* is a list of words and phrases that are to be included in an index. Instead of marking each phrase individually in a document, you can use a concordance to save time and keystrokes.

Keystrokes

1. Clear the screen, and type each word or phrase for each entry. Each phrase can be as long as you like; [HRt] codes (not [SRt]

codes) mark the end of concordance entries. The following list shows a sample concordance:

Congress
Senate
President of the United States
Senator
Representative
Legislator
Vice President
Chief Justice

2. Sort the concordance file if you want the index to be generated quickly. See "Hints" for the exact steps.

3. If you want all phrases in the concordance to be listed as major headings in the index, you do not have to mark the entries for an index. If you want some of the phrases to be used as headings and some as subheadings, mark each phrase accordingly. See "Hints" for more information.

4. Save the file as you would normally.

5. Retrieve the document to be indexed, and position the cursor at the end of it. (An index can be generated successfully only if the index definition is at the end of a document.)

6. If you want the index to begin on a separate page, insert a hard page break and label the page if desired.

7. Press Mark Text (ALT-F5).

8. Choose 5 for Define.

9. Choose 3 for Define Index.

10. "Concordance Filename (Enter = none):" appears. Enter the name of the file that contains the words and phrases to be indexed (the file you just created).

11. Type the number indicating how the page numbers are to appear in the index.

12. To generate the index, press Mark Text (ALT-F5); choose 6 for Generate, 5 for Generate Tables, Indexes, Cross-References, and so on; and then type Y to continue with the process.

Hints

When you define an index and specify a concordance file, the following code is inserted in the document:

[Def Mark:Index,*n*; *filename*]

This information tells you that the code is an index definition mark, shows the page-numbering option that was selected, and shows the name of the file that is to be used for the concordance.

A WordPerfect index can contain headings and subheadings. Each phrase found in the concordance file is used automatically as a major heading. If you want a different heading or subheading, or if you want each phrase listed in the index in several ways, mark each entry to indicate the heading or subheading to be used:

1. Use Block (ALT-F4) to block the phrase. If the phrase consists of only one word, move the cursor to the word; blocking it is not necessary.

2. Press Mark Text (ALT-F5).

3. Choose 3 for Index.

4. "Index heading:" appears with the blocked phrase (or the current word if you did not use Block). Press ENTER to accept the displayed heading, or enter a new one. (You can also edit the displayed heading and then press ENTER to accept it.)

5. "Subheading:" appears. If you edited the blocked phrase or entered a new heading, the block is again displayed as the subheading. Press ENTER to accept it as the subheading, edit the suggested subheading, enter a new one, or press Cancel (F1) if you do not want a subheading.

An index-mark code is inserted at the cursor location:

[Index:*Heading*;*Subheading*]

If you mark a phrase in the concordance, it will no longer be used automatically as a major heading by itself. The index markings will be used instead to determine the heading and subheading. Each phrase can be marked as many times as you want with different headings or subheadings. For example, you could mark the phrase "U.S. Constitution" several times, and the entries in the index might appear as follows:

```
Constitution
    U.S. . . . . . . . . . . . . . . . . . . . . . . . . . . . . . . . . . . . . .1-5
Constitution of the United States of America . . . . . . . . . . . . . . . .1-5
U.S.
    Constitution. . . . . . . . . . . . . . . . . . . . . . . . . . . . . . . . .1-5
```

If you have endnotes in a document, WordPerfect lets you specify where they will be printed. If you do not choose a specific location, endnotes are printed after the index. If you have endnotes and do not choose a specific location, you may want to press Hard Page (CTRL-ENTER) at the very end of the document so the endnotes will start on a new page and not on the same page as the index. See "Endnotes" in this chapter for more information about endnote placement.

Sorting the Concordance

Sorting the concordance alphabetically makes generating the index faster. Retrieve the concordance file to the screen if it is not already there, and follow these steps:

1. Press Merge/Sort (CTRL-F9).

2. Choose **2** to select **S**ort.

3. You are asked for the input file and the output to be sorted. Press ENTER twice to accept the default, which will sort what is displayed on the screen to the screen.

4. Choose **1** to **P**erform Action.

These steps assume that you did not make any changes to the Sort menu. WordPerfect is already set to do a line sort using the first word as the key. If you have made changes to this setup, you will need to change the Sort menu back to the original settings before typing **1** to perform the action.

Not Enough Memory

If you see the error message "Not enough memory to use entire concordance file. Continue? No (Yes)," there are a few things that you can do. First, type **N** to stop the process, and press Switch (SHIFT-F3) to see if you have another document in Doc 2. If there is one, exit that document. You can also remove all other programs (such as SideKick, ProKey, and WordPerfect Library) from memory and then try to generate the index again, or increase the amount of memory allotted with the /W option if running under Library. Second, you can type **Y** to continue, and let as much of the concordance file be used as possible. You can then save as a separate file the part of the index that was successfully generated, edit the concordance file so that it contains only words that were not yet indexed, and regenerate the index. After it has been regenerated, you can combine the two indexes.

Related Entries

     Index
     Sort and Select

CONDENSE DOCUMENTS

See "Master Document" in this chapter.

CONDITIONAL END OF PAGE

The Conditional End of Page feature keeps a specified number of lines together.

Keystrokes

Count the number of lines to be protected before completing the following steps, because when you enter the number of lines to be protected, you are in a menu and cannot see the text.

1. Position the cursor on the line just above the section of lines to be kept together. This line does not have to be blank.

2. Press Format (SHIFT-F8).

3. Choose 4 for Other.

4. Choose 2 for Conditional End of Page. The message "Number of Lines to Keep Together:" appears.

5. Enter the number of lines, including any blank spaces caused by double-spacing.

6. Press Exit (F7) to return to the document.

Hints

The conditional end of page code [Cndl EOP:n] is placed in the document, where n is the number of lines to be protected. This command will not allow a soft page break to fall within the specified number of lines. If the protected lines fall near the end of a page, the page break will occur just after the [Cndl EOP:n] code and right before the protected lines. The section of text is protected from soft page breaks, but a hard page break can be inserted at any location with CTRL-ENTER.

Conditional End of Page protects a specific number of lines, whereas Block Protect protects a block of text. When trying to decide which feature is better for a particular situation, first determine whether it is important to keep certain lines together (as with a heading and the first two lines of a paragraph), or if the block of text must be kept together regardless of the amount of text added or deleted from the block.

If you have double-spaced or even triple-spaced text, the Conditional End of Page feature takes any blank lines into consideration. For example, if you are using double-spacing and you want to protect the heading and first two lines in a paragraph, enter **6** (not 3) as the number of lines to keep together.

You may also be pleased to note that a hard return [HRt] code following a soft page break will be converted to a dormant hard return [Dorm HRt] code, which means that it will not produce a blank line at the top of the page.

Applications

Conditional End of Page is most often used to keep a title or heading with the first two lines of a paragraph or to keep three-line paragraphs together (the Widow/Orphan Protection feature will not protect you in these types of situations). Depending on how often you use such a feature, you might consider placing the steps in a macro, which can then be executed before each paragraph heading. Be sure to take the spacing into consideration (as noted in "Hints").

Because the steps for specifying the number of lines to be kept together are quite involved, you might want to consider creating the following macro, here named ALT-C for Conditional End of Page.

1. Press Macro Define (CTRL-F10).

2. Enter the name of the macro (ALT-C is a suggestion).

3. Enter a description (such as "Keep heading with text") or press ENTER to skip this step.

4. While "Macro Def" is flashing, press Format (SHIFT-F8), choose **4** for **O**ther and **2** for **C**onditional End of Page and then enter a number such as 6, 8, or 10. The higher the number, the better the chance you have of protecting the heading with the following text, even if you are working in double-spacing.

5. Press Exit (F7) to return to the document, and then press Macro Define (CTRL-F10) to finish the macro.

To use this macro, scroll through a document and find headings that are split from the following text by a page break. Move the cursor to the line just above the heading, and press ALT-C (if you named the macro with a different name, use that name to start the macro).

Related Entries

Block Protect
ENTER Key
Widow/Orphan Protection

CONFIG.SYS

The CONFIG.SYS file is checked each time you start your computer and helps configure your system. To run WordPerfect, this file needs to contain the command FILES=20, which enables WordPerfect to create up to 20 open files at once. If you are also running WordPerfect Library or Office, increase the number of files to 40. Even if you are not running one of these programs, increasing the number of files may speed up WordPerfect.

When you install WordPerfect, you can have the Install program check the CONFIG.SYS file and add the FILES=20 command for you. If the file does not exist, it will create it for you.

Increasing the number of buffers with the BUFFERS command will also help speed up some operations such as printing. To do so, retrieve the CONFIG.SYS file as a DOS text file and include the command, BUFFERS=25 (adjust if necessary).

CONTINUOUS PAPER

See "Paper Size/Type" in this chapter.

CONTROL PRINTER

Formerly called Printer Control in version 4.2, this menu helps you manage the print jobs that are waiting to be printed. You can cancel, display, and rush print jobs, or you can stop and restart the printer from this menu.

Keystrokes

1. Press Print (SHIFT-F7).

2. Choose 4 for Control Printer. The menu shown in Figure 3-31 is displayed. The status of the current job is shown at the top of the screen, giving information about the current page and the copy being printed, the type of paper needed, and the location of that type of paper. The jobs waiting in the queue are listed in the middle of the screen.

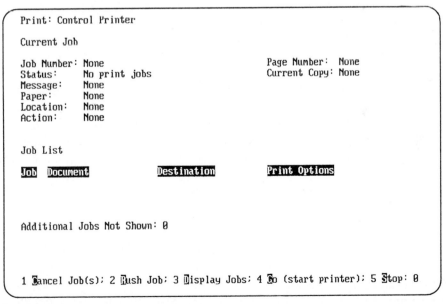

```
Print: Control Printer

Current Job

Job Number: None                        Page Number:  None
Status:     No print jobs               Current Copy: None
Message:    None
Paper:      None
Location:   None
Action:     None


Job List

Job  Document              Destination        Print Options




Additional Jobs Not Shown: 0



1 Cancel Job(s); 2 Rush Job; 3 Display Jobs; 4 Go (start printer); 5 Stop: 0
```

Figure 3-31.   Control Printer menu

3. After making the desired changes, press ENTER to return to the document.

Options

The following options are available in the Control Printer menu.

Cancel Job(s)

You can cancel any or all print jobs with this option. If you choose 1 for Cancel Job(s), the current job number is automatically displayed. Press ENTER to cancel that job, enter a different job number, or type an asterisk (*) and then **Y** to cancel all print jobs. If the printer does not respond immediately, press ENTER; the temporary print files are deleted from the disk. Turn the printer off and then on to empty the printer's buffer. Follow any instructions telling you to reset the top of the form at the printer, and send the printer a Go if necessary by choosing 4 for **G**o.

Rush Job

When you choose 2 for **R**ush Job, the last print job number is displayed automatically as the job to be rushed. Press ENTER to rush that job, or enter a different job number. You can either interrupt the printing of the current document or place it next in the queue. "RUSH" is added to the column labeled "Print Options" to indicate that the job was rushed.

Display Jobs

Information about the current print job is displayed in the upper section of the Control Printer menu. The next three jobs in the job list (queue) are listed in the middle of the screen. The job number, document to be printed, destination, and print options are listed for each job, as shown in the following screen:

```
Job List

Job  Document          Destination    Print Options
 1   (Screen)          LPT 1          Copies=3
 2   C:\CONTRACT\AMEND  LPT 1
 3   C:\BOOK\CHAPTER.9  LPT 1          Graphics=High, Binding=.5"

Additional Jobs Not Shown: 4




1 Cancel Job(s); 2 Rush Job; 3 Display Jobs; 4 Go (start printer); 5 Stop: 0
```

Note that "Additional Jobs Not Shown:" (at the bottom of the screen) shows four jobs. To display all print jobs in the queue, choose **3** for **D**isplay Jobs. A separate screen appears, which is similar to the following illustration. You may see a message saying "All print jobs are displayed" or "No print jobs" if there are less than three print jobs in the queue or no print jobs are waiting. Press any key to return to the Control Printer menu.

```
Job List

Job  Document          Destination    Print Options
 1   (Screen)          LPT 1          Copies=3
 2   C:\CONTRACT\AMEND  LPT 1
 3   C:\BOOK\CHAPTER.9  LPT 1          Graphics=High, Binding=.5"
 4   (Screen)          LPT 1
 5   B:NOTES           LPT 1          Copies=2
 6   C:\BOOK\OUTLINE   LPT 1          Text=Draft
 7   C:\LETTERS\JONES  LPT 1
```

Go (Start Printer)

If you are feeding paper, envelopes, or other types of forms into the printer manually, printing will pause at the beginning of each page. If you have a daisywheel printer and encounter font changes in the document, the printer will pause to allow you to change the print wheel. Choose **4** for **G**o to send a Go to the printer, and resume printing after inserting the paper or changing the print wheel.

If you stop the printer (with the S option on the menu), type **G** to restart the print job. If more than one page has been printed, you are asked to enter the page number from which to restart the printing. If the printer is not printing when you think it should, check the "Job Status" and "Message" lines in the upper part of the screen to see if the printer is waiting for a Go.

Stop Printing

If you choose this option, the printer may not stop right away. No further information will be sent from the computer to the printer, but the information already sent to the printer will continue printing until it is finished. If you want to stop printing immediately, switch the printer off and then back on to clear the printer's buffer. Type **G** to restart the job from a specific page.

Hints

Each print job is given a number that corresponds to the order in which it was queued. If all print jobs are canceled or printed, the order does not begin again with 1; it will start over at 1 only after you exit and reenter WordPerfect. If you see "(Screen)" listed among the print jobs, it means that the print job was queued from the screen. The print queue can contain up to 255 documents. The number of print jobs depends only on the amount of available disk space.

Related Entries

Cancel a Print Job
Display Print Jobs
Print
Restart the Printer
Rush a Print Job
Selecting a Printer
Stop Printing

CONVERT PROGRAM

The Convert program, installed with the utility files, is used to convert documents created with other software programs (such as WordStar, MultiMate, and Microsoft Word) to 5.1 format. In most cases, the reverse can also be done by converting a 5.1 document to other formats.

Keystrokes

1. If you have not already done so, you will need to run the Install program (found on the Install/Learn/Utility 1 disk) and choose the Custom option to install the Utility files. This process will copy the Convert program (CONVERT.EXE) and other utility programs to the designated drive.

2. From the DOS prompt of the drive where Convert is located, type **convert** to start the program.

3. Enter the name of the input file (the file to be converted). Be sure to include the full pathname (where the file is located) if it is not on the default drive.

4. Enter the name of the output file (the resulting file). The name cannot be the same as the input file. If the filename used for the output file already exists, you will be asked if you want to overwrite the file already on disk. Type **Y** or **N**.

5. The choices shown in Figure 3-32 (other than the first choice) can be used to convert from another format to WordPerfect.

   If you choose option **1** to convert WordPerfect to another format, the choices shown in Figure 3-33 appear.

6. Type the number corresponding to the type of conversion desired.

   If you choose the Mail Merge option (a format used by WordStar, dBASE II/III, and other programs), you are asked to supply the field delimiter, the record delimiter, and the characters to be stripped. If you do not know what to answer, type a comma for the field delimiter, {13}{10} for the record delimiter, and " for the character to be stripped. Note that delimited files can be used in a merge without converting them with this option first. See "Merge" for details.

Options

The following discussion is included to help you decide which format is best suited to your document. Note that the ASCII text file conversion is the same as the one found in WordPerfect on Text In/Out (CTRL-F5). Spreadsheet files created in Lotus 1-2-3, Excel, PlanPerfect, and Quattro can be retrieved directly into WordPerfect. See "Spreadsheet Importing and Linking" for information.

Revisable-Form-Text/Final-Form-Text (IBM DCA Format)

DCA (Document Content Architecture) is IBM's standard format for storing documents. Programs not listed as options on the Convert menu

```
Name of Input File? c:\ref\chapter.1
Name of Output File? a:chapter.1ws


0 EXIT
1 WordPerfect to another format
2 Revisable-Form-Text (IBM DCA Format) to WordPerfect
3 Final-Form-Text (IBM DCA Format) to WordPerfect
4 Navy DIF Standard to WordPerfect
5 WordStar 3.3 to WordPerfect
6 MultiMate Advantage II to WordPerfect
7 Seven-Bit Transfer Format to WordPerfect
8 WordPerfect 4.2 to WordPerfect 5.1
9 Mail Merge to WordPerfect Secondary Merge
A Spreadsheet DIF to WordPerfect Secondary Merge
B Word 4.0 to WordPerfect

Enter number of Conversion desired
```

Figure 3-32.   Convert menu

```
Name of Input File? c:\ref\chapter.1
Name of Output File? a:chapter.1ws


0 EXIT
1 Revisable-Form-Text (IBM DCA Format)
2 Final-Form-Text (IBM DCA Format)
3 Navy DIF Standard
4 WordStar 3.3
5 MultiMate Advantage II
6 Seven-Bit Transfer Format
7 ASCII Text File
8 WordPerfect Secondary Merge to Spreadsheet DIF

Enter number of output file format desired
```

Figure 3-33.   Additional choices when you choose option 1 from the main
Convert menu

might have the option of converting their documents to DCA. They can
then be converted into WordPerfect format.

When converting DisplayWrite files (FFT) to WordPerfect, column
codes are replaced with tabs.

When converting from WordPerfect to DisplayWrite (FFT), outline
and paragraph numbers are placed between "begin and end formatted
text functions" so that the outline numbers will appear without your
having to paginate the DisplayWrite document.

Navy DIF

Navy DIF is a format used by the Navy to aid in the transfer of
documents. They are considered word processing documents rather
than spreadsheet files.

WordStar and MultiMate

Documents can be transferred to and from WordStar 3.3 and MultiMate
Advantage II. If you have WordStar 2000, transfer the WordStar 2000
document to WordStar 3.3 format first and then use Convert. All possible formatting is retained.

Seven-Bit Transfer Format

WordPerfect documents can usually be transmitted electronically without any conversion. However, because some modems and communication lines can accept only 7 bits, the eighth bit will be stripped during the transfer. This can affect the format of the transferred file, because WordPerfect uses the eighth bit for program codes. If you want to retain all formatting, use this option to convert a regular WordPerfect document to 7-bit format. After it has been transferred, the person receiving the file must convert it back to WordPerfect format.

Mail Merge

Choose this option to transfer data from a database into a secondary WordPerfect file. The database file must first be converted in a delimited format, where fields and records are separated by specific characters. This option can also be used for WordStar Mail Merge data files.

Spreadsheet DIF

DIF (Data Interchange Format) is a standard format used by some spreadsheets to help transfer documents between programs. A spreadsheet file should be converted to DIF first. It can then be converted to a WordPerfect secondary merge file. A WordPerfect secondary merge file can also be converted back to DIF format. This option is necessary only if you want to convert the data to a secondary merge file. Spreadsheet files from several popular programs can be retrieved directly without conversion.

When converting a WordPerfect secondary merge file to DIF, be aware that there is a limit of 80 characters per field. If you cannot work with this limitation, consider transferring the file through PlanPerfect. The number of characters allowed in each field is then raised to 250.

WordPerfect 4.2 to 5.1

This option is similar to the conversion that is done when a 4.2 document is retrieved into 5.1. When you choose this option, you are asked for the name of the conversion resource (.CRS) file. If you press ENTER, the STANDARD.CRS file will be used by default. See "Compatibility" in this chapter for more information about creating a .CRS file.

Microsoft Word

Microsoft Word 4.0 files can be converted to WordPerfect but cannot be converted back into Word format.

ASCII Text Files

When you are converting files to ASCII (DOS text), Center, Tab, Decimal Align, Indent, and Flush Right are converted to spaces to preserve the structure of the document. Outline and paragraph numbers are also converted to regular numbers.

Shortcuts

If you know the menu selections by heart, you can enter the commands at the DOS prompt rather than going through the Convert program menus. Enter each item separated by spaces (without parentheses) at the DOS prompt, as shown here:

convert *input filename output filename n n*

The first *n* represents the option number from the first menu, and the second *n* represents the number from the second menu (if you are converting from WordPerfect to another format). For example, if you wanted to convert a file named LETTER that was created with WordPerfect to a file named LETTER.WS in WordStar format, you would type the following at the DOS prompt:

convert letter letter.ws 1 4

You can also use wildcard characters to convert multiple files. For example, entering the following command would convert all the files found on the default drive from WordPerfect to 7-bit transfer format and give the converted files an .MDM (modem) extension.

    convert *.* *.mdm 1 6

If you have chosen option **9** to convert from Mail Merge to Word-Perfect Secondary Merge, you can also add the field delimiter, record delimiter, and characters to be stripped from the file to the command line, as shown here:

    convert mailing.dbf maillist.wp 8 , {13}{10} "

Applications

The Convert program enables you to share documents with others who are using various types of software. If you are a writer, your publisher may accept text in either ASCII or WordStar format. If you convert a document to WordStar, many WordPerfect codes will be converted rather than removed (as is the case with an ASCII file).

Rather than creating a report in a database, you can export the file to a delimited (Mail Merge) format, convert it to a WordPerfect second-ary merge file, and use WordPerfect's advanced formatting features to create form letters, envelopes, and labels.

Related Entries

    dBASE
    DCA Format
    DIF
    DOS Text Files
    WordStar
    See also Appendix F, "Conversion Tables"

COPY

You can easily copy any amount of text to another location in the same document or to another document.

Keystrokes

The following is a brief explanation of how a block of text can be copied. See "Move" in this chapter for details on copying or moving sentences, paragraphs, pages, tabbed columns, and rectangular sections of text.

1. Move the cursor to the beginning or the end of the block to be moved, and press Block (ALT-F4).

2. Move to the opposite end of the block. As the cursor moves through the text, the text is highlighted.

3. Press Move (CTRL-F4).

4. Choose 1 for **Block**.

5. Choose 2 to select **Copy**. The following prompt appears on the status line:

Move cursor; press **Enter** to retrieve.

6. Move the cursor to the location where the text should be retrieved, whether this location is in the current document or another document; you can use Switch (SHIFT-F3) to move between two documents.

7. Press ENTER to retrieve the copied text.

You can press Cancel (F1) to clear the prompt at any time. You can then retrieve the copied block by pressing Move (CTRL-F4), choosing 4 to select **Retrieve**, and then typing 1 for **Block**. Another way to retrieve moved or copied text is to press Retrieve (SHIFT-F10) and then press ENTER when you are prompted for the name of the file.

Still another way to copy a block of text is to highlight the block, press Save (F10), and press ENTER. This saves the block in the same temporary file that is used to hold text that was moved or copied with Move. You can retrieve this temporary, unnamed file using the two methods just mentioned.

Hints

If you have an enhanced keyboard, you can save several keystrokes by pressing CTRL-INS to copy text after you have blocked it. If you want to move the blocked text, you can press CTRL-DEL. The same prompt telling you to move the cursor and press ENTER to retrieve the text appears.

If you do not have an enhanced keyboard, you can assign the macro commands {Block Copy} and {Block Move} to any key or key combination. See "Macros" or "Keyboard Layout" and "Mapping the Keyboard" in this chapter for details.

Moved and copied text is saved in a temporary "move" file. It remains there and can be retrieved again until another move or copy is performed or until you turn off the computer.

If the cursor is at the beginning of a sentence, a paragraph, or a page, press Block (ALT-F4) and type a period (.) to highlight the sentence, press ENTER to highlight the paragraph, or press PGDN to highlight the page. The Move option on the Move menu removes the text instead of making a copy. Moved text is saved in the same temporary file as copied text.

The Delete option on the Move menu lets you delete a sentence, a paragraph, or a page. Even though the deleted text is not saved in the temporary file, it is saved in a temporary "undelete" file, and you can retrieve it by pressing Cancel (F1) and choosing **1** for **R**estore. Remember that this method restores only the last three deletions.

Copying a Document

See "Print Options" for details about printing more than one copy. See "Copy Files" for information about copying documents from one disk to another. If you want more than one copy of a document on the screen, you can retrieve the document from disk again and again. See "Merge" in this chapter for information about creating duplicate copies when only certain information changes from copy to copy, such as in form letters.

If you find that you have more than one copy of your document on the screen and you want only one, you have accidentally retrieved the file again without first clearing the screen. If this happens often, make sure that you are not doing one of the following:

• With Save (F10), a document is saved but is not removed from the screen. If you want to save the file *and* clear the screen, use Exit (F7) before retrieving a file with Retrieve (SHIFT-F10).

• You might have entered the List Files menu while working on a document, moved the cursor to the current document filename, and chose **1** to **R**etrieve the document. A question will appear asking if you want the file to be retrieved into the current document. To see if you have a document in memory before you retrieve a file, check the upper left corner of the List Files menu. "Document size:" is displayed as part of the List Files heading. If the size is zero, there is not a document in memory.

Applications

The Copy feature can copy the name and address in a letter and place it on an envelope. If you have typed text in one document and need it duplicated in another, copy the text instead of retyping it.

Related Entries

> Merge
> Move
> Number of Copies
> Undelete

COPY FILES

You can copy files from one disk to another while in WordPerfect's List Files menu.

Keystrokes

1. Press List (F5).

2. The current default drive and directory are displayed. Press ENTER if the file or files to be copied are in that drive and directory. If not, enter the appropriate drive and directory.

3. Move the cursor to the file to be copied. If you need to copy more than one file to the same destination, type * to mark each file. Press Mark Text (ALT-F5) if you want to mark all the files in the directory.

4. Choose 8 for Copy. If you have marked files with *, you are asked "Copy marked files? No (Yes)." Type **Y** or **N**. If you type **N**, "Copy this file to:" appears, letting you copy the file that is currently highlighted.

5. Enter the drive and directory to which the file or files are to be copied. If a file with the same name already exists in the destination drive and directory, you are asked if you want to replace the existing file. Type **Y** or **N**.

Hints

You can also copy files while in DOS. To do so, exit to a DOS prompt and type **copy**. Type the name of the file to be copied, followed by the destination. For example, if you were copying a file named PROPOSAL from the current drive and directory to drive A, you would type the following:

    copy proposal a:

Related Entries

List Files

COUNT LINES

See "Line Numbering" in this chapter.

COUNT WORDS

See "Word Count" in this chapter.

CREATE A DIRECTORY

You can divide your hard disk into several directories for better organization. You can create a new directory on your disk from within Word-Perfect.

Keystrokes

1. Press List (F5). The name of the current default directory is displayed.

2. Type = to change the default directory. "New directory = " followed by the name of the current directory is displayed.

3. Enter the name for the new directory.

4. When asked if you really want to create the new directory, type **Y** or **N**.

The directory is created and the default directory remains as it was.

Hints

You can also create a new directory while in the List Files menu. If you choose **7** for **O**ther Directory and enter the name of a nonexistent directory, you will be asked if you want to create the directory you have named. Like filenames, directory names can consist of up to eight characters and an optional three-character extension.

You can also use the DOS command MD to make a new directory. To do so, exit to a DOS prompt and type **md** *directory,* where *directory* is the name of the new directory.

Related Entries

Directories
List Files

"CRITICAL DISK ERROR OCCURRED" ERROR MESSAGE

A disk error message may appear when you are trying to save or print a file.

Reason

When you save a file or print from the screen (which creates a temporary print file), WordPerfect and DOS create a new file on the disk. If that particular location on the disk is damaged, the error message will be displayed.

Solutions

Run the computer's Diagnostics test or try the DOS CHKDSK command to determine if the problem lies with the disk. If you are saving a file, you should save it to another disk or directory. You might also check to see if you have more than one copy of WordPerfect on a hard disk in different directories. If this is the case, delete the older versions of the program. If you have a memory-resident print spooler, it might be the cause of the problem. Remove the spooler from memory and see if the problem is corrected.

CROSS-REFERENCES

When you add or delete text in WordPerfect, pages are renumbered automatically. When you are adding or deleting footnotes, endnotes, paragraph numbers, and so on, the remaining numbers are renumbered automatically. Although this is definitely an advantage, it makes it difficult to refer to a specific page, footnote, paragraph number, and so on, because the numbers can always change. Because of this, a feature called Cross-Referencing lets you refer to specific page numbers, graphics boxes, footnotes, endnotes, and paragraph/outline numbers, and it automatically updates those references with the Generate option.

For example, you might want to refer to a figure on a specific page in the document. After editing the document and adding or deleting figures, the figure to which you referred might be renumbered and found on different page. Rather than going through the document and updating all the references manually, you can use the Cross-Referencing feature to update the references.

Keystrokes

Marking a Reference

1. Press Mark Text (ALT-F5).

2. Choose **1** to select Cross-**R**ef.

3. Initially, you will want to choose **3** to mark **B**oth the Reference and Target.

Options 1 and 2 give you the ability to mark either the target or the reference as you enter text, marking more than one target per reference (as in "see pages 2, 17, 30") or having more than one reference to the same target (when referring to the same figure from more than one place in the document). These options are explained under "Hints."

After choosing **3** to mark **B**oth the Reference and Target, the following sections appear:

```
Tie Reference to:

     1 - Page Number

     2 - Paragraph/Outline Number

     3 - Footnote Number

     4 - Endnote Number

     5 - Graphics Box Number

After selecting a reference type, go to the location of the item you want to
reference in your document and press Enter to mark it as the "target".
```

4. Choose the number that corresponds to the desired target (1 for Page, 2 for Paragraph/Outline Number, and so on). If you choose **5** for Graphics Box Number, you can choose from the following graphics box options:

```
1 Figure; 2 Table Box; 3 Text Box; 4 User Box; 5 Equation: 0
```

5. The next prompt that appears depends on the selection that you made. For example, if you chose to refer to a particular footnote, the prompt will appear as follows:

Cross Ref: Move to footnote; press **Enter.**

6. Position the cursor to the right of the footnote to be referenced, and press ENTER. If you are selecting a page, move the cursor next to the text to which you are referring before you press ENTER. When positioning your cursor, keep in mind that the first paragraph/outline number, footnote, endnote, or graphics box (figure, table, and so on) to the left of (before) the cursor is the target that will be used.

If you know the number of the footnote or endnote to be referenced, you can press Footnote (CTRL-F7), choose **1** for Footnote or choose **2** for Endnote, choose **2** for Edit, and then enter the number of the footnote or endnote. If the correct footnote or endnote is displayed, press ENTER. To leave a footnote or endnote without selecting it as the target, press Exit (F7). See "Hints" for more information about referencing footnotes and endnotes.

If you are referencing a graphics box, such as a figure or a table, position the cursor just after the code, not in the figure or table itself. Use Search (F2) or ←Search (SHIFT-F2) if you have difficulty finding the code.

7. You are next asked for the target name. This name is stored with both the target and the reference so that a match can be made later when the references are updated. This name is also used later when you are marking more than one reference for a particular target or marking multiple targets for the same reference.

8. After you enter the target name, the cursor is returned to the original location and the reference is inserted.

Updating the References

If you edit the document, or if a ? was inserted at the point of reference, you will need to generate the document to update the references.

1. Press Mark Text (ALT-F5).

2. Choose **6** for **G**enerate.

3. Choose **5** to **G**enerate Tables, Indexes, Cross-References, etc.

4. Choose **Y** to generate the references or **N** to cancel the procedure.

The Generate option makes several passes through the document to match references with targets having the same target name. When it finds a target for a particular reference, it updates the number in the reference. If a match is not found, a question mark (?) is inserted in place of a number.

Hints

When you mark a reference, WordPerfect inserts the code [Ref(*name*): *type n*] at that location. When you press ENTER to mark a target, the code [Target(*name*)] is inserted. *Name* refers to the target name given when you are marking a reference or a target; *type* refers to the type of reference (Pg, Par, Ftn, End, Fig, Tbl, Txt Box, Usr Box, or Equ Box) used; and n indicates the current number of that reference. If the specific target is not found (for example, when the footnote to which you referred has not yet been created), a question mark is inserted in the place of a number.

Multiple References

You can use the option to mark only a reference when you want to refer to the same target from different locations in the document. For example, you might want to refer to Figure 1 more than once from the same document (or from another document when you are working with master documents). To do this, position the cursor at the point at which you want the reference to appear, press Mark Text (ALT-F5), choose **1** for Cross-**R**ef, and then choose **1** to Mark the **R**eference only. You are then asked to identify the type of reference (page, paragraph/outline number, and so on) and to enter the target name. You can mark the target before or after this step or even include the target in another document.

As was just noted, you are asked for the type of reference (page, footnote, and so on) when marking only a reference. This feature lets you use the same target name for different types of references; you do not have to mark the target more than once. If you have a figure showing the first-quarter sales for 1990, you could mark it as a target with the target name "sales." If you wanted to refer to it later as "Figure ? on page ?" you could mark the first reference as a graphics box (figure) and the second as a page. Both could refer to the same target name, "sales." This would eliminate the need for marking both the reference and the target twice.

By using the option to mark a target, you can have multiple targets for a reference. For example, if you discussed the tax laws of 1990 three times in your document, you could mark each occurrence with the same target name, "taxes." When the single reference was updated, the entry might appear as "see pages 6, 12, 18." Unfortunately, the word "and" cannot be inserted into the sequence of numbers, because the numbers are actually one code.

Master Documents

By using the Master Documents feature, you can refer to items in other documents by marking a reference in one document and the target in another. Both would use the same target name.

To update the references, you would include the documents in one master document. To do this, press Mark Text (ALT-F5), choose 2 for Subdoc (subdocument), and enter the filename. Continue until the names of all subdocuments are included. While in the master document, you then choose the Generate option, as explained in "Updating the References." The subdocuments are expanded, references are updated, and you are asked if you want to replace the original subdocuments. Typing **Y** updates the files on disk with those containing updated references.

Referencing Footnotes and Endnotes

When you refer to a page on which a specific footnote is located, it makes no difference whether you place the code in the text just after the footnote number or in the footnote itself, because footnotes are printed on the same page in which they are referenced. If you are referring to a certain endnote, it also makes no difference where you mark the target (within the text or in the endnote itself). However, if you want to refer to the page on which the endnote is referenced, place the mark in the document just after the endnote number. If you want to refer to the page on which the endnote is to be printed, place the target code inside the endnote itself. A question mark will appear until you choose the Generate option, at which time it will be replaced with the correct page number.

Related Entries

Generate
Master Document

CTRL KEY

Like the ALT key, CTRL has no function when used alone. It is used in combination with the function keys to execute the features printed in red on the template.

You can also use the Keyboard Layout feature to assign a special character, WordPerfect function, or macro to a CTRL-key combination. See "Keyboard Layout" and "Mapping the Keyboard" and "Compose" in this chapter for more information.

Even though the Merge feature includes commands such as {DATE} to insert the current date, control codes such as ^D can also accomplish the same task. See "Merge" in this chapter for details.

Keystrokes

If a CTRL-key combination is not mapped to a special character, it will perform the following function when pressed.

^A   Displayed but not used

^B   Inserts the current page number at print time; not a merge code

^C   Merge code; pauses a merge so that text can be entered from the console (keyboard)

^D   Merge code; inserts the current date and time

^E   Merge code; ^E[HPg] marks the end of a record in a secondary file. If ^E is found in a primary file, the merge will end at that point

^F   Merge code; inserts a specific field from the secondary merge file (should appear as ^F*n*^)

^G   Merge code; starts a macro (tells it to go)

^H   Not displayed and not used

^I   Inserts a tab code into the document; former WordStar users can use this key combination instead of TAB to feel more at home

^J   Inserts a hard return [HRt] code

^K   Deletes to the end of the line. CTRL-END accomplishes the same task. If a line of text disappears because you have accidentally pressed these keys, you can press Cancel (F1) and choose **1** to **R**estore the deleted text; there is no confirmation message for this type of deletion. You can also use this CTRL-key combination to insert the [SPg] code into a search string (precede the keystroke with CTRL-V)

^L   Deletes to the end of the page; a message asks you to confirm the deletion. CTRL-PGDN is the documented WordPerfect feature to delete to the end of the page

^M   Inserts a space; can be used to insert an [SRt] code into a search string (press CTRL-V before pressing CTRL-M in this case)

^N   Merge code; tells WordPerfect to merge with the next record

^O   Merge code; used with ^C to display (output) a message (usually instructions to the user) when the merge pauses for entry from the keyboard

^P   Merge code; retrieves other primary files during a merge

^Q   Merge code; used to quit the merge operation

^R   Merge code; ^R[HRt] can be used to indicate the end of a field to separate fields in a secondary merge (data) file. If a merge pauses for input at a ^C, you must press End Field (F9) to continue

^S   Merge code; used to call another secondary (data) file during a merge

^T   Merge code; everything merged to the ^T is sent to the printer

^U   Merge code; updates the display to that point during a merge

^V   Merge code or an alternate way of displaying special characters; see "Merge Codes" and "Compose" in this chapter for more information

^W   Moves the cursor up one line

^X   Moves the cursor right one character

^Y   Moves the cursor left one character

^Z   Moves the cursor down one line

Most of the control codes are used as merge codes, even though other, more descriptive merge codes exist in version 5.1, such as {DATE}, {END FIELD}, and {END RECORD}.

Related Entries

Compose
Keyboard Layout/Mapping
Merge

CURSOR.COM PROGRAM

If you installed the utility files during installation, you can use the CURSOR.COM program to change the size or look of the cursor.

Keystrokes

1. Type **cursor** at the appropriate DOS prompt. A grid appears on the screen.

2. Move the cursor to various locations in the grid. As you move through the grid, the cursor changes size and shape.
   If you want to see how the cursor looks in a regular line of text, press the space bar. Press the space bar again to return to the grid.

3. When you are satisfied with the cursor's size and shape, take note of the column and row in the grid (displayed in the bottom left corner of the screen) and press ENTER to set the cursor and return to DOS.

Hints

The cursor will only be set until you turn your computer off. To set it again, you can enter **cursor**/nn, where the first n is the row letter and the second n is the column letter, exactly as you saw it at the bottom of the screen.
   If you want to have the cursor set each time you start your computer, add the **cursor**/nn command to the AUTOEXEC.BAT file. To do

so, press Text In/Out (CTRL-F5), choose **1** for DOS Text and **2** for **Re-trieve**, and then enter **c:\autoexec.bat**. Enter the command **cursor/***nn* anywhere in the file, as just shown. Press Text In/Out (CTRL-F5), choose **1** for DOS Text, choose **1** to Save, press ENTER to accept the displayed name, and then type **Y** to overwrite the original AUTOEXEC.BAT file. Clear the screen when you are finished.

CURSOR KEYS

WordPerfect has several options for moving the cursor through text. The major keys used to control the cursor (the arrows, END, PGUP, PGDN, −, and +) are found on the numeric keypad, or if you have an enhanced keyboard, between the regular keys and the numeric keypad. These keys can also be combined with HOME, CTRL, and ESC to move through larger sections of text.

If you have a mouse, you can use it to position the cursor anywhere on the screen or scroll through the document.

Keystrokes

Mouse

If you have a mouse, move the pointer anywhere on the screen, and click the left button to move to the cursor to that position.

To scroll through the document (either horizontally or vertically), hold down the right button and move the mouse pointer until it runs into the edge of the screen. The document will then begin scrolling in that direction.

Arrow Keys

↑	Move up one line
↓	Move down one line
→	Move right one character
←	Move left one character

HOME, CTRL, and ESC

Pressing HOME once before pressing an arrow key moves the cursor to the left or right side of the screen. Pressing HOME twice before pressing an arrow key moves the cursor to the extreme left or right side of the document. For example, HOME, HOME, ↑ moves the cursor to the beginning of the document.

The CTRL key is used with the ← and → keys to move to the previous or next word. You can also combine it with HOME and the arrow keys to move to the top or bottom of a page or from column to column when working with columns or tables.

The ESC key is a counter key, which can be used to repeat any number of keystrokes. ESC can be used with the arrow keys, PGUP, and PGDN to move in a specific direction a specified number of times.

By Word

CTRL →	Move to the beginning of the next word
CTRL ←	Move to the beginning of the preceding word

To the Edges of the Screen

HOME, ↑	Move to the top of the screen and then scroll backward one screen at a time
HOME, ↓	Move to the bottom of the screen and then scroll forward one screen at a time
HOME, →	Move to the right side of the screen (or end of the line)
HOME, ←	Move to the left side of the screen

By Screen

− or HOME, ↑	Move to the top of the screen and then scroll backward one screen at a time
+ or HOME, ↓	Move to the bottom of the screen and then scroll forward one screen at a time

By Page

PGUP	Move to the top of the preceding page
PGDN	Move to the top of the next page
CTRL-HOME, n	Go to a specific page, where n represents the page number
CTRL-HOME, ↑	Go to the top of the current page
CTRL-HOME, ↓	Go to the bottom of the current page

To the Edges of the Document

HOME, HOME, ↑	Move to the beginning of the document, after any formatting codes
HOME, HOME, ↓	Move to the end of the document
HOME, HOME, →	Move to the far right of the document (end of the line); useful for documents that are wider than the screen
END	Same as HOME, HOME, →
HOME, HOME, ←	Move to the far left of the document
HOME, HOME, HOME, ←	Move to the extreme left before any Word-Perfect codes
HOME, HOME, HOME, ↑	Move to the beginning of the document, before all text and codes

In Columns or Tables

CTRL-HOME, →	Move to the column to the right (see "Columns" or "Tables" in this chapter for more information)
CTRL-HOME, ←	Move to the column to the left
CTRL-HOME, HOME, →	Move to the far right text column
CTRL-HOME, HOME, ←	Move to the far left text column

Move n Times

ESC, ↓   Move down eight lines (can also be combined with ↑ , ← , or → to move in a specified direction eight times)

ESC, *n*, ↓   Move down a specified number of lines (can also be combined with ↑ , ← , or → to move in that direction a specified number of times)

Back to the Original Position

CTRL-HOME, CTRL-HOME   Go to the original cursor after a "major" cursor key is pressed or after a feature involving the cursor (such as Search or Replace) is executed; see "Go To" in this chapter for more information. You can also easily redefine a block by pressing Block (ALT-F4) and then CTRL-HOME, CTRL-HOME

To a Specific Character or Phrase

CTRL-HOME, *character*   Go to the first occurrence of the character

Search (F2) or   Searches for a string of characters or Word-
← Search (SHIFT-F2)   Perfect codes

Hints

If you press ← or → and the cursor does not appear to move, it is most likely moving over a WordPerfect code. The arrow keys work in Reveal Codes just as they do on the normal screen. Rather than pressing an arrow key several times in succession to move through lines or characters, you can hold it down to move more quickly.

Adjusting Cursor Speed

You can adjust the speed at which the cursor moves through text with the Cursor Speed option. See "Cursor Speed" in this chapter for details.

Related Entries

CTRL Key
ESC Key
Go To
HOME Key
Mouse Support

CURSOR SPEED

WordPerfect is automatically set to move the cursor at 50 characters per second. You can adjust this setting in the Setup menu.

Keystrokes

1. Press Setup (SHIFT-F1).

2. Choose **3** for Environment.

3. Choose **3** for Cursor Speed. The following choices are presented on the status line:

```
Characters Per Second: 1 15; 2 20; 3 30; 4 40; 5 50; 6 Normal: 0
```

4. The default setting is 50 characters per second. Select the desired cursor speed. If you choose **6** for Normal, the cursor speed will be reset at the machine's normal speed. If you already have a program that speeds up the cursor (Repeat Performance, for example), choosing Normal will let that program's settings take over. Otherwise, the cursor speed in WordPerfect will take precedence over other programs.

Programs such as Repeat Performance (produced by WordPerfect Corporation) help accelerate cursor speed and eliminate extra cursor movement after you release a cursor key.

Use the /NC startup option if you need to disable the cursor speed (WP/NC).

CUT TEXT AND COLUMNS

See "Move" in this chapter.

DASHES

Em dashes (—) and en dashes (-) can easily be inserted and printed with WordPerfect. You should also be aware of the way that you enter single (-) and double dashes (--).

Keystrokes

The following steps will help you enter an em dash, en dash, single dash, or double dash.

Em or En Dash

An em dash is equal to the width of a capital "M," and an en dash is equal to the width of a capital "N."

1. Press Compose (CTRL-2).

2. Type one of the following, depending on the type of dash needed. Note that two options are available for an em dash—choose whichever is easiest for you to remember.

    --   Em dash
    m-   Em dash
    n-   En dash

If the current font or substitute fonts do not include the em or en dash, they will be printed graphically if you have a graphics (laser or dot-matrix) printer.

Single Dash (-)

If you press the hyphen/underscore key, you will get a hyphen. This is fine if you want a hyphen, but when a hyphen is found at the end of a line, the word will be broken. When you do not want a word broken, use a dash. To use the dash, press HOME and then the hyphen key to insert a single dash or "hard hyphen." The - character is inserted, rather than the regular hyphen code [-].

Double Dash (--)

Although the em dash is more acceptable than a double dash, you may need to use a double dash if your daisywheel printer does not have an em dash.

If you press the hyphen key twice to enter a double dash, the dashes could be separated if located at the end of a line. To avoid this, make the first one a regular dash:

1. Press HOME and then the hyphen key.

2. Press the hyphen key.

If you use two regular dashes to make the double dash, the double dash could end up at the beginning of a line rather than always at the end.

Applications

Em and en dashes are used extensively in typeset documents. If you want to give your documents a more professional look, consider using them instead of single and double dashes.

In the case of compound names (such as a woman's family name and married name together), the names may be separated with a single dash. The dash prevents the compound name from being broken between lines.

Related Entries

Hyphenation

DATE AND TIME

You can use Date/Outline (SHIFT-F5) to insert the current date and time, insert a code that will update the current date and time each time a document is retrieved or printed, or change the way the date and time are displayed.

Keystrokes

Insert the Date/Time

1. Press Date/Outline (SHIFT-F5). The following menu appears:

```
1 Date Text; 2 Date Code; 3 Date Format; 4 Outline; 5 Para Num; 6 Define: 0
```

2. Choose 1 to insert the Date as Text or 2 to insert a Date Code.

The first option "types" the current date and time as text. The second option displays the current date and time as a code instead of text. The code causes the date and time to be updated each time a document is retrieved or printed.

Change the Date/Time Format

WordPerfect displays the date in the form Month Date, Year (as in November 25, 1990). Use the following steps if you want to change the way the date is displayed:

1. Press Date/Outline (SHIFT-F5).

2. Choose **3** for Date Format. Figure 3-34 shows the Date Format menu.

3. Type the string of numbers that will determine the format, including other applicable characters, such as a comma, slash, dash (hyphen), colon, or period. You can use any other text such as "Date:" or "Time:" as well. Note that you can use the following two characters as shown in the examples at the bottom of the screen in Figure 3-34:

   %   Pads numbers less than 10 with a leading zero or abbreviates the month or day of the week

   $ Pads numbers less than 10 with a space or abbreviates the month or day of the week

4. Press ENTER to set the format. The Date menu is displayed again, letting you insert the date and time.

5. Choose **1** for Date Text or **2** for Date Code, or press ENTER to leave the menu.

Hints

When the date format is changed, a code is not inserted in the document. The only code inserted is when you choose the Date Code option, which results in showing the current date format, such as [Date:3 1, 4] in Reveal Codes (ALT-F3). You can have several Date functions within a document, and each can have its own format. To do this, change the format each time before inserting a function. You can enter up to 29 characters for the date format.

If you press Cancel (F1) while changing the date format, changes are ignored and the format returns to its original setting. To change the date format permanently, press Setup (SHIFT-F1), choose **4** for Initial Settings, then choose **2** for Date Format.

Wrong Date and Time

WordPerfect uses the date and time that have been entered at DOS. Therefore, it is important that the correct date and time be entered when the computer is started. If the wrong date and time appear when

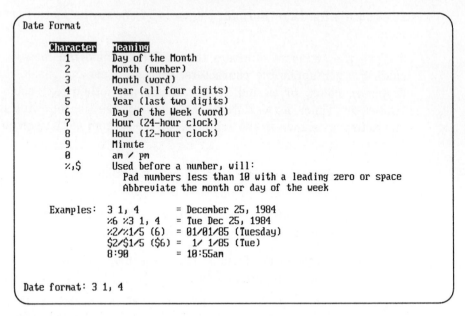

Figure 3-34.   Date Format menu

you use the Date key, exit WordPerfect and enter **date** at the DOS prompt. Enter the correct date when prompted. Next, enter **time** and then the correct time.

Some IBM compatibles have a BIOS incompatibility that resets an incorrect date and time. If you find this to be the case, make sure you have installed the Utility files, then enter **fixbios.com** at the appropriate DOS prompt to run the program. You should also include this command in your AUTOEXEC.BAT file.

Inserting the Date During a Merge

If you include the ^D or {DATE} merge code in a primary merge document, the current date and time will be inserted during the merge. These commands are exactly like inserting a date code into your document. However, rather than assigning a specific format, as is done with the Date function, the current date format is used.

Inserting the Date in a Different Language

WordPerfect comes with a language resource file (WP.LRS) that contains information for over 21 languages. This information is used to translate a date into the appropriate language and format.

This feature can be useful for inserting the proper date if you regularly write correspondence in a language different from your own. Each time the date is inserted with Date/Outline (SHIFT-F5), WordPerfect looks for a language code. If one is found, the text and date format are translated accordingly.

If you don't like the way the month and day of the week are abbreviated, you can also change the abbreviation in the WP.LRS file.

See "Languages" in this chaper for information about inserting a language code and editing the WP.LRS file.

Viewing the Current Date and Time

The Date function does not work like a clock; the time is updated only when a file is retrieved or printed. If you want to see the current date or time, press List (F5) and then ENTER. The date and time are displayed in the upper left corner of the screen.

Applications

You can include the date text or the Date function as part of a letter or memo macro. If you are including the date in a primary merge document, use ^D or the {DATE} merge code. If you insert the date as text, you will have to change the date manually in the document each time you do a merge.

Related Entries

List Files
Merge
Setup

dBASE

You can convert the data created with dBASE to a WordPerfect second-ary merge file, where the fields are separated by {END FIELD} and records are separated with {END RECORD} and a hard page break [HPg] code.

Keystrokes

1. While in dBASE, enter the USE command in this format:

    use *name*

2. After this process is finished, enter the following command in this format:

    copy to *filename* delimited

The new filename should be different from the original filename; it can include the drive and directory where the new file is to be stored. The extension .DBF is automatically added to the filename. See "Hints" for other options.

3. Exit dBASE. You can now use this file as it is in a merge or continue with the steps that follow to convert it to a WordPerfect secondary merge file.

4. Start the Convert program at DOS. If you are not sure about the exact steps, see "Convert Program."

5. Enter the input filename (the file to be converted) and the output filename (the file that will hold the converted data). Remember to enter the full pathname if necessary (for example, **b:mailing.dbf** or **c:\dbase\ mailing.dbf.**

6. Type **9** to convert a Mail Merge file to WordPerfect secondary merge format.

7. Enter a comma (,) as the field delimiter. If you specified a different character as the delimiter, enter that character.

8. Enter **{13}{10}** as the record delimiter.

9. Enter " as the character to be stripped from the file.

Using a dBASE Report in WordPerfect

You can print a report to disk and retrieve it into WordPerfect for advanced formatting before printing:

1. Open the database file with the dBASE USE command:

   use *name*

2. Next, give dBASE the REPORT FORM command:

   report form *reportname* to file *filename*

The extension .TXT is assigned unless you specify a different one.

3. Exit dBASE and enter WordPerfect.

4. Change the margins if necessary by pressing Format (SHIFT-F8) and choosing **1** for **L**ine and then **7** for **M**argins.

5. Press Text In/Out (CTRL-F5), choose **1** for **D**OS Text, and then choose **2** or **3** to retrieve the file. (See "DOS Text Files" or "Text In/Out" in this chapter for more information.)

Hints

If you want to have the files sorted in dBASE before converting them, enter the following command instead of USE *name*:

use *name* index *index files to be used*

This command opens a database file and sorts the records according to the specified index.

If you use the COPY TO *filename* DELIMITED command, fields are delimited with commas, character fields are further delimited with quotation marks, and records are delimited with a carriage return/line-feed. If you want to specify a different field delimiter, you can enter the following command:

copy to *filename* delimited with *delimiter*

If you want to specify which fields are to be included, you can enter a command such as the following:

copy to *filename* fields *field list* delimited

There are also options for selecting the records to be included in the copy. See "COPY" in your dBASE manual for further information.

Related Entries

Convert Program
Text In/Out

DCA FORMAT

DCA (Document Content Architecture) is the standard text format used by IBM. The Convert program can convert documents to and from DCA format.

Keystrokes

There are actually two DCA formats: Revisable-Form-Text and Final-Form-Text.

1. Start the Convert program from DOS. If you are not sure about the exact steps, see "Convert Program" in this chapter.

2. Enter the input filename (the file to be converted) and the output filename (the file that will hold the converted data). Remember to enter the full pathname if necessary (for example, **b:contract** or **c:\dca\contract.12**).

3. If converting a WordPerfect document to DCA, choose **1**, and then choose **1** for Revisable-Form-Text or **2** for Final-Form-Text.
    If you are converting from Revisable-Form-Text to WordPerfect format, choose **2** from the main menu. Type **3** if you are converting from Final-Form-Text to WordPerfect format.

Hints

The following functions are retained during the WordPerfect-DCA conversion:

    Hard/soft returns
    Hard/soft page breaks
    Tab/indent/tab align
    Bold
    Underline
    Center
    Flush right
    Right justification on/off
    Hard space
    Hard/soft hyphens
    Superscript/subscript
    Tab set
    Margin set
    Spacing set
    Left margin release
    Hyphenation zone reset
    Lines per inch
    Underline style
    Page number set
    Page number inserted
    Top margin
    Header/footer
    Footnotes
    Set footnote number
    Auto outline
    Strikeout on/off
    Extended characters

If a feature is not converted, it is most likely because DCA does not have a code for the function. Sometimes DCA has multiple codes for a particular function. For example, IBM 5520 uses one format for centering text, and Displaywrite uses another. WordPerfect can successfully convert all types of formats into WordPerfect but must choose one type when converting back to DCA. In earlier versions of WordPerfect, the code for centering was converted to the IBM 5520 method. Because of a high demand, centering is now converted to the code used by DisplayWrite.

Related Entries

Convert Program

DECIMAL/ALIGN CHARACTER

A decimal point is used by Tab Align (CTRL-F6) and the Decimal Tabs and Math features to align numbers. Follow the steps given here if you want to change the decimal character.

Keystrokes

1. Press Format (SHIFT-F8).

2. Choose 4 for **O**ther.

3. Choose 3 for **D**ecimal/Align Character.

4. Choose the new decimal character.

5. Change the thousands separator if desired.

6. Press Exit (F7).

Hints

The code [Decml/Algn Char:*n,n*] is inserted into the document and will change the decimal character and thousands separator from that point forward. The new character will be used to align numbers when you use the Tab Align, Decimal Tabs, and Math features or decimal justification in tables.

Related Entries

Decimal Tabs
Math
Tab Align
Tables

DECIMAL TABS

You can use Tab Align (CTRL-F6) to align numbers at a decimal point. You can also set decimal tabs and use the TAB key to align numbers.

Keystrokes

Choose the method that you prefer. If you have a large table of numeric columns, setting decimal tabs is probably preferable, because it means that you can just press TAB each time instead of Tab Align (CTRL-F6).

Tab Align

1. Press Tab Align (CTRL-F6). The cursor moves to the first tab setting and displays the following message:

Align Char = .

2. Type the number. Characters are pushed to the left until the decimal point is typed. The remaining numbers are inserted to the right.

3. Press Tab Align (CTRL-F6) to enter another number at the next tab setting, or press ENTER to return to the left margin.

If you want to insert a dot leader from the cursor's current position to the tab setting, press HOME twice before pressing Tab Align (CTRL-F6). The keystrokes would then be HOME, HOME, Tab Align (CTRL-F6), which would produce the following:

```
Breakfast. . . . . . . . . . . . . . . . . . . . . .4.98
Lunch . . . . . . . . . . . . . . . . . . . . . . .10.56
Dinner . . . . . . . . . . . . . . . . . . . . . .27.21
```

Set Decimal Tabs

1. Press Format (SHIFT-F8), choose 1 for Line, and choose 8 for Tab Set.

2. Delete all tabs if necessary by pressing HOME, HOME, ← and then Delete to End of Line (CTRL-END).

3. Enter the setting for the tab. Remember that the measurement that you enter is the amount from the left margin, not the left side of the page. If you want to set tabs from the left side of the page, choose **T** for Type and then **1** for Absolute.

4. Type **D** to change the regular, left-aligned tab to a decimal-aligned tab. Continue until you have set all the tabs.

5. Press Exit (F7) to return to the document.

When you press TAB to go to a decimal tab setting, "Align Char = ." appears at the bottom of the screen and numbers are aligned at the decimal point.

Hints

If you press Tab Align (CTRL-F6), the code [DEC TAB] is inserted. If you use decimal tabs, the code [Dec Tab] is inserted. The uppercase [DEC TAB] code indicates that you inserted the code manually with Tab Align, and it will not change, even if the type of tab changes (from decimal to left-, right-, or center-aligned).

The [Dec Tab] is inserted because of the current decimal tab setting. This code can change if you change the tab type in the Tab Set menu.

If you need to change a regular, left-aligned tab to a decimal tab, move the cursor just before the text to be affected, enter the Tab Set menu, and change the D setting to L (or any other setting such as R or C). Text will automatically be realigned as the tab type changes.

Related Entries

Tab Align
Tabs

DEFAULT DIRECTORY

The default directory is used to save and retrieve files, unless you specify another directory. This means that when you save or retrieve a file, you can enter just the filename instead of the full pathname.

Keystrokes

To set the default directory, follow these steps:

1. Press Setup (SHIFT-F1).

2. Choose **6** for Location of Files.

3. Choose **7** for Documents.

4. Enter the full pathname (drive and directory) where files should be saved to and retrieved from.

5. Press Exit (F7) when you are finished.

Hints

You can change this setting at any time. To change the setting for a single editing session, press List (F5), type =, and then enter the name of the new default directory.

DEFAULT SETTINGS

See "Initial Settings" in this chapter.

DELETE

Any of the following keystrokes can be used to delete text and codes.

Keystrokes

BACKSPACE	Delete text to the left
DEL	Delete text at the cursor; continue pressing to delete text to the right
CTRL-BACKSPACE	Delete the word at the cursor; continue pressing to delete words to the right of the cursor
HOME, BACKSPACE	Delete from the cursor to the beginning of the current word; press both again to delete words to the left of the cursor
HOME, DEL	Delete from the cursor to the end of the current word; press both again to delete words to the right of the cursor
CTRL-END	Delete text from the cursor to the end of the line
CTRL-PGDN	Delete text from the cursor to the end of the page; you are asked to confirm this type of deletion

Hints

Press Block (ALT-F4) to highlight a larger section of text, and then press DEL or BACKSPACE to delete the block. You will see "Delete Block? No

(**Yes**)." Type **Y** to delete the block, or press any other key to leave the block. If you decide to leave the block, it will remain highlighted. Press Block (ALT-F4) to turn off Block.

You can use Move (CTRL-F4) to delete a sentence, a paragraph, or a page:

1. Place the cursor in the text to be deleted, and press Move (CTRL-F4).

2. Choose **1** for the current **S**entence, **2** for the **P**aragraph, or **3** for the entire **P**age. The appropriate text will be highlighted.

3. Choose **3** to **D**elete the highlighted section.

You can also use Move to delete a tabbed column or rectangle. See "Move" in this chapter for more information. If you accidentally delete text, you can restore it by pressing Cancel (F1) and choosing **1** for **R**estore. Type **2** to display the **P**revious deletions (for a total of three deletions).

Applications

Deleting text and then undeleting it with Cancel (F1) can be used to move text. Instead of the usual five or more keystrokes, you can delete the text, move the cursor to the new location, press Cancel (F1), and choose **1** for **R**estore. Remember that you can restore only the last three deletions; therefore, it is best to undelete as quickly as possible.

Related Entries

BACKSPACE Key
Block
Cancel
Move

DELETE A DIRECTORY

You can delete a directory from the hard disk while in DOS or Word-Perfect.

Keystrokes

A directory must be empty before it can be deleted. You must also be in the parent directory to delete a directory. See "Directories" in this chapter for an explanation of parent directories.

1. Press List (F5).

2. Enter the name of the parent directory of the directory to be deleted.

3. When the list of directories and files appears, move the cursor to the directory to be deleted. Directories are marked with "<Dir>."

4. Choose **2** for **D**elete.

5. Choose **Y** or **N** to confirm the deletion.

Hints

Instead of typing the entire name of a directory after pressing List (F5), you can edit the displayed name or press ENTER to see the default directory. You can then move to the parent directory and press ENTER twice to move into it. Because a directory has to be empty before it can be deleted, you can list the files in that directory, press Mark Text (ALT-F5) to mark all files, type **2** for **D**elete, and confirm the deletion of all files. After the files are deleted, move the cursor to ".. Parent <Dir>," press ENTER twice, move to the <Dir> to be deleted, choose **2** for **D**elete, and confirm the deletion.

You can remove a directory from the DOS prompt with the RD (Remove Directory) command. First, change to the parent directory of the directory to be deleted, and then enter the RD command

RD *directory*

where *directory* is the name of the directory to be deleted. Remember that the directory must be empty before it can be deleted.

Related Entries

Directories

DELETE CODES

You can delete WordPerfect codes the same way that you delete regular text.

Keystrokes

1. Press Reveal Codes (ALT-F3). The screen is split, showing the regular screen above and the text and codes below.

2. Move the cursor to the code to be deleted. You can use any of the cursor movement keys.

3. Press BACKSPACE if the code is to the left of the cursor or DEL if the cursor is on the code itself (the code is shown in reverse video if the cursor is resting on it).

Hints

After you have spent some time with WordPerfect, you can usually tell the approximate location of a code by the appearance of the text on the screen. For example, if the margins change on the screen, there is probably a Margin Set code or an indent code at that location. Text that is boldfaced, underlined, or centered will also have codes close by.

Sometimes, when you use ← and → , the cursor does not appear to move and the position number in the lower right corner of the screen does not change. When this happens, you are moving over a code. If you are deleting text with BACKSPACE or DEL and run into a code, you are usually asked for a confirmation similar to the following:

Delete *Code*? No (**Yes**)

Type **Y** to delete the code, or press any other key (including the DEL key) to move past the code. Some codes that are easy to insert, such as [Tab], [Indent], and a hard return [HRt], do not ask for confirmation.

If you delete with keys other than BACKSPACE or DEL, codes are automatically deleted with the text. This includes a word delete, block delete, delete to the end of a line, delete to the end of a page, and so on.

Search for a Code

You can use the Search feature in the normal screen or in Reveal Codes to locate a code quickly:

1. Press Search (F2) or ←Search (SHIFT-F2), depending on whether you want to search forward or backward. It might be advisable to move to the top of the document with HOME, HOME, ↑ and then use Search (F2).

2. Press the appropriate function key to insert the code. For example, if you are searching for bold codes, press Bold (F6). If you need to search for margin settings, press Format (SHIFT-F8), choose **1** for Line, and then choose **6** to insert [L/R Mar] as the search string.

3. Press Search (F2) to start the search.

You can combine text and codes in the search string. Codes are boldface in the string. You cannot search for a code just by typing the characters; you must press the function key and choose options if applicable. When the search string is found, the cursor is always to the right of the code. You can always press BACKSPACE to delete the code and confirm the deletion without having to enter the Reveal Codes screen to check its location.

Delete Codes with the Replace Feature

You can use replace (ALT-F2) to search for codes and replace them with nothing, thus deleting them. You can also selectively delete codes by asking to confirm each "replacement."

1. Press Replace (ALT-F2).

2. If you want to confirm the deletion of each code, type **Y** in answer to the question "w/Confirm? No (Yes)." If you want each code deleted automatically, type **N**.

3. Press the appropriate function key (and choose an option from a menu if necessary) to insert the code.

4. Press Search (F2) twice: once to enter the search string and once to enter nothing as the replacement string.

If you asked to confirm each replacement, the cursor will stop at each code found. Type **Y** to delete the code or **N** to leave the code. With the exception of a few codes, such as [Tab], [BOLD]/[bold], [UND] /[und], [Center Pg], [Center], [Flsh Rgt], and [→Indent], and [→Indent←], you cannot replace one code with another. To get around this limitation, you can use the Styles feature. A style is a collection of codes that can be attached to different sections of text throughout the document. If you wanted to replace one code with another (for example, to change to a different font), you can edit the style, and the text that was marked with that style would be updated automatically. You can also create a macro that searches for a code, deletes it, and inserts a new code. You can execute this macro *n* times by using the ESC key or chain the macro to itself so that it will continue until it cannot find any other codes.

Applications

If you are having problems with a document, you should be able to find the code causing the problem with Search or Replace and then delete it. These features are also helpful when you are editing another person's documents. If you have single- and double-spacing or various margin settings throughout a document and want to return to the default settings, use Replace to search for the codes and delete them.

Related Entries

Codes
Delete
Replace
Reveal Codes
Search
Styles

DELETE FILES

You can delete files from the List Files menu in WordPerfect or from DOS.

Keystrokes

1. Press List (F5).

2. Press ENTER to see the list of files in the displayed directory, or enter the name of a different directory. If you know the name of the file to be deleted, you can add the name of the file to the directory name.

3. When you are in the List Files menu, move the cursor to the file to be deleted. If you want to delete more than one file, type * to mark each file.

4. Choose **2** to **D**elete the file or files.

5. If you marked files, you are asked

Delete marked files? No (Yes)

Type **Y** or **N**. If you type **N** or if no files were marked, you are asked to confirm the deletion of the highlighted file. Type **Y** or **N**. If you type **Y** to delete all marked files, a second confirmation is required when the following prompt appears:

Marked files will be deleted. Continue? No (Yes)

Hints

You can also delete files while in DOS. From the DOS prompt, enter **del** or **erase** (depending on your preference) and the name of the file to be deleted. To delete more than one file, you can use wildcard characters. For example, if you want to delete all files ending with the extension .DOC, enter **del *.doc**, using the * wildcard character to indicate any number of characters. To delete all files, enter **del *.***. You are asked to confirm this type of deletion.

You can also use wildcard characters in WordPerfect to specify all documents or particular documents to be deleted. After you press List (F5), the current directory is displayed, followed by *.*. All files will be displayed. If you want to mark all the files for deletion, press Mark Text (ALT-F5). Choose **2** for **D**elete and confirm the deletion. If you want only the files that have the .DOC extension deleted, press List (F5) and enter *.DOC as the "listing." Mark all the displayed files and delete them as just described.

Related Entries

Delete a Directory
List Files

DICTIONARY

See "Spell" in this chapter.

DIF

Some spreadsheet programs (including Lotus 1-2-3) can save their files as DIF (Data Interchange Format) files. These files can be converted to a WordPerfect secondary merge file and back again.

If you want to retrieve a spreadsheet into WordPerfect and do not plan to use the information in a merge, you can have the data retrieved into a table. See "Spreadsheet Importing and Linking" in this chapter for details.

Keystrokes

The following steps require that you have converted a spreadsheet file to DIF first:

1. Start the Convert program at the DOS prompt. (See "Convert Program" in this chapter for the exact steps.)

2. Enter the name of the input file (the file to be converted) and the name of the output file (the file that will contain the converted data).

3. Type **A** to convert the DIF file to the WordPerfect secondary merge format.

Hints

If you are using Lotus, you should first run the Translate utility (from the Access menu) to convert a 1-2-3 worksheet to DIF. If converting a file from a WordPerfect secondary merge file to DIF, you will need to run the Translate utility (after Convert) to translate it to a 1-2-3 file.

Each row in the DIF file is considered a record, while each column in the row is considered a field. In a WordPerfect merge file, records are separated with an {END RECORD} merge code and a hard page break, and fields are separated with an {END FIELD} merge code and a hard return.

Navy DIF Standard, option 4, is used by the Navy as an intermediate file transfer format. This format is used to transfer files among word processors, not spreadsheets. If you choose option 4, the file is converted to a normal WordPerfect document instead of a secondary merge file.

PlanPerfect (a spreadsheet produced by WordPerfect Corporation) can import and export files in WordPerfect, WordPerfect secondary merge, Lotus, DIF, dBASE, and other formats. If you have PlanPerfect, you can use it to retrieve a file in one format and save it in another.

Related Entries

Convert
Spreadsheet Importing and Linking

DIRECTORIES

You can divide your hard disk into several directories for better organization. When a disk is formatted, it contains only one directory, the root directory. Since only a limited number of files can be saved in the root directory, you will want to divide it into several directories. These directories act as large files that can hold several other files. They are named as you would name any other file, but they appear in a list of files with the label "< Dir >," indicating that each is a directory.

The root directory is named with a single backslash (\). The DOS prompt naming the drive and directory would appear as C:\. The names of directories are separated with a backslash. For example, if you have a directory named WP51, the pathname would appear as C:\WP51. The name of a directory called LETTERS created within the WP51 directory would be C:\WP51\LETTERS.

The term "parent directory" is used to identify the directory just above a directory in hierarchy. In the examples just given, WP51 is the parent directory for LETTERS, and the root directory is the parent directory for WP51. There is no parent directory for the root directory.

Figure 3-35 shows one possible organization of directories on a hard disk. Although you can divide the disk into as many subdirectories as you want, if you use many subdirectories, it takes DOS a little longer to find programs or commands, because it has to search through longer pathnames.

WordPerfect's List Files menu can be used to manage the directories. It lets you move "up" into the parent directory or "down" into subdirectories. Figure 3-36 shows the directory information available in the List Files menu. You can use List (F5) to create (make) directories, change directories, delete directories, and list the files in each directory. When in the List Files menu, you can press Print (SHIFT-F7) to print a listing of the directory.

Related Entries

Change Directory
Create a Directory
Default Directory
Delete a Directory
List Files

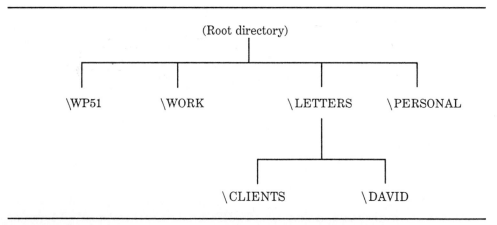

Figure 3-35.   A sample organization of a hard disk

```
11-20-89  03:42p          Directory C:\*,*
Document size:     460   Free: 32,229,376 Used:  1,011,187      Files:        81

      Current    <Dir>          ..    Parent     <Dir>
BACKIT   ,       <Dir>  07-29-89 03:47p   BOOK    ,       <Dir>  07-29-89 03:47p
CLIENTS  ,       <Dir>  07-29-89 03:48p   CNEW    ,       <Dir>  08-29-89 03:37p
COMDEX   ,       <Dir>  11-19-89 08:12p   DOS     ,       <Dir>  07-24-89 07:59a
DRAW     ,       <Dir>  07-28-89 10:31p   GAMES   ,       <Dir>  07-29-89 03:48p
GRAPHICS,        <Dir>  10-07-89 05:47p   INSET   ,       <Dir>  09-18-89 02:00p
KAREN    ,       <Dir>  07-29-89 03:49p   LETTERS ,       <Dir>  10-07-89 05:48p
LIBRARY  ,       <Dir>  07-29-89 03:50p   MACROS  ,       <Dir>  07-29-89 04:23p
MOUSE    ,       <Dir>  07-29-89 12:05p   NEW     ,       <Dir>  08-29-89 02:46p
NEWBOOK  ,       <Dir>  08-03-89 12:33p   NEWDATA ,       <Dir>  07-29-89 04:23p
PERSONAL,        <Dir>  07-29-89 04:24p   PLAN    ,       <Dir>  07-28-89 10:24p
REF      ,       <Dir>  10-30-89 05:05p   SCREENS ,       <Dir>  09-12-89 05:40p
TOOLS    ,       <Dir>  10-21-89 05:01p   USA     ,       <Dir>  11-04-89 04:41p
UTILITY  ,       <Dir>  07-24-89 08:00a   WP50    ,       <Dir>  07-29-89 04:25p
WP51     ,       <Dir>  07-28-89 10:19p   ZAP     ,       <Dir>  07-29-89 04:41p
ALTR    ,PLM       67   08-13-89 09:02p   ALTR    ,MAC       21  05-14-87 06:01a
ALTU    ,PLM       67   08-13-89 09:00p   ANSI    ,SYS    9,105  10-06-88 12:00a
APPEND  ,EXE   11,154   10-06-88 12:00a   ARC     ,       12,242 04-27-07 12:00a
ATARI   ,       1,216   02-02-88 03:06a ▼ AUTOEXEC,BAT      152  09-20-89 06:29p

1 Retrieve; 2 Delete; 3 Move/Rename; 4 Print; 5 Short/Long Display;
6 Look; 7 Other Directory; 8 Copy; 9 Find; N Name Search: 6
```

Figure 3-36. A list of files and directories in the root directory

"DISK FULL" ERROR MESSAGE

When saving a file or printing from the screen, you may encounter the error message "Disk Full—strike any key to continue," indicating that there is no available space on the disk.

Reasons

If you retrieve a large file from disk and attempt to replace the original file, you might get this error message even when it seems that there should be plenty of disk space available. What actually happens is that the original file is renamed with the extension .BK!, the current file is saved, and then the original is deleted. (If you have chosen to back up the original document, the .BK! file is not deleted.)

If you want the file to be saved on the same disk, you can enter the List Files menu and delete the original copy of the file from the disk. However, if there is a power failure during this process, you could lose your document. It is safest to use a new disk.

When you print from the screen, a copy of the document is saved to the disk with a temporary filename and is then printed. However, if there is not enough room on the disk, you will get the "Disk Full" error message. If this happens, save the file to disk first and then print from the disk using the Print menu or List Files menu.

Solutions

If you see the "Disk Full" error message, press any key to return to the document. You have two options. Either replace the data disk with one containing more space and save the file again, or press List (F5) and ENTER, and then choose 2 to Delete unnecessary files. Press Exit (F7) to return to the document and save the file again.

Another option for future documents is to use the /NB (No Backup) startup option. If you use this option to start WordPerfect (enter **wp/nb** to do so), the backup file (.BK!) will not be created. If you have the Original Backup feature on, the /NB startup option will be ignored.

As you saw in Figure 3-36, the heading on the List Files menu tells you how much disk space is available and how much is needed for the current document. See "Disk Space" in this chapter for more information.

A WP{WP}.SPC file is created each time WordPerfect is started. This temporary file occupies 4K of space on the disk so that if a "Disk Full" error message occurs, WordPerfect lets you fix the situation and try again.

Related Entries

Backup
Disk Space
"File Creation Error" Error Message

DISK SPACE

WordPerfect's List Files menu tells you how much disk space is available, how much disk space is being used by each file, and the size of the document in memory.

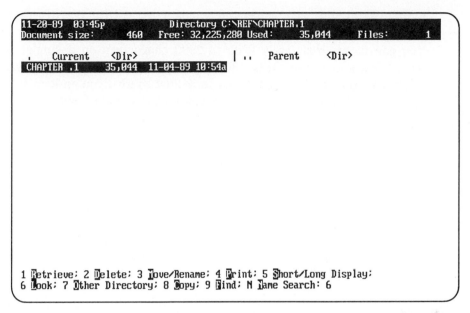

```
11-20-89  03:45p          Directory C:\REF\CHAPTER.1
Document size:     460   Free: 32,225,280 Used:      35,044     Files:      1

.     Current    <Dir>            | ..    Parent     <Dir>
CHAPTER .1        35,044  11-04-89 10:54a











1 Retrieve; 2 Delete; 3 Move/Rename; 4 Print; 5 Short/Long Display;
6 Look; 7 Other Directory; 8 Copy; 9 Find; N Name Search: 6
```

Figure 3-37.   The List Files menu with the file size shown to the right of the
                     filename

Keystrokes

    1. Press List (F5).

    2. Press ENTER to look into the displayed directory, or enter the
name of the drive and directory in question. A screen similar to the
one shown in Figure 3-37 appears. The file size is also displayed if
you use the Long Display feature.

    Each file in the directory is displayed with the file size as well as the
date and time that it was last edited. In the heading, "Document size:"
indicates the size of the document currently in memory, and "Free:"
displays the amount of space that is available on the disk.

Hints

The numbers displayed are in bytes. A two-sided, double-density disk
usually contains 360K, which is actually 368,640 bytes (1K = 1024

bytes). As a rule, each character equals 1 byte. In a WordPerfect file, each code takes at least one byte but usually consists of several bytes. You can fit approximately 2800 to 2900 characters on a single-spaced page. This allows for about 130 single-spaced pages per disk, without taking WordPerfect codes into account. Just to give you an idea, a [HRt] code is equal to 1 byte, whereas an Align code equals 5 bytes.

See "'Disk Full' Error Message" for options that are available when the disk is full.

Related Entries

"Disk Full" Error Message
List Files

DISPLAY PITCH

The Display Pitch option on the Setup menu helps the screen display properly; it has nothing to do with the pitch in which a document will be printed.

The Display Pitch feature lets WordPerfect sense when text is overlapping on the screen and make an adjustment by decreasing the number of characters that can be displayed per inch. For example, if you use a proportionally spaced font and are working with columns or tables, the text from column to column might overlap because of varying line lengths. WordPerfect would sense that two characters were trying to display in the same position and would make the adjustment. If the amount of space given to a tab or indent seems out of proportion, or if columns are so spread out that you cannot easily scan from one column to the next, you will want to follow the steps presented here to set the display pitch manually.

Keystrokes

1. Press Format (SHIFT-F8).

2. Choose **3** for **Document**.

3. Choose **1** for **Display Pitch**. The following appears:

```
Format: Document

    1 - Display Pitch - Automatic Yes
                        Width     0.1"
```

4. You can leave the setting on Automatic and let WordPerfect do the adjustments, or you can type **N** to turn off the automatic adjustment.

5. The next option asks for the width. This can be set even if the display pitch is set for automatic adjustments as a starting point. See "Hints" for suggestions.

6. Press Exit (F7) to return to the document.

Hints

The standard setting is .1″, which displays 10 spaces per inch. You will probably not want to set the display pitch to anything larger than this. If you need to expand the amount of space between columns, decrease the measurement (.07″ is a common setting) so that more spaces will be required to make one inch.

Applications

The only reason you would need to make a change to this setting is if there is too much space given to tabs, indents, or the space between columns. Also, if text is overlapping on the screen, the display pitch is too large. Follow the keystrokes just presented and change the width to a smaller number.

Related Entries

Pitch

DISPLAY PRINT JOBS

The first three jobs waiting to be printed are displayed automatically in the Control Printer menu. However, all print jobs can be displayed.

Keystrokes

1. Press Print (SHIFT-F7).

2. Choose 4 for Control Printer.

3. Choose 3 to Display all print Jobs. The screen displays a list of the print jobs that are waiting (including the three that are automatically displayed in Control Printer).

4. Press any key to return to the Control Printer menu.

5. Press ENTER to return to the document.

Hints

Although you can queue up to 255 documents for printing, only 24 can be listed at one time. If you have more, the screen will scroll to show you the last 24 jobs in the queue. Print jobs are assigned numbers. The jobs are numbered from 1 upward each time WordPerfect is started. If some print jobs are printed or canceled, the remaining jobs are not renumbered from 1 but will continue, showing the total number of print jobs queued during that editing session.

Applications

The option to display all print jobs is useful when you need to know how many documents (and which documents) are waiting to be printed. If you need to cancel or rush a print job, you can use this feature to see the number assigned to the job.

Related Entries

Cancel a Print Job
Rush a Print Job

"DIVIDE OVERFLOW" ERROR MESSAGE

The message "Divide overflow—strike any key to continue" can be caused by too many characters within set boundaries.

Reasons

This message should never occur, but it could. You may see it when working with parallel columns and Block Protect. If you enter characters between the [BlockPro:Off] and [Col Off] codes, the message is displayed because an attempt was made to fit characters within set boundaries. This message could also appear when characters are entered between the [BlockPro:On] and [Col On] codes.

Solutions

When a situation creates a problem, WordPerfect makes every attempt to correct it and let you return to your document after the message is displayed. If you encounter this error message, contact WordPerfect Corporation and report the date and version number (displayed in the upper right corner of the help screen). If your computer locks up, the document will be lost. Thus, it is important to set the Timed Backup feature. See "Backup" in this chapter for more information.

DOCUMENT COMPARE

See "Compare Documents" in this chapter.

DOCUMENT FORMAT

The Document Format menu controls the display pitch, initial codes, and initial font for a document as well as the redline method and the document summary.

Keystrokes

1. Press Format (SHIFT-F8).

2. Choose **3** for **Document**

3. Type the number for the desired option, and make any changes.

4. Press Exit (F7) to return to the document.

Options

Display Pitch

WordPerfect determines if characters are going to overlap on the screen and adjusts the amount of space. (Overlap can occur, for example, with proportionally spaced text in columns, where the characters are displayed in a fixed pitch, but more characters are allowed on the line because they are formatted for a proportionally spaced font.) You will need to use the Display Pitch option only if you think the amount of space given to tabs, indents, or the space between columns is too small or too large. This option does not affect the pitch at the printer. See "Display Pitch" in this chapter for details.

Initial Codes

If you used the Initial Settings option in the Setup menu to insert initial codes for all documents, those codes will be copied to each document but will be kept in the document header (sometimes called a "prefix"). If you look in Reveal Codes while you are at the beginning of a document, you will not see these initial codes. This Document Initial Codes option, however, lets you see the codes, delete those that are not applicable for the particular document, and add more if necessary. This is also a good location for any formatting codes in a primary merge file, because they will not be duplicated for each record, but will set the format for the entire document. See "Initial Codes" in this chapter for details.

Initial Base Font

The Initial Base Font setting from the current printer selection is copied to each document when it is created. Use this option to change the initial font for the document.

Redline Method

When text is marked for redline, the printer definition decides how the text will be printed (usually with a font change or a shaded background). You can choose Printer Dependent, with a character in the left margin, or you can have the character alternate between the left and right margins, depending on whether it is being printed on an odd or an even page.

See "Redline" in this chapter for details.

Document Summary

A document summary lets you enter information about a file, such as a descriptive filename, the name of the author, the typist, the subject, and the account number. See "Document Management/Summary" in this chapter for details.

Related Entries

Display Pitch
Initial Codes
Initial Font
Redline
Summary

DOCUMENT MANAGEMENT/SUMMARY

WordPerfect has many options that can help you manage your documents. Items in the Document Summary help you identify documents by creation date/time, descriptive name, type, author, typist, subject, account number, keywords, and text in an abstract.

Two options in the List Files menu help manage your documents based on the information found in the document or in Document Summary. The first option, Short/Long Display, lets you list documents by descriptive document names and types in addition to the standard DOS filename. The second option, Find, is like the Word Search feature found in version 5.0 and helps you find specific documents easily.

If you are serious about managing your documents, you should first select the appropriate Document Management/Summary options in Setup. The steps in the following section offer information about this as well as creating a document summary, displaying documents by their long or short filenames, and finding specific files.

Keystrokes

Document Management/Summary Setup

1. Press Setup (SHIFT-F1) and choose 3 for Environment.

2. Choose 4 for Document Management/Summary. The options shown in Figure 3-38 appear.

3. Choose the applicable options from the menu (a description of each option follows).

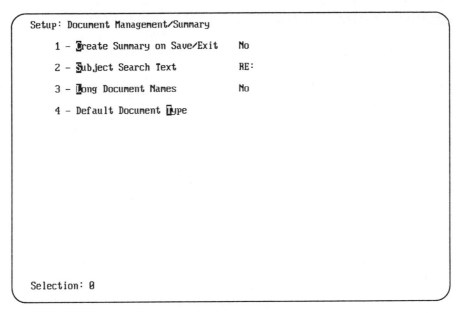

```
Setup: Document Management/Summary

      1 - Create Summary on Save/Exit      No

      2 - Subject Search Text              RE:

      3 - Long Document Names              No

      4 - Default Document Type




Selection: 0
```

Figure 3-38.   Document Management/Summary options in Setup

Create Summary on Save/Exit This option provides an "automatic document summary." If you answer "Yes" to this option, the Document Summary screen will appear the first time a document is saved with either Save (F10) or Exit (F7). If you do not want to fill in the summary at the time the document is saved, you can press Exit (F7) without entering any information.

Subject Search Text Instead of manually entering the subject, you can press Retrieve (SHIFT-F10) while in the Document Summary and have WordPerfect insert the appropriate text for you. WordPerfect does this by searching through the first 550 characters of the document for "RE:" and copying the text (from that point up to the first hard return [HRt] code) into the Subject section of the summary.

If you normally use a different term for the subject of your documents (such as "SUBJECT:," "SUBJ:," or "Subject:"), you would enter that text for this option. Since these terms are case sensitive, enter the terms exactly as you want them to appear in the document.

Long Document Names If you answer "Yes" to this option, you will be allowed to enter a descriptive name and document type (in addition to the standard DOS filename) each time you save a document. This name and document type appear in the Document Summary and in the List Files menu when you choose the Long Display option.

When you enter a descriptive name and document type, WordPerfect abbreviates them and suggests them as the DOS filename. For example, if the long document name is "Financial Statement for 1989" and the document type is "Memo," FINA-STAT.MEM is suggested as the filename. (The first three characters of the document type are used as the filename extension.) You can enter a different filename if you want to.

If this option is set to Yes, files will also be displayed by their long descriptive name in the List Files menu. This, too, can be changed to "Short Display" with option 5 for Short/Long Display in the List Files menu.

Default Document Type   A document type can consist of up to 39 characters. The text entered here will automatically be copied to each document Summary. If necessary, you can change or edit the document type when creating the summary.

Again, the first three characters of the document type will be suggested as the DOS filename extension when you save the document. For example, if "Chapter" is the document type, .CHA would be suggested as the filename extension.

4. Press Exit (F7) when finished.

Creating or Editing a Document Summary

1. Press Format (SHIFT-F8) and choose 3 for Document.

2. Choose 5 for Summary. Because the cursor moves to the beginning of the document, you may have a short delay if you are near the end of the document. The menu shown in Figure 3-39 appears.

3. Choose any or all items and enter the necessary information.

You should also be aware of an option that can retrieve certain information into the Summary for you. While at the main "Selection: 0" prompt (not while entering text for a specific item), press Retrieve (SHIFT-F10). The following message appears:

Capture Document Summary Fields? No (Yes)

If you type **Y**, WordPerfect will copy certain information into the following items listed below:

Author/Typist	Retrieves the names of the author and the typist that were entered in another summary during the current editing session. If none have been entered, no names will be inserted.
Subject	Searches for "RE:" in the document (unless you specified a different subject search text in the Setup menu) and copies the text from that point up to the next [HRt] code.
Abstract	Copies the first 400 characters from the document and inserts them into the Abstract portion of the Summary.

See the "Hints" section for other options and limitations on the number of characters that you can enter for each item.

4. Press Exit (F7) when you are finished. The cursor returns to the original location in the document.

```
Document Summary

        Revision Date

    1 - Creation Date   11-29-89 04:17p

    2 - Document Name
        Document Type

    3 - Author
        Typist

    4 - Subject

    5 - Account

    6 - Keywords

    7 - Abstract




Selection: 0                  (Retrieve to capture; Del to remove summary)
```

Figure 3-39.   Document Summary options

Short/Long Display

WordPerfect automatically displays files by their short DOS name. If you have the Long Document Name option in Setup set to "Yes," files will automatically be listed by their long document names.

An option in the List Files menu lets you switch between the long display (listing files by their descriptive names and document types in addition to their standard DOS name), or returning to the short display, which lists files by their DOS filename.

1. Press List (F5) and press ENTER.

2. Choose 5 for Short/Long Display.

3. Choose 1 for Short Display or 2 for Long Display.

4. The name of the current directory will be displayed on the status line. To change the display and remain in the same directory, press ENTER. If you want to enter another directory or list selected files, edit the pathname and press ENTER.

5. Press Exit (F7) when you are finished.

Finding Specific Documents

The Find option in the List Files menu lets you use the information entered in the Document Summary to help you find specific files. You can also search the first page or the entire document for a certain phrase. See "Find Files" in this chapter for more information.

Hints

If you use the long display, only WordPerfect document files will be displayed. In addition, the files are sorted first by their descriptive names and then by their DOS names. If a document does not have a descriptive name, the file is sorted by its DOS filename.

Summary Options

The Look feature in the List Files menu displays the summary at the beginning of the document. Enter the List Files menu, move the cursor to the file in question, and press ENTER to look at the document. If a summary exists, it is displayed in the first screen.

You can use the Find feature in the List Files menu to locate specific files based on the information entered in a Document Summary. A description of each item follows.

Creation Date   When you create a Document Summary, the current date and time are inserted into this section. (This does not necessarily coincide with the actual date on which the file was first saved but is the date on which the summary itself is created.) If you want this date to be the date when the file was actually created, choose "Create Summary on Save/Exit" in the Setup menu to create the summary when you save the document.

If you want to change the date, choose option 1 and enter the new date and time. If you do not enter the time, 12:00a is inserted for you.

Document Name   This option lets you enter a descriptive name of up to 68 characters. If you choose the long display in List Files, only the first 30 characters are displayed.

If you answered Yes to the Long Document Name option in the Setup menu, you will be prompted to enter or verify the long document name and document type each time you save a document.

Document Type   You can enter up to 20 characters to identify the document type. The first nine characters will appear in the List Files menu if you choose the Long Display option.

If you normally create the same type of document (letters, for example), you can specify LETTERS as the document type in the Setup menu. LETTERS would then be inserted as the document type when the Document Summary is created. You can always change the name if necessary.

Author/Typist   You can enter up to 60 characters for each item. If you prefer, you can press Retrieve (SHIFT-F10) while the cursor is resting on the status line (not while you are entering text for an item) and type **Y** in answer to the question "Capture Document Summary Fields? No (Yes)." By doing so, you will copy the names of the last author and typist that was entered in another summary during that editing session. For example, if you are always the author and a certain secretary is always the typist, you can enter the names once during the day and use Retrieve (SHIFT-F10) on all subsequent summaries.

Subject   Up to 160 characters will be accepted for the subject. If you press Retrieve (SHIFT-F10) while the cursor is resting on the status line, you can have WordPerfect search the first 550 characters of the document for "RE:" and copy any text from that point to the next hard return [HRt] code. If you want WordPerfect to search for a different subject search text (such as "SUBJECT:"), enter the Setup menu and make that change.

Account   You can enter up to 160 characters for the account. You can enter a name or a number, such as an employee or a social security number.

Keywords   Enter as many keywords as you would like (up to 160 characters).

Abstract   You can enter up to 780 characters in this section. If you press Retrieve (SHIFT-F10) from the status line (not while entering text in the abstract), and answer **Y** to the question "Capture Document Summary Fields?" the first 400 characters from the document will be copied into the abstract.

Saving, Deleting, or Printing a Summary

To save the summary to a file, press Save (F10) while in the Summary menu. If the file already exists, you will be asked if you want to replace it or append the summary to the end of the existing file. The summary is saved as text; not as another summary.

To delete a summary, enter the Document Summary menu, press DEL, and confirm the deletion.

A Document Summary can be printed either while you are in the summary or when you are specifying to print certain pages of a document. To print from within the summary, press Print (SHIFT-F7). If printing a document from List Files, or with the Document on Disk or Multiple Pages options in the Print menu, type **S** for Summary when you are asked for the page number.

Related Items

Find Files

DOCUMENT SIZE

WordPerfect displays the size of a document in the List Files menu.

Keystrokes

1. Press List (F5).

2. Press ENTER to see the displayed directory, or enter another directory name. If you know the name of the file in question, enter the name. The size of the file is indicated just after the filename.

Hints

To find the size of the document currently being edited, press List (F5) then press ENTER. "Document size:" in the heading indicates the size of the current document. Note that the document size is for either document 1 or document 2, not both. The document size is shown for the name of the document where the cursor was located when you pressed List (F5). Document size is indicated in bytes.

If you are in the List Files menu and decide to retrieve a file, check the document size at the top of the menu first. By making sure that it shows zero, you will ensure that you are not retrieving a copy of one document into another already in memory. If there is another document on the screen, you are asked if you want to retrieve the file into the current document.

You can have approximately 100 to 130 single-spaced pages on a double-sided, double-density disk (approximate because of the size of the document header or prefix).

Related Entries

Disk Space
List Files

DOCUMENT SUMMARY

See "Document Management/Summary" in this chapter.

DOS COMMAND

WordPerfect lets you go to DOS while the program is still running or start a single DOS command from within WordPerfect.

Keystrokes

Go to DOS

1. Press Shell (CTRL-F1).

2. Choose **1** to **G**o to DOS. If WordPerfect Library or Office is running, option 1 reads "Go to Shell." You would then need to choose option **1** from the Shell menu to go to DOS.

3. When finished at DOS, type **exit** and press ENTER to return to WordPerfect or the Shell menu. If you are returned to the Shell, choose the WordPerfect option on the menu to return to Word-Perfect.

Single DOS Command

1. Press Shell (CTRL-F1).

2. Choose **5** for DOS Command. If you are not running Word-Perfect Library or Office, option **2** is listed as the correct choice for starting a single DOS command. However, option 5 works in both cases to provide consistency for macros.

3. Enter the DOS command (for example, **md letters** would make a new directory named "letters").

4. Press any key when you are finished.

Hints

The error message "Not enough memory" may appear when you choose this option. This is because an extra copy of COMMAND.COM has to be loaded into memory.

You should not use the CHKDSK (check disk) command or load any Terminate Stay-Resident (TSR) programs while WordPerfect is running.

If you are running Shell, you can press ALT-SHIFT-space bar as a shortcut to go to the shell menu.

Related Entries

Go to DOS
Shell

DOS TEXT FILES

WordPerfect can save and retrieve DOS text files (text without codes) for use with other software programs.

Keystrokes

Save a DOS Text File

1. With the document that is to be converted to a DOS (ASCII) text file currently on the screen, press Text In/Out (CTRL-F5).

2. Choose 1 for DOS Text.

3. Choose 1 for Save.

4. Enter the name of the file, or press ENTER to use the displayed name.

Be aware that the file remains on the screen after you save it as a DOS file. When exiting the file, do not save it again unless you want to save it as a WordPerfect file. If you do, use a different filename, or the DOS text file will be overwritten with the WordPerfect version.

WordPerfect codes are stripped from the file, and soft returns are converted to hard returns. Tabs, indents, and centering are maintained with spaces.

Retrieve a DOS Text File

1. Set the page size and margins to match the line length of the file being retrieved. For example, since many DOS text files are 80 characters wide, change to a 10-pitch font and change the margins on each side to 1/4".

2. Press Text In/Out (CTRL-F5).

3. Choose **1** for DOS **T**ext.

4. Choose **2** to **R**etrieve a file with all CR/LF (carriage returns/linefeeds) converted to hard returns, or choose **3** to **R**etrieve a file and convert CR/LFs falling within the hyphenation zone to soft returns.

You can also retrieve a DOS text file normally with Retrieve (SHIFT-F10). If you do so, all CR/LFs are converted to hard returns automatically.

See "Macros" for a macro that can be used to strip out unnecessary hard returns at the end of each line.

Hints

As a safety measure, WordPerfect will not let you retrieve some files, such as files with the extensions .COM, .EXE, and .WPM (WordPerfect macros).

After you save a file as a DOS text file, it remains on the screen. Use caution when saving the file again, because you could replace the previously saved file with the WordPerfect file on the screen.

You can also use the ASCII text file option in the Convert program to convert WordPerfect files to ASCII text.

Codes that contain text (such as headers, footers, footnotes, styles, and line numbering) are stripped out when you save a file as a DOS text file. If the file contains Styles, you can first delete the styles, but leave the contents (codes) so the document will be formatted correctly. See "Styles" in this chapter for details.

If you want to keep the text included in headers, footers, and footnotes, print the file to disk instead. See "Print to Disk" in this chapter for more information.

If you want tab settings to be converted to DOS tabs rather than spaces, press Text In/Out (CTRL-F5), choose **3** for Save As, and choose **1** for Generic. See "Text In/Out" in this chapter for more information.

Applications

You can use this feature to edit DOS text files (batch files, CONFIG.SYS, and so on) or program source files. When you retrieve this type of file, the ^Z marking the end of the file is removed. When a file is saved as an ASCII file, the ^Z is added to the end of it (do not reenter it). If you do not want word wrap, it may be necessary to change the paper size to 11" x 8.5" instead of 8.5" x 11", change the margins, or use a smaller font.

If you use the Program Editor included with WordPerfect Library (a utility program produced by WordPerfect Corporation), you do not have to go through a separate procedure for saving and retrieving text files, and words will not wrap.

Related Entries

Convert Program
List Files
Print to Disk
Text In/Out

DOT LEADER

A dot leader (. . .) can precede any type of tab. You can also add a dot leader to centered text or text that is flush against the right margin.

The Table of Contents, Tables of Authorities, Lists, and Index features all have options for inserting a dot leader preceding the page number.

Keystrokes

Center or Flush Right

To create a dot leader for text that is centered or flush right, press Center (SHIFT-F6) or Flush Right (ALT-F6) twice. If you have already centered or aligned the text with the right margin, move the cursor within the text and press the applicable function key again.

Tab Settings

While in the Tab menu, press the period (.) on any tab setting to change it to a dot-leader tab. When you enter text and press TAB, a dot leader is inserted from the cursor's current location to that tab setting.

You can also insert a dot-leader tab on a one-time basis without having to set special tab settings. Press HOME twice (HOME, HOME) and then one of the following keys to insert a dot leader and create a specific type of tab, regardless of the current tab setting.

TAB	Regular, left-aligned tab
Center (SHIFT-F6)	Centered tab
Tab Align (CTRL-F6)	Decimal-aligned tab
Flush Right (ALT-F6)	Right-aligned tab

Hints

As you add or delete text, the dot leader appears or disappears, depending on how much is needed to fill the space.

Applications

Press Flush Right (ALT-F6) twice to create the following type of list or when creating your own table of contents or index.

Name	**Phone Number**
Bob Jones.	555-2121
Suzanne Parker	555-9898
Sandra J. Fallows	555-7309

Press Center (SHIFT-F6) twice and Flush Right (ALT-F6) twice (after the titles on the left) to create programs in which the following is needed:

Musical Number. . . . ."Theme from Tara". . . . . . . Bruce Johnson
Reading . . . . . . Excerpt from "Gone with the Wind" . . . . . . Kay Hill
Musical Number . . . ."Tomorrow" . . . . Annie McGuire

Related Entries

    Center Text
    Flush Right
    Index
    Lists
    Table of Authorities
    Table of Contents
    Tabs

DOUBLE SPACING

See "Spacing" in this chapter.

DOUBLE UNDERLINING

WordPerfect can print a double (or single) underline. You can also choose the way double underlining is displayed on the screen with the Colors/Fonts/Attributes menu.

Keystrokes

1. Press Font (CTRL-F8).

2. Choose **2** for **A**ppearance.

3. Choose **3** for **D**bl Und (double underline).

4. Type the text to be underlined.

5. Press → to move over the [dbl und] code (you can also return to the Appearance menu and select the option again to turn it off).

Hints

WordPerfect automatically underlines spaces, but it does not underline the space between tabs. If you want to change these settings, move the cursor to the position at which this change is to occur, press Format (SHIFT-F8), choose **4** for **O**ther, and select option **7** for Underline Spaces/ Tabs. You can then choose **Y** or **N**, depending on whether or not you want spaces or tabs underlined.

Related Entries

Underline

DOWNLOADING FONTS

See "Initialize Printer" in this chapter.

DRAWING LINES AND BOXES

See "Line Draw," "Graphics Boxes," and "Tables" in this chapter.

EDITING DOCUMENTS

You can use several features to edit and revise text.

Keystrokes

See "Delete" in this chapter for options to delete and restore text. The following is a list of other features that can be used for editing.

Block (ALT-F4)

Use Block to move, delete, and give attributes to text that has already been entered (boldface, underline, uppercase, center, superscript, and so on).

Comments

When several people are editing a document, you can use the Comment feature to insert nonprinting comments in the document. Each can be labeled with the editor's name and date so changes can be made later if the author agrees with the suggestions.

To insert a comment, press Text In/Out (CTRL-F5) and choose 4 for Comment and 1 to Create a comment. After entering the text, press Exit (F7).

Search (F2) and Replace (ALT-F2)

Search for text and WordPerfect codes with the Search feature; to replace or delete them, use the Replace feature.

Switch (SHIFT-F3)

When working with two documents, you can use Switch (SHIFT-F3) to move between the two. This is the best method for moving text between documents.

Mark Text (ALT-F5)

The Redline and Strikeout features, found on the Font (CTRL-F8) key, are useful for marking text to be added to or deleted from a document. You can then use the Remove feature, found on Mark Text (ALT-F5) to remove redline markings and text that was struck out.

See Chapter 2, "WordPerfect Basics," for other general information about editing documents.

Related Entries

Block
Comments
Move
Redline
Replace
Search
Strikeout
Switch
See also Chapter 2, "WordPerfect Basics"

EDIT-SCREEN OPTIONS

Edit-Screen options are found in the Setup menu and control various aspects of the editing screen, including whether or not to display the filename of the document, comments, or merge codes, and how much of the screen to dedicate to Reveal Codes when it is on.

Keystrokes

1. Press Setup (SHIFT-F1).

2. Choose **2** for **D**isplay.

3. Choose **6** for **E**dit-Screen Options. The options shown in Figure 3-40 appear.

4. Select any options that need to be changed, and answer any questions that follow.

5. Press Exit (F7) when you are finished.

Options

The following items are included in the Edit-Screen Options menu.

Automatically Format and Rewrite

WordPerfect automatically reformats your document as you add and delete text. If you want to increase the editing speed, you can turn this option off. The document would then be reformatted as you move the cursor through it. You can also rewrite the screen manually at any time by pressing Screen (CTRL-F3) twice.

Comments Display

If you use the Comment feature found on Text In/Out (CTRL-F5) to insert nonprinting comments in a document, they will automatically appear on the screen. Choose this option if you do not want them displayed. See "Comments" in this chapter for more information about this feature.

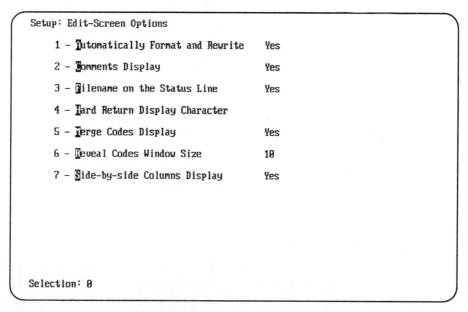

Figure 3-40.   Edit-Screen Options

Filename on the Status Line

WordPerfect displays the name of the current document at the bottom left corner of the screen. If you would prefer that the filename not be displayed, you can turn this option off.

Hard Return Display Character

Any character can be displayed on the screen to represent a hard return. This character will not be printed. See "Hard Return Display Character" in this chapter for details.

Merge Codes Display

Merge codes are always displayed unless this option is set to No. You may want to select this option to see how a merge document would normally be formatted without the merge codes. Any text accompanying the merge codes remains on the screen. For example, if a merge document contains the merge code {FIELD}Name~, turning off the display of merge codes would leave "Name~" but would remove {FIELD} from the screen.

Reveal Codes Window Size

When you press Reveal Codes (ALT-F3), WordPerfect normally uses the bottom ten lines of the screen for the Reveal Codes screen. You can increase or decrease this amount by selecting this option and entering the appropriate number of lines.

If you enter **1** as the number of lines, only the current code or character will appear in the Reveal Codes screen.

Side-by-Side Columns Display

You can greatly increase the speed of working in columns if you change this option to No. The columns will be separated by a page break, with one column on each page. They will keep their relative horizontal position on the screen, however; for example, column 2 would not be against the left margin but would be in the middle of the screen, just as it would appear if the columns were displayed side by side on the screen. See "Columns" in this chapter for more information.

Related Entries

Columns
Hard Return Display Character
Merge
Reveal Codes
Rewrite the Screen

ENCRYPTING A FILE

See "Password Protection" in this chapter.

END KEY

The END key, found on the numeric keypad, is used to move to the far right end of a line.

Keystrokes

Pressing END is the same as pressing HOME, HOME, →. It moves the cursor to the end of a line—even when the text goes beyond the edge of the screen.

To delete to the end of a line, hold down the CTRL key and press END. All text and codes are deleted from the cursor to the end of the line. To restore the deleted text, press Cancel (F1) and choose 1 for Restore.

Related Entries

Cursor Keys

ENDNOTES

Endnotes are like footnotes, but they are printed together as a group (usually at the end of the document) instead of at the bottom of the page on which they are referenced.

Keystrokes

Create an Endnote

1. Press Footnote (CTRL-F7).

2. Choose 2 for Endnote.

3. Choose 1 for Create. The Footnote/Endnote screen appears, and the appropriate note number is inserted.

4. If you want any type of indentation, press the space bar twice, and then press TAB, or Indent (F4). Type the footnote or endnote text.

5. Press Exit (F7) when you are finished.

After you create the endnote, the number is placed in the document at the cursor position. If you have chosen a color, a font, or another screen attribute to represent superscript, that characteristic will appear on the screen. Unless you have a Hercules graphics card with RamFont, the number will not be superscripted on the screen; it will, however, be superscripted when printed.

Edit an Endnote

1. Press Footnote (CTRL-F7).

2. Choose **2** for **E**ndnote.

3. Choose **2** for **E**dit. "Endnote number?" is displayed with the number of the next endnote.

4. Press ENTER to edit the displayed endnote, or enter the number of the note to be edited.

5. Press Exit (F7) when you are finished editing.

You can use Search (F2) to search for an endnote by code but not by a specific number. See "Hints" for more information about searching for endnote codes.

Delete an Endnote

1. Position the cursor at the number of the endnote to be deleted.

2. Press DEL. If the endnote is to the left of the cursor, press BACKSPACE.

3. Type **Y** or **N** in answer to the question "Delete [Endnote:n]? No (Yes)."

Endnote Placement

Endnotes are printed at the end of the document unless you specify a different location. To do so, follow these steps:

1. Move the cursor to the location at which the endnotes are to be printed.

2. Press Footnote (CTRL-F7).

3. Choose **3** for Endnote **P**lacement.

4. The question "Restart endnote numbering? Yes (No)" appears. Type **Y** if you want the endnotes to begin with number 1, or type **N** to leave them numbered as they are. This option is useful if you have a document containing many chapters and you want the endnotes to be printed at the end of each chapter beginning with num-

ber 1, instead of at the end of the document. If you type **Y**, a [New End Num:1] code is inserted after the [Endnote Placement] code.

5. The following comment appears on the screen:

```
Endnote Placement
It is not known how much space endnotes will occupy here.
Generate to determine.
```

If you want to see how many pages will be taken up by endnotes, press Mark Text (ALT-F5), choose **6** for Generate; choose **5** for Generate Tables, Indexes, Cross-References, etc.; and then type **Y** to replace existing tables and indexes.

After the endnotes have been generated, you will see this message:

```
Endnote Placement
```

Even though the note looks small, it actually takes up the exact amount of space needed for the endnotes to be printed there. All endnotes from the previous endnote placement code (or from the beginning of the document, if there are no other placement codes) are included when you generate them.

You will need to generate the document before printing.

Hints

When you create an endnote, a code similar to the following is inserted:

[Endnote:1;[Note Num]Text]

The code specifies whether this is a footnote or an endnote, the number of the note, and then the text of the note. Up to 50 characters of text are shown with the code.

There is no practical limit on the amount of text that can be included in a footnote or endnote. Each can contain up to 16,000 lines.

Endnotes are printed in the document's initial base font—not necessarily in the current font. If you set any endnote options, the font that is current when the [End Opt] code is inserted is used for endnotes. To check the initial base font, press Format (SHIFT-F8) and choose 3 for Document. The initial base font is displayed under option 3. Choose 3 for Initial Base Font if you want to change the font.

Assign a New Number to an Endnote

WordPerfect automatically numbers endnotes and renumbers them when others are added or deleted. However, if a footnote or endnote must have a specific number—for example, when you are continuing the numbering from one chapter to another—you can give it one by pressing Footnote (CTRL-F7), choosing 2 for Endnote, and 3 for New Number, and entering the number for the next note. The code [New End Num:*n*] is inserted into the document, and the following endnotes are numbered according to the specified number. Remember, however, that you can use the Master Document feature so that several documents are included together and numbering (page numbering, footnotes, endnotes, and so on) continues from one document to the next.

Options

WordPerfect has chosen a specific format for endnotes. To view or change the current settings, press Footnote (CTRL-F7), choose 2 for Endnote, then choose 4 for Options. The menu shown in Figure 3-41 appears.

If changes are made, an [End Opt] code is inserted at the cursor location, and endnotes from that point forward are affected. To make changes that will affect all endnotes, move to the beginning of the document before entering the menu.

Because you will probably want the endnote format options to be changed for all documents, consider making the changes in the Initial Codes section of Setup (SHIFT-F1). The code would then be inserted for all documents.

Spacing   Notes will automatically be single-spaced, with .167″ between each note. Spacing can also be set in the endnote itself if you want the spacing to vary from note to note. For future reference, .167″ is the line height for a 12pt (10-pitch) font.

If you want WordPerfect to control the spacing between notes, do not press ENTER after typing the text. Pressing ENTER will insert extra blank lines.

Amount of Endnote to Keep Together   If an endnote is longer than the space available on a page, it will continue on the next page. Because the Widow/Orphan feature does not affect endnotes, option 2 lets you specify the amount of text that should be kept together if the note continues onto other pages. The default measurement is .5″. Note that this setting is set in an amount rather than in number of lines.

Style for Numbers in Text and Note   Options 3 and 4 determine how an endnote number will appear in the text of a document and in the note itself. WordPerfect has been set to display the text reference number for endnotes as a superscripted number. The number within an endnote is followed by a period and is not superscripted.

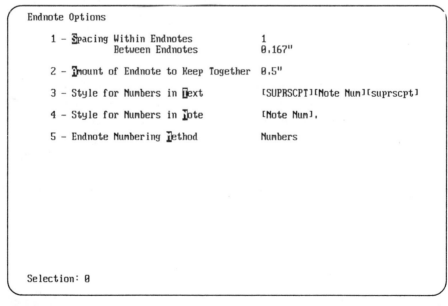

Figure 3-41.   Endnote options

To change this preset format, select the option that applies. "Replace with:" appears on the status line with the current text and codes. Delete unnecessary codes and add others. To insert the [Note Num] code, press Footnote (CTRL-F7), choose **2** for **E**ndnote, then choose **2** for Number Code to insert the [Note Num] code.

If you don't make any other changes, choose option 4 and add two spaces to the end of the style; otherwise, you will need to add them each time you create an endnote. Tabs and indents cannot be used as part of the style. Although WordPerfect lets you enter almost any code, it may not accept it once you press ENTER.

Endnote Numbering Method   A number (rather than a letter or a character) is used by default to number endnotes. Choose option 5 to change the option for endnotes. The following options appear:

1 **N**umbers: 2 **L**etters: 3 **C**haracters: 0

Press ENTER or choose **1** to use the default setting of **N**umbers, **2** for **L**etters ("A" through "Z"), or **3** for **C**haracters. If you choose option 3, the cursor is placed to the right of the option, and you can enter the characters to be used. If you press ENTER without entering characters, WordPerfect will default to numbers. You can enter a single character or as many as 20 characters. WordPerfect uses the indicated characters and then starts at the beginning of the list, first doubling and then tripling the characters. Common characters are asterisks and daggers († and ††). If your printer can print daggers, you can enter them by pressing Compose (CTRL-2) (the 2 on the top row of keys, rather than the 2 on the numeric keypad) and then entering **4,39** for a single dagger or **4,40** for a double dagger. You will not see a prompt to help you while entering these characters. If you enter characters correctly, you should see a small box representing the character. See "Compose" in this chapter for more information about other special characters that you can use.

Margin Settings for Endnotes

Endnotes all use the same margin setting (determined by the default margin setting) or, if you have an Endnote Options code, the margin setting to the left of that code.

Columns and Notes

You can create endnotes but not footnotes while in columns. If you reformat text containing footnotes into columns, the footnotes are automatically converted to endnotes. In fact, if you want to change all footnotes to endnotes, you can define columns, turn them on, go to the end of the document to reformat the text, and then move back to the beginning of the document and delete the [Col Def:] and [Col On] codes. If you want only some of the footnotes converted, move through only that portion of the text before deleting the columns codes.

Master Documents and Endnotes

Master documents allow you to include the names of several documents (such as chapters in a book) in one document and then print that one document so that all numbering (for pages, footnotes, endnotes, and so on) will continue through the subdocuments as if they were one document. You can use the Endnote Placement command effectively in this situation if you want to include endnotes at the end of each chapter or at the end of the entire book (master document). If you want to use the Generate option to see how much space will be used in the endnotes, you do not have to expand the document first. Remember also that you can choose to have the endnotes restart at number 1 with each endnote placement code. See "Master Document" in this chapter for more information.

Search for Notes

Endnotes and their associated codes are sometimes difficult to find. If you want to set endnote options, it is usually best to set them at the beginning of the document; this also makes the code easier to find in the future. If you are assigning a new number to an endnote, you would most likely specify the new number right before the endnote. However, if you cannot find the correct code, go to the top of the document, press Search (F2), press Footnote (CTRL-F7), and then choose 2 for Endnote.

The following options appear:

```
1 Note; 2 Number Code; 3 New Number; 4 Options: 0
```

Choose 1 to search for the first Note (you cannot choose specific notes), 3 for New Number if you want to search for a [New End Num] code, or 4 for the endnote Options code, [End Opt]. Although you can search for the second option, Number Code, it will not be found unless you do an Extended Search, because it is inside the endnote itself.

If you want to search for or replace text that might be found within a footnote or an endnote, use the Extended Search or Extended Replace feature. Press HOME before pressing Search (F2) or Replace (ALT-F2). The document, notes, headers, footers, and text in graphics boxes will be searched during an extended search.

Viewing Notes

The View Document feature lets you see exactly how footnotes and endnotes will appear on the printed page. If you just want to see how the endnotes will appear, go to the end of the document and view the last page.

To view the page, press Print (SHIFT-F7) and then choose 6 for View. If you have a graphics monitor, you will see an exact representation of the page. Choose the options at the bottom of the screen to scale the document up to 100 percent or 200 percent. If you have a text monitor, you will not see an exact representation or be able to scale the page, but you will still be able to see the text and its location on the page.

Printing Endnotes

If you want to print the endnotes on a separate page, go to the end of the document and press Hard Page (CTRL-ENTER). Or, if you have used the Endnote Placement feature, place a hard page break before (and after the code if necessary).

If you want to print only the endnotes, position the cursor on the last page (or the blank page at the end of the document), and print the page by pressing Print (SHIFT-F7) and choosing 2 for Page.

Change Footnotes to Endnotes

As mentioned previously, if you format text into columns, all footnotes are automatically converted to endnotes. After defining and turning on columns, you can move through the text where the footnotes are located and then return to the beginning of the document and delete the column definition and columns-on codes to return the text to normal. The footnotes remain as endnotes. See "Columns" in this chapter for more information about defining columns.

WordPerfect also includes a macro that will convert endnotes to footnotes and vice versa. These macros are installed during installation if you answer "Yes" to the question, "Install Keyboard Files?" To use the macros, press Macro (ALT-F10) and enter **endfoot** to convert endnotes to footnotes or **footend** to convert footnotes to endnotes.

Related Entries

Footnotes
Search
View Document

ENTER KEY

WordPerfect refers to the RETURN key (or the Carriage Return key) as the ENTER key. It is used to end short lines, create blank lines, execute commands, and leave menus. If you are using the pull-down menus, you can press ENTER to make a selection.

Keystrokes

To end a line before the right margin or to add blank lines, press ENTER, and a hard return is inserted. In Reveal Codes, a hard return code is shown as [HRt].

Before a command can be executed, you may be prompted for information such as the name of a file, a macro, or a directory. After you type the information, press ENTER to indicate the end of the name and execute the command. If you find yourself waiting for the computer to do something, you may have forgotten to press ENTER after entering a command or information.

If you are in a menu (except List Files), you can press ENTER to leave the menu. If you are several levels deep, pressing ENTER will return you to the previous menu, whereas pressing Exit (F7) should return you directly to the document. You can also use the space bar to exit most menus, including the List Files menu.

Hints

With WordPerfect's automatic word wrap, you do not have to press ENTER at the end of each line. If you type more text than will fit within the margins, WordPerfect automatically wraps the text to the next line, and inserts a soft return (shown in Reveal Codes as [SRt]). In contrast to a typewriter's Return key, if you press ENTER to move downward through text, blank lines are added. If you want to move downward through the text, use the down arrow key instead. If you accidentally press ENTER, you can use BACKSPACE to delete the blank lines above the cursor. If the blank lines are after the cursor, press DEL to delete them.

The following is a summary of various "return" codes and how they are inserted.

Hard Return [HRt]

Inserted when ENTER is pressed.

Soft Return [SRt]

Inserted by WordPerfect during word wrap.

Invisible Soft Return [ISRt]

You can insert this type of return by pressing HOME, then ENTER. It is most commonly used after em or en dashes and slashes so that the line will break at that point if necessary. If it is not needed to break the word or phrase (such as Colors/Fonts/Attributes) at the dash or slash, it remains invisible.

Dormant Hard Return [Dorm HRt]

If a [HRt] code comes directly after a [HRt-SPg] code (soft page break), it is automatically converted to a dormant hard return. Because two hard returns are usually placed between columns, the first one may be converted to a soft page break at the end of the page. This would normally leave the next hard return at the top of the next column. The [Dorm HRt] code eliminates these blank lines at the tops of pages and columns.

Deletable Soft Return [DSRt]

If hyphenation is off, you may find that WordPerfect places a [DSRt] code in the middle of a word and wraps part of it to the next line. If the font is too large, the margins too narrow (usually when you are working in columns), and hyphenation is off, WordPerfect is forced to break words at some point and inserts the [DSRt] code where necessary. These codes will disappear when you increase the amount of space in the line (decrease the margins), change to a smaller font, or turn on hyphenation.

Related Entries

Carriage Return
Hard Return Display Character

ENVELOPES

You can easily print on envelopes from within WordPerfect by selecting "Envelope" from the list of available types of paper.

Keystrokes

1. Press Go To (CTRL-HOME), and then press ↑ to go to the beginning of the page if you are not already there.

2. Press Format (SHIFT-F8).

3. Choose **2** for **Page**.

4. Choose **7** for Paper Size/Type.

5. Move to the form labeled "Envelope" and press ENTER to select it. If an envelope is not listed, see "Hints" for instructions about adding it to the list.

6. Choose **1** and type **Y** to Center the Page (text on the envelope) from top to bottom, *or* choose **5** for **Margins** and enter **2** for the top margin and leave **1"** for the bottom margin.

7. Press ENTER to return to the general format menu.

8. Choose **1** for Line and **7** for Margins (left and right).

9. Enter **4.5"** as the left margin, and leave the right margin at **1"**. Press Exit (F7) to return to the screen.

10. Enter the name and address, and then press Hard Page (CTRL-ENTER) to go to the next envelope. If you need to return to standard paper, repeat steps 2 through 4 and select Standard 8.5" x 11" paper.

See "Hints" for tips on how you can avoid setting the margins each time.

Hints

Note that because the size of the form was changed, the amount of text that could fit on one "page" decreased accordingly.

The MACROS.WPK keyboard contains a macro that automates the process of creating an envelope. To use this macro, you must first select the MACROS keyboard by pressing Setup (SHIFT-F1), choosing **5** for Keyboard Layout, moving the cursor to the MACROS keyboard on the list and choosing **1** to Select it. Press Exit (F7) to return to the document. You need to do this only once, unless you change keyboards in the future.

To use the macro, move the cursor to the first line of the address in the letter and press CTRL-E. (If you are not on the first line, you will be prompted to move there and press ENTER.)

Adding an Envelope to the List

Most printers have a predefined envelope among the list of paper types. For example, the HP Series II definition has set up envelopes to print with a landscape font (because it is fed into the printer sideways) and has "manual" feed chosen for the location. To create one of your own, follow these steps:

1. Press Format (SHIFT-F8).

2. Choose **2** for **Page**.

3. Choose **7** for Paper Size/Type.

4. Choose **2** for **Add**.

5. When prompted for the paper type, choose **5** for **Envelope**.

6. Choose **1** for Paper Size, and then **5** for **Envelope**. If you have envelopes that aren't the standard size of 9.5″ x 4″, type **O** (not zero) for **O**ther and enter the width and height of the envelope.

7. Change the Font Type, Prompt to Load, and Location options if necessary, and press Exit (F7) until you return to the document.

You have to follow these steps only once for each printer definition that does not already have an envelope form defined.

Margin Tips

To avoid the extra steps of inserting margin changes each time you select an envelope, edit the envelope paper definition as follows:

1. Press Format (SHIFT-F8), and choose **2** for **Page**.

2. Choose **7** for Paper Size/Type.

3. Move the cursor to the envelope definition to be edited, and choose **5** for **E**dit.

4. Then choose option **8** for Labels, and type **Y** for Yes.

5. Choose **5** for Label Margins and enter the left, right, top, and bottom margins for the envelope.

6. Then press Exit (F7) until you return to the document.

Because you did not specify a certain number of columns and rows of labels, it assumes the entire envelope is a "label" and sets the margins for that one label.

Related Items

Paper Size and Type

ENVIRONMENT

The Environment category found in Setup (SHIFT-F1) controls different aspects of the program that are related to the environment in which you work. They affect items such as backup, cursor speed, hyphenation, and units of measurement.

Keystrokes

1. Press Setup (SHIFT-F1).

2. Choose 3 for Environment. The options shown in Figure 3-42 appear.

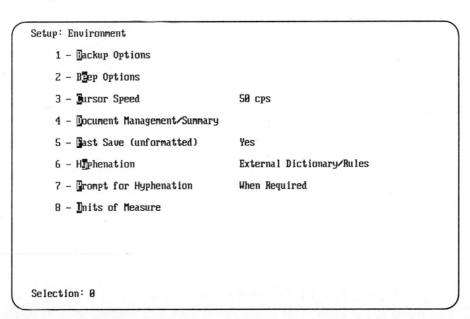

```
Setup: Environment
      1 - Backup Options
      2 - Beep Options
      3 - Cursor Speed              50 cps
      4 - Document Management/Summary
      5 - Fast Save (unformatted)   Yes
      6 - Hyphenation               External Dictionary/Rules
      7 - Prompt for Hyphenation    When Required
      8 - Units of Measure



Selection: 0
```

Figure 3-42.   Environment Setup options

3. Choose the applicable options and press Exit (F7) when you are finished.

Options

The following is a summary of all the options that appear under the Environment category of the Setup menu. Each option is also included in this chapter under its own heading. See that entry for details.

Backup Options

If you choose this option, you will be allowed to set or change the Timed Backup feature (WordPerfect is preset to back up the current document every 30 minutes) or turn on Original Backup.

Timed Backup saves your documents to a temporary file at specified intervals, while Original Backup saves the last copy of a document with a .BK! extension instead of deleting as it normally would. See "Backup" in this chapter for details.

Beep Options

Normally, WordPerfect causes the computer to beep when a hyphenation decision needs to be made. You can change this option to avoid hearing a beep during hyphenation, or you can ask that the computer beep when an error occurs or a search fails. See "Beep Options" in this chapter for details.

Cursor Speed

The cursor speed is preset to 50 characters per second. This option lets you choose between 15, 20, 30, 40, 50 (characters per second), and Normal. This setting affects the speed at which the cursor moves when it is scrolling through the document or deleting text. See "Cursor Speed" in this chapter for more information.

Document Management/Summary

Items found under this menu option help you manage your documents. You can choose from a number of items, which include the following:

creating a document summary the first time a document is saved, assigning a long document name and document type each time you save a document, and specifying a default document type (which can be overridden, of course).

Another option lets you specify a word or phrase that you normally use in letters or memos to indicate the subject matter. This word is then used by WordPerfect when it is copying the subject matter into the document Summary. The text currently entered is RE:, but you can change it to SUBJECT:, SUBJ:, and so on. See "Document Management/Summary" in this chapter for details.

Fast Save

WordPerfect is automatically set to save your documents without first making sure they are reformatted. The only disadvantage to using this setting is that it will take a little longer to print a file from disk because it has to be retrieved "in the background," be reformatted, and then be printed.

Fast Save may also slightly increase the size of your documents until you retrieve them again. See "Fast Save" in this chapter for more information.

Hyphenation

The first option dealing with hyphenation lets you choose whether you want to use the internal hyphenation rules that are built into Word-Perfect (an algorithm that is approximately 90 percent correct) or if you want to use the external (spelling) dictionary. If you leave the setting as it is, WordPerfect will reference the spelling dictionary for all hyphenation points. If there is not an acceptable hyphenation point within the hyphenation zone, the internal rules will be used.

The second option lets you choose whether you always want to be prompted for hyphenation, never prompted, or prompted only when required (when the hyphenation zone does not allow a correct hyphen, or when a word is not recognized by the spelling dictionary).

Hyphenation is turned on from within the document when you press Format (SHIFT-F8) and choose 1 for Line and then 1 for Hyphenation. See "Hyphenation" in this chapter for the exact steps.

Units of Measurement

WordPerfect is automatically set to accept settings in inches and displays the cursor location on the page in inches. With this option, you can choose to enter measurements in centimeters, point sizes (72 per inch), WordPerfect 4.2 units, or 1200ths of an inch.

Even if you do not change the type of measurement to be used at all times in this menu, you can enter any setting in any of these types of measurements on a one-time basis. For example, if you want to set the left margin at 3 centimeters, you can enter **3c**, regardless of the current setting. WordPerfect would then automatically convert it to the current unit of measurement.

You can also enter measurements as fractions. Entering **3/16″** would convert automatically to .188″ if inches were the default unit of measurement.

Related Entries

Backup
Beep Options
Cursor Speed
Document Management/Summary
Fast Save
Hyphenation
Units of Measurement

EQUATIONS

In WordPerfect 5.1, equations are not only easy to enter and format using certain commands, they can also be printed on any graphics-type printer (laser or dot matrix) without purchasing special scientific or math fonts.

WordPerfect formats equations according to accepted guidelines of the math and scientific community. Numbers and functions are printed in a normal font, while variables such as x and y are printed in italics.

Superscripted numbers are printed in a smaller font, and division lines and square root radicals grow to fit the size of an equation.

Equations are entered much like you would say them. After pressing a single key, WordPerfect displays the equation and then prints it on any graphics printer. If a character or symbol does not exist in the printer, WordPerfect creates and prints it graphically.

Figure 3-43 shows an example of an equation and how it was entered. The lower portion of the window is used to enter the equation while the upper portion of the screen, called the display window, is used to display the equation. The area to the right is referred to as the "palette" and can be used to list screen after screen of commands and special symbols that can be inserted into an equation.

The equation in Figure 3-43 could be translated as "the tangent of x equals 2 plus or minus the square root of 4 plus 4 over 2." The ' character represents a thin space and braces, { }, are used to represent items that should be treated as a group.

Please note that you can use the equation editor to format equations, but it cannot actually do the calculations.

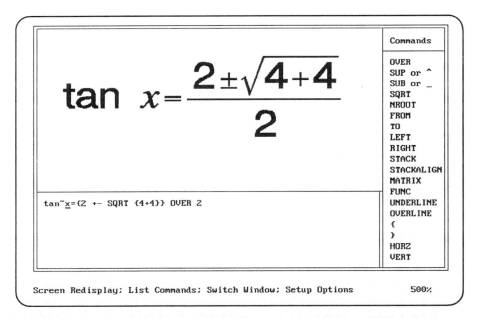

Figure 3-43.   Equation editor showing a sample equation and how it was entered

Equations can include any or all of the following:

Variables (*a*, *b1*, *xy*, etc.)
Numbers (1, 33, 45365, etc.)
Math operators (+, −, =, ±, >, etc.)
Greek characters (alpha, beta, gamma, etc.)
Binary and relational symbols (infinity, subset, <<, etc.)
Miscellaneous symbols (ellipses . . ., primes ' '', arrows, etc.)
Diacriticals (dot, bar, vec, hat, etc.)
Large operators (sum, integral, product, union, etc.)
Dynamic operators that grow with the size of the equation (brackets, square root radical, lines, etc.)

Keystrokes

The following steps help you create an equation. You can find details about the many options available in the equation editor under "Hints."

1. Press Graphics (ALT-F9). The following choices appear:

> 1 **F**igure; 2 **T**able Box; 3 Text **B**ox; 4 **U**ser Box; 5 **L**ine; 6 **E**quation: 0

2. Choose **6** for **E**quation and **1** to **C**reate. Even though you can use any type of graphics box to create an equation, this type has been designed specifically for them.

The menu shown in Figure 3-44 appears. Note that item **2** for Contents says "Equation." If you choose another type of graphics box, you will need to select this option first and choose Equation, or the equation editor will not be used.

3. You can enter a caption, change the anchor type (page, paragraph, or character), adjust the vertical and horizontal positions, or change the size. See "Graphics Boxes" in this chapter if you need assistance with the options found on this menu.

```
Definition: Equation

    1 - Filename

    2 - Contents            Equation

    3 - Caption

    4 - Anchor Type         Paragraph

    5 - Vertical Position   0"

    6 - Horizontal Position Full

    7 - Size                6.5" wide x 0.723" (high)

    8 - Wrap Text Around Box Yes

    9 - Edit




Selection: 0
```

Figure 3-44.   Graphics box menu used to insert an equation into the document

4. To create or edit an equation, choose **9** for **E**dit. The equation editor shown in Figure 3-43 appears.

5. Type the equation. To select commands, symbols, and functions from the list at the right side of the screen, press List (F5) and use the arrow keys to move through the commands or symbols. Pressing PGDN or PGUP displays a different section. The sections are named Commands, Large, Symbols, Greek, Arrows, Sets, Other, and Functions. The contents of these sections are described under "Hints." Move the cursor to the appropriate command, function, or symbol and press ENTER to insert it into the equation.

If a symbol has been assigned a keyword (such as ± for PLUSMINUS), the keyword will be inserted. If you already know the keyword, you can type it instead of selecting it from the list at the right. If a symbol does not have a keyword (look at the bottom of the screen for the word in uppercase letters), the symbol is inserted instead. You can also press CTRL-ENTER to insert a special character instead of its keyword.

You can use either the keyword or the symbol; both cause the symbol to be used in the equation. However, you may want to use the keyword whenever possible so that if the equation is later saved to a file, you can easily see the keyword that represents a symbol instead of a box (which will appear if it is a nondisplayable character in the regular editing screen).

6. When you are finished, press Screen (CTRL-F3) or F9 to display the equation in the upper section of the screen. If you have not followed the proper syntax for entering the equation, you may see the message, "ERROR: Incorrect format." If this happens, the cursor is placed at the point at which the error occurred and lets you try again. After making editing changes, press Screen (CTRL-F3) or F9 to redisplay the equation above.

The upper part of the screen usually displays an equation 500 percent larger than normal to make it legible. As the equation grows to fit the upper part of the screen, the percentage is reduced to enable you to see as much of the equation as possible. This percentage has nothing to do with how large the equation is when it prints. Press Switch (SHIFT-F3) if you find it necessary to scale the equation up (PGUP) or down (PGDN) in size to see a section of the equation in greater detail or view the entire equation at once. You can also use the arrow keys to move the equation from side to side or up and down. To return the equation to its original state, press Go To (CTRL-HOME).

A double line at the right side of the "current" box tells you which window the cursor is in. In Figure 3-43, you can see that the cursor is in the lower box because its right side is a double line. Press Switch (SHIFT-F3) or Exit (F7) when you are finished to move back to the lower section if you want to continue editing the equation.

7. Press Exit (F7) when you are finished. You will remain in the menu shown in Figure 3-44.

8. Make any necessary adjustments to this menu and press Exit (F7) again. The graphics box labeled "EQU n" (where n is the number of the equation) is inserted into the document.

Hints

WordPerfect equations have been preset to print without a border and will take all the space between the left and right margins. This does not mean that the equation will be stretched to fit the margins but that text from the document will not print to one side or the other.

Equations are preset to print as graphics. They will be printed in either a Helvetica, Times Roman, or Courier font—whichever most closely matches the document's initial base font (or the font that is current if an equation options code [Equ Opt] is inserted into the document). Other options for printing—such as the size of font used for printing, the placement of the equation, and borders—will be discussed in "Printing Equations" and "Setup Options" later in this section.

This section gives you all the options you need to enter an equation. First, you will learn the rules, or "syntax," that need to be followed to reduce the chances of getting the "ERROR: Incorrect format" message.

Next, you will find a list of all symbols and special characters, and the options available for entering them into an equation. Among these options is choosing a specific keyboard layout that can be used to insert special characters directly from the keyboard instead of selecting them from the list or entering their names.

A section on printing is next, followed by a section that tells you how to save equations to a file so they can be retrieved and used in another equation later.

Entering Equations

You can type spaces and press ENTER to help format an equation and make it more readable; however, they have no effect on the equation when it is displayed and printed. If you want a space included in the equation, you need to use the following commands.

~   Insert a space

`   Insert a thin space (1/4th of a normal space)

If you need to insert a tilde (~) or grave (`) character into an equation, you can use the literal command (\) first. This tells the equation editor to take the next character and insert it as is without translating it. For example, \~ would insert a tilde and \` would insert a grave without translating them as spaces.

ENTER is used only to format an equation in the editing screen (the lower section of the equation editor) and cannot be used to start a new line. If you need to insert a new line, use # instead. Other commands such as OVER, BINOM, STACK, STACKALIGN, and MATRIX cause equations or parts of equations to be placed over one another. See "Commands" in this chapter for details.

If you want several items in the equation to be treated as a group, place braces { } around them. For example, a minus sign and a number are treated as two separate items. If the number includes a decimal point, the decimal point is also viewed as a separate item. To make items one group, use braces, as in $\{-234.56\}$.

If you want to find the square root of **a+b**, you would use the command SQRT, meaning square root. If you type it in the equation editor as **sqrt a+b**, you will get the example on the left. If you want **a+b** to be treated as a group, enter it as **sqrt {a+b}** (with braces) to display the result shown on the right.

$$\sqrt{a} + b \qquad\qquad \sqrt{a + b}$$

If you want to insert a left or right brace as part of the equation and not indicate a group, you can use the "literal" (backslash) command.

The following operators are not available from the list of commands at the right, but you can type them directly into any equation:

+	Plus
−	Minus
*	Multiply
/	Divide
=	Equal
<	Less than
>	Greater than
!	Not

Other characters that you can enter as operators are ? . ¦ @ " , and ;.

If you prefer an "x" instead of "*" to represent multiplication, you can use the TIMES command (type **times**) to insert a graphical "x" that will display and print in the regular font. If you do not use TIMES, but type an x instead, it is considered a variable and will print in italics.

Some of these operators can also be combined to create other operators such as + − (plus minus ±), > = (greater than or equal to ≥), or ! = (not equal ≠).

Commands

The commands included in the list on the right side of the screen in the equation editor are used to format the equation. These commands can be inserted into the equation by typing them (uppercase or lowercase is acceptable) or selecting them from the list at the right. Press List (F5), move the cursor to the command, and then press ENTER.

The following is a list of commands and a description of their functions. All the commands are in uppercase to make them more recognizable. They can, however, be entered in uppercase or lowercase, because WordPerfect is not case sensitive. The commands are listed in the order in which they are found in the list.

Examples of common structures and how they should be entered appear under "Applications" later in this section.

OVER   **Fraction**

OVER places one variable over another to create a fraction. A dynamic line (one that will be sized according the length of the variables) will be drawn between them. In the following equation

{a + b} OVER {(x − y)(2x − 4xy + y)}

the group **{a + b}** is placed over the groups **{(x − y)(2x − 4xy + y)}**. Notice that braces were used to indicate which sections were to be used. If braces were not included, it would appear as if the "b" were over the "(".

$$\frac{a+b}{(x-y\ (2x-4xy+y)}$$

The OVERSM command is exactly like the OVER command, but it is printed in a font that is one size smaller.

SUP and SUB, ^ or _   Superscript and Subscript

SUP or ^ is used to indicate that the next variable (or group) is to be superscripted. SUB or _ (underscore character) indicates that the next variable (or group) is to be subscripted. If you are using SUP or SUB, you need to include a space before and after the command (x SUP y, for example). If you are using the characters ^ or _ instead, a space is not required (**x^y**).

   If you want a character to be both superscripted and subscripted, use the subscript command first. In the following equation,

$$X_y^{2-z}$$

x has both a superscript and a subscript. Notice the order and the braces that indicate a group:

   x_y^{2−z}

You can also use SUP and SUB on functions and large operators to indicate upper and lower limits. For example, if you want to show an equation that says "integral from 0 to infinity," but you want to have the zero and infinity symbol printed at the sides, you would type the equation **int _ 0^inf**. It would then appear as:

$$\int_0^\infty$$

The "from" and "to" parts of the equation (either a single character or a group) are placed in the normal location (upper side and lower side). Two other commands, FROM and TO, are also used to indicate upper and lower limits, but the limits are printed on the *top* and *bottom* instead of on the side. See "FROM and TO" in this section for more information.

SQRT and NROOT   Square Root and Nth Root

Use the SQRT command to indicate a square root or the NROOT command to indicate the *n*th root of a variable. Both are sized horizontally and vertically to fit the size of the variable.

To indicate the square root of **x+y**, enter the equation, **SQRT {x+y}**. Notice that braces are used to indicate that x and y are treated as one item. The syntax for entering NROOT is NROOT n x (where n is the nth root) and x is the variable or group. Both are used in the equation

NROOT 3 {{SQRT {a+b}} OVER {r−s}}

with the result shown here:

$$\sqrt[3]{\frac{\sqrt{a+b}}{r-s}}$$

FROM and TO   **Limits**

You can use FROM and TO to set upper and lower limits on a function, written in the following manner: **x FROM y TO z**. Both y and z would be printed in a smaller font above and below x. For example, the equation

INT FROM 0 TO INF (integral from 0 to infinity)

would print as follows with the upper and lower limits printed on the top and bottom of the integral symbol:

$$\int_{0}^{\infty}$$

You do not have to match the FROM and TO commands. For example, many equations include only the FROM statement to print the lower limit under the function or symbol, as shown in the equation **SUM FROM {n−1}**:

$$\sum_{n-1}$$

LEFT and RIGHT   **Left and Right Delimiters**

You can use LEFT and RIGHT to place left and right delimiters (such as parentheses, brackets, or lines) around parts of an equation or the whole equation. The delimiter automatically increases or decreases according to the size of the equation it encloses. When you use either command, follow it with one of the following characters or commands (taken from the Large category in the equation editor):

(	Left parenthesis
)	Right parenthesis
[	Left bracket
]	Right bracket
/	Slash
LINE	Single vertical line (│)
DLINE	Double vertical line (║)
LBRACE	Left brace ({)
RBRACE	Right brace (})
LANGLE	Left angle bracket (<)
RANGLE	Right angle bracket (>)
LCEIL	Left ceiling (⌈)
RCEIL	Right ceiling (⌉)
LFLOOR	Left floor (⌊)
RFLOOR	Right floor (⌋)

The following equation

LEFT [{SQRT {a+b}} OVER {x−y} RIGHT]

would display as follows:

$$\left[\frac{\sqrt{a+b}}{x-y} \right]$$

Always use LEFT and RIGHT together. However, if you want one side open, you can follow LEFT or RIGHT with a period (as in **LEFT .** or **RIGHT .**). This type of example might be useful if you want to use a large right angle bracket (>) on the right side to indicate that part of the equation is greater than another part. The left side, however, would be open.

STACK and STACKALIGN   Vertical Stack and Stack with Align

Because ENTER is used to format equations in the lower part of the screen and does not actually insert a new line, you can use the pound sign (#) to act as the ENTER key to start a new line.

You can also use STACK and STACKALIGN to stack equations or parts of equations on top of each other. The difference between the two commands is that STACKALIGN can be used to stack equations *and* align them.

The syntax for entering the STACK command is **STACK {x # y}** where x and y represent different equations. The # tells the equation editor where to break the line (a row delimiter). Even though only two equations are used in this example (x and y), you can stack as many groups as you want by using # to indicate where each section should break (**STACK {a+b # c−d # x+y}** would stack three equations).

STACKALIGN uses the & symbol to indicate where the equations should be aligned. If you enter

STACKALIGN {2x+60&=180 # 2x&=180−60 # 2x&=120 #
    x&=60}

the various parts of the equation will be aligned at the & from line to line (appearing to be aligned at the equal sign):

$$2x + 60 = 180$$
$$2x = 180 - 60$$
$$2x = 120$$
$$x = 60$$

Remember that you can press ENTER and use spaces to help format the equation. If it is easier for you to see the rows as you intend them to be displayed, you can press ENTER after the # symbol. The equation would then appear as follows in the lower section of the screen:

STACKALIGN {2x + 60& = 180 #
2x& = 180 − 60 #
2x& = 120 #
x& = 60}

If STACK had been used in the example instead of STACKALIGN, the equations would each be centered on the line. If you want to align sections differently (align equations at the left or right, for example), you can use the ALIGNL and ALIGNR commands. (Although you can use these commands with STACK, they should not, however, be used with STACKALIGN, because they would conflict with the alignment character.) The following equation

STACK {4x − 300 # (x − y)(2x + 8xy − 4y)(3x + 5y)}

would be printed with the upper section of the equation centered over the lower section as shown here:

$$4x - 300$$
$$(x - y)\ (2x + 8xy - 4y)\ (3x + 5y)$$

If you want the upper section aligned at the lower section's left or right "margin," you can use the ALIGNL or ALIGNR command before the section to be aligned, as shown in the following equation:

STACK {ALIGNL 4x − 300 # (x − y)(2x + 8xy − 4y)(3x + 5y)}

$$4x - 300$$
$$(x-y)\,(2x+8xy-4y)\,(3x+5y)$$

Because equations are normally centered, the ALIGNC command would only be repetitious. It is used only in conjunction with the MATFORM command. MATFORM decides how each column of a matrix is to be aligned, and even if a column is to be centered, it must be specified with the ALIGNC command.

MATRIX and MATFORM   Matrix and Matrix Format

The MATRIX command formats an equation into rows and columns. The MATFORM command is optional and lets you specify the alignment by which the matrix is to be formatted.

The syntax for entering a matrix is

MATRIX {x & y # a & b}

where & is used to separate columns and # is used to separate rows. The equation

```
MATRIX {1 &0  &⋯ &0  &0  &⋯ &0 #
        0 &1  &~ &⋅⋅ &⋅⋅ &~ &~ #
        ⋮ &~ &⋱ &⋮  &⋮  &~ &⋮ #
        0 &~ &⋯ &1  &0  &⋯ &0}
```

would appear as:

$$
\begin{matrix}
1 & 0 & \cdots & 0 & 0 & \cdots & 0 \\
0 & 1 & & & & & \\
\vdots & & \ddots & \vdots & \vdots & & \vdots \\
0 & & \cdots & 1 & 0 & \cdots & 0
\end{matrix}
$$

Notice that when a column should remain blank, a space (~) is used. If you do not use a space, you will see the error message "Incorrect format" because some type of character must be entered.

Because most matrix equations usually require some type of left and right bracket (delimiter), you might consider using the LEFT command at the beginning of the equation and the RIGHT command at the end. Of course, LEFT and RIGHT would be followed by one of the delimiters listed in "Left and Right Dilimeters" ([ ], ( ), and so on).

Each column in a matrix is centered by default. If you want to change the alignment for any or all columns, use the MATFORM command. MATFORM is used within the MATRIX command and tells the equation editor how to align each column (using ALIGNL, ALIGNC, and ALIGNR). It would be entered as follows:

MATRIX {MATFORM {ALIGNL & ALIGNC & ALIGNR}
    x & y & z # a & b & c}

with an alignment command for each column. Since there are three columns in the example, three alignment commands are needed. The column separator (&) is used to separate them.

FUNC   User Function

The FUNC (function) command lets you specify that the text following it should be printed in the base font. Variables such as a, $b1$, and xyz are normally printed in italics, while functions are printed in the base font. For example, if you typed the letters **cos**, they would be recognized as a function and would be printed in the base font. However, if you prefer typing **cosine**, the equation editor would not recognize it as a valid function (recognizing only cos, Cos, or COS as valid) and would print it in italics, as it would any other variable.

To correct the situation, you would place the FUNC command in front of the text in question. Entering **FUNC cosine** would cause the word "cosine" to be treated as a function and would print it in the base font.

If you want to italicize a function that is normally printed in the base font, you can use the ITAL command (see "Bold and Italic" in this section).

UNDERLINE and OVERLINE   Underline and Overline

The UNDERLINE and OVERLINE commands let you place a line under or over part of an equation. (If you want a line between two items, consider using the OVER command, which formats parts of an equation as a fraction.)

To use the commands, enter **Underline** or **Overline** and then the text to be underlined or overlined. Groups of items should be enclosed in braces { }. In the following example, the words "one" and "two" are considered single items, and they do not need braces. The equation

$$t = \{OVERLINE\ x\_one - OVERLINE\ x\_two\}\ OVER\ s\_D$$

would print as follows:

$$t = \frac{\overline{x}_{one} - \overline{x}_{two}}{s_D}$$

If you wanted to place the overline above each x without including the subscripted "one" and "two," you would enter the equation as

$$t = \{\{OVERLINE\ x\}\_one - \{OVERLINE\ x\}\_two\}\ OVER\ s\_D$$

Note that a new set of braces has been included around the OVER-LINE command and x so that only that character is overlined.

{ and }   Start and End a Group

As previously discussed, items should be grouped with braces if you want them to be treated as a single unit. In the following illustrations you can see how important it is to designate groups and how much they can change the meaning of an equation if you have not used braces. In the example on the left the equation reads **underline a + b**. The equation on the right was entered as **underline {a + b}**.

$$\underline{a} + b \qquad \underline{a + b}$$

Remember to place braces around negative numbers and numbers containing a decimal point. Because the minus sign and decimal points are considered separate items, they are not treated as one group unless you place them between braces as shown here:

$\{-10\}$, $\{10.03\}$, or $\{-1.489\}$

Braces are also used to indicate the sections of the equation to be affected by other commands, such as STACK, MATRIX, and OVER.

HORZ and VERT   Horizontal and Vertical Movement

The HORZ and VERT commands can be used to move sections of an equation or an entire equation up, down, left, or right. Pressing Switch (SHIFT-F3) to enter the upper section of the screen and using the arrow keys to move the equation does not affect printing as these commands will; it only moves the equation so you can see parts of it more easily.

The commands are entered as **horz** n and **vert** n with n representing the amount of space to be moved in 1200ths of an inch *to the right* or *up*. For example, **horz 600** would move the following part of the equation one-half inch to the right. You can use negative numbers to move down or to the left. For example, **vert$-$300** would move the affected part of the equation down one-quarter inch.

Entering the following

STACK $\{Q\_KS\ (0) = 1\ \#\ VERT\ -100\ Q\_KS\ (inf) = 0\}$

would put more space between the stacked upper and lower parts of an equation and would print as follows:

$$Q_{KS}(0)\ = 1$$

$$Q_{KS(\infty)} = 0$$

~ and `   Normal and Thin Space

When you type a space in an equation, it has no effect when the equation is displayed or printed. It is used to separate items and format the text to make it readable.

If you need to insert a space into the equation, type a tilde (~). You can enter a thin space (1/4 the size of a normal space) by typing the backward accent mark ` (you might refer to it as a grave).

If you need these characters in the equation, you can use the backslash (\) just before them. For example, \~ would insert a tilde instead of a normal space and \` would insert a backward accent mark.

BINOM   **Binomial**

You can use BINOM to create a binomial. Enter it as **BINOM** x y. It will be displayed and printed with the x on top and the y on the bottom. The binomial will automatically be placed between left and right parentheses without having to use the LEFT (and RIGHT) commands.

BINOMSM creates a binomial that will be printed in a font one size smaller than normal. The equation following

x + BINOM a b= y−{BINOMSM a b} OVER 2

illustrates how both can be used:

$$x + \binom{a}{b} = y - \frac{\binom{a}{b}}{2}$$

& and #   **Column and Row Separators**

As shown in previous examples, # is used with STACK, STACKALIGN, and MATRIX to show where the row should be broken. It can also be used alone, outside any of these structures, to indicate a new line.

The & sign indicates a new column in the MATRIX and MATFORM commands. A & is also used with STACKALIGN to indicate where the rows should be aligned. See "Vertical Stack and Stack with Align" and "Matrix and Matrix Format" in this section for details.

MATFORM   **Matrix Format**

This command is optional and can be used with the MATRIX command to indicate how the columns within a matrix are to be aligned (at the

left, center, or right) with ALIGNL, ALIGNC, and ALIGNR. See
"Matrix and Matrix Format" in this section for more information.

ALIGNL, ALIGNC, and ALIGNR   Align Left, Center, and Right

When using STACK, OVER, FROM, TO, and MATRIX, the variables
or groups are automatically centered over each other. If you want any
other type of alignment (left or right), you can use either ALIGNL or
ALIGNR to align them at the left or right margin. Although the use of
ALIGNC would be redundant in most cases, you need to use it with
MATFORM for columns that you want centered (some type of alignment must be entered for all columns).

If you wanted to display the equation **sum FROM a TO b**, the a and
b would be centered exactly over the Greek summation symbol. If you
wanted them aligned at the left, you would enter

SUM FROM ALIGNL a TO ALIGNL b

as shown here:

$$\sum_{a}^{b}$$

See "Vertical Stack and Stack with Align" and "Matrix and Matrix
Format" for other examples of how the ALIGN commands can be used.

PHANTOM   Place Holder

The PHANTOM command is entered as **PHANTOM** x, where x is the
variable or group that should be reserved as blank space and not
printed. It is useful when you need to reserve a specific amount of space
equal to x. For example, when you are using STACKALIGN, you can

indicate only one place of alignment per row. To get around that problem, you can use the PHANTOM command to force space that will not print, as shown in the following equation and example:

STACKALIGN {2x − 420& = 360 #
2x PHANTOM {− 420}& = 360 + 420 #
2x PHANTOM {− 420}& = 780 #
PHANTOM 2 x PHANTOM {− 420}& = 390}

$$2x - 420 = 360$$
$$2x \quad\quad = 360 + 420$$
$$2x \quad\quad = 780$$
$$x \quad\quad = 390$$

You can also use PHANTOM to trick the equation editor into thinking that a variable or character is present. For example, both SUB and SUP need some type of symbol or variable to which they can be attached. Therefore, you cannot use _0^9 T_3^8 to create superscripts and subscripts on both sides of the "T." Instead, you could use the PHANTOM command, as shown in the equation

{PHANTOM .}_0^9 T_3^8

Note that the entire PHANTOM command is enclosed in braces so that it is treated as one character. A period was used as the phantom character, because it is small and does not take up much space.

$$^{9}_{0} T \, ^{8}_{3}$$

No Delimiter

A period is used with either the LEFT or RIGHT command to indicate that there is no matching delimiter (left or right bracket) being used. See "Left and Right Delimiters" earlier in this section for details.

\   **Literal**

You can place a backslash before $\sim$, `, {, }, (or any other symbol that has a function in the equation editor) to insert it as a symbol and not as a function. For example, typing \$\sim$ would insert the tilde character instead of a space. You can also use LBRACE and RBRACE instead of \{ or \} if you want the braces to grow with the equation.

BOLD and ITAL   Bold and Italic

These two commands can be used to boldface or italicize part of an equation. It will boldface or italicize the next variable or group enclosed in braces. **BOLD x + y** would only bold the x. **BOLD xy** would bold both the x and the y, because they would be considered as one variable (a variable begins with an alphabetic character and ends with a nonalphabetic character such as a space or a symbol). To bold **x + y**, you would enclose them in braces as in **BOLD {x + y}**. **BOLD x^2** would bold both the x and superscripted 2 because they are considered one unit.

Variables (a, bc, and $x1$) are usually italicized, and functions (cos, tan, and so on) are not. If you want to italicize something that is not normally italicized, use the ITAL command. Enter it using the same rules mentioned for BOLD.

OVERSM and BINOMSM   OVER and BINOM in a Smaller Font

OVERSM and BINOMSM are commands that work exactly like OVER and BINOM, except that they cause the resulting fraction or binomial to print in a smaller font.

LINESPACE   Vertical Line Spacing

Instead of using the VERT command to add or decrease space between specific parts of an equation, you can use the LINESPACE command to control all vertical spacing in STACK, STACKALIGN, and MATRIX structures. If you used # to start a new line outside one of the structures, LINESPACE will not affect the vertical spacing between those lines; only STACK, STACKALIGN, and MATRIX are affected.

When entering the LINESPACE command, follow it with a number from 0 to 400, indicating the percentage of line spacing (100 is 100 percent, meaning normal). For example, **linespace 50** would decrease the spacing by half, and **linespace 400** would increase it to four times the normal amount.

The command must come before a STACK, STACKALIGN, or MATRIX command, or it will not affect the line spacing within those structures.

Special Characters, Functions, and Symbols

In this section is a list of characters, functions, and symbols that are available in the list at the right in the equation editor. To view or select them while in the equation editor, press List (F5), and then PGUP or PGDN to scroll through the lists. Included is their keyword (if applicable), function or description, and WordPerfect character number.

There are several ways to insert the symbols, characters, or functions into an equation:

• Type the keyword (available for all categories except arrows). Keywords for all categories except Greek are not case sensitive, meaning that you can enter them in uppercase or lowercase. Uppercase or lowercase Greek characters are inserted based on whether the keywords are entered in uppercase or lowercase.

• Press List (F5), move to the symbol, and press ENTER to insert it. If no keyword is available, the character will be inserted instead.

• From the list of symbols, press CTRL-ENTER to insert the symbol—not the keyword.

• Use Compose (CTRL-2) and type the character set and character number.

• Use the Equations keyboard layout to enter common symbols with a single keystroke (ALT-A for the alpha character, ALT-B for beta, and so on). Instructions for using a keyboard layout in equations is discussed in "Using a Keyboard Layout" later in this section.

If you are in the list at the right and want to leave it without inserting the current character, symbol, command, or function into the equation, press Cancel (F1) or Exit (F7).

The symbols are divided into sections in the order in which they are found: Large, Symbols, Greek, Arrows, Sets, Other, and Functions.

Large   The symbols listed in Table 3-2 are from the Large category. There are usually two sizes of the same symbol available. Typically, you would use the larger symbols within a line (a character graphics box). In that case, you might want to consider using the smaller symbol to give it less impact on the line height.

Symbols   The Symbols category contains a list of miscellaneous items, including primes, binary, and relational symbols, as shown in Table 3-3.

Greek   This is the only category in which the keyword is case sensitive. If the keyword is entered in uppercase, the uppercase Greek character will be inserted. If entered in lowercase, the lowercase Greek character will be inserted. For example, type **gamma** to insert γ or **GAMMA** to insert Γ. See Table 3-4 for a list of available Greek symbols.

Arrows   This category contains 34 arrows, 14 triangles, and other symbols such as hollow circles and squares. Keywords are not available for these symbols, as shown in Table 3-5, with two exceptions. To display the single left arrow and single right arrow, you can enter either $\leftarrow$ or $\rightarrow$.

Sets   The Sets category contains a variety of set symbols, relational operators, and some Fraktur and hollow letters. See Table 3-6 for the choices in this set.

Other   The Other category contains miscellaneous symbols such as diacriticals (vec, hat, bar, and so on) and ellipses. See Table 3-7 for a list of these symbols.

Functions   The following is a list of mathematical functions available in the functions screen. You can type each in uppercase or lowercase, and they will appear in the equation as they are typed. If you select them from the list, they are inserted as lowercase.

$\sum$	SUM	Summation	7,73
$\sum$	SMALLSUM	Small Sum	7,6
$\int$	INT	Integral	7,76
$\int$	SMALLINT	Small Integral	7,9
$\oint$	OINT	Contour Integral	7,77
$\oint$	SMALLOINT	Small Contour Integral	7,10
$\prod$	PROD	Product	7,74
$\prod$	SMALLPROD	Small Product	7,7
$\coprod$	COPROD	Coproduct	7,75
$\coprod$	SMALLCOPROD	Small Coproduct	7,8
$\cap$	CAP	Intersection	7,62
$\bigcap$	BIGCAP	Big Intersection	7,145
$\cup$	CUP	Union	7,61
$\bigcup$	BIGCUP	Big Union	7,144
$\uplus$	UPLUS	Multiset Union (U Plus)	7,146
$\biguplus$	BIGUPLUS	Big U Plus	7,147
$\sqcap$	SQCAP	Square Intersection	7,221
$\bigsqcap$	BIGSQCAP	Big Square Intersection	7,222
$\sqcup$	SQCUP	Square Union	7,148
$\bigsqcup$	BIGSQCUP	Big Square Union	7,149
$\vee$	OR	Logical Or	7,152
$\bigvee$	BIGVEE	Big Vee	7,153
$\wedge$	AND	Logical And	7,150
$\bigwedge$	BIGWEDGE	Big Wedge	7,151
$\oplus$	OPLUS	Circle Plus	7,156
$\bigoplus$	BIGOPLUS	Big Circle Plus	7,157
$\ominus$	OMINUS	Circle Minus	7,180
$\bigominus$	BIGOMINUS	Big Circle Minus	7,181
$\otimes$	OTIMES	Circle Multiply	7,154
$\bigotimes$	BIGOTIMES	Big Circle Multiply	7,155

Table 3-2.   Symbols Found in the Large Category

⊘	ODIV	Circle Divide	7,182
⊕	BIGODIV	Big Circle Divide	7,183
⊙	ODOT	Circle Dot	7,158
⊙	BIGODOT	Big Circle Dot	7,159
(	(	Left Parenthesis	
)	)	Right Parenthesis	
[	[	Left Bracket	
]	]	Right Bracket	
⟦	LDBRACK	Left Double Bracket	7,184
⟧	RDBRACK	Right Double Bracket	7,191
{	LBRACE	Left Brace	7,21
⟨	LANGLE	Left Angle	7,128
⟩	RANGLE	Right Angle	7,132
		LINE	Vertical Line	7,11
‖	DLINE	Double Vertical Line	7,16

Table 3-2.   Symbols Found in the Large Category (*continued*)

SYMBOLS

′	'	Prime	6,45
″	''	Double Prime	6,46
‴	'''	Triple Prime	6,113
∞	INF	Infinity	6,19
∂	PARTIAL	Partial Derivative	6,44
∇	GRAD	Nabla (Gradient)	6,43
×	TIMES	Multiplication Sign (x)	6,39
÷	DIV	Division Sign	6,8
±	+-	Plus Or Minus	6,1
∓	-+	Minus Or Plus	6,42
·	CDOT	Center Dot	6,31
⊻	XOR	Logical Exclusive Or	6,87
≤	< =	Less Than Or Equal	6,2
≥	> =	Greater Than Or Equal	6,3
≪	< <	Much Less Than	6,77
≫	> >	Much Greater Than	6,78

Table 3-3.   Items Found in the Symbols Category

≪	LLL	Much Much Less	6,123
≫	GGG	Much Much Greater	6,124
≠	!=	Not Equal	6,99
¬	NOT	Logical Not	6,20
≺	PREC	Precedes	6,117
≻	SUCC	Succeeds (Follows)	6,119
≼	PRECEQ	Precedes Or Equals	6,118
≽	SUCCEQ	Succeeds (Follows) Or Equals	6,120
≡	==	Equivalent	6,14
≢	NEQUIV	Not Equivalent	6,100
~	SIM	Similar	6,12
≃	SIMEQ	Similar Or Equal	6,115
≈	APPROX	Approximately Equal	6,13
≅	CONG	Congruent	6,116
∝	PROPTO	Proportional To	6,4
≐	DOTEQ	Equal by Definition	6,175
∥	PARALLEL	Parallel	6,17
⊥	PERP	Perpendicular To	6,89
∀	FORALL	For All	6,122
∃	EXISTS	There Exists	6,121
∴	THEREFORE	Therefore	6,102
∵	BECAUSE	Because	6,101
∷	IDENTICAL	Identical	6,103
∔	DSUM	Direct Sum (Dot Plus)	6,174
≟	QEQUAL	Questioned Equality	6,217
≒	IMAGE	Image (Falling Dots Equals)	6,176
≓	RIMAGE	Reverse Image	6,177
⋈	ISO	Isomorphic	6,178
⋫	NISO	Not Isomorphic	6,210
⋍	ASYMEQ	Asymptotically Equivalent	6,179
≭	NASYMEQ	Not Asymptotically Equivalent	6,207
⌣	SMILE	Smile	6,141
⌢	FROWN	Frown	6,142
≬	BETWEEN	Between (Quantic)	6,182
≀	WREATH	Wreath Product	6,183
⊤	TOP	Top	6,88
⊢	ASSERT	Assertion	6,91
⊣	MASSERT	Mirrored Assertion	6,92
⊨	MODELS	Models	6,100
∠	ANGLE	Angle	6,79
∡	MSANGLE	Measured Angle	6,168
∢	SANGLE	Spherical Angle	6,169
∟	RTANGLE	Right Angle	6,218
°	DEG	Degree	6,36

Table 3-3.   Items Found in the Symbols Category (*continued*)

α	alpha		8,1	χ	chi		8,47
β	beta		8,3	ψ	psi		8,49
γ	gamma		8,7	ω	omega		8,51
δ	delta		8,9	A	ALPHA		8,0
ε	epsilon		8,11	B	BETA		8,2
ε	varepsilon	epsilon (variant)	8,61	Γ	GAMMA		8,6
ζ	zeta		8,13	Δ	DELTA		8,8
η	eta		8,15	E	EPSILON		8,10
θ	theta		8,17	Z	ZETA		8,12
ϑ	vartheta	theta (variant)	8,62	H	ETA		8,14
ι	iota		8,19	Θ	THETA		8,16
κ	kappa		8,21	I	IOTA		8,18
λ	lambda		8,23	K	KAPPA		8,20
μ	mu		8,25	Λ	LAMBDA		8,22
ν	nu		8,27	M	MU		8,24
ξ	xi		8,29	N	NU		8,26
o	omicron		8,31	Ξ	XI		8,28
π	pi		8,33	O	OMICRON		8,30
ϖ	varpi	pi (variant)	8,64	Π	PI		8,32
ρ	rho		8,35	P	RHO		8,34
ϱ	varrho	rho (variant)	8,65	Σ	SIGMA		8,36
σ	sigma		8,37	T	TAU		8,40
ς	varsigma	sigma (variant)	8,39	Y	UPSILON		8,42
τ	tau		8,41	Φ	PHI		8,44
υ	upsilon		8,43	X	CHI		8,46
φ	phi		8,45	Ψ	PSI		8,48
φ	varphi	phi (variant)	8,67	Ω	OMEGA		8,50

Table 3-4.   Greek Symbols

←	Left Arrow	6,22	↓	Down Harpoon Right	6,157
→	Right Arrow	6,21	↩	Hook Left Arrow	6,145
↑	Up Arrow	6,23	↪	Hook Right Arrow	6,146
↓	Down Arrow	6,24	↦	Maps To	6,147
↔	Left & Right Arrow	6,25	◁	Triangle Left	6,170
↕	Up & Down Arrow	6,26	▷	Triangle Right	6,171
⇇	Two Left Arrows	6,259	△	Triangle Up	6,172
⇉	Two Right Arrows	6,158	▽	Triangle Down	6,173
⇄	Left & Right Arrows	6,55	◁	Small Triangle Left	6,138
⇄	Right & Left Arrows	6,54	▷	Small Triangle Right	6,139
⇐	Double Left Arrow	6,57	△	Big Triangle Up	6,136
⇒	Double Right Arrow	6,56	▽	Big Triangle Down	6,137
⇑	Double Up Arrow	6,58	◀	Solid Triangle Left	6,28
⇓	Double Down Arrow	6,59	▶	Solid Triangle Right	6,27
⇔	Double Left & Right Arrow	6,60	▲	Solid Triangle Up	6,29
⇕	Double Up & Down Arrow	6,61	▼	Solid Triangle Down	6,30
↗	North East Arrow	6,62	△	Defined As	6,110
↘	South East Arrow	6,63	▲	Corresponds To	6,181
↙	South West Arrow	6,65	⋈	Bowtie	6,140
↖	North West Arrow	6,64	★	Solid Star	6,112
↝	Curly Right Arrow	6,144	★	Big Solid Star	6,184
↼	Left Harpoon Up	6,148	◇	Diamond	6,95
↽	Left Harpoon Down	6,149	◆	Solid Diamond	6,96
⇀	Right Harpoon Up	6,150	◇	Hollow Diamond	6,111
⇁	Right Harpoon Down	6,151	○	Big Circle	6,143
⇋	Left & Right Harpoons	6,153	∘	Circle.	6,109
⇌	Right & Left Harpoons	6,152	∘	Small Circle	6,33
↿	Up Harpoon Left	6,154	•	Small Solid Circle	6,34
↾	Up Harpoon Right	6,155	□	Square	6,93
⇃	Down Harpoon Left	6,156	■	Solid Square	6,94

Table 3-5.   Symbols Found in the Arrows Category

\	SETMINUS	Set Minus (Figure Backslash)	6,7
⊂	SUBSET	Proper Subset	6,67
⊃	SUPSET	Proper Superset	6,68
⊆		Reflex Subset (Contained In)	6,69
⊇		Reflex Superset (Contains)	6,70
⊊		Subset But Not Equal	6,126
⊋		Superset But Not Equal	6,127
⊏	SQSUBSET	Square Proper Subset	6,130
⊐	SQSUPSET	Square Proper Superset	6,133
⊑		Square Reflex Subset	6,131
⊒		Square Reflex Superset	6,134
⊑		Square Subset, Not Equal	6,132
⊒		Square Superset, Not Equal	6,135
ε	IN	Member (Element)	6,15
∉	NOTIN	Not a Member	6,209
∋	OWNS	Owns (Contains As A Member)	6,71
∅	EMPTYSET	Empty Set	6,72
⋃		Double Union	6,160
⋂		Double Intersection	6,161
⟨		Double Subset	6,162
⟩		Double Superset	6,163
⊄		Not Subset	6,197
⊅		Not Superset	6,198
⊈		Not Reflex Subset	6,199
⊉		Not Reflex Superset	6,200
⋢		Square Not Subset	6,201
⋣		Square Not Superset	6,202
⋤		Square Not Reflex Subset	6,203
⋥		Square Not Reflex Superset	6,204
≮		Not Less Than	6,185
≰		Not Less Than or Equal	6,186
≯		Not Greater Than	6,187
≱		Not Greater Than or Equal	6,188
≁		Not Similar	6,189
≄		Not Similar or Equal	6,190
≇		Not Congruent	6,191
≉		Not Approximately Equal	6,192
⊀		Does Not Precede	6,193
⋠		Neither Precedes nor Equals	6,194
⊁		Does Not Follow	6,195

Table 3-6. Symbols Available in the Sets Category

⊀		Neither Follows nor Equals	6,196
∦		Not Parallel	6,205
∤		Does Not Divide	6,206
∄		There Never Exists	6,208
ℜ	REAL	Real (R Fraktur)	6,52
ℑ	IMAG	Imaginary (I Fraktur)	6,51
ℭ		C Fraktur	6,106
ℨ		Z Fraktur	6,107
℘		Weierstrass	6,53
℘		Capital Weierstrass	6,108
ℏ		Planck's Constant	6,50
ℒ		Laplace Transform (Script L)	6,105
ℰ		Script E	6,211
ℱ		Fourier Transform (Script F)	6,212
ℂ		Complex Number (Hollow C)	6,213
𝕀		Integer (Hollow I)	6,214
ℕ		Natural Number (Hollow N)	6,215
ℝ		Real Number (Hollow R)	6,216
℧	MHO	Mho	6,167
Å	ANGSTROM	Angstrom	6,35

Table 3-6.   Symbols Available in the Sets Category (*continued*)

→	VEC	Vector Above; x VEC	6,47
‾	BAR	Bar (Overline); x BAR	1,21
^	HAT	Hat (Above); x HAT	1,3
´	ACUTE	Acute Accent; x ACUTE	1,6
`	GRAVE	Grave Accent; x GRAVE	1,0
˘	BREVE	Breve Accent; x BREVE	1,22
˙	DOT	Dot Above; x DOT	1,15
¨	DDOT	Double Dot Above; x DDOT	1,7
⃛	DDDOT	Triple Dot Above; x DDDOT	6,224
˚	CIRCLE	Circle Above; x CIRCLE	1,14
~	TILDE	Tilde Above; x TILDE	1,2
⃛	DYAD	Dyad Above; x DYAD	6,225
⋯	DOTSAXIS	Ellipses (centered	6,220
…	DOTSLOW	Ellipses (on baseline)	6,221
⋮	DOTSVERT	Ellipses (vertical)	6,222
⋰	DOTSDIAG	Ellipses (diagonal)	6,223

Table 3-7.   The Other Category Includes Diacriticals and Ellipses

Functions are displayed and printed in the base font and are not italicized. If you prefer typing the entire name instead of the abbreviation that is recognized by the equation editor, use the FUNC command first, followed by the name you prefer (for example, **func cosine**). It will then be recognized as a function instead of a variable and will print in the base font instead of being italicized.

Keyword	Description
cos	Cosine
sin	Sine
tan	Tangent
arcos	Arc cosine
arcsin	Arc sine
arctan	Arc tangent
cosh	Hyperbolic cosine
sinh	Hyperbolic sine
tanh	Hyperbolic tangent
cot	Cotangent
coth	Hyperbolic cotangent
sec	Secant
cosec	Cosecant
exp	Exponent
log	Logarithm
ln	Natural logarithm
lim	Limit
liminf	Limit inferior
limsup	Limit superior
min	Minimum
max	Maximum
gcd	Greatest common denominator
arc	Arc function

det   Determinant

mod   Modulo

Using a Keyboard Layout

An option in Setup (SHIFT-F1) lets you select a keyboard that will be used when you are entering equations in the equation editor. To make editing easier, you can assign common functions, symbols, and characters to a single key combination. The selection of a keyboard for equation editing has no effect on the keyboard normally selected through Setup (SHIFT-F1).

A keyboard that contains many common symbols and characters needed in an equation has been included with WordPerfect. After installation, you should find it on the disk or directory specified for macros and keyboards under the name EQUATION.WPK. If you cannot find it and want to use or edit it, run Install and copy the Keyboard Files.

Table 3-8 lists the key assignments in the Equation keyboard layout.

To select this or any other keyboard as the one to be used in the equation editor, follow these steps:

1. Press Setup (SHIFT-F1) and choose 4 for Initial Settings.

2. Choose 3 for Equations. The options shown in Figure 3-45 appear.

3. Choose 5 to select Keyboard for Editing. A list of keyboards appears. If the Equations keyboard is not on the list, you will need to copy or install it into the directory that is designated to store macros and keyboards (via Location of Files in Setup).

4. Move the cursor to the keyboard to be used (Equations, for example), and press ENTER to select it. The name of the selected keyboard is displayed next to the option Keyboard for Editing.

5. Press Exit (F7) when you are finished.

While in the equation editor, press the appropriate keys to insert the characters or text assigned to that key. See "Keyboard Layout" in this chapter for information about assigning characters or macros to keys.

Key	Character or Text Inserted	Description
ALT-TAB		Right arrow
ALT-,	< =	Less than or equal to
ALT-.	> =	Greater than or equal to
ALT-'	SIMEQ	Similar or equal to
ALT--	CONG	Congruent
ALT-=	!=	Not equal to
ALT-\	LINE	Line
ALT-A	α	Alpha
ALT-B	β	Beta
ALT-D	δ	Delta
ALT-E	ϵ	Epsilon
ALT-F	ϕ	Phi
ALT-G	γ	Gamma
ALT-I	INF	INFINITY
ALT-L	λ	Lambda
ALT-M	μ	Mu
ALT-N	η	Eta
ALT-O	ω	Omega
ALT-P	π	Pi
ALT-R	ρ	Rho
ALT-S	σ	Sigma
ALT-T	θ	Theta
ALT-Z	SUP	Superscript
CTRL-TAB	$\leftarrow$	Left arrow
CTRL-B	BAR	Bar
CTRL-D	Δ	DELTA (capital)
CTRL-E	IN	Member (element)
CTRL-F	FROM/TO	From to
CTRL-G	GRAD	Nable (gradient)
CTRL-I	INT	Integral
CTRL-L	OVERLINE	Overline
CTRL-N	GRAD	Nable (gradient)
CTRL-O	OVER	Over
CTRL-P	PARTIAL	Partial
CTRL-Q	SQRT	Square root
CTRL-S	SUM	Sum
CTRL-Z	SUB	Subscript

Table 3-8.   Key Assignments for the Equation Keyboard Layout

```
Setup: Equation Options
      1 - Print as Graphics     Yes
      2 - Graphical Font Size   Default
      3 - Horizontal Alignment  Center
      4 - Vertical Alignment    Center
      5 - Keyboard for Editing




Selection: 0
```

Figure 3-45.   Equations options in Setup

Printing Equations

An equation is preset to print with the following characteristics:

• Equations print graphically (instead of using fonts from the printer).

• Functions (cos, lim, tan, and so on) are printed in the base font (see notes about the font type later).

• Variables (x, $y1$, abc, and so on) are printed in italics.

• Superscripts, subscripts, the small versions of BINOM (BINOMSM) and OVER (OVERSM), and the limits set with the FROM and TO commands will print two-thirds smaller than normal. If a superscript has been superscripted or any other third-level character exists, it will print at one-half the size of the base font.

If the equation is set to print as text instead of graphics, superscripts and other second-level characters will print in the font selected as the superscript font. Third-level characters will print in the superscript font of the superscript font.

• The equation box takes up the space from the left margin to the right margin.

• The equation is centered horizontally and vertically within the graphics box.

• No border lines are placed around the box.

• The graphics box attaches itself to the current Paragraph instead of being placed at an exact location on a page or flowing with the text as a character.

Setup Options

As mentioned previously, you can choose the Setup options for all equations created in the future by pressing Setup (SHIFT-F1) while in the normal editing screen to see the menu in Figure 3-45. To change any of the settings for a single equation, press Setup (SHIFT-F1) while in the equation editor.

Print or Graphics   The first Setup option lets you choose whether to print the equation graphically or as text. Choose Text if your printer cannot print graphics (for example, if you have a daisy-wheel printer). If an equation is printed as text, WordPerfect will search the base font for the characters found in the equation. If a character is not found, automatic font changes and substitute fonts are then searched (see Chapter 5, "Printer Program," for directions on specifying automatic font changes and substitute fonts). If a character or diacritical is not found in either location and your printer can print graphics, it will be printed graphically.

If, for some reason, you want to suppress all graphics printing, press Print (SHIFT-F7), type **G** for **G**raphics Quality, and choose **1** for Do Not Print.

Graphical Font Size   The second option, Graphical Font Size, lets you choose the size of the equation being printed. Equations are normally printed in the same size as the document's initial base font, but you can change the size for all equations or a single equation with this option. Choose the default font size or enter a point size of your own (72 points = 1″).

Note that Graphical Font Size takes effect only if you are printing an equation as graphics. If the option Print as Graphics is set to No, the equation is printed in the document's initial base font.

See "Applications" for a way to use this ability to scale fonts to any size in the equation editor for other applications, such as creating banners, flyers, large headings, and place cards.

Headings   The other options not previously mentioned let you choose how the equation will be placed inside the graphics box. When choosing 3 for Horizontal Alignment, you can choose Left, Center, or Right. Option 4, Vertical Alignment lets you choose Top, Center, or Bottom. Equations are centered both horizontally and vertically by default.

Remember that you can change these options for all equations or a single equation.

Font for Equations   If an equation is set to print graphically, Word-Perfect scans backward through the document for an equations options [Equ Opt] code. If one is found, it checks the current font at that code and then creates the equation in that same size and uses one of the following types of fonts based on the type of font that is current:

Helvetica
Times Roman
Courier

If an equations options [Equ Opt] code is not found, the document's initial base font is used as a guide for the font type and size. To change this font, press Format (SHIFT-F8), choose 3 for Document, and then choose 3 for Initial Base Font.

You can change the size of all equations or a single equation by pressing Setup (SHIFT-F1) from the regular editing screen (affecting all equations created from that time forward), or Setup (SHIFT-F1) from the equation editor (affecting that equation only).

   If you would rather not change the initial base font for the entire document, change the font, insert an [Equ Opt] code by pressing Graphics (ALT-F9), choose **6** for **E**quation and **4** for **O**ptions, press Exit (F7), and then change back to the original font.

Borders and Location

The Equations Options menu affects such things as borders, the amount of spacing inside and outside the box, and the caption. After pressing Graphics (ALT-F9), choose **6** for **E**quation, and then **4** for **O**ptions. The choices made in the menu shown in Figure 3-46 will affect all equations from that point forward.

   As you create each equation, the graphics box menu shown in Figure 3-44 includes options that let you decide whether the equation will be anchored to the current paragraph or a certain position on the page, or whether it will flow with the text as if it were a regular

```
Options: Equation

    1 - Border Style
            Left                         None
            Right                        None
            Top                          None
            Bottom                       None
    2 - Outside Border Space
            Left                         0.083"
            Right                        0.083"
            Top                          0.083"
            Bottom                       0.083"
    3 - Inside Border Space
            Left                         0.083"
            Right                        0.083"
            Top                          0.083"
            Bottom                       0.083"
    4 - First Level Numbering Method     Numbers
    5 - Second Level Numbering Method    Off
    6 - Caption Number Style             [BOLD](1)[bold]
    7 - Position of Caption              Right side
    8 - Minimum Offset from Paragraph    0"
    9 - Gray Shading (% of black)        0%

Selection: 0
```

Figure 3-46.   Options and settings for equations graphics boxes

character (which is useful for in-line equations). See "Graphics Boxes" in this chapter for additional information about creating any type of graphics box, including those containing equations.

Saving and Retrieving Equations

While in the equation editor, you can press Save (F10) to save the current equation to a regular WordPerfect file. You can then retrieve the file in the normal editing screen so you can use some of WordPerfect's editing features, such as Block, Move, and Undelete. If you need to use the equation in another document or need to include it as part of another equation, you can retrieve it into the equation editor by pressing Retrieve (SHIFT-F10) and entering the name of the file.

Equations are automatically saved to and retrieved from the directory specified for documents in the Setup: Location of Files menu. When you press Save (F10), the proper pathname is automatically displayed. If you choose to save it in this directory, press END to go to the end of the pathname and enter the name of the file.

If the equation contains a special character instead of its keyword, it will be retained in the file as a special character. The character will be displayed on the screen if possible; if it cannot be displayed, it will appear as a small box. Regardless of how it is displayed on the editing screen, the character set and number can always be displayed in Reveal Codes (ALT-F3).

Because some special characters cannot be displayed, it might be preferable to use keywords when available so the character is more easily recognized while you are editing in the normal screen.

Applications

Table 3-9 shows a list of common structures found in equations and how you enter them. The next section contains several examples of real equations or parts of equations. If you are entering similar equations, you can study these examples and use them to solve a problem that you might be having when you are entering and formatting equations of your own.

Syntax	Description	Sample Equation	Printed Sample
{ }	Create a group	{2x+y} over {3x-2xy+4y}	$\dfrac{2x+y}{3x-2xy+4y}$
a^x	Superscript x	x^2	x^2
a_x	Subscript x	H_2O	H_2O
a y^x	Simultaneous superscript and subscript (subscript first). Useful for printing upper and lower limits at the side	INT_1^INF	$\int_1^\infty$
a FROM x	Lower limit printed at the bottom	SUM FROM {n-1}	$\sum_{n-1}$
a FROM x TO y	Lower and upper limits printed at the bottom and top	SUM FROM {n-1} TO INF	$\sum_{n-1}^{\infty}$
a diac	Diacriticals (where diac = hat, bar, dot, etc.)	x hat x bar x dot	$\hat{x}$ $\bar{x}$ $\dot{x}$

a'	Primes (where prime can be ' '' or ''')	x' x'' x'''	x' x'' x'''
x OVER y	Fraction	x OVER y	$\dfrac{x}{y}$
BINOM x y	Binomial	BINOM x y	$\dbinom{x}{y}$
SQRT x	Square root of x	SQRT {x+y}	$\sqrt{x+y}$
NROOT n x	Nth root of x (where n is the nth root)	NROOT 10 x	$\sqrt[10]{x}$
LEFT delim RIGHT delim	Left and right delimiters to enclose equations	LEFT[x OVER y RIGHT]	$\left[\dfrac{x}{y}\right]$

Table 3-9.   Common Structures and Examples

Syntax	Description	Sample Equation	Printed Sample
a # b # c or STACK {*a # b # c*}	Stack a, b, and c (# separates rows)	a-2 # b+3 # c TIMES 4	$a-2$ $b+3$ $c \times 4$

STACKALIGN {*a & b #*
    x & y}
	Stack and align on & (i.e., decimal align)	STACKALIGN {x-2&=4 #
		    x&=6}
			$x-2=4$
			$x=6$

MATRIX {*a & b & c #*
    x & y & z}
	Create a matrix where & separates columns and # separates rows	MATRIX {2 & 4 & 8 #
		    16 & 32 & 64 #
		    128 & 256 & x}
			2 4 8
			16 32 64
			128 256 x

ALIGNL, ALIGNC, ALIGNR	Align section within other sections	ALIGNR 0 over ALIGNR 100	$\dfrac{0}{100}$
PHANTOM *x*	Reserve space for x, but don't print	x-2=4 # x PHANTOM {-2} =6	$x-2=4$ x -6
BOLD *x*	Bold x	3.45 = BOLD x	$3.45 = x$

ITAL x	Italicize x	H_ITAL 2O	H_2O
FUNC x	Print x in the base font	FUNC {H_2O}	H_2O
UNDERLINE x	Underline x	Total = UNDERLINE {87.00}	$Total\text{-}\underline{87.00}$
OVERLINE x	Overline x	t = OVERLINE x_one	$t\text{-}\overline{x}_{one}$
{UNDERLINE x}	Underline (or overline) only x without including subscripts or superscripts that may be attached	t = { OVERLINE x}_one	$t\text{-}\overline{x}_{one}$
VERT, HORZ, and LINESPACE	Change amount of space. LINESPACE only valid in STACK, STACKALIGN, or MATRIX structures.	Total: HORZ 100 1,345	$Total:$ 1,345

Table 3-9.   Common Structures and Examples *(continued)*

In each case, the equation is displayed first, with the text used to create the equation shown below.

$$x^2 \qquad y_i^2 \qquad \int_0^{\pi/6} \qquad \int\limits_{i-0}^{\infty}$$

$$\frac{1}{n+1} \qquad \bar{x} \qquad {}_2F_3 \qquad ((x^2)^3)^4 \qquad 2^{x^{2^4}}$$

x^2   y_i^2   INT_0^{pi/6}   INT FROM {i=0} TO INF
1 OVER {n+1}   x bar   {PHANTOM.}_2F_3   ((x^2)^3)^4   2^x^2^4

$$S = \sum_{r \neq s} \left| \alpha_{rs} \right|^2$$

S = SUM FROM {r!=s} ~ LEFT LINE alpha_rs RIGHT LINE^2

$$Q_s^T \;=\; P_1^{(s)} \cdot P_2^{(s)} \cdots P_{n-1}^{(s)}$$

Q_s^T ~ = ~ P_1^{(s)} CDOT P_2^{(s)} DOTSAXIS
P_{n-1}^{(s)}

$$\begin{pmatrix} A & -B \\ B & A \end{pmatrix} \cdot \begin{pmatrix} u \\ v \end{pmatrix} = \lambda \begin{pmatrix} u \\ v \end{pmatrix}$$

LEFT (MATRIX {A & -B # B & A} RIGHT) ~CDOT~
LEFT (STACK   {u # v} RIGHT) ~ = ~ lambda ~
LEFT (STACK   {u # v} RIGHT)

$$h(f) = \int_{-\infty}^{\infty} H(t) e^{-2\pi i f t} \; dt$$

h(f) = INT_{-INF}^INF H(t)e^{-2 pi ift}~dt

$$h(t) = \Delta \sum_{n=-\infty}^{+\infty} h_n \frac{\sin[2\pi fc(t-n\Delta)]}{\pi(t-n\Delta)}$$

h(t)= ΔSUM FROM {n=−INF} TO {+INF} h_n {sin [2 pi fc(t−nΔ)]} OVER {pi(t−nΔ)}

$$\Psi = \sqrt{\frac{y_2^2}{x_{3i+1}^{2ke^z}} + \sqrt[x^7+1]{\int \frac{3\pi}{\arctan(x^2-1) \times \left(\frac{\operatorname{arcsec} \mathcal{L}(x^2+i)}{\sin 4\theta}\right)}}}$$

PSI=SQRT{y_2^2 OVER x_{3i+1}^{{2ke}^z} +
{NROOT {x^7+1} {INT {3pi} OVERSM {arctan LEFT(x^2−1 RIGHT)
TIMES BINOMSM {func arcsec``` £ (x^2+i)} {sin~4 theta}}}}}

$$\int_0^{4\pi} \frac{dx}{2+\sin x} = \frac{2}{\sqrt{3}} \tan^{-1} \frac{2\tan\frac{x}{2}+1}{\sqrt{3}} \Bigg]_0^{4\pi}$$

$$= \frac{2}{\sqrt{3}} \left[\tan^{-1} \frac{2\tan 2\pi+1}{\sqrt{3}} - \tan^{-1}\frac{2\tan 0+1}{\sqrt{3}} \right]$$

STACK
{ALIGNL
INT_0^ {4 pi} dx   OVER   {2~+~sin``x}
~=~2   OVER   SQRT 3 ``tan^{-1}``
   LEFT . {2``tan``{x OVER 2}~+~1} OVER {SQRT 3}``
   RIGHT]_{``0}^{``4 pi}
#ALIGNL
vert −150 = ~2 OVER SQRT 3 ``
     LEFT [
      {tan^{−1}`{2``tan`2pi~+~1} OVER SQRT 3 ``
  −``tan^{−1}`{2``tan`0   ~+~1} OVER SQRT 3 }
     RIGHT] }

$$a = \begin{bmatrix} \int_0^{\infty} \pi^{\,x} & \dfrac{x-1}{y} & \dot{c}^{\,2} \\[2em] \sqrt[x-1]{b^{2^{3^4}} - c} & t_r^{\,y} & \dfrac{r \times \dfrac{lo}{j}}{y-1} \\[2em] e_i^{\,//} & \underset{d<c-1}{\overset{a=\breve{b}}{\underline{bc}-1<0}} & \sum_{i=1}^{\infty} i^2 \\ a & a \end{bmatrix}$$

a= LEFT (MATRIX {MATFORM {ALIGNL & ALIGNC & ALIGNR}
  INT_0^INF pi^x & {x−1} OVER y & c DOT^2 #
  NROOT {x−1}{b^2^3^4 −c} & t_r^y & {r TIMES lo OVERSM j}
OVER {y−1} #
   a VERT 100 e_i '' & a^STACKALIGN {a = &b BREVE #
     UNDERLINE bc−1< &0 # d< &c−1}
          & sum FROM {i=1} TO INF i^2
} RIGHT]

Printing Text in Any Size

Even if you do not work with equations, you can use the equation editor's ability to scale fonts to any point size for other applications. For example, you can create signs, banners, or place cards with the equation editor.

The following example was created with **Richard~C.~Oliver** as the equation.

Richard C. Oliver

A Times Roman font was chosen as the Document's initial base font so that it would not print in Courier or Helvetica, and the graphical font size was set to 30pt. In review, press Setup (SHIFT-F1) while in the equation editor, choose **2** for Graphical Font Size, choose **2** for Set Point Size, and then enter the point size. Press Exit (F7) to return to the equation editor.

Remember to use a tilde (~) if a space is needed. You can also control the amount of spacing with the thin space (`) as shown in the following example:

WordPerfect`ITAL {5.1}:~~FUNC {The~Complete~Reference}

WordPerfect 5.1:   The Complete Reference

In the example above, the ITAL and FUNC commands were used to indicate where italics and the base font (FUNC) should be used. Normally, the entire phrase would have been printed in italics because the equation editor assumes that the text is a variable. The number "5.1" would have printed in the normal base font, because it is a number, and all numbers are usually printed in the base font. The ITAL and FUNC commands give you more control. You can also use the BOLD and UNDERLINE commands when necessary.

See "Tables" in this chapter for another example of how this feature was used. A calendar was created with the Tables feature, while an equation was used to print the month in a larger font than was available in the printer.

Related Items

Setup
Tables

ERASE

See "Delete" in this chapter.

ERROR MESSAGES

From time to time, you will see error messages at the bottom of the screen. Most are related to the feature being used. If this is the case, check the feature entry in this chapter for possible solutions. If you see a specific error message, such as "Disk full — strike any key to continue," refer to the entry in this chapter that covers that message.

Hints

DOS and WordPerfect Error Messages

If you see a number preceding an error message while you are in WordPerfect, it is most likely coming from DOS. These numbered messages are usually referred to by DOS as extended error codes. See the DOS manual's index to locate the description of a specific error message.

To help distinguish further between DOS and WordPerfect, WordPerfect displays "ERROR:" before all error messages. Here is an example:

ERROR: File not found — FILENAME

If DOS sends an error message, it is usually associated with the inability to read the drive that was specified. This could be due to a bad disk, a write-protect tab, or an open drive door. For example, if you were in DOS and tried to copy a file from one disk to another, and the drive door was not closed, you would see a message similar to the following:

Not ready error reading drive A. Abort, Retry, Ignore?

If you receive a message such as this one while saving a document in WordPerfect and type **A** to abort, you will lose the current document and be returned unceremoniously to DOS. However, WordPerfect captures the "critical errors" sent from DOS and gives you the opportunity to correct the situation. The following message would be displayed instead of the DOS error message:

Drive not ready reading drive A. **1 R**etry; **2** Cancel: **1**

WordPerfect Corporation also includes a complete list of error messages in Appendix E of the WordPerfect manual.

Related Entries

"Are Other Copies of WordPerfect Running?" Error Message
"Can't Find Correct Copy of WP" Error Message
"Critical Disk Error Occurred" Error Message
"Disk Full" Error Message
"Divide Overflow" Error Message
"File Creation Error" Error Message
"Not Enough Memory" Error Message
"Put WP 2 Disk Back in Drive" Error Message

ESC KEY

ESC acts as a counter key to determine how many times a keystroke is to be repeated. It can also be used to "escape" from a WordPerfect prompt or menu.

Keystrokes

When you press ESC, "Repeat Value = 8" appears on the status line, indicating that a keystroke will be repeated eight times. You can change the default for a single procedure, for one editing session, or permanently.

Change the Repeat Value for a Single Procedure

1. Press ESC.

2. Type the new number (do not press ENTER or the value will be changed permanently for that editing session).

3. Press the keystroke to be repeated.

Change the Repeat Value for One Editing Session

1. Press ESC.

2. Type the new number.

3. Press ENTER.

Change the Repeat Value Permanently

Use the Setup menu to change the repeat value permanently.

1. Press Setup (SHIFT-F1) to go to the Setup menu.

2. Choose 4 for Initial Settings.

3. Choose 6 for Repeat Value.

4. Enter the new number.

5. Press Exit (F7) to return to the document.

A code is not placed in the document; the change is stored in the WP{WP}.SET file. Repeat the steps if you want to return the repeat value back to the default setting of 8.

Keys That Repeat

Any character	Types the character n times
Space bar	Inserts n spaces
↑ or ↓	Moves the cursor up or down n lines

← or →	Moves the cursor left or right n spaces
PGUP or PGDN	Moves the cursor backward or forward n pages
Macro (ALT-F10) or ALT-*macro*	Repeats the named macro n times
Delete EOL (CTRL-END)	Deletes n lines from the cursor down
DEL	Deletes n characters to the right of the cursor.

Hints

If you press ESC accidentally or decide not to repeat a keystroke, press ESC again or press Cancel (F1).

You can also use the ESC key to escape from any WordPerfect menu (including the pull-down menus) except Help or List Files. Press ENTER or the space bar to leave the Help menu, and press Exit (F7) to leave List Files.

If you prefer to have ESC work exactly like the Cancel key, you can assign the Cancel function to ESC with the Keyboard Layout feature on the Setup menu. See "Keyboard Layout" in this chapter for details.

Applications

Some users prefer to use ESC, ↑ or ESC, ↓ to move through a document, rather than using "screen up" or "screen down." If you want the first or last line of a screen to appear in the preceding or next screen, change the repeat value to 21 or 22 for single-spacing and to 10 or 11 for double-spacing. Pressing ESC, ↑ or ESC, ↓ will then move partial screens, giving you the desired overlap.

Repeat Macros

The ESC key is commonly used to repeat macros. If you want a macro to repeat a certain number of times, press ESC, type the desired number (do not press ENTER), and start the macro. If you want the macro to repeat until it reaches the end of the file, estimate the number of times it should repeat, and type the number after pressing ESC. If you have a search as part of the macro, the macro will stop when it cannot find further occurrences and quit the macro, regardless of the ESC value. You can enter a high number such as 1000 to ensure that it will reach the end of the file. This feature is similar to chaining a macro to itself. See "Macros" in this chapter for more information.

Related Entries

Cancel
Keyboard Layout
Macros

EXCEL

WordPerfect 5.1 can import Excel spreadsheets. See "Spreadsheet Importing and Linking" in this chapter for details. Charts created in Excel can be placed in a WordPerfect graphics box with the directions below.

Keystrokes

1. Enter the Port section of Excel's WIN.INI file.

2. Define an output file (OUTPUT.PRN, for example).

3. Enter Excel's CONTROL.EXE program and install the HP Plotters.

4. Start Excel, select the HP 7475A as the plotting device, and connect the plotter to the output file that was previously defined.

5. Select one pen for the plotter. This forces the chart to be printed in patterns.

6.Print the chart. An HPGL plotter file (named OUPUT.PRN in this example) is created on disk.

7.Exit Excel and start WordPerfect.

8.Press Graphics (ALT-F9), choose the desired type of box (Figure, Table, Text Box, or User Box), and then choose 1 for Create.

9.Choose 1 for Filename, and enter the name of the ouput file (OUTPUT.PRN in this example).

10.If you want to view the chart, choose 9 for Edit. Make other selections from the menu if necessary, and press Exit (F7) when you are finished.

Related Items

Spreadsheet Importing and Linking

EXIT

You can use Exit (F7) to leave a document as well as the WordPerfect program. If a WordPerfect menu is on the screen, you can use it to exit that menu. If you want to save the document and have it remain on the screen, use Save (F10).

Keystrokes

1. Press Exit (F7). You are always asked if you want to save the current document. If you have not changed the document since you last saved it, you will see the following message in the lower right corner of the screen, which means that you do not have to save the document again:

(Text was not modified)

2. Type **Y** or **N** in answer to the question, "Save document?" If you type **N**, skip to step 3. If you type **Y**, "Document to be saved:" is displayed. If you have saved the file before, the name of the document is shown. Press ENTER to accept the name or enter a new one. If you enter the name of a file already on disk, type **Y** or **N** to replace the former file.

3. The following prompt appears on the status line, depending on whether you have one or two documents in memory: "Exit WP? **No** (**Yes**)" or "Exit doc 1 (or 2)? **No** (**Yes**)." Type **N** to exit the document and remain in WordPerfect, type **Y** to exit WordPerfect, or press Cancel (F1) to cancel the exit procedure and remain in the document.

If you type **Y** and have two documents in memory, the cursor goes to the second document. Repeat the steps to exit WordPerfect.

Hints

Although it might seem time consuming and involves several keystrokes intensive to exit a document or WordPerfect, many built-in safety features protect you from losing your documents.

Remember that you can press Cancel (F1) to cancel the procedure and keep the document on the screen up to the very last step.

If you press Save (F10) to save the document and then use Exit (F7), you are still asked if you want to save the document. As mentioned previously, the message "(Text was not modified)" is displayed in the lower right corner to let you know that the document does not need to be saved again.

You can also use Exit (F7) to leave any WordPerfect menu except Help. Press ENTER or the space bar to leave the Help menu.

Related Entries

Save

EXPANDED MEMORY

WordPerfect needs at least 384K of memory to run. This means that your computer would need to have 512K of memory, because you also need to run DOS. It is suggested that you have 640K for more flexibility.

The advantage to having more memory is that you can edit larger files in memory without having them go to disk as quickly. When you edit a document, as much of it as possible remains in memory. However, when memory is filled, WordPerfect creates temporary files on disk to hold the extra pieces of the document that will not fit. As you scroll through the document, WordPerfect swaps unneeded parts of the documents into these overflow files and leaves the part of the document being edited in memory.

Even though WordPerfect requires only 384K of memory, it will take all the conventional memory that is available in your computer. It cannot use extended memory, but will use expanded memory if it is available.

If you have added an expanded memory board to your computer that complies with the 4.0 or 3.2 Lotus/Intel/Microsoft (LIM) specifications, WordPerfect will automatically use that memory when you edit large documents. It will also help speed up hyphenation, spell checking, and looking up words in the Thesaurus.

You can also use expanded memory to load all the WordPerfect program files into memory so it can run much faster and eliminate any disk access for overlay files. To do so, you can start WordPerfect with the /R startup option (enter **wp/r**).

If you have a memory expansion board that supports the 3.2 LIM specifications, WordPerfect will support it but will not be able to use it to the extent that it would if you had 4.0 LIM. More information follows about upgrading your 3.2 memory board to version 4.0 so you can take advantage of the additional memory support.

Hints

When you start WordPerfect with the /R option (WP/R), it checks to see if you have expanded memory that complies with the 3.2 and 4.0 LIM specifications. If so, it will take advantage of it in the following manner.

Version 3.2

If you have version 3.2 LIM, WordPerfect 5.1 will place the virtual files (temporary files that are created when WordPerfect is started) into expanded memory (as is done in WordPerfect 5.0). You can also load the overlay file (WP.FIL) into memory with the /R startup option.

WordPerfect will use approximately 1.5 MB of expanded memory if you are not running under WordPerfect Library's Shell program. If Shell is running, WordPerfect will use approximately 512K. This can be controlled with the /W startup option to specify the amount of memory to be used by WordPerfect (/W −1000 to use 1 MB of memory or /W −* to use all the expanded memory available).

Version 4.0

In you have an expanded memory board that supports LIM 4.0 specifications, all virtual files will be handled in expanded memory. The overflow files created by large documents will flow from the edit buffer (usually 32K to 64K) to expanded memory, and then to disk if necessary. In addition, the Speller and hyphenation code will be loaded into expanded memory.

With 4.0 LIM, WordPerfect will access up to 90 percent of the available expanded memory. If you have WordPerfect Library's Shell loaded, up to 50 percent of all expanded memory can be accessed. The amount of expanded memory used by WordPerfect can be controlled with the /W startup option:

WP/W −[conventional memory],[expanded memory]

You can use an asterisk to specify that all available memory be used by WordPerfect: **WP/W −*,*.**

Upgrading from 3.2 to 4.0 LIM

Approximately 90 percent of those who have a memory expansion board that supports 3.2 LIM specifications can upgrade to 4.0 by obtaining an updated "driver" free from the memory board's manufacturer. This driver is contained in the file REMM.SYS and is also available on many bulletin board systems, such as CompuServe.

Most memory boards manufactured after the announcement of LIM 3.2 were built to support EEMS 3.2 (including many of the memory boards produced by AST, Quadram, Tecmar, and Intel). Since 4.0 is basically an adaptation of EEMS 3.2, you will most likely be able to upgrade boards that support EEMS.

In a few cases, a hardware upgrade may be necessary and may cost more than you want to spend. Some computers, including the AT&T 6300 and 6300Plus, cannot use the LIM 4.0 specifications due to hardware limitations.

If your expanded memory board is not fully compatible with 4.0 LIM, but "tells" WordPerfect that it is, you may have problems using it with WordPerfect. If this happens you can start WordPerfect with the / NE option (meaning "No Expanded" memory) or, if you have a version of WordPerfect dated later than 1/19/90, you can use the / 32 startup option which forces WordPerfect to use only 3.2 calls.

Related Items

RAM Drives
Start WordPerfect

EXTENDED SEARCH/REPLACE

Headers, footers, footnotes, endnotes, and text in graphics boxes are not searched during a normal search, reverse search, or replace operation. If you want to include them in the search, press HOME before pressing Search (F2), ←Search (SHIFT-F2), or Replace (ALT-F2). See "Search" in this chapter for more information.

EXTRA LARGE PRINT

Instead of choosing a font manually, you can have WordPerfect make automatic font changes based on the current base font. If you use the size options, it is easy for WordPerfect to transfer documents from printer to printer, because when it finds a command for large, extra large, or fine print, it will print with the current printer's definition of large, extra large, and so on.

Keystrokes

1. Press Font (CTRL-F8).

2. Choose **1** for **S**ize.

3. Choose **7** for **E**xt Large. The codes [EXT LARGE] and [ext large] are inserted, with the cursor resting on the [ext large] code.

4. Type the text to be printed in the extra large font.

5. Press → to move the cursor over the [ext large] code and return to normal.

You can also follow steps 1 to 3 again to turn Extra Large off instead of pressing →.

Hints

You can change a section of existing text to extra large by defining a block, pressing Font (CTRL-F8), and choosing **1** for **S**ize and then **7** for **E**xt Large. The [EXT LARGE] code would be placed at the beginning of the block, and the [ext large] off code would be inserted at the end of the block.

If you have a Hercules card with RamFont, you will probably see a representation of the extra large font on the screen. The text will appear in a different color if you have a color monitor. To change the way the extra large font is displayed on your screen, see "Colors/Fonts/Attributes" in this chapter.

When you select a printer or update cartridges and fonts, Word-Perfect displays a message to the effect that the fonts are being up-dated. WordPerfect checks the Size Attribute Ratio setting in the Setup menu and selects the fonts that are to be used for Extra Large (and other attributes) at that time. If you do not like the way WordPerfect is printing the extra large font, you can select a new base font. You can also edit the printer definition (.PRS file) using the Printer (PTR) program. For details, see "Size Attribute Ratios" and "Automatic Font Changes" in this chapter and Chapter 5, "Printer Program."

Related Entries

Automatic Font Changes
Fonts
Size Attribute Ratios
See also Chapter 5, "Printer Program"

FAST SAVE

When you save a document, WordPerfect 5.1 "fast saves" it, which means that it does not reformat the file first. This makes it much faster to save a document.

Keystrokes

The following keystrokes help you turn the feature on or off.

1. Press Setup (SHIFT-F1) and choose 3 for **E**nvironment.

2. Type **5** for **F**ast Save (unformatted).

3. Type **Y** or **N**.

4. Press Exit (F7) when you are finished.

Hints

If you want a file to take up as little disk space as possible, turn off Fast Save. When a document is saved with Fast Save on, WordPerfect does not take the time to rewrite the prefix (a hidden part of the document containing information about initial codes, the initial font, the current printer selection, and so on) to eliminate unnecessary information. However, when you save a document in the normal fashion, that prefix is purged so that it takes up as little space as possible.

For example, if you are editing a document and change the document's initial font, initial codes, or select a different printer for the document, the old information in the prefix is marked for deletion and the new information is added. If the file is then Fast Saved, the old information (while remaining marked for deletion) is not deleted and takes up unnecessary disk space. The next time you retrieve the file (whether Fast Save is on or not), the prefix is updated and the file size goes down again. If you are not worried about disk space, you can leave Fast Save on.

If you print a document that is Fast Saved, it is retrieved "behind the scenes," reformatted, and then sent to the printer, which takes a little more time than normal. If you print from the screen instead of disk most of the time, you will probably want to leave Fast Save on, because it saves a substantial amount of time.

FIGURES

WordPerfect 5.0 has four categories of graphics boxes: Figures, Tables, Text Boxes, and User-Defined Boxes. Each category has exactly the same functionality, but some of the default options have been changed. Instructions for creating figures are included under "Graphics Boxes" in this chapter. You will also learn how to change the options for a figure, including the border style, caption style, and shading. Figures are numbered and renumbered automatically as you add and delete them.

To create a list of figures for a document, you can define List 6 at the beginning of the document; the captions for all the figures, and the page numbers on which they are found, will automatically be included in that list (you do not have to mark each caption for inclusion in the list). See "Lists" in this chapter for details.

The Cross-Referencing feature lets you refer to a specific figure from within the document. For example, you can enter the text "see Figure 3 on page 14" in the document and then update the reference when you have made all the editing changes. If the figure or page number changes, it will be updated with the Generate option on Mark Text (ALT-F5). See "Cross-References" in this chapter for details.

For other examples of how to use figures in your documents, see Chapter 4, "Desktop Publishing with WordPerfect."

Related Entries

Cross-References
Graphics Boxes
Lists
See also Chapter 4, "Desktop Publishing with WordPerfect"

"FILE CREATION ERROR" ERROR MESSAGE

"File creation error" is a DOS error message that is sometimes displayed when you are trying to save or print a file. If you attempted to use illegal characters in a filename, the new file cannot be created.

The following characters are acceptable for use in filenames:

A-Z 0-9 ! @ # $ % X ' ' ( ) − _ / ^ & ~ .

You cannot use the following in filenames:

* + = [ ] " < > ? ¦ ,

Be careful with the *, ?, and , characters. Even if they seem allowable, you should never use them.

Most operating systems have a limit on the number of files that the root directory can contain (usually 112), even if ample disk space is available. If you have reached this limit, you have two options: You can delete or move files from the root directory, or you can create a new directory for further storage. (You can divide floppy disks into directories with the same commands used for a hard disk.) See "Directories" and "Create a Directory" in this chapter for more information about creating directories.

If you see the error message while you are trying to replace a file on a network, check to see if the file is marked "read only" and cannot be replaced.

When you print the document or part of the document on the screen, a copy of the document is saved to a temporary file in memory and then printed. After available memory is filled, print jobs are kept on the drive and directory where WP.EXE resides. It is unlikely that you will get this error message during this procedure, but if you do, it is possible that the temporary print file exceeded the limit of the number of files in the root directory (you either have a floppy disk system or have WordPerfect stored in the root directory on the hard disk). If this happens, delete or move files from the WordPerfect disk, or install WordPerfect in a subdirectory where there is no limit to the number of files that you can create.

FILENAMES, LONG AND SHORT

You can save documents with a descriptive name of up to 68 characters in addition to the standard DOS filename. WordPerfect then lets you display files by their descriptive names in List Files. See "Long Document Names" and "Document Management/Summary" in this chapter for details.

FILING DOCUMENTS

WordPerfect has several features to help you file documents. Among them are the List Files menu, Save, and Retrieve. You can also create different directories on a hard disk for different types of documents.

You can set options in the Setup menu that will help you organize and find documents at a later time. See "Document Management/Summary" and "Long Document Names" in this chapter for more information.

Related Entries

Directories
Document Management/Summary
Find Files
List Files
Long Document Names
Retrieve
Save

FIND FILES

The Find option in List Files helps you find files by date of creation, revision, author, typist, subject, long document name, account number, and so on. This feature replaces Word Search found in previous versions of WordPerfect.

Using Search (F2) in List Files, you can also look for a forgotten filename by entering the part that you remember.

Keystrokes

Finding a Filename

While in the List Files menu, you can type **N** for Name Search, and then type the name of a file to move quickly to that file. If you don't remember the entire name of the file, but remember parts of the filename, you can use Search (F2) to find files that contain the letters entered (whether they are found at the beginning of the filename or not). For example, if you search for **count**, the file ACCOUNT.ING would be found first. If you continue searching, COUNTING.$ and VISCOUNT would also be found.

1. Press List (F5).

2. Press ENTER to see a list of files in the current directory, or enter the name of a different directory.

3. Press Search (F2).

4. When prompted, enter the part of the filename that you know. (You do not have to use wildcard characters as substitutes for the characters you do not know.)

5. Press ENTER or Search (F2) to start the search.

This feature takes different amounts of time, depending on the number of files in the directory. You can also search in the reverse direction by pressing ←Search (SHIFT-F2).

Finding Files

1. Press List (F5). The name of the current (default) directory is displayed.

2. Press ENTER to look at all files in that directory, or edit the pathname to view only selected files (C:\DOCS*.LET would display all the files in the DOCs directory ending with the extension .LET).

3. When in the List Files menu, choose **9** for Find. The following options appear.

Find: 1 Name; 2 Doc Summary; 3 First Pg; 4 Entire Doc; 5 Conditions; 6 Undo: 0

4. Option **1** lets you search for a specific file by **Name**. When prompted for the Word Pattern, you can enter the characters that you know, and WordPerfect will display the list of files which includes the characters in the filename. Only the DOS filename is searched. If you want to search for text found in the Long Document name, use the Conditions menu to enter the information for the Document Name category.

This option is similar to doing a Search (F2) for a file, but it will display all the files that match the conditions instead of moving to them one by one.

Choose **2** to search the Document Summary, **3** to search the First **P**age (or first 4000 characters, whichever comes first), or **4** to search the Entire document for a specific word pattern. Option **5** lets you vary the Conditions that are to be met in any or all of the Document Summary, First Page, and Entire Document options. See "Hints" for details.

Option **6** lets you Undo the search. After you have done a search, you can choose the Undo option to return to the previous list of files. In fact, you can Undo up to three times (display the three previous lists) with this option.

5. When asked for a Word Pattern, enter up to 39 characters, including any of the following wildcard characters or operators:

Wildcard Characters

?	Represents any single character
*	Represents any number of characters up to a hard return [HRt] code

Operators

; or a space	Searches for files containing both words
,	Searches for files containing either word
—	*Excludes* files containing the word pattern following the dash from the list

Enclose a phrase in quotation marks if it contains a space, comma, semicolon, minus sign (−), or other quotation marks; otherwise, the space, comma, semicolon, minus sign, or quotation mark will be considered an operator. See "Hints" for more information.

6. Press ENTER to start the process. If you are in the Conditions menu, choose **1** for Perform the Search.

Only those files meeting the specifications will remain in the List Files screen.

Hints

The more files that are listed on the List Files screen, the longer it takes Find to search through each file. To limit the number of files to be searched, note the following suggestions:

• After pressing List (F5), you can enter a filename pattern to limit the files that are displayed. For example, enter ***.ltr** to view all the files that end with the extension **.LTR**. If you have several files for a specific client, enter **jones*.*** to list all the documents containing that name.

• After entering the List Files menu, you can mark files by typing an asterisk (*) while the cursor is on the file. When you do a Find, only the marked files will be included in the search.

After finding a group of files with the same unique word or phrase, you can press ENTER while the cursor is resting on the filename to look into it without retrieving it. You can also use Search (F2) while in Look.

In versions previous to 5.1, you could use an asterisk or a dash (* or −) as wildcard characters to represent several characters. In 5.1, a dash or minus sign is used to exclude files that contain the word pattern following the dash from the list. For example, if you want to list all files except the ones from 1989, and "89" was used as the filename extension for those files, you could use the pattern −.89.

Conditions

When you choose the Conditions option under Find, you will see the menu that is shown in Figure 3-47. The number of files that are displayed in the upper right corner is the number of files in the directory or the number of files that you have marked (in this case 248).

You can use the options on this menu to set multiple conditions. For example, instead of searching through the first page only, you can search through the first page *and* search for specific items found in the Document Summary.

Perform Search   Choose 1 to select this option after you have entered all the conditions.

Reset Conditions   To reset all the conditions at once, select option 2.

Revision Date   Option 3 lets you search for files edited between certain dates. Choose 3 and enter a beginning and ending date. Enter the month, day, and year with slashes (/) between each option. You do

```
┌─────────────────────────────────────────────────────────────┐
│  Find: Conditions                         Files Selected:  248│
│                                                               │
│      1 - Perform Search                                       │
│      2 - Reset Conditions                                     │
│                                                               │
│      3 - Revision Date - From                                 │
│                          To                                   │
│                                                               │
│      4 - Text - Document Summary                              │
│               First Page                                      │
│               Entire Document                                 │
│                                                               │
│      5 - Document Summary                                     │
│          Creation Date - From                                 │
│                          To                                   │
│          Document Name                                        │
│          Document Type                                        │
│          Author                                               │
│          Typist                                               │
│          Subject                                              │
│          Account                                              │
│          Keywords                                             │
│          Abstract                                             │
│                                                               │
│  Selection: 1                                                 │
└─────────────────────────────────────────────────────────────┘
```

Figure 3-47.   Conditions used to find files

not have to enter leading zeros. For example, 9/1/89 and 09/01/89 are both acceptable. You can leave the month, day, or year empty if necessary, but should still enter the slash. For example, //89 would include all files in 1989, 9/1/ would include all files edited on that date regardless of the year, and 9// would find all files edited during September of any year.

Text   The Text option lets you search the Document Summary, First Page, or Entire Document for specific text. You can also include wildcard characters to create word patterns. All the word patterns must be found in the appropriate locations for the file(s) to be found.

If you are using this option to search through the Document Summary, all text found in the summary (not just specific items) will be searched.

Document Summary   If you want the search to be limited to a specific entry (creation date, long document name, author, typist, and so on), you can enter the word pattern in this category. Note that the date of creation in the summary is the date on which the summary was created for the document (not necessarily the date on which you created the document). Press ↑ and ↓ to move from one option to another.

Related Items

Document Management /Summary
Long Document Names

FINE PRINT

Instead of choosing a smaller font, you can choose the fine print attribute. This feature is similar to bold and underlining, where it puts an "on" and "off" code around the text to be printed in fine print. Word-Perfect will then make an automatic font change based on the current font.

Keystrokes

1. Press Font (CTRL-F8).

2. Choose **1** for Size.

3. Choose **3** for Fine. The codes [FINE] and [fine] are inserted, with the cursor between them.

4. Type the text to be printed in the fine print font.

5. Press → to move the cursor over the [fine] code and return to normal.

Hints

You can change a section of existing text to fine print by defining a block and pressing Font (CTRL-F8), and then choosing 1 for Size and 3 for Fine Print. The [FINE] code would be placed at the beginning of the block, and the [fine] off code would be inserted at the end of the block.

If you have a Hercules card with RamFont, you will be able to see a representation of the fine print font on the screen. The text will appear in a different color if you have a color monitor. To change the way that fine print is displayed on the screen, see "Colors/Fonts/Attributes" in this chapter.

When you select a printer or update cartridges and fonts, Word-Perfect displays a message to the effect that the fonts are being updated. WordPerfect checks the Size Attribute Ratio setting in the Setup Menu and selects the fonts that are to be used for fine print (and other attributes) at that time. If you do not like the way WordPerfect is printing text marked for fine print, you can select a specific base font instead. You can also edit the printer definition (.PRS) file using the Printer (PTR) program. See "Size Attribute Ratios" and "Automatic Font Changes" in this chapter and also Chapter 5, "Printer Program."

Related Entries

Automatic Font Changes
Fonts
Size Attribute Ratios
See also Chapter 5, "Printer Program"

FIXED LINE HEIGHT

See "Line Height" in this chapter.

FLUSH RIGHT

Pressing Flush Right (ALT-F6) lets you align lines of text at the right margin with or without a dot leader (. . .).

By choosing right justification, you can align several lines of text at the right margin without pressing Flush Right (ALT-F6) at the beginning of each line. Instead, each line of text can be aligned at the right margin as it is typed or after it is typed.

Keystrokes

Flush-Right a Line

1. To make a single line flush right, press Flush Right (ALT-F6).

2. After typing the line, press ENTER to turn off Flush Right. Pressing Flush Right (ALT-F6) again does not turn Flush Right off. Instead, a dot leader is inserted from the left margin (or text at the left) up to the text that is being aligned.

If you have already typed the line, move the cursor to the beginning of that line and press Flush Right (ALT-F6). If the line does not appear to be aligned properly, move to the end of the line and press ENTER. A [HRt] code is inserted, which is needed to turn Flush Right off.

Flush-Right Multiple Lines

You can choose right justification if you want to align several lines of text at the right margin:

1. Press Format (SHIFT-F8) and choose **1** for Line.

2. Choose **3** for Justification. You will see the following selections:

```
Justification: 1 Left; 2 Center; 3 Right; 4 Full: 0
```

3. Choose **3** for **R**ight.

4. Press Exit to return to the document and begin typing. Each line of text will begin at the right margin and will be aligned regardless of whether the line is followed by a hard or a soft return.

If you want to return to Left or Full justification (justified at both the left and right margins), repeat the steps above and select the appropriate option.

Flush-Right Existing Text

1. Move the cursor to the first line of the section of text that is to be aligned at the right margin.

2. Press Block (ALT-F4) and define the block of text to be affected.

3. Press Flush Right (ALT-F6). The following question appears:

[Just:Right]? **No** (**Yes**)

4. Type **Y** to right-justify that block of text, or type **N** if you change your mind.

The [Just:Right] code will be inserted at the beginning of the block, and the current justification setting (left, center, or full) is entered at the end of the block.

Flush-Right a Line With a Dot Leader

1. Press Flush Right (ALT-F6) twice.

2. Type the text to be aligned at the right margin.

To add a dot leader after you have typed the text, move the cursor anywhere in the line that is flush right against the margin, and press Flush Right (ALT-F6).

Right-Aligned Tabs

You can insert a right-aligned tab at anytime, regardless of the current tab setting. Press HOME, and then Flush Right (ALT-F6) to move the cursor to the next tab setting and right-align any text typed thereafter. If you want to insert a dot leader as well, press HOME, HOME, and then Flush Right (ALT-F6). The [RGT TAB] code is inserted if you use this feature.

Hints

The [Flsh Rgt] code is inserted at the beginning of a line that is marked for flush right. A hard return [HRt] code marks the end.

By choosing right justification instead of flush right for multiple lines, you can more easily edit the text that is right-aligned. Right justification also lets the words wrap with a soft return or a hard return, and they will still remain aligned at the right margin.

Applications

If you do not care to use WordPerfect's Table of Contents or Index feature, or if you need to add an entry to an existing table of contents or index quickly, you can press Flush Right (ALT-F6) twice to create a dot leader and then type the page number or a similar entry. This is much easier than the previous method: figuring where the right margin is, entering the Tab Set menu, and then setting a right-aligned decimal tab.

This feature may also be useful when you are creating musical programs or playbills that are similar to the following:

CAST

Characters	**Played by**
Mr. Thomas Bill	Galvan Steel
Mrs. Platapus	Jane Mann
Suzanne	Sally Shocker

Related Entries

    Dot Leader
    Justification
    Tabs

FONTS

A font is a set of characters that have similar attributes, such as size, weight, slant, and the character set being used. In fact, the term "font" comes from the early days of typesetting, when documents were set by hand and each set of characters was kept in a container called a font.

When you are selecting a font, you do not have to select a pitch (the number of characters per inch) because that information is part of the font definition.

You can select from fonts that are already included in the printer (internal fonts), those that are included in a cartridge (laser printers, Texas Instruments 855, and the IBM Quietwriter all use cartridges), or soft fonts. Soft fonts are fonts stored on disk (software) and are downloaded to the printer before printing. Cartridges and soft fonts are usually purchased separately.

When you select a printer, it automatically selects all fonts that come standard with the printer. If you have purchased separate cartridges and fonts, you will need to tell WordPerfect that they are available before you can use them. The instructions for doing so are included in this chapter under "Cartridges and Fonts."

Keystrokes

This section tells you how to change fonts within a document. See "Hints" for more information about the initial base font that is used to decide how page numbers, headers, footers, footnotes, endnotes, text in graphics boxes, and captions for those boxes are to be printed.

Selecting Fonts in a Document

There are two ways to select fonts: You can choose the base font from a list of fonts, which affects the text from that point forward (until another font change is encountered), or you can select one of the font attributes, such as Large, Extra Large, or Fine print, which affects the text between the on and off codes (similar to bold and underline).

To choose a specific font, follow these steps:

1. Press Font (CTRL-F8). The one-line menu shown here appears:

1 Size; 2 Appearance; 3 Normal; 4 Base Font; 5 Print Color: 0

2. Choose **4** for Base **F**ont. You will see the list of fonts that are available for your printer, with the cursor resting on the initial base font (see "Hints" for more information about the initial base font).

Figure 3-48 shows a list of sample fonts that would be displayed. This list will vary, depending on your printer and the available fonts.

3. Move to the font that you want to select, and press ENTER. You can also type **N** for **N**ame Search, and then type the name of the font so you can move to that point in the list more quickly.

The font change is inserted into the document at that point; to see the code, press Reveal Codes (ALT-F3).

The second method lets you choose from several attributes (Fine, Small, Large, Very Large, Extra Large, Italics, Shadow, Outline, and so on), and WordPerfect will make the font changes based on the current base font. For example, if the base font is Times Roman 12pt and you choose the Italics attribute, the Times Roman 12pt Italics font will be used if it is available. If you did not select it when you selected the fonts

```
Base Font

    CG Times  6pt (WP)
    CG Times  8pt (WP)
    CG Times  8pt Bold (WP)
    CG Times  8pt Italic (WP)
    CG Times 10pt (WP)
    CG Times 10pt Bold (WP)
    CG Times 10pt Italic (WP)
  * CG Times 12pt (WP)
    CG Times 12pt Bold (WP)
    CG Times 12pt Italic (WP)
    CG Times 14pt (WP)
    CG Times 14pt Bold (WP)
    CG Times 14pt Italic (WP)
    CG Times 18pt Bold (WP)
    CG Times 24pt Bold (WP)
    Courier 10cpi
    Courier 10cpi Bold
    Line Draw 10cpi (Full)
    Line Printer 16.67cpi
    Univers 14pt (WP)
    Univers 18pt (WP)

1 Select; N Name search: 1
```

Figure 3-48.   A sample list of fonts

and cartridges, WordPerfect will search for the next best font and use it instead. (If your printer does not have an italics font selected, italicized text will be underlined, and boldfaced text will be overstruck.)

If you use an attribute (such as Fine, Small, or Italics) instead of changing the base font, you will be able to see exactly where the change occurred if you have assigned a different color, font (if you are using Hercules RamFonts), or some other screen attribute (reverse video, underline, bold, and so on) to the print attribute. See "Colors/ Fonts/Attributes" in this chapter for more information.

When you choose one of these attributes, on and off codes are inserted (similar to those for bold and underline). This requires that you turn off the attribute later or press → to move over the off code, which is not necessary with a font change. You can also block the text first and then choose an attribute for the block.

To use this method, follow these steps:

1. Press Font (CTRL-F8). If you are choosing an attribute for a block, define the block first.

2. Choose **1** for Size or **2** for Appearance. If you choose Size, the following appears:

1 Suprscpt; 2 Subscpt; 3 Fine; 4 Small; 5 Large; 6 Vry Large; 7 Ext Large: 0

The Appearance category includes the following choices:

1 Bold 2 Undln 3 Dbl Und 4 Italc 5 Outln 6 Shadw 7 Sm Cap 8 Redln 9 Stkout: 0

3. Type the number or letter of the desired choice. When you choose an option from the Size or Appearance category, on and off codes are inserted. For example, [FINE][fine], [ITALC][italc], and [LARGE][large]. The cursor remains between the codes. If you defined a block, the codes are placed at the beginning and the end of the block.

4. If you did not define a block, type the text to be affected, and then press → to move past the off code. You can also reenter the menu and choose the option again to turn it off, or choose option **3** for **N**ormal, but you might find it more convenient to use the → key.

Hints

When you select a printer, WordPerfect automatically selects an initial base font that it will use for all documents. You can override this setting by choosing an initial base font for the document, or change the base font at any location in the document to affect text from that point forward.

The Document's initial base font is used for the following:

- Page numbers

- Headers and footers

- Footnotes and endnotes

- Text in graphics boxes

- Captions for graphics boxes

If you have chosen "options" for these items (excluding page numbers, headers, and footers), the font that is current at that time will be used. If you entered the Options menu for Footnotes, the font that is current when you insert the [Ftn Opt] code is the one that will be used for all footnotes from that point forward.

Headers and footers are printed in the font that is current when they are created. Page numbers are always printed in the document's initial base font.

You can change the font for any of the items above except page numbering by inserting a font change inside the header, footer, footnote, endnote, graphics box, or caption. However, if you want to change the font for all footnotes at one time, you can change to the font to be used for footnotes, insert a footnote options code, and then change the font back to the one used for the rest of the document.

Initial Base Font

You can change the initial base font for all subsequent documents or just change it for the current document (press Format (SHIFT-F8), Choose 3 for Document, then 3 for Initial Base Font). See "Initial Base Font" in this chapter for more details.

Downloading Soft Fonts

Before printing a document that uses soft fonts, press Print (SHIFT-F7) and choose 7 for Initialize the Printer. All soft fonts marked as being present when the print job begins will be downloaded to the printer. If you see the message "File not found," you probably have not specified the correct path for the downloadable fonts. If this is the case, type **S** for Select Printers, move to the appropriate printer, and choose 3 for Edit. Choose 6 for Path for Downloadable Fonts and Printer Command Files, and enter the correct path for downloadable soft fonts.

When you initialize the printer, the soft fonts are downloaded as if they were a normal print job. You can queue several documents after initializing the printer, but they will not be printed until the "download" print job is completed.

Automatic Font Changes

To see which fonts have been selected as small, large, extra large, outline, redline, and so on, print the PRINTER.TST file.

If you neglected to select corresponding fonts (for example, if you selected Times Roman 12pt, you would also want to select Times Roman 12pt Bold and Times Roman 12pt Italics), you can return to the Cartridges and Fonts option and do so.

You can use the Size Attribute Ratios option in the Setup menu to specify the percentage that WordPerfect should use when it selects the fonts for Extra Large, Large, Small, and so on. You can also specify the exact font to be used by editing the printer definition (.PRS) file with the

Printer (PTR) program. For more information, see "Size Attribute Ratios" in this chapter and Chapter 5, "Printer Program."

Line and Page Breaks

WordPerfect formats the document for the selected font as you enter text. If you select a small 6pt font, many more characters will fit on the line before it breaks. If you type in a 30pt font, you would get very few characters on a line, because it wouldn't take as many characters to fill the line.

The same rule applies to vertical spacing. If you are using a large font, the page break will occur much more quickly than if you were using a smaller font. If you have a large font and a small font on the same line, the line height will be adjusted for the larger font.

You can adjust the word spacing and line height manually or continue to let WordPerfect do the adjustments automatically. For more information, see "Word and Letter Spacing," "Line Height," and "Leading" in this chapter.

Changing Printers

If you retrieve a file with a different printer selected, the fonts will be converted to the ones that best match it in the new printer selections. An asterisk will appear in the font change code to indicate that it has been converted. If you return to the original printer selection, the font will be converted back to the original font.

Related Entries

Cartridges and Fonts
Initial Base Font
Initialize Printer
Leading
Line Height

Word and Letter Spacing
Size Attribute Ratios
See also Chapter 5, "Printer Program"

FOOTERS

A footer is a section of text that is printed at the bottom of every page or selected pages. WordPerfect lets you have as many as two footers per page and an unlimited number of lines in each footer.

Keystrokes

Before inserting a footer, you must be at the very beginning of the page. Press Go To (CTRL-HOME), then ↑ to move the cursor there.

1. Press Format (SHIFT-F8).

2. Choose 2 for **P**age.

3. Choose 4 for **F**ooters.

4. Choose 1 for Footer **A** or 2 for Footer **B**. Although you can use either one, both are available so that you can have footers on alternating pages.

5. When the following selections appear, choose 2 to place the footer on Every **P**age, 3 for **O**dd Pages only, or 4 for **E**ven Pages. There are also options to discontinue or edit a footer.

> 1 Discontinue; 2 Every Page; 3 Odd Pages; 4 Even Pages; 5 Edit: 0

6. Type the text for the footer. If you want to include the current page number in a footer, press CTRL-B to insert ^B. This code will insert the current page number when it is printed.

7. Press Exit (F7) when you are finished.

Hints

WordPerfect automatically subtracts the number of lines in a footer from the total number of lines on a page. The footer will not be printed in the bottom margin, regardless of the number of lines. If you want to change the amount of space reserved for the bottom margin, press Format (SHIFT-F8), choose **2** for **Page**, and then choose **5** to set the top and bottom **Margins**.

To print text at the top of every page or just selected pages, see "Headers" in this chapter.

Applications

If you want the page number to include text (as in "Page -1-") or to be in a different font, you can either create a footer and include a CTRL-B (^B), or you can define a page number style. See "Page Numbering" in this chapter for details.

You can also include graphics lines in a footer if you want to include a "border" at the bottom of each page, as shown here:

Page 2

===

Related Entries

Headers
Page Numbering
Paper Size/Type

FOOTNOTES

Footnotes are printed on the page where they are referenced. If you want footnotes at the end of the document, see "Endnotes" in this chapter.

Keystrokes

1. Press Footnote (CTRL-F7).

2. Choose 1 for Footnote.

3. Choose 1 to Create. The footnote/endnote screen appears, and the appropriate number is inserted.

4. Type the text to be included in the footnote.

5. Press Exit (F7) when you are finished.

After you create a footnote, the number is placed in the document at the cursor's location. If you have chosen a color, font, or other screen attribute to represent superscript, it will appear with that characteristic on the screen. Unless you have a Hercules graphics card with RamFont, the number will not be superscripted on the screen; it will, however, be superscripted when it is printed.

Edit a Footnote

1. Press Footnote (CTRL-F7).

2. Choose 1 for Footnote.

3. Choose 2 for Edit. The message "Footnote number?" is displayed with the number of the next available footnote.

4. Press ENTER to edit the displayed footnote, or enter the number of the note to be edited.

5. Press Exit (F7) when you are finished editing.

Delete a Footnote

1. Position the cursor on the footnote number that is to be deleted.

2. Press DEL. If the footnote is to the left of the cursor, press BACKSPACE.

3. Type **Y** or **N** in answer to the question "Delete [Footnote:*n*]? No (**Y**es)."

You can use Search (F2) to search for a footnote by code, but not by a specific number. See "Hints" for more information about searching for footnote codes.

Hints

When you create a footnote, a code similar to the following is inserted:

[Note:Footnote:1;[Note Num]Text]

The code indicates whether the note is a footnote or endnote, the number of the note (n), and the text of the note. Up to 50 characters of text are shown with the code.

There is no practical limit to the amount of text that can be included in a footnote or endnote. Up to 16,000 lines are available for each footnote or endnote.

Assign a New Footnote Number

WordPerfect automatically numbers footnotes and renumbers them when other footnotes are added or deleted. However, if a footnote must have a specific number (such as when you want to continue numbering from one chapter to another), press Footnote (CTRL-F7), choose 1 for Footnote, 3 for New Number, and enter the number for the next note. The code [New Ftn Num:n] is inserted into the document, and the footnotes that follow are numbered according to the specified number.

Instead of specifying a new footnote number at the beginning of each chapter, you can use the Master Document feature to combine several subdocuments. The numbering (for pages, footnotes, and so on) will continue from one subdocument to the next.

Options

WordPerfect has chosen a specific format for footnotes. To view or change the current settings, press Footnote (CTRL-F7), choose 1 for Footnote, and then 4 for Options. The menu shown in Figure 3-49 appears.

```
┌─────────────────────────────────────────────────────────────────┐
│  Footnote Options                                                 │
│                                                                   │
│       1 - Spacing Within Footnotes         1                      │
│                  Between Footnotes         0.167"                  │
│                                                                   │
│       2 - Amount of Note to Keep Together  0.5"                   │
│                                                                   │
│       3 - Style for Number in Text         [SUPRSCPT][Note Num][suprscpt]  │
│                                                                   │
│       4 - Style for Number in Note               [SUPRSCPT][Note Num][suprscpt  │
│                                                                   │
│       5 - Footnote Numbering Method        Numbers                │
│                                                                   │
│       6 - Start Footnote Numbers each Page  No                    │
│                                                                   │
│       7 - Line Separating Text and Footnotes  2-inch Line         │
│                                                                   │
│       8 - Print Continued Message          No                     │
│                                                                   │
│       9 - Footnotes at Bottom of Page      Yes                    │
│                                                                   │
│                                                                   │
│  Selection: 0                                                     │
└─────────────────────────────────────────────────────────────────┘
```

Figure 3-49.   Footnote options

If you make changes, [F'tn Opt] code is inserted at the cursor's location, and footnotes from that point forward are affected. To make changes that affect all footnotes, move to the beginning of the document before making changes to the menu. Because you will probably want the footnote format options to be changed for all documents, consider making the changes in the Initial Codes section of Setup (SHIFT-F1). The code is then inserted for all documents.

Spacing   Notes are automatically single-spaced, with .167 of an inch between them. You can set spacing within the footnote if you need to vary the spacing from note to note. For future reference, .167″ is the line height for a 12pt (10-pitch) font.

If you want WordPerfect to control the spacing between notes, do not press ENTER after you type the text. Pressing ENTER inserts extra blank lines.

Amount of Note to Keep Together   If a footnote is longer than the space available on a page, it will continue to the next page. Because the

Widow/Orphan feature does not affect footnotes and endnotes, option 2 lets you specify the amount of text that should be kept together if the note continues to other pages. The default measurement is .5″. Note that this is set by using a certain amount of space, instead of by the number of lines.

Style for Numbers in Text and Note   Options 3 and 4 determine how a footnote number will appear in the text of a document and in the note itself. WordPerfect has been set to display the text reference number for footnotes as a superscripted number. The number within a footnote is followed by a period and is not superscripted.

To change this preset format, select the option that applies. ″Replace with:″ appears on the status line with the current string. Delete any unnecessary codes and add others. To insert the [Note Num] code, press Footnote (CTRL-F7), choose 1 for Footnote, and then choose 2 for Number Code. Although you can insert a code into the style initially, it might not be accepted as part of the style once you press ENTER.

Before superscripting was readily available, typists would indicate a footnote in the following manner: 1/. Even though superscripting is now standard with most word processors, some people like to use the underline and the slash. If you decide to use this style, you can substitute it for the default style. Keep in mind, however, that if you want to include the superscript code, the underline will remain in the normal underline position and will not be superscripted with the number.

To get this type of style, enter the Footnote Options menu and press the listed keystrokes to enter the following codes:

[UND][Note Num][und]/

1. Choose **3** for Style for Number in Text.

2. Press DEL to delete the [SUPRSCPT] code.

3. Press Underline (F8) to insert the [UND] code.

4. Move the cursor once to the right, just past the [Note Num] code.

5. Press Underline (F8) to insert the [und] code, which turns off underlining.

6. Type the slash character (/).

7. Press ENTER when you are finished.

Even if you do not make any other changes, you may want to choose option 4 for Style Number in Note and add two spaces to the end of the style; otherwise, you will have to add them each time you create a footnote. You cannot use tab and indent codes as part of the style.

Footnote Numbering Method   A number (rather than a letter or character) is used by default to number footnotes. Choose option 5 if you want to change the numbering method to letters ("a" to "z") or use other characters.

When you choose 5 for Footnote Numbering Method, the following options appear:

```
1 Numbers; 2 Letters; 3 Characters: 0
```

Press ENTER or choose 1 to use the default setting of Numbers, 2 to use Letters (lowercase letters are used), or 3 to use Characters. If you choose 3, the cursor is placed to the right of the option, and you can enter the characters to be used. If you press ENTER without entering characters, WordPerfect will set the default back to numbers.

You can enter a single character or as many as 20 characters. WordPerfect uses the indicated characters and then starts at the beginning of the list, doubling and then tripling the characters. The most commonly used characters are asterisks and daggers (single and double). If your printer can print daggers, you can enter them by pressing Compose (CTRL-2)—the 2 on the top row of keys, rather than the 2 on the numeric keypad—and then entering 4,39 for a single dagger (†) or 4,40 for a double dagger (‡). You will not see a prompt while you are entering these steps. If you entered the characters correctly, you should see a small box representing the character. By pressing Reveal Codes (ALT-F3) and moving the cursor to the box, you will see the numbers that represent that character. See "Compose" and "Special Characters" in this chapter for more information about other special characters that you can use as well as how to print them.

Start Footnote Numbers Each Page   Option 6 has been set to No so that footnotes are numbered consecutively in a document. However, some publishers and universities require that the footnotes on each page begin with number 1. If this is the case, select this option and type **Y**.

Line Separating Text and Footnotes   WordPerfect is preset to separate the document and footnotes with a 2-inch horizontal line. You can choose from the following choices:

```
1 ]o Line; 2 2-inch Line; 3 ]argin to Margin: 0
```

Print Continued Message   You can use option 8 if you have foot-notes that wrap to the next page and you want "(continued. . .)" printed at the end of a footnote on the first page and at the beginning of the continuation on the next page. If you want to use this option, type **Y**.

If you have a language code indicating that you want to use the Speller, Thesaurus, and hyphenation rules for a different language in the document's Initial Codes, the "(continued. . .)" message will also be printed in that language.

The Language Resource file (WP.LRS) determines how the "(continued . . .)" message will print, either in your own or another language. If you want to make changes, see "Languages" in this chapter for more information about editing this file.

Footnotes at Bottom of Page   By default, footnotes are printed at the bottom of the page instead of just below the last line. If you type **N** after selecting this option, footnotes are printed just under the last line on the page.

Margin Settings for Notes

The default margin setting is used for all footnotes (1" if no margin set code is found in the Document's Initial Codes). For example, if you change the left and right margins to 1.5 inches, footnotes will still have margins of 1 inch if that was the default setting. If you want the footnotes to reflect the new margin changes of 1.5 inches, you will need to move the cursor just beyond the Margin Set code, [L/R Mar:*n,n*], enter the Footnote Options menu by pressing Footnote (CTRL-F7) and choosing 1 for Footnotes and then 4 for Options. Just entering and exiting the menu inserts the needed code; you don't have to make any changes. All footnotes then take on the margins that were set just before the [Ftn Opt] code. You can also change the default margin setting by pressing Format (SHIFT-F8), choosing 3 for Document and 2 for Initial Codes, and then setting the margin there.

Columns and Notes

Although you can create an endnote while in columns, you cannot create a footnote in columns. If you reformat text that contains footnotes into columns, the footnotes are automatically converted to endnotes.

Search for Notes

Although you would usually set footnote options at the beginning of the document or assign a new number to a footnote just before that footnote, footnotes and their associated codes are sometimes difficult to find. If you cannot find the right code, move to the top of the document, press Search (F2), press Footnote (CTRL-F7), and then choose 1 for Footnote. The following options appear:

```
1 Note; 2 Number Code; 3 New Number; 4 Options: 0
```

Choose 1 for Note to search for the first [Footnote] code (specific notes cannot be chosen), 3 for New Number to search for a [New Ftn Num] code (used when reassigning a number to a footnote), or 4 for a [Ftn Opt] code (Footnote Options menu changes). Option 2 for Number Code works only if you are doing an extended search, because it finds the [Note Num] code within the footnote itself.

If you want to search for or replace text that might be found within a footnote or endnote, use the Extended Search or Extended Replace feature. Press HOME before pressing Search (F2) or Replace (ALT-F2). The document, notes, headers, and footers are searched during an extended search, whereas a regular search looks through only the immediate document.

View Notes

By pressing Print (SHIFT-F7) and choosing **6** for View, you can view the page to see exactly how the footnotes and endnotes will appear on the printed page. This will help you see if the footnotes will print with the correct font, margins, and options (such as the type of separating line and style as well as for the note).

Change Footnotes to Endnotes

If you format text into columns, all footnotes are automatically converted to endnotes. You can then delete the column definition and columns-on codes to return the text to normal. The endnotes remain endnotes. See "Columns" in this chapter for more information about defining columns.

A macro is also included with WordPerfect that converts footnotes to endnotes and vice versa. If you want to use this macro, install the Keyboard Files (which includes both keyboard files and macros) if you have not already done so.

To use the macro, press Macro (ALT-F10) and enter **footend**. If the macro is not found, you may need to tell WordPerfect where it is with the Location of Files option on the Setup menu.

Related Entries

Search
Spell
Thesaurus
View Document

FORCE ODD/EVEN PAGE

You can insert a code into your document that will ensure that the current page will be either an odd or an even page.

Keystrokes

1. Press Go To (CTRL-HOME) and then ↑ to move the cursor to the beginning of the page.

2. Press Format (SHIFT-F8).

3. Choose 2 for **P**age.

4. Choose 2 for **F**orce Odd/Even Page.

5. Choose 1 for **O**dd or 2 for **E**ven.

6. Press Exit (F7) when you are finished.

Hints

Depending on which option you chose, the [Force:Odd] or [Force:Even] code is inserted at the cursor's location. The change is also reflected in the "Pg" prompt number on the status line.

When the document is printed and two odd or two even pages are found together, a blank page will be printed between them.

Applications

Because the first page of every chapter usually begins on an odd page, you can select this feature at the beginning of each chapter. If you are using a style to determine the format of your chapters, you could also include this code in the style. See "Styles" in this chapter for more information.

Related Entries

Page Numbering
Styles

FOREIGN LANGUAGES

WordPerfect comes in several languages. You can easily type in a different language by remapping the keyboard and assigning special characters to keys on the keyboard. See "Keyboard Layout" and "Compose" in this chapter for information about composing special characters.

WordPerfect also lets you use a different Speller and Thesaurus, depending on the language you have specified. For example, if you were doing translations from English to French, you could insert a "language" code into the document that tells WordPerfect when to switch to the Speller or Thesaurus for that language. For more information, see "Languages" in this chapter.

FORMAT

All formatting options are found on Format (SHIFT-F8). Margins, spacing, tabs, page numbering, and justification are only a few of the available formatting options.

Keystrokes

1. Press Format (SHIFT-F8). The menu shown in Figure 3-50 appears, showing how each format option is categorized. The four categories listed are Line, Page, Document, and Other.

2. Choose **1** for **Line**, **2** for **Page**, **3** for **Document**, or **4** for **Other**. Figures 3-51 through 3-54 show the menus that appear for each category.

3. You can change any of the options listed on these menus.

4. Press ENTER to return to the previous menu to make other selections, or press Exit (F7) to return to the document.

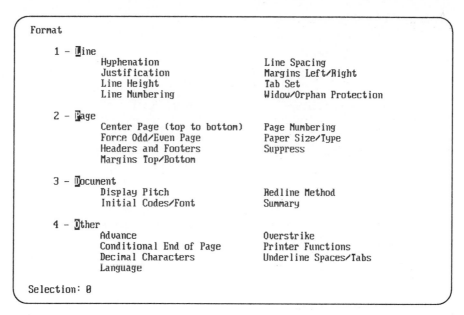

Figure 3-50.   Opening Format menu listing the features found under each category

Options

All the options listed on the format menus are explained in this chapter. Refer to the appropriate section for a description of the feature and the steps necessary to use it. The following is a general discussion of each category.

The Format: Line menu shown in Figure 3-51 controls formatting features that affect individual lines, such as tabs, margins, and spacing. Hyphenation, justification, line height, line numbering, and widow/orphan protection are also included on this menu because they deal with lines.

Figure 3-52 shows the Format: Page menu. The options listed here let you choose from many page "extras" that will help to determine where the page breaks will fall. WordPerfect checks the paper size, the top and bottom margins, and, depending on the height of the font(s) being used, WordPerfect will decide the number of lines that will fit on the page. Headers, footers, and page numbers also determine how many lines are subtracted from the total number available for the page. You should place most of these options at the beginning of the page or

```
Format: Line

    1 - Hyphenation                      No

    2 - Hyphenation Zone - Left          10%
                          Right          4%

    3 - Justification                    Full

    4 - Line Height                      Auto

    5 - Line Numbering                   No

    6 - Line Spacing                     1

    7 - Margins - Left                   1"
                  Right                  1"

    8 - Tab Set                          Rel: -1", every 0.5"

    9 - Widow/Orphan Protection          No


Selection: 0
```

Figure 3-51.   Line Format menu

```
Format: Page

    1 - Center Page (top to bottom)      No

    2 - Force Odd/Even Page

    3 - Headers

    4 - Footers

    5 - Margins - Top                    1"
                  Bottom                 1"

    6 - Page Numbering

    7 - Paper Size                       8.5" x 11"
                  Type                   Standard

    8 - Suppress (this page only)



Selection: 0
```

Figure 3-52.   Page Format menu

```
Format: Document

     1 - Display Pitch - Automatic Yes
                         Width     0.1"

     2 - Initial Codes

     3 - Initial Base Font        Courier 10cpi

     4 - Redline Method           Printer Dependent

     5 - Summary




Selection: 0
```

Figure 3-53.   Document Format menu

```
Format: Other

     1 - Advance

     2 - Conditional End of Page

     3 - Decimal/Align Character   .
         Thousands' Separator      ,

     4 - Language                 US

     5 - Overstrike

     6 - Printer Functions

     7 - Underline - Spaces       Yes
                     Tabs         No




Selection: 0
```

Figure 3-54.   Other Format menu

document so they will take effect on the current page. For example, if you define a header while in the second paragraph, it will not take effect until the next page.

Most formatting options in WordPerfect are set at the cursor's location and determine the format from that point forward. However, a few features are set for the entire document. The Format: Document menu shown in Figure 3-53 lets you change these types of formats. With option **2**, Initial Codes, you can edit the initial codes that were saved with the document when you created it. The codes were determined by the Initial Codes option in Setup (SHIFT-F1). Another advantage to using the Initial Codes feature is that the codes are not visible in Reveal Codes, which eliminates many of the codes at the beginning of the document. See the corresponding section in this chapter for details about each option.

The Format: Other menu shown in Figure 3-54 contains miscellaneous options that may not often be used in a document or settings that you might choose (in Setup) as default settings for the entire system. One feature used often in desktop publishing applications is Advance, which advances the printer up, down, left, or right from the current cursor location, or to an exact position on the page.

Option **6**, **Printer Functions**, leads to another submenu. The options listed there let you turn on kerning, insert a printer command, or choose the amount of space between letters and words.

If you have a version of WordPerfect dated 1/19/90 or later, you will also see an Option 8 on the Format: Other menu which lets you change the width, shading, and spacing of border lines used in graphics boxes and tables.

Hints

Note the mnemonic choices on each menu, and use them if you prefer. In fact, you will probably get to the point where you can make selections without even looking at the menus. For example, after pressing Format (SHIFT-F8), you can type **L** for Line and **S** for Spacing, and then enter the amount of spacing desired.

Most options selected from these menus insert a code in the document, which you can see by pressing Reveal Codes (ALT-F3). A code affects the document from that point forward until the cursor reaches another code that changes the setting.

When you enter a measurement or setting in these menus, Word-Perfect assumes that you want to set that measurement in inches unless you specify otherwise in the Setup menu. You can use the decimal equivalent (.5 for one-half) or fractions (1/2 for one-half) when you are entering these measurements.

Of course, you can always override the current unit of measurement by entering one of the following abbreviations after the measurement:

" or i = inches
c = centimeters
p = points
w = 1200ths of an inch
u = WordPerfect 4.2 Units (Lines/Columns)

For example, you could enter **3 1/2c** or **3.5c** for 3 1/2 centimeters. It would then be converted to the default unit of measurement. For example, if inches were the default, it would be converted to 1.38".

Most of the features in the Format: Line menu have some way of making their presence known. Margins, spacing, and so on show immediately on the screen. However, not all features appear on the screen. You can always enter the menu and see what the current setting is, or if you want to see page numbering, headers, footers, justification, line numbering, and other features on the screen, press Print (SHIFT-F7) and choose **6** for View Document. Although you can move the cursor while in View, you cannot make editing or formatting changes. Press Exit (F7) to return to your document.

If you are using the pull-down menus, you will find the format options under the **L**ayout category. See "Pull-Down Menus" in this chapter for more information.

Other items, such as columns and outlining, can be considered formatting features. Refer to a specific feature in this chapter for step-by-step instructions on its use.

Related Entries

Advance
Center Page from Top to Bottom

Columns
Conditional End of Page
Decimal/Align Character
Display Pitch
Footers
Force Odd/Even Page
Headers
Hyphenation
Initial Codes
Justification
Kerning
Language
Line Format
Line Height
Line Numbering
Margins, Left and Right
Margins, Top and Bottom
New Page Number
Other Format Options
Outline
Page Format
Page Numbering
Paper Size/Type
Printer Command
Pull-Down Menus
Redline
Spacing
Summary
Suppress
Tabs
Underline
View Document
Widow/Orphan Protection
Word and Letter Spacing

FORM LETTERS AND FORMS FILL-IN

See "Merge" in this chapter.

FORMS

WordPerfect 5.1 no longer uses the term "form" to describe the type and size of paper used for printing. See "Paper Size/Type" in this chapter for details about selecting or defining a specific size or type of paper.

FUNCTION KEYS

A template provided by WordPerfect Corporation is used to label the ten function keys that WordPerfect applies to various commands. If you misplace the template, press Help (F3) twice to see the screen shown in Figure 3-55. Press ENTER or the space bar to leave the help screen. Pressing Exit (F7) or Cancel (F1) will not exit help, but will display help screens for the Exit and Cancel keys.

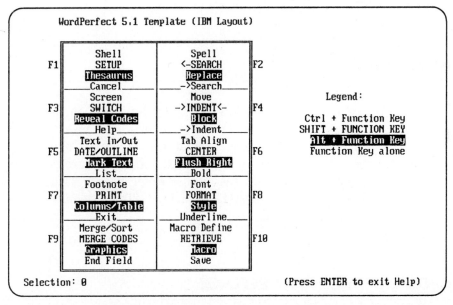

Figure 3-55.   The Function key template that is displayed when you press Help (F3) twice

If your function keys are in a row at the top of the keyboard, you can use an alternate template provided in the WordPerfect package. This type of template is not displayed in the help screen, however. If neither template that came in your package fits your particular keyboard, contact WordPerfect Corporation to find out about templates for your keyboard.

Four "levels" of commands are listed on each template. In general, the features used most often are assigned so that you can press a function key by itself to obtain that feature. On keyboards that have function keys arranged down the left side, related features are placed together. For example, the →Indent and Indent← functions are on F4, which is adjacent to the TAB key. With the introduction of the function keys across the top of the keyboard, some key assignments make less sense; for example, Bold is not next to Underline.

If a feature is printed in black on the template, press the function key by itself to use the feature. If it is printed in green, press SHIFT with the function key. For blue features, use the ALT key, and for features printed in red, use the CTRL key. Refer to the template for the color code, or place the colored stick-on labels provided with WordPerfect on the SHIFT, ALT, and CTRL keys.

GENERATE

The Generate option on Mark Text (ALT-F5) lets you compare the document on the screen with a document on disk and insert redline and strikeout marks automatically; expand and condense a master document; generate tables, lists, and an index; and update cross-references.

For more information, see "Cross-References," "Compare Documents," "Lists," "Index," "Master Document," "Table of Authorities," and "Table of Contents" in this chapter.

GLOBAL SEARCH AND REPLACE

See "Replace" in this chapter.

GO TO

WordPerfect's Go To feature lets you go to a specified page or character. When you are working in text columns or tables, you can use Go To to move from one column to the next.

Keystrokes

Go to a Specific Page

1. Press Go To (CTRL-HOME).

2. Type the number of the page. The cursor will move to the top of that page.

Go to Top or Bottom of Page or Column

1. Press Go To (CTRL-HOME).

2. Press ↑ to go to the top of the current page or column, or press ↓ to go to the bottom of the current page or column.

Go to a Column

When you are working in text columns (newspaper or parallel) or tables, you can use Go To to move to the next or preceding column or to the far left or right column.

1. Press Go To (CTRL-HOME).

2. Press → to move to the column to the right or ← to move to the column to the left.

You cannot use HOME, → to move to the far right column as you can in regular text—it moves to the "right margin" of the current column. To move to the far right column, press Go To (CTRL-HOME) and then press HOME, →. Press Go To (CTRL-HOME), HOME, ← to move to the far left column.

If you have an enhanced keyboard, you can use ALT and the arrow keys to the left of the numeric keypad to move quickly to the column to the left or right. If you do not have an enhanced keyboard, you can assign the macro commands {Item Left} and {Item Right} to any key on the keyboard to do the same thing. There are also commands for {Item Up} and {Item Down} (ALT-↑ and ALT-↓ on an enhanced keyboard) that are useful if you are working in parallel columns or tables, because you can use them to go to the set of parallel columns or the cell above or below.

See "Macros" in this chapter for more information.

Go to a Character, End of Sentence, or End of Paragraph

1. Press Go To (CTRL-HOME).

2. Type the character, and the cursor will go to the next occurrence of that character if it is within the next 2000 characters.

Instead of typing a character, type a period (.) to go to the end of a sentence, or press ENTER to go to the end of the paragraph (which actually finds the next occurrence of a hard return).

Go to Original Position

After pressing a cursor key such as PGUP, PGDN, Screen Up (−), Screen Down (+), HOME followed by an arrow key; pressing Block (ALT-F4); or doing a Search or Replace, you can press Go To (CTRL-HOME) twice to return the cursor to its original position.

This is helpful if you press a cursor key such as PGUP or PGDN by mistake and are not quite sure of your original location.

Go to Beginning of Block

If you turn on Block and begin highlighting text, but then decide that you have defined the block incorrectly, you can press Go To (CTRL-HOME) twice to return to the point at which you turned Block on. Block stays on so you can start again.

If you want to perform more than one function on a block of text, you will have to redefine the block because Block is turned off automatically after each function. For example, if you want to bold and underline a block of text, you would have to define the block twice. To quickly redefine the block, press Block (ALT-F4) and then press Go To (CTRL-HOME) twice.

Hints

Use Search (F2) when you want to go to the next occurrence of a string of characters rather than a single character. If you press a cursor key by mistake, press Go To twice to return to the original position. You can also press Go To twice in macros to go to the last location.

Related Entries

> Block
> Columns
> Cursor Keys
> Macros
> Search
> Tables

GO TO DOS OR SHELL

You can press Shell (CTRL-F1) to go to DOS temporarily. You do not exit WordPerfect; it is kept in memory.

Keystrokes

1. Press Shell (CTRL-F1).

2. Choose 1 for **G**o to DOS (or press Shell if WordPerfect Library or Office is running).

3. After completing the DOS functions, type EXIT and press ENTER to return to WordPerfect.

Hints

If you want to use a single DOS command, you can choose 2 for DOS Command. (This option is number 5 for DOS Command if the shell from WordPerfect Library or Office is running.) You can then use a single DOS command and return to WordPerfect when you press any key after the operation.

When you go to DOS while in WordPerfect, another copy of DOS (COMMAND.COM) is loaded. WordPerfect adds the message "Enter 'EXIT' to return to WordPerfect" to the DOS prompt. Type **exit** and press ENTER.

You must have enough memory (RAM) available to load the additional copy of DOS. When in DOS, you can use most commands, such as DIR, COPY, and DEL. If you want to use another program while in DOS, you must have sufficient memory available. For example, the Format and Diskcopy programs require additional memory.

Although you can run most programs when you go to DOS, do not try to load memory-resident (TSR) programs while WordPerfect is running. If you plan to load memory-resident programs, use Exit (F7) to leave WordPerfect first.

To return to WordPerfect, remember to enter **exit** at the DOS prompt. If you go to DOS from WordPerfect Library or Office, you can press Exit (F7) to return to WordPerfect. Do not enter **wp**, or (if you have expanded memory) another copy of WordPerfect will be loaded into memory. If this happens, you are asked if other copies of WordPerfect are running. Press Cancel (F1) to return to DOS if you do not want another copy of WordPerfect loaded.

One advantage to using the Go To DOS feature is that any documents in memory remain in memory. When you return to WordPerfect, your cursor returns to the point in the doucment at which you were last working.

If you are running the shell from WordPerfect Library or Office, you can press ALT-SHIFT-space bar as a shortcut method of going to the shell. See "Shell" in this chapter for more information about using the shell from WordPerfect Library or Office. This section tells you how to save graphics images or text to the clipboard and then use the information in WordPerfect documents, graphics boxes, or merge.

Related Entries

DOS Command
Exit
Shell

GRAPHICS BOXES

WordPerfect lets you place graphics boxes anywhere in a document. Figure 3-56 shows how this feature can be used to insert a graphics image into a document. You can also use these boxes for text and equations. The Graphics key (ALT-F9) also has an option that lets you place vertical or horizontal graphics lines anywhere on a page. See "Graphics Lines" in this chapter for details.

WordPerfect has several categories of graphics boxes: Figures, Table Boxes, Text Boxes, User-Defined Boxes, and Equation boxes. Each type of graphics box has identical capabilities but slightly different default settings. For example, figures automatically have a single-line border on all sides and place the caption "Figure n" below the box if a caption is selected where n is the number of the figure. A text box is shaded and has thick upper and lower borders. The caption for a table box appears in Roman numerals (as in "Table I") above the box. You can change any of these options for a single box or all boxes in the document.

WordPerfect also separates graphics boxes into different categories so you can have separate lists generated for each type of box (for example, a list of figures, list of equations, and so on). The list would include the captions for that type of box and the page numbers on which they appear. All figures are automatically included in List 6, all table boxes are included in List 7, and so on; you do not have to mark each caption for inclusion in the list. See "Lists" in this chapter.

Happy Birthday!

*Please come and help us celebrate
the company's first birthday!*

November 25, 1990

7:00 p.m.

Ivy Tower
345 N. Mountainway Drive

Figure 3-56. A sample page that includes a graphics image

The term "graphics box" refers to all types of graphics boxes. Differences are identified when applicable.

Keystrokes

Creating or Editing a Graphics Box

Before creating a graphics box, be aware of the cursor's location. If the graphics box is to be anchored to a certain position on a page, move the cursor to the top of the page (press CTRL-HOME and ↑ to move the cursor to the beginning of the page). If the graphics image will be positioned within columns, place the cursor just after the [Col On] code. If the graphics image is to remain with a certain paragraph, place the cursor within that paragraph. If you want the graphics image to flow with the text as a regular character, move the cursor to that location in the text. You will select the type of graphics box (paragraph, page, or character) when you are creating the graphics box.

You can also place a graphics box or a line in a header, footer, footnote, endnote, or style. If you want a graphics box or line repeated from page to page, consider placing it in a header or footer. If a text box is to be repeated at different locations within a document, consider placing it within a style. Keep in mind that you can only include a character graphics box (a graphics box that will wrap with the text as a single character) in a footnote or endnote. You will also not be able to include a caption in a header, footer, footnote, or endnote. See the "Applications" section and see Chapter 4, "Desktop Publishing with WordPerfect," for several examples of how you can use graphics boxes in your documents.

1. After positioning the cursor, press Graphics (ALT-F9). The following choices appear:

```
1 Figure; 2 Table Box; 3 Text Box; 4 User Box; 5 Line; 6 Equation: 0
```

2. Although you can choose options **1** through **4** or **6** to insert a graphics box (the only difference between the five options are a few default settings), you might want to choose **1** for **F**igure to insert a graphics image, **2** for **T**able Box to insert a table (either created in

WordPerfect or brought in from a spreadsheet program), 3 for Text Box if the box is to include text, 4 for User Box if you want to create a box with no graphics or text, or 6 for Equation if you want to create equations. Option 5 for Line is explained in "Graphics Lines" later in this chapter.

If you want to change the type of graphics box later, you can enter the definition menu, press Graphics (ALT-F9), and select the new type of graphics box.

3. After you make your selection, a menu similar to the following appears:

```
Figure: 1 Create; 2 Edit; 3 New Number; 4 Options: 0
```

The same menu would appear for the other options but would display "Table Box," "Text Box," "User Box," or "Equation" instead of "Figure."

4. Choose 1 to Create the chosen graphics box. Note that you can always edit the settings for a graphics box that has already been created by choosing 2 for Edit and then entering the number of the graphics box.

5. The menu shown in Figure 3-57 appears. Some of the settings will differ depending on the type of graphics box chosen. For example, if you choose to create an equation, option 2 for Contents will display "Equation" instead of "Empty," as it would normally.

The Contents option decides what will be displayed when you choose 9 for Edit: the graphics editor, with which you can move, scale, or rotate graphics images; the text editor, which lets you enter text; or the equation editor which formats equations as you enter them.

Choose each option that needs to be changed, and enter the correct information. (Each item is explained in the "Options" part of this section.) It is best to start at the beginning of the menu and change each option in the order in which it is listed.

```
Definition: Figure

     1 - Filename

     2 - Contents            Empty

     3 - Caption

     4 - Anchor Type         Paragraph

     5 - Vertical Position   0"

     6 - Horizontal Position Right

     7 - Size                3.25" wide x 3.25" (high)

     8 - Wrap Text Around Box Yes

     9 - Edit




Selection: 0
```

Figure 3-57.   The menu used to create a figure

6. Press Exit (F7) to return to the document. As you type text, a box will be displayed on the screen to show you where the graphics box will appear in relation to the text. The box will also be labeled according to the type of box being used (FIG, TBL, TXT, USR, or EQU). The number of the box is also displayed (1, 2, 3, or I, II, III, and so on). If you answered No to the option "Wrap Text Around Box," you will not see the box.

Assigning a New Number to a Graphics Box

If you want to start the graphics boxes in a certain category with a specific number, move the cursor just before the box or boxes to be affected and follow these steps:

1. Press Graphics (ALT-F9).

2. Choose the type of graphics box to be renumbered.

3. Choose 3 for **New Number**.

4. Enter the new number for the first graphics box. If the graphics box uses Roman numerals or letters, you will need to enter the new number in that format, or it will be ignored. For example, if "Figure A" is the style being used and you want the next figure to be numbered as Figure C, you would not enter 3 as the new number; you would enter C.

If you are using two-level captions, you can enter the new number for both levels with a hyphen (dash) separating them. For example, if a figure is numbered Table I.a and you want the next number to be Table III.a, you can enter the number as III-a.

Changing the Graphics Box Options

Table 3-10 gives a comparison of the options set for each type of graphics box. If you want to change any of these options, place the cursor just before the graphics box or boxes to be affected. All graphics boxes in that category will be affected until another options code is encountered.

1. Press Graphics (ALT-F9).

2. Type the number for the desired graphics box.

3. Choose 4 for Options. The options for each type of graphics box are listed in Table 3-10.

4. Choose any options and make the necessary changes. (Each option is described in the next part of this section.)

5. Press Exit (F7) to return to the document.

Options

This section is divided into two parts. The first part explains the items that are listed when you create a single graphics box (as shown in Figure 3-57). The second part explains the options that are found on the Graphics Box Options menu (as shown in Table 3-10). The second group of options affects all graphics boxes following the options code.

	Figure	Table Box	Text Box	User Box	Equation
Border Style					
Left	Single	None	None	None	None
Right	Single	None	None	None	None
Top	Single	Thick	Thick	None	None
Bottom	Single	Thick	Thick	None	None
Outside Border Space					
Left	.167"	.167"	.167"	.167"	.083"
Right	.167"	.167"	.167"	.167"	.083"
Top	.167"	.167"	.167"	.167"	.083"
Bottom	.167"	.167"	.167"	.167"	.083"
Inside Border Space					
Left	0"	.167"	.167"	0"	.083"
Right	0"	.167"	.167"	0"	.083"
Top	0"	.167"	.167"	0"	.083"
Bottom	0"	.167"	.167"	0"	.083"
First Level Numbering Method	Numbers	Roman	Numbers	Numbers	Numbers
Second Level Numbering Method	Off	Off	Off	Off	Off
Caption Number Style	[BOLD]Figure 1[bold]	[BOLD]Table 1[bold]	[BOLD]1[bold]	[BOLD]1[bold]	[BOLD](1)[bold]
Position of Caption	Below, outside	Above, outside	Below, outside	Below, outside	Right side
Minimum Offset from Paragraph	0"	0"	0"	0"	0"
Gray Shading (% of black)	0%	0%	10%	0%	0%

Table 3-10.   Graphics Box options

If you enter the Options menu, WordPerfect will use the current font for captions and any text in a graphics box created from that point in the document forward. Otherwise, the Document's initial base font is used. You can override these settings by inserting a specific font change in the caption or in the text in the graphics box.

Definition Options

The following options appear when you are creating or editing a single graphics box.

Filename   The first item lets you retrieve a WordPerfect text file, graphics image, or equation into the box. Enter the name of the file, including the drive and directory if necessary. If you forget the name of the file, you can press List (F5) to display the name of the directory specified for Graphics Files, press ENTER, move the cursor to the desired file, and choose **1** for **R**etrieve.

If you have WordPerfect Library or Office running, you can press Shell (CTRL-F1) and retrieve text or a graphics image from the clipboard.

If you are retrieving an equation, choose **2**, **C**ontents, and make sure that it displays "Equation." If you retrieve an equation and the Contents option is set to Empty or Text, the equation will be retrieved as text instead of being interpreted as an equation.

WordPerfect includes 30 graphics figures on disk that were created with DrawPerfect, a drawing program to be released by WordPerfect Corporation in early 1990. These images are stored in WordPerfect's graphics format with the filename extension .WPG. Appendix E includes a printout of each graphics image and its filename.

The types of graphics that are supported by WordPerfect are listed in Table 3-11. When you enter the name of a graphics file, you do not have to specify the format of the file. WordPerfect looks at the file, determines the format, and then converts it to WordPerfect's format so the image can be scaled, moved, and rotated by WordPerfect. These options are discussed in the "Editing Documents" section later in this chapter.

If you prefer, you can manually enter text into the box instead of entering a filename. Choose **9** for **E**dit, and then enter up to a page of text. While entering text, you can use Block, Move, Center, Flush Right, Bold, Underline, Fonts, and many other WordPerfect features. If you did not set the height of the box, it will increase or decrease, depending on the amount of text that you enter.

CGM	Computer Graphics Metafile
DHP	Dr. Halo PIC Format
DXF	AutoCad Format*
EPS	Encapsulated PostScript (only on PostScript printers)
GEM	GEM Draw Format
HPGL	Hewlett-Packard Graphics Language Plotter File
IMG	GEM Paint Format
MSP	Microsoft Windows Paint Format
PCX	PC Paintbrush Format
PIC	Lotus 1-2-3 PIC Format
PNTG	Macintosh Paint Format
PPIC	PC Paint Plus Format
TIFF	Tagged Image File Format
WPG	WordPerfect Graphics Format

If your particular format is not listed, your graphics package may be able to save the image in one of the formats listed above. If not, you can use the screen capture utility, GRAB.COM. See "Graphics Utilities" for more information.

PlanPerfect 3.0 graphics are not directly supported. You will need to upgrade to PlanPerfect 5.0, which creates graphics in WPG format or obtain the META.SYS graphics driver (GSS Metafile format) from WordPerfect Corporation that will produce CGM files.

*DXF files must first be converted to WPG format with the GRAPHCNV.EXE program before they can be used. See "Graphics Utilities" for more information about converting graphics images.

Table 3-11.   Graphics Formats Supported by WordPerfect

You can change the name of the file to be retrieved into the box at any time. For example, if you decide that a different graphics image or text file is appropriate, you can choose **1** for Filename and enter a new filename. You are then prompted with "Replace contents with FILE-NAME? **No (Yes).**" Typing **Y** would replace the contents of the box with the new file. You can also delete the filename shown by typing **1** for Filename and pressing CTRL-END to delete to the end of the name.

Contents   All graphics boxes except Text Boxes and Equations are automatically set to Empty. Text Boxes are set to "Text" and Equation graphics boxes are set to "Equation" so that the equation editor will be used when you choose **9** for **E**dit.

If you choose **1** for Filename and enter the name of a text file, the Contents option is changed to Text. If you retrieve a graphics image, "Graphics" appears. If you do not retrieve a file into the graphics box and choose **9** for **E**dit, you will be able to enter text; the Contents option would then change to Text as well.

Another option available for Contents is Graphics on Disk, which retrieves a graphics image only when you are editing, viewing, or printing. This option lets you "point" to a graphics image instead of saving it with the document. This reduces document size, retrieves the latest version of the graphics image (useful when retrieving graphs from spreadsheet programs where the data is constantly changing), and is the only way to include a graphics image in a style. If you try to retrieve a graphics image in a graphics box while creating a style, the Contents will automatically change to "Graphics on Disk."

Be aware that if you choose Graphics on Disk, you will need to have that graphics image in the directory specified as the graphics directory or in the default directory. If you want to use this option, you might want to consider converting the graphics image to WPG format with GRAPHCNV.EXE so it does not have to convert it each time it is "retrieved" for editing, viewing, or printing and will speed up the process.

If you want to use any graphics boxes for equations, you will first need to change the Contents to Equation, or the equation editor will not appear when you choose **9** for **E**dit. If you are retrieving an equation from disk to be placed in the graphics box, you will first need to change the Contents to Equation, or the equation will be interpreted as text.

To change the contents at any time, choose **2** for Contents and choose one of the following:

```
Contents: 1 Graphic; 2 Graphic on Disk; 3 Text; 4 Equation: 0
```

If you change the contents of a graphics box to a setting that does not match the current contents, WordPerfect assumes that you want to delete the current contents and asks for confirmation.

Caption   Even though WordPerfect has a caption style and a location for each type of graphics box, a caption is not included with the box unless you choose **3** for Caption; the default caption is then displayed (the number is updated with each box that is created). The following list explains the various default captions that are used for each type of graphics box. The type of numbering and location can be changed in the Options menu for each type of box.

Type of Box	Caption	Location
Figures	Figure 1	Below box, outside border
Table Box	Table I	Above box, outside border
Text Box	1	Below box, outside border
User Box	1	Below box, outside border
Equation	(1)	Right side (inside box)

When the caption is displayed, you can add text, delete the default caption by pressing BACKSPACE, enter new text, or reinsert the default caption by pressing Graphics (ALT-F9). You can also use Center (SHIFT-F6), Flush Right (ALT-F6), Bold (F6), Underline (F8), and choose from the list of Fonts (CTRL-F8) while editing the caption.

WordPerfect will center, flush-right, or wrap the text in the caption according to the width of the graphics box.

You cannot create a caption for a graphics box if it is part of a header, footer, footnote, or endnote.

Anchor Type   Before creating a graphics box, determine whether it will be placed in a specific position on the page, stay with a particular paragraph, or flow with the text as a regular character. As mentioned previously, place the cursor in the appropriate position, as shown here:

Page	Top of page or after columns on [Col On] code
Paragraph	Anywhere in the paragraph
Character	Where the graphics box will appear (in the document, footnote, or endnote)

If you create a paragraph graphics box, the graphics box code will be placed at the beginning of the paragraph or just after the last Hard

Return [HRt] code. The Page and Character options will insert the code at the cursor's location. If you are planning to insert a graphics box in columns, the cursor should be positioned after the columns on [Col On] code.

If a page graphics box is not found at the beginning of the page, you can place it on the next page, depending on its vertical position. For example, if you are in the middle of the page and request that the graphics box be placed at the bottom of the page, it will be printed on that page. However, if you are in the middle of the page and ask that it be placed at the top of the page, it will go to the next page instead.

While defining the graphics box, choose 4 for Anchor Type and choose one of the following options:

```
Anchor Type: 1 Paragraph; 2 Page; 3 Character: 0
```

If you choose 2 for Page, you are prompted for "Number of pages to skip." Because future editing could move a graphics box code from the top of a page, you could go to the beginning of the document before creating the graphics box and then specify how many pages need to be skipped. This would eliminate the problem of a graphics box code being moved to another page.

If you want the graphics box to appear on the current page, press ENTER to accept the default answer, 0. If you want to have the graphics box print on page 21 and you are on page 1, you would need to enter 20 as the number of pages to skip. If you enter a number that is greater than the total number of pages in the document, the graphics box will print on a page *after* the last page of the document.

Vertical Position   Select the type of graphics box (paragraph, page, or character) before choosing the vertical or horizontal position, because the options differ according to the type of graphics box that is selected.

If you choose a paragraph graphics box, the current position of the cursor in relation to the beginning of the paragraph is displayed. If the cursor is at the beginning of the paragraph, 0″ is displayed as the amount of offset from the top of the paragraph. If the cursor is a few lines down in the paragraph, the corresponding amount of space is displayed. For example, if you are 1 inch down in the paragraph, 1″ will be displayed as the vertical position. If you set the measurement to 0″, the border or the box will be placed at the top of the paragraph. Otherwise, the outside border space is placed at that location.

If the paragraph is too close to the bottom of the page to allow the graphics box to stay on the page with the paragraph, it checks the Minimum Offset from Paragraph measurement found in the Options menu and tries to move the graphics box further up into the paragraph so they can both be on the same page. Because the minimum amount is set to 0″ by default, you could move the graphics box to the top of the paragraph if that would help keep it together with the paragraph. If the box is still too large, it will be printed on the next page.

If you have chosen a page graphics box, the vertical position will be changed to Top, which means that the graphics box will be placed at the top of the page unless you choose another option. Choose **5** for **Vertical Position**, and then choose any of the options shown here:

```
Vertical Position: 1 Full Page; 2 Top; 3 Center; 4 Bottom; 5 Set Position: 0
```

Choose **1** for **Full Page** if you want the graphics box to span the distance between the top and bottom margins. The second, third, and fourth options place the graphics box at the top, center, or bottom of the page, respectively. The options to place the box at the top or bottom of the page do not interfere with page numbers, headers, footers, or footnotes. For example, the box will be printed below a header or above a footer. If you choose **5** for **Set Position**, the current distance from the top of the page to the cursor is displayed. Enter the exact measurement that you want from the top of the page. The top of the graphics box will be placed at that position.

If you selected Character as the graphics box type, you will see the following options when you choose **5** for **Vertical Position**:

```
Character Box Alignment: 1 Top; 2 Center; 3 Bottom; 4 Baseline: 0
```

If you choose **1** to align the text with the **T**op of the box, the top of the box will be placed at the highest point possible for the line. For example, if you are using a 12pt font, the line height will be approximately 14 points. The top of the box would then be placed 14 points above the baseline.

Choosing **3** for **B**ottom aligns the border at the bottom of the graphics box with the line of text. Choosing **4** for **Ba**seline aligns the baselines of both the text on the line and the text in the graphics box. The Baseline option is best if you have one line of text (such as an in-line equation) in the graphics box. If there is more than one line of text, the baseline of the last line in the graphics box is used.

Horizontal Position   You can change the horizontal position only if you have chosen a page or paragraph graphics box. A character graphics box will be placed at the cursor location.

If you choose Paragraph as the type, the following choices appear:

```
Horizontal Position: 1 Left; 2 Right; 3 Center; 4 Full: 0
```

The default selection is "Right" for all types of graphics boxes except equations. Equations are set to "Full" so they will span the distance between the left and right margins.

If you choose **1** for Left, WordPerfect places the graphics box against the current left margin. If the text is indented, WordPerfect places the box at the left of the indented text. If you have defined columns, WordPerfect places the box at the left of the paragraph in the current column, even if the column is not at the left side of the paper. The same principle applies when you choose option **2** to place the graphics box at the **R**ight of the paragraph.

If you choose **3** to Center a graphics box in a paragraph, the text will wrap only on the left side of the box. If you want text to wrap on both the left and right sides of the box, you will need to define columns and place a page graphics box between the columns.

Choosing **4** for **F**ull spreads the graphics box between the left and right margins of the paragraph. If you do not set a specific width for the box, it will be adjusted if the margins of the paragraph change. When the box is placed between the left and right margins, only the top line of the graphics box is displayed on the screen, regardless of the box's height. The correct amount of space is still reserved for the box.

When choosing the horizontal position for a page graphics box, you will see the following selections:

```
Horizontal Position: 1 Margins; 2 Columns; 3 Set Position: 0
```

If you choose **1** for **Margins**, the graphics box can be placed at the left or right margin, centered between the margins, or span the distance between the left and right margins (exactly like the paragraph option).

The second option, **2** for **Columns**, works the same as the Margins option, except that it relates to a particular column or columns. To use this feature, you have to position the cursor within columns before you create the graphics box (check the status line for the "Col" indicator). If you choose **2** for **Columns**, you are asked for the column or columns that will be affected by the box. If more than one column is involved, separate the column numbers with a hyphen (for example, entering **2-4** would affect columns 2, 3, and 4). The example shown in Figure 3-58 shows how a graphics image was centered between columns 1 and 2. When asked for the columns to be affected, **1-2** was entered.

After entering the columns to be affected, you are given the same horizontal choices that are given with the Margins option; remember that these settings relate to the columns just specified. In Figure 3-58, **3** for **Center** was selected. This lets you wrap text on both sides of a graphics box.

You can also choose **3** for **Set Position** to set an exact horizontal position. If you choose this option, the distance from the left side of the page to the cursor is displayed. Press ENTER to accept that measurement, or enter a different setting.

Size   As you select the vertical and horizontal positions, the size of the graphics box may also change. For example, if you request that a box be placed at the right margin of column 2, the box will decrease in size to fit that space. If a graphics image is enclosed in a box, it will be scaled to fit the new size automatically.

As you look at the measurement being used for the size of the box, either the width or the height is enclosed in parentheses. The parentheses indicate that WordPerfect will automatically calculate the width or

WordPerfect Corporation began unofficially in the summer of 1977 when Alan C. Ashton, a computer science professor at Brigham Young University, put a design for a word processing program on paper. The design was a significant departure from the Wang standard, and included such innovative features as modeless editing, auto insert, and a clean screen showing formatted text that matched what was printed.

During the same time period, Bruce W. Bastian was working on a Masters degree in Computer Science at the university. For his thesis project, he tied three computers together to generate marching band movements in 3-D graphics from any perspective within a football stadium.

Ashton and Bastian officially joined forces in 1979.

His creative and elegant programming caught the eye of Dr. Ashton, sparking interest in what would prove to be a very productive and rewarding partnership.

The two men joined forces in early 1979 and wrote a version of WordPerfect to run on Data General minicomputers. Their goal for the project was straightforward enough; make it easy, elegant, and powerful. Sharing computer time with local city administrators kept them in constant touch with the word processing needs of the marketplace which further refined their approach to WordPerfect, making it the number-one selling word processing software in the U.S. and many foreign countries.

Figure 3-58.   A page graphics box placed in the center of columns 1 and 2

the height for you. For example, if the graphics box is placed between the left and right margins, the width of the box has already been determined by the margins, and the height will be calculated according to the contents of the box. If you have text in the box, the height will be adjusted for that text, regardless of the number of lines. In fact, if you choose **9** to **E**dit a box containing text and add a few lines of text, the height of the box will change when you return to the menu.

Because text can be rotated on the page, WordPerfect lets you set the height of the box, and the width will then be adjusted according to the number of lines in the box. However, if you set the height to an exact setting and the number of lines entered in the text box exceeds that amount of space, the extra text will not be printed.

When you choose **7** for Size, the following options appear:

```
1 Set Width/Auto Height; 2 Set Height/Auto Width; 3 Set Both; 4 Auto Both: 0
```

You can choose **1** to set the **W**idth and have the height adjusted according to the text or graphics image, choose **2** to set the **H**eight and have the width adjusted, or choose **3** to set **B**oth the width and the height. Choosing **4** for Auto Both, sets the width and height according to a graphics image's original dimensions.

If WordPerfect will not let you change the size of the box, it is because the size of the box is figured according to what you have chosen earlier. For example, if the box is to be placed between the left and right margins, it would not make sense to adjust the width of the box, because that setting is already dependent on the current margins.

Wrap Text Around Box   WordPerfect automatically wraps text around a graphics box. If you do not want the text wrapped, but want it printed over the box instead, choose **8** for **W**rap Text Around Box, and then type **N**. In this case, the graphics box is not displayed on the screen.

The "Applications" section lists examples of how this feature can be used to wrap text manually around odd-shaped graphics images or to place a border around a page.

Because the graphics box will not appear on the screen when this option is set to No, it is easy to overlay graphics boxes by mistake. If you have a graphics monitor, use the view option to view the document frequently if you have a question about the location of the graphics (press Print (SHIFT-F7) and type **6** for View).

The number of graphics boxes that can be placed on a page is limited only by the printer's ability to print them (memory requirements may be restrictive). Although WordPerfect will wrap text around all boxes, it can display the wrapped text for only 20 boxes.

Edit   When you choose **9** for **E**dit, you will see a different screen, depending on the contents of the box. If the box contains a graphics image and you have a graphics monitor, you will see the image on the screen, complete with the selected border style, as shown in Figure 3-59. If you have a monochrome monitor that does not have graphics capability, you will see a pattern of dots representing the graphics image, as shown in Figure 3-60.

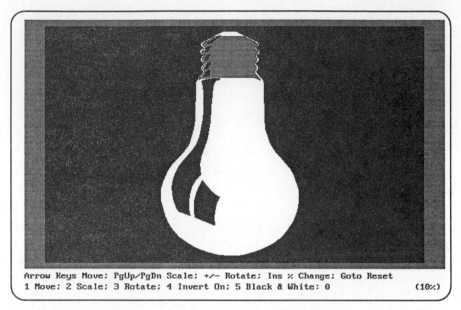

Arrow Keys Move; PgUp/PgDn Scale; +/- Rotate; Ins % Change; Goto Reset
1 Move; 2 Scale; 3 Rotate; 4 Invert On; 5 Black & White: 0   (10%)

Figure 3-59.   Editing a graphics image with a graphics monitor

If the box contains a text file, the text will be displayed on the screen, and you can edit the text. If you did not enter a filename, the screen will be blank and you can enter text at that point.

If the box contains text, the following message is displayed at the bottom of the screen:

Box: Press Exit when done, Graphics to rotate text   Ln 0" Pos 0"

The option to rotate text in a text box is available to those who have a PostScript printer or a laser printer that can combine two or more of the following orientations on the same page: portrait, landscape, reverse portrait, or reverse landscape. To have more than one orientation on the same page as in Figure 3-61, the graphics box must be a "Character" type of box.

To rotate the text in the graphics box, press Graphics (ALT-F9). The following choices appear:

```
Rotate Text: 1 0°; 2 90°; 3 180°; 4 270°: 1
```

Option 2 rotates the text 90 degrees counterclockwise (reverse landscape). The text in the box will be printed sideways from the bottom of the page to the top, as shown in Figure 3-61. Option 3, 180, prints in reverse portrait, and option 4, 270, prints in landscape orientation.

If a graphics image is included in the box, you will see the following options for moving, scaling, and rotating the image:

```
Arrow Keys Move; PgUp/PgDn Scale; +/- Rotate; Ins % Change; Goto Reset
1 Move; 2 Scale; 3 Rotate; 4 Invert On; 5 Black & White: 0          (10%)
```

There are two methods that you can use. The options on the first line tell you that you can use the arrow keys to move the image, PGUP and PGDN to scale (increase or decrease the size of) the image, and the + and − keys on the numeric keypad to rotate the image.

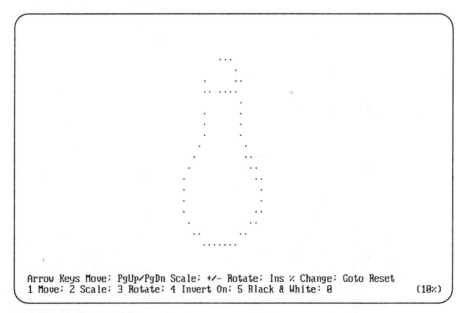

```
Arrow Keys Move; PgUp/PgDn Scale; +/- Rotate; Ins % Change; Goto Reset
1 Move; 2 Scale; 3 Rotate; 4 Invert On; 5 Black & White: 0          (10%)
```

Figure 3-60.   Editing a graphics image with a monochrome monitor

The News

Plans for Recreation Center Underway

The Board of Directors announced today that we will be adding an 8,000 square foot recreation facility to our campus. They have long felt that physical fitness will add to all employees' well-being and productivity on the job.

The recreation center will boast an indoor lap pool, jogging track, weight room, aerobics area, and basketball and racquetball courts. The center will be open from 5:00 a.m. to 10:00 p.m. six days a week.

Construction should be underway by the beginning of next month. The facility should be completed by the end of the year.

Purchasing Requests

The end of the fiscal year is quickly coming to an end. We encourage you to look closely at your budgets and your department needs and make any necessary purchasing requests as soon as possible.

If you plan to purchase computer hardware or software, you will also need to attach a C-458 form. We encourage standardization throughout our company and prefer that you purchase the products listed on the back of that form.

The deadline for these purchase requests is the end of the month.

Volunteers Needed in the Community

The personnel department has had several requests lately for volunteers in the community. Organizations need volunteers to take physically handicapped teenagers swimming, read to the blind, or help with a literacy program.

If you can donate a couple of hours a week to any of these worthy causes, please call Colleen at extension 4567.

Insurance Update

If you are admitted to a hospital for any reason, please specify your employer upon admittance. The billing departments of all hospitals in the area have been advised of our insurance coverage and are aware of the information needed to process a claim.

Don't forget that, when filing your first claim each year, one fully completed claim form must be submitted for each family member. Subsequent claims may be submitted with only a receipt for services rendered (unless the claim is accident-related, in which case a fully completed claim form is required).

All questions regarding company insurance policies—coverage, eligibility, and reimbursements—should now be directed to Mary in Accounting at extension 3042.

Figure 3-61.   A sample graphics box in which the text is rotated 90 degrees

These keys move, scale, and rotate the image by a specific increment, shown in the lower right corner of the screen. The default increment is 10 percent. You can change the percentage by pressing INS. It will then display "5%," "1%," and "25%," in that order. When you reach the percentage that you want to use, stop pressing INS. The selected percentage affects each of the options. If 10 percent is the default, the image will move 10 percent of the distance, increase or decrease 10 percent of the current size, or rotate by 10 percent (36 degrees).

Pressing Go To (CTRL-HOME) resets the image to the original location, size, and rotation.

The next line provides five options that offer more control over moving, scaling, and rotating because you enter an exact percentage or amount rather than using the interval shown at the bottom right corner.

If you choose **1** for **M**ove, you are asked for the horizontal and vertical positions. Enter a positive number to move the image up or to the right, or a negative number to move the image down or to the left. Always consider the starting position as 0″, with all other settings beginning from that point.

WordPerfect automatically scales the image according to the amount of available space in the box. Choosing **2** for **S**cale lets you change the amount of scaling for the x (horizontal) and y (vertical) axes independently. You can enter 80 percent for the x axis and 120 percent for the y axis to create a tall, narrow graphics image similar to the one shown in the following illustration. The graphics image at the left is set at the normal 100 percent scaling and the one at the right is set to 80 percent for the x axis and 120 percent for the y axis.

Scaling is not always effective for a bit-mapped image, because random bits are turned on or off to try to expand or compress the image. Because of the random selection, the image can become distorted.

Choosing **3** for **R**otate lets you rotate a graphics image (with the exception of bit-mapped graphics) by a specific percentage. Entering **90** would rotate the graphics 90 degrees counterclockwise so that the graphics image will print on its left side. Entering **180** would print the graphics image upside down, and **270** would print it with the right side pointing downward. Entering **0** or **360** would return the image to an upright position. The following example shows how an image was rotated 36 degrees:

After entering the degree of rotation, you are asked if you want a mirror image of the graphic. If you type **Y**, the graphics image will be reversed, just as if it were held up to a mirror:

You can also invert a bit-mapped image. When you choose **4** for Invert, each color is changed to its complementary color. Black is replaced with white, white with black, yellow with purple (magenta), green with red, blue with orange, and so on. Because most printers cannot print graphics images in color, the bit-mapped image will look like a negative of the original if you choose the Invert option. See "Hints" for more information about bit-mapped images.

You cannot invert text boxes so that the text will print in white on a black background. If you have a PostScript printer, you can, however, set the shading in the box to 100 percent (discussed in the next section, "Options Menu") and change the text color to white: Press Font (CTRL-F8), choose **5** for Print Color, and then choose **2** for **W**hite. See the next section for more information about shading.

The fifth option on the menu used to edit a graphics image is Black & White. This option lets you print and display the image in black and white. If you choose to use this option, the colored areas of a vector or line graphics image (all WPG graphics images) will print in solid black rather than in a pattern. If you are editing a bit-mapped image, this option will force it to be displayed in black and white, but it will not affect the printing.

Options Menu

After you press Graphics (ALT-F9) and choose a type of graphics box, you can choose **4** for Options. After selecting from the options on the menu, a code such as [Fig Opt] or [Tbl Opt] is inserted into the document and will affect all graphics boxes in that category from that point forward. Because of this, it is important to place the cursor before the graphics box(es) to be affected.

When setting options, remember that the options vary slightly from category to category. These differences are outlined in Table 3-10 (found earlier in this section).

The choices included in the Options menu are explained in the following sections.

Border Style   When you choose **1** for Border Style, you will see the following choices displayed at the bottom of the menu:

1 None; 2 Single; 3 Double; 4 Dashed; 5 Dotted; 6 Thick; 7 Extra Thick: 0

Select any of the border styles for each side. If you want to create a three-dimensional effect, choose Thick or Extra Thick for two adjoining sides and Single for the other two adjoining sides. For example, the following borders were selected to produce the example shown in Figure 3-62. Note that Extra Thick was chosen for two adjacent sides (right and bottom).

Left	Single
Right	Extra Thick
Top	Single
Bottom	Extra Thick

Choose the border style that you want to use for each side. The type of border that you select will appear in the Edit screen if the box includes a graphics image and you have a graphics monitor.

Figure 3-62. A three-dimensional border created by choosing the Extra Thick option on the right and bottom sides

If your version of WordPerfect is dated 1/19/90 or later, the Format: Other menu includes an option letting you change the thickness, shading, and spacing for each type of border style (single, double, and so on).

Outside Border Space   This setting refers to the amount of space that will be reserved around the border. If you enter 0, the text in the document can be wrapped right up to the edge of the box.

If you place a box at the top, bottom, left, or right margin, the outside border space on that side does not take effect: The border is printed flush against the margin.

Inside Border Space   This option determines the amount of space to reserve between the border and the contents of the graphics box. If you have increased the size of a graphics image to fill the graphics box, this setting will override the graphics image and cut it back if necessary. Of course, if the option is set to 0, the contents of the box can fill the box completely. If you have not selected a border style, the amount of space is still reserved. This option is more effective than using Indent, Tab, or spaces to try to add space between the image (or text) and the border.

First Level and Second Level Numbering Method   Options 4, 5, and 6 work closely together. Type either 4 for First Level or 5 for Second Level Numbering Method. The following selections appear:

```
1 Off; 2 Numbers; 3 Letters; 4 Roman Numerals: 0
```

Option 2, Numbers, refers to regular Arabic numbers (1, 2, 3, and so on). If you select Letters for the first level, uppercase letters (A, B, C, and so on) will be used. If you choose letters for the second level, lowercase letters (a, b, c, and so on) will be used. Roman numerals appear as I, II, III, IV, and so on for the first level and i, ii, iii, iv, and so on for the second level.

Although you might have selected the numbering method for both levels, neither method will be used unless you change the caption number style. If both levels are included in the caption number style, they will both be displayed at the top of the box that is placed in a document to identify the type and number of the graphics box.

Caption Number Style Enter the text that will be used for all captions in that category, and include the number **1** to represent the first level, **2** to represent the second level, or both **1** and **2**. Since you can enter any type of punctuation, you could enter **1.2**, **1-2**, or **1(2)**.

If both levels are included in the caption number style, only the second-level number will change from figure to figure until you reach the maximum number of "31." For example, if you are numbering figures for a specific chapter, you might want to enter **Figure 1-2** as the style. At the beginning of each chapter, you would choose the New Number option to start the next group of graphics boxes with a new number. If the chapter was Chapter 4, you could enter **4-1** as the new number. The figures would then be numbered "Figure 4-1," "Figure 4-2," "Figure 4-3," and so on until they reached number 4-31. At that point, the figures would be numbered 5-1, 5-2, 5-3, and so on.

Position of Caption When you choose this option for any type of graphics box except equations, you are first asked whether you want the caption placed below or above the box and then whether the caption should be outside or inside the border.

If you are in the Equations Options menu and choose this option, you are given the following choices:

```
Caption Position: 1 Below Box; 2 Above Box; 3 Left Side; 4 Right Side: 4
```

If you choose the left or right side, the caption is placed inside the box with the equation. If it will not fit in the box with the equation, it will be moved just below the box.

Minimum Offset from Paragraph   If you choose a paragraph graphics box, you can specify the amount of space that the graphics box should be offset from the top of the paragraph when you are creating the graphics box. However, if the paragraph is too close to the bottom of the page to allow the graphics box to stay on the page with the paragraph, it checks the measurement entered for this option and tries to move the graphics box further up into the paragraph so that the text and graphics box can remain together on one page. Because the minimum amount is set at 0″ by default, the graphics box could move to the top of the paragraph if this would help keep it and the paragraph together. If the box is still too large, it will be printed on the next page.

Increase this setting if you do not want a graphics box to be placed on the first line of the paragraph. Entering .5″ would let the graphics box be placed no more than a half-inch from the first line.

Gray Shading (% of Black)   If your printer can shade a graphics box, you can enter a setting from 0 to 100 percent, with 0 percent for white and 100 percent for black. The darker you make the shading, the more you should be aware of a ″halo″ effect around letters. A moderate amount of shading is provided by 20 to 30 percent. Text boxes are preset to print a shaded background of 10 percent.

If your printer can print white letters on a black background, you can choose 100 percent to make the background black and then change the print color to white by pressing Font (CTRL-F8), choosing **5** for Print Color, and then choosing **2** for White.

This type of effect will not appear when you view the document unless you have the ″View Screen Options″ in the Setup menu set to Black and White.

Hints

When you insert a graphics box into the document, a code resembling [Fig Box:*n*; *Filename*;*Caption*] (*n* represents the figure number) is inserted at the cursor location. The filename is displayed if you have retrieved a file (text, graphics, or equation) into the graphics box. Part of the caption also appears in the code if you have inserted a caption.

[Box Num] will appear as part of the caption to represent the Caption Number Style set in the Options menu.

The other codes would appear as [Tbl Box:], [Txt Box:], [Usr Box:], and [Equ Box:]. If you chose to renumber a graphics box, a code similar to [New Fig Num:*1a*] appears in Reveal Codes; *1* represents the first-level number, and *a* represents the second-level number. If one or the other is not used in the caption number style, it will not appear in this code.

When you change the options for a group of graphics boxes, the codes [Fig Opt], [Tbl Opt], [Txt Opt], [Usr Opt], and [Equ Opt] are inserted.

To search for any of these codes, press Search (F2) or ←Search (SHIFT-F2), press Graphics (ALT-F9), choose the category, and then select one of the options shown here. Keep in mind that the menu is customized for each category.

1 Figure; 2 New Figure Number; 3 Figure Options; 4 Box Number: 0

The first option searches for the next graphics box of that type. If you want to find a box by its number, you can press Graphics (ALT-F9), choose the appropriate category, choose **2** for **E**dit, and then enter the number of the graphics box to be edited without doing a search.

Option **2** on the search menu searches for a **N**ew Number code, and option **3** searches for an **O**ptions code. The fourth option applies only if you have included the automatic figure number in a caption. Even then, you need to do an extended search (press HOME before pressing a Search key) to find the code. The cursor would be placed within the caption if the code is found.

Columns, Tables, and Graphics Boxes

Because WordPerfect tables created with Columns/Tables (ALT-F7) cannot be included in columns, you can include them in a graphics box. Columns can also help you place several graphics boxes side by side and provide a way of wrapping text around a table. Any type of graphics box can also be inserted in a WordPerfect table (but not if the table is already inside a graphics box). See "Tables" in this chapter for an example of how to include graphics and equations in a table.

Graphics Types

There are basically two types of graphics images: vector and bit-mapped. A vector (or line) graphics image consists of lines drawn from point A to point B. If you move, rotate, or scale a vector graphics image, you are changing only the location of point A and point B; the line will still be drawn between them. The graphics images provided with Word-Perfect are examples of vector graphics. These are displayed in Appendix E.

A bit-mapped graphics image is quite different. Separate, tiny bits are turned on or off to create the image. A bit-mapped graphics image can be moved but not rotated (unless you have a PostScript printer). If you try to scale the image, random bits are turned on or off in an attempt to keep the same image, but because of this, distortion can occur. Scanned images (TIFF format) and PIC files produced by paint programs are examples of bit-mapped images.

Table 3-11 contains a list of graphics formats supported by Word-Perfect. If you want to use DXF format, the file will first need to be converted with the GRAPHCNV.EXE program. See "Graphics Utilities" in this chapter for details.

Printing Graphics

If you have a large graphics image or several smaller images on the screen, your printer might not have enough memory to print them. You can help the situation by decreasing the quality of the graphics or by printing the graphics and text separately and combining them at the copy machine or running the pages through the printer twice.

WordPerfect is preset to print graphics at medium quality. If you need to make a change, follow these steps:

1. Press Print (SHIFT-F7).

2. Type **G** for **G**raphics Quality.

3. Select one of the following options:

```
Graphics Quality: 1 Do Not Print; 2 Draft; 3 Medium; 4 High: 3
```

This setting will remain with the current document and will be reset to Medium when you start a new document. To change it permanently, press Setup (SHIFT-F1) and choose **4** for Initial Settings, **8** for Print Options, and **3** for Graphics Quality.

Lists

If you want a list of the captions for all figures, table boxes, text boxes, user boxes, and equations, along with the page numbers on which they can be found, define a list in the following manner:

1. Move the cursor to the location at which the list should appear.

2. Press Mark Text (ALT-F5).

3. Choose **5** for **Define**.

4. Choose **2** to Define a List.

5. When prompted, enter the number for the list using the following numbers as a guide:

6	Figures
7	Table boxes
8	Text boxes
9	User boxes
10	Equations

6. Choose the style of page numbering to be used for the list.

7. Normally, you would block and mark the text to be included in a list. However, if you use lists 6 through 10, you do not have to mark the captions; WordPerfect automatically includes them in the appropriate list.

8. After editing the document, press Mark Text (ALT-F5); choose **6** for **Generate**; then choose **5** to Generate Tables, Indexes, Cross-References, and so on; and then type **Y** to continue.

The captions for each type of graphics box will be placed in the appropriate list. If a figure does not have a caption, it will not be included in the list.

Applications

All applications in this section were created with the graphics images that are included in the WordPerfect package. Chapter 4, "Desktop Publishing with WordPerfect," has other examples.

Wrapping Text Around an Odd-Shaped Image

Even though WordPerfect cannot wrap text right up to an odd-shaped graphics image, you can do this manually, as shown in Figure 3-63. First eliminate the border with the Options menu. Then, when creating the graphics box, type **N** in answer to the "Wrap Text Around Box" prompt. If you have a graphics monitor, you can press Print (SHIFT-F7) and choose **6** to View the document and see approximately where the lines should break. Press Exit (F7) to return to the document, and use ENTER to break the lines manually. You can also use the same method for graphics that you want placed at the left margin, or in the center between margins, by adding space at the beginning of the line or in the middle of the line. Please note, however, that this process can be time consuming.

Combining Text and Graphics

By changing the option to "Wrap Text Around Graphics" to No, you can combine text and graphics images, as shown in the following example:

Wrapping Text Around
an Odd-Shaped Graphics Image

Although it is time consuming, you can wrap text around an irregular shaped object by eliminating the borders of the figure and typing **N** to the question, "Wrap Text Around Box." The box will not appear on the screen as it would if the answer to the question were Yes. After you have made all corrections to the text (it is extremely difficult to make changes after wrapping the text around the figure manually), you can look at the document in View mode (press Print (SHIFT-F7) and type **6** for **V**iew) to see where the line should break.

If you cannot read the text, increase the scaling 100% or 200% instead of using the Full Page display. After returning to the regular editing screen, you can find the exact location and press ENTER to insert a [HRt] to force the rest of the line to wrap. Even though this is time consuming and difficult to edit the text after the process is complete, it is faster than cutting and pasting by hand.

By the way, it is necessary to have a graphics display to take advantage of this feature because View in text mode will not display the line breaks accurately.

Figure 3-63. Wrapping text around an odd-shaped graphics image

Use the Advance feature to position the text in an exact position by pressing Format (SHIFT-F8), and choosing **4** for **O**ther and then **1** for Advance. In this case, the BURST-1.WPG image was used.

You can also include a border around a page by creating an empty figure in a header and setting the "Wrap Text Around Box" option to No. If you want to use the border image already provided with WordPerfect, create a user box (no borders are defined for this type of box) and retrieve the file "BORDER-8.WPG" into the graphics box. See "Borders" in this chapter for more information about how to set the graphics box menu items and how to include the graphics box in a header so that it will print on every page and not interfere with the document's margins.

Drop Cap

You can use a graphics box with no borders or border space to hold a large character at the beginning of a paragraph. You can then wrap several lines around the character (box) as shown here:

T his example shows how a 30pt font was placed in a User Box (which has no borders) to create a large letter at the beginning of a paragraph (sometimes called a "drop cap"). The regular text appears in 8pt to create the contrast between the large and small letters. Before inserting the box, the User Box Options menu was displayed and the Outside Border Space was changed to 0" on all sides. The box was created as a paragraph box, with the Horizontal Position set at the left margin. The width and height of the box was set to .3" and .35" respectively.

Graphics in Styles

You can create an overhead presentation like the one shown in Figure 3-64 using a style. You would then use the style for each item to avoid repeating the steps for inserting the checkbox graphic. To create the document, follow these steps:

1. Type the heading for the overhead or handout.

2. Press Style (ALT-F8).

3. Choose 3 for Create.

4. Choose 1 to enter a Name for the style (such as Checkbox).

5. Choose 4 for Codes.

6. Create a graphics box that points to the CHKBOX-1 graphics image included with WordPerfect. To do so, press Graphics (ALT-F9); choose 4 for User Box (no borders are defined for a user box), 1 for Create, and 1 for Filename; then enter the full pathname where

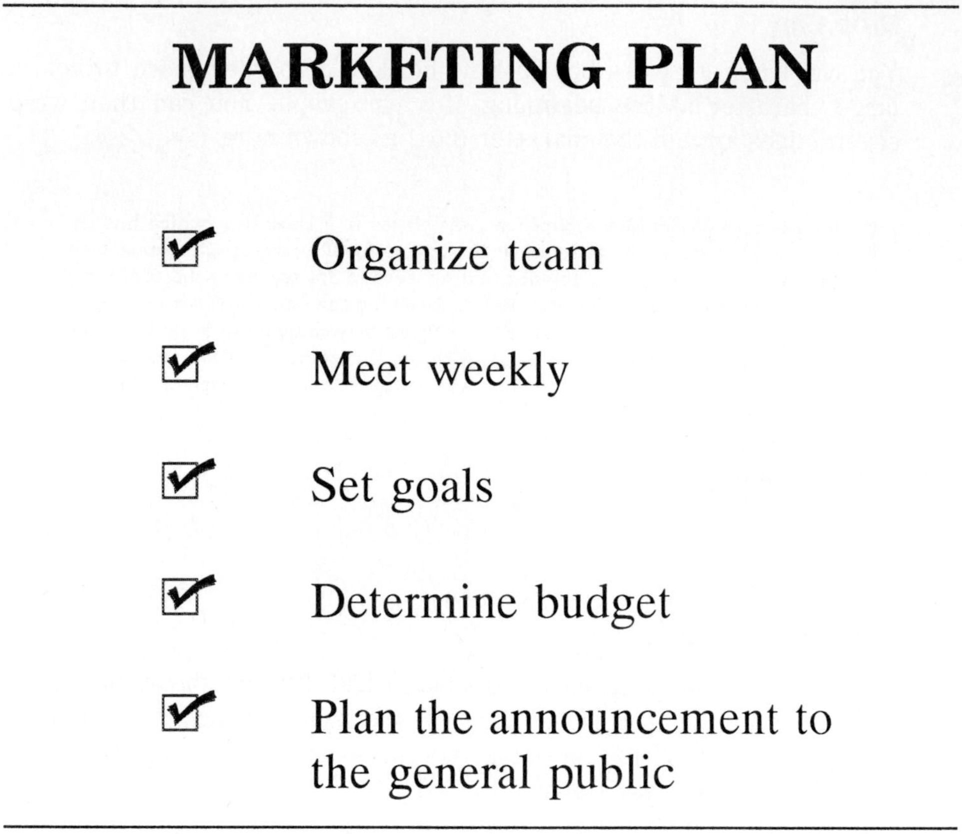

MARKETING PLAN

☑   Organize team

☑   Meet weekly

☑   Set goals

☑   Determine budget

☑   Plan the announcement to the general public

Figure 3-64.   Graphics boxes in styles

CHKBOX-1.WPG is located. Because you are in a style and cannot retrieve a graphics image (you can only point to one on disk), the contents are automatically changed to "Graphics on Disk."

7. Choose **4** for Anchor **T**ype and **3** for Character so that it will be inserted as a regular character. The last option that needs to be changed is the size. Try .4″ or .5″ for both the width and height, or experiment with settings of your own. Press Exit (F7) when you are finished.

8. Add a TAB or Indent (F4) code before the [Comment] code and two [HRt] codes after (press ENTER twice) to add space between items.

9. Press Exit (F7) to return to the checkbox style menu.

10. Choose 5 for **Enter**, and then choose 3 for Off/On. Pressing ENTER will turn the style off and back on again to make it easier to enter each item.

11. Press Exit (F7) to return to the list of styles.

12. Press ENTER to turn on the style, type the text for the first entry, and then press ENTER. WordPerfect should turn the style off and back on again. When you are finished, press → to move past the style-off code and turn off the style.

You could also use this method to include an empty figure that measures .2″ by .2″ for a small, empty box that can be used as a checkbox for forms.

If you might be using this style often, enter the Styles menu (ALT-F8), press Save (F10), and enter the name of a file that can be used for the style, such as BOX. You can then retrieve the style from that file while in the Styles menu in another document.

The examples used in this section on graphics boxes should help you when you need to insert graphics boxes of your own. See additional examples in Chapter 4, "Desktop Publishing with WordPerfect."

Related Entries

Columns
Footers
Graphics Lines
Graphics Utilities
Headers

Keyboard Layout
Lists
See also Chapter 4, "Desktop Publishing with WordPerfect"
See also Appendix E, "Graphics Images"

GRAPHICS LINES

WordPerfect can place a horizontal or vertical graphics line anywhere on a page, between columns, or in headers, footers, and styles.

Often referred to as "rules" in desktop publishing, graphics lines can help dress up your documents. Figure 3-65 gives an example of how horizontal lines can be used in a header and footer, and how vertical lines can be used between columns.

Keystrokes

Because you can choose both horizontal and vertical positions for vertical lines, it might be best to move the cursor to the beginning of the page so that WordPerfect will recognize the command before it reaches that location at print time. If you plan to place the graphics lines between columns, move the cursor into the columns area (after the [Col On] code).

1. After positioning the cursor in the correct position, or while creating a header, footer, or style, press Graphics (ALT-F9). As you are positioning the cursor or making selections, be aware that text will not wrap around graphics lines.

2. Choose 5 for Line.

3. Choose 1 to create a Horizontal line or 2 to create a Vertical line. (You can also choose 3 to edit the first Horizontal Line code to the left of the cursor or 4 to edit the first Vertical Line code to the left of the cursor. If a horizontal or vertical line is not found to the left of the cursor, WordPerfect searches in a forward direction.)

Corporate Update

Welcome to the New Year!

1989 was a very good year and all indications point to 1990 being even better. We are predicting sales to double and profits to soar.

During 1989 we opened several overseas offices, built three new buildings, introduced several new products, and received rave reviews on our old ones.

We wish you every success in your personal goals and career and are grateful to have you as part of the winning team. May 1990 be our best year ever!

New Home for Marketing

As of January 15, the Marketing department will move into building six.

All mail normally sent to the marketing department should be addressed to building six. A new phone book will be distributed before the end of the month, listing new addresses and phone numbers for those involved in the move.

Insurance Update

If you are admitted to a hospital for any reason, please specify your employer upon admittance. The billing departments of all hospitals have been advised of our insurance coverage and are aware of the information needed to process a claim.

Don't forget that, when filing your first claim each year, one fully completed claim form must be submitted for each family member. Subsequent claims may be submitted with only a receipt for services rendered (unless the claim is accident-related, in which case a fully completed claim form is required.

Insurance Questions?

All questions regarding company insurance policies—coverage, eligibility, and reimbursements—should now be directed to Mary in Accounting at extension 304.

Business Card Orders

All employees who will be attending the computer convention and need to reorder business cards are requested to do so before January 25. Please call Laurie with your order.

Travel Policies

Due to recent changes in the company travel policies and procedures, an authorization number is needed before airline tickets can be issued. If you will be traveling for the company, please have your travel form filled out and signed by your supervisor prior to submitting it to May in Accounting. She will then give the authorization number to the travel agent.

Training Classes

The next session of product training classes begins on February 8, but classes are beginning to fill up now.

Figure 3-65.   A page in which horizontal graphics lines appear in a header and footer, and vertical graphics lines are placed between columns

After selecting option **1** or **2** to create a graphics line, the following choices appear:

```
Graphics: Vertical Line
     1 - Horizontal Position      Left Margin
     2 - Vertical Position        Full Page
     3 - Length of Line
     4 - Width of Line            0.013"
     5 - Gray Shading (% of black) 100%
```

This screen is for vertical lines. Note that the line will be placed at the left margin and extend down the full page. The default settings for a horizontal line are: at the baseline and the full distance between the left and right margins.

4. Make any necessary changes. All options are explained in the next section.

5. Press Exit (F7) to return to the document, header, footer, or style. If you decide not to include the line, press Cancel (F1) to leave the menu.

By default, a horizontal line .013 inch thick would be drawn at the cursor's position, from the left to the right margin. If you choose a vertical line without making changes to the menu, a vertical line .01 inch thick will be drawn at the left margin from the top of the page to the bottom (full page). The lines will not appear on the normal editing screen, but they will be displayed when you view the document with a graphics monitor or print it.

Options

The following options appear on the Horizontal Line and Vertical Line menus.

Horizontal Position

When you are creating a horizontal line, the following selections are available for the horizontal position:

```
Horizontal Pos: 1 Left; 2 Right; 3 Center; 4 Full; 5 Set Position: 0
```

You can choose 1 to start the horizontal line at the Left margin, 2 to have the line end at the Right margin, 3 to begin the line at the Center point of the page, 4 for Full to span the page from the left and right margins, or 5 for Set Position to start the line from a specific position from the left side of the page. If you choose option 4, Full, you will not be able to specify the length of the line, since it will be calculated automatically depending on the margins.

Depending on the option chosen, the length of the line may change. For example, if you choose Center, the length of the line is set to 0″. You then need to choose the Line Length option and set it at the desired length.

If you choose 5 for Set Position, the current measurement from the left side of the page is displayed as the default.

If you are creating a vertical line, the selections are different, as shown here:

```
Horizontal Position: 1 Left; 2 Right; 3 Between Columns; 4 Set Position: 0
```

You can choose **1** to place the vertical line at the **L**eft margin, **2** for the **R**ight margin, **3** to place the line **B**etween Columns, or **4** to **S**et the Position from the left edge of the page. If you choose option **3** to place it between columns, you will see a "Place line to right of column:" prompt. Enter the number of the column. If you have more than two columns, you will need to create separate lines for each column. If the cursor is not within columns when a vertical line is defined, the line will be placed at the right margin.

If you have a graphics image or text box between columns, the graphics line could print through the box. You will probably want to create two vertical lines in this case, one above and one below the box. Use the Set Position option for both horizontal and vertical positions and manually calculate the length of the line.

If you choose **4** for Set Position, the current distance from the left side of the page is displayed as the default setting. Press ENTER or enter a new setting.

Vertical Position

By default, a horizontal line is drawn at the current baseline (the bottom edge of a line of text). You can either use the Advance feature to go to the exact vertical position on the page and then insert a horizontal line, or you can choose this option (Vertical Position) and choose **2** for Set Position, as shown in the following options:

```
Vertical Position: 1 Baseline; 2 Set Position: 0
```

If you choose **2** for Set Position, the cursor's current position on the page is displayed. Press ENTER to accept that setting or enter a different one.

If you choose Vertical Position while creating a vertical line, you are given the following choices:

```
Vertical Position: 1 Full Page; 2 Top; 3 Center; 4 Bottom; 5 Set Position: 0
```

If you choose option **1** for Full Page, the line will be drawn from the top margin to the bottom margin. You can also select **2** to have the vertical line start at the **T**op, **3** to have the line **C**entered halfway down the page, **4** to start the line at the **B**ottom of the page, or **5** to **S**et the exact vertical position from the top of the page. If you choose this option, the current distance from the top of the page to the cursor is displayed as the default. The length of the line may also change as you change the vertical position.

Length of Line

If a horizontal line spans the distance between the left and right margins, or if you have chosen a full-page vertical line, you will not be able to change this option; the length is determined by the current margins. The length of the line may change depending on the values entered for the Horizontal Position or Vertical Position option. The length is usually calculated as the distance from the cursor to the margin (left or right) selected as the horizontal position. However, if you choose to center a horizontal line between the left and right margins, the length of the line is changed to 0″. Choose this option and enter a different setting if necessary. You can extend the line into the margins if necessary.

Width of Line

Lines will be .013 inch thick unless you specify otherwise. The following illustration shows the difference between settings for .013, .03, .05, .1, and .5 inch:

Gray Shading (% of Black)

All lines are automatically 100 percent black. You can decrease the amount of shading by entering a new percentage. If you used a wide, shaded line over existing text, it will look similar to a shaded text box with no border.

Hints

The codes [HLine:*HPos,VPos,Length,Width,Shading*] and [VLine:*HPos, VPos,Length,Width,Shading*] are inserted at the cursor's current location.

When you are inserting a horizontal line at the baseline, you will need to press ENTER *twice* before you enter the next line of text. The first time you press ENTER, the cursor moves down only the width of the line. The second ENTER is needed to move the cursor down a full line so that the text on the line below or another graphics line will not print right next to the graphics line above. If you have a horizontal line that is two-tenths (.2″) of an inch wide, pressing ENTER once would move the cursor down the page .02 (to return to the original baseline). You would then need to press ENTER again to move down to the next line. Pressing ENTER the second time inserts the amount of space given to the Line Height setting. You can, of course, use the Advance feature found on the Format: Other menu to advance down a specific amount of space.

Applications

WordPerfect includes a style in the file LIBRARY.STY that uses vertical lines to create a ″pleading″ paper style, as shown in Figure 3-66. Two thin vertical lines are placed in a header so they will print on every page. To use this style, you must have installed the Style file during installation. You can return to the Install program and copy the file at any time.

You may want to delete the numbers that are included in the style and use line numbering instead. If you have an early version of 5.1, you may need to edit the header in the style and delete the first two hard

Figure 3-66.   Pleading paper created with the "pleading" style found in the
LIBRARY.STY file

return [HRt] codes to make it print properly. See "Styles" and "Line Numbering" in this chapter for details.

If you have a company logo and an address at the top right corner of your business letterhead, you can insert a horizontal line at the right margin to set off the logo from the body of the letter, as follows:

Just Desserts

You can place horizontal lines in headers and footers to create an upper and lower "border" for the page. You can also combine horizontal lines with page numbers in a header or footer (press CTRL-B to insert ^B as the current page number). In the following illustration, Advance was used to advance the lines to specific positions.

Page 2

Figure 3-67 shows you how you can use horizontal lines in a style. Each heading was created with a paired style that inserted a .013-inch-thick horizontal line against the left margin and a font change in the beginning of the style, with a .03-inch-thick horizontal line and an Advance command at the end of the style. See "Styles" in this chapter for more information about creating such a style. See Chapter 4 for other examples of how to use graphics lines in your documents.

Related Entries

Footers
Headers
Styles
See also Chapter 4, "Desktop Publishing with WordPerfect"

AMENDMENTS

AMENDMENT 1

Congress shall make no law respecting an establishment of religion, or prohibiting the free exercise thereof; or abridging the freedom of speech, or of the press; or the right of the people peaceably to assemble, and to petition the Government for a redress of grievances.

AMENDMENT 2

A well regulated Militia, being necessary to the security of a free State, the right of the people to keep and bear Arms, shall not be infringed.

AMENDMENT 3

No Soldier shall, in time of peace be quartered in any house, without the consent of the Owner, nor in time of war, but in a manner to be prescribed by law.

AMENDMENT 4

The right of the people to be secure in their persons, houses, papers, and effects, against unreasonable searches and seizures, shall not be violated, and no Warrants shall issue, but upon probable cause, supported by Oath or affirmation, and particularly describing the place to be searched, and the persons or things to be seized.

AMENDMENT 5

No person shall be held to answer for a capital, or otherwise infamous crime, unless on a presentment or indictment of a Grand Jury, except in cases arising in the land or naval forces, or in the Militia, when in actual service in time of War or public danger; nor shall any person be subject for the same offense to be a wit-

ness against himself, nor be deprived of life, liberty, or property, without due process of law,; nor shall private property be taken for public use, without just compensation.

AMENDMENT 6

In all Criminal prosecutions, the accused shall enjoy the right to a speedy and public trial, by an impartial jury of the State and district wherein the crime shall have been committed, which district shall have been previously ascertained by law, and to be informed of the nature and cause of the accusation; to be confronted with the witnesses against him; to have compulsory process for obtaining witnesses in his favor, and to have the Assistance of Counsel for his defense.

AMENDMENT 7

In suits at common law, where the value in controversy shall exceed twenty dollars, the right of trial by jury shall be preserved, and no fact tried by a jury, shall be otherwise re-examined in any Court of the United States, than according to the rules of the common law.

AMENDMENT 8

Excessive bail shall not be required, nor excessive fines imposed, nor cruel and unusual punishments inflicted.

AMENDMENT 9

The enumeration in the Constitution, of certain rights, shall not be construed to deny or disparage others retained by the people.

Figure 3-67.   Horizontal lines used in a "heading" style to set off each heading

GRAPHICS SCREEN TYPE

WordPerfect includes several graphics screen drivers that support most of the graphics monitors on the market today. WordPerfect automatically selects the best graphics driver when you first start the program.

The Graphics Screen Type selection is used when you are editing a graphics image or viewing a document. In addition to selecting a certain type of graphics driver, you can change the resolution and display more or fewer colors.

The Text Screen Type is a different setting and controls how many lines and colors are available while you are editing the document in text mode. See "Text Screen Type" in this chapter for more information about this setting.

Keystrokes

1. Press Setup (SHIFT-F1) and choose **2** for **D**isplay.

2. Choose **2** for **G**raphics Screen Type. The options displayed in Figure 3-68 appear. More screen drivers may be added in later releases.

3. Type the number corresponding to the name of your graphics monitor. You will then be placed in a submenu that lets you select different resolutions for that monitor. If you have a color monitor, you can often choose to have more colors but less resolution or vice versa. For example, the following options appear when you select an IBM VGA or compatible:

```
Setup: Graphic Screen Driver

    VGA 320x200 256 color
*   VGA 640x480 16 Color
    VGA 640X480 2 color
```

```
Setup: Graphic Screen Driver

   AT&T
   ATI
   Compaq Portable
   Hercules (& compatibles)
   Hercules InColor
   IBM 8514/A
   IBM CGA (& compatibles)
   IBM EGA (& compatibles)
   IBM MCGA (& compatibles)
 * IBM VGA (& compatibles)
   MDS Genius
   Paradise
   Text (No Graphics)
   Toshiba Portable
   Video 7




 1 Select; 2 Auto-select; 3 Other Disk; N Name Search: 1
```

Figure 3-68.   Graphics Screen Type selections

4. If you are unsure about a selection in either menu, choose **2** for Auto-Select, and WordPerfect will select the choice that best fits your hardware.

Hints

The graphics screen drivers are kept in the following files: STAN-DARD.VRS (which contains several drivers), 8514A.VRS, GE-NIUS.VRS, PARADISE.VRS, VIDEO7.VRS, ATI.VRS, and IN-COLOR.VRS. The STANDARD.VRS file is installed with the Word-Perfect program. To copy the other files, you need to answer Yes during installation to the question "Install Graphics Drivers?"

If your graphics driver is not on the list, contact WordPerfect Corporation or the manufacturer of the monitor to see if it will be supported in the future. Again, no changes should be needed for this selection, unless you want to change the resolution and the number of colors that are available with an EGA or a VGA, if you have one of the drivers not included as standard in the list, or if you have two monitors connected to the same computer and need to select a different driver.

GRAPHICS UTILITIES

WordPerfect provides two utility programs to help you deal with graphics images from other programs. The first is the Graphics Conversion utility (GRAPHCNV.EXE), which lets you convert graphics images saved in another format to WordPerfect's own graphics (WPG) format. This conversion utility is necessary only if you need to use graphics images that are in DXF format (they must be converted before they can be inserted in a WordPerfect graphics box).

If you intend to use the "Graphics on Disk" feature, you can point to a graphics image on disk instead of retrieving it into a graphics box. Pointing to a graphics image on disk lets you reduce the document size because the image is then not stored within the document.

Each time a graphics image is retrieved into a WordPerfect graphics box, it is converted to WordPerfect's graphics (WPG) format. If you are pointing to a graphics image on disk, each time you edit the graphics image, view, or print the document, it needs to convert the image. If you are not satisfied with the speed, you may want to use the Graphics Conversion program to convert it to the WPG format. See "Hints" for a list of the graphics formats that you can convert.

The second utility, GRAB.COM, lets you capture a graphics image from the screen and insert it into a WordPerfect graphics box. Because the resolution can only be as good as the resolution on your screen, it is best to save a graphics image in a format that is supported by WordPerfect's graphics feature (for a current list of supported graphics types, see "Graphics" in this chapter). If you have a software program that cannot save a graphics image in a compatible format, you can use the GRAB utility.

Keystrokes

If you did not install the utility files when you installed WordPerfect, you will need to do so before continuing. Both GRAB.COM and GRAPHCNV.EXE will be copied to the same directory where WP.EXE is located if you are installing to a hard disk or to the Utilities Disk if you are installing to a floppy.

Graphics Conversion

The following steps tell you how to convert graphics to WordPerfect's graphics format.

1. At the DOS prompt where GRAPHCNV.EXE is located, type **graphcnv.**

2. When prompted, enter the name of the file containing the graphics image to be converted. Include the full pathname (drive and directory) where the file is located if it is not found in the default directory.

3. When you are asked for the output filename, enter the name of a file that will be used to store the graphics image after it has been converted. Be careful not to enter the same filename if you do not want to overwrite the original. If you do enter the name of a file that already exists, you are asked if you want to replace the original file.

When you are finished, a message will inform you that the graphics conversion was successful.

GRAB.COM

The following steps help you start the screen capture utility (GRAB.COM) and capture a graphics screen:

1. At the DOS prompt of the directory where the GRAB utility (GRAB.COM) is located, type **grab** to load it into memory. See "Hints" for other startup options.

2. Enter the graphics program that is used to display the graphics images to be captured.

3. Press ALT-SHIFT-F9. If you are in graphics mode, you will hear a chime and a box will appear on the screen. If you are in text mode, you will hear a low buzz, which means that you will not be able to capture the screen with the GRAB program.

If you are running WordPerfect Library's Shell program, you can press ALT-SHIFT-HYPHEN (-) to capture the screen and send the result to the Clipboard instead of saving it in a file. When you are creating a graphics box, you can press Shell (CTRL-F1) to retrieve the graphics image from the Clipboard when asked for the filename.

4. A box appears on the screen. Use the arrow keys to move the box on the screen and the SHIFT-arrow keys to change the size of the box.

5. When the box is surrounding the part of the screen to be captured, press ENTER. Another chime will sound when it is finished.

The file containing the graphics image is named GRAB.WPG. If that file already exists, files are numbered consecutively as in GRABn.WPG where n represents the number of the captured image.

Hints

To get the latest options and help for each of the utilities, type **/h** after the program name, as in **GRAB/H** and **GRAPHCNV/H**. Cancel (F1) works in both programs to cancel the process at any time. The following sections tell you about each of the graphics utilities.

GRAPHCNV

The graphics conversion utility will convert the following formats:

AutoCad (DXF)
Computer Graphics Metafiles (CGM)
Dr. Halo
Encapsulated Postscript (EPS)
GEM (IMG)
Hewlett-Packard plotter files (HPGL)
Lotus (PIC)
Macintosh Paint
Microsoft Paint
PC Paint and PC Paint Plus
PC Paintbrush and Publishers Paintbrush (PCX)
TIFF format (commonly used by image scanners)

To skip the prompts, type **graphcnv** *input output,* where *input* is the name of the file to be converted and *output* is the name of the converted file. If you want to convert more than one file at a time, you can use the wildcard characters * and ?. You can have an asterisk (*) represent one or more characters and the question mark (?) represent single characters. For example, typing **graphcnv *.dfx** converts all the files ending with the extension .DFX to files having the same names but with the extension .WPG. Note that an output filename is not used in this example.

You can also use other startup options listed here. For example, **graphcnv/b = 0/c = w** would change the background to black and all the colors to white.

/L   When a file is converted, a message tells you the name of the input and output file, and whether or not the conversion was successful. Use the /L option (as in **graphcnv/l**) to send this message to the printer. Type **/l = filename** if you want to have the messages sent to the named file instead, to help track conversions.

/O   When you enter the name of a file to be used for the converted graphics image, the GRAPHCNV program checks to see if a duplicate file exists. If so, it will ask if you want to replace the original. If you do not want to be prompted, but want all original files replaced, use the /O startup option. This option will also let the graphics conversion program run unattended.

/B = n   The background color for a .WPG converted file is intense white. If you want to change the color, use the /B option. Type **graphcnv/B = n,** where *n* represents one of the following:

    0 = Black
    1 = Blue
    2 = Green
    3 = Cyan
    4 = Red
    5 = Magenta
    6 = Brown
    7 = White

/C=W   Use /C=W to convert all colors to white. This command is useful only if you have changed the background with the previous command. You cannot use this option with bit-mapped images.

/C=B   All colors are converted to black (cannot be used with bit-mapped images).

/C=2   Use this command to convert colors to monochrome (black and white).

/C=16   This option converts colors to the standard WordPerfect 16-color palette.

/C=256   If you have a graphics monitor that is capable of displaying 256 colors, you can use this option to convert colors to the standard WordPerfect 256-color palette.

/G=16   This option converts colors to the standard 16 shades of gray in the WordPerfect standard gray palette.

/G=256   If you have a graphics monitor that is capable of displaying 256 colors, you can use this option to convert colors to the 16 shades of gray in the WordPerfect standard 256-color palette.

GRAB.COM

The GRAB program works in graphics mode only. However, if you have WordPerfect Library, you can use the Clipboard's cut-and-paste feature to send whole or parts of text screens to the Clipboard, where they can then be retrieved into any program that supports the Shell.

To avoid compatibility problems, be sure to load GRAB before any other type of program.

The following are startup options for GRAB.

/D   Screens captured with GRAB are normally kept in the current directory. To specify a different directory, type **grab/d=*directory,***

where *directory* is the name of the drive and the directory that will be used for the GRAB.WPG files.

/F   Captured screens are kept in files named GRAB*n*.WPG, where *n* represents the number of screens captured. If you want to change the first part of the filename from GRAB to another name with four characters, use the /F option. For example, type **grab/f=*book*** to start the names of the captured files with the word "book."

/I   /I ignores the DOS-busy flag, enabling it to run under some applications that may not normally allow it.

/Cn   Another option available to help with incompatibilities is the /C*n* option, where *n* is any number from 0 to 5 and represents the number of keyboard interrupt attempts. /C by itself represents one try. If you are using SideKick and the computer hangs, use /C0 (zero, not the capital letter "O").

Starting GRAB with the /C0 option before other TSR programs also lets you use the shifted non-numeric arrow keys on the enhanced keyboard to change the size of the grab box.

/K   Once you change the size of a box, you can keep that size from screen to screen when you start GRAB with the /K option. If you change it during a capture, the new box size will be displayed in the next screen.

/M   If you have a color monitor, but want to capture the screen and have it converted to a monochrome bit-mapped image, use the /M option.

/R   Type **grab/r** to remove GRAB from memory.

/S   You can normally use the arrow keys to move the box on the screen and SHIFT with the arrow keys to size the box. The /S option causes the space bar to toggle between using the arrow keys to move *or* size the box.

/8   If you have an 8514A graphics card, start GRAB with the /8 option.

HAND-FED PAPER

If your printer does not have a paper tray, a tractor feeder, or a sheet feeder, you probably feed paper manually. WordPerfect lets you define any number of paper sizes or types that can be fed manually, with a sheet feeder, or as continuous paper. See "Paper Size and Type" in this chapter for more information about defining a manually fed form.

If the selected form is to be fed into the printer manually and is not initially present, WordPerfect will pause the printing at the beginning of each page and wait for you to send the printer a "Go" with the Control Printer menu.

Sending the Printer a "Go"

When you are printing with a form that is manually fed, the printer stops for you to insert each page (even if you are printing only one page) and sends a beep to the computer, telling you to give the printer a "Go." Press Print (SHIFT-F7), choose 4 for Control Printer, and type **G** to send the printer a "Go." If you print with hand-fed paper often, consider putting the steps into a macro (ALT-G is a suggestion) so that you will not have to leave the document to send a "Go" to the printer. The Macros keyboard has an ALT-G macro that includes these steps.

Top Margin

When you define hand-fed or manually fed forms for the printer, Word-Perfect looks at the Text Adjustment setting for the top edge of that particular type of paper. Most manually fed forms should have an adjustment moving text up 1 inch, because you will be feeding in the form at least 1 inch. If the top adjustment is set to 1 inch, you cannot set the top margin at anything less than 1 inch. If you set the top margin at 1.5 inches, WordPerfect checks the amount of text adjustment (usually 1") and moves down an additional 1/2 inch.

Hand Feeding with Laser Printers

WordPerfect lets you define a form that can use the manual feeder that is available for most laser printers. You can even mark the form as initially present so you do not have to send the printer a "Go" if the form (envelope, letterhead, and so on) is already waiting in the manual-feed tray.

Related Entries

Paper Size and Type

HANGING PARAGRAPHS AND INDENTS

A hanging paragraph or hanging indent is a paragraph or group of lines in which all lines except the first line are indented.

Keystrokes

1. Press →Indent (F4) to indent all lines.

2. Press Left Margin Release (SHIFT-TAB) to return the first line to the margin.

3. Enter the text for the paragraph.

Hints

A hanging indent is formatted according to the current tab settings. The paragraph will be indented every half inch if you leave the tab settings as WordPerfect has set them. Remember that Left Margin Release (SHIFT-TAB) returns to the previous tab. If you do not have a tab setting at the left margin, the keystrokes just listed will not work.

Another way of creating a hanging indent is to set the left margin farther to the right (where the paragraph should be indented). You would then only need to press Left Margin Release (SHIFT-TAB) to go to a previous tab setting to the left of the left margin. If you use this option, remember that there must be a tab setting in the margin area. Press

→Indent← (SHIFT-F4) instead of →Indent (F4) if you want to indent from both the right and left margins. If you want the paragraph indented more on the left, press →Indent (F4) until you reach the desired location, and then press Left Margin Release (SHIFT-TAB) an equivalent number of times.

Applications

Hanging paragraphs are often used for bibliographical entries, as shown in the following example:

Smith, Robert J., and Kathryn Morris. "Raising the Two-Year Old." *The Joy of Children,* November 25, 1987, 40-43.

If you have numbered items, it is easier to type the number (or use the Paragraph Numbering feature) and press → Indent (F4) as shown here:

1. Contact Mr. Rogers about visiting our child-rearing group sometime in the spring of next year.

Creating a Hanging Indent Style

If you use a hanging indent often, you might consider creating a hanging indent style. You could place the style in the Style Library to make it available for all documents, in which case you would need to create it only once. This also helps you enter several indented paragraphs at once without having to reenter the format each time. Although you can accomplish the same task with a macro, it would have to be turned on at the beginning of each hanging paragraph, whereas a paired style could turn off and back on each time you press ENTER. If you later decide to change the hanging paragraphs to numbered paragraphs, you can edit the style and make the necessary changes, and the affected text will be updated automatically.

1. While in the file being used for the Style Library, or from within the current document, press Style (ALT-F8).

2. Choose **3** to **C**reate a style.

3. Choose **1** for **N**ame, and enter **Indent** as the name of the style.

4. Since this will be a paired style (with beginning and ending codes), option **2** for **T**ype will remain as it is.

5. Choose **3** for **D**escription, and enter **use for hanging, indented paragraphs**.

6. Choose **4** for **C**odes. You will see a Reveal Codes screen, with a comment representing the text within the hanging paragraph.

7. Press →Indent (F4) and then Left Margin Release (SHIFT-TAB) to insert the [→Indent] and [←Mar Rel] codes. Move the cursor over the comment (the comment represents the text in the paragraph) and press ENTER twice. This leaves a blank line between indented paragraphs.

8. Press Exit (F7) to leave the Codes screen.

9. Choose **5** for **E**nter, and then choose **3** for Off/On (to have ENTER turn the style off and back on again when you press it).

10. Press Exit (F7) and you will see the newly created style added to the list of styles.

11. Choose **1** to turn **O**n the style, and begin typing the indented paragraph.

12. When you have finished with the first paragraph, press ENTER once. The style will be turned off (two [HRt] codes are inserted) and then back on. Continue until you have entered all hanging paragraphs.

13. To turn off the style, you can press → to move over the style-off code, or press Style (ALT-F8) and choose **2** to turn it Off.

Related Entries

Indent
Left Margin Release
Styles

HARD HYPHEN

You can use a hard hyphen as a minus sign or a dash. Unlike a regular hyphen, it can also be used to keep hyphenated words (such as "Carolyn Smith-McBride") from being separated at the end of a line.

Keystrokes

Press HOME and then the hyphen key.

Hints

When you press HOME, HYPHEN, the dash character (-) is inserted into the document. WordPerfect considers the dash a regular character and will not use it as a hyphen. Pressing the hyphen key alone inserts a required hyphen that will be used to break hyphenated words if necessary. Pressing CTRL and the hyphen together inserts a soft hyphen, the same type of hyphen used by WordPerfect during automatic or assisted hyphenation. This type of hyphen is not displayed on the screen if the word no longer needs to be hyphenated (for example, after editing changes have been made). A required hyphen appears as [-] in Reveal Codes, and a soft hyphen appears as a boldface hyphen -.

Applications

Use a hard hyphen between two last names that are used together or between cumulative page numbers in a bibliographical entry. The hard hyphen will prevent the hyphenated text from being broken between lines.

You can also use a hard hyphen as part of a dash. Pressing two regular hyphens does not guarantee that they will always be kept together. Instead, press HOME, HYPHEN, HYPHEN to insert --. See "Dashes" in this chapter for more information. You can also use a hard hyphen as a minus sign so that the formula containing the minus sign will not be broken between two lines.

Related Entries

Dashes
Hyphenation

HARD PAGE

Sometimes called a "new page" by other word processors, a hard page is used to insert a page break and start a new page. When you are working in columns, a hard page break is used to divide columns and pages.

Keystrokes

Press Hard Page (CTRL-ENTER).

Hints

A dashed double line is used to indicate a hard page [HPg] code. WordPerfect uses a single dashed line to indicate soft page breaks entered automatically. WordPerfect will adjust soft page breaks but not hard page breaks. If you want to remove a hard page break, position the cursor just below the page break at the left margin and press BACKSPACE, or position the cursor just above the line (at the right margin) and then press DEL.

Applications

Use a hard page break to end short pages and manually decide where the page break will occur. For example, if you want a section of text to be printed on a page by itself, you could precede and follow it with a hard page break. However, because the text will not flow over that page, you might want to use a full-page graphics box to reserve the space and have text flow onto the next page.

Related Entries

Page Breaks

HARD RETURN

Pressing ENTER inserts a hard return [HRt] code. Unlike a soft return [SRt] code, which is inserted by WordPerfect when it is wrapping text to the next line, an [HRt] code cannot be deleted by WordPerfect.

However, WordPerfect may, in certain situations, cause a hard return to become dormant if it is found at the top of a page or columns so it will not create a blank line at the top of the next page or column.

For example, if you separate paragraphs with two hard returns to create a blank line between paragraphs, and the first hard return falls at the end of the page, it will be converted to an [HRt-SPg] code and cause a soft page break to be inserted. The second hard return would cause the blank line to be placed at the top of the next page. Instead, WordPerfect changes the second [HRt] code to a dormant hard return [Dorm HRt] code.

Keystrokes

If you press ENTER as you near the end of a page, it may be converted to a soft page break with the [HRt-SPg] code. If this happens, the next time you press ENTER, the cursor will not appear to move down an additional line. It may be a little disconcerting at times, because it may not appear that ENTER is entering blank lines as it normally does. However, if you press Reveal Codes (ALT-F3), you will see the [Dorm HRt] code just after the soft page break.

Hints

Because soft page breaks are also used to separate columns, a dormant hard return will also eliminate the blank line at the top of a column. This feature should reduce editing time when you are checking for correct page or column breaks.

If the hard return [Dorm HRt] code no longer follows a soft page break after you have made editing changes, the dormant hard return returns to its original status as a regular hard return.

Hard return [HRt] codes following a hard page [HPg] break will not be affected. Keep in mind that this feature changes only a single hard return to a dormant hard return. If three or four hard returns are found after a soft page break, only the one immediately following the page break will be converted.

Another feature in WordPerfect lets you change the leading (the amount of space between lines) for hard returns and soft returns. See "Leading" in this chapter for details.

Related Items

Leading

HARD RETURN DISPLAY CHARACTER

WordPerfect lets you have a nonprinting character represent hard returns on the screen.

Keystrokes

1. Press Setup (SHIFT-F1).

2. Choose **2** for **D**isplay.

3. Choose **6** for **E**dit-Screen Options.

4. Choose 4 for **Hard Return Display Character**.

5. Press ALT and type **17** (using the numeric keypad) for ◀, press ALT and type **27** for ←, press ALT and type **174** for «, or use ALT with any other value for a special symbol, including **249** for • or **250** for •. You can use Compose (CTRL-2) to insert the special character. See Appendix A, "WordPerfect Character Sets," for a chart of special characters and the keystrokes used to display them.

6. Press Exit (F7) to return to the document.

If you decide not to display a character, follow the steps just given, but press the space bar in step 5 instead of entering a character. Pressing ENTER will not reset the option to nothing. Figure 3-69 shows a sample screen with « as the hard return display character.

```
                          November 25, 1990«
«
«
«
Mr. Robert J. Smith«
4567 Westview Drive«
Los Angeles, CA  94949«
«
Dear Mr. Smith:«
«
Thank you for your letter of October 15.  We were pleased to find
that our proposal was accepted by your firm.«
«
We will be in touch by phone within the next few days to make
further plans.«
«
                          Sincrely,«
«
«
«
                          Ms. Sue Sullivan«



                                        Doc 1 Pg 1 Ln 1" Pos 1"
```

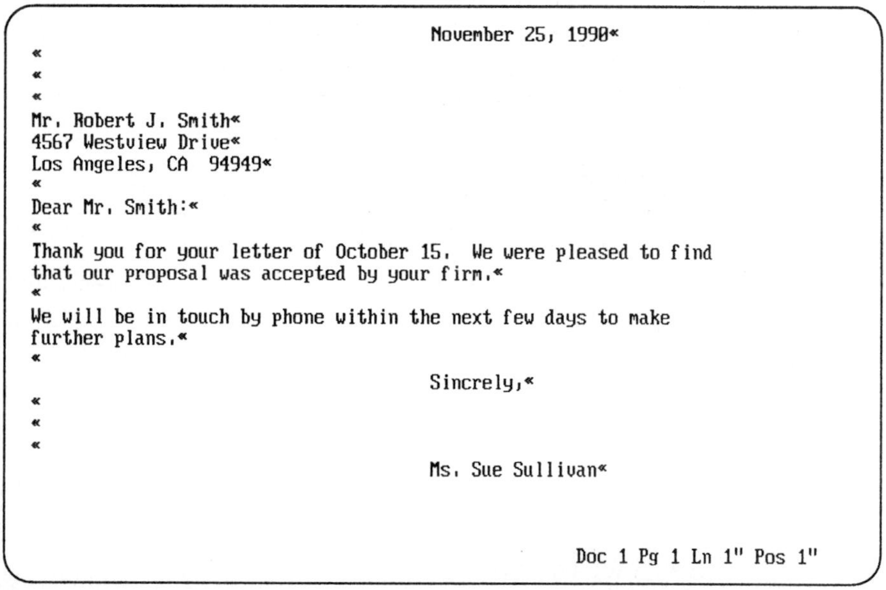

Figure 3-69.   A sample screen with « chosen as the hard return display character

Related Entries

ENTER Key
See also Appendix A, "WordPerfect Character Sets"

HARD SPACE

A hard space is sometimes called a "required space" and is used to keep separate words together as one word.

Keystrokes

Instead of pressing the space bar to insert a regular space, press HOME and then the space bar.

Hints

In Reveal Codes, a space appears as a space. A hard space appears as a space in brackets, indicating that it is a hard space [ ] code.

Applications

Use a hard space to prevent the separation of words or other text entries that you want to keep together on the same line. For example, if you did not want the phrases "Robert L. Smith," "November 25, 1990," or "x + y = z" to break at the end of a line, you would use hard spaces instead of regular spaces. A hard space can be inserted as you type or after you have finished typing.

You can also use a hard space to help provide consistency in a file that is to be sorted. For example, if you want to sort by the last name (which might be the last word in the line) and you have some names that appear as "Robert L. Smith, M.D." or "Richard Charles III," the last word in the line would not necessarily be the person's last name. You could use a hard space in this case to connect the last and second to the last words so that the Sort program treats them as one unit. See "Sort and Select" in this chapter for details about using that feature.

Related Entries

Sort

HEADERS

Headers are printed at the top of the page, and footers are printed at the bottom of the page. You can use headers and footers to print such items as a running title, the company name, a date, or a page number. See Figure 3-70 for a sample header and footer.

Keystrokes

1. Move to the top of the document or to the top of the page on which the header (or footer) is to first appear.

2. Press Format (SHIFT-F8).

3. Choose **2** for **P**age.

4. Choose **3** for **H**eaders.

5. Choose **1** for Header **A** or **2** for Header **B**. Either one can be used, but both are available so that you can have different headers on alternating pages.

6. When the following selections appear, choose **2** to place the header on Every Page, **3** for **O**dd Pages only, or **4** for Even Pages. Other options are available to discontinue or edit the header:

1 Discontinue; 2 Every Page; 3 Odd Pages; 4 Even Pages; 5 Edit: 0

7. Type the text for the header. If you want to include the current page number in a header, press CTRL-B to insert ^B. This code will insert the current page when it is printed.

8. Press Exit (F7) when you are finished.

Hints

When a header or a footer is created, a code similar to the following is placed in the document at the cursor location:

[Header A:*n*;*Text*]

The letter (A or B) indicates whether header A or header B was chosen. The number indicates the occurrence. Up to 50 characters of the header are then displayed. If there are more characters in the header or footer, "..." is displayed at the end of the 50 characters.

WordPerfect automatically inserts a blank line between a header or footer and the regular text. If you want additional lines inserted, press ENTER at the end of a header or at the beginning of a footer. The extra lines are taken into consideration when the page breaks are calculated by WordPerfect.

WordPerfect automatically subtracts the number of lines in a header from the total number of lines on a page. The footer will not be printed in the bottom margin, regardless of the number of lines. If you want to change the amount of space reserved for headers or footers, change the top or bottom margin. Press Format (SHIFT-F8), choose **2** for **Page**, and then choose option **5** to set the Top and Bottom **Margins**. If you want a header to start on a specific page, define it at the top of that page. If you want it to begin on the second page, it is best to define it on the first page and then suppress it for that page.

You can create a footer at any location on the page, and it will take effect from that point forward. Unfortunately, if you add or delete text, the code moves with the text. You might consider placing a hard page break (with CTRL-ENTER) before the header definition.

U.S. Constitution   September 17, 1787

Citizen of the United States, and who shall not, when elected, be an inhabitant of the State in which he shall be chosen.

Representatives and direct Taxes shall be apportioned among the several States which may be included within this Union, according to their respective Numbers, (which shall be determined by adding to the whole Number of free Persons, including those bound to Service for a Term of Years, and excluding Indians not taxed, three fifths of all other Persons.) The actual Enumeration shall be made within three Years after the first Meeting of the Congress of the United States, and within every subsequent Term of ten Years, in such Manner as they shall by Law direct. The Number of Representatives shall not exceed one for every thirty Thousand, but each State shall have at Least one Representative; and until such enumeration shall be made, the State of New Hampshire shall be entitled to choose three, Massachusetts eight, Rhode-Island and Providence Plantations one, Connecticut five, New York six, New Jersey four, Pennsylvania eight, Delaware one, Maryland six, Virginia ten, North Carolina five, South Carolina five, and Georgia three.

When vacancies happen in the Representation from any State, the Executive Authority thereof shall issue Writs of Election to fill such Vacancies.

Page 2

Figure 3-70.   A sample header and footer

Editing Headers

1. Press Format (SHIFT-F8).

2. Choose 2 for **Page**.

3. Choose 3 for **Headers**.

4. Choose 1 to edit Header **A** or 2 to edit Header **B**.

5. Choose 5 for **Edit**.

6. When you have finished your editing changes, press Exit (F7).

When you ask to edit a header or footer, WordPerfect searches backward for the last (most current) header or footer. If you move to the top of the document, the first header or footer definition is displayed for editing.

Because it takes so many keystrokes to edit a header or footer, you might want to consider selecting the SHORTCUT keyboard layout and using the ALT-E macro to edit the current code.

A header or footer can contain most format settings, including left and right margins, and font and spacing changes. However, you cannot set the top and bottom margins in a header. You can use the Date function (SHIFT-F5) to insert the date and time. You can also include merge codes in a header or footer.

If a margin change is not found within the header or footer, Word-Perfect uses the margin setting that was current when the header or footer is created. You can use the Speller and Thesaurus features while you are creating or editing a header or footer.

Deleting, Discontinuing, or Suppressing a Header or Footer

There are several options for deleting, discontinuing, or suppressing a header or footer. First, if you want to have several headers and footers within the same document, you can redefine them at the applicable locations. You do not have to discontinue the original one first. For example, if you want to have a header for the introduction of a book, define header A at the beginning of the document. Then, when you reach the first chapter, define header A again to include different header information. This new definition does not affect the previous header; it only changes header A from that point forward.

If you want a header or footer printed on several pages and then discontinued for the rest of the document, go to the point in the document at which the header or footer is to be discontinued (be sure you are at the top of the page) and do the following:

1. Press Format (SHIFT-F8) and choose **2** for **P**age.

2. Choose **3** for **H**eaders or **4** for **F**ooters.

3. Select the header or footer to be discontinued.

4. Choose **1** to **D**iscontinue the header or footer from that point forward.

If you have defined a header or footer for the entire document but do not want it to be printed on selected pages (on the title page and pages containing only tables and charts, for example), you can suppress the printing for the current page. The following steps accomplish that task:

1. Press Go To (CTRL-HOME) and ↑ to go to the beginning of the page.

2. Press Format (SHIFT-F8) and choose **2** for **P**age.

3. Choose **8** for **S**uppress (this page only). The menu shown in Figure 3-71 appears.

4. Select each option that is applicable, or more than one option, and type **Y** if you want the option suppressed. This method lets you suppress more than one option if necessary.

5. Press Exit (F7) to return to the document.

To delete a header or footer from a document, delete the code. Use the Search feature (see the next section), press BACKSPACE, and type **Y** or **N** when you see the message "Delete [Header A:Every page]? No (**Y**es)." The message will change, depending on which header or footer you are deleting.

Searching for Headers and Footers

As previously mentioned, if you ask to edit a header or footer, Word-Perfect searches backward to find the most current definition. You can

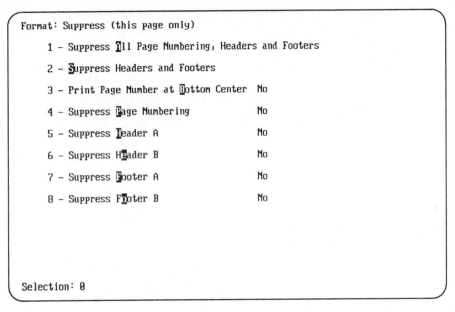

```
Format: Suppress (this page only)

      1 - Suppress All Page Numbering, Headers and Footers

      2 - Suppress Headers and Footers

      3 - Print Page Number at Bottom Center   No

      4 - Suppress Page Numbering              No

      5 - Suppress Header A                    No

      6 - Suppress Header B                    No

      7 - Suppress Footer A                    No

      8 - Suppress Footer B                    No




Selection: 0
```

Figure 3-71.   Menu to suppress printing of a header or footer on the
current page

also search for a specific header or footer. Press Search (F2) or Reverse
Search (SHIFT-F2), press Format (SHIFT-F8), choose **2** for **Page**, and then **3**
for **Hdr** (or **4** for **Ftr**), and then choose **A** or **B**. The code will be inserted
as the search string. Press Search (F2) again to begin the search.

When you use Search, Reverse Search, or Replace, WordPerfect
does not search the text in headers, footers, footnotes, and endnotes. If
you want the text in these features to be searched, use the Extended
Search feature. To start an extended search, press HOME before pressing
Search (F2), Reverse Search (SHIFT-F2), or Replace (ALT-F2). Note that you
press HOME and then the Search key. Do not hold HOME down, or you will
start a regular search.

Too Many Lines

A header or footer can contain up to a page of text. If you forget to
press Exit (F7) after the header or footer and continue typing the
document, you might exceed the page limit. If this happens, the message

"ERROR: Too many lines" is displayed, and the cursor is placed at the end of the header or footer. To correct the problem, turn on Block (ALT-F4), highlight the text that does not belong in the header or footer, press Move (CTRL-F4), choose **1** for **B**lock, and then choose **1** to **M**ove the text. Exit the header or footer, move the cursor to the correct location, and then press ENTER to retrieve the text in the document. See "Move" in this chapter for help with moving text from one place to another.

Alternating Headers or Footers

The option of having two headers and two footers makes it possible for them to appear on alternating pages. For example, you could place one header flush right on odd-numbered pages and the other at the left margin on even-numbered pages.

If you look at the tops of the pages in this book, you will notice that the header at the left contains a bolded page number and the name of the book. This header is printed on even-numbered pages only. The header at the right contains the chapter heading or current entry in that chapter, with a bolded page number flush against the right margin. This header prints on odd pages.

Previewing and Printing Headers and Footers

Headers and footers do not appear on the regular editing screen. If you want to see how they will look, you can view a page or the entire document before printing by pressing Print (SHIFT-F7) and choosing **6** to View the Document.

Remember, too, that the header or footer code displays the first 50 characters in the Reveal Codes screen.

If a page number and a header or footer are selected in the same location (for example, a header on line 1 and page number at the top left of the page), they will overlap when they are displayed during View and when printed. To have both a page number and text in a header or footer, insert a ^B in the header or footer to print the current page numbers. If you choose both headers or both footers for the same page, avoid overprinting them by inserting blank lines or by placing one at the left and the other at the right of the page.

Applications

Printing a header on alternating pages is useful for bound documents. See "Binding Width" in this chapter.

Using Headers or Footers to Number Pages

If you want to include text with a page number, you do not have to create a header or footer; you can create a page number style that contains both the text and the page number. However, if you need the page number to print in bold or some other attribute, you will need to create a header or footer, because attributes are not allowed in a page number style.

To print the current page number within a header or footer, press CTRL-B. This inserts a ^B, which inserts the current page number when you print the document.

You can use the {SYSTEM} macro command to create a header containing the text "Page n of n" so you can see the current page number along with the total number of pages in the document. The steps in the macro are listed below with comments to the side of each line to document the macro. If you do not know how to create an advanced macro, see "Macros" in this chapter or see Chapter 6, "Advanced Macro and Merge Commands."

{DISPLAY OFF}	{;}	Turn off the display ~
{Home}{Home}{Down}	{;}	Go to the bottom of the document ~
{ASSIGN}last ~{SYSTEM}page ~ ~	{;}	Get the page number and assign it to the variable named "last" ~
{Home}{Home}{Home}	{;}	Go to the top of the document ~
{Format}phap	{;}	Create header A for every page--change "h" to "f" if you want to create a footer instead ~
{Center}Page·{^B}·of·{VARIABLE}last~	{;}	Insert "Page n of" text and the number of the last page, which was stored in the "last" variable" ~
{Exit}{Exit}	{;}	Exit the header and the Format menu~

Headers for Letters and Memos

When you are creating letters or memos that are longer than one page, you might want to place a header on subsequent pages to identify the recipient of the letter, the recipient's address, the current date, and the page number. This process can be automatic if you are doing a merge, because you can place merge codes within a header or a footer. The header would then appear something like the following:

```
{FIELD}Name~
{FIELD}Address~
{DATE}
^B
```

You should also include a command on the first page of the primary file (letter) to suppress the header on the first page.

If you are not doing a merge but always place the name and address in the same place, you could have a macro block and move the name or address, retrieve it into a header, use the Date key (SHIFT-F5) to insert the date, and use ^B to insert the current page number. The last step in the macro should suppress the header on the first page.

Related Entries

Footers
Macros
Page Numbering
Paper Size/Type
Suppress
See also Chapter 6, "Advanced Macro and Merge Commands"

HELP

Help (F3) can display a description of each feature, tell you what keystrokes activate a feature, and display an on-screen WordPerfect template.

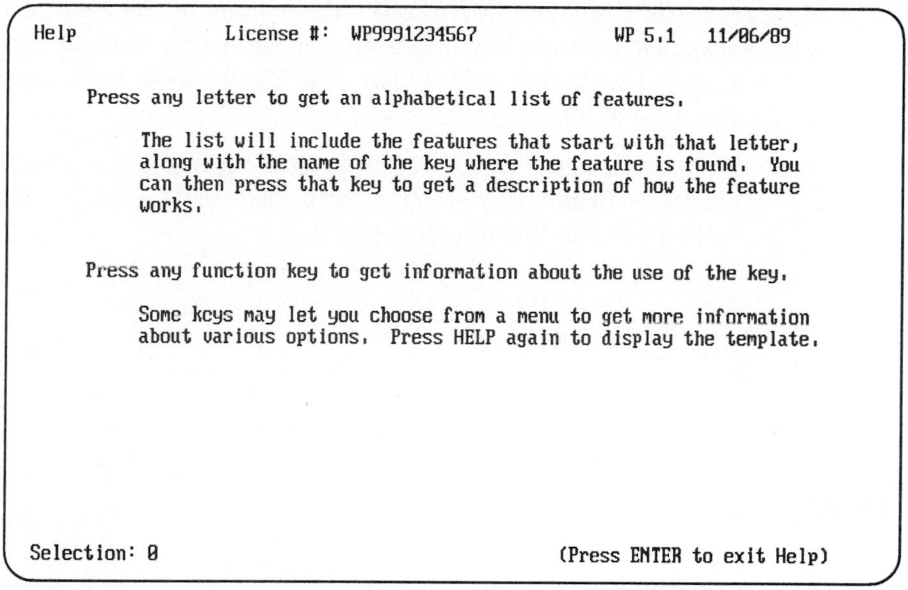

```
┌─────────────────────────────────────────────────────────────────┐
│ Help            License #:  WP9991234567        WP 5.1   11/06/89 │
│                                                                   │
│    Press any letter to get an alphabetical list of features.      │
│                                                                   │
│       The list will include the features that start with that     │
│       letter, along with the name of the key where the feature    │
│       is found.  You can then press that key to get a description  │
│       of how the feature works.                                   │
│                                                                   │
│                                                                   │
│    Press any function key to get information about the use of the │
│    key.                                                           │
│                                                                   │
│       Some keys may let you choose from a menu to get more         │
│       information about various options.  Press HELP again to      │
│       display the template.                                       │
│                                                                   │
│                                                                   │
│                                                                   │
│                                                                   │
│                                                                   │
│                                                                   │
│ Selection: 0                            (Press ENTER to exit Help) │
└─────────────────────────────────────────────────────────────────┘
```

Figure 3-72.   The initial help screen

Keystrokes

1. Press Help (F3). A menu describing the help options appears, as shown in Figure 3-72. If you did not install the help file during installation, or if you are using two floppy disk drives, you will see a message telling you that the WPHELP.FIL file is not found and asking you to type the letter of the drive containing it. If you are using two floppy disk drives, insert the WordPerfect 1 disk in drive B and type **B**. If you are using a hard disk, you will want to return to the Install program and install the help file.

2. Do one of the following:

• Type a letter to see an alphabetical listing of WordPerfect features and their keystrokes (see Figure 3-73).

• Press a function key to see a description of the feature that is assigned to that key. Instructions for using each feature are included with this help option. See Figure 3-74 for a sample of this type of help.

• Press Help (F3) again to display the template on screen. This option is useful if you have misplaced the template that was included in the WordPerfect package.

3. Press ENTER or the space bar to leave the help screens. Exit (F7), Cancel (F1), and ESC display information about their particular functions, rather than letting you exit the help screens.

Hints

WordPerfect also provides context-sensitive help. While you are using a particular feature, you can press Help (F3), and the appropriate help

```
Features [U-V]                    WordPerfect Key   Keystrokes

Undelete                          Cancel            F1,1
Underline Spaces and Tabs         Format            Shft-F8,4,7
Underline Text                    Underline         F8
Underline Text                    Font              Ctrl-F8,2,2
Units of Measure                  Setup             Shft-F1,3,8
Unlock a Document                 Text In/Out       Ctrl-F5,2
Update Spreadsheet Link           Text In/Out       Ctrl-F5,5,4,3
Update Printer Driver             Print             Shft-F7,s,7
Update References                 Mark Text         Alt-F5,6,5
Upper/Lower Case (Block On)       Switch            Shft-F3
User-defined Box                  Graphics          Alt-F9,4

Variable                          Macro Commands    Ctrl-PgUp
Very Large Print                  Font              Ctrl-F8,1,6
View Codes                        Reveal Codes      Alt-F3
View Document                     Print             Shft-F7,6
View-Document Options             Setup             Shft-F1,2,5




Selection: 0                              (Press ENTER to exit Help)
```

Figure 3-73.   A help screen showing a partial alphabetical list of Word-Perfect features and their locations on the keyboard

```
Font

      Allows you to change the current font and/or the size, appearance, or
      color of text at the printer. The way font attributes are displayed on the
      screen depends on how they were defined with the Color/Fonts/Attributes
      feature on the Setup key.

      The current font is the font in which normal text is printed. All other
      font sizes and appearances are usually variations of the current font. For
      example, if the current font is Helvetica 10 point, then bolded text is
      usually Helvetica Bold 10 point.

      The appearance of text depends on which attributes your printer supports.
      You can discover which attributes are available on your printer by
      printing the PRINTER.TST file.

      1 - Size
      2 - Appearance
      3 - Normal
      4 - Base Font
      5 - Print Color



  Selection: 0                              (Press ENTER to exit Help)
```

Figure 3-74.   A sample help screen that appears when you press a
function key

screen explaining the options found on that menu appears. Instructions
may also appear telling you to press a key for more specific information.

When you first start WordPerfect, you are asked if you want to
enter your customer registration number. If you choose to enter the
registration number, it is displayed at the top of the help screen. The
version number and the date on which your copy of WordPerfect was
released are displayed in the upper right corner of the help screen. Both
types of information are helpful to report when you call WordPerfect's
customer support.

Many features are "hidden" in submenus. If you cannot find a
feature on the template, press Help (F3) and type the first letter of the
feature. You may also want to consider using the pull-down menus if you
are having trouble finding features. All features are divided into fewer
categories and are more easily displayed on the screen. See "Mouse
Support and Pull-Down Menus" in this chapter for a list of features
found under each category.

Applications

Help (F3) can also be used to help you learn the program. You can press Help and any function key. After reading the instructions, press ENTER to return to the screen and experiment. You can also stay in help and continue pressing function keys to learn about each WordPerfect feature.

Related Entries

Error Messages
Function Keys

HIDDEN TEXT

See "Comments" in this chapter.

HIGHLIGHTING TEXT

Use Block (ALT-F4) to highlight a section of text in reverse video. Among many other options, you can move, copy, or delete the block.

Bold (F6) displays text in a higher intensity on the screen and in darker print at the printer.

Related Entries

Block
Bold

HOME KEY

The HOME key has no feature of its own, but it is used with other features to extend their function.

Keystrokes

Move to the Edges of the Screen

You can combine HOME with any arrow key to move the cursor to the edges of the screen. HOME, ↑ moves the cursor to the top of the screen, HOME, ← moves the cursor to the left edge of the screen, and so on.

Move to the Extreme Edges of the Document

Pressing HOME twice before an arrow key moves the cursor to the extreme edges of the document. HOME, HOME, ↑ moves the cursor to the top of the document; HOME, HOME, ↓ moves the cursor to the bottom of a document; HOME, HOME, → moves the cursor to the far right margin (which is useful for text that is wider than the screen); and so on. Pressing HOME, HOME, HOME, ↑ or HOME, HOME, HOME, ← moves the cursor to the beginning of a document or beginning of the line *before* all codes.

Move Within Columns and Tables

Combining Go To (CTRL-HOME) and an arrow key lets you move from column to column. Pressing Go To (CTRL-HOME), HOME, and then ← or → moves the cursor to the far left or right column, respectively.

Go To

Pressing CTRL-HOME displays "Go to" at the bottom of the screen. Enter a number to go to a specific page, or type a character to go to the next occurrence of that character. See "Go To" in this chapter for a list of options.

Extended Search, Reverse Search, and Replace

Search (F2), Reverse Search (SHIFT-F2), and Replace (ALT-F2) do not search through headers, footers, footnotes, or endnotes. Pressing HOME before starting a Search or Replace operation extends the selected feature into these areas. If the search stops in a header, footer, footnote, or endnote, you can press HOME and then the Search key to continue the extended search, or press Exit (F7) to leave the header, footer, footnote, or endnote and return to the document.

Hard Space

A hard space is used to combine two or more words as one unit so that they will not be broken at the end of a line. Press HOME and the space bar together to insert a hard space.

Hard Hyphen

If you want to insert a dash or minus sign, press HOME and then the hyphen key (HOME, -). Its function, like that of a hard space, is to prevent a word or phrase from breaking at the end of a line.

Cancel Hyphenation

If you do not want a word to be hyphenated, you can move to the beginning of the word and press HOME, /. A [/] code is inserted, meaning that hyphenation should be canceled for that particular word.

Invisible Soft Return

If you do not want a word to be hyphenated, but need it to be broken at a certain place, you can press HOME, and ENTER. You can do so after an em dash, an en dash, or a slash to break a word at that point. If the word no longer falls at the end of a line after you have made editing changes, the invisible soft return [ISRt] code is not used to break the line.

Hard Tabs

You can press HOME before any of the following keys to insert the indicated type of tab, regardless of the current type of tab setting. For example, you can insert a regular, left-aligned tab, even if the tab setting is set to be a centered tab.

TAB	Left-aligned tab
Center (SHIFT-F6)	Centered tab
Flush Right (ALT-F6)	Right-aligned tab
Tab Align (CTRL-F6)	Decimal-aligned tab

Pressing HOME twice before the keys above inserts a hard tab and a dot leader as well. Because TAB is normally used to go to the next level in a outline or to the next cell in a table, you can press HOME, TAB to insert a regular tab at any time.

Related Entries

Cursor Keys
Go To
Hard Hyphen
Hard Space
Hyphenation
Search
Tabs

HORIZONTAL LINES

See "Graphics Lines" in this chapter.

HYPHENATION

WordPerfect provides automatic or assisted hyphenation.

Keystrokes

Turn Hyphenation On/Off

WordPerfect comes with hyphenation off, but you can turn it on or off at any point in the document. You can either turn on hyphenation and make hyphenation decisions while typing, or wait until you have entered the document and then go to the top of the document and turn on hyphenation; you can then make all your hyphenation decisions at once.

1. Go to the beginning of the document or to the location at which hyphenation is to be turned on or off.

2. Press Format (SHIFT-F8).

3. Choose **1** for **Line**.

4. Choose **1** for **Hyphenation**.

5. Choose **Y** or **N**.

6. Press Exit (F7) when you are finished.

If you are presented with a hyphenation decision, position the hyphen with the left and right arrow keys, and press ESC when you are satisfied with the position. If you do not want to hyphenate a word, press Cancel (F1).

Setting Up Hyphenation

Hyphenation is automatically set to use the "External Dictionary/Rules" (using the spelling dictionary WP{WP}US.LEX and hyphenation code file WP{WP}US.HYC) and will only prompt you for hyphenation decisions when necessary. To change either of these options, follow these steps:

1. Press Setup (SHIFT-F1) and choose **3** for **Environment**.

2. If you want WordPerfect to use its own internal rules to make hyphenation decisions, choose **6** for **Hyphenation**. The following options appear:

> Hyphenation: 1 █xternal Dictionary/Rules; 2 █nternal Rules: 1

3. Choose **2** for Internal Rules (or **1** for External Dictionary/Rules if you changed the setting to Internal Rules at an earlier time).

4. Choose **7** to decide when WordPerfect should Prompt for Hyphenation. The following options appear:

> Prompt for Hyphenation: 1 █ever; 2 █hen Required; 3 █lways: 2

5. Select the appropriate option, and press Exit (F7) when you are finished.

Hints

When hyphenation is turned on or off, a [Hyph On] or [Hyph Off] code is inserted into the document. However, it does not store a code telling you if it is manual or automatic. That setting is determined in the Setup menu.

If you want hyphenation on for all documents, press Setup (SHIFT-F1), choose **4** for Initial Settings, and then choose **5** for Initial Codes. Repeat the steps under "Turn Hyphenation On/Off" above to include the [Hyph On] code in the Initial Codes section. Hyphenation will then be on for every document created from that point forward.

If you want to turn hyphenation off temporarily while scrolling (HOME, HOME, ↓) or searching, press Exit (F7) when you are asked for a hyphenation decision. As soon as you are finished scrolling or searching, hyphenation will be turned on again.

Canceling Hyphenation

If you are asked to confirm a hyphenation decision and you prefer not to hyphenate the displayed word (proper names, for instance, should not be hyphenated), press Cancel (F1). A cancel hyphenation code [/] is inserted at the beginning of the word, indicating that that particular word should never again be presented for a hyphenation decision.

If you have requested that you never be prompted, you may find words being hyphenated that you would prefer not be hyphenated. If you try to delete the hyphen, WordPerfect will "automatically" insert the hyphen again.

To avoid this, move to the beginning of the word and press HOME, /. This will insert the cancel hyphenation code [/]. You can then delete the hyphen from the word and it will not be hyphenated again.

Hyphenation Zone

The hyphenation zone surrounds the right margin. Both the hyphenation zone and the right margin are used to determine where a line should break.

WordPerfect uses percentages to determine the hyphenation zone. The default setting is 10 percent for the left side and 4 percent for the right, meaning that 10 percent of the current line length is used to determine the left hyphenation zone, and 4 percent of the line length is used to determine the right hyphenation zone. Note that if you have a very short line (such as when you are working in columns), you may want to increase the size of the hyphenation zone, or you may get three- or four-letter words presented for hyphenation decisions (10 percent of a short line is not as much as 10 percent of a long line).

If hyphenation is on, the hyphenation zone is used to determine whether a word should be hyphenated or wrapped to the next line. If a word starts before the left side of the hyphenation zone and extends past the right side, it will be hyphenated or presented to you for a hyphenation decision. If hyphenation is off, a word fitting this description would be wrapped to the next line instead of being hyphenated.

Figure 3-75 shows the area in which hyphenation decisions are made. The size of the hyphenation zone also determines exactly where the hyphen can occur. For example, with the default hyphenation zone set at 10% and 4%, the hyphen can fall anywhere within that zone. If you decrease the size of the hyphenation zone, there will be less space for a possible hyphen and, therefore, less chance of accurate decisions. If you increase the hyphenation zone, you broaden the possibilities for

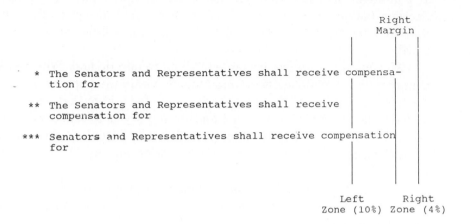

* Hyphenation on. Note that the word would have extended over the left
and right sides of the hyphenation zone, so it was hyphenated.

** Hyphenation off.

***Hyphenation on. Note that the word only extends over the left side of
the hyphenation zone, not the left and right side. Therefore, it was not
hyphenated.

Figure 3-75.   The hyphenation zone determines where a hyphen will be placed

correct placement but will have a more jagged edge or space fill when
justification is on. Follow these steps to change the hyphenation zone:

1. Press Format (SHIFT-F8).

2. Choose 1 for Line.

3. Choose 2 for Hyphenation Zone.

4. Enter the percentage of the line length to be given to the left
hyphenation zone. Remember that the shorter the line length, the
more you should allow for hyphenation.

5. Enter the percentage of the line length to be given to the right
hyphenation zone. The right hyphenation zone setting will be ignored if your printer cannot compress a line; many dot-matrix
printers are only able to expand a line by inserting white space
between characters.

If you have requested that you never be prompted for a hyphenation decision (automatic), and WordPerfect cannot find an appropriate location for a hyphen within the hyphenation zone, it will not hyphenate the word.

If you asked to be prompted when required, and WordPerfect cannot find a suitable location for a hyphen within the hyphenation zone, it checks to the left of the hyphenation zone for a hyphenation point. If it finds one, it displays the word and prompts you to make a hyphenation decision. If no hyphenation point is found in either place, Word-Perfect places the hyphen at the right margin and again prompts you for a decision.

If you have an extra-small hyphenation zone, WordPerfect still reserves a minimum of two characters so there will be some flexibility for hyphenation.

A word consisting of 5 characters or fewer will not be hyphenated (even if a hyphenation point exists for the word), unless it extends from margin to margin (which sometimes happens in very narrow columns).

Related Hyphenation Codes

The following is a description of other codes that are related in some way to hyphenation.

Invisible Soft Return   You can use an invisible soft return [ISRt] to cause a word to break without using a hyphen or space. For example, if you have words that are joined by an em dash (character 4,34 in the WordPerfect character set) and there are no spaces on either side of the em dash, the word will not break naturally at the em dash but will be presented for a hyphenation decision. Since you don't usually want to add a hyphen, canceling the hyphenation would wrap the entire phrase, leaving an unacceptable amount of space at the right margin. Instead, you can use the [ISRt] code to break the line after the em dash. To do so, move the cursor to the right of the em dash and press HOME and then ENTER.

If the [ISRt] code enters the hyphenation zone, it will be used to break the word at that point; if not, it will remain invisible. You can also use this technique after en dashes (WordPerfect character 4,77) and slashes (/). For example, in the phrase Math/Scientific, you could move the cursor to the "S" in "Scientific" and press HOME, ENTER to insert the [ISRt] code.

Deletable Soft Return   The deleteable soft return [DSRt] code is inserted and deleted by WordPerfect. It is usually inserted because hyphenation is off and the margins are too narrow to allow the word to wrap naturally (in narrow columns, for example). Since you have turned hyphenation off, WordPerfect has to break the word somewhere, so it does so with a [DSRt] code. Since you cannot manually delete the [DSRt] codes, either increase the margins, change to a smaller font size, or turn on hyphenation so that WordPerfect will delete the [DSRt] codes.

Soft Hyphen   Pressing CTRL-hyphen inserts a soft hyphen that is identical to the hyphen inserted by WordPerfect during hyphenation. If it is no longer needed after editing, it is not displayed as a hyphen on the screen. However, it is not deleted, but remains intact in the event that it is needed in the future.

Hyphen   If you type a hyphen while entering text, WordPerfect will use that hyphen if that word needs to be hyphenated. WordPerfect will not insert a soft hyphen in this case. The hyphen would appear as [-] in Reveal Codes.

Dash or "Hard Hyphen"   If you do not want the word to break at the hyphen, but want it treated as a regular character (such as a dash or a minus sign), you will need to insert it by pressing HOME and then hyphen. If you look at this type of hyphen in Reveal Codes, it will appear as a normal dash character (-).

Getting a Smoother Right Margin

If you want a more even right margin without right justification on, turn on hyphenation. Decreasing the hyphenation zone will create an even smoother right margin; however, keep in mind that because the hyphen must be placed within the zone, it should not be too small. Remember that you can always press Cancel (F1) if a hyphen cannot be placed accurately.

Less Space During Justification

Because some printers can provide right justification only by inserting more space between words, you might want to turn off justification for these types of printers. If you do not want to give up justification, try turning on hyphenation and possibly decreasing the hyphenation zone. You can also experiment with the Word Spacing Justification Limits to determine how much space is to be given to the space character to accomplish justification. See "Word Spacing Justification Limits" and "Justification" in this chapter for details.

Adding Hyphenated Words to the Dictionary

When you check the spelling of a document and choose the option Add to add a word to the dictionary, the added words are kept in the supplementary dictionary. This is a regular WordPerfect file named WP{WP}US.SUP, which can be retrieved and edited like any other file.

If you want to add the words in the supplementary dictionary to the main dictionary, WP{WP}US.LEX, you can do so with the SPELL.EXE program. Before adding the words, however, you might want to edit the file and insert hyphens where appropriate.

To use SPELL, go to DOS and change to the directory where SPELL.EXE is located, type **spell**, and choose the option Add to add words to the main dictionary. If you add words from the keyboard, insert the hyphens as you type the words. Otherwise, you can enter the name of the supplementary dictionary, WP{WP}US.SUP, which may already contain the words to be added and their hyphenation points.

Two Disk Drives

If you are using WordPerfect on a two-disk drive system, you might prefer using the internal rules for hyphenation. Otherwise, you will need to replace the data disk in drive B with the Speller disk so that the hyphenation points can be found in the dictionary. You might want to check the spelling and hyphenate at the same time. Just before you check the spelling, insert the Speller disk in drive B, go to the top of the document, and turn on hyphenation. Hyphenation decisions will then be made during the spell check.

Related Items

Justification
Spell Program
Word Spacing Justification Limits

HYPHENATION ZONE

See "Hyphenation" in this chapter.

INCHES

WordPerfect has been set to make all formatting changes in inches. The Units of Measure option in the Setup menu lets you change this to centimeters, points, or WordPerfect 4.2 units. See "Units of Measurement" in this chapter for details.

INDENT

You can use the Indent feature to indent any line or group of lines in a paragraph without changing the margins or pressing TAB for each line.

Keystrokes

Indents are dependent on the current tab settings.

1. Set tabs if necessary. Press Format (SHIFT-F8), choose 1 for Line, and choose 8 for Tab Set. After setting tabs, press Exit (F7).

2. Press →Indent (F4) to indent the left side of the paragraph only. Press →Indent← (SHIFT-F4) to indent equally from the left and right margins.

3. Press ENTER to end the indent and return to the left margin.

Hints

When you press →Indent (F4), an indent code, [→Indent], is inserted. When you press →Indent← (SHIFT-F4), the [→Indent←] code is inserted. Text will wrap within the temporary margins set by the indent codes until you press ENTER or a [HRt] code is encountered.

Use TAB to indent a single line or just the first line in a paragraph. If all lines are to be indented, use one of the Indent keys. If you use TAB for multiple lines and make editing changes, the text will not be formatted correctly. When you use →Indent← (SHIFT-F4), an equal amount of space is subtracted from the right side, regardless of the tab settings. Therefore, you only need to be concerned with the tab settings for the left-indented margin.

Applications

Use →Indent (F4) for numbered paragraphs. As you can see in the following illustration, the number is at the left margin. After typing the number, press →Indent (F4) to indent to the first tab setting.

1. In which city and state was the U.S. Constitution signed?

2. Name at least five people who signed the U.S. Constitution.

You can choose bullets (•, ○, −, +, and so on) for indented items by pressing Date/Outline (SHIFT-F5), choosing **6** for **D**efine, and **5** for **B**ullets. You can also use option **6** for **U**ser-defined on that menu to select the characters to be used as bullets. After choosing bullets as the type of paragraph numbering to be used, insert the "paragraph number" (bullet) in the document by pressing Date/Outline (SHIFT-F5), choosing **5** for **P**ara **N**um, and then pressing ENTER. Then press →Indent (F4) to indent the text.

You can create indented quotations where left and right margins are brought in with →Indent← (SHIFT-F4), as shown here:

ARTICLE II.

> Section 1. The Executive Power shall be vested in a President of the United States of America. He shall hold his Office during the Term of four Years,and, together with the Vice President, chosen for the same term, be elected,as follows.

Each State shall appoint, in such Manner as the Legislature thereof may direct, a number of

Electors, equal to the Whole Number of Senators and Representatives to which the State may

To create hanging indents or paragraphs, as shown in this sample bibliography entry, press →Indent (F4), then the Left Margin Release (SHIFT-TAB):

Schuler, Robert B. Our American Heritage. Boston, MA: Harvard University Press, 1976.

If you use styles for indented items, you can change the style by editing the codes in the style. All text marked with that style will then be updated automatically. For example, you might prefer numbered items, while another person might prefer hanging paragraphs. By changing the style, all numbered items would change automatically to hanging paragraphs. See "Hanging Paragraphs and Indents" in this chapter for a sample style or "Styles" for help in creating styles.

Related Entries

Hanging Paragraphs and Indents
Styles
TAB Key
Tabs

INDEX

WordPerfect can generate an index with headings and subheadings for a single document or several documents. The index is sorted alphabetically, and the page number for each entry marked in the document is listed.

Keystrokes

There are three basic steps to building an index: creating a concordance (or manually marking each item in the document), defining the way page numbers are to appear in the index, and generating the index.

Marking Entries

You can either search for a word or phrase that is to be included in the index and mark it manually, or you can include a list of words or phrases in a concordance. WordPerfect will then generate an index for the words or phrases included in the concordance so you do not have to mark each occurrence in the document. Although you can write a macro to help automate the procedure for marking each item within a document, the fastest, easiest way is to use the concordance. Because the Concordance feature was designed to eliminate much of the manual labor, this book documents that feature. If you decide to mark each item individually within the document rather than create a concordance, use steps 2 through 6 in the following list.

1. Type a list of the entries as you want them to appear in the index. Each entry should be separated with a hard return [HRt] code. If the entry wraps to the next line, it is still considered the same entry, because a soft return [SRt] code is not considered a separator.

   If each entry is to be used as a heading and there are to be no subheadings in the index, skip to step 8. The next six steps concern marking the heading and subheading to be used for each entry.

2. If the entry consists of one word, place the cursor anywhere in the word. If the entry should include an entire phrase, move to one end, press Block (ALT-F4), and move to the opposite end.

3. Press Mark Text (ALT-F5).

4. Choose **3** for **I**ndex.

5. The current word or blocked phrase appears following "Index Heading:". Press ENTER to accept it as the heading, edit the displayed heading, or enter a new one.

6. If you edited the heading or entered a new one, the original is displayed as a possible subheading. Press ENTER to accept it as the subheading, edit the displayed subheading, enter a new one, or press Cancel (F1) if no subheading is desired.

7. You can mark each entry more than once with different headings and subheadings. Continue until you have marked all entries. Remember that if an entry is to be a heading with no subheading, you do not have to mark it.

8. Press Merge/Sort (CTRL-F9), choose **2** for **S**ort, press ENTER twice, and choose **1** for **P**erform Action (sort the concordance file). If you complete this step, the index will be generated more quickly.

9. Save the file and clear the screen.

Defining the Page Number Listing Style

1. Retrieve the document to be indexed, and go to the end of the document (press HOME, HOME, ↓). If you want to create one index for several documents, create a master document and go to the end of that document. See "Hints" and "Master Documents" for information about creating an index for more than one document.

2. If you want the index to be generated on a separate page, press Hard Page (CTRL-ENTER). Type a heading for the index if desired.

3. Press Mark Text (ALT-F5).

4. Choose **5** for **D**efine.

5. Choose **3** for Define the **I**ndex.

6. When you are prompted, enter the name of the concordance file. If you marked each entry in the document and are not using a concordance, press ENTER. The Index Definition menu shown in Figure 3-76 is displayed.

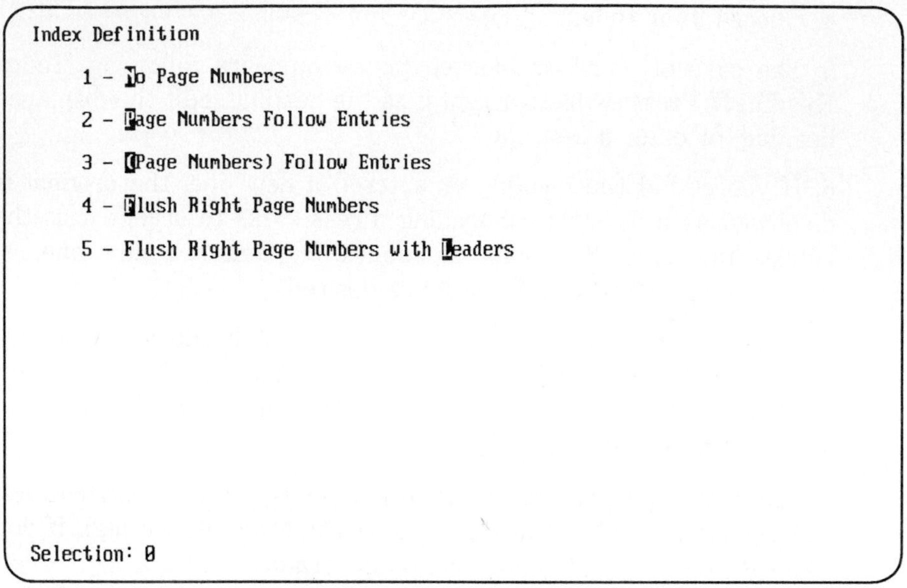

```
Index Definition

     1 - To Page Numbers

     2 - Page Numbers Follow Entries

     3 - (Page Numbers) Follow Entries

     4 - Flush Right Page Numbers

     5 - Flush Right Page Numbers with Leaders




Selection: 0
```

Figure 3-76.   The Index Definition menu

7. Select the style of page numbering to be used. See "Hints" for more information about page numbers.

Generating the Index

1. Press Mark Text (ALT-F5).

2. Choose **6** for **G**enerate.

3. Choose **5** to **G**enerate Tables, Indexes, Cross-References, etc.

4. Choose **Y** or **N** in answer to the question "Existing tables, lists, and indexes will be replaced. Continue? Yes (**N**o)."

You will be notified of the progress with a "Pass" and "Page" indicator at the bottom of the screen. When WordPerfect generates an index, it makes several passes to collect the data and the corresponding page number. This counter informs you of its progress.

If you are generating an index for a master document, WordPerfect expands the master document by retrieving all subdocuments and then generates the index all at once. Because this process can take quite a bit of the computer's memory and time, be patient. If you find mistakes after generating an index, you can make corrections to the index markings in the concordance (or document) and regenerate the index.

Hints

When you mark an entry for an index, the following code is inserted:

[Index:*heading*;*subheading*]

When you define an index (concordance and page number listing style selected), the definition code

[DefMark:Index,*n*;Concordance]

appears. This code indicates the type of definition mark, (Index), the page number style selected (*n*), and the name of the concordance file being used (if one is being used).

Indexes are sorted according to the current Language code (some languages place accented characters within unaccented characters, and others place them after the Z's). See "Languages" in this chapter for information about changing the codes.

When you generate an index, an [EndDef] code is placed at the end of the index. If you generate the index again, the [DefMark] and [End-Def] codes are used to determine which index will be replaced. If you delete the [EndDef] mark, and it is not found during the next Generate, the previously generated index is considered as text and will not be deleted. You can use this to your advantage if you want more than one index generated for the document.

If you have more than one [DefMark] code for an index, you will get unpredictable results. If you decide to change the page number style or the name of the concordance file, delete the previous [DefMark] code and redefine the index.

It is best if you always place the index definition mark [DefMark] at the end of the document, or entries appearing after the definition mark will not be included. If you are using a concordance, however, all entries will be included in the index, even if they happen to fall after the index. See "Concordance" in this chapter for more information about using a concordance file.

Index and Endnotes

If you have endnotes in your document, they will be printed after the index. If you want them to be printed before the index, you will need to use the Endnote Placement feature to tell WordPerfect the exact location. It is best to precede and follow endnotes and the index with a hard page break (press CTRL-ENTER) and have them appear on a page by themselves.

Master Documents

If you want to create an index for several documents at once, such as many chapters of a book, create a master document. This is just a regular document with the names of all the separate documents entered as subdocuments. If your computer does not have enough memory or disk space to hold all the documents when the master document is expanded, you will see an error message. If you run into this problem, you can try to delete a few of the subdocuments and see if the master document is generated successfully. See "Master Document" in this chapter for details.

Page Numbering

When you define an index, you select an option telling WordPerfect how the page number is to appear in the list, such as with a dot leader, flush right against the margin, and so on.

If you want the page number in the index to include the section or chapter number, you can do so by including the section or chapter number as part of the page number style on the Page Numbering menu. This style is also used for the page numbers that appear in a Table of Contents, Tables of Authorities, Lists, and Cross-References.

Normally, the page number style is simply ^B, meaning the current page number. If you want to include text with the page number, move to the beginning of the section or chapter and follow these steps:

1. Press Format (SHIFT-F8), and choose **2** for **Page**.

2. Choose **6** for **Page Numbering**.

3. Choose **2** for Page Number Style and enter the text to be used in the style. For example, if you are currently in Chapter 3, you might want to type **3-^B** so that the reader will know to look in Chapter 3 for the page number. To insert the ^B, press CTRL-B. If you do not include it as part of the style, it will be inserted at the end of the style automatically.

4. Press Exit (F7) to return to the document.

You can also include text such as "Chapter 3-^B," but you may not want this much text included in the index, tables, and lists.

When the index is generated, it will include the section or chapter number, as shown in the following illustration:

```
Constitution . . . . . . . . . . . . . . . . . . . . . . . . . . . . 1-1,  3-10,  3-24
Statehood  . . . . . . . . . . . . . . . . . . . . . . . . . . . . . . 3-52,  3-98
Union . . . . . . . . . . . . . . . . . . . . . . . . . . . . . 2-11,  3-26,  3-55
```

Related Entries

Concordance
Mark Text
Master Document
Page Numbering

INITIAL BASE FONT

After selecting a printer and the fonts that are available for that printer, you can choose the font that will be the initial font when you are creating a document.

You can override this base font for an entire document by selecting a new Document Initial Base Font, or you can override both settings by choosing a base font any time within the document.

Keystrokes

Selecting an Initial Base Font

1. Press Print (SHIFT-F7).

2. Choose S for Select a Printer.

3. If you have already selected a printer, move the cursor to the name of the printer and choose 3 for Edit. If you have not selected a printer, choose 2 for Additional Printers and select the printer. After reading the help messages for that printer and pressing Exit (F7), you will see the menu used for editing the printer definition.

4. If you have not already done so, choose 4 for Cartridges and Fonts, and select all the fonts you have available. See "Cartridges and Fonts" in this chapter for details. After you exit the list, WordPerfect will display the message "Updating fonts" as it stores the information about each font.

5. The name of the font currently being used as the initial font is displayed next to option 5 for Initial Base Font. Choose 5 if you want to change this font. The list of available fonts (the ones that were selected in the previous step) are displayed.

6. Move the cursor to the font to be used, and press ENTER. The name of the new font is displayed next to the Initial Base Font option.

Hints

The Initial Font is copied into each new document and stored in the document "header" or prefix. You can change the Initial Base Font for a single document by pressing Format (SHIFT-F8), choosing 3 for Document, and then choosing 3 for Initial Base Font. WordPerfect formats a document according to the initial font until you select another one.

You can also change the font at any time in the document by pressing Font (CTRL-F8), choosing 4 for Base Font, moving to the desired font, and pressing ENTER to select it.

The Document's Initial Base Font is used for page numbers, text within graphics boxes, captions for those boxes, footnotes, and endnotes. If you have selected the Options menu for any of these features, the font that is current at the time an [Opt] code is inserted will then be used. In other words, you can change the font for all these features by changing the Document's Initial Base Font, or you can change to a particular font and enter the Options menu for that feature. You do not have to select an item from the menu. Just enter the Options menu, then exit, and the [Opt] code will be inserted.

Related Entries

Cartridges and Fonts
Fonts

INITIAL CODES

If you prefer default settings that are different from the ones set by WordPerfect, you can specify initial codes to be inserted in every document. Table 3-12 shows several default settings used by WordPerfect.

Keystrokes

1. Press Setup (SHIFT-F1).

2. Choose 4 for Initial Settings.

3. Choose 5 for Initial Codes. The Reveal Codes screen is displayed, so you can see the codes as you insert them.

4. Use the same keystrokes to insert a function code as you would use when creating a document. For example, press Format (SHIFT-F8), choose 1 for Line, choose 7 for Margins, and enter the margins to be used as the default.

5. After entering all codes, press Exit (F7) twice to return to the document.

Hints

If you change the initial codes with a document on the screen, the change will not affect that document; it will affect the next one that you create. It will not affect any documents created before the change. If you retrieve a document that was created before you changed the initial codes settings, it will retain its previous initial codes settings. If you retrieve one document into another, the initial codes of the first document on the screen are used, and the others from subsequent documents are ignored.

The initial codes are copied into each document and are stored in a special "header" or "prefix." If you press Reveal Codes (ALT-F3) at the beginning of the document, you will not see the codes, but you can view or change them by editing the document's initial codes. To do so, press Format (SHIFT-F8), choose 3 for Document, and then choose 2 for Initial Codes.

Hyphenation	No
Justification	Full
Margins	1″
Page Size and Type	Standard, 8.5″ x 11″
Page Number Style	^B (meaning the current page number)
Page Numbering	None
Spacing	Single
Tabs	Every .5″
Underline Spaces	Yes
Underline Tabs	No
Widow/Orphan Protection	No

Table 3-12.   Default Settings for a Few WordPerfect Features

The default for any option that does not insert a code cannot be changed. For example, you will not be able to decide the default for Insert/Typeover mode. Keep in mind, however, that there are other options on the Initial Settings menu that can be changed to affect all documents (such as setting the repeat value for ESC and changing the graphics and text print quality).

All changes in the Setup menu are kept in the WP{WP}.SET file. See "Initial Settings" in this chapter for details.

Applications

You might want to change justification to left and turn Widow/Orphan Protection on if you find yourself changing these options frequently. If you want to use different option settings for footnotes, endnotes, or graphics boxes (figures, tables, and so on), or if you want a page number to be placed on each page automatically, you can have these codes inserted into each document automatically by inserting them as initial codes.

Related Entries

Codes
Document Format
Initial Settings

INITIAL SETTINGS

The Initial Settings menu lets you make universal changes to most format settings that can affect all documents created from that point on. All changes that differ from the standard defaults are saved with each document.

Keystrokes

1. Press Setup (SHIFT-F1).

2. Choose 4 for Initial Settings. The menu shown in Figure 3-77 appears.

3. Choose any of the options and make necessary changes.

4. Press Exit (F7) until you return to the document.

Options

The options found on the Initial Settings menu are explained here.

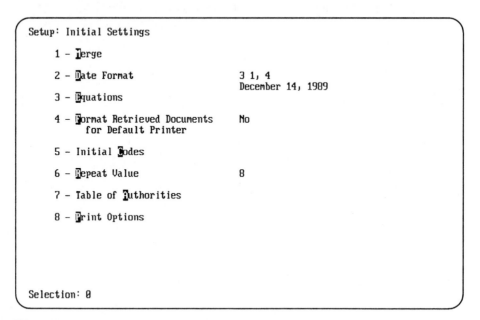

```
Setup: Initial Settings

    1 - Merge

    2 - Date Format                    3 1, 4
                                       December 14, 1989
    3 - Equations

    4 - Format Retrieved Documents     No
          for Default Printer

    5 - Initial Codes

    6 - Repeat Value                   8

    7 - Table of Authorities

    8 - Print Options




Selection: 0
```

Figure 3-77.   The Initial Settings menu in Setup

Merge

During a merge, you can enter the name of a DOS text file to be used as the secondary file in a merge. If you do, a menu similar to the one shown here appears, letting you enter the field and record delimiters (characters or codes used to separate fields and records). As shown, WordPerfect assumes that fields are separated by commas and that records are separated by carriage returns.

```
Setup: Merge DOS Text File

     1 - Field Delimiters  - Begin
                             End    ,

     2 - Record Delimiters - Begin
                             End   [CR]
```

If you use a database or another type of program that exports text files with different delimiters, you can change the delimiters in this menu rather than each time you do a merge.

To insert a line feed [LF], press ENTER. To insert a carriage return [CR] code, press CTRL-M. See "Merge" for more information.

Date Format

You can choose the default date format for all documents with this option. This is particularly useful if you live in a country that has a different format, or if your documents need to include the time as well as the date.

Equations

In the Equations Setup menu shown here, equations are usually printed as graphics in the size of the default font and are centered both vertically and horizontally in an equation box.

```
Setup: Equation Options

     1 - Print as Graphics     Yes

     2 - Graphical Font Size   Default

     3 - Horizontal Alignment  Center

     4 - Vertical Alignment    Center

     5 - Keyboard for Editing
```

You can change these options for each equation by pressing Setup (SHIFT-F1) while you are creating or editing an equation. However, if you prefer to change the settings for all equations at once, you can change them in this Setup menu. Only equations created in the future will be affected.

The last option on the menu, Keyboard for Editing, is the only option on this menu that you cannot change for each equation. With this option, you can choose a keyboard layout that you can use to insert special characters or commands with a remapped key. For example, you could press ALT-A to insert the alpha character.

You may want to install a keyboard named EQUATION, which is installed along with other keyboard files during installation. This keyboard includes several redefined keys common to equations. See "Equations" or "Keyboard Layout" in this chapter for information about using a keyboard for editing equations.

Format Retrieved Documents for Default Printer

This option can be set to format documents for the default or current printer, regardless of which printer was used when you saved the document.

Normally, when a document is retrieved, WordPerfect automatically uses the printer that was used when the document was created, so that all fonts are kept intact. If you later want to reformat the document for another printer, you can select a different printer, and the document will be reformatted.

This option can be used to avoid the extra steps of selecting a different printer. If you set the option to Yes, WordPerfect will automatically reformat the document for the current printer selection. This is useful for those who are in a network situation and share documents. If you retrieve a document created by another employee and then print it, it normally goes to the original printer that was selected at the time the document was saved. With this option set to Yes, you can retrieve any number of documents and have them reformatted for and printed on your particular printer.

Initial Codes

If you want each document to start with certain defaults, you can choose the codes that are to be included with this option. You can also change these codes for a particular document by pressing Format (SHIFT-F8) and choosing 3 for **D**ocument, and then 3 for Initial Codes.

Repeat Value

When you press ESC, "Repeat Value = 8" appears on the status line. The next key pressed will be repeated eight times. This includes cursor keys, single character keys, and macros. If you prefer a different number, enter the number here. The change will be reflected the next time you press ESC.

Table of Authorities

WordPerfect lets you have 16 different sections, or tables, in the Table of Authorities feature. The formats for these sections can vary from section to section. The initial default for each section displays a dot leader between the authority and the page number, does not allow underlining, and inserts a blank between each authority. If you want underlining to be available in all sections, or if you want to make any other changes to the table of authorities sections, use this option.

Print Options

The options found on this menu are shown in Figure 3-78. The first four options also appear in the Print (SHIFT-F7) menu so that you can change them for individual print jobs. Common changes include changing Text

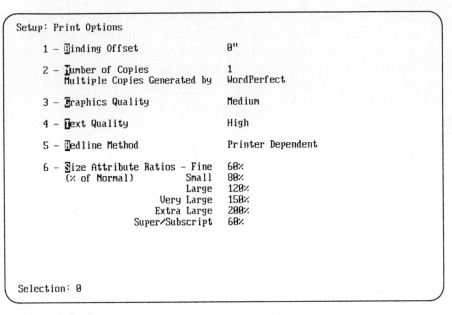

Figure 3-78.   Print Options

Quality to Draft or Graphics Quality to High, depending on the print quality of the documents that you normally produce.

You can set the Redline Method to determine how WordPerfect should print text that is marked for redline.

The last option on this menu lets you choose the percentages to use when WordPerfect decides on the fonts for the size attributes (Extra Large, Large, Small, and so on). For example, if you have a 10pt font, WordPerfect will choose a 20pt font (200%) for Extra Large if it is among the list of available fonts.

The current size attributes are not affected unless you have a PostScript printer. See "Size Attribute Ratios" or "Automatic Font Changes" in this chapter for details on updating the size attributes.

Related Entries

Date and Time
Automatic Font Changes
Equations

ESC Key
Initial Codes
Merge
Print
Size Attribute Ratios
Table of Authorities

INITIALIZE PRINTER

When you are selecting soft fonts, you can determine which fonts will be available when a print job begins and which ones can be loaded during the print job. Before printing, you will need to have those fonts down-loaded to the printer. The Initialize Printer option accomplishes this task.

Keystrokes

1. Press Print (SHIFT-F7).

2. Choose **7** for Initialize Printer.

3. Choose **Y** to proceed or **N** if you decide not to go ahead with the installation.

If you look in the Control Printer menu, you will see that a "print job" has been sent to the printer, which is used to download the fonts.

Hints

Initializing the printer erases all previously downloaded soft fonts—do not initialize the printer unless you want this to happen.

WordPerfect notes which fonts need to be downloaded and checks the directory specified in the printer definition menu for those fonts. If you have not entered a pathname to indicate where the soft fonts can be found, perform the following steps:

1. Press Print (SHIFT-F7).

2. Choose **S** for Select a Printer.

3. Move the cursor to the printer in question, and choose **3** for **Edit**.

4. Choose **6** for Path for **D**ownloadable Fonts and Printer Commands.

5. Enter the name of the drive and directory in which those fonts can be found.

If you are using two disk drives, you will need to insert the disk containing the soft fonts in drive B before you choose the option to initialize the printer, or you will see a "File not found" error message when it tries to print.

The .PRS file contains the information about the filename being used for each soft font. If you want to create soft font definitions of your own, you will need to enter downloading information at that time. See Chapter 5 for more information about using the Printer program.

Related Entries

Cartridges and Fonts
Fonts
See also Chapter 5, "Printer Program"

INS KEY

The INS key is used to toggle between inserting text (Insert mode) and replacing text (Typeover mode).

Keystrokes

WordPerfect is designed to insert text as it is typed. If you want to type over existing text, press INS. "Typeover" is displayed on the status line, indicating that characters at the cursor will be replaced.

Hints

Typeover mode does not allow you to type over codes. Likewise, codes cannot replace characters. Some keys, such as TAB and BACKSPACE, work differently in Typeover mode. When you press TAB, the cursor moves over text to the next tab setting, rather than inserting a tab code. The BACKSPACE key deletes the character at the left of the cursor and inserts a blank space in its place.

Applications

When you use Line Draw, spaces are inserted between lines and boxes. If you want to include text in a chart or a box, you can use Typeover mode so that the spaces will be replaced. If you insert text, you will need to delete the same number of spaces so that the lines and boxes align properly.

Related Entries

Typeover

INSTALL

See Chapter 1, "Installation and Setup," for assistance with installing WordPerfect for the first time. If you elected not to install certain files and later find that you need them, you can run Install again. Appendix B, "WordPerfect Files," lists all files that come with WordPerfect and with which group they will be installed.

Keystrokes

1. Go to DOS.
2. Insert the Install/Learn/Utility 1 disk in drive A (or drive B).

3. Choose **a:install** (or **b:install** if the disk is in drive B).

4. Choose **2** for Custom.

5. Choose **3** for Install Disks.

6. Install will ask you if you want to copy certain files. Choose **Y** or **N** and follow the instructions that are displayed.

7. Press Exit (F7) when finished.

Related Entries

Chapter 1, "Installation and Setup"

ITALICS

Many people prefer to use italics instead of underlining to add emphasis. You can either italicize text as you type or italicize it after you have entered it.

Keystrokes

1. Press Font (CTRL-F8).

2. Choose **2** for Appearance.

3. Choose **4** for Italics.

4. Enter the text to be italicized.

5. Press → once to move over the italics-off code. You can also reenter the Font Appearance menu and select Italics again to turn it off, but moving over the code is more convenient.

To italicize existing text, block the text using Block (ALT-F4) and repeat steps 1 through 3.

Hints

When you select the Italics option, the italics-on [ITALC] and italics-off [italc] codes are inserted, with the cursor remaining between the two. Text inserted between the codes will be printed in italics. To turn off italics, press → to move over the italics-off [italc] code.

Your printer will print italics if WordPerfect finds an italic font that is the same size and typeface as the current font. For example, if you are printing with a 12pt Times Roman font and choose italics, Word-Perfect will try to find a 12pt Times Roman Italics font. If WordPerfect cannot find a similar italic font, the text will be underlined instead.

If you have a daisywheel printer and you select Cartridges and Fonts, you will mark one print wheel as being present when the print job begins (*) and then mark others that can be loaded during the print job (+). If you selected an italic print wheel as being available for loading during the print job, the printer will stop when it reaches the italics code and prompt you in the Control Printer menu to insert the correct print wheel and send the printer a "Go." Press Print (SHIFT-F7), choose 4 for Control Printer, and then type G to do so. See "Macros" in this chapter for a quick macro that you can use to send the printer a "Go."

If you have a color monitor, italics will appear in a different color. If you have a monochrome monitor, you can use a variety of screen attributes to indicate italics: reverse video, boldface, underline, or a combination of screen attributes. Remember that if you choose under-line, only the screen displays it; it does not affect printing. See "Colors/Fonts/Attributes" in this chapter for instructions on how to change the color, font, or attribute for italics and other attributes.

Applications

If you use italics often, you might consider placing the keystrokes for turning italics on and off in a macro. If you do not use a particular

WordPerfect feature such as Tab Align, you might consider assigning italics to that function key, CTRL-F6, with the Keyboard Layout feature. See "Keyboard Layout" in this chapter for more information.

Related Entries

Fonts
Keyboard Layout

JUSTIFICATION

WordPerfect lets you justify or align text with the left margin, right margin, center it between margins, or justify text fully between margins, creating a smooth left *and* right margin.

Figure 3-79 shows all types of justification.

Keystrokes

1. Press Format (SHIFT-F8).

2. Choose **1** for **L**ine.

3. Choose **3** for **J**ustification. The following options are presented:

Justification: 1 Left; 2 Center; 3 Right; 4 Full: 0

4. Select one and press Exit (F7).

This text is left justified, which
means the text at the left margin is
even, leaving a jagged right
margin. Most people prefer left
justified text because it looks more
personal and less "computerized."

Center justification centers each line
automatically as you type, leaving a
jagged left and right margin. This
type of justification could be used
for invitations, announcements, and
flyers.

Right justification aligns text at the
right margin, leaving a jagged edge
at the left. By using right
justification, you do not have to
continually press Flush Right before
typing each line.

Full justification creates an even left
and right margin by expanding or
compressing the text on the line to fit
into space that is available.

Figure 3-79.   Examples of all types of justification

Any text appearing after the code will be justified accordingly.

Center or Right Justify Existing Text

If you want to center or right-justify existing text, follow these steps:

1. Press Block (ALT-F4) and highlight the block of text to be centered
or aligned with the right margin.

2. Press Center (SHIFT-F6) or Flush Right (ALT-F6).

3. Choose **Y** in answer to the question "[Just:Center]? No (Yes)" or
"[Just:Right]? No (Yes)."

The appropriate type of justification code will be inserted at the beginning of the block, and a justification code returning the text to its original justification is inserted at the end of the block.

Hints

After choosing center or right justification, each line starts at the center of the screen or at the right margin, depending on which selection you made. A line can wrap normally or you can press ENTER to insert a hard return [HRt] code, and the cursor again starts at the center or right margin. If it seems awkward to enter text in this manner, enter the text first and then block the text and select Center (SHIFT-F6) or Flush Right (ALT-F6), as explained above.

Note: If you change left or fully justified text to center or right justification, all tab, indent, tab align, center, and flush right codes are stripped from the text. You also cannot hyphenate text that is centered or right-justified.

The codes [Just:Left], [Just:Center], [Just:Right], and [Just:Full] are used to indicate the type of justification that you choose.

Left justification is equal to "no justification" in previous versions of WordPerfect, while full justification is equal to "justification on." Center and right justification make it possible to center or flush-right large sections of text without inserting codes at the beginning and end of each line. You can edit text more easily, and word wrap still functions normally.

How Full Justification Is Accomplished

Some printers use horizontal motion index (HMI) to adjust for extra space, while others use microspace units. HMI lets the printer adjust each character to the left and right; microspacing can adjust only in a forward direction.

With HMI, WordPerfect counts the number of characters on the line and calculates how much space is needed to spread or squeeze characters to meet the right margin. The space is divided equally between characters. If you are printing with a proportionally spaced font, the width of each character is taken into account, and the extra spacing is divided accordingly.

If your printer supports microspacing, the printer inserts the extra space between words instead of spreading or squeezing characters. Printing may be slower when you are using full justification or proportional spacing because extra time is required to make the necessary calculations and adjustments.

Adjusting the Amount of Space Between Words

When using full justification, you can squeeze characters tighter together as well as spread them out to create a smooth right margin if your printer supports HMI. Currently, WordPerfect presets the hyphenation zone at 10 percent on the left and 4 percent on the right. This means that words can end within the last 10 percent of the line or extend past the right margin, up to 4 percent of the length of the line, when justification is off. If your printer cannot squeeze characters to meet the right margin, the right hyphenation setting is ignored. You can set the hyphenation zone so that you have less "space" to fill in and more or fewer characters to squeeze in from the right. If you find that there is an unacceptable amount of white space between words, try one or all of the following:

- Turn on hyphenation at the beginning of the document or where you want hyphenation to begin. When hyphenation is off, longer words that would have required hyphenation wrap to the next line, creating more space that must be taken into account during justification. If you plan to use hyphenation often, insert the hyphenation-on code in the Initial Codes section of the Setup menu. (However, most writers prefer to write without interruption and make the hyphenation decisions later.)

- Decrease the hyphenation zone. (If you have short lines, you may want to increase the hyphenation zone because 10 percent and 4 percent may be too small.) You can also do this permanently by changing it in the Initial Codes section of the Setup menu. Keep in mind that if you make the total hyphenation zone smaller, you will have fewer locations in which to place a hyphen.

• Adjust the Word Spacing Justification Limits. Press Format (SHIFT-F8), choose **4** for **O**ther, and then choose **6** for **P**rinter Functions. The fourth option on that menu lets you decide how much the "space character" between words can be compressed or expanded to achieve right justification. The default setting lets WordPerfect decrease the amount of the space character to 60 percent of its original size or expand it to as much as 999 percent, or approximately nine times its normal size, if necessary. You can adjust these settings to practically any percentage. However, any setting over 999 percent is considered unlimited. If WordPerfect needs to increase the space to more than the maximum allowed, it will achieve justification by inserting space between individual characters.

Applications

Use full justification and proportional spacing in newspaper-style columns to create a typeset look.

Most letters and memos are written without justification. Many people feel that right justification creates a less personal, more computerized look, especially when proportional spacing is not available.

You can create and edit programs, flyers, invitations, ads, title pages, and many other types of documents using the center and right justification options.

Related Items

Center Text
Flush Right
Hyphenation
Proportional Spacing
Word and Letter Spacing
Word Spacing Justification Limits

KEEP TEXT TOGETHER

There are three options for preventing a section of text from being split between pages: Widow/Orphan Protection, Block Protect, and Conditional End of Page.

Widow/Orphan Protection can be used to protect single lines from appearing at the top or bottom of a page. However, it cannot keep titles with the following paragraph or protect three-line paragraphs.

Block Protect is used to keep a block of text from being split between pages. It is best used for text that needs to be kept together when the number of lines in the block might increase or decrease during editing changes.

Conditional End of Page should be used to keep a specific number of lines together. Choose this option when you want to keep a title with the first few lines of text in a paragraph so that it will never appear on a page by itself.

See the applicable entries for step-by-step instructions on how to use these options.

Related Entries

Block Protect
Conditional End of Page
Widow/Orphan Protection

KERNING

Kerning allows you to control the amount of space between two characters. For example, when you normally print the letter "A" followed by "V," there is a gap between the two characters because of the amount of space allotted to each character and the shapes of the characters. Using kerning, you can print the second character closer to the first. The following illustration shows letter combinations that can be kerned on the top and the effect of kerning them on the bottom:

Ta Va WA LT
Ta Va WA LT

Keystrokes

1. Move the cursor to the point at which kerning should be turned on or off.

2. Press Format (SHIFT-F8).

3. Choose **4** for **O**ther.

4. Choose **6** for **P**rinter Functions.

5. Choose **1** for **K**erning.

6. Type **Y** or **N**, depending on whether you want kerning turned on or off.

Hints

WordPerfect will insert the code [Kern:On] or [Kern:Off], depending on the selection that you make. Text is affected from the point of the code forward, until another kerning code is reached.

Kerning is probably the only WordPerfect feature that does not affect the formatting of a document when it is being created. The effect is seen only at the printer. Turning on kerning does not affect the speed of formatting, but it does slow printing.

WordPerfect Corporation has not defined kerning tables for most fonts. You may find that the larger fonts are the only ones, if any, that include kerning information. Therefore, kerning may not have any effect on the document. You can use the Printer (PTR) program to create these kerning tables for specific pairs of characters. See Chapter 5, "Printer Program," for more information about using the Printer program to create these tables.

The Advance feature can be used to advance characters to the left slightly and accomplish kerning automatically. See "Advance" for details.

Applications

Use kerning to create a more typeset-looking document. If you do not want to use kerning for the entire document, consider using it with titles or headings that use a large font. In fact, you can create a paired style to be used for headings that turns on kerning and changes to a large font. When the style is turned off, kerning is also turned off, and the text is returned to the normal font.

Related Entries

Advance
Styles
See also Chapter 5, "Printer Program"

KEYBOARD LAYOUT

WordPerfect lets you reconfigure your keyboard completely, if desired. You can reassign the function keys to other function keys, assign a special character to any key or key combination, or have any key perform a series of keystrokes (a macro).

You can create any number of keyboards, each with its own key assignments. For example, you can have French, German, and English keyboards if you create documents in all three languages.

Those who feel more comfortable using F1 for help in other programs can use the ALTRNAT keyboard layout included with WordPerfect that reassigns help from F3 to F1. ESC is also used as the Cancel key in that keyboard layout.

Keystrokes

Selecting a Keyboard

1. Press Setup (SHIFT-F1). The current keyboard is displayed to the right of option **5**, Keyboard Layout. If no keyboard name is displayed, the original WordPerfect keyboard is being used. See "Hints" for details about the original key assignments.

2. If you want to change the selection, type **5** for **K**eyboard Layout, and you will see a list of available keyboards. If there are no keyboards listed, you have not yet defined any or you have not told WordPerfect where to find them.

If the latter is the case, press Cancel (F1) to return to the Setup menu. Choose **6** for **L**ocation of Files and then choose **2** for **K**eyboard/Macro Files. If you are using two disk drives, you will need to specify drive B:, remove the data disk in drive B, and insert the Macros/Keyboards disk.

After completing this step, press ENTER to leave the Location of Files menu, and then choose **5** for **K**eyboard Layout to return to the list of keyboards.

3. Move the cursor to the keyboard layout to be used and press ENTER or choose **1** to **S**elect that keyboard. Choose **6** if you decide to use the **O**riginal WordPerfect keyboard.

4. After you select the keyboard, you will be returned to the Setup menu. The keyboard that you select will appear next to option 5. If you selected the original WordPerfect keyboard, no name is displayed.

Creating or Editing a Keyboard

1. Press Setup (SHIFT-F1).

2. Choose **5** for **K**eyboard Layout. The menu shown in Figure 3-80 appears. The list of keyboards provided by WordPerfect Corporation is included in this screen. See "Hints" for more information about using these alternate keyboards. If you have other keyboards already defined, they will also appear on this menu.

3. To create a new keyboard, choose **4** for **C**reate, and enter the name of the keyboard (up to 8 characters).

4. You now have two options for editing the new keyboard or an existing keyboard. You can either choose **7** for **E**dit or **8** for **M**ap. The following gives the differences:

Edit   If you choose **7** for **E**dit, you will see a list of all keys that have been redefined, as shown in Figure 3-81. This option lets you redefine any key on the keyboard, including function

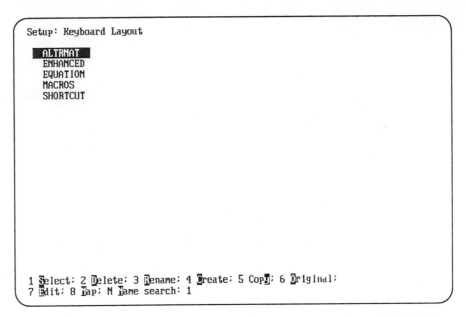

```
Setup: Keyboard Layout

    ALTRNAT
    ENHANCED
    EQUATION
    MACROS
    SHORTCUT












  1 Select; 2 Delete; 3 Rename; 4 Create; 5 Copy; 6 Original;
  7 Edit; 8 Map; N Name search: 1
```

Figure 3-80.   Main Keyboard Layout menu listing the keyboards included with WordPerfect

keys, cursor keys, and delete keys. You can also save the keystrokes from a certain key to a macro file (saved with the extension .WPM) and retrieve a macro file and assign it to a key.

If you assign a command such as {Home} or {GoTo}, it appears as such in the "Action" column, as shown in Figure 3-81. If you assign a macro to a key, it is given the label {KEY MACRO n}, where n is a consecutive number depending on the order in which the macro was created. If you assign a special character to a key with Compose (CTRL-2), you will see the character (or a small box if your monitor cannot display the character) along with the character set and character number (see Appendix A, "WordPerfect Character Sets," for a list). An example is [■: 4,5].

A description of each key is listed in the right column if you have entered one.

Map   The map option lets you see the definitions and make reassignments for letters, numbers, and symbols, as shown in

```
Keyboard: Edit

Name: ENHANCED

Key              Action            Description

Home             {KEY MACRO 1}     Home Home Home Left Arrow
Num 5            {Home}            Home
Shft-F11         {KEY MACRO 2}     Italics
Shft-F12         {KEY MACRO 3}     Retrieve Block
Ctrl-F11         {KEY MACRO 4}     Large
Ctrl-F12         {KEY MACRO 5}     Move Block
Alt-F11          {KEY MACRO 6}     Very Large
Alt-F12          {KEY MACRO 7}     Copy Block
Ctrl-Num 5       {Goto}            Go To
Alt-Up           {KEY MACRO 10}    Move Up by Sentence
Alt-Left         {KEY MACRO 8}     Move Left One Column
Alt-Right        {KEY MACRO 9}     Move Right One Column
Alt-Down         {KEY MACRO 11}    Move Down by Sentence




 1 Action; 2 Dscrptn; 3 Original; 4 Create; 5 Move; Macro: 6 Save; 7 Retrieve: 1
```

Figure 3-81.   Edit menu listing redefined keys from the ENHANCED
keyboard layout

Figure 3-82. It does not let you reassign function keys, cursor
keys, and delete keys. You would need to use the Edit menu
instead.

The menu shows the various combinations of these keys:
lowercase (near the bottom), uppercase (above the lowercase
letters), numbers and symbols, and at the top, the keys combined
with CTRL and ALT.

This menu makes it easy to assign special characters to a
CTRL- or ALT-key combination. It also clarifies which characters can
be used with the ALT and CTRL keys.

If a special character is assigned to a key, it will be displayed. If your monitor cannot display the character, a small box
appears instead.

A "C" indicates a command (which may either be the original
function of the key, such as ^B for CTRL-B, or the command for a
WordPerfect function, such as {Cancel}). An "M" indicates that a
macro (more than one keystroke) is assigned to the key.

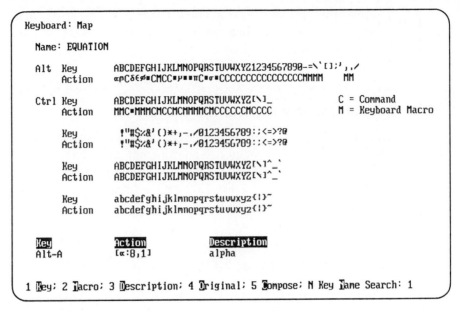

Figure 3-82. Map menu (from the EQUATION keyboard), which shows the definition of letters, numbers, and symbols at a glance

The space near the bottom of the map menu shows the current key (where the cursor is located in the map above) along with its action and description as you would see them in the Edit menu, as shown in Figure 3-81.

5. Continue creating or editing specific keys with either of these menus, as explained in the next sections.

6. When you have finished reassigning keys, press Exit (F7) to return to the list of keyboards. You can also press Cancel (F1) to cancel all changes made to the keys. The list will be returned to its previous state.

The "Hints" section contains a description of all the other options in this menu.

7. Move the cursor to the keyboard that is to be used, and press ENTER. If you want to use the original WordPerfect keyboard instead, choose **6** for Original.

Creating or Editing a Key with the Edit Menu

You can create or edit a key in either the Edit or Map menu. Since the keystrokes in these two menus are so different, they have been divided into two sections. Instructions for using the Map menu are given later in this section. After choosing **7** for **E**dit and entering the menu shown in Figure 3-81, follow these steps:

1. Choose **4** to **C**reate a new key. If you are editing a key, move the cursor to that key, choose **1** for **A**ction, and then go to step 4.

2. When prompted for the "Key:", press the key or key combination that is to be given a new assignment. For example, if you are assigning the character "á" to the lowercase "a," you should type **a**. If you want to assign it to CTRL-A or ALT-A, you would press that key combination. If you wanted to reassign Help to the F1 key, for example, you would press F1.

3. Enter a description for the key, or press ENTER to skip this step. The description appears in the list of redefined keys so you can see what its function is.

4. The macro editor appears with the name of the key and the description listed above and the current function of the key listed in the "Action" screen.

   You can now delete the previous function of the key and add a new one. The following options are available:

   Command If you are reassigning a WordPerfect function or command to the key, press that function key. The command should be inserted in braces, as in {Block}.

   If you need to insert the commands {Enter}, {Tab}, {Exit}, {Cancel}, any of the cursor commands such as {Up} or {Left}, or delete keys such as {Del} or {Backspace}, you will need to first press CTRL-V, or the function key will perform its normal Word-

Perfect function to help edit the keystrokes in this window instead of inserting the command. CTRL-V tells WordPerfect not to interpret the key, but to let the function be inserted instead.

Special Characters If you are assigning a special character to a key, you can enter it in one of three ways. If it is part of the IBM character set, you can hold down the ALT key and type the decimal value for the character on the numeric keypad. For example, pressing ALT and typing **20** displays the paragraph symbol (¶). You can also create the key with WordPerfect's Compose feature. Press Compose (CTRL-2) using the 2 on the top row of the keyboard—not the 2 on the numeric keypad—and then type the two characters to create the special character. You can create the character "á" by pressing CTRL-2 and typing **a** and then '. A list of characters that can be created when you type two other characters is included under "Compose" in this chapter.

The third method also uses the Compose feature, but instead of typing two characters, you would enter the character set number and individual character number as assigned by WordPerfect. Appendix A, "WordPerfect Character Sets," lists each special character available in WordPerfect, along with the character set number and the individual character number. After pressing Compose (CTRL-2), enter the number of the section, a comma, and then the character number. If the screen cannot display the character, a small box will be inserted instead. See "Compose" in this chapter for details.

Macros If you want to assign a number of keystrokes to a key, it becomes a macro. In fact, the editor that you see is actually the same editor used to edit macros. However, the macros created here are different from file macros, because they are saved in one keyboard file that has the extension .WPK, while file macros are saved in separate files that have the extension .WPM. See "Hints" for details about key and file macros.

While entering or editing the keystrokes for a specific key, you can press CTRL-PGUP to display a list of macro commands in the upper right corner. Move the cursor to the command that is to be inserted into the macro, and press ENTER. Press Cancel (F1) to return to the window without inserting a command. See "Macros" in this chapter and Chapter 6, "Advanced Macro and Merge Commands," for more information about using the macro commands.

5. Press Exit (F7) when you are finished to return to the list of keys and descriptions. If you change your mind and want to cancel the changes you have made in the window editor, press Cancel (F1) and confirm that all changes made should be canceled.

All other options on the Edit menu are described in the following paragraphs.

Action   If you want to edit a key, choose option **1** for **Action**. You will be placed in the macro editor, where you can edit the keystrokes assigned to the key.

Description   Choose **2** for **Description** to change the description of the currently highlighted key.

Original   If you want to return a key to its original state, choose **3** for **Original**. Because this is the same as deleting the function assigned to a key, you are asked to confirm the deletion. The key is then removed from the list.

If you accidentally delete a key's function and return it to its original state, you can press Cancel (F1) and type **Y** to cancel all changes made to the keyboard.

Create   Use Option **4** for **Create** to create a new key definition. You will be asked for the key to be redefined and a description for the key. You are then placed in the macro editor so you can assign any command, special character, or macro to the key.

Move   Option **5** for **Move** lets you move the command, special character, or macro to another key. If you choose this option, you are asked for the new key. After pressing that key, the keystrokes are moved to that key, and the old key is removed from the list. If you ask to move the definition to a key that is already on the list, you are asked if you want to replace the current definition for that key. Type **Y** to do so or **N** to change your mind and choose a different key.

This option lets you move the definition from one key to another within the same keyboard layout. See "Hints" for a method that you can use to move a key definition from one keyboard to another.

Macro: Save   With option **6** for Save, you can save the current key definition to a file macro (one with a .WPM extension). After choosing this option, you are asked for the name of the macro to be defined. Enter the name of a macro (up to eight letters). If the macro already exists, you are asked if you want to replace the existing macro.

Macro: Retrieve   You can also assign an existing file macro (one with the extension .WPM) to a key. To do so, choose **7** for **R**etrieve. Before entering the name of the macro to be retrieved, you are asked for the key that will be used for the macro. Press any key or key combination. If you press a key that has already been defined, you will see a message asking if you want to replace the previous definition.

When prompted for the name of the macro, enter the drive, the directory, and the name of the macro. If you are assigning an ALT-key macro, you can press that keystroke combination. If it is found on a drive or directory other than the default, enter the name as ALT and the letter. For example, if you were reassigning the ALT-A macro to a key, enter **alta** as the macro name after the drive and directory.

The new key is added to the list. If you entered a description when you created the macro, that description will also appear.

Creating or Editing a Key with the Map Menu

From the main keyboard layout menu shown in Figure 3-80, you can choose **8** for **M**ap to see an overall "map" of the keys that have been redefined on the keyboard. This list does not include function, cursor, or delete keys. After entering this menu, you can use the following steps to edit this map.

1. Use the arrow keys to move to the key to be redefined. The section at the bottom of the screen displays the action and a description for the current key.

2. Choose one of the options, which are described in the following paragraphs.

3. Continue redefining other keys if necessary, and press Exit (F7) when you are finished.

Key   Choose 1 for **K**ey if you want to assign a single key or Word-Perfect function to the current key. For example, if you wanted to assign {Cancel} to CTRL-C, you would choose **1** for **K**ey, and then press {Cancel} when you are asked for the key. You can also type any other letter, number, or symbol when you are prompted for the key.

Macro   Choose option **2** for **M**acro to assign a series of keystrokes (a macro) to the key. You will be placed in the Action screen (macro editor), where you can enter the series of keystrokes. Press Exit when you are finished.

Description   Option **3** for **D**escription lets you change or enter a new description for the current key.

Original   If you want to delete the definition from a key and return it to its original function, choose **4** for **O**riginal. You are asked to confirm the deletion only if a macro is assigned to the key or if the key contains a description.

Compose   To assign a special character to a key, choose **5** for Compose. When the "Key =" prompt appears, enter the character set number, a comma, and then the character number. All special characters are listed in Appendix A, "WordPerfect Character Sets."

You can also type two characters to make the special character. For example, typing two asterisks (**) makes a bullet character (●), typing **/** and **2** makes the one-half symbol (½), and typing **e** and ` creates an accented e (è). See "Compose" in this chapter for a complete list.

Key Name Search   To move quickly to a specific key, type **N** for Key Name Search and enter the key. For example, press CTRL-X to move directly to that key.

Hints

You can always press CTRL-6 (using the 6 on the top row of the keyboard instead of the 6 on the numeric keypad) to return to the original

WordPerfect keyboard at any time for that editing session. The next time you start WordPerfect, it will again select the appropriate keyboard. To deselect a keyboard permanently and return to the original layout, choose **6** for Original in the Keyboard Layout menu. WordPerfect will not let you reassign CTRL-6 (or any other CTRL-# key) to provide this type of protection. If, for some reason, you want to disable the use of CTRL-6 to return to the original keyboard, you can start WordPerfect with the /NO (no original) option. To do so, enter **wp/no**.

Before you can edit the keys on the keyboard, you will need to have the files KEYS.MRS and WP.MRS in the directory where WordPerfect is kept. If they cannot be found when you try to edit or create a key, you will see the message "ERROR: File not found -- KEYS.MRS." These files are copied with the WordPerfect program files during installation. If you are using a two-disk drive system, they are kept on the WordPerfect 2 disk.

All keyboard filenames have the extension .WPK. That extension, however, does not appear with the keyboard name in the list of keyboards.

The keyboards on the default directory are automatically displayed. If you want to use keyboards from other directories, you will need to choose **6** for Location of Files on the Setup menu and enter the drive and directory where they can be found.

Five keyboards are provided by WordPerfect Corporation. They are copied during installation if you answer Yes to the question "Install Keyboard Files." Table 3-13 lists the keys that have been redefined and their descriptions. Many of the key definitions are macros.

Deleting or Renaming a Keyboard

In addition to selecting, creating, and editing keyboards, you can delete or rename them. When you see the list of keyboards—press Setup (SHIFT-F1) and choose **5** for Keyboard Layout—move the cursor to the keyboard in question and choose **2** for Delete or **3** for Rename. Type **Y** to confirm the deletion, or enter a new keyboard name. You can also perform the same functions from the List Files menu.

Copying a Keyboard

While in the Keyboard Layout menu, you can make a copy of an existing keyboard and then make changes to the copy. To do so, move the cursor

ALTRNAT Keyboard

Key	Description
F1	Help
F3	Escape
ESC	Cancel

ENHANCED Keyboard

Key	Description
HOME	Home, Home, Home, ←
*Num 5	Home
SHIFT-F11	Italics
SHIFT-F12	Retrieve block
CTRL-F11	Large
CTRL-F12	Move block
ALT-F11	Very Large
Alt-F12	Copy block
*CTRL-Num 5	Go to
ALT-↑	Move up by sentence
ALT-↓	Move down by sentence
ALT-←	Move left one column
ALT-→	Move right one column

EQUATION Keyboard

Key	Description
ALT-,	$\leq$ (Less than or equal to)
ALT-.	$\geq$ (Greater than or equal to)
ALT-`	SIMEQ (Similar or equal to)
ALT--	CONG (Congruent)
ALT-=	!= (Not equal to)
ALT-\	LINE (Line)
ALT-A	alpha
ALT-B	beta
ALT-D	delta

* Num followed by a number indicates the key on the numeric keypad.

Table 3-13.   List of Key Definitions Included in the ALTRNAT, ENHANCED, EQUATION, MACROS, and SHORTCUT Keyboards

Key	Description
ALT-E	epsilon
ALT-F	phi
ALT-G	gamma
ALT-I	INF (infinity)
ALT-L	lambda
ALT-M	mu
ALT-N	eta
ALT-O	omega
ALT-P	pi
ALT-R	rho
ALT-S	sigma
ALT-T	theta
ALT-Tab	$\longrightarrow$ (Right arrow)
CTRL-Tab	$\longleftarrow$ (Left arrow)
CTRL-A	SUP (Superscript)
CTRL-B	BAR (Bar)
CTRL-D	DELTA (uppercase)
CTRL-E	IN (Member element)
CTRL-F	FROM TO (x From a To b)
CTRL-G	GRAD (Nabla, Gradient)
CTRL-I	INT (Integral)
CTRL-L	OVERLINE (Overline)
CTRL-N	GRAD (Nabla, Gradient)
CTRL-O	OVER (Over)
CTRL-P	PARTIAL (Partial)
CTRL-Q	SQRT (Square Root)
CTRL-S	SUM (Sum)
CTRL-Z	SUB (Subscript)

MACROS Keyboard

Key	Description
ALT-B	Restore the previous block
ALT-C	Capitalize the first letter of the current word
ALT-D	Delete a line
ALT-E	Return to main editing screen
ALT-F	Find the bookmark (see ALT-M)
ALT-G	Gives printer a Go

Table 3-13.   List of Key Definitions Included in the ALTRNAT, ENHANCED, EQUATION, MACROS, and SHORTCUT Keyboards (*continued*)

Key	Description
ALT-I	Insert a line
ALT-M	Insert a bookmark << MARK >>
ALT-N	Edit the next or previous note
ALT-R	Replace Size, Attribute, or Text
ALT-T	Transpose two visible characters
CTRL-C	Calculator
CTRL-D	Generate a Memo, Letter, or Itinerary
CTRL-E	Print name and address on an envelope
CTRL-G	Glossary macro — expand abbreviations
CTRL-P	Pointing mode when entering formulas
CTRL-R	Recalculate all formulas in a table
CTRL-F8	Font key

SHORTCUT Keyboard

Key	Description
ALT-A	Add an attribute
ALT-B	Subscript
ALT-D	Double underline
ALT-E	Edit a code
ALT-F	Fine
ALT-G	Go Printer
ALT-I	Italics
ALT-L	Large
ALT-O	Outline
ALT-P	Superscript
ALT-R	Redline
ALT-S	Small
ALT-T	Strikeout
ALT-V	Very large
ALT-W	Shadow
ALT-X	Extra large
CTRL-B	Base font
CTRL-C	Define columns
CTRL-D	Double spacing
CTRL-E	Endnote create
CTRL-F	Footnote create

Table 3-13. List of Key Definitions Included in the ALTRNAT, ENHANCED, EQUATION, MACROS, and SHORTCUT Keyboards (*continued*)

Key	Description
CTRL-G	Graphic — create a graphics figure
CTRL-H	Header A — create
CTRL-I	Document initial codes
CTRL-J	Justification
CTRL-L	Left/right margins
CTRL-M	Margins top/bottom
CTRL-O	Footer A — create
CTRL-P	Paper size/type
CTRL-Q	Equation create
CTRL-S	Single spacing
CTRL-T	Tab set

Table 3-13.   List of Key Definitions Included in the ALTRNAT, ENHANCED, EQUATION, MACROS, and SHORTCUT Keyboards (*continued*)

to the keyboard to be copied and choose 5 for Copy. When you are prompted for the keyboard filename, enter a name of up to eight letters. If a keyboard with that name already exists, you are asked if you want to replace the existing keyboard.

Name Search

When selecting a keyboard, you can choose **N** for Name Search and type the name of the keyboard to be selected. The cursor then moves directly to that keyboard. Press ENTER to turn off the Name Search feature, and then press ENTER to select the keyboard.

Unless you have several keyboards, moving the cursor to the keyboard will probably be faster than using the Name Search feature. However, if you are defining a macro that selects a keyboard, use the Name Search feature. This feature would find the desired keyboard regardless of its position in the list (which could change if you add or delete other keyboards in the future).

Combining Keys from Several Keyboards

The following steps will help you copy key definitions from one keyboard to another. For example, you may want to combine several key definitions from each of the keyboards provided by WordPerfect into one single keyboard of your own so you don't have to switch between keyboard layouts to get those functions.

1. Press Setup (SHIFT-F1) and choose 5 for **K**eyboard Layout.

2. Move the cursor to the keyboard that contains the desired keys.

3. Choose 1 to **S**elect the keyboard. The cursor is returned to the Setup menu.

4. Choose 5 for **K**eyboard Layout to reenter the list of keyboards.

5. Move the cursor to the keyboard that is to receive the new key assignments, and type 7 for **E**dit. (If the keyboard does not yet exist, choose 4 to **C**reate the new keyboard, enter the name when you are prompted to do so, and then choose 1 for **E**dit.)

6. Choose 4 to **C**reate a new key that will receive the new key assignment, and then specify the new key.

7. Enter a description when prompted.

8. Press CTRL-V.

9. Press the key from the other keyboard that contains the desired key assignment. For example, if you want to copy a macro assigned to ALT-A in the other keyboard, press ALT-A. A copy of the definition is inserted at the cursor.

10. Press Exit (F7) to return to the list of keys. Continue until you have copied all the desired key assignments from the other keyboard.

11. Press Exit (F7) to exit to the list of keyboards. Repeat the entire process if you want to add keys from other keyboards.

12. After completing the process, remember to select the correct keyboard.

Keyboards Provided by WordPerfect

WordPerfect includes five keyboard layouts: ALTRNAT, ENHANCED, EQUATION, MACROS, and SHORTCUT. All the keys and their definitions are listed in Table 3-13.

Of special note is the ALT-E key on the SHORTCUT keyboard. This powerful macro can be used to edit most WordPerfect codes. A list of these codes is included in Table 3-14.

To use the macro, position the cursor on the code to be edited — press Reveal Codes (ALT-F3) to locate the code if necessary — and then press ALT-E. The macro takes you into the appropriate menu so you can then make the necessary changes. This saves many keystrokes and helps reduce the number of duplicate codes in your document.

If you have an enhanced keyboard, you can use the following key assignments without selecting a keyboard — they are included with the "Original" keyboard. If you do not have an enhanced keyboard, you can create a macro that includes the necessary macro commands. See "Macros" in this chapter for details or refer to Chapter 6, "Advanced Macro and Merge Commands."

Most of these keys have different functions depending on which feature is being used. Any cursor keys used are those to the left of the numeric keypad.

Key	Description	Macro Command
CTRL-INS	Copy the current block	{Block Copy}
	Insert a row if in a table	
CTRL-DEL	Move the current block	{Block Move}
CTRL-↑	Move up one paragraph	{Para Up}
CTRL-↓	Move down one paragraph	{Para Down}
ALT-↑	Move up one cell in a table	{Item Up}
	Move to previous section of Parallel Columns	
	Move to previous paragraph number of the same level	

Key	Description	Macro Command
ALT-↓	Move down one cell in a table	{Item Down}
	Move to the next section of Parallel Columns	
	Move to next paragraph number of the same level	
ALT-←	Move left one cell in a table	{Item Left}
	Move to the column to the left	
	Move to the previous paragraph number of any level	
ALT-→	Move right one cell in a table	{Item Right}
	Move to the column to the right	
	Move to the next paragraph number of any level	

File Macros vs. Key Macros

The following is a discussion of the differences between file macros (those ending with the extension .WPM) and macros included in a keyboard (a file with the extension .WPK).

A keyboard can contain several macros. It also lets you assign macros to ALT *and* CTRL keys, whereas a file macro can only be assigned to an ALT-key combination. A keyboard macro takes precedence over a file macro. If you try to use an ALT-key file macro and have selected a keyboard that has redefined the same ALT key, the keyboard macro will be used. You could still use the ALT-key file macro, however, by pressing Macro (ALT-F10) and typing **altx**, where *x* represents the key that is combined with ALT.

A file macro takes up less space than a keyboard file. However, if you have several small file macros, they will each take a minimum

Codes Edited by ALT-E

Advance
Attributes On/Off (all)
Auto Reference
Base Font
Baseline for Typesetters
Center Page
Colors
Column Definitions
Comments
Conditional End of Page
Date
Decimal Align
Equation Options
Equations
Footer A/B
Footnotes/Endnotes
Force Even/Odd
Graphics Lines
Graphics Options (all types)
Graphics Boxes (all types)
Header A/B
Hyphenation On/Off
Hyphenation Zone
Justification
Justification Limits
Kerning
Language
Leading
Line Height
Line Numbering
Line Spacing
Margins L/R
Margins T/B
Math Definitions
Outline Styles
Overstrike
Page Number, New

Table 3-14.   List of Codes That Can Be Edited with the ALT-E Macro Included
in the SHORTCUT Keyboard

Codes Edited by ALT-E (*continued*)

Page Number Position
Page Number Insert
Page Numbering Style
Paper Size/Type
Paragraph Number Definition
Suppress Page Formats
Tab Sets
Tables
Targets (Automatic Reference)
Underline Spaces and Tabs
Widow On/Off
Word and Letter Spacing

Table 3-14. List of Codes That Can Be Edited with the ALT-E Macro Included in the SHORTCUT Keyboard (*continued*)

amount of disk space, regardless of their size. If you find these small files using up valuable disk space, it may be best to combine them into a keyboard file.

Macros created in a keyboard layout are assigned a number according to the order in which you defined them. For example, {KEY MACRO 1} means that it was the first macro defined for that keyboard. These macros can be included in other keys or macros when you select the keyboard that contains the macro and then press the appropriate key. You may want to use caution when doing so, however, because you could get unpredictable results if a different keyboard is selected. If you used a key that inserted {KEY MACRO 9} in the macro, for example, and then selected a different keyboard, you would get the {KEY MACRO 9} from the newly selected keyboard.

WordPerfect 5.0 Keyboards

All keyboards defined in WordPerfect 5.0 are compatible with those of version 5.1. Individual macros may not, however, be compatible because some keystrokes have been changed in the new version.

If you plan to use a keyboard layout from version 5.0 that redefined the ALT-= key, you will need to move that definition to a different key so you can use the pull-down menus.

Applications

If your fingers are accustomed to another word processor's keyboard, you can reassign WordPerfect's functions to those keys. For example, if you have used WordStar for years, you can reassign the cursor keys to the WordStar diamond, create a macro that deletes an entire line and assign it to CTRL-Y, or use CTRL-T to delete the word to the right.

Even if you have not used another word processor, you may be more familiar with another program's commands and interface. For example, in many programs, HOME goes to the far left of the screen. You could assign the keystrokes HOME, ← to the HOME key. Number 5 on the numeric keypad could then become the new HOME key.

As was mentioned previously, you can have different keyboards set up for each language that you use. You can create macros that switch between keyboards and even insert the appropriate language code, telling WordPerfect which language is being used (for Speller and Thesaurus purposes). See "Languages" in this chapter for more information.

If you accidentally delete or replace a function such as Cancel or Exit, you can always return to the original keyboard with CTRL-6.

Related Entries

Macros

LABELS

WordPerfect lets you store the information about the size of the label, the number of labels on a sheet, the distance between labels, and the margins for each label so the information can print within those boundaries.

Keystrokes

The following steps help you define and select labels. If you prefer, you can use the Labels macro, included with WordPerfect, which lets you choose from several popular types of labels made by Avery and 3M. See "Hints" for instructions on using this macro.

Defining Labels

1. Press Format (SHIFT-F8) and choose **2** for **P**age.

2. Choose **7** for Paper Size/Type. You will see a list of predefined paper sizes and types, as shown in Figure 3-83. This list varies from printer to printer.

3. Choose **2** to **A**dd to this list.

4. You are first asked to choose the type of paper. Choose **4** for Labels so it is easier to identify later when selecting the form. You can also type **O** for **O**ther and enter any name that will help you identify your particular set of labels from the list.

The menu shown in Figure 3-84 appears. You can enter specific information about the paper and where it is located.

```
Format: Paper Size/Type
                                                  Font  Double
  Paper type and Orientation    Paper Size    Prompt Loc   Type  Sided  Labels

  Envelope - Wide               9.5" x 4"       No   Manual  Land  No
  Legal                         8.5" x 14"      No   Contin  Port  No
  Legal - Wide                  14" x 8.5"      No   Contin  Land  No
  Standard                      8.5" x 11"      No   Contin  Port  No
  Standard - Wide               11" x 8.5"      No   Contin  Land  No
  [ALL OTHERS]                  Width ≤ 8.5"    Yes  Manual        No
```

```
  1 Select; 2 Add; 3 Copy; 4 Delete; 5 Edit; N Name Search: 1
```

Figure 3-83.   Paper Size/Type menu containing predefined paper sizes

5. If the sheet of labels is not 8.5″ by 11″, choose **1** for Paper Size and choose the appropriate size. If the correct size is not on the list, type **O** for Other and enter the outside dimensions.

Width   Measure and enter the width of the page. If you are using labels on a tractor feeder, measure only the width of the actual labels (excluding the holes on the sides). Include the space for the holes, however, if you will be feeding this type of label through the manual feed slot of a laser printer.

Height   Measure and enter the height of the page. If you are using labels on a tractor feeder, enter the height of a single label as the height of the page. If there is any space between labels, include the space either above *or* below the label as part of the height. If you will be feeding tractor-fed labels through the manual feed slot of a laser printer, decide how many labels will be torn off and fed through at a time, and then enter the total measurement as the height.

6. If necessary, choose **5** to change the Location of the labels.

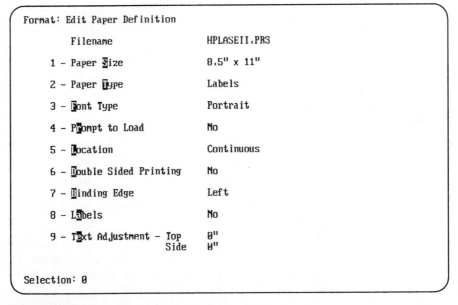

Figure 3-84.   Edit Paper Definition menu

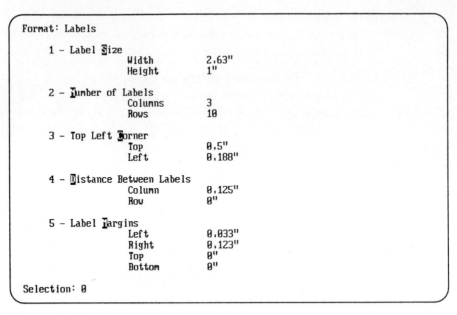

Figure 3-85.   Labels menu

7. Choose 8 for Labels, and then type **Y** to indicate that the sheet of paper contains labels. The menu shown in Figure 3-85 appears. Some measurements may already be entered in this menu. Based on the paper size, WordPerfect makes some assumptions about the number of labels that might fit on the page and enters common settings for more popular labels.

8. Make changes to the menu if necessary. The following is a guide about the type of information that you should enter. Note that you can also enter measurements in fractions (9/16, 1-1/4, and so on) and WordPerfect will convert them to their decimal equivalents.

Label Size   Enter the width and height of one label.

Number of Labels   Count the number of labels across the page, and enter that number as the number of columns. If there is only one across, enter **1** as the number of columns.

Count the number of labels down the page, and enter that number as the number of rows. If you are using tractor-fed

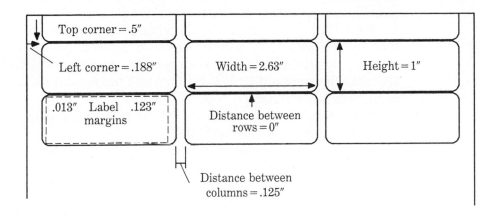

Figure 3-86.   Example of settings for a standard three-across sheet of labels

labels, enter **1** as the number of rows. If you are feeding tractor-fed labels through a laser printer, count the number of labels that you will be feeding through the manual feed slot at one time, and enter that number (you should have determined the amount earlier when you entered the height of the page).

Top Left Corner   If there is no space between the upper left corner of the page and the label, enter **0**. This would be the case if you were using labels on a tractor feeder.

   If you have a sheet of labels similar to the one shown in Figure 3-86, enter the distance from the top and left sides of the page to the corner of the first label.

Distance Between Labels   If there is any type of gutter space between columns or rows, enter that distance. In the example shown in Figure 3-86, the gutter space between columns is .125″, but there is no space (0″) between rows.

   If you are using labels on a tractor feeder, the amount of gutter space between rows should have already been included as part of the paper height.

Label Margins   Enter the left, right, top, and bottom margins for one individual label. If you enter margins that are too small for the printer's unprintable region, you will see a message that the margins have been adjusted to compensate for your printer's unprintable region when you try to exit the Labels Definition menu. WordPerfect will then add the required amount of space to the margin(s).

To avoid having WordPerfect adjust your top and bottom margins, you can choose to skip the first and last label. You will have to adjust the number of rows and the distance from the top left corner if you choose to do this.

Note: You do not have to change the left, right, top, and bottom margins in the document before printing a sheet of labels. WordPerfect automatically adjusts them according to the current label definition.

9. Press Exit (F7) twice to return to the list of paper sizes and types available. If you see an error message telling you that the labels will not fit on the paper size, double-check all measurements.

The new labels definition is highlighted in the list. The number of labels per sheet is displayed for you at the far right for easier identification.

10. To insert that definition into your document, choose 1 for Select. To exit the menu without selecting a Labels form, press Exit (F7).

Selecting Labels

You can follow these steps before or after you type the names and addresses. However, it might be easier if you select the labels definition before entering the names, so you can tell if you are typing too many characters for the line or too many lines for the label.

If you are doing a merge, you should select the label definition after the merge is finished so that the Paper Size/Type code is not duplicated with each record.

1. Move the cursor to the top of the document (press HOME, HOME, ↑).

2. Press Format (SHIFT-F8) and choose **2** for **Page**.

3. Choose **7** for Paper Size/Type.

4. Move the cursor to the desired labels definition and choose **1** to Select it.

5. Press Exit (F7) to return to the document.

If you print the labels and find that adjustments are necessary, you will need to delete the previous Paper Size/Type code, edit the labels definition, and reselect it from the list; otherwise the changes will not be in effect when you print the labels.

Hints

The text that is to appear on each label is separated with a page break. When you are entering the text for labels, separate each "label" with a hard page [HPg] break (CTRL-ENTER). If you are merging, this is automatically done for you. A soft page break will also cause the information following the page break to be printed on the next label. However, entering a hard page break will ensure that the right information will be printed on each label.

If the number of lines exceeds the height of the label, a soft page break will be inserted, indicating that you have entered the boundaries for the next label. Likewise, if the line wraps prematurely, you will know that you have exceeded the width of the label and should make adjustments if you don't want the line to wrap when the labels are printed.

There are several things you can do to avoid these problems. The easiest solution is to change to a smaller font size if one is available. Another is to decrease the line height (found on the Line Format menu) so that you can print more lines in the same amount of space. The last solution is to enter the labels definition menu and, if possible, adjust the left, right, top, and bottom margins for the label.

When you select a paper definition containing labels, a code similar to [Paper Sz/Typ:8.5" x 11",Labels,2.63" x 1"] is inserted. Note that the dimensions of a single label are also displayed.

To center text on each label, you must insert a center page code at the beginning of each label. This is easier to do if you are doing a merge, because you can insert this code at the beginning of the primary file before the merge is done so that it will be duplicated with each record or label. If you are not doing a merge, you can use Replace (ALT-F2) to search for the [Hpg] code and replace it with a [Hpg] and [Center Pg] code. To center text between the left and right margins of each label, use the Center Justification option. See "Applications" for an example and keystrokes for centering text horizontally and vertically on a label.

If you change the size of the paper after defining labels, you will most likely see an error message stating that the labels information will need to be updated for the current paper size. This error message means that you have changed the paper size and that the labels previously defined can no longer fit in those boundaries. Choose the Labels option from Edit Paper Definition, and WordPerfect will update the measurements to fit the paper size. You may then need to make additional changes.

Printing Labels

The labels information just defined is kept in the current printer's .PRS file. If you change printers, you will need to define the labels again for the new printer.

Before printing the labels, you may want to View the document—press Print (SHIFT-F7) and choose **6** to View—to see how they will print.

Insert the labels in the correct location in the printer (continuous, manual, and so on), and then print the full document as you would normally. If you hear a beep, it means that you have chosen manual feed or that you have asked to be prompted to insert the proper type of paper. Press Print (SHIFT-F7), choose **4** for Control Printer, and then choose **4** to send the printer a **G**o.

Labels Macro

WordPerfect Corporation has included a Labels macro that lets you select your type of labels from a list. It then creates the labels definition for you. This macro only defines the labels; it does not select them for the current document.

```
┌─────────────────────────────────────────────────────────────┐
│ ████████████████████████████████████████████████            │
│         Label Page/Size Definitions                         │
│ ██████████████████████████████████████████████             │
│  Mnu  Label Sizes      # of labels per..                    │
│  ltr   H x W          Sheet Row Column    Examples          │
│   A   1" x 2 5/8"       30    3    10    Avery 5160/5260     │
│   B   1" x 4"           20    2    10    Avery 5161/5261     │
│   C   1 1/3" x 4"       14    2     7    Avery 5162/5262     │
│   D   2" x 4"           10    2     5    Avery 5163          │
│   E   3 1/3" x 4"        6    2     3    Avery 5164          │
│   F   2/3" x 3 7/16"    30    2    15    Avery 5266          │
│   G   1/2" x 1 3/4"     80    4    20    Avery 5267          │
│   H   2 3/4" x 2 3/4"    9    3     3    Avery 5196          │
│   I   1 1/2" x 4"       12    2     6    Avery 5197          │
│   J   8 1/2" x 11"       1    0     0    Avery 5165          │
│   K   1" x 2 5/8"       30    3    10    3M 7730             │
│   L   1 1/2" x 2 5/6"   21    3     7    3M 7721             │
│   M   1" x 2 5/6"       33    3    11    3M 7733             │
│   N   2 1/2" x 2 5/6"   12    3     4    3M 7712             │
│   O   3 1/3" x 2 5/6"    9    3     3    3M 7709             │
│   P   11" x 8 7/16"      1    0     0    3M 7701             │
│  (↑↓), (Mnu Ltr), or (*), then Press Enter; More=PgDn        │
│  Selection: B                                               │
└─────────────────────────────────────────────────────────────┘
```

Figure 3-87.   List of common labels displayed with the Labels macro

The macro (named LABELS.WPM) is copied with the keyboard files during installation. If copied, it will be found in the directory specified for Keyboard/Macro Files.

To use the macro, follow these steps:

1. Press Macro (ALT-F10) (you do not have to clear your screen first).

2. When prompted for the name of the macro, enter **labels**.

3. The menu shown in Figure 3-87 appears, giving a list of common label sizes and types.

4. Move the cursor to each type of labels that you will be using, and mark them with an asterisk (*). To see more labels, press PGDN. PGUP will return you to this list.

5. After you have marked all the labels you need, press ENTER. You are asked to verify the selection of the marked labels. If you type **N**, you are asked if you want to set up the label that is currently highlighted. Typing **Y** for either question causes the macro to define the selected labels. Typing **N** returns you to the LABELS macro menu.

You can press Cancel (F1) or Exit (F7) at any time to stop the macro. If you press Format (SHIFT-F8), and then choose 2 for **Page**, and 7 for **Paper Size/Type**, you will see the newly defined label(s) among the list.

Using Merge

Following are the steps for merging names and addresses from a secondary file so they can be printed on labels. You may also want to read "Merge" in this chapter for details.

These steps assume that you have already created the secondary file and that the first few fields contain the name and address. The following steps include creating the primary file and merging the two files together:

1. Clear your screen.

2. Press Merge Codes (SHIFT-F9).

3. Choose 1 for **Field**, and then enter the number (or name if you have named the fields) of the field containing the person's name.

4. Press ENTER to go to the next line.

5. Repeat steps 2 to 4 to insert the necessary fields in their appropriate locations. If the city, state, and ZIP code are in separate fields, you do not have to press ENTER to go to the next line.

The primary file might look like the following if the fields are numbered:

```
{FIELD}1~
{FIELD}2~
{FIELD}3~, {FIELD}4~    {FIELD}5~
```

If a Company field needs to be inserted, but some of the records do not have a company name, you normally get a blank line. To solve this, you can enter the name of the field followed by a question mark (?). The command would then look like this on your screen: {FIELD}Company?~ or {FIELD}2?~. See "Merge" in this chapter for other solutions that are available when you are checking for and dealing with blank fields.

6. When you have finished inserting all the fields to be placed on the label, save the document and clear the screen.

7. Press Merge/Sort (CTRL-F9). Enter the name of the primary file (the file just created), and then enter the name of the secondary file containing the names and addresses.

8. When the merge is finished, press HOME, HOME, HOME, ↑ to go to the top of the document before all codes.

9. Press Format (SHIFT-F8), choose **2** for **P**age and **7** for **P**aper Size/Type, and then move to the desired labels form and type **1** to Select it.

10. Insert the labels in the correct location at the printer, press Print (SHIFT-F7), and then choose **1** to print the Full Document.

Logical Page Concept

The Labels feature works on a "logical page" concept, which defines each label as a logical page. A hard page break between labels will print the information on a single label instead of a single page. The entire page (containing one or more labels) is considered the "physical page."

Because of this new concept, you can use the labels feature for other types of applications, such as printing two "pages" side by side on one physical page. See "Applications" for an example.

Applications

Following are examples of how you can use the labels feature in other situations.

Name Badges

The following example shows how you can center text horizontally and vertically on a label. Narrow labels were used to print names for name badges. A [Center Pg] code was used to center the text on each "page" vertically. Because the code needs to be at the top of each page, it was placed at the beginning of the primary file *before* the merge was done. If you are entering the names without doing a merge, you can place a hard page break and [Center Pg] code between each label, either manually or with a macro.

To insert the [Center Pg] code, press Format (SHIFT-F8), choose 2 for **Page** and 1 for **Center Page** (top to bottom), type **Y**, and then press Exit (F7).

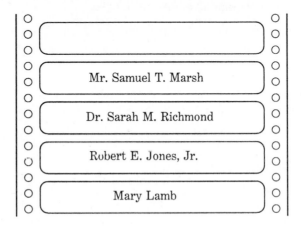

The names were also centered horizontally on each label with the Center Justification feature. This code was placed once at the beginning of the file. To insert this code, go to the top of the document after the merge, press Format (SHIFT-F8), and then choose 1 for **Line**, 3 for **Justification**, and 2 for **Center**. Press Exit (F7) when you are finished.

You can use this technique for any type of labels. In fact, if you will be using these commands, you may want to leave the individual margins for the labels at 0".

Note that the top label was skipped because of an unprintable zone at the top margin. Because this would have interfered with the top margin settings for all labels, the distance from the top left corner was adjusted to skip that label. The top and bottom labels were not included in the total number of labels.

Programs or Newsletters

Most programs and some newsletters are printed so that two "pages" appear side by side on the same physical page. An example of this is shown in Figure 3-88. To accomplish this, you would define the paper

Class
of 1990
Commencement

Program

Pledge of Allegiance .... Mark Anderson

School Song .... Senior Chorus
"Our Old Grand High" *Accompanied by Ms. Summer*

Salutatory Address .... Clark Basil
Class of 1990 Salutatorian

Commencement Address ...... Governor George Cannon

Valedictory Address .... Kimberly Jones
Class of 1990 Valdictorian

Closing Remarks .... Principal Theron Johnson

June 1, 1990

Figure 3-88. Program with side-by-side pages on one physical page

size as standard landscape (the text would print lengthwise), and the font type as landscape (if you have a laser printer). The labels definition would consist of two columns and one row. Figure 3-89 shows the measurements that you would enter for this type of labels definition. Note that the width of the "label" is equal to one-half of the 11" page.

Insert this Paper Size/Type code at the beginning of the regular document, and each page (separated by a hard or soft page break) will print within the correct boundaries.

Related Entries

Merge
Paper Size/Type

LANDSCAPE PRINTING

Laser printers can usually print in two directions: portrait (normal) or landscape. Landscape means printing down the length of the page

```
Format: Labels

    1 - Label Size
                    Width           5.5"
                    Height          8.5"

    2 - Number of Labels
                    Columns         2
                    Rows            1

    3 - Top Left Corner
                    Top             0"
                    Left            0"

    4 - Distance Between Labels
                    Column          0"
                    Row             0"

    5 - Label Margins
                    Left            0.5"
                    Right           0.5"
                    Top             0.75"
                    Bottom          0.75"

Selection: 0
```

Figure 3-89.   Sample labels definition for printing two pages side-by-side or newsletters

instead of printing across the width of the page, as is normally done.

If you do not have a laser printer, you can still print down the length of the page by turning the paper before inserting it into the printer. However, you must also let WordPerfect know that you plan to print this way so that it will allow more text on the line.

Keystrokes

1. Press HOME, HOME, HOME, ↑ to go to the beginning of the document, before all codes. If you are printing only one or a few pages of the document in landscape, go to the top of the first page to be affected.

2. Press Format (SHIFT-F8).

3. Choose **2** for **P**age.

4. Choose **7** for Paper Size/Type. You will see a list of predefined paper sizes, as shown in Figure 3-90. The list may be different for your type of printer.

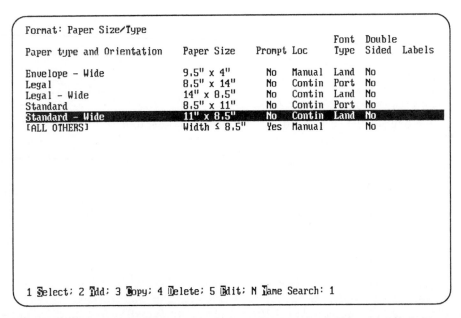

Format: Paper Size/Type						
Paper type and Orientation	Paper Size	Prompt	Loc	Font Type	Double Sided	Labels
Envelope – Wide	9.5" x 4"	No	Manual	Land	No	
Legal	8.5" x 14"	No	Contin	Port	No	
Legal – Wide	14" x 8.5"	No	Contin	Land	No	
Standard	8.5" x 11"	No	Contin	Port	No	
Standard – Wide	11" x 8.5"	No	Contin	Land	No	
[ALL OTHERS]	Width ≤ 8.5"	Yes	Manual		No	

1 Select; 2 Add; 3 Copy; 4 Delete; 5 Edit; N Name Search: 1

Figure 3-90.   Paper Size/Type menu with the standard-wide paper definition highlighted

5. Find the paper definition that includes the desired paper size (shown in the second column) and indicates that it is set for "wide" printing in the first column. In Figure 3-90, the standard wide form is highlighted. The dimensions read 11" by 8.5", which is a standard 8.5" by 11" piece of paper turned on its side.

6. Choose **1** to **S**elect the wide form. Press Exit (F7) to leave the Format: Page menu and return to the document.

Hints

If you need to add a landscape form to the list, see "Paper Size/Type" in this chapter for step-by-step instructions. If you have a laser printer, when you are defining the form, you will need to specify that the font type is landscape instead of portrait.

When you are selecting a landscape or "wide" form that is set to print with landscape fonts, only landscape fonts will appear when you press Font (CTRL-F8) and choose 4 for Base Font.

Related Entries

Paper Size/Type

LANGUAGE

WordPerfect is available in many languages, and others are continually being added. Most languages include a spelling dictionary, a thesaurus, and a hyphenation dictionary that you can purchase separately from WordPerfect Corporation.

If you type documents in another language, you may want to create a keyboard layout that inserts the characters from the other language into your documents. See "Keyboard Layout" in this chapter for details.

You can insert language codes into your documents so that Word-Perfect will know to use that language's dictionary, thesaurus, and hyphenation rules. Indexes and text sorted with the Sort feature will also be sorted according to the rules for the current language.

A file named WP.LRS comes with WordPerfect and is used by WordPerfect as a language resource file. Included in this file is the date format commonly used by each country, the translated text to be used for the date, the text for the "(Continued . . .)" message included in footnotes that are longer than one page, and the translated terms "Figure" and "Table" for use with graphics box captions.

The WP.LRS file also determines how the Document Summary prompts appear when they are printed and how the date and time are displayed in the List Files menu.

Keystrokes

Follow these steps to insert a language code into a document:

1. Move to the point in the document at which the language is to change.

2. Press Format (SHIFT-F8) and choose 4 for Other.

3. Choose 4 for Language.

4. Enter one of the following language codes:

Catalan	CA
Czechoslovakian	CZ
Danish	DK
Dutch	NL
English-Australia	OZ
English-United Kingdom	UK
English-United States	US
Finnish	SU
French-Canada	CF
French-France	FR
German-Germany	DE
German-Switzerland	SD
Greek	GR
Icelandic	IS
Italian	IT
Norwegian	NO
Portuguese-Brazil	BR
Portuguese-Portugal	PO

Russian	RU
Spanish	ES
Swedish	SV

5. Press Exit (F7) when you are finished.

Hints

During a spell check, hyphenation, or when using the Thesaurus, Word-Perfect checks for the current language code. It then searches for the dictionary, hyphenation dictionary (if separate), and thesaurus that match that language. For example, when it is checking the spelling of a document created with the U.S. version of WordPerfect, it searches for and uses the dictionary named WP{WP}US.LEX.

If you create your own dictionary with the SPELL.EXE program (included with WordPerfect), you will need to name it **wp{wp}xx.lex**, where *xx* stands for two characters of your choice. You would then need to insert a language code using these two characters so that Word-Perfect will find your dictionary.

You can purchase additional dictionaries, hyphenation dictionaries, and thesauri for different languages from WordPerfect Corporation. Call (801) 225-5000 for more information.

Indexes are sorted according to the rules of the current language. Blocks of text are sorted according to the language that is current at the beginning of the block.

When you insert the Date Text or Date Code with Date/Outline (SHIFT-F5), the text and format for the current language is inserted.

The "(Continued . . .)" message, "Figure," and "Table" are translated only if the language code is part of the document's initial codes, not just part of the document. To insert the code as an initial code, press Format (SHIFT-F8), and then choose **3** for **D**ocument and **2** for Initial Codes. Follow the previous steps for inserting a language code. Press Exit (F7) when you are finished until you return to the document. You must also enter the Footnote Options menu and choose Print Continued Message, because it is not automatically set to print.

The prompts in the Document Summary and the date/time format for the List Files menu can only be changed for the default language. If you have the U.S. version of WordPerfect, you will need to make changes for those items under the "US" section in the WP.LRS file.

WP.LRS File

As previously mentioned, the WP.LRS file contains various information and translated text for each language. If you want to change the information for any language, you can edit the WP.LRS file as you would any other WordPerfect file.

The file is in a secondary merge file format separated into fields and records. Each language is a record, while the information for each language is divided into fields. This file is formatted with the merge codes found in version 5.0 instead of 5.1, so it can also be edited in WordPerfect Library's (or Office's) Notebook program. Remember, however, that merge codes from version 5.0 are 100 percent compatible in version 5.1.

1. With a clear screen, press Retrieve (SHIFT-F10).

2. Enter the full pathname where WP.LRS is found. During installation it is copied to the same directory used by WP.EXE. If it were copied to the WP51 directory, you would enter **c:\wp51\wp.lrs**.

3. The beginning of the file contains "header" information used by the Notebook program. Pressing PGDN moves you through each page (information for each language often takes more than a page, but each language begins on a new page). To go to the appropriate section of the file quickly, press Search (F2), enter the code for the language you want to edit (**US** would search for the U.S. record), and press Search (F2) to start the search. Enter the language code in uppercase so that WordPerfect will find the language code (US) instead of any occurrence of a lowercase "us."

4. Move through the fields and change any of the information, being careful not to disturb any merge codes (^Rs and ^Es). A list follows, showing the information contained within each field.

1	Language Code
2	Date format
3	Months of the year
4	Abbreviated months of the year
5	Days of the week
6	Abbreviated days of the week
7	"(Continued . . .)" text
8	"(. . . continued)" text

9-20	Document Summary prompts
21	Order in which the month, day, and year are displayed for each filename in List Files. 1 = Day Month Year, 2 = Month Day Year, and 3 = Year Month Day
22	The two characters used to separate the month, day, and year in List Files (-/. and so on.)
23	Display time in List Files according to a 12-hour or 24-hour clock.
24	Character used to separate hours from minutes in List Files (: . and so on) and the letters used to indicate a.m. or p.m.
25	Thousands' separator used for the file size in List Files (, . ' space, and so on.)
26	"Figure" text
27	"Table" text

If there is more than one entry per field, a [HRt] code (new line) separates each entry. Be sure to maintain this format when you are editing the file. If you want to insert a dash at any time, press HOME and then hyphen (-). Pressing hyphen (-) alone inserts a hyphenation character, whereas HOME, hyphen (-) inserts a regular dash character.

5. When you are finished, save the file and exit WordPerfect.

6. When you restart WordPerfect, the changes for the current language will be in effect.

Applications

One thing that you may want to change in the WP.LRS file is the format of the date when it is inserted with Date/Outline (SHIFT-F5). Go to the second field in the record, and change the numbers (based on the selections in the Date Format menu). You can also change the way the names of the months and the days of the week are abbreviated. For example, you may want to have Sunday abbreviated as "Sun." or September abbreviated to "Sep" or "Sept."

To insert the abbreviation of a month or a day of the week, choose a date format that includes a $ or % in front of the applicable number. For example, the format %6, %3 1, 4 would print the date as "Wed, Nov 25, 1990," with both the day of the week and month abbreviated.

You can also change the way the date and time are displayed in List Files if you are accustomed to a different format. For example, if you prefer military time, change field 23 in the WP.LRS file from 12 to 24. See fields 21 through 25 in the previous list for other changes that you can make to the List Files menu.

Remember that changes to these fields do not take effect until the next time you start WordPerfect.

From time to time, WordPerfect Corporation may update this file to add other features.

Related Entries

Date
Document Management/Summary
List Files

LARGE PRINT

If your printer has a variety of font sizes, you can mark text for large print with Font (CTRL-F8) and it will be printed in a large font automatically.

Keystrokes

1. Press Font (CTRL-F8).

2. Choose 1 for Size.

3. Choose 5 for Large.

4. Choose the text to be printed in large print.

5. Press → to move past the ending code and return to the normal font to resume typing.

Hints

You can also assign a large font to a block of text by defining the block with (ALT-F4) and then pressing Font (CTRL-F8), and choosing **1** for Size and **5** for Large. When you select the Large option, a beginning and ending code are inserted. The beginning code appears in uppercase as [LARGE], and the ending code is displayed in lowercase as [large]. Text is inserted between the two codes. If you assign large print to a block of text, the beginning and ending codes will be inserted at the beginning and the end of the block.

You can always press Font (CTRL-F8) and choose option **3** to return to the normal font, or you can enter the size menu and select the Large option again to turn off the feature. However, it is easiest to press → to move over the ending code and return to the previous font.

The large font and other font attributes are selected when you choose Cartridges and Fonts. As WordPerfect displays the message "Updating Fonts," it is storing the information about each font so that it can select the appropriate font for Large (normally 120 percent of the base font). Print the PRINTER.TST document to see how Large has been defined.

See "Automatic Font Changes" in this chapter for more information about how automatic font changes are determined. If you want to choose the exact font that is to be used for large print instead of having WordPerfect select the font, you can do so with the Printer (PTR) program. See Chapter 5 for more information.

Related Entries

Automatic Font Changes
Fonts
Size Attribute Ratios
See also Chapter 5, "Printer Program"

LEADING

Leading (pronounced "ledding") is the amount of space between the base of one line of text and the top of the next line down. By default, 2 points of leading are added to every font except monospaced fonts (10 pitch, for example).

You can change the amount of leading for hard returns [HRt] and soft returns [SRt] independent of each other. You can then have one type of spacing within paragraphs and another between paragraphs. See "Applications" for an example.

Keystrokes

1. Press Format (SHIFT-F8) and choose **4** for **Other**.

2. Choose **6** for **Printer Functions**.

3. Choose **6** for **Leading Adjustment**.

4. The current setting is "0." This does not mean that there is no leading added to the current font; 2 points of leading are already included as part of the line height if the font is proportionally spaced.

5. Enter the measurement for the primary [SRt] code and then the secondary [HRt] code.

If you have the default unit of measurement in inches, you will see the current setting in inches. Because most fonts are measured in points, you may want to enter the measurement in points. To do so, type **p** after the number. For example, entering **4p** would enter the exact setting of 4pts; WordPerfect would then convert it automatically to its equivalent in inches (.056").

6. Press Exit (F7) when you are finished.

Hints

Line Height, found on the Format: Line menu (press Format (SHIFT-F8), and then choose **1** for **Line** and then **4** for **Line Height**) already includes 2 points of leading. This new Leading option lets you *add* to that measurement. Because you can add leading to a hard return or a soft return, you can have a different amount of spacing within paragraphs and between paragraphs.

When you are entering a leading measurement, you can enter a positive or negative number. By entering a negative measurement, you can reduce the amount of space between each line instead of adding to it.

Applications

People who double-space text usually enter two hard returns between paragraphs (pressing ENTER twice), but they may prefer not to have quite so much space between paragraphs. By leaving the leading for soft returns at 0″ and decreasing the amount given to a hard return, you can decrease the space between paragraphs.

If you want to reduce the amount of space given to a hard return by 50 percent, you can check the current line height and divide it by half to obtain the negative amount.

You find the current line height setting by pressing Format (SHIFT-F8) and then choosing 1 for Line, 4 for Line Height, and 2 for Fixed. Make a note of the current line height and press Cancel (F1). If you press ENTER instead, the line height will be changed from Auto to Fixed.

You can also enter **.5v** to indicate half of the current unit of measure instead of checking the current line height.

If you want to leave a document single-spaced on the screen, but want it double-spaced at the printer, enter the current line height (or 1v) as the amount of leading to be added to both soft returns and hard returns. For example, if you are using a 12pt font, the current line height would be 14pts. Enter this measurement as the amount (or 1v) for the soft and hard returns, and the document will print double-spaced.

If you have a list of items that are single-spaced with no spacing between items, you can add the amount of spacing by increasing the leading given to hard returns. Enter 0″ for soft returns and the current line height measurement for the amount of leading to be given to hard returns.

Related Entries

Line Height

LEAVING WORDPERFECT

Press Exit (F7) to leave WordPerfect. You are always asked if you want to save the document before exiting. Never turn off the computer before exiting properly. As soon as you see a DOS prompt (or the Shell menu if you are using WordPerfect Library), you can turn off the computer. See "Exit" in this chapter for complete details.

LEFT INDENT

To indent text from the left margin, use → Indent(F4). To indent text from both the left and right margins, use → Indent← (SHIFT-F4).

Press TAB if you want only the first line of a paragraph indented. See "Indent" and "TAB Key" in this chapter for more information.

LEFT MARGIN RELEASE

Pressing Left Margin Release (SHIFT-TAB) moves the cursor backward to the previous tab setting. If the cursor is at the left margin, Left Margin Release moves into the left margin if there is a tab setting in the left margin area.

Keystrokes

Press Left Margin Release (SHIFT-TAB) to move back to the previous tab setting.

Hints

After you have pressed Left Margin Release, the [←Mar Rel] code appears.

If you delete a left margin release code, the cursor will move forward rather than backward, as it does when you are deleting other codes. If you are confused when deleting these codes, enter Reveal Codes (ALT-F3) and delete the codes from there.

This feature is dependent on tab settings. If you want to release the left margin, you must have tabs set in the margin. For example, if the left margin is set at 1 inch, and you want to release the margin by 1/2 inch, a tab must be set at the .5″ position. You should have no problem releasing the margin 1/2 inch or even a full inch if you are using WordPerfect's default tab settings, because they begin at position 0 and are set every half inch (.5″).

To create a hanging indent (as used in bibliographies), either press Left Margin Release (SHIFT-TAB) while at the left margin to move the first line to the left, or press → Indent (F4) and then SHIFT-TAB. The first method places the first line outside the left margin. Use the second method if you want the first line of the entry to stay within the margins. Both methods are shown in the following illustration:

Himstreet, William C., and Wayne Murlin Baty. <u>Business</u>
    <u>Communications: Principles and Methods.</u> Belmont, CA:
    Wadsworth, 1977, pp. 305-308.

    Himstreet, William C., and Wayne Murlin Baty. <u>Business</u>
        <u>Communications: Principles and Methods.</u> Belmont, CA:
        Wadsworth, 1977, pp. 305-308.

Related Entries

Bibliographies
Indent
TAB Key

LETTER SPACING

You can control the amount of spacing between letters and words from within WordPerfect. For more information, see "Word and Letter Spacing" in this chapter.

LETTERHEAD

The only reason that you would need to inform WordPerfect that you are planning to print on letterhead paper is if your letterhead is kept in a different location from where you usually keep your regular paper. For example, if you have a sheet feeder and keep letterhead in one bin and standard paper in another, you should let WordPerfect know the location of the letterhead so it will select the appropriate type of paper during printing.

If the letterhead paper definition is not set as initially present in the printer, WordPerfect will prompt you to insert letterhead into the printer when the document is printed.

See "Paper Size/Type" in this chapter for step-by-step instructions for defining letterhead.

Two-Page Letters

If your letter is more than one page in length, you will probably want to change back to standard paper for the rest of the pages. You could insert the code somewhere on the first page, other than at the very beginning, so that it will not take effect until the next page. Because the code could move during editing changes, you might want to do the following: Place the letterhead paper definition code at the beginning of the document, press TAB, press Left Margin Release (SHIFT-TAB) to cancel the TAB, and then insert a "standard" paper definition code. Because there are codes ([Tab] and [←Mar Rel]) between the two paper codes, it will print the first page on letterhead and then set the paper to "standard" for the following pages.

Creating Letterhead

If your printer supports graphics, you can create letterhead by using a scanned image of your company's logo in a header and centering the address and phone number (printed in a smaller font) in a footer. See "Graphics Boxes" in this chapter for instructions about including a graphics image into your document.

You can also use fonts to create your logo, as shown in Figure 3-91. The Advance feature was used with the large font to move some letters to the left for manual kerning (two characters can be moved closer together or farther apart to control the space between them). For example, the "o" was advanced slightly to the left to move it closer to the capital "W" and give the appearance of tighter kerning. The word "CORPORATION" was stretched using the Word and Letter Spacing feature. See "Advance" and "Word and Letter Spacing" in this chapter for instructions.

Related Entries

Graphics Boxes
Word and Letter Spacing

LINE DRAW

You can use the Line Draw feature to draw single or double lines. You can also use any other character with Line Draw to create boxes, diagrams, simulated graphs, borders, and so on.

Because you cannot print line-drawing characters using a proportional font, you may want to consider using the Tables or Graphics feature when you need lines drawn around proportionally spaced text. Both of these features use graphics instead of line-drawing characters. The boxes will grow to fit the amount of text entered, and editing the text inside a box will not interfere with the graphics lines. See "Hints" for more information.

WordPerfect

C O R P O R A T I O N

1555 N. Technology Way, Orem, Utah U.S.A 84057 — (801) 225-5000 — Telex 830618 — FAX (801) 227-4588

Figure 3-91.   Sample letterhead created at the printer

Keystrokes

Drawing Single Lines

1. Press Screen (CTRL-F3).

2. Choose **2** for Line Draw. The following menu appears at the bottom of the screen:

```
  1 |; 2 ||; 3 *; 4 Change; 5 Erase; 6 Move: 1              Ln 1" Pos 1"
```

3. WordPerfect is set to use single lines as shown by the 1 at the end of the line. If any other number is displayed, choose **1** for Single lines.

4. Use the arrow keys to draw the lines. To draw the lines more quickly, press HOME before pressing the appropriate arrow key. The line would then be drawn to the next non-blank character or to the edge of the screen in the direction of the arrow. For example, if you are drawing a line across the screen and there is a vertical line halfway across the screen, the line will be drawn to that line. Pressing HOME, ↓ with no text below will draw a line approximately 100 characters long.

5. Press Exit (F7) to leave the Line Draw menu.

WordPerfect inserts spaces to preserve the space between lines, and [HRt] codes are inserted at the end of each line.

Changing the Line-Drawing Character

If you want double lines, choose **2** from the Line Draw menu. If your printer does not have line-drawing capabilities, you can use option **3** to print an asterisk as the line character. The following steps will let any other character be used:

1. Press Screen (CTRL-F3).

2. Choose **2** for **L**ine Draw.

3. Choose **4** for **C**hange. The following menu is presented:

1 ▐; 2 ▓; 3 ▐; 4 █; 5 ▄; 6 |; 7 ┆; 8 ▀; 9 **O**ther: 0

4. Type the number of the desired option. If you want to use a character that is not displayed, choose **9** for **O**ther. You are asked for the "Solid character." Type any character found on the keyboard. If you want to use a special character not on the keyboard, hold down the ALT key and type the ASCII decimal value on the numeric keypad or use Compose (CTRL-2) to create a special character. See "Compose" in this chapter or see Appendix A for possible characters.

5. The original Line Draw menu reappears, with option 3 displaying the newly selected line-drawing character. Option 3 is also automatically selected as the default, so you can use the arrow keys immediately to begin drawing with that character.

Erasing Line Drawing

If you want to erase line drawing (or any other character encountered), choose **5** for **E**rase in the Line Draw menu. Instead of just erasing a character, a space is inserted to replace the character so that the format of the remaining text and lines is preserved.

Moving the Cursor

Choose option **6** for **M**ove if you want to use the arrow keys as regular cursor keys. You can use only ↑ , ↓ , → , and ← . All other cursor keys, such as HOME, → are disabled.

When you are in WordPerfect, the arrow keys will not move beyond text unless there are [HRt] codes or spaces in which to move. With option **6** on the Line Draw menu, you can move the cursor anywhere, and it creates spaces and blank lines where needed.

Hints

When using the Line Draw feature, arrows indicate the direction of the line. A half-line is printed in their place when the document is printed. If you want to extend these half-lines to full lines, enter Line Draw, move the cursor to the arrow, and then press END. The arrow will be replaced with a regular line-drawing character.

Boxed Text

Lines will not print correctly when you are using a proportionally spaced font. Instead, you will need to use a line-drawing or monospaced font (such as Courier 10 pitch).

If you must draw a box around proportionally spaced text, consider placing the text in a graphics box, where the top and bottom borders will grow to fit the text in the box.

Another option for placing a box around text is the Tables feature. When you are ready to type the text to be placed in a box, press Columns/Tables (ALT-F7), choose **2** for **T**ables, choose **1** to Create, and then enter **1** as the number of columns and **1** as the number of rows. Press Exit (F7) and begin entering the text in the box. When you are finished, move the cursor out of the box and continue with the rest of the document.

The lines of the box will print only if you have a printer that can print graphics (laser or dot matrix).

The lines around the box will automatically print as double lines. To change the style, move the cursor inside the box (table), press Columns/ Tables (ALT-F7), choose **3** for **L**ines and **6** for **O**utside, and then choose the style you prefer (single, dashed, dotted, thick, or extra thick). Press Exit (F7) to return to the screen. See "Tables" in this chapter for available options.

Graphics Lines

Another alternative to Line Draw is using horizontal or vertical graphics lines. You can print these lines anywhere on the page. In fact, you can choose the thickness, length, and shading of the lines. You can also place them in headers, footers, styles, or between columns. See "Graphics Lines" in this chapter for more information.

Miscellaneous Line-Drawing Notes

If you are using Line Draw and want to combine it with text, it is usually easier to type the text and then use Line Draw when you are finished. If you want to draw the lines and boxes first and insert the text later, press INS to turn on Typeover mode. Characters will not be inserted but will type over existing spaces. If you insert characters rather than typing over them, the lines will be misaligned and you will have to delete as many spaces as the characters that you inserted.

If you turn on boldface or underlining (or insert any other code) when typing in a box, characters will be inserted even if you have Typeover on (codes will not type over characters). If you want to insert boldface or underlined text, type the text first using Typeover, and then boldface or underline the text using Block (ALT-F4).

Creating Duplicate Boxes

If you need several boxes that are the same size (as in an organizational chart), create a single box and copy it with the Rectangular Copy feature found on the Move (CTRL-F4) menu. See "Move" in this chapter for details.

Dashed Lines

Most printers can draw lines only if they are in single spacing or one-half line spacing (.5). If you are still getting spaces between each vertical line character, try decreasing the line spacing or line height.

Related Entries

Graphics Boxes
Move
Tables

LINE FORMAT

Selections on the Line Format menu control the options that are associated with lines, such as line spacing, line numbering, margins, justification, and tabs.

Keystrokes

1. Move the cursor to the position at which the formatting change is to take place.

2. Press Format (SHIFT-F8).

3. Choose 1 for Line. The menu shown in Figure 3-92 appears.

4. Make all applicable changes.

5. Press ENTER to return to the main Format menu and make other selections, or press Exit (F7) to return to the document.

```
Format: Line

     1 - Hyphenation                    No

     2 - Hyphenation Zone - Left        10%
                           Right        4%

     3 - Justification                  Left

     4 - Line Height                    Auto

     5 - Line Numbering                 No

     6 - Line Spacing                   2

     7 - Margins - Left                 1"
                   Right                1"

     8 - Tab Set                        Rel: -1", every 0.5"

     9 - Widow/Orphan Protection        Yes


Selection: 0
```

Figure 3-92.   Options on the Line Format menu

Options

The following is a brief description of each option listed on the Line Format menu. See the appropriate entries in this chapter for instructions on using each feature.

Hyphenation

If you want WordPerfect to hyphenate your document for you, change option 1 for Hyphenation to Yes. The Hyphenation Zone (option 2), figured as a percentage of the total line length, surrounds the right margin and determines if words will be wrapped or hyphenated.

An option in the Environment category of the Setup (SHIFT-F1) menu decides how hyphenation will be done: automatically or manually, and whether to use the spelling dictionary or internal rules (an algorithm that is approximately 90 percent correct). See "Hyphenation" for details.

Justification

WordPerfect is preset for full justification, meaning that the text at both the left and right margins is smooth and even. This is accomplished by inserting small amounts of space between words and, in some cases, between letters.

Other options include left justification (leaving the right margin jagged), right justification (leaving the left margin jagged), or center justification (centering text between the left and right margins).

You can use the Center and Right justification options when you want to center or flush-right multiple lines instead of pressing Center (SHIFT-F6) or Flush Right (ALT-F6) at the beginning of each line. See "Center Text" and "Flush Right" in this chapter for more information.

See "Hints" for details about changing to left justification for all documents.

Line Height

WordPerfect will automatically adjust the line height (measured from the bottom of one line to the bottom of the next) to fit the largest font on the line. You can use the Line Height option to set the line height a fixed amount (if your printer supports settings other than 6 lines per inch) or leave it at automatic. WordPerfect will use the line height, page length, and top and bottom margins to calculate the number of lines that will fit on the page.

Line Numbering

The Line Numbering feature lets you print line numbers within the left margin. These numbers will appear only when you view or print the document.

Line Spacing

Line spacing lets you determine the number of lines that will be inserted for a soft return and hard return. The default, 1, means that the document will be single-spaced. You can choose any number (2, 3, 4, 10, and so on), and you can even specify a fraction of a line (1/2, 1.5, 1.75, and so on). The amount of spacing is multiplied by the line height, which is usually dependent on the height of the current font unless you have set a fixed line height.

Margins, Left/Right

Margins are measured from the left side of the page and the right side of the page. If you want half-inch margins, you would enter .5″ for both settings. Top and bottom margins are set in the Page Format menu.

Tab Set

Tabs are set at every 1/2 inch. You can use this option to clear and set new tab settings that will then take place from that point forward in the document.

Widow/Orphan Protection

If you type **Y** in answer to the ″Widow/Orphan Protection″ option, WordPerfect will not allow the first or last line of a paragraph to appear at the top or bottom of a page. Titles and headings are not automatically protected. Use Conditional End of Page to keep a title and the first few lines of a paragraph together.

Hints

If you want to change any of these settings for all documents, you can do so by inserting them in the Initial Codes section of the Setup menu. For example, if you want left justification for all documents (which you can also change from document to document, of course), you can press Setup (SHIFT-F1), choose **4** for Initial Settings and **5** for Initial Codes, and then follow the steps that you would normally use to insert the code. All codes in this screen would then be copied to each document created in the future.

If you are used to seeing a "format line" that shows margins and tabs, consider displaying the ruler on the screen. To do this, press Screen (CTRL-F3), choose **1** for Window, and enter **23** for the number of lines in the window. Current margins and tab settings are displayed with brackets [ ] and triangles (▲). If a tab and a margin are in the same location, a brace ({ or }) is shown instead.

Related Entries

Hyphenation
Justification
Line Height
Line Numbering
Margins, Left and Right
Spacing
Tabs
Widow/Orphan Protection

LINE HEIGHT

Line height is measured from the base of one line to the base of the next line. WordPerfect determines the line height according to the current font. For example, if you are using a small font, the line height will be adjusted accordingly. If you use a large font and a small font on the same line, the line height will be adjusted for the larger font. If you do not want WordPerfect to adjust the line height automatically, you can set a fixed line height.

Two points of "leading" or space are automatically added to proportionally spaced fonts. Monospaced fonts, such as 10- or 12-pitch fonts, do not have extra space added because the amount of space is already built into those types of fonts.

Keystrokes

1. Press Format (SHIFT-F8).

2. Choose 1 for Line.

3. Choose 4 for Line Height.

4. Choose 1 for Auto or 2 for Fixed. If you type 2 for Fixed, the current line height is displayed. Enter the new setting, using the type of measurement of your choice, and the setting will be converted to the default unit of measurement automatically. If you are working with fonts that are measured in points, you might want to enter the line height in points. For example, if the default unit of measurement was inches and you entered 16p as the fixed line height, it would be converted to .22".

5. Press Exit (F7) to return to the document.

Hints

When you choose the Line Height option, the code [Ln Height:n] is inserted, where n indicates a fixed-amount setting (if you entered one) or "Auto" if you are returning to automatic line height.

Three WordPerfect features can help adjust the amount of space between lines: Line Height, Line Spacing, and Leading. Line Height changes the amount of space from one baseline to the next, Leading lets you add or subtract the amount of space given to soft returns and hard returns, and Line Spacing is multiplied by the line height to determine how much space to insert between each line. See "Spacing" and "Leading" in this chapter for more information.

Applications

If you are switching between two or more fonts of different sizes, you can set a fixed line height to create a more consistent look from line to line.

If you are using Line Draw on a dot-matrix printer and are getting small amounts of space between vertical lines, you can decrease the line height to solve the problem.

You must also choose to have a fixed line height if you are using the Baseline Placement for Typesetters option. See that entry for more information.

LINE NUMBERING

The Line Numbering feature is used to number the lines of a document when it is printed. The line numbers are not visible on the screen, unless you use the View Document feature on the Print menu.

Keystrokes

1. Move the cursor to the point in the document at which you want line numbering to begin.

2. Press Format (SHIFT-F8).

3. Choose **1** for **Line**.

4. Choose **5** for Line Numbering.

5. Choose **Y** or **N**, depending on whether or not you want the lines numbered. If you type **Y**, the Line Numbering menu appears, as shown in Figure 3-93.

6. Select any options that might be applicable (see "Options").

7. Press Exit (F7) to return to the document.

Options

The following options are found on the Line Numbering menu.

Count Blank Lines

The default is set to count blank lines. If you want to count the exact number of lines actually typed, type **N** for this option. For a macro that will count the total number of lines in the document for billing purposes, see "Applications."

Number Every n Lines

Every line will be numbered unless you change this option. To number every other line, enter **2**. You can enter any number.

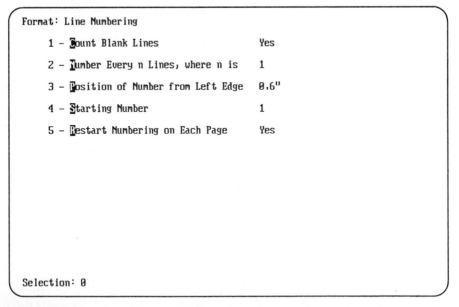

```
Format: Line Numbering

    1 - Count Blank Lines                    Yes

    2 - Number Every n Lines, where n is     1

    3 - Position of Number from Left Edge    0.6"

    4 - Starting Number                      1

    5 - Restart Numbering on Each Page       Yes




Selection: 0
```

Figure 3-93.   Line Numbering menu

Position of Number from Left Edge

This option decides how far from the left edge of the page (not the left margin) the line number will be printed. The default setting is .6″.

Starting Number

This option lets you change the starting number from 1 to any other number.

Restart Numbering on Each Page

Leave the option at **Y** to restart numbering on each page. Changing this option to **N** would put cumulative numbers throughout the document.

Hints

When you select the Line Numbering option, the code [Ln Num:On] or [Ln Num:Off] is inserted, depending on whether you typed **Y** or **N**.

You can turn the Line Numbering feature on and off at any location in a document to affect the text from that point forward. Line numbering begins with the number 1, regardless of the location of the code on the page. If you turn it off and then turn it back on later in the document, the numbering will start over with 1.

Line Numbering numbers the lines in footnotes but not in headers or footers.

View Line Numbering

Line numbering occurs at the printer, not on the screen. You can use the View Document feature, however, to see a copy of the document as it will appear when printed. Press Print (SHIFT-F7) and then choose **6** for View.

Single- or Double-Space Limitation

The Line Numbering feature does not have a spacing option; therefore, it works together with the spacing that is set in the document. For example, if you want every other line numbered and have both single- and double-spacing in the document, every other single-spaced line is numbered, and every other double-spaced line is numbered. The line numbers cannot be printed either single-spaced or double-spaced if the document itself is not consistent in its spacing.

For example, if you have created a legal pleading paper with single-spacing for the heading information (attorney, plaintiff, case number, and so on) and double-spacing for the text below, numbering cannot be double-spaced down the left side of the page. A way of getting around this limitation is to print the line numbers (and line drawing, if desired) first and then print the document on the same piece of paper or create a header that includes regular numbers. The form then needs to be created and saved only once. This avoids the use of preprinted forms whose typeface does not match that of the document.

Applications

Use the following steps to create a form like the one shown in Figure 3-94, which you can use to print legal pleading papers.

These steps assume that you will be printing the line numbers in the same font used for the document. Insert the proper font change as the first step if necessary.

1. On a clear screen, press Format (SHIFT-F8).

2. Choose 2 for **P**age and then 5 for **M**argins, Top/Bottom.

3. Leave the top margin as it is, but change the bottom margin to .75″.

4. Press ENTER to return to the main Format menu, and then choose 1 for **L**ine.

5. Choose 5 for Line **N**umbering, and type **Y**.

6. Press ENTER to return to the main Format menu.

7. Choose 6 for Line Spacing and then enter 2 for double-spacing.

8. Press Exit (F7) to return to the document.

9. Press ENTER until you reach the end of the page (approximately 27 times, however, the number will depend on the size of font being used). If you go past the page break, press BACKSPACE to delete the page break.

10. Press HOME, HOME, ↑ to go to the top of the document.

11. Press Format (SHIFT-F8) and choose 1 for Line and then 7 for Margins, Left/Right. Decrease the left margin by approximately .15″ (set it to .85″ if the regular margin will be 1″). The setting you enter will be the position of the line at the left. Be aware that the line could print over the numbers if the margin is too small.

12. Press Exit (F7) to return to the document.

13. Press Graphics (ALT-F9) and choose 5 for Line and then 2 for Vertical.

14. If you want a slightly thicker line, choose 4 for Width of Line and enter .03″. You can adjust this setting later if necessary. If you want another vertical line, insert one with the horizontal position set at .88″ so the lines will print .03″ apart.

15. Press ENTER to return to the document.

16. Save this form (PLEADING.FRM is a suggested filename). You can print several copies at once with the Number of Copies option on the Print menu and then print the regular document on the form.

If you do not care about the line numbering not being spaced consistently (all double-spaced or all single-spaced), you can still include the vertical line on every page by doing the following:

1. Create a header that will print on every page.

2. Decrease the left margin slightly.

3. Insert the vertical graphics line as just described.

4. Press Exit (F7) twice to exit from the header and the format menus.

A vertical line will be printed slightly to the left of the regular left margin on every page.

Count Lines with Line Numbering

The Line Numbering feature can be used to help count the lines in a document. Remember that headers and footers are not included, but the lines in footnotes are. If you need to count lines often, consider putting the steps in a macro. The following procedure sets up such a macro:

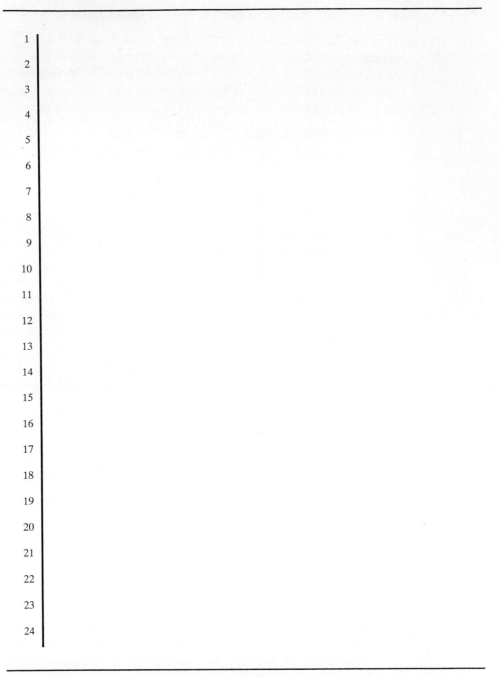

Figure 3-94.   Pleading paper created with line numbering and a vertical graphics line

1. To define a macro, press Macro Def (CTRL-F10) and enter the name of the macro (COUNT is a suggestion). Enter a description for the macro.

2. Press HOME, HOME, ↑ to move to the beginning of the document.

3. Press Format (SHIFT-F8) and choose 1 for Line.

4. Choose **5** for Line Numbering, and type **Y** to turn it on.

5. Choose **5** for **R**estart Numbering on Each Page, and answer **N**.

6. Press Exit (F7) to return to the document.

7. Press HOME, HOME, ↓ to go to the end of the document.

8. Press Print (SHIFT-F7), and choose **2** to print the last page of the document. You cannot view the document because consecutive line numbering does not work in View.

9. The number assigned to the last line is the total number of lines typed. Blank lines are not included in this count.

10. Press Exit (F7) to return to the document.

11. Press HOME, HOME, ↑ to go to the top of the document. Press Reveal Codes (ALT-F3) and delete the line numbering code. Press Reveal Codes (ALT-F3) again to return to the normal editing screen.

12. Press Macro Def (CTRL-F10) to end the macro definition.

Related Entries

Graphics Lines
Headers
Paragraph Numbering
View Document
Word Count

LINES PER INCH

See "Line Height" in this chapter.

LIST

You can use the List (F5) key to display the List Files menu if you are in the regular screen in WordPerfect. If you are in the equation editor, you can use it to enter the list of commands and symbols. When importing a section of the spreadsheet (a range), you can use List (F5) to list the ranges available in that spreadsheet so that you can easily select the correct one.

WordPerfect also lets you enter the List Files menu from almost any menu in which a filename is requested. When entering the name of a graphics image, you can press List (F5) to enter the directory where the graphics files are stored (see "Location of Files" in this chapter for instructions on specifying a directory for graphics files). When retrieving an equation, you can press List (F5) to display the files in the Documents directory. When entering the names of the primary and secondary files to be used in a merge, you can press List (F5) and retrieve a file from the list.

There are other situations in which List (F5) is allowed, including when you press Retrieve (SHIFT-F10) from the main editing screen. You will know if the alternative is available when you see the prompt "(**List Files**)" in the lower right corner.

Related Entries

Equations
List Files
Location of Files
Merge
Spreadsheet Importing and Linking

LIST FILES

The List Files menu helps organize and manage your files.

Keystrokes

1. Press List (F5).

2. The name of the current default directory is displayed. You have several options:

- Press ENTER to see the files in that directory.

- Enter a different drive and directory. Be sure to precede the name of the directory with a backslash (\). Entering a new directory this way will not change the default directory.

- Type = and enter the name of a different drive and directory. This option changes the default directory.

- Type the name of a single file, or use the wildcard characters * and ? to display a group of files. For example, if you want to display a file named SMITH.LTR, enter that as the file to be displayed. If you want to list all the files ending with .NOV, enter ***.NOV**.

- Press List (F5) again to see the list of files that was previously displayed (only applicable if you last looked at a directory on the hard drive, not a floppy disk drive). This option is useful if you just looked into a different directory or at a specific list of files and you do not want to enter the filename pattern again. See "Hints" for more information.

3. You will see a different screen if you selected Long Document Name in the Setup menu. The regular, short display listing files by their regular DOS name is displayed in Figure 3-95. Figure 3-96 shows how the same list files screen would appear if you selected Long Document Name. See "Options" for details about switching between the two displays.

4. Press Exit (F7), Cancel (F1), or the space bar to leave the List Files menu. The ENTER key will not return you to the document as it normally does; it is set as the default for looking at a file or directory.

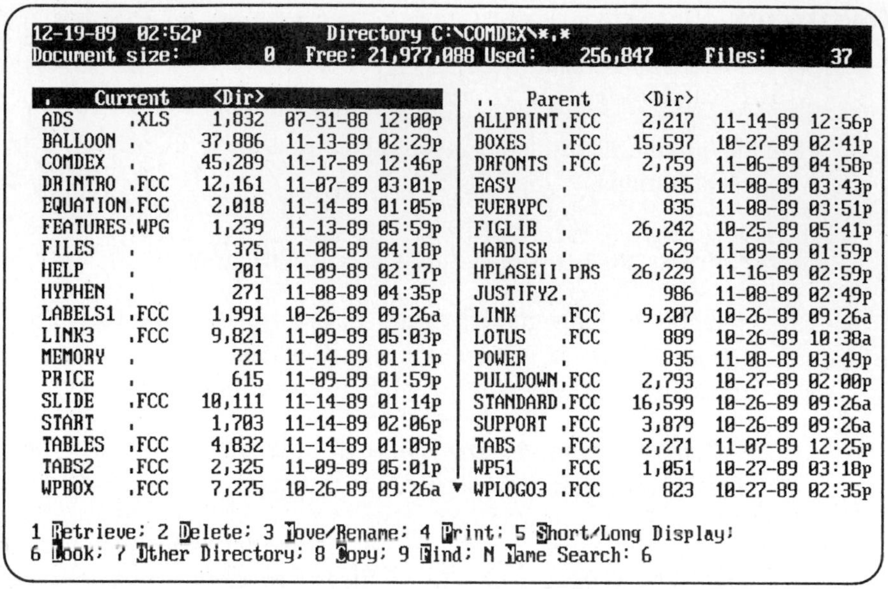

```
┌─────────────────────────────────────────────────────────────────────────┐
│ 12-19-89  02:52p            Directory C:\COMDEX\*.*                       │
│ Document size:      0   Free: 21,977,088 Used:     256,847   Files:    37 │
│                                                                           │
│ .    Current   <Dir>                 ..    Parent     <Dir>               │
│ ADS      .XLS    1,832  07-31-88 12:00p   ALLPRINT.FCC    2,217  11-14-89 12:56p │
│ BALLOON  .      37,806  11-13-89 02:29p   BOXES   .FCC   15,597  10-27-89 02:41p │
│ COMDEX   .      45,289  11-17-89 12:46p   DRFONTS .FCC    2,759  11-06-89 04:58p │
│ DRINTRO  .FCC   12,161  11-07-89 03:01p   EASY    .          835  11-08-89 03:43p │
│ EQUATION .FCC    2,018  11-14-89 01:05p   EVERYPC .          835  11-08-89 03:51p │
│ FEATURES .WPG    1,239  11-13-89 05:59p   FIGLIB  .       26,242  10-25-89 05:41p │
│ FILES    .          375  11-08-89 04:18p   HARDISK .          629  11-09-89 01:59p │
│ HELP     .          701  11-09-89 02:17p   HPLASEII.PRS   26,229  11-16-89 02:59p │
│ HYPHEN   .          271  11-08-89 04:35p   JUSTIFY2.          986  11-08-89 02:49p │
│ LABELS1  .FCC    1,991  10-26-89 09:26a   LINK    .FCC    9,207  10-26-89 09:26a │
│ LINK3    .FCC    9,821  11-09-89 05:03p   LOTUS   .FCC      889  10-26-89 10:38a │
│ MEMORY   .          721  11-14-89 01:11p   POWER   .          835  11-08-89 03:49p │
│ PRICE    .          615  11-09-89 01:59p   PULLDOWN.FCC    2,793  10-27-89 02:00p │
│ SLIDE    .FCC   10,111  11-14-89 01:14p   STANDARD.FCC   16,599  10-26-89 09:26a │
│ START    .       1,703  11-14-89 02:06p   SUPPORT .FCC    3,879  10-26-89 09:26a │
│ TABLES   .FCC    4,832  11-14-89 01:09p   TABS    .FCC    2,271  11-07-89 12:25p │
│ TABS2    .FCC    2,325  11-09-89 05:01p   WP51    .FCC    1,051  10-27-89 03:18p │
│ WPBOX    .FCC    7,275  10-26-89 09:26a ▼ WPLOGO3 .FCC      823  10-27-89 02:35p │
│                                                                           │
│ 1 Retrieve; 2 Delete; 3 Move/Rename; 4 Print; 5 Short/Long Display;       │
│ 6 Look; 7 Other Directory; 8 Copy; 9 Find; N Name Search: 6               │
└─────────────────────────────────────────────────────────────────────────┘
```

Figure 3-95.   Sample List Files screen (short display)

Hints

The List Files menu displays general information such as the current date and time, the full pathname of the directory and files being displayed, the size of the current document in memory, the total amount of space taken by the files that are listed, and the amount of space that is available on the disk. The items that show the size of the current document and the amount of space available on the disk are especially helpful if you are wondering whether you have enough room on the disk to save the current document.

The full pathname of the current directory at the top of the menu tells you the name of the drive, directory, and group of files that are displayed. The *.* indicates that all files in the directory are being shown. If you had entered *.ltr after pressing List (F5), you would see the default drive and directory with all of the .LTR files.

When asked to enter the name of the directory, you can enter up to 80 characters. This is useful when you have many levels of subdirectories (for example, C:\PROGRAMS\WP51\LEARNING\DOCU-

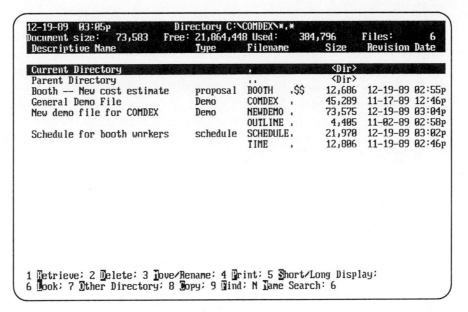

Figure 3-96.   Long Display in the List Files menu only WordPerfect documents are listed in this type of display

MENTS\LETTERS\BOB . . .). If there are more files in the directory than will fit on the screen at one time, you will see a small triangle at the top or bottom of the separating line, indicating that there are more files to be displayed. The separating line is displayed only when you are using the Short Display option.

Long Display

If you are using the Long Display option, you will see only WordPerfect files in the list. If you need access to files that are not WordPerfect files, or if you want a more accurate list of the files in the directory, use the Short Display option.

A long descriptive filename is shown in the left column, and the document type is shown in the second column only if you entered them in the Document Summary or if you saved the document with the Long Document Name option.

To enter a long descriptive filename and document type each time you save the file, press Setup (SHIFT-F1) and choose 3 for **E**nvironment, 4 for **D**ocument Management/Summary, and 3 for **L**ong Document Names. Type **Y**, and then press Exit (F7) to return to the document. Each time you press Save (F10) or Exit (F7), you are asked for a long document name and document type. If you do not want to enter them at that time, you can press ENTER to bypass the prompts. See "Document Management/Summary" and "Long Document Names" in this chapter for more complete information.

Directory Organization

If you are using a hard disk, List Files can be especially helpful in organizing directories. You can also print the contents of a directory by pressing Print (SHIFT-F7) while you are in the List Files menu.

The root or main directory is indicated by a single backslash. If you have directories created under the root directory, they are listed by name on the menu, with "< Dir >" added to indicate a directory. If you divide one of these directories, it is considered a parent directory and will list its own directories on the List Files menu.

You can move the cursor to "Parent < Dir >" and press ENTER twice to move up to that directory. You can then move the cursor to any "< Dir >" and press ENTER twice to move down into that directory. (If you use option 7 for **O**ther Directory after highlighting a "< Dir >," instead of just pressing ENTER, the default directory will be changed.) See "Directories," "Change Directory," and "Create a Directory" in this chapter for details.

File Information

Each file in the List Files menu is listed alphabetically from left to right. If you are in the Long Display, files are listed from top to bottom.

To the right of each filename is the number of bytes in the file. Each character is equal to 1 byte (with the exception of special characters, which are 3 bytes), and WordPerfect function codes vary in the amount of bytes used. If you retrieve a graphics image into a document, it will be included as part of the file size. If you want to decrease the size of files, you can use the Graphics on Disk option to point to a graphics image and not have it retrieved into the document.

Files will be displayed as containing no bytes until you press a single key. If you then look into the List Files screen, you will see that the document is at least 100 to 200 bytes in size because of the document header or prefix that is created. The prefix is used to store the initial codes, a Document Summary, the name of the printer that was used to create the document, the initial font, and so on.

Also displayed with each filename is the date and time on which it was last edited.

Mark Files

If you want to delete, print, copy, or do a "find" on selected files, press * to mark the current file. If you mark a file by mistake, press * again to unmark the file. To mark all the files in a directory, press Mark Text (ALT-F5) or HOME,*. Pressing those same keys again will unmark the files. Files are also unmarked when you exit the List Files menu. However, if you leave the menu and decide to return to the same menu and have the same files marked, you can press List (F5) twice. The previous list, complete with marks, is then displayed. If there are files that have been marked and you choose 2 for Delete, 4 for Print, or 8 for Copy, you are asked to confirm that you want to delete, print, or copy the marked files.

Options

Ten options are listed on the List Files menu. A short description of each follows.

Retrieve

Option 1 for **R**etrieve lets you retrieve the highlighted file to the screen. Before retrieving a file, take note of the current document size (shown at the top left of the List Files menu). If a number other than zero is displayed, there is another document in memory. If this is the case, you will be asked to confirm that you want to retrieve the highlighted document into the document currently on the screen.

Delete

If you choose option 2 for **D**elete, you are asked to confirm the deletion of the file. Type **N** to leave the file or **Y** to delete it. If you delete it, you cannot undelete it from within WordPerfect. You may be able to restore it with the aid of a program such Norton Utilities.

You can mark more than one file with an * for deletion. If you select option 2 for **Delete** and files have been marked, you are first asked if you want to delete all the marked files. If you type **Y**, you will be warned that all marked files will be deleted, and you will be asked for a second confirmation. If you type **N**, you are asked to confirm the deletion of the file that is currently highlighted.

Move/Rename

Option 3 for **Move/Rename** lets you move or rename the highlighted file. If you just enter a new filename without specifying a different directory, the file will be renamed. If you enter a name that already exists in that directory, you will see the message "ERROR: Can't rename file." If you include another drive or directory with the filename (the filename does not have to be different from that of the original file), the file will be moved to the new location.

Print

If you choose 4 for **Print** a file, you are asked for the page numbers to be printed. Press ENTER to print all pages, enter a range (2-4, for example), or indicate particular pages to be printed (1,3,5, and so on).

If you are editing the same file on the screen and want to print the most recent copy, print from the screen or save the document to disk first.

You can mark more than one file for printing. If marked files are found, you are asked if you want to print all the marked files. If you type **Y**, they are all queued. If you type **N**, none of the documents will be sent to the printer.

Short/Long Display

If you have selected the Long Document Name option in the Setup menu, you automatically see files listed by their long descriptive names, as shown in Figure 3-96. If you want to switch to either type of display, you can do so at any time by choosing **5** for **S**hort/Long Display, and then choosing **1** for **S**hort or **2** for **L**ong. The current directory and filename template (*.*, *.LTR, and so on) are displayed. Press ENTER to list those files again, or enter a different directory and/or filename template.

If you have chosen the Long Display option, it will take quite a bit longer to list the files on the screen. This is because WordPerfect searches each file to see if it is a WordPerfect file. It then checks the Document Summary for each file for a long document name and document type so it can display it in the List Files menu. See "Long Document Names" in this chapter for more information.

Look

Choose option **6** for **L**ook (or press ENTER) to look at the contents of a file or to look into another directory. If you look into a document that contains a Document Summary, it is also displayed in the Look screen. Press any cursor key to scroll through the file. While in Look, you can even use Search (F2) or Reverse Search (SHIFT-F2) to search for a particular phrase. The phrase will be highlighted if it is found.

While in Look, you can also choose **1** to look at the **N**ext document or **2** to look into the **P**revious document. Press Exit (F7) to return to the List Files menu.

You can look into a directory without changing the default directory using this option. Position the cursor on a directory name (labeled with "<Dir>"), and choose **6** for **L**ook or press ENTER. The full pathname of the directory is displayed and can be edited. Press ENTER to go into the directory.

The Look option is set as the default in the List Files menu. If you press ENTER, the highlighted file is displayed. The Look feature is useful when you are cleaning up your disk if you are not sure of the contents of a file. See "Look at a File" in this chapter for details.

Other Directory

Choose option **7** for **O**ther Directory to change the default drive within the List Files menu. As mentioned before, you can change the default drive without entering the List Files menu: Press List (F5), type =, and then enter the name of the default drive. You can also use this option to create new directories. If you enter the name of a nonexistent directory, you are asked if you want to create the new directory.

Copy

If you choose option 8 for Copy, you are prompted with the "Copy this file to:" message. Enter the drive, the directory, and a different filename if desired. If the filename exists on the other drive or directory, you are asked to confirm the replacement of the existing file.

If you want to copy more than one file, mark all applicable files with an asterisk (*) and choose 8 for Copy. You are asked if you want to copy all the marked files. If you type **Y**, enter the destination for the files. If you type **N**, you are given the opportunity to copy only the currently highlighted file.

You can also create a directory with this option. If you enter the name of a nonexistent directory as the destination for a file, you are asked if you want to create the new directory.

Find

While in the List Files menu, you can press Search (F2) or Reverse Search (SHIFT-F2) to search for a specific file. When you see the "Search" prompt on the screen, enter the part of the filename that you know; you do not have to use the wildcard characters * or ?. For example, you can enter **count** to find the file DISCOUNT, because those characters are found in the filename. If you continue searching, the next file containing those characters will be found.

Another option for finding files is **9** for Find. This feature lets you search the files in the directory for a specific phrase or word pattern. You can narrow the search further by marking specific files to be searched with an asterisk (*).

If you choose **9** for Find, you will see the following prompt:

```
Find: 1 Name; 2 Doc Summary; 3 First Pg; 4 Entire Doc; 5 Conditions; 6 Undo: 0
```

Option **1** for **Name** does the same thing as pressing Search (F2), except that only files meeting the criteria will remain on the screen after the process is finished.

```
┌─────────────────────────────────────────────────────────────┐
│  Find: Conditions                        Files Selected:   29 │
│                                                               │
│      1 - Perform Search                                       │
│      2 - Reset Conditions                                     │
│                                                               │
│      3 - Revision Date - From                                 │
│                          To                                   │
│                                                               │
│      4 - Text - Document Summary                              │
│             First Page                                        │
│             Entire Document                                   │
│                                                               │
│      5 - Document Summary                                     │
│          Creation Date - From                                 │
│                          To                                   │
│          Document Name                                        │
│          Document Type                                        │
│          Author                                               │
│          Typist                                               │
│          Subject                                              │
│          Account                                              │
│          Keywords                                             │
│          Abstract                                             │
│                                                               │
│  Selection: 1                                                 │
└─────────────────────────────────────────────────────────────┘
```

Figure 3-97.   Conditions that can be used to find files

If you want to have WordPerfect search for a particular word or phrase, choose 2 to search through the Document Summary, 3 to search through the First Page, or 4 to search through the Entire Document. The word search will be much faster if you are using option **1**, slightly slower with options **2** and **3**, and slowest with option **4**. Option **5** lets you change the Conditions of the search. As shown by the menu in Figure 3-97, you can narrow the search by entering specific file dates and entering a word pattern for each entry in the Document Summary. See "Find Files" in this chapter for details. Option **6** lets you Undo the last "find," meaning that it will return to the previous list of files before the last search.

Name Search

Use any cursor movement key to move the cursor to a filename listed in the menu: ↑ , ↓ , → , ← , PGUP, PGDN, or Screen Up (−) and Screen Down (+).

If you know the name of a file, you can move to it more quickly by choosing **N** for **N**ame Search and typing the name of the file. As you type, the cursor moves to the files beginning with those letters. Continue typing to narrow the selection. To reset Name Search, press ENTER or any arrow key, and the List Files menu will reappear. The space bar will not reset Name Search.

If you delete characters from the name search string, the cursor will jump backward to the appropriate location.

If you don't know the name of a file, but know part of the name, you can press Search (F2) and enter the part of the filename that you know. WordPerfect will then find the file(s) containing that set of characters in the name.

Changing the List Files Display

With the U.S. version of WordPerfect, filenames greater than 1,000 bytes use a comma as a thousands' separator. Instead of displaying the time according to a 24-hour clock (where 5:00 p.m. would be displayed as 17:00), WordPerfect displays the time according to a 12-hour clock with "a" and "p" indicating a.m. and p.m. Dashes separate the month, day, and year instead of slashes. Both the date and time in the header and the date and time indicating when a file was last saved are affected.

Other languages have different options set depending on the accepted format in their country. The WP.LRS file gives you complete control over these and other options. The information in the file is stored in a secondary merge format and can be edited from within WordPerfect. If you have the U.S. version of WordPerfect, you would need to edit the U.S. record in the WP.LRS file. Retrieve the file (located in the same directory where WP.EXE is located), and search for the U.S. record: press Search (F2), enter **US** in uppercase letters, and then press Search (F2) again.

Fields 21 through 25 contain the items affecting List Files. Move to those fields and change them according to the following information:

21   Order in which the month, day, and year are displayed

        1 = Day Month Year

        2 = Month Day Year

        3 = Year Month Day

22   The two characters used to separate the month, day, and

year (- / . and so on)

23   Display time according to a 12- or 24-hour clock

24   Character used to separate hours from minutes

        (: . and so on) and the letters used to indicate a.m. or p.m.

25   Thousands' separator used for the file size (, . ' space, and so on)

If there is more than one entry per field (as in field 24), follow each entry with an [HRt] code. If you are using dashes, enter them by pressing HOME, hyphen (-) instead of pressing the hyphen (-) key by itself (WordPerfect interprets a hyphen as a required hyphen used in hyphenation, whereas HOME, hyphen inserts the regular dash character).

See "Languages" in this chapter for other options that you can change in the WP.LRS file.

Related Entries

Change Directory
Copy Files
Create a Directory
Delete Files
Directories
Document Management/Summary
Document Size
Find Files
Languages
Long Document Names
Look at a File
Print
Rename a File
Retrieve

LISTS

For each document, you can generate up to ten lists for illustrations, figures, tables, charts, equations, and so on.

Keystrokes

There are three basic steps in creating a list. First, you mark the text to be referenced in the list. Then you define the type of page number style in the list and the location of the list. Finally, you generate the list. If you have figures, table boxes, text boxes, user boxes, or equations with a caption for each, you can include the captions in a list without having to mark them.

Mark the Text for the List

If you want figure captions, table captions, and so on to be included in different lists, you do not have to mark them. To mark all other text, follow these steps:

1. Move the cursor to the text to be referenced, and press Block (ALT-F4). Remember that any code included in the block (such as bold, underline, or center codes) will also appear in the list when it is generated.

2. Move the cursor to the opposite end of the text to be referenced.

3. Press Mark Text (ALT-F5).

4. Choose **2** for List.

5. Type the number of the appropriate list. Even though there are up to ten lists available, list 6 is reserved for figure captions, list 7 is reserved for table box captions, 8 is for text box captions, 9 is for user box captions, and 10 is for equation box captions. If you have only figures in the document, you can use any of the lists except 6.

The code [Mark:List,n] is inserted at the beginning of the block and [EndMark:List,n] is inserted at the end. These codes are visible when you press Reveal Codes (ALT-F3). The n included in the code can be any number from 1 to 10 and indicates the list in which the entry is to be included.

Define the Page Numbering and Location

A list can appear anywhere in the document. Usually, it is included at the beginning of the document, just after the table of contents. If you want it to appear at the beginning of the document, include a New Page

Number code at the beginning of the regular text, following the table of contents and list definitions. Otherwise, a reference on page 1 might appear on page 3, because the table of contents and the list are occupying pages 1 and 2.

If you are using a master document, the same principles apply. If the list definition code is found in the master document, lists will be compiled from all subdocuments listed instead of from just one document.

1. Move to the location at which the list is to appear.

2. If you want a heading for the list, enter the heading.

3. Press Mark Text (ALT-F5).

4. Choose **5** for **D**efine.

5. Choose **2** for Define **L**ist.

6. Enter the number of the list being defined. If you want a list of figure captions, choose **6**. Choose **7** for table box captions, **8** for text box captions, **9** for user box captions, or **10** for equation captions.

7. Select a page number listing option from the List Definition menu (shown here):

```
List 1  Definition

     1 - No Page Numbers

     2 - Page Numbers Follow Entries

     3 - (Page Numbers) Follow Entries

     4 - Flush Right Page Numbers

     5 - Flush Right Page Numbers with Leaders
```

8. If you want the list to be generated on a separate page, press Hard Page (CTRL-ENTER).

9. Move the cursor to the first regular text page of the document. Press Format (SHIFT-F8) and choose **2** for Page, **6** for Page Numbering, and then **1** for New Page Number. The current page number is displayed. Enter **1** to begin numbering on page 1. Press Exit (F7) twice to return to the document.

If you want to number the pages containing the lists (and other introductory pages) with lowercase Roman numerals (such as i, ii, xiv, and so on), go to the beginning of the document and repeat step 9. However, when entering the page number, enter it as a Roman numeral (for example, enter **i** as the Roman numeral for page 1).

The code [Def Mark:List,*n:n*] appears in Reveal Codes at the cursor's location. The first *n* indicates the list number, and the second *n* indicates the page numbering style for the list.

Generate the List(s)

A table of contents, the tables of authorities, lists, the index, and cross-references are all generated at once.

1. From anywhere in the document, press Mark Text (ALT-F5).

2. Choose **6** for **G**enerate.

3. Choose **5** to **G**enerate tables, indexes, cross-references, etc. (Lists are included in this operation.) The following message appears:

```
Existing tables, lists, and indexes will be replaced.  Continue? Yes (No)
```

This message is a warning that other tables, lists, and indexes previously generated will be replaced.

4. Choose **Y** to continue or **N** to cancel the procedure.

As WordPerfect generates these items, it makes several passes through the document. You will be informed of the current pass and page number as it progresses. Remember that if you defined list 6 and you have figures with captions, all those captions will be placed in list 6 automatically. The same applies to lists 7 through 10 for table boxes, text boxes, user boxes, and equation boxes. If a figure, table, or box does not have a caption, it will not be included in the list. A sample of a

---

Articles

Article I 1

Article II 5

Article III 7

Article IV 8

Article V 8

Article VI 9

Figure 3-98.   List with dot leader

finished list that was defined with option **5**, Flush Right Page Numbers with **Leader**, is shown in Figure 3-98.

Hints

If you want to delete a mark, press Reveal Codes (ALT-F3), move to the [Mark:List,n] or [EndMark:List,n] code, and delete either one. If you make changes to marks or to the text included in a marked entry, generate the list again.

Entries are entered into the list in the order in which they appear in the document. This is similar to the Table of Contents feature. If you have more than one list, you do not have to define the lists in any particular order. The numbers 1 through 9 are used only to group entries into the various lists.

You can redefine the page number listing style after a list has been generated. Choose the new option and generate the list again. If you choose option **2** or **3** as the page number listing style, the number is placed two spaces after the entry, with or without parentheses, depending on the option that you selected. Options **4** and **5** place the number flush against the right margin. The dot leader included with option **5** will adjust automatically if you add or delete text from the list after it is generated.

Section or Chapter Numbers

If you want to include a section or chapter number with the page number in the list, you can do so by going to the beginning of each section or chapter and selecting a page number style from the Page Numbering menu. The current page number style (different from the one that you selected when you were defining a list) is set to print the page number only (represented by ^B). You can change the style and add text, as shown in "3-^B." The 3 would be the chapter number and ^B represents the current page number. See "Page Numbering" in this chapter for details.

Related Entries

Index
Mark Text
Master Document
Table of Authorities
Table of Contents

LOCATION OF FILES

If you installed WordPerfect using the Basic option, the Install program copied all the files into the same directory (C:\WP51). If you chose to do a custom installation, you were given the opportunity of specifying the directory for each type of file: Graphics, Dictionary/Thesaurus, Keyboard/Macro Files, Documents, and so on. Otherwise, they would all Key be kept in the directory where WP.EXE is located.

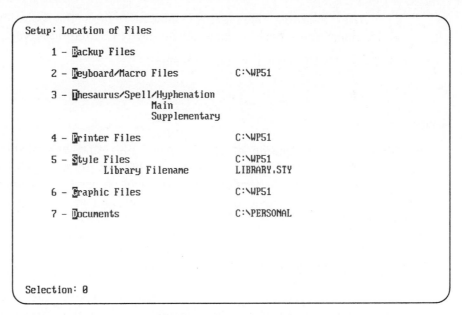

```
Setup: Location of Files
     1 - Backup Files
     2 - Keyboard/Macro Files        C:\WP51
     3 - Thesaurus/Spell/Hyphenation
                        Main
                        Supplementary
     4 - Printer Files               C:\WP51
     5 - Style Files                 C:\WP51
           Library Filename          LIBRARY.STY
     6 - Graphic Files               C:\WP51
     7 - Documents                   C:\PERSONAL




Selection: 0
```

Figure 3-99.   Location of Files menu with sample entries

The names of the directories were copied to the Location of Files menu under Setup (SHIFT-F1) as part of the installation procedure.

Keystrokes

To review or change the directories, follow these steps:

1. Press Setup (SHIFT-F1).

2. Choose **6** for **L**ocation of Files. The menu shown in Figure 3-99 appears with sample entries.

3. Make any necessary changes to the menu. If you enter the name of a directory that does not exist, an error message will be displayed. If this happens and you want to use that particular directory name, you can leave the menu, press List (F5), type =, and then enter the name of the directory to be created. Type **Y** when you are asked if you want to create the new directory.

After following these steps, you can reenter the Location of Files menu and enter the name of the newly created directory.

4. Press Exit (F7) when you are finished.

Hints

Following is a description of the types of files that are saved and retrieved from each directory. These are referred to as the "default directories," which means that the directory will be used unless another is specified when a document, macro, equation, and so on is saved or retrieved.

Backup Files

This directory is used to store the timed backup files named WP{WP}.BK1 and WP{WP}.BK2, depending on whether the current document is in Doc 1 or Doc 2. If your computer fails, you can restart WordPerfect and retrieve the backup file from this directory.

Keyboard/Macro Files

When you are using the Keyboard Layout feature, WordPerfect will look to this directory for files ending with the extension .WPK and display them on the Keyboard Layout menu. New keyboards will automatically be saved to this directory.

When starting a macro, WordPerfect searches this directory first. If the macro is not found, WordPerfect searches the directory in which WP.EXE is located. Any new macros are saved automatically to this directory unless you specify otherwise.

Thesaurus/Spell/Hyphenation

WordPerfect will search the Main directory for the main dictionary WP{WP}US.LEX, Thesaurus WP{WP}US.THS, and hyphenation file WP{WP}US.HYC when doing a spell check, using the Thesaurus, or hyphenating the document.

The second directory (Supplementary) will be used to store the supplementary dictionary WP{WP}US.SUP (the file used to store all words that are added to the dictionary during a spell check).

Printer Files

When you are installing WordPerfect, printer files ending with the extension .ALL are copied to this directory. They contain several printer definitions, usually related by the type of printer (laser, PostScript, dot matrix, daisywheel, and so on).

When you are selecting a printer, WordPerfect searches this directory for a list of printer (.ALL) files and displays the list of all printer definitions contained within those files. Any printer selections (ending with the extension .PRS) are also kept in this directory.

Style Files and Library Filename

WordPerfect uses this directory when you choose the Save or Retrieve option in the Styles (ALT-F8) menu.

You can enter the name of any file containing styles as the Library Filename. If a document does not contain any styles, the styles contained in the Style Library will be retrieved if you press the Styles (ALT-F8) key. This lets you use a standard set of styles from one document to another.

Graphic Styles

This directory will be used when you are retrieving or saving files from within a graphics box menu (figures, tables, text box, user box, or equation). If you choose the Filename option but then cannot remember the name of the file, you can press List (F5) and the name of this directory will be displayed as the default graphics directory.

Documents

Enter the name of the directory to be used for saving and retrieving files from the regular editing screen. The name of this directory will also be displayed as the default directory when you press List (F5).

Related Entries

Backup
Hyphenation
Keyboard Layout
Macros
Spell
See Chapter 1, "Installation and Setup"

LOCK AND UNLOCK DOCUMENTS

You can protect, or lock, sensitive documents with a password. If you transfer files electronically, you can lock them before sending them. The person receiving the file can then retrieve it by using the same password. Even if a file is intercepted by an unauthorized person, he or she cannot unlock it without the password.

Keystrokes

Lock a Document

1. With the document on the screen, press Text In/Out (CTRL-F5).

2. Choose **2** for **P**assword.

3. Choose **1** for **A**dd/Change a password.

4. Enter the password. You can use up to 24 characters (including spaces).

5. Reenter the password when prompted. This precaution guards against mistakes. If the two passwords do not match, the error message "Incorrect password" is displayed. You can then try again. Be aware, however, that if you enter the password incorrectly both

times (if your hands are not positioned correctly, for example), you will lock the file under an unknown password.

When you save the document, the password is saved with information in the document header or prefix.

Retrieve a Locked File

When you retrieve a file with Retrieve (SHIFT-F10) or List (F5), you will be prompted for the password before the file can be retrieved. If the password is incorrect, you are given another chance to enter the password. If it is still incorrect, the message "ERROR: File is locked -- FILENAME" is displayed on the screen. If you were using Retrieve (SHIFT-F10), you will be prompted with the Retrieve message "Document to be retrieved:" along with the name of the file so you can try again. If you were in the List Files menu, you will be returned to the document.

Remove a Password

Use the following steps to remove a password from a document:

1. With the locked file on the screen, press Text In/Out (CTRL-F5).
2. Choose 2 for Password.
3. Choose 2 to Remove the password.

You will want to be sure to save the version of the document without the password, or the previous version saved to disk will still have the password.

Hints

A file remains locked until the password is removed. Retrieving a file does not unlock it. All files associated with the locked document will also be locked. These include the backup files WP{WP}.BK1, WP{WP}.BK2, and temporary files that might have been created to move or copy text.

This provides added security on a network system and keeps someone from "undeleting" a readable temporary file from your disk.

Be aware that locking a document does not keep it from being deleted from the disk.

A locked file is encrypted. If you try to retrieve the file with any other editor or try to use the DOS TYPE command to retrieve the file, you will see a jumble of special characters and control characters, not the documents.

Passwords

If you use a different password for each document, you can easily forget a password and lose the document. Instead, consider using the same password for all of your locked files.

The longer the password, the harder it is to "break." It is even harder when you put spaces in unexpected places. If you forget the password, the document is lost.

Look at or Print a Locked Document

If you want to look at a file in the List Files menu, you are required to enter the password. If you choose the Find option in the List Files menu, you are also asked to enter the password for the locked document if you want WordPerfect to search through that file. You can also print a locked file from disk after entering the correct password.

Related Entries

Retrieve
Save

LONG DOCUMENT NAMES

By choosing the Long Document option in the Setup menu, you can save your documents with names of up to 68 characters (in addition to the standard 11-character DOS name). You can also enter the long document name in the Document Summary.

Setting the Long Document name option also displays the files by their descriptive names in the List Files menu. You can also use the Short/Long Display option in the List Files menu to display files by their long names.

Keystrokes

Prompt for Long Document Name

If you want to be prompted for a long document name each time you save a document, follow these steps:

1. Press Setup (SHIFT-F1) and choose **3** for Environment.

2. Choose **4** for Document Management/Summary.

3. Choose **3** for Long Document Names and type **Y**.

4. Press Exit (F7) to return to the document.

After you have changed the setting to Yes, you will be prompted for a long document name and document type (such as book, chapter, draft, and so on) each time you save a document. You are also asked to enter a standard filename (8 characters with an optional 3-character extension).

Document Summary

If you prefer not to be prompted each time you save a document, you can enter the long document name in the Document Summary.

1. Press Format (SHIFT-F8) and choose **3** for Document.

2. Choose **5** for Summary.

3. Choose **2** for Document Name, and enter a name of up to 68 characters.

4. Choose any other options from this menu, and press Exit (F7) when you are finished.

Displaying Long Document Names

If you have set the Long Document Name option in Setup (SHIFT-F1) to Yes, the List Files menu will automatically display files with their long document names.

If you do not have the Long Document Name option set to Yes, you can still display files by their long document names following these steps:

1. Press List (F5) and then ENTER to display the files in the displayed directory.

2. Choose **5** for Short/Long Display. The following choices are displayed:

1 Short Display; 2 Long Display: 2

3. Choose **2** for Long Display. If you have Long Display on and want to change back to the regular display where files are listed by their short names, choose **1** for Short Display.

4. The name of the current directory is displayed. Press ENTER to accept that directory, or enter a different one.

5. The files will be listed and sorted according to their long document names (as shown in Figure 3-100) until you choose the Short Display option.

Hints

Only WordPerfect documents will be displayed if you choose the Long Display option.

Up to 30 characters of the long document name are displayed in the List Files menu, even though you can enter 68 characters for the name. Keep in mind that if Long Display is on, documents will be sorted in the list according to their long document names. If a document does not have a long name, it is sorted by its short name.

Related Entries

Document Management/Summary
List Files

LOOK AT A FILE

When you are maintaining your files (deleting, copying, and so on), you can quickly check the contents. List Files has an option that lets you

```
12-19-89  03:05p           Directory C:\COMDEX\*.*
Document size:   73,583   Free: 21,864,448 Used:       384,796      Files:        6
Descriptive Name                  Type      Filename        Size     Revision Date

   Current Directory                        .        <Dir>
   Parent Directory                         ..       <Dir>
   Booth -- New cost estimate     proposal  BOOTH    .$$   12,686   12-19-89 02:55p
   General Demo File              Demo      COMDEX   .     45,289   11-17-89 12:46p
   New demo file for COMDEX       Demo      NEWDEMO  .     73,575   12-19-89 03:04p
                                            OUTLINE  .      4,405   11-02-89 02:58p
   Schedule for booth workers     schedule  SCHEDULE.     21,970   12-19-89 03:02p
                                            TIME     .     12,806   11-19-89 02:46p












1 Retrieve; 2 Delete; 3 Move/Rename; 4 Print; 5 Short/Long Display;
6 Look; 7 Other Directory; 8 Copy; 9 Find; N Name Search: 6
```

Figure 3-100.   List Files menu listing files by long document names

```
File: C:\BOOK\CONST.USA              WP5.1      Revised: 12-19-89 03:17p
Name: Constitution of the United States    Proposal   Created: 09-17-87 12:00a

                    THE CONSTITUTION OF THE UNITED STATES

                                  PREAMBLE

        We the people of the United States, in Order to form a more perfect Union
   establish Justice, insure domestic Tranquility, provide for the common defense,
   promote the general Welfare, and secure the Blessings of Liberty to ourselves a
   Posterity, do ordain and establish this Constitution for the United States of A

   ARTICLE I.
        Section 1.  All legislative Powers herein granted shall be vested in a Co
   of the United States, which shall consist of a Senate and House of Representati
        Section 2.  The House of Representatives shall be composed of Members cho
   every second Year by the People of the several States, and the Electors in each
   shall have the Qualifications requisite for Electors of the most numerous Branc
   the State Legislature.
        No Person shall be a Representative who shall not have attained to the Ag
   twenty five Years, and been Years a Citizen of the United States, and who shall
   when elected, be an inhabitant of the State in which he shall be chosen.
        Representatives and direct Taxes shall be apportioned among the several

   Look: 1 Text Doc; 2 Prev Doc; 3 Look at Document Summary: 0
```

Figure 3-101.   The screen after choosing to look at a file

look at a file without actually retrieving it. You can also use the Look
feature to view the list of files in other directories without changing the
default directory.

Keystrokes

Look at a File

1. Press List Files (F5).

2. Press ENTER to enter the displayed drive or directory, or to enter
a different directory.

3. Move the cursor to any filename.

4. Choose **6** for **L**ook or press ENTER to look at the file. The screen
will be similar to the one shown in Figure 3-101. If you created a
Document Summary for the file, it would appear first on a screen by
itself, as shown in Figure 3-102. As soon as you press ↓, the text will
appear.

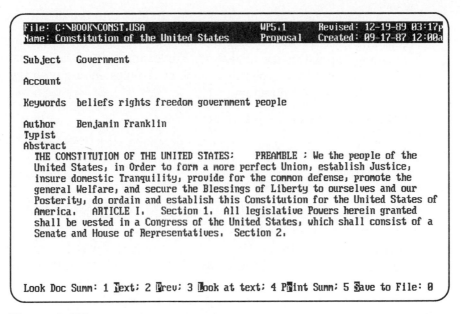

Figure 3-102.   Document Summary in the Look screen

5. You can use ↑ , ↓ , → , ← , + and −, to move through the text. You can also use Search (F2) or Reverse Search (SHIFT-F2) to search for a particular word or phrase. Pressing **S** will start a continuous scroll; press any other key to stop the scrolling.

You can also choose **1** to look into the Next document or **2** to look into the Previous document in the list of files. PGUP and PGDN will also look into the Previous and Next document.

6. Press Exit (F7) to return to the List Files menu.

Look at a Directory

If you press List (F5) and enter the name of a different drive and directory, you can look at the files without changing the default drive. You can also use the Look feature within the List Files menu to look at the files in a directory.

1. Move to any directory name in the List Files menu. (Each directory is labeled " < Dir > .")

2. Choose **6** for Look, or press ENTER to look into the directory.

3. The name of the highlighted directory is displayed, allowing you to edit the pathname if desired. For example, you can press HOME, BACKSPACE and then type **nov** to look at the files ending with the .Nov extension in that directory.

4. Press ENTER again to look at the files.

Hints

When you are looking at a file, the full pathname of the file is displayed along with the size of the file in bytes. Pressing ↑ or ↓ moves up or down one line at a time. Screen Down (+) and moves down one screen at a time, while Screen Up (−) moves up one screen at a time. When you are moving one screen at a time, one line from the previous screen overlaps so that you will not lose your place in the document.

If a file contains a Document Summary, it is displayed on the screen by itself. Pressing ↓ or typing **3** to Look at Text will move down into the text. You cannot return to the Document Summary unless you use Exit (F7) to go back to the List Files menu and choose option **6** to look at the file again. Also note the additional options displayed in Figure 3-102 that let you look at the summary for the next or previous document, look at the text, print, or save the summary.

You can better understand the structure of your hard disk by wandering through the directories with the Look feature. For example, in the List Files menu, if you place the cursor on "Parent <Dir>" and press ENTER once, the name of the parent directory is displayed. Pressing ENTER again lists the files in that directory. Any subdirectories are also listed in the List Files menu. You can also move down through the levels using Look.

Related Entries

Change Directory
Default Directory
Directories
Retrieve

LOOK UP A WORD

See "Spell" in this chapter.

LOTUS 1-2-3

See "Spreadsheet Importing and Linking" in this chapter for details about how to retrieve a Lotus 1-2-3 spreadsheet file into a WordPerfect Table.

LOWERCASE TEXT

See "Switch" in this chapter.

MACROS

You can use macros to eliminate the extra time and keystrokes necessary to perform a certain function more than once. A macro is like a tape recorder: You turn it on, press the keys to be recorded, and then turn it off. You can then play back the recorded keystrokes at any time. The only difference is that you give a macro a name.

If you are upgrading from version 4.2 to 5.1, be aware that Word-Perfect 5.1 cannot use version 4.2 macros; they will have to be redefined in version 5.1 or converted with the MACRCONV.EXE program that is installed with the utility files. Text, cursor keys, delete keys, and any key that has not been changed in 5.1 will be converted. Macros created with 5.0 are compatible with version 5.1, but some keystrokes may need changing because of menu differences.

There are two types of macros: those saved to disk in a file (which is given the extension .WPM) and those that are grouped together in a single keyboard layout file (with the extension .WPK). Both have the same capabilities and perform the same types of functions; the only difference is in the way they are stored.

You might find it more convenient to define a file macro (one with the .WPM extension). However, if you are concerned about disk space, you might want to keep all macros in a keyboard file. Single files take up a certain amount of space on disk (usually 512 bytes), regardless of the file's size. If the file is larger than 512 bytes, it takes another block of space. Because macro files are usually quite small, the remaining space (up to 512 bytes) is still reserved. If you have many macros, they can take up quite a bit of disk space. Depending on the version of DOS being used, even more space might be allocated for each file.

Because you can have more than one keyboard layout, you can use the same key or key combination for many different macros; the current macro would depend on the keyboard that is currently selected. You can use ALT key combinations, CTRL key combinations, function keys, and any other keys for macros if you place them on a keyboard layout. However, if you seldom use a macro and thus want to give it a descriptive name, a .WPM file macro might be more advantageous.

Macros included in a keyboard layout take precedence over file macros. For example, if you have a file macro named ALT-A and the current keyboard layout has a macro assigned to the ALT-A combination, the keyboard macro will be used.

In this section, macros saved in a single file with the .WPM extension are called *file macros*. Those saved with a keyboard layout are referred to as *key macros*.

Keystrokes

Define a File Macro

1. Press Macro Def (CTRL-F10). "Define macro:" appears on the screen.

2. Name the macro using one of the following methods:

   • Press ALT and a letter from "A" to "Z" for an ALT key combination macro. This type of macro is saved to disk with a .WPM extension (for example, ALTA.WPM). If you have selected a keyboard containing the same ALT key combination, you will not be able to use that combination easily.

   • Enter up to 8 characters. This type of macro is also saved to disk with a .WPM extension (for example, FORMAT.WPM).

   • Press ENTER or the space bar when you are asked for the macro name. It will be saved under the name WP{WP}.WPM. You can use either key to create the macro, but not both.

If you enter the name of a macro that already exists, the following message is displayed:

```
ALTX.WPM Already Exists: 1 Replace; 2 Edit; 3 Description: 0
```

Choose **1** to **R**eplace the original macro, **2** to **E**dit the keystrokes in the macro, or **3** to change the **D**escription. See "Editing Macros" for details.

3. When "Description:" appears, enter a description of up to 39 characters for the macro. Press ENTER if you want to skip this option. The description will appear in the Macro editor or when you use the Look option to look at the macro file in the List Files menu.

4. "Macro Def" flashes on the screen. (If you are using a Hercules Graphics Card Plus or a Hercules InColor Card with RamFont, "Macro Def" will not blink.) Enter the keystrokes to be recorded. Do not worry about making mistakes; the corrections will also be recorded.

At any time during the macro definition, you can press CTRL-PGUP and select from the following, which are described later under "Options":

```
1 Pause; 2 Display; 3 Assign; 4 Comment: 0
```

5. Press Macro Def (CTRL-F10) to end the macro definition.

If you have specified a location for macros with the Location of Files option on the Setup menu, the macro will be stored there. If not, it will be stored in the default directory. See "Hints" for more information.

Sometimes you will want to use only the advanced macro commands that are available in the macro editor when you are defining a macro and have little need for recording exact keystrokes from the screen. To do so, you can enter the macro editor immediately when you are first defining a macro by pressing HOME before pressing Macro Define (CTRL-F10). You are asked for the macro name and description and are then placed directly inside the macro editor.

Start a File Macro

If you defined an ALT key macro, press the ALT key combination (hold down the ALT key and press the letter) to start the macro. Use the following steps to start a named macro:

1. Press Macro (ALT-F10).

2. Enter the name of the macro. If you named the macro with ENTER or the space bar, press either as the name of the macro.

WordPerfect will first look for the macro on the drive and directory specified in the Location of Files option on the Setup menu. If you did not specify a drive or directory in the Location of Files option, Word-Perfect will first look in the default directory before checking the directory in which WP.EXE is kept.

You can press Cancel (F1) to stop a macro at any time.

Define a Keyboard Layout Macro

It is usually easiest to define a regular file macro first and then assign it to a key on a keyboard later. Otherwise, you have to know the exact keystrokes while you are defining the key. Both methods are described here.

1. Press Setup (SHIFT-F1).

2. Choose **5** for **K**eyboard Layout.

3. Choose **4** to **C**reate a new keyboard, or if you already have a keyboard defined and want to place the macro on that keyboard layout, move the cursor to the keyboard and choose **5** for **E**dit.

   If you are creating a keyboard, enter a name for the keyboard (you can use up to 8 characters) when you are prompted to do so.

4. If you are editing a keyboard layout, you will see a list of keys that have already been defined. Choose **6** to **R**etrieve a macro or **4** to **C**reate a new key.

5. When you are prompted, press the key or key combination that will be used for the macro. You can use SHIFT, ALT, and CTRL with any key to create a key combination.

   If you chose option **6** to **R**etrieve a macro, enter the macro

```
Key: Action

      Key              Alt-B

      Description      Insert a bullet and indent

  ┌──────────────────────────────────────────────────────┐
  │ {ALT B}                                               │
  │                                                       │
  │                                                       │
  │                                                       │
  │                                                       │
  │                                                       │
  │                                                       │
  │                                                       │
  │                                                       │
  │                                                       │
  └──────────────────────────────────────────────────────┘

 Ctrl-PgUp for macro commands;  Press Exit when done
```

Figure 3-103.   Macro editor

name when you are prompted to do so. The macro will be copied to the key *and* will remain on disk.

　　If you chose option 4 to Create a new key, the screen shown in Figure 3-103 appears, displaying the key and the key's current action in the window editor.

6. Delete the previous function (if necessary), enter new keystrokes for the macro, or edit the macro that was retrieved.

　　You can press TAB and ENTER to format the macro so that it looks more organized. Other keys (such as cursor keys and delete keys) are also used for editing the macro. If you want to enter TAB, ENTER, a cursor key, a delete key, or other selected WordPerfect functions such as Cancel or Exit (which would cancel or exit the macro), press CTRL-V before pressing that key, and the command will be inserted. See "Hints" for other available options.

　　While defining the macro, you can press CTRL-PGUP to display a list of macro commands in the upper right corner of the screen (see Figure 3-104). Move to the command to be inserted and press ENTER, or press Cancel (F1) to leave the commands without inserting one into the macro. Macro commands and editing features are covered in Chapter 6, "Advanced Macro and Merge Commands."

7. Press Exit (F7) to leave the macro editor and return to the list of keys.

8. After you have finished defining or editing other keys in that keyboard layout, press Exit (F7) to return to the list of keyboards.

9. Move to the keyboard layout that is to be used and press ENTER to select that keyboard, press Exit (F7) to use the same keyboard that was selected before making any changes, or choose **6** to use the Original WordPerfect keyboard.

If you press Exit (F7), you will be returned to the document. If you chose another keyboard or the original WordPerfect keyboard, you will be returned to the Setup menu. The keyboard that is currently selected is displayed to the right of option **5**, **K**eyboard Layout. If you selected the original keyboard, no name will appear. Press Exit (F7) once more to return to the document.

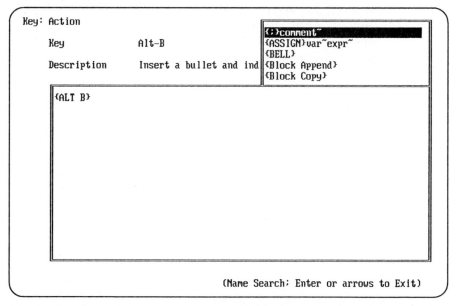

Figure 3-104.   Macro commands that are displayed in the upper right corner of the screen when you press CTRL-PGUP

Starting a Keyboard Layout Macro

Because a keyboard layout macro is assigned to a key or key combination, pressing that key or key combination will start the macro. Remember that the applicable keyboard needs to be selected before the macros on that keyboard can be used. Press Setup (SHIFT-F1), and look to the right of option 5, Keyboard Layout, for the current keyboard selection. If no keyboard is displayed, the original keyboard is being used. To change keyboard layouts, choose 5 for Keyboard Layout, move the cursor to the keyboard to be selected, and press ENTER. You will be returned to the Setup menu. Press Exit (F7) to return to the document.

Editing Macros

WordPerfect includes a small macro editor. It is not as sophisticated as the dedicated macro editor found in WordPerfect Library (for example, you cannot move or copy a block of commands or edit PlanPerfect or Library shell macros), but it is sufficient for editing any WordPerfect command that is less than 5K in size. The macro editor found within WordPerfect also has many macro programming commands available.

To make changes to a keyboard layout macro, follow the same steps described for defining the macro, but choose option 1 for Action to edit the macro instead of 4 to Create a new key. When the screen shown in Figure 3-103 is displayed, you can edit the macro.

To edit a file macro, follow these steps:

1. Press HOME and then Macro Define (CTRL-F10).

2. Enter the name of the macro or press the ALT key combination.

3. Verify the description by pressing ENTER, or enter a new description.

4. You will be placed in the macro editor. Make any necessary changes, and press Exit (F7) when you are finished.

You can also edit a macro by going through the steps to define the macro. When you try to define a macro that already exists, you can choose to replace that macro or edit it.

If you want to edit a macro named with the ENTER key, remember to press HOME before Macro Define (CTRL-F10) as described above or the original macro will be overwritten and replaced.

While you are editing a macro in the macro editor, you can access the advanced macro commands by pressing CTRL-PGUP. When you are finished, press Exit (F7) until you return to the document.

Entering Commands in the Macro Editor

Most WordPerfect commands are inserted immediately when you press the corresponding key. For example, if you press Block (ALT-F4), the {Block} command is inserted into the macro. However, many keys will not insert a function, because they are used to edit and format the document. These keys include TAB, ENTER, cursor keys, delete keys, Cancel (F1), and Exit (F7).

There are two ways to enter these commands. First, you can press CTRL-V before pressing the desired key, or press Macro Def (CTRL-F10) to toggle between two "modes" (similar to Typeover or Insert). The Default mode lets you use the keys mentioned above for editing and formatting the macro, and the other mode inserts the key's function, such as {Cancel}, {Enter}, and so on.

If you are inserting a single function or two, you might want to press CTRL-V to enter the function. If you are entering many functions at once, press Macro Def (CTRL-F10) and insert them. When you press that key, the following message appears at the bottom of the screen:

```
Press Macro Define to enable editing
```

To return to editing, press Macro Def (CTRL-F10) again. You can also press Cancel (F1) at any time to cancel the changes made to the macro. When you are asked the question "Cancel changes? No (Yes)," type **Y** or **N**.

Options

The Pause, Display, Assign, and Comment commands that you can use while creating a macro are explained here. Chapter 6, "Advanced Macro and Merge Commands" contains a list of macro programming commands and examples of how to use those commands. You do not have to understand these advanced programming commands to use macros successfully, however. They are useful for those who want to create customized applications or want more power out of their macros. In fact, you may see little use for some of the commands until you actually have an application in mind. Chapter 6 gives several examples.

Pausing a Macro

During the definition process, you can insert a pause so that when the macro is run, it can stop at that point and wait for you to enter more information. For example, you can create a macro to save the current document as a DOS text (ASCII) file. Because you would probably want to use a different name for each file, you could pause the macro at that point so you could enter a unique filename.

You can create a memorandum macro that pauses for you to insert the variable heading information ("TO:", "FROM:", "SUBJECT:", and so on). Then, when you run a macro, it would allow you to enter any amount of text as long as you do not press ENTER. For example, the "SUBJECT:" entry could be several lines long. You can press any key except ENTER to insert, delete, and correct the text. When you have finished, press ENTER, and the macro will continue.

1. During the macro definition, press CTRL-PGUP.

2. Choose 1 to **P**ause the macro at that point. If you must enter information at this point (for example, you would need to enter a "dummy" filename in the first example), you will need to enter it and then delete it by editing the macro in the macro editor later.

3. Continue with the remaining keystrokes, and end the macro definition.

As mentioned in step 2, you will sometimes have to enter information while you are defining a pause in a macro. For example, if you pause at a prompt (as you do with the Search, Save, and Retrieve features), you usually have to enter some type of information or you will get an error message and not be able to continue the macro. See "Keystrokes" for the steps used to edit a macro so that you can delete those keystrokes.

When you run a macro that contains a pause, the computer will not beep to draw your attention to the screen. If you want to add this command, you will need to edit the macro and add the {BELL} command just before the {PAUSE} command. To do so, press CTRL-PGUP while in the macro editor, move to {BELL} command, and press ENTER.

When you encounter the {PAUSE} command in a macro, WordPerfect will wait for you to enter text. As soon as you press ENTER, the macro will continue. If you are selecting a menu option during a pause, remember that you still have to press ENTER to make the macro continue.

If you want to use ENTER to insert more than one line of information during a pause, you should use the macro command called {PAUSE KEY}. This command lets you specify a different key that you can press to end a pause. For example, you can use Exit (F7) instead. In doing so, you would want to also include a {PROMPT} command that tells the user which key to press after he or she enters the information. See Chapter 6 for more information about these and other advanced macro commands.

Display

A macro is usually "invisible" when it is run, meaning that menus and prompts are not displayed on the screen. In fact, when you first define a macro, the {DISPLAY OFF} command is automatically inserted at the beginning of the macro.

If you want to pause a macro in a menu or at a prompt, you will need to make the macro display just before the pause so that the necessary menu or prompt is displayed on the screen. The display can again be turned off after the pause. To turn the display on or off, use the following steps:

1. While defining the macro, press CTRL-PGUP.

2. Choose **2** for **D**isplay.

3. Type **Y** to display the steps in the macro as they are played back or **N** to not display the steps.

4. Continue with the remaining keystrokes and end the macro definition.

Remember that if a macro is not pausing in a menu or at a prompt as it should, you need to insert a step that makes the macro display just before the pause.

Assign

While defining a macro, you can assign any value to a variable. Consider a variable as a storage place that is used to keep a piece of information for later use. When selecting the Assign option, you will be asked for the variable name and the information that should be stored there. You can use any number from 0 to 9 as the variable's name, or you can name the variable with a name of up to seven characters.

The value assigned to a variable can then be used later in the macro. For example, you could assign your name to a variable called "name." At another time in the macro (or in other macros), you could use that variable—your name—in the closing of a letter, in a memo, or other documents.

To assign a value to a variable, follow the steps given here. See Chapter 6 for other options that are available for assigning information to a variable.

1. While defining the macro, press CTRL-PGUP.

2. Choose 3 for Assign.

3. When you are prompted for the variable, type a number from 0 to 9 or enter the name of the variable (up to 7 characters). When you need the information at a later time, you will refer to it by this name or number.

4. Enter the value (information to be stored) when you are prompted to do so.

5. After you have finished defining the macro, press Macro Define (CTRL-F10) to end the definition.

You can use the information stored in the variables 0-9 any time by pressing ALT with those keys. For example, if you stored your name under the variable "1," you could press ALT-1 to retrieve the information to the screen.

Even though the ALT number keys are not available as ALT key macros, you can assign a value to them by pressing CTRL-PGUP during normal editing (not when defining a macro), typing a number from 0 to 9 when asked for the variable, and then entering the value.

You can also block a small section of text, press CTRL-PGUP, and type the number of the variable to be used. Only the first 128 characters in the block will be assigned to that variable. All WordPerfect codes are stripped from the block except for [HRt], [Tab], [→Indent], and [HPg], as well as a required hyphen (entered with the regular hyphen key). If an [→Indent←] code is encountered, it will be converted to an [→Indent] code.

The information that is entered into variables is temporary; it is lost when you exit WordPerfect. In other words, variables can double as temporary macros.

Comment

You can insert comments to document your macro at any time with this command. The comments are ignored when the macro is run, and they are visible only in the macro editor.

Because you cannot insert many of the macro commands into a macro while you are defining it from the regular keyboard, you can insert comments that will remind you to do so later when you are editing the macro. You can also document your macros easily with this feature. The comments will appear when you edit the macro.

1. While defining the macro, press CTRL-PGUP.

2. Choose 4 for Comment. "Comment:" will appear on the status line.

3. Enter the comment at this point. You can use up to 39 characters.

4. Continue defining the macro, and press Macro Def (CTRL-F10) when you are finished.

Repeating and Chaining Macros

If you want a macro to be repeated a specific number of times, press ESC, type the desired number (do not press ENTER after the number), and then start the macro. It will be executed the specified number of times or until a search condition is no longer found.

You can also chain (link) a macro to itself to create a repeating macro. If the macro contains a search, and the search condition is not found, the macro automatically stops. If the macro does not include a search, the macro will continue until you press Cancel (F1). Since a macro does not stop at the end of a replace, you can include as many replaces as you want in a macro. Perform the following steps to chain macros:

1. Press Macro Def (CTRL-F10), name the macro, and enter a description.

2. Define the macro.

3. At the very end of the macro definition, press Macro (ALT-F10) and enter the name of the macro to be chained. If it is an ALT key macro, you will need to press Macro (ALT-F10) and then press the ALT key combination. If you forget and press the ALT key combination without first pressing Macro (ALT-F10), you will nest the macro instead, which means that when the macro is run, WordPerfect will start the ALT key macro at that point and then return to this original macro. This may or may not make any difference in your situation.

4. Press Macro Def (CTRL-F10) when you have finished.

You can use the same steps to chain many macros. In fact, you can ask to start macros that have not yet been defined. Of course, they must be defined before the macro can be run successfully.

When you press Macro (ALT-F10) during macro definition and enter the name of another macro, only the keystrokes are stored. The macro is not started during the definition procedure. If you want to chain several macros, it is best to store the keystrokes that start one macro while defining another. In other words,

Macro A calls Macro B
Macro B calls Macro C
Macro C calls Macro D

and so on. Continue until all are chained, with only one being started in each macro. A chained macro does not begin until the first macro is finished. Even if you put the chained macro first in the sequence of steps, it is placed in a buffer and won't be started until after the first macro finishes.

You can also use the {CHAIN} macro command in the macro editor to chain macros.

Nested Macros

You can nest ALT key macros within other macros. You can also use the {NEST} macro command (inserted with the macro editor) to nest other types of macros (those named with 1 to 8 characters).

WordPerfect will run the first macro, run the nested macro at the point at which it is inserted, and return to the first macro to finish it.

Before you nest an ALT key macro within another macro, you should define it first. If you want to use a macro named with up to eight characters, you will need to use the {NEST} command in the macro editor.

1. While defining the first macro, press the ALT key combination for the macro to be nested at the point where you want it to be started.

2. Continue entering the keystrokes for the first macro, and press Macro Def (CTRL-F10) when you are finished.

Conditional Macro

The advanced macro commands {IF}, {CASE}, and {ELSE} are just a few of the commands that you can use to create conditional macros — ones that do different tasks, depending on certain conditions. For example, you could write a macro that says, "If the printer is waiting for a go, send it a go. If not, create the envelope for this letter."

See Chapter 6 for examples on how to use the {IF}, {CASE}, {ELSE}, and other advanced macro commands.

Hints

If you are defining a macro that is to do certain things under certain conditions, you need to define the macro when those conditions exist. For example, you cannot create a "transpose word" macro unless you have at least two words on the screen. You cannot define a macro that searches for a bold code if there is no boldface text in the current document.

An unsuccessful search will end a macro, but an unsuccessful replace will not.

If you start a merge while defining a macro, the merge starts immediately and the macro definition is ended. You do not have to press Macro Def (CTRL-F10) to end the definition. You can end the macro definition while in a WordPerfect menu or prompt by pressing Macro Def (CTRL-F10).

Location of Macros

When you define a macro, it is saved automatically to the directory specified in the Location of Files section of the Setup menu. To change that directory, follow these steps:

1. Press Setup (SHIFT-F1).

2. Choose **6** for **Location of Files.**

3. Choose **2** for **Keyboard/Macro Files.**

4. Enter the drive and directory in which the macros should be kept. Keyboard layouts (those files with the .WPK extension) will also be kept there.

5. Press Exit (F7) when you are finished.

If you do not specify a directory, the macros will be saved in the default directory unless you specify a different path. If you want to define an ALT key macro and have it saved elsewhere, type the full pathname, and then type ALT and the letter of the macro. For example, if you want to save an ALT-F macro to the drive and directory where you keep WordPerfect, enter **c:\wp51\altf** if you keep WP.EXE in a directory named WP51.

When you start a macro, either with an ALT key combination or with Macro (ALT-F10), and the drive and directory are not specified, the following places are searched in the order listed:

1. Memory

2. The drive and directory specified in the Location of Files option or the default drive and directory

3. The drive and directory in which you keep WP.EXE

When you run a macro for the first time, it is loaded into memory. The next time it is needed, it is immediately available without having to access the disk.

If you have not specified a drive and directory in the Location of Files option and you invoke an ALT key macro, it will be taken from the default directory. Later, if you change the default directory and try to use an ALT key macro with the same name, the original will be used because it is found in memory. To use the macro from the new default directory, press Macro (ALT-F10) and enter the name of the new directory along with the ALT macro name (C:\LEGAL\ALTF) so that WordPerfect looks in that directory first before searching RAM (memory).

If you want a macro started each time you start WordPerfect, enter **wp/m-***macroname* (instead of **wp**), where *macroname* is the name of the macro to be started (do not include the .WPM extension). Place the command in a batch file, or enter the following SET command in the AUTOEXEC.BAT file:

SET WP=/M-*macroname*

This commands sets the DOS environment so that when you type **wp**, it starts the macro without your having to enter the /M option.

Because WordPerfect uses the extensions .WPK and .WPM for keyboards and macros, do not use these extensions for regular Word-Perfect files. In fact, WordPerfect will not let you retrieve files with these extensions. If WordPerfect will not retrieve the file, enter the List Files menu and rename the affected file by deleting or changing the extension.

Converting 4.2 Macros to 5.1

You can use the MACROCNV.EXE program that is included with WordPerfect to convert macros created with version 4.0, 4.1, and 4.2 to

5.1 format. This file is copied with the other utility files during installation. If you chose not to install the utility files, you will need to do so before you can use this program.

Only text, cursor keys, delete keys, and the function keys that have not changed between versions (such as Cancel, Exit, Search, and Save) will be converted. All other functions in the macro will be converted to comments that do not affect the operation of the macro. You would then want to edit the converted macros and add the new keystrokes or commands used in version 5.1.

If the macro is longer than 5K, the MACROCNV program will automatically break it up into smaller sections and chain those smaller macros together.

To use the MACROCNV program, follow these steps:

1. Exit WordPerfect and go to DOS.

2. Change to the directory containing the WordPerfect program files (for example, **cd \wp51** will change to the WP51 directory).

3. Enter **macrocnv** *macroname* (where *macroname* is the name of the macro being converted).

After the macro has been converted, you will see a message telling you that the conversion is finished and informing you of any problems, such as functions that were not converted properly. You can then reenter WordPerfect and edit the macro.

Converted macros are given the extension .WPM and are saved in the directory where the original macro file was located. If the macro was larger than 5K and the macro conversion program had to break it into smaller files, numbers are added to the filenames (for example, FORMAT .MAC would be converted to the files FORMAT1.WPM, FORMAT2 .WPM, and so on). If your macro name was already 8 characters long, MACROCNV will change the filename to allow room for the numbers.

If you want to convert more than one file, you can use the wildcard characters * and ?. The ? character can be used to represent a single character in the filename, and the * is used to represent one or more characters. For example, if you wanted to convert all 4.2 macros with the extension .MAC, you would enter **macrocnv *.mac**.

Enter **macrocnv/h** if you want to read a help screen giving more information about the macro conversion program. Other options for starting the program include /m, /o, and /p. A description of each of these follows:

/M   Use this option only if you have defined a 5.0 or 5.1 macro that is too large to be edited in the macro editor (for example, if you defined a macro and then typed quite a bit of text to be stored in that macro). This option will break the macro into smaller sections and then use the {CHAIN} command to chain the sections together. Macros created in 4.2 files are automatically broken into smaller files if necessary without using this command.

Another option for editing large macros is to use the macro editor that comes with WordPerfect Library or Office.

/O   If you are converting a macro but another macro with the same name exists, you are asked if you want to replace or "overwrite" the original macro. You can use this option to overwrite the original without confirmation.

/P   You can have the message that appears on the screen after converting macros sent to a file or the printer instead. To do so, start the MACROCNV program with **/p**, type the name of the macro to be converted, and then enter >*filename* or >**prn**, where *filename* is the name of the file that will be used to contain the status report. If you use >PRN, the report will be sent to the printer connected to the first parallel port (LPT1).

Applications

You can use macros to insert commonly typed text, search for one type of code and replace it with another, or reduce the number of keystrokes needed to accomplish a certain feature, such as defining a header or footer.

If WordPerfect does not have a feature to do a specific task, such as transposing characters or words, you can write a macro to do it. A macro (or style) can set up the format for a letterhead, an envelope, or any other type of document. If you find yourself repeatedly doing a specific chore, consider defining a macro that will do it automatically.

For those who have difficulty remembering the keystrokes that perform a certain function, create a macro and give it a name that you can remember easily. For example, a file macro called KEEP could use the Conditional End of Page feature to keep a title with the first two lines of the paragraph. You can start the macro when the cursor is on the title with very few keysrokes instead of having to place the cursor above the title, count the lines, press Format (SHIFT-F8), choose **4** for Other and **2** for Conditional End of Page, enter the number of lines to keep together, and then press Exit (F7) to return to the document.

Additional applications follow, including information about how to set up a macro library.

Macros for Moving the Cursor

If you have an enhanced keyboard, you can use several keystrokes to move the cursor more quickly or to help edit text (copy and delete a highlighted block of text, for example). If you do not have an enhanced keyboard, you can write a macro that includes the macro command shown in the right column to perform the same function.

Keystroke	Function	Macro Command
CTRL-INS	Copy the current block	{Block Copy}
	Insert a row if in a Table	
CTRL-DEL	Move the current block	{Block Move}
CTRL-↑	Move up one paragraph	{Para Up}
CTRL-↓	Move down one paragraph	{Para Down}
ALT-↑	Move up one cell in a table	{Item Up}
	Move to a previous section of Parallel Columns if you are using that feature	
	Move to previous paragraph number of the same level	
ALT-↓	Move down one cell in a table	{Item Down}
	Move to the next section of Parallel Columns if you are using that feature	
	Move to the next paragraph number of the same level	

Keystroke	Function	Macro Command
ALT-←	Move left one cell in a table	{Item Left}
	Move to the column to the left if you are using any type of columns	
	Move to previous paragraph number of any level	
ALT-→	Move right one cell in a table	{Item Right}
	Move to the column to the right if you are using any type of columns	
	Move to next paragraph number of any level	

The following steps represent the easiest way to define such a macro:

1. Press HOME and then Macro Define (CTRL-F10).

2. Enter the name of the macro, or press the ALT key combination to be used.

3. Enter the description, or press ENTER to skip this step.

4. The cursor is now in the macro editor. Press Macro Commands (CTRL-PGUP), and type the name of the macro command. For example, if you want to move to the command {Item Down}, type that name and the cursor will move directly to it.

5. Press ENTER to insert that command into the macro.

6. Press Exit (F7).

To use the macro, press the ALT key combination. If you entered a name instead, press Macro (ALT-F10), and then enter the name of the macro.

Macros to Replace Codes with Codes

Although you can search for any WordPerfect code, you cannot always replace it with another code. For example, if you decide to change all of the small caps codes to italics codes, or all bold codes to underline codes, you cannot do so with a simple Replace operation. However, you can write a repeating macro to accomplish this task. Remember that you must have at least one occurrence of the code that is being replaced in the document before you define the macro.

1. Press Macro Def (CTRL-F10), name the macro, and enter a description.

2. Press Search (F2).

3. Insert the code that is to be searched for and replaced. Press the function key and select any necessary options to insert the code. For example, you would press Font (CTRL-F8), choose **2** for Appearance, and then select the attribute from the list. Choosing **7** for Sm Cap would insert the code [SM CAP].

4. Press Search (F2) to start the search.

5. Press Block (ALT-F4) to turn Block on.

6. Press Search (F2) and repeat step 3 twice to insert both the beginning and ending code.

7. Press ← once to move the cursor between the two codes, and then use BACKSPACE to delete the beginning code.

8. Press Search (F2) again to block to the ending code.

9. Assign the new attribute to the block by pressing Font (CTRL-F8), choosing **1** for Size or **2** for Appearance, and then typing the letter for the desired attribute.

10. Press ← once to move past the new attribute's ending code, and then press BACKSPACE and type **Y** to delete the previous attribute.

11. Press Macro (ALT-F10) and enter the name of this macro to chain the macro to itself.

12. Press Macro Def (CTRL-F10) to end the macro.

When you start this macro, it will repeat until the search fails and it cannot find any more attribute codes. Unfortunately, you cannot search for parameters within a code. For example, you can search for a font change code but not for a specific font change. You can use the Styles feature instead. For example, you can attach a style to a section of text and then change the codes within the style; the affected text is updated automatically.

Macros That Edit Documents

If you have a file from another program that needs extensive editing, you can use a macro, because the editing changes are usually consistent from one line to the next or one record to the next. For example, if you imported text from a database and a person's first name and last name were in separate fields, but you wanted them listed in the same field, you could write a macro to find the first name field, insert it before the second name, and remove the extra {END FIELD} merge command.

You can use macros and Switch (SHIFT-F3) to help create a second document. For example, if you have a legal document that consists of standard paragraphs that you can use in a specific type of brief, you can define a macro (such as ALT-P for "Paragraph") that copies the current paragraph, switches documents, retrieves the paragraph, goes to the bottom of the document with HOME, HOME, ↓, and then returns to the first document. While scrolling through the first document, you can press ALT-P when you want a paragraph to be copied to document 2, and the steps will be done for you. After scrolling through the first document, you can switch documents and see the finished product.

If you are creating the macro for editing purposes, you might consider naming it with ENTER or the space bar, since you may only use it under unique circumstances and it would not need a descriptive name.

Creating a Macro Library

WordPerfect's new Keyboard Layout feature lets you have libraries of macros that you can use under different circumstances. For example, you might want to have a LEGAL keyboard, where you keep all macros associated with creating legal documents. Another keyboard, named EDITING, might hold all the special macros for editing any type of document.

You can see a list of the key definitions (macros) and their descriptions by pressing Setup (SHIFT-F1), choosing 5 for Keyboard Layout, moving to the desired keyboard layout, and choosing 7 to Edit the keyboard.

If you want to see a list of available file macros, you can press List (F5), enter the drive and directory being used to store the macros, and enter the filename pattern *.WPM. For example, if the directory being used was named MACROS, you could enter **c:\macros*.wpm**. You can move to any of the macro files and press ENTER to "Look" at a description of the macro (if one was entered when you defined the macro).

You can also use a "master" macro to list many of the other macros on the screen and then chain (go to) the selected macro. You can accomplish this using the advanced macro commands. Another method uses the Merge feature. This method is a little easier, because you can easily edit the list of macros on the screen in a regular document without using the macro editor.

Figure 3-105 shows a sample macro library in which the name and description of each macro is listed (the description needs to be entered again manually; the one that you entered while defining the macro cannot be displayed here).

You can use the following steps to create your own macro library. It should look something like Figure 3-106 when you are finished.

```
                          MACRO LIBRARY


    GO          Send printer a "Go"

    LETTER      Retrieve the format for a business letter

    ENV         Print an envelope for the current document

    MEMO        Create a memo

    PLEADING    Create the format for pleading paper

    NUMBER      Number pages in "Page n of n" format


     *** If you do not want to make a selection, press Cancel (F1). ***


    Macro:
```

Figure 3-105.   Sample macro library

1. On a clear screen, make a list of your macros and enter a description for each one. You will need to use spaces to format the text on the screen; tab, indent, and center codes are not used when the message is displayed during the merge.

Limit the list to one screenful, and label the list "Macro Library" if you want to.

2. The last line should include a message similar to the following:

*** If you do not want to make a selection, press Cancel (F1).***

3. Press HOME, HOME, ↑ to go to the top of the screen.

4. Press Merge Codes (SHIFT-F9) twice, type **prompt** to move the cursor to the {PROMPT} command, and press ENTER to select it.

5. Press ENTER again when you are asked to enter the message (the contents of the screen are the "message" that will be displayed).

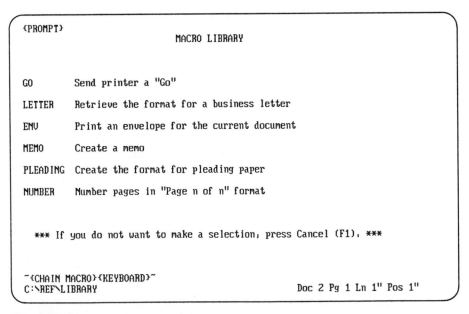

Figure 3-106.   The screen after creating a macro library

6. Press BACKSPACE to delete the tilde (~) that is inserted automatically when you press ENTER.

7. Press HOME, HOME, ↓ to go to the bottom of the screen. Remember that the list should not be longer than one screen, or it will scroll off when it is displayed during the merge.

8. Type the tilde (~) to mark the end of the "message."

9. Press Merge Codes (SHIFT-F9) twice, type **chain macro** to go to the {CHAIN MACRO} command, and then press ENTER.

10. When you are asked for the name of the macro, press ENTER (you will supply the name of the macro when the merge pauses).

11. Press ← once to move between the {CHAIN MACRO} command and the tilde (~).

12. Press Merge Codes (SHIFT-F9) twice, type **keyboard** to go to the {KEYBOARD} command, and then press ENTER to select it.

13. Press Exit (F7) and save the file ("LIBRARY" is a suggested name). Clear the screen, but do not exit WordPerfect.

During the merge, the text between the {PROMPT} command and tilde (~) will be displayed on the screen. The {CHAIN MACRO} command is used to start a macro, and the {KEYBOARD} command causes the merge to stop and let you enter the macro name from the keyboard. When you have entered the name of a macro (you can even enter one that is not displayed on the screen), the menu disappears and the macro is started.

The following steps help you display the macro library with a minimum of keystrokes. If you did not use these steps, you would have to start a merge each time you wanted to use the macro library.

1. Press Macro Def (CTRL-F10).

2. Name the macro (ALT-L for "Library" is a suggestion) and enter a description ("Call up Macro Library" is a suggestion).

3. Press Merge/Sort (CTRL-F9).

4. Choose **1** for **Merge**.

5. Enter **library** as the name of the primary file. If you used a different name, enter that name instead.

6. Since there is no secondary file to merge, press ENTER when you are asked for the name of the secondary file.

7. The macro definition ends automatically when the merge takes place. Press Cancel (F1) to cancel the procedure.

Running the Macro Library

If you followed the steps for creating a macro library, you can press ALT-L, and the menu will be displayed. Enter the name of a macro on the menu or any other macro. The merge ends, and the macro is started.

When you want to change items on the menu, retrieve the LIBRARY file and edit it. As long as you do not disturb the merge codes, you can add and delete macros or change the entire look of the screen. The ALT-L macro does not have to be adjusted; it will always use the most recent LIBRARY file.

Because you can have single-character macros, you could number the items on the screen and then start a macro by entering the number instead of entering a name. Figure 3-107 shows a sample macro library in which you can enter numbers (instead of names) to start macros. See "Merge" in this chapter and Chapter 6 if you have further questions about the merge codes used in this example.

Macros and Merges

The Merge feature includes many of the same advanced programming commands found in macros. Some of the commands work a little differently, and there are some commands unique to each feature.

You can mix macros and merges. For example, you can have a macro start a merge. Macros can also be nested in a merge, meaning that when the command to start a certain macro is encountered, WordPerfect processes the macro, then returns to the merge. You can also chain macros and merges, as shown in the macro library example. When a macro is chained, all control goes to that macro; it does not return to the merge.

```
                    MACRO LIBRARY


   1.  Send printer a "Go"

   2.  Retrieve the format for a business letter

   3.  Print an envelope for the current document

   4.  Create a memo

   5.  Create the format for pleading paper

   6.  Number pages in "Page n of n" format



  *** If you do not want to make a selection, press Cancel (F1). ***


Macro:
```

Figure 3-107.   Numbering each item can save time entering macro names

See Chapter 6 for a description of the differences between the two features and examples for using each macro and merge command.

Related Entries

Keyboard Layout
Merge
Search
See also Chapter 6, "Advanced Macro and Merge Commands"

MAIL MERGE

See "Merge" in this chapter for details about how to perform a Word-Perfect merge.

Mail Merge is a format used by WordStar to store data files. Database programs can usually convert their files to a delimited Mail Merge format. Fields are separated with a comma (some programs can specify a different character), and records are separated with a carriage return and a linefeed. Fields that normally include commas, such as city and state, have quotation marks around them.

You can use these types of files in a WordPerfect merge by entering the name of the file when you are prompted for the secondary file. You can also use the Convert program to convert these types of files to WordPerfect merge format.

See "Convert Program" and "Merge" in this chapter for details about using or converting these types of files.

Related Entries

Convert Program
Merge

MAILING LABELS

See "Labels" in this chapter.

MAPPING THE KEYBOARD

See "Keyboard Layout" in this chapter.

MARGIN RELEASE

See "Left Margin Release" in this chapter. You cannot release the right margin without resetting the margins.

MARGINS, LEFT AND RIGHT

The left and right margins are set a specific distance from the left and right sides of the paper. You can change them in a document as many times as you want. The left and right margin settings are found under the Line option on the Format menu.

Keystrokes

1. Press Format (SHIFT-F8).

2. Choose **1** for **Line**.

3. Choose **7** for **Margins, Left and Right**.

4. Enter the measurement for the left margin, and then enter the right margin setting.

   You can specify any unit of measurement after the number (″ for inches, ″c″ for centimeter, or ″p″ for points). You can even enter the measurement using fractions (for example, **1 3/8** or **5/16**), and they will be converted to the decimal equivalent.

5. Press Exit (F7) to return to the document.

If you have a laser printer, there is usually a small amount of space along the sides of the paper called ″nonprintable regions.″ If you enter margins smaller than this amount, they will be increased to the amount of the nonprintable region (because you cannot print in that space).

Hints

An [L/R Mar:*n,n*] code is inserted at the cursor position. The first number in the code is the left margin, and the second number is the right margin.

If the cursor is not at the left margin, a hard return [HRt] code is inserted just before the [L/R Mar:] code, and the cursor is returned to the left margin on the next line. The new margin remains in effect until it encounters another left or right margin code.

If you enter left and right margins that overlap because of the current paper width, you will see the message "ERROR: Margins overlap."

WordPerfect uses the paper size, margins, and current font to determine how many characters will fit on a line. If you need more characters across a page (as is the case when you are importing text from a spreadsheet), decrease the size of the font so that more characters will fit between the margins, decrease the margins, or increase the paper size. Choose the 11″ by 8.5″ paper size if you have a printer that will print in landscape mode or if you can turn the page on its side for printing.

If you have changed to 4.2 units to display and enter settings, be aware that margins are not set as they were in 4.2. Instead of entering a setting such as 12 and 90, you would set margins of 12 and 12, because you are specifying the distance from the right side of the page rather than the distance from the left side of the page.

Also, if you are using 4.2 units for the status line display, the line will not necessarily break at position 74. The "Pos" number displays the number of characters that will fit on the line, given the current font. Consider changing the unit of measurement for the status line display to the same unit of measurement being used to change format settings. Press Setup (SHIFT-F1), choose **3** for **Environment**, **8** for **Units of Measure**, and **2** for **Status Line Display**; and then enter the same unit of measurement used for option 1 (usually ″ for inches). WordPerfect can then give you an accurate report about how far the cursor is from the left side of the page instead of displaying the number of characters on the line.

To change the margin setting permanently, insert the [L/R Mar] code as an initial code in the Setup menu. See "Initial Codes" in this chapter for more information.

When you press Reveal Codes (ALT-F3), the ruler separating the regular text above from the text and codes below shows the current margin (and tab) settings in relation to the screen. Margin settings appear as [and] on the ruler line. If a tab is set in the same position as a margin, that margin setting appears as { or }. Tab settings appear as triangles. If you want to see the ruler on the screen at all times, press

Screen (CTRL-F3), choose **1** for **Window**, and press ↑ once. You can also enter a number less than the total number of lines on screen to see more than one document. If you do, the *current* document's tabs and margins are shown in the ruler line.

Margin Release

When you are at the left margin, press Left Margin Release (SHIFT-TAB) to release the left margin for the current line only. You cannot release the right margin temporarily; you would need to decrease the right margin instead.

Using Indent for Temporary Margins

You can use →Indent (F4) or →Indent← (SHIFT-F4) to set temporary left, or left and right, margins. The amount of space the margins move inward depends on the current tab settings. The temporary margins stay in effect until you press ENTER or until a [HRt] code is encountered.

Change Margins for DOS Text Files

Before you retrieve a DOS text file, it is important to change the margins and font to accommodate an 80-character line. To do this, change both the left and right margins to .25″, and change to a 10-pitch font. This is especially important if you want to use the DOS Text Retrieve option, which converts all hard returns that fall within the hyphenation zone to soft returns.

Related Entries

Indent
Left Margin Release
Margins, Top and Bottom

Paper Size/Type
Ruler Line
Setup
Text In/Out

MARGINS, TOP AND BOTTOM

The top margin is the amount of space at the top of the page where no text will be printed. The bottom margin is similar, but it is measured from the bottom of the page. You cannot print headers, footers, and footnotes in the top and bottom margins. The top and bottom margin settings are found under the Page option of the Format menu.

Keystrokes

1. Go to the beginning of the document if the entire document is to be affected, or press Go To (CTRL-HOME), ↑ to go to the top of the current page if that is the page that you want to change.

2. Press Format (SHIFT-F8).

3. Choose **2** for **P**age.

4. Choose **5** for **M**argins, Top and Bottom.

5. Enter the measurement for the top margin and then the bottom margin. You can use any unit of measurement. Type ″ after the number if the margins are to be set in inches, **c** for centimeters, or **p** for points. You can even set the margins using fractions, such as **1 3/8** and **5/16**, and they will be converted to the decimal equivalent.

6. Press Exit (F7) to return to the document.

Hints

When you set the top and bottom margins, the code [T/B Mar:n,n] is inserted in the document at the cursor position. It affects all the pages from that point forward until a new top and bottom margin code is encountered.

WordPerfect figures the number of lines that will fit on the page according to the length of the page, the top and bottom margins, and the height of the current font. If the top and bottom margins decrease, more lines will fit on the page. If you have a small font, many more lines will fit on the page than if you have a very large font.

If you have set the status line to display lines and positions in version 4.2 units, the page may or may not break at line 54 as it did in version 4.2. Consider changing the unit of measurement for the status line display to the same unit of measurement being used to change format settings. WordPerfect can then give you a more accurate report about the distance between the top of the page and the cursor, instead of displaying the number of lines on the page. See "Units of Measurement" for more information.

If you want headers, footers, footnotes, or graphics lines to be printed closer to the top or bottom of the page, decrease the size of the top and bottom margins, and add more space within the header or footer if necessary.

Text Adjustment

If you find that the top margin of the text is not printing where you expected it would, you can edit the current Paper Size/Type definition, choose the Text Adjustment option, and enter the amount of space to add or subtract (enter a negative number if subtracting) for the top text adjustment.

Related Entries

Margins, Left and Right
Paper Size/Type

MARK TEXT

You can use Mark Text (ALT-F5) to create cross-references, work with master documents, compare two documents and insert redline and strikeout markings automatically, and create a table of contents, a table of authorities, up to ten lists, or an index.

Keystrokes

There are actually two Mark Text menus; the one that is displayed depends on whether you have Block (ALT-F4) on or off. If Block is off, you use the Mark Text menu to turn some features on and off or to select options for other features. The following is the Mark Text menu with Block off:

```
1 Cross-Ref; 2 Subdoc; 3 Index; 4 ToA Short Form; 5 Define; 6 Generate: 0
```

If Block is on, the Mark Text menu lets you mark the blocked text for use with a specific feature. The following is the Mark Text menu with Block on:

```
Mark for: 1 ToC; 2 List; 3 Index; 4 ToA: 0
```

A few of the options listed on the first menu have submenus. The next section gives general information about each feature. For detailed instructions, see each entry by name in this chapter.

Options

The options have been divided into the two sections described above: with and without block on.

Mark Text Menu with Block Off

The following discussion summarizes the features listed on the Mark Text menu when Block is off.

Cross-Ref   The Cross-Reference feature lets you refer to pages, paragraph or outline numbers, footnotes or endnotes, and graphics boxes — and have those references updated after you have made editing changes. Some examples are "see Figure 16 on page 52," "in paragraph 1.11," "continued on page 34," or "see the same reference mentioned in footnote 10." You can update the references after you have made editing changes by choosing the Generate option on this menu.

Subdoc   If you have a large project that includes several files on disk, you can create a master document that lists the names of the subdocuments. Later, you can generate a table of contents, an index, lists, cross-references, and so on for the entire master document. You can also print the one master document, and it will print the subdocuments in the proper order, with consecutive pages, footnotes, endnotes, line numbers, paragraph numbers, and so on.

When you are creating the master document, you choose the Subdoc option and enter the filename (including the drive and directory, if necessary). A small box containing the filename will appear, indicating that a subdocument exists in that location. If you expand the master document, the contents of the subdocument will be retrieved into the master document. Markers are placed at the beginning and end of the subdocument so that when the master document is compressed, editing changes can be saved in the original files.

Index   This option is used to mark an individual word as an index entry. You specify the heading and subheading when you are marking. The code [Index:*heading*; *subheading*] is inserted at that point.

If you want to mark a phrase (not just the current word), first define it as a Block with (ALT-F4), press Mark Text (ALT-F5), and then choose the Index option.

You can also create a concordance so that you only have to mark each entry once instead of each time it occurs in the document. See "Concordance" in this chapter for more information.

ToA Short Form   A short form is part of the Table of Authorities feature. When text is blocked and marked for a table of authorities entry, it is treated as the full form that will actually appear in the table of authorities. At that time, you also assign a short form, which you can use as a nickname for the entry. Whenever you come to a citation that should be included in the table of authorities, you can mark the entry with the Short Form option. A [ToA:;*short form*;] code is inserted in the document and is used when the table is generated.

Define   If you choose option **5**, **Define**, you will see the following options:

```
Mark Text: Define

    1 - Define Table of Contents

    2 - Define List

    3 - Define Index

    4 - Define Table of Authorities

    5 - Edit Table of Authorities Full Form
```

These options let you choose the location and numbering style for tables, lists, and the index, or you can edit the nearest table of authorities full form to the left of the cursor.

Generate   The Generate selection displays the following choices:

```
Mark Text: Generate

    1 - Remove Redline Markings and Strikeout Text from Document

    2 - Compare Screen and Disk Documents and Add Redline and Strikeout

    3 - Expand Master Document

    4 - Condense Master Document

    5 - Generate Tables, Indexes, Cross-References, etc.
```

With the second option, you can compare a document on the screen with one on the disk. Phrases that exist in the document on the screen but not on the disk (ones that have been added) are marked with redline markings. Phrases that are missing from the document on the screen are "retrieved" from the document on the disk with strikeout markings added. You can also add redline and strikeout to a document by pressing Font (CTRL-F8) and choosing option **2** for **Appearance** and then **8** for **Redln** (redline) or **9** for **Stkout** (strikeout).

You can choose the first option on the menu to leave the redlined text, but remove the redline markings and delete the text marked with strikeout.

You can use options 3 and 4 to expand or condense master documents. When a master document is expanded, each subdocument listed is retrieved into the master document, with markers at the beginning and end of the subdocument. When a master document is condensed, the subdocuments can be saved back to disk and include any editing changes that you have made. See "Master Document" in this chapter for details.

The last option generates the table of contents, tables of authorities, lists, cross-references, and the index for the current document.

Mark Text Menu with Block On

After you block (highlight) text, you can apply the following Mark Text options to the block.

ToC   You have to mark each entry for the table of contents with this method. After you have selected this option, you are asked to indicate the level (1 through 5) for the entry. Major headings are classified as level 1 entries, subheadings as level 2 entries, and so on. A [Mark:ToC,n] code is inserted at the beginning of the block and an [EndMark:ToC,n] code is inserted at the end, with n being the level number.

List   WordPerfect has ten available lists. If there are figures in the document, the captions for those figures will automatically be included in list 6, table box captions in list 7, text box captions in list 8, user box captions in list 9, and equation box captions in list 10. The captions do not have to be marked; they are included automatically if the appropriate list is defined.

You should block and mark text with the List option that is to be included in lists 1 through 5. At that time, you are asked for the list number. The codes [Mark:List,n] and [EndMark:List,n] are inserted at the beginning and end of each block, with n representing the number of the list.

Index   This option is identical to the one found on the "Block off" Mark Text menu, but it is used to mark a block of text as an entry in the index rather than marking a single word.

ToA   You have to block and mark each entry with this option if it will appear in a table of authorities. After entering the section number (as many as 16) for the table, the blocked text is placed in a separate editing screen and is considered the full form. After editing the full form and pressing Exit (F7), you are asked to enter a short form (nickname) for the entry. You can then use the short form to mark future occurrences of the citation. A [ToA:*n;shortform;*<Full Form>] code is inserted at the cursor location. The <Full Form> in the code is used to indicate the blocked entry; *n* indicates the section of the table of authorities to be used.

Hints

Remember that any codes included in a block that has been marked for a table of contents, table of authorities, or list will appear with the entry when the tables and lists are generated. The steps for creating tables, lists, and the index are the same: Mark each entry, define the location and format with the Define option, and then generate it with the Generate option.

Related Entries

Compare Documents
Concordance
Cross-References
Index
Lists
Master Document
Outline
Paragraph Numbering
Redline

Remove Redline and Strikeout
Strikeout
Table of Authorities
Table of Contents

MASTER DOCUMENT

If you are working on a large project that consists of smaller files, you can create a master document that will tie all files or subdocuments together. You can then create a table of contents, an index, lists, and so on, for all documents as if they were one. This feature also lets you continue all types of numbering (page numbers, line numbers, footnotes, endnotes, and graphics boxes) throughout all subdocuments as if they were one.

Keystrokes

Creating the Master Document

A master document can contain a title page, introductory information, a table of contents, an index, or list definition marks, and a page numbering code or any other formatting code. When you reach the location for each subdocument, follow these steps:

1. Press Mark Text (ALT-F5).

2. Choose 2 for Subdoc. The prompt "Subdoc Filename:" appears at the bottom of the screen.

3. Enter the name of the file to be placed at that location, including the drive and directory in which it can be found. The following appears on the screen to indicate that a subdocument has been inserted:

```
Subdoc: C:\BOOK\CHAPTER.1
```

4. Continue until all subdocuments have been inserted into the master document. If a formatting command is found in a subdocument, it will be in effect until the same format command with a different setting is found in either the master document or another subdocument.

If the first code in the master document is a subdocument code and you want to move to just before that subdocument, you will need to press HOME, HOME, HOME, ↑. Even though the box containing the name of the subdocument looks like regular text, it is actually a code, and HOME, HOME, ↑ will not move before codes.

Expanding or Condensing the Master Document

You can generate such items as a table of contents, lists, an index, and cross-references as they are, or you can expand the document before you generate them. If you do not expand the document and use Generate, WordPerfect will expand it for you. After the Generate process is complete, WordPerfect asks you if you want to save the changes in the subdocuments. If you have included cross-references, you will want to type **Y** and confirm the replacement of the original documents. You will then be asked to confirm the replacement of each subdocument, or you can choose an option to replace all subdocuments without being prompted. (This is explained in greater detail later.)

When you want to print the document, you will need to expand it first; otherwise, it will be printed as you see it on the screen. Another reason you might want to expand the master document is that if you need to replace a certain word or phrase throughout all the subdocuments, you might find it easier to expand the master document, do a replace procedure, and then condense the document again, rather than retrieving each subdocument one at a time and making the change in each individual file. You can then save all changes back into the original files (subdocuments) when the master document is condensed.

1. With the master document on screen, press Mark Text (ALT-F5).

2. Choose **6** for **G**enerate.

3. Choose **3** for **E**xpand Master Document. Markers are placed at the beginning and end of each subdocument. They look similar to the ones shown here:

```
Subdoc Start: C:\BOOK\CHAPTER.1
```

This would be the text for Chapter 1.

```
Subdoc End: C:\BOOK\CHAPTER.1
```

4. Make the necessary changes to the document. You can use Generate at this time or wait until the document is condensed again. If you need to print the master document, do so at this time.

5. When you have finished making changes to the entire document, press Mark Text (ALT-F5) and choose **4** for **C**ondense Master Document.

6. You will see the prompt "Save Subdocs? Yes (No)." Type **Y** to save the changes in each subdocument before removing the contents of the subdocuments from the screen. Type **N** to ignore any changes that you may have made, and remove the contents of the subdocuments from the screen.

If you typed **Y** to save the subdocuments, the name of each file is displayed on the screen, one at a time, and you are asked if you want to replace the original file. The prompt looks like this:

```
Replace C:\BOOK\CHAPTER.1? 1 Yes; 2 No; 3 Replace All Remaining: 0
```

This process is similar to replacing a file that already exists on the disk. If you type **1** for Yes, the original on the disk is replaced with the subdocument on the screen. If you type **2** for **N**o, the name of the file is displayed, letting you edit it or enter a different filename. Typing **3** for **R**eplace causes the current subdocument and all remaining subdocuments to be replaced without continuing to prompt you.

Hints

When you insert a subdocument, a box that represents that subdocument is displayed. The code that is displayed in Reveal Codes is similar to [Subdoc:*filename*]. When the document is expanded, the codes inserted at the beginning and end of each subdocument appear as [Subdoc Start:*filename*] and [Subdoc End: *filename*]. If you delete a starting or ending code, WordPerfect will not be able to condense the master document correctly.

If you want to use the Cross-Referencing feature to refer to a page, outline, or paragraph number, or to a footnote, endnote, or graphics box (figure, table, and so on) in a different document, you can mark the reference in one document and the target (page, footnote, and so on) in the second document, using the same ID. Include both documents in a master document, and then use Generate. The cross-references will then be updated across documents.

If you prefer, you can save the master document in its expanded form. If you do so, you are informed that the document is expanded, and you are asked if you want to condense it. If you type **Y**, the process to condense the document is started. If you type **N**, the document remains expanded and you will not be asked the question when you save the document in the future. However, you can still use the Condense Master Document option on the Generate menu.

It is possible that you will not have enough memory or disk space for the entire master document when it is expanded. If this happens, you will see the error message "Not enough memory," and the process will end. As a solution to the problem, you can divide the master document into two or more master documents or you might consider purchasing more memory or a hard disk.

Applications

This feature is most frequently used for books that contain many chapters. However, because a master document can also be a subdocument that is included in yet another master document, you can use it as a kind of outline feature with which you can expand or condense different levels.

For example, if you have a different "to-do" list for each day of the week, you can include seven subdocuments in a master document, each with the name of one day of the week (Sunday, Monday, and so on). You can then expand that document to see the week at a glance. If you want to include detailed information about each item on the list but not necessarily display this information at all times, you can keep it in separate files with the subdocument codes included in the "day of the week" file. You can then expand the subdocuments when the need arises.

Related Entries

Cross-References
Generate
Index
Lists
Table of Authorities
Table of Contents

MATH

You can use WordPerfect's Math feature to calculate subtotals, totals, and grand totals for columns. You can also combine addition, subtraction, multiplication, and division for calculations across columns. For simple addition, see "Addition" in this chapter. Although the Math feature lets you perform four-function calculations, you may want to consider using the Tables feature instead. The Math feature included in Tables lets you use the information from any cell instead of being limited to performing calculations across a row or adding numbers in a column. In addition, the Tables feature always assumes that Math is on, so you don't have to turn it on and off. See "Tables" in this chapter for more information.

Note: If you want to use advanced spreadsheet applications, consider using PlanPerfect or another spreadsheet program such as Excel or Lotus 1-2-3. You can retrieve a spreadsheet from any of these programs directly into WordPerfect, and it will automatically be placed in a table. You can, however, use the Math feature to accomplish many calculations without having to buy another program. For quick calculations, you can use the calculator provided with WordPerfect Library or the calculator macro (CTRL-C) included as part of the MACROS keyboard. See "Keyboard Layout" in this chater for details.

Keystrokes

The following are the basic steps for using the Math feature, which are described in more detail in the next sections:

1. Set tabs for each column.

2. Enter titles for the columns if applicable.

3. Define the math columns.

4. Turn on Math.

5. Enter text, numbers, and math operators. (An operator is the symbol that indicates the type of calculation to be performed.)

6. Calculate.

7. Turn off Math.

Set Tabs for Each Column

1. Press Format (SHIFT-F8).

2. Choose 1 for **Line**, and then type 8 to set **T**abs. See "Tabs" in this chapter if you need further assistance in setting tabs.

3. When you are finished, press Exit (F7).

The first tab setting is considered the first column. You can enter text at the left margin, but any numbers entered there will not be considered during calculation.

You do not need to set decimal tabs for numeric columns, because you can use the Math definition to decide which columns should be aligned at the decimal point. Be aware that when you set tabs for numeric columns, the decimal point will be placed at the tab setting.

Be careful to set tabs so that text or numbers will not overlap from one column to another. When setting the tab closest to the right margin setting, allow enough room at the right margin for any calculations so that they will not wrap to the next line.

Headings for the Columns

You can type headings for each column. It is important to enter the headings before turning on Math, or the letters "T," "t," and "N" will not print. (As explained later, these characters are considered math operators if they are found in a numeric column.) You can always wait and enter the headings after you have typed the columns so that you can better estimate their placement. Just be sure to place the cursor before (to the left of) the [Math On] code.

Define Math

You can define Math as many times as you want to in a document. You can even define Math more than once between a [Math On] and [Math Off] code if you need different parts of the same section to be calculated differently.

1. Press Columns/Tables (ALT-F7). The following one-line menu is shown:

```
1 Columns; 2 Tables; 3 Math: 0
```

2. Choose 3 for Math. The options available for the Math feature are displayed as shown below:

```
Math: 1 On; 2 Off; 3 Define; 4 Calculate: 0
```

3. Choose 3 for Define. The menu shown in Figure 3-108 is displayed.

4. Use the arrow keys to move to the items that need to be changed, and enter the new values. The following discussion contains detailed information about each option.

Each tab setting is considered a column. The left margin (even though there may be a tab setting in the same position as the left margin) is not considered a column. You can have up to 24 columns. As you can see in the menu shown in Figure 3-108, each column is "numbered" from "A" through "X." The attributes (type of column, how negative numbers are to be displayed, and the number of digits to be displayed to the right of the decimal point) are listed below each column.

Type of Columns   There are four types of columns: text, numeric, calculation, and total. You can use up to 4 of the 24 columns for calculations. Numeric is the default type for all columns.

A text column can contain text or numbers and is not considered in calculations. If you have a column that contains the date or item numbers (1, 2, 3, and so on), define it as a text column.

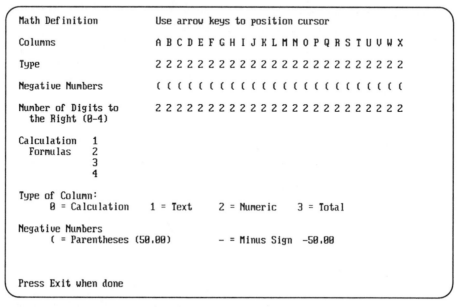

Figure 3-108.   Math Definition menu

You cannot combine WordPerfect's Newspaper or Parallel Columns feature with the Math feature; if there is more than one line in a column, you will have to wrap each line manually or use the Tables feature.

If you choose to have a calculation column, the cursor is placed at "Calculation Formulas." You can then enter a formula, using letters to indicate specific columns, numbers, and the following operators, which are used to perform the calculation:

+	Add (as in A + B)
−	Subtract (as in A − B − C)
*	Multiply (as in B * 1.06)
/	Divide (as in C/3)

You can combine as many operators as you want. Calculations are made from left to right unless you enclose part of the formula in parentheses. If parentheses are found, the calculations within the parentheses are performed first, from left to right. If you want to use a fraction, you will need to enter (for example, .75) its decimal equivalent.

If you include the calculation column in the calculation itself, the number from the previous line in that column will be used. See "Applications" for an example of how to use this feature.

You can also use the following operators alone in a calculation column. You cannot use them with any other letters, numbers, or operators. The first two deal with numeric columns, and the last two deal with total columns.

+	Total of all numeric columns
+/	Average of all numeric columns
=	Total of all total columns
=/	Average of all total columns

A total column uses the numbers from the column to the left and those above in the same column to calculate subtotals, totals, and grand totals. Column 3 in Figure 3-109 is a total column.

If you type **t** or **T** at the beginning of a number, it identifies the number as a subtotal or total that has been entered manually and is used in the final calculation. An **N** is used to indicated that a number should be subtracted.

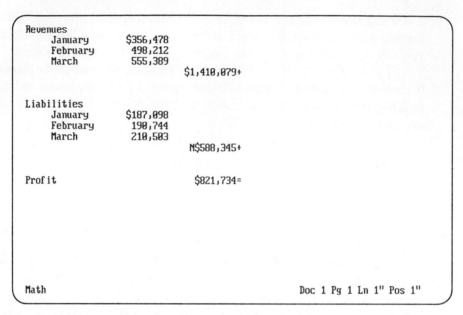

Figure 3-109.   Example of a total column in column 3

Numbers in numeric, total, and calculation columns are automatically aligned at the decimal point when you press TAB. A [DEC TAB] code (meaning a decimal tab) is inserted.

Negative Numbers   You can manually enter a negative number with a minus sign (−), enclose it in parentheses ( ), or type **N** before the number. However, WordPerfect needs to know how to display negative numbers after they are calculated. You can either use the default (enclosing a negative number in parentheses) or change it so that it is displayed with a minus sign (−).

This option is included so that the results in calculations can match your style of entering negative numbers. You cannot use the N as an option in this menu, because it is used to indicate that the number immediately following it should be negative in the following totals.

Number of Digits to the Right   You can manually enter any number with as few or as many digits to the right of the decimal point as you want, but only the first four will be considered in any calculation.

The Number of Digits to the Right option is used to determine how many digits will be displayed for a calculated result. Numbers can be rounded to the fourth digit.

Turning Math On

1. After making changes to the Math Definition menu, press Exit (F7). A [Math Def] code is inserted at that point, and the original one-line menu is displayed again.

2. Choose 1 to turn On Math. "Math" is displayed in the lower left corner of the screen, and a [Math On] code is inserted.

Enter Text, Numbers, and Math Operators

1. Press TAB to enter the text or numbers in each column. Notice that numbers are automatically aligned at the decimal point and text is aligned at the left.

   If you have a calculation column, pressing TAB will insert an exclamation mark (!). This mark indicates that WordPerfect will perform the calculation for you. The ! is considered a code and will not be printed.

2. Enter additional math operators if you want subtotals, totals, or grand totals calculated down the columns. Again, these operators will not print and are displayed on the screen to indicate that WordPerfect is calculating those particular numbers and that they were not entered manually.

The following is a list of operators that you can use to produce a total:

+	Subtotal	Adds numbers listed above that were not previously summed. If found in a total column, a + will add the numbers from above and to the left.
=	Total	Adds all subtotals above that were not previously totaled. If found in a Total column, an = will add the subtotals from above and to the left.

*	Grand Total	Adds all totals above that were not previously totaled. If placed in a total column, an * will add the totals from above and to the left. If more than one "+," "=," or * is found in the same column, the totaling will not overlap. Instead, it will total only the numbers from that code to the next.

Use the following operators if you want to insert an additional subtotal or total in a column manually:

t	Subtotal	t$45.00
T	Total	T$1,299.76

These numbers are included in total calculations, as previously described. If you want to force a number to be a negative number without typing the − or ( ) symbol, you can type **N** before the number, as in **n$52.10**. A minus sign and parentheses will print, whereas the letter "N" is considered a math operator and will not print. The N operator is especially useful when you need to force a number to be negative when it is a positive result of a WordPerfect calculation. The example in Figure 3-109 shows how a positive total can be used as a negative in further calculations.

Calculate

1. Press Columns/Tables (ALT-F7).

2. Choose **3** for **M**ath.

3. Choose **4** for Calculate.

If you have changed any of the numbers in the math section, recalculate so that all the calculations will be updated. If calculations are not performed properly, check the operators in Reveal Codes (ALT-F3), and make sure that they are shown in boldface and in brackets. If they are not, they will be considered characters, and you will need to reenter them.

Turning Math Off

This step is not necessary if the entire document is a math document. However, if you intend to continue with a regular document, turn off Math where appropriate.

1. Press Columns/Tables (ALT-F7).

2. Choose 3 for Math.

3. Choose 2 to turn Math Off.

You can turn the Math feature on and off as many times in a document as you want. Use the previous Math Def code for future calculations, or define Math columns again.

Hints

It is not necessary to define columns if you have only numeric columns and are calculating totals down those columns. If you did not make any changes to the menu, all calculations will be rounded to two digits to the right of the decimal, and negative numbers will be displayed within parentheses.

Aligning on a Different Character

Numbers are automatically aligned on a decimal point, but you can change the alignment character before the math portion of the document. For example, if you want to align numbers on a comma (European format), define that character (or any other character) as the alignment character.

1. With the cursor above the math portion of the document, press Format (SHIFT-F8).

2. Choose **4** for **Other**.

3. Choose **3** for **Decimal/Align** Character and Thousands' separator.

4. Type a comma (,) or another character for the decimal/align character and a period or another character for the thousands' separator.

5. Press Exit (F7) to return to the document.

The code [Decml/Algn Char:*n*,*n*] is inserted into the document and is used to align all numbers in numeric, total, and calculation columns.

Applications

The Math feature is best used when you need to do simple calculations for invoices and statements or when you find it necessary to insert a calculated table of figures into a document.

You can use the following checkbook-type example to register debits and credits in one column and have a running total in the next column:

Number	Date	Description	Debit or Credit	Balance
				453.25
101	11/25	Architect	(200.00)	253.25
102	11/30	Charge card payment	(125.88)	127.37
--	11/30	Deposit--paycheck	1,350.00	1,477.37
103	12/2	Christmas gifts	(98.62)	1,378.75

The following instructions assume that you are entering format settings in inches:

1. Set tabs for each column. Remember that you do not have to make the last two columns decimal tab settings if you don't want to, because the Math feature automatically aligns numbers on the decimal point. See "Tabs" in this chapter if you need assistance.

2. Enter the headings for each column, as shown in the example.

3. After pressing ENTER once or twice (depending on whether or not you want space between the headings and the columns), press Columns/Tables (ALT-F7), choose 3 for **Math** and then choose 3 for **Define.**

4. Without moving the cursor, type **1, 1, 2,** and **0** to indicate the types of columns being used (text, text, numeric, and calculation). Remember that the column at the left margin is not considered a column.

5. After you type the **0** for calculation, you are placed in the area for specifying the formula. Enter **c-d.** When you enter the letter of the calculation column in the formula (the letter "d" in this case), Word-Perfect uses the number from the previous line in that column for the calculation.

6. Press Exit (F7) to leave the Math Definition menu, and choose **1** to turn Math **On.**

7. Press TAB four times to reach the "Balance" column. A ! will be inserted in that column. Press BACKSPACE to delete it, and enter the beginning balance.

8. Enter several sample entries, and remember to place parentheses around debits. (You can also type a minus sign before a number to indicate that it is a debit.) Press TAB to go to the fourth column each time so the ! will be inserted. Do not enter a number; it will be calculated later.

9. When you are ready to calculate, press Columns/Tables (ALT-F7) and choose 3 for **Math** and then 4 for Calculate.

As you enter new entries or make changes, you can repeat the last step to calculate the current balance at any time.

Debits and credits can also appear in separate columns. If column C were used for credits, column D for debits, and column E for the balance, the calculation formula would be $C - D + E$. This would also eliminate the need to enclose a negative number in parentheses or precede it with a minus sign.

Related Entries

Addition
Spreadsheet Importing and Linking
Tables

MENU OPTIONS

The Menu Options screen under Display in Setup (SHIFT-F1) lets you choose how the menu selections will be displayed. For example, Word-Perfect has assigned a number and a letter to each menu option. In most cases, the letter assigned is the first letter in the first word. For example, "m" is used for margins, "t" for tabs, "s" for spacing, and so on. WordPerfect automatically displays the mnemonic choice in boldface. If you do not care for the mnemonics, you can return the display to normal or change it to a different attribute such as underline.

Other options let you decide how the menu bar and pull-down menus will be displayed on screen (colors, bold, underline, and so on).

Other options let you decide if you want the ALT key to bring up the menu bar or if you want to display it at all times (instead of pressing ALT-= or the right button on a mouse).

Keystrokes

1. Press Setup (SHIFT-F1) and choose **2** for **D**isplay.

2. Choose **4** for **M**enu Options. The menu shown in Figure 3-110 appears (the first option in the menu is usually displayed as Bold instead of Strikeout).

3. Choose any options that you want to change. If you choose options 1, 2, 3, 5, or 6, you can choose any of the attributes that you can normally choose when you press Font (CTRL-F8), as shown below.

```
1 Size; 2 Appearance; 3 Normal: 0
```

The Size menu lets you choose from Large, Extra Large, Small, and others, while the Attributes selection lets you choose from Bold, Underline, Redline, Strikeout, and so on. Normal is also available.

```
┌─────────────────────────────────────────────────────────────┐
│  Setup: Menu Options                                         │
│                                                              │
│      1 - ▟enu Letter Display          ▐SUPRSCPT▌             │
│  Pull-Down Menu                                              │
│      2 - ▟ull-Down Letter Display     REDLN                 │
│      3 - Pull-▟own Text               SHADW                 │
│      4 - ▟lt Key Selects Pull-Down Menu No                  │
│  Menu Bar                                                    │
│      5 - Menu Bar ▟etter Display      REDLN                 │
│      6 - Menu ▟ar Text                SHADW                 │
│      7 - Menu Bar ▟eparator Line      No                    │
│      8 - Menu Bar Remains ▟isible     No                    │
│                                                              │
│                                                              │
│  Selection: 0                                                │
└─────────────────────────────────────────────────────────────┘
```

Figure 3-110.   Menu Options in Setup

Options 4, 7, and 8 are yes/no questions and decide if the menu bar should be displayed when you press ALT by itself, if it should have a line separating it from the text, or if it should appear at the top of the screen at all times.

4. Press Exit (F7) when you are finished.

Hints

The attributes that you choose for each of the options in the menu reflect what you have set up in the Colors/Fonts/Attributes section of the Setup menu. For example, if Extra Large is displayed in orange on your screen, choosing Extra Large for one of the menu options will cause it to be displayed in orange as well.

If you have a color monitor and want a certain color, make a note of the attribute using that color and select that attribute. If you have a Hercules Graphics Card with RamFont, you can choose one of the fonts for the mnemonic choice; extra large or underline are suggestions.

If you are using an EGA or VGA monitor, you can have underline, italics, or small caps if you want to give up 8 of the 16 available colors. You can also use these attributes for the menu letter display if you have selected them. See "Colors/Fonts/Attributes" in this chapter for information about changing the colors, fonts, and screen attributes.

Related Entries

Colors/Fonts/Attributes
Menus and Messages
Mouse Support

MENUS AND MESSAGES

WordPerfect offers two types of interfaces: pull-down menus and the use of function keys. If you are familiar with versions of WordPerfect previous to version 5.1, you may want to continue using the function key interface because it may be faster. The pull-down menus are advantageous if you enjoy using a mouse or are new to WordPerfect (you do not need to have a mouse to use the pull-down menus). See "Pull-Down Menus" and "Mouse Support" in this chapter for more information about using this type of interface.

Whether you use the pull-down menus or function keys to choose a feature, you will be placed in the same WordPerfect menus or will see the same prompts. This section discusses how to work with those menus, prompts, and messages.

Mnemonic Choices

WordPerfect uses numbers *and* letters for each item on a menu (including the options on the pull-down menus). For example, you can type **m** instead of **7** for Margins if you find that easier. Some menus have more than one feature starting with the same letter. In that case, the second letter or a letter with a prominent sound in the word is chosen. Word-Perfect tries to keep that same mnemonic selection for different menus. For example, you can always type **Y** when choosing Hyphenation—whether it is in the Line Format menu or the Setup menu.

The mnemonic letter choice is displayed in bold on the screen. See "Menu Options" in this chapter if you want to change the screen attribute, color, or font used to display the mnemonic choice or if you want to return it to "Normal" so that the mnemonic choice is not displayed.

Some menus offer more than nine choices. In such cases, letters are used instead of numbers (usually the same letter as the mnemonic choice) so that you can press a single key to select an option. This could not be done if you had 10, 11, and so on in the menu, because you would have to type the numbers and press ENTER to indicate that you were finished.

Prompts and Messages

If you press Save (F10), Search (F2), Macro (ALT-F10), List (F5), or other similar keys, you are prompted for more information. "Document to be saved:," "Srch:," "Macro:," and "Dir C:\WORK" are among the prompts that appear.

Some prompts display an "answer" that you can use, edit, or change. For example, if you have done a search and press Search (F2) again, the last search string is displayed. If you have previously saved a document and you press Save (F10), the name of the document is displayed.

You can press ENTER to accept the displayed characters, or you can enter something completely different. If you begin typing, the previous string is cleared and the new one is entered. If you press a cursor key first, you can edit the string of characters by adding and deleting text where necessary. For example, if you press List (F5) and you see "Dir C:\LETTERS," you can press the right arrow key or END to go to the end of the string and add *.JCN to list only those files ending with a .JCN extension in the C:\LETTERS directory.

Yes/No Questions

WordPerfect displays the safest answer as the default to any Yes/No question. For example, if you press Exit (F7), you will see the following:

Save document? Yes (No)

The default answer is shown first. The other option is shown in parentheses. You can either move the mouse pointer to one of these options and click the left button, or you can type **Y** or **N**.

Because Yes is the default answer, you can type any key except **N** to save the document. This includes ENTER, the space bar, or even Exit (F7). You would have to specifically type **N** or choose it with the mouse to avoid saving the document.

Exiting a Menu

All menus have a default answer for most options. Most show a 0 as the default option, which means that you can exit by pressing ENTER, the space bar, ESC, Exit (F7), Cancel (F1), or any other key that is not listed as an option on the menu. For example, you could even type **M** to leave a menu if it is not listed as an option.

Some menus, such as Column Definition and Math Definition, require that you press Exit (F7), because ENTER is used to enter values into the menu. You can press Cancel (F1) to leave any menu without making changes or inserting codes in the document. You cannot use ENTER to leave the List Files menu, because the Look option is the default selected.

Inserting Codes and Changing Modes

Most menu options insert a code into the document. Some insert an "On" code and change the mode of operation, as with the Columns, Math, and Hyphenation features. You can choose another option to insert an "Off" code and return to the standard settings. Some keys only change the mode, as with INS or CAPS LOCK.

If codes are inserted, those codes will affect text from that point forward in the document. Therefore, it is important to note the location of the cursor before you enter a menu and make a change. See Chapter 2, "WordPerfect Basics," for more information about how WordPerfect is designed.

MERGE

You can use WordPerfect's Merge feature to merge two or more documents. You can merge a list of data (referred to as a secondary merge file) with form letters, mailing labels, or envelopes (referred to as a primary merge file). Merge can assist you in filling out preprinted forms or compiling a document from standard paragraphs already saved to disk.

A merge can use files from previous versions of WordPerfect, DOS text delimited files that were created with other programs (such as dBASE or other database programs), or data that has been sent to the Clipboard (only applicable if you have WordPerfect Library or Office).

If you are using files from WordPerfect 4.2 or an earlier version, they will need to be converted to WordPerfect 5.1 format. To do so, retrieve the file into WordPerfect 5.1 and then save the file. Files from version 5.0 do not have to be converted.

If you have used a previous version of WordPerfect, you may be accustomed to pressing CTRL-D to insert a ^D (used during a merge to insert the date) or any other CTRL key to insert other merge codes. You can still use these combinations if you feel more comfortable with them.

How Merge Works

There are three elements to a merge: the primary file(s), the secondary file(s), and the merged file that results. The primary file is the "form" that contains merge codes. These codes indicate what information is to be merged into the document at that point. Figure 3-111 shows an example of a form letter that contains the merge codes that will be used to retrieve the name and address from a secondary file during the merge.

The secondary file contains the data to be merged into the primary file, as shown in Figure 3-112. This file usually contains a list of names, addresses, or information about an account, but it can contain any type of information. The list is divided into records (imagine each person having a record) and each record is divided even further into fields (the name, address, and phone number could be three fields in that record). Note that {END FIELD} and {END RECORD} codes are used to divide the fields and records. You will learn how to create this type of file later. You do not always need a secondary file, because the merge can pause for "input" from the keyboard, a delimited DOS text file, or text from the Clipboard (if you are using WordPerfect Library or Office).

When you press Merge/Sort (CTRL-F9), you are asked to enter the name of the primary file (form) and secondary file (data). WordPerfect retrieves the primary file to the screen, opens the secondary file, and positions the cursor on the first record. WordPerfect scans the form (primary file) for merge codes; when it finds one, it inserts the appropriate data. When WordPerfect reaches the end of the primary file and all merge codes have been processed, a hard page code is inserted, the pointer goes to the second record in the secondary file, and the same primary file is retrieved. The process is repeated until the end of the secondary file is reached or until another secondary file is specified.

```
{DATE}


{FIELD}First Name~ {FIELD}Last Name~
{FIELD}Address~
{FIELD}City~, {FIELD}State~  {FIELD}ZIP~

Dear {FIELD}First Name~:

Thank you for your interest in our products. We have enclosed a
brochure which lists each of the items we sell, along with their
wholesale and suggested retail price.

Please let us know if we can help fill your order in the near
future.

Sincerely,




                                        Doc 1 Pg 1 Ln 1" Pos 1"
```

Figure 3-111.   A form letter used as the primary file in a merge

Keystrokes

The following is divided into different sections describing how to create a primary file, a secondary file, and how to merge the two.

Creating a Secondary File

The file containing the data, such as names and addresses, is referred to as the secondary file in a merge. It contains records (imagine each person as having a record) with each record divided into pieces of information called fields. For example, a record might contain the following fields:

Fields	Example
Name	Joe Jones
Address	456 Springwood Drive Lincoln, NE 95672

```
{FIELD NAMES}First Name~Last Name~Address~City~State~ZIP~Phone~~{END RECORD}
================================================================================
Bob{END FIELD}
McDowell{END FIELD}
4567 N. Viewcrest{END FIELD}
Kalamazoo{END FIELD}
MI{END FIELD}
59595{END FIELD}
(555) 232-2398{END FIELD}
{END RECORD}
================================================================================
Linda{END FIELD}
Sullivan{END FIELD}
23 E. Center Street{END FIELD}
Fort Sutter{END FIELD}
CA{END FIELD}
12891{END FIELD}
(112) 555-1234
{END RECORD}
================================================================================
Bart{END FIELD}
Johnson{END FIELD}
Crestview Apartments, #12{END FIELD}
Oklahoma City{END FIELD}
                                        Doc 1 Pg 1 Ln 1" Pos 1"
```

Figure 3-112.   A sample list of names and addresses used as the secondary file in a merge

Fields	Example
Phone Number	(101) 555-9999
Date of Birth	11/25/55
Social Security Number	090-09-0909

You can divide the address even further into more fields:

Field	Example
Street Address	456 Springwood Drive
City	Lincoln
State	NE
ZIP Code	95672

Before entering the information into a file, determine how many fields you will have and what information will fit into each field. To help you decide if a field should be separated into smaller fields (such as "Name" into "First Name" and "Last Name"), ask yourself if you would ever want to use the information in a field by itself. You might also want to use the Sort feature to sort records by the information in a particular field, such as "Last Name" or "ZIP Code". If so, place that information in a field by itself, or use it in a consistent location (always as the last word in the third line of the address). Remember that when you are merging, you can combine the information from several fields later.

If you don't have information for one of the fields (for example, you may have a "Company" field, but some people in your list are not associated with a particular company), leave the field blank and end it with a single {END FIELD} command. Keep the order and number of the fields consistent from record to record.

As you are entering each field, WordPerfect will display the field number in the bottom left corner of the screen. If you would rather be prompted with the field's name, you can use the {FIELD NAMES} command to tell WordPerfect the name of each field; it will then prompt you with those names instead of numbers. If you don't want to be prompted with the field name, you can skip the first four steps. If you do not assign names to the fields, however, you will need to use the field's number instead.

1. Press Merge Codes (SHIFT-F9). If you are using a mouse or the pull-down menus, you will find Merge Codes under Tools. See "Mouse Support" for more information.

2. Choose **6** for **More**. If you are using the keyboard instead of a mouse, you can press Merge Codes (SHIFT-F9) again so you don't have to remember which option to choose from the menu.

You will see a list of merge codes in the upper right corner of the screen. Type **field names** to move the cursor to that point in the list. The screen should look like the one shown in Figure 3-113.

3. Press ENTER to select the command.

4. As you are prompted for each field, type the name of the field and press ENTER. When you are finished, press ENTER again to discontinue the prompts. Your screen should look something like this:

```
{FIELD NAMES}First Name~Last Name~Address~City~State~ZIP~Phone~~{END RECORD}
=================================================================================
```

Note that WordPerfect inserts a tilde (~) to separate each field. The entire statement is ended with two tildes (~~) and an {END

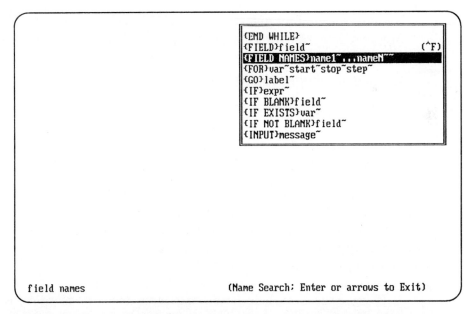

Figure 3-113.   The Field Names merge command among the list of merge commands

RECORD} command. If doing so would make it more readable, you can move past each tilde and press ENTER. The same list would then look like the following:

```
{FIELD NAMES}First Name~
Last Name~
Address~
City~
State~
ZIP~
Phone~~{END RECORD}
=============================================================================
```

You can edit this list of fields as you would any other type of text. If you add or delete fields, be sure to type a tilde (~) to separate them. If you edit the list, go to the beginning of the file (press HOME, HOME, ↑) before entering new records so that the new list of field names will be displayed on the status line.

5. Type the information for the first field (a field can include any number of lines and hard returns [HRt]), and press End Field (F9). The code {END FIELD} is inserted.

6. Continue until all fields in the record have been entered. Press Merge Codes (SHIFT-F9), and choose 2 for End Record. An {END RECORD} code and hard page break are inserted.

7. Continue until all records have been entered into the file.

8. Save the file and clear the screen.

Creating a Primary File

You can merge the information from a secondary file into any type of format. The primary file decides what the format will be. You can create form letters, memos, envelopes, labels, invoices, and many other types of documents to use in a merge. The following steps give you the instructions needed to set up a simple form letter:

1. If you need to include formatting codes (such as margins, tabs, font changes, and so on), insert them as initial codes for the docu-

ment so they won't be included in every copy of the form letter (and thus reduce the size of the resulting merged document).

To insert formatting codes in the Initial Codes section of the document, press Format (SHIFT-F8) and choose **3** for **Document**. Choose option **3** to change the Initial Base Font if necessary, and then select option **2** for Initial Codes and enter the margins, tab settings, justification, hyphenation, and other codes there. Press Exit (F7) until you return to the document.

You can use the {LABEL} and {GO} commands to eliminate the problem of duplicating formatting codes (see "Hints" for information about using these commands). Another option is to do the merge and *then* add the formatting commands to the beginning of the file.

2. Move the cursor to the point at which you want the date inserted. Press Merge Codes (SHIFT-F9) twice to display the list of merge commands. Type **date** to move to that command in the list. Press ENTER to insert the {DATE} command into the document.

3. Press ENTER four times to move the cursor to the point at which you want the inside address printed.

4. Press Merge (SHIFT-F9). The following options are displayed:

```
1 Merge; 2 Sort; 3 Convert Old Merge Codes: 0
```

5. Choose **1** for **Merge**. The following options are displayed:

```
1 Field; 2 End Record; 3 Input; 4 Page Off; 5 Next Record; 6 More: 0
```

6. Choose **1** for **Field**. The other options are explained later.

7. Enter the number (or name) of the field from the secondary file. For example, if the first field in the secondary file is "First Name," enter **1** or **first name**. The {FIELD} command will appear with the field name or number and will end with a tilde, as shown here:

```
{DATE}



{FIELD}First Name~
```

8. Continue creating the document and inserting each field at the correct location until it looks something like the one shown previously in Figure 3-111. You can use a field more than one time, and you can use fields in any order.

9. Save the file and clear the screen.

Merging the Two Documents

1. With a clear screen, press Merge/Sort (CTRL-F9).

2. Choose **1** for Merge.

3. When prompted, type the name of the primary file (the name of the form or main document indicating where the fields are to be inserted) and press ENTER.

You can also press List (F5) and ENTER to display the List Files menu for the default directory. Move the cursor to the desired filename and choose **1** to **R**etrieve it as the primary file.

If you have WordPerfect Library or Office and you have a document in the Clipboard that is to be used for the primary file, press Shell (CTRL-F1).

4. Enter the name of the secondary file (containing the list of names and addresses). You can press List (F5) and select a file from the List Files menu, or press Shell (CTRL-F1) to use the contents of the Clipboard.

If you enter the name of a delimited DOS text file, you will see a menu asking you to confirm the field and record delimiters (characters or codes used to separate fields and records). For more information about using DOS text files, see "Hints."

5. When the merge is finished, the cursor will be at the bottom of the document. If you need to insert formatting codes, return to the beginning of the document and do so. Print the document and clear

the screen. It is not advisable to save the merged document, because it will take up valuable disk space and can easily be merged again if necessary.

Stopping a Merge

If you have started a merge but want to stop the process, you can press Cancel (F1). If you or someone else has placed a {CANCEL OFF} merge command in the file, disabling the use of the Cancel key, you can press CTRL-BREAK to stop the merge.

If the merge pauses and is waiting for information, pressing Cancel (F1) will work as an Undelete key and will let you restore text that has been deleted instead of ending the merge. In that situation, you can press Merge Codes (SHIFT-F9) and choose **3** for Stop. If you choose Quit, the remaining part of the unmerged primary file will be displayed on the screen.

Simple Merge Options

This section gives several examples and applications for merge. All commands found on the Merge Codes (SHIFT-F9) key are also described throughout this section.

Envelopes or Labels

If you want to create envelopes or mailing labels from the information in your secondary file, follow these steps:

1. Create a primary file similar to the one shown in the following illustration. Do not enter any formatting codes at this time.

```
{FIELD}First Name~ {FIELD}Last Name~
{FIELD}Address
{FIELD}City~, {FIELD}State~  {FIELD}ZIP~
```

2. Press Merge/Sort (CTRL-F9) and choose **1** for **Merge**. Enter the name of the primary file that you just created and then the name of the secondary file containing the names and addresses.

3. When the merge is finished, move the cursor to the beginning of the document.

4. Press Format (SHIFT-F8), and choose **2** for **Page**. Choose **7** for Paper Size/Type. If you will be printing envelopes, select an envelope form. If one is not already defined, choose the option to add it to the list and then select it.

   If you are printing labels, choose a form that has labels defined. If one does not exist, add one to the list and select it. If you need assistance in defining a Labels form, see "Labels" in this chapter for step-by-step instructions.

5. If you have selected a Labels form, you can skip this step, because it is not necessary to change the margins or define columns first.

   If you have selected an Envelope form, you will want to change the margins so that the address will print in the correct location. Change the left and right margins by choosing the Line option on the Format (SHIFT-F8) key. You can change the top and bottom margins by choosing the Page option, also found on the Format (SHIFT-F8) key. The suggested margins for a standard, business-size envelope are as follows:

   Left = 4.5"
   Right = 1"
   Top = 2.5"
   Bottom = .5"

6. Print the envelopes or labels, and clear the screen.

Merging with Information from the Keyboard

At times you will want the merge to pause at a certain location in the document so you can type the information at that time. This type of feature is useful when you are filling out a form, creating a quick memo (pausing for the To: and From: information), or when you are inserting a unique piece of information into a form letter. In fact, you can use merge without having a secondary file at all. Instead, the primary file would contain {INPUT} merge commands that would cause the merge to stop at that point, prompt you for the necessary information, and wait for you to enter text from the keyboard.

This command is similar to the {INPUT} command in a macro. The only difference is that the merge command waits for you to press the End Field (F9) key before continuing with the merge, whereas the macro command waits for you to press the ENTER key before continuing with the macro. If you find it inconvenient or awkward to press the End Field (F9) key each time, you might want to consider using a macro for the application.

To insert the {INPUT} command into your primary file, follow these steps:

1. Move the cursor to the point at which you want the merge to stop and let you enter information.

2. Press Merge Codes (SHIFT-F9).

3. Choose 3 for Input.

4. When prompted, enter the message (up to 59 characters) that you want to have appear at the bottom of the screen during the merge.

Save the document, clear the screen, and start the merge. When the merge stops, enter the necessary information (you can also retrieve another document at this point), and press End Field (F9) to continue.

If you want to use merge to insert information for a preprinted form, trying to place the prompts in the proper location can be frustrating. The best solution is to measure the form with a ruler and then use the Advance feature to advance to a specific horizontal and vertical position. See "Advance" in this chapter for more information.

If you have multiple-line entries (such as an address) at the left side of the form, you can enter each line of the address and press End Field (F9) when you are finished. However, if a multiple-line entry occurs at a location other than the left margin, you can choose one of the following options:

• Advance down to the proper line (the distance from the top edge of the form), set a tab at the correct horizontal position, and then use →Indent (F4). This option is best for entries that end at or near the right margin.

• If a multiple-line entry needs to be placed somewhere between the left and right margin, you can advance down to the proper line and then set the margins accordingly. On the next line, you can reset the margins back to the normal setting.

Boilerplating

Some refer to the ability to create a document from several previously saved standard paragraphs as "boilerplating." When you are creating a document, you can always press Retrieve (SHIFT-10) and enter the name of the document to be retrieved at that point. You can merge several documents with this method.

If you want to automate the process, you can use the {INPUT} command throughout the primary file, where the different files should be retrieved. When you start the merge and it pauses for information, press Retrieve (SHIFT-F10), and enter the name of the file to be retrieved.

If you want the paragraphs to be automatically numbered as they are brought in, include a [Par Num:] code at the beginning of the paragraph that is saved to disk. They will all display the same number in their own file, but when they are retrieved into the completed document, they will be numbered appropriately. See "Paragraph Numbering" in this chapter to learn how to insert a paragraph number and change the numbering style.

Sounding a Bell During a Pause

If you want to alert the person doing the merge that it has stopped and is waiting for them to enter information, you can add the {BELL} command just before the {INPUT} command.

1. Press Merge Codes (SHIFT-F9) twice.

2. Type **B** to move to that point in the list, and press ENTER to select the {BELL} command.

Creating a List

When WordPerfect merges two documents, it normally takes the first record from the secondary file, merges the information from each field into the specified location in the primary document, inserts a page break, and continues.

If you do not want to have a page break inserted between each record, but want a list of records on the same page, you can use the {PAGE OFF} command at the beginning of your document. (This command replaces the ^N^P^P codes used at the end of primary files in previous versions of WordPerfect.)

1. Press Merge Codes (SHIFT-F9).

2. Choose 4 for **P**age Off to insert the {PAGE OFF} command.

3. Insert the {FIELD} commands, specifying where the information from each field is to be inserted. Your primary file could look something like this:

```
{PAGE OFF}
{FIELD}Last Name~, {FIELD}First Name~              {FIELD}Phone~
```

When you merge the files, you will not get a page break between each record.

Adding a Title to the List

The above example will work as long as you don't put a title in the primary file or headings at the top of each column. If you do, you would get a document that includes the title or column headings between each record. This happens because the entire primary file (title and all) is being duplicated for each record.

To alleviate the problem, you can use the {GO} and {LABEL} commands. You would place these commands after the title, in the following manner:

TITLE

```
{LABEL}Top ~
{FIELD}Name ~                               {FIELD}Phone ~
{NEXT RECORD}
{GO}Top ~
```

The {LABEL} command lets you name a specific location in the document so that other commands can refer to that location. The {GO} command tells WordPerfect to go to a named location. In this example, the merge "retrieves" the title and merges the name and phone number from the first record. The {NEXT RECORD} command tells Word-Perfect to position the cursor on the next record in the secondary file. The {GO} command then tells it to go to a place named "Top." The merge then returns to the place in the document that you have named "Top" and repeats the merge, this time using the information from the next record. This continues until all the records from the secondary file have been used. Because the title is not included in this loop, it will not print with each record.

These commands are also useful if you want to include all formatting codes at the beginning of the document but don't want them included with each merged record.

To access the {LABEL} and {GO} commands, press Merge Codes (SHIFT-F9) twice, move to the commands in the list, and press ENTER to select the command. Enter the label when prompted. To insert the {NEXT RECORD} command, press Merge Codes (SHIFT-F9) and choose **5** for Next Record.

"Not Enough Memory" Error Message

When you are merging large documents or are using secondary files that have a large number of records, you may get the error message "Not Enough Memory." This means that there is not enough room in memory (or on the hard disk) for the merged file.

You can remedy this problem by using the {PRINT} command at the end of your primary file. This instructs WordPerfect to print each "document" as it is merged (you would normally wait until the merge is finished and then print the entire file at once).

If you use this command, you must place a {PAGE OFF} command *before* the {PRINT} command, or you will get a blank sheet of paper between each record.

1. Retrieve the primary file, and press HOME, HOME, ↓ to move to the end of the document.

2. Press Merge Codes (SHIFT-F9) twice.

3. Type **print** to move to that point in the list, and press ENTER to select the {PRINT} command.

If you prefer, you can press CTRL-T (^T) as you did in previous versions of WordPerfect.

Hints

The examples and explanations in the previous section should help you tackle the more common merge applications. If you want to include prompts, error checking, conditional merging, branching, and looping to accomplish more sophisticated tasks, see Chapter 6, "Advanced Macro and Merge Commands," for more information. You will also learn the similarities and differences between macros and merges, and how each can best be used in a particular situation.

When you are creating the secondary merge file, do not include extra spaces, blank lines, or hard page breaks. If you do, Merge (and Sort) will not perform properly.

When you are creating the primary document, it is easy to forget the number of a field from the secondary file. Therefore, it is advisable to use the {FIELD NAMES} command. You can also retrieve the secondary file into document 2 so that you can switch between the two documents — press Switch (SHIFT-F3) — or you can split the screen by pressing Screen (CTRL-F3), choosing **1** for Window, and then entering the number of lines for the current window (entering **11** would divide the screen equally). You can then view the fields in the secondary file on the same screen while you are creating the primary file.

Eliminating Blank Lines

When you are specifying the field to be merged, type a **?** after the field name or number so that if that field is empty, a blank line will not be printed.

Remember, however, that **?** was designed to be placed in a field that is on a line by itself. If you follow it with other fields or text, they will be deleted. If you need to have more text on the line, you could use the {IF NOT BLANK} merge code to print the field only if it is not blank. See Chapter 6 for more information about using this and other advanced merge codes.

Selective Merging

Although WordPerfect includes many advanced merge commands for conditional merging, you can use WordPerfect's Sort feature to sort and select specific records to be included in the merge. See "Sort and Select" in this chapter for details.

The Notebook included with WordPerfect Library can do a simple sort and will let you select the records to be merged either manually or with selection criteria.

Using Data from Other Software Programs

As was mentioned, you can use information from other sources for the merge. The following is a discussion of some of the available options:

WordPerfect Files   You can merge files from any version of Word-Perfect. You can also mix versions (a primary file created in 4.2 and a secondary file from 5.0, for example). If you want to use a file from version 4.2 or earlier, you will need to retrieve the document into WordPerfect and save it as a 5.1 document.

The "control-type" merge codes (such as ^D, ^O, and ^C) are still supported and do not need to be converted. However, if you prefer the new commands, you can convert the old commands to the new format by pressing Merge (CTRL-F9) and choosing **3** for **C**onvert Old Merge Codes.

DOS Text Files   Many database and spreadsheet programs can save a report to disk with delimiters (separators) between each field and record. This type of file is often referred to as a delimited DOS text file and might look like this:

> Robert S. Johnson,3550 E. Oak,Monticello,VA,48484
> Susanne Rae Victor,5 Mountainway Dr.,Sunnyvale,CA,33343
> Richard Kinross,234 N. Center St.,Cedar Hills,UT,23090

Note that a comma separates each field, and each line (record) ends with a hard return (carriage return/linefeed).

When you are asked for the name of a secondary file, you can enter the name of a delimited DOS text file. WordPerfect will automatically display a menu (as shown in Figure 3-114) so you can verify the field and record delimiters.

```
Merge: DOS Text File

     1 - Field delimiters  - Begin
                             End

     2 - Record delimiters - Begin
                             End        [CR]

















  Selection: 0
```

Figure 3-114.   Menu showing field and record delimiters

If the delimiters need to be changed, choose **1** for Field delimiters or **2** for Record delimiters, and enter the characters. To enter a linefeed [LF] code, press ENTER. You can insert a carriage return [CR] code by pressing CTRL-M.

You can enter the beginning delimiter as well as the ending delimiter. If you have quotation marks around fields, you can enter them as the beginning delimiters. You would also add a quote (") just before the comma for the ending delimiter so that it would appear as ",.

Press ↓ instead of ENTER to move to the ending delimiter. If you use ENTER, you will insert a linefeed [LF] code. This is different from most WordPerfect menu options.

If you have a DOS text file that contains ^Rs and ^Es, WordPerfect will assume that it is a WordPerfect 4.2 file and will retrieve it normally. If it is a DOS text file and happens to include ^Rs and ^Es, you can press Text In/Out (CTRL-F5) to override the detection of ^Rs and ^Es, and use it as a DOS text file. Press Text In/Out (CTRL-F5) when you are prompted for the secondary file. When doing so, you will be prompted for the name of the "DOS Text delimited file." After you enter the name of the file, WordPerfect will let you verify the field and record delimiters before it continues with the merge.

WordPerfect assumes that a comma separates each field and a carriage return (CR) separates each record. If you have a program that uses other delimiters, and you don't want to change them in the menu each time you merge with a DOS text file, you can enter them in the specific setup menu so that those delimiters always appear as the default. To do so, follow these steps:

1. Press Setup (SHIFT-F1).

2. Choose **4** for Initial Settings.

3. Choose **1** for Merge.

4. Choose **1** for Field Delimiters or **2** for Record Delimiters, and enter them.

5. Press Exit (F7) when you are finished.

The new delimiters that you just entered will always appear in the menu when WordPerfect asks you to verify the delimiters for a DOS text file.

Using "Notebook"   If you have WordPerfect Library or Office, one of the smaller programs included with that package is Notebook. This program is a simple database program that you can use to create and manage secondary merge files.

You can set up the fields and enter the data as you would in a database program. Each field is labeled on a type of "form," making it easy to move from field to field. The most convincing reason to use Notebook, however, is that it automatically stores the records and fields in the correct format. You can then use the file without converting it.

You can do a merge with any file created with Notebook. You can also mark specific records within those files with an asterisk (*) and save them to a separate file or to the Clipboard so that they can then be used in the merge. When asked for the name of the secondary file, you can press Shell (CTRL-F1) and the contents of the Clipboard will be used.

You can also write a shell macro to enter Notebook, pause so that you can mark a name, and start a merge with that record. (Shell macros are like WordPerfect macros, but they are available with WordPerfect Library or Office, and you can use them to help with integration between programs.)

If you are using Library 1.1, you will need to retrieve the Notebook file into 5.1 and then save it as a 5.1 document before you can use it in a merge.

Information from the Clipboard

As was just mentioned, if you have WordPerfect Library or Office, you can use information previously saved to the clipboard as a primary file or secondary file. This lets you merge information from other types of programs without first saving it as a WordPerfect file.

For example, you can send a file or a report from PlanPerfect, Notebook, or DataPerfect (or any other program that supports Word-Perfect Library) to the Clipboard to be used as the secondary file. Because you can use a shell macro across applications, you can start one program from the shell, enter the conditions upon which to search (all those living in Maryland, for example), send the resultant file to the Clipboard, enter WordPerfect, and start the merge using a primary file on disk and the information from the Clipboard as the secondary file.

Spreadsheets or Other Database Programs   If you already have lists of records created with another program and they cannot be used as delimited DOS text files (such as a DIF spreadsheet file), use the Convert program to convert the file into a secondary merge file. See "Convert Program" in this chapter for more information.

Merge versus Macros

Many of the same applications can be done using either a merge or a macro. Both can be used to set up formats and pause for information. A macro records keystrokes, whereas a merge combines text from a number of sources.

It does not usually matter whether you use a merge or a macro for a particular application. For example, you can create a memo with either feature. Merge lets you pause by using the {KEYBOARD} command, while a macro uses the {PAUSE} command. However, you need to press End Field (F9) to continue a merge after a pause, whereas pressing ENTER continues a macro.

Although both features are useful for repetitive tasks, a macro records keystrokes and a merge compiles text. In the above example, the macro would have recorded every keystroke it took to create the memo format and would have stored it in a file with a .WPM extension. If you want to edit the form, you need to edit the macro. When the macro is started, it will insert the keystrokes as they were stored and pause for the necessary information.

The Merge feature uses a regular WordPerfect file. If editing changes are necessary, you can retrieve the file and make the changes as you would in any other file. When a merge is started, it calls up that file as the "primary" file and uses the merge commands to tell it what other text to use or retrieve into certain locations.

A merge cannot send a "Go" to the printer. You can, however, record those keystrokes in a macro and use the {NEST MACRO} or {CHAIN MACRO} command to tell the merge to start that macro at a certain point. A macro can only merge text by retrieving sections of text into a single document. However, a macro can store the keystrokes that *start* a merge. By combining the two features, nearly any type of application is possible.

If you are familiar with the advanced macro commands that were introduced in version 5.0, it should be easy for you to create some complex and powerful merge applications with the advanced merge commands. Many of the commands are the same, some with subtle differences. See Chapter 6, "Advanced Macro and Merge Commands," for a list of commands and how they can be used.

Error Messages

If you get an error message such as "Not enough room on WP disk to retrieve text," "Not enough memory," or "WP disk full -- Strike any key to continue," the merged document is too large to fit into memory and into the extra space on the WordPerfect disk reserved for virtual files. If this happens, you can try several things:

- Use Block (ALT-F4) and Save (F10) to save sections of the secondary merge file into separate files. You can then merge each of these smaller files separately with the primary file.

- Use the {PAGE OFF}{PRINT} merge code at the end of the primary file. As each record is merged, it is sent directly to the printer, the screen is cleared, and the process begins again. The only drawback to using these commands is that both the computer and the printer are tied up, and no other operation is possible until the merge is finished. If you need to interrupt the merge, you can press Cancel (F1).

- Increase the amount of memory or disk space. Since WordPerfect will use up to 64K for document 1 and 32K for document 2, make sure that you use document 1 when merging so you can have the maximum amount of memory available.

Related Entries

Convert Program
Envelopes
Labels
Macros

Paragraph Numbering
Sort and Select
See also Chapter 6, "Advanced Macro and Merge Commands"

MERGE CODES

You enter the codes to be used in a merge document with Merge Codes (SHIFT-F9). See "Merge" in this chapter for more information.

MERGE/SORT

You can use Merge/Sort (CTRL-F9) to start a merge or to use the Sort feature. The Merge and Sort features are associated because you can use Sort first to sort and select the records to be merged. See "Merge" and "Sort and Select" in this chapter for details.

MINUS KEY

The minus key on the keyboard is used as a required hyphen in Word-Perfect. To get a minus (negative) sign or a dash, press HOME, hyphen.

See "Dashes" and "Hyphenation" in this chapter for more information.

MODE COMMAND

MODE is a DOS command that you can use if you are having difficulty with colors not holding in WordPerfect. Some programs change the mode from CO80 (color, 80 columns) to BW80 (black and white), because they cannot run in color. These programs might not return to the original mode and thus would not allow WordPerfect to display colors.

Keystrokes

From DOS, enter **mode co80**. If you see the message "File not found," copy the MODE.COM file from the original DOS disk to the hard disk or boot disk. If colors are displayed upon entering WordPerfect, you have corrected the problem. If this does not work, check the switches on the graphics adapter card. The system board might also have switches that need to be set for color.

Hints

Consider placing the MODE CO80 command in a batch file that starts WordPerfect. You can also place it at the end of the batch file used to start another program that changes the mode.

Related Entries

Colors/Fonts/Attributes

MODEMS

You can send WordPerfect files with a modem.

Keystrokes

You can send a WordPerfect file over a modem in binary format or DOS text (ASCII) file format. If you use the latter format, all WordPerfect codes will be stripped from the file. The following steps help you convert the files so they can be sent intact.

Convert Program

If you want to send a file that contains WordPerfect codes over a 7-bit modem or communications line, all codes will be stripped because they use 8 bits. If you want to keep the codes, use the Convert program to convert the file to 7-bit format before sending it. The recipient of the file must then convert it back to WordPerfect format through the Convert program.

1. Start the Convert program from DOS. If you are not sure about the exact steps, see "Convert Program" in this chapter.

2. Enter the name of the file that you want to convert.

3. Enter the name of the file that will hold the converted data. If the file exists, you will be asked if you want to replace the original file. Type **Y** or **N**.

4. If you are converting from WordPerfect to 7-bit format, choose **1** for WordPerfect and then **6** for Seven-Bit Transfer Format. To convert a file back to WordPerfect format, choose option **7** from the Main Convert menu. No other information is needed to perform this conversion.

DOS Text (ASCII) File

You can strip out all WordPerfect codes by saving the file as a DOS text (ASCII) file.

1. Press Text In/Out (CTRL-F5).

2. Choose **1** for DOS Text.

3. Choose **1** to Save the file.

4. Enter the name of the file. Be careful not to overwrite the original WordPerfect file if you do not want it replaced.

Print to Disk

Some codes that are stripped contain text, such as headers, footers, and footnotes. If you want to retain all the text, print the file to disk. Step-by-step instructions are included under "Print to Disk."

Edit the printer selection, and change the port to be used for printing. When you see the port choices, choose **8** for **O**ther, and then enter the filename to be used to receive the "printed" file. Be sure to include the drive and directory so that you will know where it will be saved.

It is also best if you select the DOS Text Printer definition (return to the Install program and do so if necessary) so that no extra printer codes will be included with the text. See "Print to Disk" in this chapter for details.

After selecting the printer definition to be used for printing to disk, retrieve the file, press Print (SHIFT-F7), and choose 1 to print the Full document. It will be printed to the file that you specified when you chose the port.

Related Entries

DOS Text Files
Print to Disk
Selecting a Printer

MOVE

You can use the Move (CTRL-F4) key to move or copy text, such as a sentence, a paragraph, or a page. You can also use Move (CTRL-F4) to move or copy a highlighted block of text, a tabbed column, or a rectangular section of text. If you have an enhanced keyboard, you can highlight the text and then use two shortcut keys: press CTRL-INS to copy or CTRL-DEL to move the block of text.

You can also delete any amount of text and then use Cancel (F1) to undelete the text in a new location. The keystrokes that follow cover all methods for moving or copying text.

Keystrokes

Move (CTRL-F4)

Use Move (CTRL-F4) by itself if you want to move or copy a sentence, a paragraph, or a page.

1. Position the cursor in the sentence, paragraph, or page to be moved, and press Move (CTRL-F4).

2. Choose **1** for **S**entence, **2** for **P**aragraph, or **3** for **P**age. The appropriate section of text is highlighted.

3. Choose **1** to **M**ove or **2** to **C**opy the section. Option 3 will **D**elete the highlighted block, and option 4 will let you **A**ppend the highlighted section of text to a file on disk.

   If you choose to move the highlighted text, it will be deleted from the screen; if you choose to copy the text, a copy is made. The following prompt then appears at the bottom of the screen:

```
Move cursor; press Enter to retrieve.              Doc 1 Pg 1 Ln 1" Pos 1"
```

4. Move the cursor to the new location, and press ENTER to retrieve the text.

If you find that you need to make editing changes before reaching your destination, you can press Cancel (F1) to remove the prompt. You can then press ENTER, and it will not retrieve the moved or copied text. When you are ready to retrieve the text, press Retrieve (SHIFT-F10), and then press ENTER when you are asked for the filename (do not enter a filename). See "Hints" for other alternatives.

Block (ALT-F4)

You can highlight any amount of text with Block (ALT-F4) and then move or copy the text with Move (CTRL-F4).

1. Position the cursor at one end of the text to be moved or copied.

2. Press Block (ALT-F4).

3. Move the cursor to the opposite end of the block. You can also press any character key to highlight text to the next occurrence of that character, press the space bar to highlight to the next space, press ENTER to highlight to the next [HRt] code, or press PGDN to highlight to the next page.

4. Press Move (CTRL-F4).

5. Choose **1** for **B**lock.

6. Choose **1** for **M**ove or **2** for **C**opy.

7. Move the cursor to the location at which the moved or copied text is to be retrieved, and press ENTER.

If you have an enhanced keyboard, you can eliminate steps 4 through 6 by pressing CTRL-INS to copy the highlighted block, or press CTRL-DEL to move the highlighted block. If you do not have an enhanced keyboard, you can write a macro that includes the command {Block Move} or {Block Copy} to do the same thing. Another option is to assign these commands to a key. See "Macros" or "Keyboard Layout" in this chapter for specific instructions.

You can press Cancel (F1) so that pressing ENTER will not retrieve the moved or copied text. You can then retrieve the text by pressing Retrieve (SHIFT-F10) and then ENTER. See "Hints" for other alternatives.

Restore Deleted Text with Cancel (F1)

A simple way to move text is to delete it, move the cursor to a new location, and undelete it there. Be aware, however, that you can restore only the last three deletions. Be cautious when you are using this method.

1. Delete any amount of text.

2. Move the cursor to a new location.

3. Press Cancel (F1). The last deletion is displayed and highlighted.

4. Choose **1** to **R**estore the text.

If necessary, choose **2** to see the **P**revious Deletion. Because you can restore only the last three deletions, you may want to restore the deleted text immediately.

Move or Copy a Tabular Column

Use the following steps only for tabbed columns (columns separated with [Tab], [DEC TAB], or [→Indent] codes). If you want to delete text from parallel or newspaper columns, use the regular Block Move method just described. See the next section for details about moving text in a rectangle (from one corner to another).

1. Move to the first character in the column to be moved or copied.

2. Press Block (ALT-F4) to turn on Block.

3. Move straight down the column if only that column is to be affected. If you want to move or copy more than one column, move the cursor to the right into the applicable column(s). At this point, it will not seem that the proper text is being highlighted, as shown in Figure 3-115; be patient until the next step.

4. Press Move (CTRL-F4) and choose **2** for Tabular Column. The column is now highlighted, as shown in Figure 3-116. Note that the [Tab] codes preceding each line in the column are also highlighted as part of the column. If you moved the cursor into columns to the right when you were defining the block, those columns will also be highlighted.

```
                    PHONE DIRECTORY


        Employee                Title                Phone

   Jeanette Alexander      Claims Processor          392-6767
   Gern Blanston           Assistant Manager         223-7675
   Ted Blumenthall         Production Supervisor     549-2920
   Susan Broadbent         Customer Service          392-1392
   Ned Finney              Director of Development    374-8475
   June Hill               Executive Secretary       443-2827
   Chris Nichols           Customer Service          328-8759
   Ben Richards            Exec. Vice President      290-4985
   Julie Ross              Claims Processor          239-5489
   Gloria Rubenstein       Customer Service          484-9439
   Norrin Shepard          President                 549-9398
   Nina Turpin             Legal Secretary           394-9238
   Gary Wagner             Customer Service          395-9838




   Block on                              Doc 1 Pg 1 Ln 4" Pos 3.5"
```

Figure 3-115.   First step of highlighting a tabbed column to be moved or copied

5. Choose **1** for **M**ove or **2** for **C**opy. Option **3** will **D**elete the column(s), and option **4** will **A**ppend the column(s) to a file on disk. If you chose to move or delete the column(s), the remaining columns are moved to the left to fill the void. If you do not want the columns at the right to be moved to the left and fill the void, use the option to move or copy a rectangle instead. These steps are covered in the next section.

6. Move the cursor to the left margin, after the last column, or just after the last character in the column to the left of where the column(s) should be retrieved and press ENTER.

Remember that a [Tab] code was included as part of the column. If you retrieve a column at the left margin, it will be retrieved at the first tab setting. Delete the [Tab] code at the beginning of each line if necessary to move the column to the left margin.

If you want to retrieve the column(s) later, you can press Cancel (F1) to remove the Retrieve prompt from the screen. When you are ready to

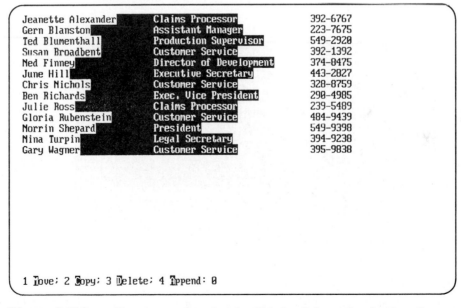

Figure 3-116.   The screen after choosing Tabular Column showing how the column and the tabs before the column are highlighted

retrieve the column(s), position the cursor, press Move (CTRL-F4), choose **4** for **R**etrieve and then **2** for Tabular Column.

Move or Copy a Rectangle

You can move or copy a rectangle, which is defined as a block of text from the top left corner to the bottom right corner.

1. Place the cursor at one corner (the upper left or bottom right), and press Block (ALT-F4).

2. Move to the opposite corner. A regular block is highlighted until the next step.

3. Press Move (CTRL-F4) and choose **3** for **R**ectangle. The screen will appear as shown in Figure 3-117.

4. Choose **1** for **M**ove or **2** for **C**opy. You can use option **3** to **D**elete the rectangle, or you can use option **4** to Append the rectangle to a file on disk.

```
Jeanette Alexander    Claims Processor        392-6767
Gern Blanston         Assistant Manager       223-7675
Ted Blumenthall       Production Supervisor   549-2920
Susan Broadbent       Customer Service        392-1392
Ned Finney            Director of Development  374-8475
June Hill             Executive Secretary     443-2827
Chris Nichols         Customer Service        328-8759
Ben Richards          Exec. Vice President    290-4985
Julie Ross            Claims Processor        239-5489
Gloria Rubenstein     Customer Service        484-9439
Morrin Shepard        President               549-9398
Nina Turpin           Legal Secretary         394-9238
Gary Wagner           Customer Service        395-9838




1 Move; 2 Copy; 3 Delete; 4 Append: 0
```

Figure 3-117. A highlighted rectangle

If you included the [Tab] codes before or after a rectangle (if you are working in columns), all remaining columns are moved to the left. If not, the space remains vacant.

5. Position the cursor anywhere on the screen, and press ENTER to retrieve the rectangle at that point. If necessary, WordPerfect inserts spaces so that the format of the rectangle is retained.

If you prefer, you can press Cancel (F1) to remove the Retrieve prompt from the screen. When you are ready to retrieve the rectangle, position the cursor, press Move (CTRL-F4), choose 4 for **R**etrieve and then 3 for **R**ectangle.

Hints

Moved and copied text is saved to the same unnamed temporary file. The section of text remains there until another section of text is moved or copied, letting you retrieve it in several places. This is useful if you chose 1 for **M**ove instead of 2 for **C**opy. You can immediately retrieve the text back into the original location and then move to the new location and retrieve it again. This feature is also useful if you need to retrieve several copies of a certain block of text onto the screen.

Text that is deleted is kept in a separate place (buffer) from text that is moved or copied. You can use both features to move two separate sections of text without overwriting one or the other.

If you prefer, you can retrieve a moved or copied block of text by pressing Retrieve (SHIFT-F10) and then ENTER. This retrieves the "unnamed" block in memory that is used to store the moved or copied text. You can only use this option to retrieve a normal block of text, a sentence, a paragraph, or a page. You cannot use it to retrieve a tabular column or a rectangle, because the text for each type of operation is kept in separate temporary files.

If you delete a block, a tabular column, or a rectangle with option 3, **D**elete, you can restore the text by pressing Cancel (F1) in another location. However, the block, tabular column, or rectangle will not be inserted correctly as it would if you had used the Retrieve Tabular Column option or the Rectangle option. If you chose the Delete option accidentally, you can restore text at the left margin and then move or copy it as a tabular column or rectangle.

If you choose the option to append, you are asked for the name of the file to which the text should be appended. If you enter the name of a file that does not exist, one will be created with that name.

The amount of text that you can move or delete and restore is limited only by the amount of disk space available.

If you want to remember only one method for moving or copying, use the Block method. If the cursor is at the beginning of a sentence, a paragraph, or a page, you can press Block (ALT-F4) and type a period (.) to highlight the sentence, press ENTER to highlight a paragraph, or press PGDN to highlight the page.

If you press Switch (SHIFT-F3), you can retrieve a second document into memory. After choosing to move or copy text, you can press Switch (SHIFT-F3) again and retrieve the moved or copied text into the other document.

Move (CTRL-F4)

When you are using Move (CTRL-F4) alone, a sentence is defined as a block of text from the first letter in a sentence up to and including at least three spaces after a period (.), a question mark (?), or an exclamation mark (!). (However, there are usually only one or two spaces at the end of a sentence.)

A paragraph is defined as a block from one [HRt] code up to and including the next [HRt] code. A single line or sentence preceded and followed by a [HRt] code can be considered a paragraph. Note that only the ending [HRt] is included with the paragraph.

A page is defined as a block of text from one hard page [HPg] break or soft page [SPg] break, up to and including the next hard or soft page break. Only the ending page break is included with the page.

Block (ALT-F4)

If you highlight a block of text, you can press Save (F10) and then press ENTER to save the block of text to the same unnamed block used for moved and copied text. Another way to retrieve the unnamed block is to press Retrieve (SHIFT-F10) and then ENTER.

Restore Deleted Text

Any group of consecutive deletions is considered a single deletion. You can press Delete Word (CTRL-BACKSPACE), DEL, Delete to End of Line (CTRL-END), and BACKSPACE, and they would all be considered one deletion. The single deletion is stored in memory as soon as you press any other nondeleting key.

If you press BACKSPACE or DEL and encounter a code that needs confirmation before it can be deleted, you can type **Y** and the deletion continues. If you skip over the code without typing **Y**, the consecutive deletion ends at that code.

Columns and Rectangles

If you want to move a column but leave the space empty, use the Rectangle option without including the [Tab] codes before or after the column.

If you do not plan to include the [Tab] codes, the last line in the rectangle must be the longest line in the rectangle, or at least as long as the longest line. If this is not the case, you will need to add spaces to the last line to make it the longest.

Line Draw

When you draw a box with Line Draw, you can create it at the left margin first and then use the Move Rectangle method to move it anywhere on the screen. This method can also be useful if you are creating an organizational chart with several boxes and want to copy the box to different locations on the screen.

If you have a rectangular piece of a formula to remove, you can cut or delete the rectangle, and the rest of the formula will be readjusted to fill the vacant space.

Related Entries

Append
Block
Cancel
Columns
Copy
Switch
Undelete

MOUSE SUPPORT AND PULL-DOWN MENUS

WordPerfect 5.1 includes mouse support and pull-down menus, which may make it easier for a beginner to find features that may otherwise seem hidden on a function key. You use the mouse to select options from any of the menus, block text, position the cursor, and scroll through the document. If you do not have a mouse, you can still use the pull-down menus by pressing other keys on the keyboard.

Keystrokes

If you have not already selected the mouse from within WordPerfect, as explained in Chapter 1, "Installation and Setup," see "Setting Up the Mouse" under "Hints."

As soon as you move the mouse, a reverse video block called the mouse pointer appears on the screen. The pointer is used to point to items that need to be selected or blocked and to mark the location to which you want the cursor moved (instructions are given here). If you move the mouse accidentally and the block appears on the screen, press any key and the block will disappear.

Pull-Down Menus

1. Click the right mouse button to display a menu bar across the top of the screen, as shown here. If you click the right button again, the menu will disappear.

```
┌──────────────────────────────────────────────────────
│ ▐File▌ Edit Search Layout Mark Tools Font Graphics Help
```

If you do not have a mouse, you can press ALT-= to display the menu bar. Pressing ALT-= again removes the menu bar.

2. Move the mouse pointer to the proper category, and click the left button to display the pull-down menu. You can also type the mnemonic (**E** for Edit, **L** for Layout, and so on), or you can use the arrow keys to move across categories and then press ↓ to move into a pull-down menu.

Figure 3-118 shows an example of a pull-down menu. For a list of features under each category shown on the menu bar, see "Hints."

Instead of moving to an item and clicking the left mouse button, you can hold down the left button while dragging the mouse. When you release the left button on a menu item, that item is selected. By holding down the left button and dragging the mouse, you can move across the menu bar to display each pull-down menu

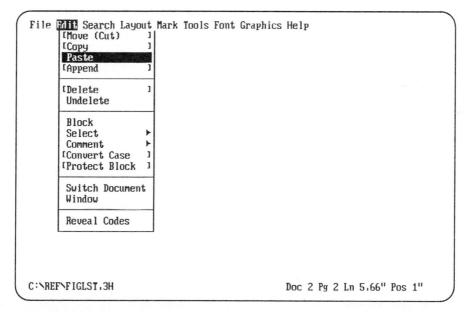

Figure 3-118.   Sample pull-down menu

as the pointer reaches it; this may help you find a feature more quickly if you don't know the appropriate category. If you are dragging the mouse and decide that you do not want to select an option, move the mouse pointer so that it is not on an item, and then release the left button.

3. To make a selection, move the mouse pointer to the desired feature and click the left mouse button. To exit a menu, click the right mouse button. (After you use the right button to display the menu bar, you can use it as the EXIT key.)

Some pull-down menu options are displayed in brackets, such as [**M**ove] and [**C**opy]. You cannot select these options unless Block is on. (If Block is on, the features that cannot be used with Block are shown in brackets.)

You can also use the cursor keys to move from one menu to the next, or you can type the mnemonic letter (usually displayed in bold) for the desired feature.

See "Hints" for other alternatives for displaying the menu bar and pull-down menus.

Menu Selections

After you select a feature from a pull-down menu, WordPerfect will most likely display a full-screen or one-line menu—the same one that appears when you are using the function keys. Exceptions to this are the Thesaurus, Switch, Window, and other features that take immediate action when they are selected.

Move the pointer to the desired selection on the menu, and click the left mouse button. If a question asks Yes or No, the cursor will be placed on the default answer. The alternative answer will be shown in parentheses. For example, if you select the Exit option from the File category, you are asked the following:

Save Document? Yes (**N**o)

If you choose **Yes** or press any key other than **N**, the document will automatically be saved.

Double Clicking to Select

In a list of items, clicking the left mouse button once will move you to the item but it will not select it.

In other situations, WordPerfect displays the name of a file when saving, or the name of the directory before entering the List Files menu. If you click the left mouse button while the pointer is on the name, the cursor will move to the position of the mouse instead of selecting it.

Instead of pressing ENTER to select the items from a list, to look into a file in the List Files menu, or to select the current filename or pathname, you can double-click the left mouse button (click twice quickly). This action is the same as clicking on the item once and pressing ENTER to select it.

Blocking Text

1. Move the mouse pointer to one end of the block, and press the left button on the mouse.

2. Hold the left button down while dragging the mouse pointer over the text to be blocked. Block will be turned on at that point, and the text will be highlighted.

3. Release the left mouse button. Block will stay on. If you want to cancel the block and turn off Block, click the left button again. (The right button will not cancel the block in this case; it will display the menu bar.)

If you need to adjust the size of the block after releasing the left button, you will either need to redefine the block or use the arrow keys on the keyboard to change the size.

4. Select an option for the block using the function keys, or click the right button to display the menu bar. Continue to move through the menus, and select an option with the left button as you would normally. Only the items that can be used with a block of text are selectable. Others (shown in brackets) are passed over as if they weren't there.

Once you have selected an item for the block, the block will no longer be highlighted and Block will be turned off.

Positioning the Cursor

One of the most useful features of the mouse is its ability to move the cursor to an exact position quickly. It is especially useful in columns or tables, where the keystrokes may seem somewhat complicated (for example, you need to press CTRL-HOME and then the right or left arrow to move from one column to the next). If you have split the screen so you can see two documents at once—Screen (CTRL-F3), option 1—you can use the mouse to move the cursor from one window to the other.

1. Move the mouse pointer to any location on the screen.
2. Click the left mouse button.

The cursor immediately moves to the new location.

Scrolling Through the Document

Normally the right button is used to display the menu bar. If the menu bar is already displayed, you can use the right button to exit menus.

To scroll through the document, however, you can hold down the right button on the mouse and move it in any direction. If the mouse pointer runs into the edge of the screen, the document begins scrolling. For example, if you hold down the right button and drag the mouse pointer to the bottom of the screen, it will continue to scroll through the document until you release the right button. This feature also applies to horizontal scrolling, which can be useful if your document is wider than the screen.

Hints

If you have a three-button mouse, you can use the middle button to cancel an action. If you have a two-button mouse, pressing the left and right buttons simultaneously will act as Cancel.

When you press Retrieve (SHIFT-F10), you will see the message "(**List Files**)" in the right corner. This message also appears when Word-Perfect asks you to enter a filename. You can press List (F5) to enter the List Files menu, or you can move the mouse pointer to "List" and click the left button.

If you are in the equation editor, you can use the mouse to make selections from the bottom of the screen. For example, you can click the left button on the word "List" to list the commands at the right. You can then click on PGUP or PGDN to view the categories of commands and symbols, and then double-click on the command or symbol of your choice.

Using the Pull-Down Menus Without a Mouse

If you do not have a mouse, or if you prefer using the keyboard, press ALT-=. The menu bar will appear, and you can use the arrow keys to move through the options. Pressing ← and → will display the pull-down menus to the left or right, and ↑ and ↓ will move the cursor from one item to the next within the pull-down menu.

Press ENTER to select an option, and press Cancel (F1) or Exit (F7) to back out of the menus.

Features on Pull-Down Menus

The features on the pull-down menus are grouped differently from those of the function keys. Table 3-15 shows each category on the menu and its features.

Setting Up the Mouse

Options found on the Setup menu let you select the type of mouse being used and make other selections that control the timing of menus, clicking, and moving.

Other options available on a different menu let you choose to have the ALT key bring up the menu bar, display the menu bar at all times, or separate the menu bar from the document with a double line.

1. Press Setup (SHIFT-F1).

2. Choose **1** for **M**ouse. The menu shown in Figure 3-119 appears.

3. Choose **1** for **T**ype. You will see a list of mouse drivers that are built into the WordPerfect program, as shown in Figure 3-120. Other mouse drivers may be added in the future.

The default selection is Mouse Driver (MOUSE.COM). The file MOUSE.COM is a mouse driver that comes on disk with your

File
Retrieve
Save
Text In
Text Out
Password
List Files
Summary
Print
Setup
Goto Shell
Exit

Edit
Move (Cut)
Copy
Paste
Append
Delete
Undelete
Block
Select
Comment
Convert Case
Protect Block
Switch Document
Window
Reveal Codes

Search
Forward
Backward
Next
Previous
Replace
Extended
Goto

Layout
Line
Page
Document
Other
Columns
Tables
Math
Footnote
Endnote
Justify
Align
Styles

Mark
Index
Table of Contents
List
Cross-Reference
Table of Authorities
Define
Generate
Master Documents
Subdocument
Document Compare

Tools
Spell
Thesaurus
Macro
Date Text
Date Code
Date Format
Outline
Paragraph Number
Define
Merge Codes
Merge
Sort
Line Draw

Table 3-15.   Pull-Down Menu Categories Listing Each Feature

Font	Graphics
Base Font	Figure
Normal	Table Box
Appearance	Text Box
Superscript	User Box
Subscript	Equation
Fine	Line
Small	
Large	**Help**
Very Large	Help
Extra Large	Index
Print Color	Template
Characters	

Table 3-15.   Pull-Down Menu Categories Listing Each Feature (*continued*)

```
Setup: Mouse

    1 - Type                          Mouse Driver (MOUSE.COM)

    2 - Port

    3 - Double Click Interval (1 = .01 sec) 70

    4 - Submenu Delay Time (1 = .01 sec)    15

    5 - Acceleration Factor            24

    6 - Left-Handed Mouse              No

    7 - Assisted Mouse Pointer Movement  No








Selection: 0
```

Figure 3-119.   Mouse Setup menu

```
Setup: Mouse Type

    CH Products Roller Mouse (PS/2)
    CH Products Roller Mouse (Serial)
    IBM PS/2 Mouse
    Imsi Mouse, 2 button (Serial)
    Imsi Mouse, 3 button (Serial)
    Kensington Expert Mouse (PS/2)
    Kensington Expert Mouse (Serial)
    Keytronic Mouse (Bus)
    Keytronic Mouse (Serial)
    Logitech Mouse (Bus)
    Logitech Mouse (Serial)
    Logitech Mouse, 3 button (PS/2)
    Microsoft Mouse (Bus)
    Microsoft Mouse (Serial)
  * Mouse Driver (MOUSE.COM)
    Mouse Systems Mouse, 3 button (Serial)
    MSC Technology PC Mouse 2 (Serial)
    Numonics Mouse (Serial)
    PC-Trac Trackball (Serial)



  1 Select; 2 Auto-select; 3 Other Disk; N Name Search: 1
```

Figure 3-120.   List of mouse types

mouse and will work just as well as any of the other drivers on the
list. However, if you want to save the amount of memory usually
taken by MOUSE.COM, and if you do not use the mouse with
another program, you can select a driver from within WordPerfect.
If you use the Mouse Driver option, you will have to load the
MOUSE.COM program before you start WordPerfect.

4. Move the cursor to the appropriate mouse driver, and choose **1** to
Select it. If you have a mouse that does not appear on the list, you
can check the documentation that came with your mouse to see if
you can select another driver.

    The menu lists some mice more than once, because of the way
they are attached to your computer. Choose the Serial option if the
mouse is connected to a serial port, or choose the Bus type if the
mouse is connected to its own bus card.

    You can also choose **2** for Auto-select to have WordPerfect
select the mouse driver that it thinks is appropriate. Option **3** for
Other Disk lets you look on another disk for a mouse driver (in case

WordPerfect or other companies provide additional mouse drivers in the future). **N** for **Name** Search lets you type the name of the mouse to move to that item in the list instead of using the cursor keys.

5. After selecting the type of mouse, you are returned to the Mouse menu. If you have a serial mouse, choose **2** for **Port** to select COM1, COM2, COM3, or COM4. Refer to your computer's documentation, or experiment until you find the right type. It will most likely be COM1 or COM2. If you have a bus-type mouse, the Port option is not applicable.

6. Choose **3** for **Double** Click Interval if you want to change the amount of time between two clicks so that WordPerfect will sense a double-click rather than two single clicks. (Remember that a double-click is the equivalent of clicking on an item and then pressing ENTER to select it.)

This option is helpful to people who are physically impaired and cannot double-click within the .70 (70/100ths or 7/10ths) of a second that is the current default. If you select items from the menu more quickly, you might want to reduce the amount of time so that two single clicks are not interpreted as a double-click. Enter this setting in one-hundredths of a second.

7. The items on the pull-down menus containing triangles have submenus. If you are holding down the left button and are dragging the mouse over the pull-down menus, and you encounter an item that has a right-pointing triangle, it displays the submenu within the default setting of .15 (15/100ths) of a second.

If you want to change the amount of time that it takes to display a submenu, choose **4** for **Sub-Menu** Delay Time, and enter a different number in one-hundredths of a second. If you find it annoying to have the submenus pop up while you are dragging the mouse, increase the delay time so that they won't be displayed immediately. If you want more response time, decrease the number.

8. Moving the mouse quickly makes it travel farther. If you want to increase the acceleration to make it move even more quickly (or decrease it so that it will not), choose **5** for **Acceleration** Factor, and enter a number from 1 to 1200 (the default setting is 24).

9. You can choose **6** for **Left-Handed Mouse** to switch the functions of the right and left mouse buttons. If you choose Yes for this option, the left button will display the menu bar, and the right button will be used to select options from the menus.

10. When a menu or option is displayed on the screen, the mouse pointer remains at its previous location, and you move it to the selection. If you want WordPerfect to move the mouse pointer automatically to the first selectable item on a menu, you can choose **7** for **Assisted Mouse Pointer Movement** and type **Y**. If you choose an option from a menu that then lists another set of choices, the mouse is moved to the first selectable item on that list.

The Assisted Mouse Pointer Movement helps those who feel uncoordinated using the mouse—it moves the mouse pointer for you. However, you may find that because the mouse pointer is moved for you, you may have to lift the mouse more often so that it does not move off the pad or table.

11. Press Exit (F7) when you are finished.

Another menu in Setup deals with the menu bar and pull-down menus.

1. Press Setup (SHIFT-F1), and then choose **2** for **Display**.

2. Choose **4** for **Menu Options**. The menu shown in Figure 3-121 appears.

3. You can choose options 2, 3, 5, and 6 to change the way the text and mnemonic selections are displayed on the screen. For example, the "F" is bolded in **File**, "E" in **Edit**, and so on. If you want to change the color, font (if you have a graphics card that supplies different screen fonts), or attributes (such as bold, underline, and redline), choose the text that you want changed and select the appropriate attribute. See "Menu Options" in this chapter for more information.

Options 4, 7, and 8 affect the way the menu bar and pull-down menus are displayed. If you want to have the ALT key select the pull-down menus, select option **4** and type **Y**. After you select this option, you can press ALT, and *then release it* to display the menu bar.

If you want a line to separate the menu bar from the regular text, as shown below, choose **7** and then type **Y**.

```
┌ File Edit Search Layout Mark Tools Font Graphics Help
│ ═══════════════════════════════════════════════════════
```

To have the menu bar displayed at all times, choose 8 and then type **Y**. This option is very useful if you have a mouse. If you are using the pull-down menus without a mouse, you will still have to press ALT-= to access the menu bar.

4. Press Exit (F7) when you are finished.

Defining Macros

When you are defining macros with a mouse, all selections are recorded as keystrokes, except when you use the mouse to position the cursor. For example, if you select the Search feature with the mouse, it will be inserted as the {Search} command in the macro. Macros defined with the mouse can be edited with the macro editor.

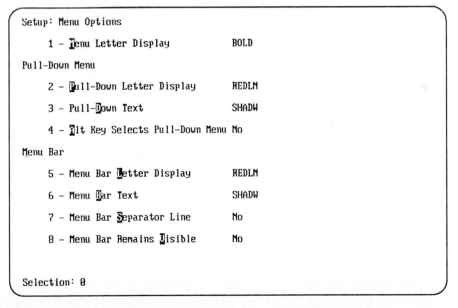

```
Setup: Menu Options
        1 - Menu Letter Display          BOLD
Pull-Down Menu
        2 - Pull-Down Letter Display     REDLN
        3 - Pull-Down Text               SHADW
        4 - Alt Key Selects Pull-Down Menu No
Menu Bar
        5 - Menu Bar Letter Display      REDLN
        6 - Menu Bar Text                SHADW
        7 - Menu Bar Separator Line      No
        8 - Menu Bar Remains Visible     No

Selection: 0
```

Figure 3-121.   Setup options for menu bar and pull-down menus

MOVING THE CURSOR

See "Cursor Keys" in this chapter.

MULTIPLE COPIES

You can specify the number of copies to be printed by pressing Print (SHIFT-F7) and typing **N** for **N**umber of Copies. See "Number of Copies" in this chapter for details.

Another option on the Print menu lets you have either WordPerfect or your printer control the number of copies that are printed. It is usually faster if the printer is in control. If you are on a network, you can let the network control the number of copies that are sent to the printer to increase the speed.

Keystrokes

1. Press Print (SHIFT-F7).

2. Choose **U** for **M**ultiple Copies Generated by.

3. Choose **1** for **W**ordPerfect, **2** for **P**rinter, or **3** for **N**etwork (if you are on a network). If you choose Printer and your current printer selection does not support this feature, the default will return to WordPerfect.

4. Choose **N** for **N**umber of Copies, and enter the number to be printed.

5. Print the document as you would normally.

Hints

The setting entered affects only the current document. If you want to change the setting permanently, you can do so in the Setup menu: press

Setup (SHIFT-F1) and choose 4 for Initial Settings, 8 for **Print** Options, and then **2** for **Number** of Copies/Multiple Copies Generated by.

If you let the printer or the network control the number of copies that are printed, all copies of the first page are printed first, and then all copies of the second page, and so on. This means that if you have a three-page document and ask for five copies, five copies of page 1 will print, and then five copies of page 2, and so on. If you let WordPerfect control the number of copies, they will be collated so that you can have pages 1 through 3 printed five separate times.

Related Entries

> Number of Copies
> Print

MULTIPLE PAGES

You can print specific pages from the document being edited. You do not have to save a document first and then print selected pages from disk.

Keystrokes

1. Determine which pages need to be printed before you follow the next steps.

2. Press Print (SHIFT-F7).

3. Choose **5** for **Multiple Pages**.

4. Enter the numbers of the pages to be printed, or press ENTER to print all the pages.

> To indicate a range of pages, type the beginning page, a hyphen, and then the ending page. If you are printing separate pages that are not in a range, separate them with spaces or commas. For example, you could enter **1-3, 6-10, 7** to print pages 1 through 3, 6 through 10, and 7. Entering **10-** would print from page 10 to the end of the document, and **-3** would print from the beginning to page 3.

Hints

If you have used the New Page Number feature to assign a particular number to a page, use the new page number (displayed on the status line) when you enter the pages to be printed.

If you have used the New Page Number feature several times throughout the document, you will need to tell WordPerfect which "section" is being used. For example, if you used the New Page Number feature three times, and three pages are numbered as "1," you can enter **3:1** to print the first page of the third section. If you have chosen to number the pages with a Roman numeral (i, iv, or xi, for example), those sections are considered separate from the regular sections in which Arabic numbers were used. For example, if you have an introductory section in the document that uses Roman numerals and the index also uses Roman numerals, but all the chapters between use Arabic numbers, you would enter **2:3** to print the third page of the index — not the third page of the first chapter after the introduction.

After sending the pages to the printer, you may see a message telling you that the document may need to be generated first and asking you to confirm that you want it printed. Type **N** if you want to return to the document and generate the table of contents, index, automatic references, or any other feature included on Mark Text (ALT-F5).

If you hear a beep, or if the printer is not printing, press Print (SHIFT-F7), choose **4** for Control Printer, and check the status of the printer. If it is waiting for a "Go," choose **4** for **G**o.

Related Entries

Print

NAME SEARCH

In the List Files menu and in other menus that list styles, fonts, and printers, WordPerfect includes a Name Search feature. You can type the name of the file, font, or printer, and the cursor will move directly to it without your having to move the arrow keys.

Keystrokes

If you see the Name Search option on a menu, you can access it by doing the following:

1. Choose **N** for **N**ame Search, or press Search (F2).

2. Choose the first character of the file, font, or printer. The cursor will move to the items that begin with that character.

3. Continue typing the name to narrow the selection.

4. To exit Name Search and return to the menu options, or to reset Name Search so you can try again, press ENTER or any arrow key.

Hints

The space bar will not reset the Name Search feature; you will need to press ENTER or any arrow key.

While entering a string of characters as part of a Name Search operation, you can press BACKSPACE to delete characters from the string, and the cursor will move back to the appropriate position in the list.

Applications

If you are defining a macro that selects an item from a list, use Name Search to go directly to that item, because the order and number of items in a list can change. After finding the item, press CTRL-ENTER if you want the macro to check if the item matches what you typed. You could then use the {ON NOT FOUND} macro command to check if the item really exists.

Related Entries

Fonts
List Files
Selecting a Printer
Styles

NETWORK SUPPORT

WordPerfect 5.1 includes the information needed to run WordPerfect on a network; you do not have to buy a separate "network version." You do, however, need to buy additional stations from WordPerfect Corporation so you can have a license to run WordPerfect on each station attached to the network.

When you install WordPerfect, an option on the menu appears for network installation. You are asked to select the type of network on which WordPerfect will be running and the directory in which the users' setup files will be stored. These instructions are all that are necessary to run WordPerfect on a network. See "Selecting a Printer" in this chapter if you need additional instructions about printing on a network.

Options

The following pages discuss other options that can help make using a network easier.

Username

If you are on a network, you are asked for a 3-character username each time you start WordPerfect. These characters are used to name your setup file (WP*xxx*}.SET, where *xxx* is the username), supplementary dictionary, and other files that are needed to run WordPerfect. Use the same three characters in the future so that you will always have the same setup selections (colors, mouse selection, location of files, and so on) and supplementary dictionary.

If you do not want to be prompted for the username each time you start WordPerfect, you can use the /u startup option. Enter this option as **wp/u-***xxx* where *xxx* is the 3-character username. You can also retrieve the AUTOEXEC.BAT file into WordPerfect, add the command **set wp=/u-***xxx*, and then save the file as a DOS text file with Text In/Out (CTRL-F5). See "DOS Text Files" if you need assistance. This command tells DOS that whenever you type **wp**, it should also include the command /u-*xxx*. You can then type **wp** in the future, without including the username.

Personal Settings

When you enter the username, a setup file is created so that each person can have his or her own default settings.

The file starts out containing defaults from the "master" setup file, including the printer selections, dictionary location, and format settings. You can override these settings by pressing Setup (SHIFT-F1) and choosing your own.

Universal Settings

Before anyone runs WordPerfect from the network, the network supervisor should select the network printers and decide any default selections for all users. As each new person starts WordPerfect for the first time, these settings are copied into their personal setup files.

If you need to make changes that will affect everyone on the network (such as changing the printer selections), follow these steps:

1. Change to the directory in which the setup files are stored (the same directory that you specified when you were installing Word-Perfect on the network). If you do not know the name of this directory, retrieve the file WP{WP}.ENV, note the directory after the /ps- command, clear the screen without saving the file, and then exit to DOS and change to that directory.

2. Start WordPerfect by entering **wp/u-{wp**. This option lets you access the "master" setup file, WP{WP}.SET.

3. Make any changes to the printer selections, the location of files, the initial codes, and other settings in the Setup (SHIFT-F1) menu.

4. Exit WordPerfect, and make sure that all other users have also exited.

5. Type **nwpsetup** to start the network setup program for Word-Perfect. If the file is not found, include the full pathname where the file can be found. The menu shown in Figure 3-122 appears.

6. Answer **Y** or **N** to each of the questions, depending on the type of information that needs to be updated in each user's setup file. You can also press Help (F3) for more information about each option.

7. After you have answered **Y** or **N** to each option, the process is started. If you do not have setup files in the current directory, an error message will appear telling you that none were found.

WP{WP}.ENV File

A network environment file is created during installation; it is called WP{WP}.ENV. This file contains the network number or letter that was selected during installation (for example, you would see /NT-1 if the

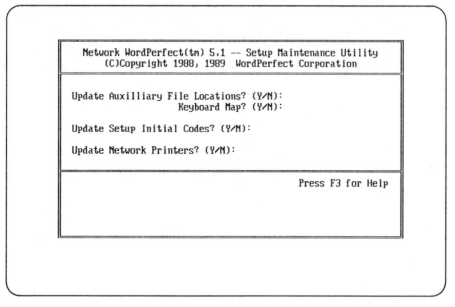

Figure 3-122.   The menu that appears when you run NWPSETUP, the network setup program

Novell NetWare option on the menu was chosen) and the directory in which the users' setup files will be stored (/PS-U:\USERS, for example). If this file is deleted, WordPerfect will not be able to run on the network, unless you start WordPerfect with the option **wp/nt-**n where n is the number or letter of the network.

You can change the commands in this file at any time by using Text In/Out (CTRL-F5) in WordPerfect to retrieve and save the file as a DOS text file.

The following is a list of networks and their corresponding numbers. Other networks may be added to this list in the future.

0 - Other
0 - Nexos
1 - Novell NetWare
2 - Banyan VINES
3 - TOPS Network
4 - IBM LAN Network
4 - LANsmart
4 - PC NOS
4 - Invisible Network
5 - Nokia PC-Net
6 - 3COM 3+
7 - 10NET
8 - LANtastic
9 - AT&T StarGROUP
A - DEC PCSA
B - 3COM 3+ OPEN

Running Stand-alone

If you need to run WordPerfect stand-alone (without using the capabilities of the network), you can start WordPerfect with **wp/sa**. Using this option, you are telling WordPerfect to ignore the presence of the WP{WP}.ENV file.

Other options that are unique to using WordPerfect on a network are discussed under their specific topics. For example, see "Selecting a Printer" in this chapter for information about selecting a network printer, or see "Retrieve" in this chapter for information about retrieving files that are being edited by other users.

Related Entries

> Retrieve
> Selecting a Printer
> Setup
> See Chapter 1, "Installation and Setup"

NEW PAGE

You can force a page break by pressing Hard Page (CTRL-ENTER). Otherwise, WordPerfect will break the page automatically when the bottom of the page is reached.

When working with columns, you also use Hard Page (CTRL-ENTER) to end one column and begin another.

See "Hard Page" in this chapter for more information.

NEW PAGE NUMBER

WordPerfect can be set to number pages automatically. However, if you need to assign a specific number to a page, you can choose the New Page Number option. This feature is also used to choose between Arabic or Roman numerals as the style for page numbering.

Keystrokes

1. Move the cursor to the beginning of the page that is to be renumbered. If it is the current page, press Go To (CTRL-HOME), ↑ to move to the top of the page.

2. Press Format (SHIFT-F8).

3. Choose **2** for **Page**.

4. Choose **6** for Page Numbering.

5. The current page number is displayed at the top of the menu. To change this, choose **1** for New Page Number.

6. Enter the new page number as a regular Arabic number (1, 2, and so on) or as a Roman numeral (i, ii, XVI, and so on). If you type the Roman numeral in uppercase or lowercase, the page number will be printed in uppercase or lowercase, respectively.

7. Press Exit (F7) when finished.

Hints

A [Pg Num:n] code is inserted into the document, where n displays the selected page number. If you enter iv as the new page number (in Roman numerals), the code will appear as [Pg Num:iv]. The new page number is reflected on the status line (shown in Arabic numbers only). You can always view the current style and number by repeating the steps above (do not choose option **1** for New Page Number unless you intend to change it, however). The code takes effect until a new code is encountered.

Printing with Renumbered Pages

When you print a file from disk, you can specify which pages are to print. Each time a new page number is assigned, WordPerfect considers it a "section." When entering the number of a specific page or pages to be printed, you can include the section, a colon, and then the page(s) found within that section. If you used Roman numerals, you can enter the page numbers in that format.

You can combine entries by separating them with a space or a comma. You can also specify ranges within or across sections. See "Print" in this chapter for details.

Page Numbers in Tables, Lists, and the Index

When you generate a table of contents, a table of authorities, lists, or an index, the page number where the entry is located is included. These features take new page numbers into account and display both regular Arabic numbers and Roman numerals when applicable.

If you insert several hard page breaks so that tables and lists will be generated on separate pages, those pages are also considered. If a new page number [Pg Num:] code is not found immediately after these extra pages, the numbers that are generated will not be accurate (unless, of course, you want the front matter to be included in consecutive numbering). In fact, when a Table of Authorities is generated, you will see a message warning you if a new page number was not found just after the Table of Authorities' definition mark. To remedy the situation, insert a new page number and generate the Table of Authorities again.

Applications

You can number introduction or front matter pages with lowercase Roman numerals. At the beginning of the first "real" page, you can insert another [Pg Num:] code, specifying that it should be considered as a new page 1 in the document and should be printed with regular Arabic numbers.

You can easily continue consecutive page numbering from one document to another using WordPerfect's Master Document feature. For example, you could have a regular file named BOOK and specify all the "subdocuments" that should be included in that document. You could specify INTRO, CHAPTER.1, CHAPTER.2, and so on as subdocuments by pressing Mark Text (ALT-F5), choosing 2 for Subdocuments, and then entering the name of the file that is to be included in the master document. When the master document is expanded and printed, the page numbering will continue from document to document as if they were one. A [PgNum:] code can be included in the master document or in any subdocuments; it will remain in effect until the next [PgNum:] code is encountered in any of the subdocuments.

If you do not use the Master Document feature but want to continue page numbering from one document to another, you can do so with the New Page Number option. For example, if you have two large documents and the first one ends with page 130, you can insert a new page number at the beginning of the second document to start with page 131. However, because of possible editing changes in the first file, you might have to update the page number at the beginning of the second file. Consider using the Master Document feature instead. See "Master Document" in this chapter for details.

Related Entries

Index
Lists
Master Document
Page Numbering
Print
Table of Authorities
Table of Contents

NEWSPAPER-STYLE COLUMNS

You can use the Columns feature to create newspaper-style columns or parallel columns. See "Columns" in this chapter for details.

"NOT ENOUGH MEMORY" ERROR MESSAGE

The error message "Not enough memory" may be displayed if you try to retrieve two large documents in memory at once (using both Doc 1 and Doc 2). It may also be displayed when you try to use the Speller, Thesaurus, Sort, and Equations; edit keyboard layout files; view a document; generate tables, lists, and so on.

Reasons

WordPerfect requires that you have at least 512K of RAM to run the program. You actually need 384K, but some features that require additional memory may not work if you have large documents in memory or are printing while you are using the features.

When WordPerfect is loaded, half of the available memory is reserved for editing the documents in Doc 1 and Doc 2. The other half is allocated as a memory cache, which is used during a cut or copy operation, for undelete buffers, virtual files, macros, and other operations that normally require disk access. The cache enables WordPerfect to run much faster because the text used in these operations is kept in memory.

If you have loaded other memory-resident (TSR) programs and you have a total of 512K, they may be using some of the RAM needed to run WordPerfect.

If you press Switch (SHIFT-F3) or to try to split the screen with Screen (CTRL-F3) and see this error message, WordPerfect cannot find the minimum 11K of RAM needed for document 2.

Sorting, viewing, and generating (for tables, lists, and the index) operations all need to have a second document available. If the two document screens are occupied, WordPerfect creates a document 3 to perform these functions. It is possible to have enough memory space for two documents in memory but still be unable to complete certain operations because there is not enough memory left for the third document.

The Thesaurus and Equations features do not use the third document but still require a considerable amount of memory.

Solutions

There are a few things you can try if you get this message.

First, exit WordPerfect, and then restart the program. This resets the memory addresses and may solve the immediate problem.

Another solution is to remove all other memory-resident programs (such as SideKick, Turbo Lightning, or any other program that comes up with a hot key) by rebooting with a regular DOS disk (without an AUTOEXEC.BAT file).

If you can load two documents but cannot run a Sort, View, or Generate operation, load only one document into memory. The memory normally used for document 2 can then be used for the operation. You can also try loading the document in Doc 2 and leaving Doc 1 empty. The 64K usually allotted to the document in Doc 1 is then available (instead of only 32K for document 2).

Use the /w startup option to specify the amount of memory to use for WordPerfect. Entering **wp/w-*** will specify that all available memory be used.

Other options include deselecting any keyboard layout, mouse driver, text or graphics screen driver, and turning off hyphenation. You can also wait until printing is finished, or edit your printer selection to include fewer fonts. Another option is renaming the WP.DRS file and using WPSMALL.DRS instead. You would then not see all the extended characters supported by WordPerfect in View.

Finally, you can increase the amount of memory in your computer. WordPerfect will take advantage of expanded memory if it is available, but it cannot use extended memory. However, you can use a program such as PCTools to create a RAM drive (extra cache) from the extended memory.

NUM LOCK KEY

You can press NUM LOCK to toggle between using the numeric keypad to enter numbers or to move the cursor. The numeric keypad is useful for entering numbers into a table or when using the Math feature.

Keystrokes

Some computers have both a numeric keypad and a middle section that you can use to move the cursor. In this type of situation, Num Lock usually is turned on automatically when the computer is started.

To turn Num Lock on or off, press NUM LOCK. If Num Lock is on, "Pos" will flash temporarily. If you want to stop "Pos" from flashing, press ENTER. Num Lock remains on even if "Pos" stops flashing. Press NUM LOCK again to turn off Num Lock.

If numbers appear on the screen when you are trying to move the cursor, you might have accidentally pressed NUM LOCK. Press it again to turn off Num Lock.

NUMBER OF COPIES

You can change the number of copies for a single print job or for several print jobs.

Keystrokes

1. Press Print (SHIFT-F7).

2. Choose **N** for **N**umber of Copies.

3. Enter the number of copies.

4. Choose **1** to print the **F**ull document or **2** to print the **P**age; or press Exit (F7) to return to the document.

Hints

All print jobs queued from that point will be affected until the number of copies is changed or until you exit WordPerfect. You can change the setting permanently in Setup (SHIFT-F1). See "Print Options" or "Setup" in this chapter for details.

If your printer can control the number of copies printed (laser printers usually can), you can print more than one copy of a document more quickly. If you are on a network, you can have the network control the number of copies for faster printing.

To do so, press Print (SHIFT-F7), choose **U** for **M**ultiple Copies Generated by, and then choose **2** for **P**rinter (or **3** for Network if you are running on a network). If the current printer selection cannot generate more than one copy, it will not allow you to change to "Printer," but will remain at "WordPerfect." See "Multiple Copies" in this chapter for more information.

Related Entries

Multiple Copies
Print

NUMBERING LINES

See "Line Numbering" in this chapter.

NUMBERING PARAGRAPHS

See "Paragraph Numbering" in this chapter.

ORIENTATION

Orientation refers to the direction of printing. As you are looking at an 8 1/2- by 11-inch page, portrait (or normal) orientation prints from the left to the right across the page, while landscape prints from the bottom of the page to the top of the page. The following illustrates the differences between the two orientations:

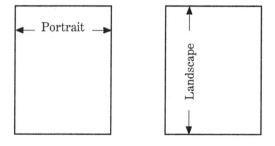

See "Landscape Printing" in this chapter for more information about printing in landscape orientation.

ORIGINAL DOCUMENT BACKUP

See "Backup" in this chapter.

OTHER FORMAT OPTIONS

When you press Format (SHIFT-F8), you are given four choices: Line, Page, Document, and Other. Other is a collection of miscellaneous formatting options that may be used less frequently than the other available formatting options.

Keystrokes

1. Press Format (SHIFT-F8).

2. Choose 4 for Other. The options shown in Figure 3-123 appear.

3. Make a selection from the menu, and then press Exit (F7) to return to the document.

Options

The following is a brief description of the options found on the Other menu. For instructions, see each item listed separately in this chapter.

Advance

When selected, this feature lets you advance up, down, left, or right a specified amount of space from the current cursor location. You can also advance to a specific horizontal or vertical position on the page. This

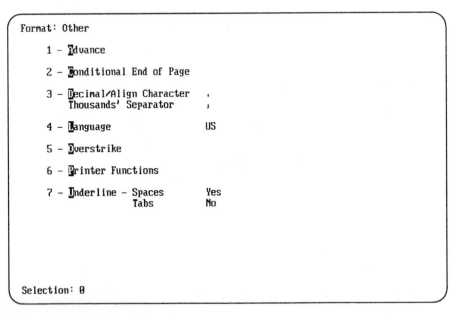

```
Format: Other

      1 - Advance

      2 - Conditional End of Page

      3 - Decimal/Align Character      .
          Thousands' Separator         ,

      4 - Language                     US

      5 - Overstrike

      6 - Printer Functions

      7 - Underline - Spaces           Yes
                      Tabs             No




Selection: 0
```

Figure 3-123.   Formatting options available on the Format: Other menu

feature is used often by desktop publishers. You can also use it to advance to an exact position for filling in forms.

Conditional End of Page

The Conditional End of Page feature keeps a specified number of lines together so they will not be split by a page break. It can be used to keep a section heading with the first few lines of the first paragraph in that section. You can also use Block Protect to protect a block of text rather than protecting a certain number of lines.

Decimal/Align Character and Thousands' Separator

The decimal point is the character used by Tab Align (CTRL-F6), Decimal Tabs, Math, and decimal align in tables to align numbers. A comma is used as the thousands' separator in Math. With this option, you can change the decimal character and thousands' character.

Language

WordPerfect Corporation offers spellers, thesauri, and hyphenation modules for various foreign languages. You can use the Language option to insert a language code into your document so the appropriate speller, thesaurus, and/or hyphenation module will be used for the text that follows that code. This feature is useful for people who create documents in different languages (for example, translators). See "Language" in this chapter for information about how to use this code.

Overstrike

You can print two or more characters in the same location with Overstrike. After choosing this option, you are presented with the Create and Edit options. After choosing the Create option, type all the characters to be printed in the same location, and then press ENTER. You can later use the Edit option to edit the characters found in the overstrike code to the left of the cursor.

Printer Functions

If you choose this option, you will see yet another menu containing more infrequently used printer functions, as shown in Figure 3-124. Each option on the menu has an entry that includes all the information about that feature. Please refer to the specific entry for more information.

Underline Spaces and Tabs

With this option, you can choose whether or not spaces or tabs will be underlined when you turn on the Underline or the Double Underline feature.

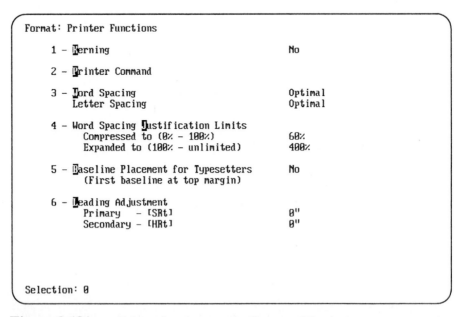

```
Format: Printer Functions

    1 - Kerning                              No

    2 - Printer Command

    3 - Word Spacing                         Optimal
        Letter Spacing                       Optimal

    4 - Word Spacing Justification Limits
        Compressed to (0% - 100%)            60%
        Expanded to (100% - unlimited)       400%

    5 - Baseline Placement for Typesetters   No
        (First baseline at top margin)

    6 - Leading Adjustment
        Primary   - [SRt]                    0"
        Secondary - [HRt]                    0"




Selection: 0
```

Figure 3-124.   Printer functions on the Format: Other menu

Related Entries

Advance
Baseline Placement for Typesetters
Conditional End of Page
Decimal/Align Character
Kerning
Leading
Overstrike
Printer Command
Underline
Word and Letter Spacing
Word Spacing Justification Limits

OUTLINE PRINTING

Some printers can print an outline font. A sample is displayed here:

This is a sample of outline printing

Keystrokes

1. Press Font (CTRL-F8).

2. Choose **2** for **Appearance**.

3. Choose **5** for **Outline**.

4. Enter the text to be printed in the outline font.

5. Press → to move over the Outline off code.

Hints

When Outline printing is selected, the beginning and ending codes [OUTLN] and [outln] are inserted, and the cursor is on the Outline off code. When you enter text, it appears between the two codes. You can repeat the steps just given to turn off Outline printing, but pressing → to move over the ending code is more convenient.

You can also define a block of text and assign Outline printing to it by pressing Font (CTRL-F8), choosing 2 for Appearance, and then choosing 5 for Outline.

You can select a color, a font, or another screen attribute to indicate that you have selected Outline. The position number on the status line will reflect the screen attribute. See "Colors/Fonts/Attributes" in this chapter for details about how to change the color or screen attribute.

Print the file PRINTER.TST to see how outline printing has been defined for your printer. Most printers (except PostScript printers) do not have true outline printing. If your printer has an outline font available, it will be used.

Related Entries

Colors/Fonts/Attributes
Fonts

OUTLINES

WordPerfect can help create outlines by automatically numbering each entry (up to eight levels). When you add or delete items, the outline is renumbered automatically. The following illustration shows the default numbering style assigned to each level:

```
I.  Level  1
    A.     Level  2
        1.     Level  3
            a.     Level  4
                (1)    Level  5
                    (a)    Level  6
                        I)     Level  7
                            a)     Level  8
```

Keystrokes

The following pages contain information about creating an outline, changing the type of numbering used for the outline, and moving sections or "families" of an outline. For information about using Outline Styles and other options related to the Outline feature, see "Hints" and "Options."

Create an Outline

1. Press Date/Outline (SHIFT-F5).

2. Choose 4 for **O**utline.

3. Choose **1** for **O**n. "Outline" appears in the lower left corner of the screen.

4. Press ENTER to insert the first number. A [Par Num:Auto] code is inserted, and the appropriate number is displayed.

   You can do one of the following:

   • Press →Indent (F4), →Indent← (SHIFT-F4), or HOME-TAB to insert a "hard tab," and then type the text for the outline entry.

   • Press TAB to move the number to the next tab setting, thereby changing the level number.

   • Press Left Margin Release (SHIFT-TAB) if you need to move the number back to the previous level number.

   • Press ENTER as many times as you want to add space between each item. (The first time you press ENTER, the number is inserted. If the cursor is just to the right of the number, ENTER inserts [HRt] codes as it normally does. If you want to insert a regular [HRt] code at any time without entering a new outline number, you can press CTRL-V, and then press ENTER.)

   Remember if you need to move back a level, press Left Margin Release (SHIFT-TAB).

5. Press Date/Outline (SHIFT-F5), and then choose **4** for **O**utline and **2** for **O**ff to turn off outlining.

Change the Type of Outline Numbering

You can choose between paragraph numbering (1. a. i. (1), and so on, using no uppercase arabic or Roman numerals), outline numbering (the default selection shown previously), legal (each level is separated by a period, as in 1.1.1), bullets (•, ○, -, and so on), or User-defined (any combination of numbers, letters, or symbols).

1. Move the cursor to the beginning of the outline (you can do this either before or after you have typed the entries).

2. Press Date/Outline (SHIFT-F5).

3. Choose **6** to **D**efine paragraph and outline numbering. The menu shown in Figure 3-125 appears, with the current definition displayed in the middle of the screen.

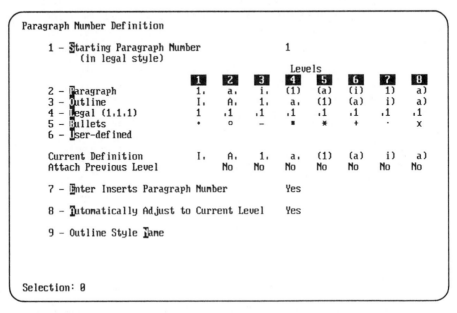

```
Paragraph Number Definition

    1 - Starting Paragraph Number          1
        (in legal style)
                                              Levels
                              1     2     3     4     5     6     7     8
    2 - Paragraph            1,    a,    i,    (1)   (a)   (i)   1)    a)
    3 - Outline              I,    A,    1,    a,    (1)   (a)   i)    a)
    4 - Legal (1,1,1)        1     ,1    ,1    ,1    ,1    ,1    ,1    ,1
    5 - Bullets              •     o     –     ■     *     +     ·     x
    6 - User-defined

    Current Definition       I,    A,    1,    a,    (1)   (a)   i)    a)
    Attach Previous Level          No    No    No    No    No    No    No

    7 - Enter Inserts Paragraph Number       Yes

    8 - Automatically Adjust to Current Level  Yes

    9 - Outline Style Name



Selection: 0
```

Figure 3-125.   Paragraph/Outline Definition menu

4. Choose **2** for **Paragraph**, **3** for **Outline** (already chosen by default), **4** for **Legal**, or **5** for **Bullets** (to have each level "numbered" with a different character).

You can also choose **6** for **User-defined**, and specify numbers, letters, or symbols of your own. If you choose this option, you are placed at the "Current Definition" line, where you can enter the new style by example. Choose from the options listed at the bottom of the screen (also shown here):

```
1 - Digits, A - Uppercase Letters, a - Lowercase Letters
I - Uppercase Roman, i - Lowercase Roman
X - Uppercase Roman/Digits if Attached, x - Lowercase Roman/Digits if Attached
Other character - Bullet or Punctuation
```

If you enter a character other than 1, A, a, I, or i, it will be used as a bullet character or punctuation. Entering **X** or **x** by itself will display either an uppercase or lowercase Roman numeral. If it is attached to the previous level, it will appear as a digit (a regular Arabic number such as 1, 2, 3, and so on). In other words, the X or x options let you have legal style numbering beneath a Roman numeral heading, as shown here:

```
I   Level  1
   1.1   Level  2
       1.1.1   Level  3
```

After entering the type of numbering for each level, you are asked if you want the current level attached to the previous level. In the example above, levels 2 and 3 are attached. If you choose Legal numbering, each level will be attached to the previous one by default.

5. When you are finished, make any other necessary changes to the menu (other options on the menu are discussed under "Options"), and press Exit (F7) to return to the document.

Move, Copy, and Delete Families

A "family" is defined as the current level and any sublevels for that level. For example, if you had the following outline, and the cursor was resting on the "B," it would move, copy, or delete all entries to "C."

> I. Marketing Concepts
>   A. Packaging
>   B. Advertising
>   1. TV
>   2. Radio
>   3. Newspapers
>   C. Sales Representatives

To move, copy, or delete families, follow these steps:

1. Move the cursor to the top level that is to be moved, copied, or deleted. The cursor can be anywhere in that level. For example, if the item has more than one line, the cursor can be on any line.

2. Press Date/Outline (SHIFT-F5).

3. Choose **4** for **O**utline.

4. Choose **3** to **M**ove, **4** to **C**opy, or **5** to **D**elete. The family is highlighted at that time. If you chose the Delete option, you are asked to confirm the deletion. Type **Y** or **N**. If you chose to Copy, a copy of the block is made and highlighted.

5. If you have chosen Move or Copy, you will see the message "Press **Arrows** to Move Family; **Enter** when done." Press any arrow key (↑, ↓, ←, or →) to move the highlighted block to the new location, and press ENTER when you are finished.

Hints

When you turn Outline on and off, the codes [Outline On] and [Outline Off] are inserted. You will also see "Outline" in the lower left corner of the screen to indicate that whenever you press ENTER, a new automatic paragraph number [Par Num:Auto] code is inserted. Each time you turn outlining on, the new outline will begin with the number 1. See the instructions included later in this section under "Starting Paragraph Number" for starting an outline with a different number.

When you change the Paragraph/Outline Numbering definition, a [Par Num Def] code is inserted into the document, which affects the paragraph numbering codes from that point forward.

You can change the Paragraph/Outline definition any time in an outline as well. You can change the option "Enter Inserts Paragraph

Number" in that menu to No and return its function to insert hard returns without actually turning off outlining.

ENTER and TAB

When Outline is on, pressing ENTER inserts a new outline number. If you want to start a new line without inserting an outline number, you can press CTRL-V and then ENTER. If you want to make ENTER insert new lines (hard returns) for an indefinite amount of time, you can press Date/Outline (SHIFT-F5), choose **6** for **D**efine and **7** for **E**nter Inserts Paragraph Number, and then type **N**.

If you need to insert a hard page break, pressing CTRL-ENTER will insert one as well as a paragraph number. If you want only a hard page break, press CTRL-V before pressing CTRL-ENTER.

Pressing TAB moves the cursor to the next tab setting and changes the paragraph number to the next level. If you want to insert a regular tab, press HOME first (HOME-TAB). Remember that when you press Left Margin Release (SHIFT-TAB), the number is pushed back to the previous tab setting and changes to the previous level.

Deleting a Paragraph Number

You can delete a paragraph number on the regular editing screen or in the Reveal Codes (ALT-F3) screen with any of the deleting keys.

Because the "number" is really a code, you can press BACKSPACE or DEL once, instead of several times, to delete the number 12. The remaining numbers are updated automatically.

Outline Number Positions

The level of a paragraph number is decided by tab settings. If the physical position of the levels needs to be changed, change the tab settings by pressing Format (SHIFT-F8) and choosing **1** for **L**ine and then **8** for **T**ab Set.

Outlining versus Paragraph Numbering

The Outline and Paragraph Numbering features use the same codes: [Par Num] and [Par Num Def]. When Outline is on, the [Par Num] codes (numbers) are inserted automatically when you press ENTER — hence the [Par Num:Auto] code.

If you want to choose the placement of the number and the level to be assigned, use the Paragraph Numbering feature. This feature is helpful for situations in which you need to choose the exact position and level of the number. The following illustration shows where you would use Paragraph Numbering to number a centered title with the first level:

ARTICLE III

AMENDMENT, REVOCATION, AND ADDITIONS TO TRUST

3.1   <u>Rights of the Undersigned</u>. As long as the Undersigned
is alive, the Undersigned reserves the right to amend, modify, or
revoke this Trust in whole or in part, including the principal,
and the present or past undisbursed income from such principal.

If you had used Outline to insert the number "III" in this example, it would have been numbered as the seventh level, because the code fell after the seventh tab setting. By choosing Paragraph Numbering, you can enter the specific level number.

You can actually use both features. Just remember that Paragraph Numbering is used to assign an automatic number, whereas Outline inserts the number and decides on the level according to tab settings. If you need to add an item to an outline at a later time, you can also use a single paragraph number.

Options

The following section gives instructions about using outline styles and other options included in the Paragraph/Outline Numbering Definition menu.

Paragraph Number Definition

The Paragraph Number Definition menu (shown earlier in Figure 3-125) decides how paragraph numbers are to be displayed in the document when you use either the Outline feature or Paragraph Number feature. A brief description for each item on the menu follows.

Starting Paragraph Number   The number entered for option 1 will affect the next paragraph or outline number in the document. Enter it in the legal style of numbering (1, 1.2, 1.3.10, and so on), even if you have selected a different style. This option is especially useful if you want to create more than one outline or section of numbering and want each section to start numbering from the beginning.

Type of Numbering   Options 2 through 6 determine how the paragraph/outline numbers will appear in the document. An example is displayed next to each option. If you want to create your own type of paragraph numbering, choose **6** for **User-defined**, and enter letters, numbers, or any other character for each level. You can also add punctuation, such as periods or parentheses. The current selection is displayed in the middle of the screen.

Attach Previous Level   If you want to attach each level to the previous level (a third-level number would appear as I.A.3. instead of 3., for example), you can either choose Legal numbering, in which No will change to Yes automatically, or select the User-defined option. After entering the numbers, letters, or characters to be used for each level, the cursor moves to the line so you can specify whether or not you want to attach the previous level. Type **Y** or **N**.

Enter Inserts Paragraph Number   If you change this option to No, pressing ENTER will not insert a new paragraph/outline number when you are in an outline. If you turn it off, you can insert a new paragraph manually by pressing Date/Outline (SHIFT-F5), choosing **5** for **Paragraph Number**, and then pressing ENTER to insert an automatic paragraph number or enter the number of the level to be inserted.

This option may be useful if you are in an outline and need to use ENTER to insert new lines instead of paragraph/outline numbers. You can change it back to the original setting later when you are finished entering the new or blank lines.

Automatically Adjust to Current Level   When this option is set to Yes, pressing ENTER inserts a new paragraph/outline number at the current level, instead of automatically returning to the left margin (as it did in versions of WordPerfect prior to 5.1).

If you want to return to the way it was done in previous versions, change this option to No. Pressing ENTER will then insert the next paragraph/outline number at the left margin, regardless of the current level.

Outline Style Name   In addition to the regular Styles feature found on ALT-F8, you can now create styles just for outlines. This feature lets you determine how each level of the outline is to be formatted. For example, you can have the first-level outline number bolded and followed by an indent code and the second level with the outline number and a Tab (so that only the first line is indented). You can also control the number of blank lines that follow a certain level by adding additional hard return [HRt] codes to the style.

The style is automatically included with the outline number when you press ENTER. Not only will it save keystrokes; it will help keep the format of the outline consistent.

Styles can be open or paired, which means that you can have codes inserted at the beginning of a level, or both at the beginning and end of each level. For example, an open style might insert an outline number and an indent code at the beginning of the level. A closed style could do the same thing but could also include codes such as extra hard returns [HRt] to create more space after that level.

An outline style can also solve the problem of having to press HOME, TAB when you want to insert a tab because a regular [Tab] code can be placed inside a style. You can also define a style that aligns the outline numbers as they are inserted.

The following steps lead you through the process of defining and selecting an outline style:

1. Press Date/Outline (SHIFT-F5).

2. Choose **6** for **D**efine.

3. Choose **9** for Outline Style **N**ame. You are placed in a menu similar to the one shown in Figure 3-126. If you installed and are using the Style Library, you will see additional outline styles that have already been defined. Note that the default style is to use paragraph numbers only.

4. Choose **2** to **C**reate a new style. (Other options on this menu are discussed later.) The menu shown in Figure 3-127 appears. Eight levels are listed, because one style affects all eight levels. However, each level can have its own individual format.

5. Choose **1** for **N**ame, and enter the name of the style. You can use the name of a specific project or try to describe the type of task for

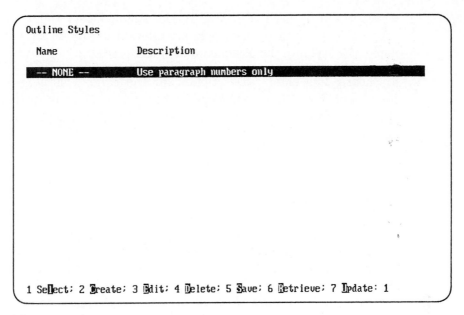

Figure 3-126.   Outline Styles menu

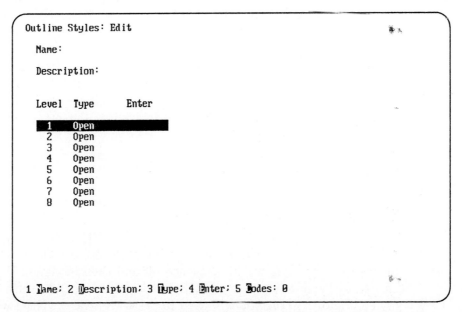

Figure 3-127.   The menu that is used to edit or create an outline style

which it will be used (General, To-Do, Aligned, and Indented are suggestions). Up to 12 characters are allowed. If you do not enter a name, the style will be assigned a number.

6. Choose **2** to enter a **D**escription for the style. This step is optional, but it can help you identify the type of style from the list shown in Figure 3-126. You can use up to 54 characters in the description.

7. Before deciding the format for each level, determine whether the style for that individual level should be open or paired. As mentioned previously, open inserts the format at the beginning of a level, whereas paired inserts codes at the beginning and end of each level.

Because of the nature of Outline, pressing ENTER will insert a new number. If you choose Paired, pressing ENTER can mean something entirely different. It can be used to insert a regular hard return [HRt] code, turn the style off, or turn the style off and then on again. If you change the meaning of ENTER, make sure that you are outside the [Outline Style Off] code before you use ENTER to insert the next outline number. If you choose to have ENTER turn the style off, pressing ENTER once will turn it off. After it is outside the [Outline Style Off] code, ENTER will again insert the next outline level. If you have ENTER set to insert a [HRt] code or to turn the style off and then on again, pressing the right arrow ($\rightarrow$) will move the cursor over the [Outline Style Off] code. You may want to leave the type open until you get used to how styles work.

If you want to change the **T**ype, type **3**. Choose **1** for **P**aired or **2** for **O**pen. The change will be displayed in the menu for the selected level.

8. If you choose Paired, you will see [HRt] inserted in the Enter column. This means that pressing ENTER will insert a [HRt] code as it would normally instead of inserting the next level. Choosing **4** for **E**nter will not let you make a selection if the type is open. If it is paired, you can choose to have ENTER insert a [HRt] code as it would outside of outlining, have ENTER turn the style off, or off/on, which means that the style would be turned off and then on again. If you choose to have ENTER insert a [HRt] code, or have ENTER turn the style off and then on, you will need to press right arrow ($\rightarrow$) when

typing the outline before you can use ENTER to insert a new outline number.

9. Choose **5** for Codes to enter the format for the current level. You are immediately placed in a Reveal Codes type of screen, with a paragraph number at the top and codes at the bottom. If you have chosen to create a paired style, a comment appears in the upper part of the screen and a [Comment] code appears in the Reveal Codes area of the screen, as shown in Figure 3-128. Place any codes that you want inserted at the beginning of the Outline item before the [Comment] code. Place the codes that are to be inserted at the end of the outline level after the [Comment] code.

10. Begin entering text and codes that will determine the format or style of that particular level. Each style already has a "fixed" paragraph number inserted within the style. A fixed paragraph number will insert the specific level number, regardless of the current tab setting. By contrast, an automatic paragraph number will change levels according to the current tab setting.

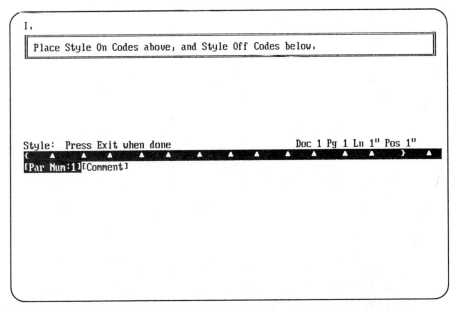

Figure 3-128.   The Reveal Codes screen used to create a paired style

Each level is preset to insert the outline number at the left margin. If you do not insert [Tab] or [→ Indent] codes before the paragraph number code in the style, that number will appear at the left margin instead of being indented. This feature gives you complete control. For example, you can have level one insert the paragraph number at the first tab setting by placing a [Tab] code before the [Par Num] code in the style. In fact, you might want to have all levels inserted at the same tab settings. An example of this would be for those who do legal numbering (1, 1.2, 1.2.1) and want each number, regardless of the level, inserted at the same location.

Some examples of outline styles follow:

• **Bolded paragraph number and indented text**

[BOLD][Par Num:1][bold][→ Indent]

I. This is an example of a bold paragraph number with indented text. If you have more than one line in the entry, each line will be indented to the first tab setting.

• **Indent the first line of the text and insert a blank line between this and next level**

[Par Num:1][Tab][Comment][HRt]

[HRt]

I. This is the outline entry as shown above. Because a [Tab] code was included, only the first line is indented. Two hard returns separate this entry and the following entry.

II. This would be the second entry, also including a tab and two hard returns.

• **Align first level numbers and indent text**

[DEC TAB][Par Num:1][→ Indent]

I. This is the first level entry, aligned at the next tab setting. The text following it is indented at the next tab setting. You may want to adjust your tab settings if you use this style.

II. This is the second item.

III. And the third. All are aligned at the decimal point.

- **Indent second level and follow with a tab**
  [→Indent][Par Num:1][Tab]

     a.   This is a second-level entry with an indent code
before the number and a [Tab] code following it.

Notice that the second example is a paired style. In the third example, [DEC TAB] was inserted by pressing Tab Align (CTRL-F6). In the last example, an [→Indent] code was used to place the second level number at the first tab setting. The difference between using it and [Tab] is that the paragraph number will be inserted, and the first line of information will be indented to the next tab setting; subsequent lines in that entry will be indented just under the paragraph number.

11. Press Exit (F7) when you are finished entering all codes. You are then returned to the menu shown in Figure 3-127, where you can repeat steps 7 through 10 for each level. Remember to place the correct number of tab or indent codes before the paragraph number if you want each level indented.

12. Press Exit (F7) when you are finished. You will return to the menu shown in Figure 3-126.

13. Among other options, you can create more styles, select a style to be used in the document from that point on, or, more importantly, save the styles to a file that you can use for more than one document. You can also retrieve the outline styles from another document so you don't have to create them again. See notes about this later in "Sharing Styles Between Documents" for information on saving and retrieving styles.

14. To select an outline style, move the cursor to the style, and choose 1 to Select it. You are returned to the Paragraph Number Definition menu, and the name of the selected outline style appears next to option 9, Outline Style Name.

15. Make any other changes in the Paragraph Number Definition menu as explained previously under "Options," and press Exit (F7) when finished.

16. You are then returned to the Date/Outline menu. Choose 4 for Outline and then 1 for On.

17. Enter the text of the outline. Press ENTER to insert the next number, press TAB to change the number to the next level, or press SHIFT-TAB to change to the previous level. If you have paired styles and you have defined ENTER to insert an [HRt] code or to turn the style off/on, you will need to press the right arrow → to move past the [Outline Style Off] code before ENTER will insert the next outline number.

Outline styles can also be used to format regular paragraph numbers. See "Paragraph Numbering" in this chapter for details.

Styles (ALT-F8) and Outline Styles

Because outline styles are stored with the regular styles, you can view them when you press Style (ALT-F8). You can create, edit, delete, save, or retrieve outline styles from this menu; however, you cannot select them at this point. Instead, you need to select styles by choosing the Outline Style Name option on the Paragraph Number Definition menu. As a way around this, you can create a style that would include a paragraph number definition code that specifies what outline style to use.

See "Styles" in this chapter for more information about changing regular styles to outline styles.

Sharing Styles Between Documents

To avoid creating the same outline style for each document, you can share styles by using the Save and Retrieve options in either the Styles (ALT-F8) or Outline Styles menu.

With the Save option, you can save all the styles in the current document (regular styles and outline styles) to another file. When you choose the Save option (they are numbered differently on the two menus), you are asked for a filename. Enter the name of a file that does not exist. (If the file exists, you are asked if you want to replace the original file. If you type **Y**, the original file is deleted; styles *and* text are replaced with the current list of styles. Instead, type **N** and enter the name of a different file.)

A disadvantage of using the Save option is that you cannot save a few styles from the list to another file—all styles are saved. Another disadvantage is that if the file already exists, the styles will not be appended to the other list of styles. Instead, the original file will be replaced if you type **Y** in answer to "Replace filename," and you will lose that file.

A better option is to clear the screen and retrieve the file where the styles are to be copied. Press Style (ALT-F8), or enter the Outline Styles menu and choose the Retrieve option (numbered differently on the two menus). You can then enter the name of the file that contains the desired styles. These styles will then be added to the list of styles already defined, instead of overwriting them as they would with the Save option. If, while retrieving styles, two styles have the same name, you are asked the question "Style(s) already exist. Replace?" If you type **N**, all files that do not have the same name are retrieved. If you type **Y**, all styles are retrieved, overwriting the current styles that have the same name.

You can use the Style Library feature in Setup to specify the name of a file that will always be retrieved when you press Styles (ALT-F8), unless styles already exist in the document. This file could contain all the styles that you normally use from document to document. The Update option in either style menu lets you update the styles in the document with those in the Style Library. To specify the name of the Style Library, press Setup (SHIFT-F1) and choose **6** for **L**ocation of Files and then **5** for **S**tyle Files/Library Filename. The directory entered will be used as the directory when you are saving and retrieving styles. Next enter the name of the file to be used as the style library.

Deleting a Style

If you choose to delete a style, you are given the following choices:

```
Delete Styles: 1 Leaving Codes; 2 Including Codes; 3 Definition Only: 0
```

Choose **1** for **L**eaving Codes to delete the definition and leave the codes. The definition is deleted, and the style-on codes are deleted from the document. However, the text and codes that were included in the style are inserted into the document at that point.

This option is useful if you decide to save the file as a DOS text file but want to keep all the text, paragraph/outline numbers, and indentation intact. Because styles would normally be deleted when you are saving a DOS text file, you can choose to delete the style and leave the codes, and then save the document.

Choose **2** if you want to delete the definition and the codes. This is the opposite of the option just described.

Choose **3** to delete the definition only. If you wanted to delete all styles except those currently being used in the document, use this option to delete all style definitions from the menu. You can then press HOME, HOME, ↓ to move through the document and press Styles (ALT-F8) to see an accurate list of the styles being used (current styles are added back into the menu as you move past them.

Related Entries

Paragraph Numbering
Tabs

OVERSTRIKE

The Overstrike feature allows two or more characters to be printed in the same position.

Keystrokes

1. Press Format (SHIFT-F8).

2. Choose **4** for **O**ther.

3. Choose **5** for **O**verstrike.

4. Choose **1** for **Create**. The overstrike [Ovrstk] code is displayed on the status line.

5. Type all the characters that will be printed in the same position, and then press ENTER.

6. Press Exit (F7) to return to the document. The last character typed will be the character that is displayed on the screen.

Hints

When you select Overstrike, an [Ovrstk:n] code is inserted, where n represents the characters that will be printed over each other in the same location. Only the last character typed will appear on the screen; type the character that you want visible last. For example, if you created the characters "ã" and "õ" and typed the tilde last, you would not be able to tell the difference between the two on the screen. They would both appear as ~. You would have to press Reveal Codes (ALT-F3) to display the characters in the overstrike code.

If you need to change the characters included in the overstrike code, position the cursor just after the code, press Format (SHIFT-F8), and then choose **4** for **Other**, **5** for **Overstrike**, and **2** for **Edit**. Add and delete characters, and then press ENTER when you are finished. Pressing Exit (F7) will return you to your document.

You can overstrike as many characters as you want. Overstrike is a code that tells WordPerfect to back up and print another character in the same position (or, with some printers, to make a second, third, or even fourth pass).

WordPerfect also has a feature that strikes through several characters with a dash (-). See "Strikeout" in this chapter for details.

Applications

Overstrike is best used to overstrike more than two characters in the same position. With WordPerfect's printing capabilities, very few characters are not directly supported. You access these characters with the Compose feature. For example, you can press Compose (CTRL-2) and type two characters, such as **a** and ", to create the character ä.

Because not all characters are composed as easily, each character has been assigned a section and a character number within that section. Appendix A, "WordPerfect Character Sets," lists all the characters supported and the number that is assigned to each. You can press Compose (CTRL-2), type the section number of the character and a comma, and then enter the character's number. If the computer cannot display the character, a small box is displayed in its place. If you move the cursor to the small box in Reveal Codes (ALT-F3), it will "expand" to show you the section number and character number for each special character. See "Compose" for details about using this alternative.

If your printer will not print a special character, you might find that you can create and print it with the Overstrike feature.

If you use an overstrike combination often, you can assign the keystrokes to a key on the keyboard using the Keyboard Layout feature.

Strikeout is another WordPerfect feature that is similar to Overstrike. It uses a dash to strike out text that is considered for deletion. If you want to use a different character, such as a slash, consider changing the strikeout character to a slash in the printer definition (.PRS file). Instructions for using the Printer program are given in Chapter 5.

Related Entries

Compose
Strikeout
See also Chapter 5, "Printer Program"

PAGE BREAKS

WordPerfect automatically inserts a page break when the end of a page is reached. This type of page break is called a soft page break. You can enter a hard page break at any location by pressing Hard Page (CTRL-ENTER). The codes that can be seen in Reveal Codes (ALT-F3) appear as [SPg] and [HPg].

A soft page [SPg] code is inserted when a space or soft return ends the page. [HRt-SPg] indicates that a hard return has been converted to a soft page break. [HPg] is used when you press CTRL-ENTER to insert the hard page break.

Hints

WordPerfect is automatically set for 8 1/2- by 11-inch paper. The top and bottom margins are preset for 1 inch each. Rather than having the status line display the number of lines that currently fit on a page (as was done in version 4.2), WordPerfect displays page breaks more accurately in inches. The "Ln" number on the status line will display the distance from the top edge of the page. With WordPerfect's default settings, the page break will be inserted when the "Ln" number is approximately 10 inches.

If you have a header, footer, page number, or footnotes on the page, the page break will come much sooner; WordPerfect automatically subtracts the space taken by those features from the total amount available on the page. WordPerfect also subtracts an extra line for spacing between a page number, header, footer, footnotes, and the text.

If you want to increase or decrease the amount of space available on the page, change the top and bottom margins or the paper size and type. See "Margins" or "Paper Size/Type" in this chapter for more information.

You can move freely across page breaks with any cursor key, and you can see the text from one page to the next. There are no limitations to the amount of text that you can move or copy between pages.

Move to a Specific Page

Press PGUP or PGDN to move the cursor to the top of the previous or next page. To go to a specific page, press Go To (CTRL-HOME), and enter the page number. The cursor moves to the top of that page.

If you want to go to the top or bottom of the current page, press Go To (CTRL-HOME) and ↑ or ↓. The following chart summarizes these keystrokes:

Action	Keystroke
Previous page	PGUP
Next page	PGDN
Go to page n	Go To (CTRL-HOME), n
Go to the top of the page	Go To (CTRL-HOME), ↑
Go to the bottom of the page	Go To (CTRL-HOME), ↓

Applications

Insert a hard page break manually if you want the text that immediately follows to always begin on a new page. You can also use a hard page break to end a short page. In fact, you can use a hard page in a style so that when you turn on the style, a hard page is automatically inserted. A style containing a hard page break and other formatting commands can be useful for the beginning of each chapter in a book or when you are creating an envelope after a letter.

If you are generating a table of contents, a table of authorities, lists, or an index, you can create a separate page for those features before they are generated. Place the [Def Mark] codes in the new page so that the table, list, or index will be generated there.

Related Entries

Go To
Margins, Top and Bottom
Paper Size/Type

PAGE FORMAT

When you press Format (SHIFT-F8), you will see several categories of formatting options, including one for page options. Most of these options appear only when you view or print a document. Among them are options for page numbers, headers, footers, top and bottom margins, and centering text on the page. Another option lets you specify the size and type of paper being used for the document.

Keystrokes

1. Move the cursor to the position at which the change is to take place (usually at the beginning of a document or page).

2. Press Format (SHIFT-F8).

3. Choose 2 for **P**age. The menu shown in Figure 3-129 appears, with all current settings displayed to the right of each option.

4. Select from the options until you have made all the desired choices.

5. Press Exit (F7) to return to the document.

```
Format: Page

    1 - Center Page (top to bottom)     No

    2 - Force Odd/Even Page

    3 - Headers

    4 - Footers

    5 - Margins - Top                   1"
                  Bottom                1"

    6 - Page Numbering

    7 - Paper Size                      8.5" x 11"
             Type                       Standard

    8 - Suppress (this page only)




Selection: 0
```

Figure 3-129.   Page Format menu

Options

Center Page from Top to Bottom

This code must be placed at the top of a page before any text.

When you ask to center the page from top to bottom, the option changes to Yes and remains so until you move to the next page. A [Center Pg] code is also inserted in the document at that point.

Force Odd/Even Page

WordPerfect lets you force a page to be an odd- or even-numbered page. For example, the first page of each chapter in a book usually starts on an odd page. If, by choosing this option, two odd- or two even-numbered pages are found together, a blank page will be "printed" between them.

Headers

This option lets you print information at the top of each page, odd pages, or even pages. Two headers are available so that alternating headers and footers are possible.

Instead of using the Page Number Position option, you can include a page number in a header. In fact, you have more flexibility if you put the page number code (^B) in a header, because you can decide the exact placement and how much space to put between the number and the text.

A header can be up to a page long. WordPerfect automatically subtracts the amount of space for a header from the total space available on the page. A blank line is automatically inserted between the header and the rest of the text on the page. If you want more space, insert extra lines at the end of a header.

Footers

Footers are identical to headers, except that they are printed at the bottom of the page.

Margins, Top and Bottom

The top and bottom margins are preset for 1 inch. Choose this option if you want to increase or decrease the top or bottom margin.

If you manually feed 1 inch of paper into the printer and Word-Perfect moves down an additional inch before printing, edit the form being used and enter a top text adjustment of 1″. This informs Word-Perfect that 1 inch of the paper has already been fed into the printer. The top margin cannot be less than the top offset.

Page Numbering

WordPerfect is preset to have pages unnumbered. However, with this option you can choose automatic page numbering at any time. You can choose to have the page number at the top left, center, or right; the bottom left, center, or right; or alternating left and right on the top or bottom of each page.

You can also specify a new page number or change the page number style. See ″Page Numbering″ in this chapter for details.

Paper Size and Type

This option lets you select from a list of paper sizes and types (envelopes, legal, letterhead, standard, and so on) or add new paper definitions to the list. When you define a form, you will tell WordPerfect its size, paper type, where the ″form″ is located (manual feed, continuous, or fed with a sheet feeder), and the type of fonts that can be used (landscape or portrait orientation).

The size of the paper determines where lines wrap and where page breaks are inserted. If you choose a type of paper with landscape as the orientation, you can turn the paper on its side in the printer, or you can print with a landscape font in a laser printer.

Suppress

This code must appear at the beginning of the page so that it can affect headers and page numbers that might be printed at the top of the page. You can turn off any combination of features, or you can choose to print the page number at the bottom center of the current page, even if you previously chose another position.

Hints

Page format codes usually belong at the beginning of a page. For example, if you define a header in the middle of a page, it cannot appear at the top of that page, because the printer will not have received the code in time. You should also define footers at the top of a page with WordPerfect 5.1.

You can change most of the page format options permanently in the Setup menu. See "Setup" in this chapter for details.

Related Entries

> Center Page from Top to Bottom
> Footers
> Force Odd/Even
> Headers
> Margins, Top and Bottom
> Page Numbering
> Paper Size/Type
> Suppress

PAGE NUMBERING

You can turn on page numbering by selecting a page number position or by including a ^B code in a header, a footer, or anywhere else on a page.

You can also change the page number style to include text with the page number (as in Page 3, -3-, or Chapter 2-3). In versions before 5.1, you had to create a header or footer if you wanted text included with the page number. When generating a table of contents, lists, an index, or cross-references, the entire page number style (text and page number) will be included.

Keystrokes

Turning on Page Numbering

WordPerfect is set to print without page numbers. To print them, you need to select the position for the page number:

1. Move the cursor to the location in the document where page numbering is to begin. If the entire document is to be affected, move to the top of the document by pressing HOME, HOME, HOME, ↑. This step moves the cursor before any text or codes. If you want page numbering to begin with the current page, press Go To (CTRL-HOME), ↑ to go to the top of the page.

2. Press Format (SHIFT-F8) and choose **2** for **P**age.

3. Choose **6** for Page Numbering. The following menu appears.

```
Format: Page Numbering

    1 - New Page Number       1

    2 - Page Number Style     ^B

    3 - Insert Page Number

    4 - Page Number Position No page numbering
```

4. Choose **4** for Page Number Position. Other options on this menu are discussed in the following two sections. The menu shown in Figure 3-130 is displayed.

5. Make a selection from the menu, depending on where you want the page number to print. If you choose option 4 or 8, the page number will print at the left margin on even pages and at the right margin on odd pages (this is useful when you are printing or copying pages on both sides of the page).

6. Press ENTER to return to the page numbering menu and make further changes, or press Exit (F7) to return to the document.

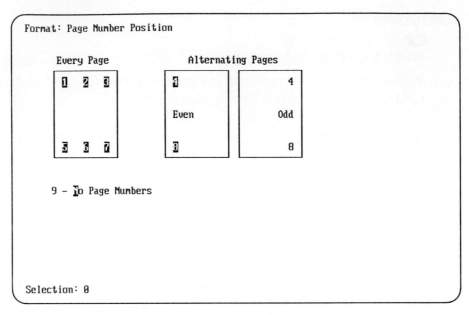

Figure 3-130. Menu used to select the page number position

Selecting a New Page Number

You can continue consecutive page numbering from one document to another by selecting a new page number. Selecting a new page number is also useful if you have front matter at the beginning of a document and want to have it numbered in lowercase Roman numerals (i, ii, and so on). You would then go to the first page that needs to begin with an Arabic numeral 1 and select that as the new page number.

1. Follow steps 1 through 3 in the previous section to enter the page numbering menu if you are not already there.

2. The current page number is displayed next to option 1. Choose **1** for New Page Number to change the number.

3. Enter the new page number in Arabic form (1, 36, 230, and so on), or in uppercase or lowercase Roman numerals (i, x, xiv, or I, X, XIV, and so on). The page number on the status line reflects the new page number, but it does not display it in Roman numerals.

4. Press Exit (F7) when you are finished, or remain in the menu to make further selections.

Changing the Page Number Style

A page number will normally appear by itself, without any other text. To change this and also have the text included in the table of contents, table of authorities, lists, the index, or cross-references, follow these steps:

1. Enter the page numbering menu if you are not already there by pressing Format (SHIFT-F8) and choosing **2** for Page and then **6** for Page Numbering.

2. The current Page Number Style (option 2 on the menu) is displayed as ^B; this code represents the current page number. You can add text or other numbers to this style by choosing **2** for Page Number Style.

3. Enter the new page number style. If you are at the beginning of the third chapter, for example, you might want to type **3-^B** (press CTRL-B to insert ^B) for the page number style so that the number will be preceded by the chapter number. When you reach the fourth chapter, you would change the style to **4-^B**. If you do not enter ^B in the page number style, it will automatically be added at the end of the style when you press ENTER. You cannot select a font or attribute for a page number; see "Hints" for alternatives.

4. Changing the page number style does not turn on page numbering. You will still need to choose **4** to select the Page Number Position.

5. Press Exit (F7) when you are finished.

Choosing **3** will Insert the Page Number into the document at any location. The current page number style will be inserted at that point; if you need to make changes to the style, do so before selecting this option.

Hints

The following codes are inserted into the document when you select the corresponding feature:

[Pg Num:*n*]
[Pg Num Style:*n*]
[Insert Pg Num:*n*]
[Pg Numbering:*n*]

Any text included with a page number style will be included in the table of contents, table of authorities, lists, index, and cross-references when they are generated, even if page numbering is off.

Changing the Appearance

The page number is always printed in the document's initial font. You can either change the initial font or include the page number along with a specific font in a header or footer.

To change the initial font, press Format (SHIFT-F8), choose **3** for Document, **3** for Initial Base Font, and then select a different font from the list.

You can also create a header or footer that includes font or attributes (such as Bold). Include ^B in the header or footer where the page number should print (press Center (SHIFT-F6) or Flush Right (ALT-F6) if desired). If you want to include the page number style, repeat the steps given in "Keystrokes" while in the header or footer. Choose a page number style, and then choose **3** for Insert Page Number.

Page Number in a Header or Footer

To include a page number in a header or footer (or anywhere else on the page), press CTRL-B to insert a ^B code. If a special character, macro, or other function has been "mapped" to CTRL-B with the Keyboard Layout feature, you will get that special character, macro, or function instead. If this happens, you may want to either press CTRL-6 to deselect the keyboard layout or insert the page number from the Page Numbering menu.

Among the choices for page number positions are top or bottom and alternating left and right. Although you can do something similar with headers and footers, it takes a few more steps. For example, for the pages in Chapter 1 of a book, you could define header A to print "Chapter 1-^B" at the left margin of even-numbered pages and define header B to print "Chapter 1-^B" at the right margin of odd-numbered pages.

If you want more than one blank line between the page number and the text, consider placing ^B in a header or footer. To add the extra space, press ENTER at the end of the header or the beginning of the footer.

If you request both a header or footer and a page number, they will most likely be printed on the same line. To avoid this, insert a blank line in the header or footer so that the page number can be printed in that space, or place a ^B in the header or footer.

Using ^N for a Page Number

In versions of WordPerfect prior to 5.1, you could use ^N (instead of ^B) to insert the current page number in a header or footer. In version 5.1 you cannot use ^N to insert a page number, because it is considered as a merge code (meaning "next record"), and merge codes can be included in a header or footer.

Page Numbers in Macros and Merge

The Macro and Merge features include a command called {SYSTEM} that can be used to detect current settings or situations in a document. For example, it can detect the state of the printer, the current filename, and even the current page. See "Applications" for uses of this command.

Applications

Different Page Number Styles

If you decide that you want page numbers that read "Chapter 3-^B," but you do not want the word "Chapter" included in lists, tables, index, and cross-references, you can do the following. Enter **3-^B** as the page number style. Do not turn on page numbering by selecting a page number position. Instead create a header or footer that includes "Chapter 3-^B." The header or footer will then be used to print the page number instead of the page number style. The page number style will still be in tables, lists, and so on.

Printing "Page n of n"

At times, you may want to print "Page *n* of *n*" as the page number when you need to know the current page number and the total number of pages in a document.

The following macro uses the {SYSTEM} command to accomplish such a task. This is what you might call an "advanced" macro, but if you follow the keystrokes step by step, you should be able to create it. When finished, the macro should look something like the following. You may or may not have the same commands on the same lines; the important thing to notice is the number and location of tildes ($\sim$). If you already know how to create an advanced macro, you can use the following example as a guide without following the steps that have been provided (centered dots indicate a space).

```
{DISPLAY OFF}
{Home}{Home}{Down}
{ASSIGN}pg~{SYSTEM}page~~
{Home}{Home}{Up}
{Format}pfbp{Center}Page·{^B}·of·{VARIABLE}pg~{Exit}{Exit}
```

1. Press HOME and then Macro Def (CTRL-F10) to start defining the macro (pressing HOME first lets you enter the macro editor immediately after entering the name and description).

2. Enter a name for the macro; **page** is a suggestion.

3. Enter a description, or press ENTER to skip this step.

4. The cursor appears in the macro editor at the {DISPLAY OFF} code. Move the cursor to the right with →, and press ENTER to move to the next line.

5. Press Macro Def (CTRL-F10) to enter the following keystrokes as themselves (otherwise, they will be used for moving the cursor and editing). If you make a mistake and need to delete it, press Macro Def (CTRL-F10) before pressing BACKSPACE, or it will not delete the character to the left; it will instead insert the {Backspace} command. You will be switching between Macro Define on and off in subsequent steps.

6. Press HOME, HOME, ↓ so the macro will move to the bottom of the document. The commands {Home}{Home}{Down} will be inserted.

7. Press Macro Def (CTRL-F10), and then press ENTER to go to the next line.

8. Press CTRL-PGUP to list the macro commands.

9. Move the cursor to the {ASSIGN} command, and press ENTER to select it.

10. Type **pg** as the name of the variable (at the place where the following information will be stored and later used). Type a tilde (∼) immediately after **pg**.

11. Press CTRL-PGUP to enter the list of macro commands, and then type **system** to move the cursor directly to that command. Press ENTER to select it.

12. Type **page** so that the system command knows that it is supposed to "get" the current page number. Type two tildes (∼∼) immediately after **page**: one to end the {SYSTEM} command and another to end the {ASSIGN} command. Press ENTER to go to the next line.

13. Press Macro Def (CTRL-F10) and then HOME, HOME, ↑ so the macro will move to the top of the document during the next step. The commands {Home}{Home}{Up} are inserted. Press Macro Def (CTRL-F10) and then ENTER to move to the next line.

14. Insert the following keystrokes to create Footer B on every page: Press Format (SHIFT-F8) to insert {Format}, and then type **pfbp**.

15. Press Center (SHIFT-F6) to insert {Center}, and then type **Page ^B of**, with a space following "of." Insert ^B by pressing CTRL-B.

16. Press CTRL-PGUP to enter the macro commands. Type **variable** to move to that command, and then press ENTER to select it.

17. Type **pg** as the name of the variable to be inserted. Type a tilde (~) after **pg**.

18. Press Macro Def (CTRL-F10) and then Exit (F7) twice to insert two {Exit} commands. This will cause the macro to exit the footer and the format menus.

19. Press Macro Def (CTRL-F10) and then Exit (F7) to leave the macro editor and end the macro definition.

When you want to run the macro, press Macro (ALT-F10) and type **page** (or the name that was used for the macro). If you want to update page numbering at any time, go to the top of the document, delete the [Footer B] code, and then run the macro again.

Related Entries

Footers
Headers
Macros
New Page Number

PAGE UP/DOWN

Press PGUP to move to the beginning of the previous page in the document, or PGDN to move to the beginning of the next page.

If you want to move up or down screen by screen instead of page by page, press the gray minus or gray plus key on the numeric keypad.

You can also press Go To (CTRL-HOME) and enter a specific page number to move to that page. You can also move quickly to the top or to the bottom of the current page by pressing Go To (CTRL-HOME) and then ↑ or ↓.

See "Cursor Keys" in this chapter for more information.

PAGINATION

Repagination is not necessary in WordPerfect; documents are automatically reformatted when you add or delete text. See "Page Numbering" in this chapter for instructions on numbering a document.

PAPER SIZE/TYPE

To format a page properly, WordPerfect needs to know the size of the paper. For example, if you plan to print lengthwise across the page, you will need to select a landscape (wide) paper definition from the Paper Size/Type menu. You can also specify the type of paper being used—letterhead, legal, envelope, labels—or you can give the paper definition a "name" of your own to identify it easily from the list.

Keystrokes

If you do not have a printer selected and try to select a paper definition, you will be asked for the paper size and then the paper type (similar to the method used in version 5.0). The information is then converted to the closest paper definition it can find when you select a printer. If you have not selected a printer, do so before continuing.

Selecting a Paper Size/Type

To choose a particular size/type of paper, follow these steps:

1. Press Format (SHIFT-F8),and choose **2** for **Page**.

2. Choose **7** for Paper Size/Type. You will see a menu similar to the one shown in Figure 3-131. The items on the list have been predefined by WordPerfect Corporation and have been customized to your printer's capabilities. Your list of paper definitions may be different from the one shown in Figure 3-131.

3. Move the cursor to the desired paper size/type, and choose **1** to Select it. You are returned to the document, and a [Paper Sz/Typ:*n*] code is inserted, where *n* indicates the type and size of paper selected.

Adding to the List

If you do not see the desired size or type of paper on the list, you can add it while in the menu. The following keystrokes guide you through the process:

1. While in the Paper Size/Type menu (follow the previous steps 1 and 2 if you are not already there), choose **1** for **A**dd and continue with step 2.

```
Format: Paper Size/Type
                                                    Font  Double
Paper type and Orientation      Paper Size   Prompt Loc   Type  Sided  Labels

Envelope - Wide                 9.5" x 4"    No    Manual Land  No
Legal                           8.5" x 14"   No    Contin Port  No
Legal - Wide                    14" x 8.5"   No    Contin Land  No
Standard                        8.5" x 11"   No    Contin Port  No
Standard - Wide                 11" x 8.5"   No    Contin Land  No
[ALL OTHERS]                    Width ≤ 8.5" Yes   Manual       No




1 Select; 2 Add; 3 Copy; 4 Delete; 5 Edit; N Name Search: 1
```

Figure 3-131.   Paper Size/Type selections

If you want to use another paper definition on the list as a model because only one or two items need to be changed, move to that item and choose 3 for Copy. An identical paper definition appears in the list. You can then choose 5 for Edit and make the necessary changes, as explained in step 3.

2. When adding a new paper definition, you are first asked to select the paper type, as shown in Figure 3-132. If you cannot find one on the list that fits your description, choose 9 for Other, and enter a name of your choice using up to 39 characters. The type (or name that you enter) will appear in the first column in the list of paper definitions shown in Figure 3-131.

3. The menu used to edit a paper definition appears, as shown in Figure 3-133. Select each applicable option, and make the necessary changes. See "Hints" for a description of all the options.

4. Press Exit (F7) when you are finished.

5. Select the new paper definition, or press Exit (F7) to return to the document without making a selection.

```
Format: Paper Type

      1 - Standard

      2 - Bond

      3 - Letterhead

      4 - Labels

      5 - Envelope

      6 - Transparency

      7 - Cardstock

      8 - [ALL OTHERS]

      9 - Other




Selection: 1
```

Figure 3-132.   Paper types available

Hints

Each new paper definition that you add to the list is saved with the printer selection (in the printer's .PRS file). The name of this file is displayed at the top of the Edit Paper Definition menu shown in Figure 3-133. If you select a different printer, a new set of paper definitions will appear in the list, and any existing paper size/type codes already in the document will be converted to the paper definition it can find. If a close match cannot be made, the [ALL OTHERS] form is selected.

If your WordPerfect package is different from the U.S. version, the default paper size/type selection matches the standard size in that country. For example, if you have the UK version, the default selection will be Standard, but the size will match the size of the A4 paper.

Adding/Editing Paper Definitions

The following is a description of each item found on the menu that is used to edit a paper definition. Refer to Figure 3-133 to see where each option appears.

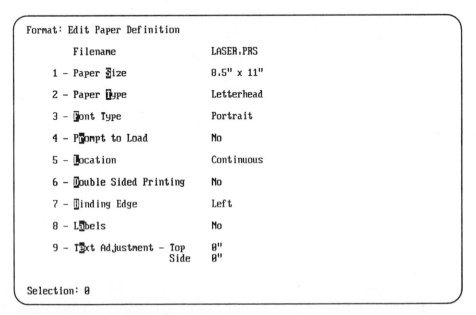

```
Format: Edit Paper Definition

        Filename                LASER.PRS

    1 - Paper Size              8.5" x 11"

    2 - Paper Type              Letterhead

    3 - Font Type               Portrait

    4 - Prompt to Load          No

    5 - Location                Continuous

    6 - Double Sided Printing   No

    7 - Binding Edge            Left

    8 - Labels                  No

    9 - Text Adjustment - Top   0"
                         Side   0"

Selection: 0
```

Figure 3-133.   Edit Paper Definition menu

Paper Size   If you need to change paper size or change to landscape printing (so the text will be printed along the length of the form instead of the width), choose **1** for Paper Size. If your particular paper size is not included in the list shown in Figure 3-134, type **O** for **O**ther, and enter the width and the height of the paper.

Paper Type   You selected the type of paper when you added the paper definition to the list. Choose **2** for Paper Type to change it if necessary. Figure 3-132 contains a list of available paper types. Choose **9** for **O**ther if you want to give the paper definition a descriptive name.

Font Type   Laser printers usually have both portrait and landscape fonts. Landscape means that the printhead inside the printer can change and print down the page, while portrait prints across the page. You would choose Landscape as the font type for paper definitions in which a "landscape" (wide) form is selected.

```
Format: Paper Size              Width  Height

    1 - Standard               (8.5" x 11")

    2 - Standard Landscape     (11" x 8.5")

    3 - Legal                  (8.5" x 14")

    4 - Legal Landscape        (14" x 8.5")

    5 - Envelope               (9.5" x 4")

    6 - Half Sheet             (5.5" x 8.5")

    7 - US Government          (8" x 11")

    8 - A4                     (210mm x 297mm)

    9 - A4 Landscape           (297mm x 210mm)

    o - Other

Selection: 0
```

Figure 3-134.   Paper Size selections

If you have a dot-matrix or daisywheel printer, leave this selection at Portrait. Although you can change the orientation of the paper within the printer and print in landscape orientation, the actual printhead does not change orientation.

To change this option, choose **3** for Font Type, and select from the following orientations:

```
Orientation: 1 Portrait; 2 Landscape: 0
```

If your printer can print both on the same page, you will see an additional option for choosing both portrait and landscape orientations.

Prompt to Load   If you want to be prompted by WordPerfect to insert the paper during printing, choose **4** for Prompt to Load, and type **Y**. If you answer Yes to this question and you are printing on this type of paper, WordPerfect will cause the computer to beep. Upon entering the Control Printer menu, you can see which type of paper is being requested, load it into the proper location, and then choose **4** to send the printer a **Go**.

Location   To specify the location of the paper definition, choose **5** for Location. You will see the following choices:

```
Location: 1 Continuous; 2 Bin Number; 3 Manual: 0
```

If you choose **2** for Bin Number, you will be prompted for the sheet-feeder bin that will be used to hold that type of paper.

If you choose **3** for Manual, you will be prompted to load each sheet (with a beep from WordPerfect), and you will need to send the printer a "Go" before each page is printed. If you have a laser printer and do not want to be prompted for each page, you can choose **1** for Continuous and still feed the paper through the manual feed tray.

Choose Continuous if the paper is automatically fed into the printer without an electronic cut-sheet feeder. This includes tractor feeders for perforated paper and laser printers that have a paper tray. When you are printing with perforated continuous paper, position the printhead at the perforation.

Double-Sided Printing   If you have a printer, such as the HP Series IID, which can print on both sides of the page (called duplex printing), you can select option 6 for Double Sided Printing, and then type **Y** to take advantage of that feature.

Binding Edge   Option 7 for Binding Edge lets you choose Top or Left binding. This selection is affected only if you have also chosen the "Binding Width" option in the Print (SHIFT-F7) menu.

Labels   You can select option 8 if the paper contains Labels. The menu shown in Figure 3-135 appears, letting you enter the number of labels, their size, and other information that is necessary for Word-Perfect to print the information in the right location. If you choose this option, you do not have to adjust margins or define columns to print on labels.

WordPerfect prints each "page" of the document on a single label. See "Labels" in this chapter for details.

```
Format: Labels

    1 - Label Size
                    Width         2.63"
                    Height        1"

    2 - Number of Labels
                    Columns       3
                    Rows          10

    3 - Top Left Corner
                    Top           0.5"
                    Left          0.188"

    4 - Distance Between Labels
                    Column        0.125"
                    Row           0"

    5 - Label Margins
                    Left          0.033"
                    Right         0.123"
                    Top           0"
                    Bottom        0"

Selection: 0
```

Figure 3-135.   Labels definition menu

Text Adjustment   This option is most useful if you are inserting paper manually into a dot-matrix or daisywheel printer, but you can use it for other situations in which the text is not printing in the proper location. When inserting manually fed paper, you will usually feed it up approximately 1″ so it fits under the paper bail. To compensate for feeding the paper up 1″, you can adjust the printing up 1″.

To change the adjustment, choose 8 for Text Adjustment. The following options appear:

```
Adjust Text: 1 Up; 2 Down; 3 Left; 4 Right: 0
```

If you are feeding paper manually, choose **1** for **Up** (it will otherwise print down too far). Enter 1″ (or any other appropriate measurement) when you are prompted for the amount of adjustment to be made.

Related Entries

Labels

PARAGRAPH NUMBERING

You can assign numbers to paragraphs, and the numbers will be updated automatically when a paragraph is added or deleted. Up to eight levels of numbering are supported.

Keystrokes

1. Move the cursor to where the paragraph number is to appear.

2. Press Date/Outline (SHIFT-F5).

3. Choose 5 for **Para** Num. You will see the following prompt:

Paragraph Level (Press Enter for Automatic):

4. Press ENTER if you want WordPerfect to choose the level automatically (levels are decided by tab settings), or enter the level number (1 through 8) if you want the paragraph to be assigned a specific level.

Hints

A [Par Num:] code is inserted at the cursor position. It can either be an automatic paragraph number (which means that WordPerfect assigns the level number according to the existing tab settings) or a fixed paragraph number (when you have assigned a specific level to the number).

The two codes differ slightly in appearance when you press Reveal Codes (ALT-F3). [Par Num:Auto] is the code that is used when WordPerfect assigns the level; it is the same code that appears when you use the Outline feature. When you specify a level, a paragraph number code is inserted in the form of [Par Num:n], where n indicates the level to be used.

The Outline and Paragraph Numbering features use the same codes and the same style of numbering. Outline inserts the numbers automatically when you press ENTER and determines the level according to the current tab settings. Paragraph numbers are automatic numbers that are inserted manually; you also have the option of assigning a specific level of numbering. Both are automatically renumbered when other [Par Num:] codes are added or deleted.

The level number is determined by tab settings. If a paragraph number is placed between tabs, the preceding level will be used. If you insert a [Tab] that pushes the code to the next tab setting, the number will change to that level (unless you have assigned a specific level to the number).

If the position of the levels needs to be changed, change the tab settings by moving the cursor above the paragraph numbers, pressing Format (SHIFT-F8), choosing **1** for Line, and then **8** for Tab Set.

If you use paragraph numbering often and do not want to repeat the four or five steps it takes to insert a paragraph number, define a macro to do the same thing (ALT-P is a suggested name).

The following illustration shows a sample legal document that uses three numbering styles:

ARTICLE 4

<u>OFFICERS</u>

<u>Section 4.1 The Chairman of the Board</u>. The Chairman of the Board, if there is such an officer, shall have the following powers and duties:

(a)   He shall preside at all stockholders' meetings.

(b)   He shall preside at all meetings of the Board of Directors.

(c)   He shall be a member of the Executive Committee, if any.

Only the third level of numbering, which uses (a), (b), and so on, can be automatic. You must assign the rest a particular level when you insert the paragraph number. If WordPerfect had assigned the level, "ARTICLE 4" would have been numbered as the seventh level, because the code fell after the seventh tab setting. "Section 4.1" would have been given a third-level number, because it falls between the third and fourth tab settings.

Change the Numbering Style

WordPerfect has been preset to number each level in an outline format, as shown here:

```
I. Level 1
   A. Level 2
      1.   Level 3
         a.   Level 4
            (1)   Level 5
               (a)   Level 6
                  i)   Level 7
                     a)   Level 8
```

You can use this style; change to paragraph style, legal numbering, or bulleted style; or choose a format of your own. You can change the style before you type the numbers, or you can change it after you have entered the numbers. Regardless of when it is done, you first need to move the cursor before the numbers to be affected and then follow these steps:

1. Move the cursor to the beginning of the document or to the beginning of the section of text to be numbered.

2. Press Date/Outline (SHIFT-F5).

3. Choose **6** for **Define**. The menu shown in Figure 3-136 appears, with the current definition displayed in the center of the screen.

4. To change the style, choose **2** for **Paragraph**, **3** for **Outline** (the default), **4** for **Legal**, or **5** for **Bullets**.

You can also type **6** for **User-defined** and specify numbers, letters, or symbols of your own. If you choose this option, you are placed at the "Current Definition" line, where you can enter the new style by example. Choose from the options listed at the bottom of

```
Paragraph Number Definition

    1 - Starting Paragraph Number                    1
        (in legal style)
                                        Levels
                             1   2   3   4   5   6   7   8
    2 - Paragraph            1.  a.  i.  (1) (a) (i) 1)  a)
    3 - Outline              I.  A.  1.  a.  (1) (a) i)  a)
    4 - Legal (1.1.1)        1   .1  .1  .1  .1  .1  .1  .1
    5 - Bullets              •   o   -   ■   *   +   ·   x
    6 - User-defined

    Current Definition       I.  A.  1.  a.  (1) (a) i)  a)
    Attach Previous Level        No  No  No  No  No  No  No

    7 - Enter Inserts Paragraph Number               Yes

    8 - Automatically Adjust to Current Level        Yes

    9 - Outline Style Name


Selection: 0
```

Figure 3-136.   Paragraph Number Definition menu

the screen, which are also shown here:

```
1 - Digits, A - Uppercase Letters, a - Lowercase Letters
I - Uppercase Roman, i - Lowercase Roman
X - Uppercase Roman/Digits if Attached, x - Lowercase Roman/Digits if Attached
Other character - Bullet or Punctuation
```

If you enter a character other than 1, A, a, I, or i, it will be used as a bullet character or punctuation. Entering **X** or **x** will display either an uppercase or lowercase Roman numeral if it appears alone. If attached to the previous level, it will appear as a digit (a regular Arabic number, such as 1, 2, 3, and so on). See the next paragraph for more information about attaching levels. The X and x options let you have legal style numbering beneath a Roman numeral heading, as shown here:

I   Level 1
   1.1   Level 2
      1.1.1   Level 3

This would allow the example given earlier in this section to appear in the more accepted form shown here:

ARTICLE IV

OFFICERS

Section 4.1 The Chairman of the Board. The Chairman of the Board, if there is such an officer, shall have the following powers and duties:

After entering the type of numbering for each level, you are asked if you want the current level attached to the previous level. In the previous example, level 2 is attached. If you choose Legal numbering, each level will be attached to the previous one by default.

5. Before leaving the menu, be aware that by setting a new paragraph number definition, the next paragraph number will be set to "1." If you do not want this to happen, choose 1 for Starting Paragraph Number, and enter the appropriate number in legal style (1, 2.1, and so on).

A [Par Num Def] code is inserted, and it affects the style of paragraph numbering from that point forward in the document.

Outline Styles

You can also use option **9** for Outline Style **N**ame to determine the format of each level of paragraph number. For example, you can include a [Tab] or [→Indent] code with the paragraph number in the style so that it is inserted automatically when the paragraph number is inserted. A [Dec Tab] inserted with Tab Align (CTRL-F6) could also be used before a paragraph number to align it at the decimal point. See "Outlines" in this chapter for complete instructions about using outline styles.

Applications

If you have created an outline with the Outline feature and need to go back and add an entry, you have the option of doing so manually with a paragraph number. This might be easier than turning on the Outline feature and trying to place the entry in the correct location.

Automatically Numbering Lines

WordPerfect has a feature that numbers lines in the left margin. However, these numbers do not appear until printed, and there is no choice of numbering style.

If you have a list of items that you want numbered, you can create the following macro to insert the numbers. Go to the beginning of a list before defining this macro.

1. Press Macro Def (CTRL-F10), enter the name for the macro (NUM is a suggestion), and then enter a description.

2. Press Search (F2), ENTER (to insert a [HRt] code), and Search (F2) again to start the search. If you have paragraphs to be numbered instead of lines, press ENTER twice to insert two [HRt] codes as the search string.

3. Press Date/Outline (SHIFT-F5), and choose **5** for **P**ara Number.

4. Press ENTER to choose the automatic paragraph level.

5. Press →Indent (F4).

6. Press Macro Def (CTRL-F10) to end the macro.

To run the macro n times to number n lines, press ESC, type the number of lines to be numbered (do not press ENTER), press Macro (ALT-F10), and enter the name of the macro. This is the safest method; otherwise, if text follows the list of lines or paragraphs, that text will also be numbered each time a [HRt] code is found.

If the document consists only of the lines or paragraphs to be numbered, you can insert an extra step between steps 5 and 6 to create a repeating macro: Press Macro (ALT-F10) and enter the name of the macro being defined. This step allows the macro to run until it cannot find any more [HRt] codes and saves you the step of pressing ESC and specifying the number of lines or paragraphs to be numbered.

Related Entries

Outlines
Tabs

PARALLEL COLUMNS

You can use WordPerfect's parallel columns for situations in which text must wrap within a column but must always be kept parallel on a page with other related columns.

Scriptwriters use parallel columns to show several related activities, such as action, words, and lighting. When text is added to or deleted from a column, the group of columns below are not reformatted; they move as a group to accommodate the text changes in the preceding group.

Newspaper-style columns do just the opposite; text flows down the page, then up into the next column; text additions or deletions result in reformatting the text that follows.

You can also use the WordPerfect table feature to keep sections of text parallel. This feature lets you easily move, copy, or delete columns, which is not an easy task when you are using parallel columns.

See "Columns" or "Tables" in this chapter for more information.

PASSWORD PROTECTION

You can lock files with a password so that only the author of the file can retrieve, print, or look at the document. The Password option is found on Text In/Out (CTRL-F5). See "Lock and Unlock Documents" in this chapter for details.

PATH FOR DOWNLOADABLE FONTS AND PRINTER FILES

If you have downloadable soft fonts for your printer, WordPerfect can download them for you. Before doing so, however, it needs to know where the fonts are located. You can also store other printer files in the same directory.

To specify the path for downloadable soft fonts, edit the printer selection and choose option 6 for Path for Downloadable Fonts and Printer Files. If you need further assistance, see "Cartridges and Fonts" in this chapter.

Each time you want to download the soft fonts, press Print (SHIFT-F7) and choose 7 to Initialize the printer. If you have a two-disk-drive system, insert the disk containing the desired soft fonts and printer command files in drive B before you initialize the printer.

Related Entries

Cartridges and Fonts
Initialize Printer

PITCH

Instead of selecting the pitch in WordPerfect, you will select a font that indicates the number of characters that will be printed in an inch (the pitch). For example, you could select a font named "Courier 10cpi (characters per inch)" for a 10-pitch font.

Proportionally spaced fonts are not set by pitch. Instead, WordPerfect checks the width of each character for the current font to determine how many characters will fit on the line. If you have a PostScript printer and select a font, you are asked for the point size, which is the height of a character rather than the width. If you have fixed-pitch fonts (nonproportionally spaced), the pitch is listed with the font name, as was just mentioned. See "Fonts" in this chapter for more information.

If you must set the pitch to an exact setting, you can do so with the Word and Letter Spacing feature. Another feature, "Display Pitch," controls the horizontal spacing on the screen—not at the printer. See either of these entries for more information.

POSTSCRIPT PRINTING

WordPerfect takes advantage of the added features and capabilities offered by PostScript printers.

Setting Up the Printer

If your PostScript printer is a serial printer, rather than a parallel one, and uses XON/XOFF protocol, you will need to specify this when selecting a serial port for the printer. Hardware handshaking, also known as DTR or DSR, lets the computer, printer, and cable control when data should be sent (whereas XON/XOFF turns control over to the software).

You can select XON/XOFF when you select the printer. The following steps guide you through the process:

1. Press Print (SHIFT-F7).

2. Choose **S** to Select a Printer.

3. Move the cursor to the printer in question, and choose **3** to **E**dit the printer selection.

4. Choose **2** for **P**ort.

5. When you see the list of port options, choose **4** for COM 1. If you have more than one serial port, you might need to specify a different COM port.

6. Enter the information for each of the options on the menu (baud, parity, stop bits, and character length).

7. Choose **5** for XON/XOFF, and type **Y**.

8. Press Exit (F7) to return to the menu used to edit the printer selection. Continue making changes if necessary, and then press Exit (F7) until you return to the document.

When you select a PostScript printer during installation, the supplementary file EHANDLER.PS is also installed. If you are having problems printing with your PostScript printer, copy this file to the printer from DOS. After you exit WordPerfect and see the DOS prompt, enter **copy ehandler.ps** *port,* where *port* is the name of the port being used by your printer.

Soft Fonts

Soft fonts are downloaded on a PostScript printer, just as they are on any other printer. When editing the printer selection, choose option **7**, Path for **D**ownloadable Soft Fonts and Printer Files, and enter the drive and directory in which the soft fonts will be kept. Select option **4**, Cartridges and Fonts, select Soft Fonts, and change the amount of memory available if necessary; then select the desired soft fonts.

To download the soft fonts, press Print (SHIFT-F7), and choose **7** to Initialize the Printer.

Advantages of a PostScript Printer

When you press Font (CTRL-F8) and choose option **4** for Base **F**ont, you are asked to specify the point size. Because the fonts can be scaled, you can choose any size up to 200 points. The font will then be created just before the document is printed, but it will be stored in the printer's memory until the printer is turned off. Therefore, printing may be a bit slow the first time you use a font.

Automatic font changes (fine, small, large, very large, and extra large) are scaled by a certain percentage, as listed here:

Fine	60%
Small	80%
Large	120%
Very large	150%
Extra large	200%
Super/subscript	60%

You can change the percentage at any time to affect printing from that point forward by following these steps:

1. Press Setup (SHIFT-F1).

2. Choose **4** for **I**nitial Settings.

3. Choose **8** for **P**rint Options.

4. Choose **6** for **S**ize Attribute Ratios.

5. Enter the new percentages, and press Exit (F7) when you are finished.

You can also get true outline and shadow fonts with a PostScript printer.

You can use PostScript printers to print white text on a black background. To do so, set the percentage of shading in graphics boxes or tables to 100 percent, and then choose white as the print color.

If you create or edit a font with the Printer program, you will find two additional options in the Size and Spacing menu. The first option, Width Scaling Factor, lets you change the height or width of the font. This option is usually set to 1, which means that the width is directly proportional to the height. You could choose .5 to scale the width to half its normal size and increase the height proportionally. Changing this setting to 2 would increase the width to double its normal width and decrease the height proportionally.

The second option that is different for PostScript printers on the Size and Spacing menu is Amount to Slant. This option is usually used to create an italic font.

Related Entries

Selecting a Printer
See Chapter 5, "Printer Program"

PREVIEW A DOCUMENT

See "View Document" in this chapter.

PRINT

You can print a block of text, a page, selected pages, or the entire document from the screen. There are also options for printing all or selected pages of a file already saved to disk.

Keystrokes

Print a Page or Document from the Screen

1. With the document to be printed on the screen, press Print (SHIFT-F7). The menu shown in Figure 3-137 is displayed.
   The currently selected printer is displayed in the lower half of the menu as well as other print options controlling the binding width, number of copies, and text and graphics quality. Change these options if necessary. (See "Hints" for more information.)

2. Choose **1** to print the Full Document or **2** to print the current **Page**.

```
┌─────────────────────────────────────────────────────────────┐
│  Print                                                        │
│                                                               │
│         1 - Full Document                                     │
│         2 - Page                                              │
│         3 - Document on Disk                                  │
│         4 - Control Printer                                   │
│         5 - Multiple Pages                                    │
│         6 - View Document                                     │
│         7 - Initialize Printer                                │
│                                                               │
│                                                               │
│  Options                                                      │
│                                                               │
│         S - Select Printer              HP LaserJet Series II │
│         B - Binding Offset              0"                    │
│         N - Number of Copies            1                     │
│         U - Multiple Copies Generated by  WordPerfect         │
│         G - Graphics Quality            Medium                │
│         T - Text Quality                High                  │
│                                                               │
│                                                               │
│                                                               │
│  Selection: 0                                                 │
│                                                               │
└─────────────────────────────────────────────────────────────┘
```

Figure 3-137.   Print menu

If you are using manually fed paper or if you have chosen a different paper type (letterhead, envelope, and so on), the computer will sound a bell each time the printer is ready for a "Go." You can press Print (SHIFT-F7) to enter the print menu, and choose 4 for Control Printer menu if you are not sure what type of paper is needed. If you are prompted, insert the new type of paper and type **G** to send the printer a "Go" (start the printer).

You can use an ALT-G macro that is part of the "MACROS" or "SHORTCUT" keyboard to send the printer a "Go" without having to press as many keys. For more information for selecting this keyboard, see "Keyboard Layout."

Print a Block

A block of text can consist of a word, a few lines, or several pages of text.

1. At the beginning (or end) of the block to be printed, press Block (ALT-F4).

2. Move the cursor to the opposite end of the block.

3. Press Print (SHIFT-F7) to print the block.

4. Type **Y** or **N** in answer to the question "Print Block? No (**Yes**)."

Print a File or Selected Pages from Disk

You can print an entire document or selected pages of a document from the List Files menu or with options on the Print menu. You can print either a document that has been saved to disk or print the one currently on the screen. If you are not sure of the filename or need to print more than one file, use the List Files menu, as described in this section.

To print a document from disk with the Print menu, follow these steps:

1. Press Print (SHIFT-F7).

2. Choose **3** to print a **D**ocument on Disk.

3. Enter the filename of the document to be printed. Include the drive and directory if the file is not found on the default drive.

4. The following prompt appears at the bottom of the screen:

Page(s): (All)

Press ENTER to print all the pages in the document, or enter the numbers of the pages to be printed. Separate individual pages with commas or spaces (as in 3,5,10), and indicate a range of pages with a dash (as in 10-13). You can combine these options to print selected pages and ranges (as in 3,5,7-9,12). Type **s** if you want to print the Document Summary. See "Hints" for details.

To print selected pages from the current document (not one that you have previously saved to disk), press Print (SHIFT-F7), choose **5** for Multiple Pages, and then enter the pages to be printed.

To print from the List Files menu, follow these steps:

1. Press List (F5).

2. Press ENTER to see a list of files from the displayed drive and directory, or enter a new drive/directory name.

3. Move the cursor to the file to be printed. If you want to queue several files at once, move to each filename and type * to mark the files.

4. Choose **4** for **Print**.

5. When asked for the pages to be printed, press ENTER to print all the pages of the document, or enter the selected pages (separated with a comma) or a range of pages (separated with a dash).

   If you marked several files, "Print marked files? **No** (**Yes**)" appears. If you type **Y**, you are asked for the pages to be printed. Press ENTER to print all pages from all marked documents or to specify the pages to be printed. If you specify page 1, only the first page of all marked files will be printed. Specifying **s** would print the Document Summary of all marked files.

   If you type **N** so as not to print the marked files, you are asked if you want to print the current file. Type **Y** or **N** and continue.

6. Press Exit (F7) when you are finished.

The marked files are placed in the queue in the order in which they appear in the List Files menu (alphanumeric order).

   If you want to print all files, press Mark Text (ALT-F5) or press HOME and type * to mark all the files in the menu, and then choose **4** to **Print**.

   If you want to print a list of the filenames for the current directory, enter the List Files menu with List (F5), and then press Print (SHIFT-F7). A list of all of the files in that drive/directory will be printed.

Hints

When printing a page or block, WordPerfect scrolls through the document up to the point of the page or block, searching for formatting commands so the text will be formatted correctly. If you are queuing a single page near the end of a large document, it will not begin printing immediately. In fact, you can go into the Control Printer menu and watch the "Page Number:" specification change as WordPerfect moves through each page.

   Printing will be faster if you are at the end of the current document before you send it to the printer.

The printer will be slow to start when printing from disk if you saved the document with the Fast Save option on (the default setting). When a document is Fast Saved, it is not formatted; WordPerfect needs to retrieve the document in the background (not to the screen), move through the document to reformat it, and then send it to the printer. See "Fast Save" in this chapter if you want to change this option to No. Doing so, however, will affect the speed at which documents are saved.

If you are editing a document and want to print the latest copy, print from the screen because the version on the disk will not be the most recent. If you want to print from disk, save the document on the screen first.

You might want to view a document (with the View option on the Print menu) before printing to avoid wasting paper. You can then see the location and contents of headers, footers, footnotes, page and line numbering, and right justification. If you have a graphics monitor, you will see the difference in font sizes and typefaces as well as text and graphics. In Graphics mode, the View option lets you see the page exactly as it will appear when it is printed. If your printer can print a particular character, it will appear in Graphics mode during View. If it cannot print a character, it will not appear in View. If you have chosen a laser printer, the document will look different from how it would look if you had selected a dot-matrix printer. In other words, the document is formatted for the currently selected printer. See "View Document" in this chapter for more information.

Controlling the Printer

After sending a document to the printer, you are returned to the document. If you want to cancel a print job, send a "Go" to the printer, rush print jobs, or check the status of the current print job, press Print (SHIFT-F7) and choose 4 for Control Printer. The menu shown in Figure 3-138 appears. See "Control Printer" in this chapter for information about all the options in this menu.

Downloading Soft Fonts

If you are using soft fonts, you will need to download them to the printer before printing. To do so, press Print (SHIFT-F7), and then choose 7 to Initialize the Printer. This step is necessary only if you turn the printer off and then on.

Text and Graphics Quality

If you do not have enough memory to print text and graphics, or if your printer cannot switch between text and graphics on the same page, you can adjust the quality of print for either selection. Decreasing graphics and/or text to draft quality may help. You can also request that graphics not be printed, print the document, and then reverse the selections so that graphics will be printed instead of text when you feed the paper through the printer again. To speed up the printing of tables, set Graphics Quality to draft; the quality of the graphics lines will not be affected.

Information about Print menu options is available in this chapter under "Control Printer," "Type Through," "View Document," "Initialize Printer," "Selecting a Printer," "Binding Options," "Number of Copies," and "Quality of Print."

Error Messages

The following error messages may appear when you print.

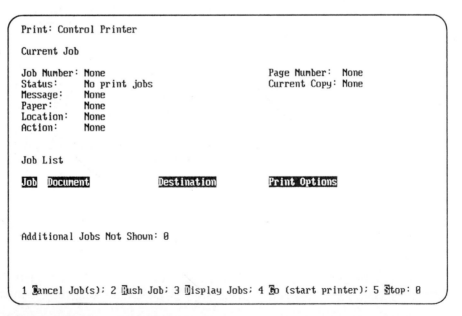

Figure 3-138.   Control Printer menu

Printer Selection Not Properly Set Up   If you created a document with a certain printer selection and then deleted that .PRS file without selecting another, WordPerfect will display the name of the original printer selection, even if it is not present. If you try to print or view the document with this setup, you will see this error message. You may also see the message if you are trying to print a file without having selected a printer. To solve the problem, select another printer. See "Selecting a Printer" in this chapter for instructions.

Document May Need to Be Generated. Print? No (Yes)   If you have defined a table of contents, a table of authorities, lists, or an index, or if you have used automatic references or the Endnote Placement option but have not generated the document, you will see this error message when you are sending the document to the printer. You can either type **Y** and have the document printed as it is, or you can type **N** to return to the document, generate, and then print. Typing **Y** will not automatically generate the document before you print it.

Not Enough Memory   Page printers, such as laser printers, "build" a page at a time before printing, rather than printing line by line. If you have a lot of graphics on one page, your printer may not have enough memory to print the document. This can also happen if you have several font changes or special characters on a page.

If this error message appears, you can decrease the Text and/or Graphics Quality options on the Print menu to medium or draft. You may even have to select the "Do Not Print" option for Graphics Quality, print only the text, reverse the options so that the graphics print instead of the text, and then feed the same page into the printer. You may still have to print graphics at draft quality. See "Quality of Print" in this chapter for more information.

The Print Queue

When you give the command to print a document, it is assigned a number and is then placed in the queue. The list of documents, their location, destination, type of paper (standard, letterhead, envelope, and so on), location of the paper (manual, continuous, or sheet-feeder bin number), and print options are listed in the queue file WP}WP{.Q.

WordPerfect displays this queue in the lower section of the Control Printer menu in the form of a job list. Only the first three print jobs are listed. If you want to see all the jobs that have been queued, choose **3** to **D**isplay the print jobs on a separate screen.

See "Control Printer" in this chapter for information about managing the print jobs in the queue.

Printing from the Screen

When you print from the screen, a copy of the document is saved in a temporary file that is then used for printing. This feature, often called "background printing," lets you edit that document or a different one while printing. If you have sufficient memory, the temporary print file is held in memory. Once you fill memory, the temporary print files are saved to disk in the default drive and directory.

The temporary print files are named WP}WP{.1, WP}WP{.2, and so on. If you look in the Control Printer menu, you will see "(Screen)" instead of a filename as the document to be printed. Because you do not need to give a document a name before it can be printed, you can type a document, print it, and clear the screen without ever saving and naming the document.

The temporary print files are automatically deleted when the job is printed. If you want to delete a print job, do so from the Control Printer menu instead of deleting the WP}WP{ files. See "Cancel a Print Job" in this chapter for details.

If you try to exit WordPerfect before it has sent the print files, you are asked the question "Cancel all print jobs? **N**o (**Y**es)." If you type **Y**, the print jobs are deleted. If you type **N**, you will remain in WordPerfect until they are printed.

If you try to print but get the message "Disk full," it means that the temporary print file cannot be saved on the disk. This will most likely happen when you are moving through the document and queue several separate pages to be printed. A copy of the document up to that point is saved in the temporary file; if you are working with a large file and are queuing several pages near the end of the document, the file will be duplicated each time, taking up a lot of disk space. Instead, save the file to disk and specify the pages to be printed from the Control Printer menu.

Printing Specific Pages or a Range of Pages

If you print a file from disk or choose the option to print Multiple Pages, you are asked to specify the pages or range of pages to be printed.

Press ENTER to print (All) pages in the document, or enter single page numbers separated with a comma or space. A range of pages is indicated with a dash. The following list illustrates the options that you can use to indicate which pages are to be printed. You can use these options in combination with each other.

1-10	Prints pages 1 through 10
S-	Prints the Document Summary
1 3 5	Prints pages 1, 3, and 5
1,3, 5	Prints pages 1, 3, and 5
1-3, 5-7	Prints pages 1 through 3, and 5 through 7
1-3,7,9	Prints pages 1 through 3, page 7, and page 9
2,13-	Prints page 2 and from page 13 to the end of the document

If you have assigned new page numbers in the document, Word-Perfect considers that a new "Section." When specifying the pages to be printed, you can also specify the section in which they are found by using a colon(:) to separate the section and page number(s). The following list includes several examples of how to specify pages when new page numbers are assigned:

1	Prints the first page in the first section
i	Searches for the first occurrence of a Roman numeral page change and prints the first page
1:1	Similar to the first example, in that it prints the first page unless it finds a Roman page change at the beginning of that page. It then searches for the first Arabic page change and prints the first page
1:i	Same as the second example, in that it prints the first page of a Roman page change
2:1	Searches for the second occurrence of an Arabic page change and prints the first page
2:i	Searches for the second occurrence of a Roman page change and prints the first page

You can combine sections and page numbers. For example, 2:3-5,3:1 means "print pages 3 through 5 of the second section," and "print page 1 of the third section."

Location of Paper

If the paper is to be fed into the printer manually, or if you choose a paper definition that is not initially present, the computer will sound a bell and display a message telling you to insert the form and send the printer a "Go."

If the paper is set for continuous printing, start printing with the print head at the perforation. WordPerfect will feed in the appropriate amount of paper for the top margin.

If you are manually feeding paper into a printer that has a platen and paper bail, choose the Text Adjustment option when defining the paper, and have the text moved up 1 inch. WordPerfect will then know that the paper will be fed 1 inch into the printer. If the top margin in WordPerfect is set to less than 1 inch, feed in the paper accordingly; if it is set for more than 1 inch, feed in the paper only 1 inch. WordPerfect will move down the additional space. See "Paper Size/Type" in this chapter for details.

Using Your Printer as a Typewriter

An optional Type Through program is available from WordPerfect Corporation that lets you type directly from WordPerfect to the printer. You cannot use this feature with a laser printer, but it is useful for printing on forms or envelopes if you have a daisywheel or dot-matrix printer.

Printing Problems

You can determine many of your printer's capabilities and limitations by printing the PRINTER.TST file that is installed with the PTR program files.

If you do not think your printer is set up properly, or if you see an error message confirming this, see "Selecting a Printer" in this chapter for more information. You can also refer to Chapter 5, "Printer Program," for details about creating or editing a printer definition.

The following is a list of possible printing problems that you may encounter and some solutions.

Printer Will Not Print   If the printer has printed before, there is usually a good explanation for why it is not currently printing. Do the following:

1. Make sure that the printer is on line. If the on-line light is not on, press the on-line button to turn it on.

2. Check to see if there is paper in the printer.

3. Check to see if the ribbon has broken or if it has run to the end of the spool.

4. Make sure that the cables are securely fastened to both the computer and the printer.

5. Look in the Control Printer menu—press Print (SHIFT-F7) and choose 4 for Control Printer—to see if there are print jobs waiting and to check the status of the current print job. You may have to give the printer a "Go" (type **G** from the menu) or cancel the print job(s), turn the printer off and then on, and send the print job again.

If the printer has never printed, check the following items in addition to the ones just listed:

1. Check the printer selection and make sure it is correct.

2. Make sure that you have selected the correct port from within WordPerfect. Parallel printers use an LPT port, and serial printers use a COM port. Even if a printer has both a parallel and serial interface, they cannot both work at the same time. Check the printer DIP switches or the control panel to be sure that you have chosen the correct interface.

3. Make sure the printer cable is attached to the correct port.

4. Check the cable to make sure that it is the correct type. (Tandy printers usually need Tandy cables.)

5. See if the printer will print from DOS. If you have a parallel printer, press SHIFT-PRTSC to print the contents of the screen. If you have a serial printer, exit to DOS, insert the original Program 1

disk in drive A (or B), and enter **copy a:readme.wp com1** at the DOS prompt (substitute "a" with "b" if you are using drive B). If the file does not print, try **com2**, **com3**, or **com4** in place of **com1** to check the serial ports.

6. If you have a serial printer, make sure that you selected the correct baud, parity, stop bits, and character length.

Printer Prints Random or Stray Characters   Check the following items if your printer prints random characters or if it stops after printing part of a document:

1. Make sure that the cables are securely attached. If they are loose, some bits can be lost.

2. If a serial printer stops at approximately the same point in each document, it could be the result of a buffer overflow. Make sure that you have the correct cabling.

3. See if the printer supports only XON/XOFF. If it does, you will need to choose XON/XOFF when selecting the serial port for the printer.

4. If you have chosen proportional spacing on a daisywheel printer, you should be using a PS print wheel.

5. If the same characters are being printed at the top and/or bottom of each page, you might have defined a sheet feeder when you really do not have one, or you may have selected the wrong sheet feeder. Consequently, the codes for the sheet feeder would not be interpreted correctly and would print as characters.

Printer Double Spaces Text   If your printer is printing text double spaced when you have chosen single spacing, turn off the auto line feed switch on the printer. This option will also help if boldfaced or underlined text is printing on two lines instead of one.

Advance and Superscript/Subscript Problems   If advance, Superscript, or Subscript is not working correctly, detach the tractor feeder and test the printer. Sometimes the tractor feeder will not let the paper advance. You might be able to partially solve this problem by releasing the tension on the tractor feeder.

Text Wraps to the Next Line Prematurely   If you have an 80-column printer but have margins that exceed that setting, the text past that point will be wrapped to the next line during printing. To solve the problem, increase the width of the left and right margins in Word-Perfect to make the lines shorter or change to a smaller font.

Related Entries

Binding Options
Cancel a Print Job
Control Printer
Display Print Jobs
Initialize Printer
Number of Copies
Print to Disk
Quality of Print
Selecting a Printer
Type Through
View Document

PRINT FORMAT

If you are converting to WordPerfect 5.1 from version 4.2, you will soon discover the absence of a Print Format key. The functions formerly assigned to CTRL-F8 have been incorporated into the single Format key (SHIFT-F8) with the exception of fonts. With Font (now the CTRL-F8 key), you can select a font (referred to as the base font) from a list of available fonts or choose attributes that are dependent on the base font. You will no longer choose pitch, because WordPerfect checks the width of each character to see how many characters will fit on a line.

Lines per Inch has been replaced by the Line Height feature found on the Line Format menu. Justification and Line Numbering are also selections on that menu. The Format: Other menu contains a feature that lets you choose whether or not to underline spaces and tabs, and the Printer Functions option on that menu leads to the Printer Command option.

A sheet-feeder bin is no longer selected directly. Instead, when you define types of paper (letterhead, envelopes, and so on), you will specify the location of the paper, which can include a sheet-feeder bin. Defining and selecting different types of paper is done through the Paper Size/ Type option on the Page Format menu.

PRINT OPTIONS

You can set the binding offset, number of copies, how the multiple copies are generated (WordPerfect, Printer, or Network), graphics quality, text quality, and redline method so that they will affect every document created thereafter.

To enter this menu, press Setup (SHIFT-F1), choose 4 for Initial Settings, and then 8 for Print Options. The menu shown in Figure 3-139 appears.

Although these options affect printing, they are also saved in the document. For example, if you change the Graphics Quality to High for a particular document and then save the document, that setting is saved with the document; it will print in high quality the next time you print it.

Another option on this menu affects the percentages that are used by WordPerfect to determine which fonts should be chosen for extra large, large, small, fine, and other size attributes. This option does not affect individual documents, but is referred to when you select or update your list of fonts. See "Automatic Font Changes" and "Size Attribute Ratios" in this chapter for details.

PRINT TO DISK

WordPerfect lets you print a document to a file on disk with any printer definition. The document would include all printer commands normally sent to the printer. You could then print the file at any time from DOS by copying it to the printer. This is useful when WordPerfect is not available.

You can also print to disk using the DOS Text Printer definition. Although it is similar to saving a DOS text (ASCII) file, this method retains all text that is normally included in codes (such as headers, footers, and footnotes) but does not include printer commands. It also includes spaces to fully justify text, if applicable, and includes such features as page numbering, line numbering, and redline markings.

Keystrokes

Changing the Printer Selection to Print to Disk

If you are going to print to the DOS Text Printer definition, you will need to install that particular printer during Installation. If you have not done so, return to the Install program, choose the Custom option,

```
Setup: Print Options

    1 - Binding Offset                      0"

    2 - Number of Copies                    1
        Multiple Copies Generated by        WordPerfect

    3 - Graphics Quality                    Medium

    4 - Text Quality                        High

    5 - Redline Method                      Printer Dependent

    6 - Size Attribute Ratios - Fine        60%
        (% of Normal)            Small      80%
                                 Large      120%
                            Very Large      150%
                           Extra Large      200%
                        Super/Subscript     60%




    Selection: 0
```

Figure 3-139.   Print Options in the Setup menu

and then choose the option to Select a printer. Move to and select "DOS Text Printer" from the list. When you are finished, start WordPerfect and follow these steps:

1. Press Print (SHIFT-F7).

2. Type S for Select Printer.

3. Move the cursor to the printer that will be used for printing to disk, and choose 3 to Edit the printer definition.

If you print to disk often, you might consider creating a printer selection specifically for that purpose. To do so, choose 2 for Additional Printers, and select the desired printer from the list. Press Exit (F7) after you read the help information about the printer, and continue to the menu that lets you edit the printer definition.

4. Choose 2 for Port.

5. Choose 8 for Other.

6. When you are prompted for the device or filename, enter the full pathname (drive, directory, and filename) that will be used for the printed file.

7. When you return to the Printer Definition Edit menu, you might want to choose option 1 for Name and enter a name that indicates that this printer selection can be used to print a file to disk.

8. Press Exit (F7).

9. When you have returned to the list of printers, choose 1 to Select the new printer definition.

Printing to Disk

1. Press Print (SHIFT-F7) and confirm that the correct printer definition is selected. If it is not, type S for Select Printer, move to the appropriate printer, and choose 1 to Select that printer.

2. Print the document as you usually do, choosing 1 to print the Full document or 2 to print just the Page. If the document is on disk, you can use option 3 to print the Document on Disk.

3. After printing to disk, be sure to change the printer selection immediately to avoid printing another file over the original.

Hints

When selecting the "device or filename," be sure to include the drive and directory where the file will be saved. Otherwise, it will be saved in the default directory.

If you use a printer definition other than the DOS Text Printer definition, the exact printer codes will be included in the file along with the text. For example, if you have a section of boldface text, the printer codes for bold on and bold off will be included.

Applications

One reason to print to disk with a printer other than the DOS Text Printer definition is that this allows you to print a document later with that particular printer and without having WordPerfect on the computer. For example, if someone in your office (who does not use Word-Perfect) has a different printer with a specific font that you need, you can type and format a document for that printer, and then print the document to disk with that printer definition. After the file is printed to disk, you can take the disk to that computer and, from DOS, copy the file to the appropriate port. If the file was saved on the disk in drive A and the printer was attached to LPT1, the exact command would be **copy a:filename lpt1**. If the printer is attached to a different port, use that port instead of LPT1.

Related Entries

DOS Text Files
Print
Selecting a Printer

PRINTER COMMAND

Each time you select a WordPerfect feature—whether it is a Margin setting, Bold, Full Justification, or Center—you are inserting a printer command through WordPerfect. During printing, the current printer definition is used to translate the WordPerfect codes into printer commands.

The Printer Command option on the Format: Other menu lets you insert a printer command directly into the document. You can also use it to send a file to the printer.

Keystrokes

1. Move the cursor to the point at which the printer command is to be inserted.

2. Press Format (SHIFT-F8).

3. Choose **4** for **O**ther.

4. Choose **6** for **P**rinter Functions.

5. Choose **2** for **P**rinter Command. The following appears:

1 Command: 2 Filename: 0

6. Choose **1** to insert a Command, and enter the command as it is found in the printer manual, using decimal form. See "Hints" for the exact format.

If you want to send a file to the printer, choose **2** for Filename, and enter the full pathname (drive, directory, and filename) of the file to be sent.

7. Press Exit (F7) to return to the document.

Hints

If you press Reveal Codes (ALT-F3) after inserting a printer command, you will see a code similar to [Ptr Cmnd:*n*], where *n* represents the printer command or filename.

If you are sending a file to the printer, it will need to be located in the directory specified in the "Path for Downloadable and Printer Command Files." To check or change this path, edit the printer selection and choose that option.

You will usually find printer commands listed as Escape sequences (ESC Q or ESC 1A are examples) or in a BASIC format such as CHR$(27);"E";CHR$(15). They should be translated and inserted in decimal format.

Escape Sequences

As a rule, any number less than 32 or greater than 126 should be entered between angle brackets (< and >). Because the decimal value for ESC is 27, it must be entered between the brackets. Pressing ESC when entering the printer command cancels the procedure.

You can enter all other characters as themselves, or you can translate them to a decimal value and enter them between angle brackets. For example, you could enter ESC Q as <27>Q or <27><81>, because 81 is the decimal value for "Q."

The following lists commonly used commands, their abbreviations, and their decimal values:

Backspace	BS	<8>
Line feed	LF	<10>
Form feed	FF	<12>
Carriage return	CR	<13>
Escape	ESC	<27>

Converting BASIC to Decimal

You may have a BASIC file to be downloaded or find the printer command listed in a BASIC format, such as the one illustrated here:

```
10 LPRINT CHR$(15);CHR$(24);CHR$(34);
20 LPRINT CHR$(27);"E";CHR$(15);
```

Use the following rules to convert the file to the decimal format used by WordPerfect:

- Replace all parentheses with angle brackets.

- Delete any quotation marks, but do not change the text found between the quotation marks.

- Delete any other text, such as the line number, LPRINT, CHR$, and semicolons (;).

The previous example would then appear as

```
<15> <24> <35>
<27>E<15>
```

Printer Program

If you do not like the way a feature is defined for your printer, you can change it by inserting new printer commands with the Printer program. For example, if you prefer to have underlined text printed in italics, you can enter the printer commands necessary to turn italics on and off where the underline commands are to be entered.

Other Options

As you have learned, you can send a file to the printer with a Printer command. If you have several commands to send, you can type the commands on a blank screen and save them in a text file with Text In/Out (CTRL-F5). You can then download the file to the printer at once, instead of entering each command separately.

Related Entries

See Chapter 5, "Printer Program"

PRINTER CONTROL

The Printer Control menu has been renamed the Control Printer menu in versions 5.0 and 5.1. See "Control Printer" in this chapter for more information.

PRINTER SELECTION

See "Selecting a Printer" in this chapter.

PROPORTIONAL SPACING

WordPerfect can easily print proportionally spaced characters. When you print in proportional spacing, narrow characters such as the letter "l" or "i" and punctuation take up less space than characters such as "w" and "m" and capital letters.

If your printer supports proportionally spaced fonts, they will be listed when you press Font (CTRL-F8) and choose 4 for Base Font. When a proportionally spaced font is selected, WordPerfect checks the width of each character and breaks the line accordingly. If there are many capitalized letters on a line, the line will be broken sooner, because capitalized letters are wider than regular characters. You do not have to adjust margins.

If you have graphics capability, the View Document feature will let you see proportionally spaced text on the screen exactly as it will be printed. If you have a monochrome monitor, you can view the document, but you will not see proportional spacing on the screen.

Kerning is also supported in WordPerfect. It is the ability to fit the characters closer together by squeezing one character into the width allowed for the other character, such as in "We" and "To." Some proportionally spaced fonts have kerning tables predefined by WordPerfect, but the majority do not. These tables can be modified or created with the Printer (PTR) program if they do not exist. See "Kerning" and Chapter 5 for details.

Printers either adjust for proportional spacing and right justification by using HMI (horizontal motion index) or by microspacing a specific number of units at a time. Printing proportionally spaced fonts or right-justified text is slower and sometimes more "jumpy" than that of nonjustified, nonproportionally spaced text.

Adjusting the Amount of Space Between Words

If there is an unacceptable amount of space between words, you can do one or more of the following:

- Turn on hyphenation.

- Decrease the hyphenation zone for a more even right margin.

- Turn off right justification.

- Adjust the amount of word and letter spacing. If you have justification on, you can adjust the word spacing justification limits. Options for both of these adjustments can be found by pressing Format (SHIFT-F8) and choosing 4 for **O**ther and 6 for **P**rinter Functions. See "Word and Letter Spacing" and "Word Spacing Justification Limits" in this chapter for more information.

Related Entries

Fonts
Justification
Kerning
Word and Letter Spacing
Word Spacing Justification Limits
See Chapter 5, "Printer Program"

PROTECT A BLOCK OF TEXT

You can prevent a block of text from being split between pages with Block Protect and Conditional End of Page. You can use Block Protect to protect a block of text in which the number of lines may change after editing. Use Conditional End of Page to protect a specific number of lines. See "Block Protect" and "Conditional End of Page" in this chapter for details.

PROTECT A DOCUMENT

See "Lock and Unlock Documents" in this chapter.

PRTSC KEY

Most computers have a PRTSC key, which is used to print the contents of the screen to a parallel printer. It is usually used with the SHIFT key so that you do not do a "screen dump" by mistake.

If you press SHIFT-PRTSC, it will print all text on the screen, including the status line. If you have a laser printer, you will need to press the Form Feed button on the printer panel on the front of the printer to eject that page after printing the screen.

WordPerfect lets you print a block of text or a single page without the status line. See "Print" in this chapter for more information.

PULL-DOWN MENUS

You can use the new pull-down menus with or without a mouse. If you have a mouse, see "Mouse Support and Pull-Down Menus" in this chapter for details.

The following instructions are for people who do not have a mouse but still want to use the pull-down menus. The features in WordPerfect may appear less hidden on the pull-down menus than they are on the function keys, which should help people who are unfamiliar with the program.

Keystrokes

1. Press ALT-= to display the menu bar across the top of the screen, as shown in the following illustration. See "Hints" for other options that you can use to display the menu bar.

```
 File Edit Search Layout Mark Tools Font Graphics Help
```

If you want to remove the menu bar from the screen, press ALT-= again. You can also use Exit (F7), Cancel (F1), or ESC.

2. Each option on the list usually has a mnemonic letter selection that is displayed in Bold (or a different color). To go to a particular item in the menu bar quickly, type the letter, and the pull-down menu for that item will appear.

You can also move to a particular selection with the arrow keys ($\leftarrow$, $\rightarrow$, $\uparrow$ and $\downarrow$). If you move to an item on the right, you can then press $\downarrow$ to display that item's pull-down menu.

3. Type the mnemonic letter selection, or move to the desired feature using the arrow keys and press ENTER to select it. A triangle indicates that a submenu is associated with that feature (as shown in Figure 3-140). The submenu will appear when the cursor is moved to that feature.

When you select an option, the pull-down menus disappear. If you do not want to make a selection, press Exit (F7) to remove the menus from the screen, or press Cancel (F1) to return to the previous menu.

Hints

Options in Setup (SHIFT-F1) let you customize the way the menu bar and pull-down menus are displayed. You can also choose to have the menu bar displayed at all times (which is more useful when you are using a mouse) or displayed when you press the ALT key.

To make changes to these options, press Setup (SHIFT-F1), and choose 2 for **D**isplay and then 4 for **M**enu Options. The menu shown in Figure 3-141 appears.

Options 2, 3, 5, and 6 control the way the regular text and mnemonic letter selections appear in the menu bar and pull-down menus. If you select any of these options, you will see the categories Size and Appearance as well as Normal. These options let you choose to have the regular text or mnemonic selection appear in bold, underline, normal, a different color (if you have a color monitor), or screen font (such as large if you have a graphics card that provides screen fonts). The selections that you make match the colors, fonts, or attributes that are normally displayed when you use those features in a document. For example, if you use yellow to represent Strikeout, you can select Strikeout for the attribute, and it will appear yellow as well.

Option 4 lets you use the ALT key to select the pull-down menus as an alternative to pressing ALT-=. If you choose this option, you would press ALT and then *release* it before the menu bar would be displayed.

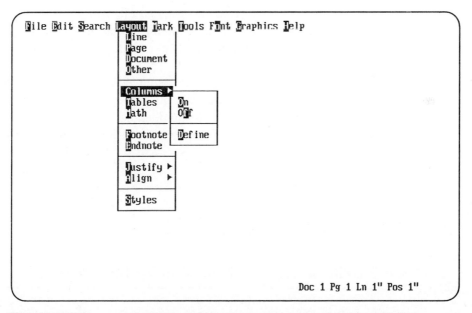

Figure 3-140.   A sample pull-down menu with a triangle indicating that a submenu is available

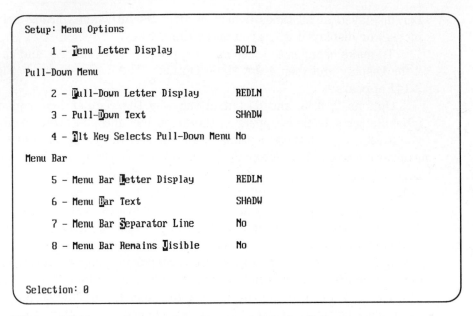

```
Setup: Menu Options

     1 - Menu Letter Display          BOLD

Pull-Down Menu

     2 - Pull-Down Letter Display     REDLN

     3 - Pull-Down Text               SHADW

     4 - Alt Key Selects Pull-Down Menu No

Menu Bar

     5 - Menu Bar Letter Display      REDLN

     6 - Menu Bar Text                SHADW

     7 - Menu Bar Separator Line      No

     8 - Menu Bar Remains Visible     No


Selection: 0
```

Figure 3-141.   Setup options for menu bar and pull-down menus

Option 8, Menu Bar Remains Visible, is useful if you are using a mouse. Mnemonic letter selections are turned off, and you can enter the text in the document without making menu selections. You would still need to press ALT-= (or ALT if you made that change in the Setup menu) to enter the menu bar.

If you decide to have the menu bar displayed at all times, you might want to consider selecting option **7**, Menu Bar Separator Line, so that a line will separate the menu bar from the document.

After making the necessary changes, press Exit (F7) to return to the document.

Related Entries

Mouse Support and Pull-Down Menus

"PUT WP 2 DISK BACK IN DRIVE" ERROR MESSAGE

You might see this error message if you have removed the WordPerfect 2 disk from the drive and WordPerfect is trying to access the program files. The most common reason for this error message is removing the disk and then trying to exit WordPerfect.

Reasons

Overflow files are usually kept where the WP.EXE and WP.FIL files are. If you redirected the overflow files to another disk drive with the /D option and then removed the disk from that drive, you could get the error message.

If you have expanded memory, you can press Shell (CTRL-F1), go to DOS, and try to start WordPerfect again (instead of typing **exit** to return). If you do this, you are asked if other copies of WordPerfect are running. If you type **N** but there is another copy running, WordPerfect will overwrite the overflow files for the first copy. If you then exit the second copy of WordPerfect and return to the first copy, it will not find the temporary files when it tries to access the disk and will display the error message. You will have to reboot the computer.

This error message can also occur if you go to DOS and delete the temporary WordPerfect files—marked with }WP{ as part of the file-name—and then reenter WordPerfect. If you have different versions of DOS on your computer, you might also see this message.

Solutions

Place the WordPerfect disk into the appropriate disk drive, and press any key to continue. If you have redirected the overflow files to another disk drive, insert that disk into the appropriate drive.

If you want to load the WordPerfect program into memory and redirect the overflow files to a RAM drive, you can remove the Word-Perfect disk and use the drive for the Speller or Thesaurus disk to eliminate disk switching.

If you go to DOS with Shell (CTRL-F1), return to WordPerfect by typing **exit** at the DOS prompt. While you are at DOS, do not start another copy of WordPerfect or you could overwrite the overflow files or delete the temporary files from DOS.

Related Entries

Start WordPerfect

QUALITY OF PRINT

You can easily choose the print quality for text or graphics. You can also choose not to print either text or graphics if you need a quick draft of a document or if you do not have enough memory in the printer to print both on the same page.

If you want to increase the speed at which tables are printed, you can decrease the Graphics Quality to draft and not actually see a difference in the quality of the graphics lines.

Keystrokes

1. Press Print (SHIFT-F7).

2. Type **G** for **G**raphics Quality or **T** for **T**ext Quality. The following options appear for both:

```
Text Quality: 1 Do Not Print; 2 Draft; 3 Medium; 4 High: 4
```

3. Choose the appropriate selection.

Hints

A selected option affects only the current document. When you clear the screen, the default settings are again in effect.

As a default, Text Quality is set to High, and Graphics Quality is set to Medium. You can change the default settings for these and other print options in the Setup (SHIFT-F1) menu. To do so, press Setup (SHIFT-F1) and choose 4 for Initial Settings and then 8 for Print Options. After changing the applicable settings, press Exit (F7) to return to the document.

The current settings are saved with the document. If you make a change and then save the document, you will not have to change the setting the next time it is printed.

If you choose "Do Not Print" for either Text or Graphics Quality, special characters that are not available in the current font, and are therefore created and printed graphically, will not print. If Text Quality is set to High, the special characters will print in high quality. If Text Quality is set to anything less than High, the graphics characters will print in the quality set for Graphics Quality.

Applications

Besides the obvious application—being able to print a draft or final version of a document—these options may be necessary, because some printers cannot print both text and graphics on the same page. If this is the case, you can choose not to print graphics, print the text of the document, and then feed the paper back through the printer while printing only graphics.

Some page printers, such as laser printers, compose an entire page before printing it instead of printing line by line. If you have a large amount of graphics on the page, you may see the message, "Not enough memory" when printing. If this happens, you can either decrease the quality of print for both text and graphics or print them separately on the same page.

QUIT PRINTING

See "Stop Printing" and "Cancel a Print Job" in this chapter.

RAM DRIVES

You can use a RAM (random access memory) drive to speed up Word-Perfect. A better option, however, is to use expanded memory and/or a "cache" that places often used information in memory and cuts down on disk access. Programs such as PC Tools can be used to create extra "cache."

See "Expanded Memory" in this chapter for more information about using expanded memory to increase the speed of WordPerfect.

RECTANGULAR MOVE AND COPY

WordPerfect lets you define a rectangular block of text from one corner to the opposite corner. You can move or copy the rectangle to another location or delete it. See "Move" in this chapter for details.

REDLINE

The Redline feature marks text that is being considered for addition. Usually, a shaded background is printed behind redlined text or a vertical bar is printed in the margin to indicate that a change has been made on that line. You can also have the vertical bar alternate between the left and right margins. If the printer can print in color, redlined text may print in red.

You can mark redlined text manually, or you can have WordPerfect check each phrase in your document for additions and have the redline marks inserted automatically (see "Compare Documents" in this chapter for more information).

Keystrokes

You can manually redline text as you type or after you have typed it.

Redline As You Type

1. Press Font (CTRL-F8).

2. Choose **2** for **A**ppearance.

3. Choose **8** for **R**edln.

4. Type the text to be redlined.

5. Press → once to move past the redline-off code.

Redline Text After You Type It

1. Move the cursor to one end of the text to be redlined, and press Block (ALT-F4) to turn on Block.

2. Move the cursor to the opposite end of the text.

3. Press Font (CTRL-F8).

4. Choose 2 for Appearance.

5. Choose 8 for Redln. The codes [REDLN] and [redln] are inserted at the beginning and end of the block.

Automatic Redline and Strikeout

WordPerfect can check the document on the screen against a document on disk, and mark all additions with redline and all deletions with strikeout.

1. Retrieve and make changes to a document.

2. Press Mark Text (ALT-F5).

3. Choose 6 for Generate.

4. Choose 2 for Compare Screen and Disk Documents and Add Redline and Strikeout.

5. "Other Document:" will appear on the status line, with the filename of the document on the screen. Press ENTER to compare the document on the screen with the named file, or enter a different filename.

A counter will appear at the bottom of the screen to let you know that progress is being made. After the process is finished, you will be returned to the document.

Hints

When you turn on Redline, the redline-on and redline-off codes, [RED-LN] and [redln], are both inserted. If you have chosen a different screen attribute, color, or font to represent redlined text, the position number on the status line will change to indicate that redline is currently on.

Although redline does not show on the normal editing screen, you can see the effect if you view the document by pressing Print (SHIFT-F7) and choosing **6** for View. Press Exit (F7) when you are finished.

Changing the Redline Method

WordPerfect will print redlined text according to the current printer definition. If the printer has the capability, it will print the text on a lightly shaded background, as shown here:

The townhouse located at 3982 E. Oak Street will be available as of November 25, 1990. Monthly rent is $640 with a $150 deposit. There will be an additional $50 deposit if the person renting has pets.

If you have a color printer, the Redline feature can be defined to print the text in red. You can print the PRINTER.TST document (installed with the PTR Program files) to determine how your printer is defined to print redline. To change the current method of redline printing, follow these steps:

1. Press Format (SHIFT-F8).

2. Choose **3** for **D**ocument.

3. Choose **4** for **R**edline Method. The following choices appear:

```
Redline Method: 1 Printer Dependent; 2 Left; 3 Alternating: 1
```

4. Choose **1** for **P**rinter Dependent to use the method as it has been entered in the printer definition, **2** to print a redline character in the

Left margin, or 3 for **A**lternating to print the redline character in the left margin on even pages and in the right margin on odd pages.

5. If you choose option 2 or 3, you are asked to enter the character to be used as the redline character. The ¦ symbol is displayed as the default character; press ENTER to accept it, or enter a symbol of your own.

If you prefer another method, you can change the codes in the printer definition (.PRS file) with the Printer program. See Chapter 5 for more information.

See "Strikeout" in this chapter for a similar feature, which strikes through text being considered for deletion.

If you decide that the redlined text should be added to the document and the redline marks removed, you can press Mark Text (ALT-F5), choose 6 for Generate, and then choose 1 for **R**emove Redline Markings and Strikeout Text from Document. The Remove feature is used to remove all redline marks (and to delete the strikeout text). If you want to remove only the redline marks, use the Replace feature to search for the [REDLN] codes, and replace them with nothing (thus deleting them and the ending codes). You can be selective about which marks to remove by confirming each replacement. See "Replace" and "Remove Redline and Strikeout" in this chapter for details.

Related Entries

Remove Redline and Strikeout
Replace
Strikeout
See also Chapter 5, "Printer Program"

REFERENCES

WordPerfect has a feature that automatically updates references to specific pages, footnotes, endnotes, paragraph and outline numbers, and graphics boxes. See "Cross-References" in this chapter for more information.

REFORMATTING

You do not have to repaginate or reformat with WordPerfect. If you make a change to a document, the text is reformatted automatically when you press any cursor key.

You can turn off the Automatically Format and Rewrite option so that the text will reformat only as you move the cursor through it. To rewrite the screen quickly, you can press Screen (CTRL-F3) twice. See "Automatically Format and Rewrite" and "Rewrite the Screen" in this chapter for more information.

REMOVE REDLINE AND STRIKEOUT

An option on the Mark Text Generate menu lets you remove all redline marks and delete the text marked for strikeout.

Keystrokes

1. Press Mark Text (ALT-F5).

2. Choose **6** for **G**enerate.

3. Choose **1** for **R**emove Redline Markings and Strikeout Text from Document.

4. Type **Y** or **N** in answer to the question "Delete redline markings and strikeout text? No (Yes)."

You will remain in the Generate menu until the process is complete; the cursor will then be placed at the end of the document.

Hints

You can selectively remove only redline marks, only text marked for strikeout, or selected redline marks and selected sections of strikeout text.

Remove All or Selected Redline Markings

You can use the following steps to delete all redline markings or selected markings:

1. Move the cursor to the beginning of the document with HOME, HOME, ↑, and then press Replace (ALT-F2).

2. Type **Y** when asked if you want to replace with confirmation (if you want to delete only selected redline marks), or type **N** if you want all redline marks removed.

3. When "→ Srch:" appears, press Font (CTRL-F8), choose **2** for Appearance, and then choose **8** for **R**edln to insert the [REDLN] code as the search string.

4. Press Search (F2) twice to start the Replace feature. Don't use a replacement string so that the code will be deleted.

5. If you typed **Y** to confirm each replacement, the cursor will pause at each [REDLN] code and ask if it should be replaced. Type **Y** to delete the code or **N** to leave it.

Delete All or Selected Strikeout Text

If you want to delete only selected sections of strikeout text, you can use Replace as you would with redline marks as explained above. Type **Y** in answer to the question "w/Confirm?", and instead of searching for [REDLN] codes, search for [STKOUT] codes. Although it may seem confusing, type **Y** to replace (delete) the [STKOUT] code and thus leave the text in place. If you want the text removed with the Remove feature, type **N** to leave the [STKOUT] code.

When finished, follow the steps for Remove to delete the text that remains and is marked with the [STKOUT] codes.

If you want to delete all the strikeout text but leave the redline marks intact, you will need to define a macro. Replace can delete the [STKOUT] codes but not the text between the codes.

The macro should search for the strikeout-on [STKOUT] code, turn Block on, search for the strikeout-off [stkout] code, and delete the block. You can then chain the macro to itself so it will repeat until no other occurrences of [STKOUT] are found.

Related Entries

Redline
Replace
Strikeout

RENAME A FILE

The List Files menu in WordPerfect lets you rename a file without having to leave WordPerfect and use the DOS RENAME command. You can either rename the file and leave it in the same directory or move it to a different directory.

Keystrokes

1. Press List (F5). The default drive/directory is displayed.

2. Press ENTER to see a list of the files in that directory, edit the displayed drive/directory and press ENTER, or enter the name of a different directory.

3. Move the cursor to the file to be renamed.

4. Choose 3 for **Move/Rename**.

5. Enter the new filename; a directory name is not required to rename the file. If you enter the name of a directory other than the one currently listed along with the same filename, the file will be moved to that directory, with no confirmation.

6. Press Exit (F7) to leave the List Files menu.

Hints

If you enter the name of a file that already exists, or if you use illegal characters, you will see the error message "Can't rename file."

If you want to move a file to a different directory but also leave the original where it is, you can copy a file from the List Files menu. After moving the cursor to the file to be copied, choose 8 for Copy, and enter the full pathname (including the new filename).

If you want to rename a file from DOS, exit WordPerfect and enter **rename** *oldfilename newfilename* at the DOS prompt.

Related Entries

List Files

REPEAT VALUE

You can repeat a key or macro any number of times with the ESC key. When you press ESC, you will see "Repeat Value = 8." This repeat value can be changed temporarily or permanently. See "ESC Key" in this chapter for more information.

REPLACE

You can use Replace to search for text or WordPerfect codes and replace or delete them. You can confirm each replacement (or deletion) if desired.

Keystrokes

Move the cursor to the point at which the Replace feature is to begin. Replace can work in both directions.

1. Press Replace (ALT-F2). If you also want to replace headers, footers, footnotes, endnotes, text boxes, and graphics box captions, press HOME just before pressing Replace (ALT F2) to do an extended search and replace.

2. Type **Y** or **N** in answer to the question "w/Confirm? **No** (**Yes**)."

3. "→ Srch:" appears. If you want to change the direction of the search and replace, press ↑.

4. Type the characters for the search string. If you want to include a WordPerfect code, press the function key that you normally use to start the feature. See "Hints" for more information about searching for WordPerfect codes.

5. Press Search (F2) to continue. Do not press ENTER to enter the search string; a [HRt] code will be inserted instead.

6. "Replace with:" appears. Type the characters to be used as the replacement string. You can also use a limited number of codes; see "Hints" for more information. If you want to delete the search string without replacing it, leave the replacement string blank.

7. Press Search (F2) to start the process. (Avoid pressing ENTER, or a [HRt] code will be inserted.) If you decide against the replacement, press Cancel (F1).

Hints

In earlier versions of WordPerfect, ESC was used to insert the search or replacement string and to begin the procedure. You can still use ESC for that purpose; any search or replace keys can be used to start the process as well.

After a replace is finished, the cursor remains at the last successful replacement. To return the cursor to its original location before you used Replace, press Go To (CTRL-HOME) twice.

Replace Within a Block

Replace works only in a forward direction when you use it for a defined block. If you have a section within the document to be affected, define a block first, and then follow the steps just described.

Case-Sensitive Replace

WordPerfect will search for both uppercase and lowercase characters if lowercase is entered as the search string. If you enter the search string in uppercase, however, only uppercase occurrences will be found.

The replacement string will be inserted exactly as you type it, with one exception. If the search string is found in uppercase, the first character of the replacement string will automatically be capitalized.

Whole-Word Search and Replace

WordPerfect does not have an option for whole-word searches. Instead, you must place a space before and after a word to indicate that it should be searched for as a whole word and not as part of another word. For example, if you wanted to search for "and" but did not include spaces, you would find occurrences of "band," "demands," "landmark," and so on.

When you include spaces before and after, the search string will not be found if the word is at the beginning of a paragraph or at the end of a sentence; instead, it will be preceded by a [HRt] or a [Tab] code or followed by some type of punctuation.

Wildcard Characters in a Search String

You can include the wildcard character ^X as part of the search string to match any character. However, you cannot use it as the first character in the string.

To insert ˄X into the search string, press CTRL-V first and then CTRL-X. The ˄X will appear in boldface, because it is considered a code rather than text.

Using WordPerfect Codes in Replace

You can search for any WordPerfect code, but you must enter it correctly. You cannot type a facsimile of the code; you must enter it with the appropriate function key. For example, if you want to search for the bold-on code [BOLD], you would press Bold (F6) when you are prompted for the search string. To search for an off code, press the applicable function key twice: once to insert the on code and again to insert the off code. If only the off code is needed, move the cursor to the on code and delete it. For example, if you want to search for the bold-off code [bold], press Bold (F6) twice and then delete the [BOLD] code.

Often, when pressing a function key to insert a code, you will see a menu of choices. Type the number of the desired code to insert it into the search string.

The following is a list of functions that you may want to search for. The keystrokes on the right are sometimes preceded by CTRL-V. If you press the CTRL-V combination, you are asked "Key =," whereupon you should press the second keystroke combination.

Hard return [HRt]	ENTER
Soft return [SRt]	CTRL-V and then CTRL-M
Hard page [HPg]	CTRL-ENTER
Soft page [SPg]	CTRL-V and then CTRL-K

You cannot search for specific parameters within codes. You can search for margin changes or font changes, but you cannot search for specific margin changes (where the left margin changed to 2 inches, for example) or specific font changes. However, if you use the Program Editor provided with WordPerfect Library, you can identify the codes used for each function and then search for the codes and replace them. If you cannot decide which function code to use, contact WordPerfect Corporation for a list.

Although you can search for all WordPerfect codes, you can use only certain codes in the replacement string. The following list shows a few codes that you can use in the replacement string:

[Tab] (any type of tab; see "Tabs" in this chapter)
[→Indent]
[→Indent←]
Bold
Underline
Center
Flush right
Hard return
Hard page
Cancel hyphenation (HOME, /)
Invisible soft return (HOME, ENTER)
Hyphen (-)
Hard hyphen (HOME, -)
Soft hyphen (CTRL, -)

You can use other codes as well. Try inserting a code as the need arises. If the code is not accepted, you cannot use it with Replace, but you may be able to use a macro, as described next.

Using Macros to Replace a Code with Any Other Code

Although you cannot always use Replace to replace one code with another, you can define a macro to search for a code, delete it, and then insert the new code. The macro can then be chained to itself so that it will repeat until no further occurrences of the search string are found. See "Macros" in this chapter for details.

Using Replace in a Macro

If you include Search in a macro, and the search string is not found, the macro is automatically ended. Because a macro will not end when a replace is finished, more than one replace can be included in a macro.

Applications

If you have created a letter or a document and later find that the same letter or document needs to be sent to other people, you can use Replace to search for all occurrences of one name and replace it with another, rather than setting up the letter for a merge.

One of the most powerful features of Replace is that it allows you to search and delete if you leave the replacement string empty. This feature is useful for deleting all margin changes in a document, various spacing settings, and bold and underline codes. If you are having a problem with a document, you can use Replace to search for a possible offending code and delete all occurrences of that code.

Related Entries

Macros
Search

RESTART THE PRINTER

While printing, WordPerfect may stop so you can insert a new sheet of paper or a different type of form, or change the print wheel. Typing **G** while you are in the Control Printer menu will send a "Go" and restart the printer. You can also use this command if you have stopped printing a document from the Control Printer menu.

Keystrokes

1. Press Print (SHIFT-F7).

2. Choose 4 for Control Printer.

3. Type **G** to send a "Go" and restart the printer.

4. Press ENTER to return to the document.

Hints

If you are using manually fed paper or are changing print wheels often, you might consider defining a macro that will send the printer a "Go" without leaving the current document. To define the macro, press Macro Def (CTRL-F10), name the macro (ALT-G is a suggestion), enter a description, and then enter the keystrokes just listed. When finished, press Macro Def (CTRL-F10) again to end the macro definition. To use the macro, press ALT-G when you hear the computer beep.

If you stop the printer on the first page and then restart it by sending a "Go," it will resume printing at the beginning of the document. If more than one page was printed, you will see "Restart on page:" with the last page number sent to the printer displayed as the default. Enter the page number to start with.

Related Entries

Control Printer
Stop Printing

RESTORE DELETED TEXT

You can delete any amount of text and then restore it with Cancel (F1). In fact, you can restore the last three deletions. See "Undelete" in this chapter for details.

RETRIEVE

You can use Retrieve (SHIFT-F10) to retrieve a file to the screen or to retrieve moved or copied text.

You can also retrieve files from the List Files menu, or press Move (CTRL-F4) to retrieve text that you have moved or copied.

Keystrokes

Retrieve a File with Retrieve (SHIFT-F10)

If you do not want to retrieve a new document into one already on the screen, clear the screen first with Exit (F7). See "Exit" in this chapter for more information.

1. Press Retrieve (SHIFT-F10).

2. Enter the name of the file. If it is not saved in the default drive and directory, enter the drive and directory in which the file can be found.

If the file is not found, you will see the error message "File not found," and you will be prompted to try again. If the file is found, it will be retrieved at the cursor's position.

Retrieve a File from the List Files Menu

If you do not want to retrieve a file into the document currently on the screen, clear the screen first using Exit (F7).

1. Press List (F5).

2. Press ENTER to see a list of the files in the displayed directory, edit the directory name and press ENTER, or enter the name of a different directory. If you know some of the characters in the filename, you can enter a template with wildcard characters; for example, if you know that the file starts with the name "Smith" but you are not sure of the exact extension, enter **SMITH.***.

3. Move the cursor to the file to be retrieved.

4. Check "Document Size" in the upper left corner of the menu before choosing **1** to **R**etrieve the file. If the number shown is 0, there is not a document on the screen, and the files will not be combined. If there is any other number for the current document size, retrieving the file will insert it where the cursor was positioned in the document.

5. If there is a document currently in memory, you will see "Retrieve into current document? No (Yes)." Type **Y** to confirm that you want to retrieve the file into the current one, or type **N** to cancel the request.

Retrieve Moved or Copied Text

When you move or copy text, you can retrieve it immediately by moving the cursor to the correct position and pressing ENTER. However, if you do not want to retrieve the text immediately, you can press Cancel (F1) and then retrieve it later with Retrieve (SHIFT-F10) or Move (CTRL-F4). These two methods are described here:

• Move to the new location, press Retrieve (SHIFT-F10), and then press ENTER instead of entering a filename. This procedure will only retrieve a moved or copied block, not a tabular column or rectangle.

• Move the cursor to the new location, press Move (CTRL-F4), choose 4 for Retrieve, and then choose 1 to Retrieve the moved or copied Block, 2 to retrieve the Tabular Column, or 3 to retrieve the Rectangle.

Hints

When you retrieve a file, a copy of the file is retrieved. The original remains on the disk so you can return to it if necessary. When you save the copy on the screen with Save (F10) or Exit (F7), you are asked if you want to replace the original on disk with the copy on the screen. If you type **Y**, the original is renamed with the extension BK!, the copy is saved, and the original is deleted. If you have the Original Backup feature on, the original is kept on the disk instead of being deleted. If you do not have Original Backup on and want to save both the original and the copy, type **N** and enter a different name for the copy.

While in the List Files menu, you can check the contents of a file before retrieving it. Press ENTER or choose 6 to Look at the file. If the document includes a Document Summary, it is displayed at the beginning of the file. If you know part of the filename or a unique term used in the file—the author, typist, or date of creation, for example—but you cannot remember the filename, you can use option **9** for **F**ind on the List Files menu.

If you press Retrieve (SHIFT-F10) and cannot remember the filename, you can press List (F5) and then press ENTER to see a list of files in a specific drive and directory.

You can also use Retrieve (SHIFT-F10) or the Retrieve option in the List Files menu to retrieve a locked document. If the file is locked, you are asked for the password. After you enter it, the file is retrieved at the cursor's location.

Text that you have moved or copied is saved to the same unnamed file until you perform another move or copy. When you retrieve the moved or copied text, only a copy is retrieved. You can retrieve the same text several times in different locations.

Retrieving a Document with a Different Printer Selection

When you save a document, WordPerfect stores the name and the date of the printer definition (.PRS file) in the document header. When you retrieve the document, WordPerfect checks the document header to see which printer was selected and compares this selection to the current printer selection. If you have selected a different printer in the meantime, WordPerfect will search for the original .PRS file and reselect it for you. When you exit the document, WordPerfect returns to the previously selected printer definition.

If the original .PRS file is not found, WordPerfect will format the document for the printer that is currently selected. While doing so, WordPerfect displays the message "Document formatted for default printer." When this is done, WordPerfect checks the available fonts in the current printer selection and converts the fonts in the document to ones that are the closest match. It will also try to match the paper size and type to one that is closest to the original selection.

When you look in Reveal Codes, an asterisk appears at the beginning of the Font or Paper Size/Type code to indicate that it is a converted font; for example, [Font:*Century Schoolbook 11pt (SA)] would be a converted font. If you return to the original printer selection, the fonts and paper size/type will be converted back to the original selections.

An option in the Setup (SHIFT-F1) menu lets you format all documents for the current printer, regardless of the printer definition saved with the file. To select this option, press Setup (SHIFT-F1), choose 4 for **I**nitial Settings and then 4 to **F**ormat Retrieved Documents for Default Printer. As each document is retrieved, it is formatted for the current printer selection. This is useful when you have switched printers or when you are working on a network. See "Print Options" or "Initial Settings" in this chapter for more information.

Types of Files That You Can Retrieve

You can retrieve WordPerfect 5.0 and 4.2 files directly into WordPerfect 5.1 without converting them. See "Compatibility" in this chapter for information about other options that are available when you are retrieving files created with earlier versions of WordPerfect.

You can also directly retrieve spreadsheets created in PlanPerfect, Excel, and Lotus 1-2-3 without converting them first. You can retrieve the spreadsheet as a table (see "Tables" in this chapter) or text. Refer to "Spreadsheet Importing and Linking" in this chapter for details.

You can retrieve a DOS text (ASCII) file as you would any other file, or you can use the Text In/Out (CTRL-F5) option to save or retrieve a DOS text file. See "DOS Text Files" in this chapter for more information.

You can use the Convert program included with WordPerfect to convert files created with other programs to WordPerfect format. See "Convert" in this chapter for more information.

Related Entries

Backup
Compatibility
Initial Settings
Lock and Unlock Documents
Move
Print Options
Spreadsheet Importing and Linking
Tables

RETRIEVE TEXT FROM THE CLIPBOARD

If you have WordPerfect Library running and press Shell (CTRL-F1), you will see the following menu:

```
1 Go to Shell; Clipboard: 2 Save; 3 Append; 4 Retrieve; 5 DOS Command: 0
```

Choose **4** to **R**etrieve text that has been saved to the Clipboard by WordPerfect and other products. See "Shell" in this chapter for more information.

RETURN

WordPerfect uses several types of "returns" to break the line at the right margin. See "ENTER Key" in this chapter for details.

REVEAL CODES

WordPerfect displays text on the screen with an appearance as close as possible to that of the printed document. Codes are not shown on the regular screen. However, Reveal Codes (ALT-F3) lets you look "behind the scenes" at the codes that you have inserted.

Keystrokes

1. Press Reveal Codes (ALT-F3).

2. The screen is divided into upper and lower halves by a ruler line that shows margin and tab settings as brackets, braces, and triangles. The top of the screen displays the regular text; both text and codes are displayed in the lower half. Figure 3-142 shows a sample Reveal Codes screen.

3. The location of the cursor is represented by a reverse video block. If the cursor is on a character or code, that character or code will appear in reverse video, which is the opposite of normal text. You can use any of the cursor keys to move the cursor, including Search (F2) and Reverse Search (SHIFT-F2). When you move the cursor, it changes position on screen both above and below the ruler line.

4. Press Reveal Codes (ALT-F3) to leave the Reveal Codes screen.

```
                  THE CONSTITUTION OF THE UNITED STATES

                             PREAMBLE


       We the people of the United States, in Order to form a more

perfect Union, establish Justice, insure domestic Tranquility,

provide for the common defense, promote the general Welfare, and
                                        Doc 1 Pg 1 Ln 1" Pos 1"
[   ▲    ▲    ▲    ▲    ▲    ▲    ▲    ▲    ▲    ▲    }    ▲    ▲
[Ln Spacing:2][Center][BOLD]THE CONSTITUTION OF THE UNITED STATES[bold][HRt]
[Center][UND]PREAMBLE[und][HRt]
[HRt]
[Tab]We the people of the United States, in Order to form a more[SRt]
perfect Union, establish Justice, insure domestic Tranquility,[SRt]
provide for the common defense, promote the general Welfare, and[SRt]
secure the Blessings of Liberty to ourselves and our Posterity, do[SRt]
ordain and establish this Constitution for the United States of[SRt]
America.[HRt]
[HRt]

Press Reveal Codes to restore screen
```

Figure 3-142.   Sample Reveal Codes screen

Hints

All keys work in the Reveal Codes screen exactly as they do in the normal screen. If you press Exit (F7), you will see the prompts asking if you want to save the document before exiting. Cancel (F1) will cancel a menu or undelete as it would in the normal screen. Even these two keys will not let you exit Reveal Codes. The only key that will return you to normal editing is Reveal Codes (ALT-F3).

While in the Reveal Codes screen, you can press Block (ALT-F4) so you can see which codes to include or exclude when defining the block. See "Codes" in this chapter for an explanation about each code.

Going into Reveal Codes lets you see a ruler line that indicates the position of margins and tabs temporarily. This is a convenient way to display the current margin and tab settings briefly. If you prefer to have the ruler line at the bottom of the screen during an editing session, press Screen (CTRL-F3), choose option **1** for Window, press ↑ once, and then press ENTER.

Changing the Size of Reveal Codes

The Reveal Codes screen usually uses ten lines of the screen. An option in the Setup menu lets you change the size of the Reveal Codes screen to show more or less text. You can also set the Reveal Codes screen to show only the current code or cursor.

1. Press Setup (SHIFT-F1).

2. Choose **2** for **D**isplay.

3. Choose **6** for **E**dit-Screen Options.

4. Choose **6** for **R**eveal Codes Window Size, and enter the number of lines to be given to the Reveal Codes window. If you enter **1**, you will see only the current code or character in the Reveal Codes screen.

5. Press Exit (F7) when finished.

Related Entries

Block
Codes

Cursor Keys
Ruler Line
Search

REVERSE SEARCH

You can use Reverse Search (SHIFT-F2) to search for text or WordPerfect codes backward from your present location in a document. To search in a forward direction, use Search (F2). See "Search" in this chapter for details.

REWRITE THE SCREEN

When you use any cursor key, WordPerfect rewrites the screen from the cursor down.

Keystrokes

If the screen does not appear to reformat correctly or if you want to rewrite the entire screen (not just from the cursor down), use the following steps:

1. Press Screen (CTRL-F3). The following menu appears:

```
1 Window; 2 Line Draw; 3 Rewrite: 3
```

2. Press ENTER or the space bar, or choose 3 to Rewrite the screen.

Another shortcut is pressing Screen (CTRL-F3) twice.

Hints

If you want to turn off automatic reformatting and rewrite (it is preset to on), press Setup (SHIFT-F1), choose 2 for Display, 6 for Edit-Screen Options, and 1 for Automatically Format and Rewrite; and then type **N** to turn it off. If you turn this option off, text will still be reformatted automatically, but you will be required to move the cursor through the text with ↓, Screen Down (+ on the numeric keypad or HOME, ↓) or PGDN. You can also use the steps listed in "Keystrokes" to rewrite the entire screen.

Applications

Turning off automatic reformatting and rewriting increases the speed of the text display slightly. It is particularly useful when you are working in side-by-side newspaper columns, where there is constant reformatting when text is added or deleted.

Related Entries

Columns

RIGHT ALIGN TEXT

You can align text at the right margin with Flush Right (ALT-F6). You can also right-align text at a tab setting by setting a right-align tab. See "Flush Right" and "Tabs" in this chapter for more information.

RIGHT INDENT

You can use →Indent← (SHIFT-F4) to indent text equally from the left and right margins. See "Indent" in this chapter for details and options.

RIGHT JUSTIFICATION

See "Justification" in this chapter.

ROTATE TEXT

You can define a type of paper in the Paper Size/Type menu that will let you print with a landscape font, or you can define an 11" by 8.5" form, turn the paper on its side in the printer, and print with a portrait (regular) font, or rotate text in a graphics box. See "Landscape Printing," "Fonts," and "Graphics Boxes" in this chapter for more information.

RULER LINE

You can display a ruler that shows the current margins and tab settings temporarily with Reveal Codes (ALT-F3) or during a single editing session with Screen (CTRL-F3).

Keystrokes

Display the Ruler Line Temporarily

1. Press Reveal Codes (ALT-F3). The screen is divided by the ruler line, as shown in Figure 3-142 (see "Reveal Codes" in this chapter).

2. Press Reveal Codes (ALT-F3) again to remove the ruler from the screen and return to the normal editing screen.

Display the Ruler for a Single Editing Session

1. Press Screen (CTRL-F3).

2. Choose 1 for Window. The following appears at the bottom of the screen:

```
Number of lines in this window: 24
```

3. Press ↑ once to move the ruler line up to the bottom of the screen, and press ENTER. The ruler is displayed just below the status line, as shown here:

Doc 1 Pg 1 Ln 1" Pos 1"

Margins are shown as square brackets ([and]), and tab settings are displayed as triangles. If a margin and a tab occur in the same location, the margin is displayed as a brace ({ or }).

Removing the Ruler

1. Press Screen (CTRL-F3).

2. Choose **1** for **Window**.

3. Press ↓ once to remove the ruler from the screen, and press ENTER.

Hints

When you display the ruler at the bottom of the screen, it is displayed at the bottom of both document 1 and document 2. If the ruler is not displayed at the bottom of the screen, it is used to split the screen and display both documents at once. They are shown in two separate "windows" divided by the ruler.

Applications

The ruler helps ease the adjustment period for people who are accustomed to seeing a ruler or a format line in other word processing programs. The ruler is also helpful when you are working with tables, tabbed columns, math columns, or newspaper or parallel columns. In fact, if you are working with tables or columns and display the ruler on the screen, it will show the left and right margins for each column, as shown here:

Related Entries

Windows

RUSH A PRINT JOB

You can move a job to the beginning of the print queue so it will be printed next, or you can interrupt the current job being printed so it can print immediately.

Keystrokes

1. Press Print (SHIFT-F7).

2. Choose 4 for Control Printer.

3. Type **R** for **R**ush a Print Job. The following message appears in the Control Printer menu, with the number of the last print job in the queue displayed as the default:

Rush which job? 3

4. Press ENTER to rush the displayed print job, or enter the number of another job to be rushed.

5. If a job is already printing, you are asked "Interrupt current job? No (Yes)." If you type **N**, the job is placed next in the queue. If you type **Y**, you will see the message "Completing page—press **Enter** to interrupt job immediately." If you press ENTER, the current page will be ejected, and the rushed job will begin printing.

Related Entries

Control Printer

SAVE

You use Save (F10) to save a document and leave it on the screen for further editing. You can also use it to save a block of text to a separate file. If you want to save a document and clear the screen, use Exit (F7) instead.

Keystrokes

Save a Document

1. Press Save (F10) to save the current document. "Document to be saved:" appears on the status line, prompting you for the name of the file. If the file has been saved before, that filename is displayed, as shown here:

```
Document to be saved: C:\PERSONAL\LEASE.AGR
```

2. Enter the name of the file, or press ENTER to use the displayed filename. Include the drive and directory if necessary.

3. If you press ENTER to use the same filename, or if you enter the name of a file already saved on the disk, you are asked "Replace filename? No (Yes)." Type **Y** to replace the file or **N** to save the file with a different name. If you type **N**, the same prompt will appear with the name of the current file. Enter a different filename.

Save a Block of Text

1. Move the cursor to one end of the block to be saved, and press Block (ALT-F4).

2. Move to the opposite end, and press Save (F10). "Block Name:" appears.

3. Enter the filename for the block.

Instead of entering a name for the block, you can press ENTER to save it as an "unnamed" block. You can retrieve an unnamed block by pressing Retrieve (SHIFT-F10) and then pressing ENTER, without first typing a filename.

Hints

When you save a file and do not specify a drive or directory, it will be saved to the default drive. If you are not sure which drive or directory is the default, press List (F5) to display the name at the bottom of the screen. To change the default drive or directory, type = after pressing List (F5) and enter the name of the new drive and directory to be used. See "Default Directory" in this chapter if you need further assistance.

When you save a file and type **Y** to replace the previous version, the original file on disk is renamed with a .BK! extension, the copy on the screen is saved, and the .BK! file is deleted. If you have turned on the Original Backup feature, the .BK! file will be kept on the disk instead of being deleted. If you are short on disk space and do not want the .BK! file to be created, you can start WordPerfect with the /NB for "no backup" option (enter **wp/nb** when you start WordPerfect). See "Backup" in this chapter for more information.

If you have retrieved more than one document to the screen, the filename of the first file retrieved is displayed as the filename to be used. Enter a different filename if necessary.

You do not have to save a document when you are using WordPerfect. You can edit and print without giving the file a name. If it is a quick, temporary document, you can create, edit, and print it, and then clear the screen without taking up space on the disk.

If you try to append a block of text to a file that does not exist, the file will be created at that time. This works just as Save (F10) does for saving a block of text as a new file.

Long Document Names

You can save documents with longer filenames containing up to 68 characters. At the same time, you are also asked for the document type. You can then display the long document name and document type in the List Files menu by choosing the Long Display option. See "Long Document Names" in this chapter for details.

Using Exit (F7) to Save

Save (F10) saves the file and leaves it on the screen for further editing. Use Exit (F7) to save the document and clear the screen. If you have just saved a document with Save (F10) and then press Exit (F7), you are again asked, as a precaution, if you want to save the document. If you have not made any changes to the document since using Save (F10), the message "(Text was not modified)" is displayed in the lower right corner of the screen, letting you know that you can safely exit the document without saving it again.

If you press Exit (F7) to save a document, but decide you want to leave it on the screen, press Cancel (F1) when asked, "Exit WP? **No** (Yes)."

Error Messages

If you see the "Disk full" error message, strike any key until you return to the document. Replace the disk with one that has more space, or enter the List Files menu and delete unwanted files.

If you are replacing a file on disk with one on the screen, you might get the error message even if it seems that there is sufficient room for the file. When you replace a file on disk, the original file is renamed, the new one is saved, and the original is deleted. You can stop the .BK! original file from being created by starting WordPerfect with the /NB (no backup) option.

If you are not sure how much disk space is available and how much is needed, enter the List Files menu and find the information at the top of the screen under "Free" and "Document size." Another option that is available to you if you did not start WordPerfect with the /NB option is to delete the original file on disk and then save the file. If you did this, you would not have both the original and the new file taking up space on the disk during the save. Be warned, however, that in the case of a power failure during the process, the file would be lost.

Other error messages such as "Sector not found" could mean that you have a damaged disk. The "Drive door may be open" message and others will also let you recover and correct the situation.

Save in Other Formats

Text In/Out (CTRL-F5) lets you save a WordPerfect 5.1 document in several formats: DOS Text (ASCII), Generic, WordPerfect 4.2, or WordPerfect 5.0.

DOS Text File   If you press Text In/Out (CTRL-F5) and choose option 1, DOS Text, you should then choose 1 for Save. Only text is saved to the file on disk. Although all WordPerfect codes are removed, some codes (such as indent, center, align, and paragraph numbering) are converted to ASCII text. Soft returns and hard returns are converted to carriage return/linefeeds, and tabs are converted to spaces.

Save Generic   This option on the Text In/Out file is similar to saving the file as a DOS text file, where all codes are removed and only text remains. However, tabs are kept as tabs, and soft returns are converted to spaces to aid with word wrap in the other word processor. To select this option, choose 3 for Save As and then 1 for Generic.

WordPerfect 5.0   Although you can retrieve a 5.1 document directly into 5.0 (and vice versa), all the new 5.1 codes not recognized by 5.0 will be converted to [Unknown] codes. These [Unknown] codes are then restored when you retrieve the document back into 5.1.

If you want to convert the document back to a true 5.0 document and strip out any unknown codes, use this option: Choose **3** for Save As and then **2** for WordPerfect 5.0.

WordPerfect 4.2   Files created in WordPerfect 4.2 can be retrieved directly into 5.1. However, you cannot retrieve 5.1 documents into Word-Perfect 4.2. Instead, choose **3** for Save As, and then type **3** for Word-Perfect 4.2.

Locking a Document

The Text In/Out menu also has an option to lock and save a document with a password. When you retrieve the document later, you are asked for the password. See "Lock and Unlock Documents" in this chapter for details.

Fast Save

When you save a WordPerfect document, it is saved in an unformatted state, which saves a great deal of time, especially for larger files. If you want a file to take as little disk space as possible, turn off Fast Save. When a document is Fast Saved, WordPerfect does not take the time to rewrite the prefix (a hidden part of the document containing information about initial codes, the initial font, the current printer selection, and so on) to eliminate unnecessary information. However, when you save a document normally, that prefix is purged so that the document takes up as little space as possible.

For example, if you are editing a document and change the document's initial font, initial codes, or select a different printer for the document, the old information in the prefix is marked for deletion and the new information is added. If you then Fast Save the file, the old information (while remaining marked for deletion) is not deleted and takes up unnecessary disk space. The next time you retrieve the file (whether Fast Save is on or not), the prefix is updated and the file size goes down once again. If disk space is of no concern, it will not be a disadvantage to leave Fast Save on. See "Fast Save" in this chapter for keystrokes and details.

Document Summary

You can insert a Document Summary to identify the subject, account, author, typist, and so on, and to give the file a descriptive filename. You can also include notes about the file. To create a Document Summary, press Format (SHIFT-F8), choose 3 for Document, and then choose 5 for Summary.

Setup (SHIFT-F1) has an option that automatically displays the document summary whenever you wish to save a file. See "Document Management/Summary" in this chapter for more information.

Related Entries

Backup
Block
Compatibility
Document Management/Summary
DOS Text Files
Fast Save
List Files
Lock and Unlock Documents
Long Document Names
Setup

SCREEN

Screen (CTRL-F3) displays a few miscellaneous options that affect the look of the screen. These features include Rewrite, Window, and Line Draw.

Keystrokes

1. Press Screen (CTRL-F3).

2. Select an option from the following menu:

```
1 Window; 2 Line Draw; 3 Rewrite: 3
```

Options

The options on the Screen (CTRL-F3) key are described next.

Windows

You can use the Window option to place a ruler showing the current margin and tab settings at the bottom of the screen or to split the screen so you can see document 1 and document 2 at once. Choose 1 for Window, and enter the number of lines to be given to the current document.

Line Draw

Choose option 2 for Line Draw to draw single or double lines, or to create lines and boxes using any character.

Rewrite

WordPerfect automatically reformats the document, from the cursor's location down, when you press any cursor key. To rewrite the entire screen (or if the screen does not appear to be formatted correctly), press Screen (CTRL-F3). Then press ENTER or the space bar, or choose 3 to Rewrite the entire screen. Pressing Screen (CTRL-F3) twice will also quickly rewrite the screen.

4.2 Options

Three options previously found on this menu—Ctrl/Alt Key Mapping, Colors, and Auto Rewrite—have been moved to Setup (SHIFT-F1).

The Keyboard Layout feature (option 5 on the Setup menu) has replaced Ctrl/Alt Key Mapping, letting you assign any special character, WordPerfect function, or macro to any key or key combination on the keyboard. The Compose feature lets you compose special characters. See "Keyboard Layout" and "Compose" in this chapter for details.

To set colors, press Setup (SHIFT-F1), choose 2 for Display, and then choose 1 for Colors/Fonts/Attributes. See "Colors/Fonts/Attributes" in this chapter for more information.

If you want to turn off automatic reformatting and rewriting, press Setup (SHIFT-F1); choose 2 for Display, 6 for Edit-Screen Options, and 1 for Automatically Format and Rewrite; and then type **Y** or **N** to turn it on or off. See "Rewrite the Screen" in this chapter for details.

Related Entries

Colors/Fonts/Attributes
Compose
Line Draw
Rewrite the Screen
Windows

SEARCH

You can use Search (F2) and Reverse Search (SHIFT-F2) to search for text or WordPerfect codes. You can also do an extended search, which also searches through headers, footers, footnotes, endnotes, captions, and text in graphics boxes.

Keystrokes

You can do a search from the regular editing screen or from the Reveal Codes screen.

1. Press Search (F2) to search from the cursor forward or Reverse Search (SHIFT-F2) to search from the cursor backward. If you want to do an extended search (searching through headers, footers, footnotes, endnotes, and text and captions contained in graphics boxes), press HOME before pressing a Search key.

"→Srch:" or "←Srch:" will appear on the status line, with the last search string displayed if there was one. If you are doing an extended search, ″→Extended srch:″ or ″←Extended srch:″ appears. You can press ↑ or ↓ to change the direction of the search.

2. Type up to 59 characters and/or WordPerfect codes, or move the cursor and edit the displayed string. If you are searching for Word-Perfect codes, you have to enter them with the appropriate function keys; they are limited in number by the available room on the status line. See ″Hints″ for details.

3. Press Search (F2) to start the search in either direction. Do not press ENTER to start the search, or you will enter a hard return [HRt] code into the search string. If you press ENTER, you can delete the code with BACKSPACE.

If the search is successful, the cursor will be placed just after the search string. If the search string was not found, you will see ″* Not Found *″ on the status line, and the cursor will be returned to its original position.

Hints

To begin a search, you can press ESC, Search (F2), Reverse Search (SHIFT-F2), or Replace (ALT-F2).

If you want to cancel the search, press Cancel (F1) at any time, and the cursor will return to the original position. Pressing ESC will not cancel the search. You can return the cursor to its original position after a search is finished by pressing Go To (CTRL-HOME) twice.

Case-Sensitive Search

If you enter the search string in lowercase letters, all uppercase and lowercase occurrences of the string will be found. If you enter the search string in uppercase letters, only uppercase occurrences will be found. The search string ″Constitution″ would find any occurrence of the word ″constitution″ as long as the first character was capitalized. All other letters in this example could be in uppercase or lowercase.

Whole-Word Searches

WordPerfect does not have an option for whole-word searches. Instead, you must place a space before and after a word that should be considered a whole word and not part of another word. For example, if you wanted to search for "and" but you did not include spaces, you would find occurrences of "band," "demands," "landmark," and so on.

If you include spaces before and after the word, however, be aware that the search string will not be found if the word is found at the beginning of a paragraph or at the end of a sentence; it would be followed by some type of punctuation.

Wildcard Characters in a Search String

You can include the wildcard character ^X as part of the search string to match any character, but it cannot be the first character in the string.

To insert the ^X code, you will need to press CTRL-V first and then CTRL-X. It will appear in boldface, because it is considered a code rather than text.

Using WordPerfect Codes in a Search String

You can search for any WordPerfect code, but it must be entered correctly. You cannot type a facsimile of the code; it must be entered with the appropriate function key. For example, if you want to search for the bold-on [BOLD] code, press Bold (F6) when you are prompted for the search string.

To search for an off code, press the applicable function key twice: once to insert the on code and again to insert the off code. If only the off code is needed, move the cursor to the on code and delete it.

Often, when you are pressing a function key to insert a code, you will see a menu of choices. Be aware that some of the codes are hidden beneath more than one menu. For example, if you wanted to search for a spacing code, you would press Format (SHIFT-F8), and then choose 1 for Line, 5 for Line again, and 3 for Line Spacing.

Press the keys listed on the right to search for the codes on the left:

Hard return [HRt]	ENTER
Hard page [HPg]	CTRL-ENTER
Soft return [SRt]	CTRL-V and then CTRL-M
Soft page [SPg]	CTRL-V and then CTRL-K

Unfortunately, you cannot search for a hard return that has been converted to a soft page break, [HRt-SPg].

You also cannot search for specific parameters within codes. For example, you can search for margin or font changes but not for specific margins (such as [L/R Mar:2″,2″]) or specific font changes.

Using Search to Define a Block

When defining a block, you can press either Search key to search for the previous or next occurrence of text or a code. If the search string is found, the block will be highlighted to that point.

Search in Macros

If you include a search in a macro, the macro will end if the search string is not found. This feature is useful in creating macros that will repeat until no further occurrences of the search string are found. A macro will not end when a replace is finished; you can do several search and replaces without ending a macro.

You can also write conditional macros using the {IF} and {ELSE} macro commands. See "Macros" in this chapter for details.

Applications

When editing a document from a hard copy, you can search for a specific word or phrase to find that section of the text quickly, which virtually eliminates scrolling through the document to make editing changes.

If a document is not formatted as it should be, search for the codes that might be affecting the format. For example, codes that are inserted with the Leading and Word and Letter Spacing features do not have any effect on the screen; it is difficult to find them unless you use Search (F2) to search for them.

You may want to search in the Reveal Codes screen so that you can see the parameters of the code without having to press Reveal Codes (ALT-F3) each time.

Related Entries

Block
Macros
Replace
Reveal Codes

SEARCH AND REPLACE

See "Replace" in this chapter.

SEARCH FOR A FILE

You can use Search (F2) while in the List Files menu to find a specific file. After pressing Search (F2), enter the characters that you remember, then press Search (F2) or ENTER.

The List Files menu also has a Find feature that lets you search through multiple files for a unique word or phrase. See "Find Files" in this chapter for more information.

SELECTING A PRINTER

During installation, you are allowed to select up to ten printers. At the end of the installation process, Install starts WordPerfect, selects the appropriate printer definitions, displays any hints about the printer, and then exits WordPerfect.

If you need to install more than ten printer definitions, you can start the Install program again (see Chapter 1, "Installation and Setup," if you need assistance) and select additional printers. If you are installing WordPerfect on a network, you may want to use the Copy option on the main menu of the Install program to copy all files (including all printer files) so you can select any printer at any time without running the Install program again.

When you select a printer in the Install program, WordPerfect copies a file with .ALL as the filename extension; it contains several printer definitions. You can later select other printer definitions from that .ALL file.

WordPerfect does not select the cartridges and fonts, or the sheet feeder, and it may not have selected the correct port (LPT1 is selected by default). You may want to edit the printer selection as explained in the next section.

If you do not select a printer as part of the installation, Word-Perfect formats documents for a 10-pitch font and 1-inch margins on a standard size page. However, you will not be able to view or print the document without first selecting a printer.

Keystrokes

Be sure that you have specified which printers are to be selected during installation. If you have not done so, refer to Chapter 1 for instructions.

1. Press Print (SHIFT-F7).

2. Type **S** for Select Printer. If you have already selected printers, you will see a screen similar to the one shown in Figure 3-143. The list of printers indicates which definitions you have selected. An asterisk appears next to the printer that is currently selected. No printers will appear in this list if you have not previously selected printers.

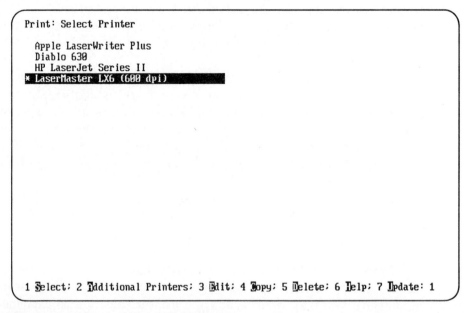

Figure 3-143.   List of selected printers

3. If the desired printer selection is among the list, move the cursor to the one to be selected and choose **1** for Select. You will be returned to the Print menu, with the newly selected printer definition displayed next to the Select Printer option.

If you want to edit the printer selection and choose the port, cartridges and fonts, or a sheet feeder, type **S** for Select Printer, choose **3** for **E**dit, and then skip to step 8.

4. If the printer is not on the list, choose **2** for **A**dditional Printers. The printer definitions in any .ALL files found in the drive or directory specified in the Setup (SHIFT-F1) menu under Location of Files will be displayed at this point. See "Location of Files" in this chapter for the steps needed to change the location.

5. Move the cursor to the printer definition to be selected, and choose **1** for Select. The Name Search feature is available on the printer selection menus; you can type **N** for Name Search and type the name of the printer so the cursor can move to that point quickly.

If you do not see your printer on the list, replace the original Printer disk with a different one, choose **2** for **O**ther Disk, and enter the same drive name.

6. When you select a new printer definition, WordPerfect suggests a filename that will be used to contain the printer definition. You can either press ENTER to accept that filename or enter one of your own (up to eight characters). The extension .PRS will be added as the filename extension if you do not enter it.

The .PRS file contains the basic printer commands needed to drive the printer: the printer name, port, sheet feeder information, types of paper available (as defined in the Paper Size/Type menu), a list of available cartridges and fonts, the initial font, and the pathname for downloadable soft fonts and printer command files.

If a file with the same name exists on disk, you are asked if you want to replace the original file. Type **Y** to replace it, or type **N** and enter a different filename. "Hints" provides more information about having more than one .PRS file for a single printer.

7. After you enter a printer filename, WordPerfect begins to store information about each internal font while displaying the message

```
┌─────────────────────────────────────────────────────────────────────┐
│ Printer Helps and Hints:  HP LaserJet Series II                      │
│                                                                       │
│ 11/6/89                                                               │
│ Initializing the printer will delete all soft fonts in printer memory and │
│ those fonts marked with an asterisk (*) will be downloaded.           │
│                                                                       │
│ Additional font support for this printer is available on a supplementary │
│ diskette.  To order this diskette, call WP Corp. at (801)225-5000.  There │
│ will be a $10 shipping fee.                                           │
│                                                                       │
│                                                                       │
│                                                                       │
│                                                                       │
│                                                                       │
│                                                                       │
│                                                                       │
│                                                                       │
│                                                                       │
│                                                                       │
│ Press Exit to quit, Cursor Keys for More Text, Switch for Sheet Feeder Help │
└─────────────────────────────────────────────────────────────────────┘
```

Figure 3-144.   Help screen for a printer

"Updating font: n," where n is the total number of internal fonts. As the information about each font is stored, the number decreases until it reaches the last one.

During this process, you will see a help message about that particular printer. An example of a help screen is shown in Figure 3-144. Printer limitations, information about setting up a serial printer, printer switch settings, and font information could all be included in this screen. You can scroll through the help message with ↑ and ↓, or press Switch (SHIFT-F3) to display help information about a sheet feeder if it is defined. When you have finished reading the help information, press Exit (F7). As you exit the help screen, the menu shown in Figure 3-145 is displayed.

8. The name of the printer, as it appeared in the printer list, is displayed next to option **1**, Name. This name appears in the list of selected printers shown in Figure 3-143. If you have more than one .PRS file for the same printer, choose this option and enter the name of the printer to reflect the purpose of that specific .PRS file. If you do not, the name of the printer will appear twice in the list, and you will have a difficult time determining which definition to

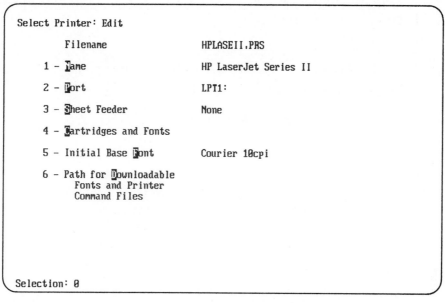

```
Select Printer: Edit

        Filename                HPLASEII.PRS

    1 - Name                    HP LaserJet Series II

    2 - Port                    LPT1:

    3 - Sheet Feeder            None

    4 - Cartridges and Fonts

    5 - Initial Base Font       Courier 10cpi

    6 - Path for Downloadable
        Fonts and Printer
        Command Files




Selection: 0
```

Figure 3-145.   Menu used to edit a printer selection

use. For example, you might want to use a certain set of cartridges, fonts, and forms for newsletters, and a different set of fonts that contain special characters and symbols for more technical documents. The name of one .PRS file could be "Newsletter Printer Definition," while the other could be "Technical Printer Definition." The other options available are described below:

Port   If your printer is attached to a port other than the first parallel port (LPT1), choose **2** for Port. The following selections are presented at the bottom of the screen:

```
Port: 1 LPT 1; 2 LPT 2; 3 LPT 3; 4 COM 1; 5 COM 2; 6 COM 3; 7 COM 4; 8 Other: 0
```

Select a COM port if you have a serial printer. Use option **8**, Other, if you want to print a document to a file on disk or to a different device (used to print to some types of networks, such as Novell Netware). If you choose a COM port, you will need to specify some additional settings, as shown here:

```
Select Printer: COM Port
        1 - Baud                      9600

        2 - Parity                    None

        3 - Stop Bits (1 or 2)        1

        4 - Character Length (7 or 8) 8

        5 - XON/XOFF                  No
```

You can find the correct settings in your printer manual. If they are set incorrectly, your printer might print random characters, stop after printing a few lines, or not print at all.

Option 1, Baud, lists the following choices:

```
Baud: 1 19200; 2 150; 3 300; 4 600; 5 1200; 6 2400; 7 4800; 8 9600: 0
```

This setting determines the rate at which data is sent from the computer to the printer. One of the most common settings is 1200 baud, but laser printers usually print at 9600 baud. If you choose option 1 for 19,200 and your printer does not support that baud rate, 110 will be used.

Option 2 for Parity, is an error-checking system in which None, Odd, or Even are the choices. In general, if you have 8 set as the Character Length (data bits), you will have no parity. Other settings depend on how your printer is set up.

Stop bits are the number of bits used to separate each byte (a character is considered 1 byte and is made up of 7 or 8 bits). Find the correct setting in your manual, choose 3 for Stop Bits, and type 1 or 2 (1 is the most common setting).

Character length (sometimes known as data bits) can be set either to 7 or 8, depending on what your printer will accept. Choose 4 for Character Length, and change this setting if necessary.

The last option for serial printers is XON/XOFF. Most printers use hardware handshaking, in which the printer sends signals to the computer to let it know when to send data and when to stop temporarily because the printer's buffer is full. Choose option 5 for XON/XOFF, and change it to Yes if you have an Apple LaserWriter or another printer that uses XON/XOFF protocol.

When you have finished with the selections, press ENTER to return to the menu that lets you edit the printer selection (shown in Figure 3-145).

Sheet Feeder   Choose option 3 if you have a Sheet Feeder attached to your printer. The paper tray in a laser printer is not considered a sheet feeder. Each .ALL file contains the sheet-feeder definitions that can be used by the various types of printers. Move to the appropriate sheet feeder on the list. Press ENTER to select it, or choose 2 for None. You will then see a help message for the selected sheet feeder. Most of the messages remind you to define or edit the paper definitions and include the sheet-feeder bin number for the "location" or where the paper will be found. See "Paper Size/Type" in this chapter for more information about defining and selecting different types of paper.

Cartridges and Fonts   When you select a printer, the fonts that are found within the printer are automatically saved in the .PRS file. If you have additional print wheels, cartridges, or soft fonts, choose 4 for Cartridges and Fonts. If your printer does not have additional fonts or cartridges available, you will see a message stating so. If more are available, you will see a list of resources. You can choose option 2 to change the **Quantity** (for example, you might have one or two cartridge slots, or want to change the amount of printer memory for soft fonts) and choose option 1 to Select the print wheels, cartridges, or soft fonts. See "Cartridges and Fonts" in this chapter if you need additional help.

If soft fonts are involved, you should mark as initially present those that should be downloaded to the printer before printing begins. Just before printing, you can press Print (SHIFT-F7) and choose 7 to Initialize the printer. WordPerfect will then download the soft fonts.

When you are finished, press Exit (F7) until you return to the printer definition menu. Information about each selected font will be stored while the message "Updating Font: n" appears at the bottom of the screen. The information will be used later to determine which fonts will be used for automatic font changes (fine, small, large, italics, and so on).

Initial Base Font After selecting the available print wheels, cartridges, and fonts, you can choose the font that is to be selected by default each time a document is created. When you choose **5** for Initial Base Font, you will see a list of fonts that were just selected with the Cartridges and Fonts option. Move to the font to be selected, and press ENTER.

Path for Downloadable Fonts If you have selected soft fonts, you will need to specify the path (location) where the soft fonts can be found. WordPerfect can then download them automatically when you choose Initialize Printer from the Print menu. Choose **6** for Path for **D**ownloadable Soft Fonts and Printer Command Files, and then enter the drive and directory in which the soft fonts can be found. This path is also used for printer command files (see "Printer Commands" in this chapter for more information).

9. When you have finished with all options, press Exit (F7). You will be returned to the list of selected printers, with the newly selected printer among the list.

10. You can continue the process and select any number of additional printers, or move the cursor to the printer that is to be selected for creating future documents and choose **1** for Select.

11. You are returned to the Print menu. The name of the currently selected printer is displayed next to the Select Printer option.

12. Press Exit (F7) to leave the Print menu.

Hints

When you are selecting printers, WordPerfect looks in the drive and directory specified in the Location of Files option of the Setup menu. When you choose Other Disk, the same drive and directory is displayed, but you can enter another one. The drive and directory entered in Location of Files is also used for the .PRS files that are created when a printer definition is selected.

When you select printers and choose 2 to see a list of Additional printers, you are looking at a list of the printer definitions found in the .ALL files. If you want to select a .PRS file that has already been defined but does not appear on the initial list of printer selections, you can choose 4 to List Printer Files while viewing the additional printers.

If you select a printer definition and later delete it (discussed later), only the name of the printer is removed from the list; the .PRS file remains on disk. The List Printer Files option will display these .PRS files so that they can be once again selected.

Using More Than One Printer

When you create and save a document, the name and date of the .PRS file that is currently selected is stored with that document in a document header. If you later select a different printer definition or retrieve the document on a machine that has a different .PRS file, WordPerfect will search for the original .PRS file and reselect it if it is found. If it is not found, you will see a message telling you that the original .PRS file is not found and that the document is being formatted for the default printer.

If WordPerfect encounters a font change or paper size/type change while reformatting the document, it searches the current .PRS file for the font that most closely matches the original font and changes it automatically. In Reveal Codes, you will see [Font:*Font Name] or [Paper Size/Type:*n]. The asterisk is added to indicate that the font or paper size/type was converted. If you return to the original .PRS file, WordPerfect converts the font or paper back to the original selection.

If you are exchanging files with others and want the document formatted exactly as it was originally, give them the corresponding .PRS file so they can copy it to their disk before retrieving the file.

If you want WordPerfect to use the default printer selection automatically and not revert back to the original, you can do one of two things:

• Delete the printer selection from the list of printers and delete the .PRS file from the disk from List Files menu. This method forces WordPerfect to use the default printer selection, because it cannot find the original .PRS file.

• Change the option found in the Setup menu that lets you retrieve files and automatically format them for the default printer, regardless of the printer that was selected when the document was saved. Press Setup (SHIFT-F1), choose **4** for Initial Settings, and choose **4** for Format Retrieved Documents for Default Printer and answer Yes.

Of course, you can always change the printer selection after you have retrieved the document; it will then be reformatted for the newly selected printer definition.

Hints for Using the Printer Selection Menus

While you are selecting from the lists of printer and sheet-feeder definitions, the menus at the bottom of the screen all have a few options in common. You can usually move to any of the printers or sheet feeders on the list and type **H** for Help. You will then see the help message that is normally displayed when you select a printer or sheet feeder.

Name Search is another option that you can use to move quickly to a specific printer, sheet feeder, or font in the list. Type **N** for **Name** Search, and then begin typing the name of the printer, sheet feeder, or font. As you type each letter, the search narrows. For example, if you type **T**, the cursor moves directly to the items in the list that begin with the letter "T." As you add other characters, the cursor moves to the name in the list that most closely matches the letters that you have typed.

Pressing ENTER or any arrow key will reset the Name Search feature but will leave the cursor at the same position. You can then try again or use the arrow keys to move to the correct selection.

In addition to choosing the option from the bottom of the menu (usually **1** for Select) you can type an asterisk (∗) to make a selection.

Deleting a Printer Selection

1. Press Print (SHIFT-F7).

2. Type **S** for Select Printer.

3. Move the cursor to the printer that is to be deleted, and choose **5** for **Delete**.

4. When asked to confirm the deletion, type **Y** to delete it or **N** if you decide not to delete it.

The name of the printer selection is removed from the list, but the .PRS file is not deleted from the disk. You can reselect it later by choosing option **2** for Additional Printers and then **4** for List Printer Files. If you do not plan to use the .PRS file again, it is best to delete it from the disk with the List Files menu or it will be reselected for any document originally created with that .PRS file.

Creating Two or More .PRS Files for the Same Printer

If you have more cartridges than you have cartridge slots, or if you have more soft fonts available than you have printer memory, you might want to select the same printer more than once and then select different cartridges and fonts for each printer.

You can either select the same printer definition again or use the "copy" option in the list of printers. When you select the same printer or choose **4** to Copy, the same .PRS filename will be suggested. Enter a different name, and change the "name" of the printer to reflect the name of the .PRS file in the menu used to edit the printer definition. If you do not change the name of the printer, the printer will be listed more than once on the list, and it will be difficult to determine which printer definition should be used for a particular document.

Having more than one printer definition will also let you use your printer resources effectively. You can have different printer selections for different types of documents so that you do not have to search through more fonts than necessary when making font selections. The fonts that are listed could also have something in common, such as foreign characters, technical symbols and characters, and so on.

Updating a Printer Definition

If you have received an updated printer definition from WordPerfect Corporation, you can choose option **7** for Update, which lets you update all the information in the .PRS file. You are also asked if you want new automatic font changes and substitute fonts selected.

Using the Printer (PTR) Program

You can use the Printer program to edit or create printer definitions. See Chapter 5 for details.

Related Entries

Cartridges and Fonts
Paper Size/Type
Print
Sheet Feeders
See also Chapter 5, "Printer Program"

SELECT RECORDS FROM A MERGE FILE

See "Sort and Select" in this chapter.

SET TABS

See "Tabs" in this chapter.

SETUP

WordPerfect comes with certain defaults set. You can use the Setup menu from within WordPerfect to customize the defaults.

You can choose backup options; set the cursor speed; choose the colors, fonts, attributes, and other display options for the screen; specify initial settings; reconfigure the layout of the keys on the keyboard; specify the location of certain files; and choose the default unit of measurement.

Keystrokes

1. Press Setup (SHIFT-F1). The options shown in Figure 3-146 appear.

2. Select any options that you need to change.

3. Press Exit (F7) until you return to the document.

Options

The following is a brief summary of the options found on the Setup menu. Some of the options lead to submenus and additional items in that category. For an overall "map" of the options included in the Setup menu, see Table 3-16.

Most of the items are also listed as separate entries in this book. See those entries for more information.

Mouse

With the first option, you can select the type of mouse, the port where it is attached, and how responsive you want the mouse to be. There are

```
Setup

    1 - Mouse

    2 - Display

    3 - Environment

    4 - Initial Settings

    5 - Keyboard Layout

    6 - Location of Files

Selection: 0
```

Figure 3-146.   Main Setup Menu

1 - Mouse
    1 - Type
    2 - Port
    3 - Double-Click Interval
    4 - Submenu Delay Time
    5 - Acceleration Factor
    6 - Left-Handed Mouse
    7 - Assisted Mouse Pointer Movement

2 - Display
    1 - Colors/Fonts/Attributes
    2 - Graphics Screen Type
    3 - Text Screen Type
    4 - Menu Options
        1 - Menu Letter Display
        2 - Pull-Down Letter Display
        3 - Pull-Down Text
        4 - Alt Key Selects Pull-Down Menu
        5 - Menu Bar Letter Display
        6 - Menu Bar Text
        7 - Menu Bar Separator Line
        8 - Menu Bar Remains Visible
    5 - View Document Options
        1 - Text in Black & White
        2 - Graphics in Black & White
        3 - Bold displayed with color
    6 - Edit-Screen Options
        1 - Automatically Format and Rewrite
        2 - Comments Display
        3 - Filename on the Status Line
        4 - Hard Return Display Character
        5 - Merge Codes Display
        6 - Reveal Codes Window Size
        7 - Side-by-Side Columns Display

3 - Environment
    1 - Backup Options
        1 - Timed Document Backup
        2 - Original Document Backup

Table 3-16. Categories in the Setup Menu and the Options Found Under Those Categories

2 - Beep Options
    1 - Beep on Error
    2 - Beep on Hyphenation
    3 - Beep on Search Failure
3 - Cursor Speed
4 - Document Management/Summary
    1 - Create Summary on Save/Exit
    2 - Subject Search Text
    3 - Long Document Names
    4 - Default Document Type
5 - Fast Save (unformatted)
6 - Hyphenation
7 - Prompt for Hyphenation
8 - Units of Measure

4 - Initial Settings
    1 - Merge
        1 - Field Delimiters
        2 - Record Delimiters
    2 - Date Format
    3 - Equations
        1 - Print As Graphics
        2 - Graphical Font Size
        3 - Horizontal Alignment
        4 - Vertical Alignment
        5 - Keyboard for Editing
    4 - Format Retrieved Documents for Default Printer
    5 - Initial Codes
    6 - Repeat Value
    7 - Table of Authorities
        1 - Dot Leaders
        2 - Underlining Allowed
        3 - Blank Line Between Authorities
    8 - Print Options
        1 - Binding Offset
        2 - Number of Copies
            Multiple Copies Generated by
        3 - Graphics Quality

Table 3-16. Categories in the Setup Menu and the Options Found Under Those Categories (*continued*)

4 - Text Quality
5 - Redline Method
6 - Size Attribute Ratios

5 - Keyboard Layout
6 - Location of Files
   1 - Backup Files
   2 - Keyboard/Macro Files
   3 - Thesaurus/Spell/Hyphenation
   4 - Printer Files
   5 - Style Files
       Library Filename
   6 - Graphics Files
   7 - Documents

Table 3-16. Categories in the Setup Menu and the Options Found Under Those Categories (*continued*)

additional selections for people who are left handed or who want WordPerfect's assistance in moving the mouse to the first selectable option when menus are displayed.

Display

If you choose option 2 for Display, you will see the options shown in Figure 3-147. Each of these options relates to the display of text on the screen. Look for the appropriate headings in this chapter for information about these options. The following is a summary of each.

Colors/Fonts/Attributes With this option you can select colors, fonts (Hercules RamFont), or screen attributes (boldface, underline, reverse video, blink, and so on) for the various WordPerfect attributes (bold, underline, italics, small print, double-underline, superscript, extra-large print, and so on). If you have an EGA or VGA monitor, you can also display underline, italics, small caps, or 512 characters (instead of 256) on the screen. Only one of these options is available at a time.

If you have a Hercules graphics card with RamFont, you can select from 12 screen fonts that will appear on the screen while you are

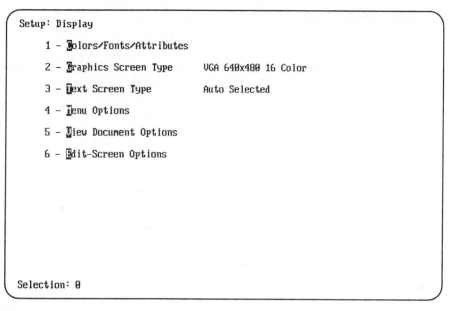

```
Setup: Display

        1 - Colors/Fonts/Attributes

        2 - Graphics Screen Type        VGA 640x480 16 Color

        3 - Text Screen Type            Auto Selected

        4 - Menu Options

        5 - View Document Options

        6 - Edit-Screen Options




Selection: 0
```

Figure 3-147.   Display options in the Setup menu

editing. This lets you see italics, superscript, extra large, double-underline, and much more while editing, without having to view the document. You can also choose to display only 6 of the Hercules fonts and have 512 characters available in each of those fonts.

The options listed in this menu are customized for each type of system. If the menu does not give you the options you expect, you may need to select a different graphics screen type. You can do so by choosing Graphics Screen Type, which is discussed next.

Graphics Screen Type   WordPerfect automatically senses the type of graphics display being used (monochrome, EGA, Hercules graphics card with RamFont, and so on) and sets the colors, fonts, and screen attributes accordingly. If you see errors when you are trying to view a document or edit a graphics image, or if you are running WordPerfect on two monitors, you may need to change the graphics screen type with this option.

Because some graphics displays have different options, such as one to display more colors but with less resolution, you may then be asked to select the type of resolution desired.

Text Screen Type   The text screen type lets you select a certain number of characters and lines for the screen. For example, if you have an EGA monitor, you can choose to display either 25 or 43 lines of text. Other options on this menu are available for those who have problems with the colors not holding, the screen changing sizes after returning from a graphics screen, or the cursor disappearing.

Menu Options   With this menu you can select the way the mnemonic letter is displayed (if you wanted it changed from bold, for instance). The screen attribute, color, or font assigned to the Word-Perfect attribute is the one that will be used. For example, if you have chosen the color red to represent italics on the screen, you can choose italics to display the mnemonic selection in red.

You can also select the colors or other attributes for the menu bar and pull down menus, including the mnemonic letter selections in those menus. Other options about how and when the menu bar and pull-down menus are displayed are also included in this menu, as illustrated in Figure 3-148.

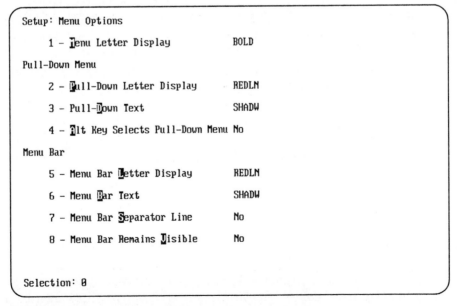

Figure 3-148.   The Menu Options category in Setup

View Document Options   If you have a color monitor, you may want to choose the options found on this menu, which let you view the text or graphics in black and white rather than in color. This gives a more accurate representation of how the document will be printed. It also lets you decide if you want bold to be displayed in color or not.

Edit-Screen Options   The menu shown in Figure 3-149 lets you choose options that affect the way the main editing screen appears. You can turn off the display of some features, such as comments, the document filename, merge codes, and side-by-side columns. You can also choose not to have WordPerfect automatically reformat each time you press a cursor key, choose a character to represent a hard return, or change the number of lines displayed in the Reveal Codes screen.

Environment

When you select option 3 for Environment from the main Setup menu, you will see the menu shown in Figure 3-150. The options found on that menu are discussed next.

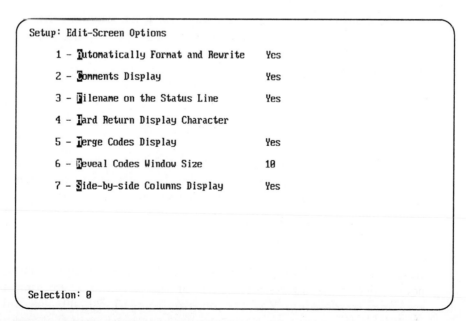

```
Setup: Edit-Screen Options

     1 - Automatically Format and Rewrite    Yes

     2 - Comments Display                     Yes

     3 - Filename on the Status Line          Yes

     4 - Hard Return Display Character

     5 - Merge Codes Display                  Yes

     6 - Reveal Codes Window Size             10

     7 - Side-by-side Columns Display         Yes




Selection: 0
```

Figure 3-149.   Edit-Screen Options

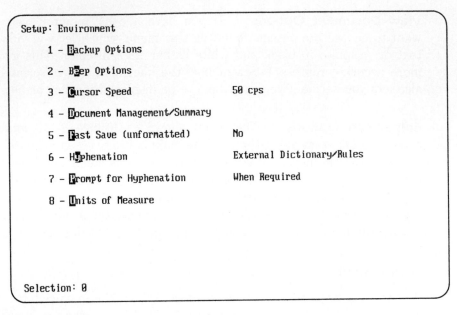

```
Setup: Environment
      1 - Backup Options
      2 - Beep Options
      3 - Cursor Speed                    50 cps
      4 - Document Management/Summary
      5 - Fast Save (unformatted)         No
      6 - Hyphenation                     External Dictionary/Rules
      7 - Prompt for Hyphenation          When Required
      8 - Units of Measure




Selection: 0
```

Figure 3-150.   Environment options

Backup Options   A Timed Backup option lets you save the current document at a specific interval. The second option, Original Backup, saves the last revision of a document instead of automatically deleting it.

   If you choose Timed Backup, you can also choose the Location of Files option on the Setup menu and specify where the timed backup files should be kept. The original backup files are kept in their original location. See "Backup" in this chapter for details.

Beep Options   WordPerfect causes the computer to beep when a hyphenation decision needs to be made. It is not set to beep when an error occurs or when a search is finished. You can use this option to reverse the selections if you want to be alerted to any or all of these conditions.

Cursor Speed   The speed of the cursor has been set to 50 characters per second. This affects the speed of the cursor for entering text, scrolling, or deleting. You can choose from 15, 20, 30, 40, and 50 characters per second, or if you already have a program that increases the cursor speed (such as Repeat Performance), you can change the setting to normal and let the other program control the cursor speed.

Document Management/Summary   The options found on this menu can be set to have a Document Summary created automatically when you first save a document. Other options let you indicate the text that you normally use for the "subject" in letters and memos (the default is "RE:") so that WordPerfect can find and insert the subject into the Document Summary if you so request.

This menu also lets you select the Long Document Name feature, which lets you save each document with a descriptive name of up to 68 characters and a document type. Setting this option to Yes also displays files with their long document name and document type in the List Files menu.

Fast Save (Unformatted)   WordPerfect is set to save your documents in an unformatted state because it takes less time. However, printing a document from disk takes a little longer because it is actually "retrieved" into a temporary file, reformatted, and then sent to the printer. Documents may also appear larger in size if Fast Save is on.

Hyphenation   WordPerfect uses the spelling dictionary to decide where to place hyphens. You can also use the internal rules (an algorithm that is approximately 90 percent correct) if you do not want to spare the additional memory needed by the spelling dictionary during hyphenation.

Prompt for Hyphenation   WordPerfect automatically makes hyphenation decisions and prompts you only when it cannot find a word in the dictionary. You can change this option so that you are always prompted or never prompted. See "Hyphenation" in this chapter for details.

Units of Measure   WordPerfect has been set to display the current position of the cursor in inches. You will also make any changes to the format (margins, tabs, page size, and so on) in inches.

With this menu option, you can change the unit of measurement to centimeters or points, or you can return to the method used in 4.2, in which the settings are based on the number of characters in a line or lines on a page. You can also use ″ or ″i″ to represent inches. The w option stands for WordPerfect units (1200 to an inch). Regardless of the unit of measurement chosen, you can make any format changes using any unit of measurement by adding the abbreviation (″, i, c, p, u, or w) just after the number. See ″Units of Measure″ for details.

Initial Settings

If you choose option 4, Initial Settings, you will see the menu shown in Figure 3-151. Any changes made to the initial settings affect all documents that are created after that time. Documents previously created are not affected.

Merge WordPerfect's merge feature can use DOS text files that have fields and records separated by some type of delimiter. If you have a database program that uses delimiters other than a comma to separate fields and a carriage return to separate records, you can change the information in this menu once rather than change it each time you do a merge.

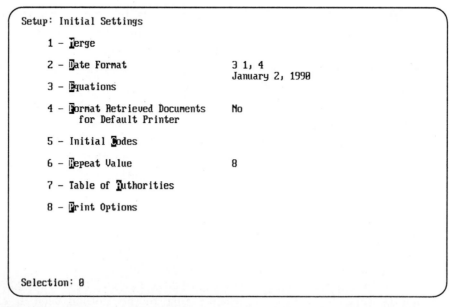

```
Setup: Initial Settings

     1 - Merge

     2 - Date Format                    3 1, 4
                                        January 2, 1990
     3 - Equations

     4 - Format Retrieved Documents     No
             for Default Printer

     5 - Initial Codes

     6 - Repeat Value                   8

     7 - Table of Authorities

     8 - Print Options




Selection: 0
```

Figure 3-151.   Initial Settings in the Setup menu

Date Format   WordPerfect automatically inserts the date in the format: month, day, year (for example, November 25, 1990). You can reverse the order of the month and day, use the current time in addition to the date, or insert the date in numeric form (as in 11/25/90). Abbreviations and leading zeros are also available.

The format chosen will be used when you press Date/Outline (SHIFT-F5) and choose 1 or 2 to insert the date as Text or as a Code. You can change the format at any time for a single document with option 3, Date Format, on the Date/Outline key. See "Date and Time" in this chapter for more information.

Equations   If you do not have a graphics printer, you can change an option on this menu so that equations will print as text instead of graphics. You can also decide whether to leave the font size for the equation at the default or set a specific size for all equations created from that time forward. Other options let you determine the horizontal and vertical placement of an equation inside the equation box and which keyboard layout (if any) is to be used when you are creating equations.

You can change all the options (with the exception of the Keyboard for Editing) for the current equation by pressing Setup (SHIFT-F1) while in the equation editor.

Format Retrieved Documents for Default Printer   You can set this option to Yes if you want to have all documents formatted for the default (current) printer, instead of the one that you selected when you saved the document. Only documents that are retrieved to the screen will be affected.

Initial Codes   If you choose this option, you are presented with a Reveal Codes screen. If you prefer different settings from those chosen by WordPerfect Corporation, you can make the changes as you would in the document. For example, if you prefer to have Left Justification and Widow/Orphan Protection on for all documents, you can select those options, and the WordPerfect codes will be inserted in every document created from that point on. Although the codes are not visible from within the document when you press Reveal Codes (ALT-F3), you can view and change them by pressing Format (SHIFT-F8) and typing 3 for Document and 2 for Initial Codes.

Because these codes are stored with the document, the document will be formatted correctly if you share files with others having different initial settings. However, be aware that a document is also formatted for a specific printer. If the .PRS file that was used when the document was created is not found, the document will be formatted for the printer that is currently selected. If you want the document to remain formatted exactly as it was when you created it, provide the original .PRS file with the document.

See "Initial Codes" and "Initial Settings" in this chapter for more information.

Repeat Value   When you press ESC, the message "Repeat Value = 8" appears on the screen to indicate that the next key pressed will be repeated eight times. You can temporarily change the repeat value from 8 to any other number by entering a new number when you press ESC, or you can change it permanently.

Table of Authorities   Because 16 tables of authorities are available, you might want to change the style for all the tables at once, instead of changing each one individually. The default settings insert a dot leader between each authority in the list and the page number, remove any underlining, and insert a blank line between each authority. You can choose not to have a dot leader, to allow underlining, or not to have a blank line inserted between each item.

Print Options   You can permanently set all options included on the lower half of the Print (SHIFT-F7) menu with the Print Options menu in Setup. This includes the binding offset, number of copies, and the quality of print for both text and graphics. You can also select the method used for redlined text and the size attribute ratios, which are the percentages that are used when you are deciding which fonts to use for Extra Large, Very Large, Large, Small, Fine, and Super/Subscript.

Keyboard Layout

You can define many keyboard layouts for different types of projects or preferences. You can create a WordStar, Dvorak, French, Spanish, or any other type of keyboard with this feature.

You can reassign macros, special characters, and WordPerfect features to any key on the keyboard. See "Keyboard Layout" in this chapter for more information.

Location of Files

By choosing option **6** for **L**ocation of Files, you will see the menu shown in Figure 3-152. If you copy the Speller, Thesaurus, printer files, and so on to a different directory from the one used by WP.EXE, choose this option and enter the path where those files can be found.

You should also use this menu to specify where keyboard and macro files and graphics files are to be kept. In addition to selecting the location for style files, you can specify which style file should be used as the default Style Library.

The last option lets you specify the default directory where documents will be saved to and retrieved from if you do not specify another directory. See "Location of Files" in this chapter for more information.

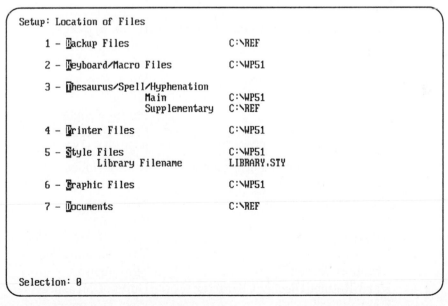

Figure 3-152.   Location of Files menu

Hints

The selections made in the setup menus are kept in a single file named WP{WP}.SET. No alterations are made to WP.EXE. If you are using a network version of WordPerfect, the "{WP" part of the filename is replaced with the initials that you used when you entered WordPerfect. Each user can have his or her own default settings. For example, if your network username is ABP, the setup file would be called WPABP}.SET.

Some of the defaults that have been set in WordPerfect are listed in Table 3-17. You can change these settings until they meet your needs.

Returning to the Original Defaults

If you need to return to the original default settings for a single editing session (until you leave WordPerfect), enter **wp/x** instead of **wp**. If you want to return to the original default settings permanently, enter **wp/x**, and then enter the Setup menu. You can also delete the WP{WP}.SET file from the disk. Be sure to do so from DOS rather than from within the List Files menu, however. The next time you enter WordPerfect, a new WP{WP} SET file is created.

Related Entries

Automatically Format and Rewrite
Backup
Beep Options
Colors/Fonts/Attributes
Columns
Comments
Cursor Speed
Date and Time
Document Management/Summary
Environment
Edit-Screen Options
Equations
ESC Key
Fast Save
Graphics Screen Type
Hard Return Display Character
Hyphenation
Initial Codes

Initial Settings
Keyboard Layout
Location of Files
Menu Options
Merge
Mouse Support
Print Options
Redline
Reveal Codes
Size Attribute Ratios
Spell
Summary
Table of Authorities
Text Screen Type
Thesaurus
Units of Measure
View Document

Feature	Default
Hyphenation	Off
Hyphenation zone	
Left	10% of line length
Right	4% of line length
Justification	Full
Margins	1″
Tabs	Every 1/2″
Widow/orphan protection	No
Page numbering	None
Paper size/type	8.5″ x 11″, Standard
Underline	
Spaces	Yes
Tabs	No
Decimal/align character	.
Thousands' separator	,
Units of measure	″
Backup	Every 30 minutes
Cursor Speed	50 cps
Fast Save	Yes
Long Document Names	No
Text Quality	High
Graphics Quality	Medium
Beep	
On error	No
On hyphenation	Yes
On search failure	No
Repeat value	8
Table of authorities	
Dot leader	Yes
Underlining allowed	No
Blank line between authorities	Yes

Table 3-17.   Several Default Selections in WordPerfect

SHADING

You can choose a percentage of shading for a graphics box, tables, and the amount of gray shading for a graphics line.

A text box is the only type of graphics box that is preset for shading (10%). Graphics lines are preset to print 100% black. If your printer can print text in white (PostScript printers have this capability), you can shade a box 100% black and print the text white.

If you request shading in a table, the percentage of shading will also be 10% by default. You can change this setting through the Options menu when you are editing a table. To shade cells in a table, you first need to edit the table, block the cells to be shaded, choose the Lines option, and then select Shading.

See "Tables," "Graphics Boxes," and "Graphics Lines" in this chapter for more information.

SHADOW BORDERS

You can create a shadow border around a graphics box to give it a three-dimensional look. You will need to enter the Options menu for the desired type of graphics box, and then set the Border Style so that two adjoining lines are set to Single and the other two adjoining sides are set to either Thick or Extra Thick. See "Graphics Boxes" in this chapter for more information.

SHADOW PRINTING

Some printers, including PostScript printers, can print in shadow printing. Here is an example:

This is an example of shadow printing on a PostScript printer

If your printer cannot create a shadow font for the current font, or if there is no shadow font available in your printer, text marked for shadow printing will be printed three or four times to create a darker print (darker than boldface). Some printers will print the text where it should be and then print the text again, offsetting it slightly to create the shadow look.

Keystrokes

1. Press Font (CTRL-F8).

2. Choose **2** for Appearance.

3. Choose **6** for Shadow.

4. Type the text to be affected.

5. Press → to move past the shadow-off code and turn off shadow printing.

You can also block the text to be affected, press Font (CTRL-F8), choose **2** for Appearance, and then **6** for Shadow.

Hints

When you select shadow printing, the shadow-on and shadow-off codes [SHADW] and [shadw] are inserted, with the cursor on the shadow-off code. Any text typed will be inserted between the two codes. You can enter the menus and select the option again to turn it off, but it is easiest to press → to turn off the feature.

To see how text marked for shadow printing will print, print the PRINTER.TST file that is installed with the PTR Program.

SHEET FEEDERS

WordPerfect supports sheet feeders that have from one to seven bins. See "Sclecting a Printer" in this chapter for details about selecting a sheet feeder when you select the printer. The following keystrokes help you select a sheet feeder after the printer has already been selected.

Keystrokes

1. Press Print (SHIFT-F7).

2. Choose **S** for Select a Printer.

3. Move the cursor to the printer for which a sheet-feeder definition should be selected.

4. Choose **3** for **E**dit.

5. Choose **3** for Sheet Feeder. The sheet feeders that were included as part of the printer's .ALL file are listed.

6. Move the cursor to the sheet feeder to be selected, and choose **1** for Select. To deselect a sheet feeder at any time, choose **2** for **N**one.

7. After reading the help screen for that sheet feeder, press Exit (F7) until you return to the document.

You should now edit each type of paper defined in the Paper Size/Type menu: Press Format (SHIFT-F8) and choose **2** for **P**age and then **7** for Paper Size/Type and change the location to reflect the bin number where it can be found. For example, if you have standard paper in bin number 1, letterhead in bin number 2, and envelopes in bin number 3, you would move to those paper definitions, choose **5** for **E**dit, **5** for Location, and **2** for **B**in Number, and then enter the bin number. WordPerfect will then know which bin to use for each form. When you are finished, press Exit (F7) until you return to the document.

Hints

When you select a sheet feeder, the sheet-feeder definition is copied to the selected printer's .PRS file.

You choose the sheet-feeder bin by choosing the appropriate form. For example, if you have defined an envelope form and specified that it is located in bin 3, choosing an envelope by pressing Format (SHIFT-F8), choosing 2 for Page and 7 for Paper Size/Type, and then selecting an envelope will automatically insert the envelope from bin number 3.

Always select the paper size and type at the very top of a page so that WordPerfect can feed the sheet of paper from the appropriate bin at the beginning of the page.

If you do not have a sheet feeder but selected a sheet-feeder definition, or if you select the wrong sheet feeder, you might see extra characters printing at the top or bottom of the page. These characters are usually the result of incorrectly interpreted Escape codes. Select a different sheet feeder, or change the location of the form to Continuous if the printer uses an internal paper tray (as is the case with laser printers).

If you do not see your sheet feeder among the list, it may be a single-bin mechanical sheet feeder that does not accept Escape codes for inserting and ejecting pages. This type of sheet feeder should usually be defined as Continuous.

You can also create a new sheet-feeder definition by using the Printer program, but a knowledge of programming commands is required to do so. See Chapter 5 for information about starting and working with the program. You might also want to check with Word-Perfect Corporation to see if the company has added your sheet feeder to the list since its initial release.

Related Entries

Paper Size/Type
Selecting a Printer
See Chapter 5, "Printer Program"

SHELL

If you do not have WordPerfect Library, Shell (CTRL-F1) is used to suspend WordPerfect in memory and go to DOS so you can format a floppy disk or do some other type of DOS command.

If WordPerfect Library's shell program is running, the Shell (CTRL-F1) key provides several other options. You can go directly to DOS for a single command without having to go through the shell menu or you can save or append the current file to the Clipboard.

You can also start shell macros from a WordPerfect macro if you have WordPerfect Library or Office version 2.1.

Keystrokes

1. Press Shell (CTRL-F1). The following menu appears:

```
1 Go to DOS; 2 DOS Command: 0
```

If you have WordPerfect Library's shell running, you will see the following prompt:

```
1 Go to Shell; Clipboard: 2 Save; 3 Append; 4 Retrieve; 5 DOS Command: 0
```

2. Choose **1** to **G**o to DOS (or **G**o to Shell if you have WordPerfect Library or Office running).

If you only want to do a single DOS command, you can skip the shell menu and return more quickly after the command is finished. Choose **2** or **5** to do a single DOS Command if you are not running shell, or **5** if you are. Even though option **5** is not shown on the menu when shell is not running, it is still available to provide consistency (when you are writing shell macros, for example). After doing the single DOS command, you are prompted to press any key to continue and return to WordPerfect.

If you are running WordPerfect Library, three other options are provided that let you save, append, and retrieve the contents of the Clipboard. Any program that supports WordPerfect Library or WordPerfect Office can save to or retrieve from the Clipboard, making it easy to share data between programs. If you choose the Save or Append option, the current document is saved or appended to the Clipboard. If you want to save only a portion of the document, block it first with Block (ALT-F4), press Shell (CTRL-F1), and choose the Save or Append option. Retrieve will retrieve the data from the Clipboard and place it into the document at the cursor's location.

Hints

If you go to the shell menu, the WordPerfect entry is marked with an asterisk as shown in Figure 3-153 to indicate that it is still in memory. Option 1 on the shell menu lets you Go to DOS from there. You would then enter **exit** to return to the shell menu. To return to WordPerfect, select the WordPerfect option from the menu.

If you go to DOS, the DOS prompt is altered to let you know that WordPerfect is still running, as shown here:

```
Microsoft(R) MS-DOS(R) Version 4.01
         (C)Copyright Microsoft Corp 1981-1988

Enter 'EXIT' to return to WordPerfect
C:\REF Tue 01-02-1990
->
```

Remember to type **exit** to return to WordPerfect—do not type **wp**, because it is already loaded in memory.

When you go to DOS, another copy of COMMAND.COM is loaded into memory. If you do not have enough memory available, you may see the message "Not enough memory to load COMMAND.COM," whereupon you are returned to WordPerfect.

You can access shell macros from version 2.1 of WordPerfect Library or Office from a regular WordPerfect macro by using the {SHELL MACRO} command. See "Macros" in this chapter for details.

Do not run the CHKDSK/F command while in DOS; it will interfere with the open files that WordPerfect creates while it is running. Also be careful not to delete any WordPerfect files while in DOS.

Load any TSR (Terminate-Stay Resident) programs before starting the WordPerfect program. They should not be loaded when you go to DOS temporarily.

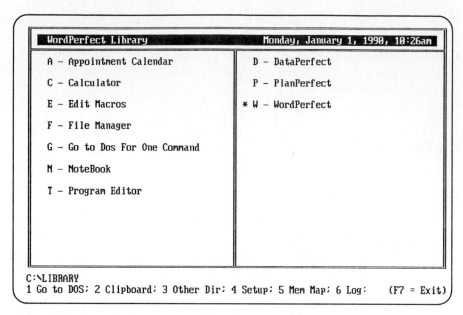

Figure 3-153.   Sample shell menu

Applications

If you have a document to be saved and run out of disk space, you can go to DOS with Shell (CTRL-F1) and format a disk.

To use the contents of the Clipboard as the secondary file in a merge, press Shell (CTRL-F1) instead of entering a filename when you are prompted for the name of the secondary file. This feature lets you extract data from another program (such as DataPerfect, Notebook, or PlanPerfect) and then merge it without first saving it as a WordPerfect file. In fact, if you have WordPerfect Library or Office 2.1, you can write shell macros that leave WordPerfect, enter another program, run a report or extract data, send the result to the Clipboard, reenter Word-Perfect, and then start a merge that will use the data in the Clipboard. See "Merge" in this chapter for details about using the Merge feature.

If you are running WordPerfect Library, you can go to the shell menu and run other programs if you have enough memory. Expanded memory is supported by both WordPerfect and Library.

Related Entries

> Go to DOS or Shell
> Macros
> Merge

SHORT FORM

The Short Form option is found on the Mark Text (ALT-F5) menu and is used in conjunction with the Table of Authorities feature. Each entry in a table of authorities has a full form, which will be the actual text printed in the table. The short form is a nickname that you can use to mark each subsequent occurrence of the full form. See "Table of Authorities" in this chapter for details.

SIZE ATTRIBUTE RATIOS

When you press Font (CTRL-F8) and choose **1** for Size, WordPerfect lets you choose from Superscript, Subscript, Fine, Small, Large, Very Large, and Extra Large. When you select your printer and the cartridges and fonts that are available for that printer, WordPerfect checks the list of available fonts and assigns fonts to each size according to a list of percentages in the Setup menu.

Figure 3-154 shows the percentages that are used by default. For example, if you are using a 12-point base font, WordPerfect would normally choose a similar 24-point font for Extra Large (if one is found in the list of fonts) because it is 200%, or twice the size. If a 24-point font is not available, the next closest font will be chosen.

You can use this menu to specify your own percentages. The new selection will take effect when you select or change the cartridges and fonts for the printer selection, unless you have a PostScript printer, in which case, the percentages take effect immediately.

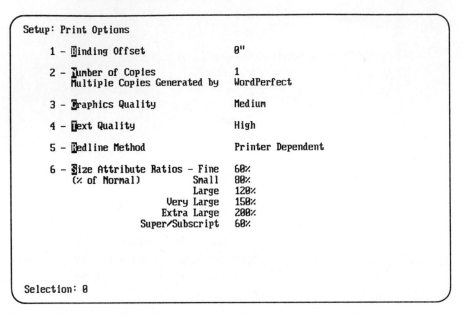

Setup: Print Options

    1 - Binding Offset   0"

    2 - Number of Copies   1
        Multiple Copies Generated by   WordPerfect

    3 - Graphics Quality   Medium

    4 - Text Quality   High

    5 - Redline Method   Printer Dependent

    6 - Size Attribute Ratios - Fine   60%
        (% of Normal)   Small   80%
                  Large   120%
            Very Large   150%
          Extra Large   200%
       Super/Subscript   60%

Selection: 0

Figure 3-154.   Percentages used by WordPerfect to select fonts for the Size attributes

Keystrokes

1. Press Setup (SHIFT-F1).

2. Choose 4 for **Initial Settings.**

3. Choose 8 for **Print Options.** The selections appear at the bottom of the menu, as shown in Figure 3-154.

4. Choose 6 for **Size Attribute Ratios.**

5. Enter a new percentage for each setting, or press ENTER to bypass any option. Enter a percentage higher than 100% to increase the size and lower than 100% to decrease the size.

6. Press Exit (F7) when you are finished.

Hints

Remember that if you do not have a PostScript printer, you will need to update the list of fonts so that the new percentages will be used when

WordPerfect selects the automatic font changes. See "Cartridges and Fonts" or "Automatic Font Changes" in this chapter for details.

After selecting the fonts that are available, you will see the message "Updating Fonts: n" on the screen. WordPerfect checks the current size attribute ratios and selects fonts that fit the specifications.

You can also use the Printer (PTR) program to select the exact fonts that are to be used for the automatic font changes. See Chapter 5, "Printer Program" for details.

Applications

This feature is especially useful for people who use PostScript printers, because of the capability of those printers to scale fonts to an exact setting. For example, if you choose 600% for Extra Large, a PostScript printer will increase the size of the current font exactly 600%.

Related Entries

Automatic Font Changes

SIZE OF PRINT

When you press Font (CTRL-F8), the first option listed is Size. The choices found in this category are as follows:

```
1 Suprscpt; 2 Subscpt; 3 Fine; 4 Small; 5 Large; 6 Ury Large; 7 Ext Large; 0
```

Note that options for superscript and subscript are found on this menu. The size of print is sometimes altered for superscripted or subscripted text.

You can turn the other options on and off, or you can block text and assign a size of print to that block. You may find this easier than making font changes, because you cannot assign a certain font to a block of text without defining a style or using a macro included as part of the Macros keyboard (see "Keyboard Layout" in this chapter for details).

The size of print is determined by the current base font and the fonts that were chosen when the printer was selected. When you selected a printer, you saw the message "Updating Font: n" while Word-Perfect stored information about each font so it could make intelligent choices about which fonts to use for automatic font changes.

You can use the Size Attribute Ratio menu to specify the exact percentages of the base font that is to be used when you are deciding the size of fonts to use. See "Size Attribute Ratios" in this chapter for more information.

You can also have complete control over the fonts chosen by using the Printer (PTR) program to select the Automatic Font Changes from the list of available fonts. See Chapter 5 for details.

Remember that the size and type of font depend on the fonts that are available in your printer. If you print the document on a different printer, the size attributes will be printed according to that printer's available fonts.

WordPerfect lets you choose how the attributes will appear on the screen. If you have a monochrome monitor, you can choose to display the different selections in boldface, underline, reverse video, or blinking characters. You may find blinking not acceptable for most attributes, but it could be effective for superscript or subscript, because they are usually a single character.

If you have a color monitor, you can select a different color for each attribute. If you have a Hercules graphics card with RamFont, you can use the Fine, Small, Large, Very Large, and Extra Large screen fonts so you can see the differences on the screen while you are editing. These screen attributes affect the screen display only; they do not affect printing. See "Colors/Fonts/Attributes" in this chapter for more information about changing the display.

Related Entries

Colors/Fonts/Attributes
Fonts
Size Attribute Ratios
See Chapter 5, "Printer Program"

SKIP LANGUAGE

If you use a language code in your document and then check the spelling, use the thesaurus, or turn on hyphenation, WordPerfect looks for the dictionary, thesaurus, or hyphenation module for that particular language. If it is not found, a message asking if you want to skip the language is displayed.

If you have the appropriate files, change the Location of Files setting in the Setup menu so that WordPerfect will be able to find them. If you do not have the files, you might want to remove the code, or you will need to choose the option to skip the language. WordPerfect will then skip over the text until it finds another language code. See "Language" in this chapter for more information.

SMALL CAPS

WordPerfect has an option on the Font (CTRL-F8) Appearance menu that lets you print in small caps. If you have an EGA, VGA, or Hercules graphics card with RamFont, you can display small caps on the screen while you are editing.

Keystrokes

1. Press Font (CTRL-F8).

2. Choose **2** for Appearance.

3. Choose **7** for Small Caps.

4. Type the text to be printed in small caps.

5. Press → to move past the small caps-off code to turn off small caps.

You can also block any amount of text, press Font (CTRL-F8), choose **2** for Appearance, and then choose **7** for Small Caps to print that section of text in small caps.

Hints

When you select small caps, [SM CAP] and [sm cap] codes are inserted, with the cursor resting on the [sm cap] off code. As you type, text is inserted between the codes. You can choose Small Caps again to turn off the feature, but it is easiest to press → to move past the off code.

You can assign a screen attribute, color, or screen font to represent small caps on the screen. The screen attribute is used only for the display; it does not affect printing. If you have an EGA or VGA monitor, you usually have 16 colors available. If you give up 8 colors, you can choose to have small caps, underline, italics, or 512 characters displayed instead (only one of these options can be displayed at a time). If you have a Hercules graphics card with RamFont, you can choose small caps as a screen font and also have the other options available. See "Colors/Fonts/Attributes" in this chapter for more information.

Related Entries

Appearance
Colors/Fonts/Attributes
Fonts

SMALL PRINT

See "Size of Print" in this chapter.

SOFT PAGE

When the maximum number of lines fills a page, WordPerfect automatically inserts a soft page break (a single dashed line). A space at the end of a line is usually converted to a soft page break, represented by [SPg] in Reveal Codes (ALT-F3). If a hard return [HRt] happens to fall at the end of the page, it will be converted to a soft page break, and the code [HRt-SPg] would be inserted.

WordPerfect automatically calculates the number of lines that are allowed on a page and takes into account the length of the page, headers, footers, page numbers, and footnotes.

If text is added or deleted, the soft page break will automatically be updated (repagination is unnecessary with WordPerfect). You can see across both soft and hard page breaks, and you can move to specific pages with PGUP, PGDN, or Go To (CTRL-HOME).

A hard page break is displayed as a double dashed line and is manually inserted when you press Hard Page (CTRL-ENTER).

Related Entries

Page Breaks

SORT AND SELECT

You can sort information in lines, paragraphs, or a secondary merge file. If you are in a table, you can sort the information in a table.

WordPerfect uses a database concept for sorting and selecting records by viewing each line, paragraph, or merge record as a record. Each record is further divided into fields, lines, and words. For example, if you have a list of clients, each client will be considered a record. Each bit of information about that client (such as address, phone number, or birth date) is considered a field.

You can use Sort to sort the records by one or more of the bits of information (sort by last name or ZIP code, for example) or to select records that fit into the same category (such as all those who attended last year's benefit and have donated more than $50 during the year).

When reading the following sections, keep in mind that while there are many options available with the Sort feature, few changes (if any) need to be made to the Sort menu when you are sorting a list of items.

Keystrokes

Sort a File

If you want to sort a file that appears on the screen, retrieve the file first.

1. Press Merge/Sort (CTRL-F9). The following prompt appears:

```
1 Merge; 2 Sort; 3 Convert Old Merge Codes: 0
```

2. Choose **2** for Sort. You are asked for the name of the input file.

3. Press ENTER to sort the contents of the screen, or enter the name of a file to be sorted. Include the drive and directory if necessary.

4. When you are prompted for the name of the output file, press ENTER to display the results on the screen, or enter the name of the file that will be used to hold the sorted data. If you enter the name of a file that already exists, you are asked if you want to replace the original file. Type **Y** to replace the file, or type **N** and enter a different filename.

5. The Sort menu appears, as shown in Figure 3-155. It has already been set to sort lines by the first word in each line. Make changes to the menu if necessary. See "Options" for information about the options on this menu.

6. Choose **1** for **P**erform Action.

The number of records involved are counted at the bottom corner of the screen during the sort. When the sort is finished, the Sort menu disappears from the screen.

Sort a Block

Use a block sort if you want to sort part of a document or if you have a list of items but do not want to include any headings in the sort.

1. Retrieve the file containing the block to be sorted.

2. Move the cursor to one end of the block, and press Block (ALT-F4).

3. Move the cursor to the opposite end to highlight the block.

4. Press Merge/Sort (CTRL-F9). The menu shown in Figure 3-155 appears.

5. Change options on the Sort menu if necessary; see "Options" for details.

6. Choose 1 for **P**erform Action.

Sort in a Table

You can use the Sort feature to sort rows in a table. See "Tables" in this chapter for instructions on creating a table.

1. Move the cursor into the table (the location is not important).

2. Press Merge/Sort (CTRL-F9). The Sort menu shown in Figure 3-156 appears. Note that the Type is set to "Tables" and the Keys section includes the word "Cell."

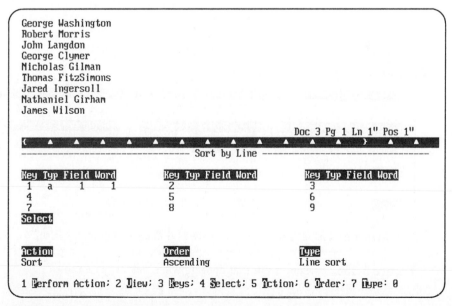

Figure 3-155.   Sort menu

3. If you want to sort all rows by the information in the first cell of each row, you do not have to make any changes to this menu. Choose 1 for **P**erform Action, and all rows in the table will be sorted. See "Hints" for other options.

Unfortunately, you cannot sort a block of cells in a table; instead, the entire table will be sorted, which may place a heading in an undesirable place. To avoid this situation, you may want to create the table with no heading. After sorting, move to the top row of the table, press Columns/Tables (ALT-F7), press INS to insert, choose 1 for **R**ow, and then enter the number of rows to be added to the top of the table.

Options

The Sort menu shown in Figure 3-155 displays numbered options at the bottom of the screen. These options are used to enter or change the information that is displayed in the menu.

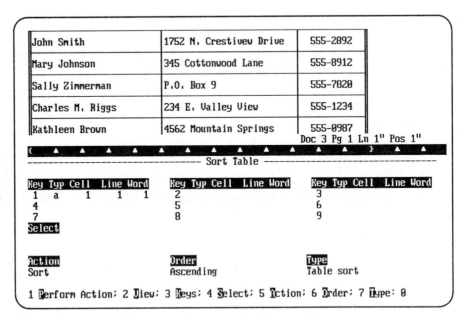

Figure 3-156. Sort menu that appears while you are in a table

The beginning of the menu displays the keys. A key is the item (word) by which the lines, paragraphs, rows, or records are sorted. WordPerfect asks you to identify whether the "word" is alphanumeric or numeric, and where it is located. You can define up to nine keys for subsorting. Keys are also used to help determine the selection criteria.

The rest of the menu displays the current selections. Each option is explained in detail below.

Perform Action

After you have made all the selections, choose 1 for Perform Action. The term "action" means sort, select, or sort *and* select. The current selection is displayed on the menu. The Action can be changed with option 5.

View

Option 2 for View lets you view the text to be sorted. You can use any of the cursor keys to move through the text. After viewing the text, press Exit (F7) to return to the Sort menu. If you are sorting a merge file and each record is larger than the amount of space at the top of the screen, you can use this option to check the field, line, or word number when defining the keys.

Keys

Before specifying the keys, verify that the type of sort is correct. Option 7 for Type is used to choose between a Line, Paragraph, or Merge sort. If you are in a table, the type of sort is automatically changed to a "Table sort" and cannot be changed to any other type of sort.

Each type of sort has its own key selection. A Line sort asks for the field and word, as shown in the following example. If you have tabbed columns on a line, each column is considered a field. Words are separated by a space, slash (/), or hard hyphen (press HOME, HYPHEN).

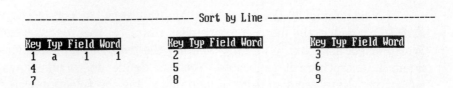

A Paragraph sort asks you to identify the line, field, and word, as shown here:

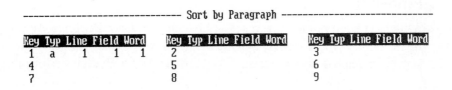

The Merge sort asks for the field number first, the line number, and then the word to be used, as indicated in the menu shown here:

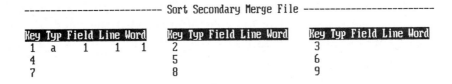

When sorting a table, "Cell" is added to the list, as shown here. This would be the cell in the row (column) that is to be used for sorting. For example, if the last name was in column 2 and you wanted to sort by last name, you would enter 2 so WordPerfect would use the second cell.

```
----------------------------- Sort Table -----------------------------
Key Typ Cell  Line Word    Key Typ Cell  Line Word    Key Typ Cell  Line Word
 1   a   1     1    1       2                           3
 4                          5                           6
 7                          8                           9
```

In a merge record, each field is separated from the next one by an {END FIELD} code. In lines and paragraphs, the fields are divided with a tab or indent code. Each column in a table divides fields.

Dealing with Variable Lines and Words   Each record (line, paragraph, or individual merge record) should always contain the same number of fields. However, there are not always the same number of words from record to record. For example, some records might have names consisting of a first name and a surname, while others have a first name, a middle name, and a surname.

In these types of situations, use a negative number to identify the word from the opposite direction. For example, if the ZIP code is in the same field as the city and state, it could be the third word in "Topeka, Kansas 89898," the fourth word in "Bismarck, North Dakota 23232," or the fifth word in "Salt Lake City, Utah 56565." However, it will always be the last field in any of these situations. The same situation would be true if you wanted to sort a list of names by the last name. In both of these cases, you would use a negative 1 (-1) to identify the word, counting from the right instead of the left.

Figure 3-157 shows the Sort menu when three keys have been defined for a merge file having an inconsistent number of words per field. Note that the negative number has been used in all three situations to sort by ZIP code, state, and then surname.

Entering the Keys   When you select option 3, Keys, you will see a one-line message at the bottom of the screen, as shown in Figure 3-157. This message prompts you to type **A** for an Alphanumeric sort or **N** for a Numeric sort. If the numbers to be sorted all have the same number of digits (as in a ZIP code or a telephone number), you can use either **A** or **N**. If there is an unequal number of digits, use the numeric sort. If you were to use the alphanumeric sort, unequal numbers could be sorted incorrectly (1000 would be sorted before 7, because 1 comes before 7). A numeric sort compares the numbers from the right instead of beginning at the left.

When you are defining the keys, use the arrow keys to move to each item. When you press →, the information (**a 1 1**) is automatically inserted. You can move freely through the keys with any of the arrow keys and type a new letter or number to replace the existing option. To delete all the information in the last key, move to any previous key and press DEL.

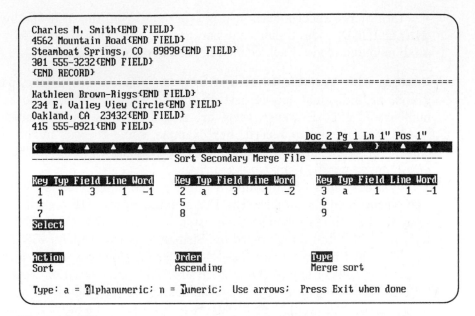

```
Charles M. Smith<END FIELD>
4562 Mountain Road<END FIELD>
Steamboat Springs, CO  89898<END FIELD>
301 555-3232<END FIELD>
<END RECORD>
================================================================
Kathleen Brown-Riggs<END FIELD>
234 E. Valley View Circle<END FIELD>
Oakland, CA  23432<END FIELD>
415 555-8921<END FIELD>
                                        Doc 2 Pg 1 Ln 1" Pos 1"
```

```
------------------------ Sort Secondary Merge File --------------

Key Typ Field Line Word    Key Typ Field Line Word    Key Typ Field Line Word
 1   n    3     1   -1      2   a    3     1   -2      3   a    1     1   -1
 4                          5                          6
 7                          8                          9
Select


Action              Order               Type
Sort                Ascending           Merge sort

Type: a = Alphanumeric; n = Numeric;  Use arrows;  Press Exit when done
```

Figure 3-157.   Instead of counting from the left, you can use negative numbers to identify words from the right

When you have finished entering the keys, press Exit (F7) to return to the menu.

Select

You can use the Select option to select all records that have a particular item in common. For example, you could select all the records for people from age 25 to 30 who are living in St. Louis. In all but a global select (discussed later), you should define the keys before entering the select statement.

When you choose option 4 for Select, you see the Select options at the bottom of the menu shown in Figure 3-158. When entering the select statement, you will identify the key to be used, the operator, and the condition to be met. You can combine keys with * and + to select all records that satisfy either condition or both conditions, respectively. You can place parentheses around entries to identify groups and to change the order of the selection (usually done from left to right). Use spaces between keys, but not within keys. Table 3-18 describes each operator that you can use in a select statement.

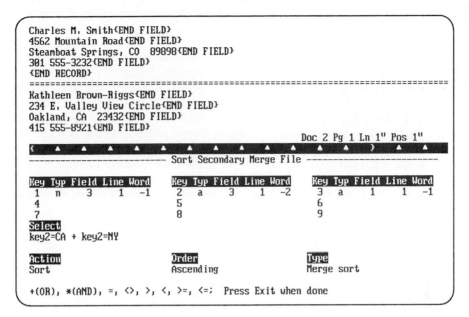

Figure 3-158.   Sort menu showing a Select statement

Symbol	Function
+ (or)	Place between keys to select records that meet one condition *or* the other
* (and)	Place between keys to select records for which *both* conditions exist
=	Equal to
< >	Not equal to
>	Greater than
<	Less than
> =	Greater than or equal to
< =	Less than or equal to
( )	Place parentheses around keys that should be considered one group; Sort considers the keys within parentheses first and then sorts from left to right

Table 3-18.   Operators Used in Select Statements

Select Statement	Explanation
key1 = Johnson	Select all records for the Johnson family reunion mailing
key2 > 54700 * key2 < 75600	Select all records having a ZIP code greater than 54700 but less than 75600
key1 > = a * key1 < = n	Select records where the last name starts with a letter "A" through "M" (or a last name consisting *only* of "N")
key6 > = $75,000	Select all records that list a salary greater than or equal to $75,000
key < > CA	Select all records except those from California
(key3 = Toledo + key3 = Columbus) * (key5 > = 25 * key5 < = 30)	Select records for all people between the ages of 25 and 35 living in Columbus or Toledo

Table 3-19.   Select Statements Showing the Use of Operators and Parentheses

As shown in Figure 3-158, you must identify a key for each option (key2 = CA + key2 = NY). You could not have used the select statement "key2 = CA + NY." Use + and * only between keys, not within keys.

Table 3-19 includes samples of select statements that should clarify how operators and parentheses are used. In the second, third, and sixth examples, * is used instead of +. To understand why, look at the second example. If a + would have been used in this situation, all the records greater than 54700 or less than 75600 would have been included. In essence, all records would have been included because either condition could be met. If you correctly use the * operator, both conditions must be met, limiting the number of records between the two numbers.

Global Select   WordPerfect can select all records that contain a specific word anywhere in the record. For this reason, you do not have to identify the exact key.

You can use only one word in a global select, and you can enter the condition in either uppercase or lowercase. Unlike Search, Select finds both uppercase and lowercase occurrences if just uppercase is used in the condition; lowercase will also find both uppercase and lowercase.

An example of a global select statement is "keyg = esq", which will select all records that contain "Esq." after a person's name or a company name. The statement "keyg > = esq" would select all records that mention "Esq," "Esq.," or "Esquire," because those phrases are greater than or equal to "Esq."

Action

If you have not entered a select statement, the action is considered to be a Sort. Option 5 for Action is then disabled. If you have entered a select statement, the action automatically changes to Select and Sort. You can choose option 5 for Action, and make a choice between Select and Sort, or Select only.

Order

Option 6 for Order lets you determine whether records will be sorted in ascending or descending order.

Type

If you choose 7 for Type, three choices appear: Merge, Line, and Paragraph with Line (the default choice). You cannot change the type to Table. However, if you are in a table when you enter the Sort menu, the type is changed to a Table sort and you cannot change it to any other type of sort.

A Line sort is set as the default and is discussed first.

Line Sort   Use the Line option to sort lines that end with a hard or soft return. If there are blank lines between any of the lines, they are extracted and placed at the very beginning of the list after it is sorted. If you have used tabs or indents in the line, each tab or indent code separates a field.

Both of the following examples could be sorted by line. In the first example, each entire line is considered field 1, because there are no tab or indent codes. If you wanted to sort by the last name, you would specify −1 because of the inconsistent number of words in each record:

```
Charles Grover
Kathleen Brown
Wallace M. Cleveland
Richard Washington
Jane S. Fremont
```

The second Line sort example contains three fields in each record because of the tabs separating each column:

```
Charles Grover          301 555-7878    Consultant
Kathleen Brown          212 555-9893    Training Manager
Wallace M. Cleveland    415 555-3212    Distributor
Richard Washington      213 555-3456    Consultant
Jane S. Fremont         301 555-7654    Distributor
```

Paragraph Sort   Any group of text separated by two or more hard returns, or a hard or soft page break, is considered a paragraph. A paragraph can be up to one page in length. When specifying a key for a paragraph sort, you need to identify the line, the field (items separated with a tab or indent code), and the word.

Merge Sort   If you are sorting a secondary merge file with fields separated by {END FIELD} codes and records by {END RECORD} codes, use the Merge option. If there are any extra lines in this type of file, it will be sorted incorrectly. When you define a key for this type of sort, specify the field number and the line within that field, and finally the word.

Hints

The last set of sort and select criteria is kept in the Sort menu until you change it or exit WordPerfect.

If you select records from a block or file and the result is a blank screen, no records were found. To restore the original text, press Cancel (F1) and choose **1**.

Sorting by Last Name

If a last name appears at the end of the line, remember to specify −1 as the "key" word to be used for the sort. WordPerfect will then start counting from the right end of the line instead of from the left.

If you have two or more words that you want considered as one word during a sort, insert a hard space (HOME, spacebar) between each word instead of a regular space. This is useful when you need to sort by a last name but have an abbreviation or title, such as M.D., Ph.D., or Jr., after the last name. If you did not use a hard space between the last name and the abbreviation and entered −1 as the word to be used for the sort, the abbreviation will be considered the last name.

Sorting by Date

If you have dates in the format "November 25, 1990," you can easily sort by day or year. However, if you enter dates as "11-25-90" with regular hyphens (-), the hyphens will be ignored and the sort will treat the entire date as one word.

Because words can be separated by a space, slash (/), or a hard hyphen (press HOME, HYPHEN), you would need to enter dates as "11/25/90" or with a hard hyphen (pressing HOME, HYPHEN between the month, day, and year).

If you wanted to sort in true chronological order, you would define key1 to sort by year (the third word), key2 to sort by month (the first word), and key3 to sort by day (the second word).

Not Enough Memory

If the document to be sorted is in document 1, document 2 is used to sort the information. If both documents are filled, document 3 is used. Document 3 is used only for features such as Sort and View, and for the generation of a table of contents, lists, index, and so on.

You may get a message telling you that the other document must be cleared before you can continue because of the lack of available memory. Because there is twice as much memory allotted to document 1 as document 2, you can leave document 1 empty and use document 2 as the document to be sorted. WordPerfect will then perform the sort in document 1 and can use the extra memory available there.

Also check the amount of disk space that is available if you see the message "Not enough memory." You should have available at least 2.5 times the amount of disk space as the file to be sorted.

Sorting Sequence

A block is sorted according to the current language code. For example, if you have selected a U.S. or European language, accented characters will be sorted with the unaccented characters. If a Scandinavian language code is active, the accented characters will be sorted *after* the unaccented characters.

Applications

Sort is considered by many to be as powerful as a database when it comes to sorting and selecting records. It is especially useful when you keep all your merge records in one file and want to select records to target specific groups and markets. The Merge feature itself can also do conditional merges, meaning that it can also select records based on certain criteria. See "Merge" and Chapter 6, "Advanced Macro and Merge Commands."

To take advantage of bulk mailing rates, you must presort envelopes or newsletters according to ZIP code. Use Sort to accomplish this instead of doing it by hand.

You can easily sort bibliographies using a paragraph sort. Enter each reference at random, and then do the sort later. If items are added, do the sort again.

When you send copies of a letter to others, you usually put the abbreviation "cc:" at the bottom of the letter, with the names of those to receive copies after it. You can block and sort the list to place them in alphabetical order.

If you sort a list that has been numbered with WordPerfect's Paragraph Numbering feature, the list will be renumbered correctly after the sort.

Related Entries

Language
Merge
Tables

SPACING

WordPerfect lets you specify any amount of line spacing, including fractions of a line.

Keystrokes

1. Move the cursor to the location at which spacing is to change.

2. Press Format (SHIFT-F8).

3. Choose **1** for Line.

4. Choose **6** for Line Spacing.

5. Enter the new spacing number (**2** for double-spacing, **1/2** for half-line spacing, **1 3/4** for one and three-quarter line spacing, and so on).

6. Press Exit (F7) to return to the document.

Hints

When you change the line spacing, the code [Ln Spacing:n] is inserted into the document, where n is the amount of spacing entered. Text from that point on is affected until another spacing change is encountered.

The amount entered for line spacing is multiplied by the current line height. When the Line Height specification is set to Automatic, a specific line height is used for different sized fonts. If you want to vary the amount of spacing between the lines, increase or decrease the line spacing slightly (1.1 or 9.0, for example) instead of changing the line height. If you choose a fixed line height to change the spacing instead, it will be used for every font, regardless of the height. Because the line spacing is multiplied by the line height, you can change the overall line spacing without affecting each font.

Printers that can print only six lines per inch may not be able to make many changes to line spacing.

You can enter the setting in decimal form (.5, 1.75, and so on) or you can use fractions.

If you get double-spacing at the printer where you specified single-spacing, make sure that the auto line feed (LF) switch is off at the printer. Check the printer manual to find the location of the switch.

Spacing for Headers, Footers, Footnotes, and Endnotes

Changing the spacing in a document does not affect the spacing in a header, footer, footnote, or endnote. You can change the spacing within an individual header or footer. Change the spacing for footnotes and endnotes through the Footnote or Endnote Options menu: Press Footnote (CTRL-F7), choose **1** for **F**ootnote or **2** for **E**ndnote, and then choose **4** for **O**ptions. You can change the spacing of the notes as well as the amount of space between each note.

You can increase the amount of space between a header or footer and subsequent text by inserting more space at the end of a header or the beginning of a footer.

Changing the Line Spacing for Special Elements

Usually, the same line spacing is used throughout a document. However, if you type double-spaced documents containing indented, single-spaced quotations, you can easily change the spacing before and after the quotation. If this is a common application for you, consider placing the steps in a macro or style. The macro could change to single-spacing and indent the paragraph, and then it would pause for you to enter the text. After you entered the text and pressed ENTER to continue the macro, it would create the necessary space between the quotation and the text, and then return to double-spacing. A style would do basically the same task. However, it is easier to make global format changes to indented text with a style rather than a macro.

If vertical lines in Line Draw do not exactly match when printed, decrease the amount of line spacing slightly.

Related Entries

Leading
Line Draw
Line Height

SPECIAL CHARACTERS

If you have a graphics printer (laser or dot matrix), you will be able to print over 1500 special characters with WordPerfect 5.1.

A list of these characters appears in Appendix A. You will find the characters grouped into 12 WordPerfect Character Sets, with each character assigned a number in that set.

Keystrokes

1. To insert a special character, press CTRL-2 (CTRL-V from the main editing screen).

2. Find the character in Appendix A, and then enter the character set number, a comma, and the number assigned to the character.

If the character cannot be displayed on your monitor, a small square box is inserted instead. Pressing Reveal Codes (ALT-F3) and moving your cursor to the small box displays the character set and character number that were entered. See "Hints" for an option that lets you see more than 256 characters on some types of graphics monitors.

Another way to insert a special character is to press CTRL-2, and then type the two characters that make up the special character. For example, typing ** will insert a bullet (•), /2 will insert ½, and a" will insert ä. For a list of these options, see "Compose" in this chapter.

Hints

Printing Special Characters

You do not have to do anything special to print a special character. WordPerfect has created and stored each character in a file named WP.DRS and will use that character if it is not found in the printer. If you are having difficulty printing special characters, you may not have installed the WP.DRS file. Return to the Install program and type **Y** when you are asked if you want to install the Graphics Driver files.

The following is an explanation of the process used to print special characters for those who have a printer that can print graphics.

If a special character is not found in the current font, WordPerfect checks the list of automatic font changes to see if a font has been entered for that particular character set. If not, it begins scanning the substitute fonts for the special character. See Chapter 5, "Printer Program," for more information on automatic font changes and substitute fonts. If the character is not found in either location, WordPerfect prints the character (or the part of the character that cannot be found) in graphics.

If either the Text or Graphics Quality in the Print (SHIFT-F7) menu is set to High, the character will be printed in high quality. If both are set to any setting less than high, the character will be printed in the quality selected for graphics quality. If either is set to Do Not Print, the graphics characters will not print.

Be aware that characters printed graphically take up memory in the printer. If you hear a beep during printing, press Print (SHIFT-F7), and then choose 4 for Control Printer to check for a "Not Enough Memory" error message. If you continue the print job, the remaining characters that could not be printed because of lack of memory will be printed as a space instead.

Displaying Special Characters

If a special character is not available and a small block is displayed instead, you can move to the small block and press Reveal Codes (ALT-F3) to see the section and character number for the special character.

If you have an EGA, VGA, or Hercules graphics card with RamFont, you can display an additional 256 characters for a total of 512 characters. Press Setup (SHIFT-F1), choose 2 for Display and then 1 for Colors/Fonts/Attributes. The list of choices for an EGA or VGA monitor lets you display attributes in 16 colors, or you can give up 8 of those colors and choose to have underlining, italics, small caps, or 512 characters instead. If you want to see more than 256 characters on the screen, choose this last option.

If you have a Hercules graphics card with RamFont, you can choose to have 12 fonts consisting of 256 characters, or 6 fonts consisting of 512 characters. If you are willing to give up 6 fonts, you can display 512 characters in each of the remaining 6 fonts. If you give up 6 fonts, the ones that remain include normal, double-underline, italics, superscript, subscript, and small print. Bold, underline, strikeout, and reverse are standard and are always available.

Choosing ALT- and CTRL-Key Combinations

See "Keyboard Layout" in this chapter for the steps that you can use to assign characters to a combination that is easy to remember. For example, you could use CTRL-H for 1/2 and CTRL-F for 1/4.

You can also define ALT-key macros for the special characters. See "Macros" in this chapter for more information.

Related Entries

Compose
Keyboard Layout
Macros

SPELL

With its 125,000-word dictionary, WordPerfect can help check the spelling of a word, a page, a document, or any size block of text. This dictionary includes approximately 25,000 legal and medical terms.

Keystrokes

Check a Word, a Page, or a Document

WordPerfect checks the spelling of a document while it is on the screen.

1. If you are checking a word or a page, move the cursor to that word or page.

If you are using WordPerfect on a two-disk-drive system, remove the data disk from drive B and insert the Speller disk.

2. Press Spell (CTRL-F2). The following menu appears:

Check: 1 **W**ord; 2 **P**age; 3 **D**ocument; 4 **N**ew Sup. Dictionary; 5 **L**ook Up; 6 **C**ount: 0

If you did not install the Speller during installation, or if you have inserted a language code and WordPerfect cannot find the spelling dictionary for that language, you will see a message telling you that the dictionary is not found. Choose 3 for Exit Spell, and see "Hints" for solutions.

3. Choose **1** to check the current **W**ord, **2** to check the current **P**age, or **3** to check the entire **D**ocument. See "Options" for details about the other options listed.

4. The appropriate selection is checked. If a word is not found in the spelling dictionary, the word is highlighted, and possible correct spellings are displayed, as shown in Figure 3-159.

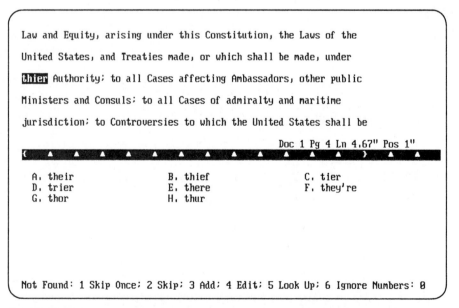

Law and Equity, arising under this Constitution, the Laws of the
United States, and Treaties made, or which shall be made, under
thier Authority; to all Cases affecting Ambassadors, other public
Ministers and Consuls; to all Cases of admiralty and maritime
jurisdiction; to Controversies to which the United States shall be

Doc 1 Pg 4 Ln 4.67" Pos 1"

A. their   B. thief   C. tier
D. trier   E. there   F. they're
G. thor   H. thur

Not Found: 1 Skip Once; 2 Skip; 3 Add; 4 Edit; 5 Look Up; 6 Ignore Numbers: 0

Figure 3-159.   Spell menu suggesting possible correct spellings

Note that you can see the status line above the choice of words so that you can always tell your position in the document.

5. If the correct spelling is on the list, type the letter assigned to the word. The correctly spelled word will automatically replace the highlighted word. If the correct word is not displayed, press ENTER or the space bar to display other choices. If other choices are not available, the current list of words is displayed again.

If the word is not listed and is correctly spelled (your name, for example), choose 1 to Skip the word Once, 2 to Skip further occurrences of the "misspelled" word in that document, or type 3 to Add the word to the supplementary dictionary. Option 4 for Edit lets you correct the misspelling yourself, and option 5 lets you Look Up the word in the dictionary according to the phonetic spelling or word pattern. Mnemonic letter selections are not available in this menu, because letters are used to select from the list of choices shown in Figure 3-159.

For more information about these choices, see "Options."

6. The next misspelling is highlighted, and the process continues.

7. When you are finished, a word count or the one-line Speller menu is displayed (depending on whether you checked the word, page, or document). Press any key to leave the Word Count feature, or press ENTER to leave the one-line Speller menu.

8. If you have a two-disk-drive system, be sure to replace the Speller disk with the data disk, and save the document on the original disk.

To stop spell checking at any time, press Cancel (F1) until you return to the document.

Check a Block of Text

1. Move the cursor to one end of the block to be checked, and press Block (ALT-F4).

2. Move the cursor to the opposite end of the block to highlight the block. There is no limit in size.

3. Press Spell (CTRL-F2). The spelling dictionary automatically starts checking the block of text.

4. Make corrections as previously indicated.

5. When you are finished, the total word count of the block is displayed. After pressing any key, you are returned to the document.

Options

Initial One-Line Speller Menu

When you first press Spell (CTRL-F2), the Speller menu appears. Each menu option is discussed in detail here.

Word   Choose **1** to check the current **W**ord. The cursor must be in the word or at the space just after the word to be checked. If the word is correct, the cursor moves to the next word and displays the Speller menu again so that you can make another choice. Press ENTER if you want to leave the menu and return to the document.

Page   To check the spelling for the current **P**age, choose **2**. When you are finished, the total number of words on the page is displayed. After you press any key to erase the word count, the one-line menu is displayed again. Make another choice from the menu, or press ENTER to return to the document.

Document   After you check the entire document, a final word count is displayed. Press any key to return to the document.

New Sup. Dictionary   WordPerfect uses two dictionaries to check a document. The main dictionary, WP{WP}US.LEX, is included on the Speller disk. The supplementary dictionary, WP{WP}US.SUP, is automatically created when the Speller is first used and is a regular WordPerfect file that is used to store the words that you add to the dictionary. If you choose **4** for **N**ew Sup. Dictionary, you can enter the name of a different file, which will then be used as the supplementary dictionary. If the supplementary dictionary is found in a different location from the one entered in the Setup menu's Location of Files menu, enter the drive and directory in which the file can be found. After you choose a new dictionary, the Speller menu is displayed again to enable you to check the appropriate section of text.

This option is useful if you are working on a special project that involves a particular set of technical terms. You can enter those words in a regular WordPerfect file and use that file as the supplementary dictionary.

Look Up   Option 5 lets you Look Up a word in the dictionary without first typing the word on the screen. Upon choosing this option, "Word or word pattern:" is displayed. You can type a phonetic spelling (enter it as it sounds) or enter a word pattern using wildcard characters for "missing" characters. For example, entering "sikadelik" would display the correct spelling, "psychedelic." When entering a word pattern, enter the characters that you are sure of, filling in the blanks with the wildcard characters ?, *, or -, as shown here:

?   Represents any single character

* or -   Represents any number of characters

For example, if you do not know how many c's and r's are in the word "occurrence" or if it ends with "ance" or "ence," you can enter **oc-r-nce** to display the correctly spelled word.

You are then given the opportunity to enter another word or word pattern. Press ENTER to leave the prompt if you do not want to look up another word. The Speller menu is again displayed. Make a choice or press ENTER to exit the speller.

Count   After a block, page, or document is checked, the number of words is displayed at the bottom of the screen, as shown here:

```
Word count: 246      Press any key to continue
```

Option **6** Counts all the words in the document without checking the spelling first.

Not Found Menu

When a word is not found in the dictionary, possible choices are displayed and labeled with the letters "A" through "X." Type the letter assigned to the correct spelling, and the misspelled word will be automatically replaced. The options listed in the "Not Found" menu are described in the following paragraphs.

Skip Once   Choose **1** to Skip the misspelled word Once. This option is useful if a word is misspelled within a quotation and must therefore remain misspelled. The next occurrence of that misspelling would be highlighted.

Skip   Choose **2** to Skip the word for the rest of the document. Use this option when a word is spelled correctly but is not found in the dictionary. It is useful if you do not want to stop on the word again in a document, but do not want to add the word to the dictionary.

Add   Choosing option **3** Adds the highlighted word to the supplementary dictionary. WP{WP}US.SUP is used as the name of the supplementary dictionary, unless you specified another name with option **4** from the Speller menu to change to a New supplementary dictionary.

Edit   If you want to edit the word yourself, choose **4** for Edit. You can also edit the word by pressing → or ← and then typing the correct spelling. When you are finished, press ENTER or Exit (F7) (you may find ENTER more intuitive even though Exit is the only choice given). The word is checked again before the Speller continues.

Look Up   WordPerfect uses as much of a word pattern as possible to display the choices on the screen. If you want to enter a specific word pattern using the wildcard character ?, *, or -, choose this option. You can also enter a word as it sounds (phonetic spelling). Words that match the word pattern or phonetic spelling are displayed. You can choose one of the choices from the menu, or you can press ENTER to return to the Not Found menu and make another selection.

Ignore Numbers   If a word contains a number, the Speller will stop on that word. The Speller will not stop on words that contain *only* numbers. For example, the Speller will not stop on the U.S. ZIP code 84532 but will stop on the Canadian ZIP code 4R2 C5T. Choose **6** to Ignore Numbers if you don't want the Speller to stop on these types of words.

Other Options

The spelling dictionary will also check for double words (two identical words side by side) and words with an irregular case (when it finds a capital letter anywhere but at the beginning of a word).

Double Words

If you have two identical words next to each other, both are highlighted, and the following menu is displayed:

```
Double Word: 1 2 Skip; 3 Delete 2nd; 4 Edit; 5 Disable Double Word Checking
```

Make the appropriate selection and spell checking continues. If you choose **5** to Disable Double Word Checking, the speller will not stop on this type of occurrence later in the document.

Irregular Case

WordPerfect checks for irregular uppercase letters. For example, if you start the word "SCott" with two capital letters, WordPerfect will highlight the word and display the following menu:

```
Irregular Case: 1 2 Skip; 3 Replace; 4 Edit; 5 Disable Case Checking
```

If the word is capitalized correctly, choose **1** or **2** to Skip the word. If either the first or second letter is already capitalized and you choose **3** for Replace, the first letter will remain capitalized. Otherwise, the entire word changes to lowercase. If all of the word is uppercase except the first letter, the entire word will be converted to uppercase. The following list shows the four types of irregular case that are checked for and what the replacement would be for each.

SCott	Scott
sCott	Scott
scOtt	scott
sCOTT	SCOTT

If there is a two-letter word in uppercase (such as the state postal code UT), WordPerfect will not stop on the word. However, if it appears as "uT," WordPerfect will change it to "Ut"—not to UT.

Hints

The possible spelling choices are not always spelled correctly. WordPerfect offers phonetic choices and words that match some type of word pattern, and it adds, deletes, and transposes characters to display possible choices.

When you replace a misspelled word that was capitalized, the first letter of the replacement word will also be capitalized. However, only the first letter remains capitalized, even if every letter of the misspelled word was found in uppercase.

When you make a choice from the menu to replace a misspelled word, all subsequent misspellings of the same word are automatically replaced.

The Speller will skip the following characters when they appear in a word, because they are considered word delimiters:

( ) , . \ / ` [ ] { } " < > ; : ~ - = + ¦ ! @ # $ % ^ & *

If you have pressed one of these keys accidentally, the Speller will not stop on the word unless the section of the word before or after the character is spelled incorrectly.

If you are asked for hyphenation decisions during the spell checking of a document, you can press Exit (F7) to leave the decisions until later.

Dictionary Not Found

If you did not install the Speller files during installation, or if you have inserted a language code and the dictionary for that language is not found, you will see the following message:

```
WP{WP}US.LEX not found: 1 Enter Path; 2 Skip Language; 3 Exit Spell: 3
```

If you installed the spelling dictionary, but have since copied it to another location, choose **1** to Enter the **P**ath (the drive and directory) where the dictionary can be found. If you are using the Language feature, you can choose **2** to **S**kip the current Language and go on to the next language or choose **3** to **E**xit the speller. See "Using Personal or Foreign Dictionaries" for more information about using the language code.

If you did not install the Speller files, return to the Install program and do so. If you have installed the Speller, but copied it to a different location, press Setup (SHIFT-F1), choose **6** for **L**ocation of Files and **3** for **T**hesaurus/Spell/Hyphenation, and then enter the drive and directory in which the main dictionary can be found so that you will not be asked for the location again.

How Spell Works

There are two word lists in the WP{WP}US.LEX file: the common word list, which contains about 2500 of the most commonly used words, and a main word list of approximately 120,000 words. You can view a list of the common words with the Speller utility (SPELL.EXE); see "Speller Utility" in this chapter for details. When you check the spelling of a document, the following occurs:

1. The common word list from WP{WP}US.LEX and the words from the supplementary dictionary WP{WP}US.SUP (unless another is specified) are loaded into memory.

2. Each word in the document is checked against the words in memory (common word list and supplementary dictionary) and then against the words in the main word list. "Please wait" is displayed on the screen while words are checked.

3. If you choose option **2** or **3** to Skip or Add the word, the word is given a special tag that identifies it as a skipped or added word, and it is placed into memory along with the common word list and the supplementary dictionary.

When skipping or adding words, you could eventually fill the amount of memory allotted. If this happens, skipped words will no longer be stored in memory. Because added words take priority, you can continue to add words (skipped words are deleted to make room as you add words) until memory is filled. When this finally happens, you will see the message "Dictionary Full." Exit the Speller at that point, and the words will be moved from memory to the supplementary dictionary. You can then block the rest of the document and continue spelling.

4. When you are finished checking the spelling of a document, the supplementary dictionary is rewritten. All the words tagged as added words and those belonging to the supplementary dictionary are sorted alphabetically and are saved in the file WP{WP}US.SUP (unless another was specified).

Using Personal or Foreign Dictionaries

The Language feature lets you insert a code into your document that tells WordPerfect which language will be used from that point on until the next language code is encountered. WordPerfect Corporation provides a speller, thesaurus, and hyphenation module for several languages (at an additional cost) that you can use for that particular section of text.

WordPerfect automatically looks for the WP{WP}US. LEX file if no language is specified. If you inserted the **fr** language code by pressing Format (SHIFT-F8), choosing 4 for Other, 4 for Language, then entering **fr**,

WP{WP}FR.LEX would be used. Note that "FR" replaced "US" in the filename. See "Language" in this chapter for the languages that are supported.

If you see a message telling you that a certain dictionary is not found, you can choose **2** to Skip the language and move on to the next language code if you do not have that particular dictionary. Contact WordPerfect Corporation if you want to purchase more dictionaries.

If you want to create a dictionary of your own with the Spell Program (SPELL.EXE), name it in the format WP{WP}*xx*.LEX, where *xx* are two characters of your choice. To use the dictionary, you will need to insert those two characters as a language code so that Word-Perfect will use your dictionary. See "Spell Program" in this chapter for details about creating and editing a personalized dictionary.

You can also use the supplementary dictionary, as explained in this section, to include words of your own. See the next section for details.

Adding and Deleting Words in the Dictionary

When you choose the option to Add a word to the dictionary during a spell check, it is automatically added to the supplementary dictionary. You can add or delete words any time from the dictionary by retrieving and editing the WP{WP}US.SUP file just as you would any other Word-Perfect file.

To add or delete words in the main dictionary, use the Spell Program (SPELL.EXE). See "Spell Program" in this chapter for more information about this and other dictionary options.

Computer Locking Up During a Spell Check

If you have problems with the computer locking up during a spell check, you most likely have memory that is incorrectly installed. Check the installation, and try checking the memory with a utility program (Word-Perfect offers a memory checker called TESTMEM that you can purchase for $15; the normal diagnostics test will usually not find the problem). If the problem persists, contact WordPerfect Support for a solution.

"Dictionary Full" Error Message

The main dictionary is limited in size only by the available disk space. A supplementary dictionary is limited only by the amount of memory available. If you see the message "Dictionary Full" when you are trying to add words during a spell check, it means that there is not enough memory to hold the additional words. First, make sure that only one document is loaded into memory; thereby freeing up the additional memory ordinarily used by the second document. If you still get the error message, edit the supplementary dictionary or consider adding some or all of the words to the main dictionary.

Hyphenation

Hyphenation points are included in the spelling dictionary so hyphenation can be 100% accurate. See "Spell Program" in this chapter if you want to add words *and* their hyphenation points to the dictionary. If you look up words with the Speller program, the hyphenation points are also displayed.

You can either use the dictionary for hyphenation or the internal hyphenation algorithm used in previous versions of WordPerfect. You might not want to use the dictionary if you are on a floppy disk system, because you would need to leave the Speller disk in when hyphenation is on. A better solution is to use the spelling dictionary, but wait to turn on hyphenation until the document is checked for spelling so that you can do both at once.

To determine how hyphenation is to be done, press Setup (SHIFT-F1) and choose 3 for Environment. Option 6 for Hyphenation determines if the dictionary or internal rules are used, and option 7 for Prompt for Hyphenation lets you decide whether you want to always be prompted, never be prompted, or prompted only when necessary, when hyphenation decisions are being made. See "Hyphenation" in this chapter for details.

Applications

In addition to correcting spelling errors, authors can use Spell (CTRL-F2) to get an accurate word count for articles. And, although this is certainly not its primary function, you can use the Look Up feature to help solve crossword puzzles. Just enter the letters you know and a question mark (?) in place of each letter that you do not know. A six-letter word for "smart" would be "cl?ve?" (clever).

Related Entries

Hyphenation
Language
Setup
Spell Program
Word Count

SPELL PROGRAM

The Spell program is used to customize the spelling dictionary. Among many other things, it lets you add words, delete words, and combine two dictionaries. If you want to use a spelling dictionary from version 5.0, it does not have to be converted first. A dictionary from version 4.2, however, must be converted with the Spell program before it can be used in version 5.1.

Keystrokes

If you did not install the utility files during installation, you will need to do so before continuing. If WordPerfect is running, exit to the DOS prompt.

1. Change to the directory in which SPELL.EXE is located. Both SPELL.EXE and WP{WP}US.LEX are kept in the same directory as WP.EXE (C:\WP51 was the suggested name of the directory), unless you specified a different directory. In this case, you would enter **cd /wp51** to change to that directory.

2. Enter **spell** at the DOS prompt. If WP{WP}US.LEX is not found, you will see a message asking if you want to create a new dictionary with that name:

```
Dictionary WP{WP}US.LEX not found.
Create a new dictionary named WP{WP}US.LEX (Y/N)? n
```

Type **Y** to create one with that name, or type **N** to create a dictionary with a different name.

If you type **N**, you are prompted for the name of the new dictionary. The name WP{WP}US.LEX is displayed, reminding you to use this format when entering a new name. For example, you could use the name WP{WP}ME.LEX, substituting "ME" for "US."

Be aware that if you enter a name other than "US," you will need to insert a language code (using the two characters that you selected) at the beginning of your documents so WordPerfect will know which spelling dictionary to use.

3. Select options from the menu shown in Figure 3-160. The options are explained under "Options."

4. When you are finished, type **0** to Exit the Spell program.

If you are running WordPerfect with two disk drives, insert the Speller disk in drive B and the Install Utilities disk in drive A. Enter **a:** to change to drive A, and then enter **spell b:** to start the Speller program.

Options

The following options are available in the Speller program.

Change/Create Dictionary

WP{WP}US.LEX, displayed in the upper right corner of the Speller Program menu, is the file used for all options. If you want to use a

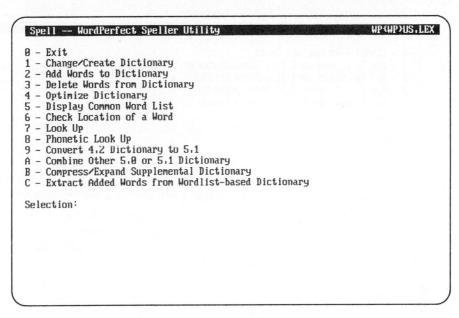

```
┌──────────────────────────────────────────────────────────────────┐
│ Spell -- WordPerfect Speller Utility                  WP{WP}US.LEX │
│ 0 - Exit                                                           │
│ 1 - Change/Create Dictionary                                       │
│ 2 - Add Words to Dictionary                                        │
│ 3 - Delete Words from Dictionary                                   │
│ 4 - Optimize Dictionary                                            │
│ 5 - Display Common Word List                                       │
│ 6 - Check Location of a Word                                       │
│ 7 - Look Up                                                        │
│ 8 - Phonetic Look Up                                               │
│ 9 - Convert 4.2 Dictionary to 5.1                                  │
│ A - Combine Other 5.0 or 5.1 Dictionary                            │
│ B - Compress/Expand Supplemental Dictionary                        │
│ C - Extract Added Words from Wordlist-based Dictionary             │
│                                                                    │
│ Selection:                                                         │
│                                                                    │
└──────────────────────────────────────────────────────────────────┘
```

Figure 3-160.   Spell program's main menu

different dictionary, choose option **1** for Change/Create Dictionary. You are asked if you want to change/create the main dictionary or the supplementary dictionary. You will need to choose supplementary dictionary if you want to use option B, Compress/Expand the Supplemental Dictionary.

After choosing Main or Supplementary Dictionary, a message tells you that it is permissible to switch disks at this time and asks for the name of the dictionary. If the dictionary file is not found on the disk, you are asked if you want to create a new dictionary with that name.

Remember to use the format WP{WP}*xx*.LEX for the main dictionary, where *xx* represents two characters of your choice. You will also need to enter these two characters as a language code into your documents in order to use the new dictionary. The supplementary dictionary should be named with the format WP{WP}*xx*.SUP.

Add Words to Dictionary

When you choose **2** to Add words to the dictionary, the following menu appears:

```
┌─────────────────────────────────────────────────────────────────┐
│ Spell -- Add Words                                   WP{WP}US.LEX │
│ 0 - Cancel - do not add words                                     │
│ 1 - Add to common word list (from keyboard)                       │
│ 2 - Add to common word list (from a file)                         │
│ 3 - Add to main word list (from keyboard)                         │
│ 4 - Add to main word list (from a file)                           │
│ 5 - Exit                                                          │
│                                                                   │
│ Selection:                                                        │
```

You can choose any or all of the options to add words to the common word list and main word list from the keyboard or a file. If there is more than one file of words to be added, choose options **2** and **4** more than once. When you enter words from the keyboard, separate them with spaces. If you want the words to include hyphens, insert them as you type the words.

After you have finished entering all the words or filenames, type **5** to Exit (and update the dictionary). Type **0** if you want to Cancel the operation. The entire dictionary will be recopied, each new word will be inserted where it belongs and the phonetic information will be created for that word.

If you are using two disk drives or if your hard disk is full, you will see a message letting you know that there is not enough room for the temporary files. If you have two disk drives, make sure that you have a disk in drive B with sufficient space, and type **B** (do not remove the disk in drive A). If there is not enough room on the disk in drive B, you will see the message again. You must correct the situation before the process can continue. A file named WP{WP}US.BAK is created on the new disk to aid in the process.

When you add or delete words, messages notify you of the progress. It takes approximately 20 minutes (or less) to add words, depending on whether you have a hard disk or floppy disk drives. If you have a RAM drive, consider copying the SPELL.EXE and LEX.WP files to the RAM drive to increase the speed.

Hyphenation Points

Because the spelling dictionary is also used for hyphenation, you can add words with hyphenation points already inserted in the proper locations. If you do not want a word to be hyphenated (such as a proper name), you can add it without hyphenation points.

If you want to add words from a file to the dictionary and include hyphens, retrieve WP{WP}US.SUP (or the name of your supplementary dictionary) or enter the words on a blank screen. Move to the places where hyphens are to be inserted, and press the hyphen key. Save the file and exit WordPerfect.

Start the Spell program, and choose the option to add words from this file to the dictionary.

Delete Words from Dictionary

When you choose option 3 to delete words from the dictionary, the following menu appears:

```
┌─────────────────────────────────────────────────────────────┐
│ Spell -- Delete Words                            WP{WP}US.LEX │
│                                                               │
│ 0 - Cancel - do not delete words                              │
│ 1 - Delete from common word list (from keyboard)              │
│ 2 - Delete from common word list (from a file)                │
│ 3 - Delete from main word list (from keyboard)                │
│ 4 - Delete from main word list (from a file)                  │
│ 5 - Exit                                                      │
│                                                               │
│ Selection:                                                    │
```

Choose any or all of these options to delete words from the common word list or main word list. You can enter the words to be deleted from the keyboard (separate each word with a space), or you can specify a file that contains the words to be deleted.

After you have chosen all applicable options, choose **5** to Exit (and update the dictionary) or choose **0** to Cancel the procedure. If you have two disk drives, you will see a message telling you that there is not enough room on drive A to create the temporary files. Confirm that there is a disk in drive B, and type **B** as the drive to be used.

Messages are displayed to keep you informed of the status. It takes the same amount of time to delete words from the dictionary as it does to add them, but you cannot add and delete at the same time.

Optimize Dictionary

After creating a new dictionary (with options **1, 2,** and **3**), choose option **4** to Optimize the dictionary. The dictionary is rewritten in a format that makes it smaller and faster. After optimizing, you can press ENTER to see lists of the words in the dictionary, or press Cancel (F1) to return to the main menu.

Display Common Word List

Option 5, Display Common Word List, lets you view the words in the common word list. Press any key to continue viewing each screen, or press Cancel (F1) to return to the main menu.

Check Location of a Word

After choosing option 6 to Check the Location of a Word, you are asked to enter a word. A message tells you whether the word was found in the common word list or the main word list. Continue checking words until you have finished, and then press Cancel (F1) to return to the main menu. The next option will also help you determine if a word is in the common word list or the main word list.

Look Up

You can use the Speller utility to look up words according to parts of a word or a word pattern. You can use the wildcard characters ?, *, and - in the place of unknown characters:

?	Represents any single character
* or -	Represents any number of characters

In Figure 3-161, you will see a sample list of words beginning with "end." Notice that hyphenation points are also displayed in this list.

Phonetic Look Up

Enter a phonetic spelling (spell the word the way it sounds) to display other words in the dictionary that sound similar to that word.

Convert 4.2 Dictionary to 5.1

You cannot use a 4.2 dictionary with WordPerfect 5.1, because of the differences in their formats. If you have customized a dictionary in 4.2 and do not want to repeat the process for version 5.1, you can use this option to convert the dictionary instead.

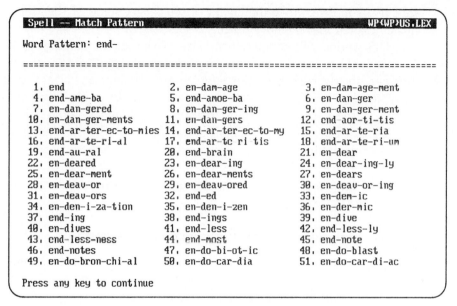

```
┌─────────────────────────────────────────────────────────────────────────┐
│ Spell -- Match Pattern                                        WP{WP}US.LEX │
│ Word Pattern: end-                                                         │
│                                                                            │
│ ==========================================================================│
│                                                                            │
│    1. end                    2. en-dam-age         3. en-dam-age-ment      │
│    4. end-ame-ba             5. end-amoe-ba         6. en-dan-ger          │
│    7. en-dan-gered           8. en-dan-ger-ing      9. en-dan-ger-ment     │
│   10. en-dan-ger-ments      11. en-dan-gers        12. end-aor-ti-tis      │
│   13. end-ar-ter-ec-to-mies 14. end-ar-ter-ec-to-my 15. end-ar-te-ria      │
│   16. end-ar-te-ri-al       17. end-ar-tc ri tis   18. end-ar-te-ri-um     │
│   19. end-au-ral            20. end-brain          21. en-dear             │
│   22. en-deared             23. en-dear-ing        24. en-dear-ing-ly      │
│   25. en-dear-ment          26. en-dear-ments      27. en-dears            │
│   28. en-deav-or            29. en-deav-ored       30. en-deav-or-ing      │
│   31. en-deav-ors           32. end-ed             33. en-dem-ic           │
│   34. en-den-i-za-tion      35. en-den-i-zen       36. en-der-mic          │
│   37. end-ing               38. end-ings           39. en-dive             │
│   40. en-dives              41. end-less           42. end-less-ly         │
│   43. end-less-ness         44. end-most           45. end-note            │
│   46. end-notes             47. en-do-bi-ot-ic     48. en-do-blast         │
│   49. en-do-bron-chi-al     50. en-do-car-dia      51. en-do-car-di-ac     │
│                                                                            │
│ Press any key to continue                                                  │
└─────────────────────────────────────────────────────────────────────────┘
```

Figure 3-161.   Sample list of words beginning with "end" that can be displayed in the Spell program

When you choose this option, you are prompted for the name of the 4.2 dictionary and then the name of the 5.1 dictionary. When the process is finished, you are returned to the main menu.

Combine 5.0 and 5.1 Dictionaries

By choosing option **A**, you can combine two 5.1 dictionaries, or a 5.0 dictionary and a 5.1 dictionary. This option is most useful for those who have used version 5.0 and have added words to that 5.0 dictionary.

During the process, hyphenated words in the 5.1 dictionary will overwrite the same unhyphenated words in the 5.0 dictionary. Words that you added to the 5.0 dictionary that are not in the 5.1 dictionary will not be hyphenated unless you add them with the hyphenation points.

Compress/Expand Supplemental Dictionary

Normally, words in the supplementary dictionary are not suggested as replacement words during a spell check. Another possible problem is that if a supplementary dictionary is too large, some of the words may not be loaded into memory during a spell check.

This option will compress the size of the supplementary dictionary so that it takes less room in memory, loads all words into memory, and includes the words from the supplementary dictionary in the list of possible choices. By compressing a supplementary file, all words are stored in the document header (prefix) and cannot be edited in Word-Perfect as they can be normally. If you need to edit the file again, you can use this option to expand the supplementary dictionary.

Before selecting this option, you need to choose option **1** to Change/ Create Dictionary and specify which supplementary dictionary you would like to use.

Extract Added Words from Wordlist-based Dictionary

You can extract words that have been added to the dictionary by selecting this option. During the process, you are asked for the name of the wordlist-based dictionary, the name of an algorithmic dictionary, and the name of the supplementary dictionary where the extracted words are to be copied.

WordPerfect then compares the two dictionaries and saves any words not found in the algorithmic dictionary to the supplementary dictionary.

Hints

If you have a RAM drive, copy the SPELL.EXE and WP{WP}US.LEX files to it to increase the speed of updating the Speller. You can add and delete words in the supplementary dictionary WP{WP}US.SUP (or any other file) by retrieving it into WordPerfect and editing the file as you would any other.

When the supplementary dictionary becomes too large for memory, you can either compress the file or add the words to the main dictionary until the disk is filled.

Related Entries

Dictionary
Language
Spell

SPLIT THE SCREEN

See "Windows" in this chapter.

SPREADSHEET IMPORTING AND LINKING

You can retrieve spreadsheets created with PlanPerfect, Lotus 1-2-3, and Excel into WordPerfect documents without first converting them. If you have a version of Wordperfect dated later than 1/19/90, you can also import Quattro and Quattro Pro files. You can find the date in the upper right corner of the Help (F3) screen. These files can be retrieved as text (in a tabular format) or as a table with lines dividing each cell.

You also have the option of importing or linking them. To import means that the data is retrieved into the WordPerfect document with no ties to the original spreadsheet. The Link option lets you create a link to the original file so that the data can be periodically updated with the latest information from the spreadsheet.

You can import or link an entire spreadsheet or a part of the spreadsheet (called a range).

Keystrokes

The following discussion will help you retrieve a spreadsheet from the following programs: PlanPerfect 3.0 and 5.0, Excel 2.*x*, and Lotus 1-2-3. Spreadsheets created in any version of Lotus are supported. However, if you have Lotus version 3.0, you will first need to save the spreadsheet as a .WK1 file. By using the .WK1 extension, Lotus saves it as a one-dimensional spreadsheet (.WK3 saves it as a three-dimensional spreadsheet).

Retrieving an Entire Spreadsheet

If you do not want to create a link, and you want to retrieve the entire spreadsheet, you can retrieve the spreadsheet as you would a regular WordPerfect document. It will automatically be placed in a table rather than being imported as text in tabular form. If you want to import it as text in tabular form, see "Importing or Linking a Section of a Spreadsheet."

Before starting the following keystrokes, move the cursor to where the spreadsheet should be retrieved. You may also want to change to a smaller font if the spreadsheet is large so that it will have a greater chance of fitting between the margins.

1. Press Retrieve (SHIFT-F10).

2. Enter the name of the spreadsheet file to be retrieved, including the full pathname (drive and directory where the file is located).

3. The spreadsheet will be imported into a table, as shown in Figure 3-162. Much of the alignment and formatting in the original spreadsheet are retained.

If the spreadsheet is wider than the current margins, you will see a message warning you that the table extends beyond the right margin. If this happens, the entire spreadsheet will still be imported and displayed on the screen; however, you will not be able to view or print the portion that extends beyond the right margin. To solve the problem, you can wait until the spreadsheet is imported and then change the Paper

	January	February	March	April
Mail	$1,750.00	$1,950.00	$2,000.00	$2,375.00
Miscellaneous	$862.50	$1,547.50	$1,237.50	$1,700.00
Office Supplies	$3,125.00	$2,125.00	$1,650.00	$1,125.00
Payroll	$150,000.00	$150,000.00	$150,000.00	$150,000.00
Phone	$1,125.00	$1,062.50	$1,250.00	$1,375.00
Rent	$8,250.00	$8,250.00	$9,000.00	$9,000.00
Taxes	$6,250.00	$6,250.00	$5,625.00	$5,625.00
Utilities	$875.00	$862.50	$725.00	$687.50
Totals	$172,237.50	$172,047.50	$171,487.50	$171,887.50

Figure 3-162. Sample spreadsheet retrieved as a table

Size/Type so that you can place the table on wider paper (choose Landscape, for example), decrease the margins, or decrease the size of the font just before the [Tbl Def] code, block and delete the table, and then retrieve the table again. If these options still do not allow you to view or print the entire table, you may want to delete some of the columns. To do so, follow these steps:

1. Move the cursor into the table if it is not already there.

2. Press Columns/Tables (ALT-F7), and choose **1** for Size.

3. Choose **2** for Columns. The number of columns currently in the table is displayed.

4. Enter the number of columns that will fit between the margins. If 15 columns were imported and you want to change the table size to 5 columns, columns 6 to 15 would be deleted.

Importing or Linking a Section of a Spreadsheet

Except for one keystroke, the steps for importing or linking all or part of a spreadsheet are identical. Use the steps for importing if you want to import part of a spreadsheet or if you want to have a choice between importing it as a table or text in tabular form. Linking gives you the same choices but creates a link to the original file that you can use to update the information in the document at a later time.

1. Move the cursor to the point where the spreadsheet is to be retrieved.

2. Press Text In/Out (CTRL-F5).

3. Choose **5** for Spreadsheet. The following options appear.

```
Spreadsheet: 1 Import; 2 Create Link; 3 Edit Link; 4 Link Options: 0
```

4. Choose **1** to Import or **2** to Create Link. Options **3** and **4** are discussed in the next section. The same menu (with slightly

different wording) appears. The following menu is the Import menu. If you chose the Link option, the word "Import" is changed to "Link."

```
Spreadsheet: Import

   1 - Filename

   2 - Range

   3 - Type                    Table

   4 - Perform Import
```

5. Choose **1** for **F**ilename and enter the name of the file to be imported. You can enter the name of a spreadsheet not yet created. Because of this, you will not see the familiar error message "File not found" if the file does not exist. Instead, you can tell if the file exists by whether or not "<Spreadsheet>" appears as the range.

If you cannot remember the name of the file, press List (F5), enter the pathname (drive and directory) where the spreadsheet can be found, and press ENTER to see a list of files in that directory. Move to the one to be imported and choose **1** to **R**etrieve it.

The file is not actually retrieved at this point. You are first given an opportunity to choose the range (the section of cells to be imported) and type (either table or text). Option **4** (discussed later) actually does the importing or linking.

After entering the filename, the following menu will appear:

```
Spreadsheet: Import

   1 - Filename              C:\PLAN\EXPENSES.PLN

   2 - Range                 <Spreadsheet>        A1:O11

   3 - Type                  Table

   4 - Perform Import
```

Note that the Range option displays "<Spreadsheet>" as the range or section to be retrieved. If you have not yet created the spreadsheet, "<Spreadsheet>" will not appear. The numbers at the right indicate the upper left cell and the lower right cell of the spreadsheet.

6. If you want to import or link a section of the spreadsheet, choose **2** for **R**ange. The upper left and lower right cells of the spreadsheet are displayed.

Enter a different range: separate the upper left cell and lower right cell with a colon, a period, or two periods (A1:F6, A1.F6, or A1..F6).

If you have named ranges in the spreadsheet, you can enter the name of the range or press List (F5) to display a list of named ranges that are in the spreadsheet. Figure 3-163 shows a list of ranges that were named in a PlanPerfect spreadsheet. The first item on the list displays the range for the entire spreadsheet. The next four items in this example were named to indicate first, second, third, and fourth quarters. If you want to select a range, move the

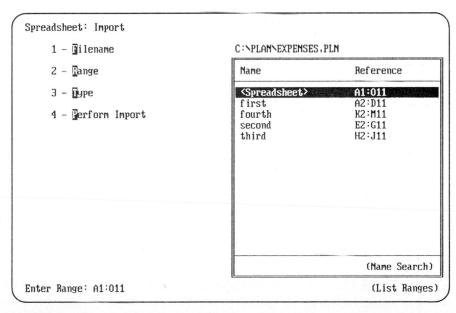

Figure 3-163.   List of named ranges in a PlanPerfect spreadsheet

cursor to the range in the list and press ENTER. If you don't find the desired range, press Cancel (F1) to return to the menu and specify any other range of cells.

7. All spreadsheets are normally retrieved as tables. If you prefer having them retrieved as tabular text, choose 3 for Type, and then choose 1 for Table or 2 for Text.

If you import a spreadsheet as text, you can import only 20 columns. The column limit is 32 if you are importing it as a table.

If you choose Text and the spreadsheet is wider than the margins, each line is wrapped to the next line with a soft return [SRt] code. To correct the problem, select a wider paper size/type (landscape, for example) or decrease the margins or size of the font before doing the importing or linking.

8. When you are finished with all the options, choose 4 for Perform Import (or Link).

If a Link was performed, you will see comments displayed above and below the spreadsheet indicating that it is a link and not an import. These comments show the beginning and end of the link, including the filename and the range that was used.

```
Link:   C:\PLAN\EXPENSES.PLN  first


    Contents of the spreadsheet

Link End
```

These comments do not affect the spacing and do not print. If you prefer not to have them displayed, follow the steps in "Link Options" to turn them off.

Editing a Link

If you need to edit a link (change the filename, range, or type), move the cursor to just after the Link, press Text In/Out (CTRL-F5), and choose 5 for Spreadsheet and then 3 for Edit Link. WordPerfect will search to the left until it finds a [Link] code and displays the information in the menu used to create the link. You can make any changes, and then choose 4 to **Perform** the Link so the changes will be updated. If a [Link] code is not found to the left, it finds the next [Link] code to the right.

Updating a Link and Other Options

When you press Text In/Out (CTRL-F5) and choose 4 for Link Options, the following options are displayed:

```
Link Options:

    1 - Update on Retrieve        No

    2 - Show Link Codes           Yes

    3 - Update All Links
```

Links are not updated automatically. If you want the links to be updated each time you retrieve the WordPerfect file, choose 1 for Update on Retrieve. You can also choose option 3 for Update All Links. To update a single link, edit the link and choose 4 for Perform Link.

During an update, all text and codes between the [Link] and [Link End] codes are deleted and then replaced with new information. This means that any changes you make to the text or format of the table will be lost. If you want to keep any of the format changes that you have made to the table, perform an import first, then move to the first cell in the table, create a link to the spreadsheet, then perform the link. Because the link codes are in the first cell, the table definition code will not be affected by any future updating.

Link Codes are always displayed unless you choose option 2 for Show Link Codes and turn them off. If you choose to not display them, the codes [Link:Filename;Range;*UL:LR*] (where UL means upper left cell and LR means lower right cell in the range) and [Link End] will still be displayed in Reveal Codes to indicate the beginning and the end of the link.

Hints

You can import or link up to 32 columns of a spreadsheet if you import the spreadsheet as a table. If you import the spreadsheet as text, the column limit is 20. This limit is set to 20, because when a spreadsheet is imported as text, WordPerfect sets two tabs (a left- and right-aligned tab setting) for each column, and only 40 tabs can be set at one time in WordPerfect.

If you prefer, you can create a table and then import the spread-sheet. If you use this method, be sure that the cursor is in the first cell to be used by the spreadsheet (usually the first cell) and change the type to table. If text is chosen, the entire spreadsheet is retrieved into one cell. If there is information already in the table, it will be overwritten with the new information.

Formatting a Spreadsheet

If you retrieve a PlanPerfect spreadsheet, WordPerfect keeps much of the original formatting, such as bold, underline, center, and other types of alignment. If you retrieve another type of spreadsheet, WordPerfect right-aligns numbers and left-aligns text.

If you retrieve a spreadsheet as text, WordPerfect sets left- and right-aligned tabs for each column so that the text and numbers can be aligned properly. Text that was aligned in the center changes to left-aligned text.

You can always change the width of the columns, change the alignment (called justification in tables), and format the columns after you have imported the spreadsheet. To do so, move the cursor inside the table, and press Columns/Tables (ALT-F7). Move the cursor to the cell or column to be affected, or use Block (ALT-F4) to block a section of cells and choose the options from the "Table Edit" menu. See "Tables" in this chapter for details about all options.

Converting a Table to Text

If you want to change a table to text, press Reveal Codes (ALT-F3) and delete the [Tbl Def:] code. A [Tab] code is then inserted between each column. However, the tab settings are not set automatically as they are when you import the spreadsheet as text. If your tabs are set at the standard 1/2", the table may not be displayed properly. Therefore, you may want to set tabs above the table before deleting the [Tbl Def:] code. To do so, press Format (SHIFT-F8), and choose 1 for **L**ine and then 8 for **T**ab Set.

To change text (with each column divided by a single tab) to a table, block the entire section, press Columns/Table (ALT-F7), and choose 1 for

Create. You are then asked if you want to create a table from tabular columns or parallel columns. Choose 1 for Tabular Columns or 2 for Parallel Columns.

Related Entries

Tables

START A NEW PAGE

To start a new page, press Hard Page (CTRL-ENTER). See "Hard Page" in this chapter for more information.

START WORDPERFECT

The following procedures will start WordPerfect. Choose the one that applies to your system, depending on whether you have two disk drives or a hard disk.

Keystrokes

Hard Disk

You should be able to start WordPerfect by entering **wp**. If you have not set up WordPerfect correctly on the hard disk, the error message "Bad command or file name" might appear. If this happens, you did not have the Install program add the path (drive and directory where WordPerfect is located) to the AUTOEXEC.BAT file. If you did, you may not have rebooted your computer since it was added. Turn the computer off and on again, and try starting WordPerfect again.

You can always start WordPerfect by changing to the directory where WordPerfect is located (entering **cd\wp51** would change to the "WP51" directory) and typing **wp**.

Two Disk Drives

1. Insert the WordPerfect 1 disk in drive A. (Do not insert the Program 1 disk—you must install WordPerfect first. See Chapter 1, "Installation and Setup," if you have not installed WordPerfect and do not have a disk labeled WordPerfect 1).

2. Insert a data disk into drive B.

3. Enter **B:** to change the default drive to B. (When you save or retrieve files, drive B will be used unless another is specified.)

4. Enter **a:wp** to start WordPerfect from drive A.

5. Remove the WordPerfect 1 disk, and insert the WordPerfect 2 disk into drive A.

6. Press any key to continue.

Options

When you start WordPerfect, you can enter startup options to perform certain functions when the program is started. If WordPerfect will not start, you may have a TSR program loaded into memory that conflicts with the Cursor Speed feature in WordPerfect, or your keyboard may not be a true enhanced keyboard. In this case, you may need to use the /NC (no cursor speed) and/or the /NK startup options (described later) to start WordPerfect. To do so, enter **wp/nc/nk**.

If you have expanded memory that is not compatible with Word-Perfect, you may need to start WordPerfect with **wp/ne** (meaning no expanded memory). The following is a description of each available startup option:

Filename (Retrieve a File)

Type **wp** *filename* to start WordPerfect and immediately retrieve the named file.

/CP-Code Page

The code page number tells WordPerfect which code page your hardware system (BIOS) uses. Setting this option lets you access the proper keyboard and 256-character ASCII character set for which your system is preset. You do not need to use this option if your version of Word-Perfect is preset to your code page (for example, you have the Icelandic version of WordPerfect and your hardware is using the Icelandic code page number 861). You also do not have to use this option if you have DOS 3.3 or higher and have placed a COUNTRY command in your CONFIG.SYS file.

The complete command to start WordPerfect with a specific code page is **wp/cp**$=n$ where n can be one of the following:

437	English
850	PC Multilingual
851	Greek
8510	Greek Alternate
860	Portuguese
8600	Portuguese (Brazil)
861	Icelandic
863	French (Canada)
865	Norwegian and Dutch

If you use this option to enter a code page for which your system is not preset, you may be able to print characters for the code page you entered, but you cannot change the way characters are displayed on the screen. A character is displayed according to the system code page.

/D-drive/directory (Divert)

Overflow files are automatically kept where WP.EXE is located. If you want to keep them elsewhere, use the /D option and specify the name of the drive and directory to be used.

Although the use of a RAM drive is not strongly recommended, you can redirect the overflow files to a RAM drive to increase the speed of the program. If the RAM drive is D:, the command would be **wp/d-d:**. If the files are redirected elsewhere and the WP/R option is used to load WordPerfect into memory (an option only if you have expanded memory), you can remove the WordPerfect 2 disk from a two-disk-drive system.

/F2

If you are using the /SS startup option to select the number of lines and columns for the screen size, that size may change when you are switching between text and graphics modes in WordPerfect or when you exit to DOS. If this is the case, try the /F2 option when you are starting WordPerfect (enter **wp/ss = lines,columns/f2**).

Before using this option, however, refer to "Text Screen Type" in this chapter for more information about setting the number of lines and columns from within WordPerfect.

/M-macroname (Start a Macro)

Type **wp/m-***macroname* to start the named macro when you start WordPerfect. (Do not include .WPM in the macro name.)

/MONO

This option causes WordPerfect to assume that you are using a monochrome monitor. If you are using a plasma, LCD, or composite display, entering **wp/mono** makes text more readable.

If you have a Hercules Graphics Card Plus or a Hercules InColor Card, /MONO prevents you from changing colors (InColor card) or the preselected font (RAMFont modes).

/NB (No Backup)

If you save a file and choose to replace the original, WordPerfect renames the original file with a .BK! extension, saves the new document, then deletes the .BK! file. Although this protects the file during a save, it takes twice as much disk space as the original file.

Use this option (**wp/nb**) if disk space is tight and you do not want the BK! file to be created.

/NC (No Cursor Speed)

The Cursor Speed feature on the Setup menu may interfere with TSR programs or your particular hardware setup. You may need to use this option type (**wp/nc**) to disable the Cursor Speed feature and successfully load WordPerfect.

/NE (No Expanded Memory)

If you do not want to use expanded memory, start WordPerfect by entering **wp/ne**. This option may be necessary if your type of expanded memory is not compatible with WordPerfect. Contact the manufacturer to see about a possible upgrade that will make it 4.0 LIM compatible.

With the 1/19/90 release of WordPerfect 5.1, /32 is available for those who have a 3.2 LIM memory that is manifesting itself as 4.0 LIM. See Appendix G, "Latest Enhancements," for more information.

/NF (Non-Flash)

Start WordPerfect by entering **wp/nf** when you are using Windows or another type of windowing program. Also use this option if text disappears (or only appears) when you press Reveal Codes (ALT-F3).

/NK (No Keyboard)

Use this option if you are unable to start WordPerfect. Entering **wp/nk** tells WordPerfect not to interpret your keyboard as an enhanced keyboard.

/NO (No Original)

You can normally press CTRL-6 at any time to deselect a keyboard layout and return to the original keyboard. If you want to prohibit users from doing so because you are in a network situation and want everyone to use a standard keyboard layout, you can disable CTRL-6 by starting WordPerfect with **wp/no**.

/NT-n (Network)

When installing WordPerfect on a network, you are asked to specify the network by number. This setting is stored in a file named WP{WP}.ENV and is used when you are starting WordPerfect for the network. For more information, see Chapter 1, "Installation and Setup", or see "Network Support," in this chapter.

/PS-Drive/Directory (Place for Setup File)

The /PS option is usually used in a network environment and directs WordPerfect to look for and create the setup (.SET) files in a certain directory. It can also be used in a single-user environment to direct

WordPerfect to a different .SET file residing in a directory other than where WP.EXE is located. You will want to use this option when you use /R so that any changes to the Setup menu will be saved to disk.

/R (RAM Resident)

If you have expanded memory, you can use this option to load the entire WordPerfect program into memory. WP.EXE is automatically. loaded into memory, but WordPerfect will look to disk for WP.FIL, which contains overlay files, menus, messages, and other parts of the program. If you use the /R option, the contents of WP.FIL will be kept in memory and there is no disk access, which greatly increases the speed of Word-Perfect.

If you are using a two-disk-drive system, you can use the /R and /D options and remove the WordPerfect 2 disk.

/SA (Standalone)

If you have installed WordPerfect on a network but find that you need to run WordPerfect in standalone mode (on a single machine) because the network is down, you can do so by entering **wp/sa**.

/SS-x,y (Screen Size)

The /SS option lets you specify the number of rows of lines (x) and columns (y) that are available on the screen. See "Text Screen Type" in this chapter for information about changing the number of lines and columns from within WordPerfect.

If you use the /SS option with the number of rows and columns available, the exact format that you should use is **wp/ss-rows,columns**. You can set the screen size only to a size that is available. If you attempt to set a different screen size, the text will not be displayed correctly.

/U-xxx (User Initials)

If you are using WordPerfect on a network, you can start WordPerfect with **wp/u-xxx** where xxx is any three characters (usually initials) that help keep each individual's temporary files separate. If you do not use this option, you will be prompted for the three characters when you start WordPerfect on a network.

/W-n,n (Workspace)

You can use the /W startup option to specify the amount of conventional and expanded memory used by WordPerfect. Enter **wp/w-*n,n*** where the first number indicates how much conventional memory is to be used and the second number indicates the amount of expanded memory to be used. You can type asterisks (*) if you want to use all available memory: **wp/w-*,*.**

/X

This option returns WordPerfect to the defaults set by WordPerfect Corporation for the current editing session only. To change it permanently, enter **wp/x** and enter the Setup menu. You can also delete the WP{WP}.SET file from DOS. It will be recreated when you enter WordPerfect again.

Hints

If you use the same keystrokes to start WordPerfect each time, consider storing them in a batch file (a file containing a batch of commands). You would then need to enter only the name of the batch file, instead of having to type all the keystrokes each time. Do not use **wp** as the name of the batch file, however, or it may cause the computer to hang, depending on your setup. The following are the commands entered from DOS at the C:\> prompt to create a batch file named "work."

```
copy con work.bat
wp/nc/nk/m-format
^Z
```

To use the batch file, enter **work** at the C:\> DOS prompt.

If you do not want to use a batch file, you can change the DOS environment with the SET command so that each time you enter WP, the other commands will be recognized as part of the command. You will want to make the SET command part of your AUTOEXEC.BAT file. Here is an example:

Set wp = wp/nc/nk/m-format

If you have WordPerfect Library, you can install WordPerfect on the Shell menu so that you only have to choose an item from the menu and never have to deal with DOS. In the Shell's setup menu, you can specify the startup options to be used.

Related Entries

Setup
Shell

STATUS LINE DISPLAY

The position of the cursor appears on the status line at the bottom right corner of the screen. The current document (1 or 2), page, line (the distance from the top of the page), and position (distance from the left side of the page) are displayed, with the last two measurements in inches.

You can choose to display the settings in centimeters, points, 1200ths of an inch, or WordPerfect 4.2 units. See "Units of Measure" in this chapter for details.

STOP PRINTING

One of the options on the Control Printer menu lets you stop the printing of a document.

Keystrokes

1. Press Print (SHIFT-F7).

2. Choose 4 for Control Printer.

3. Type S to Stop Printing. The following message is displayed:

WARNING: If you use this option, you will need to initialize your printer before you can continue printing. You will also need to make sure all forms are in their original positions. Are you sure? No (Yes)

A second message requests that you adjust the paper or advance the paper to the top of the page and send the printer a "Go" when you are ready to continue. You can also type **C** to cancel the print job. You may then be requested to "Reset printer (press RESET or turn printer OFF and ON)." If you reset the printer or turn it off and then on, you may lose the downloaded soft fonts, and you will have to initialize the printer again.

Printing will not stop immediately but will continue until the printer's buffer is emptied of data. To stop printing immediately, turn the printer off and then back on again to clear the buffer. However, this would also delete soft fonts from the printer's memory and they would need to be downloaded again.

4. After you have readjusted the paper and have reset the printer (if necessary), type **G** to send the printer a "Go" or type **C** to cancel the print job. If you send the printer a "Go" and only the data for the first page was sent to the printer, printing will start again with the first page. If the data for more than one page was sent, you will be asked to specify the page on which to resume printing. The last page sent is displayed as the default.

Hints

If you want to pause printing without using WordPerfect commands, press the on-line or ready button on the printer to take the printer off-line. Press it again to return it to on-line status and resume printing.

If you want to cancel one or more print jobs instead of stopping the printer temporarily, choose the Cancel Print Job(s) option on the Control Printer menu. You can turn the printer off and then on to clear the buffer if it does not stop printing immediately.

Related Entries

Cancel a Print Job

STRIKEOUT

You can use the Strikeout feature to print a dash through text being considered for deletion.

Keystrokes

1. Press Font (CTRL-F8).

2. Choose **2** for Appearance.

3. Choose **9** for Strikeout.

4. Type the text to be considered for deletion.

5. Press → to move past the strikeout-off code and turn off the feature.

A more common way to mark text to be deleted (since it has usually been entered already) is to block the text first with Block (ALT-F4), press Font (CTRL-F8), choose **2** for Appearance, and then choose **9** for Strikeout.

Hints

When you choose the Strikeout feature, the codes [STKOUT] and [stkout] are inserted at the cursor location. If you mark a block of text for strikeout, the strikeout-on code is inserted at the beginning of the block, and the strikeout-off code is inserted at the end of the block.

Although you can repeat the steps to turn off the feature, pressing → to move past the code is easier.

You can choose the screen attribute, color, or font that will be displayed for strikeout with the Colors/Fonts/Attributes option under Display on the Setup menu.

Redline, a feature used to mark text being considered for addition to a document, is commonly used with the Strikeout feature. You can use the Compare feature to compare the document on the screen with one on the disk. WordPerfect will insert redline marks where text has been added to the document on the screen, find any phrase that had text deleted from it, retrieve it, and place strikeout marks through it. See "Compare Documents" in this chapter for details.

Strikeout is usually used to suggest deletions to others. After their approval, you can use the option Remove Redline Markings and Strikeout Text from Document found on the Generate menu of the Mark Text (ALT-F5) key. This option will then delete all text marked with Strikeout. See "Remove Redline and Strikeout" in this chapter for the exact keystrokes.

Most printers are defined to print text marked for strikeout with a dash through the text. Others, such as the Canon laser printer, print strikeout text with white lettering on a black background. If you want to change the character to be used or assign a different font to that feature, use the Printer program (see Chapter 5).

Overstrike is a feature that you can use to print more than one character in the same position. See "Overstrike" in this chapter for details.

Related Entries

Compare Documents
Overstrike
Redline
Remove Redline and Strikeout

STYLES

Using a style is a way to assign a specific format to various sections of text. Styles differ from macros in that once you run a macro, the codes and text are inserted into the document, whereas a style inserts a style code (which can include codes and text) into the document. If you want to make changes to the codes or text inserted with a macro, you have to search and replace, make the changes manually at each location, or write additional macros to make the editing changes for you. If you use a style, you can edit the codes within the style itself, and then all text marked with that style will be changed automatically. See "Applications" for examples of how to use this feature.

Before creating and using styles, you should understand that there are two types of styles available: open and paired. When an open style is inserted into a document, it affects text from that point forward, just as a margin or tab setting would. This type of style is not turned off. However, you can insert new settings in the document to override the settings in an open style.

A paired style has "on" and "off" codes similar to bold and underline. Codes inserted in the "on" section of the style affect text inserted between the "on" and "off" codes. For example, if you entered a Helvetica 18pt font in the "on" section of the style, the text marked with that style would be changed to the Helvetica 18pt; text after the "off" code would remain in the font that was current before the style code was turned on. This is exactly like a bold or underline code where only the text between the "on" and "off" codes are bolded or underlined. This type of style is best used for headings or smaller sections of text—not entire documents.

Codes inserted in the "off" section affect text from that point forward, which is similar to an open style. This might be useful if you wanted a heading in a certain font but always wanted the text immediately following that level to be single-spaced. The next level heading might use a different font but double-spacing following that heading.

```
Styles

   Name         Type      Description

   Bibliogrphy  Paired    Bibliography
   Doc Init     Paired    Initialize Document Style
   Document     Outline   Document Style
   Pleading     Open      Header for numbered pleading paper
   Right Par    Outline   Right-Aligned Paragraph Numbers
   Tech Init    Open      Initialize Technical Style
   Technical    Outline   Technical Document Style












   1 On; 2 Off; 3 Create; 4 Edit; 5 Delete; 6 Save; 7 Retrieve; 8 Update: 1
```

Figure 3-164.   Styles menu

Keystrokes

Creating a Style

1. Press Style (ALT-F8). If you chose to install the Style Library during installation, you may see a few predefined styles already in the menu, as shown in Figure 3-164. See "Hints" for instructions about creating a Style Library of your own.

2. Choose 3 for Create a style. The menu in Figure 3-165 appears. The following discussion covers each option on the menu.

Name   Choose 1 to enter a Name for the style. You can enter up to 12 characters. This name will appear along with the type of style and the description on the list of styles. If you do not choose this option and enter a name, WordPerfect will give the style a number in the order in which it was created.

Type   Option 2 for Type lets you choose between paired and open styles. It will also let you create outline styles (styles that can be used with outlines and paragraph numbering to format each of the eight levels of numbering available). Although you can create and view outline styles in the regular Styles screen, you cannot select them directly from the Styles menu, but rather from the Paragraph Number Definition menu. See "Hints" for a way around this limitation.

If you choose an open style, it does not need to be turned off; option 5 for Enter (giving various options for turning off a style) is removed from the menu.

Description   Choose 3 to enter a Description for the style so you can easily identify it without entering the codes section to find out what is contained in the style. The description appears in the list of styles next to the style name and type.

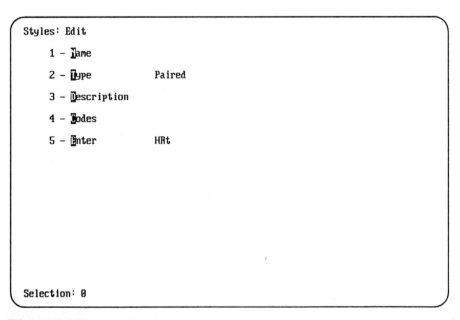

```
Styles: Edit

    1 - Name

    2 - Type            Paired

    3 - Description

    4 - Codes

    5 - Enter           HRt










Selection: 0
```

Figure 3-165.   Menu to create or edit a style

Codes   Choose 4 to enter the Codes (and text if applicable) for the style. You will see a Reveal Codes type of screen that allows you to see the codes as they are inserted. If you select an open style, the screen appears as follows:

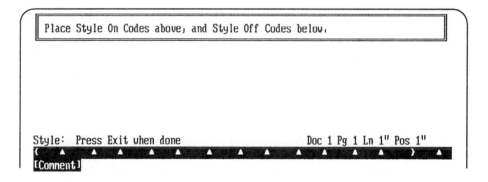

If you select a paired style, the screen displays a comment at the top with the [Comment] code in the "codes" section below telling you to place the style-on code above (before) the comment and the style-off code below (after).

The comment represents the text that will be inserted between the style-on and style-off codes. Any codes that are inserted at this point will be inserted just before the comment and will be included in the style-on code. Press → to move the cursor over the comment and insert the codes that should be included in the style-off code.

If you turn on bold in the style-on section, you do not have to turn it off; the style does that automatically. If you insert a font change in the style-on section, you do not have to change back to the original font at the end of the style; WordPerfect automatically makes the change. Other formatting options, such as margin

and spacing changes, will also be returned to their original settings. However, if you want some type of formatting to take
effect after the style-off code, you can include those codes in the
style-off section. The style-off section is also a good place to
insert extra [HRt] codes to insert blank space between headings
or items in a list.

If you need to mark the [Comment] (remember the comment
represents the text that will be typed later between the "on" and
"off" codes) for a table of contents entry, table of authorities
entry, and so on, move the cursor to the left of the [Comment]
code, press Block (ALT-F4) to turn on block, and then move the
cursor over the [Comment] code and select the appropriate
feature.

When you are finished entering codes, press Exit (F7).

Enter   If you are creating a paired style, choose **5** for Enter
(option 5 does not appear on the menu for open styles). This
option lets you choose various ways to turn off a style. The
following choices are displayed:

```
Enter: 1 Hrt; 2 Off; 3 Off/On: 0
```

Choose **1** for Hrt if you want ENTER to insert a [HRt] code as it
would normally. If you think you may need to press ENTER to start
a new line or paragraph while the style is on, leave it set to
[HRt]. If this is the case, you press → to move past the style-off
code to turn it off or enter the Styles menu, move to the appropriate style, and choose 2 to turn it Off.

Type **2** to have ENTER turn the style Off. You can use this
option in a heading or subheading style where you usually type
the text and then press ENTER to move down to the regular text.
Multiline headings or subheadings will not be adversely affected
if you let them wrap naturally with a [SRt] code. If you find that
you need a [HRt], you can copy one from another location,
because the [HRt] code itself does not turn off a style—the ENTER
key does. See "ENTER Options" later under "Hints" for details.

Choose **3** for Off/**O**n if you want to have ENTER turn the style off and then on again. This option is best if you have a number of items affected by the same style. For example, you can create a style for a numbered, indented item. If you usually have several numbered, indented items together, you can press ENTER to end one item and begin the next. At the end of the items, you would press → to move past the style-off code and end the process, or enter the Styles menu, move to the appropriate style, and choose **2** to turn it Off.

3. Press Exit (F7) when you have finished creating the style. You will be returned to the Styles menu, with the newly created style listed on the screen.

4. If you are not going to use the style immediately, press Exit (F7) to return to the document. Pressing ENTER or choosing **1** will turn the style **O**n.

WordPerfect can also create a style "by example." If you have used a certain format in the document that you want to repeat throughout the document, save it in a style by doing the following:

1. Move to the beginning of the section of codes, and press Block (ALT-F4).

2. Move the cursor just after the codes to be included.

3. Press Style (ALT-F8).

4. Choose **3** to **C**reate a new style.

5. Enter the name and description and choose **4** for **C**odes to see the codes that have been inserted from the document. The codes at the beginning of the block, up to the first character, are included before the comment; any codes found at the end of the block, after the last character, are placed after the comment.

6. Edit the codes, and make changes as needed.

7. Press Exit (F7) when you are finished.

The new style will be placed among the list.

Marking Text with a Style

1. Move the cursor to the location where you want the style to be turned on.

2. Press Style (ALT-F8).

3. Move the cursor to the style in the list, and press ENTER or choose 1 to turn On the style.

4. If the style is an open style, you are finished at this point. If the style is a paired style, enter the text to be affected.

5. There are several ways to turn off a style. If you chose to have ENTER turn the style off, or off and then on again, press ENTER. If you want to end the style without turning it off and then on again, press → to move over the style-off code. You can also press Style (ALT-F8), and choose 2 to turn the style Off, but you might find pressing → easier.

If you want to mark text with a paired style after you have entered it, block the text to be affected with Block (ALT-F4), press Style (ALT-F8), move to the appropriate style, and press ENTER to turn the style On. The style-on and style-off codes will be inserted at the beginning and end of the block of text.

This procedure is similar to the way in which desktop publishers tag sections of text with styles.

Hints

The codes that are inserted for a style appear as [Open Style:*name*] or [Style On:*name*] and [Style Off:*name*], where *name* is the name of the style. If you move the cursor to a style code, the code expands to show you the text and codes that are included. For example, the [Style On] code might appear as

[Style On:Heading;[Font:Tms Rmn 14pt][UND]]

Editing or Copying a Style

You can edit a style at any time by pressing Style (ALT-F8), moving the cursor to the style to be edited, and choosing 4 for Edit. After making changes to the codes and other options, press Exit (F7) twice to return to the document. Any text marked for that style is changed at that point.

If you change the name of the style, you are asked if you want to rename the styles in the document. If you type **Y**, all styles in the document will be renamed. If you type **N**, the codes in the document keep the same name. As soon as you scroll past one of these codes in the document, the style is inserted in the Styles menu again so you have some way to edit the style in the future.

By typing **N**, you can essentially copy a style. You can then make adjustments to that style and use it throughout the document, knowing that the original style is not lost.

Using Macros to Turn On Styles

If you plan to use a macro to turn on a style, it is best to use the Name Search feature so that it will select the correct style. When defining the macro, press Style (ALT-F8) and Search (F2), and then type the name of the style. By doing so, the cursor will move directly to that style and select it, regardless of its position in the list.

Deleting a Style

To delete a style from the list, press Style (ALT-F8), move to the style to be deleted, and choose 5 for Delete. The following options appear:

```
Delete Styles: 1 Leaving Codes; 2 Including Codes; 3 Definition Only: 0
```

Choose option **1** for Leaving Codes if you want to delete the style but leave the codes (contents of the style). This is a type of "freeze" feature that inserts all codes and text that were included in the style into the document. Because the style code is deleted, you cannot modify the format again. This option is useful if you want to save the file as a DOS Text file. Because all codes are stripped out when a DOS Text file is saved, everything within a style is also deleted. To avoid this, you could choose this option to delete the style but leave the text and codes and then save the document as a DOS Text file.

Option **2**, Including Codes, deletes the style and all the codes included in the style from the document. You can use this option if you want to return the document to its original format before any styles were used.

Option **3**, **D**efinition Only, deletes only the style definition from the menu. It leaves the style codes and their contents intact in the document. As soon as you scroll past a style code in a document, it is added to the style menu again.

This option is most useful if you want to delete extra styles that are not being used, but you are not sure about which ones are used in the document. You can delete all style definitions from the list, scroll through the document, and then enter the styles menu again to see the list of styles actually included in the document.

Sharing Styles Between Documents

Styles are saved with the current document. If you want to share styles between documents, you can use option **6** to **S**ave styles to another file or **7** to **R**etrieve styles from another file.

When you choose option **6**, **S**ave, you are asked for a filename. Enter the name of a file that does not exist. If the file exists, you are asked if you want to replace the original file. If you type **Y**, the original file is deleted; text and all styles are replaced with the current list of styles. Instead, type **N** and enter a different filename.

A disadvantage of using the Save option is that you cannot save only a few styles from the list to another file—all styles are saved. Another disadvantage is that if the file already exists, the styles will not be appended to the other list of styles. Instead, the original file will be replaced if you type Y in answer to "Replace filename" and you will lose that file.

A better option is to clear the screen and retrieve the file where the styles are to be copied. Press Style (ALT-F8), type **7** for **R**etrieve, and enter the name of the file that contains the desired styles. These styles would then be added to the list of styles already defined, instead of overwriting them as they would with the Save option. Text would not be affected.

If the two files both contain a style with the same name, you are asked the following question:

```
Style(s) already exist. Replace? No (Yes)
```

If you type **Y**, the styles in the current file with the same name will be replaced with the styles being retrieved. If you type **N**, files not having the same name are retrieved, and the original styles stay intact.

Styles are automatically saved to and retrieved from the directory used by WP.EXE unless you specified another one in the Location of Files menu. To change the directory, press Setup (SHIFT-F1), and choose **6** for Location of Files and then **5** for Style Files. Enter the pathname (drive and directory) for the styles. Enter the Library Filename if you want to see a list of default styles when you press Styles (ALT-F8). See the next section for a discussion about style libraries and how to use them.

Using a Style Library

You can create a regular WordPerfect file that contains the most commonly used styles so that you can use them for all documents. To do so, create the styles in a regular WordPerfect file (it may or may not contain text) or enter the Style menu and choose option **7** to **R**etrieve all styles from other applicable documents. Delete the styles that are specific to a particular file and that have no use in other files. Exit the Style menu, and save the document.

Press Setup (SHIFT-F1), and choose **6** for Location of Files and **5** for Style Files. Enter the drive and directory for the Style Library, and then enter the name of the file that you just created. Note that the Style Library must be kept in the directory that you just specified or WordPerfect will not be able to find it. Press Exit (F7) when you are finished.

When you press Style (ALT-F8) and there are no styles defined for the current document, the styles in the Style Library are retrieved. If the document already contains a list of styles, you can choose **8** for Update, and the styles from the library will be retrieved at that point. If there are styles from the Style Library with the same name, they will replace the styles saved in the document without confirmation. In other words, you are updating the styles in the file with those in the Style Library. If you want to then save the newly updated list, you can choose option **6** for Save, and enter the name of the original Style Library file. Type **Y** to replace the file.

A sample Style Library named LIBRARY.STY has been included with WordPerfect and is copied to the directory used by WP.EXE, unless you specified another during installation. The following is a list of the styles included in this file and what type of codes are included. Note that some of them are Outline styles, while others are Open styles that select the Outline styles. This is the method by which you can select Outline styles from the regular Styles menu.

- **Bibliogrphy [sic]** *Paired*

This style creates hanging indents, which are normally used in bibliographies. [Comment] represents the text in the bibliography entry. The codes are as follows:

[→Indent][←Mar Rel][Comment][HRt]
[HRt]

Note that there are two hard returns following the entry. The ENTER key has been set to turn this type of style off and on again to make it easier to insert a list of entries. Once you turn the style on, you can press ENTER at the end of each entry to insert the two hard returns and start the next entry automatically.

- **Doc Init** *Paired*

This style defines a table of contents containing three levels, defines a hard page break to separate the table of contents from the regular text, initializes (selects) the "document" in the form of a paragraph number definition code, and then turns on outlining. Because the "document" style is an outline style, you cannot normally select it from the regular styles menu. The paragraph number definition code, which in turn includes the outline style, is included in this style, as shown here:

[Def Mark:ToC,3:5,5,5][Comment][HPg]
[Par Num Def:Document][Outline On]

- **Document** *Outline*

The Document style is an outline style that includes various types of formats for each level in an outline, including codes that mark each level of the outline for different levels in the table of contents. You can select this type of style in the Paragraph Number Definition menu.

- **Pleading** *Open*

You can place this style at the top of a document that is to be formatted for pleading paper with line numbers and two vertical bars in the left margin. You may need to modify this style to suit your needs.

- **Right Par**   *Outline*

Also an outline style, this style right-aligns paragraph and outline numbers.

- **Tech Init**   *Open*

This style initializes (selects) the "Technical" style (explained next). Again, because the "Technical" style is an outline style, you can only select it through the regular styles menu by using a paragraph number definition code to select the outline style.

- **Technical**   *Outline*

This outline style defines a different format for each level of an outline.

Changing the Type of Style

You can use option 2 for **T**ype in the menu used to edit a style and change a style from open to paired, and vice versa. You can change either type to an outline style, but you cannot change an outline style to either an open or paired style.

If you change the type of style from paired to open, all codes contained in the style-off section of the style are deleted. If you change a style from open to paired, a [Comment] code is inserted, but no codes are included in the style-off section. You can, of course, edit the codes and change this if necessary.

If you change either type of style to an outline style, enter a name for the style (or press ENTER to accept the current name), and then enter the level of paragraph/outline numbering for which the style is to be used (the codes in the style can only affect one level of numbering). You can then edit the outline style and add styles for the remaining levels of numbering.

ENTER Options

You can choose to have ENTER turn off a style. If you later decide that you need an [HRt] code within a style, pressing ENTER at that point will insert the style-off code there and turn off the style prematurely. To avoid this problem, you can copy or delete an [HRt] code from another location in the document and then retrieve or undelete it within the style at the proper location.

Inserting the [HRt] code with this method does not turn off the style prematurely, because it is not the code that turns off the style, but the ENTER key itself.

Including Graphics in a Style

You can include a graphics image in a style if you set the contents of the graphics box to Graphics on Disk. Because a graphics image is not allowed in a style, you can point to the graphics image on disk and still be able to include it in a style. See "Graphics Boxes" in this chapter for an example of a style that uses a checkbox for each item in a list.

Applications

This section includes a few examples to illustrate how to use the different types of styles.

Open Style

You can define an open style to be used at the beginning of a letter, memo, or report. Remember that codes and text can be included.

However, if you want to pause and enter variable text ("To," "From," "Subject," and so on), you will want to use a macro that pauses for the information instead. If you do not feel that you will need to update the style of your letters, memos, or reports, a macro may be best. If you do need to update them occasionally, you may find styles easier to edit.

An open style was used to create the heading for the newsletter shown in Figure 3-166. It included the horizontal lines and advance codes to advance to the correct position, and then it entered "Corporate Update." Since the text in the masthead does not change each time the style is used, it is best to include it in the style.

If you have a book or report that has several chapters or sections, each starting with a specific style, you can use an open style at the beginning of each chapter or section. If the format changes for any reason, you can edit the style; the changes will be made at the beginning of each chapter or section automatically.

Corporate Update

Volume III, Number 40   Internal Communication   November 1, 1990

GENERAL

Inter-Office Mail Reminder

For those employees who use the numbering system when addressing inter-office mail, please be advised that the Accounting Department has now been changed to #11. For those of you who are not using the numbering system, please write employees' first and last names and departments legibly.

PERSONNEL

Vacation Schedule Correction

In an employee vacation schedule distributed with the December 15, 1989 edition of the newsletter, the Thanksgiving holiday is marked as Thursday, November 15, 1990, which is incorrect. The correct date for the holiday is Thursday, November 22, 1988.

Insurance Update

If you are admitted to a hospital for any reason, please specify your employer upon admittance. The billing departments of all hospitals have been advised of our insurance coverage and are aware of the information needed to process a claim.

Don't forget that, when filing your first claim each year, one full completed claim must be submitted for each family member. Subsequent claims may be submitted with only a receipt for services rendered (unless the claim is accident-related, in which case a fully completed claim form is required.

Insurance Questions?

All questions regarding company insurance policies (for example, coverage, eligibility, and reimbursement) should now be directed to Mary in Accounting at extension 304.

TRAVEL

Business Card Orders

All employees who will be attending the computer conventions and need to reorder business cards are requested to so before December 15. Please call Laurie with your order.

Travel Policies

Due to recent changes in the company's travel policies and procedures, an authorization number is needed before airline tickets can be issued. If you will be traveling for the company, please have your travel form filled out and signed by your supervisor

prior to submitting it to Fran in Accounting. She will then give the authorization number to the travel agent.

TRAINING

Training Classes

The next session of product training classes begins on December 8, but classes are beginning to fill up now. If you have questions regarding possible enrollment, please see the receptionist in your building for a list of registered participants.

POTPOURRI

Software Registration

The Testing Department is compiling a list of all software products currently owned by the company. If you have such a product in your office, please send a memo to Gary in Testing. Include the name, a brief description of the product, manufacturer, and version number. If you have no need for the program in your office please forward the entire package to Gary.

Printer Planner

Melinda in Engineering is the one to call if you need to borrow a printer from another

Figure 3-166.   Newsletter showing an open style for the masthead and paired styles for headings and subheadings

The style at the beginning of each chapter could include a hard page [HPg] code, force the page to be an odd page with [Force:Odd], start page numbering at page 1 with [Pg Num:1], and suppress the page number on that page with [Suppress:PgNum]. Later, if you decide to have continuous numbering throughout the document, you can remove the [Pg Num:1] and [Suppress:PgNum] codes from the style, and the change will be made throughout the document.

Paired Style — ENTER Turns the Style Off

In the sample newsletter shown in Figure 3-166, styles are used to create the headings and subheadings. The codes that are included in the heading style are as follows:

[Block Pro:On][HLine:Left,2.15″,0.01″,100%][HRt]
[AdvDn:0.06″][Font:Helv 14pt Italics][Comment][AdvDn:0.1″]
[HLine:Left,2.15″,0.03″,100%[HRt]
[AdvDn:0.06″][Block Pro:Off]

The Block Protect codes ensure that the entire heading will not be broken by a page break. Advance codes were used for the exact positioning of the horizontal lines and the text between the lines.

The codes included in the subheading style are shown here:

[Block Pro:On][Font:Helv 12pt Bold][Comment][HRt]
[Block Pro:Off]

Note that there is not a font change in the style-off section of either of these styles, because the style-off code returns to the previous font automatically.

Both styles have been defined to have ENTER turn the style off, because it is natural to type a heading or subheading and press ENTER to continue with the remaining text. If you wanted to insert a [HRt] code within the heading or subheading to force text to another line, you would need to delete or copy a [HRt] code from another location in the document and then undelete or retrieve it within the style.

Paired Style — ENTER Turns the Style Off and On

Numbered lists or bibliographies are two applications in which you might want to use paired styles that are turned off and then on again, because they usually contain more than one entry. The "Bibliogrphy"

[sic] style described earlier that is included in the LIBRARY.STY file is a good example of how to use the Off/On feature.

A numbered, indented item might use the following style:

[Par Num:Auto][→Indent][Comment][HRt]
[HRt]

When you turn on the style, the style-on codes are inserted. In the example above, the appropriate number would be inserted, and you would be ready to type the text. After typing the entry, you would press ENTER to insert the two [HRt] codes (included in the style-off code) and insert the beginning codes for the next entry. After you had finished with the entire list or bibliography, you can press → to move past the last style-off code and turn off the style without turning it back on again.

Later, if you want to change the [→Indent] code to a [Tab], you can do so in the style, and each entry will change. The automatic paragraph number can be replaced with a bullet if you want bulleted items (press CTRL-2 and then type ** to insert a bullet). Of course, if you decide that you do not want double-spacing between each entry, you can edit the style and remove one [HRt] code. When you return to the document, all items will be changed to reflect the style automatically.

Scriptwriter Styles

Scripts usually have more than one character. You can create a paired style for each character that centers the name for each character and inserts two [HRt] codes to create space between the character name and the dialogue in the style-on section. The style-off section contains two or more [HRt] codes, so the cursor will be placed correctly for the next character's dialogue.

If the dialogue for a character continues onto the next page, you may want to include a header at the top of that page, giving the name of the character and the word "Continued." You can include a header in the style-on section of the style that centers the character's name along with the word "Continued," and then discontinue the header in the style-off section of the style. If the text between the style-on and style-off codes crosses a page break, a header will be printed with the name of the current character and the word "Continued." It is then turned off at the end of that particular section of dialogue, so the header will not continue to print. If the dialogue does not cross a page break, the header will not print.

These are only a few samples of the possibilities that are available with styles. You can find more examples in Chapter 4.

Related Entries

Graphics
Outlines
See Chapter 4, "Desktop Publishing with WordPerfect"

SUBDOCUMENTS

A subdocument is a regular WordPerfect document that happens to be part of a master document. When creating a master document, you press Mark Text (ALT-F5), choose **2** for **S**ubdoc, and then enter the full pathname (drive, directory, and filename) for the document that is to be included as part of the master document. You can then expand the master document so that all subdocuments are retrieved into one document. You can make global changes to the master document; start the Generate feature to create a table of contents, an index, or lists; update cross-references; and then print. You can then condense the master document and save all the changes back into their individual files. See "Master Document" in this chapter for more information.

SUMMARY

See "Document Management/Summary" in this chapter.

SUPERSCRIPT AND SUBSCRIPT

You can raise or lower characters above or below the regular line of type with the Superscript and Subscript feature.

Keystrokes

1. Press Font (CTRL-F8).

2. Choose 1 for Size.

3. Choose 1 for Superscript or 2 for Subscript.

4. Type the text to be superscripted or subscripted.

5. Press → to move past the superscript-off or subscript-off code.

Hints

When you choose the Superscript option, the codes [SUPRSCPT] and [suprscpt] are inserted in the document; [SUBSCPT] and [subscpt] are used for subscript. Note that all text between the two codes will be affected, not just a single character.

You can repeat the steps to turn the option off again, but pressing → is easier.

Superscript and subscript characters are usually printed up or down one-third of a line. Some dot-matrix printers print a compressed character on the upper or lower half of the line. If you want to print the character up or down a specific amount, use the Advance feature to advance up or down a specific amount from the cursor.

If you have a NEC 3550 printer and the text prints in the left margin after you print a superscripted or subscripted character (footnote numbers are included), check the SW2-5 switch; it should be turned on.

Applications

Superscripts are often used for footnote numbers. However, Word-Perfect has a Footnote feature that automatically inserts a super-scripted number, lets you create the footnote, and then keeps track of the number of lines allowed per page. You can use Superscript if you need to reference a footnote more than once on a page. For example, the first reference for the first footnote could be the regular footnote number inserted by WordPerfect (footnote number[1]). The second time it is referenced, you can insert a superscripted 1 manually (second reference[1]) or use the Cross-Reference feature, superscripting the reference number.

The Superscript and Subscript features can be used in formulas or equations, such as H_2O and 10^5. The Equation feature in WordPerfect also has a superscript and subscript feature. See "Equations" in this chapter for details.

Related Entries

Equations
Footnotes

SUPPLEMENTARY DICTIONARY

WordPerfect uses two dictionaries when it checks a document for spelling: WP{WP}US.LEX and WP{WP}US.SUP. The first file contains the words included by WordPerfect Corporation, and the second is the supplementary dictionary that is used to hold the words added during the spell check.

You can enter words into any WordPerfect file and use that as a supplementary file instead. After pressing Spell (CTRL-F2), choose **4** for New Sup. Dictionary, and enter the name of the new file to be used.

See "Spell" in this chapter for additional information.

SUPPRESS

An option on the Page Format menu lets you suppress the printing of a header, footer, or page number for the current page or lets you print the page number at the bottom of the page.

The Suppress option is especially useful for title pages (it allows the page number to be printed at the bottom of that page) or for a page that contains a table or chart.

Keystrokes

You should be at the top of the page before you choose this feature so that it can suppress any headers or page numbering that might be printed at the top of the page.

1. Press Go To (CTRL-HOME), and then press ↑ to go to the top of the current page.

2. Press Format (SHIFT-F8).

3. Choose 2 for **P**age.

4. Choose 8 for **S**uppress (this page only). The menu shown in Figure 3-167 appears.

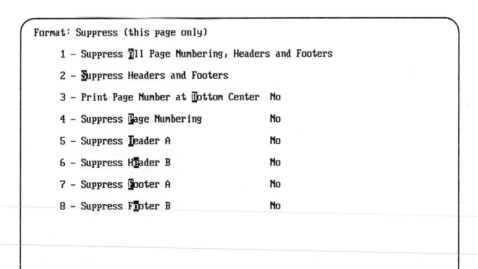

```
Format: Suppress (this page only)

    1 - Suppress All Page Numbering, Headers and Footers

    2 - Suppress Headers and Footers

    3 - Print Page Number at Bottom Center   No

    4 - Suppress Page Numbering              No

    5 - Suppress Header A                     No

    6 - Suppress Header B                     No

    7 - Suppress Footer A                     No

    8 - Suppress Footer B                     No




Selection: 0
```

Figure 3-167.   Suppress menu

5. Choose **1** to suppress **All** page numbering, headers, and footers. Choose **2** to Suppress all headers and footers. If you want to have the page number printed at the **Bottom Center** of the page, then choose **3**, and type **Y** for Yes.

You can suppress any combination of headers, footers, or page numbers by choosing from the remaining options and typing **Y** if you want them suppressed.

6. Press Exit (F7) twice when you are finished to return to the document.

Hints

When you choose the Suppress option, the code [Suppress:n] is inserted, where n can be any combination of the following:

PgBC	Print page number at bottom center
PgNum	Suppress page numbering
HA	Suppress header A
HB	Suppress header B
FA	Suppress footer A
FB	Suppress footer B

If you ask that page numbering be suppressed, you cannot then ask that the page number be printed at the bottom center of the page. You would have to change that option to **N** before you would be allowed to make the change.

If you choose option **1** or **2** to suppress all options or just headers and footers, the remaining Yes/No options change automatically to reflect the current change. You can then change any individual option.

If you want a header, footer, or page number to begin printing on the second page, it is better to define those items on the first page and then immediately suppress them. If you place the header, footer, or page number code at the top of the second page, the code could change location after you make editing changes and yield unpredictable results.

If you often type two-page letters or memos, consider placing the header on the first page, followed immediately by the command to suppress the header for that page only.

Related Entries

Footers
Headers
Page Numbering

SWITCH

Switch (SHIFT-F3) is used to switch between document 1 and document 2. If Block is on, Switch (SHIFT-F3) gives you the option of switching the block to uppercase or lowercase.

Keystrokes

Switch Documents

Press Switch (SHIFT-F3) to switch between the two document screens.

Switch to Uppercase or Lowercase

1. Move the cursor to one end of the text to be changed, and press Block (ALT-F4).

2. Move the cursor to the opposite end to highlight the text.

3. Press Switch (SHIFT-F3). The following options appear:

```
1 Uppercase: 2 Lowercase: 0
```

4. Choose **1** to change the block to Uppercase or **2** to change it to Lowercase.

5. Press Block (ALT-F4) to turn off Block.

Hints

When you switch documents, the cursor remains in its original position in the document. For example, if you were in document 1 and the status line read "Doc 1 Pg 10 Ln 3″ Pos 4.5″," and then you switched to document 2, moved through document 2, and then switched back again, the status line would still read "Doc 1 Pg 10 Ln 3″ Pos 4.5″."

If you split the screen with the Windows option on Screen (CTRL-F3), you can see both documents on the screen at once. Pressing Switch (SHIFT-F3) moves the cursor between the two. If you have a mouse, you can move the mouse pointer to a new location in either document and click the left button to move the cursor to the new location.

When you are switching to lowercase, the first word of the sentence remains capitalized if any end-of-sentence punctuation just before that word is included as part of the block. For example, if the block is highlighted, as shown in the following illustration, and is then switched to lowercase, the first letter of the sentence will remain capitalized.

```
of the Persons voting for and against the Bill shall be entered

on the Journal of each House respectively. IF ANY BILL SHALL NOT

BE RETURNED BY THE PRESIDENT WITHIN TEN DAYS (SUNDAYS EXCEPTED)

AFTER IT SHALL HAVE BEEN PRESENTED TO HIM, THE SAME SHALL BE A

LAW, in like Manner as if he had signed it, unless the Congress

by their Adjournment prevent its Return, in which Case it shall
```

Having two documents in memory makes it easier to cut and copy text from one document to another with Block (ALT-F4), Move (CTRL-F4), and Switch (SHIFT-F3).

Remember that you can view the effects in both documents when you use the Windows feature on Screen (CTRL-F3).

Related Entries

Capitalization
Windows

TAB ALIGN

Tab Align (CTRL-F6) moves the cursor to the next tab setting and aligns text or numbers at a decimal point (period). You can change the alignment character so that text can be aligned at a character other than a decimal point.

Keystrokes

Aligning the Text

1. Set tabs if necessary with the Tab Set option on the Line Format menu. See "Tabs" in this chapter if you need assistance.

2. Press Tab Align (CTRL-F6). The cursor moves to the next tab setting, and "Align char = ." appears on the status line, meaning that the text will be aligned at the decimal point.

3. Type numbers or text. The characters are inserted to the left of the cursor until you type the decimal point (period). Any text after the decimal is inserted to the right.

Changing the Decimal/Align Character

1. Press Format (SHIFT-F8).

2. Choose 4 for Other.

3. Choose 3 for Decimal/Align Character and Thousands' Separator.

4. Type the new character to be used for each option.

5. Press Exit (F7) to return to the document.

There is no immediate indication that the alignment character is changed. For reassurance, you can press Reveal Codes (ALT-F3) to see the code [Decml/Algn Char:x,y], where x represents the new decimal/align character and y represents the new thousands' separator. If you changed the decimal/align character to a comma and the thousands' separator to a decimal point, the code would appear as [Decml/Algn Char:,.].

Hints

When you press Tab Align (CTRL-F6), the code [DEC TAB] is inserted. If you have decimal tabs set and press TAB to align the text at the decimal tab, the code [Dec Tab] (in lowercase) is inserted. The uppercase code indicates a "hard" decimal tab, meaning that it will remain a decimal tab even if you change the type of tab setting. A [Dec Tab], however, will change to reflect a new type of tab setting. For example, if you change a decimal tab to a right-aligned tab, [Dec Tab] would change to [Rgt Tab].

Tab Align is best used when you are aligning text at such characters as a colon, dash, or a parenthesis (see "Applications" in this section). It can also be used effectively as a quick decimal tab. However, if you are using decimal tabs extensively, it is best to set decimal tabs (see "Tabs" in this chapter). You can then use the TAB key rather than Tab Align (CTRL-F6), as was explained earlier.

You can use any character on the keyboard as the alignment character, including a space (just press the space bar when you are asked for the alignment character). You cannot use special characters from the extended character set (ASCII decimal values 1 through 31 and 127 through 254).

Applications

Use a colon (:) as the alignment character for a memo heading, as shown here:

MEMO

```
    Date:
      To:
    From:
 Subject:
```

Align numbers at a comma rather than decimal point for European-formatted columns of numbers, as follows:

3.456,18	427,32	532,36
87,03	1,98	2.000.000,00
,76	2.079,21	7.584,33
264,00	74,77	49,06

Related Entries

Decimal Tabs
Math
Tabs

TAB KEY

Pressing the TAB key moves the cursor to the next tab setting.

Keystrokes

The TAB key is on the left part of the keyboard in about the same position as on a typewriter. It may be labeled "TAB" or it may have two arrows pointing in opposite directions ⇄ .

Hints

Usually, when you press TAB, a [Tab] code is inserted and is visible when you press Reveal Codes (ALT-F3). If you have set any type of tab other than a left-aligned tab, you will get that type of tab code inserted. For example, if you have set a centered tab, [Cntr Tab] will be inserted. A right-aligned tab will insert the code [Rgt Tab] and a decimal tab will insert [Dec Tab].

If you want to insert a hard tab (meaning a left-aligned tab that will never change, even if the type of tab setting changes), press HOME and then TAB. The code [TAB] (in uppercase) is then inserted. If you retrieve a document created with an earlier version of WordPerfect, all tabs will be retrieved as hard tabs.

If you want to go to an exact position, it is safest to use TAB rather than the space bar. A tab setting is an exact position, whereas the amount of space produced with the space bar varies from printer to printer, especially when you are using proportional spacing or full justification.

Pressing SHIFT-TAB moves the cursor to the previous tab setting. Named "Left Margin Release," SHIFT-TAB inserts the code [←Mar Rel]. You can press →Indent (F4) and then Left Margin Release (SHIFT-TAB) to create a bibliographic entry.

Tabs in Outlines and Tables

When you use the Outline feature and press TAB to move to the next level, a hard tab [TAB] is inserted. SHIFT-TAB changes to the previous level. If you want to insert a tab in an outline rather than change levels, press HOME and then TAB.

If you use WordPerfect's Tables feature, you can press TAB to move forward from cell to cell and SHIFT-TAB to move backward from cell to cell. If you want to insert a [TAB] within a cell without moving to the next cell, press HOME and then TAB.

TAB and Typeover

While Typeover is on (press INS to turn Typeover on and off), you can use TAB to move over existing text to the next tab setting instead of inserting [Tab] codes. This is especially useful in statistical typing when you want to move quickly from one column to another.

When you reach the end of a line of text and there are more tab settings, pressing TAB will insert [Tab] codes as it normally does.

TAB and Indent

Use TAB to indent the first line of a paragraph. If all lines in a paragraph are to be indented, use →Indent (F4) or →Indent← (SHIFT-F4) instead of TAB. If you use TAB to indent each line manually, extensive editing may be necessary when text is inserted or deleted. Here are some examples:

When the first line of a paragraph needs to be indented, useTAB, as shown in this example. A [Tab] code is inserted when you press TAB.

→Indent (F4) was used to indent this paragraph, because each line should be indented. When this option is used, you do not have to indent each line individually. Use this option just after the number in numbered paragraphs.

To bring both the left and the right margins in temporarily, use →Indent← (SHIFT-F4). This option is useful for indented paragraphs that will return to the normal margins when you press ENTER.

Related Entries

Indent
Left Margin Release
Tabs

TABLE OF AUTHORITIES

The Table of Authorities feature lets you mark citations throughout a document and generate up to 16 sections for cases, statutes, and so on. See Figure 3-168 for a sample table of authorities.

Although the Table of Authorities feature was designed for legal professionals, many other people have found uses for this powerful feature. Accountants use the feature to cite tax laws, and others have used it to create bibliographies that list the page numbers for each reference.

Each section in a table of authorities is sorted alphanumerically (with numbers appearing before letters), similar to an index, and each section can have its own format.

Keystrokes

There are four basic steps to creating a table of authorities. Each is discussed in detail in the sections that follow.

1. Decide what each section will be used for: cases, statutes, items from the U.S. Constitution, civil rights acts, and so on.

2. Mark each authority (sometimes referred to as a "citation"), and indicate the section in which it is to be included. Mark each subsequent occurrence of an authority with the short form. Use Search (F2) to help you find further occurrences.

3. Define the location and format for each section of the table of authorities.

4. Generate the table.

TABLE OF AUTHORITIES

Cases   **Page(s)**

Carlsberg Resources Corp v. Cambria Savings & Loan Assoc.
554 F.2d 1254 (3d Cir. 1977 10

Chapman v. Barney
129 U.S. 677 (1889) 6, 10, 11

Coal Co. v. Blatchford
78 U.S. (11 Wall.) 172, 175 (1870) 8

Navarro Savings Association v. Lee
446 U.S. 458 (1980) 7-12, 14, 16

Strawbridge v. Curtiss
7 U.S. (3 Cranch) 267 (1806) 4

Trent Realty Assoc. v. First Federal Savings & Loan Assoc.
657 F.2d 29 (3d Cir. 1981) 10, 11

United Steelworkers v. R.H. Bouligny
382 U.S. 145 (1965) 5, 9

Satutes

28 U.S.C. Section 1332(a)   1
28 U.S.C. Section 1332(c)   4, 5

Fed. R. Civ. P. 17(b)   11
Fed. R. Civ. P. 82   3, 11

Revised Uniform Ltd. Partnership Act
    Section 303, 6 U.L.A. 224 (Supp. 1984)   13
    Section 403, 6 U.L.A. 230 (Supp. 1984)   8

Miscellaneous

C. Wright, The Federal Courts
    Section 7 at 22 (4th ed. 1983)   4

Figure 3-168.   Sample table of authorities

Determine What Sections Will Be Used

After typing a document, you will usually know what types of authorities were used in that document. Although you can make up the list as you mark items, it is sometimes easier to first list the major sections that will be included in the table. Making the decision beforehand helps speed up the process when you are marking each item.

Mark Each Authority (Citation)

When you mark an item for the first time, you will be asked to specify the section number, the full form (what will actually appear in the table after it is generated), and the short form (a nickname for the full form). When you mark the item again, you need to specify only the short form.

1. Move the cursor to one end of the authority to be included in the table, and press Block (ALT-F4).

2. Move the cursor to the opposite end of the text until the authority is highlighted.

3. Press Mark Text (ALT-F5). The following menu is displayed:

```
Mark for: 1 ToC; 2 List; 3 Index; 4 ToA: 0
```

4. Choose 4 for ToA. A new menu is displayed:

```
ToA Section Number (Press Enter for Short Form only):
```

5. Enter the section number. You can also press ENTER to mark the item with a short form. However, if you are marking the first item, the short form has not yet been created. The "Short Form Only" option is used to mark subsequent authorities.

6. The full form (highlighted text) is placed in a separate editing screen. You can then format the text until it looks exactly as it should in the table. You can use bold, underline, and most other

formatting commands. An option in the Definition menu deletes underlining when the table is generated. If underlining should not be included, you do not have to manually delete it.

If you want the authority to appear in a hanging indent format, go to the beginning of the citation and press →Indent (F4), and then press Left Margin Release (SHIFT-TAB).

7. Press Exit (F7) when you have finished editing the full form.

8. You are then asked to enter the short form that will be used to mark subsequent entries. This is an abbreviated form for the full reference. Up to 40 characters of the highlighted block are automatically displayed for the short form, as shown in the following illustration:

```
Short Form: 17 U.S.C. 4516(f)
```

Edit the displayed text and press ENTER, or enter a new short form of your own choice. Each short form must be unique, or you will see an error message when the table is generated.

9. Continue to mark each subsequent authority with the Short Form, as described in the following example.

You can use Search (F2) or Extended Search (HOME, F2) to search for the next occurrence of the authority. Extended Search includes headers, footers, footnotes, and endnotes in the search, whereas Search does not. When the next occurrence of the authority is found, mark it with the short form only.

1. Press Mark Text (ALT-F5).

2. Choose 4 for ToA Short Form. The last short form used is displayed.

3. Press ENTER to use the displayed short form.

4. Continue searching and marking all subsequent occurrences of the authority.

Define the Location and Format of the Sections

1. Move the cursor to the point in the document at which the table of authorities is to be generated.

2. Press Hard Page (CTRL-ENTER) if you want to generate the table on a separate page.

3. You must enter the major heading and each section heading manually. Press Center (SHIFT-F6) and enter the title for the table, and then type the headings for each section at the left margin, as shown in Figure 3-169.

4. Move the cursor below the first section heading (where the first section should be generated), and press Mark Text (ALT-F5).

5. Choose 5 for **D**efine.

6. Choose 4 for Table of Authorities.

```
                    TABLE OF AUTHORITIES

Cases                                          Page(s)


Statutes


Miscellaneous






                                   Doc 1 Pg 1 Ln 1" Pos 1.1"
```

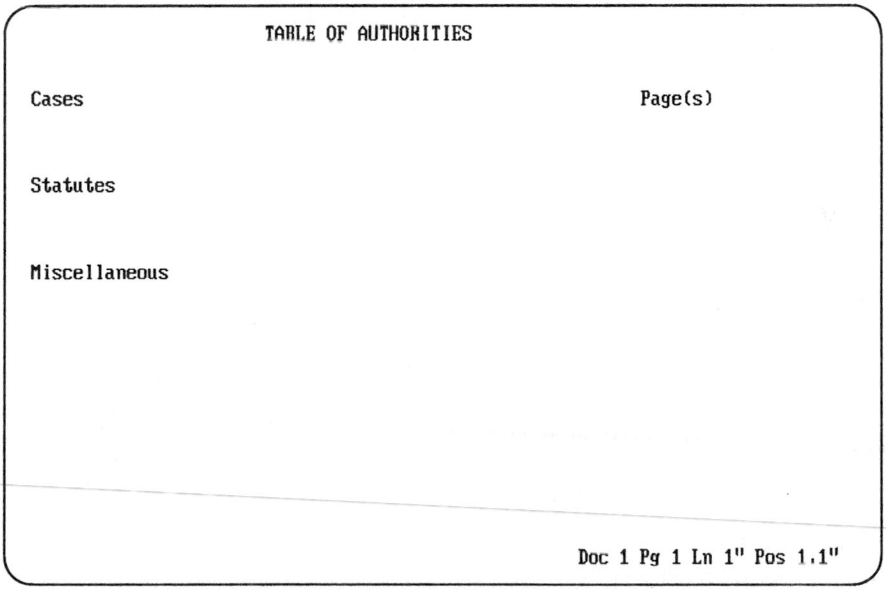

Figure 3-169.   Headings for table of authorities

7. Enter the number of the section being defined. The Table of Authorities options are displayed, as shown here:

```
Definition for Table of Authorities 1

    1 - Dot Leaders                        Yes

    2 - Underlining Allowed                No

    3 - Blank Line Between Authorities     Yes
```

8. Change any of the options necessary for that section. Remember that all sections are defined separately, and each can have its own selections.

9. Press Exit (F7) to return to the document.

10. Repeat the steps for each section under each section title.

11. Press Hard Page (CTRL-ENTER) after the table if you want the text in the document to start on a separate page.

12. To make sure that the page numbers are accurate before the table is generated, press Format (SHIFT-F8) and choose **2** for **P**age, **6** for Page **N**umbering, and **1** for New Page Number. Enter the page number for the first page of text (usually 1). If you neglect this step, you will see a message informing you that a new page number was not found when the table was generated. Insert the new page number and generate the table again.

Generate the Table of Authorities

1. Press Mark Text (ALT-F5) from anywhere in the document.

2. Choose **6** for **G**enerate.

3. Choose **5** to **G**enerate your Tables, Indexes, Cross-References, and so on.

4. The message "Existing tables, lists and indexes will be replaced. Continue? Yes (No)" is displayed. Type **Y** to continue or **N** to return to the document.

A counter is displayed on the status line, showing you that progress is being made. Since the process may require several passes through the document, the counter will increment at varying rates. The table of authorities, table of contents, lists, cross-references, and the index are all generated at the same time.

Hints

When you mark the first authority, the code [ToA:*n*;shortform;Full Form] is inserted at the cursor location, where *n* is the number of the section in the table. When only the short form is used, the code [ToA:;shortform;] is displayed. The section number and "Full Form" are not displayed in this code because the short form is all that is needed.

When you define the location and format for each section, the code [DefMark:ToA,*n*] is inserted, with *n* again being the number of the section. After a section is generated, an [End Def] code is placed at the end of each section. If the table is generated a second time, these codes are used to block and delete the previous section so the newly generated table can be displayed in its place.

When you generate a table of authorities, all full forms are found and their page numbers noted. WordPerfect then searches for the authorities marked with a short form, matches them up with the applicable full form, and combines all the page numbers. If the same authority is marked on three or more consecutive pages, the page numbers are shown as a range rather than as single pages.

If you have selected a page number style in the Page Numbering menu, the entire style will be included with the page number when the table is generated. In other words, if the page number style is 1-^B because it is in chapter one, the page numbers will appear in the table of authorities as 1-3, 1-5, and so on. See "Page Numbering" in this chapter for more information.

You can edit the table after you have created it. If you chose the Dot Leader option for listing page numbers, a dot leader is placed between the text and the page number. If text is added or deleted, the dot leader is automatically adjusted.

Editing the Full Form or the Short Form

You can always edit the full form in the table after it has been generated. However, if you plan to regenerate the table at any time, edit the full form code in the document; then you will not have to change the entry in the table each time it is generated.

You cannot edit a short form. Instead, you must delete the previous [ToA] code and mark the entry again with the new short form.

Use Search (F2) or Extended Search (HOME, F2) if you need to find the [ToA] codes. Both the full form and short form are considered [ToA] codes. When one is found, you can press Reveal Codes (ALT-F3) to see the code and determine if it is the one you are searching for.

To make changes to the full form or to change the section number, use the following steps:

1. Move the cursor to just after the authority you want to edit.

2. Press Mark Text (ALT-F5).

3. Choose **5** for **D**efine.

4. Choose **5** for **E**dit Table of Authorities Full Form. The last authority marked with a full form (just to the left of the cursor) is displayed. If an authority is not found before the cursor, the next full form to the right is found.

5. Make the changes, and press Exit (F7) when you are finished.

6. Enter the section number for the item.

If you have not assigned a unique short form to a full form, delete the entire [ToA:*n*;shortform;Full Form] code and mark the item again. If you want to change the short form for a particular item, delete the [ToA:;shortform;] code and mark it with a new short form.

When you are marking each item, the last short form entered is displayed. This makes it easier to mark each item by just pressing ENTER when that short form is displayed. However, when you are changing short forms, the appropriate short form is not usually displayed. You can use the standard method already listed by entering the short form manually, or blocking and marking the text for the short form (if it is found in the document).

1. Move to one end of the text to be used in the short form, and press Block (ALT-F4).

2. Move to the opposite end of the short form to highlight the text.

3. Press Mark Text (ALT-F5).

4. Choose 4 for ToA.

5. Press ENTER for the short form only. The highlighted block is displayed as the short form to be used.

6. Press ENTER to use the displayed short form, or edit the text and press ENTER when you are finished.

After making changes to full forms and short forms, generate the table again.

You can create a table of authorities for more than one document by including a list of subdocuments in a master document and then generating the table of authorities for the master document. See "Master Document" in this chapter for details.

Error Messages

The following are possible error messages that you might see when a table of authorities is being generated.

"Not Enough Memory"   WordPerfect uses document 2 (if available) to generate the tables, lists, and index. If it is not available, document 3 is used. If you get the error message "Not Enough Memory," exit document 2 so that the memory for that document can be used. If you still get the message, retrieve the document into document 2, and leave the document 1 screen clear. Generate can then use the additional memory in document 1 (twice as much memory as that allotted to document 2).

"No [DefMark] Found"   If you forget to define the location and format of the table, you will see the error message "No [DefMark] Found." Correct the situation and regenerate the table.

"Can't Find End of Table of Contents, Lists or Index Text"   When you first generate a table, an [EndDef] code is placed at the end of the table. Each [DefMark] code then has a corresponding [EndDef] code. If you regenerate a table and the [DefMark:ToA,n] mark is accidentally deleted, but the [EndDef] code is found, the message "Can't find end of table of contents, lists, or index text" is displayed.

If the [EndDef] code is deleted, that section of the table will be generated again, without deleting the first table. You would then get duplicate tables in the same location. If more than one [DefMark] code exists for the same section, the table will be generated in both locations.

"New Page Num Not Found. . ."   If you neglect to insert a New Page Number code between the table of authorities and the first authority marked, this message will be displayed as a warning that page number listings may not be accurate. Go to the first page of the text after the table of authorities, press Format (SHIFT-F8), choose **2** for **Page**, **6** for Page **Numbering**, **1** for **New** Page Number, then enter a new number for that page. When you are finished, regenerate the table.

"Non-Unique Short Form(s) Found"   If you use the same short form for more than one full form, this error message will be displayed to remind you that there must be a unique short form for each full form. The table will still be generated, but asterisks will appear instead of page numbers in the entries that are affected.

If you use a short form that is not assigned to a full form, the short form will be displayed in the table with an asterisk marking that item.

Related Entries

Block
Search

TABLE OF CONTENTS

You can use the Table of Contents feature to mark up to five levels of headings or titles and to generate a table of contents that lists the page numbers for each item. Figure 3-170 shows a sample table of contents contains three levels.

```
                          TABLE OF CONTENTS

The Constitution of the United States. . . . . . . . . . . . . .1
        Preamble. . . . . . . . . . . . . . . . . . . . . . . .1
        Article I . . . . . . . . . . . . . . . . . . . . . . .1
                Section 1. . . . . . . . . . . . . . . . . . . .1
                Section 2. . . . . . . . . . . . . . . . . . . .1
                Section 3. . . . . . . . . . . . . . . . . . . .2
                Section 4. . . . . . . . . . . . . . . . . . . .4
                Section 5. . . . . . . . . . . . . . . . . . . .4
                Section 6. . . . . . . . . . . . . . . . . . . .5
                Section 7. . . . . . . . . . . . . . . . . . . .5
                Section 8. . . . . . . . . . . . . . . . . . . .6
                Section 9. . . . . . . . . . . . . . . . . . . .8
                Section 10 . . . . . . . . . . . . . . . . . . .9
        Article II. . . . . . . . . . . . . . . . . . . . . . 10
                Section 1. . . . . . . . . . . . . . . . . . . 10
                Section 2. . . . . . . . . . . . . . . . . . . 12
                Section 3. . . . . . . . . . . . . . . . . . . 13
                Section 4. . . . . . . . . . . . . . . . . . . 13
        Article III . . . . . . . . . . . . . . . . . . . . . 13
                Section 1. . . . . . . . . . . . . . . . . . . 14
                Section 2. . . . . . . . . . . . . . . . . . . 14
                                            Doc 1 Pg 1 Ln 1" Pos 1"
```

Figure 3-170.   Sample table of contents

Keystrokes

The procedure for creating a table of contents includes three basic steps. Each is discussed in detail in the sections that follow.

1. Block each item, and mark it for a specific table of contents level.

2. Define the location and format for the table of contents.

3. Generate the table.

Mark Each Item

1. Move the cursor to one end of the text to be included in the table of contents, and press Block (ALT-F4). If you include any codes in the block (such as bold, underline, or centering), they will be included in the table as well. Press Reveal Codes (ALT-F3) if you need to check the location of the codes.

2. Move the cursor to the opposite end to highlight the text.

3. Press Mark Text (ALT-F5).

4. Choose 1 for ToC.

5. Enter the number of the ToC Level (1 = major heading, 2 = heading, 3 = subheading, and so on). Each level can have its own type of page numbering and will be indented according to its level (level 1 would not be indented, level 2 would be indented to the first setting, level 3 to the second setting, and so on).

Define the Location and Format of the Table

1. Move the cursor to the location at which you want the table generated.

2. Press Hard Page (CTRL-ENTER) if you want the table of contents to appear on a separate page. Type a heading for the page if desired.

3. Move the cursor to the line at which the first line of the table of contents should appear.

4. Press Mark Text (ALT-F5).

5. Choose 5 for **Define**.

6. Choose 1 for Define Table of Contents. The following options are displayed:

```
Table of Contents Definition

    1 - Number of Levels          1

    2 - Display Last Level in      No
        Wrapped Format

    3 - Page Numbering - Level 1  Flush right with leader
                         Level 2
                         Level 3
                         Level 4
                         Level 5
```

7. Choose **1** and enter the **Number of Levels** that will be included in the table of contents (type a number indicating the number of the highest level marked).

8. If you want to have all the entries in each last level follow each other and wrap when the end of the line is reached, choose **2** for **Display Last Level in Wrapped Format**, and type **Y**. Leave the option at **N** if you want each entry left on a line by itself. The following example shows the last level being wrapped:

```
                    TABLE OF CONTENTS

The Constitution of the United States. . . . . . . . . . . . . .1
       Preamble. . . . . . . . . . . . . . . . . . . . . . . . .1
       Article I . . . . . . . . . . . . . . . . . . . . . . . .1
            Section 1 (1); Section 2 (1); Section 3 (2);
            Section 4 (4); Section 5 (4); Section 6 (5);
            Section 7 (5); Section 8 (6); Section 9 (8);
            Section 10 (9)
```

9. After you choose option **1** and indicate how many levels are to be included in the table of contents, the page number style "Flush right with leader" is inserted for the appropriate number of levels. If you want to make changes to the style, choose **3** for **Page Numbering**, and choose from the options at the bottom of the screen:

```
1 None; 2 Pg # Follows; 3 (Pg #) Follows; 4 Flush Rt; 5 Flush Rt with Leader: 0
```

If you have chosen to display the last level in a wrapped format, the page number cannot be flush against the right margin, either with or without a dot leader. Therefore, you are choosing a page number style for a wrapped level, only the first three options are displayed as choices.

The following example shows how each number listing style will appear when the table is generated:

No Page Numbers
Page Numbers Follow Entries 1; 4; 10
(Page Numbers) Follow Entries (1); (4); (10)
Flush Right Page Numbers   1, 4, 10
Flush Right Page Numbers with Leaders. 1, 4, 10

10. Press Hard Page (CTRL-ENTER) after the table of contents definition mark if you want the text of the document to start on a new page.

11. Because the table of contents will add a page and create an inaccurate page count, you can choose a new page number for the first page. To do so, press Format (SHIFT-F8), and choose **2** for **Page**, **6** for Page Numbering, and **1** for New Page Number.

Generate the Table of Contents

1. Press Mark Text (ALT-F5).

2. Choose **6** for **Generate**.

3. Choose **5** to **Generate** your Tables, Indexes, Cross-References, and so on.

4. The message "Existing tables, lists, and indexes will be replaced. Continue? Yes (No)" is displayed. Type **Y** to continue or **N** to return to the document.

A counter is displayed to let you know that progress is being made.

Hints

When you mark an entry to be included in a table of contents, the codes [Mark:ToC,n] and [EndMark:ToC,n] are inserted at the beginning and end of the block, where n indicates the level number for that item.

When you define the location of a table of contents, the code [DefMark:ToC,n:n] is inserted at the cursor location. The first n in this code indicates the number of levels chosen; the second n represents up to five numbers, each indicating the page style option that was chosen for each level. After a section is generated, an [EndDef] code is placed at the end of the table. If the table is generated a second time, these codes are used to block and delete the previous section so the newly generated table can be displayed in its place.

If you have used automatic paragraph numbering for the headings in your document, you can search for a paragraph number, block the entry, and mark it for the table of contents, rather than manually scrolling through the document. You can also create a style that includes the ToC marks in the style.

When a table of contents is generated, each item will appear in the order in which it appears in the document. You can mark additional items or delete the [Mark:ToC] codes and regenerate the table. The table of contents, table of authorities, lists, and index are all generated at once.

After the table of contents is generated, each entry will be preceded by the codes [→Indent] and [→Mar Rel]. These codes help create a hanging indent style for entries that are longer than one line. Each succeeding level has one additional →Indent code to move it to the next tab setting. If the table is not aligned correctly, you may need to adjust the tab settings. See "Tabs" in this chapter for more information.

You can edit the table after you have created it. If you choose the Dot Leader option for the page number listing, a dot leader is placed between the text and the page number. If text is added or deleted, the dot leader is automatically adjusted.

If you have selected a page number style in the Page Numbering menu, the page number style will be included as the page number in the generated table of contents. In other words, if "2-^B" is the page number style (meaning the current page in Chapter 2), "2-5," "2-10," and so on will be included in the table.

Error Messages

"Not Enough Memory"   WordPerfect uses document 2 (if available) to generate the tables, lists, and index. If it is not available, document 3 is used. If you get the error message "Not Enough Memory," exit document 2 so that the memory for that document can be used. If you still get the message, retrieve the document into document 2 and leave the document 1 screen clear. Generate can then use the additional memory in document 1 (which has twice as much memory allotted to it than document 2).

"No [DefMark] Found"   If you forget to define the location and format of the table, you will see the error message "No [DefMark] Found." Correct the situation and regenerate the table.

"Can't Find End of Table of Contents,. . ."   When you first generate a table, an [EndDef] code is placed at the end of the table. Each [DefMark] code then has a corresponding [EndDef] code. If you regenerate a table and the [DefMark:ToC,*n*] mark is accidentally deleted but the [EndDef] code is found, the message "Can't find end of table of contents, lists, or index text" is displayed.

If the [EndDef] code is deleted, the table of contents will be generated again, without deleting the first table. You would then get duplicate tables in the same location. If more than one [DefMark] code exists for the table of contents, it will be generated in both locations.

Related Entries

Block
New Page Number
Search
Tabs

TABLE BOX

A table box is a type of graphics box that you insert into a document and then have text flow around it. If the tables in your document include captions, all captions can be placed in a list automatically. You would need only to define list 7, and the captions would be inserted there after you generate the document.

See "Graphics Boxes" and "Lists" in this chapter for details.

TABLES

The Tables features is perhaps the most useful and easy to use of any of WordPerfect's new features. They can be used to format text or numbers into rows and columns (as shown in Figure 3-171), create forms, and provide an alternative to WordPerfect's parallel columns and math.

Tables can appear with or without lines or shading. Individual cells (similar to spreadsheet cells) can be bold, underlined, or assigned any other attribute available in WordPerfect. Each row can increase or decrease to fit the amount of text entered, or it can be set to a specific height. Columns can be left-, right-, center-, or decimal-aligned, and basic math (addition, subtraction, multiplication, and division) can be calculated for any number of cells in the table.

With just a few keystrokes, you can block and then convert columnar text that has already been entered with tabs or parallel columns to a table. You can also easily copy, move, or delete columns and rows.

You can insert merge codes in tables, which is especially handy for forms fill-in applications. Also, when you retrieve a spreadsheet from PlanPerfect, Lotus 1-2-3, or Excel, a table is automatically created to fit the format of that spreadsheet. See "Spreadsheet Importing and Linking" in this chapter for details.

Expenses First Quarter 1990			
	January	February	March
Mail	$1,750.00	$1,950.00	$2,000.00
Miscellaneous	$862.50	$1,547.50	$1,237.50
Office Supplies	$3,125.00	$2,125.00	$1,650.00
Payroll	$150,000.00	$150,000.00	$150,000.00
Phone	$1,125.00	$1,062.50	$1,250.00
Rent	$8,250.00	$8,250.00	$9,000.00
Taxes	$6,250.00	$6,250.00	$5,625.00
Utilities	$875.00	$862.50	$725.00
Totals	**$172,237.50**	**$172,047.50**	**$171,487.50**

Figure 3-171.   Sample table created in WordPerfect

Keystrokes

Keystrokes for creating a table, entering text, and making changes to a table are given here.

Creating a Table

1. Press Columns/Tables (ALT-F7).

2. Choose 2 for Tables.

3. Choose 1 for Create.

4. Enter the number of columns (or press ENTER to accept the number that is displayed). You can have up to 32 columns.

5. Enter the number of rows (or press ENTER to accept the number that is displayed). Up to 32,767 rows are allowed.

6. At this point, the table is created and the menu shown here is displayed at the bottom of the screen.

```
Table Edit:  Press Exit when done        Cell A1 Doc 2 Pg 1 Ln 3.31" Pos 1.12"

Ctrl-Arrows Column Widths; Ins Insert; Del Delete; Move Move/Copy;
1 Size; 2 Format; 3 Lines; 4 Header; 5 Math; 6 Options; 7 Join; 8 Split: 0
```

You can use the options on this menu to format the table, or press Exit (F7) to leave the menu and begin entering text in the table. If you need to return to the editing menu, move the cursor anywhere in the table and press Columns/Tables (ALT-F7).

Following is a discussion of the concepts involved in working with a table. Any keystrokes involved assume that you are editing the table and have the Table Edit menu displayed on the screen.

Each of the boxes in the table is called a cell. You can use the arrow keys (↑, ↓, ←, and →) to move from cell to cell. The current cell "number" is shown on the status line while in a table. Each column is lettered from left to right with A being column 1, B column 2, and so on. As shown in the Table Edit menu, Cell A1 is the cell in the first row and the first column.

When a table is created, WordPerfect checks the amount of space between the left and right margins and divides it by the number of columns. If you need to change the size of a column, you can do so by moving the cursor into any cell in the column and pressing CTRL-→ or CTRL-←. If you increase the size in one column and there is no space left between the right side of the table and the right margin, the amount of space in the columns to the right is decreased. Because the table is aligned at the left margin by default, it will not increase the amount of space in the remaining columns when a column is decreased, unless you have chosen to have the table justified "fully" between the left and right margins. See "Options" for details.

If you prefer, you can wait to change the size of the columns until you have entered all text in the table and have selected the final font. This is useful when you want to decrease or increase the size of the columns according to the amount of text in the columns. As you press CTRL-→ or CTRL-←, the text in the column readjusts automatically so that you can see how much text will fit within the boundaries.

Entering Text in a Table

After pressing Exit (F7) to leave the Table Edit menu, you can begin entering text.

You can use any key such as Bold (F6), Font (CTRL-F8), Center (SHIFT-F6), or Tab Align (CTRL-F6) to format the text in a table. However, if you want to affect all the text in a column, row, or other section of cells, you can format the cells with the Table Edit menu before or after you have entered the text. More information about formatting is included under "Options."

As you enter text, the height of a cell increases according to the number of lines entered. If you press ENTER or if the line wraps with a soft return [SRt] code, the new lines remain in the same cell. If you do not want the height to adjust to fit the amount of text entered, you can fix the row height for either single or multiple lines. If you enter a fixed row height for a single line, you can enter only one line. In this case, pressing ENTER moves the cursor to the next cell to the right. If you set the height for multiple lines, you can enter as many lines as you like; however, only the number of lines that fit in the set amount of space are printed. The Row Height option is found under the "Format" option on the Table Edit menu. See "Options" for details.

Moving the Cursor in a Table

Although there are other options for moving the cursor, TAB always moves to the next cell to the right, and SHIFT-TAB always moves to the next cell to the left. (If you need to insert a TAB into a cell, press HOME, TAB.)

If there is no text in the cell or if the cursor is on the first or last character in the cell, you can use the ← and → keys to go to the previous or next cell. If there is more than one line in a cell, ↑ and ↓ move through each line and then go to the next cell above or below.

If you have an enhanced keyboard, pressing ALT and any cursor key (not the ones on the numeric keypad) is an easy, consistent way to move from one cell to another. If you do not have an enhanced keyboard, you can write macros that include the commands {Item Up}, {Item Down}, {Item Right}, and {Item Left} and assign them to any ALT key combination. The steps for writing such a macro follow:

1. Press HOME, Macro Def (CTRL-F10). Pressing HOME lets you enter the macro editor immediately after entering the name and the description of the macro.

2. Enter the name. If you want to use an ALT key combination, press those keys. For example, if you want ALT-I to be {Item Up}, hold down ALT and type **I**.

3. Enter a description, or press ENTER to skip this step.

4. Press CTRL-PGUP to see a list of macro commands.

5. Move the cursor to the {Item Up} macro command, and press ENTER to select it. (You can move quickly to the command by typing its name).

6. Press Exit (F7) to leave the macro and return to the document.

After defining ALT-I, you can use it to go to the cell above. Use the keystrokes above to assign the other "Item" macro commands to ALT key combinations.

The keys used to move the cursor within text or parallel columns also work in tables. For example, you can press Go To (CTRL-HOME), → to go to the next column to the right and Go To (CTRL-HOME), ← to go to the next column to the left.

If you have a mouse, you can easily move the cursor to any location by moving the mouse pointer and clicking the left button.

Figure 3-172 contains a table showing which keys can be used to move to certain locations.

Location	Regular Keyboard	Enhanced Keyboard
One Cell Right	TAB or GoTo (CTRL-HOME), →	ALT-→
One Cell Left	SHIFT-TAB or GoTo (CTRL-HOME), ←	ALT-←
One Cell Up	↑ if cursor is at the top of cell	ALT-↑
One Cell Down	↓ if cursor is at the bottom of cell	ALT-↓
Beginning of Text in Cell	GoTo (CTRL-HOME), ↑	
End of Text in Cell	GoTo (CTRL-HOME), ↓	
Far Left of Row	GoTo (CTRL-HOME), HOME, ←	ALT-(HOME, ←)
Far Right of Row	GoTo (CTRL-HOME), HOME, →	ALT-(HOME, →)
Top of Column	GoTo (CTRL-HOME), HOME, ↑	ALT-(HOME, ↑)
Bottom of Column	GoTo (CTRL-HOME), HOME, ↓	ALT-(HOME, ↓)
First Cell in the Table	GoTo (CTRL-HOME), HOME, HOME, ↑	ALT-(HOME, HOME, ↑)
Last Cell in the Table	GoTo (CTRL-HOME), HOME, HOME, ↓	ALT-(HOME, HOME, ↓)

Figure 3-172.   Keystrokes used to move within a table

Making Changes to a Table

You can make changes to the table at any time: before, during, or after entering text. You can change the size of columns or change the number of rows and columns within the table; format individual cells, a block of cells, or columns; change the type of lines used in the table; add shading; specify one or more rows as a header for subsequent pages; join or split cells; and add, move, copy, or delete columns and rows.

To make changes, move the cursor into the table, and press Columns/Tables (ALT-F7). If the cursor is not in the table, you can press Columns/Tables (ALT-F7), and choose 2 for Tables and 2 for Edit. WordPerfect will then search to the left of the cursor until it finds a table to edit. If it cannot find one to the left, it searches to the right.

The Table Edit menu is displayed at the bottom of the screen, and the current cell is displayed on the status line, just as it is when the table is created. The menu is redisplayed here for future reference:

```
Table Edit: Press Exit when done        Cell A3 Doc 2 Pg 2 Ln 2.53" Pos 1.12"

Ctrl-Arrows Column Widths; Ins Insert; Del Delete; Move Move/Copy;
1 Size; 2 Format; 3 Lines; 4 Header; 5 Math; 6 Options; 7 Join; 8 Split: 0
```

Options

Because Tables are powerful and flexible, many options are available. Each of the following is optional and should not diminish the simplicity of the Tables feature.

Any keystrokes involved assume that you are editing a table and the Table Edit menu displayed above is on the screen.

Changing the Size of a Column

Move the cursor to any location in the column and press CTRL-→ or CTRL-← to increase or decrease the size of the current column.

Before you adjust the size of the columns, you may want to make sure that the correct font is selected. Any text within the table will reformat to fit the column as the width is adjusted.

If you want to set an exact width for the column, you can do so by choosing option **2** for Format, **2** for Column, and **1** for **W**idth. Press ENTER to accept the current width, or enter a new number. To set the same width for more than one column at a time, block at least one cell in each column with Block (ALT-F4) before following the previous steps.

If you want to change the size by removing cell borders, you can do so by joining two or more cells. You can also split one cell into multiple rows or columns. More about joining or splitting cells is found in "Joining/Splitting Cells" later in this section.

Adding/Deleting Rows and Columns   There are two ways to add or delete rows and columns. The first method inserts or deletes rows or columns at the right side or bottom of the table. The second inserts or deletes them within the table.

To add or delete rows or columns at the right and bottom of the table, follow these steps:

1. Move the cursor into the table and press Columns/Tables (ALT F7) to display the Table Edit menu.

2. Choose **1** for Size.

3. Choose **1** for **R**ows or **2** for Columns. The current number of rows or columns in the table is displayed.

4. Enter the new total number of rows or columns. For example, if you had ten columns and you wanted to delete the last four, you would enter **6** for the total number of columns.

To insert or delete rows or columns within the table, follow these four steps:

1. If you are adding a row or rows, move the cursor just below the point where the new row(s) are to be inserted. If you are adding a column or columns, move the cursor just after the point where the new column(s) are to be inserted. In other words, rows are inserted above the cursor, and columns are inserted to the left of the cursor.

If you are deleting rows or columns, move the cursor into the first row or column to be deleted.

2. Press INS to insert new rows or columns, or press DEL to delete rows or columns.

3. Choose **1** for **R**ows or **2** for **C**olumns.

4. Enter the number of rows or columns to be added or deleted.

If you have an enhanced keyboard, you can press CTRL-INS to insert a single row into the table at any time (even if the Table Edit menu is not displayed on the screen).

Format

When entering text into the table, you can set the format for each cell. You can also block the text in the cells and assign various attributes to those cells.

By using the Format option, however, you can format cells without inserting codes. The Format option on the Table Edit menu will also save you keystrokes. For example, instead of pressing Center (SHIFT-F6) to center text in a cell, you could have the format of the cell (or column) centered and save that keystroke. If you used the Format option, the cell would take on the formatting without inserting any codes. Use the method with which you feel most comfortable.

The Format option also provides other formatting features that are unique to tables and are not available from the regular keyboard.

When you choose **2** for **F**ormat, you will see the options to format a cell (or block of cells) and columns. You can also set the height of a row with the Format option.

```
Table Edit:  Press Exit when done        Cell A3 Doc 2 Pg 2 Ln 2.73" Pos 1.12"

Cell: Top;Left;Normal                 Col: 2.17";Left;Normal
Format: 1 Cell; 2 Column; 3 Row Height: 0
```

The format of the current cell (vertical alignment, justification, and attributes) is displayed to the left of the menu, while the format for the current column (width, justification, and attributes) is displayed to the right. In this example, text will be aligned with the top of the cell, left-justified, and will appear in the normal base font. The column width is 2.17″, it is left-justified, and it will appear in the normal base font.

Notice that there is not a Row option; only a Row Height option. If you want to affect the formatting for an entire row or a section of cells, press Block (ALT-F4), move the cursor to highlight all the cells to be affected, and then choose **2** for Format. If you choose **1** for Cell, all the cells in the block will be affected. If you choose **2** for Column, each column in the block will be affected.

Table 3-20 lists all the items that are available under each option. A brief summary of these options follows in the order in which they appear in Table 3-20.

1- Cell

Type   WordPerfect assumes that all entries in a table are numbers, so they can be included when you are calculating math. If you want to force them to be considered as text so they won't be included in any calculations (such as a phone number or a ZIP code), you can choose **2** for Format, **1** for Cell, **1** for Type, and **2** for Text.

Attributes   If you want a cell bolded or underlined, you can move to the cell and press Bold (F6) or Underline (F8) while in the Table Edit menu. You can turn off the attributes by moving to the cell and pressing the keys again. To bold or underline more than one cell, block the cells with Block (ALT-F4) first. The ″Pos″ indicator on the status line displays the attributes for a cell just as it would in a regular document.

You can use the Attribute menu option to set any of the Size or Appearance options normally found on the Font (CTRL-F8) key. Note that both cells and columns can have attributes assigned to them. You can use these attributes to bold headings and totals or to draw attention to a certain column in a table. If you turn an attribute on, it stays on until you choose the attribute again to turn it off or until you choose Normal or Reset (Reset is available only for cells and is used to force the cells to take on the attributes of the column). Normal resets all attributes in the cell back to the normal base font.

```
1 - Cell
     1 - Type
          1 - Numeric
          2 - Text
     2 - Attributes
          1 - Size
          2 - Appearance
          3 - Normal
          4 - Reset
     3 - Justify
          1 - Left
          2 - Center
          3 - Right
          4 - Full
          5 - Decimal Align
          6 - Reset
     4 - Vertical Alignment
          1 - Top
          2 - Bottom
          3 - Center
     5 - Lock
          1 - On
          2 - Off

2 - Column
     1 - Width
     2 - Attributes
          1 - Size
          2 - Appearance
          3 - Normal
     3 - Justify
          1 - Left
          2 - Center
          3 - Right
          4 - Full
          5 - Decimal Align
     4 - # Digits

3 - Row Height
     Single Line:   1 - Fixed
                    2 - Auto
     Multi-line:    3 - Fixed
                    4 - Auto
```

Table 3-20.   List of Table Format Options

Justify   The Justification option is available for both cells and columns, and it lets you choose between left-, center-, right-, full-, and decimal-aligned text. An additional option, Reset, appears for cells. As with Attributes Reset, you can use this option to return the justification of the cell(s) to the current column setting.

The Justification option would be useful to format a column of numbers so they would be right- or decimal-aligned. You could choose center justification for a row of cells that include a heading or title. The default selection is left. However, if you import a spreadsheet, the cell or column will be aligned as it was in the spreadsheet (either left or right). Remember that the Math feature in a table calculates numbers regardless of their justification.

Vertical Alignment   You can choose Top, Bottom, or Center as the vertical alignment for a cell. By default, text in all cells is aligned with the top of the cell. WordPerfect automatically leaves one-tenth of an inch (.1″) between the top of the text and the top line of the cell. To change the amount of space, choose 6 for Options from the Table Edit menu, and then choose 1 for Spacing Between Text and Lines.

If you have a row at the top of a table that contains headings for the columns, you could choose Bottom to have the bottom of the last line in the heading placed at the bottom of the cell. The Center option could be useful if you have a different number of lines in each cell in the row. Each heading would be centered vertically within its own cell, regardless of the number of lines. An example of vertically centered headings is shown in Figure 3-171 earlier in this section.

Lock   You can use the Lock option to lock a cell or a block of cells. This prevents you from entering text into the cell, changing text that already exists in the cell (you can lock the cells after you have entered the text), or moving and copying those cells. If you need to unlock the cells and edit the text, you can reenter the Table Edit menu, move the cursor to the cells in question, and turn Lock off. You would use this feature when creating a Form for forms fill-in and do not want the user to edit the text in certain cells. You could also use it to lock the cells containing a math formula. The formula would still be calculated, but the user would not be able to edit the total. See "Applications" for examples of a form in which Lock was used to protect the headings and the total.

2 - Column

Width   In the Column category, you have two options that are different from those found in the Cell category: Width and # Digits. You can use the Width option to set the current column to an exact width. If you are increasing the size of a column, the columns at the right will be decreased if necessary so that the table will continue to fit within the margins. If you decrease the size of a column, the other columns will not increase to fill the space between the margins *unless* you have set the position of the table at Full (which means full justification at both margins). To do so, choose 6 for Options from the main Table Edit menu, and then choose 3 for Position of Table and 4 for Full.

If you set the width of all columns so that they will not fit within the margins, the portion of the table that extends beyond the right margin will not print. Remember that while you are in the Format menu, the current width of a column is displayed at the right side of the screen on the status line (Col:width;justification;attributes).

 # Digits   You can specify the number of digits that should appear to the right of the decimal point after a calculation. The default setting is 2, so you can see the calculation to the penny. Enter 0 if you want calculations rounded to a whole number.

3 - Row Height

When you Choose the Row Height option, the following choices appear.

```
Row Height -- Single line: 1 Fixed; 2 Auto;  Multi-line: 3 Fixed; 4 Auto: 4
```

These options determine whether the line height should be adjusted to fit a single line or multiple lines. The option is similar to the Line

Height option on the Line Format menu; the height can either grow to fit the current font (automatic) or be fixed to a specific height. These options are invaluable when you are creating forms that are to be filled in with certain information, because you can limit the amount of space given to a line. You can also choose to allow only one line in a cell by choosing the Single Line option. If you set a cell to accept only a single line, pressing ENTER will not start a new line in the same cell, but will place the cursor in the next cell automatically.

If you set a cell that already contains text to "Single Line," the remaining lines will not be displayed or printed. However, if you return to a Multi-Line row or change the font so that more characters can fit on the line, WordPerfect remembers the text that appears to have been deleted and displays it again. If you set a Multi-Line row at a fixed height, you can enter as much text as you would like, and it will be displayed on the screen. However, the text extending past the point at which the cell was fixed will not appear when this document is viewed or printed.

See "Applications" for a form that was created with fixed row heights—both for single and multiline rows.

This concludes the many options included under the Format category of the Table Edit menu. The remaining options on the Edit menu are discussed next.

Lines and Shading

When you create a table, WordPerfect places a double-lined box around the table and single lines to form a grid separating the cells. You can change the style of the lines or turn them off in any section of the table with option 3 for Lines on the Table Edit menu. The Lines option also lets you turn on shading for a cell or block of cells.

Before choosing the Lines option, press Block (ALT-F4), and highlight all the cells that will be affected by the line change. If you are adding shading, block the cells that you want shaded. For example, if you want to include double lines around a heading, or shade the heading as shown in Figure 3-172, you would block those cells in the heading and then choose 3 for Lines from the Table Edit menu. The following choices appear:

```
Table Edit:  Press Exit when done      Cell A1* Doc 2 Pg 2 Ln 7,16" Pos 1,12"
```
```
Top=Double; Left=Double; Bottom=None; Right=None
1 None; 2 Single; 3 Double; 4 Dashed; 5 Dotted; 6 Thick; 7 Extra Thick; 0
```

Take note of the second to the last line, which tells the current "status" of each line. Even though it appears that there are single lines on the bottom and right sides, these lines actually "belong" to the cells below. In other words, a cell controls only the top and left sides. You need to know this because if you set Single for the bottom line and the cell below also has that line set to Single, you will see a slightly thicker line because two single lines will be printed together. This happens for all types of lines, not just single ones. If this happens, enter one of the cells and choose None for that side.

If you want to shade the highlighted cells, choose 8 for Shade and then 1 for On or 2 for Off. The cell number on the status line will change to reverse video to indicate when shading is on for a cell.

If you are changing the style of lines or are turning them off, choose an option from 1 to 7 in the menu above. These options let you choose the lines to be affected.

Note: You can affect the lines inside the highlighted block, outside the block, all the lines, or those on only one side of the block.

After selecting the location of the lines, you will be presented with the following choices:

1 None; 2 Single; 3 Double; 4 Dashed; 5 Dotted; 6 Thick; 7 Extra Thick: 0

If you do not want any lines displayed, choose **1** for None. Each cell will remain as an individual cell, even if the lines are not displayed. If you want the table to then be single spaced, enter the Options menu (number 6 on the Table Edit menu) and change the amount of space between text lines to 0″. The text will still appear as double spaced on the screen, but will print correctly. See ″Joining or Splitting Cells″ for an option to remove the lines and treat the cells as one.

You could use the option for removing lines (but keeping the individual cells intact) in an invoice in which each item is to occupy a single line but lines within the itemized section of the invoice should not be displayed. See ″Applications″ for an example of how this is done.

Header for Subsequent Pages

If you have a table that is longer than one page, you may want to specify which row or rows are to be used as a header. The row or rows will not be displayed on the screen, but will appear when the table is viewed or printed.

From anywhere in the table, choose **4** for Header. You are then prompted to enter the number of rows to be included in the header. If you choose **1**, the first row in the table will be used. If you type a number greater than one, WordPerfect will use that many rows, starting with the first row in the table. You can turn the headers off at any point in the table by choosing **4** for Header and entering **0** as the number of rows.

When you move the cursor into a row that is being used as a header, an asterisk (∗) is displayed next to the cell number, as shown in the illustration above.

Math

WordPerfect's main Math feature in tables is similar to WordPerfect's Math feature but is easier to use, because you can refer to specific cells instead of columns that are based on tab settings. It is also more powerful, because any cell in the table can be included in a calculation. This is different from WordPerfect's regular Math feature, in which numbers being calculated must be in the same row or column. Any number in a table can be included in a calculation, regardless of the type of alignment or "justification" chosen for the cell or column.

You can use math to calculate subtotals, totals, and grand totals. You can include the four basic math functions—addition (+), subtraction (−), multiplication (*), and division (/)—in a formula.

When you choose 5 for **Math**, the following menu appears.

```
Math: 1 Calculate; 2 Formula; 3 Copy Formula; 4 ▯; 5 ▯; 6 ▯: 0
```

Option **1** Calculates any formulas or totals in the table, **2** lets you enter a **Formula** in the current cell, and **3** lets you Copy a Formula to a specific cell or to a number of cells down or to the right.

Options **4** (+), **5** (=), and **6** (*) are used to calculate a subtotal, total, or grand total for a particular column. You must use these options from the menu; you cannot enter a +, =, or * from the keyboard, or they would be considered characters—not math operators.

Before entering a formula, move the cursor to each cell that is to be included in the formula, and make a note of its number (shown on the status line). This will make it easier when you are entering the formula so you don't have to stop and check the number of a particular cell.

To enter a formula, move the cursor to the cell that is to contain the formula (and result of the calculation), and choose 5 for **Math** and 2 for **Formula**. Enter the formula, using any cell number, regular number, or the following operators:

+	Add
−	Subtract
*	Multiply
/	Divide

Some examples of formulas are **B3+B4−F7, D4∗1.05,** and **3/.22.** You can also copy the value of one numeric cell to another by entering the number of that cell when you are asked for the formula. For example, if you wanted the number for cell A5 to be displayed in A10 as well, you could enter **A5** as the formula for A10.

Once you enter a formula, it is displayed in the lower left corner of the screen whenever the cursor is in that cell.

If you need the same formula for another cell or cells, you can copy the formula to a specific cell, down, or to the right a specific number of times. The cell numbers in the formula will change according to the new relative position. For example, if cell C1 contained the formula A1+B1, you could copy it down to cell C2, and the formula would change to A2+B2. WordPerfect looks at the relative position of the cells and changes them to match the new location.

To copy a formula, place the cursor in the cell that contains the formula, choose **5** for **M**ath, and then choose **3** for Copy Formula. (If the current cell does not contain a formula, you cannot choose the Copy Formula option.) The following menu appears:

```
Copy Formula To: 1 Cell; 2 Down; 3 Right: 0
```

Choose **1** if you want to Copy the Formula to a particular Cell, and then enter the number of that cell. To copy the formula to a number of cells to the right or down from the current cell, choose **2** for **D**own or **3** for **R**ight. When you are prompted to do so, enter the number of times to copy the formula. As you move through each cell, the new formula is displayed in the lower left corner of the screen.

If you want to have WordPerfect calculate a subtotal, total, or grand total for a particular column, use options **4 +, 5 =,** or **6 ∗,** respectively. A subtotal adds all the numbers above or until it reaches another cell that contains +, =, or ∗. If there is more than one subtotal, all the numbers are totaled from one cell containing + to the next.

A Total (=) totals all the Subtotals (+) above, and a Grand Total (∗) totals all the Totals (=). See "Applications" for an example of an invoice that uses formulas, subtotals, and totals.

Options

Item **6** for **O**ptions displays the options shown in Figure 3-173. These items control the amount of spacing between the text and lines of the cells, how to display a negative result of a calculation (with a minus sign or in parentheses), the position of the table (left, center, right, or full), and the percentage of black to use for shading. Remember that the number of digits that will be displayed after a calculation is controlled by the Column Format option.

The options found in this menu affect the entire table—not individual cells or columns. If you change the Gray Shading option, it will affect all the shading in that particular table.

Option **1** for **S**pacing Between Text and Lines shows the default settings that are normally used. If you want a table to be single spaced, change the .1″ top spacing to 0″.

If you have used parentheses to indicate negative numbers in a table, you will probably want to change option **2** to **D**isplay the Negative Results within parentheses as well. You can enter negative numbers in a table with either a minus sign or parentheses, regardless of how you set this option.

```
Table Options

        1 - Spacing Between Text and Lines
                Left                    0.083"
                Right                   0.083"
                Top                     0.1"
                Bottom                  0"

        2 - Display Negative Results    1
                1 = with minus signs
                2 = with parentheses

        3 - Position of Table           Left

        4 - Gray Shading (% of black)   10%




Selection: 0
```

Figure 3-173.   Table Options menu

When a table is created, it fills the amount of space between the left and right margins. However, if you decrease the size of any of the columns, the table will no longer fill the space between the margins unless you increase the size of another column. If you choose option 3 for Position of table, you will see the following options:

Table Position: 1 Left; 2 Right; 3 Center; 4 Full; 5 Set Position: 0

Note that although option **1**, the default, is Left, you can choose option **2** to align the table with the **R**ight margin or **3** to **C**enter the table between the margins. If you choose **4** for Full, the table will always fill the space between the left and right margins. If you decrease the amount of space in one column, the others increase automatically.

You can also enter the exact horizontal position for a table with option **5** for Set Position. After selecting this option, enter the measurement from the left side of the page.

The last option on this menu lets you select the amount of shading to be used for shaded cells. Enter any percentage between 0 and 100. If you have a PostScript printer, you can choose to print shading in 100 percent black and choose white as the text color: Press Font (CTRL-F8), and choose **5** for Print Color and **2** for White.

Joining/Splitting Cells

Two of the more important formatting options are Join and Split, which let you block a section of cells and make them one, or divide a cell into more than one row or column. You can use the Join option to join a row of cells so they can be used as a heading, and you can use the Split option to divide a cell into many smaller cells.

To join any number of cells, press Block (ALT-F4), highlight the block of cells to be joined, choose **7** for Join, and then type **Y** to confirm that you want the cells to be joined. All lines will disappear, and the cell will be treated as a single cell. The example shown in Figure 3-174 was created using the Join feature to make some cells larger than others (some classes are two-hour blocks while others are one-hour blocks).

To split a cell, move the cursor to that cell, and choose **8** for Split. Choose **1** to split it into **R**ows or **2** to split it into **C**olumns, and then enter the number of rows or columns. If you have joined cells and then split them again, they will revert to their original structure. In fact, if you split any cell, it tries to match the surrounding structure. If you block a section of cells and choose to split them, each cell within the block will be split into the specified number of rows or columns.

This may make it difficult to create a table in which one section is different from another. If this happens, you can define one section of the table and then define a second table with a different structure. The two tables appear to be separated on the screen, but they will print together as long as nothing is between the [Tbl Off] code from the first table and the [Tbl Def] code for the second table. Because a double line is normally placed around the box, you may want to change the line style so that they will appear to be one table.

The invoice in "Applications" is an example of how this was done with three different tables. It also makes use of the Join and Split features.

Moving Blocks, Columns, or Rows

When you need to move text from one cell to another, you can use the normal Move (CTRL-F4) feature. If you need to move an entire section, column(s), or row(s), you can use the Move feature within tables. This

Monday	Business Room	English/History Room	Art Room
9:00-10:00	Typing	Current Affairs	Painting
10:10-11:10	Advanced Calculus		Sculpture
11:20-12:20		History	
12:20-1:30	Lunch	Lunch	Lunch
1:40-2:40	Business Machines	English	Etching
2:50-3:50		Modern Literature	Drama
4:00-5:00	Accounting		

Figure 3-174.   Using Join to join cells for a larger block of time on the schedule

feature lets you easily move, copy, or delete the current column, row, or block. This is useful if you need to switch columns or rows in a table.

The following keystrokes help you move, copy, and delete large sections of a table:

1. Move the cursor into the table, and press Columns/Tables (ALT- F7) to display the Table Edit menu.

2. Move the cursor into the row or column to be moved, copied, or deleted. If you are moving, copying, or deleting a block of cells, rows, or columns, press Block (ALT-F4) and highlight the cells, rows, or columns to be included in the block. To affect more than one row or column, you need to block only one cell in each row or column to be affected—not the entire row or column.

3. Press Move (CTRL-F4). The following appears:

Move: 1 Block; 2 Row; 3 Column; 4 Retrieve: 0

4. Choose **1** for **B**lock (if no block is defined, only the current cell will be affected), **2** for **R**ow, or **3** for Column. The following options appear:

1. Move; 2 Copy; 3 Delete: 0

5. Choose **1** for Move, **2** for Copy, or **3** for Delete.

6. Move the cursor to the position where the row(s) or column(s) are to be retrieved. If you are retrieving a block of cells, move the cursor into the first cell that is to contain the first cell of information from the block.

7. Press Move (CTRL-F4), and choose **4** for Retrieve. The last thing that was moved or copied will be retrieved.

If you delete a block, a row, or a column, you can undelete it later by moving the cursor to the proper location, pressing Cancel (F1), and then typing **Y** when you are asked if you want to undelete the block, row, or column. Only the last deletion is remembered.

If you are moving or deleting a block, only the text in that block is moved or deleted; the empty cells remain. If you are moving or deleting rows or columns, the entire section is moved or deleted.

If you need to retrieve a section again, choose **4** for **R**etrieve. If you have not just moved or copied something, you will be asked if you want to retrieve the last row, column, or block that was moved or copied.

Hints

When you create a table, a table definition code is inserted at the beginning of the table to indicate the table number, the number of columns, and the width of each of those columns. A [Row] code is placed at the beginning of each row and [Cell] codes are used to separate each column. The code [Tbl Off] is placed at the end of the table.

In the following example, the table is numbered as number 1 (Roman numeral I), there are three columns in the table, and the widths of the columns are 1.25″, 2.5″, and 1.75″. A [Row] code is inserted for each row in the table (in this case there are four rows), and a [Cell] code indicates the number of columns in each row (in this case three).

```
[Tbl Def:I;3,1.25″,2.5″,1.75″]
[Row][Cell][Cell][Cell]
[Row][Cell][Cell][Cell]
[Row][Cell][Cell][Cell]
[Row][Cell][Cell][Cell][Tbl Off]
```

The [Row] and [Cell] codes preserve the format of the table; they cannot be deleted. You also are not allowed to delete the [Tbl Off] code. You can, however, delete the [Tbl Def] code. If you do so, each [Row] code will be converted to a hard return [HRt] code, and each [Cell] code will be converted to a single tab. The table will take on the appearance of the current tab settings. If you are going to delete the [Tbl Def] code and convert the table to tabbed text, you might consider moving above the table and setting tabs so the table will be formatted properly. You can, of course, set the tabs after the [Tbl Def] code has been deleted.

If you delete the [Tbl Def] code, you cannot undelete the definition. However, if you block the entire table and delete it, you will be able to undelete it.

Tables are numbered along with any graphics table boxes, if there are any in the document. This may be important if you are trying to keep track of the numbers that are displayed at the top of a table box. Also, the captions may be misnumbered. If you have both features in one document, you may want to consider placing the table inside a table box.

Tables can span several pages. In fact, you can press Hard Page (CTRL-ENTER) to insert a page break at any time. (The code [Hrd Row] would be inserted.) Rows are never split between page breaks (identical to parallel columns with Block Protect). When you reach a soft page break or insert a hard page break, it may seem as if the borders at the bottom of one page and top of the next will not print correctly; however, when you view or print the document, you will see that the top and bottom borders do print correctly.

You can include styles in a table and include tables in styles.

Tables and Columns

Do not try to define and turn on columns if a table is found after the cursor in the document. Your table definition will be deleted and cannot be retrieved again. You will also find that you cannot create a table when Columns is already on.

If you need to include a table in columns, create a graphics box (any type will do), and then create the table while you are in the graphics box. The position of the table will be changed to Full to keep it within the boundaries of the graphics box. This solution will also help you place two tables side by side on a page. Define two columns, and then create two graphics boxes in each column. While editing the graphics box, create the tables.

Although you can also include graphics boxes inside table cells, you cannot do so if the table is already part of a graphics box.

Merging Information into a Table

You can place merge codes in any section of a table to cause text from a secondary file to merge in certain locations, or you can use the merge's {KEYBOARD} or {INPUT} commands to pause and insert text into a form during the merge.

If you want to merge a list of data from a secondary merge file, and have the merge add the appropriate number of rows for you, you can set up the table as follows:

1. Create a table with at least two rows. You can have more rows *above* these two rows, but only two are involved in the merge.

2. Insert the merge codes as indicated here. In this example, the first three fields are being placed into columns 1, 2, and 3. All records will be placed in their own row. To insert the merge commands, press Merge Codes (SHIFT-F9) twice, type the name of the command, and then press ENTER to select it. You can select {FIELD} and {NEXT RECORD} from the one-line menu after you press Merge Codes (SHIFT-F9) once. If you need further assistance, see "Merge" in this chapter.

{LABEL}top~{FIELD}1~	{FIELD}2~	{FIELD}3~{NEXT RECORD}
{GO}top~		

3. After the merge is finished, you may also want to change the line style, because the inside lines were inserted as double lines during the merge process. Move the cursor inside the table, press Columns/Table (ALT-F7) to display the Table Edit menu, press HOME, HOME, ↑ to move the first cell in the table, press Block (ALT-F4), then HOME, HOME, ↓ to block the entire table. Choose 3 for Lines, 5 for Inside, then 2 for Single.

With the Sort feature, you can sort rows in a table according to the information in any column (see "Sort and Select" for more information).

Applications

You can also use tables as a substitute for the Parallel Columns feature. If you don't want lines separating the columns, you can turn them off.

To box a section of text, as shown in this section, create a table with one column and one row. Change the "outside" lines if necessary (in the following example they were changed to "single"), and then press Exit (F7) to leave the Table Edit menu. Start typing the text that should be inserted into the table. The height of the table will grow to fit the amount of text that you enter, up to one page of text.

> **You can easily box text by creating a table consisting of one column and one row. The height of the box will grow with the text. If you need to insert a TAB as shown at the beginning of this paragraph, press HOME, then TAB.**

You can use the Tables feature to create anything from a simple "sign-up" sheet or checklist, as shown in Figure 3-175, to a complex invoice form, as shown in Figure 3-176. Calendars can also be created easily with the Tables feature, as shown in Figure 3-177.

You can even use the Tables feature to create a crossword puzzle, as shown in Figure 3-178.

A few notes follow about each of the applications shown.

Sign-up Sheet or Checklist

Instead of filling a page with lines drawn with the Line Draw feature or inserting horizontal graphics lines, you can use the Tables feature to create the form shown in Figure 3-175.

Notice that a graphics image was included at the right side of the top cell. The height of the graphics box was set at .75", and the width was automatically adjusted to fit that height. The height of the cell grew automatically to fit the size of the graphics box. The borders for the graphics box were set to "none" so they wouldn't interfere with the lines in the table.

Invoice

The invoice shown in Figure 3-176 was created with three separate columns, one defined immediately after another to compensate for the differences in format. The lines between tables were changed to Single. Because there are two single lines together, it caused a thicker single

Bicycle Race Sign-Up Sheet				
Name	Address	Phone	F	I

Check **F** if you have paid the entrance fee; **I** if you have turned in an Insurance Form

Figure 3-175.   Sample sign-up sheet

line to print. If you do not want this to happen, you can change the border to None for one side and leave it at Single for another.

Phone-Mart Shopping

Sold To: Ship To:

Invoice	Date	Terms

Purchase Order	Ship Via	Work Order

Item No.	Description	Qty	Price	Total

	Sub-Total	+
TERMS: Net 30 Days	Sales Tax	E11*.045
Interest on Past Due Accounts	Total	E11+E12
1.5% per Month on Balances	Amount Paid	
30 Days Past Due	Amount Due	E13-E14

Figure 3-176.   Invoice created with three tables

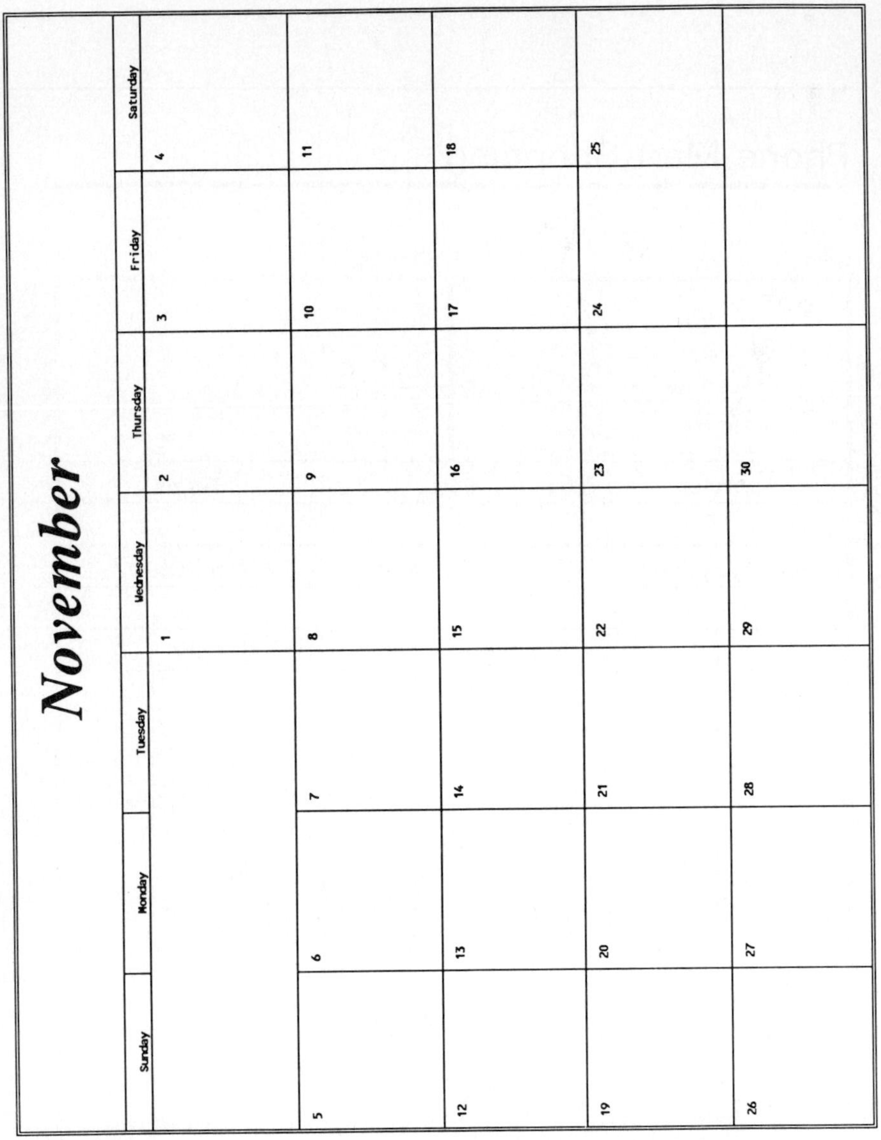

November

Sunday	Monday	Tuesday	Wednesday	Thursday	Friday	Saturday
			1	2	3	4
5	6	7	8	9	10	11
12	13	14	15	16	17	18
19	20	21	22	23	24	25
26	27	28	29	30		

Figure 3-177. You can include equations in a calendar to create a larger heading

Figure 3-178.   Crossword puzzle created with the Tables feature

Many table options were used, including Row Height (fixed single and multiline rows), Vertical Alignment, Justification in columns, Join, Split, and Math. Note that the math formulas are included in the invoice to give you an idea as to how the totals are calculated.

Calendar

A landscape type of paper was selected for the calendar in Figure 3-177 by pressing Format (SHIFT-F8), choosing **2** for **P**age and **7** for Paper Size/Type, and then selecting a "wide" 11″ by 8.5″ paper definition from the menu. Margins were set at 1/4″ to allow more room for the calendar.

Next, a table was created with seven columns and seven rows. All cells, with the exception of the cells in the top two rows, were blocked and assigned a fixed row height by choosing **2** for **F**ormat, **3** for **R**ow Height, and **3** for Multi-line Fixed. The measurement of **1.3**″ was entered. Enter a different setting if you choose.

The cells in the top row were then blocked and joined. You can also join cells for nonexistent days in the calendar. You can use this valuable space for notes, messages, or phone numbers.

To create the calendar title, exit the Table Edit menu, move the cursor to the cell in the top row, and follow these keystrokes:

1. Press Graphics (ALT-F9).

2. Choose **6** for **E**quation and then **1** to Create.

3. Choose **9** for **E**dit to enter the equation editor.

4. Type the name of the month, and press F9 to display it in the window above.

5. Press Setup (SHIFT-F1) and choose option **2** for **G**raphical Font Size and **2** for **S**et Point Size. Enter a number for the point size. Keep in mind that 72 points make an inch. The example in Figure 3-177 used 50.

6. Press Exit (F7) until you return to the table.

Print the table. The heading will print in Courier, Helvetica, or Times Roman, whichever is closest to the document's initial base font. If you want to change the initial base font, press Format (SHIFT-F8) and choose **3** for **D**ocument and **3** for Initial Base **F**ont.

Crossword Puzzle

A fun example that shows off the flexibility of tables is the crossword puzzle shown in Figure 3-178. The width of each column is set at .35″ (block all columns and set the width once), and the row height is set to a fixed single line of .35″ high (again, use Block to set the row height for all the rows at once).

All cells in the table were blocked and all lines were turned off (select None). The cursor was then moved to the proper location within the table, and Block (ALT-F4) was used to block the number of cells needed for a word. After choosing Lines, the All option was selected so that all lines inside and outside the block would be affected, and then Single was chosen for the line style.

When some of the lines appeared as thick single lines when the puzzle was first printed, the puzzle was modified so that only one single line was used instead of two.

Hopefully, these applications have given you ideas about how to use tables.

Related Entries

Merge
Sort and Select
Spreadsheet Importing and Linking

TABS

Tabs are preset for every one-half inch. WordPerfect lets you clear and set individual or multiple tabs.

Keystrokes

1. Press Format (SHIFT-F8).

2. Choose 1 for **L**ine.

3. Choose 8 for **T**ab Set. The Tab Set menu appears, as shown here:

```
L.....L.....L.....L.....L.....L.....L.....L.....L.....L.....L.....L.....L.
;     ^     ;     ^     ;     ^     ;     ^     ;     ^     ;     ^     ;
0"         +1"        +2"        +3"        +4"        +5"        +6
Delete EOL (clear tabs); Enter Number (set tab); Del (clear tab);
Type; Left; Center; Right; Decimal; .= Dot Leader; Press Exit when done.
```

4. Clear or set tabs. (See the following discussions of tab setting and clearing options for further instruction.)

5. Press Exit (F7) when you are finished.

Clear Individual Tab Settings

1. If the cursor is not on the tab setting that you want cleared, use the arrow keys to move to the tab setting that you want deleted or enter the position number. You can press ↑ or ↓ to move to the previous or next tab setting, or → and ← to move along the line. If you have an enhanced keyboard, you can use ALT-→ and ALT-← to move to the next or previous tab setting.

2. Press DEL or BACKSPACE to delete the tab.

Clear All Tabs

1. Press HOME, HOME, ← to move to the beginning of the line.

2. Press Delete to End of Line (CTRL-END) to delete all tab settings. If you have a mouse, you can point to "Delete EOL" and click the left button.

Set Individual Tabs

1. If the cursor is not where you want the tab to be set, enter the position number or use → and ← to move the cursor to the correct position. If you have to enter a fraction of an inch (for example, .25), you can enter it as a fraction (1/4), or enter it with a leading zero (0.25). If you do not enter 0 first, and type a decimal point instead, WordPerfect thinks that you want to set a decimal-aligned tab.

2. If you enter the exact position, an "L" is automatically inserted for a normal, left-aligned tab. The following list shows the types of tabs that you can set. Enter one of these letters if desired:

L   Normal, left-aligned tab

R   Right-aligned tab

C   Centered tab (text is centered at the tab setting)

D   Decimal tab (text is aligned on the decimal point at the tab setting)

After setting a tab, you can type a period (.) if you want a dot leader to appear between that tab and the previous tab. The following example shows all types of tab settings: Left, right, decimal-aligned, and centered with a dot leader.

Richard L. Anderson	Training	$500.00	.................Daily
Howard Bankett, Jr.	Consultant	$100.00	...............Hourly
Sharon F. Day	Programmer	$1,000.00	...............Weekly
Jason Weeks	Training	$150.00	...............Hourly
Elaine Johnson	Systems Analyst	$2,000.00	...............Weekly

There are also other ways to enter dot leaders on a one-time basis. See "Hints" for details.

Set Multiple Tabs

1. Clear the tabs first if necessary.

2. Enter the position for the first tab stop, a comma, and the interval. For example, entering **1,.75** would set tabs every 3/4 inch, beginning at the 1-inch mark.

Remember that if you need to set a fraction of an inch, you can enter the measurement as a fraction or with a leading zero.

Changing the Position or Type of Tab Setting

1. Move the cursor to the tab setting to be moved. Remember that you can press ↑ or ↓ to move to the next or previous tab setting.

2. Press CTRL-← to move the tab setting to the left, or press CTRL-→ to move it to the right. The text below the tab setting will change position as well, so you can see the effect immediately.

You can change tabs from one type to another, such as from left- to decimal-aligned or from center- to right-aligned and the text will automatically adjust to the new type.

Hints

When you set tabs with regular intervals, a [Tab Set] code, similar to [Tab Set:type: n'', every n''], is inserted into the document. If you set several individual tabs, it could appear as [Tab Set:type: n'',n'',n''] and so on, listing all the tab settings. Type can either be "Rel" for relative or "Abs" for Absolute.

Tabs are set so that they are relative to the left margin. This means that if you have the first tab setting at .5", it will always be one-half inch from the left margin, regardless of the left margin setting. Note that + is displayed next to each tab setting. If you move the cursor to the left side of the "0," you will see a minus sign next to each tab at the left. The numbers to the left go as far as the left margin is set (if you have set a 2" left margin, you will see numbers extending 2" to the left because that is the left side of the page).

This feature is especially useful if you change margins often, or if you use the Columns feature. If you have more than one column, the relative tab setting will be in effect for all left margins of all columns, making it unnecessary to enter the Tab Set menu and adjust the tabs for each column.

If you want to set absolute tabs that are relative to the edge of the paper, choose **Type** while in the Tab Set menu, and then choose 1 for Absolute.

If you enter the Tabs menu and decide not to make any changes, pressing Exit (F7) will still enter the [Tab Set] code into the document. To exit the menu without inserting a code, press Cancel (F1) instead of Exit (F7).

You can display a ruler on the screen to show the relative position of the tab settings without entering the Tabs menu. See "Ruler Line" in this chapter for more information. You can also press Reveal Codes (ALT-F3) to see the ruler temporarily.

Hard Tabs

By pressing HOME before TAB, Center (SHIFT-F6), or Flush Right (ALT-F6), you can insert a left-, center-, or right-aligned tab, regardless of the current tab setting. Pressing Tab Align (CTRL-F6) alone or with the HOME key has the same effect, and it sets a decimal-aligned tab, regardless of the current setting.

For example, if you have a decimal tab setting for a column of numbers, but you want to center the heading over that column, you can insert a centered tab by pressing HOME and then Center (SHIFT-F6). This is more convenient than entering the Tab Set menu, changing the tab for a single line, and then returning to the Tab Set menu for the next line.

Pressing HOME twice before each key just mentioned does exactly the same thing but includes a dot leader from the cursor to the next tab setting.

If you are in a table, pressing TAB will take you to the next cell. Press HOME, TAB if you need to insert a tab within a cell. You can also press HOME, TAB in an outline to insert a hard tab without changing levels.

The following is a summary of the keystrokes just mentioned and their functions.

Press HOME and then	To insert
TAB	Regular, left-aligned tab
Center (SHIFT-F6)	Centered tab
Align (CTRL-F6)	Decimally aligned tab
Flush Right (ALT-F6)	Flush-right tab

Remember that pressing HOME twice before one of these keystrokes inserts a dot leader as well.

Hard tabs are inserted as uppercase codes—[TAB], [CNTR TAB], [RGT TAB], or [DEC TAB]—meaning that they will never change. Tabs that are created when you press TAB while certain types of tabs have already been set are displayed in lowercase: [Tab], [Cntr Tab], [Rgt Tab], and [Dec Tab]. These types of codes change if the type of tab setting changes.

Creating Macros to Set and Clear Tabs

If you work with tabs extensively, you might want to create macros to obtain the tab settings that apply to your work. For example, to clear all tabs quickly, press Macro Define (CTRL-F10), give the macro a name and a description, follow the keystrokes for clearing all tabs, and then press Macro Define (CTRL-F10) again when you are finished. Use that macro when you need to clear all tabs quickly.

You can define another macro to set a tab in the current location. Because the cursor enters the Tab Set menu exactly where it was on the main editing screen, you can define a macro that sets a tab in the current location and mimics the Tab Set feature on typewriters. Of course, you would probably want to clear the tab settings from the menu first before using this macro.

Finally, you could define a macro that returns you to the original tab setting. This is useful if you need to change tab settings often for columns of numbers but need to return to the original tab setting for regular text. This macro would search to the left *twice* for a tab set code; once for the current tab and once for the original setting. It would then copy that tab setting to the correct location.

Related Entries

Center Text
Decimal Tabs
Dot Leader
Flush Right
Ruler Line
Tab Align
TAB Key

TARGET

See "Cross References" in this chapter.

TEXT BOXES

You can insert graphics boxes that include text and different types of borders. Most desktop publishing tasks use this type of feature to insert an enlarged quote in the middle of a page to catch the reader's attention.

See "Graphics Boxes" and Chapter 4, "Desktop Publishing with WordPerfect," for details.

TEXT COLUMNS

See "Columns" in this chapter.

TEXT IN/OUT

You can use Text In/Out (CTRL-F5) to save and retrieve files in a different format and to insert nonprinting comments.

Options

When you press Text In/Out (CTRL-F5), the options shown here appear:

```
1 DOS Text: 2 Password: 3 Save As: 4 Comment: 5 Spreadsheet: 0
```

A discussion of each of the options on this menu is listed as follows.

DOS Text

If you choose 1 for DOS Text, the following options appear:

```
1 Save; 2 Retrieve (CR/LF to [HRt]); 3 Retrieve (CR/LF to [SRt] in HZone): 0
```

You can save a file in DOS text format with the first option listed. Although all WordPerfect codes are removed, the format is retained by adding spaces. Paragraph numbers are converted to text. Tab settings are converted to spaces, and both hard returns and soft returns are converted to carriage return/line feeds (CR/LFs).

Options 2 and 3 enable you to retrieve a DOS text file and either convert a CR/LF (carriage return/line feed) to a hard return [HRt] code or to a soft return [SRt] code if it falls within the hyphenation zone. Option 3 helps retain word wrap. You can also retrieve a DOS text file with the Text In option on the List Files menu. See "DOS Text Files" in this chapter for more information.

If you want to print a file to disk, you can retain all the text that is included in WordPerfect codes, such as line numbering, headers, footers, and footnotes. See "Print to Disk" in this chapter for details.

Password

With option 2 for Password, you can add or remove a password from a document. These documents cannot be retrieved, viewed in List Files, or printed without the correct password. If you know the password, you can retrieve a locked document using the conventional methods: Retrieve (SHIFT-F10) or the Retrieve option on the List Files menu.

Save As

If you choose 3 for Save As, the following options appear:

```
1 Generic; 2 WordPerfect 5.0; 3 WordPerfect 4.2: 0
```

The Convert program lets you convert a WordPerfect document to and from WordStar, MultiMate, DCA, and Navy DIF formats. If you need to convert a document to a different format, you can use option 1 for Generic to save the current document in a generic word processor format.

The only differences between saving a file in DOS text file format and in a generic word processor format is that tabs are kept intact and each soft return [SRt] code is converted to a space (this feature aids in word wrap for the other word processor). Each hard return is converted to a CR/LF (carriage return/line feed).

You can retrieve a document created in version 5.1 into 5.0 with no conversion. However, any code that is not recognized by WordPerfect 5.0 will be converted to an [Unknown] code. If you want to strip a 5.1 file of all 5.1 features instead of having them converted to [Unknown] codes, use option 2 for WordPerfect 5.0.

A document created in version 5.1 cannot be retrieved into Word-Perfect 4.2. You will need to choose option 3 for WordPerfect 4.2. See "Compatibility" in this chapter for more information.

Comment

You can also create any number of nonprinting comments throughout the document with this option. If you choose 4 for Comment, the following options appear:

```
Comment: 1 Create; 2 Edit; 3 Convert to Text: 0
```

You can use option 1 to Create a comment, 2 to Edit the comment just before the cursor, or 3 to Convert the comment just before the cursor to regular Text.

If you block a section of text and press Text In/Out (CTRL-F5), you are asked if you want to create a comment from the text in the block. See "Comments" in this chapter for details.

Spreadsheet

You can use option 5 for Spreadsheet to import or create a link to a spreadsheet file created with PlanPerfect, Excel, or Lotus 1-2-3. See "Spreadsheet Import and Linking" in this chapter for details.

Related Entries

> Comments
> Compatibility
> Convert Program
> DOS Text Files
> Lock and Unlock Documents
> Print to Disk
> Spreadsheet Importing and Linking

TEXT SCREEN TYPE

Upon startup, WordPerfect usually senses what type of monitor you have and selects the correct text and graphics drivers from within WordPerfect. This allows text and graphics to be displayed correctly when you are using WordPerfect.

If you have problems with the text display when you exit Graphics mode (when you are editing a graphics image, exiting the equation editor, or viewing a document), WordPerfect may not have selected the correct graphics driver. You can use the Graphics Screen Type option in the Setup menu to select the exact type of driver to be used.

The Text Screen Type option lets you control the number of rows (lines) and columns (positions) that you can display on the screen. For example, if you have a VGA monitor, you can select from 80 columns and either 25, 28, 43, or 50 rows (called Extended mode).

Some graphics cards also let you create and use a different text font from the normal one. If this is the case, you can use the Text Screen Type option to "save" those settings when you enter WordPerfect and restore them when you exit. See "Hints" for more information about "Save Font" options.

Keystrokes

Several .VRS files are included with WordPerfect that contain the necessary information for both the Text Screen Type and Graphics Screen Type options. The file STANDARD.VRS is copied to the directory where WP.EXE resides; it contains information for most of the common monitors. If you want the other .VRS files to be copied, you will need to install the "Graphics Drivers Files" during installation. If you have not done so, you will need to return to the Install program and copy the files before continuing.

1. Press Setup (SHIFT-F1).

2. Choose **2** for **D**isplay.

3. Choose **3** for **T**ext Screen Type. The following list appears (more drivers may be added in the future).

```
Setup: Text Screen Driver

  ATI EGA Wonder
  Hercules Ramfont
  IBM EGA (& compatibles)
  IBM VGA (& compatibles)
  MDS Genius
  Paradise VGA Plus
```

4. Move the cursor to the name of your monitor or graphics card, and press ENTER to select it. The various options available for that card are displayed. An example of the Hercules and VGA monitor options follow to give you some idea about what is available. Others let you display 132 columns across the screen.

Hercules	**VGA**
80x25 Mono	80x25 16 Color
80x25 Mono Save 4k Font	80x28 16 Color Save Font
80x25 Mono Save 4k Font in WP	80x43 16 Color Save Font
80x43 Mono	80x50 16 Color
80x43 Mono Save 4k Font	80x50 16 Color Save Font

5. Move to the desired selection, and press ENTER to select it.

If you have any questions about which type to select, you can choose **2** for Auto-Select, and WordPerfect will try to select the correct driver.

Hints

If you have copied the .VRS files in a location other than the directory used by WP.EXE, you can use option **3** on the menu to specify the Other disk (or directory).

Save Font Options

Several choices are available for each type of text screen. Some include an option called "Save Font," "Save 4k Font," or "Save 4k Font in WP."

Some graphics cards let you select a different text font for the screen. With version 5.0, WordPerfect disregarded any font selection and would not restore the original selection when it was exited. If you want the font to be "saved" and returned when you exit WordPerfect, you can select one of the Save Font options on the list. If you have a Hercules card and select a "4k font," you can use that font within WordPerfect by selecting the "Save 4k font in WP" option.

Related Entries

Graphics Screen Type
Setup

THESAURUS

If you want to choose another word, WordPerfect's Thesaurus feature can display and substitute words that have the same or the opposite meaning (synonyms and antonyms, respectively). Many of the alternatives also have groups of associated synonyms. These groups, too, can be displayed and used as possible alternatives.

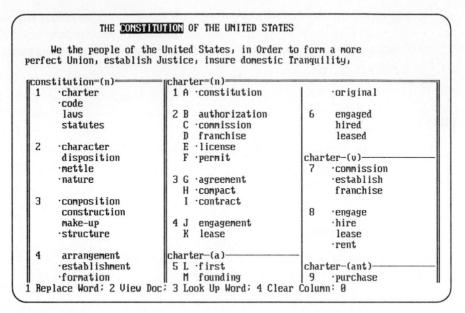

Figure 3-179.   Using the Thesaurus to choose word alternatives

Keystrokes

If you have two disk drives, remove the data disk from drive B and insert the Thesaurus disk.

1. If you want to list the alternatives for a word on the screen, move the cursor to that word.

2. Press Thesaurus (ALT-F1). See "Hints" in this section if you see an error message.

3. If the cursor is not on a word, you are prompted to enter a word. If the cursor is on a word, but that word is not found in the thesaurus, the message "Word not found" is displayed, and you are prompted to enter another word.

The list of alternatives is displayed on the screen in three columns, as shown in Figure 3-179. There are groups of nouns, verbs, adjectives, and antonyms, with each group divided further into parts of speech. Each subgroup is numbered consecutively.

4. The following options are available:

- Use → and ← to move from column to column. The boldface letters that label the words in the Thesaurus list indicate which column is current. Press ↑ and ↓ to scroll within a column.

- If you cannot find an acceptable alternative, find the next best word that has a bullet (•) by its side and type the letter for that word. A bullet indicates that the word has its own set of alternatives. In Figure 3-179, the choices for the first alternatives "charter" were displayed.

- After moving to the column that has the correct alternative, choose **1** to Replace the word in the text. If the cursor was not on a word when you pressed Thesaurus (ALT-F1), you can use option **1** for Replace to insert a word into the document. After choosing option 1, type the letter for the word.

- Only a few lines of the document are displayed above the Thesaurus screen. If you need to see more of the document, choose **2** to View the Document. Press Exit (F7) to return to the Thesaurus or to move the cursor to another word in the document, and press Thesaurus (ALT-F1) to display alternatives for that word.

- Choose **3** to Look Up another Word.

When you display other alternatives, the last column is used. To clear any of the columns, move to that column with → or ←, and choose **4** for Clear Column. BACKSPACE and DEL also clear the current column.

5. If you choose option **1** for Replace Word, you will automatically leave the Thesaurus. Otherwise, press ENTER or Exit (F7) to leave the Thesaurus and return to the document.

Hints

A word having its own group of alternatives is sometimes referred to as a "headword." Each word listed in the Thesaurus with a bullet (•) is a headword. There are approximately 10,000 headwords in the Thesaurus, with an overall word count of approximately 150,000.

The following abbreviations are used to identify different types of words in the Thesaurus:

n	Noun
a	Adjective
v	Verb
an	Antonym

Each numbered group of words on the menu is referred to as a sub-group.

The following cursor keys perform the listed functions while you are in the Thesaurus:

← and →	Move from column to column
↑ and ↓	Scroll up and down within a column
Screen Up (−) and Down (+) or Page Up (PGUP) and Down (PGDN)	Move the contents of a column up or down one screenful
HOME, HOME, ↑ and HOME, HOME, ↓	Scroll to the top or bottom of the list of alternatives in a column
GoTo (CTRL-HOME), n	Type the number of a specific subgroup to move to it

Languages

WordPerfect Corporation has produced a thesaurus for several other languages that you can purchase separately. You can then use the Language feature to insert a language code into the document to tell WordPerfect which thesaurus to use. The "US" in the thesaurus filename WP{WP}US.THS indicates that it is an English thesaurus. "FR" indicates the French thesaurus, and so on. See "Language" in this chapter for details.

Error Messages

"File not found—WP{WPUS.THS"   If you are using two disk drives and press Thesaurus (ALT-F1) without inserting the Thesaurus disk into the default drive, you will see this message, telling you that the Thesaurus file is not found.

   If you have a hard disk and plan to use the Thesaurus, copy it to the hard disk (you can use the same directory that is used by WP.EXE). Also tell WordPerfect where to find the Thesaurus file by pressing Setup (SHIFT-F1), choosing **6** for Location of Files and **3** for Thesaurus/ Spell/Hyphenation files, and then entering the drive and directory in which the file can be found.

"Not Enough Memory"   The Thesaurus takes a large amount of memory when it is started. If you see the error message "Not Enough Memory," check to make sure that document 2 is clear so that the Thesaurus can use the additional memory allotted for that document.

Related Entries

   Setup

TIMED BACKUP

   See "Backup" in this chapter.

TOTALS

   See "Addition," "Math," or "Tables" in this chapter.

TRANSPARENCIES

   WordPerfect lets you create a paper definition in the Paper Size/Type menu that is specifically used for transparencies so that WordPerfect will know where they are located when printing. For more information about creating or printing on such a form, see "Paper Size/Type" in this chapter.

TUTORIAL

WordPerfect includes an on-line, interactive tutorial. This tutorial will be copied during installation if you answer Yes to the question, "Install Learning Files?"

Keystrokes

Hard Disk

Tutorial files are copied to a directory named C:\WP51\LEARN, unless a different location was specified during installation. You should have also allowed WordPerfect to modify your AUTOEXEC.BAT file to include the \WP51 and \WP51\LEARN directories in the PATH statement. If you have not done so, return to the Install program, select Custom, choose to have the AUTOEXEC.BAT file examined, and then reboot if any changes were made.

To start the tutorial, enter **tutor** at any location.

Two Disk Drives

Place the WordPerfect 1 disk in drive A and the disk that you labeled "Learning" during installation in drive B.

1. Enter **path = a:\;b:** at the DOS prompt. This tells DOS to look first in drive A and then in drive B for any commands.

2. Enter **tutor** to start the tutorial.

3. When prompted, remove the WordPerfect 1 disk and replace it with the WordPerfect 2 disk.

Hints

The tutorial may not work on some computers that are not 100 percent IBM compatible.

TYPE THROUGH

Type Through is a separate program available from WordPerfect Corporation for those who want to use their printer as a typewriter. As you type characters or lines, they are sent to the printer. This is a useful feature for filling out forms or printing a quick envelope.

If you have a laser printer, you will not be able to use the Type Through program. Contact WordPerfect Corporation if you want to order this program.

TYPEOVER

WordPerfect is set to insert characters as you type them. You can type over existing characters by pressing INS to turn on the Typeover feature.

You can easily make corrections to a document by typing over text instead of inserting characters and deleting others. This method works especially well if characters are transposed within a word. However, when making corrections, you can use both Typeover and Insert.

Keystrokes

Press INS to switch between Typeover and Insert. "Typeover" appears in the lower left corner of the screen when Typeover is on. The following keys react differently when Typeover is on:

space bar	Replaces text to the right with spaces
BACKSPACE	Replaces text to the left with spaces
TAB	Moves the cursor over text to the next tab setting without inserting a Tab code

Hints

You cannot type over codes. If you encounter a code, text will be inserted instead. If you insert a code when Typeover is on, it will not replace text.

When you type over text, it is considered a "deletion" and can be restored with Cancel (F1).

When you are in Line Draw, Typeover is automatically turned on. This lets you draw lines around existing text (or through existing text if you are not careful).

Related Entries

INS Key
Line Draw

UNDELETE

You can use Cancel (F1) to restore any or all of your last three deletions. You can also use the Undelete feature to cut and move text with fewer keystrokes than with the conventional Move method. However, undelete the text as soon as possible, because only the last three deletions are remembered.

Keystrokes

1. Move the cursor to the location where the deletion is to be restored.

2. Press Cancel (F1). The most recent deletion is highlighted and displayed, along with the Undelete menu, as shown in Figure 3-180.

3. Choose **1** to **R**estore the deletion, **2** to display the **P**revious Deletion, or ENTER to leave the menu without making a choice.

```
┌─────────────────────────────────────────────────────────────┐
│                                                               │
│  State of New Hampshire shall be entitled to choose three,    │
│                                                               │
│  Massachusetts eight, Rhode-Island and Providence Plantations one, │
│                                                               │
│  Connecticut five, New York six, New Jersey four, Pennsylvania │
│                                                               │
│  eight, Delaware one, Maryland six, Virginia ten, North Carolina │
│                                                               │
│  five, South Carolina five, and Georgia three.                │
│                                                               │
│      When vacancies happen in the ▓Representation from any ▓State, │
│                                                               │
│  the Executive Authority thereof shall issue Writs of Election to │
│                                                               │
│  fill such Vacancies.                                         │
│                                                               │
│      The House of Representatives shall choose their speaker and │
│                                                               │
│  Officers; and shall have the sole Power of Impeachment.      │
│                                                               │
│      Section 3.  The Senate of the United States shall be composed │
│                                                               │
│  Undelete: 1 ▓estore; 2 ▓revious Deletion: 0                  │
└─────────────────────────────────────────────────────────────┘
```

Figure 3-180.   Pressing Cancel lets you restore a previous deletion

Hints

Any number of *consecutive* deletions are considered as a single deletion. For example, if you press BACKSPACE and DEL, delete a block of text, and press Delete to the End of the Page (CTRL-PGDN), it will all be considered one deletion. As soon as you press a cursor key or type a character, the "deletion" is ended.

If you are using BACKSPACE or DEL to delete and you encounter a code, you are asked to confirm the deletion. If you type **Y**, the deletion continues. If you ignore the question or type **N** to leave the code, the deletion is ended there.

When you are in Typeover mode and type over existing text, that text is saved as a deletion and can be restored with Cancel (F1).

In the Undelete menu, instead of choosing 2 to display the **Previous** deletion, you can press ↑ or ↓ to move through the three deletions.

You cannot undelete a file that has been deleted through the List Files menu. Use a file recovery program such as The Norton Utilities, Mace Utilities, or PC Tools.

Delete Without Saving

Each deletion is saved in memory until memory is filled. It then goes to temporary files, on disk. If you run out of disk space, the message "Delete without saving for Undelete? No (Yes) No" appears. Type **N** to cancel the deletion and leave the text on the screen. If you do not care about restoring the text later, type **Y**. The deletion will not be saved in this case.

Related Entries

Cancel

UNDERLINE

You can use Underline (F8) to underline text before or after it is typed.

Keystrokes

Underline Text As You Type

1. Press Underline (F8) to turn on underlining. The position number on the status line is underlined (it may be displayed in reverse video or in a different color on a color monitor).

2. Type the text.

3. Press Underline (F8) again to turn off underlining.

Underline Text After You Have Typed It

1. Move the cursor to one end of the text to be underlined.

2. Press Block (ALT-F4) to turn on Block.

3. Move the cursor to the opposite end of the text to be underlined (the text is highlighted as you move the cursor through it).

4. Press Underline (F8).

Remove Underlining

1. Move to the beginning or end of the underlined text.

2. Press Reveal Codes (ALT-F3) to view the text and the codes.

3. Locate the underline-on code, [UND], or underline-off code, [und].

4. Press BACKSPACE if the code is to the left of the cursor, or press DEL if the code is to the right of the cursor. Deleting either the [UND] or [und] code will remove the underlining.

When you become more familiar with WordPerfect codes, you can tell where the underline code is by watching the position number on the status line.

Options

Continuous vs. Noncontinuous

The spaces between words are automatically underlined, while the space between tabs is not. To change either of these, follow these steps:

1. Press Format (SHIFT-F8).

2. Choose 4 for Other.

3. Choose 7 for Underline Spaces and Tabs.

4. Change either option by choosing **Y** or **N** where applicable.

5. Press Exit (F7) to return to the document.

The code [Undrln:Spaces,Tabs] would be displayed if you chose to have the space between words and tabs underlined. If you answered Yes to only one of the options, that option alone would be displayed in the code.

Double-Underlining

You can choose double-underlining as well as single-underlining.

1. Press Font (CTRL-F8).
2. Choose **2** for Appearance.
3. Choose **3** for **D**bl Und.
4. Type the text, and then press → to turn off the feature.

You can block the text to be affected and then repeat these steps to double-underline the blocked text.

Hints

When you press Underline (F8) to turn on underlining, the underline-on [UND] and underline-off [und] codes are inserted at the same time. The cursor remains on the off code, and text is inserted between the two codes. When you press Underline again to turn off underlining, no code is inserted; the cursor moves over the code. You can use a cursor key such as →, END, or ↓ to move the cursor past the underline-off code and accomplish the same task.

Removing a Section of Underlining

If you have a section of underlined text and decide that you want only part of it to remain underlined, move the cursor to the end of the text that you want to remain underlined and press Underline (F8). An underline-off [und] code and an underline-on [UND] code are inserted, with the cursor remaining on the [UND] code. WordPerfect automatically inserts the [UND] code, because it senses that the text to the right is underlined text, and it assumes that you want to keep it that way.

Press DEL to delete the [UND] code, and type **Y** when you are asked to confirm the deletion. Underlining is removed from the text to the right of the cursor.

"Writer's Underline"

Usually a writer has to convert his or her files to ASCII (see "DOS Text Files" in this chapter) before submitting them for publication. When this conversion takes place, however, all WordPerfect codes (including underline codes) are lost. To work around this problem, many writers type an underscore at the beginning and end of text that should be underlined.

If you want to use regular underlining throughout the document, you can write the following macro, which will change WordPerfect underline codes to an underscore character after the document is completed:

1. Press Macro Def (CTRL-F10).

2. Name the macro (BROKENU is a suggestion), and enter a description.

3. Press HOME, HOME, HOME, ↑ to move to the beginning of the document.

4. Press Replace (ALT-F2) and type **N** for no confirmation.

5. Press Underline (F8) twice to insert the underline-on [UND] and underline-off [und] codes.

6. Move the cursor once to the left, and press BACKSPACE to delete the [UND] code.

7. Press Search (F2) to enter the search string.

8. When asked for the replacement string, press the underscore character (_), and insert the underline-off [und] code; insert the [und] code the same way that you did in steps 5 and 6. The replacement string should appear as " _ [und]".

9. Press Search (F2) to start the procedure.

10. Press HOME, HOME, HOME, ↑ to return to the beginning of the document.

11. Press Replace (ALT-F2) and type **N** for no confirmation.

12. Press Underline (F8) once to insert the underline-on [UND] code as the search string.

13. Press Search (F2), and type the underscore character (_) as the replacement string.

14. Press Search (F2) to complete the operation.

15. Press Macro Def (CTRL-F10) to end the macro definition.

You can start the macro anywhere in the document. All underlining will be replaced with underscore characters.

Displaying Underlining on the Screen

You can choose a color, a screen attribute, or a font to represent underlining on the screen. Underline will usually appear as underline or reverse video on a monochrome screen and in a different color if you have a color monitor. You can also start WordPerfect with the /MONO option (**wp/mono**) to ignore colors and screen fonts, and to treat your screen as if it were monochrome.

If you have an EGA or VGA monitor, you can forfeit 8 of the 16 available colors and choose to have underlining, italics, small caps, or 512 characters instead. If you have a Hercules graphics card with RamFont, you can display both underline and double-underline on the screen, regardless of whether you have a monochrome monitor or a color monitor.

To change the display, press Setup (SHIFT-F1), choose **2** for **D**isplay, and then choose **1** for Colors/Fonts/Attributes. If you need more assistance, see "Colors/Fonts/Attributes" in this chapter.

Moving Underlined Text

If text is moved from an underlined sentence or paragraph, underline-on and underline-off codes are inserted at the beginning and end of the block so the text will remain underlined when it is retrieved. However, if you retrieve the block into another underlined section of text, underlining will be turned off after the inserted block. This is because the underline-off code at the end of the block supersedes the underline-off code at the end of the original section.

Underlining at the Printer

Some printers print underlining as a solid line, while others can produce only a broken line. If you are not satisfied with the way underlined text is printed, check the printer manual for options so that you can try to modify the printer driver (see Chapter 5).

Printer Switch Settings

If underlined text prints one line below the text that should be under-lined, check the internal switch settings (sometimes referred to as DIP switches), and make sure that the switch for Auto LF (automatic line-feed) is off. If it is turned on, both WordPerfect and the printer are sending line feeds.

Related Entries

> Block
> Colors/Fonts/Attributes
> Double Underlining
> See also Chapter 5, "Printer Program"

UNITS OF MEASURE

Format settings are automatically displayed and entered in inches. The position of the cursor is also displayed in inches on the status line. The measurement next to "Ln" indicates how far the cursor is from the top of the page, and "Pos" displays the amount of space from the left of the page.

Even though the settings are set in inches by default, you can set any single setting in centimeters, points, WordPerfect 4.2 units, or in 1200ths of an inch by typing **c, p, u,** or **w** after the setting. If you are more accustomed to centimeters, points, or 4.2 units (lines and columns), you can change the unit of measurement for either option (format settings and Status Line Display).

Keystrokes

1. Press Setup (SHIFT-F1).

2. Choose **3** for **E**nvironment.

3. Choose **8** for **U**nits of Measure. The menu shown in Figure 3-181 appears, listing all available options.

4. Although you can set the two options separately, it is usually easiest to work with WordPerfect if both settings are the same.

    Choose **1** for **D**isplay and Entry of Numbers for Margins, Tabs, etc., and type the character from the lower part of the menu that

```
Setup: Units of Measure

    1 - Display and Entry of Numbers              "
          for Margins, Tabs, etc.

    2 - Status Line Display                       "


Legend:

    " = inches
    i = inches
    c = centimeters
    p = points
    w = 1200ths of an inch
    u = WordPerfect 4.2 Units (Lines/Columns)






Selection: 0
```

Figure 3-181.   Units of measurement selection

represents the desired unit of measurement. Repeat the process for option **2**, Status Line Display.

5. Press Exit (F7) to return to the document.

Hints

The status line and menus reflect the change by displaying the unit of measurement next to all measurements (for example, "Ln 3c Pos 4.5c") with the exception of 4.2 units, in which the "u" is not displayed. The "i" and " options provide two ways to display a measurement in inches; choose the one that you feel most comfortable with.

Changing a Single Setting

As mentioned previously, you can change any format setting to any of the available units of measurement. For example, if you are using inches as the default, but you want to change the line height to a fixed amount and you are familiar with typesetting, you will most likely want to make the change in points. After selecting the option, enter the points followed by the letter "p." For example, entering **20p** would set the line height at 20 points. After you enter the setting, WordPerfect will automatically convert the measurement to the default measurement. In the previous example, you would type **20p**, but as soon as you pressed ENTER, the measurement would appear as .27", if inches were the default unit of measurement.

The "c" would be used to represent centimeters, and "i" or " would be used for inches. If you plan to use WordPerfect 4.2 units, you will need to use "v" for vertical measurements and "h" for horizontal measurements. The current font determines the size of a line or column and it is not an accurate way to set measurements.

Any number entered without i, ", c, p, v, or h automatically uses the default unit of measurement. For example, if you enter **1.5** for the left margin, WordPerfect will set it in 1.5", if inches is the default. If the default measurement were centimeters, 1.5 centimeters would be used.

The w option is also available for control and accuracy. This unit of measurement is referred to as a WP 5.0 unit and lets you enter settings in twelve-hundredths of an inch. For example, 600 would be equal to 1/2", 300 would be equal to 1/4", and so on. Because it lets you set measurements in small increments, you can use this option if you want to make a slight change to a setting (for example, advancing to the left or right for manual kerning).

For future reference, WordPerfect considers a point 1/72 of an inch (publishers often refer to a point as 1/72.27 of an inch). One centimeter is equal to .39″ (it takes 2.54 centimeters to make 1″).

Fractions

You can use fractions when you are entering any measurement. For example, it you enter **5/16**, **3/4**, or **2 1/3**, it will be converted to the decimal equivalent. This type of entry is valid when you are setting margins, tabs, page size, line height, or labels, or any other time when you are prompted for a measurement.

UNLOCK A DOCUMENT

See "Lock and Unlock Documents" in this chapter.

UPPERCASE TEXT

See "Capitalization" and "Switch" in this chapter.

VERTICAL LINES

You can place vertical lines of any length and thickness in your document against the left or right margin, at the center of the page, between columns, or at a set distance from the left side of the page. See "Graphics Lines" in this chapter for details.

VERY LARGE PRINT

See "Size of Print" in this chapter.

VIEW DOCUMENT

If you have a graphics card, you can view the document to see a fairly exact representation of how it will look when it is printed. Proportional spacing, font differences, and graphics will appear in Graphics mode. You can see the entire page, increase the scaling to 100% or 200% of the printed page, or see two pages side by side on the screen.

If you have a monochrome monitor, the document will look similar to the regular document on the editing screen, but you will see headers, footers, footnotes, page numbers, line numbers, and right justification as well.

1. Press Print (SHIFT-F7).

2. Choose **6** for **View Document.** Figure 3-182 shows how a document will appear when you view it in Graphics mode.

3. Use any cursor key to move through the page or the document. You cannot edit the document in View mode. See "Options" for additional options that are available if you have a graphics card.

4. Press Exit (F7) when you are finished.

Options

The following options are displayed at the bottom of the View screen if you have a graphics card:

```
1 100%  2 200%  3 Full Page  4 Facing Pages: 3          Doc 1 Pg 1
```

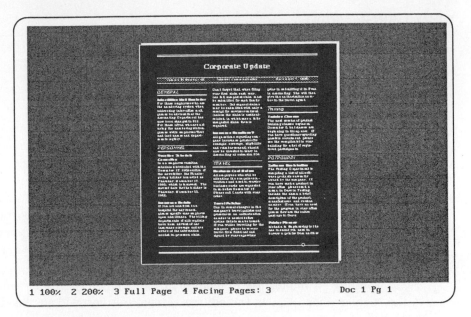

Figure 3-182.   View Document screen

WordPerfect displays the full page as the default selection. Choose **1** to see the document as it will be printed (100%), **2** to view the document at twice the normal size (200%), **4** to view facing pages, or **3** to return to the full page display.

An even-numbered page is displayed on the left, and an odd-numbered page is displayed on the right. If you have a one- or two-page document, you will not see two pages on the screen at once. If you were on page 2 and wanted to view facing pages, page 2 would appear at the left of the screen, with a blank page at the right. Pressing PGUP would display page 1 on the right side of the screen.

You can also press Switch (SHIFT-F3) to see a reversal image (for example, black switches to white).

Hints

You may see an error message while viewing a document, telling you that the chosen graphics display is not correct. Press Setup (SHIFT-F1), and choose **2** for **Display** and then **2** for **Graphics Screen Type**. Select the correct display from the list. You can also increase or decrease the resolution for some types of graphics drivers with this menu.

View Document Options

You can display text in black and white, graphics in black and white, or display bold in color. If you don't want to change the option to display in black and white permanently, you can press Switch (SHIFT-F3) in the View Document screen to switch between color and black and white.

Displaying a graphics image as black and white will give you a better idea about how it will appear when it is printed.

1. Press Setup (SHIFT-F1).

2. Choose **2** for **D**isplay.

3. Choose **5** for View Document Options. The following options appear.

```
Setup: View Document Options

    1 - Text in Black & White     No

    2 - Graphics in Black & White No

    3 - Bold Displayed with Color Yes
```

4. Choose any of the options available and press Exit (F7) when you are finished.

WIDOW/ORPHAN PROTECTION

Widows and orphans are single lines of a paragraph at the bottom and top of a page. Most style books advise against having widows and orphans in a printed document.

WordPerfect is not set to prevent these single lines from appearing automatically, but you can avoid them by turning on Widow/Orphan Protection for each document or by setting the feature permanently through the Setup menu.

Keystrokes

1. Move the cursor to the beginning of the document or to the point at which you want widows and orphans prevented.

2. Press Format (SHIFT-F8).

3. Choose **1** for **Line**.

4. Choose **9** for Widow/Orphan Protection.

5. Type **Y** to keep from having widows and orphans, or type **N** to allow them.

6. Press Exit (F7) to return to the document.

Insert the code in the Initial Codes section of the Setup menu (under the Initial Settings option) if you want to turn on Widow/Orphan Protection permanently.

Hints

When you choose the Widow/Orphan Protection option, [W/O On] or [W/O Off] is inserted, depending on your selection. Text is affected from that point forward.

WordPerfect guards against widows by moving a widow to the next page with the rest of the paragraph. It prevents orphans by moving the second to the last line of a paragraph to the next page with the orphan.

Widow/Orphan Protection will not keep a paragraph or section heading with the first two lines of the paragraph. Use the Conditional End of Page feature (found on the "Other" Format menu) instead, because it can keep a specific number of lines together.

The Widow/Orphan Protection option cannot protect three-line paragraphs. The Block Protect feature would be best in this type of situation; it can protect a specific block of text, regardless of the number of lines. To use this option, define a block with ALT-F4, press Format (SHIFT-F8), and type **Y** to protect the block.

Related Entries

Block Protect
Conditional End of Page
Keep Text Together

WINDOWS

WordPerfect lets you have two documents in memory and switch between them with Switch (SHIFT-F3). You can use the Windows feature to display both documents at once on the screen. You can easily cut and paste text from one document to the other by using Windows and Switch.

Keystrokes

1. Press Screen (CTRL-F3).

2. Choose **1** for Window. The following message appears:

```
Number of lines in this window: 24
```

The number of lines in the current window is displayed; in the example above, 24 represents the number of lines that can usually be displayed on the screen. If you have already split the screen or have already created the ruler, you will see a different number.

Also, if you changed the number of lines that can be displayed on the screen with either the /SS startup option or the Text Screen Type option in Setup, you will see that number.

3. Press ↑ and ↓ to move the ruler until it is in the desired position, and then press ENTER. You can also enter the number of lines.

If you want to divide the screen in half, and you have 24 lines, you will want to enter **11** instead of **12**, because the two status lines and the ruler line take up two lines. The screen will look something like the one shown in Figure 3-183.

4. Press Switch (SHIFT-F3) to move between the two windows.

Hints

To return the screen to its full size, follow the steps just listed. Enter **24** (or the appropriate number of lines for your screen) when you are asked for the number of lines in the window. You can also press ↓ until the ruler moves off the screen, and then press ENTER.

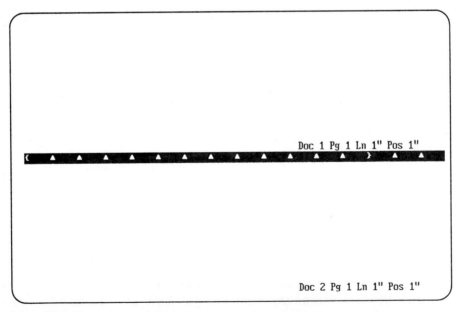

Figure 3-183.   Splitting the screen into two windows

The ruler displays the current margin and tab settings for each document. Tabs are marked with a triangle, and the left and right margins are indicated by [and] (square brackets). If a tab and margin setting are both in the same location, the margins are represented by { and } (braces). When you press Switch (SHIFT-F3), the triangles point to the document being edited.

If you need to see different parts of the same document, you can retrieve the document in both screens and scroll to the desired locations. However, you should make editing changes in only one version of the document, because changes in both cannot be written to the same file. If you need to edit both parts of the document, save them under different names and combine the edited parts later.

Related Entries

Ruler Line
Screen
Switch

WORD AND LETTER SPACING

You can adjust the amount of space between words and letters with the Word Spacing and Letter Spacing option. You can choose the recommendation of the printer manufacturer, accept WordPerfect Corporation's measurements, or increase or decrease the amount of spacing by a certain percentage. A "pitch" option lets you indicate roughly how many characters should be printed per inch.

Keystrokes

1. Press Format (SHIFT-F8).

2. Choose **4** for Other.

3. Choose **6** for **P**rinter Functions.

4. Choose **3** for **W**ord Spacing and Letter Spacing. Each is selected separately, with Word Spacing being first. The following choices are displayed at the bottom of the screen:

Word Spacing: 1 Normal; 2 Optimal; 3 Percent of Optimal; 4 Set Pitch: 2

5. Choose **1** for the **N**ormal setting (as recommended by the printer manufacturer); **2** for **O**ptimal, the setting chosen by WordPerfect Corporation (WordPerfect's recommended setting, not necessarily the maximum in this context); **3** for **P**ercent of Optimal (enter a percentage greater than 100 percent to increase the space or less than 100 percent to decrease the space); or **4** for Set Pitch.

Using the last selection, you can change the percentage of optimal letter spacing using a method that is more familiar. Word-Perfect will take the pitch entered, compare it to the current font, and figure the "percentage of optimal." If you change fonts, the percentage of optimal will still be in effect, but the pitch will not necessarily be a true pitch (characters per inch) if the font is a different size.

6. After selecting the Word Spacing choice, continue by selecting from the same options for Letter Spacing. Note that the spacing (including pitch) can be different for word and letter spacing.

7. When you are finished, press Exit (F7) to return to the document.

Hints

The code [Wrd/Ltr Spacing:Optimal,Optimal] is inserted into the document, showing the selected options. Text from that point forward will be affected until you select another word- and letter-spacing option.

The chosen pitch setting is converted to a percent of optimal for you, depending on the current font selected. If your printer cannot move the exact amount specified, it will be as close as possible.

See Chapter 5, "Printer Program," for an application of word and letter spacing.

WORD COUNT

The number of words in a block, on a page, or in a document is automatically displayed when you check the spelling of a block, a page, or a document. An option on the Spell menu lets you check the number of words in a document without checking the spelling.

Keystrokes

1. Press Spell (CTRL-F2) from anywhere in the document.

2. Choose **6** for Count.

3. When WordPerfect has finished counting, a message similar to the following is displayed in the bottom left corner of the screen:

```
Word count: 390      Press any key to continue
```

4. Press any key to return to the document.

Hints

Words that appear in headers, footers, footnotes, and endnotes are included in a word count.

Related Entries

Spell

WORDPERFECT FILES

See Appendix B for a list of WordPerfect files.

WORDPERFECT STARTUP OPTIONS

See "Start WordPerfect" in this chapter.

WORD SEARCH

See "Search" in this chapter.

WORD SPACING JUSTIFICATION LIMITS

When justification is turned on, WordPerfect increases or decreases the amount of space between words to achieve an even right margin. A space can be expanded up to 400 percent of its normal size and decreased to 60 percent of its normal size to make this adjustment. If you feel that there is too much or too little space between the words, you can change the word spacing justification limits. Once the limit has been reached, space is then added or deleted between characters.

Keystrokes

1. Press Format (SHIFT-F8).
2. Choose 4 for Other.
3. Choose 6 for Printer Functions.

4. Choose **4** for Word Spacing Justification Limits.

5. Enter the acceptable percentage that WordPerfect can use to compress and expand a space.

6. Press Exit (F7) to return to the document.

Hints

The code [Just Lim:x,y] is inserted at the cursor location; it affects the amount given to a space during justification from that point forward. The percentage of compression is indicated by an x, and the percentage of expansion is indicated by a y.

Space is not added or deleted between characters until these limits are reached.

Related Entries

Justification

WORDSTAR

The Convert program can convert WordStar version 3.3 files to WordPerfect format and back again. If you are using WordStar 2000, you will need to convert those documents to WordStar version 3.3 format before they can be converted to WordPerfect.

When converting files from WordStar to WordPerfect, the following features are not converted:

Doublestrike (only bold is supported in WordPerfect)
Margins
Merge commands
Paper length
Right justification on screen
Spacing

The features not converted when going from WordPerfect to WordStar include the following:

Center
Flush right
Footnotes and endnotes
Hard spaces
Line spacing
Margins
Mark text
Paper length
Right justification
Top margin

Center and flush right are not converted as features, but spaces are used to retain the format. Only one header and one footer will convert from WordPerfect, because WordStar allows only one per document. Many features do not convert, because WordStar does not have corresponding features.

If you are accustomed to using the "WordStar" diamond, you can reassign the functions to those keys with WordPerfect's Keyboard Layout feature.

See "Convert" and "Keyboard Layout" in this chapter for more information.

"WP DISK FULL" ERROR MESSAGE

The error message "WP Disk full" or "Not enough room on WP disk to retrieve text" may appear when you are retrieving a large file.

Reasons

When a file is retrieved, WordPerfect loads as much as possible into memory (up to 64K is allowed for document 1, and up to 32K is allowed for document 2, but less is used if the maximum amount is not available).

When memory is filled, the remaining text spills into overflow files where WP.EXE is located. Because of this, you can swap data disks or use the disk drive for the Speller or Thesaurus disks.

If the WordPerfect disk does not have enough room when you are using two disk drives, or if you have redirected the overflow files to a RAM drive and it runs out of available memory, you will see the error message.

Solutions

If you formatted the WordPerfect disk with the DOS system files by specifying **format/s**, the extra files are taking up space. Consider using a separate "boot" disk with the DOS system files to free up that much space on the WordPerfect disk.

You can usually add more memory to your system at a minimal cost. If you work with large documents regularly, consider purchasing a hard disk. If you have a RAM drive, you can redirect the overflow files there, but remember that a RAM drive takes some of the memory and forces the large document to go to the overflow files prematurely.

You can redirect the overflow files to the data disk itself with the /D option (enter **wp/d-***drive/directory* to start WordPerfect). The command **wp/d-b:** would direct the overflow files to the disk in drive B. If you redirect the overflow files, you cannot remove the disk in that drive to use the Speller or the Thesaurus.

Related Entries

Start WordPerfect

Desktop Publishing with WordPerfect

The term "desktop publishing" means having the ability to publish (or print something that is ready for publication) at your desk. In the past few years, many advances have been made toward this goal. Because it is easy to edit text, check the spelling, and use an on-line thesaurus, the actual writing is often done in a word processor. The text can then be retrieved into a page layout program, such as Ventura or PageMaker, which support many different fonts, "tags" or styles, kerning, leading, and graphics within the text.

With WordPerfect, you now have the advantages of editing text in a powerful word processor, formatting it with styles and a variety of fonts, importing graphics images, and choosing from such options as kerning, leading, and shaded text boxes.

Although it is ideal, you do not have to have a laser or PostScript printer to do effective desktop publishing. Dot-matrix printers also include a wide variety of fonts and can print graphics images and graphics lines.

This chapter introduces you to several terms used in desktop publishing and also tells you how to use those features in WordPerfect. Examples are included, with instructions for duplicating the features that have been highlighted.

Types of Documents

There is no limit to the types of documents that you can create with WordPerfect. You can produce brochures, family or business newsletters, announcements, invitations, pamphlets, catalogs, and books.

You can turn simple reports into attractive documents by choosing larger fonts for headings, drawing attention to a quote by placing it in a box, or adding a graphics image. You can choose from the 30 clip-art images provided with WordPerfect, create your own graphs with a spreadsheet program, use a graphics program to create an image, or scan a picture, logo, or signature into a file that can be used in any type of document.

Instead of using a macro to start a simple letter, you can use the same macro to retrieve a file that already contains the company logo and a thin, horizontal line (rule) that separates the logo from the text, inserts the date, moves down to insert the closing of the letter and a scanned image of your signature, and then returns to the correct position so you can finish the letter by entering the name, address, and the body of the letter. A separate macro could then retrieve an "envelope" file that already contains a smaller version of the logo and automatically inserts the name and address from the letter.

Newsletters are among the more popular applications for desktop publishing. You can use casual fonts for family newsletters and even include a scanned image of the family to avoid the costs of photo duplication. A business newsletter could include heavier fonts and enlarged quotes in shaded text boxes to draw the reader's attention to specific items.

Before experimenting on your own, look at examples that catch your eye, and try to duplicate them in WordPerfect. During the process, you can make many different choices and adjustments to create a look of your own.

Desktop Publishing Terms

This section describes common desktop publishing features in WordPerfect. After you learn more about desktop publishing terms, you will learn to create your own documents. Several sample documents, with complete instructions on how to duplicate them, are also presented in this chapter.

Fonts

The first question to ask yourself is what fonts to use for a particular project. Look through the list of available fonts by pressing Font (CTRL-F8) and choosing 4 for Base Font to decide which to use for headings, subheadings, body text, large-type quotes, and so on.

If you do not know what each font looks like, you can select each font and type a sample line of text. If you have several fonts, you could use a macro that begins at the top of the list, selects the first font, and types a line of text. The macro could then repeat itself a certain number of times until all fonts have been selected. To see how each font looks, print the document when you are finished.

There are two types of fonts: those with serifs (the decorative extensions at the ends of letters), and those without (sans serif). The following illustration shows a serif font (top) and a sans serif font (bottom):

WordPerfect Corporation

WordPerfect Corporation

Most designers use sans serif fonts for headlines and subheads, and use serif fonts for body text. Sans serif fonts catch the reader's attention, and serif fonts are easy to read in paragraph format.

However, you will often find that these rules can and should be broken. For example, you may not want a headline to jump out at the reader. A more decorative font with serifs can sometimes be attractive for headlines and can even help promote the subject matter, as shown in the following example:

The Society Page

Even though smaller fonts are often difficult to read, you can use smaller fonts if the document will be placed in multiple columns. The longer the line length, the larger the font should be. If a font still appears too small, instead of increasing the font size, you can slightly increase the amount of space in the margins or between columns to make reading easier. You can also adjust the amount of space between letters and words with the Word and Letter Spacing option.

Regardless of what fonts you choose, consider using styles for each section of text (with the exception of regular body text) so that if you want to change the font later, you can make the font change in the style itself; all text marked with that particular style will then change automatically. Styles are discussed in detail in "Styles or Tags" later in this chapter.

Word and Letter Spacing

The staff at WordPerfect Corporation who defined your printer have already set the optimal word and letter spacing; it should not have to be adjusted. However, if the page seems too dark or dense, you might want to increase the letter spacing, word spacing, or both. If you want the words or letters closer together, you can decrease the spacing.

Among the choices available with the Word and Letter Spacing option are Optimal, Normal, Percent of Optimal, or Pitch (a way of letting you enter a setting that is more familiar and having WordPerfect convert it to a "percentage of optimal" for you). Optimal is the choice made by WordPerfect Corporation, Normal is the manufacturer's suggestion, and Percentage of Optimal lets you decide if the setting should be larger or smaller than optimal. A percentage less than 100 percent will decrease the space, and a percentage greater than 100 percent will increase the space. See "Word and Letter Spacing" in Chapter 3 for details.

You can use this option to create headings such as the following:

The first line has been printed with the default letter spacing and has also been kerned (discussed in the next section). After the font was

.

changed, the letter spacing was increased to 190 percent of optimal just before the second line was typed. Of course, there will be trial and error in getting the spacing just right, but the View Document feature on a graphics monitor will help save paper during the testing period.

If you adjust the word or letter spacing for this type of effect, remember to change it back to the previous setting when you are finished.

Kerning

Kerning is the ability to squeeze two characters closer together to create a more typeset look. It is more commonly used with larger fonts, because the spaces between characters are more obvious than with smaller fonts.

Even though kerning is supported by WordPerfect, very few fonts include the necessary kerning information (tables of kerning pairs). If you select kerning by pressing Format (SHIFT-F8), choosing **4** for **O**ther, **6** for **P**rinter Functions, and **1** for **K**erning, but you do not see a difference between kerned and unkerned text, you will need to enter the information with the Printer program. Although the process can be time consuming, you can do it for a single title or headline without too much work.

You can manually kern characters with the Advance feature. For example, you could kern the letters "W" and "o" in "WordPerfect" by moving the "o" to the left slightly. Following are the steps that will help you accomplish that task:

1. Move the cursor to the character to be moved to the left (in this case "o").

2. Press Format (SHIFT-F8).

3. Choose **4** for **O**ther.

4. Choose **1** for **A**dvance.

5. Choose **4** for **L**eft.

6. Enter the amount of space to move to the left. The larger the font, the larger the setting. You may want to try anything from .02" to .05".

7. Press Exit (F7) when you are finished.

Use the View feature—press Print (SHIFT-F7), and choose **6** for View Document—often to see if you need to make additional adjustments.

If you want to enter the kerning information with the Printer program, see Chapter 5.

Leading or Line Height

When type was set by hand, the amount of space between lines was increased or decreased by placing a certain amount of lead between the lines. The amount of leading used was usually 10 to 20 percent of the size of the font.

As a rule, WordPerfect adds 2 points (there are 72 points per inch) of leading to each font. For example, a 12pt font would have 2 points of leading, making a total of 14 points for the line height setting.

When you select a font, WordPerfect automatically adjusts the line height for that font. If you have more than one font on a line, the line height is set to accommodate the largest font.

You can use the Leading feature in WordPerfect to change the amount of space between the base of one line and the top of the next line. You can change this amount separately for soft returns [SRt] and hard returns [HRt], and thus have a different amount of space within paragraphs and between paragraphs.

The line height is measured from the base of one line to the base of the next. You can leave it at automatic or change it to a fixed amount. If you want to adjust the amount of space between lines, you may want to use the Leading feature; otherwise, you would need to set a fixed line height separately for each font.

The following steps give you access to the Leading feature:

1. Press Format (SHIFT-F8).

2. Choose **4** for **O**ther.

3. Choose **6** for **P**rinter Functions.

4. Choose **6** for **L**eading Adjustment.

5. Enter the amount for soft returns and hard returns. When entering the amount, remember that 2 points have already been included with each font. You can also enter a negative number to decrease the amount of space if necessary.

6. Press Exit (F7) when you are finished.

To change the line height, follow these steps:

1. Press Format (SHIFT-F8).

2. Choose **1** for Line.

3. Choose **4** for Line Height.

4. Choose **2** for Fixed. The current line height is displayed.

5. Enter the new line height. If you want to use points to enter the setting, type the number followed by "p" for points. For example, to set the line height at 16 points, enter **16p**. The setting will be converted to the default unit of measurement.

6. Press Exit (F7) when you are finished.

You might want to change the line height setting back to Auto or adjust the height to a different setting when you are changing fonts again. If you change the line height in a paired style, it will automatically be returned to Auto when you turn the style off.

Rules or Graphics Lines

WordPerfect has a feature that lets you insert horizontal and vertical graphics lines of any thickness and shading anywhere on the page. Often called rules, these lines are often used in desktop publishing to help set off a heading or a graphics image, or define the borders of the page.

Rules are often used in headers and footers, to separate headings from text, at the left and right margins, and between columns. Each example shown later in this chapter uses some type of graphics line. In Figure 4-1, graphics lines of different thicknesses are used in a header

Corporate Update

Volume III Number 40	Internal Communication	November 1, 1990

5.1 SHIPS!

New Version of WordPerfect Now Available
For all those who have been anxiously awaiting the latest release of WordPerfect, version 5.1 is now shipping! Some of the new features that might interest you are listed below:

- Pull-down menus and mouse support, making it easy to select features, position the cursor, block text, and scroll through the document

- Tables, with their grid-like appearance, can make entering data into columns and rows much easier. Tables can also be used for forms fill-in, calendars, invoices, and much more.

- An equation editor that makes formatting and printing complex equations simple. Another related improvement lets you print *all* of the special characters supported in WordPerfect on any type of graphics printer.

Vast improvements have been made the the merge feature and additional macro commands have been included, giving you more power for your customized applications.

The Word Processing Support Department should be able to assist you with installation or other initial questions almost immediately, as our comapny was selected as a beta test site. They will be available from 9:00 a.m. to 4:00 p.m. each day.

We should be receiving our upgrade copies of the product by next week. Please confirm or place orders through Laura at extension 412.

GENERAL

Inter-Office Mail Reminder
For those employees who use the numbering system when addressing inter-office mail, please be advised that the Accounting Department has now been changed to #11. For those of you who are not using the numbering system, please write employees' first and last names and departments legibly.

PERSONNEL

Vacation Schedule Correction
In an employee vacation schedule distributed with the December 15, 1989 edition of the newsletter, the Thanksgiving holiday is marked as Thursday, November 15, 1990, which is incorrect. The correct date for the holiday is Thursday, November 22, 1988.

Insurance Update
If you are admitted to a hospital for any reason, please specify your employer upon admittance. The billing departments of all hospitals have been advised of our insurance coverage and are aware of the information needed to process a claim.

Figure 4-1.   Newsletter printed on an HP LaserJet Series II printer

and footer. The headings are created with a style that inserts a thin horizontal line in the style-on code and then includes a thicker line in the style-off code.

In WordPerfect, these graphics lines are inserted as codes, and they appear as lines only when you view the document on a graphics monitor or print the document. You need to be aware of this because you might overwrite text with these graphics lines. For example, if you place a vertical line at the left margin, it would overwrite the first character in each line. If you are going to place a vertical line at the left or right margin, you will need to narrow the margins first, insert the vertical lines, and then return to the regular margins.

Similarly, if you are placing a vertical line between columns and there is also a graphics box between the columns, the vertical line will overwrite the graphics box. To solve this problem, you need to insert two graphics lines of different lengths, starting from different positions: one above the box and one below the box.

If you want to include graphics lines between columns, you have to define the columns, and place the cursor after the column definition. Otherwise, the graphics lines will appear at the right margin.

The examples shown later in this chapter include instructions on how the graphics lines were included in each document.

Graphics Boxes

Even if you do not intend to use graphics in your document, you can enhance the appearance and interest of your document by including text in boxes. WordPerfect lets you choose from a variety of borders (none, single-line, double-line, dotted, dashed, thick, and extra-thick) for any or all sides of the box. You can change fonts and include shading in the box to draw attention to the information.

In addition to graphics, you can use these boxes for a masthead containing the names of the editors and staff that produce a particular newsletter, an enlarged quotation that draws attention to an article, or use a box to enclose the article itself. You can even place a box around an entire page.

By default, text flows around graphics or text boxes. You can choose not to have the text wrap around the boxes, and instead have the text print over the graphics image or box. You can use this feature to manually wrap text around an irregularly shaped graphics image that does not have borders or print text with a graphics image. Examples of these suggestions appear later in this chapter.

Shading or Screens

You can add shading or gray scaling to graphics boxes or lines. One of the more common settings is 10 to 20% shading. If the shading is too dark, it will create a "halo" effect around the text or image in the box.

If you have a PostScript printer, you can have 100% shading and choose white as the print color to create a reverse effect, as shown here:

> This text box is
> shaded 100%
> with white
> as the print color.

Bullets

Most desktop publishing programs do not provide automatic numbering for lists of items, but let you choose a bullet character instead. Word-Perfect offers both options. You can use the bullet characters that have already been defined (a closed circle, an open circle, a dash, and so on), or you can define your own bullet characters by pressing Date/Outline (SHIFT-F5) and choosing **6** for **D**efine and then **5** for **B**ullets or **6** for User-Defined.

After selecting numbers or bullets, you can create a paired style for the numbered items. The style-on code could insert the appropriate number of tabs, a paragraph number code (which could be a bullet), and an [→Indent] code. The style-off code could include one or two [HRt] codes, depending on whether you want the list single- or double-spaced. The "Styles" section in Chapter 3, "Commands and Features," includes this application as one of its examples.

Em and En Dashes

If your printer does not have an em dash, you can create one and assign it to a specific key with the Keyboard Layout feature. To insert an em or en dash on a one-time basis, you can follow these steps:

1. Press Compose (CTRL-2).

2. Type the following two characters, depending on what type of dash is needed. There are two options for entering an em dash; use the one that is easiest to remember.

    --   Em dash
    m-   Em dash
    n-   En dash

If you are assigning these keys to a keyboard layout or are defining a macro that will include these keystrokes, you may want to include an "invisible soft return" after the dash. Because these dashes are not treated as a regular hyphen, the "invisible soft return" [ISRt] code will break the line if necessary. For example, if you entered the phrase "The line will break after the dash—but only if you add the invisible soft return," you may be asked to hyphenate "dash—but" because Word-Perfect looks at the em dash as a regular character and treats both words as one. By moving the cursor just after the dash and pressing HOME and then ENTER, you will insert the [ISRt] code, which will be used to break the line only if the code falls at the end of the line. If the code doesn't fall at the end of the line, it will remain invisible.

Styles or Tags

Desktop publishing programs usually let you create styles, or tags, that you can assign to certain sections of text so you do not have to enter a particular format repeatedly. For example, you could have a heading style, a subheading style, a paragraph style, or a beginning of article style. WordPerfect also gives you this ability.

A style can include almost any WordPerfect code, including font or attribute codes, spacing or advance codes, and graphics lines. You can also include graphics in a style if you use the option to point to a graphics image on disk.

You can use two types of styles in WordPerfect: open and paired. An open style is appropriate for starting a chapter with a certain format, whereas a paired style might be used for headings or lists of items.

An open style does not need to be turned off—it inserts the codes and lets you continue. A paired style inserts a [Style On] and [Style Off] code, which are similar to bold on and bold off. Any codes found in the style-on section of the style are automatically turned off, or they are returned to normal in the style-off section. For example, if you included a [BOLD] code (on) in the style-on code, it would be turned off automatically in the style-off code; you wouldn't have to include the [bold] code (off) in the style.

A font change in a style-on section stays in effect until the style-off code is encountered. It then returns to the font that was in effect before the style was turned on. You can use this method to assign a font to a block of text without affecting the text that follows.

You can also use macros to insert the necessary codes. However, it is more advantageous to use a style, because you can make changes to it more easily. For example, if you decide that the font for headings is too small, you can edit the style and change the font, all text marked with that style is then updated automatically.

Styles are used extensively in desktop publishing programs. They can be used in WordPerfect to accomplish the same types of tasks.

Cross-References

You can use the Cross-Reference feature to refer the reader to a different page. For example, most magazines start an article in one place and then continue it toward the end of the magazine. You can use the Cross-Reference feature to insert the phrase "Continued on page 10," for example, and on page 10 the article would begin with the phrase "Continued from page 2." See "Cross-References" in Chapter 3 for details.

Method for Creating a Document

It is best to follow a specific process when you are producing a document. The following steps are suggested:

1. Create the text. You can add fonts and styles during this process or after you have entered the text.

2. Define the headers, footers, and page numbering. If you are going to include a footer and page number at the bottom of the page, it might be best to include both in a footer. If you are using graphics lines or a graphics box around the entire page, you might want to include them in headers or footers that have different margin settings so they will not print over the text in the document. See "Borders" in Chapter 3 for a method that you can use to create a box or border around each page in a document.

3. Change the leading (or line height, if you prefer) to create more or less space between lines or paragraphs if necessary.

4. Change the letter spacing and word spacing if necessary.

5. Define and turn on the Columns feature at the appropriate location if the document is to be in columns.

6. Start at the beginning of the document and insert graphics boxes and enlarged quotes in text boxes.

7. Turn on the Hyphenation feature at the beginning of the document, and make all hyphenation decisions at once.

8. Do a spell check and print.

Detailed instructions about each of these items is included in Chapter 3, "Commands and Features."

Sample Documents

This section includes a few sample documents, with instructions about how each one was created. After reading this section, you should be familiar with some of the tips and tricks that can be used in other applications.

Newsletters

The newsletter shown in Figure 4-1 earlier in this chapter was printed on an HP LaserJet Series II printer with Century Schoolbook and Helvetica fonts. The following tips explain how the newsletter was created.

Entering Headings and Subheadings with Styles

The text is first created. Bold and Italics are chosen in the proper places. Headings and subheadings are marked with styles. The heading style is a paired style that consists of a horizontal line extending the full distance between the left and right margins and is .01″ thick, a font change to Swiss Bold Italic 14pt (similar to Helvetica), and then an Advance Down code. In the style-off section, another Advance Down code is used for positioning, followed by another horizontal graphics line that is .03″ thick, a [HRt] code, and another Advance Down code. A block protect is placed around the entire style so that the heading will not be split by a page break.

To insert the Block Protect codes, go to the first code, press Block (ALT-F4) to turn on Block, move the cursor past the last code, press Format (SHIFT-F8), and type **Y** when asked "Protect Block? **N**o (**Y**es)." When the heading style is defined, the codes appear as follows:

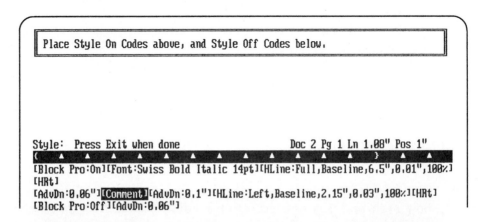

Remember that the [Comment] code represents the text that will be entered between the style-on and style-off codes (the heading).

The subheading style includes a Swiss Bold 12pt font change in the style-on section and a [HRt] code in the style-off section. The Block Protect codes were included so that a multiple-line subheading would not be split across page breaks. The style definition looks like this:

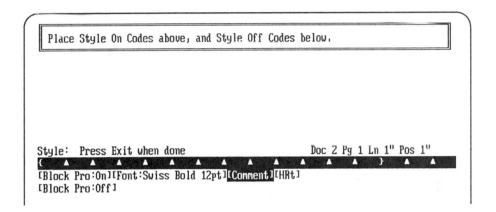

In both styles, ENTER turns the style off (option 5 on the Style Definition menu). This lets you turn on the style, type the heading or subheading, and then press ENTER to turn it off and return to normal text.

You can enter any type of style for your newsletter. If you have third- and fourth-level headings, create styles for them. You can also label the styles "Large," "Medium," and "Small" and then include the codes that make the headings the appropriate size.

Formatting the Newsletter

Because a newsletter is produced weekly or monthly, you can place the format of the newsletter (margins, column definition, hyphenation, headers, footers, page numbering, and so on) in an open style at the beginning of the newsletter or save it in a macro.

You can select this style or macro before entering the text, but it is usually easier to write and edit with normal margins and without columns and hyphenation on. After you enter the text, you can press HOME, HOME, HOME, ↑ (to move before all text and codes) and select the style, start the macro, or retrieve a file that contains only the formatting codes.

The following formatting codes were used for the newsletter shown in Figure 4-1.

Margins   The left and right margins were set to .75″, and the top and bottom margins were set to .5″. Remember while entering measurements that you can use fractions (in this example, you could enter **3/4** and **1/2**).

Headers   A single header was defined to print on every page and includes two horizontal graphics lines. The first is .01″ thick and is set to print the full distance from the left to the right margin. When possible, choose to have graphics lines extend from margin to margin so that if the margins change, the line will be adjusted according to the width of the margins. If you choose to start the line a certain distance from the left side of the page and give it a specific length, it would not be adjusted with the margins.

Pressing ENTER at the end of the first horizontal line brought the cursor down a total of only .01″—the same distance as the width of the line. Because of this, an Advance Down code was inserted to advance down .04″. The second (horizontal) line was then inserted with a width of .03″.

A [HRt] code was inserted at the end of the header to force more space between the header and the first line of text.

If you wanted to place a box around the page, as shown in the example in Figure 4-2, you could decrease the left and right margins and define an empty figure box with the following settings:

Anchor Type	Page
Vertical Position	Full Page
Horizontal Position	Margin, Full
Size	(automatically adjusted to your current margins)
Wrap Text Around Box	No

The graphics box code would then need to be followed by a left and right margin change back to the original setting so the border of the

WordPerfect 5.1

The latest version of WordPerfect is here, bringing over 4,000,000 customers a number of new and exciting features. There are also some very nice changes to some of the features that have been in the program since its conception in 1979.

Pull-Down Menus and Mouse Support

Those just learning how to use WordPerfect will most likely enjoy the new pull-down menus. Because all the features are displayed in nine menus, beginners may find it easier to select features from the menus instead of trying to find the same features on the function keys.

A mouse makes it easy to move the cursor anywhere on the screen just by clicking the left button. This will be especially helpful to those who use the columns and tables features often because it can often be confusing as to which keystrokes to use to move between columns and cells.

A mouse also makes it easy to block text (hold down the left button and drag), or scroll through the document (hold down the right button and drag).

Tables

If there is one feature that everyone will use in WordPerfect, it is the tables feature. With it, you can create grid of rows and columns for text and numbers.

Tell WordPerfect the number of rows and columns, and it will create the table automatically. If you need to change the size later, that can be done just as easily after the table has been created.

Each cell, row, or column can have their own format, shading, alignment, and more. Lines can be turned off, letting you mimic the parallel columns feature, or left on.

You can create forms, invoices, and even box a paragraph of text more easily. Cells can grow to the fit the amount of text, or you can limit the height of a cell.

Columns and rows can easily be moved, copied, or deleted. You can also add a column or row in the middle of a table with just a few keystrokes.

Hawaiian Tours					
—Travel Packages—					
	A	B	C	D	E
Oahu	✓		✓		✓
Maui	✓			✓	✓
Hawaii		✓	✓	✓	
Kaual		✓		✓	✓

If you retrieve a spreadsheet created with PlanPerfect, Lotus 1-2-3, or Excel, it will automatically be placed in a table.

Equations

The new equation editor can be used to format and print complex equations from within WordPerfect. After typing the "text" of the equation, you can press a single key to view the result. Even those who are not familiar with

$$h(t) - \Delta \sum_{n=-\infty}^{+\infty} h_n \frac{\sin[2\pi fc(t-n\Delta)]}{\pi(t-n\Delta)}$$

the equations themselves will be able to easily select from a list of 60 symbols and 300 commands.

Figure 4-2.   Sample newsletter that has a box or border around the page

box will not print over the text on the left and right margins. An extra hard return [HRt] code would be needed to create space between the top edge of the box and the first line of text. See "Borders" in Chapter 3 for step-by-step instructions if you need further help.

Footers   In Figure 4-1, two footers were created. The first one contains the horizontal graphics lines shown at the bottom of the page, and the other is used for the page number. They were created separated so that the second footer containing the page number could be suppressed on the first page.

Even though you can include text with the page number as a page number style, the page number was included in a footer so that it could be positioned between the graphics lines with the Advance Up command.

The first footer is similar to the header. The first code is a [HRt] that forces more space between the footer and the last line of text. The first and second horizontal graphics lines are .01″ thick, and the bottom line is .03″ thick. An Advance Down of .25″ was used between the first and second lines, and an Advance Down of .04″ was inserted between the second and third lines.

Footer B contains a Swiss Bold 12pt font change and the text "Page ^B." The ^B was inserted by pressing CTRL-B, which inserts the current page number at print time. Because the bottoms of both footers start at the bottom margin, an Advance Up of .1″ was inserted at the beginning of this footer to force the page number up between the lines. It may take some experimentation to find the right amount of adjustment; use the View Document feature (in Graphics mode) to help you see how much of an adjustment to make.

Footer B was then suppressed on the first page by pressing Format (SHIFT-F8), choosing **2** for **P**age, typing 8 for **S**uppress (for this page only), selecting 8 for "Suppress Footer B," and typing **Y**.

If you created a border for the page, as described earlier in this chapter under "Headers," you would need to create a footer that included a single [HRt] code. This would stop the bottom border of the box from printing over the bottom line of text on the page.

Hyphenation   The hyphenation zone was changed to 20% on the left and 10% on the right. Because the newsletter will be formatted into columns that have fairly short line lengths, the default hyphenation zone of 10% and 4% would force you to hyphenate three- and four-letter words with virtually no room to make a hyphenation decision.

Using a normal line length would give you a normal hyphenation zone, because 10% of the line would be approximately .7″ to the left, and 4% would be .25″ to the right. Therefore, when you are decreasing the length of the line with a margin change or columns, remember to increase the hyphenation zone.

If you are using text or graphics boxes throughout the document, do not turn on hyphenation at this point. You would make the hyphenation decisions and then be faced with them again while inserting graphics boxes because the length of the lines may change during the process. If you do not plan to insert text or graphics boxes, you may want to turn on hyphenation, or wait until the document is finished and make all hyphenation decisions at once.

Headlines   Entering the centered headline is the next step. An Advance to Line 1″ was inserted first, kerning was turned on, and then a Century Schoolbook 24pt Bold font was selected. After entering the headline, kerning was turned off, and the font was returned to the initial font of Century Schoolbook 11pt. If you do not see any difference in the headline when it is printed, the kerning information has not been entered into the proportional spacing table for that particular font. Step-by-step instructions for doing so using the Printer program are included in Chapter 5.

You can also use the Advance Left command to kern a headline manually. These steps are included earlier in this chapter under ″Kerning.″

Shaded Box for the Dateline   The next step includes a shaded text box for the volume, number, and date of the newsletter. Different options were chosen for the text box by pressing Graphics (ALT-F9) and choosing 3 for Text Box and 4 for Options. The top and bottom borders were changed from a thick line to a single line. The inside border space

was changed to .4" for the left and right, and .05" for the top and
bottom. Note that the amount of shading is preset to 10% for a text box.

After the Options menu was exited, a text box was created with the
selections shown in Figure 4-3. The amount of space from the top of the
page (1.5") was set for exact positioning. WordPerfect will automatically
calculate the height of the box (depending on the amount of text in the
box) so you do not have to change the size.

The text is inserted in the box when you choose 9 for Edit. After
typing the first part of the line, press Center (SHIFT-F6), and type the text
in the center of the box. Finally, press Flush Right (ALT-F6), and enter
the text at the right of the box. Do not press ENTER, or an extra line will
be inserted. Press Exit (F7) until you return to the document.

Defining Columns   Finally, you are ready to advance down to the
appropriate position and define columns. In Figure 4-1, an Advance to

```
Definition: Text Box

    1 - Filename

    2 - Contents             Text

    3 - Caption

    4 - Anchor Type          Page

    5 - Vertical Position    1.5"

    6 - Horizontal Position  Margin, Full

    7 - Size                 7" wide x 0.625" (high)

    8 - Wrap Text Around Box Yes

    9 - Edit




Selection: 0
```

Figure 4-3.   Selections for the text box containing the dateline in Figure 4-1

Line 2.25″ was used. Press Math/Columns (ALT-F7), and choose 1 for Columns and then 3 to Define the columns. Choose three newspaper columns with .25″ between each column, and then turn the columns on when you have finished.

In Figure 4-2, three columns were also used, but the margins were set manually because the third column was narrower than the first and second. The blank space makes the page look cleaner, and it can contain pull quotes and graphics boxes that extend partially from column 2 into column 3. See the next section, "Graphics Boxes," for more information.

After you have entered all these settings into a macro, style, or regular WordPerfect file, you can use the settings again at the beginning of any amount of text to decide the format for that text.

Graphics Boxes

The last step is to decide the location of text and graphics boxes. If you want to include a shaded box at the bottom left corner of the newsletter for the name of the editor and staff, you can do so as part of the format file. It will be anchored to a specific position on the page, and text will wrap around it.

If you want a text box to flow with a specific paragraph, choose Paragraph as the Type selection. The box will then be placed within that particular column. You can choose Left, Right, or Center, or you can span the distance between the left and right margins.

If you want the box to span more than one column, the type of box will need to be defined as a "Page" graphics box. The cursor needs to be after the column definition code if it is to be placed with respect to the columns. The text box shown in Figure 4-1 spans columns 1 and 2. To set this type of option, you would need to choose option 6 for Horizontal Position, 2 for Columns, enter 1-2 when asked which columns, and then choose 4 for Full (meaning the full distance between the left and right margins).

The height of the box was not set so that WordPerfect could adjust the box to fit the text. In the Options menu (set just before the text box), the inside border space was increased from 0″ to .25″ to help extend the text to the bottom of the page, and the top outside border space was changed to 0″ to eliminate extra space at the top of the box.

Also in the Options menu, the Border Style was set to a single line at the left and right, and a thick line at the top and bottom.

Note that a larger font was used for the headline in the article. To avoid overshadowing the newsletter headline, a different typeface was selected: Swiss 30pt (a regular font instead of a boldface font).

Figure 4-2 shows how a graphics box can span two columns without taking up all the space in both columns. After choosing **6** for Horizontal Position, choose **2** for Columns, enter **2-3** when asked for the columns to be affected, and then choose **2** for **R**ight (meaning at the right of columns 2 and 3). You may then want to adjust the width of the box if necessary so that it takes up more or less space in column 2.

A table was included in one of the graphics boxes. Because you cannot include a table in columns, you can "protect" it and include it if it is part of a graphics box. See "Tables" in Chapter 3 for instructions on creating a table.

You can also center a graphics box between columns by following the preceding steps but choose **3** for Center as the last step. Figure 4-4 shows what this looks like when done. It also shows how two graphics images were placed in the same location by turning off borders and setting the exact horizontal and vertical positions for the graphics boxes.

Graphics Lines

You can place graphics lines anywhere on a page, but when you are working with columns you will most likely want to place them between columns, as shown in Figure 4-4.

Before inserting vertical lines between columns, you will need to move the cursor after the columns definition and columns-on codes. You can then follow these steps:

1. Press Graphics (ALT-F9).

2. Choose **5** for Line.

3. Choose **2** for Vertical.

4. Choose **1** for Horizontal Position. The following choices appear:

Horizontal Position: 1 Left; 2 Right; 3 Between Columns; 4 Set Position: 0

Inter-Office Mail Reminder

For those employees who use the numbering system when addressing inter-office mail, please be advised that the Accounting Department has now been changed to #11.

For those of you who are not using the numbering system, please write employees' first and last names and departments legibly.

East Meets West

This past month some of our top executives traveled to Japan to meet with our sister company. While there, the group went sightseeing, ate in wonderful Japanese restaurants, and had some very productive meetings.

A few representatives from the Japanese office will be coming some time this summer for a similar visit and exchange of ideas.

Insurance Update

If you are admitted to a hospital for any reason, please specify your employer upon admittance. The billing departments of all hospitals have been advised of our insurance coverage and are aware of the information needed to process a claim.

Don't forget that, when filing your first claim each year, one full completed claim must be submitted for each family member. Subsequent claims may be submitted with only a receipt for services rendered (unless the claim is accident-related, in which case a fully completed claim form is required.

Insurance Questions?

All questions regarding company insurance policies (for example, coverage, eligibility, and reimbursement) should now be directed to Mary in Accounting at extension 304.

Business Card Orders

All employees who will be attending the computer conventions and need to reorder business cards are requested to so before December 15. Please call Laurie with your order.

Travel Policies

Due to recent changes in the company's travel policies and procedures, an authorization number is needed before airline tickets can be issued. If you will be traveling for the company, please have your travel form filled out and signed by your supervisor prior to submitting it to Fran in Accounting. She will then give the authorization number to the travel agent.

East Meets West

Training Classes

The next session of product training classes begins on December 8, but classes are beginning to fill up now. If you have questions regarding possible enrollment, please see the receptionist in your building for a list of registered participants.

Software Registration

The Testing Department is compiling a list of all software products currently owned by the company. If you have such a product in your office, please send a memo to Gary in Testing. Include the name, a brief description of the product, manufacturer, and version number. If you have no need for the program in your office please forward the entire package to Gary.

Printer Planner

Melinda in Engineering is the one to call if you need to borrow a printer from another department for any reason. When you call with your request, she will need to know the length of time the printer is needed and the purpose of requesting the printer.

2

Figure 4-4.   Vertical line between columns and a centered graphics box with two graphics images being placed in the same location

5. Choose **3** to place the line **B**etween Columns.

6. When you are prompted to "Place line to right of column:," enter the column number. In Figure 4-4, **1** was entered so that it would be placed after column 1.

If you do not want the line to start from the top margin and extend all the way to the bottom margin, choose option **2** for Vertical Position. In the example shown in Figure 4-4, for example, you would need to have two different vertical lines, or they would print over the graphics images. The first one was set to begin at the top margin and the second was set to start from the bottom margin. You would then need to decide the length of the line so that it wouldn't run into the graphics images. Use the View Document option on the Print (SHIFT-F7) menu to make adjustments before printing.

Announcement

You can create announcements, invitations, and programs with WordPerfect. The announcement shown in Figure 4-5 was created with a PostScript printer. You can create the same document on any printer by using different fonts. Use the following steps to create the example shown in Figure 4-5:

1. Change the paper size to standard wide or landscape (11 by 8.5 inches).

2. Change the margins on all sides to .5".

3. Insert the graphics image by pressing Graphics (ALT-F9) and choosing **4** for User Box and **1** for Create. Select this option so that no borders will be included by default.

4. When presented with the User Box Definition menu, choose **1** for Filename, and enter **border-8.wpg**. If the file is not found, you may not have installed the graphics image files during installation, or

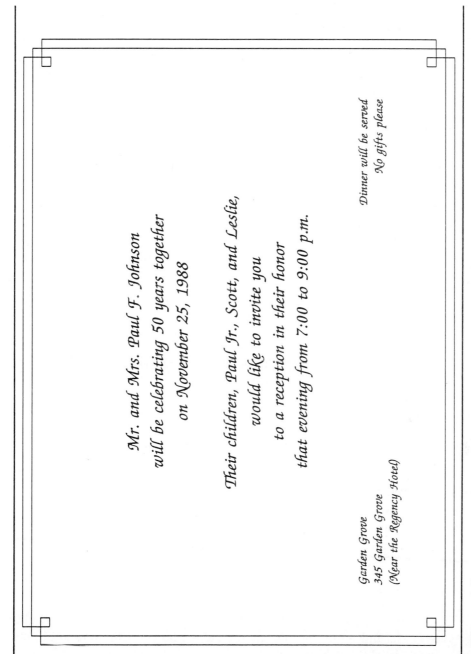

Figure 4-5.   Announcement printed on a PostScript printer

they may be in a different directory than the one that was specified in the Location of Files menu. Enter the drive and directory if necessary.

5. Choose **4** for Anchor **T**ype and **2** for **P**age. Press ENTER when you are asked how many pages are to be skipped.

6. Choose **5** for **V**ertical Position and **1** for **F**ull Page.

7. Choose **6** for **H**orizontal Position, **1** for **M**argins, and **4** for **F**ull.

8. Choose **8** for **W**rap Text Around Box, and then type **N** so that text can print over the box.

9. Press Exit (F7) to return to the document.

10. After inserting the graphics image, change the left and right margins to 1.5″.

11. Press Format (SHIFT-F8), choose **2** for **P**age, and **1** for **C**enter page (top to bottom), and then type **Y** so that the invitation will be centered between the top and bottom margins.

12. Change to double-spacing or increase the line height slightly if double-spacing creates too much space.

13. Select a font. In Figure 4-5, an ITC Zapf Chancery Italic font was used. Because the printer is a PostScript printer, the user is prompted for the point size each time a font is selected. This example uses a 20pt font for the first section of text.

14. To center the first section, press Format (SHIFT-F8), and choose **1** for **L**ine, **3** for **J**ustification, and then **2** for **C**enter. Type the first section of the announcement, and then follow the steps again, choosing **1** for **L**eft as the justification setting.

15. Reselect the same font, but this time enter 14 as the point size. Change the line height back to Auto.

16. After entering the text at the left margin, press Flush Right (ALT-F6), and enter the text at the right margin. Continue until you have finished with all lines.

17. If you have a graphics monitor, view the document to see if the placement and spacing are acceptable. You may have to decrease or increase the line height or change the font size.

18. When it looks acceptable, print the document.

Brochures

To create a tri-fold brochure, as shown in Figure 4-6, select a standard wide piece of paper (11 by 8.5), define a header that includes different types of graphics lines, and then define three columns with approximately 2 inches between each column.

The small square boxes in the header were created by calculating the exact horizontal position and then setting the length of the line equal to the width of the line.

Letterhead

You can create a simple letterhead with WordPerfect using graphics lines and various font changes. The letterhead shown in Figure 4-7 was created with 30pt Times Roman and 12pt Helvetica, with letter spacing increased to 190% of optimal. The address at the bottom was created with a Helvetica 8pt font.

You could insert a logo and place a horizontal line below it, spanning the left and right margins. If you have a PostScript printer that can print both portrait and landscape at the same time, you could place the company logo and other information at the left in a text box, rotate it so it is printed in landscape, and then insert a vertical line that prints to the right of it. Change the margins for the text in the letter, and you are finished.

Overheads and Transparencies

You can create useful overheads and transparencies by changing to the largest font available and using a landscape form if necessary.

You could use the checked box that is included with WordPerfect (CHKBOX-1.WPG) to create a to-do list, as shown in Figure 4-8. A style was used to "point" to the graphics image on disk followed by an [→Indent] code to indent the item.

Style by Design

Type of Services Offered

If you can think of it, we can create it. From business cards, to brochures to advertisements in the Wall Street Journal.

Following are just a few of the services we have provided to our customers in the past.

- Company Logos
- Stationery
- Advertisements
- Business Cards
- Corporate Identity

We can come up with solutions to any design problem. Give us a call.

At "Style by Design" we listen to our customers' ideas. We give them what they want rather than forcing them to live by "standard" rules and conventions.

We invite you to try our services. If you are not satisfied with our unique outlook on design, we gladly offer a money-back guarantee.

Please contact us when you need help designing that special brochure, advertisement, or company logo. We are at your service.

A Few of our Clients

AV&V
The Hope Chest
Just Desserts
The Springs Hotel

Awards

ADDY 1988 and 1989

Bob Moki has been featured in Adweek and Communications Arts

Designers

Bob Moki
Susan McGuiness
Randy Nelson
Rachel McDonald

Figure 4-6. Tri-fold brochure

WordPerfect
CORPORATION

1555 N. Technology Way, Orem, Utah U.S.A 84057 — (801) 225-5000 — Telex 830618 — FAX (801) 227-4588

Figure 4-7. Letterhead created with version 5.1

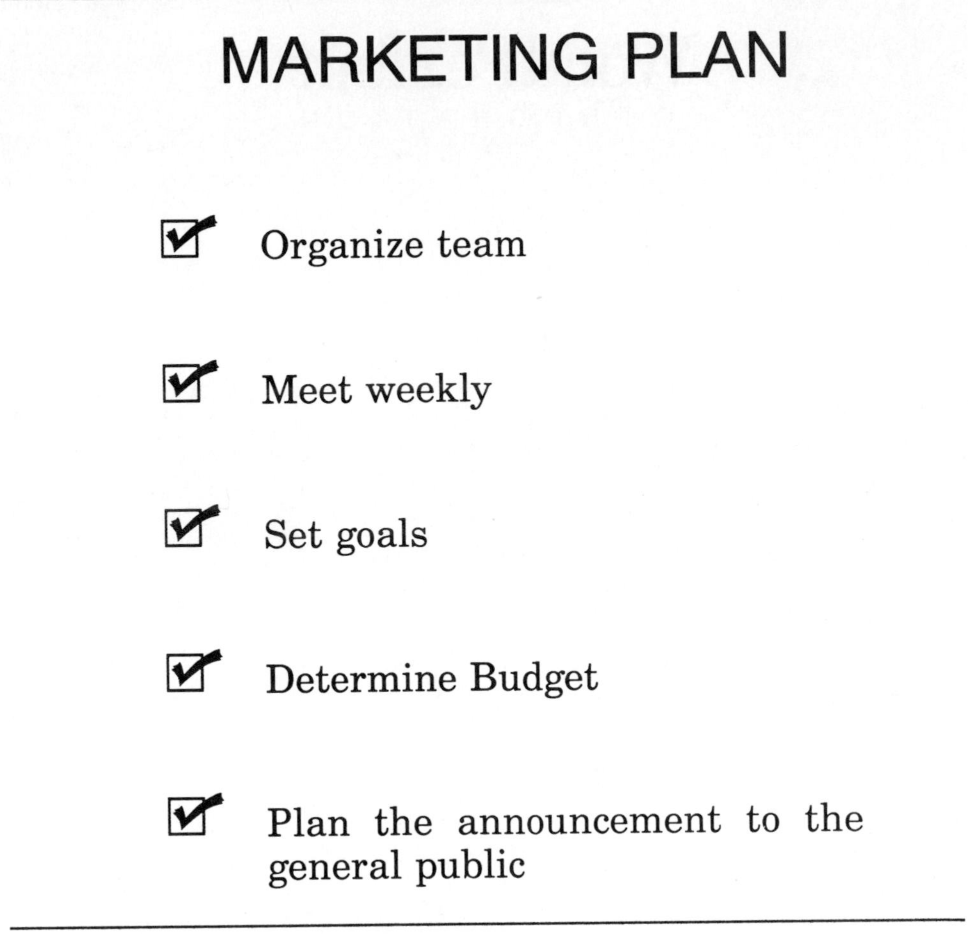

MARKETING PLAN

☑ Organize team

☑ Meet weekly

☑ Set goals

☑ Determine Budget

☑ Plan the announcement to the general public

Figure 4-8.   Overhead transparency with checkbox graphic

The examples that have been included in this chapter should give you some idea of the possibilities offered by desktop publishing with Word-Perfect. There are many other powerful features such as tables that you can use to create forms and invoices, and you can use the equation editor to create a headline of any size. See "Tables" and "Equations" in Chapter 3 for examples.

You may also want to refer to "Paper Size/Type" in Chapter 3 for a method that you can use to create and print side-by-side pages, which are useful when you are printing programs.

You can also create shadow borders that have a three-dimensional appearance by selecting Thick or Extra Thick borders for two adjoining sides of a graphics box. See "Shadow Borders" or "Graphics Boxes" in Chapter 3 for details.

If you have any problems with the steps included in this chapter, refer to the appropriate entry in Chapter 3 for step-by-step instructions.

Printer Program

The Printer program included with WordPerfect lets you customize printer definitions to fit your needs and applications. Although you may never need to change a printer definition, you can review this chapter for insights about how WordPerfect communicates with your printer.

Among other things, you can use the Printer program to convert a WordPerfect 5.0 printer definition (.PRS) file to 5.1 format, select Automatic Font Changes (the fonts used for extra large, large, small, bold, italics, and so on), and select Substitute Fonts (fonts that are searched when a special character is not found in the current font). You can also define sheet-feeder definitions, create or modify kerning tables (decide which pairs of characters to kern and the amount of movement needed to squeeze those characters closer together), and copy font libraries from one file to another.

Only the basics of the program are discussed in this chapter. For in-depth information about each option in the menus you may want to purchase the optional documentation available from WordPerfect Corporation.

Introduction

A printer definition is a preprogrammed set of instructions that tell the printer how to perform various features in WordPerfect. For example, when you create a document and choose such formatting options as page size, boldface, or right justification, codes are inserted into the text. When the document is printed, the current printer definition is used to "translate" those WordPerfect codes into commands that the printer can understand. All the codes necessary to drive the printer are included with the printer definition; you can view and change them with the Printer program.

WordPerfect has included hundreds of printer definitions so that you can, by selecting your printer, call up the set of instructions that will control the printer correctly. Moreover, you can do this without ever knowing anything about printer codes.

If your printer is not among those supported by WordPerfect, you will need to use the standard printer definition, select a definition that is compatible with your printer, or create your own printer driver using the Printer program.

In addition to changing a printer definition, you can send printer commands from within WordPerfect by pressing Format (SHIFT-F8) and choosing 4 for **O**ther, 6 for **P**rinter Functions, and then 2 for **P**rinter Command. You can then send either a command or an entire file to the printer at that point in the document. When the document is printed, the commands are sent directly to the printer without interpretation by WordPerfect. See "Printer Commands" in Chapter 3, "Commands and Features," for more information. In either case, you can find the commands in the owner's manual that is furnished with the printer.

You can also use the Printer program to edit and create fonts with appropriate character maps and proportional spacing tables or edit or create sheet-feeder definitions.

Files That Can Be Edited with the Printer Program

When you select a printer using WordPerfect's Install program, a file containing that particular printer definition (and several others) is copied to the directory specified for printer files (C:\WP51, unless otherwise specified). The file copied is named with the extension .ALL to distinguish it from other files.

Think of the .ALL file as a master file containing many printer definitions. If you want to make permanent changes to a printer definition, make the changes to an .ALL file. Such changes include adding fonts, proportional spacing tables, and character maps.

After you select a printer from the list while in WordPerfect, a printer resource file is created with the extension .PRS. Only one printer definition is kept in a .PRS file, whereas many are kept in an .ALL file.

Another difference between an .ALL file and a .PRS file is that an .ALL file does not have automatic font changes, but a .PRS file does. The automatic font changes are set up for you when you select a printer. You will see the message "Updating Font: *n*" after selecting the printer and again after selecting Cartridges and Fonts. At that time, Word-Perfect looks at all the available fonts and cartridges, and selects the ones that seem most appropriate for fine print, small print, large, very large, extra large, boldface, italics, shadow, outline, multinational, Greek, Hebrew, math, box draw, landscape, and so on. If you want to make a change to the fonts that have been selected for you or view the ones that have been selected, edit the .PRS file.

You can select the same printer definition several times from an .ALL file and keep each definition in a separate .PRS file. You can then select a different set of fonts and cartridges, forms, and initial fonts for each .PRS file. Use the Printer program if you need to make changes to these files.

If you edit your .PRS file and then enter WordPerfect and select different cartridges and/or fonts, the changes that you made to the .PRS file may be lost, because it will want to update the automatic font changes and make other changes to the .PRS file. However, you will see a warning and will be asked for confirmation before this happens.

Starting the Printer Program

Before using the Printer program, you must install it with the Install program (if you have not done so already). Start the Install program, choose Custom, choose the option to install the disks, and then answer **Y** when you are asked if you want to install the PTR Program files.

Decide which file you will be editing (.ALL or .PRS), and use the following instructions to start the Printer program. Choose the appropriate set of steps, depending on whether you have a two-disk-drive system or a hard-disk system.

See "Startup Options" later in this chapter for options that you can use when you are starting the Printer program. See "Automatic Font Changes and Substitute Fonts" later in this chapter for startup options that you can use to go directly to that point in the printer definition.

Hard Disk

1. Change to the directory where the .ALL or .PRS file to be edited is located (usually C:\WP51, unless you specified another). For example, enter **cd \wp51** if the file is found in that directory.

2. Because the Printer program (PTR.EXE) will most likely be in the same directory, enter **ptr** at the DOS prompt. You can include the name of the file to be edited after typing **ptr**. For example, entering **ptr wphp1.all** would start the Printer program and retrieve the WPHP1.ALL file.

3. If you did not include the name of an .ALL or .PRS file, press Retrieve (SHIFT-F10), and enter the name of the file to be edited.

If you do not know the name of the printer files, press List (F5). The filename template *.ALL appears along with the name of the current directory. Press ENTER to see a list of the .ALL files in that directory, or enter a different filename template, such as *.**prs**. Be sure to include the directory where the printer file(s) is found, if necessary.

Once the files are listed, move to the one to be retrieved and press ENTER.

The screen shown in Figure 5-1 appears, with the name of the file being edited displayed at the top left corner. If you are editing an .ALL file, the printer definitions included in that file are listed below. If you are editing a .PRS file, just the name of the appropriate printer definition is displayed.

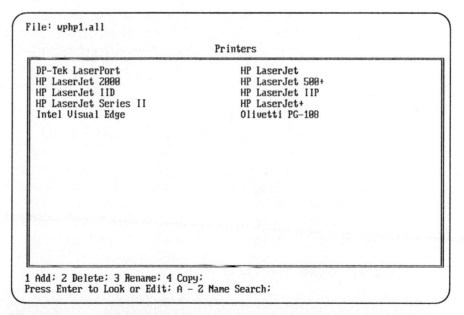

Figure 5-1.   Printer program's opening screen, listing the names of printer definitions in the .ALL file listed at the upper left corner of the screen

Two Disk Drives

1. Place the PTR Program disk in drive A and the disk containing the .ALL or .PRS file to be edited in drive B.

2. Enter **b:** to change the default directory to drive B.

3. Enter **a:ptr** to start the Printer program from drive A. You can also include the name of the .ALL or .PRS file to be edited at the same time. For example, entering **a:ptr wphp1.all** would start the Printer program and retrieve the WPHP1.ALL file from the disk in drive B.

4. If you did not include the name of the .ALL or .PRS file when you started the Printer program, press Retrieve (SHIFT-F10) and enter the name of the file to be edited.

   You can also press List (F5) after Retrieve (SHIFT-F10) to display a list of printers on drive B. See step 3 in the previous section if you need more information.

The screen shown in Figure 5-1 appears, with the name of the file being edited displayed at the top. If you are editing an .ALL file, the printer definitions included in that file are listed below. If you are editing a .PRS file, just the name of the appropriate printer definition is displayed.

Printer Files from Older Versions

If you try to retrieve a printer definition from version 5.0 or a printer file that was edited with an earlier version of PTR.EXE, you will be informed that it is a file from an older version of WordPerfect. You will also see a "warning" telling you that documents created in earlier versions of WordPerfect with the old printer definition file may have different line and page breaks when you print the same document with the converted printer file. Answer **Y** or **N** to the following question:

Convert to New Format? (Y/N) **N**

After editing the file and pressing Exit (F7) or Save (F10), *enter a different filename* for the file, or the edited file will overwrite the original. By using a different filename, you will be able to keep the original file as a backup.

If you don't want to keep a copy of the original .PRS or .ALL file for the older version of WordPerfect, you can convert the file immediately by entering **ptr/convert** *filename*.**prs**; the file will be converted without asking for confirmation. If you use this feature, remember that it overwrites the original file.

Function Keys and Help

You can press Help (F3) at any time to display a template that gives the names of the function keys, as shown in Figure 5-2. Many of the keys are in the same location as those in WordPerfect, such as Cancel (F1), Help (F3), Save (F10), Retrieve (SHIFT-F10), Exit (F7), Search (F2), Reverse Search (SHIFT-F2), Copy (CTRL-F4), Setup (SHIFT-F1), List (F5), and In/Out (CTRL-F5).

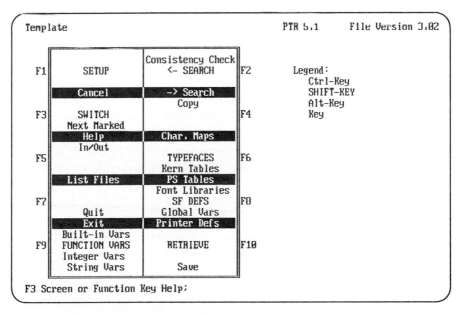

Figure 5-2.   Printer program help screen showing the function key assignments

In fact, the Printer program is similar to WordPerfect, in that you retrieve a file with Retrieve (SHIFT-F10), make changes, and then save the changes, overwriting the previous file. One minor difference is that you cannot retrieve one file into another file. You may, however, copy a printer definition from one .PRS or .ALL file to another with Copy (CTRL-F4).

Exiting the Printer Program

Although you can always use Exit (F7) to retrace your steps through submenus back to the initial screen, you can use Quit (ALT-F7) to exit from almost any location in the program. Before exiting the Printer program, press CTRL-F2 to perform a consistency check. Any errors or inconsistencies in the currently highlighted printer file are saved in a file called PRS.ERR. You will then be allowed to look at and scroll through the document. Press Exit (F7) to return to the Main menu. If you want to print the file, start WordPerfect and print it as you would any other WordPerfect file.

Help

From any screen in the Printer program, you can press Help (F3) *once* to display the template or *twice* to view help information about the current item. For example, if the cursor is highlighting the Typeface category for fonts, it will display help information about typefaces and all options contained in the Typeface menu. You can then scroll up or down in the help screen if you want to read information about related items.

While in the help screen, you can press HOME, HOME, ↑ to start at the beginning of the help file and then scroll through the file, reading the help information about every item in the Printer program. The first part of the help file lists startup options and general information for entering codes into a printer file.

Organization of the Printer Program

When editing a printer file, you can use the following function keys to go to different areas of the program more quickly instead of moving through several levels of menus.

F4	Character maps
F6	Proportional spacing
SHIFT-F6	Typefaces
ALT-F6	Kerning tables
SHIFT-F8	Sheet feeders
CTRL-F10	Font libraries
F8	Printers (return to the list of printers)

There is some overlap, however. For example, while editing fonts from within the printer definition area, you will enter the lists of character maps and proportional spacing tables to select the appropriate choice. If the desired character map or proportional spacing table has not yet been defined, you will have to enter that area and define it before you can continue defining the font.

To edit a printer definition, move the cursor to the name of the printer in the list and press ENTER. You will then see a list of categories to edit, as shown in Figure 5-3. If you are editing a PostScript printer definition, the categories change slightly, as shown in Figure 5-4. Move to the desired category and press ENTER.

In a few screens, you will enter codes immediately, such as the Printer Initialization screen, but most of the screens require you to make a choice and then go on to yet another screen (such as the Vertical Motion or Horizontal Motion screen) and add codes.

Pressing Exit (F7) lets you retrace your steps backward through the menus, while ENTER leads you farther down the path into more submenus. You can always press Quit (ALT-F7) to exit all submenus immediately.

```
File: wphp1.all

                     (Shared) Printer: HP LaserJet Series II

   Initialize and Reset
   Printer Commands
   Horizontal Motion
   Vertical Motion
   Attribute Methods
   Fonts
   Forms
   Graphics
   Helps and Hints about Printer
   Miscellaneous Numbers
   Miscellaneous Questions
   Resources
   Soft Font Format Type



 Press Enter to Look or Edit; A - Z Name Search;
 Do all that apply
```

Figure 5-3.   Categories for a printer definition

```
File: wpps1.all

                     (Shared) Printer: Apple LaserWriter

   Fonts
   Forms
   Graphics Resolutions
   Helps and Hints about Printer
   Miscellaneous Numbers
   Miscellaneous Questions
   Printer Commands
   Resources
   Soft Font Format Type




 Press Enter to Look or Edit; A - Z Name Search;
 Do all that apply
```

Figure 5-4.   Categories for a PostScript printer

Uses for the Printer Program

You should not need to make any changes to your printer definition, but if you do, see "Entering Codes" later in this chapter. The information should also help if you need to create a new printer definition.

Most WordPerfect users would probably not want to enter the Printer program. However, if you want to make changes to the Automatic Font Change selections that WordPerfect has chosen for you (fine, large, very large, italics, small caps, and so on), you would do so through the Printer program. You can also choose a list of substitute fonts so that if a special character cannot be found in the current font, WordPerfect can look through a prioritized list of fonts for the character. If you have a graphics printer, the character will be printed even if it is not found in the current or substitute fonts. You might also want to use the Printer program to adjust the kerning for a font.

Automatic Font Changes and Substitute Fonts

Before making changes to the Automatic Font Changes or Substitute Fonts selections, make sure that you have selected all available cartridges and fonts from within WordPerfect. If you make changes to the .PRS file and then return to WordPerfect and select more fonts and cartridges, you will see a message asking "Do you want automatic font changes?" or "Do you want substitute fonts?" Type **N** if you want to leave the selections that you made in the .PRS file, or type **Y** to overwrite those selections.

Editing Automatic Font Changes

When you are in WordPerfect and select all the fonts that are available for your printer, WordPerfect looks at the list and decides which fonts to use for extra large, large, small, fine, bold, italics, and so on. It does this for every font on the list.

If you are not satisfied with WordPerfect's selections, or if you want to have complete control over which fonts are selected, you can do so using the PTR program.

You can start the program, retrieve the .PRS file (you cannot modify the automatic font changes for an .ALL file), and move through several levels of menus; or you can use the following steps as a shortcut:

1. Go to DOS to change to the directory that contains the Printer program.

2. Enter **ptr/afc** *filename.***prs** at the DOS prompt, where the name of the file to be edited is *filename.prs*.

3. You are placed in the opening screen of PTR, with the name of the .PRS file being edited at the top left corner of the screen. Press ENTER to look at the fonts for that printer.

4. Move to the first font to be changed and press ENTER. You will see a screen similar to the one shown in Figure 5-5. The name of the font being affected is displayed in the top center section of the screen.

5. Move to any attributes listed, and press ENTER to select a different font. You will then see the entire list of fonts again.

6. Move to the font to be selected for that attribute, and type *.

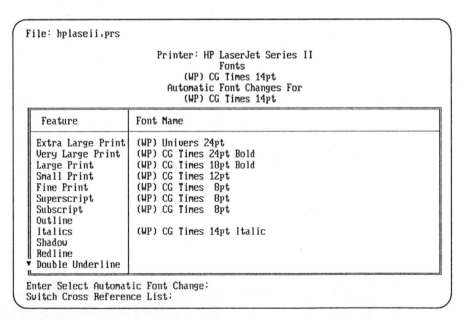

Figure 5-5.   List of automatic font changes

7. Press Exit (F7) when you are finished.

8. Continue making changes to the automatic font selections, and then press Exit (F7).

9. Move to the next font to be changed, press ENTER, and continue with steps 5 through 8.

10. Press Exit (F7) until you leave the program. Remember to save the file when you are prompted to save, or you will lose all the changes that you just made.

There are other automatic font changes besides the ones shown in Figure 5-5. Figure 5-6 shows the additional categories that you can select.

You can choose the font that will be used when you are printing characters from certain WordPerfect character sets. For example, if you have a font that contains Greek characters, select it for that automatic font change, and it will be used to print characters from the Greek character set.

If you reenter WordPerfect and make future font selections, Word-Perfect senses that you have made changes to the .PRS file and asks if you want it to reselect the automatic font changes. Type **N** if you want to keep the automatic font changes as you selected them. If you answer No, the new fonts will not have automatic font changes. Reenter the PTR program, and make the selections manually.

Selecting Substitute Fonts

When you type a special character that is not found in the current font, WordPerfect looks to see if you have entered an automatic font change for that particular character set (Greek, Math, and so on). If not, it searches through a list of substitute fonts for the character. If it cannot find it in that location, it prints the character (or the diacritical part of the character that it cannot find) in graphics. If you do not have a graphics printer, a space will print instead.

To ensure that a character will be printed normally instead of in Graphics mode (Graphics mode is slower and the text may not look as crisp), you can enter the Substitute Font section of the PTR program and enter a list of fonts to be searched if a character is not found in the current font.

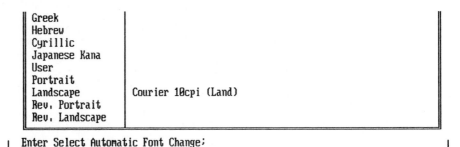

```
File: hplaseii.prs

                        Printer: HP LaserJet Series II
                                   Fonts
                            (WP) CG Times 14pt
                          Automatic Font Changes For
                            (WP) CG Times 14pt
   ┌──────────────────────┬──────────────────────────────────────┐
   │  Feature             │ Font Name                            │
   ├──────────────────────┼──────────────────────────────────────┤
   │▲ Bold                │ (WP) CG Times 14pt Bold              │
   │║ Strikeout           │                                      │
   │║ Underline           │                                      │
   │║ Small Caps          │ (WP) CG Times 12pt                   │
   │║ ASCII               │                                      │
   │║ Multinational 1     │                                      │
   │║ Multinational 2     │                                      │
   │║ Box Draw            │                                      │
   │║ Typographic Sym,    │                                      │
   │║ Iconic Symbol       │                                      │
   │║ Math                │                                      │
   │▼ Math Extension      │                                      │
   └──────────────────────┴──────────────────────────────────────┘

   Enter Select Automatic Font Change;
   Switch Cross Reference List;
```

```
   │║ Greek              │                                      │
   │║ Hebrew             │                                      │
   │║ Cyrillic           │                                      │
   │║ Japanese Kana      │                                      │
   │║ User               │                                      │
   │║ Portrait           │                                      │
   │║ Landscape          │ Courier 10cpi (Land)                 │
   │║ Rev, Portrait      │                                      │
   │║ Rev, Landscape     │                                      │
   └──────────────────────┴──────────────────────────────────────┘

   Enter Select Automatic Font Change;
   Switch Cross Reference List;
```

Figure 5-6.   Continued list of automatic font changes

You can move through several levels of menus or use the following shortcut to go to the Substitute Font section of the printer definition:

1. Go to DOS to change to the directory where the Printer program is located.

2. After following the preceding steps 1 and 2, enter **ptr/sub** *filename.***prs** at the DOS prompt, where *filename.prs* is the name of the file to be edited.

3. You are placed in the opening screen of PTR with the name of the .PRS file being edited on the screen. Press ENTER to look at the fonts for that printer.

4. Move to the first font to be changed and press ENTER. You will see a screen similar to the one shown in Figure 5-7, with the names of all fonts available in the printer among the list. The name of the font being affected is displayed at the top center section of the screen.

5. Move to the font in the list that is most likely to have the needed characters, and choose **1** to make it first in the list. Continue moving

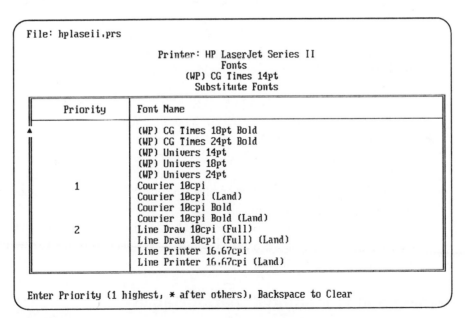

Figure 5-7.   Substitute fonts for special characters

through the list of fonts and entering numbers to indicate the search priority. You can have up to nine substitute fonts. The more fonts you select, the longer it may take to print, because Word-Perfect might need to search through all the substitute fonts for certain characters.

6. Press Exit (F7) when you are finished.

7. Move to the next font to be changed, press ENTER, and repeat steps 5 and 6.

8. Press Exit (F7) until you exit the PTR program. Remember to save the file when you are prompted to save, or you will lose all the changes that you just made.

Character Map

If you want to see which characters have been defined for a particular font, move the cursor to the Fonts category and press ENTER, and then move to the font in question and press ENTER.

When you see a list of categories for the font, move to the Character Map entry and press ENTER. You will see a list of all character maps that are being used by the fonts in that printer definition, with the cursor resting on the currently selected character map. Press ENTER to edit or look at that font.

The characters are listed by section, 0 to 12. You can press ↑ or ↓ to look at the characters in the list, or you can press Search (F2) to search for a particular character. For example, you could press Search (F2) and type **trademark** to move directly to character 22 in section 4 for the registered trademark symbol. The character will be displayed on the screen only if the character is in the computer's ROM (see Appendix A for a list of printed characters).

After you have finished looking at the characters that have been defined or you have made your changes, press Exit (F7) until you return to the name of the printer.

Kerning and Proportional Spacing Tables

The Kerning feature allows you to control the amount of space between two characters. For example, you can kern the characters "Y" and "o" so that they fit together better; "You" would be printed, instead of "You."

WordPerfect Corporation has not defined many kerning tables for smaller fonts, but it has included some kerning information for larger fonts. Kerning is part of the proportional spacing (PS) table for a font. Many fonts can share the same proportional spacing table.

You can make changes to the kerning tables by going to the font and editing the selected PS table, or you can press ALT-F6 to go directly to the kerning tables. The following steps lead you through the process of selecting and editing a kerning table for a particular font instead of editing the kerning tables in general.

1. After starting the Printer program and selecting a printer to be edited, move to the "Fonts" category and press ENTER.

2. Move the cursor to the Font Library that contains the desired font. For example, if you want to edit or create a kerning table for an AD soft font, move to that category and press ENTER.

3. Move to the font in the Font Library, and press ENTER to select that font.

4. Move to the "Size and Spacing Information" category, and press ENTER.

5. Press ↓ until you reach the last option, Proportional Spacing Table:, and press ENTER.

6. A list of PS tables appears, with the cursor resting on the currently selected PS table. Press ENTER to look at or edit the table. You will see a screen similar to the one shown in Figure 5-8.

7. Press TAB until you reach "Kerning Table" at the bottom of the screen. If a kerning table has been selected, you will see the name of the table; otherwise "None selected" will appear.

8. Move to the kerning table to be edited, and then press ENTER to select it. You can also choose 1 to Add a new kerning table to the list. If you choose to add one to the list, enter a name for the table.

9. The menu shown in Figure 5-9 appears. The character on the left is the first one in the pair to be kerned. For example, if you want to kern the characters "V" and "A," move to the "V" (as shown in Figure 5-9). You can use the arrow keys or press Search (F2), type the character, and then press Search (F2) again to move directly to the character.

```
File: C:\WP51\WPHP1.ALL

                    (Shared) Printer: HP LaserJet Series II
                    (Cartridge Slot): HP Super 8 Cartridges
                         (WP) Univers 24pt
                       Size and Spacing Information
                 Proportional Spacing Table: HP AD TmsRmn30B
  ┌────────────────────────────────────────┬─────────┬─────────┐
  │ Number Description                      │  Width  │ Adjust  │
  ├────────────────────────────────────────┴─────────┴─────────┤
  │  0,32    (Space)                            31              │
  │  0,33  ! (Exclamation Point)                40              │
  │  0,34  " (Neutral Double Quote)             41              │
  │  0,35  # (Number/Pound)                     95              │
  │  0,36  $ (Dollars)                          62              │
  │  0,37  % (Percent)                          98              │
  │  0,38  & (Ampersand)                        97              │
  │  0,39  ' (Neutral Single Quote)             31              │
  │▼ 0,40  ( (Left Parenthesis)                 40              │
  ├────────────────────────────────────────────────────────────┤
  │ Units: 300ths                       Point Size: 30          │
  │ Kerning Table: HP AC/AD/AE/AF TmsRmn Bold                   │
  └────────────────────────────────────────────────────────────┘

 Press Enter to Edit
```

Figure 5-8.   Proportional spacing table

```
File: C:\WP51\WPHP1.ALL

                    (Shared) Printer: HP LaserJet Series II
                    (Cartridge Slot): HP Super 8 Cartridges
                         (WP) Univers 24pt
                       Size and Spacing Information
                 Proportional Spacing Table: HP AD TmsRmn30B
                 Kerning Table: HP AC/AD/AE/AF TmsRmn Bold
  ┌────────────────────────────────────────┬───────────────────┐
  │ Number Description                      │  Kerning List?    │
  ├────────────────────────────────────────┴───────────────────┤
  │▲ 0,86  U                                    ←┘              │
  │  0,87  W                                    ←┘              │
  │  0,88  X                                    ←┘              │
  │  0,89  Y                                    ←┘              │
  │  0,90  Z                                    ←┘              │
  │  0,91  [ (Left Bracket)                     ----            │
  │  0,92  \ (Backslash)                        ----            │
  │  0,93  ] (Right Bracket)                    ----            │
  │▼ 0,94  ^ (Caret)                            ----            │
  ├────────────────────────────────────────────────────────────┤
  │ Point Size: 30                                             │
  └────────────────────────────────────────────────────────────┘

 Press Enter to Edit Kern Adjust Values
```

Figure 5-9.   Kerning Table menu

If a list of characters to be kerned exists, you will see an arrow pointing left. If none have been defined, you will see the marks "---". In Figure 5-9, you will see that V, W, X, Y, and Z all have had characters kerned to them.

10. To edit the list of characters to be kerned, press ENTER.

11. You will again see a list of all characters. Move to the second character in the pair to be kerned (in the example just given, it is the "A," as shown in Figure 5-10).

12. Enter the value or number of units that should be used to move the second character to the left. Enter this number as a negative number (−20, −10, −5, and so on) because the character will be moved to the left. In Figure 5-10, −20 was entered for an "A," −5 for a "C," and −5 for a "G."

In the unlikely event that you want to move a character to the right, enter a positive value.

The number of units depends on the number supported by your printer. If your printer prints 300 dots per inch, entering −20 would move 20/300ths or 1/15th of an inch to the left. If the printer supported 120 units (the common unit for daisywheel printers), entering −20 would move 20/120ths or 1/6th of an inch.

If you need to change the point size, press TAB to move to that selection at the bottom of the screen, and enter the point size for the current font.

13. Continue entering values for other characters that might be the second character in a pair, using the same character as the first letter in the pair ("We," "Wa," "Wu," and so on).

14. Press Exit (F7) to return to the list of characters in the font. Move to the next character that will be the first character in a pair, and continue with the process.

15. When you have finished with the kerning information, you will want to select the kerning table to be used for the current font; then press Exit (F7) until you exit the Printer program. Save the .PRS or .ALL file, overwriting the previous one.

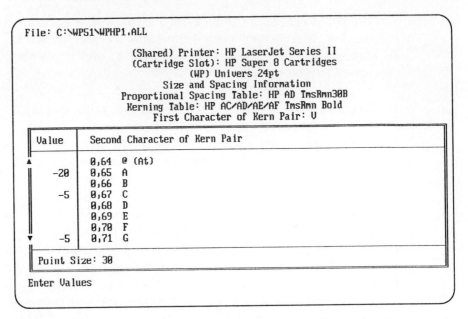

Figure 5-10.   Menu in which you enter the amount of space to move a character to the left

This process is done by trial and error. You will want to save your changes often, exit the program, enter WordPerfect, and print the KERN.TST file from the Conversion disk to see if you need to make further adjustments. This file contains a list of common kerning pairs, an example of how two characters would appear when you vary the amount of kerning from −1 to −30, and a sample of kerned and unkerned text.

Copying Fonts from One File to Another

You can use the Printer program to copy fonts from one file to another. The process will differ depending on whether you are copying fonts from a 5.1 or a 5.0 printer file.

Copy from a 5.1 .ALL File to Another 5.1 File

You can copy all fonts (font libraries) from one 5.1 file to another using the Update Startup option. You can use this option if you have customized or created fonts and then receive an updated printer definition from WordPerfect Corporation and do not want to lose the font information.

　　To copy the fonts, start the Printer program, as shown here:

　　ptr/update *source*.all *target*.all

The fonts from the *SOURCE*.ALL file will be copied to the file *TARGET*.ALL.

　　You can also use the following process to copy fonts, but the Update option is easier.

Copying Fonts from a 5.0 .ALL File

If you want to copy fonts from a 5.0 printer definition to a 5.1 printer definition, you will need to create a Font Library first. You can then copy that Font Library to another .ALL file.

　　1. Start the Printer program, and retrieve the printer definition from 5.0 that contains the fonts to be copied (usually an .ALL file).
　　　　When you are asked if you want to convert the file to the new format, type **Y**.

　　2. Move to the printer definition that contains the fonts, and press ENTER.

　　3. Move to the "Fonts" category and press ENTER.

　　4. Choose **1** to Add a Font Library, and then press CTRL-ENTER to use the default pattern.

　　5. Enter a name for the Font Library. You will be asked for the type of Font Library, as shown here:

```
Font Type 0 Built-In; 1 Cartridge; 2 Soft (KB); 3 Soft (Slots); 4 Wheel: 2
```

6. The type will usually be **2** for Soft Fonts (KB). (KB represents the soft fonts in memory.)

7. Move the cursor to the Font Library that contains the desired fonts (it usually has the same name as the printer), and press ENTER.

8. Mark each font with an asterisk (*) that is to be copied to the new Font Library.

9. Choose **4** for Copy.

10. When you are asked to which Font Library these fonts should be copied, move the cursor to the library that you just created, and press ENTER.

11. After they are copied, press Exit (F7) to return to the list of font libraries.

12. Copy that Font Library to the 5.1 .ALL file. Move to the newly created Font Library, and choose **4** for Copy.

13. Enter the name of the 5.1 .ALL file.

14. Press Exit (F7) until you are asked if you want to save the printer file. Type **Y**, and enter a different name for the file so it will not overwrite the original 5.0 .ALL file.

15. Type **N** when you are asked if you want to exit the Printer program.

16. Retrieve the 5.1 .ALL file to which you copied the new Font Library.

17. Move to the desired printer selection, and press ENTER.

18. Move to the "Fonts" category and press ENTER.

19. Move to the Font Library that you copied from the 5.0 file, and mark it with an asterisk (*).

20. Save the .ALL file and exit the Printer program.

Entering Codes

The Printer program calls a string of codes and commands an expression. You can enter the codes found in the printer manual in ASCII, decimal, hexadecimal, octal, or binary format. You will need to enclose those commands within the following delimiters:

ASCII   " "

Decimal   [ ]

Hexadecimal   < >

Octal   { }

Binary   : :

You can enter the values [32] through [126] within ASCII " " delimiters. The following is an example of each type of format and how to enter it:

Character or code	ASCII	Decimal	Hex	Octal	Binary
Escape		[27]	<1B>	{33}	:11011:
A	"A"	[65]	<41>	{101}	:1000001:

If you have more than one command to be entered in the same format, you can use one set of delimiters. Use commas to separate each value, as shown here:

String	ASCII	Decimal	Hex	Octal	Binary
Escape A		[27,65]	<1B,41>	{33,101}	:11011,1000001:
AB	"AB"	[65,66]	<41,42>	{101,102}	:1000001,1000010:

You can combine different formats when you enter the commands. For example, you can enter ESC W as [27]"W", or you can use the same format to save a little disk space, as in [27,87].

If you want to represent a constant in an expression in ASCII, enclose it in ' ' (single quotes). You can represent hexadecimal by following it with the letter "h," octal by following it with the letter "q," and binary by following it with "b." A constant entered in decimal form does not need any characters or symbols to identify it. Here are examples of each of these types of expressions:

ASCII	Decimal	Hex	Octal	Binary
	10	0ah	12q	1010b
'C'	40	28h	50q	101000b
'd'	100	64h	144q	1100100b

If you want to insert a WPDL command (a command from the WordPerfect Printer Definition Language), enter it in uppercase. You can see a list of the WPDL commands by pressing CTRL-F9 while entering an expression. If you want more information about any of the commands, move to the appropriate command and press Help (F3).

Enter all user-defined variables in lowercase. You can use them to save space and time. If you are repeatedly entering the same string, you can move to the last category, "Variables," enter a variable name, and then enter the string as the expression. You can then use the user-defined variable in place of the string when it is needed in the printer definition.

You can view all this information and more by pressing Help (F3) twice and then pressing HOME, HOME, ↑ to go to the top of the help file.

Startup Options

Other startup options, in addition to those you have previously read about—/CONVERT, /AFC (Automatic Font Change), and /SUB (Substitute Fonts)—are listed next.

/MONO

Enter **ptr/mono** if you have a plasma, LCD, or composite display so that the text will be more readable.

/UPDATE

If you have created or customized several font libraries in an .ALL file, you can use this option to copy them to another .ALL file so you don't have to recreate them. Enter the command as **ptr/update** *source target*, where *source* is the .ALL file that contains the font libraries, and *target* is the .ALL file to which you want them copied. You can use this feature if you receive an updated .ALL file from WordPerfect Corporation and want to copy any font changes from an old .ALL file to the new one.

/UNITS=n

The PTR program normally displays all measurements in inches. If you prefer using a different unit of measurement, start PTR by entering **ptr/units**=*n* where *n* can be one of the following:

c	centimeters
p	points (72 points per inch)
w	WordPerfect units (1200 units per inch)

/CP=n

A code page tells WordPerfect which code page your hardware system (BIOS) uses. Setting this option lets you access the proper keyboard and 256-character ASCII character set for which your system is preset. You do not need to use this option if your version of WordPerfect is preset to your code page. You also do not have to use this option if you have DOS 3.3 or higher and have placed a COUNTRY command in your CONFIG.SYS file.

The complete command to start PTR with a specific code page is **ptr/cp**=*n* where *n* can be one of the following:

437	English
850	PC Multilingual
851	Greek
8510	Greek Alternate
860	Portuguese
8600	Portuguese (Brazil)
861	Icelandic
863	French (Canada)
865	Norwegian and Dutch

If you use this option to enter a code page for which your system is not preset, you may be able to print characters for the code page that you entered, but you cannot change the way in which characters are displayed on the screen. A character is displayed according to the system code page.

The Printer program will give you some indication of the power of WordPerfect. However, even people who are not "experts" will be able to work with the program to make changes to their printer definitions or font selections. While working with the program, use the Help key often; the information obtained there should help describe the options more clearly.

Advanced Macro and Merge Commands

This chapter is for those who want to go beyond the simple macro or merge. Because macros and merge share many of the same advanced commands and concepts, both are included in this chapter with differences noted when necessary.

The commands used in macros and merges are fairly complex. If you have a programming background, you will be able to catch on quickly. However, these concepts *can* be learned by those who are motiviated by desire or necessity.

The first section discusses the difference between macros and merges, and how to access the commands for each. The next section tells you how to use variables and enter expressions. A description of each advanced macro and merge command is then included, with several examples to help you get started.

Differences Between Macros and Merges

Often, it does not matter whether you use a merge or a macro for a certain application. For example, you could create a memo with either feature. Merge lets you pause by using the {KEYBOARD} command, while a macro uses the {PAUSE} command. However, as mentioned before, you would need to press End Field (F9) to continue a merge after a pause, whereas pressing ENTER would continue a macro.

Although both features are useful for repetitive tasks, a macro records keystrokes whereas a merge compiles text. In the previous example, the macro would have recorded every keystroke it took to create the memo format and would have stored it in a file with a .WPM extension. If you wanted to edit the memo, you would need to edit the macro. When the macro is started, it would insert the keystrokes as they were stored and pause for necessary information.

The Merge feature would use a regular WordPerfect file. If editing changes were necessary, you could retrieve the file and make the changes as you would in any other file. When a merge is started, it calls up that file as the "primary" file and uses the merge commands to tell it what other text to use or retrieve into certain locations.

A merge could not send a "Go" to the printer. You could, however, record those keystrokes in a macro and use the {NEST MACRO} or {CHAIN MACRO} commands to tell the merge to start that macro at a certain point. You could also use a macro to store the keystrokes that *start* a merge.

Accessing Macro Commands

Defining a macro that records keystrokes is as easy as pressing Macro Def (CTRL-F10), giving the macro a name and a description, pressing the keys to be recorded, and then pressing Macro Def (CTRL-F10) to end the macro.

You can include a few macro commands during this process by pressing Macro Commands (CTRL-PGUP). The following options appear, which include very basic macro commands:

```
1 Pause; 2 Display; 3 Assign; 4 Comment: 0
```

Pause	Pause the macro for input from the keyboard
Display	Decide whether or not to display menus and keystrokes while the macro is running
Assign	Assign text to a variable (store it for later use)
Comment	Insert comments to help document the macro

If you are not defining a macro, you can still assign text to a variable (storage place) by pressing Macro Commands (CTRL-PGUP). If

Block (ALT-F4) is on at the time, the text in the block will be stored in the variable.

If you want to use any of the other advanced macro commands, you must be in the macro editor. To enter the macro editor quickly for a new macro or for one that you have already defined, follow these steps:

1. Press HOME, and then press Macro Define (CTRL-F10).

2. Enter the name of the macro.

3. Enter a description, or press ENTER to accept the description that has already been entered.

If you do not press HOME at the beginning of the process and enter the name of a macro that has already been defined, you will be asked if you want to replace or edit the macro instead of going directly into the macro editor.

While in the macro editor, you can follow these steps to access the macro commands:

1. Press Macro Commands (CTRL-PGUP). The first few macro commands are displayed in the upper right corner of the screen, as shown in Figure 6-1.

2. Type the name of the macro command; the cursor will go directly to that command. You can also use the cursor keys to move through the list if you do not know the exact name of the command.

3. Press ENTER to insert the command into the macro.

4. Enter any additional information for that command. The syntax or rules for entering the command are displayed in the list of macro commands.

For example, if you select the {ASSIGN} command, you will see the syntax (rules) for entering other needed information:

{ASSIGN}var˜expr˜

This means that after selecting the {ASSIGN} command, you will need to enter the variable's name, a tilde (~), the expression (information to be stored in the variable), and then another tilde (~). If you omit a tilde, the macro will not work properly. See "Variables" and "Expressions" later in this chapter for more information.

While in the macro editor you can press ENTER and TAB to help make the macro more readable. These keystrokes create space and new lines; they do not interfere with the macro. If you want to insert an {Enter} or {Tab} function, you must first press CTRL-V and then ENTER or TAB. You must also press CTRL-V before pressing Exit (F7) or Cancel (F1) if you want to insert the {Exit} and {Cancel} commands; otherwise, they will exit the macro editor or cancel changes to the macro. Pressing CTRL-V is also necessary before any editing keystrokes, such as DEL, BACKSPACE, HOME, and any cursor keys.

If you need to enter several editing keys at once, press Macro Define (CTRL-F10). This is like pressing CTRL-V before every keystroke. When you need to use DEL, BACKSPACE, and the cursor keys to edit and move through the macro, press Macro Define (CTRL-F10) to return to normal editing.

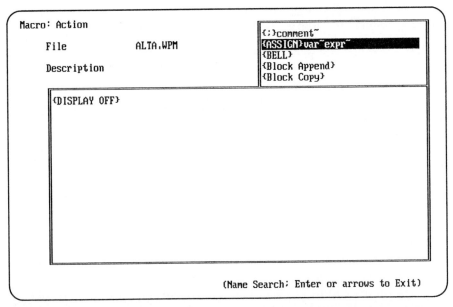

Figure 6-1.   You display macro commands by pressing Macro Commands (CTRL-PGUP) while in the macro editor

Accessing Merge Commands

Accessing merge commands is a little easier. While creating the merge document, you can press Merge Codes (SHIFT-F9) once to select from a few merge commands shown here:

1 Field; 2 End Record; 3 Input; 4 Page Off; 5 Next Record; 6 More: 0

Choose **6** for **More** to see a list of the more advanced merge commands, as shown in Figure 6-2. You can also press Merge Codes (SHIFT-F9) once more, for an easier and faster way to access the advanced merge codes;

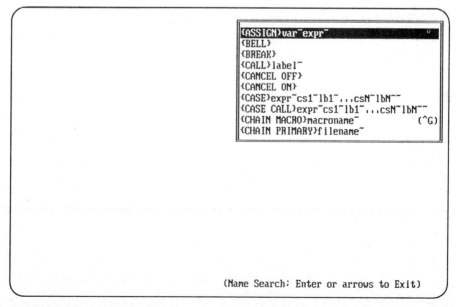

```
{ASSIGN}var~expr~                                    0
{BELL}
{BREAK}
{CALL}label~
{CANCEL OFF}
{CANCEL ON}
{CASE}expr~cs1~lb1~...csN~lbN~~
{CASE CALL}expr~cs1~lb1~...csN~lbN~~
{CHAIN MACRO}macroname~                        (^G)
{CHAIN PRIMARY}filename~
```

(Name Search; Enter or arrows to Exit)

Figure 6-2.   You display advanced merge commands by pressing Merge Codes (SHIFT-F9) twice

in other words, press Merge Codes (SHIFT-F9) twice. The following is a summary of the process of selecting merge commands:

1. Press Merge Codes (SHIFT-F9) twice.

2. Type the name of the desired merge command to go to the command more quickly. You can also use any cursor key to move through the list.

3. Press ENTER to select the highlighted command.

4. When you select a merge command, you are prompted for any additional information, and the tildes are inserted for you automatically. For example, after choosing the {LABEL} command, you are prompted to "Enter Label:". WordPerfect then inserts the tilde (~) for you.

At times, you may find it necessary to select another merge command when you are entering an expression. For example, if you wanted to store a total of several fields in a variable named "Total," you would want to enter {FIELD} commands, indicating which fields were to be included in the expression, as shown here:

{ASSIGN}Total~{FIELD}pastdue~+{FIELD}current~~

In that case, you could enter **total** when you are prompted for the name, but would need to press ENTER when you are prompted for the expression. The command would then appear as follows:

{ASSIGN}Total~~

You would then need to move the cursor between the two tildes, press Merge Codes (SHIFT-F9), choose 1 for Field, and then enter the name of the field. Note also that there are two tildes at the end of the first example: One is to mark the end of the field name or number, and the second is to end the complete expression. See the next section for more information about variables and expressions.

In a merge document, ENTER and TAB cannot be used to help format the merge command as they can in the macro editor. Because you are entering merge commands in a regular WordPerfect document, the ENTER keystrokes would create new lines and TAB would insert [Tab] codes in the finished document.

However, you can use the {COMMENT} merge command to "hide" comments and codes, such as [HRt] and [Tab] codes produced by pressing ENTER and TAB. To do so, you would select the {COMMENT} command from the list of merge codes, enter the text or codes, and then press ENTER. If you press ENTER as the first code in the comment, it will also insert the ending tilde to mark the end of the comment. You would then need to move the cursor once to the left so it is under the tilde, and then enter the remaining text and codes.

In the following example, the merge checks to see if the total field is greater than 0. If so, the customer receiving the letter is asked to send in payment.

{IF}{FIELD}Total˜>0˜Please send payment.{END IF}

Because all {IF} commands need to be paired with an {END IF} command, some people prefer to have both commands against the left margin and indent the statement included between the two commands. If you want to do the extra work needed to make the merge commands more readable, you can insert a [HRt] and a [Tab] code between the first {COMMENT} and tilde (~), and a [HRT] between the second {COMMENT } and tilde (~) as shown here:

{IF}{FIELD}Total˜>0˜{COMMENT}
    ˜Please send payment.{COMMENT}
˜{END IF}

Note: When you print a document with merge codes, the merge codes will not normally be printed. To print both the text and the codes, use the macro CODES (press Macro (ALT-F10), type **codes** and press ENTER).

Variables

Because variables are used extensively in the following commands and examples, a description and explanation about their use follows.

A variable is a place to store information. The information can be text, a numeric value, information from a specific field (when doing a merge), or the result of an arithmetic calculation.

You can use other commands, such as {IF} and {CASE}, to test the information found in a variable and act accordingly. For example, if you stored the number of "months owing" as a variable, you could then have the macro or merge test the variable to see if it is greater than a certain number. If so, that person's record might be placed in a collection file.

You can prompt the person running the merge or macro with a message asking for a single character and store it in a variable with the {CHAR} command. The {TEXT} command does the same thing but lets the user store more than one character. The {ASSIGN} command lets you enter any expression (fields, text, arithmetic calculations, or a combination of the above) in a variable. You can also assign a value to a variable with the {LOOK}, {FOR}, and {FOR EACH} commands. All six—{CHAR}, {TEXT}, {ASSIGN}, {FOR}, {FOR EACH}, and {LOOK}—let you name a variable with any number of characters, but only the first seven are recognized. These are referred to as "global" variables, and they can be used by any macro or merge. Global variables take up memory that is not released until you exit WordPerfect or store "nothing" in the same variable. For example, you could enter **{ASSIGN}Name~ ~** to insert nothing in the "Name" variable.

If you want a variable to be associated with a *specific* merge file, you can use the {LOCAL} command. It differs from the {ASSIGN} command in that you can use up to 15 characters for the variable's name; the memory used by a {LOCAL} variable is released once you exit the document in which it was defined.

See {ASSIGN}, {LOCAL}, {CHAR}, {TEXT}, {LOOK}, {FOR}, {FOR EACH}, and {VARIABLE} in this chapter for more examples on how to store and use variables.

Inserting a Variable in a Macro or Merge

In WordPerfect 5.0, you were limited to ten variables (0 to 9). With version 5.1, you can also use names for variables.

The previous section describes in general terms how information is *stored* in a variable. To insert the contents of named or numbered variables, select the {VARIABLE} command from the list of macro commands, and then enter the name or number of the variable followed by a tilde. The commands would then appear as follows:

{VARIABLE}1 ~

or

{VARIABLE}Name ~

If you have a numbered variable from 0 to 9, you can insert it (in macro only) by pressing CTRL-V, and then press ALT-*n*, where *n* is the variable number. The command would then appear as follows:

{VAR 1}

To insert the contents of a variable into a *merge* document, select the {VARIABLE} command from the list of merge commands, and enter the name of the variable when you are prompted to do so. When the merge is run, the contents of that variable will be retrieved into the finished document.

If you used the ALT-*number* method of naming a variable, you can check the contents of the variable or retrieve it to the screen at any time by pressing ALT and the number at the regular editing screen.

Expressions

An expression is used by the {ASSIGN}, {CASE}, {CASE CALL}, {IF}, {LEN}, {LOCAL}, {MID}, and {WHILE} commands to decide what information will be stored in a variable or what conditions to check for. It can include text, numbers (no larger than 2,147,483,647 or smaller than −2,147,483,647), information from specific fields or other variables, and arithmetic operations. You cannot, however, use real numbers (those containing decimals).

Some examples of valid expressions follow:

{ASSIGN}number~10*3~

{IF}{FIELD}income~>49999~

{WHILE}"{VARIABLE}Name~"!="Doug Smith"~

In the first example, the expression 10*3 (10 multiplied by 3) is assigned to the variable named "number." The second example uses the {IF} command to check the income field for an income that is greater than $49,999. The third example says that "while the 'Name' variable does not equal Doug Smith, then do the commands that follow." As soon as the merge finds Doug Smith's record, the {WHILE} routine would end.

Operators

WordPerfect offers several operators that you can use in an expression. You can use the operators to add, subtract, multiply, and divide. For example, you can add two or more variables (or fields if you are doing a merge) for a total. Another situation would be to use "equal" or "not equal to" operators to compare two values to see if they are identical and then act accordingly.

If you want to use the operators with text (not numbers), you will need to include the values in quotation marks. You can also use quotation marks for numbers; if there is any doubt, be sure to include them. You can use single (') or double (") quotation marks, but you must pair them correctly. The following is correct:

{IF}"{FIELD}First Name~"="Bob"
    .
    .
{END IF}

The following example is also correct, because the quotation marks are paired correctly:

{IF}"{VARIABLE}State~"='California'~

The logical operators that you can use in an expression are listed next.

Use the following five operators (+, −, *, /, and %) to calculate numbers. The numbers being calculated can also be taken from a variable (or field if doing a merge).

+ Add

Add two values and return the result. 1 + 1 returns 2.

− Subtract

Subtract the second value from the first and return the result. 3 − 2 returns 1.

* Multiply

Multiply two values and return the result. 2 * 3 returns 6.

/ Divide

Divide and use the remainder as the result. 10 / 5 returns 2.

% Remainder

Divide the first value by the second and return the remainder. 10 % 3 returns 1.

When you are using the next group of operators (=, !=, >, or <), the strings on both sides of the operators are compared to each other. The result will either be true or false. The macro or merge could then take one of two directions, depending on the outcome. See {CASE}, {CASE CALL}, {IF}, and {WHILE} commands in this chapter for examples of each.

=   Equal to

Compare the two values and return −1 (true) if they are equal; otherwise, return 0 (false). 1=1 returns −1, which is "true."

!=   Not equal to

Compare the two values and return −1 (true) if they are not equivalent; return 0 (false) if they are equivalent. 1!=2 returns −1 (true).

>   Greater than

Compare the values, and if the first value is greater than the second, return −1 (true); otherwise, return 0 (false). 5>2 returns −1 (true).

<   Less than

Compare the values, and if the first value is less than the second, return −1 (true); otherwise, return 0 (false). 1<10 returns −1 (true).

These next three operators are more technical because they compare the bits of each number. You do not necessarily have to understand these operators to use them. See {STATE} in this chapter for more information.

& Logical AND (Used in a Bitwise Operation)

Each number is made of 16 bits, using a combination of 1 and 0. For example, a 3 is 0000000000000011. During the & operation, the 16 bits in two numbers are compared. If there are two ones in the same position for *both* numbers, a 1 will be returned. If not, a 0 will be returned. The result would then make up a third bitwise number, as shown in the following example:

3	0000000000000011
7	0000000000000111
3&7	0000000000000011

Because there are zeros in the last two bits for both the numbers, a 1 was returned. The third to the last number did not have both a 1 or a 0, so a 0 was returned.

¦ Logical OR (Used in a Bitwise Operation)

This option is similar to the previous one, except that it only checks for a 1 in the same position for *either* number. In the following example, a 1 is returned whenever there is a 1 in either number.

3	0000000000000011
7	0000000000000111
3¦7	0000000000000111

Note that if there is a 1 in the same position in both numbers, a 1 is also returned.

! Logical NOT (Used in a Bitwise Operation)

This operation changes the bits in the number to their opposite. For example, !3 would be 1111111111111100 (the opposite of 0000000000000011).

Although the last three operators may not technically be called operators, you can use them in expressions to change the case of a number (positive or negative), change the order of evaluation, and help compare text strings.

− Change the Number to a Negative

Numbers greater than 2,147,483,647 are considered negative. You can only have a positive number up to 2,147,483,647. Instead of trying to figure out which number greater than 2,147,483,647 would be the desired negative number, insert a minus sign ($-$) in front of a number to change its sign.

You can also place the minus sign to force a negative number to be positive: $-(-10)$ would return 10.

( ) Indicate a group

Although parentheses are not technically operators, you can use them to control the order in which items are calculated. The part of the expression in parentheses is calculated first, and then the expression is evaluated from left to right, as is normally done.

For example, {VARIABLE}1~ $-3*${VARIABLE}2~ would give an entirely different result from ({VARIABLE}1~ -3)*{VARIABLE}2~, because 3 would be subtracted from variable 1 before being multiplied by variable 2.

You can also nest parentheses within each other.

" or ' Text (String) Operator

Also not technically operators, quotation marks (single or double) should be placed around any text string that is being used in comparisons. Either can be used, but they must be paired correctly. For example, you could use them in the following to check the contents of {VARIABLE}1. Because it might be "Y" (which is text, not numbers), you need to use quotation marks.

```
{IF}"{VARIABLE}1~"="Y"~
    {GO}New~
{END IF}
```

A Final Word of Caution

Be sure to include tildes ($\sim$) where needed. A tilde ($\sim$) is used to indicate that a particular value, variable, or expression is complete. If you forget to include the tildes, your macro or merge will not perform correctly.

In many cases, it may appear that only one $\sim$ is needed, but if you are including variables and fields as part of an expression, they each need their own tilde to mark the end of the variable or field name. In the following example, two tildes are inserted; one is needed for the {IF} statement and one for the {VARIABLE} command.

{IF}"{VARIABLE}Name~"="Sue"~

If you have deleted one tilde accidentally, a macro will not perform correctly or, if you are doing a merge, you will see an error message during the merge telling you that the syntax is incorrect or the merge will appear to do something different if it finds a subsequent tilde to satisfy the syntax.

If you get into an infinite loop, you can try pressing CTRL-BREAK or Cancel (F1) to get out of the loop. However, there is always the possibility that you will not be able to get out of something once the computer has started it. If this happens, you may need to reboot the computer and troubleshoot the commands used.

A Description of Each Macro and Merge Command

The following is a list of advanced macro and merge commands. They are grouped according to the type of task that they will perform. For example, although there are several ways to pause a macro or merge, it is usually easiest to see all alternatives at once so you can determine which is best for your situation. Any related commands are also included in each section. For example, you can use {BELL} to draw the user's attention to the screen during a pause, a prompt, or an error message. That particular command would be mentioned in the section for pausing.

Some of the commands are unique to macros or merge. For example {KEYBOARD} is available only in merge, but you can do the same thing with the {PAUSE} command in macros. Each command includes a statement about whether it is available in macros, in a merge, or in both.

Document a Macro or Merge

You will see {;} or {COMMENT} often in the examples found in this chapter. {;} is used in a macro, and {COMMENT} is used in a merge to help document the steps so that you can tell what is happening at each step.

{;}comment~   Macro Only

If you want to include comments to document steps in a macro, you can place the comments between the {;} command and a tilde. After selecting the {;} command from the list of macros, enter the comment, and then type a tilde to end the comment. Comments appear as follows:

```
{Format}phap    {;}Create Header A for every page~
{PAUSE}         {;}Pause for text in the header~
{Exit}{Exit}    {;}Exit from header, then format menu~
```

{COMMENT}comment~   Merge Only

The {COMMENT} command lets you insert text or codes into your merge files that will *not* be read into the final document. You can use comments to provide documentation for a primary or secondary merge file. You can also use them to "hide" [HRt] or [Tab] codes that you have used to format merge commands so that they can be more readable. (If you need to enter a [HRt] code, pressing ENTER will insert an empty {COMMENT}~ command into the document. You will then need to move the cursor between the {COMMENT} command and the tilde (~), and enter the [HRt] and other codes at that point.)

By using comments, you could format the following line

```
{IF}"{VARIABLE}1~"="1"~{DOCUMENT}memo~{END IF}
```

with the hard returns and tabs enclosed in a {COMMENT} and a tilde (~) to make the structure more readable and understandable:

```
{IF}"{VARIABLE}1~"="1"~{COMMENT}
    ~{DOCUMENT}memo~{COMMENT}
  ~{END IF}
```

Macros for Cursor and Block Shortcuts

If you have an enhanced keyboard, you can use several "shortcuts" for moving the cursor and copying or moving a block of text. For example, you can press ALT-← and ALT-→ to move from column to column or from cell to cell while in a table. You can also use ALT-← and ALT-→ to move to the next or previous outline number in an outline. You can press CTRL-DEL to move a highlighted block of text and CTRL-INS to copy a highlighted box.

If you do not have an enhanced keyboard, you can define ALT key macros (or any key using the Keyboard Layout feature) to do the same thing. For example, pressing ALT-→ is the same as the command {Item Right}. Table 6-1 gives the regular keystrokes on an enhanced keyboard, their function, and the macro command that you can use to accomplish the same task. (All arrows in Table 6-1 refer to the cursor keys found at the left of the numeric keypad.)

Key	Description	Macro Command
CTRL-INS	Copy the current block	{Block Copy}
	Insert a row if in a table	
CTRL-DEL	Move the current block	{Block Move}
N/A	Append the current block	{Block Append}
CTRL-↑	Move up one paragraph	{Para Up}
CTRL-↓	Move down one paragraph	{Para Down}
ALT-↑	Move up one cell in a table	{Item Up}
	Move to the previous section of Parallel Columns if you are using that feature	
	Move to the previous paragraph number of the same level	
ALT-↓	Move down one cell in a table	{Item Down}
	Move to next section of Parallel Columns if you are using that feature	
	Move to next paragraph number of the same level	
ALT-←	Move left one cell in a table	{Item Left}
	Move to the column to the left if you are using any type of columns	
	Move to the previous paragraph number of any level	
ALT-→	Move right one cell in a table	{Item Right}
	Move to the column to the right if you are using any type of columns	
	Move to the next paragraph number of any level	

Table 6-1.   Keystrokes Available on an Enhanced Keyboard

Inserting the Date in a Macro or Merge

{DATE}   Merge Only

This command will insert the current date at the time of the merge. You can also accomplish the same function by inserting a date code into the primary merge document: Press Date/Outline (SHIFT-F5) and choose **2** for Date Code.

If you want to insert the current date with a macro, follow the keystrokes just listed.

Pausing and Prompting for Information

You can use the commands that follow to pause a macro or merge and ask the user for some type of information. This information could then be stored in a variable so that you can use it later, or it could be displayed on the screen as the user types it.

You can use {INPUT}, {CHAR}, {TEXT}, {PROMPT}, and {STATUS PROMPT} to display messages. Most of the time, you may want only one-line messages. If you enter more than one line for the message, it will scroll upward on the screen, displaying the entire message. To learn how to place a prompt or message in a specific position on the screen (useful when simulating pop-up menus), see the last section on "Positioning Messages on the Screen" toward the end of this chapter.

The following are the commands discussed in this chapter:

{KEYBOARD}	Pause with no prompting Press End Field (F9) to continue	Merge only
{PAUSE}	Pause with no prompting Press ENTER to continue	Macros only
{PAUSE KEY}	Pause with no prompting Choose the key to continue	Macros only
{INPUT}	Pause and prompt Press F9 to continue in a merge	Macros and merge

	Press ENTER to continue in a macro	
{CHAR}	Store single character in variable	Macros and merge
{TEXT}	Store up to 127 characters in variable	Macros and merge
	Press ENTER to continue	
{BELL}	Call attention to the pause	Macros and merge

{KEYBOARD}   Merge Only

The {KEYBOARD} command is the same as the ^C merge code found in previous versions of WordPerfect. During the merge, the {KEYBOARD} command causes the merge to pause and wait for text from the keyboard. Pressing End Field (F9) continues the merge.

When you use the {KEYBOARD} command, no message is displayed on the screen to prompt the user for the desired information. If the user cannot determine the type of information to enter by looking at the preceding text in the document, as shown in the following example, he or she may want to use a {PROMPT} command just before the {KEYBOARD} command.

```
                        MEMO
DATE:       {DATE}
TO:         {KEYBOARD}
FROM:       {KEYBOARD}
SUBJECT:    {KEYBOARD}
```

Another option is to use the {INPUT} command. {INPUT} pauses the merge *and* displays a message. All text entered at that point goes directly into the document, just as it would with the {KEYBOARD} command.

If you do not want to insert the text directly into the document, but instead want to store it in a variable to be used later, use {CHAR} or {TEXT}.

{PAUSE}   Macros Only

This command causes a macro to pause temporarily so you can select items from a menu or type text into a document. Pressing ENTER ends the pause.

This type of command does not have a prompt associated with it. If you want a prompt to appear, insert the {PROMPT} or {STATUS PROMPT} command just before {PAUSE}, or use the {INPUT} command instead (which displays a message *and* pauses for input).

Many times you will want to pause a macro and press ENTER to enter several lines of text. You cannot do this with {PAUSE}, because pressing ENTER ends the pause and continues the macro. Instead, use the {PAUSE KEY} command, which lets you specify which key to use to continue the pause. See {PAUSE KEY} next for details.

{PAUSE KEY}key~   Macros Only

The {PAUSE KEY} command lets you decide which key to use to continue the macro after a pause. This is useful when you want to press ENTER during a pause (for example, when you are entering a multiline address or a list of items).

If you use this command, you may also want to use the {PROMPT} or {STATUS PROMPT} commands to display a message telling the user which key to press to continue. If you use {PROMPT}, the message is cleared when you begin typing, so you may want to use {STATUS PROMPT} instead.

In the following example, Exit (F7) is used to continue the pause. To insert the {Exit} command, press CTRL-V and then Exit (F7). An empty {STATUS PROMPT} command was used at the end to clear the message from the screen.

```
{STATUS PROMPT}Press • Exit·(F7)·when·finished.~
{PAUSE KEY}{Exit}~
{STATUS PROMPT}~
```

{INPUT}message~   Macros and Merge

The {INPUT} command is exactly like combining {STATUS PROMPT} and {KEYBOARD} (for merge) commands or {STATUS PROMPT} and {PAUSE} (for macro) commands. You can use the {INPUT} command to pause the merge or macro for input *and* display a message telling the user what type of information is needed.

When you are selecting the {INPUT} command, enter the message to be displayed. If you select the command while in the macro editor, be sure to include the ending tilde indicating the end of the message. Selecting the merge {INPUT} command automatically inserts the tilde for you.

When the {INPUT} command is encountered during a merge or macro, the message is displayed on the status line and pauses. Press End Field (F9) to continue the merge or ENTER to continue the macro. The following is an example of an {INPUT} command in a merge document:

{INPUT}Enter the address and press F9 to continue.˜

You would change "F9" to "ENTER" if the command was being used in a macro because ENTER would be pressed to continue a macro.

{CHAR}variable ∼ message ∼   **Macros and Merge**

The {CHAR} command is useful when you need to prompt the person running the merge or macro for a single character and store it in a variable. For example, if you are asking a Yes/No question or are asking for a number from 1 to 9, you can use the {CHAR} command. It is identical to the {TEXT} command, except that when the user types a character, the macro or merge continues immediately. The {TEXT} command lets you enter up to 127 characters and then requires that you press ENTER to continue the merge or macro.

You can test the character (variable) with the {IF}, {CASE}, {CASE CALL}, or {WHILE} commands to see what action to take. The following merge example asks whether the client is male or female with the {CHAR} command. It can then use that information to customize the document to either sex.

```
{CHAR}Sex˜Is {FIELD}name˜ a Male or Female?˜{COMMENT}
˜{CASE}{VARIABLE}Sex˜˜{COMMENT}
  ˜F˜Female˜f˜Female˜{COMMENT}
  ˜M˜Male˜m˜Male˜{COMMENT}
  ˜{ELSE}{STOP}˜˜{COMMENT}
˜{LABEL}Female˜ You will receive a genuine leather handbag{GO}Continue˜{COMMENT}
˜{LABEL}Male˜ You will receive a genuine leather wallet {GO} Continue˜{COMMENT}
˜{LABEL}Continue˜in the next four to six weeks.
```

You can use the same example in a macro, except that you would delete all {COMMENT}∼ commands.

The variable that is created by the {CHAR} command is considered a global variable; it can have up to 7 characters and is available to all macros and merges.

If you are using the {CHAR} command in a merge and already have a {LOCAL} variable with the same name in the merge file, the local variable will be overwritten. This principle is also true for variables created with {TEXT}, {FOR}, and {LOOK}.

{TEXT}var ~ message ~   Macros and Merge

This command is similar to the {CHAR} command in that it displays a message, pauses for you to enter text, and then stores that text in the named variable. The difference is that {TEXT} lets you enter several characters, and the {CHAR} command pauses for a single character.

{CHAR} could be used in Yes/No situations or menu selections in which one character can be entered and stored. As soon as the single character is pressed, the merge continues. {TEXT}, on the other hand, lets you enter up to 127 characters and then continues when ENTER is pressed. If you are running a merge, you can press *either* ENTER or End Field (F9) to continue the merge.

The variable that is created can then be inserted at any location in the document or tested to see what decisions need to be made based on the information found in the variable.

The {INPUT} command can also be used to prompt the user for several characters. However, these characters are inserted directly into the document instead of being stored in a variable.

In the example below, the user is prompted for their name. That information is stored in a variable named "Name," and can be inserted at any other location in the document using the {VARIABLE} command ({VARIABLE}Name~ would insert the contents of the "Name" variable).

{TEXT}Name~Enter your full name: ~

Note that a colon and two spaces were used so that the prompt and "answer" would not run together on the status line.

{PROMPT}message ~   Macros and Merge

The {PROMPT} command is used to display a message on the status line. Because the message briefly flashes on the screen, you would want to combine the {PROMPT} command with another command such as {WAIT} so it can be displayed for a specific amount of time. If you are doing a merge, you could combine it with {KEYBOARD} or, if you are doing a macro, you could combine it with the {PAUSE} command. For example,

{PROMPT}After each pause, remember to press F9.˜{WAIT}30˜

would display the message for 3 seconds (the number entered with the {WAIT} command is entered in tenths of a second).

When selecting the {PROMPT} command as a merge command, you cannot initially enter a prompt that is longer than one line. You can, however, edit the message after it has been entered and add more lines so that the prompt message will scroll upward on the screen and provide a full-screen menu or a screen of information. See "Positioning Macros on the Screen" toward the end of the chapter for more information about positioning messages and menus on the screen.

{STATUS PROMPT}message˜   **Macros and Merge**

Unlike {PROMPT}, you can use {STATUS PROMPT} to display a message on the screen until a message from another {STATUS PROMPT} or {INPUT} command replaces it. You can use this command to display a message during a merge reminding the user that the F9 key should be pressed to continue after any pause. You would enter it as:

{STATUS PROMPT}After each pause, press F9 to continue.˜

Because the {STATUS PROMPT} will remain on the screen until you exit WordPerfect (or until it is replaced by another {STATUS PROMPT} or {INPUT} command), you may want to use an empty {STATUS PROMPT} command ({STATUS PROMPT}˜) at the end of the primary file or macro.

{BELL}   **Macros and Merge**

This command will sound a beep to attract the user's attention to the screen. You can use it just before any of the previously mentioned commands that stop and require the user to enter information.

Storing and Using Information in a Variable

The {CHAR} and {TEXT} commands let you store information in a variable. You can then use that information in other places during the macro or merge, or use it to check for various conditions. Other commands that can be used to store information in a variable include {ASSIGN}, {LOCAL} (for merges only), {LOOK}, {FOR}, and {FOR EACH}. Information about {ASSIGN}, {LOCAL}, and {LOOK} is included next. {FOR} and {FOR EACH} are covered under "Looping" in this chapter.

The following is a summary of the commands discussed in this section. Be sure to read the information in the previous section about {CHAR} and {TEXT}, which pause for a character or text to be stored in a "global" variable.

{ASSIGN}var~expr~	Store the expression in a "global" variable	Macros and merge
{LOCAL}var~expr~	Store the expression in a "local" variable	Merge only
{LOOK}var~	Look to see if a key is pressed and store that key in a "global" variable	Macros and merge
{VARIABLE}var~	Retrieve the information from the named variable	Macros and merge

{ASSIGN}variable~expression~   Macros and Merge

There are several ways to "assign" information to a variable. You can select the {ASSIGN} command from the list of macro or merge commands, you can press Macro Commands (CTRL-PGUP) while at the main editing screen, or you can block the text to be stored in the variable and press Macro Commands (CTRL-PGUP).

In all cases (with the exception of using Block), you will be asked for the variable's name and then the expression. If you blocked the text, it is only necessary to enter the variable's name; the first 128 characters in the block are then stored as the "expression."

If you are entering this command in a macro, be sure to insert tildes as shown. The following is a sample of {ASSIGN} commands:

```
{ASSIGN}Name ˜Richard Kimball˜
{ASSIGN}Name˜{FIELD}First˜ {FIELD}Last˜ ˜
{ASSIGN}Total˜{VARIABLE}Pastdue˜ +{VARIABLE}Current˜ ˜
```

The first example assigns the text "Richard Kimball" to the "Name" variable. The second example could only be used in a merge and would assign the contents from the first and last name fields from *each* record to the "Name" variable. The "Name" variable would then change from record to record. The last example would add the numbers found in a "pastdue" variable to the "current" amount due (also held in a variable) and would store the total in a variable named "total."

If you are selecting the {ASSIGN} command as part of a merge document and need to enter fields or variables as part of the expression, you must press ENTER to "finish" the expression ({ASSIGN}variable ˜ ˜), then move the cursor between the two tildes and enter the fields or variables at that time.

Remember that you can use any number of characters for the variable name, but only the first seven are recognized by WordPerfect. You can use the variable in any other macro or merge until you exit WordPerfect (upon which time it is cleared from memory). If you use the same name for an {ASSIGN} and {LOCAL} variable in a merge, the {LOCAL} variable will take precedence.

If you block a section of text and assign it to a variable, the following codes on the left will be converted to the codes on the right. All other codes will be deleted.

Code	Converted to
[→Indent]	{Indent}
[→Indent←]	{Indent}
[Tab]	{Tab}
[Center]	{Tab}
[Flsh Rgt]	{Tab}
[←Mar Rel]	{Tab}

[-] (Hyphen)	- (Hard Hyphen)
[HRt]	{Enter}
[HRt-SPg]	{Enter}
[Dorm HRt]	{Enter}
[SRt]	space
[SPg]	space
[HPg]	{HPg}

{LOCAL}variable ~ expression ~   Merge Only

The {LOCAL} command is identical to the {ASSIGN} command; it stores an expression into the named variable. The only difference is that a "local" variable is available only within the merge file in which it is stored while the variable stored with {ASSIGN} is a "global" variable and can be used by any merge file or macro.

When you need to insert the variable into the document or test the contents of a variable, use the {VARIABLE} command. Enter it as follows: {VARIABLE}name ~. If you have used the same name for a "global" variable (named with {ASSIGN}) and a "local" variable (named with {LOCAL}), the "local" variable takes precedence. This means that if you inserted {VARIABLE}total ~ and there was a global and local variable with the name "total," the local variable would be used.

{LOOK}variable ~   Macros and Merge

The {LOOK} command looks to see if a key has been pressed and stores it in the named variable. The variable can then be tested to see what character was pressed and act accordingly. This command is useful for data validation (to see if the correct key was pressed), selecting items from a menu, or looking for a particular key or character.

The following is a merge example that shows how you can use the {LOOK} command to create a loop and check each character until the correct one (*) is pressed.

```
~{LABEL}Top~{COMMENT}
~{LOOK}mark~{COMMENT}
~{IF}"{VARIABLE}mark~"="*"~{COMMENT}
```

```
~*{GO}End~{COMMENT}
~{ELSE}{GO}Top~{END IF}{COMMENT}
~{LABEL}End~
```

{VARIABLE}var~   **Macros and Merge**

{VARIABLE} lets you access the information in a variable. You can use this command by itself to insert the text found in the variable, with {IF} or {CASE} to test the contents of the variable, or any other time that the information in the variable could be used.

The following test determines if the contents of the "Name" variable is "Bob." If it is, it will go to the section of the macro named "end." If not, it will continue after the {END IF} command.

{IF}"{VARIABLE}Name~"="Bob"~{GO}end~{END IF}

If you have a variable named from 0 to 9, and you are in the macro editor, you can press CTRL-V, and then press ALT and the number of the variable instead of selecting the {VARIABLE} command first. Variable "1" would then appear as {VAR 1} instead of {VARIABLE}1~. Both would perform the same function.

Data Validation

Two commands are available in both macros and merge to help check the data entered. You can check the length of an entry with the {LEN} command and use the {MID} command to extract data from the "middle" of the entry.

The following is a summary of the two commands:

{LEN}var~ or expr~	Check the length of a variable or expression	Macros and merge
{MID}var~ or expr~	Extract data from a variable or expression	Macros and merge

{LEN}expression~ or {LEN}variable~   **Macros and Merge**

The {LEN} command is used to determine the length of a variable or an expression. An expression can be any combination of fields, variables, or text. You can use it to determine if a certain amount of text will fit within a specified area (when filling in forms, for example).

By itself, the {LEN} command simply gives the number of the characters in the expression or variable. It is more useful if you use it with a command such as {IF} to prevent the user from entering too many characters, as shown in the following merge example:

{LABEL}Loop~{COMMENT}
    ~{TEXT}Desc~Enter a description of up to 20 characters: ~{COMMENT}
    ~{IF}{LEN}{VARIABLE}Desc ~~>20 ~{BELL}{PROMPT}Too many
characters were entered.~{WAIT}5 ~{GO}Loop~{END IF}

You could use the same example in a macro by removing the {COMMENT}~ commands.

If the user enters a description of more than 20 characters, he or she will hear a bell to signify an error, the message "Too many characters were entered" will be displayed for half a second, and the prompt will appear again. If the length of the "Desc" variable is less than 20 characters, the macro or merge will continue with no error messages.

{MID}expression ~ offset ~ count ~   or
{MID}variable ~ offset ~ count ~   Macros and Merge

The {MID} command is similar to {LEN}; it can be used to control the length of an entry. This command can look at an expression, start x number of characters from the beginning of the expression, and count the number of characters to be extracted. Characters that are extracted are then displayed on the screen.

If you prefer, you can use this command instead of {LEN} to take the first x number of characters and use them as the entry instead of sending the user an error message.

{TEXT}Desc~Enter a description of up to 20 characters: ~{COMMENT}
 ~{MID}{VARIABLE}Desc~~0~20~

The previous example is for a merge document, but you could duplicate it in a macro by removing the {COMMENT}~ commands.

The {MID} command looks at the "desc" variable, starts at 0, and extracts the next 20 characters to be displayed on the screen. When you are selecting the {MID} command as part of a merge, you will need to press ENTER to skip the "expr" part of the command and enter the {VARIABLE} command from the list of merge commands after you have entered the offset and count numbers.

You can also use this command to extract the last four digits of a phone number (some corporations have a common prefix and list only the employee's four-number extension in an internal phone book). The following is an example of how this would be done for a phone number in the format 555-2222. The number 4 was used as the "offset" number, because the first character is considered 0 by WordPerfect. If the area code were included, the additional number of characters would need to be added to the offset.

{MID}{FIELD}Phone ~ ~4 ~4~

Marking a Location or Subroutine

In the following sections, you will learn about branching to different parts of a macro or merge document so subroutines can be performed. For example, if you use the {CASE} command to check the contents of a variable, the macro or merge would go to and run a subroutine (a section of the macro or merge) that would be applicable to that answer. You can also use {CASE CALL}, {CALL}, and {GO} to go to a specific label. See the discussions on branching in this chapter for more information about how these commands can "go to" or "call" a section named with a label.

First, you need to know how to label a section and how to use various commands to go to that label.

{LABEL}label~	Label a section or subroutine	Macros and merge
{GO}label~	Go to a particular section named with a label, and do not return	Macros and merge
{CALL}label~	Call a subroutine named with a label and then return	Macros and merge

{RETURN}   Used with {CALL} to mark   Macros and merge
               the point at which the macro
               or merge is to return to the
               original location

{LABEL}label ~   Macros and Merge

The {LABEL} command is used to mark a place in the macro or merge
file. The {GO}, {CALL}, {CASE}, and {CASE CALL} commands are used
to indicate which sections or "labels" should be used. For example,
{GO}Top~ searches for the place in the merge file named Top
({LABEL}Top~) and continues the merge from there.

You can use any number of characters in a label, including spaces,
but the first 15 should be unique to other label names and local variable
names in a merge. The first seven characters should be unique when
used in a macro.

You will usually want to use a {RETURN} command at the end of a
subroutine named with a {LABEL} so the {CALL} and {CASE CALL}
commands will know when to return.

{GO}label ~   Macros and Merge

This command causes the macro or merge to go to a section of the file
that has been named with the {LABEL} command and continue from
that point. If you had a section in the document named "Top"
({LABEL}Top~), using {GO}Top~ would go to that section.

This command is different from the {CALL} command, because it
does not return. The {CALL} command goes to the named label and
then returns to the first command after {CALL} once it encounters a
{RETURN}.

The following macro prompts the user about whether he or she is
finished with the current document. It then uses the {IF} command to
check to see if variable 1 is Yes. If it is, the {GO} command goes to a
label named "Done" and executes the steps necessary to save the current document and overwrite the original.

```
{CHAR}1 ~ Are you finished?  ~      {;}Store Y or N in variable 1 ~
{IF}"{VARIABLE}1 ~" = "Y" ~          {;}If variable 1 is "Y",
    {GO}Done ~                            {;}Go to the subroutine labeled "Done" ~
```

```
{END IF}
    .                            {;}Middle section of the macro~
    .
    .
{LABEL}Done~              {;}The "Done" subroutine~
    {Exit}y{Enter}yy     {;}Save the document and exit~
```

If any commands are found below the "Done" label, and you do not want the macro to continue executing those steps, you should use a {QUIT} command to stop the macro at that point. Use the {STOP} command to stop a merge.

{CALL}label~   Macros and Merge

This command is similar to the {GO} command; it goes to a label in the macro or merge file and starts executing the commands found there. The difference is that once the {CALL} command goes to a label and then encounters a {RETURN} command, it returns to the first line after the {CALL} command and resumes the merge at that point. In other words, *it is absolutely necessary* to use the {RETURN} command with the {CALL} command so it will know when to return.

In the following example, the {SYSTEM} command checks to see if the current page is page 1. If it is not, the macro goes to a subroutine that makes sure the cursor in on page 1. After these steps, the {RETURN} command is encountered, and the macro returns to the point immediately after the {CALL} command (in this case, {END IF}) and then completes the remaining steps of the macro.

Note that the label "Heading" was used in the next section of the macro. No other part of the macro uses a command to go to this label; it was simply added to help identify that section of the macro.

```
{IF}{SYSTEM}page~!=1~     {;}If not on page 1~
    {CALL}Position~       {;}Call the subroutine labeled "position"
{END IF}

{LABEL}Heading~
    {Format}phap              {;}Create Header A for every page~
    Page {^B}{Enter}          {;}which contains the current page number~
    {Date/Outline}t           {;}and the current date~
    {Exit}                    {;}Exit from the header~
    uh                        {;}Suppress Header A on the first page~
    {Exit}                    {;}Exit from the format menu~
```

{QUIT}   {;}Stop the macro ~
{LABEL}Position~
   {Home}{Home}{Home}{Up}   {;}Go to the top of the document before all
                           other codes ~
{RETURN}   {;}Return and create the header for page 1 ~

{RETURN}   Macros and Merge

{CALL} and {CASE CALL} are used to go to specific labels in the merge. When a {RETURN} command is encountered, the merge returns to the point just after the {CALL} or {CASE CALL} commands. In other words, you must use {RETURN} when you are using the {CASE} or {CASE CALL} commands. See {CALL} above for an example of how to use {RETURN}.

Branching with {IF} Commands

{IF} commands (as well as the {CASE} commands described in the next section) let you have conditional merges or macros that perform certain functions based on certain conditions.

You can use {IF} commands to check for these conditions, and branch or "go to" different parts of the macro or merge, depending on what the outcome is. For example, you could check a variable to see whether the user entered a Y or an N. You could check a specific field in a merge file to see if the person lives in Ohio and if so, send them the appropriate letter. You could check the "system" to see if the printer is waiting for a "Go" and then send a "Go" if necessary.

Four {IF} commands are available in merge, and two are available for macros. The two extra commands included in merge are used to test the contents of a field to see if it is blank. {IF EXISTS} tests only to see if a variable exists but doesn't check the contents. {ELSE} is optional, but you can use it to contribute to the branching process. {END IF} must be used with all {IF} commands to mark the end of the {IF} statement.

You can nest {IF} commands several levels deep. A macro lets you have up to 30 levels and a merge up to 20 per file. Nested {IF} commands take one level each in a macro, but they do not take a level in a merge.

The following is a summary of the {IF} commands and other related commands discussed in this section:

{IF}expr~	Evaluate the expression	Macros and merge
{IF EXISTS}var~	Check to see if the named variable exists	Macros and Merge
{IF BLANK}field~	Check to see if the named field is blank	Merge only
{IF NOT BLANK}field~	Check to see if the named field is not blank	Merge only
{ELSE} (optional)	Commands after {ELSE} are used if the {IF} statement is false	Macros and merge
{END IF}	To be used to end all {IF} commands	Macros and merge

{IF}expression~   Macros and Merge

Use this command to evaluate the expression (which can be a field, variable, or any combination of the two) and execute commands based on certain criteria.

In everyday life, people perform {IF} commands without realizing it; for example, "IF the light is green, press the accelerator." The {IF} command in WordPerfect performs in a similar manner.

The {IF} statement is evaluated, and if it is true (the light is green), the instructions following the tilde (~) will be executed until either an {ELSE} or an {END IF} command is encountered. When one of these two commands is found, the macro or merge skips to the instructions following the {END IF} command and continues from that point.

If the result of the {IF} statement is false, the macro or merge skips to the {ELSE} command and executes any instructions found there until the {END IF} command is encountered. If an {ELSE} command is not included with the {IF} statement (because it is optional), the macro or merge skips to the {END IF} command and begins executing the instructions following it.

The structure of the command might be something like this merge example:

{IF}{FIELD}Owes˜ >1000 ˜ We have noticed that your balance is greater than
$1,000, so we must expect payment within the next 15 days.{END IF}

We appreciate your patronage and hope to serve you again soon.

    The extra lines between {END IF} and the following text were used
to start a new paragraph.

    In the example above, the paragraph after the {END IF} would
print whether the statement is true or not. However, if the person owes
more than $1,000, the additional sentence is inserted.

    The {ELSE} command could be used to supply another alternative if
the statement were false. For example, in the following example, a
statement is inserted for those who have a balance of less than $1,000.
The last paragraph is again printed for both situations.

{IF}{FIELD}Owes˜ >1000 ˜ We have noticed that your balance is greater than
$1,000, so we must expect payment within the next 15 days.{ELSE}We have noticed
your balance is less than $1,000. You'll have to visit us more often.{END IF}

We appreciate your patronage and hope to serve you again soon.

    Remember when you are using the {IF} command that you will need
to use the {END IF} command as well. The {ELSE} command is optional.

    See "Checking the State of WordPerfect" and "Using System
Information" in this chapter for other examples of how to use the {IF}
command.

{IF EXISTS}variable˜   Macros and Merge

The {IF EXISTS} command tests to see if a variable exists. If it does,
the merge continues after the tilde (˜). If it does not exist, it continues
after the paired {END IF} command. You can also use an {ELSE}
command as an alternative if the variable does not exist.

    When you use this command, you are saying that you are not
concerned with the contents of the variable; you just want to know if it
exists. By using this command, you can avoid overwriting a variable that
already exists. The example that follows is a macro that shows how this
could be done:

```
{IF EXISTS}Total~              {;}Check to see if there is a "total" variable~
      {QUIT}                   {;}If there is, quit~
{END IF}
{ASSIGN}Total~{VARIABLE}1~*3~  {;}If not, multiply variable 1 by 3 and
                                  store the result in a variable named
                                  "total"~
```

{IF BLANK}field~   Merge Only

{IF BLANK} checks to see if the named field is blank. If it is, the commands following the tilde will be processed. If it is not blank, the merge will continue after the {END IF} command. Another command, {IF NOT BLANK} (described next), checks to see if the opposite is true.

In the following example, the merge checks to see if the field containing the phone number is blank. If it is, the sentence asking for the information is inserted into the letter, and then the merge continues on after the {END IF} command. If the field is not blank (you have a phone number for this person), the merge skips to the instructions after the {END IF} command.

{IF BLANK}phone~Our records show that we do not have your phone number. Please notify us with this information as soon as possible so we can keep you up to date with our current interest rates.{END IF}

You can use the {ELSE} command in this situation to insert different text if the field is not blank.

{IF BLANK}phone~Our records show that we do not have your phone number. Please notify us with this information as soon as possible so we can keep you up to date with our current interest rates.{ELSE}We will contact you by phone with the current interest rates at the beginning of each month.{END IF}

{IF NOT BLANK}field~   Merge Only

When inserting a field command into a merge file, you can always include a question mark just after the field name or number to eliminate a blank line if the field is blank. The primary merge file might look like the following:

{FIELD}First~ {FIELD}Last~
{FIELD}Title?~
{FIELD}Company?~
{FIELD}Address

The only problem with including a question mark is that it not only deletes the [HRt] code but also deletes anything else on that line. In the previous example, this would not create a problem, because there is not any other text on the "Title" or "Company" line. However, in the following example, the person's last name would be deleted if he or she didn't have a title:

Dear {FIELD}Title?˜ {FIELD}Last˜:

If you omit the ? from the Title field, you get an extra space between "Dear" and the person's name if there is no title. To get around this problem, you can use the {IF NOT BLANK} command to help eliminate blank lines and spaces.

This command checks to see if the named field is not blank (if it has something in it). If it is not blank, the merge will continue after the tilde (˜). If it is blank, the merge skips past the {END IF} command and continues from there. You can also use the {ELSE} command to provide another alternative.

The first example shows how if the Company field is not blank, it prints the company's name. If it is blank, it skips past the {END IF} command and prints the Address.

{FIELD}Name˜
{IF NOT BLANK}Company˜{FIELD}Company˜
{END IF}{FIELD}Address˜

Notice that the hard return forcing a new line was placed *before* the {END IF} command. This ensures that it will not print if the field is blank.

The second example shows you how to solve the "Title" problem.

Dear {IF NOT BLANK}Title˜{FIELD}Title˜ {END IF}{FIELD}Name˜

Again, in this example, the title will print if the field is not blank. If it is blank, it will skip after the {END IF} command and print the name only. An extra space is inserted *before* the {END IF} command to separate the possible title from the name. However, it will not be inserted if the field is blank.

{END IF}   Macros and Merge

You must use {END IF} to mark the end of an {IF}, {IF BLANK}, {IF NOT BLANK}, and {IF EXISTS} statement.

{ELSE}   Macros and Merge

The {IF} commands are structured in such a way as to test a condition to see if it is true or false. The {ELSE} command is optional in any of the {IF} statements. If the condition is true, the commands following the {IF} command would be executed. The merge would then skip to the {END IF} command, and any instructions included after the {ELSE} command would be ignored. If the condition were false, the instructions after the {IF} command would be ignored, and the instructions after the {ELSE} command would be used instead. The macro or merge *then* goes to the {END IF} command and continues from that point. See {IF} and {IF BLANK} for an example of how {ELSE} can be used.

Branching with {CASE} Commands

There are two other commands that you can use to branch or go to different sections and subroutines of a macro or merge: {CASE} and {CASE CALL}.

The {CASE} and {CASE CALL} commands are similar to {IF} commands, except that you can use them to check for multiple conditions. Each condition causes a different thing to happen. You can nest several {IF} statements to achieve the same result.

{CASE} is also similar to the {GO} command, in that it "goes" to a label and does not return (depending on the condition, of course). The {CASE CALL} is similar to the {CALL} command, because it goes to a named label and returns when a {RETURN} command is encountered.

The following commands are discussed in this section:

{CASE}	Evaluate an expression and "go to" a different label for each case	Macros and merge
{CASE CALL}	Evaluate the expression, "call" a different label for each case, and then return to the first command after the ending tilde (~)	Macros and merge
{ELSE}	Optional command to offer another alternative in case an exact match is not found	Macros and merge
{RETURN}	Must be used at the end of a section or subroutine to mark when to return	Macros and merge

{CASE}expression ~ case1 ~ label ~ . . .
{ELSE} ~ label ~ ~   Macros and Merge

The expression in the {CASE} command is checked and compared with each case until an exact match is made or until there are no more cases. If the user is to type a letter from a to z, you should have the {CASE} command check for both upper- and lowercase. See the {CHAR} command earlier in this chapter for an example.

When an exact match is found, the macro or merge will go to the specified label (similar to a {GO}label ~). If no match is found, the label following the optional {ELSE} ~ command is used. If you do not use an {ELSE} command, the macro or merge will resume at the instructions following the entire {CASE} statement (marked by an ending tilde).

The following example could be used by a real estate agent who needs to send prospective home buyers a current listing of homes. The secondary file could include information such as the client's name, address, phone number, and number of bedrooms he or she would like in a home. During the merge, the Bedroom field is checked. Depending on how many bedrooms are required, the merge retrieves a different document, which gives a list of the one-, two-, or three-bedroom homes that are available. If the client wants more than three bedrooms, the document named "large" is retrieved, giving a list of larger homes.

```
{CASE}{FIELD}bedrooms~~{COMMENT}
        ~1~one~2~two~3~three~{ELSE}~large~~{COMMENT}
~{LABEL}one~{DOCUMENT}one~{STOP}
{LABEL}two~{DOCUMENT}two~{STOP}
{LABEL}three~{DOCUMENT}three~{STOP}
{LABEL}large~{DOCUMENT}large~{STOP}
```

Note the use of tildes. There is a tilde after the {ELSE} command, just as if it were another case being considered. The end of the entire case statement needs to be marked with another tilde, making a total of two tildes at the end (one for the last label and one for the end of the {CASE} statement). It is important to enter them correctly, or the merge will not work. Also note that {COMMENTS}, usually used for formatting (as they are in the upper section of the example), are optional because of the {STOP} command. Once a {STOP} command is reached, the rest of the file is ignored.

This example could also be customized for a macro by prompting for the number of bedrooms, storing that information in a variable, and then testing the variable, as shown in the following example:

```
{CHAR}bedroom~How many bedrooms do you want in the home? ~
{CASE}{VARIABLE}bedroom~~
        1~one~2~two~3~three~{ELSE}~large~~
{LABEL}one~{Retrieve}one{Enter}{QUIT}
{LABEL}two~{Retrieve}two{Enter}{QUIT}
{LABEL}three~{Retrieve}three{Enter}{QUIT}
{LABEL}large~{Retrieve}large{Enter}{QUIT}
```

{CASE CALL}expression~case1~label~. . .
{ELSE}~label~~   **Macros and Merge**

This command is exactly like {CASE}, except that it "calls" a label instead of "going to" that label. It goes to a {LABEL}, performs the commands there, and then returns to the first command after the ending tilde in the {CASE CALL} statement when it encounters a {RETURN}. It is absolutely necessary for a matching {RETURN} to be included for the {CASE CALL} command.

In the preceding example, you could cause the merge to go to a section of the primary file labeled "land" that talks about options for buying land through the agent and building a custom home of their own by using the {RETURN} command instead of the {QUIT} command. It would then look something like this:

```
{CASE CALL}{FIELD}bedrooms~~{COMMENT}
    ~1~one~2~two~3~three~{ELSE}~large~~{COMMENT}
~{GO}land~
~{LABEL}one~{DOCUMENT}one~{RETURN}{COMMENT}
~{LABEL}two~{DOCUMENT}two~{RETURN}{COMMENT}
~{LABEL}three~{DOCUMENT}three~{RETURN}{COMMENT}
~{LABEL}large~{DOCUMENT}large~{RETURN}{COMMENT}
~{LABEL}land~
```

Even though they are shown here, the {COMMENT}s at the end of each line in the lower section of the example are optional. Because of the {GO} and {RETURN} commands, the merge will go immediately to the specified location without inserting the hard return found at the end of the line. However, because {COMMENT}s will not cause any harm, it is acceptable to include them, even if they are unnecessary.

{ELSE}   Macros and Merge

When you use a CASE structure beginning with the {CASE} or {CASE CALL} command, the merge tries to find an exact match between the expression and each case. Once it finds a match, it goes to a specified label and performs the actions there. If it does not find a match, it will look at the {ELSE} command (if one is included) and go to that named label instead. If an {ELSE} command is not included, the merge goes to the first instruction after the ending tilde (~). See the preceding examples for the correct method to be used.

{RETURN}   Macros and Merge

Use {CALL} and {CASE CALL} to go to specific labels in the merge. When a {RETURN} command is encountered, the merge returns to the point just after the {CALL} or {CASE CALL} command. You *must* use {RETURN} when you are using {CASE} or {CASE CALL}. See {CASE CALL} earlier in this chapter for an example of how to use {RETURN}.

Looping

You can repeat a section or subroutine in the macro or merge by creating a loop. Always provide a way to get out of the loop, however, or you could create an infinite loop. For example, you could check for a certain condition at the beginning or end of the loop. Once that condition is found, the macro or merge would stop the loop and continue.

You can create a simple loop by using {GO} and {LABEL}, as discussed previously in this chapter under "Marking a Location or Subroutine." You can also create a loop with the {FOR}, {FOR EACH}, and {WHILE} commands, as discussed in this chapter. The following commands are discussed in this section.

{LABEL}label~	Mark a section or sub-routine	Macros and merge
{GO}label~	Go to the section or sub-routine	Macros and merge
{FOR}var~start ~stop~step~	Repeat the subroutine n number of times. {FOR} lets you indicate when to start, stop, and at how many increments	Macros and merge
{FOR EACH}var ~expr1~expr2~ ...~	Perform the subroutine for each expression	Macros only
{END FOR}	Ends the "for" loop	Macros and merge
{WHILE}expr~	Repeat the subroutine while the expression is true	Macros and merge
{END WHILE}	Ends the "while" loop	
{NEXT}	Goes to the next iteration of a "for" or "while" loop	Macros and merge

{GO}label~ and {LABEL}label~   Macros and Merge

The easiest way to create a loop is to mark a subroutine with {LABEL} and then at the end of the subroutine use a {GO} command that goes back to the same label. The subroutine repeats until a certain condition is met.

You could use the following macro to convert endnotes to footnotes. The section labeled "Repeat" will repeat until no other endnotes are found in the document. In that case, the macro would normally receive a "not found" message, and the macro would end.

```
{IF}{STATE}&512~              {;}If Reveal Codes is on~
{Reveal Codes}                {;}Turn off to ensure consistency in deleting~
{END IF}                      {;}endnotes~

{LABEL}Repeat~
{Footnote}ee{Enter}           {;}Edit next endnote~
{Right}                       {;}Move past endnote number~
{Block}{Home}{Home}{Down}{;}Block all of the text in the endnote~
{Block Move}{Exit}            {;}Move the highlighted block and exit endnote~
{Backspace}y                  {;}Delete the endnote~
{Footnote}fc                  {;}Create a footnote~
{Enter}                       {;}Retrieve the moved text~
{Exit}                        {;}Exit the footnote~
{GO}Repeat~                   {;}Repeat the process until all notes are converted~
```

See "Checking the State of WordPerfect" for an exploration of the {STATE} command.

{FOR}var~start~stop~step~   Macros and Merge

You can use the {FOR} command when you need to repeat a task a certain number of times.

1. After selecting the {FOR} command, enter the name of the variable (that will be created by the {FOR} command). This variable will be used as a "counter" to see how many times a task should be repeated.

2. Enter the starting value of the loop. If you are doing a merge, you could use a {FIELD} command so it will use the contents of the field (a number) as the starting point. Macros or merges could use a {VARIABLE} that contains a specific number.

3. Enter the Stop point (the number at which you want to stop).

4. After entering this information, you will need to specify the "Step." This refers to the increments at which the loop will be repeated. For example, if you enter 1, the loop increments *each* number between the start and stop points. If you enter 2, the loop will increment *every other* number between the starting and stopping points.

The information entered is stored in the variable and can be used as a counter to control the number of repetitions.

In the following merge example, a secondary file contains the following fields:

1	Name
2	Address
3	Phone
4	PTA member (Y/N)
5	Number of children
6-?	Variable number of fields containing children's names

Although you should be consistent in ordering your fields, you can have a variable number of fields per record. In the previous list, you can see that some people might have 2 children registered in the school, while others might have 11. Field 5 stores the number of children, and field 6 (through an indefinite number) lists the children's names.

Because there is a variable number of fields, you can use the {FOR} command to insert them all into a letter to the parents. In the following example, the number of children (field 5) is stored in a variable named "num." The {FOR} command then creates a variable named "field." Each time the loop is started, a different number is stored in the field variable, telling it which field should be inserted in the list.

The process will *start* at field 6 because that is where the list of children begins. The Stop value adds the total number of children to 5, which is the number of fields preceding the list of children and the "number of children" field. This helps the {FOR} loop determine how many children are listed (5 fields at the beginning of the record plus the number of children equals the total number of fields in the record). This, then, is where the process stops. The step number is one, telling Word-Perfect to increment by one (thus listing all the children in the record).

The last command tells WordPerfect to insert the {FIELD} number that is the result. For example, it would first insert the contents of the sixth field, the seventh, and so on, until it reaches the end of the list of children. Don't forget to include the {END FOR} command at the end of the loop.

```
{ASSIGN}num~{FIELD}5~~
Name
```

```
{FOR}field~6~{VARIABLE}num~+5~1~{COMMENT}
   ~{FIELD}{VARIABLE}field~~
{END FOR}
```

You can also use the {NEXT} command within the {FOR} loop to skip fields. In the following example, the {NEXT} command is used to eliminate field 8 from the list.

```
{ASSIGN}num~{FIELD}5~~
List of Children:
```

```
{FOR}field~6~{VARIABLE}num~+5~1~{COMMENT}
    ~{IF}{VARIABLE}field~=8~{NEXT}{END IF}{COMMENT}
    ~{FIELD}{VARIABLE}field~~
{END FOR}
```

If you had used 2 as the step, every other field (7, 9, and so on) would be inserted.

A macro could use the {FOR} command to search for the *nth* occurrence of a word. In the following example, the sixth occurrence of the word would be found:

```
{TEXT}Word~What do you want to search for? ~
{FOR}Times~1~6~1~
    {Search}{VARIABLE}Word~{Search}
{END FOR}
```

You could also prompt the user for the number of times to search for the word and then use that number as the stop value as shown here:

```
{TEXT}Word~What do you want to search for? ~
{TEXT}Number~Which occurrence of the word do you want found? ~
{FOR}Times~1~{VARIABLE}Number~~1~
    {Search}{VARIABLE}Word~{Search}
{END FOR}
```

{FOR EACH}var~expr1~...exprN~~   Macros Only

You can use {FOR EACH} to repeat a process for each expression. You are not limited to starting and stopping at a certain position, as you are with {FOR}. You are also not limited to numbers, but to any expression (text, variables, and calculations). Again, an {END FOR} command marks the end of the loop. An extra tilde marks the end of the expressions entered.

At the beginning of each loop, each expression is stored in the variable, and then the loop is repeated for each expression.

For example, let's say that you have just arranged the sale of several small companies to one larger company. The larger company now wants you to replace all occurrences of the previous owners' names with their name in a document. You would first retrieve the file and then run the following macro. The macro stores the name of each company in a variable called "Old." The loop then does a search and replace, searching for the "Old" company, and replacing it with the new one (Takeover International).

```
{FOR EACH}Old~ACME~Excel, Inc.~Scientific International~~
  {Replace}n{VARIABLE}old~Takeover International~
{END FOR}
```

This macro is especially helpful because it can do the task unattended.

Now let's say that you have four contracts that contain the names of the previous companies. You could have one {FOR EACH} loop that retrieves each of those documents, executes the {FOR EACH} loop just given for each of those documents, and then saves the documents and overwrites the original. The macro would appear as follows:

```
{FOR EACH}File~Contract.1~Contract.2~Contract.3~Contract.4~~
    {Retrieve}{VARIABLE}File~{Enter}
        {FOR EACH}Old~ACME~Excel, Inc.~Scientific International~~
        {Replace}n{VARIABLE}old~Takeover International~
        {END FOR}
    {Exit}y{Enter}yn
{END FOR}
```

{END FOR}   **Macros and Merge**

The {END FOR} command marks the end of a {FOR} or {FOR EACH} loop. As soon as the {END FOR} command is reached, it returns to the {FOR} or {FOR EACH} command. When the loop is finished, the macro (or merge) moves after the {END FOR} command and continues from there. See {FOR} and {FOR EACH} in this chapter for details.

{WHILE}expr~   **Macros and Merge**

You can use this command to test a certain condition (entered as the expression) to see if it's true. If the condition is true, the command repeats the steps between the {WHILE} and {END WHILE} commands until the condition is false, whereupon it quits and continues after the {END WHILE} command.

The following example shows how the loop will be repeated a certain number of times. The {ASSIGN} command assigns the number 1 to a variable named "Number." The {WHILE} command says that while the "Number" variable is less than 10, continue the loop. Another {ASSIGN} command in the loop increases the variable by 1 (necessary to avoid an endless loop). When it reaches 10 (repeats 10 times), the loop will stop.

```
{ASSIGN}Number~1~{COMMENT}
~{WHILE}{VARIABLE}Number~<10~
do
do
do
{ASSIGN}Number~{VARIABLE}Number~+1~{COMMENT}
~{END WHILE}
```

In the next example, the {WHILE} command is used in a merge to test the information in a field instead of using a "counter" to end the loop.

In this example, a letter is being sent to library patrons who have overdue library books. The merge uses two secondary files. One named ADDRESS contains the names and addresses of the patrons of the library. The other, CHECKOUT, contains a list of books that have been checked out along with their due dates.

When the merge is started, the ADDRESS file is specified as the secondary file to be used. The {NEST SECONDARY} command (see "Chaining, Nesting, and Substituting" later in this chapter) is used to access the list of the overdue books in the CHECKOUT file.

The merge also depends on the CHECKOUT secondary file having a "dummy" record at the end of the file with "End" inserted in the first field instead of the name of a book that has been checked out. This dummy record is used in the example instead of a counter to end the loop. The end of the CHECKOUT secondary file might look like the following:

```
Kimberly Thomas{END FIELD}
Little House on the Prairie{END FIELD}
Laura Ingalls Wilder{END FIELD}
11/25/90{END FIELD}
{END RECORD}
==========================
End{END FIELD}
{END FIELD}
{END FIELD}
{END FIELD}
{END RECORD}
==========================
```

The {WHILE} command says that while the name of a person who has checked out the book does not equal "End," to continue the loop. As soon as it finds the "End" record, it knows that it has reached the end of the nested CHECKOUT secondary file, returns to the original secondary file (ADDRESSES), goes to the point after the {END WHILE} command, and the merge continues.

{COMMENT}~ commands have been added to help document each step of this example.

```
Dear {FIELD}Name~:
The following books are now due. Please return them as soon as possible.

{ASSIGN}Patron~{FIELD}Name~~{NEST SECONDARY}checkout~
Book Name                      Due Date
_____

{WHILE}"{FIELD}Name~"!="End"~{COMMENT}while not at the end of the
checked out books
~{IF}"{VARIABLE}Patron~"="{FIELD}Name~"~{COMMENT}if this book is
checked out to the patron in question...
~{FIELD}Book~          {FIELD}Date~{COMMENT}include this
book in the list
~{END IF}{COMMENT}
     ~{NEXT RECORD}{COMMENT}and check or continue to the next book
     record
~{END WHILE}_____
     {NEXT RECORD}{COMMENT}skip the dummy "end" record~
```

{END WHILE}   **Macros and Merge**

This command is used to end a {WHILE} loop. See {WHILE} above for details.

{NEXT}   **Macros and Merge**

You can use {NEXT} in a {FOR} or {WHILE} loop to skip a step in the loop. It increases the counter by one and goes to the next cycle of the loop. See {FOR} in this chapter for an example of how to use this command.

Checking the State of WordPerfect

You can use the {STATE} command, available only in macros, to check the state of WordPerfect. For example, you can check to see whether or not Block, Typeover, or Reveal Codes is on. By checking for these conditions at the beginning of a macro, you can ensure consistency. Consistency is important, because the macro will behave differently under different conditions.

For example, if you intend to use the macro to delete WordPerfect codes, you will want to have Reveal Codes off. Otherwise, you may or may not be asked to confirm the deletion of the code, depending on whether Reveal Codes is on or off.

{STATE}   **Macros Only**

When used alone, the {STATE} command returns a number that indicates the state of WordPerfect. The numbers are listed here:

1,2,3	Which document is current
4	Normal editing screen
8	Editing structure other than main screen (headers, footers, footnotes, graphics boxes, and so on)
16	Macro is being defined

32	Macro is running (always set)
64	Merge is active
128	Block is on
256	Typeover is on
512	Reveal Codes is on
1024	Status line shows a Yes/No question
2048	In a list (List Files menu, list of macros, list of printers, list of fonts, and so on)
32,768	This state is set when it's not possible to go to shell or DOS

If you are in Reveal Codes in document 1 with the Block feature on, the state is 677 because 512 (Reveal Codes) + 128 (Block) + 32 (macro running) + 4 (main editing screen) + 1 (document 1) = 677.

If you need to know one particular state, you can perform an AND operation with the value returned by {STATE}. The resulting value will be either 0 or the value of the state. For example, if you need to know whether you are at the main editing screen (4) or in an editing structure other than the main screen (8), use the command {STATE}&12. You could use an & to compare the AND operation to the state with 12, because 4 + 8 = 12. The result will be 0, 4, 8, or 12, which indicates the state or states currently active.

The following example checks to see if Reveal Codes is on. If it is on, it turns it off to ensure consistency in deleting codes.

```
{IF}{STATE}&512~            {;}If Reveal codes is on~
        {Reveal Codes}      {;}Turn it off~
{END IF}
    .                       {;}continue from here~
    .
    .
```

Using "System" Information

The {SYSTEM} command, available for both macros and merge, can be used to give information about several variables, such as the page number, the filename, the state of the printer, the current attribute, the current column, the current cell in a table, and much more.

{SYSTEM}sysvar~   **Macros and Merge**

The following is a list of {SYSTEM} variables that can be determined. You can use either the variable's name or the number. For example, if you wanted the current page number, you could use {SYSTEM}page~ or {SYSTEM}14~. A list of all values returned for each type of variable is included after the examples of how the {SYSTEM} command can be used.

Attrib	1
Cell	2
CellAttr	23
CellState	24
Column	3
Document	4
Endnote	5
Equation	6
Figure	7
Footnote	8
Left	9
Line	10
List	11
Menu	13
Name	12
Page	14
Path	15
Pos	16
Print	17
Right	18

Row	22
ShellVer	25
TableBox	19
TextBox	20
UserBox	21

Following are a few examples of how to use the {SYSTEM} command. You can use these macros to insert "Page n of n" in a footer, insert the filename in a footer, and generate the document if it has been modified since the last generate. The last example can be used in either a macro or merge to check the state of the printer and send it a "Go" if necessary.

Page n of n

```
{DISPLAY OFF}
{Home}{Home}{Down}                           {;}Go to last page~
{ASSIGN}pg~{SYSTEM}page~~                     {;}Assign pg # to "pg" variable~
{Home}{Home}{Home}{Up}                        {;}Go to very beginning of doc.~
{Format}pfbp                                  {;}Create Footer B for every pg.~
{Center}Page·{^B}·of·{VARIABLE}pg~            {;}Center "Page n of n" in footer~
{Exit}{Exit}                                  {;}Exit footer and format menu~
```

If the number of pages changes in the document, go to the top of the document, delete the footer, and run the macro again. You can even include these steps at the beginning of the macro if you want to.

Filename in Footer

```
{DISPLAY OFF}
{Home}{Home}{Home}{Up}                        {;}Go to very beginning of doc.~
{Format}pfap                                  {;}Create Footer A for every page~
{SYSTEM}Path~{SYSTEM}Name~                    {;}Insert pathname and filename~
{Exit}{Exit}                                  {;}Exit footer and format menu~
```

You will not be able to use the {SYSTEM} command to determine the PATH (the pathname of the current document) or NAME (the current filename) in a merge, because you cannot name the file until the merge is finished.

Generate If Document Has Been Modified

{IF}{SYSTEM}Document~&4~   {;}If document status is 4 (modified since last
                                   generated)~

   {Mark Text}ggy   {;}Generate~
{END IF}

Send Printer a "Go" If Necessary

{IF}{SYSTEM}Print~=8~   {;}If printer is waiting for a "go"~
   {Print}cg{Exit}   {;}Send a "go"~
{END IF}

If you are doing a merge, you can nest a macro that sends a "Go" to the printer, as shown in the following example:

{IF}{SYSTEM}Print~&8~{NEST MACRO}Go~{END IF}

The SHORTCUT keyboard has a macro named ALT-E that uses the {SYSTEM} command extensively. This macro tests the current code and places you within the edit screen of that feature. For example, you can position the cursor on a "header" code and press ALT-E to edit the text within the header immediately, thus eliminating five keystrokes normally needed to get there. If you place the cursor on a margin setting, the ALT-E macro will change that setting and delete the old margin code to eliminate duplicate codes.

Table 6-2 lists all system variables and the values that are returned. Enter the variable on the left as the system variable ({SYSTEM}sysvar~). The numbers on the right indicate the value that is returned.

Chaining, Nesting, and Substituting

If you are doing a merge, there are many commands that you can use to chain, nest, or substitute files. An additional command lets you retrieve a document without processing any merge codes within that document.

Other commands for macros and merge help chain and nest macros.

Sysvar	Value(s)	Returned
Attrib (1)	Current font attribute:	
	1	Extra large
	2	Very large
	4	Large
	8	Small
	16	Fine
	32	Superscript
	64	Subscript
	128	Outline
	256	Italics
	512	Shadow
	1024	Redline
	2048	Double underline
	4096	Bold
	8192	Strikeout
	16384	Underline
	32768	Small Caps
Cell (2)	Current cell position in a table, such as A4, E7, and so on. This system variable is undefined if the cursor is not in a table when the command is encountered	
CellAttr (23)	Attributes of the current cell (see "Attrib" in this table for values). This system variable is undefined if the cursor is not in a table when the command is encountered	
CellState (24)	State of a cell. Divide the value returned by 256 (value returned/256) to determine the following states:	
	0	Left-justified
	1	Full-justified
	2	Center-justified
	3	Right-justified
	4	Decimal-aligned
	Mod the value returned by 256 (value returned %256) of the value returned to determine the following states:	
	1	Justify is cell specific
	2	Attribute is cell specific
	4	Cell is bottom-aligned
	8	Cell is center-aligned
	16	Contents type is "text"
	32	Contents is a formula
	64	Cell is locked

Table 6-2.   System Variables for the {SYSTEM} Command

Sysvar	Value(s)	Returned
		This system variable is undefined if the cursor is not in a table when the command is encountered
Column (3)		Current column number (numbered sequentially from left to right) in a table or in columns
Document (4)		Current modification status of the document on the screen:
	1	Document has been modified
	4	Document has been modified since last generated
	256	Document is blank (Blank documents appear in document screens 1 and 2 when you first start WordPerfect and when you exit to a clear screen. A document from which you delete all text and codes is not "blank")
	512	Cursor is between [Tbl Def] and [Tbl Off] codes (in a table)
	1024	Cursor is between [Math On] and [Math Off] or the end of the file (Math is on)
	2048	Cursor is between [Outline On] and [Outline Off] or the end of the file (Outline is on)
		All other values are undefined and not guaranteed to be 0
Endnote (5)		Number of the current endnote
Equation (6)		Number of the current equation, according to the following formula:

$$\text{Return value}/32 = \text{first level}$$
$$\text{Return value}\%32 = \text{second level}$$

For example, if the current endnote is 1.2, {SYSTEM}Equation will return 34 (34/32 = 1, 34%32 = 2)

Sysvar	Value(s)	Returned
Figure (7)		Number of the current figure, according to the formula described under system variable Equation above
Footnote (8)		Number of the current footnote
Left (9)		Item (character or code) immediately to the left of the cursor
Line (10)		Vertical position of the cursor in 1200ths of an inch
List (11)		Number of items in the current list. (For purposes of this system variable, a list is any list in WordPerfect in which you can perform a name search)
	65535	The cursor is not in a list
	0	The list is empty
	Other	The number of items in the list. In List Files, "Current" and "Parent" each count as an item on the list. Therefore, {SYSTEM}List˜ while in List Files returns 2 plus the number of files in the list (if there are 3 files in the list, {SYSTEM}List˜ returns 5; if there are no files in the list, it returns 2)

Table 6-2.   System Variables for the {SYSTEM} Command (*continued*)

Sysvar	Value(s)	Returned
Menu (13)		Number of the menu currently active (the keystrokes to get to the menu are listed next to each menu):
	65535	Main editing screen (including all editing substructures, such as footers, headers, endnotes, and styles editor)
	177	**Setup** (SHIFT-F1)
	346	**M**ouse (1)
	165	**T**ype (1)
	221	**D**isplay (2)
	187	**C**olors/Fonts/Attributes (1)
	165	**G**raphics Screen Type (3)
	165	**T**ext Screen Type (3)
	341	**M**enu Options (4)
	342	**V**iew Document Options (5)
	343	**E**dit Screen Options (6)
	347	**E**nvironment (3)
	68	**B**ackup Options (1)
	44	**B**eep Options (2)
	181	**C**ursor Speed (3)
	348	**D**ocument Summary (4)
	55	**U**nits of Measure (8)
	45	**I**nitial Settings (4)
	344	**M**erge (1)
	345	**E**quations (3)
	220	**T**able of Authorities (7)
	105	**P**rint Options (8)
	208	**K**eyboard Layout (5)
	237	**C**reate (4)
	209	**E**dit (7)
	56	**L**ocation of Files (6)
	102	**Shell** (CTRL-F1)
	17	**Spell** (CTRL-F2)
	38	**Screen** (CTRL-F3)
	30	**Move** (CTRL-F4)
	112	**R**etrieve (4)
	305	**List** (F5)
	350	**Date/Outline** (SHIFT-F5)
	79	**D**efine (6)

Table 6-2.   System Variables for the {SYSTEM} Command (*continued*)

Sysvar	Value(s)	Returned
	60	**Text In/Out** (CTRL-F5)
	70	DOS Text (1)
	249	Password (2)
	388	Save As (3)
	250	Comment (4)
	259	Spreadsheet (5)
	78	**Mark Text** (ALT-F5)
	154	Cross-Reference (1)
	32806	**Exit** (F7)
	74	**Print** (SHIFT-F7)
	0	Control Printer (4)
	153	View Document (6)
	133	Select Printer (S)
	76	Additional Printers (2)
	133	Help (3)
	47	List Printer Files (4)
	134	Edit (3)
	75	Sheet Feeder (3)
	42	Cartridges/Fonts (4)
	132	Initial Base Font (5)
	133	Help (6)
	353	**Math/Columns** (ALT-F7)
	16	Columns (1)
	33	Define (3)
	296	Tables (2)
	296	Create (1)
	298	Edit (2)
	325	Size (1)
	311	Format (2)
	306	Cell (1)
	323	Type (1)
	351	Attribute (2)
	148	Size (1)
	149	Appearance (2)
	352	Justify (3)
	308	Vertical Alignment (4)
	367	Lock (5)
	307	Column (2)
	307	Width (1)

Table 6-2.   System Variables for the {SYSTEM} Command (*continued*)

Sysvar	Value(s)	Returned
	231	Attributes (2)
	148	Size (1)
	231	Attributes (2)
	148	Justify (3)
	312	Row Height (3)
	299	Lines (3)
	338	Header (4)
	297	Math (5)
	313	Options (6)
	298	Join (7)
	302	Split (8)
	28	Math (3)
	3	**Footnote** (CTRL-F7)
	137	Footnote (1)
	67	Options (4)
	137	Endnote (2)
	135	Options (4)
	3	Endnote Placement (3)
	155	**Format** (SHIFT-F8)
	5	Line (1)
	1	Page (2)
	6	Headers (3)
	240	Header **A** (1) or Header **B** (2)
	117	Footers (4)
	240	Footer **A** (1) or Footer **B** (2)
	368	Page Numbering (6)
	9	Page Number Position (4)
	328	Paper Size/Type (7)
	327	Edit (5)
	230	Size (1)
	229	Type (2)
	330	Font Type (3)
	234	Location (5)
	327	Double Sided Binding (6)
	10	Suppress (8)
	169	Document (3)
	132	Initial Base Font (3)
	11	Redline Method (4)
	125	Summary (5)

Table 6-2.   System Variables for the {SYSTEM} Command (*continued*)

Sysvar	Value(s)	Returned
	25	Other (4)
	150	Advance (1)
	164	Overstrike (5)
	7	Printer Functions (6)
	59	**Styles** (ALT-F8)
	158	Create (3)
	59	Edit (4)
	147	**Font** (CTRL-F8)
	148	Size (1)
	132	Appearance (2)
	146	Base Font (4)
	146	Color (5)
	340	**Merge Codes** (SHIFT-F9)
	346	More (6)
	136	**Graphics** (ALT-F9)
	137	Figure (1), Table Box (2), Text Box (3), User Box (4), or Equation (6)
	138	Create (1)
	144	Options (4)
	227	Lines (5)
	224	Horizontal (1)
	226	Vertical (2)
	62	**Merge/Sort** (CTRL-F9)
	52	Sort (2)
	32809	**Save** (F10)
	237	**Macro Define** (CTRL-F10)
	264	**Pull-Down Menus**
	265	File
	273	Text In
	272	Text Out
	293	Password
	377	Setup
	266	Edit
	274	Select
	322	Comment
	267	Search
	277	Extended
	268	Layout
	276	Columns

Table 6-2. System Variables for the {SYSTEM} Command (*continued*)

Sysvar	Value(s)	Returned
	378	Tables
	286	Math
	279	Footnote
	280	Endnote
	283	Justify
	290	Align
	376	Mark
	286	Cross-Reference
	289	Table of Authorities
	285	Define
	295	Master Document
	294	DocumentC ompare
	271	Tools
	281	Macro
	284	Outline
	282	Merge Codes
	264	Font
	278	Appearance
	279	Graphics
	279	Figure, Table Box, Text Box, User Box, or Equation
	291	Line
	292	Help
Name (12)		Name of the current document (for example, JONES.LTR). Since no filename is associated with the merged document while the merge is executing, this system variable is not available in Merge
Page (14)		Current page number
Path (15)		Path to the current document (for example, C:\WP51\) (Note the slash on the end of the path.) Since no path is associated with the merged document during a merge, this system variable is not available in merge
Pos (16)		Current cursor position in WordPerfect units (1200ths of an inch)
Print (17)		Current print status:
	1	No characters have been sent to printer
	2	An attempt has been made to send characters to printer
	8	Printer is waiting for a "Go"
	16	Trying to rush job
	32	Trying to cancel job
	64	Network down
	128	Printing in progress

Table 6-2.   System Variables for the {SYSTEM} Command (*continued*)

Sysvar	Value(s)	Returned
	256	Downloading a file
	2048	Last print job aborted abnormally
	All others are undefined and not guaranteed to be 0	
Right (18)	Item on which the cursor is resting. In merge, this command will return 0 if the cursor is resting on a soft return or soft page code	
Row (22)	Current row number in a table (equals 0 if the cursor is not in a table when the command is encountered)	
ShellVer (25)	Current Shell version number (Shell is an optional WordPerfect Corporation program). The formula for determining the version from the number returned is (Major Version# * 256) + Minor Version# For example, if you were running WordPerfect under Shell version 1.1, 257 would be returned: (1*256)+1. If you were running under Shell 2.0, 512 would be returned: (2*256)+0	
TableBox (19)	Number of the current table box, according to the formula described under the Equation system variable	
TextBox (20)	Number of the current text box, according to the formula described under the Equation system variable	
UserBox (21)	Number of the current user-defined box, according to the formula described under the system variable equation	

Table 6-2. System Variables for the {SYSTEM} Command (*continued*)

The following is a discussion of the differences in chaining, nesting, and substituting.

When you ask to "chain" a new file or macro, the name of that file or macro is stored in memory. As soon as the current file or macro is finished, WordPerfect goes to the chained file or macro and does not return to the parent file.

"Nesting" means to go immediately to the named file or macro, execute the commands there, and then return to the original file or macro at the same point at which it left.

Substituting is similar to chaining, but it goes to the new file *immediately*—it does not wait until the end of the current file is reached. When you substitute a file, the merge does not return to the orginal file as it does when nesting.

You can nest 30 levels deep in a macro and up to 10 in a merge.

The following is a summary of the commands discussed in this section:

{DOCUMENT}	Retrieve a document	Merge only
{CHAIN MACRO}	Chain a macro	Merge only
{CHAIN PRIMARY}	Chain a primary file	Merge only
{CHAIN SECONDARY}	Chain a secondary file	Merge only
{NEST MACRO}	Nest a macro	Merge only
{NEST PRIMARY}	Nest a primary file	Merge only
{NEST SECONDARY}	Nest a secondary file	Merge only
{SUBST PRIMARY}	Susbstitute a primary file	Merge only
{SUBST SECONDARY}	Susbstitute a secondary file	Merge only
{CHAIN}macro~	Chain a macro	Macros only
{NEST}macroname~	Nest a macro	Macros only
{SHELL MACRO}macro~	Chain a shell macro	Macros only

{DOCUMENT}filename~   **Merge Only**

The {DOCUMENT} command retrieves the named file at that point in the document and moves on without processing any merge codes found in the document. This process can be useful for building other merge applications. For example, if you were a lawyer, you could have different sections of a deposition on disk containing merge codes such as {FIELD}name~ and {FIELD}address~ indicating where the client's name and address will be inserted. You could run a merge that used the {DOCUMENT} commands to compile the entire will (but wouldn't process the {FIELD}~ commands) and then merge the will with the secondary file to insert the name, address, and other pertinent information.

The description of the {CASE} and {CASE CALL} commands includes a simple example of how you can use the {DOCUMENT} command to insert different files, depending on how the user answers a question.

If you want to retrieve a file and have the codes processed at that time, use the {NEST PRIMARY} command instead.

{CHAIN MACRO}macroname ~   Merge Only

When this command is found, the named macro is stored in memory and is started after the merge is finished, regardless of its location in the file.

Only one macro can be started after the merge is finished. If you have more than one macro specified, the last one encountered is used. If an error ends the merge, the macro will not be started unless you use the {ON ERROR} command to guard against such an occurrence.

If you need to start more than one macro during a merge, you can use the {NEST MACRO} command instead to start the macro at that point and then return to the merge after it is finished.

{CHAIN MACRO} performs the same function as the WordPerfect 5.0 ^G merge code.

{CHAIN PRIMARY}filename ~   Merge Only

If you have two or more files to merge, you can chain them with this command. For example, if you have created a form letter named LETTER and have an envelope format (ENV) in another primary file, you can insert the {CHAIN PRIMARY}env ~ command at the end of the letter to chain them, and they will be done in one process.

After the current primary file reaches its end, the merge would switch and use the ENV file as the primary file. If you are using a secondary file, the same record just used will continue to be used for the second primary file. By chaining the ENV file to the LETTER file, you can easily create both at once.

This example is best when you are merging with the keyboard or a single record. Otherwise, the merge would go to the ENV file and would not return to LETTER. If you wanted to have them switch back and forth, you could use the {CHAIN PRIMARY}Letter ~ command at the end of the ENV file, thus creating a loop. If you do this, you *must* remember to use the {NEXT RECORD} command just before chaining back to the LETTER file, or the primary file will continue to use the same record and create an endless loop. By telling the merge to go to the next record, the merge will continue chaining until there are no more records in the secondary file; then the merge will stop.

{CHAIN SECONDARY}filename~   Merge Only

This command lets you chain to another secondary file once the end of the current secondary file is reached. You can use it at the end of one secondary file to "connect" to another, or you can enter it in the primary file.

    You can also use the command at the end of one secondary file so that it will automatically switch to a new secondary file instead of ending the merge. This is useful if you need to send the same letter to people listed in several secondary files. It could save you from starting the merge with a different secondary file each time the secondary file ended and could be left to do the merge unattended.

{NEST MACRO}macroname~   Merge Only

The {NEST MACRO} command starts the named macro where the command is encountered. After the macro is finished, it returns to the place where the macro left the cursor in the document and continues with the merge.

    Use this command instead of the {CHAIN MACRO} command if you want to start more than one macro at the end of a merge.

    Because a merge cannot do some tasks that a macro can, you can include the steps within a macro and then use the {NEST MACRO} command within the merge file. For example, if you have a table in a document that needs to be calculated, you can have the merge fill in the information and then have a macro named CALC calculate the formulas and totals for that table and continue with the merge. Such a command would appear as {NEST MACRO}calc~.

{NEST PRIMARY}filename~   Merge Only

This command is the same as the ^P command found in previous versions of WordPerfect. When the {NEST PRIMARY} command is encountered, WordPerfect starts processing that file immediately, using the current record from the secondary file (if there is one) to fill in the fields found in the nested primary file and then returns to the original file. You can nest up to ten levels of primary files.

You can use this command to assemble documents by retrieving smaller "documents" to make a larger one. Any merge codes found in the smaller documents are processed using the current record, unless a different secondary file is chosen. People who assemble contracts or legal documents that have different paragraphs for different situations may want to store the paragraphs in different documents (the paragraphs could be numbered with an automatic paragraph number so they will be numbered consecutively when they are brought together).

The main primary file might look something like the following:

```
{LABEL}Loop~{COMMENT}
~{TEXT}File~Enter the name of the paragraph to be retrieved:
~{NEST PRIMARY}{VARIABLE}File~ ~{COMMENT}
~{CHAR}Cont~ Do you have more paragraphs? (Y/N)~{COMMENT}
~{IF}"{VARIABLE}Cont~"="y"~

{GO}loop~{END IF}
```

Note that two hard returns (ending the current paragraph and inserting a blank line) follow the tilde (~) in the IF statement. If there are more paragraphs to be entered, two hard returns are inserted, and the user is prompted for the next filename.

{NEST PRIMARY}~ (without entering a filename) nests the same primary file, creating a loop. This is identical to the use of ^P^P in previous versions of WordPerfect.

{NEST SECONDARY}filename~   **Merge Only**

If you need to merge with information from a different secondary file, you can use the {NEST SECONDARY} command. At that point in the merge, the records from the new secondary file are used. When the end of the file is reached, it will return control to the original secondary file. You can nest up to ten levels of secondary files.

If you are doing this type of merge, you may want to use other merge commands such as {IF} to check each record and see if you want to use the fields from that record in the merge.

See {WHILE} in this chapter for an example of nesting a secondary file.

{SUBST PRIMARY}filename~   Merge Only

The {SUBST PRIMARY} command lets you substitute another primary file for the current one. The command is similar to {NEST PRIMARY} and {CHAIN PRIMARY}; it passes control to another primary file. {NEST PRIMARY} passes control to a new primary file and then returns to the original primary file. You can enter the {CHAIN PRIMARY} command anywhere in a primary file, but it will not take effect until the first primary file is completed. {SUBST PRIMARY} passes control to a new file immediately and does not return to the first primary file. Because the original primary file is no longer used, all local variables assigned by that primary file are emptied.

You can use the {IF} command to test a specific field or variable and substitute a new primary file, depending on the outcome. In the following example, control will be switched to the file INVOICE if the amount in the "total" variable is greater than 0.

{IF}{VARIABLE}Total~ > 0 ~{SUBST PRIMARY}Invoice~{END IF}

{SUBST SECONDARY}filename~   Merge Only

The file named as the {SUBST SECONDARY} will be used as the new secondary file as soon as the command is encountered. See {SUBST PRIMARY} above for differences between this command, {NEST}, and {CHAIN}.

This command replaces the ^S merge command in previous versions of WordPerfect.

{CHAIN}macro~   Macros Only

You can chain macros or repeat the current macro with the {CHAIN} command. If you want to chain a letter macro (LETTER.WPM) to an envelope macro (ENV.WPM), the command in the letter macro would look like the following:

{CHAIN}env~

A macro can only be chained to one macro, even if other macros are nested. However, you can have a macro chain a macro that chains a macro, and so on. The chained macro will be executed when the current macro has finished.

{NEST}macro~   Macros Only

Use {NEST} to start another macro at a particular point in the current macro and then return to the original macro when the nested macro finishes. Nesting macros is most useful to access macros that are often used by themselves but are sometimes combined with others. For example, if you have a macro that generates tables and lists, and you want to include that macro with the rest of the final formatting for a document, you could nest it as shown in the following example. After the generate macro is complete, control will return to the original macro, and a spell check will begin.

{Home}{Home}{Home}{Up}	{;}Go to the very beginning of doc~
{Style}{Search}Final	{;}Select Style and search for the Final style~
{Enter}o	{;}Turn off Name Search and turn on the style~
{NEST}generate~	{;}Generate the document~
{Spell}d	{;}Spell check the document~

{SHELL MACRO}macroname~   Macros Only

If you have WordPerfect Library or Office (version 2.1 or later), you can write "shell macros" that you can start in any program that supports the shell and can be used to go across programs. For example, you could start a shell macro from WordPerfect, have it exit WordPerfect, enter PlanPerfect, calculate a spreadsheet, send a portion to the Clipboard, restart WordPerfect, and then retrieve the contents of the Clipboard.

The {SHELL MACRO} command lets you start the shell macro at the location in which it is found in the macro. The macro is chained, not nested, which means that all control goes to the shell macro and does not return to the WordPerfect macro.

You could also use the {SYSTEM}shellver~ command to check the current version of the shell and see if the shell macro can be run. See "Using System Information" in this chapter.

Displaying a Macro or Merge

The steps in a macro or merge are not usually displayed on the screen while the macro or merge is running. You can control this with the following commands:

{DISPLAY ON}	Display the keystrokes and menus in a macro	Macros only
{DISPLAY OFF}	Do not display the macro as it runs	Macros only
{MENU OFF}	Turn off the display of WordPerfect menus	Macros only
{MENU ON}	Turn on the display of WordPerfect menus	Macros only
{REWRITE}	Display the merged document up to that point	Merge only
{SPEED}	Control the speed of the macro	Macros only
{WAIT}	Wait a specified amount of time	Macros and merge

{DISPLAY ON} and {DISPLAY OFF}   Macros Only

When you define a macro from the keyboard, the {DISPLAY OFF} command is inserted. If you enter the macro editor directly by pressing HOME before the Macro Define (CTRL-F10), it will also be inserted. However, if you are defining a macro with the Keyboard Layout feature, you will need to insert the {DISPLAY OFF} command if you do not want to watch each step of the macro. Including {DISPLAY OFF} also makes the macro run faster.

If the macro pauses in a WordPerfect menu for you to enter information, you *must* place the {DISPLAY ON} command just before the steps that display the menu, or it will not be displayed on the screen. You can then insert {DISPLAY OFF} after the menu has been displayed.

 If a macro does not work properly, you can include the {DISPLAY ON} command so you can see where it failed and correct the macro.

{MENU OFF} and {MENU ON}   Macros Only

You can use these two commands to turn the WordPerfect menus on or off at any time. They are already used internally if you use the pull-down menus so that only selected menus are displayed. For example, if you selected the Text Out option under File, you would not see the normal Text In/Out menu at the bottom of the screen, but would instead see the next pull-down menu.

 You can use these commands instead of {DISPLAY ON} and {DISPLAY OFF} if you want to remove a menu from the screen and display a message of your own with the {PROMPT} command. For example, you could use {MENU OFF}, enter the List Files menu, and then display a menu selection of your own at the bottom of the screen.

{REWRITE}   Merge Only

During a merge, the screen remains blank while the merge processes "in the background." Once the merge is finished, the screen is rewritten, showing the merge up to that point. If you want to rewrite the screen at any other point, insert the {REWRITE} command at the desired location. This command was known as ^U in previous versions of Word-Perfect.

{SPEED}100ths~   Macros Only

Use the {SPEED} command to slow the execution of a macro. Indicate the time to wait between each instruction and/or key in hundredths of a second. The larger the number, the longer is the delay. For example, {SPEED}1~ causes 1/100 of a second delay, while {SPEED}100~ causes a one-second delay.

This command is useful for running demos in which you want the keystrokes to be displayed on the screen at a speed at which people can read (remember to use {DISPLAY ON} with this command). The command is also useful when you are debugging a macro to see where it fails.

{WAIT}10ths~ **Macros and Merge**

You can use {WAIT} with {PROMPT} to display the prompt for a certain amount of time. Enter the number in tenths. In the following example, the message will be displayed for 5 1/2 seconds.

{PROMPT}After the merge is finished, print the document and clear the screen.~{WAIT}55~

Stopping, Quitting, Breaking, and Restarting

Four commands are discussed in this section: {RESTART}, {BREAK}, {STOP}, and {QUIT}. Some are unique to macros and some to merge. These commands control different ways to end a macro or merge.

{QUIT}	Quit the macro or merge at that point. If in a merge, the rest of the primary file is read in	Macros and merge
{STOP}	Stop the merge at that point, and do not read in the rest of the primary file	Merge only
{RESTART}	Stop the macro when the current macro or subroutine is finished	Macros only
{BREAK}	End a loop or {IF} statement	Macros and merge

{QUIT} **Macros and Merge**

The {QUIT} command stops a macro or merge at that point, regardless of whether it is in the main level or a sublevel (in a nested primary merge file, for example). This command is unlike {BREAK}, which stops at the parent level, unless it is encountered in a substructure. With {QUIT}, if it is contained in a substructure, control will be returned to the higher level instead of stopping.

If you have used the {CHAIN MACRO} command, the {QUIT} command will not allow the chained macro to be executed.

When using the {QUIT} command in a merge document, all text remaining in the primary file is read into the merged document, including the merge commands that have not yet been processed. If you do not want this to happen, use the {STOP} merge command instead. You can use {QUIT} to end the merge after all the merge commands have been processed, leaving only text. Using {QUIT} at that point, instead of {STOP}, is a little quicker.

For example, you may want to pause with the {KEYBOARD} command so that someone can enter the TO, FROM, and SUBJECT, information. You can then enter {QUIT} at the end of the memo so that you can enter the body of the text without having to remember to press End Field (F9) when you are finished.

                    MEMO

TO: {KEYBOARD}
FROM: {KEYBOARD}
DATE: {DATE}
SUBJECT: {KEYBOARD}

{QUIT}

{STOP}   Merge Only

The {STOP} command stops a merge at the point at which it is encountered. No further execution is allowed. The {STOP} command is different from the {QUIT} command, in that it does not read the rest of the primary file onto the screen.

{BREAK}   Macros and Merge

If you are using the {FOR} or {WHILE} command, you can use the {BREAK} command to stop the loop unconditionally. The commands {END FOR} and {END WHILE} only mark the end of (delimit) the loop.

If {BREAK} is used within a structure using {IF}, {IF BLANK}, {IF NOT BLANK}, or {IF EXISTS}, the macro or merge moves directly to the {END IF} command and resumes at that point. If {BREAK} is used outside an IF structure or FOR or WHILE loop, a merge will return to the parent file if the current file is nested. If used in a macro, it will return to the parent macro if the current macro is nested.

{RESTART}   Macros Only

You can use the {RESTART} command to end a macro or merge from within a nested macro. If you do not want the nested macro to return to the parent macro, insert the {RESTART} command anywhere in the nested macro. As soon as it is completed, the entire macro will end.

Error Checking

You can control whether or not someone can press Cancel (F1) to stop a merge or macro with the {CANCEL ON} and {CANCEL OFF} commands.

You can also use commands that determine what action should be taken if the user does press Cancel, an error occurs, or, in the case of macros, a search is not successful. The following commands are introduced in this section:

{CANCEL ON}	Let the user cancel the macro or merge	Macros and merge
{CANCEL OFF}	Disable Cancel (F1)	Macros and merge
{ON CANCEL}	Determine the action if Cancel is pressed	Macros and merge
{ON ERROR}	Determine the action if an error is found	Macros and merge
{ON NOT FOUND}	Determine the action if a search fails	Macros only
{RETURN CANCEL}	Indicates a "cancel" has occurred	Macros and merge
{RETURN ERROR}	Indicates an error has occurred	Macros and merge

{RETURN NOT FOUND}	Indicates that a search has failed	Macros only

{CANCEL OFF}   Macros and Merge

This command lets you disable Cancel so it cannot be used to stop a macro or merge. However, you will always be able to cancel by pressing CTRL-BREAK as an upper-level interrupt.

{CANCEL ON}   Macros and Merge

You can use {CANCEL OFF} in a section of the macro or merge, then use this command to allow the use of Cancel (F1) again.

{ON CANCEL}action~   Macros and Merge

Use the {ON CANCEL} command if you want to have special action taken when Cancel (F1) is pressed or signaled by a {RETURN CANCEL} condition from a subroutine or nested macro or merge.

Usually, when Cancel (F1) is pressed, a {RETURN CANCEL} condition is returned, which means "cancel the macro or merge." To specify an action other than canceling the macro or merge, use the {ON CANCEL} command. For example, if Cancel (F1) is pressed, you could tell the merge to {GO} to a section of the document that contains a {PROMPT} command prompting you with a message.

Valid commands for the action part of the {ON CANCEL} command are {BREAK}, {CALL}, {GO}, {QUIT}, {RETURN}, {RETURN CANCEL}, {RETURN ERROR}, {STOP}, {RESTART}, and {RETURN NOT FOUND}. {STOP} is unique to a merge, and {RESTART} and {RETURN NOT FOUND} are available only in a macro.

Entering {ON CANCEL}~ (without entering any type of action) will ignore Cancel (F1) when it is pressed, doing the same thing as {CANCEL OFF}. If {CALL} is specified as the action, the called subroutine is executed, and then the macro or merge will resume where the Cancel condition was indicated.

When using this command, insert it before a cancel condition could occur.

{ON ERROR}action~   Macros and Merge

This command decides what should be done if an error occurs. An error could occur because a nested, chained, or substituted file or macro is not found; if an error occurs in a nested macro; or when printing with the {PRINT} merge command. The default is {RETURN ERROR} where the error message is displayed and the macro or merge quits.

Valid commands you can use for the action of {ON ERROR} are identical to the commands that you can use for the actions of {ON CANCEL}: {BREAK}, {CALL}, {GO}, {QUIT}, {RETURN}, {RETURN CANCEL}, {RETURN ERROR}, {STOP}, {RESTART}, and {RETURN NOT FOUND}. {STOP} is unique to a merge, and {RESTART} and {RETURN NOT FOUND} are available only in a macro.

Entering {ON ERROR}~ (without entering any command as the action) will do nothing and will ignore the error message.

{ON NOT FOUND}action~   Macros Only

{ON NOT FOUND} is similar to {ON CANCEL} and {ON ERROR}. When a search fails (during a Search, Find in the List Files menu, or Name Search) {RETURN NOT FOUND} is executed, which means that you will see the message "Not found," and the macro will end.

When doing a Name Search in any WordPerfect list (such as List Files, Fonts, or Styles) the cursor will move to the item in the list that is closest to the name entered and will not generate a "not found" message. If you want to know whether or not the exact item was found in the list, you can choose Name Search, enter the name, and then press CTRL-ENTER (a {HPg} command will be inserted in the macro). If the item is not an exact match, a "not found" condition will be generated.

You can use the {ON NOT FOUND} command to specify that a different action be taken than ending the macro. Again, {BREAK}, {CALL}, {GO}, {QUIT}, {RETURN}, {RETURN CANCEL}, {RETURN ERROR}, {RESTART}, and {RETURN NOT FOUND} are available.

{RETURN CANCEL}   Macros and Merge

When Cancel (F1) or CTRL-BREAK is pressed, a {RETURN CANCEL} command is generated, which stops the merge or macro.

You can insert this command to simulate a Cancel condition and terminate the macro or merge upon returning from a subroutine. If you have used the {ON CANCEL} command, WordPerfect will capture the {RETURN CANCEL} and act according to the action entered for the {ON CANCEL} command.

Pressing Cancel (F1) or CTRL-BREAK will also stop a macro or merge.

{RETURN ERROR}   Macros and Merge

When an error is encountered, a {RETURN ERROR} command is generated, which allows the error message to be displayed. You can use this command to simulate an error and stop the macro or merge (unless you have anticipated an error message and have used the {ON ERROR} command to decide what action should be taken if an error occurs).

{RETURN NOT FOUND}   Macros Only

When a search fails, a {RETURN NOT FOUND} is generated, which displays the message "Not found," and the macro ends. You can use this command to simulate a "not found" situation and end the macro (unless you have anticipated a "not found" and have used the {ON NOT FOUND} command to decide what action should be taken).

Debugging Commands

You can use {DISPLAY ON}, {DISPLAY OFF}, and {SPEED} to display a macro or slow it down so you can see the point at which the macro fails. These commmands were discussed earlier in this chapter under "Displaying a Macro or Merge."

Two other commands, {STEP ON} and {STEP OFF}, are available to both macros and merge to aid in debugging or finding mistakes.

{STEP OFF} and {STEP ON}   Macros and Merge

If a macro or merge is not running correctly, you can insert the {STEP ON} command at the beginning of the primary file or macro, at the point at which you feel there is a problem. You can use {STEP OFF} to return to normal execution.

The next time the macro or merge is run and encounters the {STEP ON} command, it pauses and displays each character or command on the screen before it is executed. If you are doing a *merge*, you may find it useful to press Reveal Codes (ALT-F3) before starting the merge. You can then see which code or command is being processed. Press any key to continue after each character or command is displayed.

If you are using {STEP ON} in a *macro*, the next character or a command will be displayed. The commands are grouped into four sections, as shown here:

ALT X	ALT-letter macro
KEY CMD *n*	Function key, cursor key, WordPerfect command, and so on
KEY MACRO *n*	Macro from a keyboard layout
MACRO CMD	Specific macro command (such as {GO} and {BELL})

Because the KEY and MACRO commands are displayed as numbers instead of words, Table 6-3 is offered to aid in translation.

{BELL}   Macros and Merge

You can use {BELL} commands throughout macros or merge files for debugging purposes. For example, if the merge stops after the computer sounds four beeps but does not reach the fifth, the problem lies somewhere between the fourth and fifth {BELL} commands.

Converting Keys, Characters, and Numbers

When defining a macro, you may want to use the {ORIGINAL KEY} command if you think you may have a keyboard selected when the macro is run and you want to access the original function of the key.

{CTON} and {NTOC} are commands that you can use to convert characters to numbers and vice versa. These commands are only available in merge. {KTON} and {NTOK} are available only in macros and can be used to convert a key to a number and vice versa.

⌐ KEY CMD (Key Command)

1	^A
2	^B - Page Number
3	^C - Merge from Console
4	^D - Merge Date
5	^E - Merge End Record
6	^F - Merge Field
7	^G - Merge Macro
8	^H - Home
9	^I - Tab
10	^J - Enter
11	^K - Delete to End of Line
12	^L - Delete to End of Page
13	^M - Search value for [SRt]
14	^N - Merge Next Record
15	^O - Merge Output Prompt
16	^P - Merge Primary File
17	^Q - Merge Quit
18	^R - Merge End Field
19	^S - Merge Secondary File
20	^T - Merge Text to Printer
21	^U - Merge Update the Screen
22	^V - Ignore Meaning of the following Code
23	^W - Up
24	^X - Right & Search Wildcard
25	^Y - Left
26	^Z - Down
27	^[- ESC
28	^\
29	^]
30	^^ - Reset Keyboard Map
31	^_
32	Cancel
33	Forward Search
34	Help
35	Indent
36	List
37	Bold

Table 6-3.   Key and Macro Commands That Are Displayed When You Use the {STEP ON} Command

KEY CMD (Key Command)

38	Exit
39	Underline
40	Merge End Field
41	Save
42	*not defined*
43	*not defined*
44	Setup
45	Backward Search
46	Switch
47	Left/Right Indent
48	Date/Outline
49	Center
50	Print
51	Format
52	Merge Commands
53	Retrieve
54	*not defined*
55	*not defined*
56	Thesaurus
57	Replace
58	Reveal Codes
59	Block
60	Mark Text
61	Flush Right
62	Columns/Table
63	Style
64	Graphics
65	Macro
66	*not defined*
67	*not defined*
68	Shell
69	Spell
70	Screen
71	Move
72	Text In/Out
73	Tab Align
74	Footnote

Table 6-3.   Key and Macro Commands That Are Displayed When You Use the {STEP ON} Command (*continued*)

KEY CMD (Key Command)

75	Font
76	Merge/Sort
77	Macro Define
78	*not defined*
79	*not defined*
80	Backspace
81	Delete Right
82	Delete Word
83	Word Right
84	Word Left
85	Home, Home, Right (End)
86	Home, Home, Left
87	*not defined*
88	Go To (CTRL-HOME)
89	PGUP
90	PGDN
91	Screen Down (+)
92	Screen Up (−)
93	Typeover
94	Left Margin Release (SHIFT-TAB)
95	Hard Page
96	Soft Hyphen (CTRL-HYPHEN)
97	Hard Hyphen (HOME, HYPHEN)
98	Hard Space (HOME, space)
99	Para Up
100	Para Down
101	Item Left
102	Item Right
103	Item Up
104	Item Down
105	ALT-HOME
106	Delete Row (CTRL-DEL)
107	Menu Bar (ALT-=)
108	Block Append
109	Block Move
110	Block Copy

Table 6-3.   Key and Macro Commands That Are Displayed When You Use the {STEP ON} Command (*continued*)

MACRO CMD (Macro Commands)

1	{ASSIGN}
2	{BELL}
3	{BREAK}
4	{CALL}
5	{CANCEL OFF}
6	{CANCEL ON}
7	{CASE}
8	{CASE CALL}
9	{CHAIN}
10	{CHAR}
11	{;} comment
12	{DISPLAY OFF}
13	{DISPLAY ON}
14	{ELSE}
15	{END FOR}
16	{END IF}
17	{END WHILE}
18	{FOR}
19	{FOR EACH}
20	{GO}
21	{IF}
22	{LABEL}
23	{LOOK}
24	{NEST}
25	{NEXT}
26	{SHELL MACRO}
27	{ON CANCEL}
28	{ON ERROR}
29	{ON NOT FOUND}
30	{PAUSE}
31	{PROMPT}
32	{QUIT}
33	{RESTART}
34	{RETURN}
35	{RETURN CANCEL}
36	{RETURN ERROR}
37	{RETURN NOT FOUND}

Table 6-3. Key and Macro Commands That Are Displayed When You Use the {STEP ON} Command (*continued*)

MACRO CMD (Macro Commands)

38	{SPEED}
39	{STEP ON}
40	{TEXT}
41	{STATE}
42	{WAIT}
43	{WHILE}
44	{Macro Commands}
45	{STEP OFF}
46	{ORIGINAL KEY}
47	{IF EXISTS}
48	{MENU OFF}
49	{MENU ON}
50	{STATUS PROMPT}
51	{INPUT}
52	{VARIABLE}
53	{SYSTEM}
54	{MID}
55	{NTOK}
56	{KTON}
57	{LEN}
58	{~} (hard tilde)
59	{PAUSE KEY}

Table 6-3.   Key and Macro Commands That Are Displayed When You Use the {STEP ON} Command (*continued*)

{ORIGINAL KEY}	Use the original function of the key	Macros only
{CTON}	Convert a character to a number	Merge only
{NTOC}	Convert a number to a character	Merge only
{KTON}	Convert a key to a number	Macros only
{NTOK}	Convert a number to a key	Macros only

{ORIGINAL KEY}   Macros Only

The {ORIGINAL KEY} command will return the unmapped value of the last key pressed at the keyboard. If a keyboard is selected that maps a different function to a specific key, this command becomes especially useful.

{CTON}character~   Merge Only

This command converts a character to its ASCII number. For example, an "A" would be converted to "65."

You can use this command if you want to check to see if a character fits within a certain range. {CTON} could convert characters to their ASCII equivalent, {ASSIGN} or {LOCAL} could assign the result to a variable, and then the {IF} command could be used to check to see if the variable were greater than or less than a certain number.

For example, if you have a menu of choices "numbered" A through C, you could quickly check the range (65 through 67) to see if what the user entered was valid. Of course, if you wanted to let users press lowercase letters, you would also need to check the range 97 through 99.

{NTOC}number~   Merge Only

The {NTOC} command can change an ASCII number to its character equivalent. This command does just the opposite of the {CTON} command, which changes a character to its ASCII number.

If you want to convert a WordPerfect character number to its equivalent character, multiply the character set number by 256. You can then add the number of the character within that set and use the total number in the {NTOC} command. If you want to convert character 4,11 to the correct character (the British pound sign, £), you would need to first multiply 4 by 256, then add 11. This calculation can be included as part of the {NTOC} command, as shown in the following example. The example shows how you can use this command to insert the proper currency symbol from character set 4.

```
{TEXT}curr~ Enter the type of currency being used:
11 = British pounds
    12 = Japanese yen
```

57 = U.S. dollars

Selection: ˜{NTOC}4*256 + {VARIABLE}curr˜ ˜

{KTON}key˜   Macros Only

The {KTON} command can convert any key (function key, delete key, cursor key, or any character) to a unique number. For example, you can enter the command {KTON}{Block}˜ to get the number 32827.

If you enter a character, the number returned will be equivalent to its WordPerfect character set and character number. In other words, entering {KTON}%˜ will return 37. When dealing with these character set numbers, WordPerfect multiplies the character set number by 256 and then adds the character number to that. You must then divide (or have the macro divide) the number by 256. The result will be the character set number, and the remainder will be the number of the character in that set. Because 37 is less than 256, you can assume that it belongs to character set zero. Returning the number 560 would mean that it came from character set 2 and is character number 48 in that set (560/256 = 2 with a remainder of 48).

This command might be useful in checking to see if the correct key were pressed. The following example would check to see if bold were turned on.

```
{LOOK}key˜
{IF}key = 32805 ˜
     {GO}message˜
{END IF}
```

To convert a number back to a key, use the {NTOK} (number to character) command. The key or function would be inserted into the document. For example, if you converted the number 32805 to a key, bold would be turned on at that point.

{NTOK}number˜   Macros Only

The {NTOK} command changes a number to a key. This command does just the opposite of {KTON}. See {KTON} for details.

Fields and Records

All remaining commands are unique to merge. They discuss commands dealing with fields and records. The next section, "Miscellaneous Merge Commands" also deals only with merge commands.

{END RECORD}   Merge Only

This command is used to end each record in the secondary file and replaces the ^E merge code used in previous versions of WordPerfect. When this command is selected, a hard page break [HPg] is also inserted. Having each record separated makes it easy to move from record to record when you press the PGUP and PGDN keys. You can also use Go To (CTRL-HOME) to go to a specific page (record) or press HOME, HOME, ↓ to determine the total number of records by looking at the last page number.

   If you accidentally press End Field (F9) or insert an End Record (SHIFT-F9, E), you will see the "Field n" prompt on the status line. If this happens, delete the code and press HOME, HOME, ↑ to clear the "Field n" prompt.

{FIELD}field~   Merge Only

The {FIELD}field~ command is the same as the ^F used in previous versions and tells WordPerfect where to insert the information from a specific field in the secondary file. The following is a form letter that uses {FIELD} commands showing where the name and address are to be inserted.

{FIELD}first name~ {FIELD}last name~
{FIELD}street address~
{FIELD}city~, {FIELD}state~ {FIELD}zip code~

Dear {FIELD}first name~:

Any extra spaces or punctuation marks need to be outside the {FIELD}field~ commands. If they are entered with the field name or number, WordPerfect will think that the space or punctuation is part of the field name and will not find such a field in the secondary file.

You can insert the {FIELD} merge command into almost any part of a document, including headers, footers, and tables. The only exception is that you cannot enter a merge code into styles.

Another option still available from previous versions of WordPerfect is the capability of placing a question mark at the end of the field name (but before the tilde) to see if the field is blank. If it is, it deletes from the ? to the end of the line. However, because this could delete text that you did not want deleted, you can instead use the {IF NOT BLANK} or {IF BLANK} command to check the field's contents.

You can also use the {FIELD} command as part of another merge command. For example, you could use it as part of the {CASE} command to check for certain conditions in the field. See {CASE} and {CASE CALL} for examples.

{FIELD NAMES}name1 ~ . . . ~ nameN ~ ~   Merge Only

As you enter fields into a secondary file, you are prompted at the bottom of the screen for the current field by number. If you would like to have the fields identified by name instead, you can use the {FIELD NAMES} command at the beginning of the secondary file.

When selected, it will prompt you for the name of the first field. After typing the name and pressing ENTER, it will prompt you for the name of the second field, and so on. After naming all fields, pressing ENTER twice ends the command. Two tildes (~ ~), an {END RECORD} command, and a hard page break are also inserted to end the command.

The field names will appear immediately on the status line, prompting you for the appropriate information. If you want to leave a field blank, remember to press End Field (F9) to leave it blank and go on to the next field.

If you need to make changes to the list, do so, and then press HOME, HOME, ↑ to update the prompts on the status line to the new field names.

You can enter more fields than you have names for. For example, if you reach the end of the prompts but you have more fields to be entered (a list of children, for example), the remaining fields will be numbered.

Miscellaneous Merge Commands
{MRG CMND}codes{MRG CMND}

If you want to include merge commands in a primary document that should not be processed, place the {MRG CMND} commands around them. During a merge, anything between the {MRG CMND}s will be placed in the merged document without being processed as merge codes.

This command can be used to create a secondary document, as shown here:

```
{INPUT}Enter the name: ~{MRG CMND}{END FIELD}
{MRG CMND}{INPUT}Enter the phone #: ~{MRG CMND}{END FIELD}
{END RECORD}
= = = = = = = = = - - - - = = ■ = = = = - - - - = = = = = = = = = = = =
{MRG CMND}
```

{NEXT RECORD}

This command tells the merge to move to the next record in the secondary file and replaces the ^N merge command from previous versions of WordPerfect.

Because this usually happens automatically, this command is not used often. However, there may be some instances in which you need to force it to go to the next record or it will continue reading in the fields from the current record. See {WHILE} in this chapter for an example of how to use the {NEXT RECORD} command.

{PAGE OFF}

When a primary file is merged with a secondary file, WordPerfect automatically inserts a hard page [HPg] break between each "record." When you merge a letter with a list of names and addresses, Word-Perfect places a hard page break at the end of the letter and continues the merge.

If you do not want page breaks to separate records, use the {PAGE OFF} command. You can use this command to create a list of records on the same page. The following example would create a list of names and phone numbers without page breaks:

```
{PAGE OFF}{COMMENT}
~{FIELD}Name~                    {FIELD}Phone~
```

If you are using the Labels feature to print labels, do not use this command to turn off page breaks because they are needed to divide the text between labels, not pages.

This type of command replaces the ^N^P^P command used in previous versions of WordPerfect.

{PAGE ON}

If you have turned hard page breaks off with the {PAGE OFF} command, you can turn them back on at any time with the {PAGE ON} command.

{PRINT}

You may not have enough memory in your computer to merge large files successfully. If you see an error message informing you of this, you can use the {PRINT} command at the end of the primary file. This will tell the merge to print what is merged up to that point, clear the screen, and continue the merge process.

Using {PRINT} alone will print a blank page between files because of the page break that naturally occurs at the end of each merged file. To avoid the blank page between documents, use the following:

{PAGE OFF}{PRINT}

This replaces the ^T^N^P^P merge code combination that did the same thing in previous versions of WordPerfect.

{PROCESS}codes{PROCESS}

Any merge commands found between the {PROCESS} commands will be processed during a merge. This is the opposite of {MRG CMND}, which does not process the commands found between the two {MRG CMND} codes.

Because merge commands are automatically processed during a merge, the {PROCESS} command is not usually necessary. However, if you have merge commands in a secondary file, they will not be processed until they are encountered. By using the {PROCESS} command, you can have the merge commands processed as WordPerfect encounters them (during a scan of the secondary file, for example, when the merge is searching for specific records).

You may want to use this command if you have a {GO} command that tells the merge to go to a specific record, skip records, chain files, or start a macro.

Appearance of Macro Prompts

To control the appearance and display of messages and prompts in macros, you can use WordPerfect's special control characters in combination with the messages of the {CHAR}, {PROMPT}, {INPUT}, and {TEXT} commands. For example, the following prompt

{CHAR}1~{^N}{^N}1{^O}{^N}Save;{^T}2{^U} ClearScreen: 1{Left}~

will appear as follows when the macro is run:

<u>1</u> Save; <u>2</u> Clear Screen: <u>1</u>

Because of the {Left} command the cursor will be moved under the last "1." As you can see, the underline was accomplished with two different methods. These control characters—which you can create while in the macro editor by pressing CTRL-*letter*—are listed here:

Character	Code	Function
CTRL-H	{Home}	Move cursor to upper left
CTRL-J	{Enter}	Create a new line
CTRL-K	{Del to EOL}	Delete to the end of the line
CTRL-L	{Del to EOP}	Clear the screen, and move cursor to upper left
CTRL-M	{^M}	Move cursor to the beginning of the line

Character	Code	Function
CTRL-N	{^N}	Turn on the display attribute (code should be followed by an attribute code—see below)
CTRL-O	{^O}	Turn off display attribute (code should be followed by an attribute code)
CTRL-P	{^P}*cr*	Move the cursor to the specified location (*c* = column, *r* = row)
CTRL-Q	{^Q}	Turn off all display attributes
CTRL-R	{^R)	Turn on reverse video
CTRL-S	{^S}	Turn off reverse video
CTRL-T	{^T}	Turn on underline
CTRL-U	{^U}	Turn off underline
CTRL-V	{^V}	Turn on mnemonic attribute
CTRL-W	{Up}	Move the cursor up one line
CTRL-X	{Right}	Move the cursor right one character
CTRL-Y	{Left}	Move the cursor left one character
CTRL-Z	{Down}	Position the cursor down one line
CTRL-\	{^\}	Turn off bold
CTRL-]	{^]}	Turn on bold

Display attribute control codes to follow ^N and ^O (turning the following attributes on end off):

Character	Code	Attribute
CTRL-A	{^A}	Very large
CTRL-B	{^B}	Large
CTRL-C	{^C}	Small
CTRL-D	{^D}	Fine print
CTRL-E	{^E}	Superscript
CTRL-F	{^F}	Subscript

Character	Code	Attribute
CTRL-G	{^G}	Outline
CTRL-H	{Home}	Italics
CTRL-I	{Tab}	Shadow
CTRL-J	{Enter}	Redline
CTRL-K	{DEL to EOL}	Double underline
CTRL-L	{DEL to EOP}	Bold
CTRL-M	{^M}	Strikeout
CTRL-N	{^N}	Underline
CTRL-O	{^O}	Small Caps
CTRL-P	{^P}	Blink
CTRL-Q	{^Q}	Reverse video

Positioning Macros on the Screen

The {CHAR}, {TEXT}, {INPUT}, {PROMPT}, and {STATUS PROMPT} commands let you display a message on the screen. If the message consists of one line, it is displayed on the status line. If it consists of two or more lines, the message or menu scrolls up on the screen so that the entire message (up to 24 lines, or the number of lines that is available on your screen) is displayed.

If you want to control the position of the menu or message in a macro, you can use the {^P} command and enter the x and y coordinates of the position on the screen. This capability is not available in merge.

In the following example, the {Del to EOP} command clears the screen (temporarily while the message is being displayed) and places the menu in the upper left corner. Rememer to press CTRL-V before pressing CTRL-PGDN to insert the {Del to EOP} command. The small dots represent spaces.

```
{CHAR}Choice~{Del to EOP}Please·enter·your·selection:{Enter}
. . . A···Apples{Enter}
. . . B···Bananas{Enter}
. . . C···Coconuts{Enter}
Selection: ~
```

If you want to place the menu at a location other than at the upper left corner of the screen, you can use the {^P} command to determine the position. To do so, clear the screen, and type the menu as you would like it to appear—without macro commands. Next, move the cursor to the upper left corner and press ↓, counting the number of keystrokes required to reach the line where the cursor should appear. Write that number down as the y coordinate.

Now press →, counting the number of keystrokes required to reach the horizontal position. Write that number down as the x coordinate. Repeat the process for each line.

Enter the macro editor, and insert the macro commands and prompts as you normally would. At the beginning of each line, press CTRL-P. The {^P} command will be inserted. Next, hold down the ALT key, and type the number of the x coordinate (the number of characters across the screen); then let up on the ALT key. Repeat the process for the y coordinate (the number of lines down the screen) by holding down the ALT key and typing the number of the y coordinate.

Although there are other options, such as entering line 1 as {^A}, 2 as {^B}, and so on, this method is easier. Also, you do not absolutely have to clear the screen with the {Del to EOP} command before displaying such a menu, however, you may find that it look better if you do.

You can add lines around the menu to make it look more like a "pop-out" box. However, because Line Draw does not work inside the macro editor, and you cannot move a block of text into the macro editor, you will need to enter the lines with Compose (CTRL-2) or by holding down the ALT key and entering their decimal value. ALT-186 would enter the character ‖. To see a chart listing all the line characters and their decimal values, press Help and then CTRL-V from either the main editing screen or while entering the macro in the macro editor.

If you have WordPerfect Library, you can draw the line box on the regular editing screen of WordPerfect with the Line Draw feature—press Screen (CTRL-F3) and choose option 2—and then cut and paste it into the macro editor with shell's Cut-and-Paste feature. To do so, press ALT-SHIFT (HYPHEN), move the cursor to the upper left corner, press ENTER, and then move the cursor to the opposite corner and press ENTER. Choose the option to Save it to the Clipboard. Once you are in the macro editor, press ALT-SHIFT-+ to retrieve it.

WordPerfect Character Sets

WordPerfect ASCII Set

Character Set: 0
Contains: ASCII space through tilde (decimal 32 through 126)

```
           1                   2
    0 1 2 3 4 5 6 7 8 9 0 1 2 3 4 5 6 7 8 9 0 1 2 3 4 5 6 7 8 9
  0
 30       !  "  #  $  %  &  '  (  )  *  +  ,  -  .  /  0  1  2  3  4  5  6  7  8  9  :  ;
 60    <  =  >  ?  @  A  B  C  D  E  F  G  H  I  J  K  L  M  N  O  P  Q  R  S  T  U  V  W  X  Y
 90    Z  [  \  ]  ^  _  `  a  b  c  d  e  f  g  h  i  j  k  l  m  n  o  p  q  r  s  t  u  v  w
120    x  y  z  {  |  }  ~
```

Multinational 1

Character Set: 1
Contains: Common multinational characters and diacriticals

```
         0  1  2  3  4  5  6  7  8  9  1  1  2  3  4  5  6  7  8  9  2  1  2  3  4  5  6  7  8  9
                                      0                             0
  0      `  ´  ~  ^  -  /  ˊ  ¨  ˚  ˝  ¸  ,  .  °  ˛  ˇ  ˘  _  ˘  ß  ı  ȷ  Á  á  Â  â
 30      Ä  ä  À  à  Å  å  Æ  æ  Ç  ç  É  é  Ê  ê  Ë  ë  È  è  í  Í  î  Î  ï  Ï  ì  Ì  Ñ  ñ  Ó  ó
 60      Ô  ô  Ö  ö  Ò  ò  Ú  ú  Û  û  Ü  ü  Ù  ù  Ÿ  ÿ  Ā  ā  Đ  đ  Ø  ø  Õ  õ  Ý  ý  Ð  ð  Þ  þ
 90      Ă  ă  Ā  ā  Ą  ą  Ć  ć  Č  č  Ĉ  ĉ  Ċ  ċ  Ď  ď  Ě  ě  Ė  ė  Ē  ē  Ę  ę  Ǵ  ǵ  Ğ  ğ  Ğ  ğ
120      Ģ  ģ  Ĝ  ĝ  Ġ  ġ  Ĥ  ĥ  Ħ  ħ  Ì  ì  Ī  ī  Į  į  İ  ı  Ĩ  ĩ  Ĳ  ĳ  Ĵ  ĵ  Ķ  ķ  Ĺ  ĺ  Ľ  ľ  Ļ  ļ
150      Ŀ  ŀ  Ł  ł  Ń  ń  Ņ  ņ  Ň  ň  Ņ  ņ  Ő  ő  Ō  ō  Œ  œ  Ŕ  ŕ  Ř  ř  Ŗ  ŗ  Ś  ś  Š  š  Ş  ş
180      Ŝ  ŝ  Ť  ť  Ţ  ţ  Ŧ  ŧ  Ŭ  ŭ  Ű  ű  Ũ  ũ  Ų  ų  Ů  ů  Ū  ū  Ŵ  ŵ  Ŷ  ŷ  Ź  ź  Ž  ž  Ż  ż
210      ŋ  ŋ  Ď  ď  Ī  ī  Ñ  ñ  Ř  ř  Š  š  Ť  ť  Ŷ  ŷ  Ý  ý  Ď  ď  Ơ  ơ  Ư  ư
```

Multinational 2

Character Set: 2
Contains: Rarely used noncapitalizable multinational characters and diacriticals

```
         0  1  2  3  4  5  6  7  8  9  1  1  2  3  4  5  6  7  8  9  2  1  2  3  4  5  6  7  8  9
                                      0                             0
  0      .  ¨  °  ˳  ʼ  ˏ  ˄  ˭  ˉ  ᴋ  ˬ  ʾ  ˎ  ·  ˌ  ˳  ˷  ˪  ˡ  ˊ  ˏ  ̣  ˻  ̜  ˡ  ˠ  ̆  ̈  ʹ  ˮ
```

Box Drawing

Character Set: 3
Contains: All double and single box-drawing characters

```
         0  1  2  3  4  5  6  7  8  9  1  1  2  3  4  5  6  7  8  9  2  1  2  3  4  5  6  7  8  9
                                      0                             0
  0      ░  █  ▌  ▐  ▄  ▀  ▬  ▮  ─  │  ┌  ┐  ┘  └  ├  ┬  ┤  ┴  ┼  ═  ║  ╒  ╕  ╛  ╘  ╞  ╤  ╡  ╧  ╪
 30      ╓  ╖  ╜  ╙  ╟  ╥  ╢  ╨  ╫  ╔  ╗  ╝  ╚  ╠  ╦  ╣  ╩  ╬  ─  ┄  ╴  ╷  ╴  ║  ╶  ╹  ╾  ╼  ┃  ┇
 60      ├  ┝  ┠  ┣  ┯  ┰  ┱  ┲  ┥  ┨  ┩  ┪  ┷  ┸  ┹  ┺  ┿  ╂  ╈  ╊  ┽  ╀  ╇  ╉  ╆  ╅  ╃  ╄  ╁  ╇
```

Typographic Symbols

Character Set: 4
Contains: Common typographic symbols not found in ASCII

	0	1	2	3	4	5	6	7	8	9	**1**0	1	2	3	4	5	6	7	8	9	**2**0	1	2	3	4	5	6	7	8	9
0	●	○	■	•	⋆	¶	§	¡	¿	«	»	£	¥	₧	ƒ	ª	º	½	¼	¢	²	ⁿ	®	©	□	¾	³	´	'	
30	"	"	‟	–	—	‹	›	○	□	†	‡	™	SM	℞	●	○	■	□	□	–	ff	ffi	ffl	fi	fl	...	₰	₣	₢
60	₠	£	,	„	⅓	⅔	⅛	⅜	⅝	⅞	⊛	℗	☺	‰	‱	‰	№	—	'	₮	₣	₢	₤	₦	₳

Iconic Symbols

Character Set: 5
Contains: Rarely used "picture" (icon) symbols

	0	1	2	3	4	5	6	7	8	9	**1**0	1	2	3	4	5	6	7	8	9	**2**0	1	2	3	4	5	6	7	8	9
0	♥	♦	♣	♠	♂	♀	☼	☺	☻	●	♪	♫	■	⌂	‼	√	↕	⌐	¬	▢	▣	↵	☞	☎	✔	□	⊠	☺	#	♭	♮
30	☠	⊕	☒	₡	⌣																										

Math/Scientific

Character Set: 6
Contains: Non-extensible, non-oversized math/scientific characters not found in ASCII set

	0	1	2	3	4	5	6	7	8	9	**1**0	1	2	3	4	5	6	7	8	9	**2**0	1	2	3	4	5	6	7	8	9
0	−	±	≤	≥	∝	/	∕	\	÷	|	⟨	⟩	~	≈	≡	∈	∩	∥	Σ	∞	¬	→	←	↑	↓	↔	↕	▶	◀	▲
30	▼	·	·	∘	•	Å	·	μ	−	×	∫	∏	∓	∇	∂	′	″	‾	ℓ	ℏ	ℑ	ℜ	℘	⇌	⇋	⇒	⇐	⇑	⇓
60	⇔	⇕	↗	↘	↖	↙	∪	∩	⊂	⊃	⊆	⊇	∋	∅	⌈	⌉	⌊	⌋	≪	≫	∠	⊗	⊕	⊖	⊕	⊙	∧	∨	⊤	⊥
90	⌢	⊢	⊣	□	■	◇	◆	⟦	⟧	≠	≢	∴	∵	∷	∮	ℒ	ℭ	ℨ	℘	○	△	◇	★	‴	Ⅱ	≅	≡	≼	<	≤
120	≥	∃	∀	⋘	⋙	⊌	⊊	⊋	⊓	⊔	⊏	⊑	⊐	⊒	⊿	△	▽	◁	▷	⋈	⌣	◯	→	←	↦	↤	↦
150	→	→	⇀	⇁	↑	↾	↓	⇃	⇉	⇇	∪	∩	⊂	⊃	⊚	⊛	⊝	Ʊ	⊿	◁	▷	△	▽	∔	∸	⊟	≠	⋇	⊘	⊗
180	⊨	≜	∮	∣	★	≺	≼	≻	≽	∤	≠	≢	≠	⋏	⋎	⋋	⋌	⊄	⊅	⊈	⊉	⊬	⊭	⊮	⋊	⋉	⋈	⊺	℈	ℨ
210	⊹	ℰ	ℑ	ℭ	Ⅰ	ℕ	ℝ	₂	⌐	℈	⋯	...	⋮	⋱	⋰	‾	+	−	∓	∗	∕	∥	⫿	ℋ	℘

Math/Scientific Extension

Character Set: 7
Contains: Extensible and oversized math/scientific characters

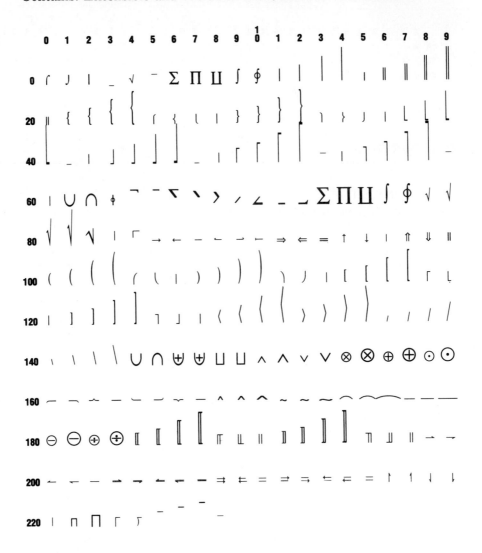

Greek

Character Set: 8
Contains: Full Greek character set for ancient and modern applications

```
          1                   2
0 1 2 3 4 5 6 7 8 9 0 1 2 3 4 5 6 7 8 9 0 1 2 3 4 5 6 7 8 9
0   Α α Β β Β ϐ Γ γ Δ δ Ε ε Ζ ζ Η η Θ θ Ι ι Κ κ Λ λ Μ μ Ν ν Ξ ξ
30  Ο ο Π π Ρ Σ σ Σ ς Τ τ Υ υ Φ φ Χ χ Ψ ψ Ω ω ά έ ή ί ϊ ό ύ ϋ
60  ώ ε ϑ ϰ ϖ ρ ϒ φ ω ˙ · ‐ ‾ ⁓ ˉ ˘
90  ᾿ ῾ ῍ ῝ ῏ ῟ ᾿ ᾿ ὰ ᾶ ᾷ ᾴ ᾳ ᾱ ᾰ ᾶ ᾷ ᾳ ᾲ ᾴ ᾶ ᾷ ᾳ ᾲ ᾴ è é ё ё
120 ė ĕ ȅ ή ή ῆ ῇ ῂ ῄ ῇ ῆ ῇ ῂ ῄ ῇ ῆ ῇ ῂ ῄ ῇ ῂ ί ί ι ΐ ί ῗ ϊ
150 ῒ ΐ ῐ ῑ ῖ ό ό ὸ ὁ ὄ ὅ ὀ ὁ ύ ύ ὺ ῠ ῡ ύ ύ ὺ ύ ῦ ῧ ώ ώ φ φ φ φ
180 ὢ ὣ ῶ ῷ φ φ φ φ ὤ ὥ ῶ ῷ φ φ ʹ ͵ ϛ Ϝ ϙ ϡ Ἀ Ἁ Ἐ Ἱ Ὀ Ὑ Ὠ
```

Hebrew

Character Set: 9
Contains: Hebrew characters

```
          1                   2
0 1 2 3 4 5 6 7 8 9 0 1 2 3 4 5 6 7 8 9 0 1 2 3 4 5 6 7 8 9
0   א ב ב ג ד ה ו ז ח ט י ך כ ל ם מ ן נ ס ע ף פ ץ צ ק ר ש שׁ ת
30  פּ ׂ ֻ ֹ ֺ ָ ֵ ִ ֱ ֳ ֲ ׳
```

Cyrillic

Character Set: 10
Contains: Full Cyrillic character set for ancient and modern applications

```
          1                   2
0 1 2 3 4 5 6 7 8 9 0 1 2 3 4 5 6 7 8 9 0 1 2 3 4 5 6 7 8 9
0   А а Б б В в Г г Д д Е е Ё ё Ж ж З з И и Й й К к Л л М м Н н
30  О о П п Р р С с Т т У у Ф ф Х х Ц ц Ч ч Ш ш Щ щ Ъ ъ Ы ы Ь ь
60  Э э Ю ю Я я Ѓ ѓ Ђ ђ Ґ ґ Є є Ѕ ѕ І і Ї ї Ј ј Љ љ Њ њ Ћ ћ Ќ ќ
90  Ў ў Џ џ Ѣ ѣ Ѳ ѳ Ѵ ѵ Җ җ
```

Japanese

Character Set: 11
Contains: Hiragana and Katakana characters

	0	**1**	**2**	**3**	**4**	**5**	**6**	**7**	**8**	**9**	**1 0**	**1**	**2**	**3**	**4**	**5**	**6**	**7**	**8**	**9**	**2 0**	**1**	**2**	**3**	**4**	**5**	**6**	**7**	**8**	**9**
0	あ	い	う	え	お	っ	ゃ	ゅ	ょ			か	け	あ	い	う	え	お	か	き	く	け	こ	が	ぎ	ぐ	げ	ご	さ	し	す
30	せ	そ	ざ	じ	ず	ぜ	ぞ	た	ち	つ	て	と	だ	ぢ	づ	で	ど	な	に	ぬ	ね	の	は	ひ	ふ	へ	ほ	ば	び	ぶ
60	べ	ぼ	ぱ	ぴ	ぷ	ぺ	ぽ	ま	み	む	め	も	や	ゆ	よ	ら	り	る	れ	ろ	わ	を	ん	〔	〕	【	】	「	」	『
90	』	.	。	、	ゝ	ゞ	〃	ー	゛	゜	゜	ア	イ	ウ	エ	オ	ッ	ャ	ュ	ョ	ヴ	カ	ケ	ア	イ	ウ	エ	オ	カ	キ	ク
120	ケ	コ	ガ	ギ	グ	ゲ	ゴ	サ	シ	ス	セ	ソ	ザ	ジ	ズ	ゼ	ゾ	タ	チ	ッ	テ	ト	ダ	ヂ	ヅ	デ	ド	ナ	ニ	ヌ
150	ネ	ノ	ハ	ヒ	フ	ヘ	ホ	バ	ビ	ブ	ベ	ボ	パ	ピ	プ	ペ	ポ	マ	ミ	ム	メ	モ	ヤ	ユ	ヨ	ラ	リ	ル	レ	ロ
180	ワ	ヲ	ン	ヽ	ヾ																									

User-Defined

Character Set: 12
Contains: 255 user-definable characters

WordPerfect Files

Files on Master Disks

The following files are stored in compressed files. They are copied as individual files during installation.

Program 1/2

WP.EXE	WordPerfect program file that is loaded into memory upon start-up
WP.FIL	Second WordPerfect program file (can be loaded into memory with /R start-up option)
WP.MRS	Macro resource file containing macro commands
WP.QRS	Equation resource file
KEYS.MRS	Keyboard macro resource file
PRINTER.TST	Printer test file
STANDARD.IRS	Input resource file containing the mouse drivers
STANDARD.PRS	Standard printer resource file
STANDARD.VRS	Video resource file containing text and graphics screen drivers

WPSMALL.DRS	Used for two-disk drive systems. Contains the IBM 256-character set instead of all characters in the WordPerfect character sets. This file is used for viewing documents if the WP.DRS file is not found
README.WP	Lists changes and enhancements to the current version of the program

Spell/Thesaurus

WP{WP}.SPW	Necessary to run Speller
WP{WP}US.HYC	Hyphenation code
WP{WP}US.LEX	Speller
WP{WP}US.THS	Thesaurus
README.SPL	Lists changes and enhancements to the latest Speller and Thesaurus files

PTR Program/Graphics

PTR.EXE	Printer (PTR) program file
PTR.HLP	Help file for PTR program
CHARMAP.TST	File used to test available characters in the printer
KERN.TST	File used to test kerning
*.FRS	Screen fonts for EGA, VGA, and Hercules cards
*.VRS	Video drivers for various graphics monitors

WP.DRS	File used during View to display all WordPerfect characters
README.PTR	Lists changes and enhancements to the files on the PTR Program/Graphics disks

Install/Learn/Utilities

INSTALL.EXE	Install program necessary for the installation of WordPerfect (can be deleted to save disk space)
CONVERT.EXE	Converts files to and from WordPerfect 5.1 format
CURSOR.COM	Program used to change the size and shape of the cursor
FIXBIOS.COM	Used to fix date and time inconsistencies in some compatibles
GRAB.COM	Program that can be used to capture an image on the screen and save it to a file for use in a graphics box
GRAPHCNV.EXE	Converts graphics to WordPerfect's WPG format
MACROCNV.EXE	Converts 4.2 macros to version 5.1 format. Converts text and keys that have not changed (cursor keys, delete keys, some function keys, and so on)
NWPSETUP.EXE	Program used to update all user's .SET (setup) files with new default settings and printer selections
SPELL.EXE	Program used to customize the Speller

STANDARD.CRS	Standard conversion resource file used to convert 4.2 documents to 5.1
WP.LRS	Language resource file
WPINFO.EXE	Provides information about your specific computer system
CHARACTR.DOC	Contains a list and description of all characters
*.PIF	Files for running WordPerfect under Microsoft Windows on a 286 or 386 machine
*.WKB	Files used in the workbook lessons
*.WPG	Graphics used in the workbook lessons
WORKBOOK.PRS	.PRS file used for the workbook lessons
*.TUT	Tutorial files
WPHELP.FIL	WordPerfect help file
*.WPK	Five keyboard layouts: ALTRNAT, ENHANCED, EQUATION, MACROS, SHORTCUT
*.WPM	Macros provided to help set up labels, print codes with text, and convert endnotes to footnotes (and vice versa)
LIBRARY.STY	File containing several styles
README.UTL	Lists the latest changes and enhancements to files on the Install/Learn/Utility disks

Files Installed to Hard Drive

During installation, all files are copied in groups. The files below are listed according to the group with which they are copied.

WP Program Files

The following files are copied to C:\WP51 unless otherwise specified:

WP.EXE
WP.FIL
WP.MRS
WP.QRS
KEYS.MRS
PRINTER.TST
STANDARD.IRS
STANDARD.PRS
STANDARD.VRS
WPSMALL.DRS

Graphics Drivers

The following files are copied to the same directory as WP.EXE:

WP.DRS
*.FRS
*.VRS

Help Files

The following file is copied to the same directory as WP.EXE:

WPHELP.FIL

Utility Files

The following files are copied to the same directory as WP.EXE:

STANDARD.CRS	MACROCNV.EXE
CHARACTR.DOC	NWPSETUP.EXE
CONVERT.EXE	SPELL.EXE
CURSOR.COM	WPINFO.EXE
FIXBIOS.COM	WP.LRS
GRAB.COM	WP51-286.PIF
GRAPHCNV.EXE	WP51-386.PIF
INSTALL.EXE	WP51.INS

Graphics Images

The following files are copied to the directory specified for "Graphic Files." If none was specified, they are copied to the same directory as WP.EXE. Appendix E, "Graphics Images," includes a printout of each of these images.

ARROW-22.WPG	FLOPPY-2.WPG
BALLOONS.WPG	GAVEL.WPG
BANNER-3.WPG	GLOBE2-M.WPG
BICYCLE.WPG	HANDS-3.WPG
BORDER-9.WPG	MAGNIF.WPG
BULB.WPG	MAILBAG.WPG
BURST-1.WPG	NEWS.WPG
BUTTRFLY.WPG	PC-1.WPG
CALENDAR.WPG	PRESNT-1.WPG
CERTIF.WPG	PRINTR-3.WPG

CHKBOX-1.WPG
CLOCK.WPG
CNTRCT-2.WPG
DEVICE-2.WPG
DIPLOMA.WPG

SCALE.WPG
STAR-5.WPG
TELPHONE.WPG
TROPHY.WPG

Learn and Tutorial

The following files are copied to the directory specified for the "Learn and Tutorial" files (C:\WP51\LEARN), unless otherwise specified.

ADDRESS.WKB
CHARACTR.WKB
CUSTOMER.WKB
EQUATION.WKB
INVOICE.WKB
MEMO.WKB
MUSICBOX.WKB
NEWSLTR.WKB
NEWSTABL.WKB
OUTLINE.WKB
PARKSPEL.WKB
REPORT.WKB
RETAIL.WKB
STORES.WKB
TABLE.WKB
BKGRND-1.WPG
BUTTRFLY.WPG
GRAPH.WPG
STAR-5.WPG
WORKBOOK.PRS
ADDRESS.TUT
ADVANCED.TUT
BANNER.TUT
BEGIN.TUT
INTRO.TUT
INTRO_1.TUT

LESS.TUT
LESS1.TUT
LESS2.TUT
LESS3.TUT
LESS4.TUT
LESS5.TUT
LESS6.TUT
LETTER.TUT
LETTER_F.TUT
LETTER_P.TUT
LETTER1.TUT
MEMO.TUT
MERGE.TUT
MERGE2.TUT
MORE.TUT
PARK.TUT
PARK1.TUT
PARKMEMO.TUT
QUIT.TUT
RESTART.TUT
TOA.TUT
TOA_1.TUT
TOA_O.TUT
TUTOR.COM
TUTOR.TUT
TUTOR_M.TUT

Keyboard/Macro Files

The following files are copied to the directory specified for "Keyboard/Macro Files." If none is specified, they will be copied to the same location as WP.EXE:

ALTRNAT.WPK
ENHANCED.WPK
EQUATION.WPK
MACROS.WPK
SHORTCUT.WPK
LABELS.WPM
CODES.WPM
REVEALCO.WPM
REVEALTX.WPM
FOOTEND.WPM
ENDFOOT.WPM

Dictionary/Thesaurus

The following files are copied to the directory specified for the "Dictionary/Thesaurus." If none is specified, they will be copied to the same directory where WP.EXE was copied.

WP{WP}US.LEX
WP{WP}.SPW
WP{WP}US.HYC
WP{WP}US.THS

Style Files

The following file is copied to the directory specified for "Style Files." If one is not specified, it will be copied to the same directory as WP.EXE:

LIBRARY.STY

Printer Files and PTR Program

PTR.EXE
PTR.HLP
CHARMAP.TST
KERN.TST
*.ALL
*.PRS

Files Installed to 720K Floppy Disks

The following is a list of files that are copied to the ten disks prepared during installation. The disks are labeled as suggested by the Install program.

WordPerfect 1

WP.EXE
WPHELP.FIL
PRINTER.TST

WordPerfect 2

WP.FIL	STANDARD.PRS
WP.MRS	STANDARD.VRS
WP.QRS	WPSMALL.DRS
KEYS.MRS	*PRS
STANDARD.IRS	

Speller

WP{WP}US.LEX
WP{WP}.SPW
WP{WP}US.HYC

Thesaurus

WP{WP}US.THS

Install/Utilities

CHARACTR.DOC	NWPSETUP.EXE
CONVERT.EXE	SPELL.EXE
CURSOR.COM	WPINFO.EXE
FIXBIOS.COM	STANDARD.CRS
GRAB.COM	WP.LRS
GRAPHCNV.EXE	WP51-286.PIF
INSTALL.EXE	WP51-386.PIF
MACROCNV.EXE	WP51.INS

Macros/Keyboards

ALTRNAT.WPK	CODES.WPM
ENHANCED.WPK	REVEALCO.WPM
EQUATION.WPK	REVEALTX.WPM
MACROS.WPK	FOOTEND.WPM
SHORTCUT.WPK	ENDFOOT.WPM
LABELS.WPM	LIBRARY.STY

Font/Graphics

*.FRS
*.VRS
WP.DRS

Learning/Images

ADDRESS.WKB	PARK.TUT
CHARACTR.WKB	PARK1.TUT
CUSTOMER.WKB	PARKMEMO.TUT
EQUATION.WKB	QUIT.TUT
INVOICE.WKB	RESTART.TUT
MEMO.WKB	TOA.TUT
MUSICBOX.WKB	TOA_1.TUT
NEWSLTR.WKB	TOA_0.TUT
NEWSTABLE.WKB	TUTOR.COM
OUTLINE.WKB	TUTOR.TUT
PARKSPEL.WKB	TUTOR_M.TUT
REPORT.WKB	ARROW-22.WPG
RETAIL.WKB	BALLOONS.WPG
STORES.WKB	BANNER-3.WPG
TABLE.WKB	BICYCLE.WPG
BKGRND-1.WPG	BORDER-9.WPG
BUTTRFLY.WPG	BULB.WPG
GRAPH.WPG	BURST-1.WPG
STAR-5.WPG	BUTTRFLY.WPG
WORKBOOK.PRS	CALENDAR.WPG
ADDRESS.TUT	CERTIF.WPG
ADVANCED.TUT	CHKBOX-1.WPG
BANNER.TUT	CLOCK.WPG
BEGIN.TUT	CNTRCT-2.WPG
INTRO.TUT	DEVICE-2.WPG
INTRO_1.TUT	DIPLOMA.WPG
LESS.TUT	FLOPPY-2.WPG
LESS1.TUT	GAVEL.WPG
LESS2.TUT	GLOBE2-M.WPG
LESS3.TUT	HANDS-3.WPG

LESS4.TUT   MAGNIF.WPG
LESS5.TUT   MAILBAG.WPG
LESS6.TUT   NEWS.WPG
LETTER.TUT   PC-1.WPG
LETTER_F.TUT   PRESNT-1.WPG
LETTER_P.TUT   PRINTR-3.WPG
LETTER1.TUT   SCALE.WPG
MEMO.TUT   TAR-5.WPG
MERGE.TUT   TELPHONE.WPG
MERGE2.TUT   TROPHY.WPG
MORE.TUT

Printer (.ALL) Files

*.ALL

PTR Program

PTR.EXE
PTR.HLP
CHARMAP.TST
KERN.TST

Other Files

The following files are created when you first run WordPerfect:

WP{WP}.SET   Contains the selections made in
                           the Setup menu and the current
                           printer selections

WP{WP}US.LCN	Contains the WordPerfect license number that you entered the first time WordPerfect was started
WP{WP}US.SUP	Supplementary dictionary that is created for words that are "added" to the dictionary during a spell check
WP{WP}.WPM	File that is created if you name a macro with the ENTER key

The following files are created each time you start WordPerfect. They are temporary files that are deleted when you exit properly with the Exit (F7) key.

WP}WP{.TV1 or TV2	Top virtual file for document 1 or 2. Text above the cursor is stored in this overflow file if necessary
WP}WP{.BV1 or BV2	Bottom virtual file for document 1 or 2. Text below the cursor is stored in this overflow file if necessary
WP}WP{.CHK	File that keeps track of the overflow files
WP}WP{.SPC	Used to reserve space on the disk in the case of a disk full error message
WP}WP{.UN0	Contains the most recent deletion
WP}WP{.UN1	Contains the second most recent deletion
WP}WP{.UN2	Contains the third most recent deletion
WP}WP{.Q	Print queue, which lists the documents waiting to be printed

WP}WP{.Q1	Print buffer sort file
WP}WP{.n	Temporary print file where n is used to indicate the number of the print job
WP}WP{.DIR	Directory listing file
WP}WP{.DI0	Print directory listing file
WP}WP{.LS1 or LS2	List manager overflow file for document 1 or 2
WP}WP{.GF1 or GF2	GIF graphics image file for document 1 or 2
WP}WP{.GFT	GIF bitmap compress file
WP}WP{.PF1 or PF2	Document prefix for document 1 or 2, where initial codes/font, printer selection, and graphics information are stored
WP}WP{.SRI	Sort input file
WP}WP{.SRO	Sort output file
WP}WP{.SRT	Sort file on screen
WP}WP{.STY	Temporary style file
WP}WP{.ARI	Automatic reference index file
WP}WP{.ART	Automatic reference text file
WP}WP{.BLK	Block file
WP}WP{.CLM	Column file

Differences Between 5.0 and 5.1

If you upgraded from version 4.2 to 5.0, you probably remember the dramatic changes made to the program. Not only were there changes made to nearly every prompt and menu, but the whole concept of measurement changed. Instead of using the number of lines and characters to calculate margins, tabs, font changes, paper length, and so on, WordPerfect 5.0 dealt with "real" units of measurement, such as inches, centimeters, and points.

If you are upgrading from 5.0 to 5.1, you will not have to make these types of adjustments. The basic structure and "feel" of the program has not changed from version 5.0. Some slight changes have been made to the menus and prompts to help make them more clear, and an alternate interface has been added for people who prefer using pull-down menus and a mouse. If you do not want to use the alternate interface, however, you do not have to.

Interface Changes

Very little of the basic interface has changed. The following should make you feel more comfortable with some of the small changes and help you understand why the changes were made.

The Template

The function key template has three minor changes:

- List Files (F5) has been changed to List, because you can now use it to list more than files.

- Math/Columns (ALT-F7) has been changed to Columns/Tables. Although math is still an option on this function key, you might find it easier to use the math capabilities provided in the new Tables feature.

- Merge R (F9) has been changed to the more descriptive End Field.

These keys still perform basically the same functions; only the names have changed.

Prompts

With the introduction of mouse support, all **Y/N** prompts have been changed to **Y**es (**N**o) to make it easier for those who use a mouse to make a selection by pointing at either choice and clicking. The cursor rests under the "default" selection, while the other choice is shown in parentheses. In the above example, if you accidentally pressed any key (except **N**), the question would be answered Yes.

No is not always the choice in parentheses. As in previous versions, the default is always the safest answer. For example, if you pressed Exit (F7), you would be asked the following:

Save document? **Y**es (**N**o)

Because Yes is the default, pressing any other key by accident does not cause you to lose the document if you wanted to save it.

Pull-Down Menus

WordPerfect 5.1 has pull-down menus to make it easier for beginners to learn the program. With the menus, more options can be displayed on the screen and thus appear less "hidden" than those assigned to the function keys.

If you prefer using the function keys, the pull-down menus and mouse support will be invisible, unless you press the ALT-= or press the right button on the mouse.

If you want to use the pull-down menus, you do not need a mouse to do so. You can move to different sections of the menus (and to selections on those menus) by pressing the cursor keys or by typing their mnemonic equivalents (for example, **F** for **F**ile). If you have a mouse, you can move to the menu option and click the left button to select it.

Through the Setup menu, you can choose to have the ALT key access the pull-down menus, instead of having to press ALT-=, or you can reassign the function to another key on the keyboard.

Mouse Support

With WordPerfect 5.1, you can use a mouse to position the cursor anywhere on the screen, scroll through the document, or mark a block of text.

To position the cursor anywhere on the screen, move the mouse "pointer" to a new location, and click the left mouse button. This is especially useful for people who often work with columns or tables and want to move the cursor quickly without having to remember key combinations.

To scroll through the document (up, down, left, or right), *hold down* the right mouse button and drag it to the edge of the screen (remember that *clicking* the right button brings up the pull-down menus). When the pointer runs into the edge of the screen, it starts scrolling through the document in that direction.

To block a section of text, hold down the left mouse button, and drag the pointer to the other end of the block. You can then select an option from the keyboard, or click the right button to pull down the menus and make a selection from there.

Entering Measurements

You can now use fractions to enter measurements in all settings (margins, tabs, line height, and so on). For example, instead of entering a measurement in tenths of an inch (which can be difficult using a standard ruler that is divided into sixteenths of an inch), you can enter it as a fraction (such as 3/16), and WordPerfect will convert it to its decimal equivalent (.188″).

New Features

This section covers most of the new features included in version 5.1.

Tables

Probably the most exciting new feature in 5.1 is Tables. Anyone who does any type of word processing will probabaly use this feature. If you have ever tried to calculate tab settings for a table of numbers, a comparison chart, or an invoice, you will know how difficult it can be. Determining how much space to give each column (considering the size of the font being used) and how much to leave between each column is more than most people want to attempt.

The Tables feature solves this problem, and it is probably the simplest feature available in WordPerfect. After choosing the option to create a table, found on Columns/Tables (ALT-F7), it prompts you for the number of columns and rows in the table. (If the number of rows or columns changes later, you can easily adjust the table.) WordPerfect then creates a grid on the screen, dividing it into boxes, or ″cells.″ Each column is given an equal amount of space that you can easily change by pressing CTRL and the left or right arrow keys.

You can easily move, copy, or delete columns and rows. In 5.0, this was difficult to do in tabbed columns and nearly impossible in parallel columns.

Options are available for joining or splitting ″cells″ in a table for headings or creating larger or smaller boxes for forms fill-in or shading sections of the table. You can choose the style of lines to be used for the grid or turn the lines off completely. By turning them off, you can mimic the Parallel Columns feature in WordPerfect, because the cell will increase and decrease in size as you add or delete text. By creating a table with one column and one row, you can easily box any amount of text. Or, if you prefer, you can set cells to a specific height and place merge codes inside a table for ease in filling in forms.

You can designate one or more lines as a header for tables that are longer than one page, and each cell, column, or row can have its own format or attributes (centered, decimal aligned, bold, enlarged font, and so on). Math in tables is even more powerful than the regular Math feature found in WordPerfect, because any cell can be used in a formula, and formulas can be copied to other cells.

You can convert tabular text or parallel columns that were created in previous versions of WordPerfect to tables instantly by blocking the text and choosing the option to create a table. If you delete a table definition, [Tab] codes are inserted to retain the structure of the table.

Spreadsheet Support

A feature that is closely associated with Tables is the ability to retrieve spreadsheets from PlanPerfect 5.0, Lotus 1-2-3, or Excel without having to convert them. After retrieving the file as you would any other Word-Perfect file, the spreadsheet is automatically placed in a table.

If you want to retrieve a small section of a spreadsheet (a range), you can do so by choosing the Text In/Out (CTRL-F5) Spreadsheet option. You can retrieve any section of the spreadsheet and choose from a list of ranges that may have been named in the spreadsheet.

Another option on the Text In/Out (CTRL-F5) Spreadsheet menu lets you create a link to an entire spreadsheet or range. This feature places markers before and after the spreadsheet to indicate that there is a link to a spreadsheet file on disk. You can then choose to have the spread-sheet updated each time the WordPerfect file is retrieved or you can use the option to "Update all links" at any time. By doing so, you can make changes to a spreadsheet and know that the data in the WordPerfect file can be updated easily without having to change the numbers manually or reimport the spreadsheet.

This feature may even be important for people who have never created a spreadsheet. If you work in a network environment and have access to spreadsheet files that have already been created, you can tell WordPerfect where the spreadsheet is and update it periodically so that you can be aware of any changes that other people have made to the data in the spreadsheet.

Equation Editor

If you place equations in text, you will appreciate the new equation editor included in WordPerfect 5.1. You can enter equations using a simple, straightforward syntax (language) and save and retrieve the equations so you can use them in more than one document.

You enter the syntax for an equation in the lower section of the equation editor, while the equation itself is displayed in the screen above. You can type all the commands or select them from a list at the right. You can access many other commands and special symbols (including Greek and math) by pressing PGUP or PGDN while in this list.

You no longer have to set half-line spacing and then use superscripts, subscripts, advance, and overstrike to achieve the format of an equation. Nor will you need to be concerned about the availability of characters in your printer. If a character is not found, WordPerfect creates and prints it graphically on a dot-matrix or laser printer (it won't print on a daisy-wheel printer unless the print wheel contains the characters used in the equation).

A special keyboard layout is included with WordPerfect to make it easier to include special characters or commands in an equation with CTRL- or ALT- key combinations. For example, ALT-A displays an alpha character, and CTRL-B inserts the bar (line) command.

Special Characters

Another feature that will benefit a large number of users is the ability to print *any* character in the WordPerfect character set as long as you have a graphics (dot-matrix or laser) printer.

You will no longer wonder which font contains the copyright ©, trademark ™, section § symbol, or international characters such as ñ or Ä. You can also print complex characters, such as those of Japanese (は) and Hebrew (ש). WordPerfect will also print the character in a size that matches the current font.

Labels and Paper Size/Type

You can now define and select a specific size of paper from the same menu instead of defining it in one menu and then trying to choose that form based on vague menus when you are creating a document. Instead of choosing a paper size and type that has no meaning, you can pick the form directly from a list, so you will immediately know what you are getting. If the form you want is not on the list, you can create it and then select it.

A new Labels option has been added to the menu that is used when you are defining a form. When answering Yes to the option for labels, you will see the menu that asks for the number of labels, the measurements and margins for each label, the distance between labels, and where the upper left corner of the first label is located. You will need to do this only once.

WordPerfect 5.1 also includes the macro LABELS.WPM, which contains several predefined label formats and leads you through the steps of choosing a labels form.

After merging or entering names and addresses (each name and address is separated by a page break), you move to the beginning of the document, select the form containing the labels definition, and print. It is not necessary (or even advisable) to set margins, columns, or line height. This feature also guarantees that you can choose any font and center the text for each label, and it will print correctly. This feature alone will save you countless hours of work.

Another task for which you can use the Labels feature is printing two pages side by side on an 8 1/2- by 11-inch (standard landscape) page. The pages can have their own headers, page numbers, and even footnotes. The label definition would specify that there are two "columns" and one "row" on a standard landscape piece of paper. The distance between labels would determine the amount of gutter space, and each page (label) can have its own set of margins.

Merge

WordPerfect has always had a Merge feature, and few changes have been made to its initial design. However, version 5.1 offers an update that should not only make it easier for beginners to use, because it has clearer prompts and merge commands, but should also offer the power that advanced customers need when they design specialized applications.

More than 60 advanced merge commands let you loop, branch, and test for specific conditions and act on the results of those tests. For example, you can include conditional statements so that different letters can be sent to clients depending on the information found in specific fields (such as income or date of birth). Combined with the power of macros (which can now be nested within a merge), there are few tasks that you cannot automate.

See "Macros" and "Merge" in Chapter 3 for basic information about macro and merge commands. Chapter 6 contains more advanced information on macros and merge.

Descriptive Filenames

If you feel that the 11-character limit on filenames is too limiting, you will be glad to know that WordPerfect now supports filenames of up to 68 characters (although a maximum of 30 can be displayed on the List Files screen). Although it is still necessary to give a document a DOS filename, you can enter the more descriptive name in the Document Summary and then display it on the List Files screen along with the DOS filename.

New options in List Files also make it easier to find a specific file by using a descriptive name, DOS filename document, type, author, subject, account, and so on.

Text Drivers

If you have an EGA, a VGA, or a Genius monitor, you will be able to select different text drivers to see more lines of text on the screen. For example, if you have a VGA monitor, you will be able to see either 28 or 50 lines at one time, instead of the standard 25.

Enhanced Features

Install

WordPerfect 5.0 included an optional installation program that helped copy the program to a hard disk. Now, because of the size of Word-Perfect 5.1, the number of disks required, and the large number of printer drivers available, all files have been compressed. This allows WordPerfect Corporation to ship WordPerfect 5.1 on fewer disks and provide more printer drivers.

Because all the files are compressed, an Install program is now *necessary* to copy the files to the hard disk and expand them while doing so. Because of this necessity, WordPerfect has put a great deal of time and effort into making the Install program completely automatic for new users and customizable for those who are more familiar with their systems. Help screens and error messages guide you through the process and tell you if you insert the wrong disk. The Install program will also check the AUTOEXEC.BAT and CONFIG.SYS files for necessary commands and add them if you want. This is a major step in helping new users feel comfortable.

Options have also been included for those who want to have more control over the program. These options include selecting your own directory names, updating only specific disks, changing your own AUTOEXEC.BAT or CONFIG.SYS files, and setting up network versions of WordPerfect.

Dictionary-Based Hyphenation

Automatic hyphenation is now more accurate, because each word in the dictionary includes hyphenation points. Combining the dictionary and hyphenation files also saves disk space.

Context-Sensitive Help

You can now press Help (F3) while in a menu or prompt to receive help on that specific feature.

Outlining

Although true outlining (expands or collapses headings and subheadings) has not yet been incorporated, WordPerfect now lets you move, copy, or delete all subheadings associated with a specific heading.

Outline styles have also been added to let you define how an outline number is to be inserted. For example, if you prefer to have all outline numbers aligned and the text following them indented, you can do so with an outline style. The style is automatically inserted when you create an outline; you do not have to select it from a menu each time you add an entry.

Relative Tabs

Tabs are now set at positions relative to the left margin. As the margins change, the tabs change accordingly. You no longer have to reset tabs when you are using more than one column. In such a case, a 1/2″ tab setting will be in effect for *all* margins of all columns.

Another welcome enhancement to tabs is the ability to change the type of tab (left, centered, right, or decimal) and have the text change automatically. In previous versions, you could only do this with a complicated macro. The text on the screen immediately reflects the changes made to the tab type and position, instead of making you wait to see the effect after exiting the Tab menu.

Dormant Hard Return

If WordPerfect finds a single hard return [HRt] code at the top of a page, it will change it to a dormant hard return so that it will not be displayed or printed. If, after editing, the [Dorm HRt] code is no longer at the top of the page, it will be changed back to a regular hard return.

This feature, combined with Widow/Orphan protection, virtually eliminates the need for scrolling through a document to check for correct page breaks. It will also help those who work with columns, because it eliminates the possibility of a blank line at the top of a column.

Justification

In previous versions, you could choose to have right justification on or off. This meant that WordPerfect would stretch or shrink the text on the line to create an even left and right margin. If you wanted to center or flush-right a block of text, you would block the text and then choose the appropriate function. Codes were placed at the beginning and end of each line, making future editing difficult.

In version 5.1, you can choose left, full, right, or centered justification. This feature lets you insert a code anywhere in your document that affects text from that point forward. To center or flush-right an entire block, you now insert the appropriate justification code at the beginning of the text to be affected, and it will automatically be adjusted. However, if you want only a section of text to be affected, you can still block the text and choose the appropriate function. The proper justification codes are inserted at the beginning and end of the block so that only the highlighted text is affected.

Graphics

You can now link to a graphics image on disk, which means that documents can be smaller (the graphics image would not be stored with the document, but would be "retrieved" when you edit, view, or print the document). Another advantage is that any changes made to the current graphics image will be included the next time the WordPerfect document is retrieved.

Because graphics are not allowed in styles, you can work around this limitation by using the option to link to a graphics image on disk and thus not actually "include" a graphics image in a style.

Another option lets you create a true shadow box by requesting a thick or extra-thick border on two adjoining sides of the graphics box.

Page Numbers

You can now include text with the page number (as in "Chapter 1-13") so that the chapter or section number will be included when you generate a table of contents, index, list, or automatic reference.

Keyboard Layout

An option included on the Keyboard Layout menu, Map, lets you see at a glance which keys have been remapped on your keyboard. It tells you if a macro, keyboard command, or special character has been assigned to a key. It also makes it easier to assign any of these items to a key.

Printing Changes

The printer drivers have been modified so that they no longer include printer-specific information about leading (the amount of space between each line). WordPerfect instead adds 2 points (72 points per inch) to each font to make it more compatible with the typesetting industry.

Another change to the printer drivers (that will not be evident to a casual WordPerfect user) is that WordPerfect stores the information about fonts and cartridges in a Font Library that can be shared by more than one printer. This decreases the amount of disk space occupied by WordPerfect, because the font information is not duplicated for each driver.

Shell Support

If you have WordPerfect Library, you will be glad to know that version 5.1 has included additional support for shell macros. You can also use files from the Clipboard during a merge.

You can now save or append an entire file to the Clipboard without having to block it first, and you can execute a single DOS command from within WordPerfect.

Differences Between 4.2 and 5.1

WordPerfect 5.1 is a different program from 4.2. It was entirely rewritten with version 5.0. However, WordPerfect Corporation has made every attempt to make the transition from previous versions as painless as possible.

This appendix explains most of the major differences to the program that were introduced with version 5.0. If you have used version 4.2 and are upgrading directly to version 5.1 without using version 5.0, you will want to know and understand the changes that were introduced with version 5.0. This appendix should explain some of those changes and how some of the new features are comparable or better than those that were used in the past.

Function Key Changes

There were four new function key assignments in 5.0, and three other function keys changed slightly. It is reassuring to know that you can still create and edit documents, save them, and exit with the same familiar keys that you have always used.

The following table covers all seven function keys and their previous and new assignments:

Function Key	Previous Assignment	New Assignment
SHIFT-F1	Super/Subscript — These features are now found on Font (CTRL-F8) under the Size option	Setup — This key includes options originally found under the WP/S Setup menu along with new features such as Keyboard Layout (replacing CTRL/ALT Key Mapping) and cursor speed
SHIFT-F5	Date — Date functions are still found on this key	Date/Outline — Outline and Paragraph Numbering have been moved to the Date key to make more room for features on Mark Text (ALT-F5)
CTRL-F8	Print Format — Applicable options are now found on Format (SHIFT-F8)	Font — This key lets you change the base font as well as the size and appearance of the font. You can also change the print color with this function key

Function Key	Previous Assignment	New Assignment
ALT-F8	Page Format—Applicable options are now found on Format (SHIFT-F8)	Styles—You can create styles for certain sections of text to maintain consistency in your documents. If a change needs to be made, you can change the codes in the style, and all text marked with that style is then updated
SHIFT-F8	Line Format—Previous functions are still found on this key, along with those previously found on Print Format and Page Format	Format—All format options are now found on this menu, including Line, Page, Document, and Other format categories
ALT-F9	Merge Codes—All merge codes (including End Record—formerly ^E) are now found on SHIFT-F9. This was done so that Graphics would be on the same key in both PlanPerfect and WordPerfect	Graphics—You can insert boxes containing text or a graphics image within documents and have text flow around them
SHIFT-F9	End Record (formerly ^E) is still found on this function key but has been combined with all other merge codes previously found on ALT-F9	Merge Codes—Previously found on ALT-F9

Menus and Messages

Quite a few changes have been made to the menus since version 4.2. You will find more submenus than before, especially on Format (SHIFT-F8) and Setup (SHIFT-F1). However, WordPerfect has been designed so that after you make your selection, you can press Exit (F7) to return to the document immediately. If you press ENTER or the space bar to exit a menu, you will retrace your steps backward through the submenus instead of returning directly to the document. Using ENTER is advantageous if you want to return to the main menu and select another submenu.

Most of the current selections also appear on the menu. For example, you can see what the current margin settings are on the Line Format menu without having to choose the Margins option.

Another major change is that instead of typing a number to make a selection, you can use a letter. For example, you can press Format (SHIFT-F8), type **L** for **L**ine, and then type **T** for **T**ab Set. This will be a welcome change for people who find it difficult to type numbers. By default, the letter that you can use to make a selection appears in boldface. If you prefer, you can change the appearance to underline, a different color, or a different font (if you are using a Hercules card with RamFont).

A change to messages has been made so that you will see "Yes" or "No" spelled out, instead of "Y" or "N" displayed as the default answer. For example, instead of seeing "Save document? (Y/N) Y," you will see "Save document? **Yes** (**No**)."

Units of Measurement

Probably the most drastic change is that the status line no longer appears in lines or column positions. The inch is now used as the default unit of measurement to show the current location of the cursor in relation to the top and left sides of the paper. Inches are also used to display and enter settings such as margins and tabs.

You can change this unit of measurement to centimeters or points (72 points per inch), or even return to WordPerfect 4.2 units, by pressing Setup (SHIFT-F1) and choosing option 3 for Environment, and then 8 for Units of Measure. However, 4.2 units do not work exactly as they used to, and you may often see fractions of a line or position, depending on the font being used. If you are using a 10-pitch, nonproportionally spaced font and you choose 4.2 units, the status line should appear exactly as it did in 4.2. However, if you change fonts often, you will probably want to leave the unit of measurement at inches, centimeters, or points instead of 4.2 units.

The following example should illustrate the reason for this. If you have selected a small font and have the standard 1-inch margins, you will be able to fit quite a few characters on the line. In fact, the screen may scroll horizontally three or four times. If the status line showed 4.2 units, you might see the line break at position 200 or 250. If you then changed to the largest font available, not as many characters would fit on the line, but the line would still break at 7.5 inches, whereas in 4.2 units the line could break after only position 30 or so.

The reason for this is that WordPerfect checks a spacing table for each character that is typed and determines whether or not it can fit on the line. It also checks the height of the font and adjusts the number of lines that can fit on the page. A large font allows fewer than 54 lines on the page. If you have chosen a smaller font, you will get more than 54 lines on the page. This eliminates the old process of manually figuring margins, tabs, pitch, line spacing, and possibly even changing the lines per inch for each font change. Instead, you set absolute margins once (left, right, top, and bottom), and WordPerfect places the appropriate number of characters on the line or page, regardless of the font.

Displaying the status line in inches also makes it easier to make format changes. If you do desktop publishing, you will want to know exactly where you are at all times, and lines and column positions do not accurately display this information.

Selecting Printers

You can select as many printer definitions as you want. You are not limited to six, nor do you print to a "printer number." The information for each printer is kept in a separate .PRS (printer resource) file. The .PRS file contains not only the basic printer driver, but also a descriptive printer name that you can change. It also contains the port selection, sheet-feeder information, and cartridge, font, and print wheel selections. If you have more cartridges than cartridge slots, or more soft fonts than you have printer memory, you can select the same printer definition more than once, select different .PRS filenames, make the printer name more descriptive, and select the appropriate fonts for each printer definition.

A document is formatted for the printer that is currently selected. The list of fonts that appears when you are selecting a font is the same list of fonts that was selected when the printer was selected. If you have a different printer selected, and you retrieve the previous document, WordPerfect will try to find the original printer definition that was used and select it again. After you finish editing the document and clear the screen, WordPerfect will return to the original printer selection. If the original .PRS file that was used to create the file cannot be found, the current printer selection will be used instead. If you need to share documents, and want a document formatted exactly as it was for your printer selection, give the person you are sharing with a copy of your .PRS file, or it will be reformatted for their printer selection.

If you want to change printer selections for a specific document, you can do one of two things. You can press the space bar in a blank screen (to make WordPerfect think you have begun creating a document and select the current printer), retrieve the file and delete the space. The document will then be reformatted for the current printer. The second method is to retrieve the file and let WordPerfect choose the previous printer selection, and then press Print (SHIFT-F7), type **S** for Select Printer, and select the new printer definition to be used. The document is reformatted at that time.

Fonts

One of the new function key assignments is Font (CTRL-F8). A printer definition is no longer limited to eight fonts. In fact, each printer selection can have up to 250 fonts, each properly named instead of numbered. When you press Font (CTRL-F8), you can choose 4 to change the Base Font. This is simply a font change. The reason it is referred to as a base font is that all other attributes listed under the Size and Appearance options (1 and 2 on that menu) are based on that font. For example, fine print will most likely be different for a Helvetica 14pt base font than it would be for a Times Roman 12pt base font.

WordPerfect determines the fonts that will be used for these various attributes when you select fonts, cartridges, and print wheels during the printer selection. After selecting the available fonts, you will see the message "Updating Fonts: n." During this time, WordPerfect quickly scans the information about each font (size, typeface, slant, orientation, character table, and so on) and determines which fonts can be used for the various attributes such as fine, small, large, very large, extra large, italics, small caps, and so on. You can change these font selections using the Printer program, as discussed in Chapter 5.

You can either change fonts by choosing a base font each time or by using the attributes to make the changes. You want to retrieve PRINT-ER.TST and print the document to see which fonts WordPerfect has selected for these attributes.

One advantage to using the attributes method is that you can block text and assign an attribute to it. This is possible because each attribute has a beginning and ending code, as in large on [LARGE] and large off [large]. You cannot do this with a base font change, unless you use a macro or the temporary font option on the font key as it has been assigned in the MACROS.WPK keyboard. Otherwise, the code is inserted and affects the document from that point forward.

Another way to get around this limitation is to place a font change in a paired style. You can turn on the style to insert the font change, and as soon as you turn the style off, WordPerfect automatically returns to the original base font that was selected just before the style was turned on. See "Styles" in this chapter for more information.

After selecting the available fonts, cartridges, and print wheels, you can choose the initial font. This selection is saved with each document in the document "prefix" and is not visible when you press Reveal Codes (ALT-F3). However, you can display and change it for each document by pressing Format (SHIFT-F8) and choosing 3 for Document and then 3 for Initial Base Font.

If you select fonts in one document and then select a different printer definition, WordPerfect will check the information for each previous font, find the best match in the new printer selection, and make the font change automatically. This type of font change will appear with an asterisk when you look at the code in Reveal Codes (ALT-F3). Word-Perfect will also change the attribute selections accordingly so that large print, for example, would be changed according to the newly selected font.

The greatest advantage to this method is that if you return to the original printer selection, WordPerfect will restore the original font changes and remove the asterisk from the font change code.

Types of Paper

Instead of choosing a sheet-feeder bin from within the document or selecting either continuous or hand-fed forms when defining a printer, you can choose from a list of paper sizes and types. When you add or edit a paper type in the Paper Size/Type menu, you will indicate the size, type, location, and orientation (portrait, landscape, or both).

The location indicates whether that particular type of form (letterhead, envelope, legal size paper, and so on) is to be fed manually, is continuous, or if it can be found in a sheet-feeder bin. You will also indicate whether or not the form is initially present when the print job begins. If the form is not initially present or is manually fed, Word-Perfect will stop and ask you to insert the form and give the printer a "Go" when ready.

Setup and Initial Settings

All information entered in the Setup menu is now kept in a single file named WP{WP}.SET. WP.EXE is no longer altered. If you are using a network version of WordPerfect, the {WP in the filename will change to reflect the user's ID (3 characters) so that each person can have individual settings. In fact, any temporary file starting with WP}WP{ follows the same rule.

In the past, you could change the initial settings, but since the settings were not kept with the document, the documents could be formatted incorrectly when retrieved with another person's copy of WordPerfect that had different initial settings. This problem has been corrected by the changes made to WordPerfect 5.0 and 5.1.

To change the default settings, you can press Setup (SHIFT-F1), and choose 4 for Initial Settings and then 5 for Initial Codes. You will see a Reveal Codes type of screen that displays the codes as you insert them. As you make selections (select Left Justification, turn on Page Numbering, turn on hyphenation, turn on Widow/Orphan Protection, and so on), the codes are inserted on the screen. When you create documents from that point on, the initial codes are copied to each new document. You will not see them in Reveal Codes (ALT-F3), but you can view and change the codes for each document by pressing Format (SHIFT-F8) and choosing 3 for Document and then 2 for Initial Codes.

The initial codes for a document are not affected if you change them in the Setup menu after the document is created. If you want to force a document to take on different initial codes, make the change in Setup (SHIFT-F1), clear the screen, and press the space bar to start creating a document and, in effect, copy the initial codes into the new document. Retrieve the document that is to have the new initial codes, and then delete the space. When documents are retrieved into an existing document, the former initial codes are ignored and are replaced by the new ones.

You can use the Format: Document initial codes to insert any other codes that you might normally place within the document. This makes Reveal Codes a little cleaner. If you are trying to find a format code and it is not in the document, check the initial codes in the Format: Document menu.

Styles

Styles help you keep consistent formats for different parts of a document or different documents. If you need to make changes to the format, you can change the style itself, and all text marked with that style will automatically be updated.

Macros do not slow formatting speed, but styles do. However, styles may be more effective than macros in many cases. If you need a certain format at different points throughout a document, you can insert the codes with a macro. However, if you wanted to make a small change to each of these sections, you would have to do so manually. Styles are easy to insert into your document, but the advantage comes when you have to make changes to the style or format. Instead of making the change throughout the document manually, you can make the change once in the style, and all text marked with that style is updated.

If you use paired styles, you can insert any formatting codes (font changes, line height, and so on) in the style. The text will be returned to the original settings as soon as the style is turned off. When you look at a style-on or style-off code in Reveal Codes (ALT-F3), it expands to show you the codes currently included in that style.

Special Characters

WordPerfect has eliminated the CTRL/ALT Key Mapping feature previously found on Screen (CTRL-F3) and has replaced it with a full keyboard mapping facility that lets you assign any special character, macro, or WordPerfect function to any key on the keyboard (not limited to CTRL or ALT key combinations). WordPerfect also supports more than 1500 characters, instead of the standard 256. Of course, the characters that you can display and print depend on your monitor and printer. If you have an EGA or a Hercules graphics card with RamFont, you can choose to have 512 characters displayed instead of 256.

You can map the characters to a key on a keyboard (you can have several different keyboards, such as Math, Greek, and German), or you can use the Compose feature to insert the characters into the document.

The characters are divided into 12 character sets, with one available for characters defined by the user. If you feel that a character can be composed using two separate characters, you do not need to know the section or character number that has been assigned to that character. You can press Compose (CTRL-2) and then type the two characters. For example, you can create most foreign characters by typing the letter and then ", ˆ, ', or a comma to create the diacritical mark. You can also create other characters, such as the copyright symbol or the British pound sign using two different characters. With this method, you could type **o** and **c** for ©, and **l** and a hyphen for £. See "Compose" in Chapter 3, "Commands and Features," for a list of characters that you can compose with two characters.

If you cannot find a combination that works, locate the character in Appendix A and note its section and character number. If you need to do this, you might want to assign the character to a key if you need to use it often and cannot easily compose it from memory. With this type of character, press Compose (CTRL-2); type the section number, a comma, and the character number; and then press ENTER.

You can also hold down the ALT key and type the decimal value of the character on the numeric keypad to insert any of the standard 256 characters. You can still access the familiar character chart found in 4.2 by pressing Help (F3) and then CTRL-V. (You can use CTRL-V instead of CTRL-2 for Compose in the normal editing screen.) If a character cannot be displayed, you will see a small box instead. If you move the cursor to the box and look at it in Reveal Codes, the section and character number are displayed. See "Compose" and "Keyboard Layout" in Chapter 3 for more information.

Macro Changes

Macros are greatly improved with version 5.1. You can edit macros, use programming commands to further customize applications, and include a group of macros in one keyboard file to save disk space.

You can still use macros as they were used in the past. You can create macros that are saved in a file with a name consisting of 1 to 8 characters (previously 2 to 8 characters, with 1-character macros reserved for temporary macros), or you can use an ALT key combination to name them. These macros now have the extension .WPM.

With 5.1, you can use the Keyboard Layout feature found on Setup (SHIFT-F1) option **5** to assign a macro to any key on the keyboard. This includes keys from "A" to "Z," SHIFT-key combinations, CTRL-key combinations, and ALT-key combinations. The macros found in each keyboard layout are saved in one file with the extension .WPK. It is probably more advantageous to use keyboard macros, because they take precedence over ALT-key file macros. They also take up less disk space by being kept in one file instead of many smaller files.

One disadvantage to using keyboard macros is that you need to know the exact keystrokes when you are creating the macro. Another alternative, however, is to create a file macro as you would normally, and then use the option on the Keyboard Layout menu to retrieve a macro and assign it to a key. You can then insert any programming commands needed and delete the .WPM macro file when you are finished. See "Macros" and "Keyboard Layout" in Chapter 3 and see Chapter 6, "Advanced Macro and Merge Commands," for more information about macros.

Converting 4.2 Macros

WordPerfect Corporation has included a macro conversion program that converts text, cursor keys, delete keys, and any other keystrokes that have not changed from version 4.2 to 5.1. The program is named MACROCNV.EXE and is installed with the utility files. Run the program from the DOS prompt by typing **macrocnv** and following the instructions that are displayed.

Converting Files from 4.2

You can retrieve a 4.2 document into 5.1 with no problems. However, if you have many font changes, they will be converted to comments that tell you to change the font manually. Some formatting codes, such as bin number changes, margins, and page size, are also lost in the conversion.

If you have heavily formatted documents with numerous font changes, margin changes, and bin number selections, you can create a .CRS (conversion resource) file that you can use when you retrieve 4.2 documents into 5.1. This file will tell WordPerfect which font in 5.1 is equal to fonts 1 through 8 in 4.2 and will make the changes for you. You can also use any attributes (such as italics) instead of selecting a font. You can include other information in this .CRS file so that margins, page size, and the appropriate form (bin number) will be selected during the process.

The procedure for creating a .CRS file is explained under the topic "Compatibility" in Chapter 3.

Conclusion

Although the changes made to WordPerfect may take some getting used to, you will soon feel as much at home with the product as you did with previous versions.

When you first converted to a word processor from a typewriter, letting WordPerfect insert page numbers rather than entering them manually was probably a small but welcome adjustment. You will find that many of the "workarounds" that you became accustomed to and accepted in previous versions have been eliminated with 5.1. Instead of doing tasks manually, see what WordPerfect 5.1 can do for you.

Graphics Images

The following 30 graphics images are included in the WordPerfect 5.1 package. They were taken from a library of over 500 images that were produced with WordPerfect Corporation's new draw program, Draw-Perfect. To order this program or additional figure libraries, call WordPerfect Corporation at 1-800-321-4566.

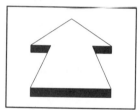
ARROW-22.WPG

BALLOONS.WPG

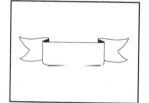
BANNER-3.WPG

BICYCLE.WPG

BKGRND-1.WPG

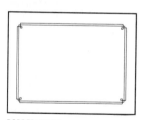
BORDER-8.WPG

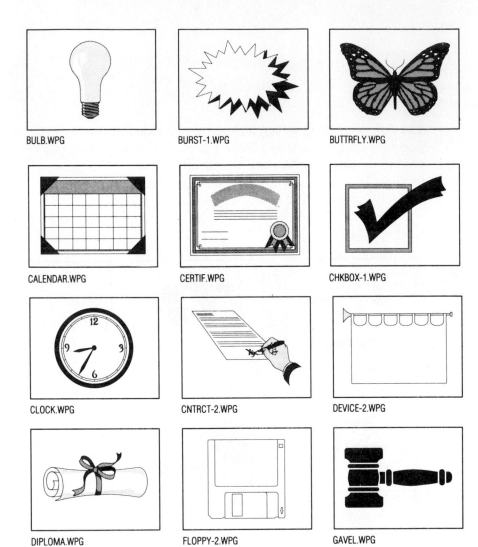

BULB.WPG

BURST-1.WPG

BUTTRFLY.WPG

CALENDAR.WPG

CERTIF.WPG

CHKBOX-1.WPG

CLOCK.WPG

CNTRCT-2.WPG

DEVICE-2.WPG

DIPLOMA.WPG

FLOPPY-2.WPG

GAVEL.WPG

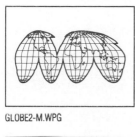

GLOBE2-M.WPG

HANDS-3.WPG

MAGNIF.WPG

MAILBAG.WPG

NEWS.WPG

PC-1.WPG

PRESNT-1.WPG

PRINTR-3.WPG

SCALE.WPG

STAR-5.WPG

TELPHONE.WPG

TROPHY.WPG

Conversion Tables

Some say WordPerfect is easy to learn if you have never used another word processor, because the transition from a typewriter to Word-Perfect is very natural.

If you have used a different word processor and are learning Word-Perfect, it can be somewhat difficult to adapt to the new environment and terminology. The tables in this appendix have been prepared to help with that adjustment period.

A table of comparable terms is provided for WordPerfect and each of the leading word processors: WordStar (Table F-1), MultiMate (Table F-2), Microsoft Word (Table F-3), and IBM DisplayWrite (Table F-4). WordStar keystrokes are included in the WordStar table because they are as familiar as the feature name to many users of WordStar.

All features in each program are listed in alphabetical order, with the comparable WordPerfect feature and keystrokes listed in parallel columns. You will find that in all but a few instances, WordPerfect matches the other programs feature for feature. Features that are available with WordPerfect but are not with the other word processors are not listed.

WordStar Professional	WS Keystrokes	WordPerfect	WP Keystrokes
Abandon file	^KQ	Exit	F7
Abort last command	^U	Cancel	F1
Alternate character pitch	^PA	N/A	
Begin block	^KB	Block	ALT-F4
Beginning of document	^QR		HOME, HOME, ↑
Block menu	^K	Block	ALT-F4
Block column	^KN	Rectangle	Block (ALT-F4), Move (CTRL-F4), 3

Table F-1. WordStar Professional/WordPerfect 5.1 Conversion Table

1269

WordStar Professional	WS Keystrokes	WordPerfect	WP Keystrokes
Boldface	^PB	Bold	F6
Bottom of screen	^QX	Screen down	+ on numeric keypad
Center text	^OC	Center	SHIFT-F6
Change logged disk	^KL or L on Main Menu	Default drive	List (F5), =, *new drive/directory*
Character left	^S	Character left	←
Character right	^D	Character right	→
Character width	.CW	N/A	
Clear tab	^ON	Tabs	Format (SHIFT-F8), 1, 8
Conditional page	.CP	Conditional End of Page	Format (SHIFT-F8), 4, 2
		Block Protect	ALT-F4, SHIFT-F8
		Widow/Orphan Protect	Format (SHIFT-F8), 1, 9
Copy a block	^KC	Move	Block (ALT-F4), Move (CTRL-F4), 1, 2
Copy a file	^KO or O from Main Menu	Copy file	List (F5), 8
Cursor keys			
Character left	^S		←
Character right	^D		→
Line up	^X		↑
Line down	^E		↓
Word left	^A		CTRL-←
Word right	^F		CTRL-→
Top of screen	^QE		HOME, ↑
Bottom of screen	^QX		HOME, ↓
Scroll up	^R or PGUP		− on numeric keypad
Scroll down	^C or PGDN		+ on numeric keypad
Left side of screen	^QS		HOME, ←
Right side of screen	^QD		HOME, →
Beginning of file	^QR		HOME, HOME, ↑

Table F-1.   WordStar Professional/WordPerfect 5.1 Conversion Table (*continued*)

WordStar Professional	WS Keystrokes	WordPerfect	WP Keystrokes
End of file	^QC		HOME, HOME, ↓
Delete	^KJ	Delete	DEL
Delete a block	^KY	Delete block	Block (ALT-F4), BACK-SPACE or DEL
Delete a file	Y from Main Menu	Delete a file	List (F5), 2
Delete character at cursor	^G	Delete character	DEL
Delete character left	DEL	Delete character Left	BACKSPACE
Delete entire line	^Y	N/A	Write a macro: HOME, ←, CTRL-END, DEL
Delete line left	^Q DEL	N/A	Write a macro: Block (ALT-F4), HOME, ←, DEL, Y
Delete line right	^QY	Delete to End of Line	CTRL-END
Delete word right	^T	Delete Word Right	CTRL-BACKSPACE
Directory	^KF	List Files menu	List (F5)
Double strike	^PD	Bold	F6
Down a line	^Z	Line Down	↓
Down screen	^C	Screen Down	+ on numeric keypad
End of block	^KK	Block	ALT-F4 and highlight to end of block
End of file	^QC	End of file	HOME, HOME, ↓
Exit to operating system	X from Main Menu	Exit	F7
		Go to DOS temporarily	Shell (CTRL-F1), 1
File directory	F on Main Menu	List Files menu	List (F5)
Find and replace	^QA	Replace	ALT-F2
Find misspelling	^QL	Spell	CTRL-F2
Find text in file	^QF	Search	F2 or SHIFT-F2
Footing	.FO	Footers	Format (SHIFT-F8), 2, 4
Heading	.HE	Headers	Format (SHIFT-F8), 2, 3
Help menu	^J	Help	F3

Table F-1.   WordStar Professional/WordPerfect 5.1 Conversion Table (*continued*)

WordStar Professional	WS Keystrokes	WordPerfect	WP Keystrokes
Hide/display block	^KH	N/A	Block does not use markers; Cancel (F1) or Block (ALT-F4) will turn off Block
Hyph-help	^OH	Hyphenation	Format (SHIFT-F8), 1, 1
Insert/overwrite	^V	Insert/Typeover	INS
Justify	^OJ	Justification	Format (SHIFT-F8), 1, 3
Last find or block	^QV	Go to original position	CTRL-HOME, CTRL-HOME
		Go to block	CTRL-HOME, ALT-F4
Left side	^QS	Left edge of screen	HOME, HOME, ←
Line down	^X	Line Down	↓
Line height	.LH	Line Height	Format (SHIFT-F8), 1, 4
Line up	^E	Line Up	↑
MailMerge	M on Main Menu merges to the printer	Merge	CTRL-F9, 1
Ask for variable	.AV	Pause for input from console (keyboard)	{KEYBOARD} command
Data file in merge	.DF	Secondary merge file	Can call another secondary file with {CHAIN SECONDARY}
Display message	.DM	Output message	{PROMPT} or {INPUT}
Eliminate blank lines	/O	Eliminate blank lines	Use question mark or {IF NOT BLANK}
Merge report variable	.RV	{FIELD}	Merge Codes (SHIFT-F9), F, *field number*
Margins	^OL and ^OR	Margins	Format (SHIFT-F8), 1, 7
Marker	^Q0-9	N/A	
Move Block	^KV	Move	Block (ALT-F4), Move (CTRL-F4), 1, 1

Table F-1. WordStar Professional/WordPerfect 5.1 Conversion Table (*continued*)

WordStar Professional	WS Keystrokes	WordPerfect	WP Keystrokes
New page	.PA	Hard Page	CTRL-ENTER
Nonbreaking space	^PO	Hard Space	HOME, space bar
Nonprinting comment	.IG	Comment	Text In/Out (CTRL-F5), 5
Omit page number	.OP	Page numbering set to Off	If on, turn off with SHIFT-F8, 2, 6
On-screen menu	^O	Format	SHIFT-F8
Open a document file	D	Begin typing on screen when program comes up or retrieve an existing file	Retrieve (SHIFT-F10)
Open a nondocument file	N	DOS text or ASCII file	Text In/Out (CTRL-F5), 1
Other ribbon color	^PY	Print Color	Font (CTRL-F8), 5
Overprint character	^PH	Overstrike	Format (SHIFT-F8), 4, 5
Overprint line	^P	Strikeout	Font (CTRL-F8), 2, 9
Page break	^OP	Hard Page or Soft Page	CTRL-ENTER for hard page; WP enters soft pages automatically
Page length	.PL	Paper size/type	Format (SHIFT-F8), 2, 7
Page numbering	.PN	Page Numbering	Format (SHIFT-F8), 2, 6
Paragraph tab	^OG	Indent	F4
Phantom rubout or phantom space	^PG/^PF	Special Characters	Compose (CTRL-F2), section number, comma, character number, ENTER
Previous position	^QP	Go To, Go To	CTRL-HOME, CTRL-HOME
Print	^KP or ^P	Print	SHIFT-F7, 1 for Full document or 2 for Page
Print display	^OD	View Document	Print (SHIFT-F7), 6
Read file into document	^KR	Retrieve	SHIFT-F10

Table F-1.   WordStar Professional/WordPerfect 5.1 Conversion Table (*continued*)

WordStar Professional	WS Keystrokes	WordPerfect	WP Keystrokes
Reform or reformat	^B	WP automatically reformats the screen after editing changes; Rewrite screen allows manual reformatting	Screen (CTRL-F3), ENTER
Release margins	^OX	Left margin release; expand right margin	SHIFT-TAB; Format (SHIFT-F8), 1, 8
Rename	^KE or E on Main Menu	Rename File	List (F5), 3
Repeat command or key	^QQ	Repeat Value	ESC, number or character
Repeat last find	^L	Search	F2, F2
Right end of line	^QD	Right side of screen	END or HOME, →
Ruler line	^OT	Ruler	Screen (CTRL-F3), 1, ↑, ENTER
Run a program	R on Main Menu	Go to DOS	Shell (CTRL-F1), 1
Run MailMerge	M on Main Menu	Merge	CTRL-F9, 1
Run SpellStar	S on Main Menu	Spell	CTRL-F2
Save (done)	^KD	Exit	F7
Save and exit	^KX	Exit	F7, Y, name of document, Y if overwriting previous file, Y to exit
Save and resume	^KS	Save	F10
Set left margin or right margin	^OL/^OR	Margins	Format (SHIFT-F8), 1, 7
Set line spacing	^OS	Spacing	Format (SHIFT-F8), 1, 6
Set tabs	^OI	Tabs	Format (SHIFT-F8), 1, 8
Soft hyphen	^OE	Soft Hyphen	CTRL-HYPHEN (-)
Spacing	^OS	Spacing	Format (SHIFT-F8), 1, 6
SpellStar	S on Main Menu	Spell	CTRL-F2
Standard pitch	^PN	Select Base Font	Font (CTRL-F8), 4
Stop a command	^U	Cancel	F1
Strikeout	^PX	Strikeout	Font (CTRL-F8), 2, 9

Table F-1.   WordStar Professional/WordPerfect 5.1 Conversion Table (*continued*)

WordStar Professional	WS Keystrokes	WordPerfect	WP Keystrokes
Superscript/sub-script	^PV/^PT	Superscript/Sub-script	Font (CTRL-F8), 1, 1 or 2
Tab, insert	^I or TAB	TAB key	TAB (or ^I)
Tabs, clear and set	^ON and ^OI	Tabs	Format (SHIFT-F8), 1, 8
Top margin	.MT	Top Margin	Format (SHIFT-F8), 2, 5
Top of file	^QR	Beginning of file	HOME, HOME, ↑
Top screen	^QE	Screen Up	− on numeric key-pad
Underscore or underline	^PS	Underline	F8
Up line	^W	Up Line	↑
Up screen	^R	Screen Up	− on numeric key-pad
Vari-tabs	^OV	Tabs	Format (SHIFT-F8), 1, 8
Word left	^A	Word Left	CTRL- ←
Word right	^F	Word Right	CTRL- →
Word wrap	^OW	Automatic	
Write block to file	^KW	Block and Save	ALT-F4, F10

Table F-1.   WordStar Professional/WordPerfect 5.1 Conversion Table (*continued*)

MultiMate Advantage	WordPerfect	WP Keystrokes
Alternate keyboard	Keyboard Mapping or Special Characters	Setup (SHIFT-F1), 6 or Compose (CTRL-2)
Background/foreground printing	Possible to print and edit a document at the same time	
Back up a document auto-matically	Backup	Setup (SHIFT-F1), 3, 1
Bold print	Bold	F6

Table F-2.   MultiMate Advantage/WordPerfect 5.1 Conversion Table

MultiMate Advantage	WordPerfect	WP Keystrokes
Bound columns	Parallel Columns	Columns/Tables (ALT-F7), 1,
Cancel printing	Stop printing	Printer (SHIFT-F7), 4, S or C
Case significance	Search (uppercase finds only uppercase; lowercase finds both)	Search (F2); Reverse Search (SHIFT-F2); Replace (ALT-F2)
Center	Center Text	SHIFT-F6
Clear place marks	N/A	
Column calculations	Math	Columns/Tables (ALT-F7), 3
Column mode (copy, move, or delete)	Move, copy, or delete columns	Block (ALT-F4), Move (CTRL-F4), 2
Copy (within document)	Copy text	Block (ALT-F4), Move (CTRL-F4), 1, 2
Copy (external) from one document to another	Copy text	Block (ALT-F4), Move (CTRL-F4), 1, 2
Create an ASCII file	DOS text or ASCII file	Text In/Out (CTRL-F5), 1
Create a new document	In WP, begin typing on a clear screen, or change an existing document and save it as a new document. You do not have to name a document until you save it	
Create a print file	DOS text or ASCII file	Text In/Out (CTRL-F5), 1; Print (SHIFT-F7), send document to disk
Cursor movement	Cursor control or arrow keys	
Custom dictionary	Spell	CTRL-F2, 4, name of new supplementary dictionary
Data file	Secondary merge file (created or a Notebook file from WordPerfect Library)	
Decimal tab	Tab Align or Tab Set	CTRL-F6 or Format (SHIFT-F8), 1, 8
Default pitch	Font	Font (CTRL-F8), 4
Delete	Block Delete	ALT-F4, DEL, Y
Delete character	Delete Character	DEL
Delete document	Delete Files	List (F5), 2, Y

Table F-2.   MultiMate Advantage/WordPerfect 5.1 Conversion Table (*continued*)

MultiMate Advantage	WordPerfect	WP Keystrokes
Delete underline	Delete Codes	Delete [UND] or [und] codes in Reveal Codes
Display directory	List Files menu	List (F5)
Document handling utilities	List Files menu	List (F5)
Document Summary screen	Summary	Format (SHIFT-F8), 3, 5
Double underscore	Double Underline	Font (CTRL-F8), 2, 3
Draft print	Text Quality	Print (SHIFT-F7), T, 2
Edit an old document	Retrieve	Retrieve (SHIFT-F10); List (F5), 1
End of page	Bottom of Page	CTRL-HOME, ↓
End of screen	Screen Down	+ on numeric keypad
Enhanced print	Text Quality (already set to High)	Print (SHIFT-F7), T, 4
Escape	ESC key (to cancel a function, set a variable number for a function, or position a hyphen)	
Footer setup	Footer	Format (SHIFT-F8), 2, 4
Footnotes	Footnotes	CTRL-F7
Format change	Format	SHIFT-F8
Format line	Format	SHIFT-F8, 1
Format page	Format	SHIFT-F8, 2
Forms fill-in	Forms Fill-In (merge)	Merge (CTRL-F9), 1
Go To	Go To	CTRL-HOME
Hard space	Hard Space (required space)	HOME, space bar
Header setup	Header	Format (SHIFT-F8), 2, 3
Help	Help	F3
Highlighting	Block	ALT-F4
Hot print	Page Print	Print (SHIFT-F7), 2
Hyphen, soft	Soft hyphen inserted by WP during automatic hyphenation	
Indent	Left Indent	F4
	Left/Right Indent	SHIFT-F4

Table F-2.   MultiMate Advantage/WordPerfect 5.1 Conversion Table (*continued*)

MultiMate Advantage	WordPerfect	WP Keystrokes
Insert (drop-down or push), usually in Typeover mode	Automatic Insert/ Typeover; preset default is Insert mode (inserts text and pushes existing text to the right)	INS (to turn on Typeover, which writes over existing text)
Insert character	Automatic	
Justification	Justification	Format (SHIFT-F8), 1, 3
Key procedures		
Build	Macro Def	CTRL-F10
Execute	Macro	ALT-F10 to invoke
Pause	Pause	CTRL-PGUP, 1
Prompt	Comments (use for messages)	Edit macro and use {PROMPT} command
Library	Boilerplates/merge	Merge/Sort (CTRL-F9) or Retrieve (SHIFT-F10)
Line and box drawing	Line Draw	Screen (CTRL-F3), 2 or Graphics (ALT-F9)
Line length	Margins	Format (SHIFT-F8), 1, 7
Line spacing	Spacing	Format (SHIFT-F8), 1, 6
Merge	Merge	Merge/Sort (CTRL-F9), 1
Merge document	Primary file	
Move	Move	CTRL-F4
Next page	Page Down	PGDN
Next word	Word Right	CTRL- →
Number of lines per page	Paper Size/Type	Format (SHIFT-F8), 2, 7
Omit line if blank (in merge)	Merge (primary file)	Merge Codes (ALT-F9), F, *field number* ?
Page break	Hard Page or Soft Page	Hard Page (CTRL-ENTER); soft page break automatically entered by WP
Page combine	N/A	
Page down	Page Down	PGDN
Page length	Paper Size/Type	Format (SHIFT-F8), 2, 7
Page numbering	Page numbering in document or in header/footer	Format (SHIFT-F8), 2, 6
Page up	Page Up	PGUP
Pound symbol (£)	Special Characters	Compose (CTRL-F2), L, -, ENTER

Table F-2.   MultiMate Advantage/WordPerfect 5.1 Conversion Table *(continued)*

MultiMate Advantage	WordPerfect	WP Keystrokes
Previous word	Word left	CTRL- ←
Print	Print	SHIFT-F7, 1, 2
Print pitch	Font	Font (CTRL-F8), 4
Printer control codes	Printer command	Format (SHIFT-F8), 4, 6, 2
Proportional spacing	Select PS Font	Font (CTRL-F8), 4
Remove a document from the queue	Cancel a Print Job	Print (SHIFT-F7), 4, C
Rename a document	Rename a File	List (F5), 3
Repaginate	Automatic	
Replace	Replace	ALT-F2
Required page break	Hard Page	CTRL-ENTER
Restart the document currently printing	"Go" (resume printing)	Print (SHIFT-F7), 4, G
Restore a backed-up document	Original backup; set in Setup (SHIFT-F1) and retrieve with .BK! extension	
Return	Enter	ENTER
Save	Save	F10
Save/Exit	Exit	F7
Screen print	Print Screen	SHIFT-PRTSC
Search	Search	F2
	Reverse Search	SHIFT-F2
	Replace	ALT-F2
Search Document Summary screens	Word Find or Look	List (F5), 9, 1; or List (F5), 6
Section numbering	Outline or Table of Contents	Date/Outline (SHIFT-F5), 4 or 5; Block (ALT-F4), Mark Text (ALT-F5), 1
Shadow print	Bold	F6
Spacing	Spacing	Format (SHIFT-F8), 1, 6
Spell check a document	Spell	CTRL-F2
Spell check a section of a document	Spell check a block	Block (ALT-F4), Spell (CTRL-F2)
Status line	Status line at bottom of screen; displays document, page, line, and position of cursor	

Table F-2.   MultiMate Advantage/WordPerfect 5.1 Conversion Table *(continued)*

MultiMate Advantage	WordPerfect	WP Keystrokes
Strikeout	Strikeout	Font (CTRL-F8), 2, 9
Strikeover	Typeover (the default in WP is Insert mode)	INS
Subscript	Subscript	Font (CTRL-F8), 1, 2
Superscript	Superscript	Font (CTRL-F8), 1, 1
System print commands	Date	SHIFT-F5, 1 or 2
	Current Page Number	CTRL-B
Tab locations	Tabs	Format (SHIFT-F8), 1, 8
Table of Contents	Table of Contents	Block (ALT-F4), Mark Text (ALT-F5), 1
Thesaurus	Thesaurus	ALT-F1
Top margin	Top Margin	Format (SHIFT-F8), 2, 5
Underline	Underline	F8
Widows and orphans	Widow/Orphan Protection	Format (SHIFT-F8), 1, 9

Table F-2.   MultiMate Advantage/WordPerfect 5.1 Conversion Table (*continued*)

Microsoft Word	WordPerfect	WP Keystrokes
ASCII files, save	DOS text or ASCII files	Text In/Out (CTRL-F5), 1
Autosort	Sort	Merge/Sort (CTRL-F9), 2
Bold	Bold On/Off	F6
	Bold block	Block (ALT-F4), F6
Cancel	Cancel	F1
Center	Center	SHIFT-F6
Columns	Columns (newspaper and parallel)	Columns/Tables (ALT-F7), 1
CONVWS and CONVERTD programs (used to convert WordStar, Delimited, DIF, dBASE, and SYLK for use with Microsoft Word)	Convert program on Conversion disk (used to convert WordStar, DIF, Navy DIF, MultiMate, Wang, MailMerge including dBASE, and DCA files for use with WordPerfect)	

Table F-3.   Microsoft Word/WordPerfect 5.1 Conversion Table

Microsoft Word	WordPerfect	WP Keystrokes
Copies, print	Copies, Number of	Print (SHIFT-F7), N
Copy	Copy	Block (ALT-F4), Move (CTRL-F4), 1, 2
Copy, retrieve	Copy, Retrieve	After Copy, move cursor and press ENTER
Delete	Delete Block	Block (ALT-F4), DEL, Y
	Move	Block (ALT-F4), Move (CTRL-F4), 1, 1
Double underline	Double Underline	Font (CTRL-F8), 2, 3
Feed, paper	Paper Size/Type, location of	Format (SHIFT-F8), 2, 7
Format command	Format	SHIFT-F8
Font name and size	Base Font	Font (CTRL-F8), 4
Footnote (create)	Footnote (create)	CTRL-F7, 1, 1
Footnote (jump to)	Footnote (edit)	CTRL-F7, 1, 2, footnote number
Footnotes/endnotes (select one option)	Footnote/Endnote	CTRL-F7, 1 for footnote, 2 for endnote
Gallery	Use macros; change settings in the Setup menu; save commonly used settings in a regular file; or use Styles	Macro Def (CTRL-F10) and Invoke Macro (ALT-F10); Setup (SHIFT-F1); Save (F10); Style (ALT-F8)
Gutter width	Binding Width	Print (SHIFT-F7), B
Hanging indent	Hanging Indent	Indent (F4), Left Margin Release (SHIFT-TAB)
Help	Help	F3
Highlight	Cursor	
Hyphenate	Hyphenation	Format (SHIFT-F8), 1, 1
Indent first line	Tab	TAB
Index, define	Index, Define	Mark Text (ALT-F5), 5, 3
Index, mark for	Index, Mark for	Mark Text (ALT-F5), 3
Insert deleted/copied text	Restore deleted text; Retrieve Move/Copy file	Cancel (F1), 1; Retrieve (SHIFT-F10), ENTER

Table F-3.   Microsoft Word/WordPerfect 5.1 Conversion Table (*continued*)

Microsoft Word	WordPerfect	WP Keystrokes
Italic	Italics	Font (CTRL-F8), 2, 4
Jump to footnote	Footnote (Edit)	CTRL-F7, 1, 2, *footnote number*
Jump to page	Go to page	CTRL-HOME, *page number*
Keep paragraph together	Conditional End of Page	Format (SHIFT-F8), 4, 2
	Block Protect	Block (ALT-F4), Format (SHIFT-F8), Y
	Widow/Orphan Protection	Format (SHIFT-F8), 1, 9
Left indent	Indent	F4
Left/right indent	Left/Right Indent	SHIFT-F4
Library	Sort	Merge/Sort (CTRL-F9), 2
	Hyphenate	LineFormat (SHIFT-F8), 1, 1
	Indexing	Mark Text (ALT-F5), 3
	Paragraph numbering	Date/Outline (SHIFT-F5), 5
	Outlining	Date/Outline (SHIFT-F5), 4
	Go to DOS	Shell (CTRL-F1), 1
	Spell	Spell (CTRL-F2)
	Table of Contents	Mark Text (ALT-F5)
Load, Transfer	Retrieve a Document	SHIFT-F10
Margins (top, bottom, left, and right)	Margins (left and right)	Format (SHIFT-F8), 1, 7
	Margins (top and bottom)	Format (SHIFT-F8), 2, 5
New page	Hard Page	CTRL-ENTER
Nonbreaking hyphen	Dash	HOME-HYPHEN (-)
Nonbreaking Space	Hard Space	HOME, space bar
Number, Library	Outline Numbering	Date/Outline (SHIFT-F5), 4
	Paragraph Numbering	Date/Outline (SHIFT-F5), 5
	Define numbering style	Date/Outline (SHIFT-F5), 6
Optional Hyphen	Soft Hyphen	CTRL-HYPHEN (-)
Options (used to show invisible codes, use printer display, turn off command menu, set the default tab width, measurement, and mute alarms)	Setup menu (used to set program defaults, control "beep," backup, and other options)	SHIFT-F1

Table F-3.   Microsoft Word/WordPerfect 5.1 Conversion Table (*continued*)

Microsoft Word	WordPerfect	WP Keystrokes
Overtype on/off	Typeover On/Off	INS
Page length	Paper Size/Type	Format (SHIFT-F8), 2, 7
Page number	Page Number	Format (SHIFT-F8), 2, 6
Pages, print	Pages, Print	Print (SHIFT-F7), 3, *filename, page numbers*
Page width	Paper Size/Type	Format (SHIFT-F8), 2, 7
Print file	Print to Disk	Select printer and change port to filename; print to that printer
Print glossary	N/A	
Print merge	Merge	Merge/Sort (CTRL-F9), 1 begins the merge; use End Field (F9) and Merge Codes (SHIFT-F9) to create secondary (data) file; use Merge Codes (SHIFT-F9) to insert Merge codes in primary document (form)
Print Options	Control Printer	Print (SHIFT-F7), 4
Print Printer (print active document)	Print Full Document	Print (SHIFT-F7), 1
	Print Current Page	Print (SHIFT-F7), 2
Printer display	Automatic	
Queued, print jobs	Automatic	
Quit	Exit	F7
Range, print	Range, Print	Print (SHIFT-F7), 3, *filename, page range*
Rename document	Rename Document	List (F5), ENTER, 3
Repaginate, print	Automatic	
Replace	Replace	ALT-F2
Required hyphen	Hard Hyphen	Hyphen (-)
Return to standard paragraph settings	Delete Codes	Reveal Codes (ALT-F3)
Right indent	Left/Right Indent	SHIFT-F4
Ruler	Ruler	Screen (CTRL-F3), 1, ↑, ENTER

Table F-3.   Microsoft Word/WordPerfect 5.1 Conversion Table (*continued*)

Microsoft Word	WordPerfect	WP Keystrokes
Run, library	Go to DOS	Shell (CTRL-F1), 1
Running head	Headers/Footers	Format (SHIFT-F8), 2, 3 or 4
Save document	Save a Document	F10
Scrap	Delete buffer	Last three deletions are kept in delete buffer. Restore by pressing Cancel (F1)
	Cut/copy buffer	Block (ALT-F4), Move (CTRL-F4) stores most recently moved/copied text in file "named" with the ENTER key. You can Save (F10) to or Retrieve (SHIFT-F10) from this file by pressing ENTER rather than entering a filename
Scrolling	Moving the cursor	Cursor movement keystrokes (see Chapter 3 for list)
Search	Search	F2
	Search	SHIFT-F2
Select text (highlight)	Block	ALT-F4
Setup, printer port	Printer Port	Print (SHIFT-F7), S to select printers. When editing printer definition, choose 1 for Port
Small caps	Small Caps	Font (CTRL-F8), 2, 7
Space before paragraph	Blank lines	ENTER
Spell	Spell (checks spelling and allows correction at the same time rather than in separate passes)	CTRL-F2
Strikethrough	Strikeout	Font (CTRL-F8), 2, 9
	Overstrike (to print more than one character in the same place)	Format (SHIFT-F8), 4, 5

Table F-3.   Microsoft Word/WordPerfect 5.1 Conversion Table (*continued*)

Microsoft Word	WordPerfect	WP Keystrokes
Style	Style	ALT-F8
Style bar	Reveal Codes	ALT-F3
Subscript	Subscript or Block Subscript	Font (CTRL-F8), 1, 2, or Block first
Superscript	Superscript or Block Superscript	Font (CTRL-F8), 1, 1 or Block first
Table, define	Table of Contents, Define	Mark Text (ALT-F5), 5, 1
Table, mark	Table of Contents, Mark (basic procedure also used for lists and tables of authorities)	Block (ALT-F4), Mark Text (ALT-F5), 1
Tabs, clear	Tab, Clear	Format (SHIFT-F8), 1, 8, HOME, HOME, ← DEL
Tabs, reset all	Tabs, Clear All	Format (SHIFT-F8), 1, 8, CTRL-END
Tabs, set	Tabs, Set	Format (SHIFT-F8), 1, 8
Transfer clear	Exit	F7
Transfer delete	Delete Files	List (F5), ENTER, 2
Transfer glossary	N/A	
Transfer load	Retrieve a Document	SHIFT-F10
Transfer merge	Retrieve one document into another	Retrieve (SHIFT-F10)
Transfer options	View and change default directory	List (F5), =, *directory name* to change default
Transfer rename	Rename documents	List (F5), ENTER, 3
Transfer save	Save a Document	F10
Underline	Underline On/Off	F8
	Underline Block	Block (ALT-F4), F8
Undo	Undelete	Cancel (F1)
Widow/Orphan control	Widow/Orphan Protection	Format (SHIFT-F8), 1, 9
Windows (up to eight)	Windows (two documents)	Screen (CTRL-F3), 1
Window close	Window	Screen (CTRL-F3), 1
Window Move	Window	Screen (CTRL-F3), 1

Table F-3.   Microsoft Word/WordPerfect 5.1 Conversion Table (*continued*)

DisplayWrite 4	WordPerfect	WP Keystrokes
ASCII copy to file	DOS text or ASCII file	Text In/Out (CTRL-F5), 1
Begin/end keep	Conditional End of Page or Block Protect	Format (SHIFT-F8), 4, 2 or, while Block is on, Format (SHIFT-F8), Y
Block edit	Move, copy, delete, or append text	Block (ALT-F4), Move (CTRL-F4)
Bold	Bold	F6
Carriage return or required carriage return	Hard return or soft return	Hard Return (ENTER); soft return automatically entered by WP
Center	Center	SHIFT-F6
Codes, display all	Reveal Codes	ALT-F3
Compress documents	N/A	
Copy documents	Copy files	List (F5), 8
Create comment	Comments	Text In/Out (CTRL-F5), 5
Create document	In WP, begin typing on a clear screen	
Cursor	Cursor control or arrow keys	
Cursor draw	Line Draw	Screen (CTRL-F3), 2
Default drive	List Files menu	List (F5), = *directory*
Defaults	Initial settings	Setup (SHIFT-F1), 5
Display options	Colors, graphics screen type, etc.	Setup (SHIFT-F1), 3
Document assembly	Boilerplates or document assembly (merge)	Retrieve (SHIFT-F10) or Merge/Sort (CTRL-F9), 1
Document comment	Comments	Text In/Out (CTRL-F5), 5
DOS commands	Go to DOS	Shell (CTRL-F1), 1
Erase documents	Delete Files	List (F5), 2
Final-form text conversion	Convert	Use Convert program on Conversion disk
Footnotes	Footnotes	CTRL-F7, 1
Format	Format	SHIFT-F8
Get	Retrieve and Text In/Out	SHIFT-F10, CTRL-F5
Go to page	Go To	CTRL-HOME, *page number*
Headers and footers	Headers/Footers	Format (SHIFT-F8), 2, 3 or 4
Hyphenation	Hyphenation	Format (SHIFT-F8), 1, 1

Table F-4.   DisplayWrite 4/WordPerfect 5.1 Conversion Table

DisplayWrite 4	WordPerfect	WP Keystrokes
Indent	Indent	F4
	Left/Right Indent	SHIFT-F4
Keyboard extensions	Keyboard Mapping	Setup (SHIFT-F1), 5
Keystroke programming	Macros	Macro Def (CTRL-F10); Macro (ALT-F10) to start
Line adjust	Automatic	
List services	List Files menu	List (F5)
Margins	Margins	Format (SHIFT-F8), 1, 7
Math	Math	Columns/Tables (ALT-F7), 3
Merge	Merge	CTRL-F9, 1
Notepad	Switch	SHIFT-F3
Outline appearance	Change Paragraph/Outline Numbering	Date/Outline (SHIFT-F5), 6
Outlines	Outlines	Date/Outline (SHIFT-F5), 4
Overstrike characters	Overstrike	Format (SHIFT-F8), 4, 5
Page ends	Hard and soft page breaks	Hard Page (CTRL-ENTER); soft page breaks are automatically entered
Page numbers	Page numbering in document or in header/footer	Format (SHIFT-F8), 2, 3 or 4 header/footer
Paginate	Widows/Orphan Protection	Format (SHIFT-F8), 1, 9
Paper clip	N/A	
Print (background/foreground)	Print (always background)	SHIFT-F7
Profiles	Setup	SHIFT-F1
Recover documents	Backup	Setup (SHIFT-F1), 3, 1
Reference areas, tables	Tables	Graphics (ALT-F9), 2
Rename documents	Rename Files	List (F5), 3
Required hyphen	Hard Hyphen	HOME-HYPHEN (-)
Required space	Hard Space	HOME, space bar
Required tab	Indent	F4
Revisable-form text conversion	Convert	Use Convert program on conversion disk
Revise document	Retrieve	SHIFT-F10
Revision marking	Redline/Strikeout	Font (CTRL-F8), 2, 8 or 9
Save document	Save Document or Save and Exit	F10 or F7
Scale line	Ruler	Screen (CTRL-F3), 1, ↑, ENTER

Table F-4.   DisplayWrite 4/WordPerfect 5.1 Conversion Table (*continued*)

DisplayWrite 4	WordPerfect	WP Keystrokes
Search	Search	F2
	Reverse Search	SHIFT-F2
	Replace	ALT-F2
Skip to line	Advance	Format (SHIFT-F8), 4, 1
Spell	Spell	CTRL-F2
Superscripts and sub-scripts	Superscript/Subscript	Font (CTRL-F8), 1, 1 or 2
Supplement	Change dictionary	Spell (CTRL-F2), 4
Tables	Tables	Columns/Tables (ALT-F7), 2
Tabs	Tabs	Format (SHIFT-F8), 1, 8
Typestyle	Font	Font (CTRL-F8), 4
Underline	Underline	F8
Utilities	List Files mneu	List (F5)
	Convert program	Use Convert program on Conversion disk
View document	View Document	Print (SHIFT-F7), 6
Working copy	Original backup file is named with .BK!	Setup (SHIFT-F1), 1

Table F-4.   DisplayWrite 4/WordPerfect 5.1 Conversion Table (*continued*)

Remember that you can reassign any WordPerfect function to any key with the Keyboard Layout feature. This can help you make WordPerfect emulate another program.

Transferring Files

You can use the Convert program to transfer data created with these word processors to WordPerfect format. There are options for converting WordStar 3.3, MultiMate, and IBM DisplayWrite files directly to WordPerfect. After converting Microsoft Word documents to revisable-form text (DCA), you can use the Revisable-Form Text option in Convert to transfer the documents to WordPerfect. See the "Convert Program" entry in Chapter 3, "Commands and Features," for details.

The Latest Enhancements

WordPerfect Corporation provides "interim releases" every few months to fix bugs in the program and include enhancements. This appendix lists the enhancements that have been made to each interim release. As of this book's printing, one release, dated 1/19/90, has been made available. You can find the date of your release in the upper right corner of the Help (F3) screen.

If you encounter a problem with the program that has been fixed with the latest release, the interim release is available at no charge. If you want to take advantage of the changes you see here, you can order the latest release of 5.1 for $15 to $25, depending on the number of disks that you need. To order the latest release, call (800) 321-4566.

You can find the latest changes by reading the README files on your original WordPerfect disks.

Border Options

When you create a graphics box of any type (figure, table box, text box, and so on), you can first enter the Options menu and specify the border style for each side of the box. The selections include Single, Double, Dashed, Dotted, Thick, and Extra Thick. The Line option in the Tables menu also lets you choose Single, Double, Dashed, Dotted, Thick, and Extra Thick for the type of lines in the table.

With the latest release of 5.1, WordPerfect includes an option on the Format: Other menu that lets you specify the width, shading, and spacing for those lines. Before following the steps below, move the cursor above any graphics boxes or tables to be affected.

1. Press Format (SHIFT-F8).

2. Choose 4 for Other.

3. Choose 8 for Border Options. The menu shown in Figure G-1 appears.

4. Make the desired selections, and press Exit (F7) when you are finished.

You can also change the length of the dashed line and the spacing between double lines, dots, and dashes.

The [Brdr Opt] code is inserted when you select any option from this menu and affects all borders in graphics boxes and tables from that point forward.

```
Format: Border Options

    1 - Single -        Width           0.013"
                        Shading         100%

    2 - Double -        Width           0.013"
                        Shading         100%
                        Spacing Between 0.013"

    3 - Dashed -        Width           0.013"
                        Shading         100%
                        Dash Spacing    0.013"
                        Dash Length     0.053"

    4 - Dotted -        Width           0.013"
                        Shading         100%
                        Dot Spacing     0.013"

    5 - Thick -         Width           0.063"
                        Shading         100%

    6 - Extra Thick -   Width           0.125"
                        Shading         100%

Selection: 0
```

Figure G-1.   Border options

Characters

Character Set 10 now has 47 additional characters, which are shown in Figure G-2.

Equations

The equation commands LONGDIV (long division) and LONGDIVS (long division straight) have been added to the equation editor. These commands are dynamic symbols that grow to fit the size of the equation (similar to OVER, which draws a fraction line to fit the size of the equation).

	0	1	2	3	4	5	6	7	8	9
100			Ҁ	ҁ	Ш	ш	Ӏ	ӏ	А	ᴀ
110	Á	á	É	é	Й	й	Ó	ó	Ý	ý
120	Ы́	ы́	Э́	э́	Ю́	ю́	Я́	я́	À	à
130	È	è	Ѐ	ѐ	Ѝ	ѝ	Ò	ò	Ỳ	ỳ
140	Ы̀	ы̀	Э̀	э̀	Ю̀	ю̀	Я̀	я̀	☐	☐

Figure G-2.   Characters added to Character Set 10

The equation **2 LONGDIV {34.15}** is displayed on the left, and the equation **2 LONGDIVS {34.15}** is displayed on the right. Note that the long division symbol is straight in the example on the right.

$$2\overline{)34.15} \qquad 2\overline{\lceil 34.15}$$

The macro named INLINE has also been added to help you format equations that will appear within a line of text. A user box is used instead of an equation graphics box in this case. The box is a character graphics box, and the baseline of the text will be aligned with the baseline of the equation. Also, because it is a user box, borders do not print.

Expanded Memory

Some expanded memory cards identify themselves as LIM 4.0-compatible even though they do not support all 4.0 functions. The /32 switch forces WordPerfect to use LIM 3.2 calls when accessing expanded memory. To use this option, start WordPerfect by entering **wp/32**.

WordPerfect can also use expanded memory on some previously unusable memory managers with this release.

Graphics

If you change the contents of a graphics box from "Graphic" to "Graphic on Disk," WordPerfect prompts you to save the current graphics image to disk. Press Cancel (F1) if you want to change the Contents option but you do not want to save the image to disk.

Also see "Border Options" earlier in this appendix.

Keyboard

If you have selected a keyboard layout, you can press CTRL-6 anywhere from within WordPerfect to deselect that keyboard temporarily and return to the original keyboard. The next time you enter WordPerfect, the previous keyboard will be selected.

The change made to this feature is that you can press CTRL-6 twice in succession at any time to enable the selected keyboard. Thus, you can deselect and then select the keyboard without having to enter the Setup (SHIFT-F1) menu.

This feature also works in the equation editor with an equation keyboard.

List Files

If you press Search (F2) or Reverse Search (SHIFT-F2), you can press ↑ or ↓ to change the direction of a search. Pressing ↑ and ↓ now works to change the direction of a search in the List Files menu or the Look screen.

Merge

If you are entering a filename for a primary or secondary merge file, and the file cannot be found, WordPerfect now returns you to the filename prompt so you can try again. Before, you had to start the entire process again.

Mouse

If you remove STANDARD.IRS from the directory where WP.EXE is located, WordPerfect loads without any mouse information. You can also unselect a mouse by highlighting the current selection and typing *.

Printing

When it cannot find a character, WordPerfect checks the list of substitute fonts and then prints the character graphically if the character is not found in those substitute fonts. In the first release of WordPerfect, fonts that were too large or too small were used for substitute fonts.

With the current release, WordPerfect will not use a font that is 6.26 percent larger or smaller than the current font for substitute fonts; the characters will be printed graphically instead.

Another change that reduces print codes, speeds printing time, and reduces required printer memory was made to treat consecutive spaces as one large space on printers that have absolute horizontal motion.

Sort

Extended characters (foreign currency symbols) are now ignored when WordPerfect sorts numeric fields.

Spell

You can use the mouse to select replacement words during a spell check.

Spreadsheet

You can now import and link with Borland's Quattro and Quattro Pro spreadsheets.

Importing Quattro Pro may be noticeably slower than importing other spreadsheets, however, because cells are stored in column order. As a result, WordPerfect makes several passes through the Quattro Pro file to convert it to row order.

Tabs

You can use the following keys to set tabs in the Tab Set menu:

/	Change the type of tab (absolute or relative)
TAB	Set a left-aligned tab
Center (SHIFT-F6)	Set a center tab
Flush Right (ALT-F6)	Set a right-aligned tab
Tab Align (CTRL-F6)	Set a decimal tab

Text In/Out

If you retrieve a file and then use Text In/Out (CTRL-F5) to save the document in a format that is different from the one in which it was originally retrieved, a default filename is not displayed. This helps you avoid overwriting the original file with the same file in a different format.

With the latest version, you can press Retrieve (SHIFT-F10) at the "Document to be saved" prompt to display the file's original filename. This only works on files retrieved with Retrieve (SHIFT-F10)—not those retrieved from the List Files menu or with Text In/Out (CTRL-F5).

Text Screen Type

The screen driver for "Text (no graphics)" has been removed from STANDARD.VRS. This driver is now a separate .VRS file with the name GTEXT.VRS and is available on the supplemental Graphics Drivers disk for $10. For ordering information, contact WordPerfect Corporation at (800) 321-4566.

Two Disk Drives

STANDARD.VRS contains several of the most common graphics/text screen drivers. If you are running WordPerfect on a two-disk-drive system and feel that STANDARD.VRS is taking up too much space on your floppy disks, you may prefer using the individual drivers available on the Graphics Drivers disk. Using only one or two of these .VRS files in place of the larger STANDARD.VRS file can free disk space. For ordering information, contact WordPerfect at (800) 321-4566.

3Com 3 + ®	3Com Corporation
3Com 3 + ® OPEN	3Com Corporation
3M®	3M
ATI EGA Wonder®	ATI
AT&T®	AT&T
AT&T® 6300	AT&T
AT&T® 6300Plus	AT&T
AT&T® Star GROUP	AT&T
AutoCAD®	Autodesk, Inc.
Banyan® Vines®	Banyan Systems, Inc.
Bitstream®	Bitstream, Inc.
CH Products Roller Mouse	CH Products
COMPAQ DeskPro 286®	COMPAQ Computer Corporation
CompuServe®	CompuServe, Inc.
DataPerfect®	WordPerfect Corporation
dBASE II®	Ashton-Tate
dBASE III®	Ashton-Tate
DEC™ PCSA	Digital Equipment Corporation
DESQview™	Quarterdeck Office Systems
DIF®	Lotus Development Corporation
DisplayWrite®	International Business Machines Corporation
Dr. Halo™	IMSI

DrawPerfect®	WordPerfect Corporation
Excel™	Microsoft Corporation
GEM® Paint	Digital Research, Inc.
Helvetica®	Linotype Company
Hercules InColor Card®	Hercules Computer Technology
Hercules Graphics Card Plus™	Hercules Computer Technology
Hewlett-Packard® Graphics Language	Hewlett-Packard Company
HP LaserJet™	Hewlett-Packard Company
HP LaserJet PLUS™	Hewlett-Packard Company
HP LaserJet™ 500 +	Hewlett-Packard Company
HP LaserJet™ 2000	Hewlett-Packard Company
HP LaserJet II™	Hewlett-Packard Company
IBM®	International Business Machines Corporation
IBM® 5520	International Business Machines Corporation
IBM® LAN Network	International Business Machines Corporation
IBM PS/2® Mouse	International Business Machines Corporation
IMSI Mouse™	IMSI Inc.
Intel® Visual Edge	Intel Corporation
Kensington Expert Mouse	Kensington
Key Tronic® Mouse	Key Tronic Corporation
LaserWriter®	Apple Computer, Inc.
Logimouse®	Logitech, Inc.
Lotus® 1-2-3®	Lotus Development Corporation
Mace Utilities®	Paul Mace Software, Inc.
MailMerge®	MicroPro International Corporation
The Genius®	Micro Display Systems
Microsoft® Paint	Microsoft Corporation

Microsoft Mouse™	Microsoft Corporation
Microsoft® Windows	Microsoft Corporation
Microsoft® Word	Microsoft Corporation
Mouse Systems Mouse®	Mouse Systems Corporation
MSC Technology PC Mouse 2	Monolithic Systems Corporation
MultiMate®	Ashton-Tate
MultiMate Advantage™	Ashton-Tate
MultiMate Advantage II™	Ashton-Tate
NetWare®	Novell, Inc.
Notebook™	WordPerfect Corporation
Numonics Mouse	Numonics
PageMaker®	Aldus Corporation
PC-Net	Nokia
PC Paintbrush®	ZSoft, Inc.
PC Paint® Plus	Mouse Systems Corp.
PC-Trac Trackball	PC-Trac
PlanPerfect™	WordPerfect Corporation
PostScript®	Adobe Systems, Inc.
ProKey™	RoseSoft, Inc.
Publishers Paintbrush®	ZSoft, Inc.
Quietwriter®	International Business Machines Corporation
Repeat Performance™	
SideKick®	Borland International, Inc.
SpellStar™	MicroPro International Corporation
SYLK®	Microsoft Corporation
Texas Instruments® 855	Texas Instruments, Inc.
The Norton Utilities®	Peter Norton Computing, Inc.
Times®	Linotype Company
TOPS®	Sun Microsystems, Inc.

A

Absolute measurement, 34-35
Absolute tabs, 1031
Abstract, entering, 275, 278
Account, entering, 278
Add (+)
    math operator, 665
    table math operator, 1014
Addition, 71-73
Adjusting text for printing, 651, 782
Advance, 73-76, 738-739
    kerning character manually with, 76,
      1075-1076
AF (Attribute Off) conversion command, 195
Align
    character, 77
    in an equation, 326
    text, 76, 979
ALIGNC equation command, 326
ALIGNL equation command, 320, 326
Alignment, vertical, for a cell, 1009
ALIGNR equation command, 320, 326
.ALL file, 1105
ALT key, 23-24, 78-79
    displaying the menu bar with, 17, 817-818
    inserting bullets with, 124-125
    naming macros, 620, 622
ALT-= key combination, 17, 37-38, 816
ALTRNAT keyboard layout, 525, 536, 540
Alternating headers/footers, 478
Anchor type, graphics box, 419-420
Announcement, sample, 1094-1097
AO (Attribute On) conversion command, 195
Appearance, 79-80, 381
    page number, changing, 770
Append, 80-81 See also Move
"Are other copies. . .running?" message, 32-33,
  81-82
Arrow keys. See Cursor keys
Arrows, 330, 335
ASCII (DOS text) files, 83
    converting, 217
{ASSIGN} command, 1152-1154
Attribute Off (AF) conversion command, 195
Attribute On (AO) conversion command, 195
Attributes, 83-84
    activating, 49
    appearance, 381
    assigning to a block, 105-106

Attributes, continued
    assigning with a monochrome system,
      161, 164, 168, 169
    cell, 1007
    choosing screen appearance, 161-169,
      874-875
    displaying, 45
    size, 381
Author/Typist, 275, 277
Auto-Install. See Install
Auto reference. See Cross-References
AUTOEXEC.BAT file, 84-85
    checking by install, 8, 9-10, 32
Automatic font changes, 87-89, 383-384
    editing, 792, 1113-1115
Automatic formatting and rewrite, 86-87, 289
Automatic word wrap, 301

B

^B code, 385, 503, 766, 769, 770-772, 774
Background printing, 800
BACKSPACE, 90-91
    deleting text to the left, 53, 252
Backup, 91-95
    files, 18, 33
    location of directory files, 608
    manual, 93-94
    original, 92-95
    retrieving files, 93
    setup option, 18, 878
    timed, 91-95, 306, 608
Backward accent mark, 325
"Bad command or file name," 945
Banners, 95-96
Base font, 50, 96-97
    checking initial, in endnotes, 295
    initial, 271, 382-383, 503-505
    selecting, 139, 866
Baseline placement for typesetters, 97-98
BASIC, converting to decimal for printer
  commands, 811-812
Basic installation option, 7-9
Batch file, starting WordPerfect, 951
BC (Beginning Codes) conversion command,
  193-194
Beep options, 99-100, 306, 878
Beginning Codes (BC) conversion command,
  193-194
{BELL} macro command, 628, 1151, 1203

{BELL} merge command, 1151, 1203
Bibliographies
    style, 966
    See also Hanging indent
Bin Number (BN) conversion command, 193
Bin Paper (BP) conversion command, 195
Binding edge, 101-102, 781
Binding offset, 101, 102-103
Binding options, 100-103, 781
BINOM equation command, 325
Binomial, creating in an equation, 325
BINOMSM equation command, 325, 328
Bit-mapped image, 437
    inverting, 431
.BK! extension, 837
Blank lines, 91, 692
[BLine:Off] code, 98
[BLine:On] code, 98
Block (ALT-F4), 103-111
    append, 107
    assign attributes to, 105-106
    attach a style to, 106-107
    bold, 105
    center, 107-108
    change case of, 108
    check spelling of, 108, 919-920
    column, in any, 109
    copy, 106, 702-703
    define, 858
    delete, 106
    deleting text, 252
    edit with, 54-55
    flush right, 107-108
    with a mouse, 103-104, 713
    move, 106, 702-703
    print, 108, 794-795
    protect from page breaks, 107,
      111-113, 815
    rectangle, 109-110
    redefine, 110, 407
    replace codes, 108
    replace text, 108, 831
    retrieve an unnamed block, 106
    save an unnamed, 107, 708-709
    sort, 108-109, 900-901
    turned off after every block
      operation, 110
    underline, 105, 1048-1049
{Block Copy} macro command, 220
{Block Move} macro command, 220
Block protect, 111-113
    comparison to conditional end of
      page, 206

Block protect, *continued*
    keeping text together, 523
Blocks, moving, in a table, 1018-1020
BN (Bin Number) conversion command, 193
Boilerplating, 688
Bold (F6), 49, 113-117
BOLD equation command, 328
Boldface, 49, 114
Borders, 117-123, 1289-1290
    for equations, 344-345
    shadow, 886
Bottom margins, 650-651, 764-765
Boxed
    comment, 186
    text, 576, 1023
Boxes
    creating duplicate, 577
    moving, 709
BP (Bin Paper) conversion command, 195
Braces { } in an equation, 314, 323-324
Branching, 1160-1168
{BREAK} command, 1198-1199
Brochure, sample, 1097, 1098
BUFFERS command, 208
Built-in fonts, 136
Bullets, 123-125, 496
    outline numbering with, 744-745

C

Cache, memory, 734
Calculations. *See* Addition, Math, Tables
Calculator, WordPerfect Library, 662
Calendar, created with tables, 1026, 1027-1028
{CALL} command, 1159-1160
Cancel (F1), 27-28, 125-126
    hyphenation code [/], 486, 489-490
    with a mouse, 125, 714
    print job(s), 210
    restoring deleted text, 66, 703
    returning to your document from any
      menu, 36
{CANCEL OFF} macro command, 1200
{CANCEL OFF} merge command, 685, 1200
{CANCEL ON} command, 1200
Canon laser printer, 955
"Can't find correct copy of WP" message, 128
"Can't find end of table of contents, lists, or
    index text" message, 991-992, 998
Capitalization, 129-130
    changing a block, 108
Caps, small, displaying, 18

Captions, 130-133, 418-419
    number style, 130-131, 434
    position, 131, 434
Carriage return. *See* ENTER key
Cartridges, selecting, 134-140, 865
{CASE CALL} command, 1167-1168
{CASE} command, 1166-1167
Case-sensitive search, 856
[Cell] code, 1020
Cell, status line indicator, 34
Cells in tables
    attributes of, 1007
    joining a row, 1017-1018
    justification of, 1009
    locking, 1009-1010
    splitting a row, 1017-1018
    types of, 1007
    vertical alignment of, 1009
[Center] code, 145
Center page
    with hand-fed paper, 141
    from top to bottom, 140-143, 764
Center (SHIFT-F6), 46, 143-146, 147
    existing block, 107-108, 519-520
    over or under graphics box, 132-133
Centered tabs, 144-145
Centered text, 145
    creating dot leader for, 144, 284-285
    line draw around, 146
Centering a line, with a dot leader, 144
Centering text, 145
Centimeters, 145, 148
CGA monitor, selecting display colors, 161,
    163-165
CH (Character) conversion command, 193
{CHAIN} macro command, 1193-1194
{CHAIN MACRO} merge command, 1190
{CHAIN PRIMARY} merge command,
    1190-1191
{CHAIN SECONDARY} merge
    command, 1191
Change directory, 148-150
Chapter numbers, including in a list, 606
{CHAR} command, 1149-1150
Character (CH) conversion command, 193
Character map in Printer program, 1118
Character sets, 1219-1224
Characters
    added to Character Set 10, 1291
    per inch, 150-151
    inserting into an equation, 329
Checklist, created with Tables, 1023, 1024

CHKDSK/F (DOS command), 224, 281, 891
    deleting lost clusters, 65
Clean screen, 35-37
Clear tabs. *See* Tabs
Clipboard, retrieving text from, 840, 890-891
Clusters, lost, 65
[CNTR TAB] code, 145
Code page number, 946
Codes, 40-42, 151-160
    deleting, 67, 91, 255-258
    deleting with replace, 257, 834
    entering in Printer program, 1125-1126
    hard, 42
    initial, 20, 271, 505-507, 511
    inserting, 676
    language, 560-562
    list of, 152-160
    macro for editing, 1135
    replace in a block, 108
    replacing one code with another, 832-833
    replacing with macros, 638-640, 833
    searching for, 256-257, 857-858
    soft, 42
    turning on/off, 41
Col, 34
[Col Off] code, 112, 176
[Col On] code, 112, 176
Color
    codes, on template, 404
    monitor, adjusting bold, 116
    selections for EGA and VGA, 874
Colors
    not holding, 168-169
    printing, 169-171
Colors/fonts/attributes
    changing, 18
    selecting, 161-169, 874
Column separator (&) in an equation, 325
Columns, 171-185
    changing the number of, 178
    converting parallel, into a table, 178-179
    copying tabular, 109
    drawing lines between, 177
    entering text in, 175
    gutter space between, 173
    increasing the speed of working with,
        177-178
    limitations, 179
    moving, 178
    moving between, 175, 176, 485
    moving cursor in, 235
    moving tabular, 109

Columns, *continued*
    moving without [Tab] codes, 709
    newspaper, 172-174
    parallel, 112, 173-174, 181, 788
    turning on and off, 174-175, 177
Columns and tables, 1021
Columns display, side-by-side, turning on/off, 290-291
Columns in a table
    adding/deleting, 1005-1006
    changing the size of, 1001, 1004-1005
    moving, 1018-1020
    number of digits in, 1010
    width of, 1010
Columns, tabular
    copying, 182, 703-706
    moving, 182, 703-706
COM port, selecting for a serial printer, 791, 863-865
.COM, reserved filename extension, 282
Command, reassigning to a key, 530-531
COMMAND.COM, 891
Commands, conversion, 192-196
Commands, equation editor, 315-329
Commands, macro, 624, 626, 1143-1215
Commands, merge, 1143-1215
[Comment] code, 187
{;} comment command, 1143-1144
{COMMENT} merge command, 1144
Comments, 185-188
    boxed, 186
    creating, 185, 1036
    changing to text, 186
    displaying, 289
    inserting in macros, 630
    searching for, 187
Common word list, 934
Compare
    deleting text marked for strikeout, 189-190
    documents, 188-190
    phrase by phrase, 189
    removing the redline markings, 189-190
Compatibility, 191-196
Compose (CTRL-2), 196-201
    creating characters, 759-760
    entering bullet characters, 123
Computer, turning off, 70
Concordance, 201-205
    creating, 498-499
    sorting, 204-205
Conditional
    end of page, 113, 205-208, 523, 739

Conditional, *continued*
    end of page macro, 207
    macros, 632
Conditions in the Find menu, 372-374
CONFIG.SYS file, 208
    checking by Install, 8, 9-10
Context-Sensitive help, 482-483
Continuous underline, 1049
Control printer, 209-213, 794, 952-954
Conversion commands, 192-196
Conversion (.CRS) file, 192
Convert program, 213-218
    converting file to seven-bit format, 699-700
    transferring data from other word processors, 1288
Converting
    4.2 to 5.1, 191-194, 216-217
    5.0 to 5.1, 13-14
    5.1 to 4.2, 194-196
    keys, characters, and numbers, 1203-1210
    multiple files, 196
Copies, multiple, printing, 722-723
Copies, number of, 735-736
Copy, 218-221
    block, 106, 701-710
    document, 220-221
    files in List Files, 221-222
    page, 701-702
    paragraph, 701-702
    sentence, 701-702
    shortcut with enhanced keyboard, 703
    text, 54
    with unnamed block method, 707
COPY (DOS) command, 222
Copy installation option, 13
Count words. *See* Word count
COUNTRY (DOS) command, 947
/CP (Code Page) startup option, 946-947
Create Summary on Save/Exit, 273
Creation date, 277
Cross-References, 225-229, 653
Crossword puzzle
    created with tables, 1028
    solving with look up, 929
.CRS (conversion resource) file, 192
{CTON} merge command, 1209
CRTL (control key), 23-24, 229-232
    combinations, list of, 230-231
    moving the cursor with, 234
    naming macros, 622
CTRL-2 (Compose), 197
    accessing master character set, 915

CTRL-6, return to original keyboard, 534-535, 949, 1293

CTRL-ALT-DEL, reboot, 70

CTRL-BACKSPACE, delete word at cursor, 28, 53, 90, 252

CTRL-BREAK, stopping a merge, 685

CTRL-DEL for move shortcut, 106, 219, 703

CTRL-END, 53, 252

CTRL-ENTER (Hard page break), 28
   inserting a special character in equations, 311-312

CTRL-HOME (Go to), go to any page, 775

CTRL-INS
   for copy shortcut, 703
   inserting a new row, 1006

CTRL-M, inserting carriage return [CR] code, 694

CTRL-PGDN, 53, 252

CTRL-PGUP, 531
   displaying list of macro commands, 623, 626
   during macro definition, 621
   pausing a macro, 627

CTRL-V, 197
   editing keyboard layout, 530-531, 540
   entering functions into a macro, 623, 626, 1132
   inserting a regular hard return in outline, 743, 747
   in normal editing screen, 915

Cursor, 33

Cursor keys, 233-237

Cursor movement, 51-52, 233-236
   in line draw, 575-576
   macros, 637-638
   with a mouse, 233, 714
   over a code, 41-42
   to original position, 236, 831
   shortcuts, 219-220, 703, 1002-1003
   in tables, 235, 1002-1003

Cursor speed, 237-238, 306, 878-879
   increasing, 236

CURSOR.COM program, 232-233

Custom installation option, 9-11

Cut text and columns. *See* Move

D

/D (Divert) startup option, 947, 1069

^D merge code, 242, 243

Daggers, printing, 297

Dashes, 238-240, 493
   em, 238-239, 1081
   en, 238-239, 1081

Dashes, *continued*
   single, 239
   double, 239

Dashed line, 577

Data bits, setting, for serial printer, 864

Data validation, 1155-1157

DataPerfect, 695

Date, 240-243
   changing format, 240-241, 881
   creation, 277
   inserting, 240
   inserting during a merge, 242
   inserting language code, 243
   sorting by, 911

Date and time
   entering in DOS, 241-242
   viewing, 243

DATE (DOS) command, 242

{DATE} merge command, 242, 243, 683, 1146

Date/Outline (SHIFT-F5), 240

dBASE files, converting, 244-246

dBASE report, using in WordPerfect, 245

.DBF, dBASE extension, 244

DCA (Document Content Architecture) format, 246-248

Dead key, 196

Debugging, 1202-1203

Decimal/Align character, changing, 248-249, 739, 979

Decimal Tabs, 249-251
   aligning with, 76-77
   hard, 980
   setting, 250

[DEC TAB] code, 250-251, 666, 980

[Dec Tab] code, 980, 981

Default answer, in a menu, 39

Default document type, 19-20, 274

Default directory, 251-252, 849
   changing, 148-150
   location of, 608-609
   specifying, 65

Default settings, 44

Default setup options, returning to, 884, 885

DEL key
   deleting text at cursor, 53, 252
   (DOS) command, 259

Deletable soft return code [DSRt], 302, 493

Delete, 52-53, 252-253
   all files in a directory, 254
   block, 91, 106
   codes, 255-258
   directory, 64, 254-255
   to end of line, 28

Delete, *continued*
    to end of page, 29
    files, 64, 258-259
    footnote, 387
    word, 28
Deleted text, restoring, 126, 703, 709, 835
Delimiter, 693-694
    field, 213-214
    record, 213-214
Delimiter, no, 327
Delimiters, left and right, in an equation, 318-319
Descriptive filenames, 1246
Desktop publishing terms, 1072-1082
Diacritical marks, 197-198
Dictionary
    adding hyphenated words to, 494
    adding words, 927, 931-932
    changing, 930-931
    combining 5.0 and 5.1, 935
    converting 4.2 to 5.1, 934-935
    creating, 930-931
    deleting words, 927, 933
    extract added words from, 936
    optimizing, 933
    personal, 926-927
    supplementary, 920-921, 935-936, 974
Dictionary, foreign, 926-927
"Dictionary full" message, 928
DIF (Data Interchange Format), 216, 260-261
Digraphs, 198-199
DIP switches, 117, 803
Directories, 261-263
    changing, 148-150
    creating, 223-224, 607-608
    deleting, 64, 254-255
    location of default, 608-609
    looking into, 617-618
    organizing, 594
    parent, 262, 594
    root, 261, 367, 594
Directory, default, 251-252
    change, 148, 849
    names, 223
    specifying, 65
Disk
    printing to, 700-701, 808-809
    space, 264-266
    switching, 46
Disk drives, running WordPerfect 5.1 with, 31-32
"Disk full" message, 62, 263-264
Disk space requirements, 3-4

Display
    character for hard return, 469-471
    pitch, 266-268, 270-271
    print jobs, 210-211, 268-269
    short/long, 64, 274, 276, 596-597
    in setup, 874-877
    special characters, 916-917
{DISPLAY OFF} macro command, 628, 1195-1196
{DISPLAY ON} macro command, 1195-1196
Display window, in equations, 309
DisplayWrite files (FFT), converting to Word-Perfect, 215
DisplayWrite 4 command conversion table, 1286-1288
Divert (/D) startup option, 947
Divide (/), math operator, 665
    table math operator, 1014
"Divide overflow" message, 269-270
Document
    copying, 220-221
    creating, 47-65
    editing, 287-288
    filing, 368-369
    format, 270-272, 399, 400
    formatted for current printer, 510-511
    formatting for the default printer, 510-511
    header, 272, 504, 506
    load. *See* Retrieve
    location of, 609
    locking, 610-612, 852
    moving cursor to edges of, 235, 485
    name, 277
    names, long, 273-274, 276, 612-615, 850
    original, backup, 92-95
    prefix, 271, 365-366, 504, 506
    printing from the screen, 793-794
    retrieving, 69
    saving, 62, 848-849
    scrolling through, with a mouse, 714
    size, 46, 68, 279
    unlocking, 610-612
    See also Documents
Document Management/Summary options, 18-20, 272-278, 306-307, 879
{DOCUMENT} merge command, 1189-1190
"Document may need to be generated" message, 799
Document Summary, 271, 853
    creating, 274-275
    deleting, 278

Document Summary, *continued*
    editing, 274-275
    entering the long document name,
      613-614
    fields, capturing, 277
    printing, 278
    saving, 278
    searching to find a file, 370
    See also Document Management/
      Summary
Document type, 277
    default, 19-20, 274
Documents
    comparing, 188-190
    condensing *See* Master document
    editing, 287-288, 640
    merging, 684-685
    switching between, 55
    See also Document
Dormant hard return [Dorm HRt] code, 207,
    301-302, 468-469, 1248
DOS
    extended error codes, 354
    Go to, 280, 407-409
    return from, 280, 891
    and WordPerfect messages, 354-355
DOS CHKDSK command, 224, 281
DOS command, executing a, 280-281
DOS COPY command, 13
    backing up files with, 94
DOS DATE command, 242
DOS DEL command, 259
DOS ERASE command, 259
DOS MD command, 224
DOS RD command, 254-255
DOS RENAME command, 828, 829
DOS text (ASCII) file, 281-283
    editing, 283
    field and record delimiters, changing, 509
    margins, changing for, 649
    merge, using in, 693-694
    retrieving, 282
    saving, 281-282
    saving a file as, 700, 851
    saving document with style codes
      as a, 963
    saving style text and codes, 758
DOS text printer definition, printing to disk
    with, 807, 808
DOS TYPE command, 612
DOS version, determining, 128
Dot leader
    centering a line with, 144
    flush-right a line with a, 377
    inserting, 250, 283-285, 1030, 1032

Double click interval, changing, 719
Double-clicking to select, with a mouse, 713
Double dash, 239
Double-sided printing, 781
Double underlining, 285-286, 1050
    with addition, 73
Double words, 923
Downloadable fonts, path for, 789, 866
Downloading fonts. *See* Initialize printer
Drawing lines around centered text, 146
Drawing lines and boxes. *See* Line draw,
    Graphics boxes, Tables
DrawPerfect, 416
Drive, default, changing, 849
Drivers
    graphics screen, 455
    mouse, 4-5, 16
    text, 1246
Drop cap, creating with a graphics box, 441
[DSRt] (Deletable soft return), 302, 493
DXF graphics format, 456

E

^E merge code, 1211
Edit-Screen options, 288-291, 877
Editing speed, increasing, 289
EEMS 3.2, 363
EGA monitors
    displaying additional characters, 874, 916
    selecting text modes, 161-166, 1246
EHANDLER.PS file, 791
{ELSE} command, 1165, 1168
Em dash, 238-239, 301, 492, 1081
En dash, 238-239, 301, 1081
Encrypting a file. *See* Password file protection
{END FIELD} merge code, 677, 905, 910
{END FOR} command, 1173-1174
{END IF} command, 1165
END key, 291-292
{END RECORD} merge code, 677, 910
{END RECORD} merge command, 1211
{END WHILE} command, 1176
Endnotes, 292-300
    changing to footnotes, 300
    creating in columns, 298
    placement, 502
    referencing, 229
    searching for, 298-299
    spacing, 295-296, 914
Enhanced keyboard, 51, 536, 540
    copy/move shortcuts, 219, 703, 1002-1003
    key assignments, 541-542, 637-638, 1145
    moving between columns with, 175

ENTER key, 300-302
  inserting a new outline number, 747
  options in a style, 967-968
  saving an "unnamed" block in memory
    with, 107
  turning off a style, 960-961
  when to press, 47-48, 67
Envelopes, 302-305
  creating, with a simple merge, 685-686
Environment file, WP{WP}.ENV, 11-12
Environment, setup (SHIFT-F1), 305-308, 877-880
[Equ Opt], 343
Equation commands, 315-329
Equation editor, 309, 311, 352-353, 1244
  making selections with a mouse, 714-715
Equation keyboard, 536-537, 540
  layout, 339-341
Equations, 308-353
  applications of, 345-353
  borders, 344-345
  creating, 310-312
  entering, 313-315
  examples, 350-352
  inserting new line, 313
  inserting spaces, 313
  keyboard for editing, 510
  list of common structures, 345-349
  location, 344-345
  operators, 314-315
  option code [Equ Opt], 343
  printing, 341-342
  retrieving, 345
  retrieving into a graphics box, 416, 418
  saving, 345
  setup, 342-344, 509-510, 881
Erase. *See* Delete
ERASE (DOS command), 259
Error checking in macros and merges,
  1199-1202
"ERROR: File not found—KEYS.MRS", 535
"ERROR: Incorrect format" in an
  equation, 312
"ERROR: Margins overlap", 648
Error messages, 32-33, 354-355, 798-799
"ERROR: Too many lines" in a header or footer, 477-478
ESC key, 355-358
  changing the repeat value, 30
  escaping from any menu except Help, 30
  hyphenation decision, 488
  moving the cursor with, 234
  moving through a document, 357
  repeating macros with, 630, 829

ESC key, *continued*
  using in replace, 830-831
Escape sequences, printer commands
  listed as, 811
Excel, importing from, 358-359, 937
.EXE, reserved filename extension, 282
Exit (F7), 359-360
  turning hyphenation off temporarily, 489
  using, to save, 62, 850
  WordPerfect, 65-66
Exit, returning from DOS, 891
Expanded memory, 361-363, 735, 1292
Expressions, 1137-1138
Extended memory, 361, 735
Extended search (HOME, F2), 477, 485-486, 855-856
Extended search/replace, 363, 830
Extensions, reserved filenames, 282
Extra large print, 363-365

F

Families, move, copy, or delete in outlines,
  745-746
Fast Save, 307, 365-366, 797, 852, 879
Features, alphabetized list of, displayed in
  Help (F3), 26-27
FF (Font Off) conversion command, 192-193
Field delimiters, 213, 509
{FIELD} merge command, 683-684, 1211-1212
{FIELD NAMES} merge command, 680-682,
  691, 1212
  in a merge file, 677, 679
Figures, 366-367
"File creation error" message, 62, 367-368
File, language resource, 243, 392
File macros, 619-622
  editing, 625
"File not found - WP{WP}US.THS", 1043
Filename
  displaying, on the status line, 290
  finding, 369-370
  retrieving, into a graphics box, 416
Filenames
  descriptive, 1246
  long and short, 368
Files
  ASCII text, 83
  backup, 18, 33
  converting 4.2, to 5.1, 191-194, 216-217,
    1262-1263
  converting 5.1, to 4.2, 194-196
  converting multiple, 196
  copying, in list files, 221-222, 598

Files, *continued*
    created by WordPerfect, 1236-1238
    deleting, 64, 258-259, 595-596
    destroying, 36
    finding, 369-374, 598-599
    5.0, using, 21-22
    installed to hard drive, 1229-1233
    installed to 720k floppy disks, 1233-1236
    listed by master disk, 1225-1228
    location of, 20-21, 606-610
    looking at, 597, 615-618
    marking, 65, 595
    moving, 596
    overflow, 46, 81-82, 819
    renaming, 596, 828-829
    retrieving, 64, 595, 836
    searching for, 859
    sorting, 900
    temporary, 81-82
    virtual, 3-4
    WordPerfect, 1225-1238
FILES=20, in CONFIG.SYS file, 208
Filing documents, 62-65, 368-369
Final-Form-Text, IBM DCA format,
   214-215, 246
Find
    conditions, 372-374
    files, 369-374
Fine print, 374-375
5.0 files, using, 21-22
5.0 printer definition, converting from 5.0 to
   5.1, 13-14
512 characters, choosing to display, 18
Fixed line height. *See* Line height
Flush right, 375-378
    aligning text, 77
    block, 107-108
    caption, 133
    right justifying existing text, 519
    text, creating dot leader for, 284-285
FO (Font On) conversion command, 192
Font
    library, 136
    outline, 741-742
    type, changing, 779-780
Font changes, automatic, 87-89, 383-384
Font equation option, 343-344
Font (FT) conversion command, 195
Font Off (FF) conversion command, 192-193
Font On (FO) conversion command, 192
Fonts, 378-385, 1073-1074
    changes 4.2 to 5.1, 1257-1258
    changing, 50

Fonts, *continued*
    copying, 14-15, 1122-1124
    downloadable, 789, 866
    outline, 792
    RAM, 45
    scaling, 791
    selecting, 15-16, 134-140, 379-382, 865
    selecting substitute, 1115-1118
    shadow, 792
    size and type displayed, 161-169
    soft, 138, 791, 865
    swapping, 136
    updating, 15
Footers, 385-386, 472-479, 1088
    spacing, 914
Footnotes, 386-394
    changing all, to endnotes, 298, 299
    protecting, 112
    referencing, 229
    referencing more than one on a page, 974
    spacing, 389, 914
{FOR EACH} macro command, 1172-1173
{FOR} command, 1170-1172
Force, odd/even page, 394-395, 764
Foreign languages, 396, 739
Form letters and forms fill-in. *See* Merge
Format, 396-402
    document, 270-272
    matrix, in an equation, 325-326
    menu, 37
Format (SHIFT-F8), 57-58
Format and rewrite, automatically, 86-87, 289
Format: Other, 737-741
    menu, 121
Format retrieved documents for default
   printer, 510-511
Forms. *See* Paper size/type
Formula in a table, 1014
Fraction
    creating in an equation, 315
    conversion to decimal equivalent of, 1056
FROM equation command, 316, 317-318
FT (Font) conversion command, 195
/F2 startup option, 948
Full form, 985, 989-991
Full justification, 68, 520-522
FUNC (Function) equation command,
   322, 338, 353
Function keys, 403-404
    changes from 4.2 to 5.1, 1252-1253
    help message for each, 26-27
    in Printer program, 1109-1110, 1111
    template, 23-25

Function, user, in an equation, 322
Functions
    inserting into an equation, 329
    mathematical, 330, 338

G

ˆG merge code, 1190
Generate, 404
    index, 500-501
    in mark text, 654-655
Generic
    file, saving, 1035
    format, saving, 191, 851
Genius monitor, 1246
Global
    search and replace. *See* Replace
    select, 908-909
    variables, 1136
Go, sending printer a, 211-212, 462
{GO} macro command, 1158-1159, 1169-1170
{GO} merge command, 690, 1158-1159,
    1169-1170
Go to (CTRL-HOME), 30, 405-407, 485
    block, beginning of, 406
    character, 406
    in columns, 405-408
    DOS, 407-409
    original position, 406
    page, 44, 66, 405, 761-762, 775
    resetting graphics image, 429
    shell, 407-409
    (twice), 110, 406, 831, 856
GRAB.COM, 456-458, 460-461
Grand total math operator, 668
GRAPHCNV.EXE (Graphics Conversion
    utility), 456-457, 458-460
Graphic styles, location of, 609
Graphical font size, changing for
    equations, 343
Graphics, 1249
    printing, 437-438
    in styles, 441-443, 968
    and text, combining, 439-440
Graphics box options, table of, 414-415
Graphics boxes, 409-443, 1079-1080, 1091-1092
    anchor type, 419-420
    assigning a new number to, 413-414
    border style, 117-119, 431-433
    caption, 130-133, 418-419
    caption number style, 130-131, 434
    caption position, 131, 434
    changing the options, 414

Graphics boxes, *continued*
    contents of, 417-418
    creating, 411-412, 413
    definition menu, 132
    drop cap, creating, 441
    editing, 412, 425
    editing a graphics image, 427
    full-page, 468
    horizontal position of, 422-423
    inside border space, 433
    lists, defining, 438-439
    minimum offset from top of
        paragraph, 435
    numbering, 433
    outside border space, 433
    protecting, 112-113
    rotating graphics image, 427-429, 430
    rotating text, 426-427
    scaling graphics image, 427, 429
    shading, 435, 1089-1090
    size of, 423-425
    tables, including, 436-437
    vertical position of, 420-422
    wrapping text around, 425
    wrapping text up to uneven graphics
        image, 439
Graphics conversion utility, 456-457
Graphics equation option, 342
Graphics formats
    converted by GRAPHCNV, 458
    table of, 417
Graphics images, 1265-1267
    inverting, 431
    mirror image of, 430
    moving, 427, 429
    printing into a graphics box, 418
    resetting, 429
    retrieving into a graphics box, 416
    rotating, 427-429, 430
    scaling, 427, 429
    types of, 437
Graphics lines, 444-453, 576-577, 1077-1079,
    1092-1094
    horizontal, 444-448, 449, 450, 452-453
    length of, 449
    shading, 450
    vertical, 444-446, 448-449, 450-451
    vertical, placing between columns,
        183-184
    width of, 449
Graphics on disk, 418, 456
Graphics quality option, 798, 820-821
    effect on printing special characters, 201

Graphics screen drivers, 455
Graphics screen type, 454-455, 875
Graphics utilities, 456-461
Grave, backward accent mark, 325
Gray shading, 450
Greek symbols, 330, 334
Group, designating in an equation, 323-324
Gutter space
    between columns, 173
    between labels, 549

H

Halo effect, 435
Hand-fed paper, 462-463
Hanging indent, 48, 49, 463-465, 497
Hanging paragraph, 463-465, 497
    style, creating, 464-465
Hard codes, 42
Hard disk, starting WordPerfect 5.1 with, 32,
    945-946
Hard hyphen, 239, 466-467, 486, 493
Hard page (CTRL-ENTER), 28, 467-468
    inserting, 760, 899
Hard page break code [HPg], 42, 43, 760, 857
Hard return, 300, 301, 468-469
    code [HRt], 42, 300, 301
    display character, 290, 469-471
    dormant, 301-302, 1248
    searching, 857
Hard space, 471-472, 486, 911
    [] code, 471-472
Hard tabs, 486-487, 981, 1032-1033
Hardware handshaking, 790, 864
Header for subsequent pages in a table, 1013
Headers, 472-480, 764, 1086
    including in a paired style, 971-972
    spacing, 914
Headings
    equation option, 343
    index, marking in a concordance, 203
    style, 1084-1085
Headword, 1041
Help (F3), 25-27, 480-484
    context-sensitive, 482-483, 1247
    displaying interim release date, 1289
    entering registration number, 483
    exiting, 484
    pressing twice for template, 403
    in Printer program, 1109, 1110
Hercules card with RamFont
    appearance of Block with a, 104

Hercules card with RamFont, *continued*
    choosing mnemonic font choice in menus,
      673-674
    displaying additional characters, 916-917
    extra large font, 364
    fine print, 375
    selecting screen fonts, 874-875
Hercules Graphics Card Plus, 45
    selecting text modes, 162-167
Hercules InColor Card, 45
    foreground/background colors setup, 116,
      162, 167
Hidden codes. *See* Codes
Hidden text. *See* Comments
Highlighting text, 105, 484
HMI. *See* Horizontal motion index
HOME, *, marking all files, 796
HOME key, 29-30, 485-487
    moving the cursor with, 234
HOME, BACKSPACE, 28, 53, 90, 252
HOME, DEL, 53, 252
HOME, HOME, inserting a dot leader, 284
HOME, HYPHEN, 466
HOME-TAB, inserting a regular tab in outline, 747
Horizontal graphics line, 444-448, 449, 450,
    452-453
Horizontal motion index (HMI)
    adjusting for proportional spacing, 814
    for justification, 520-522
Horizontal movement in an equation, 324
HORZ equation command, 324
[HPg] code, 760
[Hrd Row] code, 1021
[HRt] code, 42, 300, 468-469
[HRt-SPg] code, 468, 899
Hyphen, hard/soft, 31, 237, 466-467, 486, 493
    required, 466
Hyphen, using as a wildcard character, 60
Hyphenated words, adding to the dictionary,
    494, 932-933
Hyphenation, 487-494, 579, 928, 1089
    cancel, code [/], 126, 486, 489-490
    dictionary-based, 307, 1247
    files, location of, 608-609
    rules, internal, 307
    setting up, 307, 488-489, 879
    turning on/off, 488, 489
    with two disk drives, 494
    zone, 490-492

I

IBM DCA format, Revisable-Form-Text/Final-
    Form-Text, 214-215

{IF BLANK} merge command, 1163
{IF EXISTS} command, 1162-1163
{IF} command, 1161-1162
{IF NOT BLANK} merge command, 1163-1165
Inches, 495
Indent, 48-49, 495-497
    hanging, 463-465, 497
    left, 569
    quotations, 496-497
    right, 844
    temporary margins, 649
    using tab, 982
Index, 497-503
    creating an, entry with flush right, 378
    marking entries, 498-499, 653, 656
    page numbers in, 731-732
Initial base font, 382-383, 503-505
    changing, 505
    changing, for a single document, 271
    selecting, 139, 504, 866
    storing, 504-505
Initial codes, 20, 271, 505-507
    changing, 881-882
    storing, 506
Initial Pitch (IP) conversion command, 194
Initial Settings, 507-513, 880-882
    changes 4.2 to 5.1, 1259
    changing, for a document, 511
Initialize printer, 513-514
    downloading soft fonts, 797
Inline macro, 1292
{INPUT} macro command, 1148-1149
{INPUT} merge command, 687, 1148-1149
INS key, 514-515
    changing increment in a graphics box, 429
    switching between typeover and insert,
        47, 1045
    type over existing text, 514-515
Insert mode, 514-515
Install, 515-516, 1246-1247
    program, 6-13, 859
Interface changes 5.0 to 5.1, 1239-1242
Interim releases, 13, 1289
Invisible soft return code [ISRt], 301, 486, 492
Invoice, created with Tables, 1023-1025, 1027
IP (Initial Pitch) conversion command, 194
[ISRt] (Invisible soft return), 301, 486, 492
ITAL equation command, 328
Italics, 516-518
    choosing to display, 18
    in an equation, 328

J

Job list, printer, 799-800
Join a row of cells, 1017
[Just:Center] code, 107, 144, 520
[Just:Full] code, 520
[Just:Left] code, 520
[Just:Right] code, 107, 377, 520
Justification, 518-522, 579, 1248-1249
    aligning text, 77-78
    cells and columns, 1009
    full, 68, 520-522
    left, changing to, 507
    on, 520
    spacing, 493-494, 1066-1067

K

Kerning, 523-525, 813-814, 1075-1076, 1118-
    1122
    manually with Advance Left and
        Right, 76
KERN.TST file, 1122
Key
    creating/editing, 530-534
    in sorting, 903
Key macros. *See* Keyboard layout macros
Keyboard
    copying, 535, 539
    creating, 526-527, 528
    deleting, 535
    deselecting, 1293
    editing, 526-527, 528
    editing in equations, 510
    enhanced, 541-542, 637-638, 1145
    enhanced, copy shortcut, 219, 703
    renaming, 535
    returning to original with CTRL-6,
        534-535
    selecting, 525-526, 1293
Keyboard layout, 525-545, 1249
    selecting, 339, 525-526
    using to enter equations, 339-341
Keyboard layout macros, 619-620, 622-625
    defining, 622-624
    editing, 625
    starting, 625
Keyboard layouts provided with version 5.1,
    536-544
        ALTRNAT, 536, 540
        ENHANCED, 536, 540
        EQUATION, 536-537, 540
        MACROS, 537-538, 540

Keyboard layouts with version 5.1, *continued*
    SHORTCUT, 538-539, 540, 541, 543-544
Keyboard/Macro files, location of, 608
Keyboard mapping, 526-530
{KEYBOARD} merge command, 696, 1147
Keyboards
    combining keys from several, 539-540
    provided by WordPerfect, 536, 540-542
    WordPerfect 5.0, 544
Keypad, numeric, 233
Keys
    entering, 905-906
    function, 23-25, 26-27
    repeating, 23, 356-357
KEYS.MRS, 535
Keyword, inserting in an equation, 311-312
Keywords, entering, 278
{KTON} macro command, 1210

L

{LABEL} macro command, 1158, 1169-1170
{LABEL} merge command, 690, 1158, 1169-1170
Labels, 545-558
    centering text on, 552
    creating, with merge, 685-686
    defining, 546-550, 781
    height, 547
    macro, 552-554
    margins, 550
    new feature in 5.1, 1244-1245
    number of, 548-549
    printing, 552
    selecting, 550-551
    size, 548
    using merge with, 554-555
    width, 547
LABELS.WPM, 553-554
Landscape printing, 558-560, 737, 779-780
Languages, 560-565, 739
    skip, 897
    codes, 560-562
    resource file (WP.LRS), 243, 392, 560-561, 563-565
Large print, 565-566
Laser printers
    Canon, 955
    hand feeding, 462-463
    nonprintable regions, 647
Last name, sorting by, 911
LBRACE equation command, 328
Leading, line height adjustment, 567-569, 1076-1077

Leaving WordPerfect, 569
Left delimiters, 318-319
LEFT equation command, 318-319, 321-322
Left-handed mouse, 720
Left indent, 48, 569
Left Margin Release (SHIFT-TAB), 31, 569-570, 649, 982
    moving back to previous outline level, 743
Left margin, tabs set relative to, 1031
Left margins, 647-650
Left/Right indent, 48
Legal outline numbering, 744
{LEN} command, 1155-1156
Letter spacing, 571, 1063-1065, 1074-1075
Letterhead, 571-572, 573, 1097, 1099
Libraries, font, 136
LIBRARY.STY, 450
    sample style library, 965-967
License number, entering, 9, 10-11, 26
LIM (Lotus/Intel/Microsoft) specifications, 361, 362
LIM 3.2 (/32) startup option, 1292
Limits, indicating, in an equation, 316, 317-318
Line
    breaks, 384
    deleting to the end of (CTRL-END), 28
    flush-right, 376
    graphics, 444-453
    inserting a new, in an equation, 313
    per inch. *See* Line height
    status, 33-34
Line draw, 572-577
    around centered text, 146
    character, changing, 574-575
    combining with text, 577
    copying a box created with, 709
    erasing, 575
    moving a box created with, 709
    moving the cursor, 575-576
    selecting, 854
    using with bold, 116
Line format, 397, 398, 401, 578-581
Line height, 579-580, 581-583, 1076-1077
    setting fixed, 583
Line numbering, 580, 583-589
    counting lines, 584, 587, 589
    spacing limitations, 585-586
    view, 585
Line sort, 903-904, 909-910
Line spacing, 580, 913-914
    changing for special elements, 914
    vertical, in an equation, 328-329

Lines
    counting with line numbering, 587, 589
    dashed, 577
    drawing between columns, 177
    eliminating blank, in merge, 692
    graphics, 444-453, 576-577
    multiple, flush-right, 376
    numbering automatically, 787-788
    per inch. *See* Line height
    in a table, 1011-1013
    vertical, placing between columns,
      183-184
LINESPACE equation command, 328-329
Link to a spreadsheet, 942-943
List Files, 590-601
    change default drive, 597-598
    changing search direction, 1293
    copy, 598
    delete, 595-596
    determine default directory, 66
    display, changing, 600-601
    file information, 594-595
    find a specific file, 598-599
    look, 597
    manage files, 63-65
    menu, 279
    move/rename, 596
    name search, 599-600
    options, 595-600
    print, 62, 596
    rename a file, 828-829
    retrieve a document, 47, 220-221, 595
    short/long display, 596-597
List menu, 39, 603-604
Lists, 601-606
    defining page numbering, 602-604
    generating, 604-605
    including section or chapter numbers, 606
    marking the text, 602
    marking entries, 655
    page numbers in, 731-732
Literal (\) equation command, 313, 328
[Ln Num:On], 585
[Ln Num:Off], 585
{LOCAL} merge command, 1154
Location of
    equations, 344-345
    files, 606-610, 883
Lock
    a cell, 1009-1010
    documents, 610-612
Locked file, retrieving, 611, 838

Logical operators, 1138-1142
Logical page, 555
Long display, 64, 614
Long document names, 19, 273-274, 276, 612-
    615, 850
LONGDIV equation command, 1291-1292
LONGDIVS (straight) equation command,
    1291-1292
Look
    at a file, 615-618
    in list files, 64-65
    up a word. *See* Spell (CTRL-F2), Spell
      program
{LOOK} command, 1154-1155
Looping, 1168-1176
Lost clusters, 65
Lotus/Intel/Microsoft (LIM) specifications,
    361, 362
Lowercase text. *See* Switch
LPT port, 863

M

/M (Macro) startup option, 948
Mace Utilities, undeleting a file, 1047
Macro Commands (CTRL-PGUP), 1132
    accessing, 1130-1132
    descriptions of, 1143-1215
Macro Def (CTRL-F10), toggling between two entry
    modes, 626
Macro editor, 625-626, 1132
    control characters, 1215-1217
    entering commands, 626
    entering immediately, 621
    line draw in, with WordPerfect
      Library, 1218
    screen, 623
Macro Library
    creating, 640-644
    running, 644
Macro prompts, appearance of, 1215-1217
Macro to create conditional end of page, 207
MACROCNV.EXE, 619, 634-636
    start options, 635-636
Macros, 619-645
    assigning a file, to a key, 533
    assigning to key, 531
    assigning value to a variable, 629-630
    block shortcuts with, 1144-1145
    chaining, 630-631
    changes 4.2 to 5.1, 1261-1262
    commands, 624, 626, 1143-1215
    comments in, 630

Macros, *continued*
  conditional, 632
  converting 4.2 macros to 5.1,
    634-636, 1262
  cursor shortcuts, 1144-1145
  date, inserting, 1146
  defining, 620-624
  defining with a mouse, 721
  displaying, 628-629
  documenting, 1143-1144
  editing, 625-626
  editing documents, 640
  entering functions into a macro, 623
  file, 542, 544, 619-622
  key, 542, 544, 619-620, 622-625
  key definition, saving to a file macro, 533
  location of files, 633
  nested, 631, 632
  for moving the cursor, 637-638
  page numbers in, 771
  pausing, 627-628
  positioning on the screen, 1217-1218
  repeating, 357-358, 630
  for replacing codes, 638-640
  retrieving, 622
  searching in, 858
  starting, 622, 625
  turning on styles with, 963
Macros and merge, differences between, 644-
  645, 696-697, 1129-1135
MACROS keyboard layout, 537-538, 540
MACROS.WPK keyboard file, 303
Mail merge, 645-646
  transfer format, 216
Mailing labels. *See* Labels
Main menu, list files menu similar to, 67
Manual backup, 93-94
Mapping the keyboard. *See* Keyboard layout
Margin Bias (MB) conversion command, 194
Margin release. *See* Left margin release
Margins
  bottom and top, 650-651, 764-765
  center text between, 143
  label, 550
  left and right, 580, 647-650
  release, 31
  temporary, using indent for, 649
  top and bottom, 650-651, 764-765
Mark files, 222, 595
Mark text, 651-657
  all files, 595, 796
  backing up files with, 94
  with Block Off, 652

Mark text, *continued*
  index, lists, table of contents, 108
Master disks, files, 1225-1228
Master document, 657-661
  cross references in several documents
    with, 228
  index, creating for several documents, 502
  pages, numbering in, 732-733
MATFORM equation command, 321-322,
  325-326
Math, 661-671
  adding with, 71-73
  aligning text and numbers, 78, 669-670
  in tables, 1014-1015
Mathematical functions in equations, 330, 338
MATRIX equation command, 321-322
Matrix format in an equation, 321-322, 325-326
MB (Margin Bias) conversion command, 194
MD (DOS) command, 224
Measurement
  absolute, 34-35
  entering, 1241-1242
  units of, 308, 401, 879-880, 1053-1056,
    1254-1255
Memory
  cache, 734
  expanded, 361-363, 735, 1292
  extended, 361, 735
  minimum requirements, 4
Memory-resident (TSR) programs, 734
  loading, 408
Menu bar, displaying, 38, 721, 816, 876
Menu bar separator line, 818
{MENU OFF} macro command, 1196
{MENU ON} macro command, 1196
Menu options, 672-674, 876
Menus, 37-39, 674
  cancelling, 125
  changes 4.2 to 5.1, 1254
  exiting, 68, 676
Menus, pull-down, 17-18, 36-39, 710-721,
  815-818
  categories, list of, 716-717
  changes 5.0 to 5.1, 1240-1241
  features, 712
  using, without a mouse, 715
Merge, 677-698
  commands, 1143-1215
  date, inserting, 1146
  documenting, 1143-1144
  eliminating blank lines, 692
  with envelopes, 685-686
  error messages, 697

Merge, *continued*
    form letters, 677
    initial setting, 509
    inserting the date during, 677, 683
    with labels, 685-686
    lists, 689-690
    new feature in 5.1, 1245-1246
    page numbers in, 771
    pausing a merge for forms fill-in, 686-687
    setting up boilerplate, 688
    setting up format, 880
    sounding a bell during a pause, 688
    stopping a, 685
    using data from other software programs,
      692-693
    using, with labels, 554-555
    using WordPerfect Library, 684
Merge and macros, differences between, 644-
    645, 1129-1135
Merge codes (SHIFT-F9), 698
    display, 290, 1133-1134
Merge commands
    accessing, 1133-1135
    descriptions of, 1143-1215
Merge sort, 904, 910
Merge/Sort (CTRL-F9), 698
Merging from the keyboard, 686-688
Messages, 674, 675
    changes 4.2 to 5.1, 1254
Mice, supported by 5.1, 4-5
Microsoft Word
    command conversion table, 1280-1285
    files, converting, 217
Microspacing
    adjusting for proportional spacing, 814
    for justification, 520-521
{MID} command, 1156-1157
Minus key, 698
Mistakes, correcting, 52-53
Mnemonics
    advantages, 400
    changing display attribute, 672-674, 876
    choices in menus, 674-675
Mode co80, 168, 699
MODE (DOS) command, 698-699
    color, selecting, 116
    underlining on COMPAQ monitor, 168
Modems, 699-701
Modes
    changing, 676
    See also Menus
Monitor, COMPAQ, underlining with, 168
/MONO startup option, 169, 948

Monochrome monitor
    adjusting bold, 115-116
    screen attributes, 161, 164, 168, 169
Mouse
    defining a block with, 103-104
    left-handed, 720
    selecting a, 16
    setting up, 715, 717-721, 871, 874
    support, 710-721, 1241
    unselecting, 1293
    using a, in menus, 37-39
    using to cancel, 125
Mouse acceleration factor, 719
Mouse Driver (MOUSE.COM), external, 4, 5,
    715, 718
Mouse drivers supported, 4, 5
Mouse pointer, 710
Mouse pointer movement, assisted, 720
MOUSE.COM driver, 4, 5, 16, 715, 718
Move, 701-710 *See also* Cursor movement
    block, 54, 106, 701, 702-703
    delete and restore, 253
    rectangle block of text, 706-707
    sentence, paragraph, or page,
      701-702, 708
    shortcut with enhanced keyboard, 703
    tabular columns, 703-706
    text with undelete (F1), 703
    with unnamed block method, 707
{MRG CMND} merge commands, 1212-1213
MultiMate Advantage
    command conversion table, 1275-1280
    file conversion, 215
Multiple copies
    of a document on the screen, 70
    printing, 722-723
Multiple pages, printing, 723-724
Multiple references, 228
Multiple targets, 228
Multiply (*)
    math operator, 665
    table math operator, 1014

N

^N, inserting a page number, 771
^N merge command, 1213
Name badges, using labels to print, 555-556
Name, document, 277
Name search (in Menus), 539, 724-725, 868
    file, font, or printer, 8
    List Files, 63-64, 369-370, 599-600
Names directory, 223
Navy DIF file format, 215

/NB (No Backup) startup option, 95, 264, 849, 851, 948

/NC (No Cursor) startup option, 238, 948

/NE (No Expanded memory) startup option, 949

NEC 3550 printer, text prints in left margin, 973

Negative numbers, math, 666

{NEST} macro command, 632, 1194

{NEST MACRO} merge command, 1191

{NEST PRIMARY} merge command, 1191-1192

{NEST SECONDARY} merge command, 1192-1193

Nested macros, 631, 632

Network (/NT) startup option, 949

Network support, 726-730
    installing in a, 11-12
    setup file, 727
    setup program, 728

Networks, list of, 729

New page, 467, 730

"New page num not found" message, 992

New page number, 724, 730-733
    entering as Arabic or Roman numeral, 731, 768
    selecting, 768-769

Newsletters
    printing side-by-side pages on, 556, 558
    sample, 1084-1094

Newspaper columns, 172-174

{NEXT} command, 1176

{NEXT RECORD} merge command, 690, 1213

/NF (Non-Flash) startup option, 949

/NK (No Keyboard) startup option, 949

No backup startup option (/NB), 95, 264, 849, 851, 948

No cursor speed (/NC) startup option, 948

"No [DefMark] Found" message, 991, 998

No delimiter (.) equation command, 327

No expanded memory (/NE) startup option, 949

No keyboard (/NK) startup option, 949

/NO (No Original) startup option, 535, 949

Non-Flash (/NF) startup option, 949

Noncontinuous underline, 1049

Nonprintable regions, laser printer, 647

"Non-unique short form(s) found" message, 992

Normal space (~) in an equation, 324-325

Norton Utilities, 1047

"Not enough memory" message, 733-735, 799, 821, 891, 911-912, 991, 997, 1043

"Not enough memory," *continued*
    expanding a master document, 660
    in merge, 690-691, 697

"Not enough memory to use entire concordance file. . .", 205

Notebook (WordPerfect Library)
    using in merge, 695

^N^P^P merge code, 689

NROOT equation command, 316-317

/NT (Network) startup option, 949

Nth Root in an equation, 316-317

{NTOC} merge command, 1209-1210

{NTOK} macro command, 1210

NUM LOCK key, 735

Number of copies, 735-736

Numbering lines. *See* Lines

Numbering paragraphs. *See* Paragraph numbering

Numbers, negative, 666

Numeric keypad, 233

NWPSETUP (network setup program), 728

O

{ON CANCEL} command, 1200

{ON ERROR} command, 1200-1201

{ON NOT FOUND} macro command, 725, 1201

Open style, 956, 968-970, 1082

Operators, 1138-1142
    equation, 314
    file search, 371
    select, 907-908

Options, setup, 16-21

Orientation, printing of forms, 737

Original backup, 837

Original defaults, returning to, 884, 885

Original document, backup, 92-95

{ORIGINAL KEY} macro command, 1209

Original position, moving cursor back to, 236

Orphan protection, 1059-1061

Other format, 399, 400, 737-741

Outline and paragraph numbering, differences, 747-748

Outline font printing, 741-742, 792

Outline numbering, changing the type of, 744-745

Outline numbering definition, 124

Outline styles, 750-756, 787, 966

Outlines, 742-758, 1247-1248
    adjusting to current level automatically, 749
    attach previous level, 749

Oulines, *continued*
    bulleted, 123-124
    creating, 743-744
    inserting paragraph numbers with
      ENTER, 749
    paragraph number level, adjusting with
      tabs, 747
    saving as a DOS text file, 758
    tabs in, 982
    See also Paragraph numbering
OVER equation command, 315
Overflow files, 46, 819
    temporary, 81-82
Overheads, 1097, 1100
OVERLINE equation command, 322-323
OVERSM equation command, 315, 328
Overstrike, 739-740, 758-760

P

^P merge command, 1191
Page
    breaks, 28, 384, 467, 760-762
    center from top to bottom, 140-143, 764
    centering with hand-fed paper, 141
    conditional end of, 113
    delete to end of, 29
    deleting, 253
    force odd/even, 764
    moving cursor by, 29, 235
    moving to a specific, 761-762
    placing a border around, 119-122
    printing from the screen, 793-794
    starting a new, 945
Page format, 397, 398, 762-766
"Page *n* of *n*", printing, 772-774
Page number position, selecting, 767-768
Page number style, 479, 502-503, 766, 771-772
    changing, 769
    defining for an index, 499-500
    text included after generation, 770
Page numbers, 765, 766-774, 1249
    appearance of, changing, 770
    creating with Advance, 76
    in a header or footer, 385, 770-771
    index/lists/tables, 731-732
    in macros and merge, 771
    new, 724, 730-733
    Roman numerals, 768
    selecting new, 768-769
    turning on, 767-768
{PAGE OFF} merge command, 689, 691, 697,
    1213-1214
{PAGE ON} merge command, 1214

Page up/down, 774-775
Pages
    multiple, printing, 723-724
    printing with renumbered, 731
    ranges of, printing, 800-802
    specific, printing, 800-802
Pagination, 42, 44, 775
Paired style, 956, 970-971, 1082
Palette, equation, 309
Paper, location of, 802
Paper, hand-fed, 462-463
    loading during printing, 780
    location of, defining, 780
Paper Size (SZ) conversion command, 193
Paper size/type, 100-103, 546, 765, 775-782,
    1244-1245
    adding to list, 776-777
    changes 4.2 to 5.1, 1258
    editing, 776-782
    selecting, 775-776
Paragraph numbering and outlining, differ-
    ences, 747-748
Paragraph numbering
    changing to, 744
    definition, 744, 748-756
Paragraph numbers, 782-788
    automatic, 753, 783
    definition menu, 124
    deleting, in an outline, 747
    fixed, 753, 783
    starting, 748-749
    style, changing, 784-787
    types of, in outlines, 749
Paragraph sort, 904-910
Paragraphs
    adjusting space between, 1076
    deleting, 253
    hanging, 463-465, 497
    moving, 701-702, 708
Parallel columns, 788
    with block protect, 181
    changing the number of, 181-182
    converting to a table, 178-179
    converting to normal text, 181
    defining, 173-174
Parallel port, 863
Parent directory, 262
Parity, serial printer, 864
Password file protection, 611, 612, 789, 1035
PATH (DOS) command, 84, 85
Paths/pathnames
    downloadable fonts, 789, 866
    printer files, 789

{PAUSE KEY} macro command, 628, 1148
{PAUSE} macro command, 628, 696, 1147-1148
Pausing a macro, 627-628
PC Tools, 1047
Personal settings on a network, 727
Pg. *See* Status line
PGDN, 774
PGUP, 774
PHANTOM equation command, 326-327
Pitch, 789-790
    display, 266-268, 270-271
Place for setup file (/PS) startup option,
    949-950
Place holder in an equation, 326-327
PlanPerfect
    importing and exporting files, 261, 937
    merging from, through clipboard, 695
Pleading paper style, 450-452, 966
Point (measurement unit), 1056
Point size, specifying, 791
Pointer, mouse, 710
Port, printer, 863
Portrait printing, 558
Portrait, printer orientation, 737
Pos. *See* Status line
PostScript printing, 790-793
Prefix of a document, 271, 365-366, 504,
    506, 852
Preview a document. *See* View
Primary merge file, 677, 678, 682-684
Print, 793-805
    block, 108
    colors, 169-171
    continued message, 392
    daggers, 297
    to disk, 806-809
    equation option, 342
    extra large, 363-365
    format, 805-806
    large, 565-566
    from list files menu, 596
    menu, 61
    multiple copies, 722-723
    options, 511-512, 806, 882
    quality of, 798, 820-821
    queue, 212, 799-800
    screen, 803
    from screen, 800
    setup options, 20, 21
    size of, 895-896
Print jobs
    cancel, 126-128, 210, 954

Print jobs, *continued*
    display, 210-211, 268-269
    numbering, 212
    rush, 127, 210, 847-848
{PRINT} merge command, 691-697, 1214
Printer
    bolding methods, 117
    control, 209-213, 797, 813
    DIP switches, 803
    initialize, 513-514, 797
    problems, 802-805
    restarting, 211-212, 462, 794, 834-835
    selecting, 8-9, 859-870
    sending a "Go", 211-212, 462
    switch settings, 117
    using, as a typewriter, 802
    using more than one, 867-868
Printer command, 810-812
    converting BASIC to decimal, 811-812
    escape sequences, 811
Printer definition, WordPerfect 5.0, converting
    to 5.1, 13-14
Printer driver, updating, 12-13, 869
Printer files
    converting, from older versions,
        1108-1109
    location of, 609
    path for, 789
Printer installation option, 12-13
Printer program, 812, 1103, 1128
    exiting, 1110
    files that can be edited with, 1105-1106
    function keys, 1109-1110, 1111
    organization of, 1111-1112
    starting, 14, 1106-1108, 1126-1128
    uses for, 1113-1124
Printer resource (.PRS) file, 861-863,
    866-868, 1105
Printer selection
    changes 4.2 to 5.1, 1256
    changing, 807-808
    deleting, 868-869
    menus, 868-869
    retrieving a document with a different,
        384, 838-839
"Printer selection not properly set up" mes-
sage, 799
PRINTER.TST file, 566, 742, 824, 887
Printing, 60-62
    background, 800
    changes, 1250
    contents of a directory, 796

Printing, *continued*
    from disk, 796-797
    to disk, 808-809
    double-sided, 781
    graphics, 437-438
    labels, 552
    landscape, 558-560
    portrait, 558
    PostScript, 790-793
    range of pages, 800-802
    with renumbered pages, 731
    from screen, 800
    selected pages, 796-797
    shadow, 886-887
    special characters, 915-916
    specific pages, 800-802
    stop, 212, 952-954
    text in any size in equation editor, 352
    white letters on a black background, 435
Procedure, cancel, 125
{PROCESS} merge commands, 1214-1215
Program editor, 283
    codes key function, 832
Programs, printing side-by-side pages on, 556-558
{PROMPT} macro command, 628, 1150-1151
{PROMPT} merge command, 1150-1151
Prompts, 37-39, 675
    cancelling, 125
    changes 5.0 to 5.1, 1240
Proportional spacing, 813-814
    character tables (PS table), 1118-1122
.PRS (printer resource) file, 861-863, 866-868, 1105
PRTSC key, 815
/PS (Place for Setup file location) startup option, 949-950
PS Table. *See* Proportional spacing
Pull-Down menus, 17-18, 36-39, 710-721, 815-818, 876
    categories, list of, 716-717
    changes 5.0 to 5.1, 1240-1241
    features, 712
    using, without a mouse, 715
"Put WP 2 disk back in drive" message, 818-820

Q

Quality of print, 798, 820-821
Quattro/Quattro Pro, 937, 1294
{QUIT} command, 1187-1198
Quit printing. *See* Cancel (F1) and Stop printing
Quotations, indented, 496-497

R

/R (RAM resident) startup option, 361-362, 950
RAM drive, 821-822, 936, 947
RamFonts, 162
RBRACE, 328
RD (Remove Directory) DOS command, 254-255
RE:, identifying subject matter with, 273
Reboot (CTRL-ALT-DEL), 70
Record delimiters, 213, 509
Records in a merge file, 677, 870
Rectangular block, 109-110
    copying, 706-707
    moving, 706-707
    moving without [Tab] codes, 709
Redline, 188, 822-825
    changing, 271, 824-825
    removing, after compare, 189-190, 825, 826-828
References *See also* Cross-Reference
    marking, 225-227
    multiple, 228
    updating, 227
Reformatting, 86, 826
Registration number, entering, 483
Relative tabs, 1031, 1248
Release date, display of, 483, 1289
Releases, interim, 13, 1289
Rename file, 828-829
Renumbered pages, printing, 731
Repagination, not necessary in WordPerfect, 44, 67
Repeat
    Performance program, 129, 237
    value (ESC key), 355-356, 511, 829, 882
Repeating keys, 23, 356-357
Replace (ALT-F2), 56-57, 830-834
    within a block, 108, 831
    deleting codes with, 69, 257
    extended, 363, 485-486
    whole word, 831
Required space, 471
{RESTART} macro command, 1199
Restart printer, 834-835
Restore deleted text, 28, 52-53, 709, 835
Retrieve (SHIFT-F10), 47, 64, 835-839
    capturing document summary fields with, 277
    inserting subject search text with, 273
    in list files, 279, 836-837
    locked file, 611, 838

Retrieve text
from the clipboard, 840
copied or moved text, 54-55, 837
unnamed block, 106, 707, 708-709
{RETURN CANCEL} command, 1201-1202
{RETURN ERROR} command, 1202
Return, hard, 468-469
RETURN key, 300
{RETURN} command, 1160, 1168
{RETURN NOT FOUND} macro
command, 1202
Reveal codes (ALT-F3), 840-843
changing, to any size, 290, 842
seeing text with codes, 40, 41, 152
Reverse search (SHIFT-F2), 843, 855-856
Reverse video, adjusting, 40-41
Revisable-Form-Text, IBM DCA format,
214-215, 246
{REWRITE} merge command, 1196
Rewrite screen, 854
[RGT TAB] code, 377
Right align text, 844
Right-Aligned tabs, inserting, 377
Right delimiters, 318-319
RIGHT equation command, 318-319, 322
Right indent, 844
Right justification. *See* Justification
Right justify existing text, 519-520
Right margins, 493, 647-650
Roman numerals, entering new page numbers
as, 731
Root directory, 261
limit on number of files, 62, 367
Rotate image in a graphics box, 427-429, 430
Rotate text, 845
in a graphics box, 426-427
[Row] code, 1020
Row height in a table, 1010-1011
Row separator (#) in an equation, 325
Rows in a table
adding/deleting, 1005-1006
moving, 1018-1020
Ruler, 581, 845-847
Rules, 444, 1077-1079
Rush print job, 210, 847-848

S

^S merge command, 1193
/SA (Standalone) startup option, 729, 950
Save, 848-853
block, 107, 849
document, 62, 220, 848-849

Save, *continued*
fast, 307, 365-366, 852
Save font options, 1039
Scale an image in graphics box, 427, 429
Screen, 853-855
moving cursor by, 234
moving to edges of, 485
printing from, 800
rewriting, 826, 843-844
splitting, 55, 937
Screen edges, moving cursor to, 29, 234
Screen Size (/SS) start option, 950
Screen type
graphics, 454-455
text, 1037-1039
Screens, 1080
Scriptwriter styles, 971-972
Scrolling with a mouse, 714
Search (F2), 55-57, 855-858. *See also* Replace
and Extended
Search/Replace
case-sensitive, 856
codes, 55-56, 256-257
extended, 363, 855-856
filenames, 64, 369
in list files, 598, 859
name search (in a list menu), 539
reverse, 843
whole word, 831, 856-857
Secondary merge file, 677-682
Section numbers, including in a list, 606
Sentence
copying/moving, 708
deleting, 253
Serial printer, selecting a COM port for,
863-865
SET (DOS) command, 634, 952
.SET file, creating, on a network, 12
Sets, 330, 336-337
Settings
default, 44
initial, 507-513
personal, on a network, 727
tab, inserting dot leader, 284
universal, on a network, 727-728
Setup (SHIFT-F1), 16-21, 870-885
changes 4.2 to 5.1, 1259
choosing menu options, 672-674
edit-screen options, 288, 289
environment category, 305-308
options, 871-883
options for equations, 342-344
print options, 511-512

Seven-bit transfer format, 216
Shading (graphics boxes and lines), 450, 885-887, 1080
Shading in a table, 1011-1013
Shadow borders, 886
Shadow font, 792
Shadow printing, 886-887
Sheet feeders, 887-889
    selecting, 865
Shell (CTRL-F1), 889-893
    executing a DOS command, 280
    Go to, 407-409
{SHELL MACRO} macro command, 1194-1195
Shell support, 1250
SHIFT key, 23
    naming macros, 622
SHIFT-PRTSC, printing the screen, 803-804, 815
SHIFT-TAB, moving to previous tab setting, 982
Short form, 985-986, 990-991
Short/Long display, 64, 274, 276, 614
SHORTCUT keyboard layout, 475, 538-539, 540, 541, 543-544
Side-by-side columns display, 290-291
Sign-up sheet, created with tables, 1023, 1024
Single dash, 239
Size attribute
    choosing, 381
    ratios, 88, 893-895
Size of print, 50, 895-896
Skip language, 897
Small caps, 897-898
    choosing to display, 18
Soft codes, 42
Soft fonts, 379
    downloading, 139-140, 383, 789, 791, 797
    specifying location of, 138
Soft hyphen (CTRL-HYPHEN), 31, 466, 493
Soft page break, 42, 43, 898-899
    inserted automatically, 468-469
    searching for, 832, 857
Soft return code, 42, 301
Soft return, deletable [DSRt], 302
Soft return, invisible [ISRt], 301, 486
Sort and select, 899-912
    block, 108-109
Sorting sequence option, 912
Space
    between lines, adjusting, 582-583
    between words, adjusting, 521-522, 814
    hard, 471-472, 486
    inserting in an equation, 313
    required, 471-472

Space, *continued*
    underlining, 286, 740
Spacing, 913-914
    endnotes, 914
    footnotes, 389-390, 914
    line, 913-914
    proportional, 813-814
Special characters, 915-917, 1244
    assigning to a key, 531
    changes 4.2 to 5.1, 1260-1261
    displaying, 200, 916-917
    printing, 200-201, 915-916
{SPEED} macro command, 1196-1197
Spell (CTRL-F2), 58-60, 917-929
Spell files, location of, 608-609
Spell program, 494, 929-936
Speller menu, 59
Spelling, checking in a block, 108, 919-920
[SPg] code, 760, 898
Split a row of cells, 1017
Split screen. *See* Windows
Spreadsheet
    DIF, 216
    formatting, 944
    importing and linking, 937-945
    retrieving an entire, 937-939
    retrieving as tabular text, 942
    support, 1243
SQRT equation command, 316-317
Square root in an equation, 316-317
[SRt] code, 42, 301, 468
/SS (Screen Size) startup option, 950
STACK equation command, 319-321
STACKALIGN equation command, 319-321
Stand-alone, running WordPerfect, 729, 950
STANDARD.IRS, 1293
STANDARD.VRS, 1295
Start new page. *See* Hard page
Start WordPerfect, 31-33, 945-952
Startup options, 946-951
    for the printer program, 1126-1128
{STATE} macro command, 1176-1177
State of WordPerfect, checking, 1176-1177
Status line, 33-34, 67, 290, 952
{STATUS PROMPT} command, 1151
{STEP OFF} command, 1202-1203
{STEP ON} command, 1202-1203, 1204-1208
Stop bits, serial printer, 864
{STOP} merge command, 1198
Stop printing, 212, 952-954
Strikeout, 954-955
    automatic (compare documents), 188, 823
    deleting text marked for, 827-828

Strikeout, *continued*
  removing after compare, 189-190, 826-828
Style
  attach, to a block, 106-107
  copying, 963
  creating by example, 961
  editing, 962-963
  files, location of, 609
  graphics image, including in a, 418, 968
  library, 609, 965-967
  library filename, 757
  open, 956
  paired, 525, 956
  pleading paper, 450-452
  turning on/off, 961-962
Styles, 956-972, 1081-1082
  changes 4.2 to 5.1, 1260
  changing the type, 967
  deleting, 757-758, 963-964
  in graphics, 441-443
  outline, 750-756, 787
  page number, 769, 771-772
  sharing between documents, 756-757,
    964-965
  turning on with macros, 963
  use of, with outline styles, 756
SUB (_) equation command, 316
Sub-Menu delay time, changing, 719
Subdocument, 653, 972
Subheading style example, 1084-1085
Subheadings, index, marking in a
  concordance, 203
Subject, entering, 275, 278
Subroutine, 1157-1160
Subject search text (Document Summary), 273
Subscript, 973-974
  in equations, 316
  using with Advance, 75
{SUBST PRIMARY} merge command, 1193
{SUBST SECONDARY} merge
  command, 1193
Substitute fonts, selecting, 1115-1118
Subtotal math operator, 667
Subtract (-)
  math operator, 665
  table math operator, 1014
Summary, 278
  creating, on Save/Exit, 273
  setup options, 19, 306-307
SUP (^) equation command, 316
Superscript, 973-974
  in equations, 316
  using with Advance, 75

Supplementary dictionary, 920-921,
  935-936, 974
Suppress, 765, 974-977
Switch settings, printer, 117
Switch (SHIFT-F3), 977-978
  between two documents, 34, 55, 977, 978
  capitalizing with, 129
  changing to uppercase or lowercase in a
    block, 108, 977, 978
  disks, 46
Symbols, 330, 332-333
  inserting into an equation, 329
  large, 330, 331-332
  other miscellaneous, for equations,
    330, 337
System information, using, 1177-1180,
  1181-1188
{SYSTEM} macro command, 479, 772, 773,
  1178-1180, 1181-1188
{SYSTEM} merge command, 1178-1180,
  1181-1188
System requirements, 3-13
SZ (Paper Size) conversion command, 193

T

^T, 691
Tab Align (CTRL-F6), 77, 249-250, 979-981
TAB key, 981-983
  changing to a decimal tab, 251
  indenting with, 48-49, 982
  outline and, 747
Tab ruler, displaying, 648-649
Table box, 998
Table cells, format of, 1006-1007
Table definition code, 1020
Table of authorities, 983-992
  creating more than one for a
    document, 991
  initial settings for, 511, 882
  marking entries, 656, 985-986
  short form, 653-654, 893
Table of contents, 992-998
  creating an entry with flush right, 378
  marking entries, 655, 993-994
  style for, 966
Table sort, 904
Tables, 998-1028
  adding/deleting rows and columns,
    1005-1006
  aligning in, 78, 1017
  changing column size in, 1001, 1004-1005
  converting to text, 944-945

Tables, *continued*
    creating, 1000-1001
    effect of turning on columns above a, 179
    entering text in, 1001-1002
    header on subsequent pages in, 1013
    including in a graphics box, 436-437, 1021
    joining cells in, 1017-1018
    lines, 1011-1013
    merging into, 1021-1022
    making changes to, 1004
    math in, 1014-1015
    moving blocks in, 1018-1020
    moving columns in, 1018-1020
    moving cursor in, 235, 485, 1002-1003
    moving rows in, 1018-1020
    new feature in 5.1, 1242-1243
    options, 1016-1017
    page numbers in, 731-732
    sample applications of, 1022-1028
    shading, 1011-1013
    sorting rows in, 901-902
    splitting cells in, 1017-1018
    tabs in, 982
Tables and columns, 1021
Tabs, 1029-1033
    absolute, 1031
    aligning text, 77
    centered, 144-145
    clear with macro, 1033
    clearing, 1029
    decimal, 76-77, 249-251
    hard, 486-487, 1032-1033
    inserting a dot leader, 284, 1030
    relative to left margin, 1031, 1248
    restore previous setting with macro, 1033
    right-aligned, inserting, 377
    set at current position with macro, 1033
    settings, 580, 1030, 1031, 1295
    underlining, 740
Tabular column
    copying, 109, 182, 703-706
    moving, 109, 182, 703-706
    moving the cursor in, 182
Tags, 1081-1082
Targets, multiple, 228
[Tbl Def] code, 1020-1021
[Tbl Off] code, 1020
Template, 23-25, 403-404
    changes 5.0 to 5.1, 1240
Temporary
    files, 81-82
    margins, using indent for, 649
    print files, 800

TESTMEM, memory checker, 927
Text
    adjustment, 651, 782
    aligning, 76-79, 979
    attaching a style to a block of, 106-107
    block of, deleting, 91
    block of, moving, 701-710
    blocking with a mouse, 713
    boldfaced, 49, 114
    boxed, 576, 1023
    centering, 143-146, 147
    centering on labels, 552
    changing a comment to, 186
    changing to a comment, 186
    copying, 701-710
    creating dot leader for centered, 284-285
    creating dot leader for flush right, 284-285
    deleting, 52-53, 252
    editing, 53-57
    entering, 47-48
    entering in a table, 1001-1002
    entering in columns, 175
    flush right, 377
    and graphics, combining, 439-440
    highlighting sections of, 105, 484
    indented, 48-49
    inserting, 69
    keeping together, 523
    line draw around centered, 146
    lowercase/uppercase. *See* Switch
    marking, 108, 651-657
    printing in any size in Equation Editor, 352-353
    protecting, from page break, 815
    quality, 798, 820-821
    replacing, 108
    restoring deleted, 28, 52-53, 66, 126, 703, 709, 835
    retrieving, from the clipboard, 840
    right-align, 844
    rotating, 845
    rotating in a graphics box, 426-427, 845
    saving a block of, 849
    subject search, 273
    wrapping to next line prematurely, 805
    See also Cursor movement
Text boxes. *See* Graphics boxes
Text columns. *See* Columns
Text drivers, 1246
Text file, retrieving into a graphics box, 416
Text files
    ASCII, 83

Text files, *continued*
    DOS, 281-283
Text In/Out (CTRL-F5), 1034-1037, 1295
    saving in another format, 191, 851-852
    using with AUTOEXEC.BAT file, 84-85
{TEXT} command, 1150
Text screen type, 876, 1037-1039, 1295
"Text was not modified" message, 850
Thesaurus, 60, 1039-1043
    choosing word alternatives, 1040-1041
    foreign language, 1042
    location of files, 608-609
Thin space (') in an equation, 324-325
Thousands' separator, 739, 979
Tilde (~), in equations, 324-325
Tildes (~), inserting enough, 1142-1143
Time, 240-243
Timed backup, 91-95
TIMES command in an equation, 314
TO equation command, 316, 317-318
Top margin, 650-651, 764-765
    with hand-fed forms, 462
Totals. *See* Addition, Math, or Tables
Transfer format, seven-bit, 216
Transparencies, 1043-1044, 1097, 1100
TSR (Terminate and Stay Resident)
    programs, 408
Turning columns on and off, 174-175, 177
Tutorial, 35, 1044-1045
Type through, 802, 1045
Typeover, 47, 1045-1046
    using with bold, 116
    using tab in, 982
Typesetters, baseline placement for, 97-98
Typewriter, using your printer like a, 802
Typist, 275, 277

U

/U (User initials) startup option, 950-951
Undelete, 1046-1048
    text (F1), 27-28
Underline (F8), 49, 1048-1053
    with addition, 73
    block of text, 105, 1048-1049
    double, 285-286, 1050
    removing a section of, 1050-1051
    space between tabs, 286
    spaces and tabs, 740
UNDERLINE equation command, 322-323
Underlining, choosing to display, 18, 1052
Undo a file search, 371
Units of measure, 1053-1056
    abbreviations, 401

Units of measure, *continued*
    changing default settings, 308, 879-880,
        1055-1056
    differences, 4.2 versus 5.1. 648, 1254-1255
Universal settings on a network, 727
[Unknown] code, 22, 191, 852
Unlock documents, 610-612
Update installation option, 13
Uppercase text. *See* Capitalization and Switch
User function in an equation, 322
User initials (/U) startup option, 950-951
Username, network, 12, 726-727
Utilities, graphics, 456-461

V

{VARIABLE} command, 1155
Variables, 1135-1137, 1152-1155
    global, 1136
    inserting, 1136-1137
Vector (line) graphics image, 437
VERT equation command, 324
Vertical
    alignment for a cell, 1009
    graphics lines, 444-446, 448-449, 450-451
    line spacing in an equation, 328-329
    lines. *See* Borders, Graphics lines
    margins. *See* Margins
    movement in an equation, 324
    stacking in an equation, 319
Very large print. *See* Size of print
VGA monitors, 874, 916, 1246
View, 45, 1057-1059
    text to be sorted, 903
Virtual files, 3-4
Virtual memory, 46
.VRS files, 1038, 1039

W

w, unit of measurement, 75, 880, 1055
/W (Workspace) startup option, 362, 951
{WAIT} command, 1197
WC (WordPerfect Character) conversion com-
    mand, 195-196
{WHILE} macro command, 1174-1176
Whole-word search and replace, 831
Whole-word searches, 856-857
Widow/Orphan protection, 507, 523, 580,
    1059-1061
    block protect, conflict with, 112
Width scaling factor, 792
Wildcard characters, spell, 60, 921
Wildcards in a file search, 371

Window, display, in equations, 309
Window size, reveal codes, 290
Windows, 854, 1061-1063
Word, check location of, 934
Word count, 921-922, 1065
Word, delete, 28, 90
Word left (CTRL- ←), 29, 234. *See also* Cursor
    movement
Word, look up. *See* Spell (CTRL-F2)
Word pattern, spell checking, 60, 917-919
Word processing concepts, 35-46
Word right (CTRL- →), 234. *See also* Cursor
    movement
Word search (List Files), 369
Word spacing, 1063-1065, 1074-1075
    justification limits, 522, 1066-1067
Word wrap, automatic, 301
WordPerfect
    differences 4.2 to 5.1, 1251-1263
    differences 5.0 to 5.1, 1239-1250
    exiting, 65-66
    features, 26-27
    installing, 5-13, 515-516
    leaving, 569
    loading more than one copy of, 81-82
    options for starting, 22
    template, 23-25, 403-404
WordPerfect 4.2 format, saving as, 852, 1035
WordPerfect 4.2 to 5.1, converting, 216-217
WordPerfect 5.0 format, saving as,
    851-852, 1035
WordPerfect 5.0 keyboards, 544
WordPerfect 5.0 units. *See* Units of
    measurement
WordPerfect 5.1
    starting, 31-33, 945-952
    updating, 13
WordPerfect Character (WC) conversion com-
    mand, 195-196
WordPerfect Library or Office
    calculator, 662
    capturing a graphics screen with shell,
      457-458
    clipboard, using in merge, 695
    line draw in macro editor with, 1218
    Notebook, creating secondary merge
      file, 695
    Program Editor, 283, 832
    starting WordPerfect, 952
    support for shell, 1250
    using Shell with, 408, 889
    using, to merge, 684

WordPerfect Printer Definition Language
    (WPDL), 1126
WordPerfect release date, display of, 483
WordPerfect template, 23-25, 403-404
Words, adjusting space between, 521-522, 814
WordStar, 1067-1068
    mail merge format, 645-646
WordStar diamond, reassigning cursor
    keys to, 545
WordStar Professional, command conversion
    table, 1269-1275
WordStar 2000, converting files, 215
Workspace (/W) startup option, 951
"WP disk full" message, 1068-1069
WP 5.0 units, 75, 1055
WP.DRS file, 735, 915
WP.EXE,
    cannot fit on one disk, 32
    locating virtual files in relation to, 4
WP.FIL, 4, 32
WP51.INS file, 13
WPHELP.FIL, 481
"WPHELP.FIL not found" message, 25
WPINFO program, 84
.WPK extension, 531, 535, 608
    for key macros, 542, 619
    restriction on use of, 634
WP.LRS (Language resource) file, 243, 392,
    560-561, 563-565, 600-601
.WPM extension, 282
    for file macros, 542, 619
    restriction on use of, 634
WP/M startup option, 634
WP.MRS, 535
WP/NC (No cursor) startup option, 22
WP/NE (No enhanced memory) startup
    option, 22
WP/NK (No keyboard) startup option, 22
WPSMALL.DRS, 735
WP{WP}.BK1, 18, 33, 70, 93, 94, 608
WP{WP}.BK2, 18, 33, 70, 93, 94, 608
WP}WP{.BV1, 46
WP}WP{.BV2, 46
WP{WP}.ENV environment file, 11-12, 727,
    728-729
WP}WP{.Q, 799
WP{WP}.SET file, 16, 168, 356, 727, 884, 951
WP{WP}.SPC file, 264
WP}WP{.TV1, 46
WP}WP{.TV2, 46
WP{WP}US.HYC, 488, 608

WP{WP}US.LEX, 488, 494, 608, 920, 925-927, 974
"WP{WP}US.LEX not found", 58, 925
WP{WP}US.SUP, 494, 609, 920, 974
WP{WP}US.THS, 608
WP{WP}.WPM, 620
Writer's underline, 1051-1052

XYZ

/X startup option, 951
^X, wildcard character in a search string, 831-832, 857
XON/XOFF protocol, setting for a serial printer, 790-791, 864-865
Yes/No questions, 675-676
Zone, hyphenation, 490-492

The manuscript for this book was prepared and submitted to Osborne/McGraw-Hill in electronic form. The acquisitions editor for this project was Roger Stewart, the associate editor was Laurie Beaulieu, the technical reviewer was Jennifer Nelson, and the project editor was Kathy Krause.

Text design by Lynda Higham and Pam Webster, using Century Expanded for text body and Eras Demi for display.

Cover art by Bay Graphics Design Associates. Color separation and cover supplier, Phoenix Color Corporation. Screens produced with InSet, from Inset Systems, Inc. Book printed and bound by R.R. Donnelley & Sons Company, Crawfordsville, Indiana.